RSAC

D1440753

AUG 2004

The Invention of Racism in Classical Antiquity

The Invention of Racism
in Classical Antiquity

• *BENJAMIN ISAAC* •

PRINCETON UNIVERSITY PRESS

PRINCETON AND OXFORD

Library of Congress Cataloging-in-Publication Data

Isaac, Benjamin H.

The invention of racism in classical antiquity / Benjamin Isaac.

p. cm.

Includes bibliographical references and index.

ISBN 0-691-11691-1 (alk. paper)

1. Racism—Greece—History—To 1500. 2. Racism—Rome. I. Title.

DF135.I82 2004

320.5′6′0938—dc21

2003048610

British Library Cataloging-in-Publication Data is available

This book has been composed in Times Roman

Printed on acid-free paper. ∞

www.pupress.princeton.edu

Printed in the United States of America

1   3   5   7   9   10   8   6   4   2

· *FOR IDA* ·

• C O N T E N T S •

(following page 251)

1. Heracles and Busiris. Caeretan black-figure hydria, Late Archaic Greek, c. 510 B.C. Vienna Kunsthistorisches Museum, ANSA IV 3576. A. Furtwängler und K. Reichhold, *Griechische Vasenmalerei; Auswahl hervorragender Vasenbilder* (München 1904), Pl. 51.

2a and 2b. Greek assaults Persian (Eurymedon). Attic red-figure oinochoe, unattributed, Early Classical Greek, c. 465 B.C. Inv. No. 1981.173. Hamburg, Museum für Kunst und Gewerbe.

3. Persian Soldiers. Attic red-figure lekythos, c. 400 B.C., #695. © Copyright The British Museum

4a and 4b. Oriental ruler, probably the King of Persia, riding a camel. Attic red-figure oinochoe, towards the end of the first half of the fifth century. British Museum, London, #1912.7–9.1. © Copyright The British Museum

5a and 5b. Athenian mistress and black slave girl in cemetery. Attic white-ground lekythos, Bosanquet painter, 450–440 B.C., v.i. 3291. Antikensammlung, Staatliche Museen zu Berlin–Preussischer Kulturbesitz-.

6. Nude black boy attending Athenian older man. Attic red-figure belly amphora. Chr. VIII 320 Ptr., c. 470 B.C. Department of Classical and Near Eastern Antiquities, National Museum of Denmark.

7. Claudius and Britannia. From a series of Roman imperial reliefs found in the Sebasteion at Aphrodisias by courtesy of the New York University Excavations at Aphrodisias. Photo courtesy of the New York Excavations.

8a–b and 8c–d. Judaea Capta Coins. Silver denarii, Israel Museum Inv. No. 140 and No. 139. Collection Israel Museum, Jerusalem. Photo © Israel Museum

9. Mass execution of German prisoners. Column of Marcus Aurelius, Rome, scene 61. Photo: Eugen Petersen, *Die Marcus-Säule auf Piazza Colonna in Rom*, eds. Eugen Petersen, Alfred von Domaszewski, und Guglielmo Calderini, Text (1 Band).–Tafeln (2 Port.), (Munich, 1896), Tafel 70.

10. Vanquished Germans surrender to the Emperor. Panel relief of Marcus Aurelius, Roma, Musei Capitolini, Inv. 809/S, Archivio Fotografico dei Musei Capitolini.

• A C K N O W L E D G M E N T S •

Many people have been helpful. Erich Gruen, Ida Isaac, and Martin Ostwald have read all of the book, most of it more than once. Their comments have decisively influenced its shape and contents. I am grateful for helpful comments made by Guy Rogers and for remarks on part of the book by Margalit Finkelberg and Arthur Isaac. Glen Bowersock provided valuable assistance in many ways. I acknowledge with thanks their numerous suggestions to which I have responded and apologize for resisting others. Advice on specific points has been rendered by Daniel Benderski and Nili Cohen. An earlier version of chapter 3 was published in Hebrew as an article in the journal *Zion* and was read before publication by Tessa Rajak. Susan Weingarten assisted in editing part of an earlier version of the text. I mention with gratitude periods of study leave granted by Tel Aviv University and spent at Dumbarton Oaks in Washington, DC, Churchill College, Cambridge, and the Institute for Advanced Study in Princeton.

Financial support was provided by the Israel Science Foundation and the Luther I. Replogle Foundation.

Tel Aviv, January 2003

AJA	*American Journal of Archaeology*
ANRW	*Aufstieg und Niedergang der römischen Welt*
BAR	*British Archaeological Reports*
BCH	*Bulletin de Correspondence Hellénique*
BE	*J. et L. Robert, Bulletin épigraphique*
CAH	*Cambridge Ancient History*
CE	*Chronique d'Egypte*
CIL	*Corpus Inscriptionum Latinarum*
CJ	*Codex Justinianus*
ClJ	*Classical Journal*
CPh	*Classical Philology*
CQ	*Classical Quarterly*
CR	*Classical Review*
CTh	*Codex Theodosianus*
FGrH	*F. Jacoby, Die Fragmente der griechischen Historiker*
FHG	*C. Müller, Fragmenta Historicorum Graecorum*
GCS	*Die Griechischen Christlichen Schriftsteller der ersten drei Jahrhunderte*
Geogr. Gr. Min.	*K. Müller, Geographi Graeci Minores*
HSCP	*Harvard Studies in Classical Philology*
HTR	*Harvard Theological Review*
IEJ	*Israel Exploration Journal*
Ill. Class. Stud.	*Illinois Classical Studies*
ILS	*H. Dessau, Inscriptiones Latinae Selectae*
JEA	*Journal of Egyptian Archaeology*
JESHO	*Journal of the Economic and Social History of the Orient*
JHS	*Journal of Hellenic Studies*
JJS	*Journal of Jewish Studies*
JQR	*Jewish Quarterly Review*
JRS	*Journal of Roman Studies*
JTS	*Journal of Theological Studies*
OED	*Oxford English Dictionary*
PCPS	*Proceedings of the Cambridge Philological Society*
PG	*J.-P. Migne, Patrum Graecorum Cursus Completus: series Graeca*
PL	*J.-P. Migne, Patrum Latinorum Cursus Completus: series Latina*
RA	*Revue Archéologique*
RE	*Pauly-Wissowa-Kroll, Real-Encyclopädie der classischen Altertumswissenschaft*

REA	Revue des Etudes Anciennes
REG	Revue des Etudes Grecques
REJ	Revue des Etudes Juives
RhM	Rheinisches Museum
SCI	Scripta Classica Israelica
SEG	Supplementum Epigraphicum Graecum
SHA	Scriptores Historiae Augustae
Stern, GLAJJ	M. Stern, Greek and Latin Authors on Jews and Judaism
TAPA	Transactions of the American Philological Association
YCS	Yale Classical Studies
ZDPV	Zeitschrift des Deutschen Palästina-Vereins
ZPE	Zeitschrift für Papyrologie und Epigraphik

Introduction

LESS THAN A CENTURY AGO nobody would write or wish to read a book about racism. Indeed nobody was aware that such a thing existed, for the word does not appear in the *Oxford English Dictionary* (*OED*) of 1910.[1] The term *racialism* has been around a little longer: It first appeared in print in 1907.[2] Does this mean that racism did not exist before the twentieth century? In fact there is a consensus that it originated in the nineteenth century and has its intellectual roots in that century, although some scholars give it a somewhat longer history. Most of those who have expressed an opinion on the subject claim that racism, more precisely described as "scientific racism," was an offshoot of the ideas about evolution that developed in the nineteenth century. Since racism is thought not to be attested earlier, conventional wisdom usually denies that there was any race hatred in the ancient world.[3] The prejudices that existed, so it is believed, were ethnic or cultural, not racial. In this book I shall argue that early forms of racism, to be called proto-racism, were common in the Graeco-Roman world. My second point in this connection is that those early forms served as prototype for modern racism which developed in the eighteenth century.

Since racism, ethnic prejudice, and xenophobia are so widespread in our times and have played such a dominant role in recent history, it is obviously important to understand how these phenomena developed, as attitudes of mind and intellectual concepts. Group hatred and bigotry are found in many forms throughout human history, but I shall attempt to show that there is a red thread, or rather, that there are a number of red threads that can be followed from the fifth century B.C. onward. Racism, properly understood, can be claimed to represent sets of ideas, the roots of which may be found in Greek and Roman society. On the other hand, I certainly do not claim that we are dealing here with the specific form of scientific racism which was a product of the nineteenth century.

[1] The current edition has as its first reference: 1936 L. Dennis, *Coming American Fascism*, 109. "If . . . it be assumed that one of our values should be a type of racism which excludes certain races from citizenship, then the plan of execution should provide for the annihilation, deportation, or sterilization of the excluded races."

[2] The second reference will strike many of us as sad: 1910 *Westm. Gaz.* 11 Apr. 10/3. What appears to me to be the greatest results of the Botha-Smuts government are the abolition of racialism and the construction of roads.

[3] See George M. Fredrickson, *Racism: A Short History* (Princeton, 2002), 17: "It is the dominant view among scholars who have studied conceptions of difference in the ancient world that no concept truly equivalent to that of 'race' can be detected in the thought of the Greeks, Romans, and early Christians." I should add here that this study reached me only days before I had to submit the final version of my own work and I have therefore been unable to take sufficient account of it.

There are several recent, useful studies of ancient ethnicity and of early processes of ethnic integration, topics that attract much attention these days, but
this book is not one of those. Here the aim is to offer a systematic study of the
forms of proto-racism, ethnic prejudice, and xenophobia that are encountered in
the ancient literature in Greece and Rome from the fifth century B.C. till late
antiquity. The book analyzes patterns of thinking, intellectual and emotional
concepts as well as attitudes towards select specific peoples as encountered in
Greek and Latin literature of the period concerned. It focuses on bigotry and
social hatred in antiquity. This may not be an appealing subject, but its importance cannot be denied. This work is not concerned with the actual treatment of
foreigners in Greece and Rome, but with opinions and concepts encountered in
the literature. It traces the history of discriminatory ideas rather than acts, although the next theme traces the impact such ideas may have had in the sphere
of action.

The third major theme in this work is the relationship between such ideas and
patterns of thinking and ancient imperialism. I shall argue that there is a demonstrable connection between the views Greeks and Romans held of foreign peoples and their ideology of imperial expansion. I do not discuss the mechanisms
of ancient imperialism, but, again, the attitudes of mind that created an atmosphere in which wars of expansion were undertaken—or not undertaken. This
will lead to the conclusion that decisions about war and peace were determined,
at least in part, by commonplaces and vague ideas currently accepted, and to a
lesser degree than might seem reasonable by well-informed assessments.

For this study I shall use all the available literary sources in Greek and Latin
of the period concerned, while taking due account of the peculiarities of each
literary genre. The visual arts undoubtedly might make a contribution, but this
type of evidence is so different in kind that it is best reserved for a separate
study by an individual with the necessary qualifications.[4] I have included some
illustrations to provide an example of what such material may add to the literary sources that form the basis of this study.

The structure of this book follows from the aims described above. It is divided into two parts. The first discusses general concepts and their development, and the second deals with specific peoples as presented in the literature of
the periods considered. I shall discuss opinions about foreign nations, such as
Greek ideas of Persia, and opinions about peoples incorporated into the Roman
Empire, such as Roman ideas about Greeks. This is all the more necessary
because so many foreign nations were incorporated into the Roman Empire at
some stage.

Readers may wonder who this book might interest besides, obviously, ancient

[4] For a brief, general survey: Z. Amishai-Maisels, "The Demonization of the 'Other' in the
Visual Arts," in Wistrich (ed.), *Demonizing the Other* (1999), 44–72. For early Greece: W. Raeck,
Zum Barbarenbild in der Kunst Athens im 6. und 5. Jahrhundert v. Chr. (Bonn, 1981); Beth Cohen
(ed.), *Not the Classical Ideal* (Leiden, 2000), a volume of articles which interprets "the Other" in
the broadest possible sense; Catherine Morgan, "Ethne, Ethnicity, and Early Greek States, ca. 1200–
480 B.C.: An Archaeological Perspective," in Malkin (ed.), *Ancient Perceptions* (2001), 75–112.

historians and classicists. It is my hope that all those who care about the antecedents of the problems we have faced over the past century and are still facing
would find it instructive. These, I hope, will include some modern and early
modern historians. It is my ambition to advance our understanding of the essence of racism and ethnic prejudice in all periods and societies in some respects. Consequently, I hope the book will also be of use to those interested in
contemporary manifestations of discrimination, anti-semitism, and group hatred. The basis for this claim is my contention that racism is a phenomenon that
can assume many apparently different shapes and forms while preserving a
remarkable element of continuity which is undeniable, once it is traced over the
centuries. Racism has been with us for a long time and in various cultures,
adopting various different shapes. It continues and will continue to be with us.
If we recognize only one variety that belongs to a restricted period, we may fail
to recognize it as it emerges in an altered guise.

THE BACKGROUND

Ethnic and racial prejudice and xenophobia are forms of hostility towards
strangers and foreigners, at home or abroad. They occur in every society, but in
widely differing degrees, social settings, and moral environments. They are the
result of the human tendency to generalize and simplify, so that whole nations
are treated as a single individual with a single personality. Contemporary western society is marked by a substantial degree of sensitivity to such attitudes,
although, at the same time, the symptoms are widespread, even where there is
no public or official approval. One of the peculiar legacies of the Greek language and Greek society is the word "barbarian," still used today in English
and other modern languages. This concept has been studied extensively, as it
says so much about Greek and Roman culture in general.[5] However, what has
been lacking up to now is a general study aimed at tracing the development of
the prevalent negative attitudes towards immigrants and foreigners in Greek and
Roman society, and towards other peoples.[6] The subject is an important one, as

[5] Out of trivial curiosity, I started counting the number of academic publications on antiquity
which contain various forms of the term "barbarian" in their title. I gave up when I reached the
number sixty-five—the majority of them deal with the fourth century A.D.

[6] Note, however, the old monograph by Julius Jüthner, *Hellenen und Barbaren: Aus der Geschichte des Nationalbewusstseins* (Leipzig, 1923), which, in spite of its title, offers a brief survey of
the attitudes towards foreigners encountered in Greek, Roman, Hellenistic, Christian, and Byzantine
sources. For Greece see Edith Hall, *Inventing the Barbarian: Greek Self-Definition through Tragedy*
(Oxford, 1989); Jonathan M. Hall, *Ethnic Identity in Greek Antiquity* (Cambridge, 1997); T. Long,
Barbarians in Greek Comedy (Carbondale, 1986), esp. chapter 6: "The Barbarian-Hellene Antith-
esis"; Steven W. Hirsch, *The Friendship of the Barbarians: Xenophon and the Persian Empire*
(Hanover, 1985); Cohen (ed.), *Not the Classical Ideal*; Christopher Tuplin, "Greek Racism? Obser-
vations on the Character and Limits of Greek Ethnic Prejudice," in Gocha R. Tsetskhladze (ed.),
Ancient Greeks West and East (Leiden, 1999), 47–75; for Rome see the survey article by Karl
Christ, "Römer und Barbaren in der hohen Kaiserzeit," *Saeculum* 10 (1959), 273–288 and the

already observed. It is also an extremely delicate topic because of the current sensitivity to all forms of discrimination: any consideration of ancient preconceptions is in danger of hurting modern sensibilities. Moreover, there is a long tradition of seeing Greece and Rome, especially Greece, as the origin of liberty, spiritual and otherwise, and of constitutionalism. A systematic consideration of what we would regard as ancient forms of bigotry may not appeal to some scholars. The study of ancient ethnicity is far more popular at present than that of social hatred, but it is the latter which I have undertaken. In other words, it is not a study of self-definition and self-perception, but of views of others, primarily negative views held by Greek and Roman authors. In this work I shall not use the term "Others" frequently, because "the Other" has in recent decades acquired quite a broad meaning: "Others" include women, slaves, children, the elderly, or disfigured people. It refers to any group that is not part of the establishment, but is placed on the margin or periphery of society, or does not belong to it at all.

This work, then, is concerned with ambivalence and hostility towards foreigners, strangers, and immigrant minorities, rather than internal marginal groups. Such an attempt is as justified as any historical study of racism or social conflict and stress in later periods.[7] Indeed it is the aim of this work to contribute to an understanding of the intellectual origins of racism and xenophobia. As will be seen, some of the patterns visible in the ancient world continued to exist or have re-appeared and are still with us. Others are not. As has already been

---

subsequent monographs by A. N. Sherwin-White, *Racial Prejudice in Imperial Rome* (Cambridge, 1967) and J.P.V.D. Balsdon, *Romans & Aliens* (London, 1979); Yves Albert Dauge, *Le Barbare: Recherches sur la conception romaine de la barbarie et de la civilisation* (Brussels, 1981). These three works will be considered below. For the fourth century A.D.: Alain Chauvot, *Opinions romaines face aux barbares au ive siècle ap. J.-C.* (Paris, 1998). The necessary parameters for the study of this subject have been clearly set forth in a forthcoming article: Gideon Bohak, "The Ibis and the Jewish Question: Ancient 'Anti-Semitism' in Historical Perspective," in M. Mor and A. Oppenheimer (eds.), *Jewish-Gentile Relations in the Second Temple, Mishnaic and Talmudic Periods* (Jerusalem). Special mention may be made of Aubrey Diller, *Race Mixture among the Greeks Before Alexander* (Urbana, IL, 1937). This is a learned and thoughtful work, submitted as a Ph.D. thesis in 1930. It can perhaps be said that the author was the victim of the follies of his time, for he wrote an almost reasonable book about a misguided topic and his conclusions are nonsense: "the idea (of Greek superiority) was strongly negative. It raised a barrier between the Greeks and their neighbors that was crossed consciously, deliberately and at last wantonly. Without such a barrier there would scarcely have been an organic nation capable of maintaining and advancing a civilization of its own. Greek culture would have been contaminated and dissipated prematurely" (p. 31). "For the historical period before Alexander, therefore, we must conclude that there was not much race mixture in Greece" (p. 160). One is tempted to say that the book represents racism with a human face. It was reprinted without changes in 1971.

[7] No word of apology is found in Claude Rawson, *God, Gulliver and Genocide: Barbarism and the European Imagination, 1492–1945* (Oxford, 2001), which studies hostility and ambivalence in the attitudes towards others in the literature of the past five centuries, with special emphasis on Montaigne and Swift. "More broadly, this book is about how the European imagination has dealt with the groups which it habitually talks about killing, and never quite kills off, because the task is too difficult or unpleasant, or the victims are needed for their labour, or competing feelings get in the way" (p. viii).

noted, it is usually considered unjustifiable to speak of ancient racism.[8] None of the works on racism and ethnic prejudice which I have seen and cited assert that it precedes Columbus and European colonialism. This is also the contemporary popular perception.[9] Obviously, it did not exist in the modern form of a biological determinism which represents a distortion of Darwin's ideas, nor was there systematic persecution of any ethnic group by another. However, I shall argue that it is justified to speak of "proto-racism."[10] Modern racism has, by now, quite a long history of development. In its early stages in the eighteenth century, there was nothing like the state-imposed set of theories and applications developed later in Nazi Germany. There were various authors in search of concepts who did not necessarily agree with one another and developed different and often contradictory ideas. In this stage racism remained a fairly moderate doctrine, based on environmentalism and preoccupied with various evaluations of the relationship between the non-Europeans and their European masters. Yet no recent discussion of racism and xenophobia can ignore the many relevant works written in the period of the Enlightenment, for twentieth-century racism could not have existed without these predecessors. Indeed, many of the ideas published in the eighteenth century became part of later racism. In this connection it has been emphasized, however, that the authors of the Enlightenment constantly employ Graeco-Roman concepts and ideas, as will be discussed below. Thus one of the aims of this book is to show that some essential elements of later racism have their roots in Greek and Roman thinking.

The method applied here must also be somewhat different from the study of ethnicity, a subject which, like the consideration of individual identity, has to take into account self-perception, the views of others of oneself, and the perception of others' views of oneself.[11] It will be understood that a consideration of hostility towards, say, Egyptians in Rome, has to leave out many of the positive aspects of Roman attitudes towards Egypt. Similarly, although Greek culture was admired, studied, and imitated in Rome, the present work will concentrate more on the negative or ambivalent attitudes Rome showed towards Greeks and

[8] F. I. Zeitlin, *Playing the Other: Gender and Society in Classical Greek Literature* (Chicago and London, 1996); Brian Leigh Molyneaux, *The Cultural Life of Images: Visual Representation in Archaeology* (London, 1997), esp. B. Sparkes, "Some Greek Images of Others," 130–158; Cohen (ed.), *Not the Classical Ideal*, Introduction.

[9] See, for instance, Susan Saulny, "And there was light, and it was good?" *New York Times*, Sunday, September 2, 2001, citing various anthropologists. Thus C. Loring Brace of the University of Michigan is quoted as saying: "The concept of race does not appear until the trans-Atlantic voyages of the Renaissance." Naturally, in the United States, those who discuss racism tend to focus on skin color. The article continues: "Another way of thinking about skin color is to ask: When did Europeans start thinking of themselves as white? 'There was no whiteness prior to the 17th century,' said Manning Marable, director of the Institute for Research in African-American Studies at Columbia University." See now Frederickson, *Racism*, cited above, n. 3.

[10] The term "proto-racisme" has been used by Jean Yoyotte for Egypt according to L. Poliakov, *Ni Juif ni Grec: Entretiens sur le racisme* (Paris, The Hague, New York, 1978), preface pp. 7–22, at p. 8. Frederickson, *Racism*, applies it to the later Middle Ages.

[11] A seminal study of identity was Erik H. Erikson's *Childhood and Society* (New York, 1950).

Greece, although the former will certainly not be ignored.[12] This will inevitably result in clarifying only part of the spectrum of attitudes, for the work cannot and should not provide all the favorable or neutral judgments made by Greeks and Romans of other peoples.

This study considers how Greeks and Romans thought and wrote about others, more than how they actually behaved towards them, although clearly there is a connection between the two. If we interpret them properly, we can understand what ancient authors meant to convey or conveyed, sometimes without meaning to do so, about other peoples and about foreigners living in their midst. It does not follow that we can deduce from their writings how the Greeks and Romans treated them in practice in day-to-day life. There are several reasons for this. First, and most obviously, the authors are all men belonging to the well-to-do or upper classes, which gives them a specific perspective. Second, it is not their ambition to provide us with insights on how the others saw their position vis-à-vis the Greeks and Romans.[13] This book, therefore, aims in particular to elucidate the views encountered in Greek and Roman literature. These views pertain to various dimensions and features of social life and culture: religion, occupation, modes of life and conflict, and language. Emphasis and values may change over time, but we are always concerned with the ways one group saw another. It is not my intention to consider the economic, legal, and social realities of those concerned. This is necessarily a limited perspective, but it will be instructive all the same: we know that the Greeks in their classical age failed to build an integrated empire including non-Greeks, and we know that the Roman Empire was a multiethnic structure for centuries. This might have led us to suppose that the attitudes of Greek authors towards foreigners would have been more characterized by prejudice and hostility than the attitudes in Latin literature would have been. This appears not to be the case. It may be seen that there is

---

[12] Uffe Øystergård, 'What is National and Ethnic Identity?' in Bilde et al., Ethnicity in Hellenistic Egypt (1992), 16–38, esp. 35f. also suggests that this might be a useful approach: "We do keep talking as if national stereotypes somehow do exist out there in the 'real' world. Even the most refined scholar who would never dare enter such a word in his or her professional work lapses in or back to 'primitive ethnography' when going abroad and attending learned conferences. . . . So, why not take as a point of departure these very stereotypes and see where they lead us? Such an approach might be entitled the discursive approach." He then refers to F. Barth (ed.), *Ethnic Groups and Boundaries: The Social Organization of Cultural Difference* (Bergen, Oslo, London, 1969). This is a collection of essays by various social anthropologists on a number of specific ethnic groups. For a more recent discussion of ethnicity from an anthropological perspective: J. M. Hall, *Ethnic Identity*, esp. 17–33. I have not been able to consult the latter's recent work: *Hellenicity: Between Ethnicity and Culture* (Chicago, 2002); For ancient Greece, see now I. Malkin (ed.), *Ancient Perceptions of Greek Ethnicity* (Washington, DC and Cambridge, MA, 2001). For Greek culture and identity in the Roman Empire, see the collection of essays: Simon Goldhill (ed.), *Being Greek under Rome: Cultural Identity, the Second Sophistic and the Development of Empire* (Cambridge, 2001). Other recent works which I have been unable to consult are Tim Whitmarsh, *Greek Literature and the Roman Empire: The Politics of Imitation* (Oxford, 2001), and Erik Nils Ostenfeld (ed.), *Greek Romans and Roman Greeks* (Aarhus, 2002).

[13] There are a few important exceptions: Greek authors, such as Galen or Lucian of the second sophistic, who write about their experiences in the city of Rome, for instance.

not necessarily always a direct correspondence between social tensions, bigotry, or even hatred and the actual treatment of minorities as may be illustrated easily by a modern parallel. The Jews in mid-nineteenth-century Germany were more fully emancipated than those of any other European nation. Yet there was fierce anti-semitism at the time. Again, there was no sense then that this would lead where we now know it to have led. The existence of racism in the United States did not prevent the abolition of slavery and the gradual emancipation of the blacks in that country. I assume therefore that it is illuminating to study ideas and attitudes in their own right.

Here we touch upon a further major aim of this work. It is assumed here that an understanding of negative attitudes towards other peoples will clarify part of the underlying assumptions and attitudes of ancient imperialism. This should be true, first of all, for the stage where one nation or empire sets out to subjugate and annex or incorporate—"enslave" is the simple ancient term—another people or nation. It should clarify the Greek conquest of Persia by Alexander if we understand how fourth-century Greeks viewed Persians. The same should be true, *ceteris paribus,* for the Roman subjugation of Asia Minor. Furthermore, it is conceivable that we will be able to understand the functioning or disintegration of ancient empires better if we understand attitudes towards incorporated peoples. It is important to realize that the Roman Empire managed to become an integrated whole, in spite of Roman ambivalence towards the Greeks, and it is at least as interesting to see how it then split into two parts, a Latin- and a Greek-speaking empire, where westerners and easterners could exhibit fierce animosity towards one another. Again, the assumption is that Greek and Roman texts will convey mentalities and ideology. It is also assumed that the study of imperial attitudes towards the various peoples who inhabit an Empire will help in clarifying the underlying feelings, ambitions, and fears of those who maintain, expand, or lose an empire.

It is therefore not the intention of this book to provide an analysis of the aims and mechanisms of ancient imperialism in practice, nor of imperial strategy and military policy. I do not pretend to explain imperialism in any systematic manner, for imperialism is not only a policy, but also and even more so, an attitude of mind. It has been my aim to verify whether certain attitudes towards foreign peoples encountered in ancient literature go together with imperialist behavior. It is not my claim that attitudes steer policy, drive conquest, or even determine the treatment of subject peoples, their integration, or suppression. Considering them may help in clarifying an aspect of warfare that tends to be somewhat neglected, at least in ancient history. This may be illustrated with a recent parallel. Both France under Napoleon and Germany under Hitler invaded Russia. For both these nations these campaigns ended in the loss, not just of a battle or campaign, but of their entire wars of expansion, wars that had been successful before they attacked Russia. Whatever their aims and methods, they did so only because they were convinced that they would succeed. This means that there was an extraordinary discrepancy between their image of Russia as a country and reality. It is therefore useful in itself to consider the views of other peoples held by countries at war and their self-perception. When Alexander and his army attacked Persia successfully, he did so with the image of that country that had developed among the Greeks ever since the early fifth century. It is therefore instructive to trace what kind of image this was and how it developed. The same is true, *mutatis mutandis*, for the failed Roman attacks on Parthia in the first century B.C. Thus, besides tracing the early history of group- and ethnic prejudice this study has for its second aim to consider the interrelation between ethnic stereotypes and relations, particularly hostile relations between states. It is a truism that morale is a key factor in warfare and morale is determined in large part by the views both sides have of the other and themselves. Such views may be formed by good intelligence work and cautious evaluation, but sets of stereotypes inevitably play an important role, which is one of the explanations for disastrous failures, such as Crassus at Carrhae and the Russian invasions already mentioned.

A further and significant contribution to be made by such an examination is a better insight why certain attempts were not made. After Germanicus's campaigns in Germany the only serious war effort made there was by Domitian. We may compare this with the long series of Parthian and Sassanian expeditions down to the seventh century. The difference is remarkable and can only be explained by the difference in expected gains and expected effort to be expended. Although the Germans were regarded as fierce fighters, there was no expectation of considerable profit if they were subjugated, so the conquest of Germany never became a first priority after the reign of Augustus. Even though this is obvious in principle, it will be useful to consider the image of the Germans in Roman sources in this light.

Since we are dealing not only with peoples at war but also with integrated empires, there is a related topic that may profitably be studied. When peoples were conquered, incorporated into provinces and, in due course of time, became part of an integrated empire, this entailed a process of ethnic disintegration or decomposition. This is the essence of "Romanization." The Nabataeans, the Idumaeans, and the Commageneans in the east, the Allobroges in the west, all disappeared as ethnic entities. How this happened and what was the result is not the topic of this book, but it will be useful to see how observers at the center of the empire related to such peoples during the various stages of this development. The descendants of those vanished peoples who had become inhabitants of integrated provinces were regarded in various ways which it will be interesting to trace. How did Roman aristocrats view Greeks, Syrians, or Gauls in the second century A.D.? How much regard, disrespect, or even contempt was there for those peoples who had undergone a successful process of ethnic dissolution and imperial integration? What kind of tensions did this process engender over time?

ANCIENT INFLUENCE ON EARLY MODERN AUTHORS

Because it is one of the aims of this work to trace the ancient roots of early modern racism, it will be useful here to give a few examples which illustrate the statement made above about the conceptual links between modern racism and the ancient world. An early form of racism has been recognized in the "theory of degeneration" of Georges-Louis Buffon (1707–1788), through his work *La dégénération des animaux,* which was very influential in the eighteenth and nineteenth centuries.[14] This is essentially an application of the environmental theory: Buffon writes that the white man, meaning the normal man, who truly represents humanity, has grown progressively blacker in a tropical climate and can recover his original, normal color by returning to the temperate zone. Buffon suggested an experiment whereby a number of blacks would be transported from Senegal to Denmark and kept there in isolation and under observation. It would then become clear how long it would take for such people to turn white, blonde, and blue-eyed. The opposite experiment, of transporting Danes to Senegal, was not considered although the expectation that they would turn black was exactly the premise of the theory, white being considered the norm and black a form of degeneration.[15] Buffon, it has been observed, was probably the first to employ the term "race" in something approaching its modern sense. He defines races as varieties of the species whose characters have become hereditary as a result of the continuous actions of the same causes that produce individual differences, but he was not very consistent in his usage.[16] Note that this represents a combination of external influence (climate) and heredity. It has even been suggested that racial theoretical thinking is found fully developed in Buffon's writings.[17] Buffon writes that donkeys are degenerate

---

[14] Buffon's output and popularity was remarkable; see Jean Pivetau (ed.), *Oeuvres philosophiques de Buffon* (Paris, 1954), 527f. for titles and editions. For his ideas about *physiognomics* see below.

[15] Georges-Louis Leclerc de Buffon, *Histoire naturelle générale et particulière avec la Description du Cabinet du Roy,* vol. 4 (published in 1766), "De la dégéneration des animaux," 311–374, esp. 311–313. It was the sort of experiment which the eighteenth century found fascinating. One of the best known of these is the plan, never carried out, to raise a number of children in full isolation from birth onward; cf. Roger Shattuck, *The Forbidden Experiment: the Story of the Wild Boy of Aveyron* (New York, 1980). The second part of this title refers to the famous case of a wild boy, discovered in southern France in 1800. He was studied as representing the perfect specimen of a natural man. It is worth noting that the idea of raising infants in total isolation in order to gain essential information goes back to classical antiquity. Herodotus 2.2 tells of an experiment carried out by the Egyptian Pharaoh Psammetichus who ordered two infants to be raised in isolation. In due course of time they spontaneously started using the Phrygian word for bread, which proved to the satisfaction of the Egyptians that not they, but the Phrygians, were the most ancient people on earth. The idea was revived in the twentieth century by the behavioral psychologist B. F. Skinner, who developed the "Air-Crib," a large, soundproof, germ-free, air-conditioned box designed to house infants during the first two years of life and supposed to provide a labor-saving and optimal environment during this stage. Skinner's own daughter spent most of her first two years in such a device. According to the author, the infant seemed healthy and happy and had been free of colds and other infection; cf. B. F. Skinner, "Baby in a box; the mechanical baby-tender," *Ladies' Home Journal* 62 (1945) 62: 30–31, 135–136, 138.

[16] Gustav Jahoda, *Images of Savages: Ancient Roots of Modern Prejudice in Western Culture* (London and New York, 1999), 44.

[17] Tzvetan Todorov, *Nous et les autres: La Réflexion française sur la diversité humaine* (Paris, 1989), translated into English as *On Human Diversity: Nationalism, Racism, and Exoticism in French Thought* (Cambridge, MA, 1993), 96–106, esp. 103: "We are now in a position to note that

horses, apes degenerate men. The Negro is to man what the donkey is to the horse. The Negro is man, not animal, only because white and black can procreate together. Buffon formulates his view on the influence of climate on the characteristics of man as follows: "Ever since man began to settle under different skies and to move out of one climate into another, his nature has undergone changes . . . these changes became so great and so evident that one might think that the Negro, the Laplander, and the White are different species, were it not that on the one hand we are told that originally only one man was created, while on the other we know that the White Man or Laplander or Negro, however dissimilar, are able to unite and propagate. . . ." He furthermore considers those living in the temperate climate of his own part of the world to be the most beautiful people possible. Buffon has an obsession with the aesthetics of humanity common to other racial theorists of his times, whereby ideas of beauty and ugliness are narrowly ethnocentric and dictated largely by skin color.[18] In principle Buffon believed in monogenesis, in the unity of mankind. This had been the traditional starting point for all those who accepted the truth of the Bible. Buffon was not religious, but accepted the fact that all human beings can procreate together and must therefore belong to the same species. However, there is, in his view, a definite hierarchy of subspecies in which some peoples are closer to animals and others further removed from them.

As shown in part 1, the environmental theory, central to the work of Buffon and accepted by many or most people up to the second half of the nineteenth century, originated in the Graeco-Roman world. It was widely accepted from the fifth century B.C. until late antiquity.[19] Furthermore, ancient literature is also full of claims that people degenerated by moving from one region to another. The ancient environmental theory was Buffon's point of reference, although this does not imply that his ideas were generally accepted in his own time. There is another element in Buffon's hierarchy of humanity which, as we shall see, is prominent in ancient literature, namely the criterion of sociability. The essence

---

the racialist theory in its entirety is found in Buffon's writings." This is not to say that Buffon was the first to write a racist treatise in the narrow, biological sense of the term. Several authors are candidates for primacy in this respect: Henri de Boulainvilliers (d.1722); Lord Kames (Henry Homes, 1696–1782); cf. M. Banton, *Race Relations* (London, 1967), 28; Anthony J. Barker, *The African Link: British Attitudes to the Negro in the Era of the Atlantic Slave Trade, 1550–1807* (London, 1978), 53, 61f. Kames was a prolific author; see his *Sketches of the History of Man* (Edinburgh, 2d ed. 1778; Dublin, 3rd ed. 1779, repr. of the second ed., London, 1993). He was a man who wanted to have his cake and eat it. He based his racist ideas on a polygenist (see below) approach, which he reconciled with Old Testament authority, claiming that human differentiation was due to divine intervention at the time of the Tower of Babel. He also sought to explain the compatibility of his strictly racial ideas with the environmental theory which was generally accepted at the time.

[18] See the quotations by Todorov, *On Human Diversity*, 104.

[19] For the history of the idea of environmental determinism: Franklin Thomas, *The Environmental Basis of Society: A Study in the History of Sociological Theory* (New York and London, 1925). James William Johnson, *The Formation of English Neo-Classical Thought* (Princeton, 1967), 46–48, shows how climatic determinism as found in Greek and Latin literature directly influenced the English authors of the Enlightenment from the seventeenth century onward.

of civilized people is their social adaptation; lack of this is typical of barbarians. "A people who live without the restraint of fixed laws, or of a regular government, can only be considered as a tumultuous assemblage of barbarous and independent individuals, who obey no laws but those of passion and caprice."[20] This approach echoes that of the ancient texts: the treatise *Airs, Waters, Places* and the works of Aristotle and Strabo, among others.

Buffon's contemporary David Hume (1711–1776) expressed the view (1748) that "the Negroes, and in general all the other species of men (for there are four or five different kinds) [are] naturally inferior to the whites." Later he repeats again that "nature made an original distinction between these breeds of men."[21] He does not seem to have expressed views on how nature achieved this. Voltaire, however, seeks to show that climate could *not* account for race differences, since "Negro men and Negro women, transported to the coldest countries, still produce there animals [*sic*] of their own species."[22] Unlike Buffon, Voltaire believed in polygenesis. Being an unbeliever and ignorant of the biological evidence available in his time, he had no difficulty in rejecting the unity of mankind. The different races which he distinguished therefore did not have a common origin, in his view. His ideas were adopted by many later racists, especially those who refused to admit the principle of evolution.

Kant combined two approaches in his theory about the origin of races: ". . . it is clear that the reason for it (i.e., blackness) is the hot climate. However, it is certain that a great number of generations has been needed for it to become part of the species and hereditary."[23] This shows that Kant, like Buffon, assumed without further consideration that racial characteristics are determined by external influences (climate) and then, after many generations become hereditary (i.e., acquired characters became hereditary). This combination of environmentalism and a belief in the inheritance of acquired characters became quite popular in the nineteenth century.[24] Once again, this is an extremely common approach in antiquity. Kant observes that "The Negroes of Africa have by

---

[20] Buffon, *Histoire naturelle générale,* vol. 3, English translation (London, 1817), p. 412; cf. Todorov, *On Human Diversity,* 98: "It is clear that for Buffon the term 'barbarous' is correlated with 'independent'—that is, asocial."

[21] Cited in full, below, in chapter 1. Hume, like some other authors of the second half of the eighteenth century such as Dr. Johnson, put less credence in climatic causation: Johnson *Formation,* p. 48.

[22] Voltaire, *Essai sur les moeurs et l'esprit des nations* 1 [1756] (Paris 1963), 6; English translation: Robert Bernasconi and Tommy L. Lott, *The Idea of Race* (Indianapolis, IN, 2000), 5–7. Cf. Todorov, *On Human Diversity,* 100f. Voltaire assumes that the animality of the blacks may be due to the hot climates in which apes may have ravished girls. For other authors of the Enlightenment, notably Rousseau, who were confused as regards the distinction between blacks and apes: Shulamit Volkov, "Exploring the Other: The Enlightenment's Search for the Boundaries of Humanity," in Wistrich (ed.), *Demonizing the Other,* 148–167, esp. 153f.

[23] *Physical Geography* in vols. 2 and 8 of Kant's *Gesammelte Schriften* (Berlin, 1900–66), English trans. by E. C. Eze, *Race and the Enlightenment* (Oxford, 1997), 60.

[24] For its influence in England, see Ruth Schwartz Cowan, *Sir Francis Galton and the Study of Heredity in the Nineteenth Century* (New York and London, 1985), 15–19.

nature no feeling that rises above the trifling."[25] He cites David Hume in asserting that blacks transported elsewhere and set free have still not produced a single person who has "presented anything great in art or science or any other praiseworthy quality . . ." Kant thus definitely considers the differences between races, as he sees them, to have been determined *by nature*. Obviously, the concept *by nature* derives directly from Greek ethnography and philosophy. "So fundamental is the difference between these two races of man, and it appears to be as great in regard to mental capacities as in colour." Finally, Kant asserts that "The tallest and most beautiful people on dry land are on the parallel and the degrees which run through Germany."[26] This follows the ancient Greek and Roman tradition of considering their own peoples the best in the world as determined by geography and climate. Thus Kant's aesthetics are defined more narrowly and nationalistically than those of Buffon, who was willing to regard all of those living in the temperate climates he knew of as the most beautiful.[27] Some nineteenth-century racists still allowed for the environment to play a decisive role in the formation of race, as well as hereditary factors.[28] This is not to suggest that all early modern thinkers were racists. It is the aim of this work to trace particular forms of stereotypical thinking and this necessarily ignores many authors who resisted such patterns, for instance the remarkable and courageous philosopher Helvétius (1715–1771), who firmly denies any correlation between physical and mental characteristics.[29]

[25] Immanuel Kant, *Beobachtungen über das Gefühl des Schönen und Erhabenen* (Königsberg, 1764), reprinted in *Gesammelte Schriften* ii, translated as *Observations on the Feeling of the Beautiful and Sublime* (1764), by J. T. Goldthwait (Berkeley, CA, 1960); "On National Characteristics," 110f.

[26] Eze, 59. For Kant's racism: Allen W. Wood, *Kant's Ethical Thought* (Cambridge, 1999), 3f., 206, references on 339; Eze, *Race and the Enlightenment*, 103–140; Robert B. Louden, *Kant's Impure Ethics: From Rational Beings to Human Beings* (Oxford and New York, 2000), 93–100. It is generally acknowledged that Kant cherished racist theories, but there are shades and differences of interpretation and emphasis in the evaluation of his views.

[27] There is no point in recapitulating the history of modern racism, which is the subject of many major works cited in the footnotes here. The only early racist theorists mentioned here are those who demonstrably passed on Graeco-Roman ideas and made them an integral part of their theories. There is therefore no reason to describe the views of authors such as Renan, Le Bon, Taine, and Gobineau (all discussed, for instance, in Todorov, *On Human Diversity*).

[28] E.g., Ernest Renan, *L'Avenir de la science* (published in 1890, based on his thoughts of 1848, I refer to the edition published in Paris, 1995), 214: "Les races et les climats produisent simultanément dans l'humanité les mêmes différences que le temps a montrées successives dans la suite des développements." The introduction to this edition, by Annie Petit, pp.7–45, fails to note this aspect of Renan's thinking, while asserting (p. 45) that "*l'Avenir de la science* est à la fois aux commencements et à la fin de l'oeuvre renanienne, et l'a constamment nourrie. Et c'est un ouvrage-bilan doublement."

[29] Claude-Adrien Helvétius, *de l'esprit* (Paris 1758), ed. Moutaux (Paris 1988), 404: 'Il seroit cependant facile d'appercevoir que la différence extérieure qu'on remarque, par exemple, dans la physionomie du Chinois et du Suédois, ne peut avoir aucune influence sur leur esprit . . ." For Helvétius, see Albert Keim, *Helvétius, sa vie et son œuvre: d'après ses ouvrages, des écrits divers et des documents inédits* (Paris 1907); Mordecai Grossman, *The Philosophy of Helvétius with special emphasis on the educational implications of sensationalism* (New York, 1926); on the resistance to his ideas: D.W. Smith, *Helvétius: a Study in Persecution* (Oxford, 1965).

As modern racism has been shaped by its eighteenth-century roots, so the Enlightenment adopted ideas and modes of thinking developed and accepted in the ancient world. It will be argued here that this continuity is sufficient to allow us to speak of Graeco-Roman forms of proto-racism. It should be noted that the examples cited here from the early modern authors are much concerned with skin color, a topic not systematically discussed in this book. Skin color was important to the authors of the Enlightenment and they applied to it the ideas taken from ancient authors in connection with other groups. One of the tenets of this study is that racists adapt prototypes of stereotypical thinking to the objects of their preoccupation.

The first part of the book will discuss the development of negative or hostile ideas about groups of others in antiquity, as well as ideas of the superiority of one's own group, in a more or less systematic manner. Where appropriate, it will indicate continuity by referring to later authors who adopt the ancient concepts. Unavoidably, there are interesting, related phenomena which cannot be included in this discussion. To give just one example: Aristotle assumes that all creatures which are biologically perfect reproduce themselves.[30] Those which he classifies as imperfect, such as insects and some of the reptiles, are generated spontaneously from the earth, like plants, or are the product of the fusion of rotting matter. These ideas were taken over and extended to some groups of human beings by Paracelsus in the fifteenth century and by Andrea Cesalpino, Gerolamo Cardano, and Giordano Bruno in the sixteenth. The claim was that beings such as pygmies or the American Indians had no soul and descended from another, second Adam or were generated spontaneously from the earth.[31] They were *similitudines hominis* rather than real men.

These theories raised opposition from the church as being blasphemous and heretical, but they nevertheless enjoyed popularity well into the seventeenth century.[32] They might be discussed here, because they basically deny groups of people their humanity and reduce them to the status of a kind of animal. And indeed the denial of human status to groups of human beings is relevant to any discussion of racism and will be included in this book. However, the ideas just described do not represent anything like Aristotle's original ideas, for although Aristotle may consider some foreigners bestial or brutish, and approximate

---

[30] Aristotle, *De generatione animalium* 762a 10ff.; *Meteorologica*, 381b 10. Note, however, that there was an old and traditional belief that early man was "earthborn": Empedocles, in Diels-Kranz, *Die Fragmente der Vorsokratiker* (Berlin, 6th ed. 1951), fr.6; M. R. Wright, *Empedocles: The Extant Fragments* (New Haven, 1981), no. 53, comments on pp. 215–217; Plato, *Politicus* 269B; Aristotle, *De generatione animalium* 762b; see also Herodotus 8.55: Erechtheus is said to have been γηγενής.

[31] Lewis Hanke, *Aristotle and the American Indians: a study in race prejudice in the modern world* (Bloomington, IN, 1959); Anthony Pagden, *The Fall of Natural Man: The American Indian and the Origins of Comparative Ethnology* (Cambridge, 1982), 22f. and references in notes 37 and 38.

[32] Frederickson, *Racism*, 40–42, observes that "sixteenth- and seventeenth-century Spain is critical to the history of Western racism because its attitudes and practices served as a a kind of segue between the religious intolerance of the Middle Ages and the naturalistic racism of the modern era."

slaves to animals, he does not claim that they actually are animals. Moreover, the preoccupation with the soul and the origins of primitive man, so urgent in the sixteenth century, was neither part of the intellectual interest of Graeco-Roman antiquity, nor of later racism. There is therefore no justification in tracing such theories in a work that considers ancient ideas about foreigners and minorities, and which attempts to trace direct dependence of early modern ideas on the Graeco-Roman world. It seems clear, however, that eighteenth- and nineteenth-century western thought has many concepts in common with Greek and Roman group prejudices.

CHRONOLOGY AND SUBJECT MATTER

At this point we need to clarify the chronological limits of this study and our terminology. As for the former, the starting point is not problematic. This should be the beginning of Greek prose, notably historical prose, and therefore we can safely begin systematic analysis with Herodotus, although we may have recourse to earlier sources as needed. Herodotus is the first author to devote extensive discussion to the relationship between Greeks and non-Greeks and this must therefore be our first major point of reference. It is far harder to determine where to stop. Ideally all of antiquity should be taken into account, even though this book is rather long as it is. Lack of space is a feeble excuse which a serious author should never use, just as lack of time never is a proper reason to pass over a truly relevant topic in a lecture.[33] Clearly the Roman imperial period should be covered systematically. Fourth-century pagan literature will be included, although in a less systematic manner.[34] It was my impression that it would not be profitable to do more than that, because the essentials of the patterns analyzed in this study do not change thereafter. The next decision then was whether to include non-pagan texts of the Christian Roman Empire. Or rather: the major decision to be taken was the inclusion or exclusion of Christian literature. There is no question that this would be important and interesting. Such treatment then should also include non-patristic texts of the Christian Empire, such as legal material. Finally, it is clear that, once such sources are included, they should cover the field systematically from the beginning till late antiquity and perhaps beyond. Christian attitudes, it seems, were partly similar and partly different from the start. Paul writes: "For as many of you as were baptized into Christ have put on Christ. There is neither Jew nor Greek, there is neither slave nor free, there is neither male nor female; for you are all one in Christ Jesus. And if you are Christ's, then you are Abraham's offspring,

---

[33] A lecturer who is fortunate enough to get the undivided attention during fifty minutes of an audience, whatever the size, consisting of colleagues, students, and perhaps others who are interested, should not imply that those people ought to listen to him for a hundred minutes. The average lecturer himself does not want to listen to anybody else for more than fifty minutes.

[34] Chauvot, *Opinions romaines face aux Barbares* (1998).

heirs according to promise."[35] Whatever the interpretation of such words over the centuries and whatever the practice, it is a different starting point, a different approach that deserves attention in its own right and should not be included as a secondary issue in this study. The chronological limits therefore cover fifth-century Greece and will include Rome down to the third century with occasional forays into the fourth century. Christian texts are not considered in any systematic manner, nor are Jewish sources whatever the language because the Jews never became part of mainstream Greek and Roman society.

It is not my aim to compare the Graeco-Roman world with contemporary and non-Western societies. The literature on these subjects is massive and anyone interested in broad theoretical frameworks of racism can find them there. Related work in social science will be considered from time to time for the sake of clarification. I do not have the expertise—and it may not be possible for those who do—to describe manifestations of group hatred in antiquity in terms of mental illnesses. What would be considered delusional or paranoid in one culture may be something quite different in another. The aim here is to trace ideas and attitudes in antiquity as they developed over time, while keeping in mind the impact they may have had in more recent times. No such treatment has yet been undertaken and there is therefore no need to justify the attempt. The term "proto-racism" will be used to describe patterns of thought in antiquity, as it will be argued that ancient views of other people and the groups to which they belonged took forms that were adopted by early modern racists. It will be argued that the definitions adopted below amply justify the application of the term proto-racism to describe attitudes towards others which were widespread in antiquity.

CONCEPTS AND DEFINITIONS

The definition of terminology will serve two purposes. First, we need clearly defined terminology to apply to ancient phenomena and, second, we need to clarify our own approach. If we want to determine whether there were indeed early forms of racial prejudice and racism in Greece or Rome, it must be clearly understood what we mean by the terms *race, racism, racialism,* and *racial prejudice.*[36] Other terms which require precise definitions are *ethnic groups,*

---

[35] *Galatians* 3.27–9: ὅσοι γὰρ εἰς Χριστὸν ἐβαπτίσθητε, Χριστὸν ἐνεδύσασθε· οὐκ ἔνι Ἰουδαῖος οὐδὲ Ἕλλην, οὐκ ἔνι δοῦλος οὐδὲ ἐλεύθερος, οὐκ ἔνι ἄρσεν καὶ θῆλυ· πάντες γὰρ ὑμεῖς εἷς ἐστε ἐν Χριστῷ Ἰησοῦ. εἰ δὲ ὑμεῖς Χριστοῦ, ἄρα τοῦ Ἀβραὰμ σπέρμα ἐστέ, κατ᾽ ἐπαγγελίαν κληρονόμοι.

[36] Works consulted (a tiny selection only of the existing literature): R. Benedict, *Race and Racism* (London, 1942). While attacking racism, Benedict accepted the existence of races. Yet, Benedict largely followed the opinions of her teacher, Franz Boas, who, certainly no racist, in *The Mind of Primitive Man* (1911) argued for the precedence of culture over race. Yet he too was ambivalent: the German translation of Boas' work, *Kultur und Rasse* (Leipzig, 1914), 236f. ends with a call for racial hygiene. For a collection of his work: George W. Stocking (ed.), *The Shaping of American*

group prejudice, and *xenophobia*. Nobody would want to claim that the Elder Cato cherished an unreserved affection for his contemporary Greeks, but we can only decide if his dislike should be considered racial prejudice or another form of prejudice, or no prejudice at all, if we first decide exactly what we mean by prejudice in general, and racial prejudice in particular. Since this is a historical study the methods, the available material, and the questions asked will be essentially and conceptually different from those found in the works of social scientists or psychologists. In establishing my definitions I will follow an order of priorities which is slightly different from that of many historical studies. This book aims to explore early forms of racism. It is not concerned with race and I will therefore define *racism* before discussing *race*. As will be seen below, I have good reasons for this: I want to understand racism and this means I have to work with the concept of race as devised by racists. I accept the opinion of those who assert that "race" in the sense in which it is used by the racist does not exist. If, however, I adopt a definition of race which seems more or less reasonable or rational, then it is impossible to trace patterns of racism, which are by definition irrational.[37]

Anthropology, 1883–1911: A Franz Boas Reader (Chicago, 1974); for a brief and representative statement: "Instability of Human Types" in Bernasconi and Lott (eds.), *The Idea of Race*, 84–88. Influential works that appeared after World War II: M. Banton, *Race Relations*; *The Idea of Race* (London, 1977); *Racial Theories* (Cambridge, 1987). Banton's works certainly do not ignore history, but they represent social science and are therefore different in outlook and method from this book. See also: P. Mason, *Race Relations* (London, 1970); Robert Miles, *White Man's Country: Racism in British Politics* (London, 1984). For sociological studies of the acceptance and rejection of the concept of race: Leonard Lieberman, "The Debate Over Race: A Study in the Sociology of Knowledgy," *Phylon* (1968), 127–141; Leonard Lieberman and Larry T. Reynolds, "The Debate Over Race Revisited: An Empirical Investigation," *Phylon* (1978), 333–43; L. T. Reynolds, "A Retrospective on 'Race': The Career of a Concept," *Sociological Focus* 25 (1992), 1–14. These papers trace the reception of the concept in the various branches of the social sciences and other sciences and offer ideas about the social position of the academics involved. It should be noted that the references are exclusively to the bibliography in English and the sociological data taken only from the United States. More relevant for the present study are works about racism. For the history of racism: Léon Poliakov, *Le mythe aryen: essay sur les sources du racisme et des nationalismes* (Paris, 1971); translation: *The Aryan Myth* (New York, 1996); *Le Racisme* (Paris, 1976); *The History of Antisemitism*, 4 vols. (London, 1974–1986); George L. Mosse, *Toward the Final Solution: A History of European Racism* (London, 1978); Maurice Olender (ed.), *Pour Léon Poliakov, le racisme: mythes et sciences* (Paris, 1981); Albert Memmi, *Le racisme. Description, définition, traitement* (Paris, 1982), which was available to me only in the German translation: *Rassismus* (Frankfurt/Main, 1987); Todorov, *Nous et les autres*; Jahoda, cited above; Berel Lang (ed.), *Race and Racism in Theory and Practice* (Lanham, MD, 1999); S. E. Babbitt and S. Campbell, *Racism and Philosophy* (Ithaca and London, 1999). P. Salmon, "Racisme ou refus de la différence dans le monde gréco-romain," *DHA* 10 (1984), 75–98. Note also the recent readers: Martin Bulmer and John Solomos (eds.), *Racism* (Oxford, 1999); Bernasconi and Lott, *The Idea of Race*.

[37] Bernard Lewis, *Race and Slavery in the Middle East: An Historical Enquiry* (New York and Oxford, 1990), chapter 2, at p. 17, accepts for "race" what he describes as "current American usage." This, he says, exclusively denotes "such major divisions as white, black, Mongolian and the like." In itself this is unsatisfactory, as will be argued below. No less important, these divisions are irrelevant if we consider Graeco-Roman antiquity, and if I were to adopt this usage, it would follow automatically that there was no racism at the time. That, of course, would not worry classicists and

RACISM AND RACIALISM

It is essential to adopt a proper definition of racism. The adoption of a definition that is too narrow and too specific will result in a failure to recognize
manifestations of racism for what they are, because they do not correspond
precisely with the strict criteria imposed by the definition. A definition that is
too broad and too vague makes it possible to describe virtually every form of
discrimination as racism. Both phenomena occur frequently and are harmful for
intellectual and moral clarity. There are numerous definitions of racism, varying
from a narrow to a broad interpretation. A British sociologist who has published widely on racism, Michael Banton, defines racism and prejudice as follows: "By racism is meant the doctrine that a man's behaviour is determined by
stable inherited characters deriving from separate racial stocks having distinctive attributes and usually considered to stand to one another in relations of
superiority and inferiority." Prejudice, although related to racism, is somewhat
different: it has been defined as "a generalization existing prior to the situation
in which it is invoked, directed toward people, groups, or social institutions,
which is accepted and defended as a guide to action in spite of its discrepancies
with the objective facts."[38] This definition of racism is very precise and clearly
refers to the form encountered in modern Europe.[39] However, it ignores a number of features usually included in racism: it only refers to judgments of the
behavior of man and not to his moral qualities, inborn gifts, or physical appearance. These are almost always the subject of racist views. Thus it would deny
the qualification of racism to claims that a certain people has a distinctive smell
or an ugly skull, for instance, since these are not forms of behavior. Moreover,

---

historians who deny there was such racism, but it will indeed bother those who study, for instance,
the Nürnberger race laws. The Nazis were obsessed with groups of people who do not fit current
American usage as defined by Lewis. I should add that this is no attempt to criticize Professor
Lewis's fascinating analysis of the history of prejudice and slavery in the Middle East.

[38] Banton, *Race Relations,* 8, referring also to W. Vickery and M. Opler, "A Redefinition of
Prejudice for Purposes of Social Science Research," *Human Relations* 1 (1948), 419–428. For
discussion of Banton and Van den Berghe's definitions: see Robert Miles, "Theories of Racism,"
in Bulmer and Solomos, *Racism* (1999), 348f., reprinted from Miles, *Racism* (London, 1989). Cf. the
following definition in an anthropological textbook: Marvin Harris, *The Rise of Anthropological
Theory* (New York, 1968), 81: "According to the doctrine of scientific racism, the significant sociocultural differences and similarities among human populations are the dependent variables of group-
restricted hereditary drives and attitudes. Racist explanations thus depend on the correlation of
hereditary endowment and group behavioral specialties." This definition is concerned only with
"scientific racism," but even so I cannot find it fully satisfactory. The focus is solely on behavior,
besides ignoring the element of value judgment which is an essential feature of racism. The definition is taken from a chapter on the rise of racial determinism (pp. 80–107) which describes the
irrationality of the theory very well.

[39] Similarly, Benedict Anderson, *Imagined Communities: Reflections on the Origin and Spread of
Nationalism* (London and New York, 1983), 149–151, who sees racism as having its origin in
European ideologies of *class*, rather than in those of nation. Racism, he says, is a national phenomenon which does not extend beyond the border and outside Europe it belongs to colonialism. As will
be clear from this Introduction, I think this approach is unduly restrictive and restricted.

it describes racism as a way of looking at others and does not relate to forms of aggression or the actual behavior of the racist. Furthermore, it implies, but does not clarify explicitly, that racism is an attitude which denies the individuality of human beings. It regards them exclusively in terms of a collective and does not allow for individual differences. In any case, this definition does not in fact allow for the existence of nonwestern or ancient racism, for the phrase "stable inherited characters deriving from separate racial stocks" clearly suggests the biological determinism which characterizes modern racism.

A topic which it will not be possible to treat here is the work of fascist and national-socialist ancient historians from the 1920s till the end of World War II. Although interesting, this is not immediately relevant here. Ancient historians, such as Helmut Berve, who supported the German Nazi or Italian fascist regime and accepted their ideologies, did not trace ancient predecessors of the racist, nationalist and imperialist ideas that they supported. They tended to write about the topics favored in the classical studies of those times with a contemporary ideological slant.[40] They were racist, but did not consider the nature of Greek and Roman imperialism or the development of racist ideas in antiquity. At another level, I have not joined in the debate about Martin Bernal's *Black Athena*. Although it touches on some of my current themes, I am convinced to do so would only confuse the main issues of this study without contributing anything to the discussion of Bernal's topics.[41]

Pierre L. Van den Berghe, an American anthropologist, also gives a narrow description of racism: "It is important to stress that racism, unlike ethnocentrism, is not a universal phenomenon. Members of all human societies have a fairly good opinion of themselves, compared with members of other societies, but the good opinion is frequently based on his own creations. Only a few human groups have deemed themselves superior because of the contents of their gonads."[42] This concept of racism has clearly been determined by its use in recent history, in the 1930s and 1940s, and Banton and Van den Berghe have formulated their definition to make it fit this particular historical situation. Their approach would make it futile to look for racism anywhere but in modern,

[40] For Berve, see the interesting article by Stefan Rebenich, "Der Fall Helmut Berve," *Chiron* 31 (2000), 457–496. Berve's writing about Alexander and Caesar were colored by and adapted to the Führerkult; his view of ancient society was racist and followed the demands of National Socialism, but he did not study racism in antiquity. See further the recent issue of *The Classical Bulletin* 76 (2000) with papers by E. Christian Kopff, "Italian Fascism and the Roman Empire," pp.109–115; Peter Aicher, "Mussolini's Forum and the Myth of Augustan Rome," pp.117–140; John T. Quinn, "The Ancient Rome of Adolf Hitler," pp.141–156; Richard F. Thomas, "Goebbels' *Georgics*," pp.157–168. The other papers are concerned with matters of racism and ideology in the United States.

[41] Martin Bernal, *Black Athena: the Afroasiatic Roots of Classical Civilization*, 2 vols. (New Brunswick, NJ, 1987–1991); Mary R. Lefkowitz and Guy MacLean Rogers (eds.), *Black Athena Revisited* (Chapel Hill, NC, 1996); Wim M. J. van Binsbergen (ed.), *Black Athena: Ten Years After* (Leiden, 1996); Bernal, *Black Athena Writes Back: Martin Bernal Responds to His Critics* (Durham, NC, 2002).

[42] Pierre L. Van den Berghe, *Race and Racism* (New York, 1967), 12.

western civilization. It assumes that there are forms of chauvinism, prejudice, and discrimination everywhere among humanity, but the term racism is here applied only to discrimination on the basis of presumed biological differences.

It is striking how public perspective of the essence of racism has shifted even during the past fifty years. During the second half of the nineteenth- and the first half of the twentieth century, racist attitudes, at least in Europe, focused on groups that were physically largely undistinguishable from the majority. This was true for the Jews and for other minorities. Although much was made of presumed physical differences, it remained a fact that many or most Jews looked like their non-Jewish neighbors. Nobody would deny that the prejudices against Jews, Gypsies, and other groups constituted a form of racism. The racists themselves were convinced that these groups belonged to another race: thus the Semitic race was invented. Many Nazi Germans with family names ending in -ovits were firmly convinced that the speakers of Slavic languages belonged to a different and inferior race. After World War II, however, the emancipation of the dark-skinned population in the United States attracted particular attention, both in the United States and in Europe. Here racism had a group for its object that looked different from the majority. Such variations affect both racists and their critics. The external appearance of the body received more attention over the past decades, and people tend to forget that racism could exist just as well where physical differences are insignificant. A lucid definition of racism should take more than one variation of it into account. One can go further: racism can be understood properly only if it is recognized that it assumes many different forms, depending on the subject and target groups.[43] Sometimes it focuses on groups showing real physical and imaginary mental differences and sometimes on differences imaginary in both spheres. It is essential to adopt an understanding and definition of racism that is broad enough to encompass its varying manifestations over time, while recognizing its essential features. A failure to do so has serious consequences: it encourages people to ignore racism if it does not fit a narrow definition or it may lead to the opposite result, frequently encountered in our times. Racism then becomes a vague form of imprecation directed at a hated enemy or power.

Racism therefore should be given a broader and yet precise meaning. The sociologist Albert Memmi has carefully considered the matter of definitions. At one stage he proposed the following: "Racism is the valuation, generalized and definitive, of biological differences, real or imaginary, to the advantage of the accuser and the disadvantage of his victim, in order to justify aggression."[44] This is a definition in the narrower sense, since all racism is held to be focused on biological differences. Memmi later revised his definition: "Racism is the valuation, generalized and definitive, of differences, real or imaginary, to the

---

[43] Frederickson's *Racism* presents the development of various brands of racism while focusing on Europe, the colonies, and America.

[44] Albert Memmi, "Le racisme est la valorisation, généralisée et définitive, de diffférences biologiques, réelles ou imaginaires, au profit de l'accusateur et au détriment de sa victime, afin de justifier un aggression," in "Essai de définition du racisme," *La Nef* 19–20 (1964), 41–47.

advantage of the accuser and the disadvantage of his victim, in order to justify his privileges or aggression."[45] This definition is broader because it drops the narrow focus on merely biological differences and includes all differences. Furthermore, it does not require active aggression to be part of racist behavior, but proposes that such behavior may have the purpose of justifying existing inequality. Memmi argues that it is possible to use either definition, as long as we recognize that racism always entails the interaction of two components: fear and aggression. This is clearly an advance, since it makes it possible for us to recognize racism as a significant phenomenon outside the recent European context. A difficulty of this definition, however, is that it leaves hardly any difference between racism and ethnic prejudice. To be specific: it does not explain why it is racism to say that members of a group suffer from inborn mental inferiority, whereas it is ethnic prejudice to claim that they have bad manners. More recently it has been argued that racism cannot be identified exclusively as an ideology with a specific biological content or reference. It is thus described as "any argument which suggests that the human species is composed of discrete groups in order to legitimate inequality between those groups of people."[46] This definition has the same advantages and the same problems as Memmi's later one.

Again, both definitions, like that of Banton, only imply but do not specify the implications of such an attitude for the position of an individual. The essence of racism, and, to a lesser extent, of group prejudice, is that individuals are exclusively regarded as representatives of the group to which they belong. They are assumed to have all the characteristics usually ascribed to the group.

In any case, reducing the emphasis on the biological ingredient of racism makes it feasible to look for it, or something related to it, in nonwestern and earlier cultures. Philip Mason, a British anthropologist, describes how a broader definition allows us to use the concept of racism in analyzing nonwestern cultures:

> In a small tribe, the ruler was usually the personal choice of his subjects, from among those qualified by birth; there is a consensus of opinion in his favour so long as he governs within certain limits of custom and consultation. But where the state becomes larger, he and his officials or nobles need an impersonal sanction [. . .] surprisingly often, the rulers have hit on the same device. They have applied the sanction of religion to the social system and succeeded in establishing myths which stated or implied that the division of society into separate categories and descent was divinely ordained [. . .] These are early forms of relationships between groups

[45] Albert Memmi, *Le racisme* (1982), German translation: *Rassismus* (1987), II: Definitionen, esp. 103; 151; 164–177. See also W. J. Wilson, *Power, Racism and Privilege* (New York, 1972), cited by Bulmer and Solomos, *Racism*, 4: "racism is an ideology of racial domination based on (i) beliefs that a designated racial group is either biologically or culturally inferior and (ii) the use of such beliefs to rationalize or prescribe the racial group's treatment in society, as well as to explain its social position and acomplishment."

[46] R. Miles in Bulmer and Solomos, 350f. with reference to John Rex, *Race Relations in Sociological Theory* (London, 1970), 159.

who are really divided but the fact is that they are at different stages of development. But to the rulers, it seems—and they encourage the belief—that the differences are inherent and due to their descent. This is the beginning of race relations.[47]

Mason asserts that inequality or oppression of certain groups is often justified by the myth of a distinct lineage in the cadre of an order imposed by a divine will. According to Mason, such myths arise in many cases following the conquest of one ethnic unit by another (he gives the example of the Tutsi and the Hutu). In citing this I do not mean to imply, of course, that Graeco-Roman antiquity is not "western." It is western, but it is not modern. If it can be shown that there are forms of racism in nonwestern culture, it follows that it may also have existed in earlier stages of western society. In fact it is not hard to find Greek and Roman parallels for the phenomena described by Mason.

At this point it may be useful to add some definitions given by a number of standard works of reference, as representing commonly accepted thinking and usage. The *Encyclopaedia Britannica* defines *racism* as "the theory or idea that there is a causal link between inherited physical traits and certain traits of personality, intellect, or culture and, combined with it, the notion that some races are inherently superior to others." Here the applicability of the term racism depends on the factor of heredity. Quite clearly the concept of heredity is important in considering this subject and will have to be taken into account. However, as observed above, some of those who have written on the subject take an even wider view. In this view, presumed physical and personality traits are seen as generally immutable and stable, but not necessarily biologically determined. The essence of racism in this case is that groups are regarded as having characteristics over which they have no control of their own and which are determined by other factors, such as climate, geography, or hereditary factors that cannot be influenced by men themselves. In other words, biological determinism should not be regarded as *the* essential ingredient of racist attitudes. Environmental determinism can just as well be a key to racism, or indeed any other form of determinism, such as astrology, which ignores individuality, personal characteristics, and free will in the shaping of humanity.

The *Oxford English Dictionary* of 1910 contained no reference to the word racism, which shows what a recent concept it is. In the second edition, racism is defined as "a. The theory that distinctive human characteristics and abilities are determined by race. b. = Racialism." *Racialism*, an unfortunate word,[48] is then defined in *Oxford's* second edition as follows: "Belief in the superiority of a particular race leading to prejudice and antagonism towards people of other races, especially those in close proximity who may be felt as a threat to one's

---

[47] P. Mason, *Race Relations* 72f.

[48] H. W. Fowler and F. G. Fowler, *The King's English* (Oxford, 3rd ed. 1931), 51: "The ugly words *racial* and *coastal* themselves might well be avoided except in the rare cases where *race* and *coast* used adjectivally will not do the work . . . ; and they should not be made precedents for new formations. If *language* is better than *linguistic,* much more *race* than *racial*; . . ." The new formations appeared in spite of the Fowlers' warning and thus we are stuck with "racialism," an ugly word for an ugly phenomenon.

cultural and racial integrity or economic well-being." A slightly different definition tries to clarify the difference between racism and racialism: *"Racialism*
does not refer so much to the doctrine (sc. of racism) as to the practice of it,
though it is often loosely used to refer to activities that serve the interests of a
particular racial group."[49] Since the opposite view also exists, using racialism
for the theory and racism for the practice,[50] it would be preferable to stop using
racialism and to use racism, properly defined, in both senses. In some versions,
the definitions of racism and racialism depend on the definition of race, and we
should turn our attention to this concept also. First, however, it is appropriate to
observe that no single definition will ever satisfy everybody, for racism is not a
scientific theory or concept, but a complex of ideas, attitudes, and forms of
behavior which are themselves by definition irrational.

Racism is never based on solid facts, objectively analyzed; it changes over
time and between peoples, depending on a multitude of factors. It mixes up
inherited features with cultural phenomena and confuses reality and fantasy,
language and religion, real and nonexistent differences. In its interpretation it
always distorts the facts for its own purposes, for its aim is always to prove that
the other group is inferior and the racist superior, and that these qualities are
permanent and cannot be changed.[51] Hence it claims that the attributed characteristics are not subject to control by those so characterized. They come from
the inside, that is, from essential traits of the body, or from the outside, from
climate and geography.[52] Moreover, they are collective and override any individual differences that may be the result of education, personal circumstances
or a human will. Thus racism denies reality and is therefore almost impossible
to describe objectively in realistic terms to everybody's satisfaction. It is interesting to see that the definition of "racial discrimination" in British law works

[49] Banton, loc. cit.

[50] Todorov, *On Human Diversity*, 90: "The word 'racism' in its usual sense, actually designates
two very different things. On the one hand, it is a matter of *behavior*, . . . ; on the other hand, it is a
matter of *ideology*, a doctrine concerning human races. . . . In order to keep these two separate, I
shall adopt the distinction that sometimes obtains between 'racism', a term designating behavior,
and 'racialism', a term reserved for doctrines."

[51] Thus Ernest Renan asserts: "Les phénomènes, par exemple, qui signalèrent l'eveil de la conscience se retracent dans l'éternelle enfance de ces races non perfectibles, restées comme des tém-
oins de ce qui se passa aux premiers jours de l'homme." See Ernest Renan, *L'avenir de la science*
(Paris, 1890, edited in 1995), 214. Cf. G. Jahoda, *Images of Savages*, part 3: "The Image of the
savage as child-like," esp. 132–134: "Savagery as the infancy of humanity."

[52] For an example we may cite the racist author Gustave Le Bon, *Lois psychologiques de l'évolution des peuples* (Paris, 1894), translated as *The Psychology of Peoples* (1924, repr. New York,
1974), 37: "A negro or a Japanese may easily take a university degree or become a lawyer; the sort
of varnish he thus acquires is however quite superficial, and has no influence on his mental constitution. What no education can give him, because they are created by heredity alone are the forms of
thought, the logic, and above all the character of the Western man." Note that the reprint, published
by Arno Press in their series "Perspectives in Social Inquiry," contains no word of explanation by
the advisory editors of the series about the nature of this book, the aim of which is "to describe the
psychological characteristics which constitute the soul of races, and to show how the history of a
people and its civilisation are determined by these characteristics" (p. xvii).

well in practice thanks to the broad interpretation of "racial group" accepted in the *Race Relations Act*, which will be cited more extensively below.

A description that comes close to my views of the essence of racism was recently offered by G. M. Frederickson: '[Racism] originates from a mindset that regards "them" as different from "us" in ways that are permanent and unbridgeable. This sense of difference provides a motive or rationale for using our power advantage to treat the ethnoracial Other in ways that we would regard as cruel or unjust if applied to members of our own group."[53]

I would define racism as follows: "an attitude towards individuals and groups of peoples which posits a direct and linear connection between physical and mental qualities. It therefore attributes to those individuals and groups of peoples collective traits, physical, mental, and moral, which are constant and unalterable by human will, because they are caused by hereditary factors or external influences, such as climate or geography." The essence of racism is that it regards individuals as superior or inferior because they are believed to share imagined physical, mental, and moral attributes with the group to which they are deemed to belong, and it is assumed that they cannot change these traits individually. This is held to be impossible, because these traits are determined by their physical makeup.

ETHNIC PREJUDICE

Rien en général de plus ridicule et de plux faux que
les portraits qu'on fait du caractère des Peuples divers.
—*Helvétius*[54]

Helvétius found it obvious that one cannot characterize entire peoples over time as if they were a single individual at a specific moment. "It has been said that the French are cheerful; this is repeated forever. People fail to notice that our present adversity has forced the rulers to impose considerable taxes on the land and that the French nation therefore cannot be cheerful; since the class of the farmers constitutes by itself two thirds of the people, it is needy and the needy cannot be cheerful." Or, more succinctly: "The geographical position of Greece is always the same: why are the Greeks of today different from the Greeks of the past?"[55] The eighteenth-century French philosopher was rare in his firm and consistent rejection of collective stereotypes. He had few predecessors and few

[53] Frederickson, *Racism*, 9.

[54] Helvétius, *de l'esprit*, 409, note a.

[55] Ibid., 409. This is echoed by Paul-Henri Dietrich d'Holbach, *Le Système social: Principes naturels de la morale et de la politique, avec un examen de l'influence du gouvernement sur les moeurs* (Paris, 1773), part 3, chapter 1, which contains criticism of environmental determinism and indeed of all forms of determinism, criticizing Montesquieu in particular. He ascribes the cause of corruption and degeneracy—which is his topic in this chapter—to the form of government of nations. See Pierre Naville, *D'Holbach et la philosophie scientifique au xviii* siècle* (Paris 2d ed. 1967), "le système de la Nature," pp. 227–310.

followers. A few words must therefore be said about ethnic prejudice. This study gives pride of place among the prejudices to what I call "proto-racism." I am well aware that, in doing so, I am influenced by the fact that racism is the kind of prejudice our generations are best acquainted with. Both in Europe and in the United States the twentieth century concentrated on presumed racial differences more than on any other distinctions. It is therefore interesting in itself to trace what might be the ancient origins of racist attitudes. However, this should not lead us to ignore other forms of prejudice. Nowadays many European countries have movements hostile to immigrant minorities, who deny that they are racist. Indeed, when they demand that the immigrants conform to the traditional cultural and social values of the host country this cannot properly be called racism, since it allows for the possibility of such change. We have to describe them as intolerant and xenophobic, rather than racist.[56]

Even if this study succeeds in showing that proto-racism was a significant phenomenon in antiquity, it may well be the case that the distinction between various forms of prejudice is more important to us than it was to Greeks and Romans. It is therefore essential to give other prejudices their due, even though particular attention has to be paid to proto-racism in order to demonstrate the relevance of this concept. There should be no disagreement as to the existence of ethnic prejudice or xenophobia in antiquity, even though there may be marked differences in the evaluation of these phenomena, but the existence of proto-racism is not obvious.

First, it is important to note that one should not only consider ethnic prejudice, but also other forms of group prejudice. Whatever can be said about ethnic prejudice may also be true of prejudices regarding members of a certain religion, the inhabitants of a specific region of a country, or any other group of people assumed to have something in common. The major difference between racism and ethnic and other group prejudices is that such prejudices do not deny the possibility of change at an individual or collective level in principle. In these other forms of prejudice, the presumed group characteristics are not by definition held to be stable, unalterable, or imposed from the outside through physical factors: biology, climate, or geography. It is, of course, possible to think in racist terms without using the word "race"; another term, such as "difference," may do just as well.[57] Both racist attitudes and ethnic prejudice treat a whole nation or other group as a single individual with a single personality. The varied individuality of the members of such groups is ignored in both cases, but

[56] It is easy to see how such distinctions may become blurred, for instance in the following pronouncement by Pim Fortuyn, the assassinated founder of a Dutch anti-immigrant party: "Christian inhabitants of the Netherlands, like those on the Veluwe, morally have more rights than Islamic immigrants, because Christians have contributed for centuries to building our country" (statement made on March 2, 2002, which I translated and cited from the party's Website: www.pim-fortuyn.nl, s.v. 'Uitspraken'). Here we see that religion, curiously combined with regionalism, is regarded as the vehicle that should endow privileges to a specific group because of presumed inherited merit.

[57] Claude Lévi-Strauss, *Race et Histoire* (Paris, 1952), notes that racism focuses on imaginary characteristics of biological races and then focuses on the manner in which cultural differences tend to be perceived. This, to some extent, blurs the difference between racism and ethnic prejudice.

ethnic prejudice, as distinct from racism, maintains some flexibility towards the individual.

We should also be clear about the use of *prejudice*. I accept the following definition: "In its broad etymological sense, prejudice—prejudgment—is a term applied to categorical generalizations based on inadequate data and without sufficient regard for individual differences. . . . The stereotype is distinguished from the prejudgment only by a greater degree of rigidity. Prejudgment occurs where facts are not available. But stereotypy is a process which shows little concern for facts even when they are available."[58]

Whether our definition of racism is accepted or not, at this stage it will suffice to note that some of the other definitions are also broad enough to include forms of prejudice that are not western and not recent in date. They would certainly justify considering the existence of something called proto-racism in Graeco-Roman antiquity. After considering racism and racialism, it is now appropriate to consider whether a useful definition of race, in a sense relevant to the present study, is available.

RACE

Not all meanings of the term *race* will concern us here.[59] It may also be observed that all the authors who write about racism are careful to give a precise definition of racism as they see it, but race is less often defined in these works.[60] A particular difficulty is that the usage of the term race has changed considerably over time.[61] What these meanings have in common, however, ist that they refer to a common descent or origin. The term race is therefore no longer used in the sense of "a tribe" or "a people," as is common in some of the older literature,[62] for we no longer accept the idea that a nation or people can be seen

---

[58] Nathan W. Ackerman and Marie Jahoda, *Anti-Semitism and Emotional Disorder: A Psycho-analytic Interpretation* (New York, 1950), 3f.

[59] According to the *OED Online* (2000), the term "race" occurs first in English between 1500 and 1520 in a poem *The Dance of the Sevin Deadly Sins* by William Dunbar, *Poems* 26.50. Among those who followed the sin of Envy he lists: "And flatteris in to menis facis; | And bakbyttaris of sindry racis, | To ley that had delyte." It is used here in the sense of "a set or class of persons." In French it is first used in its modern sense by François Bernier in 1684; see "A New Division of Earth" published in the *Journal des Savants*, April, 1684, English trans. in R. Bernasconi and T. L. Lott, *The Idea of Race* 1–4. It appears in this sense in the sixth edition of the *Dictionnaire de L'Académie française* (1835): "Race, se dit, par extension, d'une multitude d'hommes qui sont originaires du même pays, et se ressemblent par les traits du visage, par la conformation extérieure. La race caucasienne. La race mongole. La race malaise. Les habitants de ce royaume, de cette province sont une belle race d'hommes." Note the characteristic insistence on aesthetics in this example.

[60] Ashley Montagu, *The Idea of Race* (Lincoln, Nebraska, 1965), 7, observes that the term is of recent and obscure origin and that concepts of race are unsatisfactory and meaningless.

[61] Bulmer and Solomos, *Racism*, 7–9.

[62] There are similar difficulties in understanding the Greek terms ἔθνος and γένος; cf. C. P. Jones, "ἔθνος and γένος in Herodotus," *Classial Quarterly* 46 (1996), 315–320.

to have a common ancestor.[63] The same goes for the traditional use of race for "a group of several tribes or peoples, regarded as forming a distinct ethnical stock." Even if it was common in antiquity to think of peoples and tribes in terms of common descent, we should avoid doing so ourselves. This book will not, therefore, use the term race to refer to a "people" or a "tribe," because it suggests common descent, sometimes with the connotation of purity of lineage. I will thus take the liberty to insert "people" instead of "race" where appropriate, even when I cite translations of ancient texts made by others. In this connection I shall also avoid the the term "race-hatred" or "racial hatred." This may be seen as purist, but it suggests that human races exist, which they do not, as will be observed below. The term racist hatred better indicates that this is an irrational hatred of something that does not exist in reality.

In order to cover various approaches to the problem it might be useful to consider legal definitions in various countries. The British *Race Relations Act* provides the following: ". . . 'Racial group' means a group of persons defined by reference to colour, race, nationality or ethnic or national origins, and references to a person's racial group refer to any racial group into which he falls."[64] Thus, racial group is a broader concept than race and includes categories which are not conceptually problematic, such as nationality and national origins. The problematic concept of race has been interpreted here as indicating "group descent, a group of geographical origin and a group history." Thus the members of a race should share a common color, and a common physique based on common ancestors, and they are to be distinguished from other inhabitants of the same region.[65] As already observed above, this definition is intended to be used in cases of racial discrimination brought before the court. As such it serves a practical purpose and may well serve the legal profession and the courts satisfactorily in spite of the fact that biologists and most social scientists would not accept it as reflecting reality. This was made clear in the verdict in an appeal in 1972, for instance, where it was noted: "within the human race, there are very few, if any, distinctions which are scientifically recognized as racial."[66]

---

[63] Lewis, *Race and Slavery in the Middle East*, note 1 on p. 109f. relates that in 1940 the British Army recognized the relevance for its recruits of "four and only four races—English, Scottish Welsh, and Irish."

[64] *Race Relations Act 1976, ss 1(1) (b), 3(1)*, cited in [1983] 1 *All England Law Reports* 1062–1072 at 1065, appeal of Mandla and another v. Dowell Lee and another before the House of Lords. This concerns the case of a Headmaster who refused to admit a Sikh boy to school unless he removed his turban and cut his hair. The appeal, which was allowed, claimed that this represented discrimination against the Sikhs as a "racial group."

[65] Speech of Lord Templeman in the case cited above, p.1072.

[66] Lord Fraser of Tullybelton, op. cit., p. 1066, citing with approval the view of Lord Simon in an earlier case (*London Borough Ealing Council v Race Relations Board* [1972] AC 342, [1972] 1 All ER 105, HL): "Moreover, 'racial' is not a term of art, either legal or, I surmise, scientific. I apprehend that anthropologists would dispute how far the word 'race' is biologically at all relevant to the species amusingly called homo sapiens." This is entirely appropriate, except that it is not just the anthropologists, but also, and even more so, the biologists who dispute the biological relevance of the word "race."

This illustrates very well how complex and slippery the idea of race continues to be. In the words of Lord Simon: "This is rubbery and elusive language—understandably when the draftsman is dealing with so unprecise a concept as 'race' in its popular sense and endeavouring to leave no loophole for evasion."[67]

These problems are again illustrated very well by a later case against the licensee of a public house, the Cat and Mutton, in London, who refused to serve gypsies, putting up a sign saying "Sorry, no travellers"[68] (travellers being a term often used for gypsies). In this case it had therefore to be shown that the gypsies are a "racial group" according to the law, meaning that they were regarded as a community recognizable as an ethnic group within the meaning of the Race Relations Act. The point was made: "No doubt, after all the centuries which have passed since the first gipsies left the Punjab, gipsies are no longer derived from what in biological terms is a common racial stock, but that of itself does not prevent them from being a racial group as widely defined in the 1976 Act."[69] It should, perhaps, worry us that an English Court of Appeal in 1988 was capable of assuming that the gypsies at some stage in the past "derived from a common racial stock" even though Lord Simon, in 1972, had been lucid on the imprecision of the concept of "race." Furthermore, it is a paradox that the legal protection of a group of people against discrimination requires them to be defined as a racial group, even if it is generally recognized that there is no such thing in the proper sense of the term. A difficulty raised in this case may be cited here: "Gipsies prefer to be called 'travellers' as they think that term is less derogatory. This might suggest a wish to lose their separate distinctive identity so far as the general public is concerned. Half or more of them now live in houses, like most other people. Have gipsies now lost their separate, group identity so that they are no longer a community recognisable by ethnic groups within the meaning of the Act?"[70] The Commission for Racial Equality duly produced expert witnesses who claimed that the gypsies were a group of persons defined by reference to ethnic origins. Their arguments were rejected by the County Court on grounds rejected in turn by the Court of Appeal. This shows that the law will protect someone against discrimination against a racial group only if he belongs to a group recognized as such. It may be useful to remember that many German Jews in the 1930s were baptized, and regarded themselves as German Christians, while the Nazi race laws regarded them as Jews. Communal identity is not necessarily a matter of consensus. To

---

[67] Lord Simon, cited by Lord Fraser, ibid. Lord Fraser then turns to the definition of "racial" in the *OED*, Supp. 1 (1972) which he considers too loose and vague to be accepted as it stands. There is no reason to cite this here, since it has been replaced in the new edition of the *OED*. Similarly, the Israel Supreme Court, in an opinion given by Justice Eliahu Mazza in a criminal appeal, *ha-Rav Ido Albeh v State of Israel*, 1831/95, accepted a broad and flexible interpretation of the concept "racism." The court explicitly rejects an interpretation of "racism" as referring exclusively to biological differences between groups.

[68] *Commission for Racial Equality v Dutton* [1989] 1 All ER 306–320.

[69] Nicholls LJ, at 313.

[70] loc. cit.

take an extreme example: modern legislation may not have the equipment to protect persons regarded as witches or sorcerers against discrimination, because witches and sorcerers are not a group defined by reference to ethnic origins.

Any modern society that wants to protect its members against racial discrimination feels a need to clarify what is meant by this and this in turn invites clarification of what is race. Once we know what race is, it is easier to define racial discrimination.[71] Thus the very need to combat racism invites precision which itself is misguided and which threatens to reinforce the idea of race where it should be discredited.[72] Ideally the law should distinguish between racism and other forms of collective discrimination of members of ethnic, national, and other groups. In practice, of course, the courts have to use existing legislation to protect individuals against abuse. For the present study, however, the consequence is that legal definitions do not help in gaining clarity and precision. It might have been more instructive if the jurists had attempted to define racism instead of race.

For our purposes the following use of race, as defined in the *OED*, is relevant—and also the one most compromised in modern history: "One of the great divisions of mankind, having certain physical peculiarities in common." It adds the following comment: "the term is often used imprecisely: there is no generally accepted classification or terminology even among anthropologists. It is first attested in this sense in 1774."[73] In theory a race is a geographically separate and genetically somewhat distinctive population within a species. Thus it has a straightforward meaning in evolutionary biology, but with regard to human beings it is emotionally charged and imprecise in popular usage. The element of descent or common origin must be considered essential in any use of the word race.

It was believed possible to classify human beings on the basis of physiological traits, on the assumption that certain groups possess hereditary traits that are sufficiently constant to characterize them as distinct human types. In practice no

[71] Racial discrimination is defined in the *Act* s 1(1) as follows: "A person discriminates against another in any circumstances relevant for the purposes of any provision of this Act if—(*a*) on racial grounds he treats that other less favourably than he treats or would treat other persons; or (*b*) he applies to that other a requirement or condition which he applies or would apply equally to persons not of the same racial group as that other but—(i) which is such that the proportion of persons of the same racial group as that other who can comply with it is considerably smaller than the proportion of persons not of that racial group who can comply with it" and (ii) which he cannot show to be justifiable irrespective of the colour, race, nationality or ethnic or national origins of the person to whom it is applied; and (iii) which is to the detriment of that other because he cannot comply with it.' (ibid., p. 1065).

[72] For the conceptual complexity of the current debate in the United States: Frederickson, *Racism*, 151.

[73] The following example may be cited here: "From the U.N.E.S.C.O. statement we can define 'race' as 'a division of man, the members of which, though individually varying, are characterized as a group by certain inherited physical features as having a common origin' (*New Biol.* 29 [1959], 69)." For the UNESCO statement, see below. Cf. *Encyclopaedia Britannica*: "*Race*: a biological grouping within the human species possessing genetically transmitted traits that are sufficient to characterise it as a distinct human type."

classification has proved satisfactory. The concept becomes even less acceptable when subdivisions are taken as the basis for an evaluation of a moral or
mental hierarchy. This idea has too often been used in combination with the
view that some races are inherently superior to others, the superior race being
one's own. Since the basis for a classification of humanity into races is one of
descent, this is naturally a biological and physiological concept.

The idea of race in its recent form is a by-product of Darwin's work.[74] Darwin's criterion for a species is that, in principle, it cannot produce fertile offspring when crossed with a representative of another species, according to his
definition.[75] Another criterion is "constancy of character." "Whenever it can be
shown or rendered probable, that the forms in question have remained distinct
for a long period, this becomes an argument of much weight in favour of treating them as a species."[76] Obviously mankind does not include a series of species. Attempts were therefore made to recognize subdivisions of the human
species, called subspecies or, simply, "races."[77] The term "subspecies" as used
by Darwin is commonly used in zoology, but has not become popular among
racial theorists. However, this is another definition of race, or subspecies, which
rests on physiological traits: skin color, eye color and eye form, hair color and
hair form, shape of the nose, stature and cephalic index. Racial differentiation is
usually assumed to depend on certain combinations of these anatomical charac-

[74] Darwin's own ideas about the social evolution of man have been discussed in numerous studies
and are the subject of remarkable disagreement with some scholars describing him as a racist,
others as a social evolutionist. See the following studies containing bibliographies: Marvin Harris,
The Rise of Anthropological Theory: A History of Theories of Culture (London, 1968); Thomas F.
Glick (ed.), *The Comparative Reception of Darwinism* (Austin, TX, 1972); Derek Freeman, "The
Evolutionary Theories of Charles Darwin and Herbert Spencer," *Current Anthropology* 15 (1974),
211–237, with fifteen commentaries and a reply by Freeman; John L. Greene, "Darwin as a Social
Evolutionist," *Journal of the History of Biology* 10 (1977), 1–27. Greene has used Darwin's annota-
tions of books and articles to review his discussion of social evolution. The following conclusions
are relevant: there is no doubt as to the centrality of race formation in Darwin's concept of human
evolution (Greene, p. 5). Like most or many of his contemporaries he cautiously believed in the
heritability of acquired mental and moral capacities and dispositions (pp. 6, 9), an assertion rejected
by some Darwin scholars. He seems to have approved of a form of environmental determinism (8)
and was impresed by Galton's discussion of the deleterious effects of negative selection in civilized
nations (11).

[75] See chapter 8 of *The Origin of Species* on Hybridism.

[76] Charles Darwin, *The Descent of Man, Selection in Relation to Sex* (London, 1877) reprinted as
volume 21 of *The Works of Charles Darwin*, ed. Paul H. Barrett and R. B. Freeman (London,
1989), chapter 8, "On the Races of Man," pp.166–199 of the original publication, pp. 172–205 of
the 1989 edition.

[77] Darwin, op. cit. (1877), 175 [(1989), 181]. He nowhere gives a precise definition of "race" or
"subspecies," but says man "has diverged into distinct races, or as they may be more fitly called,
subspecies." He concludes that "some of these [races] are so distinct that . . . they would have been
considered as good and true species." However, all the races, he says, "agree in so many unimportant details of structure and in so many mental peculiarities, that these can be accounted for only by
inheritance from a common progenitor." This attitude, it must be admitted, is virtually the same as
Buffon's, cited above, and Buffon has been called one of the first genuine racists by some historians. As noted, Darwin's own place in the debate has been the subject of much debate, mainly
because he is ambiguous on the issue in *The Descent of Man*.

teristics. In fact such combinations are never found to represent large groups. In these theories a race represents a population which reproduces without any significant addition of genes belonging to other populations. This, however, is a construct; the phenomenon does not occur on any significant scale. The reason for this is the reality of continuous migration, both individual and large-scale, and the mingling of peoples. No races do in fact exist.[78] All modern European nations, for instance, show a composite racial history as a result of migrations and mixtures of people. Furthermore, by definition, any such classification should be based exclusively on physiological characteristics.

Paradoxically, the advances of science in recent decades have made it possible to detect common physiological features among some population groups through the use of blood-typing and DNA analysis. This is a confusing development, since it might lead to claims that the old belief in the reality of race and of ethnic blood relationships was after all a scientific fact. However, even if it can be shown that there are common biological features that can be discerned in certain regions or among some peoples, this will not salvage the concept of race, for there is no connection between these and other biological features or other characteristics in the sphere of culture, language, or society, let alone of moral qualities. In other words, if it is shown that a given group of people are statistically more susceptible to a certain illness, this does not mean these people form a race, for this susceptibility is only one out of all the possible characteristics that people may have in common.[79] If no other form of proof were at hand, then it would still suffice to observe that no two scholars who wrote about race agree on the number of human races: they range from two or three or four, five, six to ten, eleven, thirteen, fifteen, sixteen, twenty-two, thirty-two, thirty-four up to sixty-three.[80] Race, then, does not exist, but it is extremely difficult to

---

[78] This is not a recent discovery. Long ago some authors were entirely lucid on these matters. Count Heinrich Coudenhove-Kalergi, *Anti-semitism throughout the Ages* (London, 1935); originally published in German: *Das Wesen des Antisemitismus* (Vienna, 1901), reprinted many times, in the Nazi period, and as recently as 1992, 31–6, argued that the term "Semitic" refers to a group of languages, not to kinship of any kind. On p. 36 he states: 'I maintain and substantiate my assertion that whether on grounds of the shape of the skull, of colour, growth of hair or of geographical settlement, it is practically impossible to establish an exact and strictly scientific classification and separation of the Semites"; see also 59–61. For the anti-antisemitic author Coudenhove-Kalergi (1859–1906), see Ritchie Robertson, *The 'Jewish Question' in German Literature 1749–1939: Emancipation and its Discontents* (Oxford, 1999), 198f., 261f. Jacques Barzun, *Race: A Study in Superstition* (first published in 1937; revised edition New York, 1965), ix: "This book is coming back into print because the idea it treats of, although repeatedly killed, is nevertheless undying." For the development of the debate about race among American anthropologists and sociologists, see the articles by Lieberman and Reynolds, cited above, n. 36.

[79] Blackburn, "Why Race is not a Biological Concept," 7, observes: "If racial differences were confined to less apparent features such as blood proteins and genes, no one outside of a few academic disciplines would be likely to use the concept of race."

[80] This point was raised already by Darwin himself, *The Descent of Man* (1877), 174; (1989), 180f.: "there is the greatest possible diversity among capable judges whether he should be classed as a single species or race, or as two (Viery), as three (Jacquinot), as four (Kant), five (Blumenbach), six (Buffon), seven (Hunter), eight (Agassiz), eleven (Pickering), fifteen (Bory St Vincent),

combat the acceptance of something that does not exist and yet is widely believed to exist.[81]

Ideas about race and racism are often hopelessly confused in basic sources of reference. Even in the Subject Index of the Library of Congress Catalog "race" is an officially recognized subject to which reference is made. That may be justified by the claim that there are books about race. However, the same cannot be said of "race awareness" which has as narrower terms "race identity of blacks" and "race identity of whites." This implies the existence of white and black races. There are subject headings "race relations" and "ethnic relations," used at random for books on ethnic relations.[82] The subject "race relations" has subheadings: "Mexican Americans" and "East Indians" which implies that Mexicans and East Indians are races. Worse, there is an official heading "race identity" with a narrower term "black nationalism." By the usual definitions this can only mean that there exists a movement on the part of the black race in favor of national independence. The Library of Congress is followed as authoritative by libraries in many countries all over the world. Indeed the same con-

---

sixteen (Desmoulins), twenty-two (Morton), sixty (Crawfurd), or as sixty-three, according to Burke." Cf. Blackburn, p. 4f. and table 1.1. L. L. Cavalli-Sforza, Paolo Menozzi, and Alberto Piazza, *The History and Geography of Human Genes* (Princeton, 1994), note that "there are clearly no objective reasons for stopping at any particular level of taxonomic splitting. . . . All populations or population clusters overlap when single genes are considered, and in almost all populations, all alleles are present but in different frequencies. No single gene is therefore sufficient for classifying human populations into systematic categories," and they conclude that "from a scientific point of view, the concept of race has failed to obtain any consensus; none is likely, given the gradual variation in existence." See now Joseph L. Graves, *The Emperor's New Clothes: Biological Theories of Race at the Millennium* (New Brunswick, NJ, 2001), which argues once again that the concept of race is invalid, not as a statement of political correctness, but on the basis of scientific reality. This is entirely convincing, but his discussion of the history of the idea of race seems too much determined by conditions in North America. As observed in Kenan Malik's review, *TLS* of Jan. 11, 2002, p. 6f.: "It is a pity that such books remain necessary." Current advances in genetics offer new dangers of regression. See, for instance, Neil Risch et al., "Categorization of Humans in Biomedical Research: Genes, Race and Disease," *Genome Biology* 2002, 3(7):2007.1–2007.12. Risch and his colleagues take issue with two publications: R. S. Schwartz, "Racial Profiling in Medical Research," *New England Journal of Medicine* 344/18 (2001), 1392f., and J. F. Wilson et al., "Population Genetic Structure of Variable Drug Response," *Nature Genetics* 29 (2001), 239f. and an editorial in the same journal: "Genes, Drugs and Race," *Nature Genetics* 97–98 (2000), all of which deny the biological relevance of race. Rice and his co-authors disagree and "strongly support the continued use of self-identified race and ethnicity," although they do recognize that a value system attached to such findings is not scientific. The claims of this study immediately reached the press: the *International Herald Tribune* of August 1, 2002, p. 7: "A geneticist argues for the idea of race." Risch and his colleagues do not intend to encourage racism; they want to improve medical care. Yet the effect of their publication can only be harmful.

[81] As I found out myself in the case of the term "limes" in Roman history.

[82] A few illustrations will suffice: under the heading "ethnic relations" we find Rodolfo D. Torres et al., *Race, Identity and Citizenship* (1999). Under the heading "race relations" we find: Jerry Boucher et al., *Ethnic Conflict: International Perspectives* (Newbury Park, CA, 1987); B. Crawford and R. D. Lipschutz, eds., *The Myth of "Ethnic Conflict": Politics, Economics, and "Cultural" Violence* (Berkeley, 1998); I. Svanberg and M. Tydén, *Multiethnic Studies in Uppsala* (Uppsala, 1988). Hundreds of books are classified without any lucid criteria.

fused subject headings regarding race may be found in the catalogues of major libraries in many countries.[83] It is quite clear that the responsible librarians at the Library of Congress have no doubt that race exists and confuse it with forms of social grouping that do exist. This is the message they help spread through their influence.

A major, but misguided effort was made to define and explain race in nonracist terms by the UNESCO in its "statement on race."[84] It is misguided because its basic assumption is the existence of races.[85] Numerous modern authors do not believe in the reality of race themselves, but they still proceed from the assumption that race exists for racists, in the sense that racists are believed to respond to real physical traits of the targets of racism.[86] Here we are back to the

[83] Let me give two absurd examples of erroneous cataloguing: Richard Walther Darré's *Neuadel aus Blut und Boden* (Munich, 1930), is a Nazi pamplet arguing for racial purity, eugenics, and the conservation of the traditional tie of the German farmer with the soil. In the Library of Congress Catalog, followed by other catalogs of major libraries in various countries, the first subject heading for this work is "Nobility—Germany." Darré, who was Reichsminister of agriculture in the Nazi years, wrote about racial purity and farmers, his own idea of an elite, not about hereditary aristocracy. Hans F. K. Günther, *Führeradel durch Sippenpflege* (Munich, 1936), which argues also for racial purity and for family values, is again listed with "nobility" for its subject. The only reasonable heading for such works is "racist" with possible subheadings. These librarians confuse nobility in the generally valid sense of the term with a racist distortion of it.

[84] Ashley Montagu, *Statement on Race* (New York, 1951). The UNESCO statement contains an attempt to define "race" very carefully and explain why the concept is so often misused. It still proceeds from the assumption that mankind is divided into races (Mongoloid, Negroid, Caucasoid).

[85] See the UNESCO statement, paragraph 3, cited by Montagu, p. 48. The Statement regards race as a scientific fact, which, however, is misused by many people in practice; cf. paragraph 5, p. 60. Note, however, Montagu's best-known work *Man's Most Dangerous Myth* (1942) and see his important paper: "The Concept of Race in the Human Species in the Light of Genetics," reprinted in Bernasconi and Lott, *The Idea of Race*, 100–107.

[86] Colette Guillaumin, *L'idéologie raciste: genèse et language actuel* (Paris and The Hague, 1972), 62; see also Guillaumin, "The Changing Face of 'Race'," in Bulmer and Solomos, *Racism*, 355–362, reprinted from Guillaumin, *Racism, Sexism, Power and Ideology* (London, 1995). For a similar observation: Gavin Langmuir, in L. Poliakov (ed.), *Ni Juif ni Grec, entretiens sur le racisme* (Paris and The Hague, 1975), 18. For authors who rejected the applicability of the term "race" at an early stage, see Robert Miles, "Racism as a Concept," cited in Bulmer and Solomos, *Racism*, 344–347; Guillaumin, ibid., 358f. On the other hand, even modern works of reference can be remarkably assertive in their presentation of the old approach, e.g., *Brockhaus Enzyklopädie: siebzehnte Auflage* (Wiesbaden, 1971), 12. Band, s.v. "Menschenrassen," pp. 406–410, includes four pages of photographs of 64 presumed races and refers, on p. 406, to works such as Egon Freiherr von Eickstedt, *Rassenkunde und Rassengeschichte der Menschheit* (Stuttgart, 1934, 2d ed. 1937); H. Weinert, *Die Rassen der Menschheit* (2d ed. 1939). For Eickstedt, see C. Zentner and F. Bedürftig (eds.), *Das grosse Lexikon des dritten Reiches* (Munich, 1985), 141: He developed a formula to establish people's race, supported by citations from Hitler and Rosenberg, with special attention to the correlation between race and character. His work ends with a call for eugenics, to fight the battle for the superior nordic races against the backward southern stock. For recent discussions: Montagu, *Man's Most Dangerous Myth;* A. Memmi, *Rassismus* (1987), 11–28; Robert Miles in Bulmer and Solomos, op. cit.; Blackburn, "Why Race is not a Biological Concept," 3–26. For a good summary of the genetic argument: Cavalli-Sforza et al., *The History and Geography of Human Genes*, chapter 1.5: "Classical attempts to distinguish human 'races'," pp. 16–18; 1.6: "Scientific failure of the concept of human races," pp.19f.

serious consequences of an insufficiently lucid understanding of the essence of racism. I repeat once more, although it should be superfluous to say so, that racism is never caused by the physical characteristics of the other.[87]

RACE DOES NOT EXIST, RACISM DOES

Since the concept of race as such is merely theoretical, since it is a quasi-biological construct invented to establish a hierarchy of human groups and to delineate differences between them, and since it does not work in practice, attempts have been made from the beginning to incorporate other features which are not physiological. The designation "race" in the sense of subspecies cannot be applied by definition to language groups (the Aryan race), national groups (the English race), religious groups (the Christian or Jewish race), groups with one or more physical features in common, such as skin color, or the entire species of humans (the human race): such usages are biologically and scientifically meaningless.[88] Similarly, culture and race have been confused. Culture clearly may change from one generation to the next. Again, those who contribute to the same culture may not have common ancestors, and people with common ancestors do not necessarily participate in a single culture. Culture therefore is not a function of what would be termed race according to any definition.

Of course, it is not meaningless that certain groups of peoples feel they belong together. This, however, is a sociological fact, not a biological one, just as it is a fact of linguistics that people speak the same language, or a fact of religion when they share a common faith, organized or not. Furthermore, it is sociologically significant when people imagine that they themselves, or another

[87] Consequently I disagree as a matter of principle with the approach of Christopher Tuplin, "Greek Racism?" in Tsetskhladze (ed.), *Ancient Greeks West and East* (1999), 47–75, at 47. Tuplin cites two definitions of racism which he rejects and asserts: ". . . and I think ordinary English usage still associates 'racism' with cases where there are relatively clear physical or genetic differences between two sets of people." He then argues that there was no Greek racism in this sense. Thus racism always is a response to real, demonstrable differences. The implication is that ordinary English usage regards white hatred of blacks as racism, but not anti-semitism for the Jews because they are not physically distinct enough from the peoples among which they live. Another disagreement with this article is the fact that Tuplin accepts the existence of race, as shown, for instance, on p. 69, where he speaks of "our idea of major racial distinctions." This, as I argue in this Introduction, precludes a proper analysis of racism. Tuplin, however, insists on the presence of strongly held ethnic prejudices among the Greeks.

[88] Poliakov, *Le Racisme,* 22: "La race dont il nous parle—qu'il s'agisse de la sienne ou de celle des autres—n'est nullement une race: dans sa bouche, ce terme désigne un groupe social donné, identifiable par des traits culturels, linguistiques, religieux, historiques, etc.—mais jamais par des traits exclusivement physiques." Cf. Guillaumin, in Bulmer and Solomos, 356–359, who cites Jean Hiernaux as one of the first to make this observation: "Race is not a fact, but a concept." Guillaumin gives a brief and lucid description of the development of the concept. In French it meant, in the sixteenth century, "family" or "family relationship" and was applied only to important dynasties. It later was applied to much wider groups.

group, share a common origin and if they attribute presumed physical or mental characteristics to this common origin. It may therefore be concluded that race is merely one of the ways in which people are popularly classified. Through the influence of modern science and biology, this clarification has taken a quasi-biological form. In recent centuries this presumed biological content has been gradually combined with other traits which have nothing to do with biology, such as language (Indo-European, Semitic), religion, social and cultural characteristics. If human races do not exist, is there a point in adopting a working definition for present purposes? The same question might have been asked if we were considering fear of ghosts, devils, or witches. We know that the ghosts and devils do not exist in reality, whereas witches are ordinary women thought to have evil magic powers and therefore, as a category, they do not exist either. Yet people are afraid of them. Is there then a point in defining ghosts, devils, or witches? The answer seems obvious. Since they exist in the minds of many people it is still necessary to define what is meant by the idea or what people think they mean.

Ashley Montagu, while recognizing that human races do not occur in reality, defines the concept as follows: races are "groups of human beings which exist in nature and are comprised of individuals each of whom possesses a certain aggregate of characters which individually and collectively serve to distinguish them from the individuals in all other groups."[89] More recently social scientists who recognize that race is not a biological reality, but also see that it is a relevant concept in social interaction, have argued that it has no fixed meaning. Instead, they suggest, it is constructed and transformed sociohistorically. They therefore propose the following definition: "Race is a concept which signifies and symbolizes social conflicts and interests by referring to different types of human bodies."[90] This definition may work well for those who attempt to understand social interaction in the modern United States, but it is less satisfactory for anyone considering, for example, Renan's hostile ramblings about all the peoples of the Near East (the "Semitic race") or Nazi anti-semitism. It will not work either for a study like the present one, which attempts to trace the development of ideas about race over time, for these ideas do not focus exclusively on the body, but on the interconnection between physical and mental, moral and spiritual characteristics. So, paradoxically, a social study which has the aim of understanding racist group dynamics should focus on joint patterns of interaction in various societies, while minimizing the importance of continuity over time in the conceptual content of racist ideas. A historical study, however, which traces the long-term development of racist intellectual concepts, will look for the continuity in the mechanisms of racist thinking.

For the present study I shall define race as "a group of people who are believed to share imagined common characteristics, physical and mental or

[89] Ashley Montagu, "The Concept of Race" in Bernasconi and Lott, *The Idea of Race*, 103.

[90] Michael Omi and Howard Winant, "Racial Formation in the United States," in Bernasconi and Lott, *The Idea of Race*, 181–212, esp. 183.

moral which cannot be changed by human will, because they are thought to be determined by unalterable, stable physical factors: hereditary, or external, such as climate or geography." A belief in the reality of race in itself is always misguided, but it is not necessarily racism. It becomes racism if the ensuing differences between peoples are the basis for the division of individuals into superior and inferior racial groups.

It is less difficult to adopt a definition of "ethnic group" which will satisfy most readers. For convenience we may refer to one that appears in the legal document, cited above: For a group to consitute an ethnic group it is essential that it should have: "(1) a long shared history, of which the group is conscious as distinguishing it from other groups, and the memory of which it keeps alive; (2) a cultural tradition of its own, including family and social customs and manners, often but not necessarily associated with religious observance."[91] Lord Fraser approved the following passage from the judgment of Richardson J sitting in the New Zealand Court of Appeal in *King-Ansell v Police*

> [a] group is identifiable in terms of its ethnic origins if it is a segment of the population distinguished from others by a sufficient combination of shared customs, beliefs, traditions and characteristics derived from a common or presumed common past, even if not drawn from what in biological terms is a common racial stock. It is that combination which gives them an historically determined social identity in their own eyes and in the eyes of those outside the group. They have a distinct social identity based not simply on group cohesion and solidarity but also on their belief as to their historical antecedents.[92]

Thus the essence of racism is that it tries to establish a hierarchy of groups of human beings, basing itself on an imagined concept: race, that is, on illusory common characteristics which override individual differentiation. Since it is based on prejudice, it is marked by an emotional and rigid attitude which it is difficult or impossible to modify by rational argument or practical experience. Racist theory has expended great effort to show that some races are superior and others inferior, based on physiological, psychological, and historical considerations. Basing itself on a distorted form of evolutionary theory, modern racism assumes that man's physical development proceeds in a straight line from his prehuman progenitors up to the highest form attained which was, of course, European man. Following this reasoning, other races represent earlier, less developed stages of this evolution and should therefore be considered of lower quality. This is an untenable construct, just as it is untenable to maintain

---

[91] Lord Fraser in [1983] 1 All ER 1062 at 1066f. In addition to those two essential characteristics, the following are considered relevant: "(3) either a common geographical origin, or descent from a small number of common ancestors; (4) a common language not necessarily peculiar to the group; (5) a common literature peculiar to the group; (6) a common religion different from that of neighbouring groups or from the gneral community surrounding it; (7) being a minority or being an oppressed or a dominant group within a larger community, for example a conquered people (say, the inhabitants of England shortly after the Norman conquest) and their conquerors might both be ethnic groups."

[92] [1979] 2 NZLR 531 at 543.

that size of the brain cavity of more intelligent people is greater than that of others. However, this complex of ideas led to the theory of "the great man," a notion that mankind is evolving into a superior, further advanced race and that some such individuals may already exist among us. However, this last set of ideas on linear progress and increasing superiority belongs to the nineteenth and twentieth centuries.[93] It should therefore not be part of a study of the ancient world.

It is, however, also clear that modern racism was not invented at one stroke.[94] It developed gradually from its beginnings in the eighteenth century, when heredity was not yet central to thinking about human development. For this earlier period the more flexible definition of racism may be applied, which speaks of "differences" in general, rather than "biological differences." The essence of early racism, as distinct from most other forms of hostility towards others, is that it seeks the cause for the differences between groups of peoples in either physiological or genetic determinism. This means that the presumed collective characteristics are unalterable by human will. They are claimed to be constant and to derive from factors over which people have no control, be it from the outside (climate and geography) or from the inside (genetic or physiological). Since many of the tenets of early racism are found in Graeco-Roman literature, it will be useful to consider whether antiquity knew comparable attitudes, which, for the sake of convenience, might be called proto-racism.[95]

It is clearly essential to distinguish between ethnic and other group prejudices and proto-racial prejudice. Although it is true that traditional English usage commonly confuses race and people, this is no longer acceptable in our times. As cited above, group prejudice constitutes "a generalisation existing prior to the situation in which it is invoked, directed toward people, groups, or social institutions, which is accepted and defended as a guide to action in spite of its discrepancies with the objective facts." An alternative definition that is also acceptable: "a belief about people that is 1) wholly derived from membership in a special group; 2) disregards the variability within the group; 3) is accompanied and sustained by negative affect."[96] This means that prejudice, although it is a form of frequently hostile generalization, does not invoke the idea that change is impossible. The traits attributed to the other are not believed to be rooted in his essential and stable physical makeup. One can change nationality,

[93] R. Benedict, *Race and Racism* passim.

[94] Note, however, Cavalli-Sforza et al., *The History and Geography of Human Genes*, 19: "Racism has existed from time immemorial but only in the nineteenth century were there attempts to justify it on the basis of scientific arguments."

[95] As noted above, note 10, I have not invented the term, but neither is it commonly used.

[96] Yaacov Schul and Henri Zukier, "Why do Stereotypes Stick?" in Wistrich, *Demonizing the Other*, 31–32, esp. 33. A serious difficulty in this definition is that it requires a negative affect. I cannot see that the example from the *Guide to Venice*, cited below, shows a negative affect. Yet it is clearly stereotypical as described under (1) and (2). Moreover, the definition, but not the accompanying explanations, ignores the important fact that stereotypical belief often, or even usually, leads to corresponding action. Note the influential older study: B. Bettelheim and M. Janowitz, *The Dynamic of Prejudice* (New York, 1950).

language, religion, and culture, but not one's inherited characteristics. Religion is a special factor. In many countries religious groups are subgroups, and prejudices against them may be fierce, but in many or most countries one can leave one religious community to join another. Nationality is a broad concept. One can be an African American, a Native American—that is, belonging to specific subgroups by birth—or a former immigrant to the United States, having received citizenship and so on. All such groups may be the target of ethnic prejudice. It is essential, however, to distinguish between prejudice regarding presumed common characteristics that are changeable at a personal or collective level and those that are considered unalterable, based as they are on factors beyond human control. Thus claims that certain peoples have no manners, cannot drive, or have a fine sense of humor are instances of group prejudice. They still allow for the possibility that individuals may be taught manners and driving, or lack a sense of humor. On the other hand, the claim that a certain people has an appalling cuisine because their sense of smell is deficient would be an example of racism. By implication, such a people will never be able to cook properly, for a sense of smell cannot be acquired. The present work will trace these sorts of patterns and attitudes in ancient sources.

It may be useful to note once again what we should and should not be looking for in Greece and Rome. Greek and Roman antiquity did not know the sort of racism that western civilization developed in the nineteenth and twentieth centuries, since they had no concept of biological determinism. There was no nationalism in the modern sense in the Graeco-Roman world, nor was there any concept that a specific ethnic group should live within defined borders. What the ancient world did have was a range of prejudices, phobias, and hostilities towards specific groups of foreigners and it is the aim of this part of the work to understand these better than has been attempted so far. Clearly, racism is not a way of looking at people based on genuine scientific observation of their physical and mental qualities. It is a construct of ungrounded theories and discriminatory commonplaces elaborated with the specific aim of establishing the superiority of one group over another, based on presumed physiological characteristics.

What we should consider, therefore, is the degree to which antiquity knew such a phenomenon, even if it lacked the biological elements of modern racism. The question to be considered is what are the explanations given in ancient literature for the presumed superiority or inferiority of specific groups. If these consist of theories regarding heredity or unalterable exterior influences, it is possible to speak of proto-racism. If the assumed causes of qualitative differences are human actions or social relations within people's own control, then we should speak of ethnic or group prejudice. In other words, if we find that a people is described as having the mentality of slaves because they are ruled by a king, then this is not racism, but ethnic prejudice. If, however, we read that people are stupid and courageous because they live in a cold climate, then it can be argued that this is a form of proto-racism, since there is an implicit assumption that these people are stupid through physical factors beyond their control. Their descendants will remain stupid, because the climate of their country will not change and thus their bodies will remain the same. Moreover, each individual belonging to such people will be assumed to have the characteristics ascribed to his group, whether inherited, or caused by the environment. This is to the point because, as we shall see, the distinction between heredity and characteristics acquired through external influences was not considered significant in Graeco-Roman antiquity. According to ancient thinking, external influences could alter physical and mental characteristics—such as the southern sun which turns white people into blacks—and these subsequently became stable and were inherited. Furthermore, if we read that people are superior because they are of pure lineage, then this is an imagined construct aimed at establishing superiority on the basis of heredity. Such theories can be qualified as an early form of racism. The term proto-racism, then, may be used when Greek and Latin sources attribute to groups of people common characteristics considered to be unalterable because they are determined by external factors or heredity.

XENOPHOBIA

One further concept has to be defined before we use it, namely xenophobia, a term not attested in ancient Greek, but, like similar compounds, a construct of recent date.[97] Although this is less complex than racism, it still needs some clarification since it is a compound used in various ways. The second element is a clinical term for an extreme, irrational fear of a specific object or situation. A phobia is classified as a type of anxiety disorder in psychiatry. Numerous more or less parallel words have been coined to specify the object of fear by prefixing "phobia" with the Greek word for the object feared. In many of these cases, the popular meaning has lost some of its clinical precision. Thus, xenophobia is defined in the *OED* as "a deep antipathy to foreigners." This definition is accompanied by a large number of examples which clearly show the term to be used commonly for a "strong dislike of foreigners" rather than a pathological fear of them.[98] The essence of the antipathy is that the objects of xenophobia are seen as people who have come from elsewhere and therefore do not belong to one's own society. It can relate both to the people themselves or their immediate ancestors. Xenophobia can, in fact, take the form either of ethnic prejudice or of racism, or a combination of the two. For the present study, then, xenophobia will be used as a term for various forms of ethnic prejudice and racism

---

[97] E.g., Frederickson, *Racism*, 6: "a term invented by the ancient Greeks . . ."

[98] As in *The Economist* of June 1, 1963, 908: "The mild xenophobia . . . which informed such *Punch* lines as 'e's a stranger: 'eave 'arf a brick at 'im'."

aimed at those seen as foreigners or immigrants, as they are commonly called today.[99]

DISCUSSION OF THE MODERN LITERATURE ON ANCIENT PREJUDICES

I hope these definitions will contribute to the clarity of this work and assist in the clarification of its conceptual framework. This is all the more important as no general work has been written about the attitudes of Greeks to other nations and peoples in the classical and Hellenistic periods.[100] The relationship between Romans and others, however, has been discussed more often in the modern literature. At this point something should be said about the existing literature we have taken into account and the methods it has employed. Three works must be mentioned at the outset because they involve essential matters of method, and the introduction is the proper place to discuss some aspects of these: A. N. Sherwin-White, *Racial Prejudice in Imperial Rome* (Cambridge, 1967); J.P.V.D. Balsdon, *Romans & Aliens* (London, 1979); and Y.-A. Dauge, *Le Barbare* (Brussels, 1981).[101] Sherwin-White's book is a short publication of lectures given in Cambridge.[102] He does not discuss theories, abstract ideas, or methods, but his views are clearly expressed throughout the work. I cannot agree with several aspects of his approach. His work consists of a systematic discussion of what a limited number of authors have to say about various peoples. Thus his historiographic method is significant and must be taken into account. However, the question of what constitutes racial prejudice is not discussed by Sherwin-White at all. He makes no distinction between racial and ethnic prejudice, which is a necessary distinction, as I have argued above. The second point to observe is that Sherwin-White has decided to ignore the commonplaces he encounters in the authors he discusses. For instance: "But in all this Tacitus is not expressing an opinion about the barbarians. He is writing literary history according to the commonplace book. His opinion or his admiration comes out unexpectedly . . ." (p. 44). Sherwin-White then gives examples of Tacitus's expressions of admiration for barbarian leaders. This, however, is not really relevant. There was a long tradition of, admiration for, and special treatment of

[99] The term should not be applied to hatred of other peoples in general, e.g., the dislike of Greeks and Romans for nomads.

[100] Note, however, Long, *Barbarians in Greek Comedy*; E. Hall, *Inventing the Barbarian*; J. M. Hall, *Ethnic Identity* (1997), and see above, n. 12.

[101] See also the brief survey by D. B. Saddington, "Race Relations in the Roman Empire," *ANRW* 2.3 (1975), 112–137 and his earlier paper: "Roman Attitudes to the External Gentes of the North," *Acta Classica* 4 (1961), 90–102.

[102] Unlike Balsdon's book, which was widely criticized, Sherwin-White received many positive reviews, apart from two highly critical discussions by W. den Boer, *ClJ* 65 (1969), 184–186, and by Ramsay MacMullen, *AJP* 90 (1969), 500f. Note also the pertinent criticism of G. W. Bowersock, *Roman Arabia* (Cambridge, MA, 1983), 124, note 4.

enemy leaders. Enemy leaders may be admired and given preferential treatment while their subjects are despised and enslaved or worse.

It is precisely the point of stereotypes and commonplaces that they deny the individuality of members of a group.[103] "The X-people are thieves" is a statement that denies the certainty that the majority of them are perfectly honest. When we come to consider individuals, the stereotype may lose some of its force: "for someone who grew up among the X, he is surprisingly honest." I therefore disagree fundamentally with Sherwin-White when he says that commonplaces do not represent opinions, including prejudices. If in our times a group of people are believed to be thieves, then this may be called a commonplace, but it is more correct to describe it as a prejudice. Such prejudices may be voiced by simple people or by famous authors. In fact, there was a period, not long ago, when highly respected social scientists confidently generalized about nations.[104] The result was a serious confusion of research and sweeping generalization. However, even when endowed with academic respectability such observations remain what they are: statements of prejudice. It is essential to interpret prejudices and collective judgments in our sources properly. Thus it is precisely when ancient authors echo common prejudice that they are valuable as an indicator of how foreigners were seen in their time. We need to search for conventional material, for it is there we shall find the ideas that give a better impression of the general views of Roman authors and their readers than the information and analysis that are unique to a specific text. Stereotypes and commonplaces are one form in which generalizations, preconceptions, and prejudices are expressed. Although they are often innocuous and their aggressive intent masked by humor, it is important to see what they are conceptually. This is not, of course, to suggest that a joke about a group is the same as a full-scale physical attack. There are also positive stereotypes. It is important, however, to recognize each statement for what it is. Let me cite a random example, taken from the *Michelin Guide to Venice* (first ed., 1996), "The Venetians": "To stereotype the flavour of Venice would be detrimental to the magic of the place and offensive to her proud inhabitants" (p. 10). The *Guide* then continues as follows:

> The Venetian is born with a **positive**[105] outlook on life that is maintained by an **imperturbable** nature in which emotional involvement is tempered, in a very gentlemanly manner, by a certain indifference to anything that lies beyond the lagoon. This leads to him being noticeably predisposed to being **tolerant**, an innate quality acquired from a knowledge of different peoples distilled over the centuries. The blend of an almost Anglo-saxon [*sic!*] *aplomb* with boundless and all-embracing curiosity renders this personality even more fascinating.

[103] Lucid remarks about stereotypes in the ancient world: E. Hall, op. cit., 102–104.

[104] Margaret Mead, Ruth Benedict and others, who studied "collective identity," "national character," and similar topics; see the brief description by Uffe Øystergård, in Per Bilde et al., *Ethnicity in Hellenistic Egypt* (1992), 19–25.

[105] Bold print and italics as in the original text.

This continues for half a page. It is a good example, because the authors are demonstrably unaware that they are spouting stereotypes—which they claim to reject. It is interesting that the rejection of stereotyping in the first sentence itself is justified by a stereotype: to stereotype Venetians would be offensive to those proud people, it is claimed, as if it is legitimate to stereotype the inhabitants of a town without magic, provided its inhabitants are not proud.[106] Venetians are *born* with a positive outlook on life and tend to be tolerant because they dispose of a reservoir of knowledge *accumulated* over the centuries. This betrays confusion between acquired and inherited characters, comparable with what we encounter in many ancient texts. Note further that all these stereotypes are positive.[107] Thus, the present study, unlike Sherwin-White's book, will focus on stereotypes in ancient literature and analyze them for what they show about mentalities.

In this connection something must be said about the use of various genres of literature in this study which is based on a broad variety of texts: historiography, philosophy, medical texts, speeches and more. It is a problem of many historical studies that they have to work with a combination of sources that cannot be described in their context without imposing an intolerable burden on the length and readability of the study. I hope I have been sufficiently cautious in interpreting the texts discussed. A first self-imposed rule in this book is that I have interpreted all the literary sources only as evidence for contemporary ideas and attitudes. Thus, for instance, I have used the historian Livy, who lived in the reign of Augustus, only as an author providing evidence for attitudes in his own times. Even though he writes about the earliest period of the existence of Rome, I have made no attempt to extract from his work evidence about periods earlier than his own. As a consequence I have not much to say about republican Rome before the mid–second century B.C., for there is not much contemporary literature. Something more needs to be said about the interpretation of satire which is especially complex. The satire is a literary form, first developed in Rome, in which prevailing human vices, follies, abuses, or shortcomings are held up to censure by means of ridicule, irony, or related methods.[108] It works by means of attack, entertainment, and preaching in varying respective doses.[109]

The genre was established by Lucilius in the second century B.C., developed by Horace and Juvenal, and taken up in Greek by Lucian of Samosata. Horace and Juvenal, however, wrote from quite different perspectives. Horace is moved to laughter and irony rather than to indignation or anger. Juvenal, writing more

---

[106] It must be admitted that the Venetians are not the only proud people around. One trait all Scandinavians have in common is their national pride, which is deeply rooted in their mentality, or so we read in the *Michelin Guide of Scandinavia and Finland* (1996), p. 31.

[107] The existence of positive stereotypes is excluded in the definition given by Edith Hall, *Inventing the Barbarian* 121: "Stereotypes project on to target groups characteristics which are the opposite of qualities admired in the group creating the stereotypes."

[108] For an ancient definition: Diomedes, *GLK* 1.485 = Kaibel, *Comicorum Graecorum Fragmenta*, 1. 55f.

[109] Niall Rudd, *Themes in Roman Satire* (London, 1986), chapter 1: aims and motives, at p. 1.

than a century later, looks with anger and indignation on the corruptions of his time. Clearly, in interpreting satire for the purpose of this study, one must be aware of the nature of the genre. Satire often exaggerates and always is meant to evoke laughter or anger. It should not be treated as portraying daily life in an accurate manner, or even as representing considered reflections. Satirists have different aims from historians and ethnographers. Satire must, however, be taken seriously as a form of commentary on the opinions of the speaker and, hence, of the current views of many of his readers. As observed by Anderson, "the poet Horace or Juvenal should not be identified totally with the character in the Satires who makes the social commentary. That character or *persona* . . . must be plausible, but he is also subject to criticism by design of the poet."[110] Or we may cite Henderson, more recently: "So these poems figure the traditionalist profile of a 'typical' adult-citizen-Roman who is 'free' to voice aggressive masculinity in the public eye."[111] "We know that, whatever else, Satire satirizes the satirist and satirizes the genre of Satire, turns on itself and on the consciousness of its voice and its readers. Its mark and mask is *self-mockery*."[112] Thus, to take one example, Juvenal complains: "Here in Rome the son of free-born parents has to give the wall to some rich man's slave."[113] This is not meant as a literal description of the movements of slaves and free men in Rome, but it definitely expresses a feeling, held by many Romans—but not necessarily a feeling held in that form by the poet himself—that the slaves of the rich humiliate free-born Romans. Again, as observed by Anderson, "in the case of these violently indignant speakers, the poet has deliberately attributed to them objectionable and offensive ways, more or less as a warning to the audience to dissociate itself from their indignation. In other words, sometimes the *persona* created by the satiric poet is so distinct from the poet's biography that the two are oppposites."[114] Juvenal, in any case, would not have written as he did, if he had not confidently expected that this was an effective way of representing a feeling shared by many of his readers. For the present study satire is thus entirely relevant. It is enough for us to observe that many Romans felt humiliated by the position of the slaves of the rich, whatever Juvenal himself may have felt, and whatever a more distant observer might have felt in observing contemporary Rome. Thus, satire may be used as a reliable reflection of contemporary readers' perception of their social environment. We may take this one step further. It is quite likely that the rulers in Rome were influenced in their policies by such perceptions. In other words, even if they themselves did not share negative feelings towards specific groups of aliens, they may still have adapted their policy to the sympathy or hostility they perceived to be prevalent.

[110] William S. Anderson, *Essays on Roman Satire* (Princeton, 1982), viii.

[111] John Henderson, *Writing down Rome: Satire, Comedy, and other Offences in Latin Poetry* (Oxford, 1999), 194.

[112] Ibid., 205.

[113] 3. 131: divitis hic servo claudit latus ingenuorum filius.

[114] Anderson, *Essays,* 9. See also pp. 293–296 on "anger in Juvenal and Seneca."

A useful discussion might also be devoted to the role of judicial and other rhetoric in promoting stereotyping. Although I use such texts throughout this study, I have decided not to discuss the genre as such for reasons of economy.

Balsdon's book is very substantial and deals with a wide range of subjects. It describes how Romans regarded other peoples and how they regarded themselves, how other peoples regarded the Romans, how they communicated and affected one another. It is based on a great wealth of material and deals with all these topics at a rapid pace. The book never stops for questions or discussion. Throughout, the book sustains a tone of cheerful cynicism, which makes it highly entertaining but sometimes hides the seriousness of the subject matter.[115] It is frequently left to the reader to decide whether the author mocks the chauvinism of the sources he cites, or accepts it. There are two major disadvantages to the book. It attempts to study at least four major topics and includes numerous interesting but secondary matters, such as eunuchs and the seven-day week. It tries to do a great deal in one volume and therefore leaves many real questions untouched, insufficiently separating essentials from mere curiosities. Second, it covers the period of the republic from the second century B.C. onward and the principate as well, as if it was one continuum. This occasionally hides major differences that may have occurred over so many years.

I must also briefly mention here Dauge's massive book about Rome and the Barbarian because its conclusions are the opposite of those reached in the present work. Four pages out of a total of 859 set forth the author's conviction that there was a total absence of racism in Rome. His view is that Rome was essentially an open society, which therefore cannot have produced racist views. This is cheerful dogma rather than well-considered analysis. An important point is undoubtedly that Dauge supports an eccentric definition of race.[116] It is remarkable that an academic work on ancient history, published in 1981, should use Italian fascist literature for its methodological approach to racism. Yet I have not seen this mentioned in any review of the book, which shows how vague contemporary thinking often is about racism. A third important problem, apart from the extraordinary length of the work, is the way in which sources are presented. As in Balsdon's work, it is frequently unclear whether Dauge is

---

[115] Elsewhere, or perhaps only in earlier years, Balsdon himself was capable of slipping: "Orientals are best impressed by oriental splendour": *The Emperor Gaius (Caligula)* (Oxford, 1934, repr. 1964), 54.

[116] Dauge, *Le Barbare*, 525: "Un «race» véritable, d'ailleurs, ne peut être qu'une création volontaire à partir d'éléments divers, par un processus continu de *dissolution* et de *concentration* qui rappelle l'opération «*solue et coagulée*», et par la conjonction des meilleurs, appelés à fusionner pour constituer une communauté sans cesse renouvelée." For this definition the author refers to Julius Evola, *Sintesi di dottrina della razza* (Milano, 1941), who designed his own quite peculiar social philosophy. Evola, (266) happily announces the formation of a race both new and old: it is the race of fascist man, the 'razza dell' uomo di Mussolini." In *Le fascisme vu de droite* (Paris, 1981), 92, Evola proudly relates that Mussolini had read his work, had received him and expressed his unreserved approval of the thesis. Supported by such company Dauge represents a confused attempt not to throw the baby away with the bathwater. He leaves us with an imaginary race, which is, however, not a race according to the definitions of racists.

simply citing Roman authors' negative views of others, or applauding them. Usually the latter seems to be the case. This, again, is a very common feature in modern works dealing with ancient judgments of others.

I have singled out these three books on the subject for discussion in the Introduction because each of them shows significant features which, I maintain, must be reconsidered if we are to attempt to understand these topics. Otherwise the text below will refer to works dealing with relevant topics in the appropriate place.[117] However, one remarkable article should be added here, Elias Bickerman's "Origines Gentium,"[118] about Greek and Jewish ideas about ethnicity in antiquity. It contains much that is relevant here, particularly the concluding sentences:

> The Greek, Hellenocentric, approach failed to solve the problem. But are modern theories much better? The "Cro-Magnon" race of our textbooks or the "Semites" as the substratum of the "Semitic" languages are fictions of a different kind but hardly of a higher value than the Trojan origin of Rome. The remarkable fact remains that Greeks conceived the idea of common inheritance of all peoples, and tried to understand the common past of mankind historically. As so often in Greek science, they failed because they attempted too much.

The present study will consider Greek attitudes towards foreigners from a rather different angle.

THE ARRANGEMENT OF THIS BOOK

Throughout this work I shall distinguish strictly between (a) those forms of prejudice and preconception which are aimed at strangers, at ethnic, or at other groups; and (b) those views of others which may be called proto-racist, as defined above. The period covered starts with the fifth century B.C. There are two parts: the first discusses a number of general themes while the second deals with specific peoples as presented in the literature of the periods considered. I shall discuss both opinions about foreign nations, for example, Greek ideas of Persia, and opinions about peoples incorporated into the Roman Empire, for example, Roman ideas of Greeks. This is all the more necessary because so many foreign nations became subjects of the Roman Empire at some stage. The study thus covers not just two different cultures, Greece and Rome, but also a very extended period and thus a variety of political and social climates. It is my claim that this is justified because consistent patterns of thinking about foreigners are encountered throughout this period. Specific ideas and attitudes occur from the fifth century B.C. through the Roman imperial period and I shall

---

[117] Such as F. W. Walbank, "Nationality as a Factor in Roman History," *Selected Papers: Studies in Greek and Roman History and Historiography* (Cambridge, 1985), 57–76.

[118] E. J. Bickerman, "Origines Gentium," *CPh* 47 (1952), 65–81; reprinted in *Religion and Politics in the Hellenistic and Roman World* (Como, 1985), 399–417.

argue that the political and social climates are responsible for minor variations only.

The first major topic considered in chapter 1 is the environmental theory, that is, the assumption that the physical environment influences or even determines group characteristics. It is essential to understand these ideas properly and to trace their history from their beginnings in Greece in the fifth century B.C. through their development over the centuries, both because they were so influential in antiquity and because of the pervasive effect they had, and still have, on opinions in later periods. From the start they served to separate "inferior" and "superior" peoples and to apportion various weaknesses to different populations. The environmental theory was often, but not always, combined with value judgments. Although authors no doubt felt that the environment decisively influenced human beings, a second factor should now be mentioned, which was also considered significant in determining human nature. It was thought that the characteristics which were acquired from the outside, through climate or other external factors, were transmitted to posterity. The heredity of acquired characters is not now a fashionable idea.[119] In antiquity it was, and it was also widely accepted in the eighteenth century. At the same time, however, there also existed an idea that people would change if they moved to another environment, an idea also raised by eighteenth-century authors. In practice, as we shall see, ancient authors believed that this change could only be for the worse. There is never any suggestion in the literature that people improve when they move to a more favorable area, while there is no lack of examples of deterioration. This was still the idea in the Enlightenment: Buffon assumed blacks were degenerated whites, having turned dark because of the activities of the sun. He never assumed whites were bleached blacks, turned white in the northern climate. Hence he proposed the experiment of sending blacks to Denmark, to see how long it would take for them to return to being whites. The development of these concepts in later periods will be traced and we shall see how they were applied in other circumstances. Clearly the environmental theory was of great interest to the Romans, who acquired an empire that extended over a wide variety of climatic zones and geographical regions. In Rome such theories were closely linked with views on the expansion of the empire, and the moral qualities and merits of the various subject peoples. The connection between theories about others and views on the expansion of the empire will be indicated where relevant in the discussion, but will not be the subject of a separate chapter.

A second important concept is considered subsequently in chapter 1, namely the effect of mixed and pure lineage. The emphasis on pure blood and the condemnation of mixed marriages in modern racism makes it unnecessary to argue at length why such a phenomenon should be considered proto-racism in

[119] The name of the theory: heredity of acquired characters is somewhat misleading when applied to the more recent version, because it seems to focus on irrelevant features such as mutilations and other nonadaptive changes. Its ancient precursor did precisely that, as will be seen below.

other periods. The idea that pure lineage results in offspring of better quality than offspring of mixed origins appears in Greek thought, notably in fifth-century Athens, and can be traced throughout the ages. The Roman view of descent and lineage is of great interest. Ideas regarding purity of lineage are important, even though the Romans never claimed a pure lineage for themselves. Nevertheless, many authors fully endorse the view that mixed marriages will produce people of inferior quality. I am not aware of the existence of a theoretical framework justifying such views in antiquity, unlike the environmental theory, which is the subject of much discussion in the ancient literature. The merits of pure blood were taken for granted.

Then follows a discussion of ancient physiognomics, an ancient science or pseudoscience, which aims "to examine and recognise the character of the personality from the character of the body." The assumption of a direct connection between external bodily features and mental traits involves stereotypes and value judgments from the start. Some of these stereotypes are explicitly linked with specific peoples. Moreover, it will be seen that ancient physiognomics tends to focus on group characteristics rather than individual features. It is a significant topic in any discussion of Greek and Roman stereotypical thinking.

Chapter 2 will consider aspects of the interrelationship between attitudes to foreign peoples and imperialist or expansionist ideologies in Greece and Rome. As already observed, this is not a systematic analysis of ancient imperialism. It is an attempt to trace the views held by Greeks and Romans of their enemies and subjects. The assumption is that it is an essential part of the study of peoples at war to understand how they regarded each other and themselves in general terms. For the ancient world, an important concept to be discussed in this connection is the doctrine of natural slavery as developed by Aristotle and widely accepted afterwards.[120] It is relevant to the discussion of ancient stereotypical thinking because it asserts that slaves are different, physically and mentally, from free men through inherited characteristics. This is applied to foreign peoples collectively and, consequently, was influential in early modern imperialist thinking. The claim that some members of humanity are born to be slaves could be described as the ultimate form of proto-racism. Aristotle's natural slaves correspond with all the features listed as characteristic of what is believed to be a race. He writes that slaves—and indeed all non-Greeks—share imagined common characteristics—physical, mental, and moral—which cannot be changed by human will, because they are determined by unalterable, stable, hereditary factors. This naturally leads to a brief discussion about the moral aspects of imperialism: conquest has to be justified, even in a period that does not believe in the equal rights of men. Aristotle's theory forms an attempt to justify both individual slavery and subjugation and enslavement of foreigners. The theory was influential, but Hellenistic and Roman attitudes towards individual slaves and vanquished enemies generally fit into a somewhat different tradition which will be traced in the sequel of chapter 2. It will be seen how

---

[120] See Peter Garnsey, *Ideas of Slavery from Aristotle to Augustine* (Cambridge, 1996).

attitudes towards foreign peoples vary over time in tandem with the prevalence of an ideology of imperial expansion. As emphasized above, this is not an attempt systematically to "explain" imperialism, its aims or ideology. It explores the attitudes of expansionist peoples towards others as an aspect of their motivation and morale.

Attempts to dehumanize foreigners, by claiming they are like animals, or are, in fact, animals, are a familiar feature of racist hatred. We shall therefore see to what extent this was common in the ancient world.

These attitudes often justify the means by which subjugation is realized: large-scale killings, various forms of bloodshed or, conversely, clemency and integration. Anyone discussing hatred of foreigners, discrimination, and racism in our times is bound to think of the pathological behavior that marked the nineteenth and, especially, the twentieth century in this respect. Although it is not the aim of this study to trace actual behavior in antiquity, but to clarify the development of ideas, it is yet unavoidable to say something about actual practice even though the conclusions are clear from the start. There was a good deal of bloodshed, mass murder, and cruelty, but no racist society as such or any systematic racist policy leading to mass murder as seen in the twentieth century.

So far all the topics discussed are related to the mechanisms whereby the Graeco-Roman world established differences between peoples and divided them into groups, superior and inferior. It is generally recognized that an integral part of ethnic prejudice and racist hatred tends to be fear of the other, hence the term *xenophobia*. Chapter 3, will therefore consider several themes in this sphere: Greek and, particularly, Roman fears of moral contamination by others, reinforced by increased contact; anxiety that their culture and empire was being undermined by the foreigners they subjected, particularly those living as immigrants or minorities among them (*Vincendo Victi Sumus*). The large-scale presence of aliens and immigrants in the imperial capital and in Italy caused social tension in the local society, familiar from our own times, which is amply reflected in the literature. The fear this influx engendered leads to regular attempts to regulate the foreign presence, through expulsions or restrictive measures. More specifically, a strong tendency to regard contact between peoples as damaging in general can be found both in Greek and in Roman literature and is frequently explicitly stated. Intercourse with foreign peoples through travel, trade, and migration is not usually described as enriching or instructive.[121] On the contrary, it is seen as corrupting, contaminating, or undermining one's own culture. In a sense this is the moral and spiritual counterpart of the belief in the value of pure lineage.

Thus it will the aim of part 1 to trace general concepts and approaches towards others in Greece and Rome in a roughly systematic manner. Part 2 represents an attempt to show how these ideas, concepts, and approaches are applied to specific peoples. After the consideration of general themes, the second part

---

[121] An exception was Solon κατὰ θεωρίην πρόφασιν ἐκπλώσας at Herodotus 1.29.1. Even if this was a pretext, it still suggests that it was a credible pretext at the time.

of this study is devoted to a survey of Greek and Roman views of selected groups of foreigners, to see how these general themes are represented in Graeco-Roman views of neighbors, minorities, and both friendly and hostile peoples. Topics to be discussed include the views held by the Greeks about Persia after their victory in the fifth century (chapter 4). This is mostly concerned with Herodotus, of course, but not exclusively. Next come the views of Persia and other eastern nations held by fourth-century authors, in particular Plato, Isocrates, and Xenophon. An important theme is the rise of the belief in the opposition of East and West, or Asia and Europe as a distinction between superior and inferior peoples. Throughout this chapter I will trace the association between the transformation of Greek attitudes towards Persia, and Greek ambition to march against Persia. It will be shown that there is a direct connection between the rise of eastward imperialism and attitudes towards Persia in the literature.

It might have seemed obvious that this sort of study should deal extensively with Alexander's attitude towards Persians, for there are numerous passages on his resorting to Persian practices, and they have been widely discussed. However, this material has almost all been preserved by authors of the Roman period, even though it is true that some of those did draw on historians who were contemporary, or near-contemporary, with Alexander. It seems enough of a challenge to analyze attitudes towards Persia in contemporary Greek and Roman sources, without attempting to deal with Roman sources on Alexander as well. We would continuously have to consider whether the attitudes encountered reflect the original sources or the Roman authors who used them. For other reasons little will be said of Hellenistic attitudes towards other peoples, a fascinating subject, which would make this study much longer than it already is. However, this would not really clarify Greek and Roman attitudes. It is true that such a study might involve a different range of attitudes and outlooks from those encountered in the present book, but that may be taken as a reason why it should be a separate work.

Rome, however, is central to the topic of this study. As will be seen, the belief in the opposition of East and West, or Asia and Europe was in Rome replaced, to some extent, or expanded, with the concept of an opposition between North and South. However, the peoples living east of Italy, Greeks, various peoples in Asia Minor, Syrians, Egyptians and others, always played a large role in the Roman perception of their empire because of their high cultural level and their ancient religious and political traditions. Chapter 5 is therefore devoted to Roman imperial attitudes towards the eastern part of the empire and the impact of expansion eastwards on imperial ideology. The discussion includes some thoughts on Cato the Elder and the Elder Pliny on Greeks and their influence on Rome. I will also look at the views of various authors on the effect of the Roman involvement in Asia Minor in the early second century as well as opinions of the inhabitants of this area and their influence on the Roman army and on Rome itself. This part of the discussion will include a consideration of ideas about the generally corrupting influence of Asiatics and their wealth. In connection with this, considerable attention will be paid to the idea that the successes of the empire bear in themselves the seeds of decline, and the related fear that the vanquished somehow subdue their Roman conquerors. It will be seen throughout this chapter how close the connection is between such ideas and the essence of ancient Roman imperialism. As already mentioned, I have not discussed the Roman republic before the mid-second century B.C., because there is not enough contemporary material.[122]

This is followed by a consideration of how the Romans responded in practice and at a conceptual level to the presence of Asiatics, Egyptians, and others in their empire in general, and in Rome in particular. It will be seen how there was a tendency to expel such peoples frequently from the city of Rome, even though they seemed to have made their way back fairly quickly. An intellectual response characteristic of both Greece and Rome in times of increasing expansion is the occurrence of frequent doubts as to the desirability of travel overseas, commerce, or indeed any contact between peoples, even though there is a basic idea that civilization is possible only through contact with others. An interesting reaction to the encounter with strangers seen as particularly barbaric is the denial of their humanity. They are described as if they are animals, not metaphorically but in reality.

The following chapters contain a survey of ancient views of specific selected groups of foreigners: first (in chapter 6) Syrians, Phoenicians, and Carthaginians. These are best considered as one group for our purposes. Then follow the Egyptians who occupied a special place among foreign nations from the classical Greek period till the Late Empire (chapter 7). Parthia / Persia must also be considered, because for the Romans it represented the only rival empire (chapter 8). Next I shall deal with the Greeks as seen by the Romans (chapter 9). A short chapter will be devoted to a category of people rather than a specific ethnic group. One of the great social divisions—between men of the mountains and those of the plains—will be examined for its relevance in the present context in chapter 10. Then we move to the western foreigners: Gauls and Germans are discussed in chapters 11 and 12. Obviously, this treatment omits many peoples about whom much has been said in the ancient literature. Much could be said about the Hispani, Britons, Pannonians, Thracians, and others, but this would not be conceptually very different from what is said about the Germans and Gauls. It has been my aim to make a selection which suffices to indicate basic patterns and avoid tedious repetition as much as possible.

An omission that will strike many readers as eccentric is systematic discussion of the attitudes towards black Africans. Ancient ideas about Africans are highly interesting. Much has been said, and may still be said about Blacks in the ancient world, but the present study is not the proper place for it, because they did not form much of an actual presence in the Greek and Roman worlds. Blacks were considered remarkable, but few of them lived among the Greeks and Romans and no country inhabited by blacks was ever part of the Greek and Roman empires. The Ethiopians are mentioned fairly frequently in some

---

[122] See in general: Tim Cornell, *The Beginnings of Rome: Italy and Rome from the Bronze Age to the Punic Wars* (London, 1995).

sources, but usually as representatives of peoples living near the edge of the world. They were present in fifth-century Athens, but as a rare and expensive type of slave which enhanced the status of the owner.[123] This only confirms the impression that their impact on the social consciousness of the fifth-century Athenians was strictly limited. I have therefore excluded Ethiopians from systematic treatment because for some authors they are clearly mythical and this study deals only with people whom the Greeks and Romans actually experienced. Ancient ideas about—and attitudes towards—Ethiopians (i.e., blacks) will frequently be mentioned and discussed where these are instructive about the manner in which Greeks and Romans thought about the causes of physical differences between peoples. For similar reasons I have decided not to treat the Scythians systematically. Finally, ancient hostility towards the Jews is discussed in chapter 13 as part of these considerations. Jews lived in substantial numbers in the Diaspora and Judaea was part of the Roman Empire from the first century B.C. till the Moslem conquest. Jews are relevant for the present study also because feelings about them were quite strong and it is therefore only natural to compare ancient attitudes towards the Jews with those current in later periods.

The advantage of this general arrangement is that it elucidates the specific attitudes and opinions regarding various peoples, for the treatment in the first part of this chapter, based as it is on thematic analysis, tends to obscure the distinct character of the attitudes towards specific peoples in various parts of the ancient world. Moreover, this will show how various ideas and preconceptions continued through time, from the fifth century B.C. till the Later Roman Empire.

CONCLUSION

The central theme of the present work is the irrational in Greek and Roman ideas about foreigners. It focuses on patterns of bigotry and social hatred in antiquity and attempts to show that some of these are prototypes of the ones familiar to us in modern times.

When the student of a social or historical phenomenon belongs to the culture in which it occurs or occurred, the choice of position is determined by the necessity to take a stand: one is either for it or against or tries to be indifferent. However, even if the student does not belong to the culture that is being studied, the analysis will still bring to it value judgments that are accepted in the student's own culture.

The demand for detachment in such studies, often encountered in the literature, is in any case unsound. It expects of the scholars a split personality which would remove all personal perspective and engagement from their activities as students. This could only result in dull and mechanical and therefore meaning-

---

[123] Margaret C. Miller, *Athens and Persia in the Fifth Century BC: a Study in Cultural Receptivity* (Cambridge, 1997), 212–217: "It appears that in slave-owning societies to have a rare type of slave conferred the same sort of status that ownership of a rare breed of dog gave latter-day aristocrats."

less analysis. In fact, it does not exist in practice. What exists, however, is a pretense at objectivity by students who often ignore the fact that their views are wholly determined and thus distorted by current consensus. Such were my considerations when I published a book about Roman frontier policy and imperialism in the East in 1990. It seemed to me only fair to say something about my personal perspective in thinking about the problems at hand. I thought a candid admission that I was intellectually and emotionally involved in the subject of my studies would show that I was aware of my limitations and tried to use my personal experience to advantage in my ruminations. I must admit that I found it surprising when a few critics, encouraged by this admission, used it against me and accused me of openly acknowledged bias in my views. It seemed to me then, and seems to me true today, that authors who are aware of their perspective have a better chance of delivering lucid analysis, than those who pretend that their experience in life plays no role in their work.

The subject itself of the present study is irrationality and hostility, which makes it even harder to maintain a reasonably dispassionate approach. It cannot be approached by serious thinkers without personal engagement or in isolation of their own social perspective. No person anywhere fails to be touched by prejudice and racism, one's own or that of others, but the manner in which this happens varies and so does one's intellectual outlook on society. Inevitably, someone like me who grew up as a Jew in Amsterdam after World War II has early been made aware of one kind of racism, whereas anyone who grew up in Washington, DC in the 1960s and 1970s has different experiences. To mention merely the most obvious difference: one form of racism focuses on people who are physically indistinguishable from other groups in the same society, the other form concentrates precisely on real physical differences. This has essential consequences for the way in which these phenomena are understood. Those who define racism in recent U.S. publications tend to concentrate on physical aspects, while those who did so in Europe in 1950 tried to understand forms of discrimination that existed in spite of the physical similarity of the discriminated. Let me state it in one sentence: U.S. blacks were never forced to wear the equivalent of a Star of David for the sake of identification. A proper analysis of the history of racism should encompass these various manifestations of it and understand its common roots. This study then represents an attempt to understand broader patterns of group tensions in the past and especially their intellectual roots in Greek and Roman antiquity. It is not a cheerful topic, yet needs to be understood. Whoever writes about it must be involved, emotionally and intellectually, and this involvement may be turned to advantage if it is used for dispassionate analysis.

My own prehistory in the Netherlands made it obvious that these are subjects worth considering. Thirty years at Tel Aviv University made it possible for me to write the book. The two stages together provided a background in which I witnessed forms of social and ethnic tension relevant to many of the topics considered in this study.

Stereotypes and Proto-Racism:

Criteria for Differentiation

Superior and Inferior Peoples

Physical and Group Characteristics

In the Introduction we defined attitudes which we described as proto-racism or pronounced forms of ethnic stereotypes. The following chapters will describe and analyze the conceptual framework which should allow us to determine to what extent Graeco-Roman antiquity used such attitudes in relating to other people. The period covered starts with the fifth century B.C. As already observed, at this time there was nothing resembling the forms of racism found in the nineteenth and twentieth centuries, which adopted or rather misused the insights of science to build an elaborate structure of reasoned discrimination.[1] Obviously, all ideas that derive from Darwinist or quasi-Darwinist constructs must be discarded for the present discussion, but we can look at ancient scholarship and popular ideas presented in the ancient texts. Even if it is clear that the Greeks and Romans never developed an elaborate conceptual framework to justify their classification of humanity, it is still important to understand their implicit and explicit assumptions regarding the differences between peoples. People always try to justify their attempts at categorizing human beings into inferior, equal, and superior groups. Such justifications are all the more prevalent in the case of highly articulate and sophisticated cultures such as Greece and Rome.

Since Greek and Roman literature exercised a profound influence on later European thinking, we inevitably recognize such ideas in more recent periods. We must trace the means by which Greeks and Romans described other peoples and explained their own superiority and the good qualities or inferiority of others. It will be necessary to understand the explanations they give for the existing differences. The sources used are historical writings, ancient works of science, and any literary works that may be relevant. This clearly requires careful distinction between the genres involved: we must distinguish between a lawyer's speech and satirical poems. But both are of value for the present study, for both lawyer's speeches and satirical poems derive their impact on their audience from the fact that they are intended to reflect commonly held opinions, values and, most important for this study, prevalent prejudices.

The first major topic to be considered is the environmental theory, in other words, the assumption that the physical environment influences or even deter-

---

[1] Modern pseudoscience is abundantly illustrated and discussed by Poliakov, *Aryan Myth*, especially in chapter 11.

mines group characteristics.[2] It is essential to understand these ideas properly and to trace their history from their first development in Greece in the fifth century B.C. over the centuries, both because they were so influential in antiquity and because of the pervasive effect they had, and continue to have, on opinions, as seen in the Introduction. From the start, they served to separate "inferior" and "superior" peoples and to apportion various weaknesses to different populations. These traits were assumed to be shared by all individuals belonging to these groups, an essential feature of stereotypical and proto-racist thinking, an important element of which is the denial of individuality. The environmental theory was often, but not always, combined with value judgments.

A second factor was also considered significant in determining human nature: it was thought that the characteristics which were acquired from the outside, through climate or other external factors, were transmitted to the next generation and would then remain stable over time. The heredity of acquired characters is not now a fashionable idea, although it does have its supporters. In antiquity, it was taken for granted, and it was widely accepted in the eighteenth century and part of the nineteenth. At the same time, however, there also existed an idea that people would change if they moved to another environment, an idea also raised by eighteenth-century authors. In practice, as we shall see, ancient authors believed that this change could only be for the worse.

The third influential idea, first attested in fifth-century Athens, is the value of pure lineage. An aggregate of theories about unmixed ancestry springing from native soil was regarded as highly significant by the Athenians themselves and taken over in various forms by later authors, most famously by Tacitus when he says that the Germans are autochthonous and of pure race.

Thus we shall encounter a combination of ideas: the influence of environment and climate, heredity, acquired heredity, and various techniques that were based upon these assumptions, all serving to establish hierarchies of peoples.

THE IMPACT OF ENVIRONMENT: GREEK VIEWS

Herodotus

The assumption that there is a direct relationship between geography and human qualities is clearly present in the work of Herodotus, although not, perhaps, to the extent claimed by several commentators.[3] Thus Macan writes:

[2] For the history of the idea of environmental determinism: F. Thomas, *The Environmental Basis of Society* (1925). Besides being an old work, its treatment of antiquity understandably has its limitations. Important for this subject is James William Johnson, *The Formation of English Neo-Classical Thought* (Princeton, 1967), esp. 46–48.

[3] See now Rosalind Thomas, *Herodotus in Context: Ethnography, Science and the Art of Persuasion* (Cambridge, 2000), 102–114; Reinhold Bichler, *Herodots Welt: Der Aufbau der Historie am Bild der fremden Länder und Völker, ihrer Zivilisation und ihrer Geschichte* (Berlin, 2000), 35; also: M. Dorati, *Le storie di Erodoto: etnografia e racconto* (Pisa and Rome, 2000), and for the two latter works, see W. Fornara, *CR* 51 (2001), 238–241.

You might almost come down to Montesquieu to find a firmer grasp on the relation of Physics and Politics, a clearer reference of institutions and arts to climate, soil, flora, fauna, than are displayed by Herodotus, notably in his accounts of Egypt, Scythia, Libya, and even Hellas. "Soft countries breed soft races" is his moral of the whole story: the sea and the mountains of Greece, the poverty of her soil, and the isolation of her valleys, made her not merely the home of liberty but the nursery of heroes.[4]

First, it is noticeable that Macan has curiously inverted the objects of his praise. Montesquieu's views in this respect are derivative. He develops the standard collection of stereotypes found in various classical sources: people living in cold climates are forceful, self-confident and courageous; those living in hot climates have less self-confidence and courage, and are more emotional. Asiatics are servile, Europeans, free men and conquerors.

Montesquieu (1689–1755), following Jean Bodin (1530–1596)[5] and John Arbuthnot (1667–1735),[6] developed these views under the influence of ancient authors who will be treated in the following pages, and it is peculiar, even for someone who accepts such ideas, to consider him as one who has a firmer grasp of these matters than the authors who serve as his model.[7] Montesquieu elaborated and expanded, but did not really add anything to the ancient environmental theories. It must be said, moreover, that Montesquieu, following Bodin and

[4] R. W. Macan in *CAH* 5 (1927), 408.

[5] Jean Bodin, *The Six Bookes of a Commonweale*, facsimile reprint of the English trans. of 1606, Kenneth Douglas McRae, ed. (Cambridge, MA, 1962), 5.1, pp. 545–568, and see Introduction A22–4. The English translation combines the original French version *Six livres de la République* (Paris, 1575) and Bodin's later Latin edition of 1586. This work superseded his earlier *Methodus ad facilem Historiarum Cognitionem* (Paris, 1566). For Bodin's influence in England: Johnson, *The Formation of English Neo-Classical Thought* (1967), 32, 48.

[6] John Arbuthnot, *An essay concerning the effects of air on human bodies* (London 1733); Richard Mead, *A Treatise Concerning the Influence of the Sun and Moon upon Human Bodies and the Diseases thereby Produced*, trans. T. Stack (London, 1748). For brief comments on the work of Arbuthnot: Thomas, *The Environmental Basis of Society* (1925), 58–62; for that of Mead, ibid., 55–58. For the influence of Arbuthnot on Montesquieu, ibid., 62f. Arbuthnot cites *Airs* but accepts the environmental theory mostly because "it seems agreeable to Reason and Experience" (p. 146). On Arbuthnot, see especially: Claude Bruneteau, *John Arbuthnot (1667–1735) et les idées au debut du dix-huitième siècle* (Ph.D. thesis, Paris 1973; publ. Lille 1974), 264–274. Bruneteau (p. 264) observes that Arbuthnot influenced Montesquieu directly—although Montesquieu hardly acknowledges his dependence—and Taine indirectly. While concluding that ". . . it seems probable that the Genius of Nations depends on that of the Air" (p. 148, § xvii), Arbuthnot affirms that "Arts and Sciences have hardly ever appeared in very great or very small Latitudes." The great authority of Arbuthnot is shown, for instance, in the lavish praise bestowed on him by Dr. Johnson, cf. J. Boswell, *Boswell's Life of Dr Johnson* (London, 1791), ed. G. B. Hill, revised by L. F. Powell (Oxford, 1950), Vol. 1.452 and note 3; also vol. 2.382; vol. 5.29. See also George A. Aitken, *The Life and Works of John Arbuthnot* (Oxford, 1892); Johnson, *The Formation of English Neo-Classical Thought* (1967), 60f. and this author's earlier paper: "Of Differing Ages and Climes," *Journal of the History of Ideas* 21 (1960), 465–480. Johnson cites numerous studies on Hippocrates and the environmental theory which were published in the first half of the eighteenth century and especially after 1720.

[7] See in particular Montesquieu, *L'esprit des lois* (1748), Book 14, Ch. 2; Book 17, Ch. 3–5.

Arbuthnot, based himself not so much on Herodotus, as Macan thinks, but rather on a number of later authors.[8] Macan is all too pleased to think he has found in Herodotus what he believes ought to have been there, but this is only partly true. Even so, the approach certainly occurs in Herodotus 9.122, the conclusion to the entire work: The Persian Artembares tries to persuade Cyrus to leave Persia after the victory over Astyages and to move from poor and rugged Persia to a better country. Cyrus then answers that they might do so, but they should not expect then to continue as rulers, "but to prepare for being ruled by others—soft countries give birth to soft men—there was no land which produced the most remarkable fruit, and at the same time men good at warfare." The Persians followed his advice "and chose rather to live in a rough land and be rulers, than to cultivate plains and be the slaves of others."[9]

This passage shows that the idea that life in a hard country, as opposed to a life of luxury, was likely to produce good warriors, was current among the Greeks of the fifth century.[10] This idea retained its influence throughout antiquity. The passage also implies a direct connection between the rise and decline of empires, and people's lifestyle. It is further relevant to observe that this theory quite emphatically includes the Asiatic Persians among the strong and dominant class of peoples. This is important, for, as we shall see below, in chapter 4, Herodotus has been credited by many modern authors with the idea that there was an essential distinction between East and West, Asia and Europe, whereby Persia was obviously part of the decadent and slavish East. The theme of climate and culture recurs along different lines in a statement about Egypt: "Not only is the climate different from that of the rest of the world, and the rivers unlike any other rivers, but the people also, in most of their manners and customs, exactly reverse the common practice of mankind."[11] Herodotus sug-

---

[8] Bodin cites Herodotus occasionally, but nowhere in support of the environmental determinism which he advocates. He refers to (Ps.?-)Hippocrates, Aristotle, Vegetius, and Vitruvius. Arbuthnot, p. 152f. cites *Airs*, but attempts to adapt the theory to contemporary advances in science.

[9] Κῦρος δέ, ταῦτα ἀκούσας καὶ οὐ θωμάσας τὸν λόγον, ἐκέλευε ποιέειν ταῦτα, οὕτω δὲ αὐτοῖσι παραίνεε κελεύων παρασκευάζεσθαι ὡς οὐκέτι ἄρξοντας ἀλλ' ἀρξομένους· φιλέειν γὰρ ἐκ τῶν μαλακῶν χώρων μαλακοὺς ἄνδρας γίνεσθαι· οὐ γάρ τι τῆς αὐτῆς γῆς εἶναι καρπόν τε θωμαστὸν φύειν καὶ ἄνδρας ἀγαθοὺς τὰ πολέμια. Ὥστε συγγνόντες Πέρσαι οἴχοντο ἀποστάντες, ἑσσωθέντες τῇ γνώμῃ πρὸς Κύρου, ἄρχειν τε εἵλοντο λυπρὴν οἰκέοντες μᾶλλον ἢ πεδιάδα σπείροντες ἄλλοισι δουλεύειν. The contrast between rugged mountaineers and cultivators in the plain recurs more than once in the work of Strabo, as noted below—and again in that of Bodin, p. 564; cf. Part 2, chapter 7. For the idea that luxury destroys empires: David Lewis, *Sparta and Persia* (Leiden, 1977), 149 and below, chapters 2 and 3.

[10] R. Thomas, *Herodotus in Context*, 107f.

[11] 2.35: Αἰγύπτιοι ἅμα τῷ οὐρανῷ τῷ κατὰ σφέας ἐόντι ἑτεροίῳ καὶ τῷ ποταμῷ φύσιν ἀλλοίην παρεχομένῳ ἢ οἱ ἄλλοι ποταμοί, τὰ πολλὰ πάντα ἔμπαλιν τοῖσι ἄλλοισι ἀνθρώποισι ἐστήσαντο ἤθεά τε καὶ νόμους. Cf. Parmenides, fr. 8.57: ἑωυτῶι πάντοσε τωὐτόν, τῶι δ' ἑτέρωι μὴ τωὐτόν and cf. *Airs, Waters, Places*, 19.1, cited below, n. 47. Herodotus is echoed by Sophocles, *Oedipus Coloneus*, 337–340; cf. Alan B. Lloyd, *Herodotus Book II*. 3 vols. (Leiden, 1975), esp. 2.146f., who points out that Herodotus's statement here accords very well with the treatise *Airs, Waters, Places*, discussed below. There is, however, little doubt that Herodotus antedates this treatise. Even J. Jouanna, *Hippocrate, Airs, eaux, lieux* (Paris, 1996), 82, who advocates a relatively

gests a parallel, and does not insist on a causal connection. Still, the point is made that the people are as unique or strange as their country. The idea that a people has habits and customs that are the reverse of what is normal will be found in later periods in connection with the Jews.

Although Herodotus occasionally expresses views indicating that he saw a connection between geography and human character, some commentators have made too much of this.[12] In Herodotus's work, as phrased by Donald Lateiner, "Historical contingency does not yield to a seductive, determinist theory. Geography does not determine history; it can only condition human existence and action." Thus Herodotus's assessment of the Ionians on the eastern shores of the Mediterranean has been misinterpreted. In 1.142 we read that the Ionians have "built their cities in a region where the weather and the seasons are the most beautiful of all the world I know." He then goes on to discuss the Ionian dialects and in the next chapter he states that, in the time of Cyrus, all of Greece was politically and militarily weak, but the Ionians were by far the weakest and least respected.[13] I can see no justification for reading into this passage that Herodotus "emphasises the Ionians' physical and moral softness: their good weather makes them weak."[14] The historian clearly had more subtle views about geography and peoples, as will be clear, for instance from 3.106, where he says that "Greece has been given a climate more beautifully tempered (than any other country)," just like the extreme regions of the world, India and Arabia—which, unlike Greece, he never visited.[15] Here the implication certainly is that a good climate is good for Greece and the Greeks. It is also the earliest passage in Greek literature to claim that the Greek climate is the best in the world, but, unlike later authors, Herodotus does not deduce from this that the Greeks are therefore people of better quality than all the others, as became common later on.

As Edith Hall observed, In Greek tragedy, a connection between environment and group character is sometimes invoked implicitly, but explicit connections

---

early date for the treatise, places it between the works of Herodotus and Thucydides. Lloyd, vol.1.165–8, discusses Herodotus in this connection and asserts that he was obviously familiar with the doctrines expounded in the treatise. I cannot see any evidence for this conclusion. It must be admitted, however, that the exact date of Herodotus's own work is not certain either. Herodotus read from his work in Athens in 445/5, a year before he was involved in the foundation of Thurii (*Kleine Pauly* vol.5, col. 470).

[12] This has been argued convincingly by Donald Lateiner, "The Empirical Element in the Methods of Early Greek Medical Writers and Herodotus: A Shared Epistemological Response," *Antichthon* 20 (1986), 1–20, esp. 16f.; and by Thomas, *Herodotus in Context*, ch. 4.

[13] 1.143: ἀσθενέος δὲ ἐόντος τοῦ παντὸς τότε Ἑλληνικοῦ γένεος, πολλῷ δὴ ἦν ἀσθενέστατον τῶν ἐθνέων τὸ Ἰωνικὸν καὶ λόγου ἐλαχίστου·

[14] Peter Hunt, *Slaves, Warfare, and Ideology in the Greek Historians* (Cambridge, 1998), 146 with reference to S. Flory, *The Archaic Smile of Herodotus* (Detroit, 1987), 48. There is no point in citing 4.142 in this connection. The Scythians may have called the Ionians "either the lowest of the free, or the faithfullest of the slaves," but one cannot without further ado treat as Herodotus's own view a caustic comment attributed by Herodotus to Scythians at a time of conflict.

[15] Cf. Thomas, *Herodotus in Context*, 106, who argues that Herodotus, in this passage, is aware of the environmental theory without taking it to the extreme lengths of *Airs*.

are nowhere drawn.[16] Furthermore, when Herodotus says in 2.77 that the Egyptians are healthy because their climate is equable this cannot really be considered as much of a theory, but it does show yet again that Herodotus was not an author who would claim that a people like the Ionians are morally soft because of their good climate.[17] Thus we encounter some elements of what was to become the environmental theory in the work of Herodotus, but they are not of central importance and they are not used in any systematic way so as to establish a hierarchy of peoples and their values.

Airs, Waters, Places

The most important ancient text for clarifying ideas regarding the relationship between man and his physical environment is the late-fifth-century treatise *Airs, Waters, Places*, one of the works ascribed to Hippocrates, but perhaps not written by him.[18] This occupies a unique place among the works belonging to the Hippocratic corpus.[19] It had an enormous influence, not only on ancient philosophers such as Plato and Aristotle, or the medical author Galen, but also on early modern authors, among others Jean Bodin, John Arbuthnot, Montesquieu, Hume, and Herder, who were influenced by their ancient predecessors.[20]

The treatise *Airs, Waters, Places* has frequently been discussed by modern

[16] Hall, *Inventing the Barbarian*, 172–174.

[17] Cf. Lloyd, *Herodotus Book II*, vol. 2.332f.; Thomas, *Herodotus in Context*, 37–39. Thomas points out that Herodotus, in his statement about Egyptian health, is voicing a Hippocratic view. For Herodotus on Ionia, Thomas, p.105, where she observes that Herodotus is not making any observations here about the health or ethnic character of the inhabitants.

[18] The best edition is Hippocrate, *Airs, eaux, lieux*, ed. Jacques Jouanna (Paris, 1996). The date is discussed in the introduction, 82. Arguments for the various dates proposed all depend on comparisons of the treatise with other works in the Hippocratic corpus or with the political views of Herodotus and Thucydides. Jouanna places the treatise "between Herodotus and Thucydides." Heinimann, *Nomos und Physis* (1945), "Anhang," pp.170–209, agrees, but thinks he can be more precise. The author is a contemporary of Herodotus. "Mit Herodot verbindet ihn auch das griechische Selbstbewustsein und Gemeinschaftsgefühl gegenüber den Barbaren." He therefore suggests a date before the beginning of the Peloponnesian War, shortly before 430. Various scholars have argued that the treatise is a combination of two works, and it has even been suggested that these two works were written by two different authors. These theories have been rejected in recent studies, cf. Jouanna, pp. 15–21. For the relationship between the treatise and Herodotus's work, see now Thomas, *Herodotus in Context*, Chapters 2 and 3, esp. 105: "We should thus draw a far sharper distinction between the type of environmental determinism of the kind visible in *Airs* and other Hippocratic works, where physiological effects are expected, and the hints of it visible in Herodotus." As for the authorship, there is no solid evidence to support or contradict the tradition attributing it to Hippocrates. For present purposes it is essential only to recognize that we have a genuine text dating to the second half of the fifth century B.C.

[19] Modern scholars have distinguished some features in the treatise which are common to elements in several other works. Jouanna, op. cit., 71–79, has argued that these are not essential, thus leaving the treatise a work *sui generis*.

[20] On these later followers, see Léon Poliakov, *Le mythe aryen: essay sur les sources du racisme et des nationalismes* (Paris, 1971); English translation: *The Arian Myth: A History of Racist and Nationalist Ideas in Europe* (New York, 1971), esp. 165–171; 176f.; E. C. Eze, *Race and the Enlightenment* (Oxford, 1997); Johnson, *The Formation of English Neo-Classical Thought* (1967).

scholarship, which tends to take many of the facts and ideas represented in the essay far more seriously than may be healthy or correct.[21] In chapter 12 the author announces: "Now I wish to show how Asia and Europe differ from one another in every respect and particularly in the physical shape of their peoples."[22] This is in itself highly significant, for it is the first time we encounter the idea of bipolarity between Europe and Asia.[23] As indicated in the beginning of this chapter, modern authors erroneously tend to assume that this concept is already

---

[21] The literature is extensive: R. Pöhlmann, *Hellenistische Anschauungen über den Zusammenhang zwischen Natur und Geschichte* (Leipzig, 1879, non vidi); F. Jacoby, "Zu Hippokrates' ΠΕΡΙ ΑΕΡΩΝ ΥΔΑΤΩΝ ΤΟΠΩΝ," *Hermes* 46 (1911), 518–567; M. Pohlenz, *Hippokrates und die Begründung der wissenschaftlichen Medizin* (Berlin, 1938); F. Heinimann, "Nomos und Physis," *Nomos und Physis: Herkunft und Bedeutung einer Antithese im griechischen Denken des 5. Jahrhunderts* (Basel, 1945, repr. Darmstadt, 1978), chapter 1, pp.13–41; Anhang, pp. 170–209; C. van Paassen, *The Classical Tradition of Geography* (Groningen, 1957), 317–328. W. Backhaus, "Der Hellenen-Barbaren-Gegensatz und die Hippokratische Schrift" ΠΕΡΙ ΑΕΡΩΝ ΥΔΑΤΩΝ ΤΟΠΩΝ," *Historia* 25 (1976), 170–185, esp. 179–181; H. Grensemann, "Das 24. Kapitel von De aeribus, aquis, locis," *Hermes* 107 (1979), 423–441. The latter is concerned with the structure of the treatise, arguing that chapter 24 is referred to in chapter 1.7, which would prove that the entire treatise is conceived as one work. Ph.J. van der Eijk, "'Airs, Waters, Places' and 'On the Sacred Disease': Two Different Religiosities," *Hermes* 119 (1991), 168–176, discusses the relationship between these two treatises, arguing that *Airs* is later and possibly by the same author. Discussion of various aspects relevant for the present study may be found in: J. A. López Férez, "Los escritos Hipocráticos y el Nacimiento de la identidad Europea," in H. A. Khan (ed.), *The Birth of the European Identity; The Europe-Asia Contrast in Greek Thought 490–322 B.C.* (Nottingham, 1994), 90–123; response by Vivian Nutton, pp.124–130. Full bibliography may be found in Jouanna's edition. Particularly relevant for us is Christopher Tuplin, "Greek Racism? Observations on the Character and Limits of Greek Ethnic Prejudice" in Tsetskhladze (ed.), *Ancient Greeks West and East* (Leiden, 1999), 47–75, at 63–69. As noted above, Introduction, n. 87. I disagree with Tuplin's assumptions as regards the nature of race and the essence of what is racism. Thomas, *Herodotus in Context*, 86–98, points out that the ethnography here is not primarily and exclusively about Greek superiority over barbarians, but about continents and general physical rules that should in theory apply to all mankind.

[22] *de aere aquis et locis* 12: Βούλομαι δὲ περὶ τῆς Ἀσίης καὶ τῆς Εὐρώπης λέξαι ὁκόσον διαφέρουσιν ἀλλήλων ἐς τὰ πάντα, καὶ περὶ τῶν ἐθνέων τῆς μορφῆς, τί διαλλάσσει καὶ μηδὲν ἔοικεν ἀλλήλοισιν.

[23] C. van Paassen, *The Classical Tradition of Geography*, 326: "Another influence went more deeply however. . . . the contrast Europe–Asia and in particular the contrast Greek–non-Greek. This contrast is found in Herodotus, but with him it is closely connected with his ethical-religious view." This approach was taken even further by Backhaus, who argues that chapters 12 and 24 of the treatise merely claim to describe an opposition between Europe and Asia, but in reality describe a contrast between Greeks and non-Greeks as the author sees it. As will be clear by now, I disagree with this interpretation. The contrast Europe–Asia is not significant in the work of Herodotus, and the contrast Greek–non-Greek, while it exists, is less marked than in later authors. In the treatise the contrast Europe–Asia *is* emphasized in chapter 12, while that between Greeks and non-Greeks is never mentioned. It is hard to achieve clarity by asserting that an author says one thing, but really means another. I agree with van Paasen, however, when he argues that the theory at the root of these views is neither philosophical nor medical. López Férez, in Khan (ed.), *The Birth of European Identity* (1994), 91f. observes that the terms "Europe" and "Asia" are used in a purely geographical sense in the treatise, although it is clear that this represents the first instance in Greek literature where these terms are used in obvious contrast: "No ostante, es la primera vez en la literatura griega en que de modo evidente se quiere hablar de Asia en contraste con Europa."

significantly present in the work of Herodotus.[24] Its first occurrence should, however, clearly be assigned to the text under discussion. The treatise then continues: "For everything in Asia is far more beautiful and grows to far greater size; the region is more cultured than the other, the character of the inhabitants is more tractable and gentle.[25] The cause of this is the moderate climate,[26] because it lies further east in the middle between the risings of the sun, and farther away from the cold." The best part of it has good water, is not too hot or too dry. Food is plentiful. "People are well nourished, of very fine physique and very tall, and hardly differ from each other in shape or length."[27] . . . "Courage, tenacity, energy and will-power could not develop under such natural conditions . . . either among the locals or among immigrants, but pleasure must dominate." The author returns to this topic in chapter 16, where an additional factor is introduced, namely the influence of the monarchy.

> As regards the lack of character and of courage among the inhabitants (sc. of Asia), the reason the Asiatics[28] are less belligerent and gentler in character than the Europeans is mostly the nature of the seasons, which do not change much towards heat or cold, but are equable. . . . Through these causes, I think the Asiatic race is feeble and also because of its institutions. Kings rule most of Asia. Now where men are not masters of themselves and free, but are ruled by despots, they are not interested in military training but intent on not appearing to be combative. For the risks are not similar.

It is important to note that this is probably the earliest text which describes the inhabitants of Asia as soft through the combined influence of climate and monarchy. The date of composition of *Airs* is uncertain, but it was definitely after Herodotus published his work and probably quite some time afterwards.[29]

[24] Always assuming that *Airs* is later than Herodotus's work. As pointed out to me by Martin Ostwald, this occurs in Herodotus's work, 1.4.9, but there it is attributed to the Persians, in the account of the Trojan war: "Thereafter they always regarded the Greeks as their enemies. For Asia and the barbarian peoples which inhabit it, the Persians consider their own, but Europe and the Greeks they view as separate." Ἀπὸ τούτου αἰεὶ ἡγήσασθαι τὸ Ἑλληνικὸν σφίσι εἶναι πολέμιον. Τὴν γὰρ Ἀσίην καὶ τὰ ἐνοικέοντα ἔθνεα βάρβαρα οἰκηιοῦνται οἱ Πέρσαι, τὴν δὲ Εὐρώπην καὶ τὸ Ἑλληνικὸν ἥγηνται κεχωρίσθαι.

[25] 12.2: καὶ τὰ ἤθεα τῶν ἀνθρώπων ἠπιώτερα καὶ εὐοργητότερα for the reading and interpretation, cf. Jouanna, p. 220.

[26] 12.3: Τὸ δὲ αἴτιον τούτων ἡ κρῆσις τῶν ὡρέων cf. Jouanna, comments on p. 294f. Some parts of Asia show greater variety of climate and geography, according to 13.2.

[27] This is typically a statement made about people one has never seen or never properly looked at. Karl Reinhardt attributes the idea that the East is more fertile than the West to Posidonius and he uses it as a significant element in his source critique (*RE* s.v. Poseidonios, col. 676). Albrecht Dihle, "Der fruchtbare Osten" in *Antike und Orient: Gesammelte Aufsätze* (Heidelberg, 1984), 47–60, argues that the idea was spread by those who participated in Alexander's conquest of India. It appears that both scholars are unaware of the fact that the idea figures prominently in the fifth-century text here discussed.

[28] The effects of the monarchy are mentioned again in 23.4. I use the term "Asiatics" as a problematic rendering of several Greek terms.

[29] See above, n. 18 and the remarks by Vivian Nutton in Khan (ed.), *The Birth of European*

As shown, in chapter 4, this idea does not occur in Herodotus; it appears extensively in Isocrates' *Panegyricus* and in the last chapter of the *Cyropaedia,* but
these were again much later, 380 and around 360, respectively. This shows that
ideas concerning the influence of the environment existed in late-fifth-century
Greece, but were not dominant. They were neither adopted by Isocrates nor
were they represented in the last chapter of the *Cyropaedia,* which describes the
Persians as effeminate because of their way of life, not because of their climate
or other external factors. Yet these works, full of confident stereotypes, could
have used them profitably. Of course, they constitute works belonging to two
different genres.[30] In the treatise now under discussion, it is significant that the
softness of the inhabitants is attributed to their climate rather than their wealth,
as in many later texts. The issues of monarchic rule and social disintegration,
which are essential arguments for Isocrates and the author of the last chapter of
the *Cyropaedia*, are mentioned only as secondary factors in the Hippocratic
treatise. The main point made by this author, however, is that the physical,
spiritual, and moral qualities of the inhabitants of Asia are all determined by the
climate in which they live. The paradox is that the climate is fine, nature prolific, the people are therefore healthy and well off—and the result is that they
are feeble. This is their collective character and in his view no other factor
contributes to it, apart from their institutions, as already observed. For Europeans, according to the treatise, the opposite is true. It is pertinent to note that
the observations about climate do not reflect reality, however interpreted. If by
Asia the author really meant the western shore of Anatolia, then he would have
known that the climate there is not much different from Greece. If he refers to
Asia in a much broader sense, then his description is obviously incorrect.[31]

Chapter 23.3–4 of *Airs* states that Europeans, unlike Asiatics, differ greatly
from each other physically.

> The same arguments pertain also to character. In such a nature arise wildness, unso-
> ciability and temper.[32] For the frequent shocks to the mind bestow wildness, destroy-
> ing mildness and kindness. For this reason Europeans, I think, are also more coura-
> geous than Asiatics. For constant similarity engenders indolence, while change
> stimulates endurance in body and soul; leisure and indolence reinforce cowardice,[33]
> endurance and labour courage. For this reason Europeans are more belligerent, and

---

Identity, 124, commenting on López Férez, p. 91. Nutton agrees with Jouanna that the treatise
cannot be dated closer than some time in the second half of the fifth century, not excluding a date
early in the fourth century. I would find the latter hard to accept.

[30] Nutton in Khan (ed.), *The Birth of European Identity*, 128f., observes that the ideas in the
treatise did not exert much influence on medical literature before Galen. Yet it will be argued below
that the environmental theory as such spread rapidly in the fourth century and afterwards.

[31] Backhaus, *Historia* 25 (1976), 179f., shows at length how the climate described in the treatise
does not correspond with reality.

[32] τό τε ἄγριον καὶ τὸ ἄμικτον (or: τὸ ἀμείλικτον) καὶ τὸ θυμοειδὲς ἐν τῇ τοιαύτῃ φύσει
ἐγγίγνεται·

[33] Cf. Euripides, *Orestes* 1350f. for "Phrygian cowards" as a stereotype which was later taken
over into Latin literature.

also because of their institutions, for they are not ruled by kings as are the Asiatics. Where kings rule, there must be the greatest cowards, as I said above. For souls are enslaved; they refuse to run risks spontaneously and at random for the sake of someone else's power. But those who are governed by their own laws,[34] running risks for their own sake and not for the sake of others, choose willingly to go into danger, for they themselves enjoy the spoils of victory. Thus institutions contribute much to the development of courage.

In fact, the treatise has little to say about Europeans and returns to what it has already observed about the Asiatics. The positive point made about Europeans is that they live in a climate with pronounced changes and this endows its inhabitants with "endurance in body and soul" and a concomitantly courageous character. A feature that will prove to be important in other later descriptions of foreign peoples by Greek and Latin authors is the lack of sociability of the Europeans (τὸ ἄμικτον, if this is the correct reading of the text). This is a quality exhibited by various mountain-dwellers and nomadic people and seen as extremely undesirable. As shown by François Hartog, in ancient literature nomads are generally described with negatives: they do not eat bread, do not work, do not sow, do not live in houses, they have no statues of their gods, not temples or altars etc.[35] They are characterized by what they are not and what they do not do. Nomads are the idlest of people, according to Aristotle (*Pol.* 1256a). However, sociability is the primary criterion in determining whether a people is considered acceptable or not. This is the case with the Cyclops in the *Odyssey* and continued to be so in Roman times. Once again, all these qualities are described as group characteristics. As noted in the Introduction, the concept of barbarous people as unsociable is echoed in the work of Buffon, one of the earliest racist theorists in the literature of the Enlightenment.

The author of *Airs, Waters, Places*, as already noted, combines two spheres of influence on people: climate and political institutions.[36] The importance of the latter, presumably, represented a consensus to such a degree that the treatise could not ignore it. In any case, it is very interesting that, in his view, the two go together: in Asia both climate and kingship result in the population being feeble and cowardly. The reverse is true for Europe. There is also a strong tendency to believe that climate and topography have an influence in a directly corresponding manner on character and physiology. Following Herodotus, the

[34] For textual problems and questions of interpretation, see Jouanna, p. 244, n. 1.

[35] François Hartog, *Le miroir d'Hérodote: Essai sur la représentation de l'autre* (Paris, 1980), 218f. Hartog argues that Herodotus tends to think in terms of inversions rather than differences or contrasts in his descriptions of Greeks and other peoples. His Persians told the truth because they were inversions of Greek liars like Polycrates. The Egyptians and Scythians were inversions of each other as well as of the Greeks. All this is probably true, but may be less valid in universal terms than the book suggests, and less typical of Herodotus than of ancient ethnography in general.

[36] R. Thomas, *Herodotus in Context*, 97: (the author) "has two contradictory agendas: (a) to show that climate is crucial; and (b) to show that continent is crucial . . . In addition he stresses a third point (c), that *nomoi* are also crucial—which confounds all."

treatise is the second work to mention a theme that was to have a long history—and will be discussed again elsewhere in this work—namely, the contrast between mountain and plain.[37]

Unlike chapters 12–22, chapter 24 of *Airs* does not refer to any specific people or named region. Having once said that the Europeans (unlike the Asiatics) are different from one another, the chapter then describes the geographical conditions and their impact on the peoples in Europe.[38]

> Those who live in a region which is mountainous, rough, high, and well-watered, where the changes of the seasons show marked differences, are likely to be tall, well suited for endurance and courage, and such natures are likely to possess quite a lot of wildness and ferocity. Those who inhabit low-lying regions,[39] that are grassy, marshy, and have more hot than cool winds, and where there is hot water, those will be neither tall nor well-shaped, but tend to be stocky, fleshy, and dark-haired; they themselves are dark rather than blonde, more susceptible to phlegm than to bile. Similarly, courage and endurance are not by nature part of their character, but the imposition of law may produce them artificially.

Climate, geography and institutions all go together in producing peoples of uniformly good or bad character. Another feature worth observing is that skin and hair color are part of the package. The fighters are light and blonde or ruddy, the weak type is dark. This passage may well be the earliest occurrence of this kind of stereotype about color and character.[40] The author then continues to describe mixed types: Those living on a mountain plateau "tend to be tall in stature and similar to one another, but rather effeminate and docile in character."[41] We may assume that the effeminate types referred to are the men. We are not told what the women were like.[42] In contrast, people living on poor and dry land where there are sharp differences between the seasons will be "hard in physique and steady, blonde rather than dark, stubborn and independent in character and in temper." By this time it should be obvious to the unprejudiced reader that all this is pure theory and not based on any actual observation in the

---

[37] See below, chapter 10.

[38] 23.1: Τὸ λοιπὸν γένος τὸ ἐν τῇ Εὐρώπῃ.

[39] κοῖλα χωρία.

[40] The same idea is found in Ps.Aristotle, *Physiogn.* 812a–b. Frank M. Snowden, *Before Color Prejudice: The Ancient View of the Blacks* (Cambridge, MA, 1983), concludes that there were generally no such prejudices in antiquity. He does not discuss the present passage in detail (85); see also: id. "Greeks and Ethiopians" in John E. Coleman and Clark A. Walz (eds.), *Greeks and Barbarians: Essays on the Interactions between Greeks and Non-Greeks in Antiquity and the Consequences for Eurocentrism* (Bethesda, MD, 1997), 103–126. For a different view: Lloyd A. Thompson, *Romans and Blacks* (London and Oklahoma, 1989). Gay L. Byron, *Symbolic Blackness and Ethnic Difference in Early Christian Literature* (London, 2002), appeared too late for me to take into account.

[41] μεγάλοι καὶ ἑωυτοῖσι παραπλήσιοι. ἀνανδρότεραι δὲ καὶ ἡμερώτεραι αἱ γνῶμαι.

[42] G.E.R. Lloyd, *Science, Folklore and Ideology: Studies in the Life Sciences in Ancient Greece* (Cambridge, 1983), 65, observes that the different responses of men and women to climatic and other factors, and different incidences of disease are noted repeatedly in the treatise.

field.[43] This follows from the general impression that the entire system fits together so nicely, but even more so from the fact that no actual people are ever described. The climates described are also entirely stereotypical, as will be obvious to anyone who has ever traveled through Turkey and the Near East.

One of the peoples described in some detail in the treatise are the Scythians. Even here it is doubtful whether any of the information is based on actual observation. Essential features in the description of the Scythians are clearly based on legend or folktales, such as the description of Scythian women as Amazons (17), the idea of Scythian sterility or impotence (19),[44] the reversal of male and female roles in their society, and the observation that all Scythians are alike.[45] The treatise explains these characteristics as the result of a combination of lifestyle and climate. The reversal of male and female roles is a familiar theme. Herodotus describes the Egyptians in such terms,[46] echoed in this by

[43] Scholarly tradition tends to emphasize the author's genuine observations. E.g., T. Clifford Allbutt, *Greek Medicine in Rome* (London, 1921), 80: "the author . . . had likewise travelled widely and observed shrewdly"; Franklin Thomas, *The Environmental Basis of Society* (1925), 32: "He was a most acute observer of natural phenomena, his inductive method is worthy of notice." van Paassen, *The Classical Tradition of Geography*, describes the work as 'a speculative generalisation which accords with medical experience and theory (320)." The former is correct, the latter clearly is not. Jouanna, in his introduction, pp. 54–71, insists on the high level and sophistication of the ethnographic observations in the treatise. However, see now the lucid observations by Rosalind Thomas, "Ethnography, Proof and Argument in Herodotus," *Histories' PCPS* 43 (1997), 128–148, esp. 140f. about the significance of τεκμήρια and the language of proof in this and *Airs* and other essays. "The context is ethnographic and in some sense scientific—in the sense that the author is trying to ascertain the truth about the physical world—but it can hardly be said to be entirely based on experience." For the relationship between Greek medicine and philosophy: G.E.R. Lloyd, *Magic, Reason and Experience* (Cambridge, 1976); W.H.S. Jones, *Philosophy and Medicine in Ancient Greece, Bull. Hist. of Medicine* Supp. 8 (1946); Lateiner, *Antichthon* 20 (1986), 1–20; see now Thomas's monograph, *Herodotus in Context*.

[44] See also the comments by Jouanna on pp. 235–240. van Paassen, 323–324, comments on their sterility and frequently occurring impotence, "which was a generally known characteristic." Apparently he accepts it as fact. Cf. Charlotte Triebel-Schubert, "Anthropologie und Norm: der Skythenabschnitt in der hippokratischen Schrift 'Über die Umwelt'," *Medizin Historisches Journal* 25 (1990), 90–103. Admittedly, Herodotus 1.105 and Aristoteles, *EN* mention a similar affliction, the latter only among the Scythian kings. Lloyd, *Magic* (1979), 26–28, observes parallels between ch. 22 and *On the Sacred Disease (Morb. sacr.)*. For Herodotus on the Scythians: Stephanie West, "Herodotus in the North? Reflections on a Colossal Cauldron," *SCI* 19 (2000), 15–34 and for the θήλεια νοῦσος see 18f. with n.12. In her paper West argues that Herodotus did not visit the region himself and had no personal acquaintance with it. The same is clearly true for the author of the treatise. See Thomas, *PCPS* 43 (1997), 141. Jouanna, 58f., however, considers the description in the treatise superior to that of Herodotus and Strabo. It is better structured and contains more picturesque detail, he says. For Herodotus on Scythians see also D. Braund, "Greeks, Scythians and Hippake, or 'Reading Mare's-Cheese'" in Tsetskhladze (ed.), *Ancient Greeks West and East* (Leiden, 1999), 521–530.

[45] How and Wells, *A Commentary on Herodotus* 1, helpfully explain that 'the sameness of appearance is common to all uncivilized peoples; so Kinglake says of the Bedouins 'almost every man of the race closely resembles his brethren'" (428). See also below, chapter 12, p. 438, on Tacitus's claim that the Germans all look alike because of their pure lineage.

[46] Herodotus 2.3. See below, chapter 7.

Sophocles (*OC* 337–341). As stated in *Airs* 19.1, the Scyths represent the extreme northern people, corresponding to the Egyptians who live farthest to the south. Both are different from all the other peoples and resemble only themselves, says the treatise.[47] However, living at opposite ends of the world, they apparently also resemble each other according to some legends.

Similarly, it seems clear that the author has never really observed the inhabitants of western Georgia (οἱ Φασιηνοί, Kolchis) or their country, which he describes in chapter 15, although he must have had some second- or third-hand information—or if he was there in fact, his description is fanciful.[48] These chapters present another contrast, which forms a secondary theme in the treatise, namely the opposition of North and South, although the material dealing with the South has been missing since antiquity.[49] In the Roman period the contrast between North and South eclipsed the contrast between Europe and Asia, as will be seen below. However, the treatise does not contain one of the concepts which quickly gained importance afterwards: the idea of an ideal environment in the middle between two extremes. A variation of this is adumbrated by Herodotus 3.106, where he says that "Greece has been given a climate more beautifully tempered (than any other country)," just like the extreme regions of the world, India and Arabia. The treatise, however, argues that the ideal climate, that of Asia, is not good for its inhabitants because it saps their vitality. That is clearly not Herodotus's idea.

It is curious and very significant that the treatise fails to mention the Greeks

[47] *Airs* 19.1: ὅτι πολὺ ἀπήλλακται τῶν λοιπῶν ἀνθρώπων τὸ Σκυθικὸν γένος, καὶ ἔοικεν αὐτὸ ἑωυτέῳ, ὥσπερ τὸ Αἰγύπτιον, cf. Parmenides, fr. 8.57, cited above, n. 11.

[48] Ch. 15: "The fruits that grow there are all weak, soft and imperfect by the excessive quantity of water and because of this they do not ripen." Cf. the *Encyclopaedia Britannica,* CD, Version 1997, s.v. "Transcaucasus" on the region of Kolkhida: "Its subtropical conditions have supported cultivation since ancient times; citrus fruits, tea, and tung are still grown, mostly on the elevated foothills surrounding the plain. The wetter lowlands at the Kolkhida's centre collect cold air, and frosts are too frequent for cultivation of more sensitive crops." For the region: D. Braund, *Georgia in Antiquity* (Oxford, 1994); esp. note, p.16 on *Airs*: "negative to the point of misrepresentation"; see also: 49, 54. Pohlenz, *Hippokrates* (1938), 16, has tried to argue that the author actually visited the places he describes. By way of argument he refers to a travel account of 1901, which I have not seen, said to show remarkable agreement with the treatise, notably the fact that the locals are still described as lazy. See Backhaus, *Historia* 25 (1976), 176f. for comments. Jouanna, 57f., believes that the author himself visited the regions here described and seems to accept these and other ethnographic descriptions as reflecting reality. Similarly: Klaus E. Müller, *Geschichte der antiken Ethnographie und Ethnologischen Theoriebildung,* 2 vols. (Wiesbaden, 1972); esp. vol. 1, 138f.; Nutton, in Khan, *The Birth of the European Identity, 127: "there can be little doubt that the reports are those of an eye-witness, of someone who has himself visited there regions and seen for himself,"* with reference to Elinor Lieber, 'Herodotus and the Hippocratic 'Airs, Waters, Places' on Eunuchs—natural and divine,' *Actes du XXXIIe* Congrès International d'Histoire de la Médécine (Antwerp, 1991), 169–173, which I have not seen.

[49] There is a major lacuna where the treatise discusses Egypt in Lybia, in chapter 12.6; see Jouanna, p. 222, note 1 and additional notes on p. 298. This lacuna existed already in the time of Galen.

themselves and how they are affected by the environment.[50] Greeks are indeed mentioned once, but only those living in Asia Minor: "All the Greeks and barbarians in Asia who are not ruled by despots, but are independent and work for themselves, are the most bellicose of all."[51] This is an interesting and quite inconsistent statement, for earlier in the same chapter we read that the uniformity of the seasons is the main reason why Asiatics are less belligerent than Europeans, the institutions being only a contributory factor. Even if the assumption was that the Greeks were immigrants, it is usually assumed that immigrants deteriorate rapidly under the influence of a different environment, as will be seen below. However this may be, the Greeks are precisely the people whom the author knew well and whose climate he had experienced himself. It is therefore significant that he does not mention them. He discusses Scythians, Egyptians, and the inhabitants of Colchis, unnamed Europeans and Asiatics, but not Greeks. It is not a solution to assume that he really does refer to the Greeks without naming them, for the author was perfectly capable of naming them had he so wished. In the case of the Greeks he could have described their interaction, based on personal observation, but he preferred to generalize and speculate about other peoples.[52] It is probably wrong to look for a specific reason why Greeks are absent from the treatise, for the same absence has been noted in all Greek geographical surveys from Hecataeus onwards and this includes the geographical sections in the historical works of Herodotus, Thucydides, Xenophon, and the *Hellenica Oxyrhynchia*. Polybius was an exception, but later authors did not follow his example.[53] In this aspect, therefore, the treatise follows the custom that was established by this time in Greek geographical discussions, of focusing on non-Greeks and ignoring the Greeks.

For us the most significant feature of the treatise, however, is that it seems to be the first work in Greek literature, or any literature for that matter, which consistently describes peoples in terms of stereotypes that are said to cover all of the individual members of the groups it describes. It leaves no room for any

[50] As López Férez, in Khan, *The Birth of European Identity* (1994), 102 and Nutton, ibid., 124, point out, since the Greeks are not mentioned in this context the treatise is, in a sense, not Hellenocentric.

[51] Ch.16: ὁκόσοι γὰρ ἐν τῇ Ἀσίῃ Ἕλληνες ἢ βάρβαροι μὴ δεσπόζονται, ἀλλ᾽ αὐτόνομοί εἰσι καὶ ἑωυτέοισι ταλαιπωρεῦσιν, οὗτοι μαχιμώτατοί εἰσι πάντων. Lloyd, *Magic*, 246, ignores the fact that the treatise does not mention the Greeks: "The fact that in certain respects this writer . . . exaggerates the contrasts between Greeks and non-Greeks does not diminish the value of his testimony as evidence of the way the Greeks themselves saw those contrasts."

[52] Backhaus, "Der Hellenen-Barbaren-Gegensatz," 185, has argued that the author not so much contrasts Europe and Asia as Greeks and barbarians. The difficulty with this theory is that the Greeks are not mentioned in the work, apart from the one reference to Greeks in Asia, mentioned in the previous note. Some authors ignore the fact that the Greeks are not mentioned and described and simply assume that they are implied. Tuplin, "Greek Racism," 68, deduces this from the occurrence of the word *polis* in the text.

[53] For this important point, see the forthcoming study by Yuval Shahar, *Josephus Geographicus: The Classical Context*. As Shahar puts it: "the classical period has left us Greek geography, but not a geography of Greece."

individuality. As such it is a significant milestone in the rationalization of discriminatory thinking.[54]

Other Authors on the Environmental Theory

A similar approach is found in Plato's *Laws* 747c–e and in Aristotle, *Politics* 1327b. In the *Laws* we find the Egyptians, Phoenicians, "and many other peoples" being accused of having an approach to wealth and to life in general which shows a narrow-minded outlook.[55] Like the author of *Airs,* Plato then considers that there may be two reasons for this. Bad lawgivers may be to blame, or natural causes. "Some localities are more likely than others to produce comparatively good (or bad) characters, and we must take care to lay down laws that do not fly in the face of such influences."[56] "Some sites are suitable or unsuitable because of varying winds or periods of heat, others because of the quality of the water; in some cases the very food grown in the soil can nourish or poison not only the body but the soul as well. But best of all will be the places where the breeze of heaven blows, where spirits hold possession of the land and greet with favour (or disfavour) the various people who come and settle there."[57] Clearly, Plato, like the author of *Airs*, is aware that climate and geography are unalterable and constant factors, while constitutions are the work of men. That is why Plato wrote the *Laws* and not a work about geography or the weather. We find the same idea in this explicit form in the *Republic* 435c–436a, where he also mentions the love of money (τὸ φιλοχρήματον) of the Egyptians and Phoenicians, the hot temper (τὸ θυμοειδές) of Thracians, Scythians, and other inhabitants of the north, and the love of learning (τὸ φιλομαθές) of the Greeks, but no causes of these presumed collective qualities

[54] Tuplin, "Greek Racism," 68f., concludes that the treatise is not racist for three reasons: (a) ethnical characteristics are not treated as directly genetic but as the result of the psychological impact of the environment. (b) "The basic problem is that our author's idea of differentiation does not match our idea of major racial distinctions." (c) Most other peoples were not very physically different. As regards (a), this conclusion insists too much on genetics as a condition for (proto-)racist thinking. As for (b), I refer to the Introduction, where I reject such ideas concerning major racial distinctions. Regarding (c), it is surprising to see it seriously asserted that racism can be directed only at people who are physically very different. As noted, Tuplin definitely recognizes the presence of strong ethnic prejudice.

[55] *Leg.* 747c, καθάπερ Αἰγυπτίους καὶ Φοίνικας καὶ πολλὰ ἕτερα ἀπειργασμένα γένη νῦν ἔστιν ἰδεῖν ὑπὸ τῆς τῶν ἄλλων ἐπιτηδευμάτων καὶ κτημάτων ἀνελευθερίας.

[56] *Leg.* 747d (trans. Trevor J. Saunders): μηδὲ τοῦθ' ἡμᾶς λανθανέτω περὶ τόπων ὡς οὐκ εἰσὶν ἄλλοι τινὲς διαφέροντες ἄλλων τόπων πρὸς τὸ γεννᾶν ἀνθρώπους ἀμείνους καὶ χείρους, οἷς οὐκ ἐναντία νομοθετητέον· In antiquity this is cited already by Galen, *Quod animi mores corporis temperamenta sequantur* 806, in a discussion of the environmental theory.

[57] *Leg.* 747e (trans. Trevor J. Saunders): τούτων δ' αὖ πάντων μέγιστον διαφέροιεν ἂν τόποι χώρας ἐν οἷς θεία τις ἐπίπνοια καὶ δαιμόνων λήξεις εἶεν, τοὺς ἀεὶ κατοικιζομένους ἵλεῳ δεχόμενοι καὶ τοὐναντίον. Whatever the θεία τις ἐπίπνοια may mean, it seems to represent a view of the ideal environment which differs slightly from that described in *Airs* 12 and 23, where we read of the weakening and softening effects of ideal natural conditions.

are given.[58] There is, however, some evidence that Panaetius and others who were Platonists asserted that a mild and well-balanced climate, such as that of Attica, is conducive to wisdom.[59] This idea also occurs elsewhere in Plato's work. In the *Timaeus* he writes that the goddess Athena herself had chosen the site of Athens, for it has "a temperate climate throughout the seasons (which) would bring forth men of surpassing wisdom."[60] In any case, the influence of *Airs* on the passage in the *Laws* is obvious, even if Plato more than the treatise seems to believe in the salutary effect of a good climate. The idea that Egyptians and Phoenicians are greedy sharpers, however, seems to be new in this period. Although it is true that the Phoenicians appear as traders—treacherous or not—already in Homer, the stereotypes above are found in explicit form again in several fourth-century texts.[61] Above we saw this idea was also represented in Isocrates' *Panegyricus*, dated to 380, but it does not occur in *Airs, Waters, Places*. In the fifth century some eastern peoples were considered famously rich, as we saw, but there was no idea that they were also greedy. Most importantly, the view that such collective qualities are caused either by a bad constitution or by the environment and in particular the climate is first encountered in *Airs*.

The essence of this concept is found in Aristotle, with some interesting variations:

> The peoples[62] of cold countries generally, and particularly those of Europe, are full of spirit, but deficient in skill and intelligence; and this is why they continue to remain comparatively free, but attain no political development and show no capacity for governing others.[63] The peoples of Asia are endowed with skill and intel-

[58] Karl Trüdinger, *Studien zur Geschichte der griechisch-römischen Ethnographie* (Basel, 1918), 57 n. 2, finds Plato's argument curious.

[59] Proclus, *in Timaeum* 50b (1.162): τὴν δὲ εὐκρασίαν τῶν ὡρῶν τὴν τῶν φρονίμων οἰστικὴν Παναίτιος μὲν καὶ ἄλλοι τινὲς τῶν Πλατωνικῶν ἐπὶ τῶν φαινομένων ἤκουσαν, ὡς τῆς Ἀττικῆς διὰ τὰς ὥρας τοῦ ἔτους εὖ κεκραμένας ἐπιτηδείως ἐχούσης πρὸς τὴν τῶν φρονίμων ἀνδρῶν ἀπογέννησιν. The idea that Greece and, particularly, Attica offer the best climatic mixture, notably the best air, and therefore produce the best possible people recurs at some length in an anonymous and undated life of Pythagoras excerpted by Photius, *Bibliotheca* 249.441a.13ff., cited and discussed by Trüdinger, *Studien zur Geschichte der griechisch-römischen Ethnographie* (1918), 51–53. Trüdinger argues that it dates to the fourth century B.C. and antedates 338.

[60] Plato, *Timaeus* 24c (trans. Donald J. Zeyl): ἡ θεὸς προτέρους ὑμᾶς διακοσμήσασα κατῴκισεν, ἐκλεξαμένη τὸν τόπον ἐν ᾧ γεγένησθε, τὴν εὐκρασίαν τῶν ὡρῶν ἐν αὐτῷ κατιδοῦσα, ὅτι φρονιμωτάτους ἄνδρας οἴσοι· Cf. Critias 109c; 111e for Attica's ideal mixture of seasons.

[61] For Egyptians and Phoenicians see also below, chapters 7 and 6.

[62] Cf. Richard Kraut (trans. and comm.), *Aristotle, Politics, Books vii and viii* (Oxford, 1997), 92: "By a 'nation' (*ethnos*) he means a social organization larger and looser than that of the *polis*. The Scythians, Thracians, Celts, and Persians (all but the last being northern Europeans) are counted as nations at VII 2 1324^{b}11–12." Kraut observes that Greece sometimes, also by Aristotle himself, is regarded as part of Europe. For Aristotle's use of the term θυμός see W. L. Newman, *The Politics of Aristotle*, 4 vols. (Oxford, 1887–1902), vol. 2, 364; Kraut, *Aristotle*, 93f.

[63] Newman, 2.365, comments: "Aristotle can hardly include the Macedonians among the "nations of Europe," for they were not unable to rule over others, but does he regard them as Greeks? He is

ligence, but are deficient in spirit; and this is why they continue to be peoples of subjects and slaves. The Greek stock,[64] intermediate in geographical position,[65] unites the qualities of both sets of peoples. It possesses both spirit and intelligence: the one quality makes it continue free; the other enables it to attain the highest political development, and to show a capacity for governing every other people—if only it could once achieve political unity. (trans. Ernest Barker)[66]

This approach is undoubtedly heavily influenced by *Airs, Waters, Places*, but unlike the latter Aristotle is not antimonarchic. He therefore expresses no opinion here about the effect of monarchy on peoples' physical and mental health. It might be said that he is more consistent, for he holds that political and social organization—important as they are—are determined by climate, and he is also more systematic. In other works Aristotle argues that there is a direct connection between bodily and mental characteristics. He asserts it in principle: "It seems to me that soul and body react on each other; when the character of the soul changes, it changes also the form of the body, and conversely, when the form of the body changes, it changes the character of the soul." And an undatable Pseudo Aristotelian chapter in *Problemata* asks: "Why are those who live in climates of extreme cold or heat brutish in manners and appearance?"[67] This text further elaborates on the favorable effect on body and mind of the "best mixture" of qualities and the harmful effects of the extreme climates. As examples of the physical effect of extreme heat, for instance, the text gives the bandy legs and curly hair of the Ethiopians and Egyptians. This is explained by analogy: just as planks are warped when they dry, so are the bodies of living beings (909a.27–32). It adds that those who live in the South have dark eyes while northern peoples have grey eyes and this is explained by the influence of the

---

probably thinking of the Scythians, Thracians, and Illyrians among other European races. He refers to Xenophon, *Cyr.* 1.1.4 and, by contrast, to Isocrates, *Pan.* 67.

[64] Kraut and others translate: "the Greek race" for τὸ τῶν Ἑλλήνων γένος. Barker's "stock" is better but not ideal.

[65] Newman, 2.366, notes that the ὀμφαλός at Delphi was regarded as the center both of Greece and of the habitable earth: Strabo 9.3.6 (c.419). Xenophon, cited below, claims the same for Athens and Strabo 6.4.1 (c.286) for Italy.

[66] Aristotle, *Pol.* 1327b: τὰ μὲν γὰρ ἐν τοῖς ψυχροῖς τόποις ἔθνη καὶ τὰ περὶ τὴν Εὐρώπην θυμοῦ μέν ἐστι πλήρη, διανοίας δὲ ἐνδεέστερα καὶ τέχνης, διόπερ ἐλεύθερα μὲν διατελεῖ μᾶλλον, ἀπολίτευτα δὲ καὶ τῶν πλησίον ἄρχειν οὐ δυνάμενα· τὰ δὲ περὶ τὴν Ἀσίαν διανοητικὰ μὲν καὶ τεχνικὰ τὴν ψυχήν, ἄθυμα δέ, διόπερ ἀρχόμενα καὶ δουλεύοντα διατελεῖ· τὰ δὲ τῶν Ἑλλήνων γένος, ὥσπερ μεσεύει κατὰ τοὺς τόπους, οὕτως ἀμφοῖν μετέχει. καὶ γὰρ ἔνθυμον καὶ διανοητικόν ἐστιν· διόπερ ἐλεύθερόν τε διατελεῖ καὶ βέλτιστα πολιτευόμενον καὶ δυνάμενον ἄρχειν πάντων, μιᾶς τυγχάνον πολιτείας. On ethnocentrism, James S. Romm, *The Edges of the Earth in Ancient Thought: Geography, Exploration and Fiction* (Princeton, 1992), 46–48, 54f. W.K.C. Guthrie, *A History of Greek Philosophy* 3 (1962), 161 n. 3, says Aristotle has added the point about the Greeks "obviously in dependence on earlier sources." This is possible, but I do not know why it is obvious.

[67] *Problemata* 909a.1 Διὰ τί θηριώδεις τὰ ἔθη καὶ τὰς ὄψεις οἱ ἐν ταῖς ὑπερβολαῖς ὄντες ἢ ψύχους ἢ καύματος; ἢ διὰ τὸ αὐτό; Cf. K. Trüdinger, *Studien zur Geschichte der griechisch-römischen Ethnographie* (1918), 54–56, where reference is made to E. Richter, *de Aristotelis problematis* (Diss. Bonn, 1885), which I have not seen.

72   · *C H A P T E R 1* ·

temperature on the balance of moisture in the body (910a.12). In a similar manner, *Airs, Waters, Places* explains various collective physical features caused by climate, but unlike the *Problemata,* it also explains collective character traits. Here too, the inhabitants of warm regions are cowardly (δειλοί) and those in the cold regions courageous (ἀνδρεῖοι).⁶⁸ The explanation given is that people who live in the cold are naturally hot and therefore brave, while those who live in the heat are naturally chilled and thus cowardly. The interdependence of body and soul, linkage between physical and mental processes and relationship between personal character and external appearance were common assumptions among Greek thinkers. This was the conceptual basis for the development of the theory of physiognomics, discussed below.

To return to the environmental theory as found in Aristotle's work, his views and concepts are essentially the same as those in *Airs,* with minor variations. Aristotle adds a contrast that is not found in *Airs:* Europeans are incompetent and stupid, while Asiatics are intelligent and skillful. Aristotle has no doubts as to the relationship between climate and people. He agrees with the bipolarity of Europe representing a cold climate and Asia representing warmth. The cold climate produces free people with spirit who are, however, stupid and incompetent,⁶⁹ a quality which extends to their political organization. The Asiatic climate produces soft people, intelligent and competent, but slaves. Elsewhere in the *Politics* Aristotle returns to this theme without specifying the causes: he claims that "Kingships [among some uncivilized peoples] possess an authority similar to that of tyrannies; but they are none the less constitutional, and they descend from father to son. The reason is that these uncivilized peoples are more servile in character than Greeks (as the peoples of Asia, in turn, are more servile than those of Europe); and they will therefore tolerate despotic rule without any complaint."⁷⁰ It could be argued that the existence of slaves implies the existence also of masters who were less soft, but neither Aristotle, nor the author of the treatise, tells us what qualities were needed to become a master in Asia. Unlike the treatise *Airs,* Aristotle introduces a third factor: the Greeks are the ideal group in the middle. As already noted, *Airs* ignores the Greeks. In Aristotle's view, Greeks combine European spirit and freedom with Asiatic intelligence and competence. Hence they would be capable of ruling all mankind—an early text, if not the first one to suggest that the Greeks should achieve universal rule. An additional argument brought forward is the presumed

⁶⁸ *Problemata* 909b.9ff.: Διὰ τί οἱ μὲν ἐν τοῖς θερμοῖς τόποις δειλοί εἰσιν, οἱ δὲ ἐν τοῖς ψυχροῖς ἀνδρεῖοι; and again 910a.40–910b.

⁶⁹ Cf. Ps.Aristotle, *Problemata* 909b: Διὰ τί οἱ ἐν τοῖς θερμοῖς τόποις σοφώτεροί εἰσιν ἢ ἐν τοῖς ψυχροῖς.

⁷⁰ *Pol.* 1285a (trans. Ernest Barker). διὰ γὰρ τὸ δουλικώτεροι εἶναι τὰ ἤθη φύσει οἱ μὲν βάρβαροι τῶν Ἑλλήνων, οἱ δὲ περὶ τὴν Ἀσίαν τῶν περὶ τὴν Εὐρώπην, ὑπομένουσι τὴν δεσποτικὴν ἀρχὴν οὐδὲν δυσχεραίνοντες. The issue here is that the monarchy among the barbarians resembles tyranny, but is not, for the ruler governs according to law and the position is hereditary, a condition made possible by the servile nature of those peoples. For the idea of "slavery by nature" or "natural slavery," see below, chapter 2. Newman, 2.365, refers for the slavishness of barbarians to *Tragicorum Graecorum Fragmenta Adespota* 359 Nauck: ἰὼ τυραννὶ βαρβάρων ἀνδρῶν φίλη.

geographical centrality of Greece. It is undoubtedly highly significant that this concept is found in a passage unambiguously stating the centrality of Greece in the world and the superiority of the Greeks over all other peoples, while the latter are described in fully stereotypical terms. It is no less important to note that Aristotle assumes that there is an immediate connection between collective superiority and empire. Here we touch upon two of the main components in Aristotle's views on empire, the other being an offshoot of his theory of natural slavery. The two are related, as may be seen in the passage just quoted, where it is said that "barbarians are by nature more slavish than Greeks and those in Asia more so than those in Europe." Natural slavery is the result of climate.

Aristotle was not the first to describe Greece as being positioned in the middle. Xenophon says of Athens: "One might reasonably think that the city lies in the middle of Greece and indeed of the entire world. For the further we travel away from her, the greater is the heat or cold we suffer."[71] Aristotle was writing after Isocrates produced his *Panegyricus,* discussed below, and also after the last chapter of the *Cyropaedia* was written, but he was certainly the first to ascribe differences between peoples to factors wholly beyond their own control. The implication of this is also that the superiority of the Greeks is ultimately a result of luck or fate: geographical and environmental advantages have created the conditions for their success. For the Greeks themselves, of course, Aristotle's views are not as simplistic. There are three things that make men what they are: nature, habit, and reason (φύσις ἔθος λόγος, *Pol.* 1332a–b). Both habit and reason can be modified by training and Aristotle therefore writes much about education in this connection.[72] It may be noted further that Aristotle ignores the other contrast, discussed extensively in the original version of *Airs, Waters, Places*, namely that between North and South.

Collective characteristics, then, are determined by climate.[73] The implication is that changes come from the outside, will remain stable, and do not occur

---

[71] Xenophon, *de vectigalibus* 1.6: οὐκ ἂν ἀλόγως δέ τις οἰηθείη τῆς Ἑλλάδος καὶ πάσης δὲ τῆς οἰκουμένης ἀμφὶ τὰ μέσα οἰκεῖσθαι τὴν πόλιν. ὅσῳ γὰρ ἄν τινες πλέον ἀπέχωσιν αὐτῆς, τοσούτῳ χαλεπωτέροις ἢ ψύχεσιν ἢ θάλπεσιν ἐντυγχάνουσιν.

[72] Cf. Carnes Lord, *Education and Culture in the Political Thought of Aristotle* (Ithaca and London, 1982); "Politics and Education in Aristotle's 'Politics'," in G. Patzig (ed.), *Aristoteles' "Politik"* (Göttingen, 1990), 202–215; see p. 203: "For the Greeks, the education of children was conceived much less as a training of the mind than as a training of the character or the soul." Plato, *Leges* 747c–d, is uncertain whether the character of the Phoenicians and Egyptians, which he describes as negative ("sharpers"), is formed the way it is by *nomos,* i.e., bad laws, education or misfortune, or by *phusis,* i.e., the environment, climate or, soil.

[73] K. J. Dover, *Greek Popular Morality in the Time of Plato and Aristotle* (Oxford, 1974), 83–87, briefly discusses heredity and environment in popular generalizations about human nature. He cites various texts which show that Greeks considered themselves morally better than *barbaroi* (and that many Greeks found themselves superior to other Greeks). He then goes on to show that Demosthenes and other orators lay much emphasis on customs and tradition in their appreciation of cities and communities. It is not certain how significant this is for the present discussion. One would expect moral rhetoric to emphasize traditions and good behavior rather than nature and inherited characteristics. The requirements of the argument usually are enough to explain the emphasis on national customs and traditions. Cf. Dover, pp. 88–95, on individuals.

through evolution or conscious choice. Individuality is ignored. This is proto-racism as defined in the Introduction, for climate and geography rather than genetics are said to determine group characteristics. Large groups of peoples, indeed entire nations, are believed to have common characteristics determined by factors outside themselves, which are, by implication, unchangeable. These presumed characteristics are then subject to value judgments, in which the others are usually rejected as being inferior to the observer, or, in rare instances, approved of as being untainted and superior. It is furthermore the case that these descriptions evidently are not based on direct observation, which characterizes them even more as ethnic stereotypes and proto-racism. Finally, and in connection with the previous observation, it should be noted that so far we have dealt exclusively with the sort of observations made about foreign peoples living elsewhere, not with foreigners living as minorities among the Greeks or Romans.

The Heredity of Acquired Characters

Before continuing to see how these ideas were taken over by later authors, it is necessary to consider the mechanisms whereby group characteristics were believed to have been formed. The treatise *Airs* in the Hippocratic corpus and Aristotle's work state unequivocally that this took place under the influence of physical factors in the environment: climate and geography. *Airs* also allows for political organization as a factor, but Aristotle sees political institutions as also dependent on the environment. This leaves no room for other factors that might also be thought to play a role: heredity, personal choice, and individual differentiation. It is precisely the element of heredity that is central in nineteenth- and twentieth-century racism, for racism in the narrow sense of the term holds that there is a causal link between inherited physical traits and traits of personality, intellect, or culture. Both ideas, ancient environmental determinism and modern collective heredity, then introduce systems that withhold from humanity any means of determining the level of their own achievements, whether this is the physical environment or inherent characteristics that are passed on from generation to generation by inheritance. The result of both is that groups of human beings are described in stereotypes, characterizing them as inferior in various ways. It could therefore be said that notions of heredity would have served such thinking in antiquity just as well as the environmental argument. It is not surprising that heredity is indeed represented in ancient thinking, although in forms different from those encountered in the nineteenth and twentieth centuries. This assertion requires explanation and justification. Two mechanisms are to be discerned here and for the first we must consider again a passage in the treatise on *Airs, Waters, Places*.

Chapter 14 in *Airs, Waters, Places* is entitled "About the Longheads" (περὶ τῶν Μακροκεφάλων).[74] Among this people, said to have inhabited the region

---

[74] F. Heinimann, *Nomos und Physis*, 141f.; Martin Ostwald, *From Popular Sovereignty to the Sovereignty of Law: Law, Society, and Politics in Fifth-Century Athens* (Berkeley and Los Angeles,

of Trapezus, long heads are considered a feature of nobility. Therefore they artificially elongated their children's heads.

> Thus originally custom achieved the effect that through force such a form developed; but as time went on this happened naturally, so that custom no longer forced it. For the seed comes from everywhere in the body, healthy seed from the healthy parts and unhealthy from the unhealthy parts.[75] If bald children usually have bald parents, grey-eyed children usually grey-eyed parents and squint-eyed children usually squint-eyed parents and if the same is true for the other physical characteristics, what prevents a long-headed parent from having a long-headed child? Now, however, it is not like in the past, for the custom is no longer in force because of intermarriage with (other) people.[76]

This is an essential passage, which expounds the idea of the heredity of acquired characters. The argument about seed expresses the idea that human seed has the qualities of the entire person as he or she is, the moment the seed is produced. This would make it possible for a man and a woman with artificially elongated heads to have children born with naturally elongated heads. It is assumed here that there is, in fact, no difference between inherited and acquired characters in their transmission to the next generation. A variation of this theory is also present, although less extensively argued, in chapter 23 of *Airs*, where the author explains that variations in the weather affect the physical characteristics of people and are thus responsible for the differences in stature and character of people in Europe, "for there develops more deterioration in the coagulation of the seed when the seasons change often than when they are similar or the same."[77]

1986), 261. The practice of deforming the heads of babies by binding them tightly so that they retained through life an elongated form is well known from various parts of the world. It is attested, for instance, in the sculpture of the Mangbetu of Central Africa and on vases of the Zapothecs of Oaxaca in Mexico (before the ninth century A.D.). See, e.g., the example in the Museo Nacional di Antropología, Mexico City, Inv. no. 10-357379.

[75] The phrase ἀπό τε τῶν ὑγιηρῶν ὑγιηρός, ἀπό τε τῶν νοσερῶν νοσερός *de morbo sacro* 2.12.

[76] *De aere aquis et locis* 14: Καὶ πρῶτον περὶ τῶν Μακροκεφάλων. Τουτέων γὰρ οὐκ ἔστιν ἄλλο ἔθνος ὁμοίως τὰς κεφαλὰς ἔχον οὐδέν. Τὴν μὲν γὰρ ἀρχὴν ὁ νόμος αἰτιώτατος ἐγένετο τοῦ μήκεος τῆς κεφαλῆς, νῦν δὲ καὶ ἡ φύσις ξυμβάλλεται τῷ νόμῳ· τοὺς γὰρ μακροτάτην ἔχοντας τὴν κεφαλὴν γενναιοτάτους ἡγέονται. Ἔχει δὲ περὶ νόμου ὧδε· τὸ παιδίον ὁκόταν γένηται τάχιστα τὴν κεφαλὴν αὐτέου ἔτι ἁπαλὴν ἐοῦσαν, μαλακοῦ ἐόντος, ἀναπλήσσουσι τῇσι χερσὶ, καὶ ἀναγκάζουσιν ἐς τὸ μῆκος αὔξεσθαι, δεσμά τε προσφέροντες καὶ τεχνήματα ἐπιτήδεια, ὑφ᾽ ὧν τὸ μὲν σφαιροειδὲς τῆς κεφαλῆς κακοῦται, τὸ δὲ μῆκος αὔξεται. Οὕτω τὴν ἀρχὴν ὁ νόμος κατειργάσατο, ὥστε ὑπὸ βίης τοιαύτην τὴν φύσιν γενέσθαι· τοῦ δὲ χρόνου προϊόντος, ἐν φύσει ἐγένετο, ὥστε τὸν νόμον μηκέτι ἀναγκάζειν. Ὁ γὰρ γόνος πανταχόθεν ἔρχεται τοῦ σώματος, ἀπό τε τῶν ὑγιηρῶν ὑγιηρός, ἀπό τε τῶν νοσερῶν νοσερός. Εἰ οὖν γίγνονται ἔκ τε τῶν φαλακρῶν φαλακροί, καὶ ἐκ γλαυκῶν γλαυκοί, καὶ ἐκ διεστραμμένων στρεβλοὶ, ὡς ἐπὶ τὸ πλῆθος, καὶ περὶ τῆς ἄλλης μορφῆς ὁ αὐτὸς λόγος, τί κωλύει καὶ ἐκ μακροκεφάλου μακροκέφαλον γενέσθαι;

[77] 23: αἱ γὰρ φθοραὶ πλείονες ἐγγίγνονται τοῦ γόνου ἐν τῇ ξυμπήξει ἐν τῇσι μεταλλαγῇσι τῶν ὡρέων πυκνῇσιν ἐούσῃσιν ἢ ἐν τῇσι παραπλησίῃσι καὶ ὁμοίῃσιν. For the custom among other peoples: Müller, *Geschichte der antiken Ethnographie*, 1.139 with note 300.

The theory is put forward here explicitly, but there can be little doubt that it was generally assumed to be a matter of course. In modern Europe this theory is associated with Lamarck (1744–1829)[78] and others,[79] notably Spencer[80] and, notoriously, Lysenko in the Soviet Union,[81] but it is not now accepted. In contemporary terms, the hypothesis suggests that there is some inherent biological property that enables organisms to pass on physical modifications to their descendants, independently of a Darwinian mechanism of selection.[82] One of the consequences of the theory could be that no animal—or race—is locked forever into its present characteristics, which is the essence of racism, as first stated by Immanuel Kant.[83]

There is another aspect of interest for our subject: when the evolutionary

---

[78] *Philosophie zoologique* (Paris, 1809; repr. Bruxelles, 1983); trans. Hugh Elliott, *Zoological Philosophy* (1914, reprinted, 1984). Lamarck was, to some extent, preceded and influenced by Pierre Cabanis (1757–1808), *Rapports du physique et du moral chez l'homme* (Paris 1802), vol. 2, 127: "If the determining causes of an early habit continue to act for several generations, a newly acquired nature will be formed" (cited by Poliakov, *Aryan Myth*, 218). Like the treatise *Airs, Waters, Places,* Cabanis combined this idea with the familiar theories on climates and geography. Cf. Conway Zirkle, "The Early History of the Idea of the Inheritance of Acquired Characters and of Pangenesis," *Trans. Am. Phil. Soc.*, NS 35 (1946), 91–151. Zirkle goes back to Aristotle. On Lamarck in general: L. J. Jordanova, *Lamarck* (Oxford, 1984); Pietro Corsi, *The Age of Lamarck: Evolutionary Theories in France 1790–1830* (Berkeley, 1988). See also Eva Jablonka and Marion J. Lamb, *Epigenetic Inheritance and Evolution: the Lamarckian Dimension* (Oxford, 1995), which represents an attempt to re-examine the role of the inheritance of acquired characters in evolution. I lack all competence in these matters.

[79] For its influence in England, see Ruth Schwartz Cowan, *Sir Francis Galton and the Study of Heredity in the Nineteenth Century* (New York and London, 1985), 15–19.

[80] For Spencer, see John Greene, "Biology and Social Theory in the Nineteenth Century: Auguste Comte and Herbert Spencer" in Marshall Clagett (ed.), *Critical Problems in the History of Science* (Madison, WI, 1959), 419–446; Derek Freeman, "The Evolutionary Theories of Charles Darwin and Herbert Spencer," *Current Anthropology* 15 (1974), 211–237.

[81] Zhores A. Medvedev, The *Rise and Fall of T. D. Lysenko* (New York, 1969); David Joravsky, *The Lysenko Affair* (Cambridge, MA, 1970); Dominique Lecourt, *Lyssenko: histoire réelle d'une «science prolétarienne»* (Paris, 1976). Lysenko became involved in these problems not out of a genuine interest in the theory of genetics, but through his work in plant breeding. His aim was to breed an improved variety of wheat in two or three years, an impossibility according to geneticists who argued that extended progeny tests are required to discover what will be the result of crossing various types. Lysenko was anti-intellectual, unlike Lamarckian scientists.

[82] Darwin proposed his own attempt to account for the acquisition of hereditary characters, which he called "pangenesis," in *The Variations of Plants and Animals Under Domestication* (1868). This was based on the Hippocratic idea cited above. Galton firmly denied the inheritance of acquired characters; see Cowan, *Sir Francis Galton* (1985), 28–30 and chapter 3.

[83] Races are "hereditary differences in animals which belong to a single phylum." These differences "constantly maintain themselves during all transpositions to other regions and through the generations. They produce mixed young when cross-bred with other races": Immanuel Kant, *Von den verschiedenen Rassen der Menschen* (1775) in *Kants Gesammelte Schriften, Band II, Vorkritische Schriften* (Berlin, 1912), 429–443, esp. 430. Kant, p. 429, says that his essay is meant as play rather than penetrating research (mehr wie ein Spiel als eine tiefe Nachforschung), but it is hard not to feel that he takes it entirely seriously all the same. For Kant's racism, see also the Introduction.

ideas of Lamarck and others were in fashion, this reinforced the authority of the environmental theory. In combination the two concepts seemed satisfactory tools for an understanding of the development of both the individual and the race. Characters acquired in a given environment were thought to be transmitted and in the course of generations these resulted in the rapid production of a constant variation. Accordingly, when the theory that acquired characters were hereditary came to be undermined, this affected the prestige of the environmental theories. In other words, the environment: climate and geography could no longer account for the development of stable variations.[84] Environmental determinism lost its authority when modern hereditary theory no longer accepted its associate theory: the heredity of acquired characters. As shown above, the two had been companions since the fifth century B.C.

Now let us return to Kant's essay, already mentioned. It is an excellent example of how such theories are inspired by irrational prejudice rather than factual observation, for Kant also has a strong belief in the environmental theory which one would assume would contradict the idea of immutability.[85] Yet he combines the two by assuming that there are germs (*Keime*) which cause the body to develop specific characteristics through influence of the environment, particularly the quality of the air and the sun. Such characteristics are lost or change if the environment changes, but when it does not, they are stable.[86] As paraphrased by Louden: "Race as Kant construes it is thus a set of latent predispositions that reside in all members of the species, parts of which then get activated depending on what sort of climate an individual lives in (and what length of time one spends in this climate). Again, according to this view, *all* human beings were potentially black, red, yellow, and white. (On Kant's view there are only four races.) Our ancestors actually became black, yellow, red, or white only by moving to a region of the earth whose climatic conditions triggered the appropriate 'race germ' to actualize itself—after which point 'the other germs obligingly retire[d] into inactivity.' "[87] Although Kant does not say so, he is here following almost literally a variation of the theory that is found in Tertul-

---

[84] The view that acquired characters are not inherited has generally been accepted on the basis of the work of Carl Nägeli (1865), August Weismann, and others in this period; cf. William M. Montgomery, "Germany" in Thomas F. Glick, *The Comparative Receptions of Darwinism* (Austin, TX and London, 1974), 81–116.

[85] Note, in this connection, also Kant's ideas about nations: Kant, *Beobachtungen über das Gefühl des Schönen und Erhabenen*, ch. 4: "Von den Nationalcharakteren" (1764) in *Sämtliche Werken* 2, 267: "Ob diese Nationalunterschiede zufällig sind und von den Zeitläufen und der Regierungsart abhängen oder mit einer gewissen Nothwendigkeit an das Klima gebunden sind, das untersuche ich hier nicht." He says this in a footnote at the beginning of a treatise which entirely consists of stereotypical descriptions of nations. Cf. R. B. Louden, *Kant's Impure Ethics* (2000), 87–93.

[86] Thus he explains that blacks may function well in the climate which suits their body, but because of the natural wealth which they enjoy they degenerate: "(Feuchte Wärme) entspringt der Neger, der seinem Klima wohl angemessen, nämlich stark, fleischig, gelenk, aber unter der reichlichen Versorgung seines Mutterlandes faul, weichlich und tändelnd ist." This, clearly, is the old idea from the Hippocratic treatise about Asiatics, transferred to blacks. It is significant that the element of moral and spiritual judgment is inserted without qualms.

[87] Louden, *Kant's Impure Ethics*, 97.

lian's *de anima*, discussed below. For racists the great advantage of this approach is that it allows for individual variation as the result of environmental
and external influences, while still leaving sufficient scope for sweeping generalizations.

At another level, this allows the combination of monogenetic views in theory
with racist opinions in practice. The basic elements of a presumed race are still
in place, whenever this is found convenient. In other words, the assumption of
the existence of germs in Kant's theory of race is a tactical but small concession
to reality that does not affect the imaginary world of racism.

The idea of inheritance of acquired characters has been described as a moderate form of environmentalism, because it avoids the extreme claim that, at the
time of birth the brain is a *tabula rasa* and that all abilities, qualities, and
characteristics possessed by a human adult have in fact been acquired during
the course of his or her own life.[88] It is easy to use ideas regarding the heredity
of acquired characters for discriminatory approaches, since they combine elements of the environmental theory with assumptions regarding heredity.[89] When
applied to human groups, this leads to a belief that their characteristics are
uniform and constant. Thus, for instance, it is claimed that a given people
displays a sluggish response because of the quality of the air. This characteristic
is also transmitted through a hereditary mechanism. According to the theory,
such people would eventually change if they move to a different environment,
but since entire peoples do not normally change their habitat this is not a meaningful element in the theory. A consequence of the existence of such theories is
therefore that ideas of concerning group characteristics which are based on
them can in some cases resemble racist ideas even by the narrow definitions
cited in the Introduction, for instance Memmi's original proposal: "Racism is
the valuation, generalized and definitive, of biological differences, real or imaginary, to the advantage of the accuser and the disadvantage of his victim, in
order to justify aggression." An important difference between ancient and nineteenth-century ideas is that the ancients, unlike modern scientists, did not consider the difference between simple heredity and the heredity of acquired characters conceptually important.[90]

---

[88] This was the position of the followers of Locke and Condillac. Cf. Schwartz Cowan, *Sir
Francis Galton* (1985), 15.

[89] For its popularity in England, Schwartz Cowan, *Sir Francis Galton*, 15–19, already cited. A
good example of the manner in which this approach has been uncritically accepted in broad circles
may be found in Seeck's description of the Egyptians. He describes how Egypt had been ruled by
despots for thousands of years, while other provinces of the Roman Empire had been governed by
emperors for a mere three hundred years: "Freilich hatte sich auch in ihnen die knechtische Unter-
würfigkeit schnell genug entwickelt, wurzelte aber doch nicht so tief *in angeerbten Instinkten* (my
italics), wie bei dem Volke, das schon seit der Zeit, wo es die Steinblöcke zu den Pyramiden
herbeischleppen musste, zur Sklaverei gezüchtet war." The Egyptians were, in other words, "a
people born for slavery" in Seeck's view: O. Seeck, *Geschichte des Untergangs der antiken Welt* 4
(2d ed.) (Stuttgart, 1922), 330f.

[90] An important feature in the difference between the older idea of heredity and the nineteenth-
century evolutionary concept is the matter of time-reckoning. The heredity of acquired characters is

It might seem speculative to build too much on a single author. It will therefore be useful to cite some further sources which also explicitly argue for the
heredity of acquired characters. It occurs in another Hippocratic treatise, *De
Semine:* "Crippled parents usually have normal children. However, in case of
an illness, the four sorts of fluid from which the semen derives, do not provide
a complete semen, but that which comes from the crippled part is weaker. It
seems therefore not surprising that the child is crippled like the parent."[91] Aristotle, in a related argument that is not relevant for present purposes, discusses
the question whether semen is drawn from the whole of the parent's body or
not.[92] One of four lines of argument which, he says, may be used to prove that
this is the case, is the following: "mutilated parents produce mutilated offspring."[93] In this connection he provides the following evidence: "Children are
born which resemble their parents in respect not only of congenital characters
but also of acquired ones; for instance, there have been cases of children which
have had the outline of a scar in the same places where their parents had scars,
and there was a case at Chalcedon of a man who was branded on his arm, and
the same letter, though somewhat confused and indistinct, appeared marked on
his child."[94] Again, the context is not important for present purposes, but there
can be no doubt that Aristotle accepts the evidence he cites as reliable.

For all these examples, as for the discussion in *Airs, Waters, Places*, it is true
that the only forms of external influence mentioned, in general or through examples, are forms of damage. As observed by Tuplin, "talk of corruption and
deterioration implies that nature's intention is homogeneity, deviation is a case
of damage."[95] This corresponds with the general absence, in antiquity, in a belief in progress and improvement over time. Change can only be for the worse.[96]
By contrast, modern thinking in general, and modern racism in particular, are
much concerned with progress.

---

a form of almost instant adaptation, unlike Darwinian evolution, which requires the sort of time
span that was inconceivable as late as the eighteenth century. Mosaic chronology assumes that the
earth was created in 3700 b.c.

[91] Hippocrates, *De Semine* 11.1 (484): ἐπὴν δέ τί οἱ νόσημα προσπέσῃ καὶ τοῦ ὑγροῦ αὐτοῦ,
ἀφ' οὗ τὸ σπέρμα γίνεται, τέσσαρες ἰδέαι ἐοῦσαι, ὁκόσαι ἐν φύσει ὑπῆρξαν, τὴν γονὴν οὐχ ὕλην
παρέχουσιν, ἀσθενέστερον δὲ τὸ κατὰ τὸ πεπηρωμένον, οὐ θαῦμα δέ μοι δοκέει εἶναι καὶ
πηρωθῆναι, καθάπερ ὁ τοκεύς. Ed. Ballière. I follow Joly in the Budé ed., who reads προσπέσῃ,
[καὶ] τοῦ ὑγροῦ.

[92] *De generatione animalium* 721b.

[93] τὸ ἐκ κολοβῶν κολοβὰ γενεσθαι. Cf. 724a: Τοῦ δ' ἐκ κολοβῶν γίγνεσθαι κολοβὰ ἡ αὐτὴ
αἰτία καὶ διὰ τί ὅμοια τοῖς γονεῦσιν. γίγνεται δὲ καὶ οὐ κολοβὰ ἐκ κολοβῶν, ὥσπερ καὶ
ἀνόμοια τοῖς τεκνώσασιν· This argument is not part of the later Lamarckian theory of the heredity
of acquired characters.

[94] Trans. A. L. Peck (Loeb). οὐ γὰρ μόνον τὰ σύμφυτα προσεοικότες γίγνονται τοῖς γονεῦσιν
οἱ παῖδες ἀλλὰ καὶ τὰ ἐπίκτητα· οὐλάς τε γὰρ ἐχόν τῶν γεννησάντων ἤδη τινὲς ἔσχον ἐν τοῖς
αὐτοῖς τόποις τῶν ἐκγόνων τὸν τύπον τῆς οὐλῆς, καὶ στίγμα ἔχοντος ἐν τῷ βραχίονι τοῦ πατρὸς
ἐπεσήμηνεν ἐν Χαλκηδόνι τῷ τέκνῳ συγκεχυμένον μέντοι καὶ οὐ διηρθρωμένον τὸ γράμμα.

[95] Tuplin, "Greek Racism," 66.

[96] Below, chapter 3.

During the reigns of Augustus and Tiberius, Strabo discusses the cause of the colour of the skin of Aethiopians and the texture of their hair, which he attributes to scorching by the sun. He then observes that the Indians "do not have woolly hair and that their skin is not so mercilessly burnt." "And already in the womb children, by seminal communication,[97] become like their parents; for congenital illnesses and other similarities are also thus explained."[98] Strabo apparently attributes the transmission of acquired characters to the father's sperm. However this may be, he takes it for granted that Aethiopians and Indians look the way they do through the fierce or slightly less extreme influence of the sun, and that their children inherit these features. Later in the first century, the elder Pliny wrote in his *Naturalis Historia* (*NH*) that the Ethiopians are "scorched by the heat of the sun which is nearby and are born with a singed appearance, with curled beard and hair."[99] Pliny has interesting observations about the transmission of characters in book seven of his work. "It is also well known that sound parents may have deformed children and deformed parents sound children or children with the same deformity, as the case may be; that some marks and moles and even scars reappear in the offspring, in some cases a birthmark on the arm reappearing in the fourth generation."[100] This statement shows unambiguously what seemed clear from the texts cited earlier, namely that transmission of acquired characteristics was considered as almost the same as other forms of transmission. Everything could be inherited and there were no clear rules. This is further emphasized in Pliny's subsequent assertion that likeness could be determined by accidental circumstances, such as "recollections of sights and sounds and actual sense-impressions received at the time of conception."[101]

In roughly the same period Seneca combines the standard environmental theory—presumably without giving much thought to the finer aspects of his reasoning—with assumptions regarding the acquisition of characteristics by birth: "For certain qualities are acquired by birth (*innascuntur*) only in better characters."[102] This is followed by a comparison of the quality of fertile soil with the

---

[97] διάδοσιν F or διαθέσιν other MSS: disposition. The same comparison, without the explanation, appears in Arrian, *Indica* 6.9. Arrian's source is a matter of speculation. Brunt, *History of Alexander and Indica* vol. 2 (LCL, Cambridge, MA, 1983), 447, suspects "that 6.4–9, though ultimately derived from Nearchos, who is not named, was taken by Arrian from Megasthenes." This is possible, but it does not assist in attributing Strabo's views here discussed to any specific Hellenistic source. For the Ethiopians in Greek tragedy, see E. Hall, *Inventing the Barbarian* (1989), 140–143; for Aristotle on the Ethiopians, see below.

[98] Strabo 15.1.24 (696) ἐν δὲ τῇ γαστρὶ ἤδη κατὰ σπερματικὴν διάδοσιν τοιαῦτα γίνεται οἷα τὰ γεννῶντα· καὶ γὰρ πάθη συγγενικὰ οὕτω λέγεται καὶ ἄλλαι ὁμοιότητες.

[99] Pliny, *NH* 2.80.189: namque et Aethiopas vicini sideris vapore torreri, adiustisque similes gigni barba et capillo vibrato non est dubium. See also Ptolemy, *Tetrabiblos* 2.2.56, discussed below.

[100] Pliny, *NH* 7.50: Iam illa vulgata s<un>t: vari<e> ex integris truncos gigni, ex truncis integros; eadem parte truncos, signa quaedam naevosque et cicatrices etiam regenerari, quarto partu.

[101] Pliny, *NH* 7.52: Similitudinum quidem inmen<s>a reputatio est et in qua credantur multa fortuita pollere, visus, auditus, memoria haustaeque imagines sub ipso conceptu.

[102] Seneca, *De Ira* 2.15.1: Quaedam enim non nisi melioribus innascuntur ingeniis, sicut valida

corresponding quality of fine trees growing in it. This means that the plants, as well as the peoples he is discussing, acquire their nature by birth and are influenced by, but under the influence of, climate and soil.

A variant of the idea may be found in a discourse of Favorinus (second century A.D.) against the employment of wet nurses, as rendered by Aulus Gellius.[103] The proposition defended here is that a child's heredity is determined partly by the male seed and partly by the milk it receives as a baby. "And there is no doubt that in forming character the disposition of the nurse and the quality of the milk play a great part; for the milk, although imbued from the beginning with the material of the father's seed, forms the infant offspring from the body and mind of the mother as well."[104] Thus a child will absorb the hereditary characteristics of whoever nurses it, be it the mother or a wet nurse. This, according to Favorinus, is especially damaging if the wet nurse "is either a slave or of servile origin and, as usually happens, of a foreign and barbarious nation, if she is dishonest, ugly, unchaste and a wine-bibber."[105] As always in antiquity, the assumption is that the only option is deterioration. It is not considered possible that the wet nurse might be superior to the natural mother. No less significant is the clear assumption that the milk transfers all characteristics, physical and mental, including even a tendency to addiction to alcohol. Third, it is of interest to see here, as will be discussed fully in chapter 2, that slaves and even descendants of slaves are regarded as inferior as a matter of course and this inferiority is hereditary. About the essence of slavishness there is more to be said in this connection.

As we shall see, the idea that the soil has a direct impact on the people born on it plays a part in the concept of autochthony. The principle of the heredity of acquired characters is only stated explicitly in relatively few sources, but once it is clear that the idea existed, it is obvious that it was, in fact, commonly assumed to operate in practice. This is clear, for instance, from the expression cited and discussed elsewhere in this book, where Cicero calls Jews and Syrians, "peoples born to be slaves" (*servituti nati*). Slavery is not a physical condition, even though Aristotle (*Pol.* 1254 a–b) considered the possibility that it might be one. The underlying assumption is that people who have been subjected become servile in spirit through their condition, and they then pass on

---

arbusta laeta quamvis neclecta tellus creat, et alta fecundi soli silva est: itaque et ingenia natura fortia iracundiam ferunt nihilque tenue et exile capiunt ignea et fervida, sed inperfectis illis vigor est ut omnibus, quae sine arte ipsius tantum naturae bono exurgunt, sed nisi cito domita sunt, quae fortitudini apta erant, audaciae temeritati que consuescunt. See below for further discussion of this passage.

[103] Aulus Gellius, *Noctes Atticae* 12.1. Favorinus is mentioned later, in this chapter for his criticism of autochthony and again on p. 156, because he was attacked by Polemon.

[104] Op. cit., 12.1.20 (trans. John C. Rolfe, Loeb): quoniam uidelicet in moribus inolescendis magnam fere partem ingenium altricis et natura lactis tenet, quae iam a principio imbuta paterni seminis concretione ex matris etiam corpore et animo recentem indolem configurat.

[105] Op. cit. 12.1.17 (trans. Rolfe): . . . praesertim si ista, quam ad praebendum lactem adhibebitis, aut serua aut seruilis est et, ut plerumque solet, externae et barbarae nationis est, si inproba, si informis, si inpudica, si temulenta est;

this quality to their children. This notion is common in several authors, such as Josephus and Tacitus, where they discuss the long-term effect of subjugation by Rome (see chapter 2). The result is an approach which, even by narrow definition, undoubtedly must be called racism, if we accept, for instance, that racism is "the theory or idea that there is a causal link between inherited physical traits and certain traits of personality, intellect, or culture and, combined with it, the notion that some races are inherently superior to others." Cicero, Josephus, and Tacitus, moreover, place emphasis on their conviction that the condition of peoples who had become used to subject status was unchangeable, which is another essential feature of racist thinking.

In summary, the heredity of acquired characters is a concept generally accepted in Greece and Rome and explicitly formulated by several authors. It is found in several Hippocratic treatises, Aristotle, Strabo, Pliny, and others and implicitly in many more authors. It is a convenient concept for the formulation of discriminatory stereotypes, since it allows the combination of elements of the environmental theory with assumptions regarding heredity. When applied to human groups it leads to a belief that their characteristics are uniform and constant once acquired, a process which could be almost instantaneous. A related idea is the theory of natural slavery, to be discussed below, which, in turn, was important in ancient imperialist thinking.

The Impact of Environment: Hellenistic and Roman Views

We must now trace the development of these ideas in later periods and see how they were applied in other circumstances. The idea of environmental influence is clearly present in Polybius 4.21, where he explains that the Arcadians have a harsh character 'resulting from the cold and sombre weather conditions usually prevailing in this region—conditions to which all men by nature must necessarily adapt; for there is no other cause why we differ to such an extent from one another in character, appearance and colour as in most of our activities in accordance with our nationality (τὰς ἐθνικὰς καὶ τὰς ὁλοσχερεῖς διαστάσεις) and the distance we are separated from each other."[106] This shows that Polybius fully accepted the approach described above. Polybius explicitly says that climate determines the physical features, characteristics, and color of entire peoples. That is to say, he regards it as self evident that there is a connection between physical and mental characteristics, for they all are determined by the climate, and he speaks in terms of collective traits. This is not the result of

---

[106] *Hist* 4.21. οὐ γὰρ δι' ἄλλην, διὰ δὲ ταύτην τὴν αἰτίαν κατὰ τὰς ἐθνικὰς καὶ τὰς ὁλοσχερεῖς διαστάσεις πλεῖστον ἀλλήλων διαφέρομεν ἤθεσί τε καὶ μορφαῖς καὶ χρώμασιν, ἔτι δὲ τῶν ἐπιτηδευμάτων τοῖς πλείστοις. Comm. F. W. Walbank, *A Historical Commentary on Polybius* I (Oxford, 1957), p. 469: Translate "in accordance with our nationality and the distance we are separated from each other."; Strachan-Davidson renders ". . . or according to yet wider diversities"; but διάστασις suggests a spatial interval. . . . and geographical separation played a part in the milieu-theory.

extensive deliberation and presentation; it is mentioned as an obvious fact that almost goes without saying.

The next author who is reported to have been greatly interested in the doctrine of a causal connection between physical environment and national character is the Stoic philosopher, scientist, and historian Posidonius (c. 135–51 B.C.). However, his work has not survived. In the first century B.C., Diodorus Siculus inserted a section on extremely cold and extremely hot climates into his third book. This follows a long tradition of special interest in the peoples of the extreme north and south.[107] His conclusion is that, given the differences, "it is not surprising that those peoples' manner of life and bodies should also be different from ours (3.34.8)." Diodorus's description of India, which may derive from the account of the Hellenistic author Megasthenes (late fourth-early third century) also attests adherence to the theory. The inhabitants of India are said to be unusually tall and massive because of their excellent food supply. They also excel in the arts because of the fine quality of the air and water.[108] A lengthy passage in the work of Vitruvius on architecture (first century B.C.) is usually assumed to derive from Posidonius, although there is no explicit evidence linking it with this author.[109] Vitruvius writes:

> This is also the reason why the races that are bred in the north are of vast height, and have fair complexions, straight red hair, gray eyes, and a great deal of blood, owing to the abundance of moisture and the coolness of the atmosphere (6.1.3). [about the influence of climate on physique, northern climates as compared with hot ones in the south] On the contrary, those that are nearest to the southern half of the axis, and that lie directly under the sun's course, are of lower stature, with a swarthy complexion, hair curling, black eyes, [strong legs,] and but little blood on account of the force of the sun. Hence, too this poverty of blood makes them over-timid to stand up against the sword, but great heat and fevers they can endure without timidity, because their frames are bred up in the raging heat. Hence, men that are born in the north are rendered over-timid and weak by fever, but their wealth of blood enables them to stand up against the sword without timidity (6.1.4). The pitch of the voice is likewise different. . . . (6.1.5) Further, it is owing to the rarity of the atmosphere that southern nations, with their keen intelligence due to the heat, are very free and swift in the devising of schemes, while northern nations, being enve-

[107] Romm, *The Edges of the Earth*, chapter 2.

[108] Diodorus 2.36.1. Dihle, op. cit., 24; 27, has no doubt that this passage and its reliance on the environmental theory derives directly from Megasthenes. While this is possible, there is nothing in the text to prove it.

[109] Trüdinger, *Studien zur griechisch-römischen Ethnographie*, 121f. and n. 2: "Vitruv VI 1.4 ist Hauptquelle und schöpft geradewegs aus Posidonius." W. Theiler, *Posidonios, Die Fragmente* (Berlin, 1982), vol. i, Fr. 71, p. 73f.; comm., vol. ii, 71–74, where it is tentatively suggested that Varro served as intermediary. It is not included in I. G. Kidd, *Posidonius I, The Fragments* (Cambridge, 1972), because Posidonius is not explicitly mentioned in the text. See Jean-Louis Ferrary, *Philhellénisme et impérialisme: Aspects idéologiques de la conquête romaine du monde hellénistique* (Rome, 1988), 382–394, who rejects the theory of Posidonian derivation with extensive discussion.

loped in a dense atmosphere and chilled by moisture from the obstructing air, have
but a sluggish intelligence. That this is so we may see from the case of snakes. . . .
(6.1.9) But although southern nations have the keenest wits, and are infinitely clever
in forming schemes, yet the moment it comes to displaying valour, they succumb
because all manliness of spirit is sucked out of them by the sun. On the other hand,
men born in cold countries are indeed readier to meet the shock of arms with great
courage and without timidity, but their wits are so slow that they will rush to the
charge inconsiderately and inexpertly, thus defeating their own devices. . . . the
truly perfect territory, situated under the middle of the heaven, and having on each
side the entire extent of the world and its countries, is that which is occupied by the
Roman people (6.1.10). In fact, the races of Italy are the most perfectly constituted
in both respects—in bodily form and in mental activity to correspond to their valour. . . . Hence it was the divine intelligence that set the city of the Roman people
in a peerless and temperate country, in order that it might acquire the right to
command the whole world (6.1.11). (trans. M. H. Morgan)[110]

This is essentially the same concept as that developed in *Airs, Waters, Places*
and adapted by Aristotle, with some variations. Instead of a contrast between
Europe and Asia, the geographical poles here are North and South, a contrast
which in *Airs* appears as a secondary theme and is also present in the work of
Diodorus Siculus.

Whereas *Airs* primarily sees the difference between uniformity and variation
in climate and geography, Vitruvius, or his source, mentions heat and cold with
their presumed effect on the quantity of blood in the body. Ideas about the
correlation between the quality of blood and the development of moral characteristics and intelligence appear in Aristotle's work. Blood that is hot, thin, and
clear is conducive to the development of courage and intelligence (*de Partibus
Animalium* 648[a]9–11) writes Aristotle, but he does not argue that the quality of

[110] 6.1.3 ex eo quoque, <quae> sub septentrionibus nutriuntur gentes, inmanibus corporibus,
candidis coloribus, directo capillo et rufo, oculis caesis, sanguine multo ab umoris plenitate caelique
refrigerationibus sunt conformati; qui autem sunt proximi ad axem meridianum subiectique solis
cursui, brevioribus corporibus, colore fusco, crispo capillo, oculis nigris, [cruribus validis,] sanguine
exiguo solis impetu perficiuntur. itaque etiam propter sanguinis exiguitatem timidiores sunt ferro
resistere, sed ardores ac febres sufferunt sine timore, quod nutrita sunt eorum membra cum fervore;
itemque corpora, quae nascuntur sub septentrione, a febri sunt timidiora et inbecilla, sanguinis
autem abundantia ferro resistunt sine timore. 6.1.9 Item propter tenuitatem caeli meridianae nationes ex acuta fervore mente expeditius celeriusque moventur ad consiliorum cogitationes; septentrionales autem gentes infusae crassitudine caeli, propter obstantiam aeris umore refrigeratae
stupentes habent mentes. hoc autem ita esse a serpentibus licet aspicere, quae, per calorem cum
exhaustam habent umoris refrigerationem, tunc acerrime moventur, per brumalia autem et hiberna
tempora abrigeratus autem contra tardiores. cum sint autem meridiane nationes animis acutissimis
infinitaque sollertia consiliorum, simul ut ad fonibus, ad armorum vehementiam paratiores sunt
magnis virtutibus sine timore, sed tarditate animi sine considerantia inruentes sine sollertia suis
consiliis refragantur. cum ergo haec ita sint ab natura rerum in mundo conlocata et omnes nationes
inmoderatis mixtionibus disparatae, veros inter spatium totius orbis terrarum regionesque medio
mundi populus Romanus possidet fines.

blood itself is determined by climate. It is possible that this connection is due to another author, writing between Aristotle and Vitruvius. The resulting stereotypes are essentially the same, however.

The extent to which Vitruvius transfers some of the traditional elements of opposition between East and West to North and South is striking. The inhabitants of the North are fair, tall, good fighters, unintelligent, and slow. They have a lot of blood and cannot stand the heat. The Southerners are small, dark, soft, and poor fighters, but intelligent and quick. The cause is that they do not have much blood, but can stand the heat. The difference in intelligence is present in Aristotle but not in the older work, and was probably taken over by Vitruvius's source, or the source of his source, from Aristotle. More important, however, is the idea that Italy and Rome are sited ideally in the middle, which makes them a suitable nucleus for universal rule.[111] The same idea is also found also in Aristotle, but in his view, naturally, Greece is the ideal land in the middle, capable of ruling the world. It is important to observe that the first Roman source which explicitly and expansively repeats the environmental idea—almost four centuries old by that time—is a technical handbook. The idea is first encountered in a medical treatise, then taken over by philosophers and historians, and now found again in a work on architecture.

The last version of this concept in antiquity that I am aware of is to be found in another technical treatise, the *Epitome of Military Science* by Vegetius (late fourth-early fifth century). The reasons Vitruvius and other Romans would have thought in terms of an opposition North–South rather than East–West are easy to understand. Vitruvius lived in the first century B.C., when Rome had fought hard wars with German and Gallic peoples living immediately north of Italy. It was Vitruvius's point that Italy was the ideal country in the middle. This was an impossible construction to express in terms of East and West, for west of Italy was Spain, which was not a suitable candidate for the powerful but dull fighters which the scheme demanded. The North–South opposition continued to be the Roman version, for instance in the works of Pliny and Vegetius, cited below. Like Polybius, Vitruvius explicitly says that climate determines the physical features, and hence their mental characteristics. He reduces the differences which he describes to a single factor: the quantity of blood in the body, which is determined by the heat of the sun. He thus regards it as self-evident that there is an immediate connection between physical and mental characteristics, all of them being determined by the climate and all of them having an equally strong impact on all of the peoples described.

The views expressed in *Airs, Waters, Places* exerted a strong influence on the work of Galen, who was the most influential medical author of antiquity. Born in Pergamum, c. A.D. 129, he was the friend and physician of Marcus Aurelius, and he died in Rome, some time after A.D. 200. He wrote a commentary on

---

[111] Cf. Greg Woolf, "Becoming Roman, Staying Greek," *PCPS* 40 (1994), 116–143, at 121.

Airs, which is extant in Hebrew.[112] In his work *My Own Books*, Galen writes that in his view this treatise should be entitled *Habitation, water, seasons and lands*.[113] He also comments on *Airs* in *The Soul's Dependence on the Body,* chapters 8 and 9 (798–805). Here he quotes several of the passages from chapters 12 and 16 which emphasize the difference between Europe and Asia, for instance the assertion that "courage, tenacity, energy and will-power could not develop under such natural conditions . . . either among the locals or among immigrants, but pleasure must dominate." Several of the passages cited by Galen are precisely those that concern the present study and have been cited above. Besides the passages from chapters 12 and 16, in chapter 24 he also includes the material on the differences between the peoples of the mountains and those in the plains.[114] Following several further direct quotations he says: "so as not to have too many of Hippocrates' sayings, we may sum up with: 'You will observe that the physical shape and the behaviour of men vary according to the nature of their country (802).' "[115] Galen then remarks that (Hippocrates) "indicates clearly the dependence, not just of character, but also of intellect and understanding, on seasonal balance,"[116] repeating later once again that intelligence and capability depend on "seasonal mixture" (803). He concludes his praise of Hippocrates, saying that this author is the most reliable witness for the close dependence of human nature on environment and the seasons (805), for everyone knows that "those living below the Bears (in the North) have a body and soul that are opposite in character of those who live near the region burnt by the sun, while those who live in a well tempered region are better than those peoples, as regards their body, the character of their soul, their intelligence and good sense."[117] Thus we see that the most influential of ancient medical writers firmly supports the essence of the environmental

---

[112] A. Wasserstein (ed.), *Galen's Commentary on the Hippocratic Treatise: Airs, Waters, Places in the Hebrew Translation of Solomon Ha-Me'ati;* edited with introd., English translation, and notes (Jerusalem, 1982).

[113] *De Propriis Libris* 35 (trans. P. N. Singer, Oxford, 1997): ὥσπερ γε καὶ τοῦ περὶ τόπων, ἀέρων, ὑδάτων, ὃ ἐγὼ περὶ οἰκήσεων καὶ ὑδάτων καὶ ὡρῶν καὶ χωρῶν ἐπιγεγράφθαι φημὶ δεῖν.

[114] *Airs* 24, = *Quod animi mores corporis temperamenta sequantur* 800f. Cf. Elisabeth C. Evans, "Galen, the Physician as Physiognomist," *TAPA* 76 (1945), 287–298, esp. 296f.

[115] Ibid. [τί γάρ] ἵνα μὴ πολλῶν αὐτοῦ μνημονεύσω ῥήσεων, ἐφεξῆς ἐρεῖ "εὑρήσεις γὰρ ἐπὶ τὸ πολὺ τῆς χώρης τῇ φύσει ἀκολουθέοντα καὶ τὰ εἴδεα τῶν ἀνθρώπων καὶ τοὺς τρόπου."

[116] 802: ἐν τούτοις πάλιν ἐδήλωσε σαφέστατα μὴ μόνον τὰ ἤθη ταῖς τῶν ὡρῶν κράσεσιν ἀλλὰ καὶ τὴν ἀμβλύτητα τῆς διανοίας ὥσπερ οὖν καὶ τὴν σύνεσιν ἑπομένην.

[117] 805: τίς γὰρ οὐχ ὁρᾷ τὸ σῶμα καὶ τὴν ψυχὴν ἁπάντων τῶν ὑπὸ τοῖς ἄρκτοις ἀνθρώπων ἐναντιώτατα διακείμενα τοῖς ἐγγὺς τῆς διακεκαυμένης ζώνης; ἢ τίς οὐκ οἶδε τοὺς ἐν τῷ μέσῳ τούτων, ὅσοι τὴν εὔκρατον οἰκοῦσι χώραν, ἀμείνους τά τε σώματα καὶ τὰ τῆς ψυχῆς ἤθη καὶ σύνεσιν καὶ φρόνησιν ἐκείνων τῶν ἀνθρώπων. Although before Galen cites literally from the text of *Airs* on this matter, here in fact he attributes views to this Hippocratic treatise which are not found there but belong to later periods. In *Airs* the opposition is between Asia and Europe, rather than between North and South. This change in emphasis is found first in Roman sources (Vitruvius). Moreover, the ideal quality of those living in the middle was expressed first by Aristotle and does not occur in *Airs*. The idea that the heat of the sun is responsible for the dark skin of some peoples living in the South also appears in Galen, *de temperamentis* 1.628.

theory. He firmly believes in the close interdependence of climate, physical shape, and mental qualities. Being Greek, he does not go to the trouble of adapting *Airs* for Roman readers. He does not convert the East–West contrast to a North–South opposition, although he cites the views on the effect of extreme cold and heat on people. He does not argue that the Romans are natural rulers of the world since they live in the ideal environment. However, the essence of Galen's observations is that the environmental theory is fully represented and fully accepted, so that he is thus representing yet another major figure in the sequence of influential authors who ensured its transmission to later periods.

Vegetius writes:

> They tell us that all peoples that are near the sun, being parched by great heat, are more intelligent but have less blood, and therefore lack steadiness and confidence to fight at close quarters, because those who are conscious of having less blood are afraid of wounds. On the other hand the peoples of the north, remote from the sun's heat are less intelligent, but having a superabundance of blood are readiest for wars. Recruits should therefore be raised from the more temperate climes. The plenteousness of their blood supplies contempt for wounds and death, and intelligence cannot be lacking either which preserves discipline in camp and is of no little assistance with counsel in battle. (trans. N. P. Milner)[118]

Vegetius omits Vitruvius's conclusion that the perfect combination of qualities was to be found in Italy and the Roman people, but draws the inference that both peoples of the North and those of the South were unsuitable for army service, so that those in the middle are the best recruits, which really means the same thing, since Vegetius quite reasonably regards recruitment as essential in building a good army.

As already observed, the two Roman sources here discussed are in essence technical treatises. It will therefore be useful to see how the environmental theory is encountered in major literary authors.

Cicero writes in *de divinatione* 2.96 (trans. W. Falconer) that natural defects may be restored by nature, surgery, or medicine. "But if such defects had been engendered and implanted by a star nothing could have changed them. Do not unlike places produce unlike men? It would be an easy matter to sketch rapidly in passing the differences in mind and body which distinguish the Indians from the Persians and the Ethiopians from the Syrians—differences so striking and so pronounced as to be incredible. Hence it is evident that one's birth is more

[118] Vegetius 1.2: Omnes nationes, quae uicinae sunt soli, nimio calore siccatas, amplius quidem sapere, sed minus habere sanguinis dicunt ac propterea constantiam ac fiduciam comminus non habere pugnandi, quia metuunt uulnera qui exiguum sanguinem se habere nouerunt. Contra septentrionales populi, remoti a solis ardoribus, inconsultiores quidem, sed tamen largo sanguine redundantes, sunt ad bella promptissimi. Tirones igitur de temperatioribus legendi sunt plagis, quibus et copia sanguinis suppetat ad uulnerum mortisque contemptum et non possit deesse prudentia, quae et modestiam seruat in castris et non parum prodest in dimicatione consiliis.

affected by local environment than by the condition of the moon."[119] This is part
of a longer attack on the "Chaldeans" and those who believe in astrology. In *De
lege agraria* Cicero explicitly asserts that human behavior is not determined by
origin or seed, but by environment and lifestyle. "Men's characters are inserted
in them not so much by origin and semen as by those things which nature itself
endows to form our way of life whereby we are fed and live."[120] "The Carthaginians are fraudulent and liars, not by origin, but because of the nature of their
site, with its port, which brought them in contact with merchants and strangers
speaking foreign languages which leads to greed and the desire to cheat. The
Ligurians, being mountaineers, are hard and boorish because of the nature of
their land. The Campanians have the best land imaginable, fertile with an abundance of crops, a healthy and beautiful town. This has made them arrogant . . .
and their luxury corrupted Hannibal himself who was invincible by arms."[121]

Unlike the passages quoted from Vitruvius and Vegetius, these are not potted
and adapted copies of something found in earlier authors—Posidonius or another Hellenistic source. In the first passage Cicero is basically criticizing the
belief in the absolute determination of astrology. In this respect, he was not
alone: astrologers and soothsayers were usually considered undesirable elements in Rome, as observed elsewhere in this study. One of Cicero's arguments
is that people can influence and improve the impact of bodily defects. The other
is that peoples differ because of the influence of the environment. He firmly
believes, following the tradition of the Hippocratic author, that the most important element in determining character and body is environmental circumstances.
Here, unlike most ancient authors, he explicitly excludes and denies heredity as
an independent, valid factor. It is interesting that he actually says that "terrarum
situs . . . ad nascendum valere." In other words: he believes that environment,
rather than the conditions of the moon, influences not just human development
but also birth itself. How this is assumed to have worked in practice he does not
say and may not have considered at all.

Cicero does not present the usual form of environmental theory or a variant,
but quite a different approach. He argues that the true determining factor is the
social environment, as shown beautifully by his example of Carthage. The Car-

[119] Cicero, *de divinatione* 2.96: Quodsi haec astro ingenerata et tradita essent, nulla res ea mutare
posset. Quid? dissimilitudo locorum nonne dissimilis hominum procreationes habet? quas quidem
percurrere oratione facile est, quid inter Indos et Persas, Aethiopas et Syros differat corporibus
animis, ut incredibilis varietas dissimilitudoque sit. Ex quo intellegitur plus terrarum situs quam
lunae tactus ad nascendum valere.

[120] Cicero, *De lege agraria* 2.95.5: Non ingenerantur hominibus mores tam a stirpe generis ac
seminis quam ex eis rebus quae ab ipsa natura nobis ad vitae consuetudinem suppeditantur, quibus
alimur et vivimus.

[121] Carthaginienses fraudulenti et mendaces non genere sed natura loci, quod propter portus suos
multis et variis mercatorum et advenarum sermonibus ad studium fallendi studio quaestus vocaban-
tur. Ligures duri atque agrestes; docuit ager ipse nihil ferendo nisi multa cultura et magno labore
quaesitum. Campani semper superbi bonitate agrorum et fructuum magnitudine, urbis salubritate,
descriptione, pulchritudine. ex hac copia atque omnium rerum adfluentia primum illa nata est arrogantia, quae a maioribus nostris alterum Capua consulem postulavit, deinde ea luxuries, quae ipsum
Hannibalem armis etiam tum invictum voluptate vicit.

thaginians had a good port. What made them into what they were, according to Cicero, was their harmful contact with strangers, not any hereditary, physical cause. Thus it was the social result of a geographical feature that made them into liars. The other examples are somewhat more traditional: the Ligurians are boorish mountaineers because of the nature of their land, and the Campanians are corrupt because of its natural abundance. In any case, Cicero has no doubt that physical environment—climate and geography—is the decisive factor in the social differentiation of humanity, not an internal factor, such as heredity or a good or bad constitution. This is taken for granted in the present passage and in others to follow.

Many questions remain, some of which it will be impossible to solve. It is, however, also important to note that Cicero is somewhat unusual in his belief in a measure of free will and individual variability. Unlike the other authors who supported the environmental theory, Cicero thinks in terms of social interaction and human factors, rather than mechanical forces like sun, mountains, and plains. Elsewhere he also accepts the environmental theory, but with serious reservations. "Nature affects some things, but others not at all."[122] This does not affect his eventual judgment, which is prejudiced and intolerant like that of so many others, but it is, in intellectual terms, quite an original approach. This makes his attitude a far less clear-cut expression of proto-racism than that of most supporters of the environmental theory. It may be better described as a mixture of three ingredients: strongly held ethnic prejudice together with elements of geographical determinism, but also a measure of individual variation and personal differentiation. Another important point is that, typically, he mentions only negative characteristics and negative influences. This may have something to do with his general tendency to xenophobia, but it is also connected with the phenomenon observed frequently in this study: the influence of foreigners and a change of climate is almost always believed to be for the worse. There is always a possibility of degeneration and deterioration, but improvement does not normally occur.[123]

Livy's account of the speech made by Cn. Manlius, the consul, before his troops in 189 B.C. is mentioned frequently in this book and will be discussed at length below, in chapter 5. In it he writes (38.17.9–10): "These are now degenerate, of mixed stock and really Gallogrecians, as they are called; just as in the case of crops and animals, the seeds are not as good in preserving their natural quality as the character of the soil and the climate in which they grow have the power to change it."[124]

---

[122] Cicero, *de fato* 4.8: Ut igitur ad quasdam res natura loci pertinet aliquid, ad quasdam autem nihil . . .

[123] This idea is found again in the work of Johann Friedrich Blumenbach, *Über die natürlichen Verschiedenheiten im Menschengeschlecht* (Leipzig, 1798, first published in 1776), 135–137; English translation (which I have not seen): *On the Natural Varieties of Mankind* (New York, 1969). Blumenbach held that all of humanity belongs to one species and has produced five races, the original and superior race being the "Caucasian." The four others are claimed to have degenerated from this ideal original race.

[124] hi iam degeneres sunt, mixti, et Gallograeci uere, quod appellantur; sicut in frugibus pecu-

This is a speech written by the historian Livy for a military commander addressing his troops two centuries earlier. The troops were about to do battle with mixed forces in Asia Minor. It is a literary speech, written for Roman readers in the age of Augustus and can have no connection with whatever the consul may have said at the time. It is indeed surprising that Livy thought it appropriate for a republican commander to discuss environmental theory in front of his troops, but he may have thought that professional farmers would be familiar with such matters, even in 189 B.C. The close connection between human nature and the soil appears already in Plato and has been noted in Cicero to some extent, as seen above. Climate and soil are considered the essential factors in determining human development and it is stated explicitly that "seed"—in other words, heredity—is a secondary factor. Or rather: seed is affected by the environment: 'Whatever grows in its own soil, prospers better; transplanted to alien soil, it changes and it degenerates to conform to the soil which feeds it."[125]

The passage under discussion, however, offers something new, for the issue here is the Gauls who established themselves in Galatia, in Asia Minor. The Gauls were famous fighters who had defeated the Romans in the past. The commander then argues that they are good fighters only in Gaul: after their migration to Asia Minor, they would have deteriorated to the level of other Asiatics. Noteworthy here is the comparison with crops and soil, which reminds us of various ideas encountered above and below which entail the strong link between human beings and the soil or earth. Sometimes these are expressed in terms of metaphors, sometimes in a more immediately physical sense, describing the earth as mother. Herodotus attributed to a Persian the statement that "there was no land which produced the most remarkable fruit, and at the same time men good at warfare." The connection between land and men was seen to be essential in the views of the author of *Airs, Waters, Places*. Most relevant for the present context is the view, widely held by the Athenians and discussed below in a separate section, that their presumed continuous occupation of their native land endowed them with superiority.

The Gauls had migrated and deteriorated. However, they had also degenerated for another reason. They were a mixed people and thus of lesser quality: *degeneres sunt, mixti . . .* or, in Florus's later paraphrase: *mixta et adulterata*, mixed and impure, bastards. This is the counterpart of the view held by the Athenians that they were superior because their ancestors were not mixed with migrants. The belief that marriage with outsiders produces offspring of lesser

---

dibusque non tantum semina ad seruandam indolem ualent, quantum terrae proprietas caelique, sub quo aluntur, mutat. Cf. the adaptation of this passage by Florus 1.27.3–4: ceterum gens Gallograecorum, sicut ipsum nomen indicio est, mixta et adulterata est: reliquiae Gallorum, qui Brenno duce vastaverant Graeciam, orientem secuti, in media Asiae parte sederunt; itaque, uti frugum semina mutato solo degenerant, sic illa genuina feritas eorum Asiatica amoenitate mollita est.

[125] 38.17.12: generosius in sua quidquid sede gignitur; insitum alienae terrae in id quo alitur, natura uertente se, degenerat. For the same idea, see Aulus Gellius, *Noctes Atticae* 12.1.16: ". . . ac saepe videas arborem laetam et nitentem, in locum alium transpositam, deterioris terrae suco deperisse."

quality appears firmly entrenched in Greece as well as in Rome. Finally, it is instructive to see how Livy adapted the description of the Gallograeci to his literary needs. In Book 37.8.4, referring to 190, a year before the consul made his speech, Antiochus III asks for support against Gallograecia, "for the inhabitants were at that time more belligerent, the original nature of the people had not yet disappeared and they preserved their Gallic spirit."[126] It would have made a difference to the Roman soldiers fighting them in 189, but for Livy it clearly was only a matter of time for the Gauls in Galatia to become soft forever. The implications of such ideas are significant: they represent obvious forms of proto-racism in their hostility to intermarriage and they constitute a form of environmental determinism, which affects Roman views of entire peoples and their place in the value system. No less important: such ideas have obvious consequences for the manner in which the Romans saw their empire and the peoples who made up its population.

Strabo, of course, is one of the most important ancient geographers and without doubt the most important in the age of Augustus.[127] Thus his views on the influence the physical environment exercises upon man are of interest. Strabo criticizes Posidonius for his acceptance of environmental determinism, explicitly rejecting the theory (2.3.7 [103]): ". . . some local characteristics of a people come by nature (i.e. location), others by custom and practice." He gives a number of examples: "For instance, it was not by nature that the Athenians were fond of literature, while the Lacedaemonians and also the Thebans, who are still closer to the Athenians, were not so; but rather by practice. . . . But Posidonius confuses all this." In at least one other passage, he rejects reports that those who drink from a spring in Halicarnassus become effeminate. "Apparently the softness of man is blamed on the air or the water; however, these are not the cause of softness, but wealth and an intemperate way of living."[128] The idea that wealth and prosperity can cause decline is present already in Herodotus and extensively in *Airs*, as was seen above. In these authors, however, the prosperity is produced by the land. Strabo here takes issue, not with this line of thought, but with authors who claim that certain types of air and water have a directly debilitating effect. Strabo, therefore, is not arguing against the environmental theory as found in *Airs* and so many other authors, but against specific theories about water and soil. In practice Strabo often, but not always, thinks along the familiar lines of environmental influences.

Strabo writes of Europe that most of it is in many ways particularly favorable

[126] 37.8.4: Etiam in Gallograeciam miserat; bellicosiores ea tempestate erant, Gallicos adhuc, nondum exoleta stripe gentis, servantes animos.

[127] The subject of four books which all appeared at roughly the same time: Katherine Clarke, *Between Geography and History: Hellenistic Constructions of the Roman World* (Oxford, 1999); Johannes Engels, *Augusteische Oikumenegeographie und Universalhistorie im Werk Strabons von Amaseia* (Geographica Historica 12; Stuttgart, 1999); Daniela Dueck, *Strabo of Amasia: A Greek Man of Letters in Augustan Rome* (London, 2000); Anna Maria Biraschi and Giovanni Salmeri (eds.), *Strabone e l'Asia Minore* (Napoli and Perugia, 2000)

[128] Strabo 14.2.16 (c.656): ἔοικε δ' ἡ τρυφὴ τῶν ἀνθρώπων αἰτιᾶσθαι τοὺς ἀέρας ἢ τὰ ὕδατα· τρυφῆς δ' αἴτια οὐ ταῦτα, ἀλλὰ πλοῦτος καὶ ἡ περὶ τὰς διαίτας ἀκολασία.

for the development of excellence in men and governments. Most of its territory is inhabitable. The cold mountainous regions are poor, but even there good government will have a civilizing effect, as is the case, for instance, with the Greeks. The Romans, too, took over many nations inhabiting unfavorable regions, brought them in contact with each other, and taught them how to live under forms of true government. According to Strabo (2.5.26 [c. 126]):

> All of Europe that is level and has a temperate climate has natural circumstances which cooperate toward these results; for while in a country that is blessed by nature everything tends to peace, in a disagreeable country everything tends to make men warlike and courageous; and so both kinds of country receive benefits from each other, for the latter helps with arms, the former with products of the soil, with arts and with character-building. But the harm that they receive from each other, if they are not mutually helpful, is also apparent. . . . However, . . . the whole of this continent has a natural advantage . . . for it is diversified with plains and mountains, so that throughout its entire extent the agricultural and civilised elements dwell side by side with the warlike element; but . . . the peace-loving element is more numerous and therefore keeps control over the whole body. . . . and the leading nations, too—formerly the Greeks and later the Macedonians and the Romans—have taken hold and helped. (trans. H. L. Jones)

The basic ingredients of environmental determinism combined with ideas regarding a constitutional component and going back to the Hippocratic treatise are obvious here. Note, for instance, the remark about the diverse geography of the continent, which has a beneficial effect on the population, an idea already stated in *Airs*.[129] Strabo, however, adds two significant elements in his analysis of European society, namely "the leading nations" that help in controlling Europe, and the existence of a useful balance between economically productive people and warlike but unproductive peoples. This is also of importance in considering processes of Romanization. Note further that for Strabo, communication, intercourse, and contact between peoples is the precondition and yardstick of civilization. This, again, was the work of the Romans. An interesting passage illustrating Strabo's insistence on the need for communications is the following: "Now one might think that the wanderings of the Greeks to the barbarian peoples are caused by the circumstance that the latter had been divided into small groups and powers which, because of their self-sufficiency, had no intercourse with one another; therefore they were weak against attackers from abroad."[130] Here he explains another aspect of the undesirability of isolation: it makes people vulnerable to invaders. This is an interesting variant view of isolation and thus of pure lineage. Strabo, indeed, claims that it does not work in practice, and goes on to show how, in fact, it is accompanied by negative characteristics: "This self-sufficiency among the Iberians was especially

---

[129] See also below, chapter 10: "Mountaineers and Plainsmen."

[130] Strabo 3.4.5 (c. 158): Τῆς δὲ τῶν Ἑλλήνων πλάνης τῆς εἰς τὰ βάρβαρα ἔθνη νομίζοι τις ἂν αἴτιον τὸ διεσπάσθαι κατὰ μέρη μικρὰ καὶ δυναστείας ἐπιπλοκὴν οὐκ ἐχούσας πρὸς ἀλλήλους κατ᾽ αὐθάδειαν, ὥστε ἐκ τούτου πρὸς τοὺς ἐπιόντας ἔξωθεν ἀσθενεῖς εἶναι.

outspoken, since they had *by nature* (italics mine) acquired a disposition that was reckless and devious."[131] Consequently they would indulge in small-scale raids and robberies rather than organize a joint defense against invaders, such as the Carthaginians and, later, the Romans. Strabo does not belong to the many ancient authors who felt that communication and contact between peoples were a threat and danger to integrity.

There is no trace of the environmental theory in these observations. The fate of the Iberians is determined by their social behavior and this, in turn, has not changed through the ages because it is steered by characteristics acquired "by nature." As already observed above, human characteristics "acquired by nature," that is, inherited and regarded as static in time, are an essential feature of a proto-racist view of humanity. In the case of Strabo we should repeat immediately that he was inconsistent in this and more often than not had a tolerant view of strangers. He tends to give more thought than others to actual or reported patterns of behavior and social interaction than to theories about the underlying causes of reported stereotypes. An interesting example of Strabo's descriptions of various peoples is the opposition between plain and mountains, a point that will be discussed further below. Strabo does not simply repeat generalities, but makes an attempt to describe how such situations are affected by Roman rule and the Roman army.

As an indication of how popular and widely accepted the environmental theory was, it is interesting to note that brief mention of it may be found in poetry. Lucan's *Bellum Civile* (*BC*), written in the reign of Nero, explains where good and poor fighters come from: "Every people born in the northern snows is fierce in wars and loves death; but as one goes towards the East and the moderate parts of the world, peoples grow softer through the mildness of the sky. There one sees both loose garments and flowing robes worn by men."[132] This shows to what extent these ideas had become a commonplace, generally accepted among the Roman establishment. The passage just cited is, in fact, part of a speech by Lentulus in response to one by Pompey which extols the military excellence of the Parthians (Lucan, *BC* 8.294–308). Thus it is clear that the general stereotype existed side by side with genuine respect for the Parthian army. Curiously, Lucan here conflates the two traditional contrasts, encountered in the literature since *Airs* in the fifth century. Lucan does not refer to North versus South and East versus West, but to North versus East. The North is inhabited by fierce fighters, the East by soft, effeminate men. In fact, this makes better sense in Roman terms, for Rome was, at the time, engaged mainly in wars in the North and East, not in the South or West.[133]

---

[131] Ibid. τοῦτο δὲ τὸ αὔθαδες ἐν δὴ τοῖς Ἴβηρσι μάλιστα ἐπέτεινε προσλαβοῦσι καὶ τὸ πανοῦργον φύσει καὶ τὸ μὴ ἁπλοῦν·

[132] Lucan, *BC* 8.363–6: omnis, in Arctois populus quicumque pruinis / nascitur, indomitus bellis et mortis amator: / quidquid ad Eoos tractus mundique teporem / ibitur, emollit gentes clementia caeli. / illic et laxas uestes et fluxa uirorum / uelamenta uides.

[133] The effeminacy and softness of some peoples in Roman eyes will be discussed below, in chapter 5.

A passage in Pliny shows yet another interesting variant of the environmental view of humanity. It has already been mentioned above because it shows a belief in the heredity of acquired characters (*NH* 2.80.189). It follows Aristotle's concept of a tripartite division of the world, consisting of two extremes and the center, substituting, as usual in this period, North and South for Asia and Europe. A similar approach with variations may be found in the work, cited below, of the second-century geographer and astronomer Claudius Ptolemaeus (Ptolemy) from Alexandria. His astrological ideas are treated in the *Apoteles-matica* (= *Tetrabiblos,* written around the middle of the second century, after Pliny's work). However, the tone and contents of Pliny's work are different from other descriptions. Instead of showing the attitudes characteristic of many of the authors here discussed who give negative and unsympathetic descriptions of at least some of the groups they discuss, Pliny has something positive to say about all three. Those living in the south (the Ethiopians, as usual) are dark, wise (*sapientes*), and tall, those in the north are white, blonde, and fierce (*truces*), while those living in the middle are of intermediate size and complexion: their environment is fertile, they are gentle (*molles*), lucid (*sensus liquidos*), and their minds are creative (*ingenia fecunda*). They also have empires, unlike the inhabitants of the extreme regions who are never subject to those in the center, because of the wildness of nature in their parts.[134] Pliny does not even say that those fortunate enough to live in the moderate regions are the Romans. On the contrary, he seems to take a broad view by stating that they have empires, in the plural. This, then, appears to be an attempt to reconcile the traditional ethnocentric view of the world with the opposing tendency to idealize the extreme parts of the world.[135] The basis for Pliny's characterizations, however, is a standard version of the environmental theory. This appears in a discussion of daylight and the way it varies at different latitudes. He explains the effect of the heat of the sun in the South and North respectively on the animals and humans inhabiting those regions. The different physical and mental characteristics that he describes are all explained by the effect of the heat on bodily fluids.

There is thus a rigid and permanent relationship between temperature, body, and spirit, which fits the definition of proto-racism. Pliny adds the familiar reference to empires being the preserve of those living in the temperate zone, whereby it is noticeable that he uses the plural, while Aristotle, who first gave this interpretation of the theory, spoke only of the Greek people, who would have been able "to attain the highest political development, and to show a capacity for governing every other people—if only it could once achieve political unity," because they lived in the ideal environment, in the geographical midpoint (*Pol.* 1327b, trans. Ernest Barker). Aristotle, of course, was merely speculating about a possible Greek empire, while Pliny lived in the Roman

---

[134] Pliny, *NH* 2.80.190: isdem imperia, quae numquam extim<is g>entibus fuerint, sicut ne illae quidem his paruerint, avolsae ac pro numine naturae urguentis illas solitariae.

[135] Cf. Romm, *The Edges of the Earth*, chapter 2.

Empire and was aware of the Hellenistic kingdoms that had existed in the past. Vitruvius, however, in his description of the theory, refers only to the Roman Empire. However this may be, Pliny clearly is one of the authors whose unreserved acceptance of the environmental theory and its proto-racist conceptual world is linked firmly with ideas about the functioning of empires.

A similar view may be found in a work that was probably written somewhat earlier, namely Seneca's *De Ira*. The author here repeats many of the traditional elements of the theory, slightly adapted for use in a work whose theme is anger.[136] He propounds the thesis that those nations which are free, such as the Germans and Scythians, are also the most prone to anger. Anger is a noble quality of those who are brave and firm, but not disciplined. Their strong character is free from softness and weakness, but may turn into overconfidence and recklessness. They are ungovernable, but also unsuited for ruling others. Seneca then briefly mentions climate as the cause for all of this: "Therefore empires are for those peoples who enjoy a milder climate. Those who dwell in cold climates in the north have wild tempers, which the poet calls 'most similar to their skies.'"[137] This represents, in essence, elements of the environmental theory which we find in Vitruvius and Pliny, but Seneca is not concerned with physiological explanations and only mentions the northerners and those in the middle, who are capable of acquiring and maintaining empires. We already saw that Seneca here combines elements of the environmental theory with assumptions about the heredity of acquired characters.

We encounter a somewhat different form of the environmental theory in Tacitus' *Agricola* 11.[138] Tacitus is uncertain if the Britons were indigenous or immigrants.

> Their physical features are various and so are the possible inferences that may be drawn from this. The red hair and long limbs of the inhabitants of Caledonia clearly indicate an origin from Germania. The dark colour of the Silures, their hair, usually curly, and the fact that they live opposite Spain suggest that the old Hiberi crossed the sea and occupied this region;[139] those who live nearest to the Gauls also resemble them, either from the lasting influence of their origin, or because in countries projecting in opposite directions and thus approaching each other, climate has produced (similar) physical characteristics.[140]

[136] Seneca, *De Ira* 2.15, relevant also for the discussion of Germans and of Romanization.

[137] *De Ira* 2.15.5: Fere itaque imperia penes eos fuere populos, qui mitiore caelo utuntur. In frigora septemtrionem que vergentibus inmansueta ingenia sunt, ut ait poeta, suo que simillima caelo.

[138] For this passage, cf. Allen A. Lund, "Zu den Rassenkriterien des Tacitus," *Latomus* 42 (1982), 845–849.

[139] Tacitus, like other ancient authors, believed that Spain was opposite and near to Britain; cf. Agricola 10.2 and Isaac, *Limits of Empire*, 405. Ogilvie and Richmond, *Tacitus, Agricola*, still repeat the theory that the dark complexion of these people derived from "the short, dark race of non-Aryan stock which was widely spread over the Mediterranean lands and beyond in the neolithic period" (175). It must be admitted that even Tacitus makes more sense than that.

[140] Tac. *Agricola* 11: habitus corporum varii atque ex eo argumenta. namque rutilae Caledoniam

Tacitus therefore considers that there are three possibilities (1) In the case of the Silures, geographical origin has determined lasting physical characteristics. Strictly speaking this is a combination of environmental influence and the heredity of acquired characters. One need not assume that Tacitus thought it through like this, but it is worth considering the underlying assumptions of these and similar statements. (2) The Britons living near Gaul look like Gauls because of common ancestors or (3) because the climate is similar it has produced similar people. Tacitus inclines to the second possibility, namely a migration of Gauls to Britain, because of certain cultural similarities: religion, language, and behavior when in danger. This is a simple historical explanation, while the third possibility again shows use of the tenets of the environmental theory. His comments on the respective courage of Gauls and Britons are the familiar ethnic stereotypes, discussed below, in the chapter on Gauls (chapter 10).

Tacitus was one of the first but by no means the last author to publish his thoughts about the origins of the British.[141] There are many elements derived from the standard environmental theory in his works, but they are scattered over them and not usually concentrated in one place. "The foremost in *virtus* among the Germans are the Batavi . . . The Mattiaci . . . resemble in all other aspects the Batavi, except that they derive a more spirited temperament from the soil and climate of the land which is still[142] their own.[143]

In this connection it will be interesting to consider two passages on this topic from Caesar's *Gallic War* which show an unconventional approach. The Volcae Tectosages were a Gallic people who had established themselves in the heart of the southern Germanic area.[144] Caesar remarks that because the Volcae live in the same economic conditions as the Germanic tribes, their pattern of life and personal physique and condition are the same as those of the Germans (6.24.2–

---

habitantium comae, magni artus Germanicam originem adseverant; Silurum colorati vultus, torti plerumque crines et posita contra Hispania Hiberos veteres traiecisse easque sedes occupasse fidem faciunt; proximi Gallis et similes sunt, seu durante originis vi, seu procurrentibus in diversa terris positio caeli corporibus habitum dedit.

[141] Poliakov, *Le mythe arien* (1971), 49–66, cites the various myths proposed over the centuries extensively. Sir Walter Scott, above all, was highly influential in portraying history in terms of race: struggles between Scottish blood and English blood, Saxon blood and French blood. Theories regarding pure blood and mixed blood alternate in the literature of this period.

[142] cetera similes Batavis, nisi quod ipso adhuc terrae suae solo et caelo acrius animantur. The meaning of *adhuc* is very doubtful. I take it tentatively with *terrae suae* to indicate that the Mattiaci, living as they do across the Rhine (*in sua ripa*), have not yet been fully incorporated into the Empire, which, however, is taken by Tacitus as going to happen in due course of time. The land is *still* their own.

[143] *Germ.* 29.3. Cf. J.G.C. Anderson, *Cornelii Taciti de origine et situ Germanorum* (Oxford, 1938), p. 148, comm. ad loc.: "The bracing highland country of the Mattiaci is contrasted with the dead level of the low-lying and humid Batavian 'island': the livelier temperament of the Rhinelanders as compared with the more stolid Dutch is still noticeable." Such is the force of the environmental theory that a twentieth-century scholar could seriously maintain that people, living two millennia apart, but in the same geographical location, must respond to the same stereotypes.

[144] See also below, chapter 10.

5). He contrasts them with the Celts of Gallia, who had developed their economic life through the propinquity of the Roman province and its supplies of consumer goods, and who gradually lost their supremacy in the skills of war (24.5–6). Thus Caesar accepts the idea that the Gauls deteriorated through contamination with Roman wealth, while the group that settled among the sober Germans maintained their quality. Perhaps superfluously it may be noted that this once more still conforms to the idea that people never improve: they either maintain their level or deteriorate. Furthermore, good warriors cannot be wealthy. The Suebi owed their huge physique to their diet of meat and milk and to their continual exercise, but partly also to their freedom of life and lack of discipline (*BG* 4.1.8–9).[145] It is interesting to observe that Caesar attributes everything to diet and lifestyle, rather than to external factors such as climate and geography. This shows unusual independence of mind, possibly because he reports his own observations rather than second- or third-hand stereotypes. Yet he also wrote under the influence of the ideas of his age, for instance the conviction that prosperity corrupts and prosperous neighbors contaminate.[146]

A variation of the environmental theory that influenced later authors is supported by Seneca. Seneca substitutes "God" (*ille deus*) for nature (*natura*), but says explicitly that the latter is merely another name for God: "the germs/seeds (*semina*) of all the ages and arts are within ourselves. God, our master, produces out of the hidden our abilities."[147] This version of the environmental theory is found again in Christian literature, notably in the work of the African Church Father Tertullian (c. 160–225), who, following Seneca, cited here, explains in his *de anima* what are the influences that bear on the nature of the soul. Citing Seneca he continues:

> germs that are contained in us and which are hidden throughout childhood, for from these mental capacity develops. The seed of the fruit have also only one form for each species, but they develop in different ways. Some develop perfectly normal, others respond even better, yet others change in accordance with the nature of the climate and the soil, the quality of the labor and care, the change of the seasons, or following random events. Thus also the soul develops, having a uniform shape as a germ, but a distinct form as it grows. Much depends on the location. It is told that in Thebes dumb and stupid people are born, but in Athens eloquent and bright people,[148] while in Kollytos the children learn to speak a month earlier because their tongues are precocious.[149] . . . Empedocles, however, determines that the causes of intel-

---

[145] Abstention from wine, drinking wine, mixed or unmixed, drinking blood, and drinking milk, these were all considered significant customs for foreigners as early as Herodotus in his description of the customs of the Scythians, cf. Hartog, *Le miroir d'Hérodote*, 179–184.

[146] For observations by Caesar following traditional concepts, see below, chapter 11 (on the Belgae).

[147] Seneca, *de beneficiis* 4.6.6: Insita sunt nobis omnium aetatum, omnium artium semina, magisterque ex occulto deus producit ingenia.

[148] Cf. Cicero, *de Fato* 4.7: Athenis tenue caelum, ex quo etiam acutiores putantur Attici; crassum Thebis, itaque pingues Thebani et valentes.

[149] Plato was born in the deme of Kollytos: Diogenes Laertius 3.3.5.

ligence and stupidity are in the quality of the blood, but he concludes that the
perfection and further development depend on teaching and discipline. Yet it is well
known that peoples have different characters. The comedians make fun of the Phrygians because they are afraid.[150] Sallust calls the Mauri unreliable[151] and the Dalma-
tians crude; even the apostle reproaches the Cretans of being liars.[152]

First, it is important to note that this Christian author has no more sense of
individuality in describing peoples than any of his pagan predecessors. He accepts without reservation the traditional stereotypes to the extent that he cites
his sources. Even more important, Tertullian has discovered an ingenious and
novel way of combining the idea of immutability, inherent in theories concerning heredity, with the environmental theory. It follows to some extent ideas
about *semen* / sperm found, for instance, in the Hippocratic corpus and in the
work of Strabo (not accepted by Cicero), discussed above. These hold that
semen / sperm or seed, is being influenced by the environment and the parents,
so that, for instance, acquired characters are transmitted to offspring. Tertullian,
however, says something different. Expanding Seneca's idea, he claims that
there are *semina*, seeds or germs, in human beings after they are born and these
germs are susceptible to external influences which affect body and mind. What
follows is then, more or less, the usual environmental theory in its simple form,
accompanied by a series of commonplaces, sanctioned by early Christian agreement with the familiar status of Cretans as liars.[153] The reference to Empedocles
reflects Tertullian's awareness that there were other views. Tertullian's germs
were in a similar sense—and without giving credit to his source of inspiration—taken up again by Immanuel Kant, as observed above. Thus they served

---

[150] See below, chapter 6 for references. The Phrygians are first described as cowards in Euripides,
Or. 1351 and this was taken over in Latin literature.

[151] Sallustius, *Hist.* fr. 2.39 (Maurenbrecher); cf. P. McGushin, *Sallust: The Histories* (Oxford,
1992), fr. 2.37 with comments on p. 49.

[152] Tertullian, *de anima* 20: Sicut et Seneca saepe noster: insita sunt nobis omnium artium et
aetatum semina, magisterque ex occulto deus producit ingenia, ex seminibus scilicet insitis et occultis per infantiam, quae sunt et intellectus. Ex his enim producuntur ingenia. 2. Porro et frugum
seminibus una generis cuiusque forma est, processus tamen uarii: alia integro statu euadunt, alia
etiam meliora respondent, alia degenerant pro condicione caeli et soli, pro ratione operis et curae,
pro temporum euentu, pro licentia casuum; ita et animam licebit semine uniformem, fetu multi-
formem. 3. Nam et hic de locis interest. Thebis hebetes et brutos nasci relatum est, athenis sapiendi
dicendique acutissimos, ubi penes colyttum pueri mense citius eloquuntur praecoca lingua, siquidem et plato in timaeo mineruam affirmat, cum urbem illam moliretur, nihil aliud quam regionis
naturam prospexisse talia ingenia pollicitam; unde et ipse in legibus megillo et cliniae praecipit
condendae ciuitati locum procurare. Sed Empedocles causam argutae indolis et obtusae in sanguinis
qualitate constituit, perfectum ac profectum de doctrina disciplinaque deducit. Tamen uulgata iam
res est gentilium proprietatum. Comici Phrygas timidos inludunt, Sallustius uanos Mauros et feroces
Dalmatos pulsat, mendaces Cretas etiam apostolus inurit.

[153] Paulus, *ep. ad Titum* 1.12: εἶπέν τις ἐξ αὐτῶν (scil. τῶν Κρητῶν), ἴδιος αὐτῶν προφήτης·
Κρῆτες ἀεὶ ψεῦσται, κακὰ θηρία, attributed to Epimenides. It is cited frequently by early Christian
authors in connection with Callimachus's hymn to Zeus 8f.: Ζεῦ, σὲ μὲν Ἰδαίοισιν ἐν οὔρεσί φασι
γενέσθαι, Ζεῦ, σὲ δ' ἐν Ἀρκαδίῃ· πότεροι, πάτερ, ἐψεύσαντο; Κρῆτες ἀεὶ ψεῦσται· See, for
instance, Origenes, *Contra Celsum* 3.43.16; Clemens Alexandrinus, *Stromata* 1.4.59.

as a theoretical basis for a racist theory, which proposed the immutability of inherited race, while still explaining variations by an adaptation of the familiar environmental theory.

At a more conventional level, in his discussion of the Novatians, the church historian Socrates (c. 380–450) explains that the austerity and good sense of the Phrygians and Paphlagonians was caused by the climate.[154] He adds that they live in the middle between the Scythians and Thracians, peoples with fierce characters, and the peoples of the East, who are the slaves of their desires.[155] Hence they are not interested in horse races or the theater and they abhor fornication.

Finally, it should be mentioned that the environmental theory was not the sole approach accepted by ancient scholars and literary men. Above, we saw that Cicero, *de divinatione* 2.96, argues against the plausibility of astrological theory. We do not have the texts with which Cicero disagreed, but the astrological approach is well known from Ptolemy's *Tetrabiblos* already referred to. Here Ptolemy states his view that group characteristics are conditioned by the astrological situation. It is worth citing Ptolemy's comments on the Middle East at some length:

> The remaining parts of the quarter, situated about the centre of the inhabited world, Idumaea, Coele-Syria, Judaea, Phoenicia, Chaldaea, Orchinia, and Arabia Felix, which are situated toward the north-west of the whole quarter, have additional familiarity with the north-western triangle, Aries, Leo, and Sagittarius, and, further-more, have as co-rulers Jupiter, Mars and Mercury (29). Therefore these peoples are, in comparison with the others, more gifted in trade and exchange; they are more unscrupulous, despicable cowards, treacherous, servile, and in general fickle, on account of the stars mentioned (30). Of these, again the inhabitants of Coele-Syria, Idumaea and Judaea are more closely familiar to Aries and Mars, and there-fore these peoples are in general bold, godless, and scheming. The Phoenicians, Chaldaeans, and Orchinians have familiarity with Leo and the sun, so that they are simpler, kindly, addicted to astrology, and beyond all men worshippers of the sun (31).[156]

---

[154] Socrates, *HE* 4.28. The Phrygians here apparently had shaken off their popular stereotype of being cowards.

[155] τῷ δὲ ἐπιθυμητικῷ οἱ πρὸς ἀνίσχοντα ἥλιον τὴν οἴκησιν ἔχοντες πλέον δουλεύουσι. This is a Christian development of the Greek tradition, going back to the fourth century B.C., which considered Orientals servile. Instead of being slaves to their kings they are now slaves to their desires. The fierce character of Scythians and Thracians is traditional and occurs already in Plato.

[156] Ptolemy, *Tetrabiblos* 2.3.65f. (29f.) (trans. F. E. Robbins, Loeb): τὰ δὲ λοιπὰ τοῦ τεταρτημορίου μέρη περὶ τὸ μέσον ἐσχηματισμένα τῆς ὅλης οἰκουμένης, Ἰδουμαία Κοίλη Συρία Ἰουδαία Φοινίκη Χαλδαϊκὴ Ὀρχηνία Ἀραβία εὐδαίμων καὶ τὴν θέσιν ἔχοντα πρὸς βορρόλιβα τοῦ ὅλου τετάρτη μορίου προσλαμβάνει πάλιν τὴν συνοικείωσιν τοῦ βορρολιβικοῦ τριγώνου, Κριοῦ Λέοντος Τοξότου, ἔχει δὲ συνοικοδεσπότας τόν τε τοῦ Διὸς καὶ τὸν τοῦ Ἄρεως καὶ ἔτι τὸν τοῦ Ἑρμοῦ. διὸ μᾶλλον οὗτοι τῶν ἄλλων ἐμπορικώτεροι καὶ συναλλακτικώτεροι, πανουργότεροι δὲ καὶ δειλοκαταφρόνητοι καὶ ἐπιβουλευτικοὶ καὶ δουλόψυχοι καὶ ὅλως ἀλλοπρόσαλλοι διὰ τὸν τῶν προκειμένων ἀστέρων συσχηματισμόν. καὶ τούτων δὲ πάλιν οἱ μὲν περὶ τὴν Κοίλην Συρίαν καὶ Ἰδουμαίαν καὶ Ἰουδαίαν τῷ τε Κριῷ καὶ τῷ τοῦ ἄρεως μᾶλλον

At the end of all this it is engaging to see that Ptolemy considered the Phoenicians and others addicted to astrology. On the geography, Menachem Stern observes that the list of countries grouped with Judaea is surprising, especially Chaldaea and the obscure Orchinia. Syria proper is not mentioned at all.[157] Stern assumes that this confused presentation must reflect the use by Ptolemy of old sources which he did not succeed in rationalizing. The other point to be observed is that Coele-Syria and Judaea are first described with others as cowards, among other qualifications, and later, with Idumaea, as bold. Stern suggests, again convincingly, that in referring to the second group Ptolemy had the Jews in mind. As a man who lived at the time of the Jewish revolts under Trajan and Hadrian, Ptolemy may have felt the Jews were bold. As for the qualifications themselves, that of being fickle or inconstant is probably most frequently assigned to unpopular others: Ptolemy's own Egypt is described as such by Tacitus. Caesar applies it to the Gauls, Lucan to the Mauri, and Cicero to the Greeks. While the Phoenicians are described as greedy traders in Homer and, particularly in texts from the fourth century onwards, eastern peoples in general also appear as servile, cowardly, and treacherous in the same period.[158]

The essence of this entire passage, however, and the reason it seemed worth citing it at length, is the appearance of so many familiar stereotypes which, in this case, are attributed to laws of astrology, wherewhereas other ancient authors firmly believe these same qualities or similar ones are caused by climate and geography.[159] The underlying assumption, which Cicero refuses to accept, is that external factors are the only ones to determine common characteristics of groups of people. The astrologers, c.q. according to Ptolemy, represent in fact

συνοικειοῦνται, διόπερ ὡς ἐπίπαν θρασεῖς τέ εἰσι καὶ ἄθεοι καὶ ἐπιβουλευτικοί· Φοίνικες δὲ καὶ Χαλδαῖοι καὶ Ὀρχήνιοι τῷ Λέοντι καὶ τῷ ἡλίῳ διόπερ ἁπλούστεροι καὶ ψιλάνθρωποι καὶ φιλαστρόλογοι καὶ μάλιστα πάντων σέβοντες τὸν ἥλιον· Cf. Müller, *Geschichte der antiken Ethnographie* 2, 172f.

[157] It is mentioned in 2.3.41: in Syria, Commagene, and Cappadocia there is much boldness, knavery, treachery, and laboriousness (τὸ θρασὺ καὶ πονηρὸν καὶ ἐπιβουλευτικὸν καὶ ἐπίπονον).

[158] It will be noted that Ptolemy himself reverses the commonplaces about east and west, whereby his own Egypt is masculine, honest, and strong in character, while the west is feminine, soft, and secretive. See further below in chapter 5. In fact, much of the second book of the *Tetrabiblos* is a stereotypical description of peoples with astrological explanations. In the discussion of individual peoples occasional reference will be made to the work.

[159] Ptolemy, although he may have been born in Ptolemais in Egypt, represents the world of Alexandrian Hellenistic scholarship, which is not dealt with in the present study, just as the Egyptian traditions hostile to the Jews will not be considered in the chapter on Jews. It is clear, however, that, in his dislike of Middle Eastern peoples he has enough in common with various Roman authors to justify considering him here. In his theoretical introduction to the work, Ptolemy argues for a connection between astrology and environmental theory in claiming that the sun, moon, and stars influence the environment which, in turn, influences human beings (*Tetrabiblos* 1.2). He elaborates on this in 2.2, which repeats many of the common features of environmental theory. This, inevitably, has been considered as deriving from Posidonius, an attribution not accepted by all (references in Stern, *GLAJJ* 2.162 n.1). In this connection it is worth observing that Ptolemy's description of the Ethiopians comes close to that of Strabo 15.1.24 (595f.), cited above. Strabo happens to refer to two of his sources in this chapter: Onesicritus and Theodectes, but he fails to mention Posidonius.

an extreme and inflexible form of environmentalism. Astrology does not leave any room for people to improve or change each other and themselves, a possibility which some of the proponents of the environmental theory do allow for, for instance the first text to develop it, *Airs, Waters, Places.* Here we found a clear statement that the constitution—monarchy or other—also makes a decisive contribution to group characteristics. Ptolemy's astrology does not take into account what happens when people move from one place to another, which according to its own tenets should decisively affect their character. Roman settlers in Berytus ought to have children with Phoenician characteristics and Phoenicians in Rome should have Roman children, according to the theory. However, this is never considered.

Ptolemy's astrology is an entirely mechanical concept which leaves no scope for individual action and temperament. Paradoxically, it leaves no room for hereditary influence either,[160] which is the basis for modern racial thinking. However, in the rigidity whereby immutable external factors, namely the position of the stars, are assumed to determine the character of entire peoples for generations, this is definitely an extreme example of proto-racism.

It is interesting to note that astrology can lead to quite different interpretations of such matters. One author who emphatically rejects the environmental theory—precisely because he believes in astrology—is the fourth-century scholar Firmicus Maternus. Whatever his shortcomings in the technical discussion of astrology,[161] he reaches the sensible conclusion that the ethnic commonplaces which he cites as widely accepted in his time were in fact only very partially applicable.[162] It has to be admitted, however, that the voice of Firmicus Maternus has had little influence against the weight of all the major authors who accept the environmental theory without qualms, perhaps precisely because he had more sense, at least in this respect.

This completes our survey of the Roman development of environmental theory. As for the discussion of Greek views, it should be noted once again that the views discussed so far apply to entire foreign peoples, living in their homeland or perhaps moving elsewhere together. We have not yet seen opinions on foreigners living as minorities in another environment. Furthermore, it will suffice to state that the Roman literature, even when we allow for individual variations and a few exceptions, accepted Greek ideas regarding the environment and its impact on group characteristics without serious reservations. Details were adapted: an opposition of North–South replaced the opposition of Europe–

---

[160] In *Tetrabiblos* 1.2 Ptolemy concedes that "differences of seed exert a very great influence on the special traits of the genus" (αἵ τε γὰρ τῶν σπερμάτων διαφοραὶ πλεῖστον δύνανται πρὸς τὸ τοῦ γένους ἴδιον). However, it is clear that this means no more than the difference between a horse and a man being determined by seed, while differences in body and soul of men are determined by place of birth. See also the general considerations in 4.10.

[161] Firmicus Maternus, *Mathesis* vol.1, ed. P. Monat (Paris, 1992), for the shortcomings: Introduction, p.16f.; 20–23.

[162] *Mathesis*, 1.2.1–4; 1.10.12.

Asia, for instance, for the reasons already indicated: unlike the Greeks, the Romans saw the world from the perspective of empire-builders. Their most formidable enemies lived north of Italy, not west of it. For the same reason, Strabo would allow for the adaptibility of, for example, mountain-dwellers, while earlier authors describe them as incapable of progress towards sociability. According to Strabo, they could be improved under the influence of good government. The essence of environmental theory and its proto-racist basis, however, was generally accepted in Rome. In fact, it appears in some form in every author who discusses climates and strange peoples.

For the purpose of the present study we should therefore point out that, ever since the renaissance, all students of the classics through the ages, whether they read Greek or Latin or both, were exposed to the environmental theory and other proto-racist views without ever encountering serious criticism or discussion. There are partial exceptions, as we have seen: Cicero, Julius Caesar, and Strabo express partially dissident views which were not developed. However, a few short passages in Cicero's *de divinatione* and *de lege agraria* surely could not counterbalance the consensus in all of the literature from the fifth century B.C. onward. We find the theory in mediaeval islamic sources in a form immediately derivative of the Greek texts.[163] It should not surprise us, therefore, if the intellectuals of the Enlightenment accepted the theory and its corollaries without serious criticism.

It will be useful to say a little more about this group and the various ways in which early modern authors took over and adapted Graeco-Roman ideas. As Diderot wrote to Catherine the Great, "The Greeks were the teachers of the Romans. The Greeks and Romans have been ours."[164] As observed by Peter Gay, "the encounter (of the 'philosophes' of the Enlightenment) with the classics, often casual or insignificant, was also decisive for them as it was for few other men."[165] "For the men of the Enlightenment, the road to independence (from Christianity) lay through the ancients."[166]

One of the concepts which the "philosophes" of the Enlightenment accepted from antiquity was the environmental theory. In this they, in turn, have exercised a tremendous influence on contemporary thinking and thus on the modern interpretation of the classics discussed here. The French political philosopher Jean Bodin (1529/30–1596) apparently was the first.[167] He devoted a chapter of

---

[163] Bernard Lewis, *Race and Slavery in the Middle East* (New York and Oxford, 1990), 45–48. Blacks are overcooked in the womb and northern people undercooked. The merit of the people of Babylon is due to their temperate climate. We encounter the familiar stereotypes regarding the mental characteristics of those peoples.

[164] Diderot, "Plan d'une université pour le gouvernement de Russie" in *Œuvres complètes* (Paris, 1875, repr. 1966), vol. 3.477. He continues: "je l'ai dit, et je le répète: on ne peut guère prétendre au titre de littérateur, sans la connaissance de leur langues." Cf. Peter Gay, *The Enlightenment: An Interpretation. The Rise of Modern Paganism* (New York, 1966), 94.

[165] Gay, *The Enlightenment*, 44. For the impact of the classics on the Enlightenment, see Book 1, chapters 1–3.

[166] Gay, *The Enlightenment*, 69.

[167] Bodin, *The Six Bookes of a Commonweale*, 5.1, pp. 545–568, and see Introduction A22–4.

his *République* to the environmental theory, quoting copiously from classical literature, including the key passages from *Airs*, Aristotle, Vitruvius, and Vegetius, analyzed above:[168] "The people therfore of the middle regions haue more force than they of the South, & lesse pollicie: and more wit than they of the North, & lesse force; and are more fit to commaund and gouerne Commonweales, and more iust in their actions."[169] Bodin was followed by John Arbuthnot (1667–1735). Best known is Montesquieu in *L'Esprit des Lois* who supported a universalistic point of view and believed that environmental influences or *nurture*, rather than permanent, inherited traits, make man what he is.[170] He certainly proclaimed the superiority of Europeans over Asiatics and others, but he assumed that this was caused by differences in climate, not by inborn qualities.[171]

These ideas were not generally accepted. The environmental theory was criticised by Helvétius (1715–1771) and D'Holbach (1723–1789).[172] Diderot discussed the customs of the South Pacific islanders, emphasizing their conception of a free society based on tolerance and developing his views on sexual freedom, all in contrast to contemporary European society.[173] David Hume, being a

---

See Etienne-Maurice Fournol, *Bodin, prédécesseur de Montesquieu: étude sur quelques théories politiques de la «République» et de «l'esprit des lois»* (Paris, 1896, repr. Genève, 1970), ch. 4, at 116f., where it is strangely suggested that Bodin himself invented the environmental theory and did not develop it under the influence of any earlier author. On p. 118 he claims that all commentators agree on Bodin's originality. It is in fact remarkable to what extent Bodin is guided by classical literature in his arguments. He does not cite many recent authors, exceptions being Francisco Alvarez, *History of Ethiopia* (1557?) and Sigmund Herberstein, *Reise zu den Moskowitern* (1526).

[168] The relevant passage from Vitruvius is cited in *The Six Bookes*, p. 447f. and both Vitruvius and Vegetius again on p. 550.

[169] Bodin, op. cit., 550 and see 552. On p. 554 Bodin argues for a causal connection between complection and character of northern and southern peoples respectively.

[170] For the influence of Bodin on Montesquieu, see Fournol, *Bodin*, ch. 5.

[171] *L'esprit des Lois*, Book 14, ch. 2; Book 17, ch. 3–5.

[172] Claude-Adrien Helvétius, *De l'esprit* (Paris, 1758), ed. J. Moutaux (Paris, 1988), devotes three chapters to a systematic refutation of environmental determinism (3.28–30). He rejects the idea that there is any correlation between location, climate, and courage and concludes (p. 414) "qu'il n'est point de Nations priviligiées en vertu, en esprit, en courage. La nature, à cet égard, n'a point fait un partage inégal de ses dons." In his view moral forces, education, and good government are essential factors and these are subject to change. Another critic, mentioned above, is Paul-Henri Dietrich d'Holbach, *Le Systeme social: Principes naturels de la morale et de la politique, avec un examen de l'influence du gouvernement sur les moeurs* (Paris, 1773), Part 3, chapter 1.

[173] Diderot, *Supplément au voyage de Bougainville* (written 1772, published 1796) ed. Gilbert Chinard (Oxford and London, 1935). In this work Diderot allegedly gives an account of the dialogue between a native of Tahiti, Aotourou, and a chaplain in the crew of Bougainville who made a journey to the Pacific in 1768–1769. The Tahitians are depicted as primitives who lived a life of innocent sexual freedom. The dialogue depicts a subtle inversion of the existing Christian norms and attributes to the Tahitian the exclamation: 'O le vilain pays! si tout y est ordonné comme ce que tu m'en dis, vous êtes plus barbares que nous.' Poliakov,*The Arian Myth*, 169, observes that Diderot also philosophized on the inferiority of the Laplander. The Laplanders were regularly the subject of comments in the literature of this period, e.g., by Blumenbach, cited below in chapter 5. It is worth observing also that the entry on intolerance in Diderot, *Encyclopédie* 3, *Oeuvres complètes* 7 (Paris, 1976), pp. 541–546, deals with religious intolerance exclusively.

polygenist, generally rejected the impact of the environment on group character, yet in his essay "On National Characters" published in 1748, he declares in passing that "there is some reason to think, that all the nations, which live beyond the polar circles or between the tropics, are inferior to the rest of the species, and are incapable of all the higher attainments of the human mind."[174]

Another thinker who undoubtedly belonged to this group was Kant's pupil Johann-Gottfried von Herder (1774–1803).[175] He considers the Hippocratic treatise important, considers the environment influential, but he also argues for the supremacy of genetic forces, being an early proponent of the heredity of acquired characters.[176] He had some sympathy for peoples living in the extreme parts of the earth—the North and the Equator. They were the victims of their environment, "What so forcibly discriminates the Negro races in Africa itself? The climate considered in the most extensive signification of the word, so as to include the manner of life and the food." They are black through the effect of the climate, which also is responsible for an increased measure of libido, which again causes the pronounced development of their sexual organs.[177] At the end of his chapter on Africa: "That finer intellect which the creature whose breast swells with boiling passions beneath this burning sun, must necessarily be refused, was countervailed by a structure altogether incompatible with it. Since then a nobler boon could not be conferred on the Negro in such a climate, let us pity, but not despise him."[178]

These quotations show clearly that group prejudice and discriminatory ideas are not restricted to ideas about inherited qualities. They can equally well focus on supposed environmental influences. Racism, according to the narrow defini-

---

[174] David Hume, "Of National Character," *Essays and Treatises on Several Subjects* (I have seen the Edinburgh ed., 1825), 521f. Now included in *Political Essays*, ed. Knud Haakonssen (Cambridge, 1994), 86; Cf. Shulamit Volkov, "Exploring the Other: The Enlightenment's Search for the Boundaries of Humanity," in R. S. Wistrich (ed.), *Demonizing the Other* (1999), 148–167, esp. 150; Eze, *Race and the Enlightenment* (1997), 32f; Poliakov, *Arian Myth*, 176f. For Hume's polygenist racism see in particular footnote f (ed. Haakonssen, p. 86), added in the second edition of this work, in which he specifically deals with blacks: "I am apt to suspect the negroes, and in general all the other species of men (for there are four or five different kinds) to be naturally inferior to the whites. There scarcely ever was a civilized nation of any other complexion than white, nor even any individual eminent in either action or speculation. . . . Such a uniform and constant difference could not happen, in so many countries and ages, if nature had not made an original distinction between these breeds of men." James Beattie published an attack on this statement in 1770, cf. Eze, 34–37. It is interesting to note that Hume's essay begins with entirely sensible criticism of national stereotypes (p.78). He adheres to the classical division between *physical* (i.e., environmental, external) and *moral* (i.e., social) causes. While merely acknowledging the importance of the former, he greatly emphasizes the role of the latter.

[175] Johann-Gottfried von Herder, *Outlines of a Philosophy of the History of Mankind*, Book VI, 270f.; see the *Sämtliche Werke,* B. Suphan, ed. (Hildesheim, 1967); for brief extracts in English: Eze, *Race and the Enlightenment*, 70–78; Bernasconi and Lott, *The Idea of Race* (2000), 23–26, citing an English translation by Thomas Nenon, 1999, which I have not seen; cf. Poliakov, *Aryan Myth*, 174, 186f.

[176] *Ideen zur Philosophie der Menschheit* 2 (1785), Ges. Schriften, vol. 13, 269–276.

[177] Op. cit. 233–235.

[178] Op. cit. 236.

tions cited in the Introduction, always entails ideas about the hereditary transmission of characteristics, but, as argued there, a broader definition includes
other essential features of it which have the same result: the classification of
groups of peoples through claims that link physical, and mental or moral characteristics. It is therefore significant for our purposes that some of the eighteenth-century environmentalists classified humanity according to color and geography. Christoph Meiners (1747–1816) is one of the authors who did so in
his popular work, the *Outline of the History of Mankind*, adding that "one of the
chief characteristics of tribes and peoples is the beauty or ugliness of the whole
body or of the face."[179] In his view only people of "Caucasian stock" (excluding
the Slavs) are beautiful. What he considered ugly races are permanently inferior
and animal-like: "The black and ugly peoples are distinct from the white and
beautiful peoples by their sad lack in virtue and their various terrible vices."[180]
Perfection or imperfection of the body and the spirit go together, and are determined by climate. "The ancients already understood, and they said so, that even
the most fertile countries weaken the forces of the spirit and the male virtues."[181]
Climate may favor the inner strength of peoples and, conversely, some environments may corrupt and and diminish the most noble human characters. He
gives a long list of particularly dangerous areas, encompassing much of the
inhabited world.[182] Not long afterwards Georges Cuvier (1769–1832) expressed
similar ideas, insisting on the beauty of the Caucasian skull.[183] He divides humanity into three races—white, yellow, and black—and subdivides these into
further groups, all of which receive marks for the beauty or ugliness of their
skull and the quality of their civilizations. Climate is assumed to be the primary
force behind these differences.[184] As observed in the Introduction, the early

[179] Christoph Meiners, *Grundriss der Geschichte der Menschheit* (Lengo, 1785), 43. For Meiners'
racist ideas, see B. Rupp-Eisenreich, "Des choses occultes en histoire des sciences humaines: le
destine de la 'science nouvelle' de Christoph Meiners," *L'Ethnographie* 79 (1983), 181–183;
Gustav Jahoda, *Images of Savages: Ancient Roots of Modern Prejudice in Western Culture* (London, 1999), 65–68.

[180] Meiners, *Grundriss,* 116.

[181] Meiners, *Grundriss,* 111 with note a, referring to Aristotle, *Pol.* 7.7, Livy 38.17, and so on.

[182] Chapter 2 contains an attempt to divide humanity into two tribes (*Stämme*) and various races,
based on physical characteristics and their geographical distribution. The introduction to the second
edition contains an explanation of an improved nomenclature, replacing a division based on tentative origin (e.g., Caucasian) by one distinguishing between the "dark and ugly" and the "white or
light-coloured and beautiful peoples."

[183] Georges Léopold Cuvier, *Le règne animal* (1797); translated into English: Baron Cuvier, *The
Animal Kingdom, Arranged after its Organization* (London, 1863, repr. 1969), 37f.: "The Caucasian
race, to which we belong, is distinguished by the beauty of the oval which forms the head; and it is
this one which has given rise to the most civilized nations,—to those which have generally held the
rest in subjection: it varies in complexion and in the colour of the hair . . . It is by this great and
venerable branch of the Caucasian stock, that philosophy, the arts and sciences, have been carried to
their present state of advancement; and it has continued to be the depository of them for thirty
centuries." By contrast, there is "The Negro race": "The projecting muzzle and thick lips evidently
approximate it to the Apes: the hordes of which it is composed have always continued barbarous."

[184] *The Animal Kingdom,* 37: "Mild climates, soils naturally irrigated and rich in vegetables, are

modern authors are far more preoccupied with skin color than the Greek and Latin authors. This did not prevent them from borrowing ancient conceptual prototypes for their racist ideas, notably the environmental theory.

These ideas influenced many people, among them Hegel (1770–1831), who goes to much trouble in reconciling his acceptance of environmental theory with a belief in the freedom of the human will. These efforts do not prevent him from declaring, the "Climate does have a certain influence, however, in that neither the *torrid* nor the *cold region* can provide a basis for human freedom or for world-historical nations. . . . All in all, it is therefore the *temperate zone* which must furnish the theatre of world history. And more specifically, the northern part of the temperate regions is particularly suited to this purpose."[185] Hegel's appendix contains full descriptions of the various races of mankind, which he distinguishes complete with familiar and less familiar generalizations regarding the physical (skull-shape and skin color), mental, and moral characteristics of each race. There is a clear hierarchy, with the Caucasian race at the top.

Johann Friedrich Blumenbach (1752–1840) held that the beauty of the human face is determined by climate. The more moderate the climate, the more beautiful the face. He does not argue that nonwhite people are inherently inferior, but that a process of degeneration leads to this result.[186] Curiously he singles out the Egyptians and the inhabitants of the Indian peninsula.[187] Here the classification follows aesthetic criteria, that is to say, the superiority or inferiority of human beings is assigned on the basis of the presumed beauty of their outward shape and this, in turn, is believed to be the result of environmental influences. Thus Blumenbach argues that the "Lapps and Hungarians belong to the same original race, but the faces of the Hungarians are more beautiful, because they live in a mild climate near Greece and Turkey."[188]

Thomas Jefferson, in his discourse about the natural inferiority of the blacks asserts that they have a lesser share of beauty than the whites, require less sleep, are superficial and transient in their emotions as compared with whites, and much inferior in reasoning, though not in memory. They have no imagina-

---

the natural cradle of agriculture and civilization; and when their position is such as to afford shelter from the incursions of barbarians, talents of every kind are mutually excited."

[185] Georg Wilhelm Friedrich Hegel, *Lectures on the Philosophy of World History*, trans. H. B. Nisbet (Cambridge, 1975), Appendix: "The Natural Context or the Geographical Basis of World History," 152ff., esp. 152–155.

[186] Blumenbach, *Über die natürlichen Verschiedenheiten im Menschengeschlecht* (1798), 135–137, cited also above.

[187] Op. cit, 135: "Die ersten Einwohner waren in einem so entnervenden Klima weichlich geworden, und wurden immer von anderen tapfereren nordischen Völker besiegt."

[188] Blumenbach, p.137. Blumenbach does not believe in the existence of human races and disagreed with Leibnitz, Linnaeus, and Buffon on this matter. He recognizes "varieties" (208f.; 212f.), namely the Caucasian, Mongolian, Ethiopian, American, and Malaysian varieties, the Caucasian being original (204). The differentiation was caused by climate and customs which resulted in the transmission of acquired characters. Thus he explains that black people have flat noses because they are carried on their mothers' backs as babies (140f.).

tion or gift for poetry. This inferiority, he says, is not the effect merely of their condition of life, but has been produced by nature. He admits that the blacks have not been studied sufficiently. "I advance it therefore as a suspicion only, that the blacks, whether originally a distinct race, or made distinct by time and circumstances, are inferior to the whites in the endowments both of body and mind."[189] Thus, it is clearly the case that humanity is classified into quality groups determined by external influences, for beauty is according to this line of thinking considered the equivalent of perfection.[190] Jefferson may admit that his observations are not based on sound study, but he has in fact no doubts about the inferiority of the blacks. He is genuinely uncertain, however, whether this is the result of external influences or heredity. It does not seem as if he finds the cause important, for it does not affect the result.[191]

Two remarkable figures in the present context are John Stuart Mill and Henry Thomas Buckle. The former in his *Principles of Political Economy* (first published in 1848), the latter in his *History of Civilization in England* (1857) are important because of their firm rejection of the racial determinism which gained ground in this period. Curiously, Buckle did so through acceptance of a strict form of environmental determinism which had become quite unusual by this time.[192]

Thus the various authors cited here have different theories about the causes of these differences, but they agree in their value judgments and assumption of a true hierarchy of races and a corresponding hierarchy of beauty. The confusion of aesthetics, physical characteristics, and merit was to remain a permanent

---

[189] Thomas Jefferson, in the chapter on Laws in his *Notes on the State of Virginia* (1787) ed. W. Peden (Chapel Hill, 1955), 138–143.

[190] An influential author exalting physical beauty through a presumed scientific method of cranial comparisons was the Dutch painter and anatomist Peter Camper (172–189), whose major work was published in 1791 and 1792. He devised a method for the classification of the shape of the skull and identified "facial angle'" as an essential feature in the representation of different races. See Mosse, op. cit., 21–24. G. Jahoda, *Images of Savages* (1999), 71–74, points out that Camper's theory was misused and distorted by others, since he denied that the range of facial angles corresponds to a scale of superiority and inferiority.

[191] A sad footnote: Walther Rathenau, *Reflexionen* (Leipzig, 1908), last chapter, "Ungeschriebene Schriften," published ruminations about the salubrious impact of the nordic environment on the nordic, Aryan race which were cited with relish in a special brochure by the Nazi ideologist R. Walther Darré, *Walther Rathenau und das Problem des nordischen Menschen* (Munich, 1933).

[192] John Stuart Mill, *Prinicples of Political Economy* (London, 1848), vol. 1, p. 390: "of all vulgar modes of escaping from the consideration of the effect of social and moral influences on the human mind, the most vulgar is that of attributing the diversities of conduct and character to inherent natural differences." Mill built on the tradition of Jeremy Bentham and his followers who, themselves, were influenced by Helvétius. Henry Thomas Buckle's major work is his *History of Civilization in England* 1 (new ed. London, 1873), with the relevant chapter 2 on environmental determinism (over a hundred pages). Environmental theory played a role also in the works of Herbert Spencer, *The Principles of Sociology*, 3 vol. (London, 1876–96) and of Friedrich Ratzel, for which see Ellen Churchill Semple, *Influences of Geographic Environment, on the Basis of Ratzel's System of Anthropogeography* (New York, 1936). For Ratzel's ideas about states and frontiers, see B. Isaac, *The Near East under Roman Rule* (1998), 403f. See also Thomas, *The Environmental Basis of Society* (1925), 78–91, for the environmental ideas of Ratzel and Spencer.

element in racist ideas. An offshoot of these assumptions is the popular pseudo(?)-science of physiognomics, about which more will be said below.

Conclusions

Thus far we have seen that many people in the Graeco-Roman world held that there was a dual process considered to be at work in shaping the character and nature of people: environment, they thought, decisively influences human beings and the characteristics thus acquired are transmitted to posterity. The former concept received a great deal of attention. Ever since the treatise on *Airs*, historians, philosophers and technical authors expressed their views on the effect climate and environment have on entire populations. The details vary considerably, but the mechanism as such is discussed and accepted. The only real variable is the role attributed to social factors, notably the political constitution. Some authors regard a monarchy as influential in emasculating people; others do not. It is also assumed—but less frequently argued explicitly—that the characteristics acquired through environmental influences become stable and are inherited, even without the influence of the environment. Such a view leaves no room for individual variation and free will. Indeed, the stability and permanence are thus doubly assured twice: climate and environment determine group characteristics and these are inherited from generation to generation. This raises the question of the effect of migration from one place to another. Here there is remarkable consensus in the sources throughout the period under consideration: there is scope only for deterioration and degeneration. Sturdy and dull-witted people who move from a harsh climate to an environment of abundance become soft. The reverse does not apply. Undoubtedly this is connected with basic ancient views on the nature of progress. According to these views, decline and dissolution are inevitable and contact between peoples can only reinforce these processes.[193] Although it is generally true that, by contrast, nineteenth- and twentieth-century thinking in general, and racism in particular, are deeply concerned with progress, there is also a corresponding preoccupation with decline. This is true, for instance, for the thinking of Gobineau, who insists on the inevitable decline of human stock because of mixed marriages. By contrast, progress was an essential feature in the philosophy of the antiracist Helvétius.[194]

Almost from the start these ideas were closely connected with visions of warfare and conquest. Thus Aristotle's environmental determinism led him to assert that the Greeks were by nature endowed with gifts which should enable them to dominate their neighbors. These neighbors, insofar as they lived in the East, were servile by nature and thus born to be subjects. These ideas were widely accepted and taken over by Roman authors who naturally made the Romans rather than the Greeks the ideal people in the middle, qualified by

---

[193] More about this, below, chapter 3, on contacts between peoples and in chapter 5, on Roman fears for the vigor of their empire.

[194] Cf. Mordecai Grossman, *The Philosophy of Helvetius* (1926), 110f.

nature to rule. However, they added some elements of their own. Thus Strabo claims that Roman control provided the natural balance between the various extremes and taught all peoples to live under forms of true government. It is a vision, furthermore, which also has an impact on Roman ideas about the dangers of empire. Expansion brings the conqueror in contact with inferior peoples which inevitably affects the conqueror, causes his decline and thus, eventually, the end of empire. The very success of an empire also carries the seeds of its decline and fall.

Finally, it has been seen how these Greek and Roman concepts profoundly influenced more recent authors and their ideas about human groups, races, regional differences between men and thus were instrumental in the shaping of early racist views.

Closely connected with these negative feelings about contact between peoples is a third and highly significant concept which remains to be considered, namely heredity as such, and in particular the effect of mixed versus pure lineage. Again, it will be clear to everyone that there is nothing in antiquity resembling recent European racist ideas, since these were formed under the direct influence of current scientific thinking, even when they were a travesty or deviant form of this. However, the way in which people saw themselves superior as a group vis-à-vis other groups is relevant and, as has been seen above, much in the environmental theory must be described as proto-racism. As such it has been actively borrowed by eighteenth-century authors. This should be distinguished from theories about ancient ethnicity, for I am not considering social identity, but self-perception and its interaction with views on others. In theories about ethnicity, descent and not heredity is the decisive factor.

DESCENT AND LINEAGE: GREEK VIEWS

Immigration, it seems, hardens hearts and softens brains like
few other issues.
—*The Economist*, September 8, 2001

The idea that people of superior quality should be of pure lineage, without a mixture of foreign elements among their ancestors, has been an extremely common conviction through the ages. Kant had no doubts on the subject: "The Spaniard [is] born of a mixture of European and Arab (Moorish) blood . . . as shown by bull-fights, his character is cruel which is proved by the auto-da-fé of former times and his taste shows that his origin lies in part outside Europe. . . . This is the judgement which one can truthfully make. The mingling of stocks (due to great conquests) little by little erodes the character and it is not good for the human race in spite of any so-called philanthropy."[195] An important ancient

---

[195] Kant's racist views are found in his essay on the subject, cited above, and in his *Schriften zur*

historian in the twentieth century fully agreed with Kant: "Hybridisation on a considerable scale involves the break up of unified races into a heterogeneous and loose mass lacking stable spiritual and moral standards. This is, of itself, a sufficient explanation for the collapse of ancient culture and the Roman Empire." This was written by Martin P. Nilsson in a chapter in which he argues at length that the Roman Empire fell because of racial contamination.[196]

It is well known that people in antiquity usually defined their social groupings in terms of common descent.[197] Common ancestry in the past justified contemporary structures, enmities, friendships, and diplomatic ties.[198] Thus descent was used to explain or justify social patterns, but it was less common to attach presumed hereditary qualities to these patterns, which would have resulted in racist approaches, according to all definitions. However, lineage was important even so, and we need to consider here several claims of people thought to have been of pure lineage. These always appear in ancient literature in connection with the land, which once again is a feature that recurs in modern racist ideas. The question usually asked is whether the same people always inhabited the land, or whether a people migrated and other peoples mixed with it. The first reference is a fragment of Parmenides which may have been coined by Hecataeus for the Egyptians: ἑωυτῶι πάντοσε τωὑτον, τῶι δ᾽ ἑτέρωι μὴ τωὑτόν (fr. 8.57). The claim is repeated for the Egyptians in combination with the Scythians in *Airs, Waters, Places* "As regards the seasons and their physical shape, the Scythian people is very different from the other men and, like the Egyptian people, it resembles only itself (19)."[199] As might be expected in this text, there is an assumption that climate and physical shape are connected, but more important, the Scythians and Egyptians, peoples of the extreme North and

---

Anthropologie Geschichtsphilophie Politik und Pädagogik (repr. Darmstadt, 1970), "Anthropologie in pragmatischer Hinsicht, Vom Erkenntnisvermögen," (1798). Cf. Léon Poliakov, *The Arian Myth*, 171f.

[196] Martin P. Nilsson, *Imperial Rome* (London, 1926), p. 363, written, it is true, in 1926, but reprinted without comments by Schocken Books, New York, 1962, while the author was alive.

[197] E. J. Bickerman, "Origines Gentium," *CPh* 47 (1952), 65–81 = *Religion and Politics in the Hellenistic and Roman World* (Como, 1985), 399–417; for the Greeks: Jonathan Hall, *Ethnic Identity in Greek Antiquity* (Cambridge, 1997), p. 32 and passim; Malkin, *The Returns of Odysseus* (1998), 60f.; I. Malkin (ed.), *Ancient Perceptions of Greek Ethnicity* (Washington, D.C., 2001); For definitions of the term "ethnicity," see Malkin, *Returns*, 55f.; for quasi-historical heroic myths of migration in this connection: J. Hall, 62f., 73, 86f., 124–128; Malkin, p.134f. See also Coleman and Walz, *Greeks and Barbarians*, esp. J. E. Coleman, "Ancient Greek Ethnocentrism," pp. 175–220. For later periods: Per Bilde et al. (ed.), *Ethnicity in Hellenistic Egypt* (Aarhus, 1992); Siân Jones, *The Archaeology of Ethnicity: Constructing Identities in the Past and Present* (London and New York, 1997) is relevant for the theory of Romanization in northwestern Europe. Influential works on modern ethnicity: N. Glazer and D. P. Moynihan, *Ethnicity: Theory and Experience* (Cambridge, MA, 1975); B. Anderson, *Imagined Communities: Reflections on the Origin and Spread of Nationalism* (London, 1983); E. Gellner, *Nations and Nationalism* (1983); E. J. Hobsbawm and T. Ranger, *The Invention of Tradition* (1983); E. J. Hobsbawm, *Nations and Nationalism since 1780* (Cambridge, 1990).

[198] Christopher P. Jones, *Kinship Diplomacy in the Ancient World* (Cambridge, MA, 1999).

[199] *Airs* 19: Περὶ δὲ τῶν ὡρέων καὶ τῆς μορφῆς, ὅτι πολὺ ἀπήλλακται τῶν λοιπῶν ἀνθρώπων τὸ Σκυθικὸν γένος, καὶ ἔοικεν αὐτὸ ἑωυτέῳ, ὥσπερ τὸ Αἰγύπτιον . . .

the South, are separate and different from all other peoples. For the Egyptians this claim has a lengthy tradition and we shall encounter it again. The ancient views of the Scythians differed widely in the works of many authors, as late as Strabo.[200]

The idea of pure lineage is generally not prominent in Herodotus.[201] However, we need to consider a special case, namely the assumption of pure lineage by the Athenians. It occurs, for instance, in Herodotus 1.56, in relation to the Lacedaemonians and Athenians, the former being Doric, the latter Ionian: "the former were a Hellenic, the latter a Pelasgic people and the latter had never emigrated, while the former had been excessively migratory."[202] The next chapter, 57, discusses the language of the Pelasgi. Herodotus concludes that they spoke a barbarian language. "If so . . . the Attic people, who were certainly Pelasgi, must have changed their language at the same time that they passed into the Hellenic community."[203] Their identity as Ionians, and more particularly, as the oldest of the Ionians was perhaps more important to the Athenians at an earlier stage, for Solon describes them as such in the sixth century.[204]

Our subject is not what modern scholarship makes of the reality of these claims and of the legendary Pelasgi.[205] The present passage is one of many which show that the matter of lineage is believed to determine one's essential social identity. The Athenians were thought to be Pelasgi, speaking a barbarian

[200] Strabo 7.3.7f. (c. 300f.); cf. Romm, *The Edges of the Earth*, 45–47.

[201] See, extensively, Enrico Montanari, *Il mito dell'autoctonia: linee di una dinamica mitico-politica ateniense* (Rome, 2d ed. 1981), Part 1.

[202] 1.56: Ἱστορέων δὲ εὕρισκε Λακεδαιμονίους τε καὶ Ἀθηναίους προέχοντας, τοὺς μὲν τοῦ Δωρικοῦ γένεος, τοὺς δὲ τοῦ Ἰωνικοῦ. Ταῦτα γὰρ ἦν τὰ προκεκριμένα, ἐόντα (or: ἔθνεα) τὸ ἀρχαῖον τὸ μὲν Πελασγικόν, τὸ δὲ Ἑλληνικὸν ἔθνος. Καὶ τὸ μὲν οὐδαμῇ κω ἐξεχώρησε, τὸ δὲ πολυπλάνητον κάρτα. For this passage, see C. P. Jones, *CQ* 46 (1996), 317f. The Pelasgi are mentioned in the Homeric epos, but it is only in Herodotus that they appear as the original population of the Aegean, such as here. In later periods they are also recorded as having colonized other parts of the Mediterranean, notably Italy. Cf.: D. Briquel, *Les Pélasges en Italie* (Rome, 1984); but not only there. Pomponius Mela 1.83 says of the Carians: alii indigenas, sunt qui Pelasgos, quidam Cretas existimant. This would imply that the Pelasgi were immigrants to Caria.

[203] 1.57: Εἰ τοίνυν ἦν καὶ πᾶν τοιοῦτο τὸ Πελασγικόν, τὸ Ἀττικὸν ἔθνος, ἐὸν Πελασγικόν, ἅμα τῇ μεταβολῇ τῇ ἐς Ἕλληνας καὶ τὴν γλῶσσαν μετέμαθε. For the argument used here by Herodotus: R. Thomas, *PCPS* 43 (1997), 146; R. A. McNeal, "How did the Pelasgians become Hellenes? Hdt. 1.56–58," *Ill. Class. Stud.* 10 (1995), 11–21, deals with the textual problems in these chapters. Thomas, *Herodotus in Context* (2000), 117–122, concludes that Herodotus takes the autochthony myth literally "and rationalizes it into current ethnic definitions. If the Athenians had always lived in Attica, unlike the later Greeks, and if the Dorians who came south were original Greeks, then it follows that the Athenians were not originally Greek and did not speak Greek until they entered the body of the Greeks." She points out that this was not current thinking in Athens at the time. See also Thomas, "Ethnicity, Genealogy, and Hellenism in Herodotus," in I. Malkin (ed.), *Ancient Perceptions of Greek Ethnicity* (Washington, DC and Cambridge, MA, 2001), 213–223, esp. 222–225.

[204] Solon, as cited in *Ath. Pol.* 5.2.6: γιγνώσκω, καί μοι φρενὸς ἔνδοθεν ἄλγεα κεῖται, πρεσβυτάτην ἐσορῶν γαῖαν Ἰαονίας κλινομένην.

[205] Another *polis* with claims of Pelasgic origins, based on Homeric evidence (*Il* 2.681) was Argos; see E. Hall, *Inventing the Barbarian* (1989), 171f.; J. Hall, *Ethnic Identity in Greek Antiquity*, chapter 4.

tongue, who joined the Hellenes and then changed their language, while still remaining Athenians because they continued to live in Attica. It is clear also that they had to speak Greek in order to become Hellenes, as Herodotus emphasizes in the next chapter: "The Hellenes have never, since they originated, changed their language."[206] In this connection we might consider the following statement by Momigliano: "Ancient ethnography gives little space to language. Comparative philology had not been invented. Ethnic groups were defined in terms of common descent and of common institutions."[207] I find this not convincing. It cannot be denied that Herodotus was convinced that an important part of the identity of the Pelasgi included the question of whether they spoke Greek or not. Furthermore, he found it obvious that the Athenians would have started speaking Greek when they joined the Hellenic community, or, rather, they could not have joined if they had not spoken Greek, for there are no Hellenes who do not speak Greek. The Hellenes had a common language but no common ancestors or institutions. Yet Herodotus at least considered them an *ethnos*. The Egyptians were also an *ethnos* and, as we saw above, Herodotus represents them as being of the opinion that those who did not speak their language were barbarians (2.158).[208] Generally speaking, language is one of the essential components of social identity.

In a famous passage cited above for other reasons, Herodotus represents the Athenians as explaining why they could not have supported the Persians: first because of the destruction of Athenian sanctuaries, second because of "the Hellenic ties (τὸ Ἑλληνικόν), that is, our relationship, common language, the joint altars and sacrifices and the common customs, which it would not be well for the Athenians to betray."[209] Thus Herodotus portrays Hellenic identity as a package consisting of a kinship, and a common language, religion, and culture. It is clear that each of these four elements is represented as an indispensable ingredient of being Greek.[210] Notably absent are references to common territory and history.

[206] 1.58: Τὸ δὲ Ἑλληνικὸν γλώσσῃ μέν, ἐπείτε ἐγένετο, αἰεί κοτε τῇ αὐτῇ διαχρᾶται, ὡς ἐμοὶ καταφαίνεται εἶναι.

[207] Arnaldo Momigliano, *Alien Wisdom* (1975), 69; similarly, Malkin, *The Returns of Odysseus*, 55–61; see also J. M. Hall, *Ethnic Identity in Greek Antiquity*, 177–81 on the role of language in ethnicity, where the topics here discussed are not mentioned. Hall points out that linguistic groups cannot be equated with ethnic groups, which might seem obvious but perhaps is not always true.

[208] See also above. Cf. Cicero, *de Rep.* 1.58: Cedo, num, Scipio, barbarorum Romulus rex fuit? {L.} Si, ut Graeci dicunt omnis aut Graios esse aut barbaros, vereor, ne barbarorum rex fuerit; sin id nomen moribus dandum est, non linguis, non Graecos minus barbaros quam Romanos puto. Thus Cicero represents Laelius as saying that barbarism can be defined in one of two ways, as the Greeks did, in terms of language or, as Laelius would prefer, in terms of customs (*mores*).

[209] Herodotus 8.144: αὖτις δὲ τὸ Ἑλληνικόν, ἐὸν ὅμαιμόν τε καὶ ὁμόγλωσσον, καὶ θεῶν ἱδρύματά τε κοινὰ καὶ θυσίαι ἤθεά τε ὁμότροπα, τῶν προδότας γενέσθαι Ἀθηναίους οὐκ ἂν εὖ ἔχοι.

[210] It is therefore an idle speculation to suggest that Herodotus gives the four criteria in what he regards as the order of their relative importance: How and Wells, A *Commentary on Herodotus*, 2.286. The phrase is not actually a "definition of Greekness," but means only "the fact that the Greek people is of one blood and one tongue," as pointed out by C. P. Jones, "ἔθνος and γένος in Herodotus" *CQ* 46 (1996), 315–320, esp. 315, n. 4. Cf. for this passage David Konstan, "To Hellēnikon ethnos," in I. Malkin (ed.), *Ancient Perceptions of Greek Ethnicity* (Washington, DC

Isocrates makes the same point again in vaguer fashion: "(Athens) has made it seem that the name 'Hellenes' is no longer one of common descent (γένος) but of thought, and that those are called 'Hellenes' who share our education (or: culture παιδεύσις) rather than our common nature (φύσις)."[211] He assumes that in the past "Hellene" was a term denoting kinship. Then the Athenians, supposedly autochthonous, and therefore no kin of the Hellenes, joined them nevertheless. Isocrates' solution is to argue that the entry of the Athenians into the Hellenic community marked a change from a kinship relationship to a cultural tie. The implication of the pronouncement, however, is also that Athenian education and culture have become normative. To be a Hellene must involve acceptance and sharing in Athenian culture and spiritual life. This then entails both a sharper contrast between Hellene and barbarian, and a narrower interpretation of what it means to be a Hellene, namely, a Greek with Attic culture.[212]

How generally this proposition was accepted is uncertain, but the least it shows is that fourth-century Greeks could be vague about the precise meaning of the concepts "Hellas" and "Hellene."[213] It is quite likely Isocrates was interested also in representing the Hellenic community in a broader sense, so that he could include the Macedonians, who were not considered Hellenes by origin, but might claim to share Hellenic culture, and would have helped promote his anti-Persian program—but he does not say so, of course. Clearly, we must not assume that Isocrates meant that barbarians could become Hellenes if they accepted Greek culture, but the opposite is certainly true: Greeks who lost their Greek culture were no longer Hellenes in his eyes or in the eyes of later authors.[214] In this connection it will be clear that it is always difficult to discuss such problems with regard to the Greeks, who were both *Hellenes* and citizens

---

and Cambridge, MA, 2001), 29–50; Jeremy McInerney, "Ethnos and Ethnicity in Early Greece," ibid., 51–73, on Herodotus, see esp. 57–59; Rosalind Thomas, "Ethnicity, Genealogy, and Hellenism in Herodotus," ibid., 213–233, esp. 214f., points out that the words in 8.144 are spoken by Athenian delegates for the benefit of Spartan envoys who feared that Athens might support Persia. They follow a declaration that Athens first resisted Persia in revenge for the destruction of Athenian temples. We cannot, therefore, take this statement as straightforward evidence for Herodotus's own views, which are not simplistic, as shown by Thomas.

[211] Isocrates, *Panegyricus*. 50: καὶ τὸ τῶν Ἑλλήνων ὄνομα πεποίηκεν μηκέτι τοῦ γένους, ἀλλὰ τῆς διανοίας δοκεῖν εἶναι, καὶ μᾶλλον Ἕλληνας καλεῖσθαι τοὺς τῆς παιδεύσεως τῆς ἡμετέρας ἢ τοὺς τῆς κοινῆς φύσεως μετέχοντας. Isocrates' passage has attracted great attention; see, e.g., J. Jüthner, *Hellenen und Barbaren* (1923), 34–39; F. W. Walbank, "The Problem of Greek Nationality," *Selected Papers* (1985), 1–19, esp. 5f.; Suzanne Saïd, "The Discourse of Identity in Greek Rhetoric from Isocrates to Aristides," in Malkin (ed.), *Ancient Perceptions of Greek Ethnicity*, 275–299, esp. 282. Strabo 1.4.9 (c. 66–67) is relevant for the period of Alexander and the third century B.C., discussed below, in chapter 4.

[212] This is the sort of thinking first enunciated in Thucydides 2.41.1: Ξυνελών τε λέγω τήν τε πᾶσαν πόλιν τῆς Ἑλλάδος παίδευσιν εἶναι.

[213] Jones, *Kinship Diplomacy*, 135, cites Isocrates in support of the assumption that the term *genos* had begun to denote "kind" or "type," without reference to birth. There may have been such a development, but this does not mean that ideas of blood relationship had lost their significance in a sort of linear development. Cf. Walbank, "The Problem of Greek Nationality," 7, and his article "Nationality as a Factor in Roman History," *Selected Papers* (1985), 57–76, esp. 58f. Physical relationship retained its importance in Greece and Rome, as I hope I have shown in this chapter.

[214] Saïd, "The Discourse," 292.

of their own political unit, whatever it was. Hellenes always spoke Greek and, as will be seen below, they could be in conflict, but then there were other norms to maintain. They could not fight a war with each other, only engage in "internal conflict" (*stasis*).[215]

The next point we shall consider here is the specific claim of Athenians that they were autochthonous, that is to say, indigenous, always having lived in their own land.[216] This is also found in a speech which Herodotus attributes to an Athenian envoy, addressing Gelo of Syracuse: "we Athenians, the most ancient people in Greece, the only Greeks who have never migrated.[217] Being the only ones who had never moved, they were naturally the oldest. The special link of the Athenians to the soil of Attica is already clearly implied in the Iliadic catalogue, where Erechtheus is described as born from the Earth, brought up by Athena and installed in her sanctuary.[218] Erechtheus was, in fact, the second king of Athens born from the earth, the first being his predecessor Cecrops,[219] a juxtaposition which emphasizes the idea of autochthony. "The two earth-born kings are mythical representatives of the whole Athenian people in their claim to autochthony."[220] Pindar's second Isthmian Ode (probably c. 470 B.C.) is the

---

[215] See J. Price, *Thucydides and Internal Conflict: Stasis as a Model for the Peloponnesian War* (Cambridge, 2001).

[216] V. J. Rosivach, "Autochthony and the Athenians," *CQ* 37 (1987), 294–306; N. Loraux, *The Invention of Athens* (London, 1986); id., *The Children of Athena: Athenian Ideas about Citizenship and the Division between the Sexes* (Princeton, 1993). Loraux argues that the idea of an earth-born origin removes women from any role in the Athenian ethnogenesis. J. Hall, *Ethnicity*, 51–56; Daniel Ogden, *Greek Bastardy in the Classical and Hellenistic Periods* (Oxford, 1996), chapter 5, pp. 166–173; H. Alan Shapiro, "Autochthony and the Visual Arts in Fifth-Century Athens," in D. Boedeker and K. A. Raaflaub, *Democracy, Empire, and the Arts in Fifth-Century Athens* (Cambridge, MA, 1998), 127–151. Edward E. Cohen, *The Athenian Nation* (Princeton, 2000), chapter 3. I cannot understand why J. Hall, 54, asserts that Aeschylus, *Agamemnon*, 536, for the first time describes the Athenians as autochthonous. The passage does not refer to the Athenians but to Troy and the adjective is used in an entirely different sense; cf. Eduard Fraenkel, Aeschylus, *Agamemnon*, 3 vols. (Oxford, 1950), comments in vol. 2, p. 272. Fraenkel, vol. 1, p. 123, following Wilamowitz and others, translates the adjective as "together with the land." Hall refers to Montanari, *Il mito dell'autoctonia*, 31. Montanari, however, recognizes that the passage is irrelevant: "tale menzione non si riferisce ad Atene, né ad alcuna stirpe greca, bensì al *genos* regale di Priamo."

[217] 7.161 ἀρχαιότατον μὲν ἔθνος παρεχόμενοι, μοῦνοι δὲ ἐόντες οὐ μετανάσται Ἑλλήνων. As pointed out by Shapiro, "Autochthony," 130f., autochthony does not mean that every individual Athenian claimed to be descended from native Athenian heroes. It means that, in a collective sense, all historical Athenians are descended from the two founding heroes, Cecrops and Erechtheus, who themselves sprang from the soil of Athens.

[218] Homer, *Il.* 2.546–9: Οἳ δ' ἄρ' Ἀθήνας εἶχον ἐϋκτίμενον πτολίεθρον δῆμον Ἐρεχθῆος μεγαλήτορος, ὅν ποτ' Ἀθήνη θρέψε Διὸς θυγάτηρ, τέκε δὲ ζείδωρος ἄρουρα, κὰδ δ' ἐν Ἀθήνῃς εἷσεν ἑῷ ἐν πίονι νηῷ. This is often assumed to be an Athenian interpolation from the sixth century. However, that is not important for present purposes. G. S. Kirk et al., *The Iliad: A Commentary* (1985–1993), 1.179f., 205; R. Parker, "Myths of Early Athens," in J. Bremmer (ed.), *Interpretations of Greek Mythology* (London, 1987), 187–214, at 193–195.

[219] Cecrops was a twisting snake below the waist: Euripides, *Ion* 1163f; Aristophanes, *Vespae* 438; cf. Shapiro, op. cit., for illustrations.

[220] Parker, 193f.; Loraux, *The Children of Athena*, 46; Rosivach, *CQ* 37 (1987), 294–306, esp.

first text in which we encounter the explicit claim that the Athenians were descendants of Erechtheus and thus were themselves descendents of someone who was born from the earth itself: "having attained to the glorious honours given by the Erechtheidai in shining Athens."[221] Autochthony here means the joint descent of all Athenians from common ancestors. All Athenians are thus relatives. At a later stage genealogy was no longer the essence of autochthony, but collective birth from the earth.[222]

Thucydides also insists on the connection with the land: "For Attica remained longest free from internal strife because of the poverty of the soil and because the same people always inhabited it."[223] It recurs in the *epitaphios logos*, where Thucydides makes Pericles remind his assembled compatriots that their ancestors, "always inhabiting the land as the same people, through their courage passed it on from generation to generation as a free country."[224] Autochthony thus became closely associated with a complex of core values: the legitimacy of possession of the soil, mutual solidarity, the equality of all citizens, and resistance to foreign domination. A subtheme here is the statement that Attica remained free from internal strife because of the poverty of the soil. Like so many other Greek and Roman authors cited in this study, Thucydides

---

295f. Rosivach argues that this is a relatively late, probably fifth-century interpretation of the Erechtheus myth. On pp. 297–301 he analyzes the term αὐτόχθων, concluding that the meaning "born from the earth" is a later addition to the original one, which is "always living in the same land." He then suggests that the chthonic origins of Erechtheus originally had no connection with the indigenous origins of the Athenians. He goes on to argue that the legend was used as part of democratic ideology, asserting the political equality of all citizens and the superiority of even the humblest citizen to any noncitizen. Shapiro, "Autochthomy," 130–133, does not accept this view, arguing that the central figures in the autochthony legend, Cecrops and Erichthonios/Erechtheus, are well attested in the archaic period, especially as represented in the arts. Rosivach's etymology of αὐτόχθων is criticized by S. Tsitsiridis, *Platons Menexenos* (1998), 200f., who refers to F. Sommer, "Zur Geschichte der griechischen Normalkomposita," *Abhandlungen der Bayerischen Akademie der Wissenschaften, Phil.-hist.Kl.* 27 (1948), 83f., where it is argued that αὐτόχθονες originally indicated people "who always had themselves owned the land as their own." This fits Thucydides, as cited below.

[221] Pindar, *Isthmia* 2.19: καὶ τόθι κλειναῖς τ᾽ Ἐρεχθειδᾶν χαρίτεσσιν ἀραρὼς ταῖς λιπαραῖς ἐν Ἀθάναις, οὐκ ἐμέμφθη ῥυσίδιφρον χεῖρα πλαξίπποιο φωτός, Cf. Sophocles, *Ajax* 201f.: including the Salaminians among the Erechtheids; Herodotus 8.44, 55; Euripides, *Ion* 20f., 266–270, 1427–1429. Erechtheus and Erichthonius are often considered identical. Pindar may have been the first to make a distinction between the two (Harpocration s.v. Αὐτόχθονες.)

[222] Cf. Ogden, *Greek Bastardy* (1996), 167.

[223] Thuc. 1.2.6: τὴν γοῦν Ἀττικὴν ἐκ τοῦ ἐπὶ πλεῖστον διὰ τὸ λεπτόγεων ἀστασίαστον οὖσαν ἄνθρωποι ᾤκουν οἱ αὐτοὶ αἰεί. This accords with the original meaning of αὐτόχθων as argued by Sommer (above, 220). As observed by A.W. Gomme, *A Historical Commentary on Thucydides* I (Oxford, 1956), 93, Herodotus, on the contrary, seems to take pleasure in pointing out that a good many noble Athenian families were descended from early "refugees" from disturbed countries coming to a safe one (the Peisistratidai, Harmodios and Aristogeiton, etc.).

[224] Thuc. 2.36.12: τὴν γὰρ χώραν οἱ αὐτοὶ αἰεὶ οἰκοῦντες. For Thucydides' speeches and those in other Greek historians: F. W. Walbank, "Speeches in Greek Historians," *Selected Papers* (1985), 242–261. For the *epitaphios logos*: P. A. Brunt, "Introduction to Thucydides, Postscript. Thucydides' Funeral Speech," in *Studies in Greek History and Thought* (Oxford, 1993), 159–180. For autochthony emphasized in other funeral orations: Ogden, *Greek Bastardy*, p.167f. and n.13.

considers poverty conducive to the health of society. In keeping with the ideology indicated by Thucydides, Pericles, in fact, took an important step to reserve Athenian citizenship for those with proper ancestors. In 451/0 he enacted the citizenship law, by which citizens' rights were bestowed only on those who could prove that both parents were Athenian citizens (ἀστοί).[225]

Not surprisingly, the modern scholarship has interpreted this law along widely diverging ideological lines.[226] In 445/4 there followed legislation which purged a very large number of persons from the list of full citizens (*politai*).[227] It is in any case worth noting that Pseudo-Xenophon, *Constitution of the Athenians*, which may have been written shortly after—and certainly not long after—the establishment of the citizenship law, still complains that "we have set up equality between slaves and free men and between metics and citizens." The reason for this is that "the city needs metics in view of the many different trades and the fleet."[228] From his point of view it is yet another example of his

[225] Aristotle, *Ath.Pol.* 26.3: καὶ τρίτῳ μετὰ τοῦτον ἐπὶ Ἀντιδότου διὰ τὸ πλῆθος τῶν πολιτῶν Περικλέους εἰπόντος ἔγνωσαν μὴ μετέχειν τῆς πόλεως, ὃς ἂν μὴ ἐξ ἀμφοῖν ἀστοῖν ᾖ γεγονώς. Plutarch, *Per.* 37.3: ἀκμάζων ὁ Περικλῆς . . . νόμον ἔγραψε, μόνους Ἀθηναίους εἶναι τοὺς ἐκ δυεῖν Ἀθηναίων γεγονότας; Aelian, *Varia Historia* 6.10: Περικλῆς στρατηγῶν Ἀθηναίοις νόμον ἔγραψεν, ἐὰν μὴ τύχῃ τις ἐξ ἀμφοῖν ὑπάρχων ἀστῶν, τούτῳ μὴ μετεῖναι τῆς πολιτείας; Suda s.v. Δημοποίητος ὁ ὑπὸ τοῦ δήμου εἰσποιηθεὶς καὶ γεγονὼς πολίτης. Περικλῆς γὰρ ὁ Ξανθίππου, νόμον γράψας τὸν μὴ ἐξ ἀμφοῖν ἀστυπολίτην μὴ εἶναι. Cf. J. K. Davies, "Athenian Citizenship: The Descent Group and the Alternatives," *CJ* 73 (1977–1978), 105–121; C. Patterson, *Pericles' Citizenship Law of 451–50 B.C.* (New York, 1981). See also Gomme, "The Law of Citizenship at Athens," in *Essays in Greek History and Literature* (Oxford, 1937), 67–88, which discusses problems less relevant for present consideration. See now Cohen, *The Athenian Nation*, chapter 2, which emphasizes that the law demands that a *polites* should be the offspring, not of two *politai* but of two *astoi*, the latter being a far broader category than the former. The main opposition, he argues, is between *astoi* and *xenoi*. For present purposes it is still true that a *polites* has to be the child of two *astoi*, and that the child of a foreigner and an Athenian cannot be a *polites*. For the question of who were *astoi*: Cohen, 70–78. Cohen's suggestions regarding the status of *astoi* and *politai* are rejected by Robin Osborne in his review of Cohen, *CP* 97 (2002), 93–98, at 94f.

[226] References and discussion in Patterson, *Pericles' Citizenship*, 97–104; her own interpretation: 104–115 and chapter 5, conclusion. The most extreme view along racist lines is found in C. Hignett, *A History of the Athenian Constitution to the End of the Fifth Century B.C.* (Oxford, 1952 with subsequent reprints), "Appendix X: The citizenship law of 451/450": 346. Hignett argues that this law was introduced to prevent the debasement of the Athenian citizenship: "Athens had admitted foreign immigrants under Solon and Peisistratos, and since the growth of Piraeus a large alien population had been residing there. These aliens included not merely Greeks from the Athenian Empire and the rest of Greece, but non-Greek elements and even Orientals. To allow citizens to intermarry with such might entail a debasement of their racial purity that would be viewed with alarm by conservatives, and the alarm might be shared by progressive statesmen who could take a long view." This view has been supported by various scholars, mentioned by Patterson in n. 8 to the introduction on p. 3. This is not the place for a discussion of this subject, but it should be noted that the Athenian insistence on the purity of their lineage must be taken into account. Patterson, p.130: "It is still profitable to view Pericles' law as a legal buttress of the solidarity of the Athenian descent group." Page 133: "With Pericles' law the Athenians isolated themselves from outsiders. . . . It was the first step on a course which would eventually require further regulations." See Ogden, op. cit., 169f. for the connection between autochthony and the citizenship law.

[227] Plutarch, *Pericles* 37.4: almost five thousand individuals were reduced in status.

[228] For this source, see above. Ps.-Xenophon, *Constitution of the Athenians* (trans. G. W. Bower-

claim that in Athens the rabble has all the advantages to the detriment of the better people. Seen in a broader context, this is an early example of the extreme xenophobia which will always find any discriminatory and hostile measures taken against foreign residents or minorities unsatisfactory because they do not go far enough.[229] It is also part of another complex, discussed below, which attributes the evils in society to the naval element and the proximity to the sea. Finally, Pseudo-Xenophon may have been among a minority of sceptics regarding the idea of autochthony, for he alleges that most Greeks speak their own dialect and have their own customs and dress, but the Athenians are the only Greeks who use a combination from the whole Greek and barbarian world.[230] This is a statement that may represent an effort to depreciate the value of racial purity.[231]

We find the idea of autochthony also in Comedy in Aristophanes' *Wasps* (first performed in 422 B.C.): "We on whom this stern-appendage, this portentous tail is found, are the genuine old Autochthons, native children of the ground; we the only true-born Attics, of the staunch heroic breed, Many a time have we fought for Athens, guarding her in hours of need; When with smoke and fire and rapine the fierce Barbarian came, Eager to destroy our waspsnests" (1075–1080) (trans. B. B. Rogers, Loeb).[232] The chorus then goes on to deny that younger Athenians deserve the traditional title of being indigenous.[233] Apparently it was an idea that was important enough to be mentioned on the most solemn of occasions, but jokes in comedy on the subject were not only acceptable but appreciated, for the *Wasps* won second prize at the *Lenaea*. This probably says more about the sense of humor of fifth-century Athenians than it indicates any loss of the force of the idea.

It also appears, probably not much later, throughout Euripides' *Ion*.[234] The

---

sock, Loeb), 1.12: διὰ τοῦτ᾿ οὖν ἰσηγορίαν καὶ τοῖς δούλοις πρὸς τοὺς ἐλευθέρους ἐποιήσαμεν καὶ τοῖς μετοίκοις πρὸς τοὺς ἀστούς, διότι δεῖται ἡ πόλις μετοίκων διά τε τὸ πλῆθος τῶν τεχνῶν καὶ διὰ τὸ ναυτικόν· As observed by Martin Ostwald, another possible view on Pericles' citizenship law is that it was directed at marriages between Athenian heiresses with foreign men, which would give foreigners control over Athenian properties.

[229] By contrast he speaks in extremely cynical terms about the miserable treatment by the Athenians of their allies (1.16–18). They have become the slaves of the Athenian people: διὰ τοῦτο οὖν οἱ σύμμαχοι δοῦλοι τοῦ δήμου τῶν Ἀθηναίων καθεστᾶσι μᾶλλον (1.18).

[230] Ps.-Xenophon, *Constitution of the Athenians* 2.8: καὶ οἱ μὲν Ἕλληνες ἰδίᾳ μᾶλλον καὶ φωνῇ καὶ διαίτῃ καὶ σχήματι χρῶνται, Ἀθηναῖοι δὲ κεκραμένῃ ἐξ ἁπάντων τῶν Ἑλλήνων καὶ βαρβάρων.

[231] As observed by Brunt, "Introduction to Thucydides," 163, n.2.

[232] *Vesp.* 1075–1080: ἐσμὲν ἡμεῖς, οἷς πρόσεστι τοῦτο τοὐρροπύγιον, Ἀττικοὶ μόνοι δικαίως ἐγγενεῖς αὐτόχθονες, ἀνδρικώτατον γένος καὶ πλεῖστα τήνδε τὴν πόλιν ὠφελῆσαν ἐν μάχαισιν, ἡνίκ᾿ ἦλθ᾿ ὁ βάρβαρος, τῷ καπνῷ τύφων ἅπασαν τὴν πόλιν καὶ πυρπολῶν, ἐξελεῖν ἡμῶν μενοινῶν πρὸς βίαν τἀνθρήνια. cf. *Lys.*1082.

[233] Cf. comm. A. H. Sommerstein (Warminster, 1983): "According to the speaker here the only true indigenous Athenians are those who have the 'sting', the waspish temper of himself and his comrades."

[234] See, e.g., Euripides, *Ion* 10–30, 267–270, 542f., 736, 1427–1429. Cf. Cohen, *The Athenian Nation*, 85–7, for an alternative interpretation of autochthony in this work.

separateness of Athenians is brought out again and again: "But listen, father, to what has been on my mind. They say that the renowned earth-born inhabitants of Athens are not a people brought in from the outside. I shall land there suffering from two disadvantages: being the son of an outsider and being myself born out of wedlock" (trans. K. H. Lee, Warminster 1997).[235] Only legitimate Athenian birth grants the right of free speech: "May it turn out that my mother is of Athenian stock so that I can enjoy freedom of speech inherited from my mother. The fact is that if an ousider lands in a city of pure blood (καθαρὰν πόλιν), then, though he be a citizen in theory, he possesses the voice of a slave and does not have freedom of speech."[236] This shows that the idea of being indigenous was used as justification for keeping immigrants in an inferior status. The notion that the foreigners are an alien threat recurs frequently in the play.[237]

It has been shown that there was in the fifth and fourth centuries an increasing preoccupation in Athens with the statuses of foreign residents and full citizens.[238] The fears of what this can entail for a state are expressed, for instance, in a speech which Thucydides attributes to Alcibiades in 415: [2] "Do not change your minds regarding the planned expedition to Sicily out of fear that you will face a great power. The cities in Sicily are peopled by a mixed rabble, and easily accept population change and immigration;[239] [3] and therefore nobody is equipped as he would be for his own fatherland with arms for the protection of the state or with permanent improvement for the cultivation of his land; everybody thinks that either by persuasive words or by civil strife he can obtain something at the public expense."[240] The sense of the speech is clear: the

[235] Euripides, *Ion* 587–92: ἐγὼ δὲ τὴν μὲν συμφορὰν ἀσπάζομαι, πατέρα σ' ἀνευρών· ὧν δὲ γιγνώσκω, πάτερ, ἄκουσον. εἶναί φασι τὰς αὐτόχθονας κλεινὰς Ἀθήνας οὐκ ἐπείσακτον γένος, ἵν' ἐσπεσοῦμαι δύο νόσω κεκτημένος, πατρός τ' ἐπακτοῦ καὐτὸς ὢν νοθαγενής. Ion has no mother or father (108 and 836f.). He, a bastard, drives the legitimate heir from the palace of Erechtheus; also 836–840; 1293–1295. Comm. Owen on 589ff. See also the relevant lines 722 (problematic) and 1048ff. For the contemporary attitude to metics cf. what is said of Parthenopaeus in *Supp.* 891–895, from which it is clear that resident foreigners in Athens should not be troublesome or disputatious, which would make them hard to tolerate as citizen and guest. However, they must join the army and fight the country's wars. See also *Medea* 824–830: ἱερᾶς χώρας ἀπορθήτου. Montanari, *Il mito dell'autoctonia*, 159–197, has shown that autochthony is central to Euripides' *Ion*; cf. Loraux, *The Children of Athena*, 184–236; Ogden, *Greek Bastardy* (1996), 170–172. Note also Euripides, fr. 50.7–10 (Austin) from the *Erechtheus*: αὐτόχθονες δ' ἔφυμεν· αἱ δ' ἄλλαι πόλεις πεσσῶν ὁμοίως διαφοραῖς ἐκτισμέναι ἄλλαι παρ' ἄλλων εἰσὶν εἰσαγώγιμοι. For the *Erechtheus,* see Montanari, 125–165.

[236] *Ion* 670–675: εἰ δ' ἐπεύξασθαι χρεών, ἐκ τῶν Ἀθηνῶν μ' ἡ τεκοῦσ' εἴη γυνή, ὥς μοι γένηται μητρόθεν παρρησία. καθαρὰν γὰρ ἤν τις ἐς πόλιν πέσηι ξένος, κἂν τοῖς λόγοισιν ἀστὸς ἦι, τό γε στόμα δοῦλον πέπαται κοὐκ ἔχει παρρησίαν.

[237] *Ion* 289–297; 813f.

[238] Davies, *CJ* 73 (1977–1978), 111f.: "the rules generated obsessions, anxieties, and inscurities." Greek tragedy contains a few episodes in which aspersion is explicitly cast against a Greek that his blood is not free from barbarian taint, as shown by Hall, *Inventing the Barbarian,* 174–177.

[239] See Gomme, *A Historical Commentary,* vol. 4, p. 250.

[240] Thucydides 6.17.2f.: καὶ τὸν ἐς τὴν Σικελίαν πλοῦν μὴ μεταγιγνώσκετε ὡς ἐπὶ μεγάλην δύναμιν ἐσόμενον. ὄχλοις τε γὰρ ξυμμείκτοις πολυανδροῦσιν αἱ πόλεις καὶ ῥαδίας ἔχουσι τῶν

Greek cities in Sicily, unlike Athens, have mixed populations. That means that they are easy to defeat, for immigrants will not be loyal to their new polis. They will not defend it against an enemy, but are only interested in material gain for themselves, at the expense of their new homeland. Alcibiades is not referring here to a mixture of Greeks and non-Greeks, but to populations of Greeks from various cities.[241] This is the logical corollary of the statement already cited above: "For Attica remained longest free from internal strife because of the poverty of the soil and because the same people always inhabited it." In this connection, we may add that Sicily has a rich soil.

The same preoccupation is apparent in Demosthenes' oration For Phormio, and the speech by Apollodorus against Phormio. These deal with the freed slave of a wealthy banker in Athens in the early part of the fourth century B.C. who took over his former master's businesses and succeeded in making them prosper. This led to actions brought against him by the sons of the banker. From the text it appears that there were quite a few such cases of freedmen taken into the business by their former owners.[242] The claimant, Apollodorus, tries to use Phormio's status as a freed slave against him, although his own father had a similar background. "Thus," says Demosthenes, "you all but taunt the Athenians for admitting to citizenship a person like yourself."[243]

That did not prevent Apollodorus from returning to the theme: "You have perhaps imagined, because he solecizes in his speech, that he is a barbarian and a man readily to be despised. The fellow is indeed a barbarian in that he hates those whom he ought to honor; but in villainy and in bringing matters to ruin he is second to none."[244] In this entire complex the matter of language was particularly important. This is also clear from Demosthenes' Against Eubulides where the defendant has to answer charges that he was no legitimate Athenian. The reason for this accusation was his father's foreign accent (ὡς ἐξένιζεν). This could be easily explained: the man had been taken prisoner, sold into

---

πολιτῶν τὰς μεταβολὰς καὶ ἐπιδοχάς. καὶ οὐδεὶς δι᾽ αὐτὸ ὡς περὶ οἰκείας πατρίδος οὔτε τὰ περὶ τὸ σῶμα ὅπλοις ἐξήρτυται οὔτε τὰ ἐν τῇ χώρᾳ νομίμοις κατασκευαῖς· ὅτι δὲ ἕκαστος ἢ ἐκ τοῦ λέγων πείθειν οἴεται ἢ στασιάζων ἀπὸ τοῦ κοινοῦ λαβὼν . . .

[241] As explained by Gomme, A Historical Commentary, p. 249f. The Greek-Sicilian rulers carried out many transplantations of populations in the beginning of the fifth century. However, between 461/69 and 415, the date of the Athenian expedition to Sicily, only one transplantation, in 423, is recorded in the sources. Although this recent case may have been prominent in the minds of Alcibiades' audience, it is clear that the speech here generalizes and plays on vague but widely accepted stereotypes regarding these distant Greeks.

[242] Demosthenes, Or. 36 Pro Phormione 28f. For the status of these freedmen: 30.

[243] Op. cit. 47.5–48 (trans. A.T. Murray, Loeb): μόνον οὐκ ὀνειδίζεις οἷον ὄντα σ᾽ ἐποιήσαντ᾽ Ἀθηναῖον.

[244] Or. 45 (Apollodorus, in Stephanum 1) 30: ὑμεῖς δ᾽ ἴσως αὐτὸν ὑπειλήφατε, ὅτι σολοικίζει τῇ φωνῇ, βάρβαρον καὶ εὐκαταφρόνητον εἶναι. ἔστι δὲ βάρβαρος οὗτος τῷ μισεῖν οὓς αὐτῷ προσῆκε τιμᾶν· τῷ δὲ κακουργῆσαι καὶ διορύξαι πράγματ᾽ 31 οὐδενὸς λείπεται. λαβὲ δὴ τὴν μίσθωσιν καὶ λέγε, ἣν τὸν αὐτὸν τρόπον διὰ προκλήσεως ἐνεβάλοντο. The Loeb edition notes: "soloikos is a word of narrower meaning than barbaros, and is applied mainly to faults of pronunciation or mistakes in grammar, especially syntax, due to foreign origin." Apollodorus mentions Phormio's status again in 73 and 80.

slavery, and spent a long time on the island of Leucas.[245] Thus the accent certainly must have been genuinely Greek, but it must have had a trace of non-Attic dialect. In both cases xenophobia is used as a weapon in the law-courts. Note that even a genuine Athenian whose father spent years elsewhere involuntarily could be attacked as a stranger. In the speeches regarding Phormio, the arguments are intricate, but the essence is clear and reminds us of similar xenophobic accusations in our own times: foreigners who are allowed to settle and work in our countries will abuse their privileges and steal from legitimate citizens. These are phobias in the full sense of the term, that is, a mental disturbance, characterized by irrational states of anxiety, which, in the case of xenophobia, usually takes the form of a combination of hatred, fear, contempt, and disgust. Because they are engendered by emotional imbalances, they are not influenced by reality. People of all periods will be certain that immigrants are job-stealers, even if, in reality, they are decent people seeking to better their lives, and usually at the same time doing jobs that locals either cannot or will not do.

Indeed, in antiquity such views are not typical of Athenians only. Aristotle considers it natural that "For practical purposes, it is usual to define a citizen as 'one born of citizen parents on both sides,' and not on the father's or mother's side only; but sometimes this requirement is carried still farther back, to the length of two, three, or more stages of ancestry."[246] He also asks whether a city should be populated by one people (*ethnos*). The reply is that, in fact, it must.[247] Furthermore, he observes that a polis with a larger population cannot be well governed. One of his arguments is: "it is easy for foreigners and resident aliens to usurp the rights of citizenship, for the excessive number of the population makes it not difficult to escape detection."[248] This shows to what extent he considers it essential to prevent the inclusion of foreigners in the body of citi-

[245] Demosthenes, *Or.* 47 (*contra Eubulidem*), 16–18.

[246] Aristotle, *Pol.* 1275b (trans. Ernest Barker): Ὁρίζονται δὲ πρὸς τὴν χρῆσιν πολίτην τὸν ἐξ ἀμφοτέρων πολιτῶν καὶ μὴ θατέρου μόνον, οἷον πατρὸς ἢ μητρός, οἱ δὲ καὶ τοῦτ᾽ ἐπὶ πλέον ζητοῦσιν, οἷον ἐπὶ πάππους δύο ἢ τρεῖς ἢ πλείους. See comments by Richard Robinson, *Aristotle's Politics Books III and IV* (Oxford, 1962), 6f., mainly for the question of what Aristotle means here when he writes about citizenship. Robinson emphasizes that Aristotle distinguishes between citizenship in the narrow sense, that is, the status of a person who has all the political privileges and duties of a citizen, which excludes women, more specifically, the right to take part in deliberative and judicial office. Citizenship in the larger sense includes women, who may be trueborn Athenians, but do not have the rights just mentioned. What matters for us is that citizenship in the narrow sense is defined here as it is: it is granted only to those with two Athenian parents. This remains true also if one accepts the views of Cohen, *The Athenian Nation*, chapter 2, cited above.

[247] *Pol.* 1276a–b. ἀλλὰ τῶν αὐτῶν κατοικούντων τὸν αὐτὸν τόπον, πότερον ἕως ἂν ᾖ τὸ γένος ταὐτὸ τῶν κατοικούντων, τὴν αὐτὴν εἶναι φατέον πόλιν, καίπερ αἰεὶ τῶν μὲν φθειρομένων τῶν δὲ γινομένων, This is translated by Robinson: "But when we have the same men inhabiting the same place, are we to say that it is the same city as long as the inhabitants are of the same stock, although some are always dying and others being born?" The question implies that the population of a city must be of the same *genos*.

[248] *Pol.* 1326b: ἔτι δὲ ξένοις καὶ μετοίκοις ῥᾴδιον μεταλαμβάνειν τῆς πολιτείας· οὐ γὰρ χαλεπὸν τὸ λανθάνειν διὰ τὴν ὑπερβολὴν τοῦ πλήθους.

zens. He repeats this point when he discusses the advantages and disadvantages for a city of accessibility from the sea (1327a, cited below). A disadvantage is that foreign trade brings about an increase in population and visits by people brought up under other constitutions. Note that Aristotle was no Athenian and he is not here discussing Athens, but *poleis* in general.

In a recent article Alan Shapiro has shown that the myth of Athenian autochthony is represented frequently on Athenian vases which show the birth of Erichthonios from the soil of Attica. It is also, indirectly, prominent through the presence of Erechtheus on the West Pediment of the Parthenon.[249]

The theme of autochthony was further developed in the fourth century and became a commonplace. It is found in the work of Lysias, in his funeral oration, undated, but presumably composed between 392 and 386. It occurs also, as might be expected, in the work of Isocrates, in his *Panegyricus* (published 380 B.C.) and then in the writings of Plato and Demosthenes. Lysias claims that "the origin of the Athenians is lawful, for most people are a mixture of various groups, occupy foreign soil from which they have expelled the inhabitants; the Athenians, however, are autochthonous and the same land is both their mother and their fatherland."[250] This is a new variant of the idea: the claim that the Athenians are the only people who lawfully live where they do, because of their pure lineage, all other peoples having taken over other peoples' land in some stage of their history. Isocrates, *Panegyricus* 20–22, takes the same theme a step further, deriving claims toward other Greek states from Athenian autochthony. He argues that Athens is entitled to *hegemonia* because of (a) its successes in war and (b) it is the oldest, greatest, and most famous city in the world. Then he raises the topic under discussion: Athens is "autochthonous": "We live in this city without having expelled others, nor having deserted it, nor being mixed with many other peoples. So beautiful and so noble are we that we have always inhabited the land from which we were born, being *autochthones* and able to call our city by the same names that one uses for ones closest relatives (24). It is fitting that we only are called nourisher (*trofos*), *patris* and mother by the Greeks (25)."[251] Besides the by now familiar arguments, Isocrates brings in a novel association of the elements of Athens nourishing and serving as fatherland for all the other Greeks.

Following Isocrates, Demosthenes speaks at length on this theme in his *Funeral Oration* (Or. 2.17.2–5 [1390–91], dated 338), clarifying that "those who came as migrants into their cities and received the citizenship are comparable to adopted children; but these men [sc. the Athenians] are by birth legitimate citizens of their fatherland."[252] The latest to insist on autochthony is Hyperides

---

[249] Shapiro, "Autochthony," 133–150.

[250] Lysias, *Epitaphios* 17: ἥ τε γὰρ ἀρχὴ τοῦ βίου δικαία· οὐ γάρ, ὥσπερ οἱ πολλοί, πανταχόθεν συνειλεγμένοι καὶ ἑτέρους ἐκβαλόντες τὴν ἀλλοτρίαν ᾤκησαν, ἀλλ' αὐτόχθονες ὄντες τὴν αὐτὴν ἐκέκτηντο μητέρα καὶ πατρίδα.

[251] Cf. Shakespeare, *Richard II*, 1.3.307: "Then Englands ground farewell: sweet soil adieu, My Mother, and my Nurse."

[252] *Epit.* 4.8 τοὺς μὲν ἐπήλυδας ἐλθόντας εἰς τὰς πόλεις καὶ τούτων πολίτας προσαγορ-

in his *Funeral Oration* of 323 (*Epitaphios* 6.7). These speeches also introduce a topic further developed and emphasized by Plato in his *Menexenus*, a problematic work of uncertain date,[253] but certainly written after the work of Isocrates and before that of Demosthenes and Hyperides, namely that the land of Attica itself was actually the mother of the ancestors of the Athenians.[254]

This theme was first developed by Lysias, early in the fourth century: Attica is both mother (μητέρα)[255] and fatherland (πατρίς) of the Athenians. A little later, Isocrates, extended this to a claim that Athens fulfills that function for all of the Greeks. Plato, in the *Menexenus*, returns to Lysias's version. The land itself, therefore, produced these men and was also the first to produce the best human nourishment, wheat, barley, and the olive.[256] This is yet another first instance of an idea that would have much influence in later periods: the assumption of an unbreakable connection between a group of people and the land that they inhabit. The idea that the soil produces a people and that the character of the soil determines the character of the people has been seen above and will be seen again below as being influential in Roman literature. In recent history, the bond between peoples and their land has often been part of nationalist ideology and it was carried to extreme lengths in combination with racist ideas. As we see, in Athens too, the claim of pure descent and the ties with the soil of the fatherland were part of the same concept.[257]

ευομένους ὁμοίους εἶναι τοῖς εἰσποιητοῖς τῶν παίδων, τούτους δὲ γνησίους γόνῳ τῆς πατρίδος πολίτας εἶναι. See also Lycurgus, *Leocrates* 41 and 100, citing *Rhesus*.

[253] For the date: Stavros Tsitsiridis, *Platons Menexenos: Einleitung, Text und Kommentar* (Stuttgart, 1998), 41–52. Note the reservations as regards the interpretation of this source expressed by Cohen, *The Athenian Nation*, 95, 100–102

[254] Cohen, chapter 3, does not accept the view that the Athenians ever seriously claimed to have been sprung from the soil of their native land. He sees the Athenian concept of autochthony as merely one of a usual type of nationalist myths found also among other nations and which should not be overinterpreted. This is not the place to discuss these matters in detail. It must be observed, however, that Athenian literature has been more influential over time than other literatures and the fact that the idea existed elsewhere does not mean it was not given great weight by the Athenians themselves. The conclusion of Cohen's chapter (p. 103) is that "classical Athenian reality—in its openness to newcomers and in its willingness to accept offspring of acculturated *astoi* as *politai*— contradicted traditional Athenian claims to homogeneity through autochthony, even in their figurative, not literal formulations." As observed in the Introduction to this study, we are here concerned with the history of ideas rather than their application in practice, and I would maintain that the Athenian idea of autochthony *was* influential, whatever the reality of its application in fifth- and fourth-century Athens, more influential, that is, than any Japanese, Dutch, or Maori parallels. Moreover, such parallels have to be used with caution. Israel's claim to the Holy Land, however expressed in biblical passages, was never based on any pretense of continuous and original presence on the land. It was a claim made in spite of regular, long-term interruptions.

[255] For the earth as mother: Tsitsiridis, *Platons Menexenos* (1998), 201 and 204f. See also above, p. 90.

[256] Plato, *Menexenus* 237e–238a. ὃ δὴ καὶ ἡ ἡμετέρα γῆ τε καὶ μήτηρ ἱκανὸν τεκμήριον παρέχεται ὡς ἀνθρώπους γεννησαμένη· μόνη γὰρ ἐν τῷ τότε καὶ πρώτη τροφὴν ἀνθρωπείαν ἤνεγκεν τὸν τῶν πυρῶν καὶ κριθῶν καρπόν, ᾧ κάλλιστα καὶ ἄριστα τρέφεται τὸ ἀνθρώπειον γένος, For the earth as nurse, see also Timaeus 40b; Leges 740a.

[257] This does not mean that mystical or religious ties with the land are always part of a racist ideology. This is a phenomenon encountered among many peoples in many periods.

The *Menexenus* has already been cited and will be cited again, below as representative of its time in the discussions of Greek imperialism and of the fourth-century attitudes regarding Persia.[258] What it has to say about purity of lineage is in keeping with this. Note the well-known words about the Athenians and their pure blood:

> That is how firm and sound the high-mindedness and liberality of our city are, how much we are naturally inclined to hate the barbarians, though being purely Greek with no barbarian taint. For people who are barbarians by birth but Greeks by law—offspring of Pelops, Cadmus, Aegyptus, Danaus and many others—do not dwell among us. Consequently, our city is imbued with undiluted hatred of foreignness. (trans. Paul Ryan)[259]

Three claims are made about the Athenians in this passage. First is the myth of pure lineage: the Athenians are a people of pure descent that was never adulterated with immigrant blood. The second claim made about them is that they had always possessed and inhabited the same land. The *Menexenus* then makes the further point that the Athenians are not only unmixed with other Greeks, but the other Greeks themselves are mixed with foreigners. Thus the Athenians are twice uncontaminated: they are not mixed with other Greeks and hence not mixed with non-Greek foreigners. They are the only pure Greeks and the only Greeks that are pure citizens of their own city. Thus only they have a healthy love of freedom and hatred of foreigners, for the other Greeks are "barbarians by nature, though Hellenes by law." Being autochthonous the Athenians are the only Greek people who have a true claim to nobility of birth (εὐγένεια).[260] Although the *Menexenus* is a text to read carefully, an exercise in rhetoric inserted into a dialogue containing some elements of satire, I believe it may still be taken as representative of the mood among many contemporary Athenians, rather like the literary creations which Thucydides attributes to Pericles.

We have seen Plato's suggestion that one of the disastrous results of a Per-

---

[258] Below, chapter 4, notes 56, 142.

[259] Plato, *Menexenus* 245c–d: οὕτω δή τοι τό γε τῆς πόλεως γενναῖον καὶ ἐλεύθερον βέβαιόν τε καὶ ὑγιές ἐστιν καὶ φύσει μισοβάρβαρον, διὰ τὸ εἰλικρινῶς εἶναι Ἕλληνας καὶ ἀμιγεῖς βαρβάρων. οὐ γὰρ Πέλοπες οὐδὲ Κάδμοι οὐδὲ Αἴγυπτοί τε καὶ Δαναοὶ οὐδὲ ἄλλοι πολλοὶ φύσει μὲν βάρβαροι ὄντες, νόμῳ δὲ Ἕλληνες, συνοικοῦσιν ἡμῖν, ἀλλ’ αὐτοὶ Ἕλληνες, οὐ μειξοβάρβαροι οἰκοῦμεν, ὅθεν καθαρὸν τὸ μῖσος ἐντέτηκε τῇ πόλει τῆς ἀλλοτρίας φύσεως. For φύσει μισοβάρβαρον see: Stavros Tsitsiridis, *Platons Menexenos* (1895), 357–359. See comments by D. Whitehead, *The Ideology of the Athenian Metic* (Cambridge Philological Society, supp. 4, 1977), 113f. Whitehead mentions this passage in a brief discussion of "race," but, he says, "the eulogy of Athenian autochthony is a *topos*," a phrase which suggests that it was therefore not taken seriously by Athenian readers, an assumption which I reject, as noted in the Introduction. He concludes, however, that "the Athenian generally felt less of a Greek than an inhabitant of Attica and an Athenian citizen."

[260] *Menexenus* 237b: τῆς δ’ εὐγενείας πρῶτον ὑπῆρξε τοῖσδε ἡ τῶν προγόνων γένεσις οὐκ ἔπηλυς οὖσα, οὐδὲ τοὺς ἐκγόνους τούτους ἀποφηναμένη μετοικοῦντας ἐν τῇ χώρᾳ ἄλλοθεν σφῶν ἡκόντων, ἀλλ’ αὐτόχθονας . . . Cf. Tsitsiridis, pp. 196–200. Note his comment on αὐτόχθονας: "Platon versteht das Wort zweifellos nicht in der einfachen Bedeutung 'eingeboren', sondern in der Bedeutung 'aus der Erde selbst stammend', wie die Darstellung der Athener als wirkliche Kinder der Erde im folgenden vermuten lässt."

sian victory in the fifth century would have been the occurrence of mixed marriages. A somewhat different but no less interesting concept is found in his *Timaeus*: "This is in fact nothing less than the very same system of social order that the goddess first devised for you when she founded your city, which she did once she had chosen the region in which your people were born, and had discerned that the temperate climate in it throughout the seasons would bring forth men of surpassing wisdom. And, being a lover of both war and wisdom, the goddess chose the region that was likely to bring forth men most like herself, and founded it first."[261] This passage, even more so than many others, should not be taken out of context, for it is clearly of the cosmology of the *Timaeus*, which depends on the assumption that the *cosmos* is a living thing. Having said this, it is still true that the passage sees the Athenians as the product of the spot where their city was situated. Athena chose the location because of its climate, which was certain to bring forth men of wisdom and war. This is therefore an explicit combination of the environmental theory and the concept of autochthony. The climate is assumed to have been responsible for the collective character of the Athenians and the location is said to have brought forth the people. Moreover, these natural laws are so certain that for the Goddess all this was predictable.

Eugenics

Plato developed a closely related idea in the *Republic*, where he proposes setting up a secret system of eugenics. He suggests applying to the breeding of the guardians, the highest class in his projected state, the methods that are applied naturally to hunting dogs, horses, and fighting birds in order to prevent deterioration of stock. He concludes "first, that the best men must have sex with the best women as frequently as possible, while the opposite is true of the most inferior men and women, and, second, that if our herd is to be of the highest possible quality, the former's offspring must be reared but not the latter's. And this must all be brought about without being noticed by anyone except the rulers, so that our herd of guardians remains as free from dissension as possible."[262] The children are to be raised by nurses in rearing pens if they are good—parents will not know the identity of their children—but the children, of

[261] Plato, *Timaeus* 24c–d (trans. Donald J. Zeyl): ταύτην οὖν δὴ τότε σύμπασαν τὴν διακόσμησιν καὶ σύνταξιν ἡ θεὸς προτέρους ὑμᾶς διακοσμήσασα κατῴκισεν, ἐκλεξαμένη τὸν τόπον ἐν ᾧ γεγένησθε, τὴν εὐκρασίαν τῶν ὡρῶν ἐν αὐτῷ κατιδοῦσα, ὅτι φρονιμωτάτους ἄνδρας οἴσοι· ἅτε οὖν φιλοπόλεμός τε καὶ φιλόσοφος ἡ θεὸς οὖσα τὸν προσφερεστάτους αὐτῇ μέλλοντα οἴσειν τόπον ἄνδρας, τοῦτον ἐκλεξαμένη πρῶτον κατῴκισεν. This passage is cited by Galen in his discussion of the environmental theory: *Quod animi mores corporis temperamenta sequantur* 806. Galen has been discussed above.

[262] Plato, *Respublica* 459d–e: Δεῖ μέν, εἶπον, ἐκ τῶν ὡμολογημένων τοὺς ἀρίστους ταῖς ἀρίσταις συγγίγνεσθαι ὡς πλειστάκις, τοὺς δὲ φαυλοτάτους ταῖς φαυλοτάταις τοὐναντίον, καὶ τῶν μὲν τὰ ἔκγονα τρέφειν, τῶν δὲ μή, εἰ μέλλει τὸ ποίμνιον ὅτι ἀκρότατον εἶναι, καὶ ταῦτα πάντα γιγνόμενα λανθάνειν πλὴν αὐτοὺς τοὺς ἄρχοντας, εἰ αὖ ἡ ἀγέλη τῶν φυλάκων ὅτι μάλιστα ἀστασίαστος ἔσται.

inferior parents, or defective children are to be hidden "in a secret and unknown place." This may or may not be an allusion to infanticide. In the *Timaeus,* Socrates recapitulates the steps to be taken and there he says that "the children of the good parents were to be reared, but those of the bad were to be sent secretly to various other parts of the city; and as these grew up the rulers should constantly watch them so that they might bring back the deserving amongst them to take the place of the undeserving."[263] In Book 3 of the *Republic* it is proposed that, where intermarriage fails to produce children of the desired quality, such low quality offspring will be transferred to a lower caste.[264] Men and women may have children only during a prescribed procreative age; if they do otherwise, the offspring will not be reared (461b). It has rightly been observed that Plato cautiously refrains from referring explicitly to infanticide, because this was a sensitive subject.[265]

The manner in which Plato proposes to persuade the city to adopt this system is remarkable. "They will tell a myth, 'a Phoenician story,' such as the poets tell and have persuaded many people to believe it too." The myth will be that "the people themselves, their weapons, and the other craftsmen's tools were at that time really being fashioned and nurtured inside the earth and that when the work was completed, the earth, who is their mother delivered all of them up into the world."[266] This will motivate the people to fight for their land and defend it and regard their compatriots as their earthborn brothers (ὡς ἀδελφῶν ὄντων καὶ γηγενῶν). This is then followed by a variation of the Hesiodean myth. The three projected classes of citizens, guardians, auxiliaries, and others: the farmers or other craftsmen, will each contain some gold, silver or iron and bronze, respectively.[267] The point of this story is to make it acceptable that some children have to be moved up or down to another caste, because they will be reported as containing metal of a caste not their own. The essence of this idea is that the metal content of the people is hereditary and that they will not marry

---

[263] *Timaeus* 19a: {ΣΩ.} Καὶ μὴν ὅτι γε τὰ μὲν τῶν ἀγαθῶν θρεπτέον ἔφαμεν εἶναι, τὰ δὲ τῶν κακῶν εἰς τὴν ἄλλην λάθρα διαδοτέον πόλιν· ἐπαυξανομένων δὲ σκοποῦντας ἀεὶ τοὺς ἀξίους πάλιν ἀνάγειν δεῖν, τοὺς δὲ παρὰ σφίσιν ἀναξίους εἰς τὴν τῶν ἐπανιόντων χώραν μεταλλάττειν;

[264] 415a–c; 434a–cf. Herbert D. Rankin, *Plato and the Individual* (London, 1964), chapters 3 and 4, with detailed analysis of the individual passages and the differences between them; J. Faris, "Is Plato's a Caste State Based on Racial Differences?" *CQ* 44 (1950), 38–43, arguing (against Popper) that citizens born into the wrong caste may be moved not only down but also upwards: Karl R. Popper, *The Open Society and Its Enemies,* I, *The Spell of Plato* (Princeton, Rev. ed., 1966), chapter 8, 140f. Faris is probably right against Popper in his interpretation of *Resp.* 434a–c and 547a, but he also claims to have shown thereby that Plato is not describing a caste society or one based on a (proto-)racist view of humanity. In my view this conclusion rests on definitions of "caste" and "racial society" that are unacceptably formalistic (see p. 38).

[265] Rankin, *Plato and the Individual,* 46–48.

[266] Plato, *Resp.* 414d–e (trans. G.M.A. Grube, rev. C.D.C. Reeve). For the "earth-born" see also *Politicus* 269b; 271a–b.

[267] 415a: ἐστὲ μὲν γὰρ δὴ πάντες οἱ ἐν τῇ πόλει ἀδελφοί, ὡς φήσομεν πρὸς αὐτοὺς μυθολογοῦντες, ἀλλ᾽ ὁ θεὸς πλάττων, ὅσοι μὲν ὑμῶν ἱκανοὶ ἄρχειν, χρυσὸν ἐν τῇ γενέσει συνέμειξεν αὐτοῖς, διὸ τιμιώτατοί εἰσιν· ὅσοι δ᾽ ἐπίκουροι, ἄργυρον· σίδηρον δὲ καὶ χαλκὸν τοῖς τε γεωργοῖς καὶ τοῖς ἄλλοις δημιουργοῖς.

outside their castes. Since the members of each caste will marry among themselves they will usually produce offspring of the same level. While it is true that Plato presents all this as part of an invented myth to be told the citizens, the conclusion is yet inescapable that the metal contents which determine the overall quality of a person are racial characteristics.

Plato returns to this subject in an important later passage, when he explains how the city will necessarily decline, like everything in nature. This is an early instance of the ancient preoccupation with the decline of states. This will happen because the leaders themselves will produce children of lower quality through carelessness. "Hence, rulers chosen from among them will not be able to guard well the testing of the golden, silver, bronze and iron races . . . The intermixing of iron with silver and bronze with gold that results will engender lack of likeness and unharmonious inequality" which in turn will cause war and civil strife.[268] This is the clearest possible statement that, in the system envisaged by Plato, mixed marriages can only produce degenerate offspring which eventually destroy the state.[269] In other words, the projected system of eugenics is central to the preservation of the city: when this breaks down and groups start to mix, decline and fall are certain.

Aristotle also devotes a full chapter of his *Politics*, Book Seven, to proposed legislation aimed at ensuring the production of healthy offspring, including demands to expose deformed children and children conceived as a result of intercourse in contravention of the regulations which he specifies. If "the regular customs" (ἡ τάξις τῶν ἐθῶν) do not permit exposure (1334b–1335), abortion must be carried out of children conceived in a manner contrary to the regulations. Aristotle also promises elucidation on "the particular kind of bodily constitution in the parents that will be most beneficial for the offspring,"[270] but he either has never written on this or it has been lost. In this connection mention must also be made of Plutarch's report on the Spartan custom of state-imposed eugenics. A committee examined each newborn infant and if it was found unhealthy or deformed it was thrown into a ravine, the argument being that it was "of no advantage either to itself or to the state."[271] Exposure of children with defects seems to have been quite common in fourth-century Athens. Although the evidence appears in Plato's *Theaetetus* as a maieutic metaphor, for an idea

---

[268] *Resp.* 546d–547a: ἐκ δὲ τούτων ἄρχοντες οὐ πάνυ φυλακικοὶ καταστήσονται πρὸς τὸ δοκιμάζειν τὰ Ἡσιόδου τε καὶ τὰ παρ' ὑμῖν γένη, χρυσοῦν τε καὶ ἀργυροῦν καὶ χαλκοῦν καὶ σιδηροῦν· ὁμοῦ δὲ μιγέντος σιδήρου ἀργύρῳ καὶ χαλκοῦ χρυσῷ ἀνομοιότης ἐγγενήσεται καὶ ἀνωμαλία ἀνάρμοστος, ἃ γενόμενα, οὗ ἂν ἐγγένηται, ἀεὶ τίκτει πόλεμον καὶ ἔχθραν.

[269] In 415c, Plato suggests inventing an oracle which will predict that the city will be ruined if it ever has an iron or a bronze guardian.

[270] Aristotle, *Pol.* 1335b: ποίων δέ τινων τῶν σωμάτων ὑπαρχόντων μάλιστ' ἂν ὄφελος εἴη τοῖς γεννωμένοις, . . .

[271] Plutarch, *Lycurgus* 16.1f.: ὡς οὔτε αὐτῷ ζῆν ἄμεινον ὂν οὔτε τῇ πόλει τὸ μὴ καλῶς εὐθὺς ἐξ ἀρχῆς πρὸς εὐεξίαν καὶ ῥώμην πεφυκός. Cf. Paul Cartledge, *Spartan Reflections* (London, 2001), 84, 114, 124f. For the views on Spartan infanticide in later periods, see Elizabeth Rawson, *The Spartan Tradition in European Thought* (Oxford, 1969), 175, 182, 259, 340, 342.

proposed in the dialogue, it clearly implies that the custom existed in ordinary practice.[272] This, however, concerns exposure by decision of the parents of the child and has no connection with ideas of eugenics as proposed by Plato and Aristotle.

There are, by definition, two types of eugenics: first, the removal of offspring considered as undesirable by the authorities, which was realized in antiquity by the exposure or killing of infants, and in modern times by forced sterilization, abortion, and euthanasia.[273] Second, there is the effort to produce a superior type of human being by selective breeding. The former, inevitably, is easier to attempt than the latter. However, this was seen as merely checking the presumed deterioration of human stock while the latter aimed at improving it.[274] As far as I am aware, nobody in antiquity ever tried to carry out such plans in any systematic way in practice, but it is significant to realize that the concept was first formulated in the fourth century B.C.

Although there were a number of predecessors, the first thorough exposition of eugenics in modern history was not made until the nineteenth century by the English scientist Sir Francis Galton. In his book *Hereditary Genius* (1869), Galton proposes that a program of arranged marriages between men of distinction and women of wealth would produce a superior race. He coined the term "eugenics" in 1883.[275] It is significant here since the idea of eugenics was inevitably supported by individuals and groups who believed in the superiority of specific classes or presumed races.[276] Galton, it should be noted, totally rejected

---

[272] Plato, *Theaetetus* 160e. For this and further evidence of the exposure of children in Greece: La Rue van Hook, "The Exposure of Infants at Athens," *TAPA* 51 (1920), 134–145, which contends that there is no sound evidence that proves the prevalence of exposure in classical Athens; A. Cameron, "The Exposure of Children and Greek Ethics," *CR* 46 (1932), 105–114. This paper contains, on p. 105, the peculiar statement that it is essential to recognize "that the cruelty involved in infanticide even by exposure is very slight, a fact which is well recognised in modern legal practice." Note also the discussion about exposure in Rome: H. Bennett, "The Exposure of Infants in Ancient Rome," *CJ* 18 (1923), 341–351; Max Radin, "The Exposure of Infants in Roman Law and Practice," *CJ* 20 (1925), 337–342.

[273] B. Anderson, *Imagined Communities*, 149: "The fact of the matter is that nationalism thinks in terms of historical destinies, while racism dreams of eternal contaminations, transmitted from the origins of time through an endless sequence of loathsome copulations: outside history."

[274] As explained by the eugenist F.C.S. Schiller: "Negative eugenics aims at checking the deterioration to which the human stock is exposed, owing to the rapid proliferation of what may be called human weeds. . . . we must look to positive eugenics, which sets itself to inquire by what means the human race may be rendered intrinsically better, higher, stronger, healthier, more capable." Cited by Donald J. Childs, *Modernism and Eugenics: Woolf, Eliot, Yeats, and the Culture of Degeneration* (Cambridge, 2001), 3.

[275] See *OED* with references to Galton's own definitions of eugenics in 1883: (1) the cultivation of race; (2) the conditions under which men of a high type are produced. Cf. Ruth Schwartz Cowan, *Sir Francis Galton and the Study of Heredity in the Nineteenth Century* (New York, 1985). For the predecessors of Galton in the nineteenth century, Lyndsay Andrew Farrall, *The Origins and Growth of the English Eugenics Movement, 1865–1925* (New York, 1985), 10–22.

[276] Such as the American Eugenics Society, which was founded in 1926 by men who believed that the white race was superior to other races and also that the "Nordic" white was superior to other whites. They successfully encouraged restrictions on immigration from nations with "inferior"

environmentalism and adopted a completely hereditarian position, as distinct from the early racial theorists and more closely approaching later ones.[277] Eugenics rapidly gained influence in Germany through the work of Wilhelm Schallmayer.[278] Best known, and the most immediate reason for the total delegitimization of the concept, is the German obsession with it in the Nazi period, where it was seen as directly connected with the idea discussed in this chapter of "Blut und Boden."[279]

Eugenics is an exception among the subjects discussed in the present work. So far we have seen, and will see further below, that many of the proto-racist concepts represented in Greek and Roman antiquity somehow found their way in altered form into later European racism via the authors of the Enlightenment. In these cases it is usually easy to show that the early modern authors refer to the Greek and Latin sources and were therefore inspired by them.

Obviously, there are also aspects of racism that did not exist in Greece and Rome, because they were engendered by developments in later thinking. The subject of eugenics is somewhat different in this respect. It clearly occurs in Greek literature as a concept and it was a fashionable idea among late-nineteenth and twentieth-century racists, but it is not significant before or during the eighteenth century. Even so there can be no doubt that the movement was inspired by the ancient ideas, for Plato's *Republic* was widely read in the nineteenth century. This is clear, for example, from the manner in which Darwin introduces a eugenic proposal of his own: "Man scans with scrupulous care the character of his horses, cattle, and dogs before he matches them, but when it comes to his own marriage he rarely, or never, takes any such care."[280] This is a direct echo of Plato's *Republic* 459a–b: "Tell me this, Glaucon: I see that you have hunting dogs and quite a flock of noble fighting birds at home. Have you noticed anything about their mating and breeding? etc. etc. . . . Dear me! If this

---

stock, such as southern and eastern Europe, and argued for the sterilization of insane, retarded, and epileptic citizens in the United States. In the United States three international conferences on Eugenics were held in, respectively 1912, 1921, and 1932. The proceedings were duly published. In the 1930s the popularity and prestige of eugenics began to decline in the United States. See Mark H. Haller, *Eugenics: Hereditarian Attitudes in American Thought* (New Brunswick, NJ, 1963, repr. 1984); Steven Selden, *Inheriting Shame: The Story of Eugenics and Racism in America* (New York, 1999). The English movement was more moderate, see: Farrall, *The Origins and Growth of the English Eugenics Movement*. See now D. J. Childs, *Modernism and Eugenics*, for the influence of these ideas on English literature, notably Virginia Woolf, T. S. Eliot, and W. B. Yeats.

[277] Cowan, op. cit., 14–20. As already noted, he also denies the heredity of acquired characters.

[278] Sheila Faith Weiss, *Race Hygiene and National Efficiency: The Eugenics of Wilhelm Schallmayer* (Berkeley, 1987).

[279] As illustrated by the title: *Neuadel aus Blut und Boden* by R. Walther Darré (Munich, 1930). There are numerous books on Nazi eugenics.

[280] Charles Darwin, *Descent of Man and Selection in Relation to Sex* (2d ed., 1877), 617, reprinted as volumes 21–22 of *The Works of Charles Darwin* ed. by Paul H. Barrett and R. B. Freeman (London, 1989), 643. See also Frederic the Great: "I find it annoying when I see to what trouble people go in this harsh climate to grow pineapple, bananas, and other exotic plants, while so little care is taken for humanity" etc. cited with approval by Darré, *Neuadel aus Blut und Boden* (1930), ch. 7.

also holds true of human beings . . .". Francis Galton was one of many whose racism was influenced by a distorted form of Darwin's ideas, and it is possible that he would have invented eugenics, even if the relevant passages from Plato, Aristotle, and Plutarch had been lost in the Middle Ages. Plato's idea of decline through degeneration resulting from mixed marriages was also a dominant theme in nineteenth-century racism, for instance in the work of Gobineau.[281] So, Greek literature probably has a share in the invention of eugenics in modern history and the same is equally true for the connection between race and the land, or "Blut und Boden," to which we shall now return.

Isocrates takes up the theme of pure blood and soil from a rather similar viewpoint to that of Plato and the earlier orators: the Athenians are the best among mankind. "For I am aware that other regions produce various fruits, trees and animals, each according to its location and some of them far better than those of other lands, so our own country is able to bear and nurture men who are not only the most able in the world in the arts and in action and speech, but they are also superior to all others in valour and virtue."[282] In other words, the soil of Attica was such that it produced a people which was the best of all mankind. Pure lineage, autochthony, and superiority are all part of the same parcel.

The Athenian idea of indigenous birth was never questioned in antiquity. We still find it endorsed by Tacitus and Plutarch[283] and fully accepted by Pompeius Trogus, who explains that the Athenians "are unique in priding themselves on their origins as well as their development. It was not immigrants or a motley rabble of people brought together at random that founded the city; rather, the Athenians were born from the land which they inhabit, and their home is also their place of origin."[284]

The Athenian concept is clearly different, for instance, from that which linked the Land of Israel with the Jewish people, for the Jewish tradition never claimed that the Jews originated there. The land was theirs by a divine decision, not because of continuous possession, or rather in spite of frequent and lengthy absences. In European culture the expression "mother country" has become so common as to make it virtually a synonym for "one's native country." The soil is the mother, the people the father in this conception. For the present discus-

---

[281] Comte Arthur de Gobineau, *Essai sur l'inégalité des races humaines,* 2 vols. (1853–1985). Much has been written about Gobineau; see, e.g., G. L. Mosse, *Towards the Final Solution* esp. chapter 4; Poliakov, *The Arian Myth,* 233–238. Darwin's attitude regarding the notion of degeneration in civilized society was ambivalent: John L. Greene, "Darwin as a Social Evolutionist," *Journal of the History of Biology* 10 (1997), 11.

[282] Isocrates, *Areopagiticus* [7] 74; cf. *Peace* 94.

[283] Tacitus, *Ann.* 2.55, cited and discussed below, in chapter 9, p. 397. Plutarch, *Theseus* 3.1.1; *Mor.* 604d (citing Euripides): τίς γὰρ εἴρηκε τῆς ἑαυτοῦ πατρίδος ἐγκώμιον τοιοῦτον, οἷον Εὐριπίδης; ἢ πρῶτα μὲν λεὼς οὐκ ἐπακτὸς ἄλλοθεν, αὐτόχθονες δ' ἔφυμεν· αἱ δ' ἄλλαι πόλεις πεσσῶν ὁμοίως διαφορηθεῖσαι βολαῖς ἄλλαι παρ' ἄλλων εἰσὶν εἰσαγώγιμοι.

[284] Iustinus *epitoma* 6.1.3 (trans. J. C. Yardley): Soli enim praeterquam incremento etiam origine gloriantur; quippe non advenae neque passim collecta populi conluvies originem urbi dedit, sed eodem innati solo, quod incolunt, et quae illis sedes, eadem origo est.

sion, it is significant because of its early occurrence in Athens and its immediate link with the concept of pure lineage.

To return to pure lineage, presumed common ancestors always determined current relationships, but this did not necessarily exclude migration and marriage with other groups. Total insistence on pure lineage is relatively rare as an idea; it was prominent among the Jews in Babylonia in the Talmudic period,[285] but even there it developed over time. Earlier Nehemiah had enacted a law against mixed marriages, which Momigliano has noted was paralleled in Athens by Pericles' similar law.[286] It is particularly interesting to see how the idea that the Athenians were indigenous developed over the years. It appears in Herodotus rather innocuously as a historical contrast with the Spartans, who had wandered a great deal. In the later fifth century it gradually came to serve a claim of superiority over all other Greeks who were not indigenous.

A subsidiary idea was attached to it in the fourth century, to the effect that the unique ties between the Athenians and their land had made them and their land into the nurse and *patris* of all Greeks. As noted also in chapter 4, in *Laws* 693a, Plato speculates about the consequences of Greek defeat in the wars with Persia. Such a disastrous result would have meant a loss of identity for the individual Greek states and the end of separation between Greek and non-Greek. This implies not only a strong belief in the importance of social and ethnic separation, but also disapproval of mixed marriages between Greeks and non-Greeks. Later in the same work Plato modifies this slightly with regard to the incorporation of Greeks from other cities. He explains that a state with a mixed population causes immense damage to peoples who enjoy a healthy society and live under good laws, for "the unfamiliar customs of the visitors rub off on to their hosts." However, this would not be true for states which are not well governed anyway (*Laws* 949e–950a).[287] Aristotle also describes the admission of large numbers of Greeks from other cities as disruptive, and a cause of civil strife.[288] One of the dangers of too large a city is that it is easy in such a community for foreigners and resident aliens to obtain citizenship.[289] It is taken for granted that this is harmful.

All the relevant fourth-century authors are convinced of the value of pure descent. The Athenians among them are agreed that the Athenians are of uniquely pure descent and superior to all other peoples of the world. The Athenians may not have been unique in their ideas regarding a special attachment to the soil and corresponding superiority, but they have had more influence than any other people thanks to the status of their literature. All the authors cited

---

[285] Cf. Aharon Oppenheimer, *Babylonia Judaica in the Talmudic Period* (Wiesbaden, 1983), 16f.

[286] Momigliano, *Alien Wisdom*, 81.

[287] Cf. David Whitehead, *The Ideology of the Athenian Metic* (Cambridge, 1977), 109–114 about "race" and especially p. 115.

[288] Aristotle, *Pol.* 1303a–b: στασιωτικὸν δὲ καὶ τὸ μὴ ὁμόφυλον. Aristotle then gives examples of conflict in cities with a population of mixed origin.

[289] Aristotle, *Pol.* 1326b: ἔτι δὲ ξένοις καὶ μετοίκοις ῥᾴδιον μεταλαμβάνειν τῆς πολιτείας. Cf. the comments of Newman, 3.349, who says it frequently happened in Athens.

above have been read widely by Romans[290] and, later, by European intellectuals ever since the renaissance. If it is accepted that the Athenians inspired western civilization with their democracy, can it be denied that they were instrumental in conveying the idea of racism? Furthermore, the value of Athenian democracy was disputed, both in Athens and by other Greeks. It does not seem as if the value of pure lineage was a subject of popular debate. It was accepted.

There are several other claims of autochthonous descent to be mentioned here, particularly the myth of the foundation of Thebes by the Phoenician Kadmos. Following orders received at Delphi, Kadmos had reached the site of Thebes in order to found a city there. He needed water and the only spring available was guarded by a dragon which Kadmos then killed. Athena now advised him to extract its teeth and to sow them. From the dragon's teeth warriors sprung from the soil, fully armed.[291] These Kadmos pelted with stones and the warriors, assuming each that one of the others was attacking them, proceeded to fight each other till only five were left. From these the nobility of Thebes derived its descent, being called *Spartoi* (sown men).[292] The myth, as told, claims again a direct extraction from the soil for the Theban nobility, just as the Athenians claimed for themselves. Thus it is another example of the importance attached to the link between ancestors and soil. The city, when founded, was peopled not with immigrants, but with men produced locally by the native soil. Kadmos, himself, was a Phoenician and that may have made it particularly attractive to the Theban aristocracy to assume that they themselves had sprung from Theban soil.[293] Above we saw that Plato, in the *Menexenus*, makes the Athenians emphasize their own autochthony, unlike that of the descendants of Pelops or Kadmos. As told, therefore, this myth is less explicit as a claim of pure lineage, for we are not informed that no stage immigrants or foreigners mixed with the *Spartoi*. It is, however, quite possible that there were such claims, for obviously we have less information about the way Theban aristocrats perceived their origins than about Athens, given the composition of our source material. The idea in itself that people might have sprung from the earth was widely accepted. Indeed, there was an old and traditional belief that in an early stage human beings were "earthborn" (γηγενεῖς).[294] As observed by M. R. Wright, Empedocles relates human to plant life and provides a nonmythi-

---

[290] See, for instance, the reference to autochthony by Cicero, *pro Flacco* 62.

[291] Ps.-Apollodorus, *Bibliotheca* 3.23f. ἀνέτειλαν ἐκ γῆς ἄνδρες ἔνοπλοι, οὓς ἐκάλεσαν Σπαρτούς; Hyginus, *Fab.* 278; Ovidius, *Met.* 3.95–136. Cf. Ruth B. Edwards, *Kadmos the Phoenician* (Amsterdam, 1979), 20, 31f.; *Lexicon Iconographicum Mythologiae Graecae* 5/1 (1990), 863–882; for Kadmos and the Spartoi: 872.

[292] See, however, Rosivach, *CQ* 37 (1987), 296 and n. 46 on p. 306. See also Pindar, Frg. Hymn. 29.1: ἢ Κάδμον ἢ Σπαρτῶν ἱερὸν γένος ἀνδρῶν.

[293] See Lucian on Kadmos, cited below.

[294] Empedocles, Diels-Kranz, *Die Fragmente der Vorsokratiker* (Berlin, 6th ed. 1951), fr.62; 57; 96; 98 = M. R. Wright, *Empedocles: The Extant Fragments* (New Haven, 1981), fr.53; 50 (with comments on p. 211f.); 48; 83; Plato, *Politicus* 269b; Aristotle, *De generatione animalium* 762b; cf. 715b, where Aristotle discusses animals that arise from rotting matter; see also Herodotus 8.55: Erechtheus is said to have been γηγενής.

cal explanation for the autochthonous traditions.[295] Aristotle, discussing the laws and customs of the first men, describes them as a matter of course as either "earth-born," or the survivors of some cataclysm."[296] Other peoples who claimed to have been autochthonous were the Arcadians and the Aiginetans[297] and the Kynourioi on the Peloponnese.[298] Of course, the Pelasgians were assumed to have been autochthonous.[299] As far as we can tell, however, only the Athenians developed a great emotional attachment to the idea and this belongs to the period of imperial expansion.

At any rate, the idea was firmly rooted in the Greek conceptual world, as is clear from the fact that it is still casually referred to by Polybius, as cited by Strabo. Polybius divides the Alexandrians into three sections: the native Egyptians, that is, 'the mercenary class," and the (true) Alexandrians, "who were also not distinctly inclined to civil life, and for the same reasons, but still they were better than those others, for even though they were a mixed people, still they were Greeks by origin and mindful of the customs common to the Greeks."[300] It is obvious that the meaning of "mixed" here is that they were descendants from assorted Greek settlers, not a mixture of Greeks with others. This is still a reason for Polybius to consider them second-rate people. Pausanias, as has been shown recently, was not particularly interested in the concept of autochthony.[301]

There is at least one Greek author who was critical of the idea and even ridiculed it, but he was Favorinus, the famous Greek orator who originated in Arelate in Gaul in the second century A.D. His Greek was excellent,[302] but we can hardly expect him to cherish the most chauvinistic of Greek concepts: "If some small number of people think that they are autochthonous, and give themselves airs for this reason, then these truly are empty boasts: I grant you, mice and other more insignificant animals are born in the earth, but it is right for humans to be born from no other source than a human. What is more, if these people affiliate themselves more closely to the earth than all others for this reason—well, one should not deal with one's own portion of the earth only, but

[295] M. R. Wright, *Empedocles*, p.216, comments on his fr. 53 (Diels-Kranz, fr. 62).

[296] Aristotle, *Pol.* 1269a.5: . . . τοὺς πρώτους, εἴτε γηγενεῖς ἦσαν, εἴτ' ἐκ φθορᾶς ἐσώθησαν . . . See also: Pindar, *Nem.* 6.1–3: "Εν ἀνδρῶν, ἐν θεῶν γένος· ἐκ μιᾶς δὲ πνέομεν ματρὸς ἀμφότεροι· Hesiod, *op. et dies* 108; see further references in Newman, comm. ad loc., 2.310.

[297] Harpocration, s.v. αὐτόχθονες δὲ καὶ Ἀρκάδες ἦσαν, ὡς Ἑλλάνικός φησι, καὶ Αἰγινῆται καὶ Θηβαῖοι. Other sources regarding the Arcadians are discussed by Rosivach, *CQ* 37 (1987), 305f.

[298] Herodotus 8.73, referring also to the Arcadians. Herodotus also mentions several non-Greek peoples as claiming themselves to be indigenous or described as such by others: the Carians and Caunians (1.171f.), and the Libyans and Ethiopians in Libya (4.197).

[299] The *Pelasgi* are described as autochthonous in many sources, cf. Montanari, *Il mito dell' autoctonia*, p. 33, n. 4; Hall, *Inventing the Barbarian*, 171.

[300] Polybius 34.14.5: καὶ γὰρ εἰ μιγάδες, Ἕλληνες ὅμως ἀνέκαθεν ἦσαν καὶ ἐμέμνηντον τοῦ κοινοῦ τῶν Ἑλλήνων ἔθους (= Strabo 17.1.12 [c.797]). See D. Delia, *Alexandrian Citizenship during the Roman Principate* (Atlanta, GA, 1991), 34–9: "The ethnic basis for status distinctions."

[301] David Konstan, "To Hellenikon ethnos," 39–43.

[302] Note, however, the verdict of Syme, *Tacitus* (1958), 505: "the nullity of Favorinus . . . is convincingly attested with reference to the tract Περὶ φυγῆς (*P. Vat. gr.* 11).

inhabit the whole earth."[303] Thus Favorinus makes the Athenian claim that they are born from the earth seem foolish. It could be true for mice, but not for men, he says, and besides, if it were true, then the earth knows no boundaries and belongs to all—like Greek language and culture, is the implication. With these arguments he focuses only on the claim of being earth-born, ignoring the issue which was more important in practice, that of descent and lineage.

To conclude this topic, clearly, the insistence on pure descent, and the measures taken to preserve a pure line, should be considered proto-racist doctrine. Unlike the environmental theory, however, it is easily covered by a narrow definition of racism, for it focuses exclusively on descent and on the maintenance of stable, uncontaminated characteristics in the physical and spiritual sphere. It has in common with all manifestations of proto-racism that it is at the same time used as an argument in favor of one's own superiority and as an excuse for the poor treatment of foreigners.

It is impossible not to say something about the insalubrious insistence on a combination of racial purity and attachment to the soil in recent history. In Nazi Germany *Blut und Boden* was a favorite slogan, but it was popularized in France before it was adopted by Germans. The nationalist author Maurice Barrès (1862–1923), a follower of Taine and Renan, wrote his most famous novel against the rational cosmopolitanism of the "uprooted" intellectuals, hence its title: *Les Déracinés* (1897). Barrès extolled the close community of a nation with its deep roots in past generations and in the ancestral soil.[304] To Barrès the individual was merely a link in the chain of generations, inevitably determined by the blood of common forefathers and defined by his part in a collective, inherited unconscious, which itself was defined by race. Like Taine, Barrès believes in the role of environment and race in fulfilling the destiny of the nation. He combines this with extreme xenophobia: "The foreigner, like a parasite is poisoning us."[305]

---

[303] A. Barigazzi (ed.), *Favorino di Arelate, Opere: introduzione, testo critico e commento* (Florence, 1966) Fr. 96,10.25f. .ε[ἰ] δέ [τι]νες ὀλίγοι αὐτόχθονες εἶν[αι ἡγούμε]νοι ἐπὶ τούτῳ μ[έγα φρον]οῦσιν, οὗτοι ὄντ[ω]ς ἀλαζον[εύονται· ἢ]ν γάρ τοι καὶ μυῶν καὶ ἄ[λλων ε]ὐτελεστέρ[ων] ζῴων [χθονογέ]νεια, ἀνθρώπῳ δὲ ὄντι οὐ καλὸν μὴ ἐξ ἀνθρώπο[υ γενέσθαι]. εἰ δ' αὖ διὰ τοῦτο πρὸς τὴν γῆν οἰκειότερον ἑτέρων [ἀπά]ντ[ων ὁμο]ιοῦνται, ἀλλ' οὐχ ὥσπερ ἐκ τρυμαλιᾶς ἐξαναδύντα χρὴ [.... ἐκ]εῖνο τὸ καθ' αὐτὸν μέρος μόνον περιέπειν, ἀλλὰ πᾶσαν τὴν γῆν οἰκεῖν ὡς πάντων μητέρα καὶ τροφὸν τὴν αὐτὴν οὖσαν. I quote the translation of Tim Whitmarsh, "Greece is the World: Exile and Identity in the Second Sophistic," in S. Goldhill (ed.), *Being Greek under Rome* (2001), 300, discussion on p. 300f. For Favorinus, see also below. According to Diodorus 1.10 the Egyptians claim that the soil of the Thebaid generates mice.

[304] E.g., M. Barrès, *Les Déracinés* (Paris, 1897), vol. 2, p. 69: "La race germaine se substitue à l'autochthone dans tout l'est de la France. Vaut-elle moins?—Oui, car elle est étrangère. Par ces immigrés, le type se modifie et se gâte." Cf. Todorov, *On Human Diversity* (1993), 229–233, 246–249.

[305] M. Barrès, "Contre les étrangers," which he later included in his book on nationalism, *Scènes et doctrines du nationalisme*, in *L'oeuvre de Maurice Barrès* 20 vols. (Paris, 1965–1969), vol. 2.161. On Hippolyte Taine, see Todorov, *On Human Diversity*, 153–157, bibliography on p. 412. For the development of this ideology in Germany: George L. Mosse, *The Crisis of the German Ideology* (New York, 1964) which I have seen in the German translation: *Ein Volk, ein Reich, ein*

Descent and Lineage: Roman Views

To begin with, we may as well state the obvious: unlike the Athenians, the Romans never attributed to themselves a pure lineage or any notion of being autochthonous.[306] Even if they had wanted to do so at any stage of their history, their founding myths made this impossible. They obviously took these myths very seriously, as witness the *Aeneid* or Claudius's speech to the senate about the acceptance of Gauls as members of that body.[307]

Admittedly, Montanari has found a few traces of autochthony in Roman legend.[308] Dionysius of Halycarnassus reports that the earliest occupants of Rome were barbarian "Sicels, a native people."[309] Thereafter the "Aborigines" established themselves there. These later changed their names to "Latins" and then again to "Romans" after Romulus founded the city (Dionysius 1.9.3). He further states that "There are some who assert that the Aborigines, from whom the Romans descend, are autochthonous Italians, a people which originated by itself."[310] One of the kings of these Aborigines was named Faunus (Dionysius 1.31.2). This may be combined with a note which calls the "Fauni indigenous, i.e. autochthonous."[311] Even if there was such a tradition, every Roman was aware that the Romans never had a consistent policy to resist the inclusion of foreigners among their citizens, and the legend cited here does not deny this either.

It has often been observed that the Romans never made a rigid distinction between themselves and others, the barbarians. Unlike the Chinese, the Greeks, and the Jews, for example, they had no general designation for aliens. At an early stage they were even prepared to accept the Greek view and consider themselves barbarians.[312] However, we cannot therefore assume that they considered lineage irrelevant, individually or collectively. Caesar emphasized his

---

Führer: die völkischen Ursprunge des Nationalsozialismus (Königstein, 1979), tracing it back to the mid-nineteenth century.

[306] T. J. Cornell, *The Beginnings of Rome* (London, 1995), 60.

[307] In the fragment of Claudius's own speech he insists on the foreign origin of Rome's kings (*ILS* 212, col. 1). Tarquinius Priscus was of "mixed blood" (*propter temeratum sanguinem*). In Tacitus's rendering of Claudius's speech, the Emperor points to the foreign origin of his own and other early aristocratic families (*Ann.* 11.24). He continues arguing that the ongoing acceptance of provincials was an essential element for the expansion and vitality of Empire.

[308] Montanari, *Il mito dell'autoctonia*, 221–229: 'Limiti de trasferibilità del tema dell'autoctonia nel mondo romano." See however, Cornell, loc. cit.: "In attempting to prove that the Romans were of the purest Greek stock, Dionysius of Halicarnassus faced a virtually impossible task."

[309] Dionysius of Halycarnassus 1.9.1: βάρβαροι Σικελοί, ἔθνος αὐθιγενές.

[310] Dionysius 1.10.1: Τοὺς δὲ Ἀβοριγῖνας, ἀφ' ὧν ἄρχει Ῥωμαίοις τὸ γένος, οἱ μὲν αὐτόχθονας Ἰταλίας, γένος αὐτὸ καθ' ἑαυτὸ γενόμενον ἀποφαίνουσιν· The last clause has been declared a gloss.

[311] Servius, *ad Aen.* 8.314: haec nemora indigenae favni 'indigenae', id est inde geniti, αὐτοχθόνες. This is a comment on Vergil's line: haec nemora indigenae Fauni Nymphaeque tenebant / gensque virum truncis et duro robore nata.

[312] Walbank, "Nationality as a factor in Roman history," 68.

descent from Venus, and Roman historians were very interested in the origins of other peoples. Some they considered inferior and others superior, and this will be our subject here.

The first author to discuss the origins of the British was Julius Caesar, who reports that the peoples of the interior of Britain were indigenous according to their own traditions, whereas those of the coastal areas immigrated from Gallia Belgica.[313] So, there were claims, at some stage, that part of the British were autochthonous. Tacitus does not mention this local tradition, either because he had not read it in Caesar's work, or because he did not consider it worth mentioning. Interesting references to pure lineage may be found again in the work of Diodorus Siculus (first century B.C.) who, apparently, was especially interested in the phenomenon. While writing under Roman rule he presumably writes from a Graeco-Hellenistic perspective. He observes that "with respect to the antiquity of the human race, not only do Greeks put forth their claims but many of the barbarians as well, all holding that it is they who are autochthonous."[314] It is not entirely clear what he means, since most of the Greeks did not claim autochthony; they believed they were descendants of the migrant Ionians, Aeolians, and Dorians.

However this may be, Diodorus clearly recognized a trend among both Greeks and non-Greeks to enhance one's dignity by claiming autochthony. He goes on to mention a few of those believed to be autochthonous: the single largest entity was all of India which is said to be like Athens: all Indian peoples and tribes are autochthonous and the population was not mixed with migrants, individuals, or settlements, nor had any Indian ever formed a settlement elsewhere.[315] His third book starts with his impression of the Ethiopians—descriptions of which we encountered in earlier authors above. As far as I know, after Herodotus (4.197) Diodorus is the only source that actually describes them as indigenous (*autochthones*), even though he says the fact is generally conceded (3.2.1). He then goes on to say that those living in the far south were also "the first to be generated by earth," which in his opinion is clear to everybody.[316] This then leads on to an idealized description of the Ethiopians which follows Homer.[317] The combination of indigenous extraction and generation by the earth itself is reminiscent of the Theban *Spartoi*, sown by Kadmos, already mentioned. Among the Athenians, too, there was an idea that they were both autoch-

---

[313] *BG* 5.12.1: Britanniae pars interior ab eis incolitur, quos natos in insula ipsi memoria proditum dicunt, maritima pars ab eis, qui praedae ac belli inferendi causa ex Belgio transierunt . . . See also above, in the section on the impact of the environment.

[314] Diodorus 1.9.3: περὶ δὲ τῆς τοῦ γένους ἀρχαιότητος οὐ μόνον ἀμφισβητοῦσιν Ἕλληνες, ἀλλὰ καὶ πολλοὶ τῶν βαρβάρων, ἑαυτοὺς αὐτόχθονας λέγοντες . . .

[315] Diodorus 2.38.1 Τὴν δ' ὅλην Ἰνδικὴν οὖσαν ὑπερμεγέθη λέγεται κατοικεῖν ἔθνη πολλὰ καὶ παντοδαπά, καὶ τούτων μηδὲν ἔχειν τὴν ἐξ ἀρχῆς γένεσιν ἔπηλυν, ἀλλὰ πάντα δοκεῖν ὑπάρχειν αὐτόχθονα, πρὸς δὲ τούτοις μήτε ξενικὴν ἀποικίαν προσδέχεσθαι πώποτε μήτ' εἰς ἀλλοεθνεῖς ἀπεσταλκέναι.

[316] Diodorus 3.2.1: ὅτι δὲ τοὺς ὑπὸ τὴν μεσημβρίαν οἰκοῦντας πιθανόν ἐστι πρώτους ὑπὸ τῆς γῆς ἐζωογονῆσθαι, προφανὲς ὑπάρχειν ἅπασι·

[317] J. Romm, *The Edges of the Earth*, 49–53.

thonous and had a special tie with the land. The Indians and Ethiopians presumably are selected because of their remoteness. Diodorus has other remarkable ideas.

About the presumed origin of the Britons, another ultimate people, he says, like Caesar, that they are indigenous and that they maintain their ancient way of life in their customs.[318] They use chariots, for instance, in their wars, even as tradition tells us the old Greek heroes did in the Trojan War. Here we see that Diodorus assumes that one can deduce origins from the level of culture of a society. If people are old-fashioned or legendary or live in very distant regions and are therefore primitive, they must be autochthonous, or so he seems to suggest. This is not a view encountered in other authors in a similar form. Diodorus mentions several other peoples, mostly legendary, whom he believes to be indigenous.[319] Ammianus, citing anonymous authors, says that "those who were first seen in Gaul were indigenous, named Celts after a beloved king."[320]

As we saw previously, Livy attributed to Cn. Manlius, addressing his troops in 189 B.C., the unambiguous statement: "These are now degenerate, of mixed stock and really Gallogrecians" (38.17.9–10). It is apparently obvious to Livy's readers that Gauls mixed with Greeks must be degenerate. Yet, unlike the Athenians, the Romans did not cultivate a myth that they were of pure lineage themselves. They were immigrants and according to their own early traditions mixed with other groups after they arrived in Italy. Even so, the view that pure lineage is better than mixed ancestry occurs frequently in Latin literature. In ancient Greek literature, seafaring had long been associated with trade, commerce, social evolution, and consequent moral decline. The Golden Age was traditionally held to be ignorant of navigation, for seafaring was dangerous.[321] This topic is also discussed in chapter 3. Here we are concerned with a pronouncement by Seneca on the benefits and harmful effects of the wind: "How about the fact that it allows trade between all peoples and has mixed peoples living far apart? It would be a great kindness of nature, if human madness did not use it to harm itself."[322] Seneca, however, has no illusions about the existence of any autochthonous people. In a lengthy discourse about the migrations of humanity in another work he writes realistically: "The causes which impel people to leave their homes are various; what is in any case beyond doubt, that is that there exists no people which has remained in its place of origin. Man-

---

[318] Diodorus 5.21.5: κατοικεῖν δέ φασι τὴν Πρεττανικὴν αὐτόχθονα γένη καὶ τὸν παλαιὸν βίον ταῖς ἀγωγαῖς διατηροῦντα.

[319] The Sicani on Sicily are indigenous (5.2.4; 5.6.1); the original Samothracians (5.47); the Rhodians (5.56); the Eteocretans (5.64); the Ichthyophagi (3.20.2); the Panchaians (the inhabitants of a legendary island in the Indian Ocean: 5.42.4); see also 5.56.4.1.

[320] Ammianus 15.9.3: Aborigines primos in his regionibus quidam visos esse firmarunt, Celtas nomine regis amabilis. . . . In the previous paragraph, 15.9.2, Ammianus claims to be using Timagenes of Alexandria as the best author on Gaul.

[321] Hesiod, *Works and Days,* 236f. cf. M. L. West, *Hesiod, Works and Days* (Oxford, 1978), 216. See also Romm, *The Edges of the Earth,* 74f.

[322] Seneca, *QN* 5.18.4: Quid quod omnibus inter se populis commercium dedit et gentes dissipatas locis miscuit? Ingens naturae beneficium, si illud in iniuriam suam non vertat hominum furor!

kind moves constantly. Each day there is a change in this big world: new cities are founded, new nations are created, while older ones disappear or are absorbed by peoples that are more powerful."[323] The two pronouncements are not mutually contradictory. Seneca recognizes the reality of migrations and movement, but finds it regrettable.

Not all Roman authors are so lucid. The classic passage regarding pure lineage—and the one with greater impact on later discussions than any other ever made, is that by Tacitus on the Germans: "The Germans themselves I would regard as indigenous, and not mixed at all with other peoples through immigration or intercourse."[324] This is taken up again in chapter 4: "For my own part, I accept the view of those who think that the peoples of Germany have never contaminated themselves by intermarriage with foreign nations, and that they appear as distinct, of pure blood, like none but themselves. Hence, too, are the same physical peculiarities throughout so vast a population. All have fierce blue eyes, red hair, and huge frames, fit only for a sudden exertion. They are less able to bear laborious work. Heat and thirst they cannot in the least endure; to cold and hunger their climate and their soil inure them."[325] These are the passages that drew more attention than any other in the work[326] and which are responsible for Momigliano's suggestion that Tacitus's *Germania,* together with the Iliad, should be given high priority among the hundred most dangerous books ever written.[327] To start with matters that are of lesser relevance to the

---

[323] Seneca, *ad Helviam de Consolatione* (*Dial.* 12 (11)) 7.5: Alios alia causa excivit domibus suis: illud utique manifestum est, nihil eodem loco mansisse, quo genitum est. Adsiduus generis humani discursus est; cotidie aliquid in tam magno orbe mutatur: nova urbium fundamenta iaciuntur, nova gentium nomina extinctis prioribus aut in accessionem validioris conversis oriuntur. Cf. 7.10: Vix denique invenies ullam terram, quam etiamnunc indigenae colant; permixta omnia et insiticia sunt.

[324] Tac., *Germania* 1: Ipsos Germanos indigenas credidierim minimeque aliarum gentium adventibus et hospitiis mixtos . . .

[325] Ipse eorum opinionibus accedo qui Germaniae populos nullis aliarum nationum conubiis infectos propriam et sinceram et tantum sui similem gentem extitisse abitrantur. etc. R. Much, *Die Germania des Tacitus* (erste Auflage, 1937; dritte Auflage, ed. by H. Jankuhn and W. Lange, Heidelberg, 1967), 105–107, provides extensive references to prove the superiority of the Germans over the Gauls; Cf. Poliakov, *The Aryan Myth*, 80.

[326] Except perhaps *Germ.* 33.2, see below, chapter 11.

[327] A. Momigliano, "Some Observations on Causes of War in Ancient Historiography," *Proceedings of the Second International Congress of Classical Studies,* I (Copenhagen, 1958), 199. The literature on the *Germania* is vast. For the text: A. A. Lund, *Germania: Interpretiert, herausgegeben, übertragen, kommentiert* (Heidelberg, 1988); H. Jankuhn and D. Timpe, *Beiträge zum Verständnis der Germania des Tacitus,* Teil I: *Bericht über die Kolloquien der Kommission für die Altertumskunde Nord- und Mitteleuropas im Jahr 1986* (Göttingen, 1989); G. Neumann and H. Seemann (eds.), *Beiträge . . .* Teil II . . . Kolloquien . . . im Jahre 1986 und 1987 (Göttingen, 1992). For the impact of the *Germania* in various periods: F. L. Borchardt, *German Antiquity in Renaissance Myth* (Baltimore, 1971); Kenneth C. Schellhase, *Tacitus in Renaissance Political Thought* (Chicago, 1976), esp. 32–47; Jacques Ridé, *L'image du Germain dans la pensée et la litterature allemandes de la redécouverte de Tacite à la fin du xvième siècle.* 3 vols., 1274 pp. (Lille and Paris, 1977), esp. 140–164; for the impact of Tacitus's statement on the origins of the *Germani*: 1058–1065; D. Kelley, "*Tacitus Noster*: The *Germania* in the Renaissance and Reformation," in T. J. Luce and A. J. Woodman, *Tacitus and the Tacitean Tradition* (Princeton, 1993), 152–167;

present discussion: Tacitus's description of the Germans does not follow the by now familiar categories encountered in those texts which present the environmental view of ethnography. Tacitus does not describe the Germans as the opposite of another people, nor does he repeat the familiar contrast between intelligent but soft, and fierce but stupid people. He gives a description of the presumed physical and mental characteristics of the Germans. They lack stamina and are fit only for spurts of exertion. Tacitus also says that they cannot stand heat, but can endure cold and hunger because their climate and soil inure them against these—a familiar line of thought taken from the environmental approach. This is the only characteristic we have encountered previously, in Vitruvius, who also says that northern people cannot stand heat. However, this is only one of the contrasting qualities which Tacitus does not take any further.[328] We may conclude that we are faced here with a different ethnographic tradition and this will be discussed below. The present passage, however, is especially significant because of its insistence on the pure lineage of the Germans. The question of what was Tacitus's source for this statement is less important for us than the fact that this view circulated among the Romans. Traditionally Posidonius has been made responsible, but as is so often the case, this claim is not based on any concrete information.[329]

The only vaguely comparable statement is found in Plutarch, *C. Marius* 11.3,

---

Ronald Mellor (ed.), *Tacitus: The Classical Heritage* (New York, 1995), xxii–xxiv; for the *Germania* as misused and misinterpreted in the third Reich: Allan A. Lund, *Gemanenideologie im Nazionalsozialismus: Zur Rezeption der 'Germania' des Tacitus im "Dritten Reich"* (Heidelberg, 1995); for the impact of the *Germania* in Germany see also Simon Schama, *Landscape and Memory* (New York, 1995), 75–134. On the *Germania* see further D. Timpe, *Romano-Germanica: Gesammelte Studien zur Germania des Tacitus* (Stuttgart and Leipzig, 1995). Recent work on the *Germania* as ethnography: A. A. Lund, "Zum Germanenbegriff bei Tacitus," in H. Beck (ed.), *Germanenprobleme in heutiger Sicht* (Berlin, 1986), 53–87; *Zum Germanenbild der Römer. Eine Einführung in die antike Ethnographie* (Heidelberg, 1990); C. Trzaska-Richter, *Furor Teutonicus. Das römische Germanenbild . . . Bochumer Altertumswissenschaftliches Colloquium 8* (Trier, 1991). For a brief and convenient text, translation into English and commentary: Herbert W. Benario, *Tacitus Germany / Germania* (Warminster, 1999); a new translation and commentary: J. B. Rives, *Tacitus: Germania* (Oxford, 1999). In spite of these two recent works, the proportion of German as compared with English works about this text is remarkable. A review of Benario in an English journal curiously describes the *Germania* as a "little-read text." Some people never learn: Rudolf Much, *Die Germania des Tacitus* (1937) represents a classic national-socialist view of the text. The third edition, revised by Wolfgang Lange and Herbert Jankuhn (Heidelberg, 1967), has been updated, but not changed where it counts, and the racist interpretation is still in place without warning or comment. Cf. Lund, *Germanenideologie*, 46f.

[328] This is repeated in part by Vegetius, cited above.

[329] E. Norden, *Die germanische Urgeschichte* (Leipzig, 4th ed. 1959), 69. For Posidonius on the *Germani* see now G. Dobesch, *Das europäische 'Barbaricum' und die Zone der Mediterrankultur: Ihre historische Wechselwirkung und das Geschichtsbild des Poseidonios* (Vienna, 1995). K. Trüdinger, *Studien zur Geschichte der griechisch-römischen Ethnographie*, 146–170, represents encomium rather than analysis of the *Germania*. Trüdinger argues that Tacitus may depend on Posidonius for details, but is superior in overall vision. He rejects a suggestion made by Wissowa (writing before Norden) that *topoi* may be traced in the description of "primitive" peoples (146, n.1).

where we read that the origin of the Teutones and Cimbri was unknown, because they had no intercourse with others and had traveled a long way. This incidentally is a variant we have not yet encountered: a people which was of pure lineage, but not autochthonous. The idea that they had no intercourse with others places them in a familiar category of ancient ethnography: that of primitive nomads, unsociable and brutish, discussed below, in chapter 2. Plutarch does not say this of the Cimbri, but the association would have been quite obvious to any ancient reader. Strabo (7.2.3 [c. 294]) says they practice human sacrifice, which places them precisely in this category.[330] Presumably they were Germans from the far North, says Plutarch, for they were tall and had blue eyes.

This does not lead us very far: the alternative view was that they were a mixture of Gauls and Scythians from the far East (*C. Marius* 11.4) or a group of Cimmerians who had split off. It is interesting to observe that Strabo, often seen as relying on Posidonius, says that the Gauls and Germans were related and had intermarried and migrated back and forth.[331] The generation of scholars who developed techniques of source-criticism reconstructed a partly imaginary tradition of the transmission of such ideas and then argued that Tacitus was untrustworthy because his way of describing the Germans has much in common with older ethnographic descriptions.[332] Today we find the traditional belief in Tacitus simplistic and subsequent disappointment in his writings in this respect naïve as well. It is, however, profitable to study the commonplaces found in such descriptions because they can tell us something about the way the Greeks and Romans in general saw foreigners.[333]

Tacitus in fact introduced the same dual claim for the Germans which the

---

[330] Human sacrifice and its significance to the Romans are mentioned frequently in this work; see especially below, Part 2.

[331] Strabo 4.4.2 (c.196), discussed also below, in the section on Celts, p. 418.

[332] J.G.C. Anderson, *Cornelii Taciti, de origine et situ Germanorum* (Oxford, 1938), introduction p. xxviii: "In the last two decades, however, many scholars have had their faith in the trustworthiness of the narrative shaken anew by the critical studies of Wissowa, Norden and others. . . . These have shown that the Germania is almost the last of a long series of descriptions of ancient peoples and that ethnography, like other kinds of literary composition, had not only created a style of its own and established a universally recognised form of treating the subject, but had also gone through a typological development." Anderson then explains the patterns of commonplaces which they found in these descriptions. He attempts to argue that criticism has gone too far. "Identical customs are often found among primitive or half-civilized peoples." It is important to recognize the essence of this disagreement for what it is. Wissowa, Norden and others understood traditions of stereotype and prejudice in terms of literary genre. Anderson rejects this and claims that the stereotypes were actually true descriptions of what he calls "primitive and half-civilized peoples." See recently K. Bringmann, "Topoi in der taciteischen Germania," in Jankuhn and Timpe, *Beiträge zum Vertändnis der Germania* I (1989), 59–78.

[333] J.-E. Bernard, "Philosophie politique et antijudaïsme chez Cicéron," *SCI* 19 (2000), 113–131, esp. 126 (on commonplaces in judicial rhetoric): "En terms techniques, les lieux communs ne sont pas autre chose que des idées générales, communes aux cas particuliers, auxquels on rapporte toutes les sources des raisonnements: ils relèvent un fond bien réel de la pensée philosophique de l'orateur." He refers to *De Oratore* 2.29.

Athenians had made for themselves: they are of pure blood, not having inter-married with others, and they have inhabited their native land forever (*ipsos Germanos indigenas credidierim*), without admitting immigrants (*minimeque aliarum gentium adventibus et hospitiis mixtos*).[334] The language leaves us in no doubt that Tacitus considered this a marked distinction: the Germans are not contaminated (*infectos*) by intermarriage and they are therefore a people that is distinct or peculiar (*propriam*) and pure or uncorrupted (*sinceram*), like none but themselves (*tantum sui similem*).[335] The latter phrase is reminiscent of the first reference we met to a people of pure lineage, probably the Egyptians, mentioned in a fragment of Parmenides cited above. It was seen again in the treatise on *Airs,* where it refers to both Egyptians and Scythians. It should not concern us here from which lost text Tacitus borrowed these claims for the Germans,[336] but it is noteworthy that Strabo does not believe in a pure German lineage.[337] It is clear, however, that the first Roman to apply the concept to the Germans transferred it from the Scythians, the barbarians farthest north from the Greeks, to the most northerly people known to the Romans, the Germans. Another point to be noted is that Tacitus in the *Germania* does not state that the German tribes were of pure lineage through a conscious choice or as a deliber-ate policy. They were uncontaminated, he says, because their land was inac-cessible and, no less important, "who would leave Asia, Africa or Italy and move to Germany with its rough terrain, bitter climate, sombre to see, unless it were one's fatherland?"[338] As in the case of the Athenians, the claim of pure lineage is obviously very important, for Tacitus returns to it in the *Histories*.

In the *Histories* the claim of pure lineage occurs in a speech attributed to the Tencteri, the people living across the Rhine opposite Colonia Agrippinensis. Envoys from the Tencteri exhort the Agrippinenses, formerly the Ubii, to join the revolt of Civilis in A.D. 69. The speech ends as follows: "Resume the cus-toms and the lifestyle of your fathers, reject the pleasures, through which, more

[334] The third edition of Much, *Die Germania des Tacitus* (revised by Wolfgang Lange and Herbert Jankuhn, Heidelberg, 1967), 45–47, argues at length that archaeological research in Northern Ger-many, Denmark, and Southern Scandinavia has shown continuity of settlement by Germans from the Neolithic period till the Roman period: "So wird man sagen dürfen, dass die Bewohner dieses Gebietes, die nach Ausweis der historischen Zeugnisse und der sprachlichen Reste in Stammes— bzw. Personennamen und in Runendenkmälern . . . Germanen waren, sich in ungebrochener Ent-wicklung bis zu den grossen Vermischungsvorgängen am Ende der Steinzeit zurückvervolgen las-sen" (46).

[335] Here Much and the editors of his third edition (1967), 94–97, disagree with Tacitus for, as they say, we know that the physical characteristics of the Germans were essentially the same for all of the Indogermans, not only the color of their skin, eyes, and hair, but also the form of their skull and face. Thus it is not true to say, as does Tacitus, that the Germans resemble only themselves. These scholars mean to say (in 1967) that all Indogermans resemble only themselves.

[336] For speculations: Anderson, *Tacitus Germania*, 54; E. Norden, *Die germanische Urgeschichte in Tacitus' Germania* (Stuttgart, repr. 1959), 54; 67ff.

[337] 4.4.2 (c. 196), discussed below, in the section on Gauls.

[338] Tac. *Germania* 2.1: quis porro . . . Asia aut Africa aut Italia relicta Germaniam peteret, infor-mem terris, asperam caelo, tristem cultu aspectuque nisi patria sit?

than through arms, the Romans dominate their subjects. A pure and uncontaminated people, forgetting your slavery, you will be equals, or even rule over others."[339] As usual, this is a rhetorical exercise by an historian who attributes to non-Roman leaders the sort of speech that a Roman reader would find convincing.

Contrary to Tacitus's pronouncements about the autochthony and pure lineage of the Germans in the *Germania* discussed above, this speech implies that there were German tribes who themselves cherished ideas of this sort. The Ubii were contaminated and the Tencteri attempted to persuade them to reverse the process. It would of course be interesting to know—but this is a futile desire—whether this speech reflects actual values espoused by the Germans at the time. However, the essence of these words for us lies in the views of Tacitus on foreign peoples, their identity and their attitudes towards Rome. Tacitus expresses his views on the mechanism of Romanization: "the pleasures through which, more than through arms, the Romans dominate their subjects" are the amenities of urban culture. The passage is cited here because it calls upon the Agrippinenses to revert to being a people *sincerus et integer et servitutis oblitus,* a pure and uncontaminated people, forgetting their servitude. In order to achieve this, the Agrippinenses are called upon to massacre all Romans in their territory and take upon themselves various other unappealing tasks. The answer contains one interesting piece of information. The Agrippinenses explain, according to Tacitus, that there are Romans who settled in the colony and married local people. So, clearly, the Ubii could no longer revert to being a pure and uncontaminated people, however much the Tencteri called upon them to do so. At least, that is what the Ubii are said to have thought. It is conceivable that the Tencteri had a solution in mind for the problem, but Tacitus does not imply this. However, Tacitus undoubtedly assumes that being of German descent is superior to being of Gallic origin and has no doubt that this was also felt by those peoples themselves, *Germ.* 28: "The Treveri and Nervii take ostentatious pride in claiming German descent as though they are removed from resemblance to the listless Gauls by the glory of this blood-relationship."[340]

Tacitus's scornful comment on the inhabitants of South-Western Germany, the *agri Decumates,* has been much discussed: "I should not count among the peoples of Germany—although they live across the Rhine and the Danube, those who cultivate the *agri Decumates:* all the wastrels of the Gauls, audacious from poverty, have occupied a land which was precariously held."[341] The

---

[339] Tac. *Hist.* 4.64.3: instituta cultumque patrium resumite, abruptis voluptatibus, quibus Romani plus adversus subiectos quam armis valent. sincerus et integer et servitutis oblitus populus aut ex aequo agetis aut aliis imperitabitis.

[340] Treveri et Nervii circa adfectationem Germanicae originis ultro ambitiosi sunt, tamquam per hanc gloriam sanguinis a similitudine et inertia Gallorum separentur. Much, *Die Germania des Tacitus,* 359–361, considers at extraordinary length the question of whether the *Treveri* and *Nervii* are of Germanic or Gallic origin without reaching a satisfactory solution, of course.

[341] *Germ.* 29.4: Non numeraverim inter Germaniae populos, quamquam trans Rhenum Danuvium-

implication is that *levissimi* and *inopia audaces* are the sort of riff-raff to be found only among displaced Gauls and not among *Germani*. In the last chapter of the *Germania,* Tacitus discusses the Peucini, Veneti and Fenni, wondering whether they should be assigned to the Germans or the Sarmatians, for their language is related to that of the Germans and they live like them in permanent settlements. They are all squalid and their leaders are indolent and through intermarriage they are now degenerating into something resembling the Sarmatae.[342] Thus we see again that Germans marrying non-Germans become something far less than Germans, even though several important components of being German are still listed: they are not nomads, but permanently settled,[343] they speak a German language, and they normally live in miserable squalor[344] under an indolent leadership. It is blood that counts more than anything else.

It is undoubtedly important for the history of racist thinking to observe which themes from Tacitus's *Germania* were taken up over the years. The Italian humanist Gian Antonio Campano appears to have been the first to impress on his German contemporaries the value of Tacitus's observations for their own ethnogenesis.[345] Machiavelli (1469–1527) in his *Discourses on the First Decad of Livy* (1.55) explains the integrity and piety of the Germans of his time partly by the fact that "they never had much intercourse with their corrupt neighbours, the Italians, French and Spanish, since they are rarely visited by them and seldom visit their neighbours themselves, but they live content with the food and clothing produced by their own country, thereby preventing all occasion of intercourse and with it the first step towards corruption."[346]

The early sixteenth-century humanists, notably Celtis, who first used Tacitus as a central source for German history, find in him an image of Germany—or *Germania Magna* (Gross Teutschland) as it is now sometimes called—and its manners in antiquity.[347] They repeat various commonplaces regarding the exter-

---

que consederint, eos qui Decumates agros exercent: levissimus quisque Gallorum et inopia audax dubiae possessionis solum occupavere. . . . Cf. Syme, *Tacitus*, 128; J.F.G. Hind, "Whatever happened to the Agri Decumates?" *Britannia* 15 (1984), 187–192.

[342] *Germ.* 46: Perucinorum Venethorumque et Fennorum nationes Germanis an Sarmatis adscribam dubito. quamquam Peucini . . . sermone cultu sede ac domiciliis ut Germani agunt. sordes omnium ac torpor procerum: conubiis mixtis nonnihil in Sarmatarum habitum foedantur.

[343] Strabo 7.1.3 (291) describes the Germans in different terms. He says they migrate easily and in fact live like Nomads.

[344] For the poverty of the Germans: cf. Strabo 7.1.3 (c. 291).

[345] G. A. Campano, *Oratio Ratisponensis* (1471) in *Opera Omnia*, fol. xciib, which I have not seen; see J. Ridé, *L'image du Germain*, 182–188; 1061–1064; for full references to the only edition, Venice 1502, Ridé, vol. 3.434; for Campano see pp.182–191. For Tacitus's impact in general: chapter X.iv.

[346] Niccolò Machiavelli, *Discorsi sopra la prima deca* 1.55 in N. Machiavelli, *Opere*, ed. M. Bonfantini (Milano, 1963), 204f.: "I che nasce da dua cose: l'una non avere avute conversazioni grandi con i vicini, perché né quelli sono iti a casa loro né essi sono iti a casa altrui, perché sono stati contenti di quelli beni, vivere di quelli cibi, vestire di quelle lane che dà il paese, d'onde è stata tota via la cagione d'ogni conversazione ed il principio di ogni corruttela."

[347] Conradus Celtis, *Germania generalis,* ed. F. Pindter (Leipzig, 1934); cf. Schellhase, *Tacitus in*

nal appearance of the German tribes: their "original rude simplicity," their loyalty, liberty, constancy, usually avoiding the criticisms found in Tacitus. The
idea that they were indigenous and linked with the land was considered important, but not all authors were much interested in Tacitus's claim that the Germans were of pure lineage.

It appears in modified form in the work of Sebastian Franck, who asserts that
the Germans before Christ's birth "were not pleased to allow any strangers to
live among them so that their land would not be polluted by foreign customs,"
nor did they migrate from elsewhere and they were not expelled by others to
Germany, for they had always lived there.[348] Franck thus makes freedom from
foreign influences into a conscious policy on the part of the early Germans, an
idea that is not present in Tacitus's *Germania* and only implied elsewhere in his
work, such as the address of the Tencteri to the Ubii, cited above. The concept
of autochthony occurs in Celtis's work, but there it is little more than a rephras-
ing of Tacitus's words: "Indigenous, no other race is more primordial. The
womb of Demogorgon spread open and scattered the race widely, where, under
the winds of the air, it was created, all together at the same moment."[349] This
theme became conceptually significant in a much more recent phase, as illustrated, for instance, by the praise of the arch-germanophile Houston Stewart
Chamberlain, who discusses the internal divisions of the old Germanic tribes
and then rambles: "But a foreigner had at once recognised the uniformity of the
various tribes, and instead of the indistinguishable babel of names . . . he had
created for the luxuriant offshoots of this strong race the uniform comprehen-
sive term 'Germanic,' and that because his eye had at the first glance discerned

---

Renaissance Political Thought, 32–47; Ridé, *L'image du Germain,* chapter IV, 193–259; Kelley,
"Tacitus Noster," 158–161. For Tacitus's impact in general: chapter X.iv. For the reception of the
Germania in twentieth-century Germany and in the Nazi period: A. A. Lund, *Germanenideologie
im Nationalsozialismus.*

[348] Sebastian Franck, *Germaniae Chronicon* or *Teütscher Nation, aller Teütscher Völcker, Herkommen, Namen, Händel, Thaten* etc. (1539): "liessen niemant frembds gern under jn wonen, damit
dz land mit fremden sitten nit verunreinigt würde." The text, which I have not seen, is cited by
Ridé, op. cit., 1085f.; for this author, see Ridé, pp. 819–841, bibliographical references: vol. 3.294,
n. 622. In another passage Franck almost approaches Thucydides' Pericles in his *epithapios logos*
(Thuc. 2.36.12) which he presumably had not seen: "die Teütschen [haben] vor vil andern Völcker
bevor das wir nit ein frembd herkommen volck, als ein unflat auss anderen Ländern aussgetriben,
herkommen, sondern von Tuiscone, Noe sun, in dem Land darinn wir seind, gefallen, gezeügt und
geporn, als dz der Teütschen Land auch der Teütschen ursprung ist" (cited by Ridé on p.1086).

[349] Celtis, *Germania generalis* 2.5–7: Indigena, haud alia ducens primordia gente, | Sed caelo
producta suo, Demogorgonis alvus | Protulerat patualas ubi cuncta creata sub auras. I cite the
translation by Schellhase, p. 39. See for this passage Borchardt, *German Antiquity in Renaissance
Myth,* 108. I cannot claim independent reading and depend here on what I have found in the
secondary literature. For instance, Ridé, *L'image du Germain,* p. 1077 and Kelly, p. 159 with n. 27,
refer to Albert Krantz, *Saxonia* (Cologne, 1520, *non vidi,* bibliographical references in Ridé, vol.
3.436), preface, who says that the Saxons are, like the other Germans: "in jhrem Lande geboren, ein
einheimisch und eingesessen Volck." This, again, follows Tacitus and makes them indigenous, but
does not stress, as Tacitus does, that they were of unmixed origin. Other sixteenth-century authors
who took up the idea, such as Heinrich Bebel and Andreas Althamer, are discussed by Ridé, pp.
1087–1094.

their common stock." Chamberlain duly cites Tacitus on their autochthony, and enthuses: "It is peculiar how much more clearly the stranger, who is not biased by details, sees the great connection of phenomena, than the man who is directly interested in them!"[350] This is a suitable conclusion to the discussion of the Germans and their pure lineage.

Below, in Part 2, chapter 9, we shall discuss indirect references to Athenian autochthony in Tacitus's work.[351]

In the ancient literature the evils of mixed stock continue to be a motif, both in the Greek East of the Empire and among those writing in Latin in the West. Dio Chrysostom, born in Prusa in Asia Minor (A.D. 40–50 till after 110) praises the citizens of Nicaea (Iznik) in Bithynia because "their city is inferior to none in the nobility of its lineage and the composition of its people, for it consists of the most distinguished descendants not of small bands of worthless immigrants from here and there, but of the first among the Hellenes and Macedonians. And what is most important, it had heroes and gods as founders."[352] Nicaea was founded by Alexander's general Antigonus and, after its subsequent destruction, refounded by Lysimachus. On one or both of these occasions, Macedonian settlers were established there. At a later stage, the city created truly Hellenic origins for itself and Dio alludes to these myths.[353]

Apparently the best and most pleasing compliment one could pay to a Hellenistic establishment in Asia Minor was to insist on the lineage of its ancestors: they were not a city of nondescript migrants but of Greeks and Macedonians of true blood. Once again, we see that such views were very common, but there were critics. Not surprisingly, one of them is Lucian of Samosata. Himself a Syrian (c. A.D. 120–after 180), he satirizes contemporary xenophobia and criticism of mixed origin in his "Assembly of the Gods":[354] "It is this peerless Dionysus, who is half human; in fact, on his mother's side he is not even Greek, but the grandson of a Syrophoenician[355] trader named Kad-

---

[350] Houston Stewart Chamberlain, *The Foundations of the Nineteenth Century* (English trans.), 2 vols. (London and New York, 1911), 1.496.

[351] See chapter 9, p. 397.

[352] Dio Chrysostom 39.1: . . . οὐδεμιᾶς ἡττωμένη τῶν ὁποίποτε ἐνδόξων γένους τε γενναιότητι καὶ πλήθους συνοικήσει, τῶν φανερωτάτων γενῶν οὐκ ἀλλαχόθεν ἄλλων συνελθόντων φαύλων καὶ ὀλίγων, ἀλλὰ Ἑλλήνων τε τῶν πρώτων καὶ Μακεδόνων· τὸ δὲ μέγιστον ἥρωάς τε καὶ θεοὺς οἰκιστὰς λαβοῦσα. Cf. C. P. Jones, *The Roman World of Dio Chrysostom* (Cambridge, MA, 1978), 89–91.

[353] Jones, op. cit., p. 89.

[354] For Lucian: Christopher Robin, *Lucian and his Influence in Europe* (London, 1980); Jennifer Hall, *Lucian's Satire* (New York, 1981); C. P. Jones, *Culture and Society in Lucian* (Cambridge, MA, 1986); R. Bracht Branham, *Unruly Eloquence: Lucian and the Comedy of Traditions* (Cambridge, MA, 1989). For more on Lucian, see below. For the *Assembly of the Gods*, see Jones, pp. 34–38; for the passage cited here see also Branham, p. 166.

[355] For the notion of a Syrophoenician: Mark 7.24; also Juvenal, *Satire* 8.159–161; see also Pliny, *NH* 7.201: Syrophoenicas ballistam et fundam (sc. invenisse dicunt). E. Courtney, *A Commentary on the Satires of Juvenal* (London, 1980), p. 408: Syrophoenicians are sometimes described in terms usually applied to Phoenicians, sometimes depicted in terms usually reserved for Syrians.

mos."[356] Kadmos is described as effeminate and womanish by nature (θῆλυς καὶ γυναικεῖος τὴν φύσιν). This is the usual stereotype of Syrians rather than Phoenicians. Criticism is also expressed of his followers, who include a Lydian and a Phrygian. Zeus himself was from Crete. There is criticism of mixed marriages of gods with mortals. Doubtful gods are Attis, Corybas, and Sabazius, Mithras "the Mede, with his caftan and his cap, who does not even speak Greek." Lucian is here satirizing common hostile attitudes to people with a mixed background. The examples of mixtures, however, do not include anything Roman, only mainland Greek and eastern elements. Lucian appears to be reacting to a social climate in Greece or among Greeks in Greece and Asia Minor, not to attitudes in Rome or Italy. Another author of this period, Apuleius (born c. 125 in Madaurus in Africa Proconsularis), is unambivalent and unapologetic in defense of his mixed origin:

> Concerning my fatherland, as you have shown on the basis of my own writings, it
> lies on the very border of Numidia and Gaetulia. I have in fact declared in my
> public declarations made in the presence of the honorable Lollianus Avitus, that I
> am half Numidian and half Gaetulian. However, I do not see what there is in this
> for me to be ashamed of, any more than there was for the Elder Cyrus, being of
> mixed origin, half Mede and half Persian. After all it is not where a man was born
> but his way of life that should be considered, nor in what region, but how he lives
> his life. . . . Have we not seen that in all periods and among all peoples different
> characters occur, while some appear more remarkable for their stupidity or their
> cleverness? The wise Anacharsis was born among the extremely foolish Scythians,
> among the intelligent Athenians, the silly Meletides. And yet I have not spoken out
> of shame for my country.[357]

Apuleius is saying several things in this passage. First, he denies the merit of pure descent. He himself is of mixed origin and says a great king like Cyrus was the same. Second, he rejects the idea that the location of one's birth or where one lives determines character or moral or other quality. Third, he ob-

---

Thus they were noted for their obsequiousness (Eunapius *Vit. Soph.* 16.2.2: καὶ ὃ πάντες οἱ Συρο-φοίνικες ἔχουσιν κατὰ τὴν κοινὴν ἔντευξιν ἡδὺ καὶ κεχαρισμένον,), a quality desirable in inn-keepers; they were also considered avaricious (Lucil. 497) and generally despised (Lucian, *Deor. Concil.* 4). More about Syrophoenicians in the secton on Syrians, Phoenicians, and Carthaginians, below.

[356] *Deor. Conc.* 7. Cf. Jones, *Culture and Society in Lucian*, 38, for the possible contemporary background.

[357] Apuleius, *Apologia* 24: De patria mea uero, quod eam sitam Numidiae et Gaetuliae in ipso confinio mei<s> scriptis ostendistis, quibus memet professus sum, cum Lolliano Auito c. v. prae-sente publice dissererem, Seminumidam et Semigaetulum, non uideo quid mihi sit in ea re puden-dum, haud minus quam Cyro maiori, quod genere mixto fuit Semimedus ac Semipersa. non enim ubi prognatus, sed ut moratus quisque sit spectandum, nec qua regione, sed qua ratione uitam uiuere inierit, considerandum est. . . . quando non in omnibus gentibus uaria ingenia prouenere, quanquam uideantur quaedam stultitia uel sollertia insigniores? apud socordissimos Scythas Anacharsis sa-piens natus est, apud Athenienses catos Meletides fatuus. nec hoc eo dixi, quo me patriae meae paeniteret, . . . see below, p. 343f.

jects to the idea that everybody should be judged by the current stereotypes attached to his people. People should be judged as individuals. Finally, he argues in the sequel, not cited here, that he has no reason to be ashamed of his people or his family. This, then, is an explicit denial of all the concepts discussed in this part of the book. It may not be surprising that there should be such a denial in an ancient text, but given that it does exist, it is surprising that it should be so rare.

It is less clear exactly what milieu the third-century senator from Asia Minor, Cassius Dio, represents when he says of the Emperor Caracalla: "Antoninus belonged to three peoples;[358] and he acquired none of their good characteristics and all of the bad qualities: the inconstancy, cowardice and impetuosity of Gaul, the harshness and fierceness of Africa, the cunning of Syria, where he originated through his mother."[359] This is far removed from Apuleius's rational approach. Perhaps these remarks should not be taken too literally. Even so, a few observations may be made. The first point to note is the fact that Caracalla's mixed origin left him with only negative characteristics, in Dio's eyes. Second, he is presented as being of Gallic origin even though he had no Gallic ancestors. He was born in Lyons, but did not grow up there, for he was raised in Rome. It is also questionable how far Lyons was Gallic in the late second century, when it was the capital of the Roman provinces of the Gauls.[360] Thus Dio implicitly attributes to Caracalla qualities or rather shortcomings, which combine inherited factors and an extreme form of environmentalism. Furthermore, it would appear that we cannot expect consistency in such matters, for Dio's extensive comments on the Emperor Claudius emphasize that emperor's cowardice without ever alluding to the fact that, like Caracalla, he too was born in Lyons.[361] It is remarkable that Dio should speak of Caracalla's Syrian background as he does, for Dio himself rose to very important posts under Severus Alexander who was himself of Syrian origin, although ashamed of it perhaps, if we trust the *Historia Augusta*.[362]

In the next section, on physiognomics, it will be seen that the second-century author Polemon and some of his fourth-century followers combined the myth of Greek pure origin with the environmental theory: those who are pure Greeks are also the most beautiful people in the world, living as they do in the middle

---

[358] It is hard to say whether Dio means "peoples" or "provinces" with ἔθνεσιν in this phrase.

[359] Dio 78 (77) 6.1a: ὅτι τρισὶν ἔθνεσιν ὁ ᾿Αντωνῖνος προσήκων ἦν, καὶ τῶν μὲν ἀγαθῶν αὐτῶν οὐδὲν τὸ παράπαν τὰ δὲ δὴ κακὰ πάντα συλλαβὼν ἐκτήσατο, τῆς μὲν Γαλατίας τὸ κοῦφον καὶ τὸ δειλὸν καὶ τὸ θρασύ, τῆς ᾿Αφρικῆς τὸ τραχὺ καὶ ἄγριον, τῆς Συρίας, ὅθεν πρὸς μητρὸς ἦν, τὸ πανοῦργον.

[360] P. Wuilleumier, *Lyons, métropole des Gaules* (Paris, 1953); A. Audin, *Lyons, miroir de Rome dans les Gaules* (Paris, 1965).

[361] Dio 60.2 indeed emphasizes Claudius's cowardice, but ascribes this to the circumstances of his youth, particularly the fact that he was surrounded by freedmen as a boy. As a result he had become a slave himself. For Claudius birth: Suetonius, *Claudius* 2.1; Seneca, *Apocolocyntosis* 6.1, where Claudius is represented as lying about his origin from Lyons, which is regarded as ridiculous. It really made him a Gaul (*Gallus germanus*, untranslatable).

[362] F. Millar, *A Study of Cassius Dio* (Oxford, 1964), 25–27.

between North and South. This is as obvious a proto-racist construct as one could expect to find in antiquity.

Finally, there is one myth of mixed origin, which it will be interesting to cite here because it became a genre with a good deal of influence well into the twentieth century. In his *bellum Iugurtinum* 17–18, Sallust inserts a brief geographical excursus about North Africa.

> In the beginning Africa was inhabited by the Gaetulians and Libyans, rude and uncivilized folk, who fed like beasts on the flesh of wild animals and the fruits of the earth. They were governed neither by institutions nor law, nor were they subject to anyone's rule. A restless, roving people, they had their abodes wherever night compelled a halt. After the death of Hercules in Spain, as the Africans believe, . . . of those who made up his army, the Medes, Persians and Armenians crossed into Africa . . . the Persians lived closer to the Ocean, intermarried (*secum miscuere*) with the Gaetulians . . . and because they often moved from place to place trying the soil, they called themselves Numidians (Nomads) . . . but the Medes and the Armenians had the Libyans as their nearest neighbours.

Thus, according to Sallust, the Medes were called Mauri by the Libyans. Persians became Numidians, who finally became masters of the greater part of North Africa. Later the Phoenicians founded cities on the coast.[363]

The historical construct offered by Sallust is familiar: the well-known and existing population of an area was preceded by "original" inhabitants who lived at a much lower level. These were overwhelmed by one or more invasions of forceful newcomers. Above, in note 139, I cited Ogilvie and Richmond regarding "the short, dark race of non-Aryan stock which was widely spread over the Mediterranean lands and beyond in the neolithic period." These aboriginal Mediterranean folk, swarthy little people, who were not Indo-Europeans, used to be a stock presence in modern books about the Mediterranean and the Near East in the period before the arrival of the Greeks. They are said to have worshipped a "Mother Goddess," usually assumed to have been imported from Asia Minor, and to have used place-names that contained the non-Greek elements of -νθ- and -σσ- (*Korinthos, Tylissos*).[364] The essence of all this is that in comparative linguistics, which reconstructs relationships between languages, ethnic origin, religion, and political culture are all treated as belonging to the same sphere, justifying generalizations.[365] The other point worth noting in

---

[363] For discussion of Sallust's possible sources (*not* Posidonius): Trüdinger, *Studien zur Geschichte der griechisch-römischen Ethnographie*, 127–129.

[364] They are still mentioned in relatively recent works such as the third edition of the *Cambridge Ancient History* vol. II, where geographical concepts (e.g., "Mediterranean"), ethnic identity, race, social class, religion, language, and the language of personal names are sometimes cheerfully mixed as if they were all one and the same thing: *CAH* II.1 (1973), pp. 419–423, by Margaret S. Drower, esp. 419: "Here, then, we have evidence of the presence among the Hurrians of a small ruling class of Indo-Aryans worshipping gods different from those of the Hurrian pantheon." See also p. 38f. (J.-R. Kupper); 230f. (O. R. Gurney); vol. II 2, 109f. (W. F. Albright).

[365] For another recent example: Claude Orrieux and Pauline Schmitt Pantel, *A History of Ancient*

Sallust's information is that he assigns a mixed eastern origin to all North African peoples. Apart from the inhabitants of the Phoenician cities on the coast, whose origin is obvious, all the others living in North Africa are said to be descendants of Medes and Persians. Sallust bases his account on a translation from the Punic books written by king Hiempsal, and claims to represent local traditions. Interestingly, Sallust does not emphasize here, as does Vergil, that the African neighbors of Carthage were formidable fighters.[366]

Thus we have seen that there is a long-standing tradition in Greek and Latin literature of idealizing the concepts of unmixed origin, pure lineage, and autochthony. This entails explicit statements that intermarriage between peoples produces descendants of inferior quality—physical, mental, and moral—while consistent marriage between men and women belonging to the same people will result in superior human beings. No rationale for these views is given, but they were strongly held all the same. Closely related is the idea, known particularly well from Athens, that autochthony produces better people, linked with their native soil. This link, valuable in itself, has the additional advantage that it is represented as a superior moral claim to possession of the land. These ideas were widespread in Rome, even though Roman legends do not make such claims for the early Romans. Athens gave citizenship only to children of two citizens. The Romans granted it liberally.

A belief in the superiority of unmixed origin is necessarily an historical fiction. (1) It reflects a conviction that the quality of an entire people is determined by lineage and origin only, and will be stable if protected against foreign contamination. (2) It regards some peoples as superior, others as inferior, solely on a random biological or genetic basis. (3) The assumption that mixed origin necessarily leads to degeneration and deterioration represents a form of xenophobia, or fear of ethnic contamination which again is based solely on biological prejudice. (4) The fiction of autochthony assumes a physical relationship between man and land which, by definition, turns an immigrant or descendant of immigrants into an inferior being and justifies keeping such people in an inferior status.

These ideas are clearly proto-racist. Moreover, these specific forms of proto-racism have been particularly influential in shaping modern racism. The idealization of pure blood, the condemnation of mixed marriages, and the myth of *Blut und Boden* all have their roots in Greco-Roman antiquity.

Greece (Oxford, 1999), 133: "The Persians were a people with an Indo-European language who originated in the Iranian province that still bears its name. . . . The common Indo-European origins of the Greeks and the Persians ('sisters of the same blood', according to Aeschylus) should not obscure the fact that, ever since Homer, the Hellenic civilization had distanced itself from the cosmic vision that continued to be exalted on Achaemenid monuments. . . . The best proof of the originality of the Persians was their choice of a Semitic language, Aramaic as their official language."

[366] Vergil, *Aen.* 1.338: sed fines Lybici, genus intractabile bello; 4.40: hinc Gaetulae urbes, genus insuperabile bello, et Numidae infreni cingunt . . . lateque furentes Barcaei.

STEREOTYPES IN PSEUDO(?)-SCIENCE AND ART:
PHYSIOGNOMICS AND THEOPHRASTUS'S "CHARACTERS"

Deine Seele ist genau so Schwarz wie dein Gesicht.
—Sarastro in Mozart's *Zauberflöte*

Sarastro is Zoroaster, who ruled the Temple of Wisdom, in Mozart's neoplatonic and masonic opera, written to celebrate beauty and wisdom. The two of them go together, just like their opposites. There is no doubt here that black is ugly. The ugly black servant is therefore as bad morally as he is ugly to look at and he himself agrees with this assessment.[367]

So far we have seen numerous texts which show how Greeks and Romans thought of others and themselves in proto-racist terms and stereotypes. It will be appropriate to conclude this chapter with a brief survey of two offshoots of stereotyping which became very popular in ancient literature and were also influential in later periods. If one assumes that climate and environment directly affect and stabilize bodily characteristics and that there is also a direct connection between these characteristics and mental qualities, then the next conceptual step could be that environment determines both external appearance and character. This assumption underlies the theory and practice of physiognomics, popular in antiquity and more recently. The aim of physiognomics as defined in a fourth-century treatise is "to examine and recognize the character of the personality from the character of the body."[368] Another definition is a little more explicit: ". . . to inquire into the character and dispositions of men by an inference drawn from their facial appearance and expression, and from the form and bearing of their whole body."[369] A modern definition: "Physiognomics is the discipline that seeks to detect from individuals' exterior features their character, disposition, or destiny."[370]

The ideas of physiognomics are attested in Mesopotamia,[371] but they gained considerable popularity through the influence of the Peripatetic and Stoic

---

[367] Monostatos: 'Und ich soll die Liebe meiden / weil ein Schwarzer hässlich ist? / Bin ich nicht von Fleisch und Blut? / . . . / Lieber guter Mond, vergebe,/ Eine Weisse nahm mich ein. / Weiss ist schön! Ich muss sie küssen;/

[368] *De Physiognomonia* ap. J. André (ed., trans., and comm.), *Traité de physiognomonie par un anonyme latin* (Paris, 1981), 2: <Profitetur> itaque ex qualitate corporis qualitatem se animi considerare atque perspicere. The term φυσιογνωμονία first occurs in Hippocrates, *De Morbis Popularibus* 2.5 and in the Pseudo-Aristotelian treatise *Physiognomonica*, 806a, where the following definition is given: ἡ μὲν οὖν φυσιογνωμονία ἐστί, καθάπερ καὶ τοὔνομα αὐτῆς λέγει, περὶ τὰ φυσικὰ παθήματα τῶν ἐν τῇ διανοίᾳ, καὶ τῶν ἐπικτήτων ὅσα παραγινόμενα μεθίστησι τῶν σημείων τῶν φυσιογνωμονουμένων.

[369] Aulus Gellius, *NA* 1.9.2 (trans. J. C. Rolfe, Loeb): uerbum significat mores naturasque hominum coniectatione quadam de oris et uultus ingenio deque totius corporis filo atque habitu sciscitari.

[370] Tamsyn S. Barton, *Power and Knowledge: Astrology, Physiognomics, and Medicine under the Roman Empire* (Ann Arbor, MI, 1994), 95.

[371] Barton, op. cit., 100f.

schools. As a science it was studied and described by medical men,[372] as an art it was considered important by the practitioners of rhetoric[373] and thence by those who wrote drama,[374] history, and biography.[375] It is usually described as "pseudoscience" but recently there appeared protestations at such a qualification.[376] We may leave it to historians of science to decide whether or not ancient physiognomics was a science from the ancient perspective, for in the present work we are concerned only with the uses of physiognomics for social purposes.

The philosopher Pythagoras (sixth century B.C.) was widely credited with inventing the discipline, but Galen claimed it went back to the father of medicine, Hippocrates.[377] However, the idea that there is a relationship between the features of a person and his character is present in Greek literature from its inception, although the systematic development only began in the fourth century B.C. In principle, physiognomics uses three tools, although the three are not always kept separate: (1) Comparisons with animals: physical features of human beings are compared with those of animals and inferences are made from the presumed nature of these animals for conclusions about the character of men and women. (2) Physical differences between peoples (ἔθνη). The outward appearance of different peoples is described, as well as the presumed mental and moral qualities of each of these peoples. Men who have these outward characteristics are assumed to have similar characters. (3) Grouping of individuals into types. Physical characteristics and facial expressions corresponding with these types are described in a more or less systematic manner.[378]

Before pursuing this further, we should note Elisabeth Evans' observations on the general popularity of physiognomic thinking in antiquity. Although it is

---

[372] Elisabeth C. Evans, *Physiognomics in the Ancient World* (Philadelphia, 1969), 19f.; Barton, *Power and Knowledge*, 97–9.

[373] Evans, *Physiognomics*, 39–46; Barton, *Power and Knowledge*, 128–131.

[374] Evans, op. cit., 28–39.

[375] Op. cit., 46–58.

[376] Barton, *Power and Knowledge* (1994), 12, 15–17. Barton's principle "is not to assume that the ancients must normally be thinking rationally in our terms but, rather, to find a rationale, to make sense of apparent nonsense" (15). This comes close to Saul Lieberman's well-known dictum: "Nonsense is nonsense, but the history of nonsense is scholarship." See, for a different approach: Maud W. Gleason, *Making Men: Sophists and Self-Presentation in Ancient Rome* (Princeton, 1995), 33: "The value of Polemo's treatise as a source for social prejudice lies precisely in the places where it fails as a science to provide an objective record of social conditions." See also p. 35: 'What purports to be an inductive science, built up from myriad specific observations, becomes a deductive science based on generalized impressions and preexisting prejudices that are confirmed by observed details—some of which can be freely discarded if they do not conform to overall impressions." For the problems in appreciating "scientific" method in "pre-scientific" society, see M. Beard, *JRS* 76 (1986), 40 and references in notes 42 and 43.

[377] For references: Evans, *Physiognomics*, 27f., notes 106 and 107. For passages in the Hippocratic corpus which deal with specific physiognomic signs: Evans, 20, n. 20. R. Foerster, *Scriptores physiognomonici graeci et latini*, 2 vols. (Leipzig, 1893) is still the most extensive collection of texts and references.

[378] This is a paraphrase of a classification in *Physiognomonica* 805a; cf. Anon., *De Physiognomonia* (André), 9, which considers the first method (comparisons with animals) the easiest and safest.

true that the formal treatises on the subject are relatively late and few in number, the fundamental ideas they embody were clearly influential and are found in many classical authors. "'Physiognomic consciousness' in descriptions of momentary physical appearance is common in many of the writers, and serves to illumine the effect of physiognomic thinking upon the art of characterization."[379]

Some of the fundamental ideas of physiognomics are found in Aristotle's work.[380] The first extant full treatise on the subject, the *Physiognomonica,* was once attributed to Aristotle but this is now generally thought to be a peripatetic text dating to the third century B.C.[381] It is not based on any general theory, but lists its observations with or without ad hoc explanations, some of them based on contemporary medical and physiological thinking.[382] Thus it is clear that physiognomics involved stereotypes and value judgments from the start. For instance, the treatise claims that birds with stiff wings are brave and those with soft ones are cowardly. The same, it continues, is true for men: "those living in the north are brave and stiff-haired, and those in the south are cowardly and have soft hair."[383] However, there are inconsistencies, for elsewhere in the same text we read: "Stiff hair on the head betokens cowardice."[384] Too dark a skin also marks a coward, and both characteristics are ascribed to Ethiopians.[385] They have stiff hair and are dark, and are therefore presumed to be cowards. The concepts here of an opposition between north and south, linked with skin color and cowardice, clearly derive from the environmental theory. Remarkable is the absence of any attempt at defining a logical connection: there is no reason why one should seek a relationship between stiff hair and bravery or cowardice.

Comparisons of human features and characteristics with those of animals are elaborated at length in the physiognomic treatises and should not be confused with the phenomenon discussed below, whereby specific human beings or peo-

---

[379] Evans, op. cit., 6.

[380] Aristotle, *Historia Animalium* 491b–492a, where the idea is already linked with the external characteristics of animals. *Analytica priora* 70b, extensively sets forth the theory. For further references: E. C. Evans, "Roman Descriptions of Personal Appearance in History and Biography," *HSCP* 46 (1935), 43–84, at 48, n. 1; *Physiognomics,* 7. Aristotle may have written a lost work about the subject mentioned perhaps by Galen, *Quod animi mores corporis temperamenta sequantur* 797: σύγγραμμα φυσιογνωμονικῶν θεωρημάτων,

[381] Foerster's edition also contains a Latin translation of this treatise by Bartholomaeus de Messana.

[382] Ps.-Aristot., *Physiogn.* 808b (trans. W. S. Hett, Loeb): Δοκεῖ δέ μοι ἡ ψυχὴ καὶ τὸ σῶμα συμπαθεῖν ἀλλήλοις· καὶ ἡ τῆς ψυχῆς ἕξις ἀλλοιουμένη συναλλοιοῖ τὴν τοῦ σώματος μορφήν, πάλιν τε ἡ τοῦ σώματος μορφὴ ἀλλοιουμένη συναλλοιοῖ τὴν τῆς ψυχῆς ἕξιν.

[383] *Physiogn.* 806b: οἱ μὲν γὰρ ὑπὸ ταῖς ἄρκτοις οἰκοῦντες ἀνδρεῖοί τέ εἰσι καὶ σκληρότριχες, οἱ δὲ πρὸς μεσημβρίαν δειλοί τε καὶ μαλακὸν τρίχωμα φέρουσιν. Cf. Anon., *De Physiognomonia* (André), 14.

[384] 812b: οἱ φριξὰς τὰς τρίχας ἔχοντες ἐπὶ τῆς κεφαλῆς δειλοί·

[385] The Egyptians also are marked as cowards because of their dark skin. As observed by Evans, *Physiognomics* 9, n. 28, these are the only two peoples singled out in the Pseudo-Aristotelian treatise in connection with an analogy as peoples rather than individuals. These assertions are repeated in Anon. *De Physiognomonia* (André), 79.

ples are compared with or described as animals in order to deny them human status, describing men, describing them as something less than human. The two traditions in fact do opposite things. Physiognomy and fables regard animals in terms of human beings. The presumed characteristics of certain animals are compared with those of men and women, and the animals are then described in anthropomorphic terms. In other words, animals are depicted as if they were human, but "no one would find it possible to say simply that a man was really like a beast; only that he resembled it to a certain extent."[386] The comparison of specific human types with animals is an attractive form of stereotyping, because all animals of a given sort are very much alike. The inference is that something similar is true of human beings. This is morally almost innocent, although psychologically undoubtedly a complex issue connected with totemism and heraldry. As an emotional process it is quite distinct from the habit of denying groups of human beings their humanity.[387] Animal comparisons in physiognomics are part of a long and venerable tradition that begins in Egyptian, Oriental, and Greek literatures, includes the fables, continues through the Middle Ages, and is later found in Balzac's *Comédie humaine*.[388] It is still with us in the novel forms of characters such as Winnie the Pooh, Mickey Mouse, and Tom and Jerry.

Ps. Aristot., *Physiogn.* 807a–b provides a remarkably detailed description of the presumed physical characteristics of brave and cowardly men. There are also descriptions of sensitive and insensitive men, those of an easy disposition, shameless men, orderly ones and men of high or, respectively, low spirits, and so on. This treatise was followed by others,[389] based on the same premises, and

---

[386] Ps.-Arist., *Physiogn.* 805b: πρῶτον μὲν γὰρ ὡς ἁπλῶς εἰπεῖν οὕτως ὅμοιον θηρίῳ ἄνθρωπον οὐδεὶς ἂν εὕροι, ἀλλὰ προσεοικότα μέν τι. A third variety, represented by the work of Semonides of Amorgos, is discussed below.

[387] For Roman attitudes towards animals: D. Goguey, "Le Romains et les animaux: regard sur les grands fauves, liens affectifs entre l'homme et l'animal," in *Homme et animal dans l'antiquité Romaine* (Centre de recherches A. Piganiol, Tours, 1995), 51–66.

[388] For Egyptian and Oriental antecedents to various Greek fables: M. L. West, "Near Eastern Material in Hellenistic and Roman Literature," *HSCP* 73 (1969), 113–134, esp. 122–125. P. 124: "In Egypt there had been since before 3000 BC a tradition of pictures, probably associated with stories, in which animals of all kinds were humorously represented as engaging in human activities." The first allusions to fable in Greek literature are Hesiodus, *Op.* 202–212 and Archilochus, fr.174 West. For Aesopic fables in Greek literature, see now Gert-Jan van Dijk, *AINOI, LOGOI, MYTHOI. Fables in Archaic, Classical, and Hellenistic Greek Literature, with a Study of the Theory and Terminology of the Genre* (Leiden, 1997), and Francisco Rodriguez Adrados, *History of the Graeco-Latin Fable*, 2 vols. (Leiden, 1999–2000); N. Holzberg, *Die antike Fabel: eine Einführung* (Darmstadt, 2001). John Henderson, *Telling Tales on Caesar. Roman Stories from Phaedrus* (Oxford, 2001), did not become available to me before this book went to press.

[389] M. Antonius Polemon (see above); Johanna Schmidt, *RE* 20.1 (1941), cols. 1064–1074, s.v. "Physiognomik" (outdated); note the articles by Evans: "Roman Descriptions of Personal Appearance in History and Biography," *HSCP* 46 (1935), 43–84, which is a revised Ph.D. thesis; "The Study of Physiognomy in the Second Century AD," *TAPA* 72 (1941), 96–108; "Physiognomics in the Roman Empire," *ClJ* 45 (1950), 277–282; "Galen, the Physician as Physiognomist," *TAPA* 76 (1945), 287–298; and see her monograph already cited above: *Physiognomics in the Ancient World* (1969); G. Dagron in *Poikilia. Études offertes à Jean-Pierre Vernant* (Paris, 1987); André, op. cit., introduction.

the concept remained popular in the Middle Ages and afterwards. Basically, physical and mental characteristics are always grouped into correlating types. This presumed discipline was very popular, both among medical authors, notably the highly influential Galen,[390] and among orators and historians. The reason for this lies in its presumption of scientific objectivity, which provided a rationalization and reinforcement of social prejudices. Galen, in fact, was the first to attempt a systematic rationalization of the presumed connections between environment, physical characteristics, and mental qualities, connections that previous authors had taken for granted. Thus he was the first to include in his argument an explicit connection between the environmental theory and physiognomics, even if earlier texts proceeded from the implicit links between the two concepts. We may add that the later texts do not pursue any further Galen's attempt to provide physiognomics with a systematic theory.

A significant strand in the physiognomical approach, closely linked with the theme of animals, mentioned above, is the opposition between perceived male and female characteristics.[391] As we have seen before, the idea of a people being effeminate occurs frequently and will be mentioned again below. It has also been noted that this represents a specific set of values where men who judge other men as weak or even impotent call them "effeminate." I am not aware of any reference to the character of women in this sort of typology, except perhaps the idea, discussed below, that Egyptian men and women exchange roles. In other words, it is not clear that authors who refer to an effeminate people had any thoughts about what the women of an effeminate people were like. The women serve only as object of negative comparison. This is also true for the later treatise on Physiognomics, where female characteristics are mentioned only as negative qualities ascribed to men. In recent history it was, and perhaps still is, not unusual to describe women with a particularly strong character as masculine. That seems to have been less common in antiquity. The Pseudo-Aristotelian treatise devotes an entire section to a division of the animal king-

---

[390] Particularly relevant is one of the works of Galen the Physician entitled Γαλήνου ὅτι τὰ τῆς ψυχῆς ἤθη ταῖς τοῦ σώματος κράσεσιν ἕπεται and in Latin: *Quod animi mores corporis temperamenta sequantur* On this text, see the article on Galen by Evans, cited in the previous note and Evans, *Physiognomics*, 24–26. While a good deal of attention is paid to physiognomics by Galen, Evans goes too far in calling it "a small handbook on physiognomy." A French translation has been published with notes by Vincent Barras et al., *Galien: L'âme et ses passions* (Paris, 1995), 75–116: "Les facultés de l'âme suivent les tempéraments du corps." As observed by Evans,*TAPA* 76 (1945), 291, Galen represents a significant effort to relate the temperaments of the body to the humors of the soul, unlike the professional physiognomists who do not ask serious questions about cause and effect, but rely on crude classification and comparison. Galen's treatise has been mentioned above for its adherence to the environmental theory. Chapter 8 contains direct quotations from the treatise on *Airs, Waters, Places.* Chapters 9 and 10 quote relevant passages from Plato's *Timaeus* and *Leges.* In this connection it is worth noting that Plato anticipates the basic tenets of physiognomics, cf. Evans, *Physiognomics*, 20–22. The connection between physiognomics and ancient medical science is central to the work of Barton, *Power and Knowledge.*

[391] Cf. M. Gleason, "The Semiotics of Gender: Physiognomy and Self-Fashioning in the Second Century C.E.," in *Before Sexuality: The Construction of Erotic Experience in the Ancient Greek World*, D. M. Halperin, J. J. Winkler, and F. I. Zeitlin (eds.), (Princeton, 1989), 389–416; *Making Men* (1995), chapter 3; Barton, op. cit. 115–117.

dom into two physical types, the male and the female, attributing positive qualities to the former and negative qualities to the latter.[392] Women are mentioned
because of their negative characteristics, which are the opposite of those of true
men: "But it seems to me that the female sex has a more evil disposition than
the male, is more forward and less courageous."[393] Then follows a description of
the female body intended to confirm this. "The males are in every respect opposite to this; their nature is as a class braver and more honest, that of the female
being more cowardly and less honest."[394] This is followed by a description of
the lion which "seems to have the most perfect share of the male type. . . . in
character he is generous and liberal, magnanimous and with a will to win; he is
gentle, just, and affectionate towards his associates."[395] In all this the lion is
assumed to have characteristics similar to the male of the human species, who
physically resembles the lion. The lion, of course, like the eagle, occupies a
special place in the symbolism of many cultures and periods. Less common: in
Greek and Roman physiognomics the panther, *reputed* to be brave, is more
female in appearance and its description ends with the words: "This is the shape
of the body, and its character is petty, thieving and, generally speaking, deceitful."[396] Many more examples are given where positive and negative mental and
moral characteristics are linked with physical features, which are then compared with similar physical features of animals reputed to have similar characters and with men and women. The positive qualities are always regarded as
male, the negative ones as female. Thus ancient texts often regard a man or
group of men as effeminate by definition, when they are reputedly cowardly.
Courage is regarded as one of the essential ingredients of masculinity, while
cowardice is by definition part of the female nature. This line of thinking resulted in the natural representation in Rome of conquered peoples as female, a
feature illustrated in figures 7 and 8. Male prejudice exists side by side with
other stereotypes, notably ethnic ones. The attitude of men towards women is
one category among many which regard certain groups of people—in this case,
half of humanity—in terms of fixed stereotypes. Physiognomics is one of the
tools developed to rationalize and classify such ideas. Individuals who look, for
instance, like Celts are also believed to have a character corresponding to current stereotypes about Celtic character. There is one remarkable point: mas-

---

[392] Ps.-Aristot., *Physiogn.* 809a–814a. Anon., *De Physiognomonia* 3–7 (André), introduction p.
18.

[393] Ps.-Arist., *Physiogn.* 809a–b (trans. W. S. Hett, Loeb): δοκεῖ δέ μοι καὶ κακουργότερα γίνεσθαι τὰ θήλεα τῶν ἀρρένων, καὶ προπετέστερά τε καὶ ἀναλκέστερα.

[394] Op. cit. 809b: τὰ δὲ ἄρρενα τοῦ τοις ἅπασιν ἐναντία, τὴν φύσιν ἀνδρειοτέραν καὶ δικαιο-
τέραν εἶναι γένει, τὴν δὲ τοῦ θήλεος δειλοτέραν καὶ ἀδικωτέραν.

[395] τούτων οὕτως ἐχόντων, φαίνεται τῶν ζῴων ἁπάντων λέων τελεώτατα μετειληφέναι τῆς τοῦ
ἄρρενος ἰδέας. . . . τὰ δὲ περὶ τὴν ψυχὴν δοτικὸν καὶ ἐλεύθερον, μεγαλόψυχον καὶ φιλόνικον,
καὶ πραῢ καὶ δίκαιον καὶ φιλόστοργον πρὸς ἃ ἂν ὁμιλήσῃ. Polemon 1.172.5–7 (Foerster). Cf.
Barton, *Power and Knowledge*, 126f.

[396] 810a: ἡ μὲν οὖν τοῦ σώματος ἰδέα τοιαύτη, τὰ δὲ περὶ τὴν ψυχὴν μικρὸν καὶ ἐπίκλοπον
καὶ ὅλως εἰπεῖν δολερόν. Polemon, 1.196.4–198.2 (Foerster). Cf. M. Detienne, *Dionysus Slain*
(Baltimore, 1979), trans. of *Dionysos mis à mort* (Paris, 1977); Barton, *Power and Knowledge* 127.

culine men are superior and effeminate men are inferior, but women themselves are not considered.

In Rome these ideas were also widely accepted, but they were taken even further towards the irrational than in Greece.[397] Forms of divination and related practices became popular, such as *metoposcopia*, which predicted the future of individuals by looking at their faces. Cicero insists on the importance of the face, and particularly the eyes, in expressing emotions: for him the eyes are the mirror of the soul.[398] Physiognomy was certainly popular by the time of Augustus.[399] Suetonius reports that Narcissus, Claudius's freedman, ordered a *metoposcopos* to examine the Emperor Claudius's son Britannicus and Vespasian's son Titus, who were being raised together. The expert correctly predicted what nobody would have expected at the time, that the latter, and not the former, would become emperor.[400]

There were sceptics: Pliny the Elder reports that physiognomists could predict the life span of people painted by the master painter Apelles (Pliny, *NH* 35.88). However, he also criticizes the practice and theory of physiognomics, for he considers the conclusions frivolous, arguing with Aristotle himself: "I am surprised that Aristotle not only believed that there are signs in the body itself predicting the length of life, but even more that he published this. Although I think that these indications are baseless and must not be divulged without hesitation, lest everybody anxiously search for these indications in himself, I will say a few words, because so great a man has considered them worthy of his teaching. . . . And he does not only observe these indications together <in every individual>, but each of them separately, frivolous things, in my view, but discussed everywhere."[401] He then criticizes another very serious author, Pompeius Trogus, for adhering to the theory (*NH* 11.273f.). Another writer who clearly did not believe in it is Petronius. In the *Satyricon*, a promiscuous lady's maid says: "I know nothing of fortune-telling, and I am not in the habit of studying the stars as the astrologers do, but I can tell what men are like by the

[397] Barton, op. cit., chapter 2, 95–131.

[398] Cicero, *De Oratore* 3.221: Sed in ore sunt omnia, in eo autem ipso dominatus est omnis oculorum . . . Animi est enim omnis actio et imago animi voltus, indices oculi. *De Legibus* 26. Cf. Ps.-Arist., *Physiogn.* 63; Anon. *De Physiognomonia,* 20 (André): Nunc de oculis disputandum est, ubi summa omnis physiognomoniae constituta est. Then follow twenty-five paragraphs on the eyes. For Cicero's ideas in this connection: Evans, *Physiognomics*, 19, n.19.

[399] Pliny, *NH* 11.274–6, cites a brief passage from the Augustan author Pompeius Trogus about physiognomics.

[400] Suetonius, *Titus* 2.1. On physiognomics in Suetonius, see Evans, *HSCP* 46 (1935), 43–84; J. Couissin, "Suétone physiognomoniste dans les Vies des XII Césars," *Rev. Ét. Lat.* 31 (1953), 234–256, makes the same point and fails to cite any secondary literature, including the earlier article by Evans.

[401] 11.273: Miror equidem Aristotelem non modo credidisse praescita vitae esse aliqua in corporibus ipsis, verum etiam prodidisse. quae quamquam vana existimo nec sine cunctatione proferenda, ne in se quisque ea auguria anxie quaerat, attingam tamen, quia tantus vir in doctrinis non sprevit. . . . 274: nec universa haec, ut arbitror, sed singula observat, frivola, ut reor, et volgo tamen narrata. He refers here to Pompeius Trogus; see above, n. 399.

expressions on their faces, and I have only got to watch how a man walks to know what is on his mind."[402] This is a caustic description of physiognomics at its most vulgar and basic level, but the implication is also that it is a bogus science even when practiced with more pretence. Another critic of the theory and practice is the second-century author Artemidorus, who preferred his own problematic discipline of the interpretation of dreams.[403]

The existence of these critics, however, should not hide the fact that physiognomics was at the height of its popularity in the late first and second centuries A.D. One of the most influential orators of his time, most able and highly arrogant, a sophist and friend of the Emperor Hadrian, was Antonius Polemon of Laodicea (A.D. 88–145). He was an active practitioner of the art and the author of an influential treatise on the subject.[404] Polemon also used the technique effectively for encomium and invective. In his discussion of eyes he observes that "Eyes that are clear and shining are good, unless other signs corrupt them . . . Of this type surely are the eyes of the Emperor Hadrian, . . . gleaming, moist, keen, large full of light."[405] Polemon describes a Celt as follows: "when the eye is open and it shows a brilliance such as that of marble, and when the vision is sharp, this is a sign of shamelessness." He further describes the Celt as a typical eunuch and adds a full page of invective. Favorinus of Arles was a competitor and enemy of Polemon's and a later source explains that all this referred to Favorinus.[406] Since the eunuch is considered to be the ultimate in effeminacy,

---

[402] Petronius, *Satyricon* 126: vides me: nec auguria novi nec mathematicorum caelum curare soleo, ex vultibus tamen hominum mores colligo, et cum spatiantem vidi, quid cogitet scio.

[403] Artemidorus, *Oneirocriticus* 2.69 cf. E. C. Evans, *TAPA* 72 (1941), 105f.

[404] Philostratus, *VS* 1.25; *RE* 21.2 (1952), cols. 1320–1357 (W. Stegmann) and references in André (ed.), *Anonyme Latin, Traité de Physiognomonie*, 28–31. Cf. Gleason, *Making Men*, chapter 2, 21–54: "Portrait of Polemo"; for Polemon as a physiognomist, 28–54.

[405] Polemon, *De Physiognomonia* 1.148–9 (Foerster): "Sunt certe oculi Hadriani imperatoris huius generis nisi quod luminis pulcri pleni sunt atque charopi acres obtutu, cum inter homines visus non sit quisquam luminosiore praeditus oculo." The text is known through a translation into Arabic (given side by side with a Latin translation, the work of Georg Hoffmann, in Foerster's edition, Teubner 1893, cited here). A new edition and translation of Polemon Arabicus is being prepared by Robert Hoyland, who observes that Hoffmann's text and translation suffer from overactive editorial interference. The anonymous Latin treatise of the fourth century also made extensive use of Polemon's original: Anonymi, *De Physiognomonia* in vol. 2 of Foerster's edition and André, *Traité de physiognomonie*; for Hadrian, see 35. Furthermore there is a Greek paraphrase by Adamantius: Ἀδαμαντίου σοφιστοῦ φυσιογνωμονικά in Foerster, vol. 1. ci–ciii, text: pp. 297–426. This version does not mention the Emperor Hadrian. For the available information on Adamantius: Evans, *Physiognomics in the Ancient World*, 11f.; 15f. Barton, *Power and Knowledge*, 102–118; and see 96f.: "For Polemo . . . physiognomical theory served as a classificatory grid to contain his political and intellectual opponents." Polemo's remarkable arrogance is illustrated by the anecdote recorded by Philostratus, *Vit. soph.* 1.25.3; cf. Syme, *Tacitus* (1958), 505.

[406] Polemon, *De Physiognomonia* 1.160f.; Anonymi, *De Physiognomonia* 40 (André); Evans, op. cit., 12–14; Barton, op. cit. 117f. Favorinus is mentioned by name only in the Arabic translation and in the Anonymous treatise. Both Favorinus and Polemon were pupils of Dio Chrysostomus, who himself expresses a firm belief in physiognomics: *Or.* 4.87f. For the conflict between Favorinus and both Hadrian and Polemon: Philostratus, *Vitae Sophistarum* 489–91; Dio 69.3.4–4.1; SHA *Hadrianus* 15.10–13; Cf. Simon Swain, "Favorinus and Hadrian," *ZPE* 79 (1989), 150–158; *Helle-*

this is the ultimate insult. Moreover, Favorinus, says Polemon, was not a castrated eunuch, but born as one, which made him a monster. Thus the accusation of effeminacy and a comparison with an animal are again brought together. Favorinus is both not male and not a man; he does not belong to mankind. Favorinus gives his own perspective of what he is in his address to Corinth.[407] Favorinus describes himself as a Roman *eques*, who adapted himself to such an extent to Greek manners, dress, and language that he deserves a bronze statue in Corinth, or so he claims. The lesson for his fellow Celts is that no barbarian needs to despair of acquiring Greek culture.

Like Pliny before him and Ptolemy after him, Polemon roughly follows the traditional division of the world, whereby—following the environmental theory as usual—he is interested particularly in the connections between climate and physical characteristics and corresponding characters. Unlike other authors, Polemon does not attempt to explain the causation between exterior and interior. He is satisfied stating reputed facts. Like other Roman physiognomists before him, he also made predictions based on his art.[408] In the fourth century Ammianus mentions physiognomics with respect (15.8.16).

There is also a full treatise on the subject by an anonymous author of the late fourth century, based largely on Polemon.[409] The manner in which the observations of physiognomists are combined with ethnic stereotypes may be illustrated by the following passage: "They first take as model the characters of nations or provinces and compare individuals with those, saying: 'Such and such resembles an Egyptian. Now the Egyptians are cunning, docile, fickle, rash, and voluptuous. Such and such resembles a Celt,[410] or a German. Now the Celts are ignorant, courageous and fierce. Such and such resembles a Thracian. Now the Thracians are unfair, lazy and drunkards.'" The treatise follows this up in practice. "Curly hair indicates a man who is very deceitful, greedy, fearful, grasping: those are found among the Egyptians, who are fearful, and among the Syrians who are greedy . . . Blond, thick, and bleached hair indicates wild and savage customs: this is the type of the Germans."[411]

---

nism and Empire: Language, Classicism and Power in the Greek World, AD 50–250 (Oxford, 1996), 44f.; Gleason, *Making Men*, chapter 1: "Favorinus and His Statue"; Tim Whitmarsh, "Greece is the World, Exile and Identity in the Second Sophistic," in S. Goldhill (ed.), *Being Greek under Rome* (2001), 269–305, esp. 294–305.

[407] Dio Chrysostom, 37.25–7. The thirty-seventh oration in the corpus of Dio Chrysostom addressed to the Corinthians is usually attributed to Favorinus. It is certainly not the work of Dio Chrysostom. Cf. for the attribution to Favorinus: Gleason, *Making Men* (1995), 16f.

[408] Cf. Gleason, *Making Men*, 48–50.

[409] Anonymi *De Physiognomonia*, printed in vol. 2 of Foerster's collection of texts; see now André's ed.; for the date: André, 32f.

[410] *De Physiognomonia* (André) 9: Nam primo gentium vel provinciarum propositis moribus ad similitudinem singulos quosque homines referebant, ut dicerent: "Hic Aegyptio est similis, Aegyptii autem sunt callidi, dociles, leves, temerarii, in venerem proni; hic Celto, id est Germano, est similis, Celti autem sunt indociles, fortes, feri; hic Thraci est similis, Thraces autem sunt iniqui, pigri, temulenti." See also ibid. 14, where Egyptians are said to be cowards and Syrians greedy.

[411] *De Physiognomonia* (André) 14: Capilli crispi nimium subdolum, avarum, timidum, lucri cu-

Skin color is also a factor: Egyptians and Ethiopians, because of their dark skins, are said to be frivolous, peaceful, cowardly, and shrewd. Peoples with light skins, living in northern regions, are said to be courageous and bold and so forth.[412] This is an extreme form of stereotyping which obviously derives from the environmental theory, for that theory holds that hair type and skin color are determined by the action of the sun. A person who is thought to fit the physical stereotype of a certain nation is thus consequently assumed to have the (mostly negative) mental and moral characteristics attributed to that nation, even if he does not belong to it. Thus not only are all Egyptians believed to be cunning, fickle, and so on, but so are all people who have curly hair like the Egyptians. The principle here applied is present already in the Pseudo-Aristotelian treatise,[413] but in this text only one example is given: Egyptians and Ethiopians, being dark, are cowards (however, women, who have light skins, are also cowards).[414] The immediate model for all such observations appears to have been Polemon's treatise.[415] He briefly mentions an opposition west–east, but is more interested in the traditional opposition of north and south, where physical and character features are contrasted: those in the North are simple, hot-tempered, have little discretion and are dull; those in the South are clever, sagacious, light-minded liars who are greedy and thievish.[416]

In the Arabic translation of Polemon's work we encounter what is understandably missing in the anonymous Latin treatise, namely the old claim that the Greeks, being in the middle, are perfect, "in so far," that is, "as they are of pure Hellenic or Ionian descent. They are men sufficiently tall, broad-shouldered, straight, firm, their skin is white, they are fair . . . they have straight legs, shapely extremities, the size of their head is just right, their neck strong,

---

pidum hominem ostendunt. Referuntur autem tales ad gentem Aegyptiorum, qui sunt timidi, et ad Syrorum, qui sunt avari. . . . Capilli flavi et crassi et albidiores indociles et indomitos mores testantur; referuntur autem ad gentem Germanorum. Cf. Adamantius 2.37 (Foerster) where this sort of hair is, in the Greek tradition, assigned to Scyths and Celts ἡ δὲ ἄγαν ξανθὴ καὶ ὑπόλευκος, ὁποία Σκυθῶν καὶ Κελτῶν, ἀμαθίαν καὶ σκαιότητα καὶ ἀγριότητα, . . .

[412] *De Physiognomonia* (André), 79: Color niger levem, imbellem, timidum, versutum indicat: refertur ad eos qui in meridiana plaga habitant, ut sunt Aethiopes, Aegyptii et qui his iuncti sunt. Color albus subrubeus fortes et animosos indicat: refertur ad eos qui in septentrione commorantur. Cf. Adamantius, 2.33 (Foerster): Δῆλον δὲ ἀπὸ τῶν προλελεγμένων, ὡς ἡ μὲν μέλαινα χροιὰ δειλίαν καὶ πολυμηχανίαν μηνύει, ἡ δὲ λευκὴ καὶ ὑπόξανθος ἀλκὴν καὶ θυμὸν λέγει . . .

[413] Ps.-Aristot., *Physiogn.* 805a: διελόμενοι κατὰ τὰ ἔθνη, ὅσα διέφερε τὰς ὄψεις καὶ τὰ ἤθη, οἷον Αἰγύπτιοι καὶ Θρᾷκες καὶ Σκύθαι, ὁμοίως τὴν ἐκλογὴν τῶν σημείων ἐποιοῦντο.

[414] *Physiogn.* 812a: Οἱ ἄγαν μέλανες δειλοί· ἀναφέρεται ἐπὶ τοὺς Αἰγυπτίους, Αἰθίοπας. οἱ δὲ λευκοὶ ἄγαν δειλοί· ἀναφέρεται ἐπὶ τὰς γυναῖκας.

[415] For Polemon on this, see Adamantius. For the theory regarding physiognomics and national characteristics: Adamantius 2.1.2 (Foerster). The peoples mentioned are, not surprisingly, the Egyptians, Ethiopians, and Scythians.

[416] Adamantius 2.31 (Foerster): ὡς δὲ ἐπὶ τὸ πολὺ οἱ μὲν ὑπὸ τῇ ἄρκτῳ οἰκοῦντες εὐμήκεις εἰσί, ξανθοί, λευκοὶ τὰς κόμας, ἀπαλότριχες, γλαυκοί, σιμοί, παχυσκελεῖς, περιπληθεῖς σαρκὶ λαγαρᾷ, προγάστορες, ἀπλοῖ, θυμοειδεῖς, ὀλιγόβουλοι, θερμόβουλοι, δυσμαθεῖς, οἱ δὲ ὑπὸ τῇ μεσημβρίᾳ μελανότριχες, οὐλότριχες, μελανόφθαλμοι, λεπτοσκελεῖς, εὐμαθεῖς, πολυγνώμονες, κουφόνοοι, ψεῦσται, κερδαλέοι, ἐπίκλοπα νοήματα ἔχοντες. Cf. the Arabic translation of Polemon, translated into Latin, 1.238, 6–12, 14–20 (Foerster) and see Barton, *Power and Knowledge* (1994), 120f.

their hair dark blonde, soft and nicely thick, their face is square, their lips are thin, nose straight, their eyes melting, bright and vigorous, catching much light. The Hellenic people has the most beautiful eyes of all."[417] As noted above, ancient physiognomics attached particular importance to the beauty of the eyes. These prounouncements may most probably be attributed to Antonius Polemon, which is interesting in itself, for he originated from Laodicea ad Lycum in Asia Minor and can hardly have imagined his own ancestors to have been purebred Hellenes. However this may be, pure lineage is here introduced as a factor in a treatise on physiognomics and it is combined with the environmental theory. The ideal people are found in the middle between north and south, but they are ideal only if they are also pure-blooded Hellenes. The physical ideal represented by those pure Hellenes is interesting, in view of comparable ideas in recent history. The anonymous Latin treatise agrees that the extreme regions are bad and the best environment is the middle. However, this author cautiously goes on to explain that there *is* no true middle, thus avoiding any ethnic allusion. He includes no reference to pure Hellenes or pure blood of any kind.[418]

Allusions to physiognomics also occur in the works of Christian scholars, e.g. Clement of Alexandria[419] and Origen.[420] While classical Greek physiognomics was chiefly descriptive, Roman and later medieval studies in particular developed the predictive and astrological side, with treatises often digressing into prophetic folklore and magic. Physiognomics is treated by such scholars as Albertus Magnus, John Duns Scotus, and Thomas Aquinas. Physiognomics was highly developed as a science in Islam, where it both continued pre-Islamic traditions and based itself on translations of the Greek treatises on physiognomics, notably Ps.-Aristotle and Polemon.[421] The element of divination is even more pronounced in Islam than it is in late antiquity.

Shakespeare's famous "There's no art / To find the mind's construction in the

---

[417] See the Arabic translation of Polemon (Latin trans.): 1.242 (Foerster): Graecorum formas describam, cum formae eorum purae sunt neque ullum genus sibi permixtum est. Est enim populus terrae suae participes habens . . . Est autem purus Graecus moderatae inter longam et brevem, latam et angustam staturae et erectae *etc.* . . . Hic typus Graecus purus est. Adamantius 2.32 (Foerster): Εἰ δέ τισι τὸ Ἑλληνικὸν καὶ Ἰωνικὸν γένος ἐφυλάχθη καθαρῶς, οὗτοί εἰσιν αὐτάρκως μεγάλοι ἄνδρες, εὐρύτεροι, ὄρθιοι, εὐπαγεῖς, λευκότεροι τὴν χρόαν, ξανθοί, σαρκὸς κρᾶσιν ἔχοντες μετρίαν εὐπαγεστέραν, σκέλη ὀρθά, ἄκρα εὐφυῆ, κεφαλὴν μέσην τὸ μέγεθος, περιαγῆ, τράχηλον εὔρωστον, τρίχωμα ὑπόξανθον ἁπαλώτερον οὖλον πράως, πρόσωπον τετράγωνον, χείλη λεπτά, ῥῖνα ὀρθήν, ὀφθαλμοὺς ὑγροὺς χαροποὺς γοργοὺς φῶς πολὺ ἔχοντας ἐν ἑαυτοῖς· εὐοφθαλμότατον γὰρ πάντων <τῶν> ἐθνῶν ⁃ὸ Ἑλληνικόν. Cf. the comment by Gleason, *Making Men* (1995), 33: "Nonetheless, in Polemo's presentation, Greek scientific tradition wins out over Roman empirical realities to put the purebred vestiges of the Hellenic race firmly in place as the central reference point for the physiognomist's racial typology."

[418] *De Physiognomonia* (André), 116, p.132f.

[419] Clemens Alexandrinus, *Stromata* 1.21.135: οἱ φυσιογνωμονοῦντες ἰατροί τε καὶ μάντεις, οἱ δὲ καὶ ὑπὸ δαιμόνων κινηθέντες ἢ ὑδάτων καὶ θυμιαμάτων καὶ ἀέρος ποιοῦ ἐκταραχθέντες· Cf. E.C. Evans, *TAPA* 72 (1941), 108 with n.63.

[420] Origenes, *Contra Celsum* 1.33.40.

[421] *Encyclopaedia of Islam*, 2.916a s.v. firāsa and 5.234b s.v. kiyafā; for the texts: M. Steinschneider, *Die arabischen Übersetzungen aus dem Griechischen* (Leipzig, 1897). Cf. T. Fahd, *La divination arabe* (Leiden, 1966).

face" (*Macbeth* 4.12) did not deter various authors from claiming precisely that. In fact Shakespeare was a contemporary of one of the earliest of those, Gianbattista della Porta.[422] Later in the sixteenth century there was the highly influential artist Le Brun with his lecture on facial expression in painting and rhetoric (1668).[423] Georges-Louis Leclerc de Buffon (1707–1788) has been mentioned above for his ideas about race. He was a pioneer anthropologist with an interest in physiognomics.[424] However, he accepted only part of the theory. He held that man's entire dignity resides in his face, but rejected the attempts to deduce an intrinsic character from external features, nor did he accept the divinatory aspects of the theory. He accepts what he calls "pathognomy," the study of the fleeting passions, as visible on the face.

The Swiss pastor Johann Caspar Lavater (1741–1801) continued the study of physiognomics—using the old Greek name—which for him was an expression of the divine in human life.[425] Unlike Buffon he fully accepted the significance of the fixed facial parts of the face as indicators of character. From the classical physiognomists he accepted the interaction of mind and body and its interpretability seeking the influences of the spirit on the features, and vice versa. In simpler terms, he believed it is possible to know men by reading their faces. He was critical, however, of the ancient system of comparing humans with animals.[426] His reputation in this field was firmly established throughout Europe.[427] His theories clearly were a step towards racist theories, for he cherished prescriptive ideals about the ideal face and corresponding soul. Like the classical treatises he also attempted to classify national physiognomies. As in antiquity there was criticism, notably by the prolific physicist and satirical writer Lichtenberg, who ridiculed physiognomics.[428] Another author to be mentioned here is the zoolo-

[422] Melissa Percival, *The Appearance of Character: Physiognomy and Facial Expression in Eighteenth-Century France* (Leeds, 1999), 16–19. Della Porta's *De Humana Physiognomonia* (1586) antedates *Macbeth*.

[423] Jennifer Montagu, *The Expression of the Passions: The Origin and Influence of Charles Le Brun's 'Conférence sur l'expression générale et particulière'* (New Haven/ London, 1994); Percival, op. cit. chapter 2.

[424] Percival, 28–32.

[425] Ernst Staehelin (ed.), *Johann Caspar Lavaters ausgewählte Werke, 2. Band: Gott schuf den Menschen sich zum Bilde*, 1772–1779 (Zürich, 1943), p. 115: "'Gott schuf den Menschen, Sein Bild! Er schuf ihn zum Gleichniss Gottes'. . . . Siehe da, seinen Körper, die aufgerichtete, schöne erhabne Gestalt! Nur Hülle und Bild der Seele! Schleyer und Werkzeug der abgebildeten Gottheit! Wie spricht sie von diesem menschlichen Antlitz in tausend Sprachen herunter!"

[426] J. C. Lavater, *Over de Physiognomie* (Dutch translation, Amsterdam, 1781), vol. 2, pp. 1–5, argues that Aristotle is highly superficial and incorrect in his comparison of humans with animals.

[427] Besides the works cited in the previous notes, see Lavater, *Physiognomische Fragmente zur Beförderung der Menschenkenntnis und Menschenliebe: eine Auswahl mit 101 Abbildungen*, 4 vols. (1775–1778; repr. Zürich 1968–1969); *L'art de connaitre les hommes par la physiognomie*, many editions. I have seen the edition by J. P. Maygrier (Paris, 1820); *Essays on Physiognomy: For the Promotion of the Knowledge and the Love of Mankind* (London, 1789, numerous later editions); Cf. Percival, *The Appearance of Character*, chapter 8.

[428] Georg Christoph Lichtenberg, *Schriften zum Physiognomik-Streit: Über Physiognomik wider die Physiognomen : zur Beförderung der Menschenliebe und Menschenkenntniss. Fragment von*

gist Georges Cuvier (1769–1832). His special admiration for the Caucasian race has been mentioned above. He finds "it is distinguished by the beauty of the oval formed by its head." His significance lies in the development of a theory whereby there was a direct connection between the shape of the skull of various races and their intelligence and sensibility. As he himself states, the link between the proportions of the head and the quality of the mind is so well known that the rules of physiognomy, based on these, have become a common-place notion.[429] His comparisons had the aim of arriving at an index of "animality" of human races. Cuvier thus made a decisive contribution to the racist theories regarding skull shapes and measurements. Better known still is the work of Cesare Lombroso (1835–1909), who tried to discern a possible relationship between criminal psychopathology and physical or constitutional defects. His chief contention was that criminality was rooted in biology and passed down through heredity.[430] Although criminality is not a significant topic in ancient literature, this continues the ancient tradition of recognizing individual or collective moral and spiritual weaknesses through physiognomics. Lombroso's theories were widely influential in Europe for a time.[431] A related biological theory of his linked criminality with body types, asserting that crime was more common among muscular, heavy, and athletic persons than among tall, thin persons or soft, rounded individuals. It will be clear then that, in spite of the difference in style and variations in arguments, there is a direct tradition, at an intellectual level, leading from the fourth century B.C. to recent abuse of the theory.

To sum up this discussion of physiognomics we may conclude that the ancient approach rests on a triple postulate: first, it is assumed that the environment has a direct, continuous impact on physical features, as extensively discussed above. Then there is the assumption of a direct and stable connection between external, physical features and mental and moral qualities. In modern or early-modern versions of physiognomics the emphasis is more on heredity than on the influence of the environment, but the second postulate is as influential in modern times as it was in the classical literature. Third, it is assumed that this connection between external factors of one kind and physical and mental characteristics is stronger than any individual variations could be. This is the denial of individuality and variation, both between individuals and generations, so

---

Schwänzen (Steinbach, 1970). Lavater, *Over de Physiognomie* (1781), vol. 2, 276–342, attempts to defend himself against Lichtenberg's attack. Cf. Percival, *The Appearance of Character*, 13, 31, 159, 169. Another influential sceptic was Immanuel Kant; see R. Louden, *Kant's Impure Ethics* (2000), 77–79.

[429] G. Jahoda, *Images of Savages* (1999), 76–79, citing E. Geoffroy St. Hilaire and G. Cuvier, *Histoire naturelle des orang-outangs* (Paris, 1795; I have not seen this), 6f. for the remark about phyiognomics.

[430] Like Lavater, Lombroso was interested in life after death: *After Death—What?: Researches into Hypnotic and Spiritualistic Phenomena* (English translation, Wellingborough, 1988).

[431] His best known works are *L'uomo delinquente* (Torino, 1876) and *Le crime, causes et Remèdes* (Paris, 1899).

characteristic of racist thinking. In antiquity as in modern racist theory, these assumptions are not based on any empirical observation or objective reasoning. They are based on belief or, rather, conviction. There is no essential difference between the belief that cowards have soft hair and the modern phantasies regarding the connection between skull size and mental characteristics, be they superior or inferior.[432] There should therefore be no doubt that these assumptions and this approach is covered by the definition of proto-racism, adopted in the Introduction. Hence we see that the ideas represented by physiognomy are as easily incorporated in their theories by diviners as by racists. Furthermore, since such an approach is first encountered in highly influential Greek authors, their theories much influenced the later ones.

Theophrastus's Characters

The explicit detail found in the works on physiognomics is repeated at the individual level to some extent in the *Characters* of Theophrastus, Aristotle's successor as head of the Peripatos. These are thirty sketches of unpleasant personalities, indisputably literary masterpieces, which combine exemplary detail with sweeping stereotype. The notion of human types and the certainty that this sort of grouping exists in real life has had a tremendous impact through the ages, and this work of Theophrastus is followed by a long literary tradition which includes Jean de la Bruyère, Thomas Overbury's *The Wife*, and John Earle's *Micro-cosmographie*. It is perhaps only in our times seen as not quite healthy, as denying individuality to people in this manner.[433] The *Characters*, however, was not an entirely new type of work when it was written. The earliest example of the genre, dating to the seventh century B.C., may be the poem about women by Semonides of Amorgos, which describes nine disagreeable kinds of women. The poem is briefly discussed below because seven of them women are said to have been made out of animals.[434]

The author of the preface to Theophrastus's *Characters*—who was not Theophrastus—asserts that he will never cease to remain surprised that not all Greeks are similar, since they live in the same climate and are raised in similar fashion.[435] In other words, he would have found it logical if all Greeks were

---

[432] Charles Dickens, *Great Expectations,* chapter 42: "'This is a terrible hardened one' they says to prison visitors, picking out me. 'May be said to live in jails, this boy.' Then they looked at me, and I looked at them, and they measured my head, some on 'em—they had better a-measured my stomach." For the beginnings of the pseudoscience of phrenology, founded by Joseph Gall in 1825, see George L. Mosse, *Toward the Final Solution,* 27–30.

[433] J. W. Smeed, *The Theophrastan Character: The History of a Literary Genre* (Oxford, 1985), traces the genre down in the literature from Theophrastus to the twentieth century. For bibliography: 339–341.

[434] Hugh Lloyd-Jones, *Females of the Species: Semonides on Women* (London, 1975), 29–33: "Character in Greek Literature."

[435] Theophrastus, *Characteres,* Pro. 1: Ἤδη μὲν καὶ πρότερον πολλάκις ἐπιστήσας τὴν διάνοιαν ἐθαύμασα, ἴσως δὲ οὐδὲ παύσομαι θαυμάζων, τί γὰρ δήποτε, τῆς Ἑλλάδος ὑπὸ τὸν αὐτὸν ἀέρα κειμένης καὶ πάντων τῶν Ἑλλήνων ὁμοίως παιδευομένων, συμβέβηκεν ἡμῖν οὐ τὴν αὐτὴν τάξιν τῶν τρόπων ἔχειν.

identical, but since they are not, they still can be categorized as belonging to collective types rather than each man representing only himself as an individual. As described by Smeed, "The subject may be described through carefully chosen behavioural details, or by a list of abstract characteristics, or metaphorically, or by a combination of all three methods. The 'character' obviously involves a typological approach to human personality: the subject, although presented to us as an individual person, must also stand for a social, moral, or psychological category."[436] Thus the tendency of type-casting, so popular in the seventeenth and eighteenth centuries and still extant today, goes back to the fourth century B.C.[437] We see that Greek literature, followed by Latin literature, has given later European civilization two highly seductive and therefore extremely powerful tools, suggesting that it is possible to classify humans into superior and inferior groups. One of these tools is seductive because of the impression of precision and scientific method it conveys, the other because of its artistic and humorous force.

Conclusions

This chapter analyzes the conceptual framework in which Graeco-Roman attitudes toward other peoples occurred, tracing the phenomena of proto-racism or pronounced forms of ethnic stereotypes, as defined in the Introduction. The period covered starts with the fifth century B.C. Obviously, there never was a form of racism resembling that of the nineteenth and twentieth centuries, which was based on a biological determinism derived from and distorting contemporary science. There are, however, other relevant patterns:

1. An almost generally accepted form of environmental determinism, first explicitly and extensively presented in the medical treatise *Airs, Waters, Places,* written at an uncertain date in the second half of the fifth century B.C. The particular form of environmental determinism first found in this work became the generally accepted model in Greece and, afterwards, with variations, in Rome. According to this view, collective characteristics of groups of people are permanently determined by climate and geography. The implication is that the essential features of body and mind come from the outside and are not the result of either genetic evolution or conscious choice. Individuality and individual change are thereby ignored. This is proto-racism as defined in the Introduction, for climate and geography rather than genetics are said to determine group characteristics. Entire nations are believed to have common characteristics de-

---

[436] Smeed, *The Theophrastan Character,* p. 2.

[437] Theophrastus's *Characters* was indubitably a new genre at the time, even though there are passages in older literature which foreshadow the work: Herodotus's description of the Despot (3.80); the Oligarchical man in Plato's *Republic* (553a), perhaps, but more important are the Magnificent man (μεγαλοπρεπής) in Aristotle's *Nicomachean Ethics* 1123a, as well as the types described in *Physiogn.,* cited above, for here we are concerned with general types of ordinary men. There is a theory that Theophrastus's selection is influenced by the "extremes" to Aristotle's "means" in the *Ethics.*

termined wholly by factors outside themselves, which are, by implication, unchangeable. As argued in the Introduction, the essence of racism is that it believes groups of people share imagined common characteristics, physical, mental or moral. These cannot be changed by human will, because they are determined by unalterable, stable physical factors: external, such as climate or geography and hereditary. These presumed characteristics are then subject to value judgments, in which others are usually rejected as being inferior to the observer, or, in rare instances, approved of as being untainted and superior. It is furthermore true as a general rule that these descriptions are not based on direct observation or when they are so based, then they are made in denial of reality. This characterizes them even more as ethnic stereotypes and proto-racism.

Aristotle developed the theory further, adding two elements that made it an essential tool for ambitious imperialists. He held that the Greeks occupied the best environment between Europe and Asia and were therefore ideally capable of ruling others. In contrast, he claimed, the inhabitants of Asia were servile by nature, or natural slaves, and therefore suited to be subjects of the Greeks. Roman authors took over these ideas, duly substituting themselves as the ideal rulers, and with some variations. Instead of the contrast between Europe and Asia, which the Greeks found essential, the geographical poles for most Roman authors are North and South.

2. A second conceptual mechanism that was generally accepted in Graeco-Roman antiquity is a belief in the heredity of acquired characters, which is explicitly propounded in some works, for instance in the treatise mentioned above, *Airs, Waters, Places,* in the work of Aristotle and elsewhere, mostly in technical treatises. However, it is clear from many implicit references that the principle was usually taken for granted, also in the Hellenistic and Roman periods.

3. As we have seen, ideas concerning environmental determinism are often combined with the belief in heredity of acquired characters. When applied to human groups, this leads somewhat paradoxically to a belief that their characteristics are uniform and constant. Climate and geography have definite effects on all people living in a given region. These effects then become permanent traits because they become hereditary in one generation. The result of this combination is a powerful incentive to discriminatory approaches.

4. In the view of many of the relevant authors there is yet another important factor. A good form of government is an essential ingredient in shaping a people. Under a ruler or government considered bad no people can function well. The most obvious example is Isocrates' firm belief that Persia must be a weak nation, because it is ruled by an overly powerful king. This, clearly, is not a racist or proto-racist concept if only because it is liable to change. The last chapter of Xenophon's *Cyropaedia* claims that Persia was strong when it had a good king, and deteriorated when the kings did. This is essentially a sociopolitical view, and is often offered in parallel to, or together with, the environmental

approach. It occurs first in *Airs,* and is repeated most emphatically by Isocrates. The essence is that Persia must be soft and feeble, because it is an absolute monarchy, while the Greeks, being free, are motivated fighters. As such it becomes a a conceptual tool in the service of imperialism, discussed further below in point 7.

5. Autochthony and pure lineage. The Athenians attached tremendous importance to the dual myth that they had lived in their own land from the beginnings of time without ever abandoning it, and that they were a people of unmixed lineage. They saw themselves as originally having sprung from the soil itself, the earth serving as their collective mother. This myth served various purposes: (a) It was used as argument that they and only they held legitimate possession of their soil. (b) They regarded themselves as a people uncontaminated by an admixture of foreign elements, and were therefore superior. The uniqueness of their origins is deemed obvious by many fifth-century authors. The citizenship law, which awarded citizenship only to the children of two citizens, was intended to preserve this purity. All the fourth-century authors who mention autochthony, mostly orators, are convinced of the value of pure descent. They are agreed that the Athenians are of uniquely pure descent and superior to all other peoples of the world. Other Greek states have produced comparable myths, but only Athens insisted on this to such a great extent. Their insistence was still accepted in the Roman period.

The idea as such, however, appealed mostly in a negative sense to other Greeks and, later, to Roman authors: intermarriage and mixed blood are considered bad and conducive to degeneration. In this form the concept of pure lineage appears in the works of many Roman authors, even though the Romans in practice liberally granted citizenship to subject peoples. Best known are Tacitus's comments on the Germans, whom he described in terms in which the Athenians describe themselves: they were "indigenous, and not mixed at all with other peoples through immigration or intercourse." Although the idea was generally accepted, there are exceptions: Lucian and Apuleius are critical.

Clearly, of all the concepts discussed in this study, this is the one that most closely approaches modern racism, for it establishes a hierarchy of peoples, based on the fiction that some are of pure lineage, while others are of mixed descent. It could even be said that the Athenians regarded themselves as a "race" in modern terms. Furthermore, it is clear that these ideas were influential later as well, for they appear in authors who were read widely ever since the renaissance.

6. Physiognomics is a discipline—if this is the proper term—that seeks to detect from individuals' external features their character, disposition, or destiny. Its value is widely accepted in ancient literature, not only in the technical treatises which are devoted to the subject, from the fourth century onward, but also by many authors of major works on other topics. It was particularly popular because of the presumption of scientific objectivity, which provided a rationalization and reinforcement of social prejudices. For the present study it is partic-

ularly relevant because of the way it is supported by and reinforces ethnic prejudice. Physiognomics uses the physical differences between peoples (ἔθνη). The outward appearances of different peoples are described, as well as the presumed mental and moral qualities of each of these peoples. Individuals who have the presumed outward characteristics of another people are supposed to have the stereotypical personality of those they resemble. It has also been seen that the theory of physiognomics was interwoven with aspects from the environmental theory. This was, in fact, rationalized by Galen.

Physiognomics always retained some popularity, but it gained particular prominence in the eighteenth and nineteenth centuries, popularized by authors, most of whom had read their classics. It is significant for the present study because it always groups physical and mental characteristics as correlating types. This is precisely one of the elements in the definition of racism adopted in the Introduction: racism postulates a direct and linear connection between physical and mental qualities.

7. The ideas here described were a significant element in ancient concepts of imperialism. As with so many other features the essence of this is first encountered in *Airs*, which insists that the inhabitants of Asia are soft because of their good climate and resources. They are less belligerent and gentler in character than the Europeans, who are more courageous and belligerent. Another contributing cause of the Asiatic feebleness is monarchic rule, whereas the Europeans are good fighters through the influence of climate and geography and also because of their institutions, for they are not ruled by kings. This idea was further developed by Aristotle: In his view the Greeks combine European spirit and freedom with Asiatic intelligence and competence. They are therefore capable of ruling all mankind—an early text, if not the first one to suggest that Greeks should achieve universal rule. Aristotle also emphasizes in this connection the presumed geographical centrality of Greece. He assumes there exists an immediate connection between collective superiority and empire. It is highly significant that these concepts gain influence in a time when the Greeks were gradually conceiving the idea of expansion eastward at the cost of Persia. This ideology clearly was an essential part of the mood in which Greek imperial expansion could be considered. This is not to say that this belief in their own superiority as such impelled the Greeks towards conquest, but it may have persuaded them that it was possible and justified.

No less important: these ideas were taken over, suitably adapted, by the Romans. We find them in Vitruvius, the Elder Pliny, Vegetius, but also in major literary authors such as Cicero and Seneca. For them, Italy was ideally situated in the middle, but now the middle was between North and South, rather than between Europe and Asia. It is to be noted that the significance of the idea lies not in the imagined centrality of the authors' own region. Most people in premodern times thought they lived in the center of the world, but not all of them saw this as an ideal precondition for the acquisition of empire.

The last significant concept to mention in connection with imperialist ideas is that of decline and degeneration. Just as there are believed to be environments which are good or even ideal for the creation of an imperial power, so there are those that are unfavorable. A related idea, which also is part of the complex of environmental theories, is that of decline as a result of migration. It is first attested in the work of Herodotus, 9.122, where Cyrus says that the Persians, if they move from rugged Persia to a better country, should not expect to continue as rulers, "but to prepare for being ruled by others—soft countries give birth to soft men. There is no land which produces the most remarkable fruit, and at the same time men good at warfare." This idea was fully accepted in Rome, for instance in the case of the Celts who established themselves in Asia Minor and, in the opinion of the Romans, subsequently degenerated. It has been séen that no account is taken anywhere of the possibility of improvement: strong people become feeble in a soft environment, the reverse does not occur. In the case of the Gauls who moved to Asia Minor another factor was thought to cause degeneration, namely mixed marriages: they had become contaminated with Asiatic blood and therefore degenerated. This is the negative corollary of the concept of pure lineage, mentioned under 5, above. Both ideas just mentioned—the harmful effects of migration and those of mixed blood—are connected with the view that a people is by nature attached to its native soil. The soil produces its people and each and every people prospers best on its native soil. Above we also saw how Plato sees in eugenics a means of delaying for some time the decline and collapse that would result from mixed marriages between members of the classes in his projected city. Mixed marriages, one might almost say interracial marriages, were the main cause of degeneration, decay, and internal conflict, he believes. He aims to make his ideas acceptable with the aid of the myth of an earth-born citizenship consisting of a golden, silver, iron, and bronze class of people.

The discussion above repeatedly showed that all these ideas were influential in later periods, in particular the eighteenth and nineteenth centuries. It has also been argued that these ancient views of others can legitimately be described as a form of proto-racism because they attribute collective and unalterable characteristics to entire groups of peoples. An entire people is described as if it were a single individual. Conversely, individuals are regarded as necessarily and inevitably having all the characteristics commonly ascribed to the group to which they belong. Moreover, these characteristics are believed to belong to the physical as well as the mental and moral spheres. They are imposed by the physical environment and transmitted from generation to generation. As in recent racist views, the other is sometimes seen as superior and sometimes as inferior. Others can be clever and immoral, or courageous but stupid. Depending on the relevant mixture, the others are seen as a greater or lesser threat. These views are not present equally strongly in all authors and there are occasional texts that disagree with specific aspects of this complex. However, they basically represent common approaches in antiquity. Of course there was no active debate on these subjects of the sort encountered over the past few centuries. Also it is essential to recognize that, in spite of the tensions engendered, proto-racism never argued for a need to exterminate a group of human beings because of their collective identity. Furthermore, pagan antiquity had not yet invented the concept of collective and inherited guilt, which in the later Christian society served as an excuse for large-scale discrimination against and persecution of the Jews.

Conquest and Imperialism

I am well aware that I may with justice be considered
ungrateful and lazy if I describe in this casual and cursory
manner a land [sc. Italy] which is at once the nursling and
the mother of all other lands, chosen by the providence of
the gods to make heaven itself more glorious, to unite
scattered empires, to soften their customs, to bring together
the harsh and coarse tongues of so many nations into contact
by community of language, to give mankind civilisation, and
in a word, to become throughout the world the single
fatherland of all peoples.[1]

THIS IS AN ALMOST programmatic statement of Roman imperialism as seen by
Pliny the Elder. The central role of the homeland in imperial ideology has been
shown as present already in fifth-century Athens. Empire, in Pliny's view, has
four functions: it unites what is scattered; it improves customs, it unifies and
links peoples through the imposition of a common language, and it civilizes.
This is not, it must be stressed, an explanation of the aims of imperialism. It is
no explanation of why Rome systematically subjugated one people after another. It shows, however, how Pliny represents the effects of the process. It is
beneficial for everybody concerned and this should justify the empire in the
eyes of the Romans and their subjects. These various elements are also viewed
in various ways by other authors, not surprisingly, for Pliny the Elder was
rather a conservative man. However, some of those authors are far more critical
and cynical than Pliny. To unite distant peoples and to bring them in contact is
viewed with ambivalence throughout antiquity, as we will discuss below, in
chapter 3. It is indeed regarded as inevitable, but also as corrupting and undermining integrity. The improvement or softening of customs may make people

---

[1] Pliny, *NH* 3.39: nec ignoro ingrati ac segnis animi existimari posse merito, si obiter atque in
transcursu ad hunc modum dicatur terra omnium terrarum alumna eadem et parens, numine deum
electa quae caelum ipsum clarius faceret, sparsa congregaret imperia ritusque molliret et tot popu-
lorum discordes ferasque linguas sermonis commercio contraheret ad conloquia et humanitatem
homini daret breviterque una cunctarum gentium in toto orbe patria fieret.

more agreeable,[2] but it is also seen as a form of degeneration into slavery, which collectively emasculates a people and, subsequently may infect the rulers as well, as shown below, in chapters 3 and 5. This process is thought to be caused by the group dynamics of slavery, the subject of this chapter. Taken together, what Pliny describes is a program of radical transformation and alteration of the subject peoples: Empire affects their customs, language, civilization, and replaces their own fatherland with that of the conquerors. Whatever we think of such claims and the reality in the empire, it is surely significant that we saw no Greek author of the fifth and fourth centuries adhering to such a proclaimed ideology.

It will, then, be useful to pay more attention to a number of particular topics, mentioned in passing in the previous chapters, namely, attitudes towards subject peoples in terms of slaves, the theory of natural slavery, and its application to entire peoples; comparisons of human beings with animals; the fear of being dominated by the vanquished; the beneficial and harmful effects of contact between peoples as viewed in ancient literature. All these topics are important for our understanding of the working of relations between peoples in antiquity, as argued in the Introduction. Views of the others and themselves are instrumental in power relations and particularly in warfare. Rulers will not readily attack an enemy deemed more powerful, more easily one regarded as weak. Such impressions are sometimes realistic and sometimes they are not. Even if a serious attempt was made to gain reliable information, the image of the enemy is often determined by complexes of stereotypes. Hence this subject is entirely relevant for the present study. This will be followed, in Part 2, by a survey of the views held by Romans of specific minorities, ethnic groups, and foreigners. This chapter therefore is a continuation of the previous one in that it analyzes how Greeks and Romans saw others, but here the focus is more narrowly how they saw those who were the target of their imperial ambition.

SUBJECT PEOPLES AND SLAVES

The existence of slavery was not a topic of discussion in antiquity, but there were arguments about specifics, notably there was a controversy about the difference in nature between free men and slaves, an issue important for the justification of slavery. If an essential difference, mentally and physically, between free men and slaves could be demonstrated, it was easier to claim that their difference in status was justified and reasonable. If there was no essential difference, slavery was harder to justify, for it would depend only on brute force. Was slavery contrary to justice and also contrary to nature? Aristotle responds to arguments along these lines by contending that slavery was both natural and just, because some human beings were so shaped by nature that they lacked some of the essential qualities of fully fledged men. They were therefore fit

[2] This is what Vergil expresses in succinct form with his *pacique imponere morem* (*Aen.* 6.852).

only to serve as instruments for those who had all those qualities. The difficulty is that the controversy is reported only in one source, Aristotle's *Politics*, where Aristotle gives us his own views on the subject, usually designated "the theory of natural slavery," together with a somewhat elliptic account of the arguments of the other side. The scope and starting point of the discussion are determined by the fact that it is part of an effort by Aristotle to fit the slaves into his model of a just and workable polis. The statement, "slaves are subhuman or lesser men while masters are superior," justifies the inferior status of slaves, whereas the claim that all men are equal leaves slavery without moral justification. Here we move from the sphere of the individual into that of the collective and the group, which makes the subject relevant for this book.

The theory of natural slavery has been discussed very often from various perspectives and, since this is not a study of concepts of ancient slavery, I shall limit myself to a number of specific issues.[3] Relevant for our subject are ideas which assign to specific groups of people an inferior place in society on the grounds that they are deficient in various ways and need therefore to be subordinated to their intellectual and moral superiors in a master/slave relationship.[4] That is to say, specific, non-Greek peoples are described as collectively having qualities which designate them as the proper material for slaves of the Greeks. Being subhuman they live best in a symbiotic relationship with fully human masters. The arguments applied by Aristotle to individual slaves and masters are easily applied to entire groups and peoples. This is clear from the terminology employed: δούλωσις and δουλεία and related forms are commonly used by Thucydides and by other authors to express the subjection of one state to another.[5] As observed by Gomme, δουλεία and δουλοῦσθαι, etc. are frequently used to denote political subjection generally; ἀνδράποδα always applies liter-

---

[3] Peter Garnsey, *Ideas of Slavery from Aristotle to Augustine* (Cambridge, 1996) contains a full bibliography; see the older study by Robert Schlaifer, "Greek Theories of Slavery from Homer to Aristotle," *HSCP* 47 (1936), 165–204; repr. in M. I. Finley, *Slavery in Classical Antiquity*, 93–132; Nicholas D. Smith, "Aristotle's Theory of Natural Slavery," repr. in David Keyt and Fred D. Miller (eds.), *A Companion to Aristotle's Politics* 142–155. Note in particular the historical study by P. A. Brunt, "Aristotle and Slavery," in *Studies in Greek History and Thought* (Oxford, 1993), 343–388; concerning the ideological question: M. Schofield, "Ideology and Philosophy in Aristotle's Theory of Slavery," in Günther Patzig, *Aristoteles' "Politik," Akten des XI. Symposium Aristotelicum, 1987*, 1–27. Schofield argues that Aristotle's theory is not to any interesting extent ideological. He defines ideology in a Marxist sense. Schofield's arguments are discussed by Charles H. Kahn, "Response to Schofield," 28–31 esp.28f. Kahn disagrees, emphasizing the ideological element in Aristotle's theory. See also Olof Gigon, "Die Sklaverei bei Aristoteles," in *La «Politique» d'Aristote* Entretiens sur l'antiquité classique 11 (Geneva, 1965), 247–276. Relevant also is the recent article by Vincent J. Rosivach, "Enslaving *Barbaroi* and the Athenian Ideology of Slavery," *Historia* 48 (1999), 129–157. For a survey of debates and issues in the study of slaves and slavery: Zvi Yavetz, *Slaves and Slavery in Ancient Rome* (New Brunswick, NJ, 1988).

[4] Garnsey's definition, p. 13.

[5] Thucydides does so in 1.98.4 (ἐδουλώθη,) of the subject cities of the empire and in 1.141.1 (δούλωσιν) and just above 2.63.1 (δουλείας ἀντ' ἐλευθερίας) of possible domination of Athens by Sparta.

ally to individual slaves.[6] It should be observed that the contrast between free man and slave, ἐλεύθερος-δοῦλος, originated in the domestic sphere and was first broadened into the realm of politics about the time of the Persian Wars. The justification of individual slavery then becomes applicable also to collective subjugation and thus becomes part of imperialist ideology. If a theory considers foreigners inferior, asserts that this inferiority is hereditary, and if it is claimed that this justifies subordinating them to their superiors, then it should be discussed here. The question to be considered therefore is to what extent the theory of natural slavery as developed by Aristotle and accepted by later authors fits a specific complex of attitudes towards others, as discussed in chapter 1. The first problem to examine is whether it can be described as proto-racist within the terms of the definition accepted in the Introduction: "an attitude towards individuals and groups of peoples which posits a direct and linear connection between physical and mental qualities. It therefore attributes to those individuals and groups of peoples collective traits, physical, mental and moral, which are constant and unalterable by a human will, because they are caused by hereditary factors or external influences, such as climate or geography." In other words, we need to explore the theory first to see whether it regards individuals as masters or slaves by nature because they are believed to share imagined physical, mental, and moral attributes with the group to which they are deemed to belong. We then have to see whether it is assumed that they cannot change these traits individually, whether these characteristics are thought to be stable throughout the group from one generation to the next. If indeed these qualities are deemed unchangeable, we then must see whether this is thought to be the case because they are determined by elementary factors beyond human control.

A start may be made, however, with the arguments Aristotle opposed, which called into question the essential difference between free men and slaves. As already mentioned, they are found in Aristotle only in truncated and edited form and they are therefore not easy to reconstruct.[7]

In his discussion Aristotle summarizes the arguments of the critics of natural slavery as follows (1255a): Slavery is unjust because it is based on law or convention rather than nature and rests on force. Slaves by convention are war-captives, held to be slaves by law, a law which is in effect rather a sort of "convention" (ὁμολογία) than a true law. This, we may add inter parentheses, was common practice as acknowledged by various authors.[8] According to Aristotle, there were now critics who claimed this is immoral, because it is based only on superior force and not on true justice. Here there is disagreement (Aristotle does not say between whom or with whom). There are those who say that war enslavement is just, but they undermine their case by adding that it makes a

---

[6] A. W. Gomme, *A Historical Commentary on Thucydides: The Ten Years' War* (Oxford, 1956), 3.646.

[7] Giuseppe Cambiano, "Aristotle and the Anonymous Opponents of Slavery," in Finley, *Classical Slavery*, 22–41.

[8] See, for instance, Xenophon, *Cyropaedia* 7.5.73 and cf. Cambiano, op. cit. 24f.

difference if a war is just or unjust, and if Greeks are captured rather than barbarians. This implies that, after all, in practice there are many slaves who ought to have been free. Aristotle concludes that the only resolution of the argument is to admit that there are natural free persons and natural slaves.

Thus the view that slavery was unjust, as it was a product of convention and rested on nothing but force is ascribed to unnamed persons. Aristotle does not identify these opponents of slavery with whom he disagrees, and the question is therefore how many of such opponents there were and whether this was a recent controversy or had been around for some time. It is impossible to say whether Aristotle refers to isolated intellectuals or a larger number.[9] The first explicit statement which may be cited with certainty was uttered by a Sophist, Gorgias' pupil Alcidamas writing probably not very long before Aristotle (c. 370 B.C.): "God made all men free; Nature has made none a slave."[10] The formulation might but need not necessarily indicate that there were others who already had asserted that Nature has made some people slaves. It is, however, possible that Alcidamas had only Greek slaves in mind, not barbarians.[11] In any event, it is quite likely that we need to consider in connection with this exchange an earlier fragment from Antiphon's *De Veritate* (c. 420 B.C.?):[12]

[9] See Cambiano, op. cit., 23, for reference to isolated intellectuals. Garnsey, *Ideas of Slavery*, 75–77; p. 77, n. 4 summarizes the thesis of the critics (as represented by Aristotle).

[10] Schol. Aristotle, *Rhet.* 1373b18 (ed. Rabe, p.74): καὶ ὡς ἐν τῷ Μεσσηνιακῷ λέγει Ἀλκιδάμας, ἐλευθέρους ἀφῆκε πάντας θεός, οὐδένα δοῦλον ἡ φύσις πεποίηκεν. Cf. E. R. Dodds, "The Failure of Greek Liberalism," in *The Ancient Concept of Progress* (Oxford, 1973), 92–105, at 101. Dodds notes that this view is echoed by a character in Philemon, frag. 95 Kock: κἂν δοῦλος ᾖ τις, σάρκα τὴν αὐτὴν ἔχει· φύσει γὰρ οὐδεὶς δοῦλος ἐγενήθη ποτέ [ἀπὸ τοῦ πάλαι πλάσαντος ἀνθρώπων γένος. ἴσην δὲ πάντων διάθεσιν τοῦ σώματος ἐποίησεν οὗτος ὡς ἐλευθέρου γένους. ἐλευθέρους ἐποίησε πάντας τῇ φύσει, δοῦλον δὲ μετεποίησεν ἡ πλεονεξία]. Since Philemon was a comic poet, a younger contemporary of Aristotle, this seems to show that the idea had become popular fairly rapidly. In *Ideas of Slavery*, Garnsey notes that the statement reads as a negative comment on the concept of natural slavery, and thus as an attack on the morality of institutional slavery (75f.). He argues that the theory of natural slavery was first developed by Aristotle and concludes that it is not yet present in the *Nicomachean Ethics*, and may be found as a new concept in the *Politics* (107–127).

[11] Brunt, "Aristotle and Slavery," 351 against earlier interpretations, e.g., by Schlaifer, "Greek Theories of Slavery," 200.

[12] Testimonia and fragments in DK 2. 334–370; Eng. trans. in R. K. Sprague (ed.), *The Older Sophists* (1972) (add *P. Oxy* 3647); J. Barnes, *The Presocratic Philosophers* (London, 1982), ch. 23 (a) with translation; P. Oxy 3647, comm in *Oxyrhynchus pap.* 52, p.4f. (Helen Cockle); F. Decleva Caizzi, in F. Adorno and others (eds.), *Corpus dei papiri filosofici greci e latini* I (Florence, 1989), 176–222; M. Ostwald, "*Nomos* and *Phusis* in Antiphon's περὶ ἀληθείας' in M. Griffith and D. J. Mastronarde (eds.), *Cabinet of the Muses: Essays on Classics and Comparative Literature in Honor of Thomas G. Rosenmeyer* (Atlanta, GA, 1990), 293–306; Basileios A. Kyrkos, *Antiphon-Kritias-Anonymus Iamblichi: Studienausgabe Ausgewählter Texte* (Ioannina, 1988), 43–53, with a German translation. For P.Oxy 11.1364: ibid., 46–59. About Antiphon: ibid., introduction, 33–41. See also H. C. Baldry, "The Unity of Mankind," *Grecs et Barbares*, Entretiens Hardt 8 (1962), 174; W.K.C. Guthrie, *A History of Greek Philosophy*, vol. 3 (Cambridge, 1962), 152f.; Michael Nill, *Morality and Self-Interest in Protagoras Antiphon and Democritus* (Leiden 1985), 52–74. I have not seen Michael Gagarin, *Antiphon the Athenian: Oratory, Law, and Justice in the Age of the Sophists* (Austin, TX, 2002).

A.(= *P.Oxy.* 1364 and 3647) [= fr. B DK].[13]

[Col.2] . . . (of more familiar societies) we understand and respect; those of distant societies (5) we neither understand nor respect. This means that we have become barbarians in our relations with one another, (10) for by nature we are all equally equipped in every respect to be barbarians and Greeks.

This is shown by examining those factors which are by nature necessary among all human beings and (20) are provided to all in terms of the same capacities; it is in these very factors that none of us is (25) differentiated as a barbarian or a Greek. We all breathe into the (30) air with our mouths and with our nostrils, and we all laugh when there is joy in our [Col. 3] mind, or we weep when suffering pain; we receive sounds (5) through our hearing; we see when sunlight combines with our faculty of sight; we work with our hands (10) and we walk with our feet . . . [gap] [Col. 4] . . . each group of men came to an (5) agreement on terms of their liking and enacted the laws.[14]

Clearly, what we have is so fragmentary that it is dangerous to say too much, although in fact a lot has been said by various scholars: the sequel may even have contained a rebuttal, by Antiphon or someone else, of what has been preserved. In what survives of the text Antiphon does not mention slavery, nor does he treat slaves and barbarians as equals. *Nomos* and *physis* are here contrasted, whereby the latter is taken as determining what is unavoidable, ineluctable, and universally valid *by nature*. The former refers to man-made prescriptions and dictates of the laws based on agreement.[15] The fragment denies the distinction between Greek and barbarian by nature.[16] The attack therefore appears to be aimed at people who lose their sense of perspective as regards the relative importance of *nomos* and *physis*. Thus, in attributing too absolute a value to their own *nomoi*, they fail to consider the fact that *physis*, nature, accords no higher rank to one society or ethnic group over another.[17] If this is

---

[13] I follow the inversion of the sequence of fragments in the *corpus dei papiri filosofici*. The translation is that given by Ostwald (296), which was adapted from that by Jonathan Barnes, *The Presocratic Philosophers* 2, 207–210.

[14] *P.Oxy* 1364a . . . ρων ἐπ[ιστάμε-]θά τε κ[αὶ σέβομεν·] τοὺς δὲ [τῶν τη]λοῦ οἰκ[ούν]των, οὔτε ἐπι[στ]άμεθα οὔτε σέβομεν. ἐν τ[ο]ύτῳ οὖν πρὸς ἀλλήλους βεβαρβαρώμεθα, ἐπεὶ φύσει γε πάντα πάντες ὁμοίως πεφύκ[α]μεν καὶ βάρβαροι καὶ ἕλλην[ες] εἶναι. σκοπεῖν δ[ὲ] παρέχει τὰ τῶν φύσει [ὄντων] ἀναγκαῖ[α ἐν] πᾶσιν ἀν[θρώ]ποις, π[οριζόμενά] τε κατὰ τ[ὰς αὐτὰς] δυνά[μεις ἅπασι,] καὶ ἐν [αὐτοῖς τού]τοις οὔτε β[άρβα]ρος ἀφώρι[σται] ἡμῶν ο[ὐδείς,] οὔτε ἕλλην. ἀναπνέομέν τε γὰρ εἰς τὸν ἀέρ[α] ἅπαντες κατὰ τὸ στόμ[α] [κ]αὶ κατ[ὰ] τὰς ῥῖνας· κ[αὶ γελῶ][με]ν χ[αίροντες τῷ] δακρύομε[ν] λυπούμενοι· καὶ τῇ ἀκοῇτοὺς φθόγγους εἰσδεχόμεθα· καὶ τῇ αὐγῇ μετὰ τῆς ὄψεως ὁρῶμεν· καὶ ταῖς χερσὶν ἐργαζόμεθα· καὶ τοῖς ποσὶν βαδ[ίζο]μεν ·υβ[] ·[] τ[] ··μ·[] λοι εἰσιν [κα]τὰ τὸ ἀρέ[σκον συν]εχώρη[σαν] ἑκαστοι·[] καὶ τοὺς νόμ[ους ἔθεν]το· κ·[·']···[]

[15] Ostwald, "*Nomos* and *Phusis*" (1990) , 296–299.

[16] Ostwald, op. cit., p.301; E. A. Havelock, *The Liberal Temper in Greek Politics* (London, 1957), 255–294, esp. 256–258, therefore makes Antiphon an early apostle of liberalism; see the criticism by P. A. Brunt in his review, reprinted in *Studies in Greek History and Thought* (Oxford, 1993), 389–394, esp. 392f.

[17] This point is made by Caizzi, "Il nuovo papiro di Antifonte," *Studi di filosofia preplatonica* (Naples, 1984), 191–208.

the case, that is, if the criticism is accepted, there is no room left for a theory which holds that part of humanity is suited by nature only to act as slaves to others. While it may go too far to claim that Aristotle, in his *Politics*, is arguing with the opinion expressed in Antiphon's fragment—we do not know who else may have published similar opinions—the present passage certainly is relevant as it disqualifies a justification of slavery which classifies slaves as an inferior subdivision of humanity.

For this study the fragment is important because it explicitly asserts that "by nature" Greeks and barbarians are not differentiated.[18] The fragment goes to some length to show that this is true in a physical sense, but it is clear that the text goes further, when it says—an apparent paradox—that "we have become barbarians (ourselves) when we deny that by nature we are all equally equipped in every respect to be barbarians and Greeks." In spite of the fragmentary nature of the text it seems fair to conclude that Antiphon—or at least the the fragmentary text quoted here—is opposed to proto-racist attitudes held by others. These others might have included the author of *Airs, Waters, Places*, discussed in chapter 1, who hardly discusses Greeks, but definitely describes Asiatic peoples in terms which might suggest that they might be seen as natural slaves. As observed, Antiphon does not mention slavery, but his views show agreement with those whom Aristotle describes as claiming "that for one man to be another man's master is contrary to nature because it is only convention that makes the one a slave and the other a freeman and there is no difference between them by nature, and that therefore it is unjust, for it is based on force." This does not imply, of course, that Antiphon was against slavery as such.

We must now return to Aristotle. In his exposition of the theory of natural slavery he inserts a grand view of a hierarchy of nature and life, wholly expressed in terms of master and slave or ruler and subject pairs. He even asserts that "it is a general law that there should be naturally ruling elements and elements naturally ruled."[19] He further asserts that in each of these cases both elements profit from the relationship.[20] Within men the soul rules the body (unless they are degenerate) and it is expedient for both body and soul that this

---

[18] Cf. Herodotus 2.158, discussed below, in chapter 4, p. 263.

[19] 1260a, 7–9: δῆλον τοίνυν ὅτι τὸν αὐτὸν τρόπον ἔχει καὶ ἐπὶ τῶν ἄλλων, ὥστε φύσει τὰ πλείω ἄρχοντα καὶ ἀρχόμενα. See the commentary by W. L. Newman, *The Politics of Aristotle*, 4 vols. (Oxford, 1887–1902), vol. 2, p. 215f., with proposals for three different interpretations, all of them referring to "those naturally ruled."

[20] *Politics* 1.2.7, 1254a20ff. The essence of this idea, that the inferior profits from being ruled by the superior, is present already in Plato, *Resp.* 590c–d. Cf. Gregory Vlastos, "Slavery in Plato's Thought," in *Platonic Studies* (Princeton, 2d ed. 1981), 147–163, esp. 147–53; reprinted also in Finley, *Slavery in Classical Antiquity*, 133–49, esp. 133–138. Vlastos argues that Plato in principle would have agreed with Aristotle on two more essential points: (a) the difference in intellectual and social status rests on a diversity of native endowment: nature is the original factor in differentiating the philosopher from the producer and *a fortiori* from the slave. (b) this difference only repeats on the human plane a pattern writ large over the cosmos. See also Vlastos, "Does Slavery exist in Plato's Republic?" *Platonic Studies,* 291–295.

should be so (1254b, 5–11). Man rules animals and that again is profitable for both, because it assures preservation. Among human beings the male is by nature superior and the female inferior, the male ruler and the female subject (1254b, 11–16). The same principle operates among mankind in general, which is divided into superior and inferior men, the former being by nature masters, the latter by nature slaves and, again, this is profitable for both. A slave must by nature belong to another—and that is why he in fact belongs to another—and he "participates in reason to the extent of apprehending it in another, though destitute of it himself."[21] He does not have the faculty of deliberation (τὸ βουλευτικόν, 1260a13). Like animals he does not share in true felicity and free choice [i.e., the attributes of good quality of life] (1280a, 32–34).[22]

The usefulness of slaves, like that of animals, lies in the physical services they render to the masters. Hence, according to Aristotle, "it is nature's intention also to erect a physical difference between the body of the freeman and that of the slave, giving the latter strength for the menial duties of life, but making the former upright in carriage and (though useless for physical labour) useful for the various purposes of civic life . . . It is thus clear that, as some are by nature free and others are by nature slaves, and for these latter the condition of slavery is both beneficial and just."[23] The physical difference between the free and the slaves is visible also in the arts, for instance in the images of black slaves, reproduced here in figures 5 and 6. Earlier in the *Politics* Aristotle describes the natural ruler as "The element which is able, by virtue of its intelligence, to exercise forethought, is naturally a ruling and master element" and the natural slave and subject as "the element which is able, by virtue of its bodily power, to do what the other element plans, is a ruled element, which is naturally in a state of slavery; master and slave have accordingly [as they thus complement one another] a common interest."[24] "The terms 'master,' 'slave' and 'freeman' signify not a form of expertise, but a certain disposition."[25] Nature as acting agent follows a rational plan, according to which the inferior

<hr/>

[21] 1254b 20–3: ἔστι γὰρ φύσει δοῦλος ὁ δυνάμενος ἄλλου εἶναι (διὸ καὶ ἄλλου ἐστίν), καὶ ὁ κοινωνῶν λόγου τοσοῦτον ὅσον αἰσθάνεσθαι ἀλλὰ μὴ ἔχειν. Newman, comm. ad loc. writes that this sentence "justifies what preceeds: the slave has just been mentioned as on a level with the brute, and now facts are adduced which show how nearly they approach each other" (146).

[22] Trans. Barker: διὰ τὸ μὴ μετέχειν εὐδαιμονίας μηδὲ τοῦ ζῆν κατὰ προαίρεσιν. For the comparison of human beings with animals, see below.

[23] 1254b 25–1255a 2, trans. Barker. The relationship is less obvious than it should be, says Aristotle, because some slaves have bodies like freemen and the beauty of the souls of freemen is not easy to recognize.

[24] 1252a, 32–5 (trans. Barker): τὸ μὲν γὰρ δυνάμενον τῇ διανοίᾳ προορᾶν ἄρχον φύσει καὶ δεσπόζον φύσει, τὸ δὲ δυνάμενον [ταῦτα] τῷ σώματι πονεῖν ἀρχόμενον καὶ φύσει δοῦλον· διὸ δεσπότῃ καὶ δούλῳ ταὐτὸ συμφέρει. Newman comments: "The sketch of the political teaching of the Peripatetics here given . . . deserves study, as being in the main a *résumé*, though a brief one, of the teaching of the Politics" (107).

[25] 1255b, 20–22: ὁ μὲν οὖν δεσπότης οὐ λέγεται κατ' ἐπιστήμην, ἀλλὰ τῷ τοιόσδ' εἶναι, ὁμοίως δὲ καὶ ὁ δοῦλος καὶ ὁ ἐλεύθερος.

element serves the superior in the framework of a well-organized pattern whereby each part profits from its symbiosis with the other.[26]

This view of nature and humanity is proto-racist by definition. Mankind and indeed all of nature are divided into superior and inferior beings, a hierarchy determined by nature and thus unchangeable and constant. Aristotle does not explain how nature achieves this, but he describes it as an empirical truth and leaves no doubt that nature has made these distinctions in order to establish the hierarchies and their functions for the benefit of all and everything. He thus asserts that this division should have and has indeed essential and permanent consequences for social relationships. His observations about the different qualities of bodies and souls of slaves and freemen posit a direct and linear connection between physical and mental qualities, which is part of racism as defined. It is important to note that the insistence on the physical peculiarity of slaves is not only Aristotle's idea. It is encountered elsewhere: Theognis, for instance, declares that no slave ever has an upright head. His head always inclines forward and his neck is bent.[27] Xenophon even claims that free men and slaves have different smells.[28] These authors thus attribute to slaves collective traits, physical, mental, and moral, which are constant and unalterable by human will, because they are caused by a stable and external organizing entity (nature). It is not made clear if this is caused by heredity or external influences, such as climate or geography. Aristotle speaks of nature as determining all for well-defined purposes and leaves the question of methods open.

So far we have seen only that Aristotle distinguishes between two categories of men: masters and slaves by nature. Who are the masters and who the slaves? Aristotle is in fact quite specific: females and slaves are by nature different, he says, in accordance with their function (1252a, 35–1252b, 5). This is true only for Greeks, it appears. "Yet among barbarians the female and the slave have the same rank; and the cause of this is that barbarians have no class of natural rulers, but with them the conjugal partnership is a partnership of female slave and male slave. Hence the saying of the poets—'Tis meet that Greeks should rule barbarians [Euripides, *IA* 1400]'—implying that barbarian and slave are the same in nature."[29]

---

[26] 1256b, 15–27: Nature produces plants for the sake of animals and animals for the sake of man. It makes nothing without purpose or in vain and therefore has made all animals for the sake of men.

[27] He continues: "nor will a rose or a hyacinth ever grow from a squill, or a free child be borne by a slave woman." Theognis 1.535–8: Οὔποτε δουλείη κεφαλὴ ἰθεῖα πέφυκεν, ἀλλ᾿ αἰεὶ σκολιὴ καὐχένα λοξὸν ἔχει. οὔτε γὰρ ἐκ σκίλλης ῥόδα φύεται οὔθ᾿ ὑάκινθος, οὐδέ ποτ᾿ ἐκ δούλης τέκνον ἐλευθέριον.

[28] Xenophon, *Symposium* 2.4, cf. Cambiano, "Aristotle and the Anonymous Opponents of Slavery," 28.

[29] 1252a, 32–1252b, 9 (trans. Barker): φύσει μὲν οὖν διώρισται τὸ θῆλυ καὶ τὸ δοῦλον (οὐθὲν γὰρ ἡ φύσις ποιεῖ τοιοῦτον οἷον οἱ χαλκοτύποι τὴν Δελφικὴν μάχαιραν, πενιχρῶς, ἀλλ᾿ ἓν πρὸς ἕν· οὕτω γὰρ ἂν ἀποτελοῖτο κάλλιστα τῶν ὀργάνων ἕκαστον, μὴ πολλοῖς ἔργοις ἀλλ᾿ ἑνὶ δουλεῦον)· ἐν δὲ τοῖς βαρβάροις τὸ θῆλυ καὶ τὸ δοῦλον τὴν αὐτὴν ἔχει τάξιν. αἴτιον δ᾿ ὅτι τὸ φύσει ἄρχον οὐκ ἔχουσιν, ἀλλὰ γίνεται ἡ κοινωνία αὐτῶν δούλης καὶ δούλου. διὸ φασὶν οἱ ποιηταὶ

Aristotle thus asserts that among the barbarians there are only two categories of human beings: male slaves and female slaves. Among them there are no masters by nature such as we find among the Greeks. Following his grand theory he immediately draws the conclusion that the barbarians should be slaves of the Greek (men) who have a category of masters among them. So far he has not stated whether there are any natural slaves among the Greeks, but it is clear that among the barbarians there are only slaves. Later in the work he says so explicitly again: "the uncivilized peoples are more servile in character than Greeks (as the peoples of Asia, in turn, are more servile than those of Europe); and they will therefore tolerate despotic rule without any complaint."[30] These are ideas that we saw in chapter 1: they first appear in explicit form in the treatise *Airs, Waters, Places* which is undated, but certainly belongs to the fifth century.

Aristotle finds common ground with the critics of natural slavery on at least one issue: "Greeks taken prisoners are not slaves, but barbarians are and thus there are people who are essentially slaves everywhere and others who are so nowhere. The same line of thought is followed in regard to nobility, as well as slavery. Greeks regard themselves as noble not only in their own country, but absolutely and in all places; but they, the Greeks, regard barbarians as noble only in their country [sc. and not among Greeks]."[31] It must be noted here that there was no consensus along these lines in fifth-fourth century Greece. Democritus has said famously: "To the wise man every land is to be travelled; for the whole world is the native land of the good soul."[32] If the good men are at home everywhere, this implies that there are good non-Greeks.

For Aristotle, however, it is clear that slaves by nature are non-Greeks and the masters by nature Greeks, which means that the division between superior and inferior men is essentially one based on ethnic identity. Since these distinctions have been created by nature for good reason, it follows that the forceful subjugation and enslavement of non-Greeks by Greeks is just and beneficial because it agrees with the nature of both groups. "From this it follows that even warfare is by nature a form of acquisition—for the art of hunting is part of it—

"βαρβάρων δ᾽Ἕλληνας ἄρχειν εἰκός", ὡς ταὐτὸ φύσει βάρβαρον καὶ δοῦλον ὄν. On the position of the barbarian husband vis-à-vis his wife Newman remarks that it assumes an unnatural form, because that which is naturally the ruling element is wanting. If the wife is a slave, it is because everybody is so. She is not worse off than her husband (110). Cp. Euripides, *Hel.* 246, where Helen says, Τὰ βαρβάρων γὰρ δοῦλα πάντα πλὴν ἑνός.

[30] *Pol.* 1285a (trans. Ernest Barker). διὰ γὰρ τὸ δουλικώτεροι εἶναι τὰ ἤθη φύσει οἱ μὲν βάρβαροι τῶν Ἑλλήνων, οἱ δὲ περὶ τὴν Ἀσίαν τῶν περὶ τὴν Εὐρώπην, ὑπομένουσι τὴν δεσποτικὴν ἀρχὴν οὐδὲν δυσχεραίνοντες. The issue here is that the monarchy among the barbarians resembles tyranny, but is not, for the ruler governs according to law and the position is hereditary, a condition made possible by the servile nature of those peoples.

[31] *Pol.* 1255a, 31–36: ἀνάγκη γὰρ εἶναί τινας φάναι τοὺς μὲν πανταχοῦ δούλους τοὺς δ᾽ οὐδαμοῦ. τὸν αὐτὸν δὲ τρόπον καὶ περὶ εὐγενείας· αὑτοὺς μὲν γὰρ οὐ μόνον παρ᾽ αὑτοῖς εὐ γενεῖ· ἀλλὰ πανταχοῦ νομίζουσιν, τοὺς δὲ βαρβάρους οἴκοι μόνον, . . .

[32] Democritus, fr. 247 (Diels); C.C.W. Taylor, *The Atomists Leucippus and Democritus* (Toronto, 1999), 37, D111: ἀνδρὶ σοφῶι πᾶσα γῆ βατή· ψυχῆς γὰρ ἀγαθῆς πατρὶς ὁ κόσμος.

which is applied against wild animals and against those men who are not prepared to be ruled even though they are born for subjection, in so far as this war
is just by nature."[33] War then is a form of acquisition, just like hunting, and the
object of this process is the procurement of slaves among those peoples who are
slaves by nature, but refuse to comply with this demand.[34] Provided certain
norms are respected, war is therefore a legitimate process aimed at reducing
inferior foreigners to the state of slavery for which nature has designed them
anyway. Thus we see that the manner in which Aristotle viewed non-Greeks
serves as justification (not explanation or encouragement) for their subjugation.
The comparison with animals here is significant.[35] Aristotle does not say that
natural slaves are animals, but he regularly makes comparisons and concludes
that in some aspects slaves are closer to animals than to their masters, as will be
seen below.

At this point it may be useful to observe that this is the second opposition
between Greeks and non-Greeks encountered in Aristotle's *Politics*. The first is
discussed above: the environmental theory, as seen by Aristotle, is responsible
for a division of mankind in Europeans, Asiatics, and those in the middle, the
Greeks. The theory of natural slavery, by contrast, divides humanity in Greeks
and non-Greeks.

It will be clear that Aristotle's entire treatment of the issue of slavery is
theoretical and abstract. Aristotle describes the polis, and slavery with it, as it
ought to be, not as it was. The idea that Greeks should not have Greek slaves
was not unusual. There may even have been a consensus of sorts. Greek states
should not enslave Greek cities and Greek individuals should not acquire Greek
slaves. They should fight barbarians.[36] Practice was rather different. Although
many slaves in Greece were foreigners, the Spartans had their helots and the

---

[33] Aristotle, *Pol.* 1256b, 23–6: διὸ καὶ ἡ πολεμικὴ φύσει κτητική πως ἔσται (ἡ γὰρ θηρευτικὴ
μέρος αὐτῆς), ᾗ δεῖ χρῆσθαι πρός τε τὰ θηρία καὶ τῶν ἀνθρώπων ὅσοι πεφυκότες ἄρχεσθαι μὴ
θέλουσιν, ὡς φύσει δίκαιον τοῦτον ὄντα τὸν πόλεμον. Cf. comments by Newman, 2.177f., showing how variously this passage has been interpreted. For clarity I cite also the translation by Newman: "hence the art of war also is in some sense by nature a form of κτητική for of the art of war
the art of the chase is a part, which ought to be used agains both wild animals and such human
beings as being intended by nature to be ruled refuse to be ruled, seeing that this kind of war is by
nature just" (178).
[34] Schlaifer, "Greek Theories of Slavery," 176–181, emphasizes the exact identity of the bases of
the legal positions of the slave, metic, and foreigner in Athens.
[35] Schlaifer, 182, regards it as a mistake to insist too strongly on the analogy between the slave
and the beast.
[36] Plato, *Resp.* 469b–471b. The dialogue between Socrates and Glaucon might be read as implying there was a consensus, 469b–c: Πρῶτον μὲν ἀνδραποδισμοῦ πέρι, δοκεῖ δίκαιον Ἕλληνας
Ἑλληνίδας πόλεις ἀνδραποδίζεσθαι, ἢ μηδ' ἄλλῃ ἐπιτρέπειν κατὰ τὸ δυνατὸν καὶ τοῦτο ἐθίζειν,
τοῦ Ἑλληνικοῦ γένους φείδεσθαι, εὐλαβουμένους τὴν ὑπὸ τῶν βαρβάρων δουλείαν; Ὅλῳ καὶ
παντί, ἔφη, διαφέρει τὸ φείδεσθαι. Μηδὲ Ἕλληνα ἄρα δοῦλον ἐκτῆσθαι μήτε αὐτούς, τοῖς τε
ἄλλοις Ἕλλησιν οὕτω συμβουλεύειν; Πάνυ μὲν οὖν, ἔφη· μᾶλλον γ' ἂν οὖν οὕτω πρὸς τὸς βαρβάρους τρέποιντο, ἑαυτῶν δ' ἀπέχοιντο. Cf. Gregory Vlastos, *Platonic Studies* (Princeton, 2d ed.
1981), "Does Slavery exist in Plato's Republic?" 291–295.

Thessalians their *penestai,* all of them Greeks who had been enslaved.[37] A recent study has shown that before the reign of Philip of Macedon, Greeks, including Athenians, were not reluctant to enslave Greek women and children taken in the towns they captured from each other, but until late in the period the adult citizen males caught in these cities typically were killed, not enslaved.[38] More important, it is quite clear that Aristotle's natural slaves and their presumed characteristics are an invention for the sake of argument,[39] which does not mean that Aristotle and others themselves believed them to be a figment of the imagination. They served a purpose in an intellectual climate which justified wars of conquest and enslavement of the enemy.[40] It will be obvious that this in

---

[37] Plato, *Leges* 776c–778a, where it is said that the Helot system "is probably just about the most difficult and contentious institution in the entire Greek world"; cf. Brunt, "Aristotle and Slavery," 349f.; Garnsey, *Ideas of Slavery,* chapter 4. Athenaeus, *Deipnosophistae* 6.263c–264c, cites Posidonius as claiming that the Mariandynians "found themselves unable to manage themselves because of the weakness of their intellect and therefore gave themselves up voluntarily to the service of more intelligent men." Cf. P. Garnsey, "The Middle Stoics and Slavery," in P. Cartledge, P. Garnsey, and E. Gruen, *Hellenistic Constructs: Essays in Culture, History and Historiography* (Berkeley, 1997), 159–174 at 166–172. This text has been regarded as Aristotelian in its approach by several commentators, cited by Garnsey, 167, n.15. However, Garnsey himself says that, in spite of appearances, it is not Aristotelian. There can be no question that Garnsey is right. Athenaeus, 265b–c, also cites Theopompus (fourth century B.C.), who states that the first Greeks to use slaves were the Lacedaemonians and Thessalians and those slaves were vanquished Greeks. The Chians were the first to purchase non-Greeks as slaves. P. Garnsey, "The Middle Stoics and Slavery," at 165f., points out rightly that this as a whole should not be taken as representing Posidonius's views. There is no reason to doubt Athenaeus's assertion, however, that the relevant passage derives from the fourth-century historian Theopompus. Seneca, *Ep.* 90.4–5, cited in the same context, does not discuss slaves but leadership in the golden age. Moreover, it is hard to distinguish here between Seneca's own thoughts and those of Posidonius which he cites. Cf. Willy Theiler, *Poseidonios: Die Fragmente* 2 (Berlin, 1982), F 448, pp. 384–390. The text is, for good reasons, excluded from Kidd's collection.

[38] Rosivach, "Enslaving *Barbaroi,*" 129–141. Soldiers taken after a battle were normally held either for ransom, to exert political pressure, or to be exchanged for prisoners on the other side (137).

[39] Cf. Garnsey's conclusions, *Ideas of Slavery,* pp. 124–127, esp. 126. "He 'discovered' a body of people who would do nicely as natural slaves. Slaves in Greece were mainly barbarians, foreigners, and there was a convention against making chattel slaves of fellow Greeks. Aristotle decided to designate them, *qua* barbarian, natural slaves. This was a crucial decision, for otherwise the category of natural slaves might be thought of as entirely academic. It was also a popular choice, if Aristotle can be believed. The Greeks, he says point-blank, prefer to use the term 'slaves' only of barbarians (*Politics* 1255a 28ff., cf. 1252b 5ff.)." I disagree with Rosivach's suggestions for the origins of these ideas in "Enslaving *Barbaroi,*" 152–157. The first foreigners whom the Athenians enslaved, according to Rosivach, were Thracians, "a people whom the Athenians could see as culturally 'primitive,' at least compared with themselves." Even more important, says Rosivach: they did not speak Greek and language was particularly important to the Greeks. This is methodically unsound. The theory of natural slavery and its immediate application to non-Greeks is irrational, like any form of racist prejudice. Since this is an emotional process, denying reality, we can not understand such irrational prejudice through tracing factual reality. Worse: in a sense it legitimizes and masks irrational prejudice by providing it with a basis in reality.

[40] Cf. Charles Kahn in Günther Patzig, *Aristoteles' "Politik"* (1990), 1–27, at 28f., concludes "that the defence of slavery satisfies all the conditions for ideology. It obviously serves a class

itself does not make the Greeks more inhumane or crueller than other peoples. Nor does the theory of natural slavery explain imperialism. It is important because this shows that the Greeks were the first to make an attempt to argue about individual slavery and imperialist conquest and subjugation at this specific rational level. This is all the more important, because there is good reason to believe that Aristotle's views on slavery are representative of those held by many Greeks of the same class.

The theory of natural slavery forms a rationalization of inequality and as such is an important element in Greek imperialist ideology. For us it should be understood that this rationalization is in fact an emotional process which denies and distorts reality as we see it. It satisfies psychological needs through its apparent justification of essential inequality. In practice it also explicitly leaves the vanquished indefinitely in an inferior status. As will be discussed in some detail in chapter 4, Aristotle apparently advised his pupil Alexander of Macedon to pursue a policy of sharp differentiation between Greeks and (eastern) enemies, who were to be ruled and treated "like plants and animals" after their subjugation.[41] This shows a similar approach to vanquished foreigners and reflects Aristotle's personal conviction. There is no claim or pretense that the subject peoples will ever be incorporated into an integrated empire. There is only the theory of mutual benefit on an unequal footing. Thus it can be said that the theory combines an imperialist ideology with an uncompromising proto-racist attitude.

We must now see how the ideas of Aristotle and other authors influenced later generations and, in particular, how the ideas about slavery interacted with those about foreign conquest and empire. Before doing so, however, we may briefly look at some famous passages in the work of Thucydides and Plato which have a bearing on the present discussion. First, there are the Athenians' pronouncements in Thucydides' Melian dialogue,[42] notably "that in normal human speech 'justice' is determined by equal compulsion on both sides, whereas a superior power acts so far as its ability allows, and the weaker perforce submits."[43] "Of the gods we believe, and of men we know, that by a necessary law of their nature[44] they rule wherever they can. And it is not as if we were the first to make this law, or to act upon it when made: we found it existing before us, and

---

interest by justifying a system of gross inequality. It is supported by a painfully bad argument which takes as its premise the assumption of a difference in kind among humans that conflicts with one of the fundamental principles of Aristotle's own philosophy."

[41] Plutarch, *Mor.* 329 b–d (= *De Fort. Alex.* 6); see below, ch. 4, n. 178.

[42] For the Melian dialogue, "the moral theory," see J. de Romilly, *Thucydides and Athenian Imperialism* (Oxford, 1963), 298–310, and see now J. Price, *Thucydides and Internal War* (Cambridge, 2001), 195–204.

[43] Thucydides, 5.89 (trans. Price, op. cit., p. 199): ὅτι δίκαια μὲν ἐν τῷ ἀνθρωπείῳ λόγῳ ἀπὸ τῆς ἴσης ἀνάγκης κρίνεται, δυνατὰ δὲ οἱ προύχοντες πράσσουσι καὶ οἱ ἀσθενεῖς ξυγχωροῦσιν.

[44] Crawley's translation "by a necessary law of their nature" may be a little misleading, but there is justification. Thucydides says that οὗ ἂν κρατῇ, ἄρχειν is a principle universally obeyed ὑπὸ φύσεως ἀναγκαίας. In the next sentence he then refers to τὸν νόμον.

shall leave it to exist for ever after us; all we do is to make use of it, knowing that you and everybody else, having the same power as we have, would do the same as we do."[45] There can be little doubt here that, in the speech attributed to them by Thucydides, the Athenians assimilate the relation between imperial states and their subjects to that between master and slave.[46] The Athenians do not claim that this is just and right, nor do they claim that both sides profit from the unequal relationship, as does Aristotle in his theory of natural slavery. The Athenians merely claim it is inevitable.[47] Again, we must add that the Athenians may actually have said something altogether different at the time, but what counts for us is that Thucydides found it plausible for Athenian representatives to speek like this on such an occasion.

Callicles, speaking in the *Gorgias*, goes a step further towards Aristotle in claiming that this is not merely inevitable, but indeed just and right:

> But I believe that nature itself reveals that it is a just thing for the better man and the more capable man to have a greater share than the worse man and the less capable man. Nature shows that this is so in many places[48] both among the other animals and in whole cities and nations of men, it shows that this is what justice has been decided to be:[49] that the superior rule the inferior and have a greater share than they . . . I believe that these men do these things in accordance with the nature of what is just—yes, by Zeus, in accordance with the law of nature, and presumably not with the one we institute.[50]

This opinion is ascribed to Callicles and not to Socrates, who refutes it (*Gorgias* 488–490). Commentators have made various tentative suggestions about what kind of view Callicles here represents.[51] It seems probable that Callicles is meant to articulate an attitude which was held by at least some influen-

---

[45] Thucydides 5.105.2 (trans. Richard Crawley): ἡγούμεθα γὰρ τό τε θεῖον δόξῃ τὸ ἀνθρώπειόν τε σαφῶς διὰ παντὸς ὑπὸ φύσεως ἀναγκαίας, οὗ ἂν κρατῇ, ἄρχειν· καὶ ἡμεῖς οὔτε θέντες τὸν νόμον οὔτε κειμένῳ πρῶτοι χρησάμενοι, ὄντα δὲ παραλαβόντες καὶ ἐσόμενον ἐς αἰεὶ καταλείψοντες χρώμεθα αὐτῷ, εἰδότες καὶ ὑμᾶς ἂν καὶ ἄλλους ἐν τῇ αὐτῇ δυνάμει ἡμῖν γενομένους δρῶντας ἂν ταὐτό. See also 1.76. 2 and 4.61.5.

[46] See the commentary by Gomme and Andrewes: A.W. Gomme, A. Andrewes, and K. J. Dover, *A Historical Commentary on Thucydides*, 4 (Oxford, 1970), 162–164. Gomme, in discussing 1.76, refers to Democritus, fr. 267 (DK): φύσει τὸ ἄρχειν οἰκήιον τῶι κρέσσονι.

[47] For imperialism in the Athenian speeches, see de Romilly, *Thucydides and Athenian Imperialism*, esp.56f.

[48] E. R. Dodds, *Plato, Gorgias: A Revised Text with Introduction and Commentary* (Oxford, 1959), 267, takes the verb δηλοῖ as impersonal.

[49] Ibid., 267: "'right' has always been assessed in these terms, viz . . ."

[50] Plato, *Gorgias* 483c–e (trans. Donald J. Zeyl): ἡ δέ γε οἶμαι φύσις αὐτὴ ἀποφαίνει αὐτό, ὅτι δίκαιόν ἐστιν τὸν ἀμείνω τοῦ χείρονος πλέον ἔχειν καὶ τὸν δυνατώτερον τοῦ ἀδυνατωτέρου. δηλοῖ δὲ ταῦτα πολλαχοῦ ὅτι οὕτως ἔχει, καὶ ἐν τοῖς ἄλλοις ζῴοις καὶ τῶν ἀνθρώπων ἐν ὅλαις ταῖς πόλεσι καὶ τοῖς γένεσιν, ὅτι οὕτω τὸ δίκαιον κέκριται, τὸν κρείττω τοῦ ἥττονος ἄρχειν καὶ πλέον ἔχειν. . . . ἀλλ᾽ οἶμαι οὗτοι κατὰ φύσιν τὴν τοῦ δικαίου ταῦτα πράττουσιν, καὶ ναὶ μὰ Δία κατὰ νόμον γε τὸν τῆς φύσεως, οὐ μέντοι ἴσως κατὰ τοῦτον ὃν ἡμεῖς τιθέμεθα.

[51] Dodds, *Plato, Gorgias*, 266f., and others seem to prefer the view that the opinions here expressed are close to Plato's own emotional reactions to democracy, although, ultimately, he rejects them.

tial Athenians in Plato's time. In this view it is just and a law of nature that the better man and the better people subjugate the inferior. The text does not say that the inferiors are so by nature, but it states explicitly that those who are inferior should be subject to the superior "through a law of nature" (κατὰ νόμον γε τὸν τῆς φύσεως), a new and at the time paradoxical phrase.[52] It can therefore be said that some statements in the work of Thucydides and Plato anticipate certain elements of Aristotle's theory. It is also to be noted that the view as formulated here—even if it is refuted later in the same dialogue—represents more of an imperial ideology than Aristotle, for it focuses less on slavery and more on inequality in general. As stated it can easily serve as the basis of an expansionist ideology.

Aristotle's theory of natural slavery influenced later writers. Several accept the natural inferiority of some peoples as a given fact and posit that this justifies their subjugation and enslavement. This was a matter of both inevitability and justice. Moreover, both sides profited from the relationship. In this form it recurs in Cicero's *de Republica*. Relevant passages, however, have been preserved only indirectly, through quotations in Augustine's *City of God,* where arguments are cited in favor of the justice of slavery and imperialism. The foundation for this is that some peoples are by nature suitable to be subject to others.

This same book, *De Republica*, advocates the cause of justice against injustice with great force and keenness. The pleading for injustice against justice was first heard, and it was asserted that without injustice a republic could neither increase nor even subsist, for it was laid down as an absolutely unassailable position that it is unjust for some men to rule and some to serve; and yet the imperial city to which the republic belongs cannot rule her provinces without having recourse to this injustice. It was replied in behalf of justice, that this ruling of the provinces is just, because servitude may be advantageous to the provincials, and is so when rightly administered,—that is to say, when lawless men are prevented from doing harm. And further, as they became worse and worse so long as they were free, they will improve by subjection. To confirm this reasoning, there is added an eminent example drawn from nature: for "why," it is asked, "does God rule man, the soul the body, the reason the passions and other vicious parts of the soul?" This example leaves no doubt that, to some, servitude is useful; and, indeed, to serve God is useful to all. And it is when the soul serves God that it exercises a right control over the body; and in the soul itself the reason must be subject to God if it is to govern as it ought the passions and other vices.[53]

---

[52] As Dodds observes, Callicles' new phrase is not to be confused with "natural law" in the Stoic sense or with laws of nature in the modern sense of an observable law relating to natural phenomena. "Callicles' 'law of nature' is not a generalization about Nature but a rule of conduct based on the analogy of 'natural' behaviour." In other words he means a regularly occurring or apparently inevitable phenomenon observable in human society.

[53] Cicero, *de re publica* 3.35ff. from Augustine, *de civitate Dei* 19.21, trans. J. F. Shaw in *Nicene and Post-Nicene Fathers,* vol. 2, ed. Philip Schaff (Edinburgh, 1886).

CHAPTER 2 ·

The third book of Cicero's *de re publica* has been preserved in a very fragmentary state. In the passage above Augustine cites a debate staged between Philus and Laelius on the question of the justice in a state, particularly in Rome, and on Rome's relations with the empire. The topic of the debate is the thesis that a state cannot be governed without injustice. Against it is argued (by Laelius) that slavery can be beneficial to some people. Augustine gives this view his backing.[54] For us the argument is noteworthy in that the conquest and incorporation of foreign peoples into provinces is seen as just because Rome protects the provincials from harm.[55] This reads like the sort of argument Cicero himself would use.[56] It contains elements which remind us immediately of Aristotle, such as the idea that the provincial benefits from his subjugation according to the same principle which makes slavery beneficial to the slaves. The analogy between masters / slaves and soul / body also echoes Aristotle. However, in other respects it is different in tone, for the Roman source is far more explicit in describing the benefits to the ruled than Aristotle ever is. The complement which is present in Aristotle's *Politics* is lacking: Cicero and Augustine do not say that by nature the rulers profit from their subjects, in the same manner in which Aristotle argues that all inferior beings exist for the benefit of superior beings. Cicero, unlike Aristotle, feels that the existence of the empire is justified because of genuine advantages to the provincials. The attitude of Cicero and other Romans comes closer to the modern concept of the "White Man's Burden"[57] than to the attitude of earlier European colonialists. Cicero is also prepared to recognize that, in practice, there may be injustice: "For there is a kind of unjust slavery, when those who are capable of governing themselves are under the domination of another."[58] Aristotle also acknowledges that some people should be slaves nowhere (*Pol.* 1255a, 31f.), Cicero's words echo Aristotle, but Cicero more explicitly recognizes that real life is not always compatible with one's ideal.[59]

Conquest and incorporation of foreign peoples into provinces are seen as just because Rome protects the provincials from harm. Thus it corresponds with

---

[54] Cf. Garnsey, *Ideas of Slavery*, 40f. Garnsey also cites Augustine, *Contra Julianum* 4.12.61 and *de Civitate Dei* 14.23 containing passages which derive from Cicero's *de Republica* with echoes from Aristotle's theory of natural slavery.

[55] Garnsey, op. cit., 40, also cites the following related passage: Isidorus, *Origines* 18.1 (early seventh century A.D.); Nonius, p. 498.13: "Those wars are unjust that are undertaken without provocation. For only a war waged for revenge or defence can actually be just . . . But our people by defending their allies have gained dominion over the whole world."

[56] Garnsey, p.42, cites Cicero, *de Off.* 2.26, describing the ideal. The empire rules the provinces as a protectorate of the world (*patrocinium*) rather than a dominion. Cf. W. Capelle, "Griechische Ethik und römischer Imperialismus," *Klio* 25 (1932), 86–113.

[57] Kipling: "Take up the White Man's burden / Send forth the best ye breed / Go, bind your sons to exile / To serve your captives' need."

[58] Cicero, *De re publica* 3.38 (quoted in Nonius, p. 109.1): Est enim genus iniustae servitutis, cum ii sunt alterius, qui sui possunt esse; cum autem ii famulantur . . .

[59] Garnsey goes on to show how the theory of natural slavery is encountered in the works of Philo of Alexandria and early Christian authors.

Aristotle's claim that slavery is beneficial to the natural slave. "Servitude may be advantageous to the provincials, and is so when rightly administered, it shows that this is what justice has been decided to be:[60] that the superior rule the inferior and have a greater share than they." Here, more explicitly than anywhere in Aristotle, do we find an explicit justification for conquest and subjugation. It is not surprising that we should find it in Cicero more than in Aristotle, for Cicero was a political leader of a successful imperial power, Aristotle the tutor of a conqueror-to-be.

In the age of Augustus, Dionysius of Halicarnassus is writing for Greeks in Greek to persuade them that Rome deserves her empire ". . . that they, the Greeks, may neither feel indignation at their present subjection, which is grounded on reason (for by an universal law of nature, which time cannot destroy, it is ordained that superiors shall ever govern their inferiors), nor rail at Fortune for having wantonly bestowed upon an undeserving city a supremacy so great and already of so long continuance."[61] This ironically brings to mind Thucydides and Plato's Callicles and their justification of imperialism. We have here a simple Graeco-Roman imperialistic interpretation of the theory of natural slavery in its popular form, but for the benefit of Roman imperialism and its subjugation of the Greeks. It does not mention benefit and profit, but states, as a matter of course, that superior men will rule inferiors through a law of nature. Superior is here clearly associated with military success.

Strabo, writing in the reigns of Augustus and Tiberius, attacks Eratosthenes (third century B.C.) for his opinions on the difference between Greeks and barbarians. Strabo here is confused and confusing.

> Now, towards the end of his [Eratosthenes'] treatise—after withholding praise from those who divide the whole multitude of mankind into two groups, namely Greeks and Barbarians, and also from those who advised Alexander to treat the Greeks as friends but the Barbarians as enemies—Eratosthenes goes on to say that it would be better to make such divisions according to good qualities and bad qualities; for not only are many of the Greeks bad, but many of the Barbarians are refined—Indians and Arians, for example, and, further, Romans and Carthaginians, who carry on their governments so admirably.[62]

Whatever Strabo may have thought he meant, so much seems to be clear: there are authors who see humanity as divided between two groups: Greeks and others. The same, or related Greeks advised Alexander to treat Greeks and non-

[60] Above, n. 49.

[61] 1.5.2: φύσεως γὰρ δὴ νόμος ἅπασι κοινός, ὃν οὐδεὶς καταλύσει χρόνος, ἄρχειν ἀεὶ τῶν ἡττόνων τοὺς κρείττονας

[62] Strabo 1.4.9 (c.66): Ἐπὶ τέλει δὲ τοῦ ὑπομνήματος οὐκ ἐπαινέσας τοὺς δίχα διαιροῦντας ἅπαν τὸ τῶν ἀνθρώπων πλῆθος εἴς τε Ἕλληνας καὶ βαρβάρους, καὶ τοὺς Ἀλεξάνδρῳ παραινοῦντας τοῖς μὲν Ἕλλησιν ὡς φίλοις χρῆσθαι τοῖς δὲ βαρβάροις ὡς πολεμίοις, βέλτιον εἶναί φησιν ἀρετῇ καὶ κακίᾳ διαιρεῖν ταῦτα. πολλοὺς γὰρ καὶ τῶν Ἑλλήνων εἶναι κακοὺς καὶ τῶν βαρβάρων ἀστείους, καθάπερ Ἰνδοὺς καὶ Ἀριανούς, ἔτι δὲ Ῥωμαίους καὶ Καρχηδονίους οὕτω θαυμαστῶς πολιτευομένους. Cf. 1.2.3 (c. 15–17) for an earlier attack on Eratosthenes. For further discussion of this text, see chapter 4, p. 299f.

Greeks as two groups, the former being his own people, the latter representing the enemy. The issue is still the one that is present also in Aristotle's Politics: Greeks are superior, non-Greeks inferior, and this has consequences for current ideas about imperialism. Eratosthenes, so we understand from Strabo, argues against the division of mankind into Greeks and non-Greeks and prefers one which distinguishes between civilized peoples with good government and those who are uncivilized and poorly governed. It is fairly certain that the most important of Alexander's unnamed advisors is Aristotle, whose views on Greeks and non-Greeks we have seen. For the present topic it is important to note that there was continued disagreement about these matters in the third century B.C., and that the topic was also being debated in the reigns of Augustus and Tiberius. It still was in the second century A.D., as appears from thoughts about the topic by Dio Chrysostomos (15.25f.). The influence of the theory on early Christian authors and on mediaeval and later thinkers is well known and need not be traced in the present study.[63]

This is the place to observe that there existed a viewpoint quite different from Aristotle's theory of natural slavery, even if this had no consequence in practice. Among the later Stoics, Seneca argues at length for the need to treat slaves well. This does not mean that he rejects or even slightly doubts the essence of slavery and its place in society, let alone that he tried to reform the institution as such when he was one of the most powerful men in Rome. It is remarkable, however, that he quite explicitly rejects the tenets of Aristotle's reasoning: "Kindly remember that he whom you call your slave sprang from the same stock, is smiled upon by the same skies, and on equal terms with yourself breathes, lives, and dies. It is just as possible for you to see in him a free-born man as for him so see in you a slave."[64] Free men and slaves, in this view, are not different in respect of heredity or environment. This means that for Seneca there is no general law that there should be naturally ruling elements and elements naturally ruled. Seneca denies Aristotle's assertion that there are natural masters and natural slaves. In his view a slave must not by nature belong to another. Anyone could through bad luck become a slave and once a slave he could still be free in spirit.[65] Seneca was aware, as anyone living at court would have been, that a few former slaves attained some of the most powerful positions in the epire and he expresses no criticism of this.[66]

This chapter so far has dealt with a complex of arguments serving to explain and justify slavery and subjugation by claiming that slaves and the vanquished are inferior by nature. The slave or the subject has been fitted by nature for his

---

[63] For the theory as represented in the works of Philo and early Christian literature, see Garnsey, *Ideas of Slavery*. For the adaptation of the theory by Aquinas, see Brunt, "Aristotle and Slavery," 345f.; some comments on Locke and Hobbes: 354–356.

[64] Seneca, *Ep.* 47.10 (trans. R. M. Gummere, Loeb): Vis tu cogitare istum quem servum tuum vocas, ex isdem seminibus ortum eodem frui caelo, aeque spirare, aeque vivere, aeque mori! tam tu illum videre ingenuum potes quam ille servum. Cf. Garnsey, *Ideas of Slavery* (1996), 67f.

[65] *Ep.* 47.17: "Servus est." Sed fortasse liber animo.

[66] 47.9 commenting on Callistus, the powerful freedman of Gaius and Claudius.

station in life and so has the master or the conqueror according to the theory. Aristotle explicitly identifies the masters with the Greeks and the slaves or the subjects with non-Greeks. The advantage of this approach is that it makes slavery morally acceptable, because both parties benefit from their station in life and both are fulfilling roles suited to their natural abilities.

We should now discuss, however, a different perspective which makes no attempt at justifying anything, nor is it a consistent theory; it is rather a set of assumptions regarding the long-term effect of slavery on a person, an approach that gained much influence in Rome.

Plato, *Laws* 776d–778a:

ATHENIAN: We know we would all agree that a man should own the best and most docile slaves he can get—after all, many a paragon of a slave has done much more for a man than his own brother or son, and they have often been the salvation of ther masters' persons and property and entire homes. We know quite well, do we not, that some people do tell such stories about slaves?

MEGILLUS (SPARTAN): Certainly.

ATHENIAN: And do not others take the opposite line, and say that a slave's soul is rotten through and through, and that if we have any sense we will not trust such a pack at all? The most profound of our poets actually says (speaking of Zeus) that "If you make a man a slave, that very day / Far-sounding Zeus takes half his wits away [*Od.* 17.322–3].[67] Everyone sees the problem differently, and takes one side or the other. Some people do not trust slaves as a class in anything: they treat them like animals (κατὰ δὲ θηρίων φύσιν), and whip and goad them so that they make the souls of their slaves three times—no, a thousand times—more slavish than they were. Others follow precisely the opposite policy."

The interest of this discussion for our purposes lies in particular in the second, negative view of slaves. It is not important here whether Plato has more sympathy for the one or for the other view. It suffices if we may assume that it represents an attitude held in broad circles in contemporary Athens. It is stated explicitly that the very status of slaves is responsible for the poor state of their mind. The more they are treated like animals, the more they become slavish in spirit. This is a view which clearly has nothing to do with the theory of natural slavery (Plato's *Laws*, of course, antedates Aristotle's *Politics*). On the contrary, this view implies that the character of a slave is formed or destroyed by his status and may be further eroded by harsh treatment. The effect, however, is related to the theory of natural slavery, for it still assumes that slaves are inferior. There is no consensus on this matter, as is clear from Plato's dialogue, and we shall see below that there was another opinion, widespread in Rome, that the best manner to reinforce the slavishness of subjects was by encouraging

[67] *Leg.* 776e–777a: {ΑΘ.} Οὐκοῦν καὶ τοὐναντίον, ὡς ὑγιὲς οὐδὲν ψυχῆς δούλης, οὐδὲ πιστεύειν οὐδέποτ᾿ οὐδὲν τῷ γένει δεῖ τὸν νοῦν κεκτημένον· ὁ δὲ σοφώτατος ἡμῖν τῶν ποιητῶν καὶ ἀπεφήνατο, ὑπὲρ τοῦ Διὸς ἀγορεύων, ὡς—ἥμισυ γάρ τε νόου, φησίν, ἀπαμείρεται εὐρύοπα Ζεὺς ἀνδρῶν, οὓς ἂν δὴ κατὰ δούλιον ἦμαρ ἕλῃσι. Cf. Garnsey, p.89 with discussion on p. 93f.

them to indulge in luxury. In any case, the inevitable conclusion is that a man, once he is a slave, will forever be a slave, for he will not be a sound and fully fledged human being any longer. The passage from Plato's *Laws* is worth citing here, because we shall see that similar ideas determined the attitudes of historians towards the newly acquired provinces of the Roman Empire: the very fact of subjugation altered the spirit of a nation and the longer it was under foreign rule, the more it became irrevocably slavish. Here too there was an idea that the attitudes of the conquerors had an impact on the spirit of the vanquished or, rather, the very state of subjugation made the vanquished servile and unfit to live as free men.

The theme is taken up at another level in a dialogue on the effect of the monarchy on the quality of rhetoric in the treatise *On the Sublime,* ascribed to Longinus, probably written in the first half of the first century.[68] A philosopher advances one view: "In our times the art of persuasion and of being brilliant in public causes no longer reaches the highest level. The reason is that democracy (i.e., the republic as opposed to the principate) supports genius and only in a democracy does one find brilliant orators. . . . Freedom feeds the thoughts of great genius, inspires their hopes and fosters competition."[69]

"But we seem to have been educated to a school of legal servitude.[70] We are merely superb flatterers. A slave can acquire various skills, but he can never be an orator, for this requires a sense of freedom of speech."[71] The author replies: "Perhaps it is not peace in the whole world which corrupts the great minds, but the interminable war . . . greed . . . the search for pleasure. . . . It is the love of riches and of pleasure which enslaves us etc."[72]

This is a debate on the impact of political freedom as opposed to the mon-

[68] "Longinus," *On the Sublime,* ch. 44. For the date: D. A. Russell (Oxford, 1964), xxii–xxx: Caligula? Henri Lebègue, *Du Sublime* (Paris, 1965), xi–xiii: probably late in the reign of Tiberius.

[69] *De sublimitate* 44.2–3: πιστευτέον ἐκείνῳ τῷ θρυλουμένῳ, ὡς ἡ δημοκρατία τῶν μεγάλων ἀγαθὴ τιθηνός, ᾗ μόνῃ σχεδὸν καὶ συν ἤκμασαν οἱ περὶ λόγους δεινοὶ καὶ συναπέθανον; θρέψαι τε γάρ, φησίν, ἱκανὴ τὰ φρονήματα τῶν μεγαλοφρόνων ἡ ἐλευθερία καὶ ἐπελπίσαι, καὶ ἅμα διεγείρειν τὸ πρόθυμον τῆς πρὸς ἀλλήλους ἔριδος καὶ τῆς περὶ τὰ πρωτεῖα φιλοτιμίας.

[70] *De sublimitate* 44.3: οἱ δὲ νῦν ἐοίκαμεν ἔφη παιδομαθεῖς εἶναι δουλείας δικαίας, Russell: "but we of the present day . . . would seem to have learned from infancy to live in justified slavery virtually swathed round right from our first tender thoughts in the same habits and customs, never allowed to taste that fair and fecund spring of literature, freedom; so that we have turned out simply a set of magnificent toadies." The topics of this chapter are found also in various other authors of the first century A.D., such as the Elder Seneca and Tacitus in his *Dialogus.*

[71] *De sublimitate* 44.4: διὰ τοῦτο τὰς μὲν ἄλλας ἕξεις καὶ εἰς οἰκέτας πίπτειν ἔφασκε, δοῦλον δὲ μηδένα γίνεσθαι ῥήτορα. εὐθὺς γὰρ ἀναζεῖ τὸ ἀπαρρησίαστον καὶ οἷον ἔμφρουρον ὑπὸ συνηθείας ἀεὶ κεκονδυλισμένον·. Russell: "the inability to speak freely and the consciousness of being a prisoner at once assert themselves, battered into him as they have been by the blows of habit."

[72] *De sublimitate* 44.6.3 ὅρα δὲ μήποτε οὐχ ἡ τῆς οἰκουμένης εἰρήνη διαφθείρει τὰς μεγάλας φύσεις, πολὺ δὲ μᾶλλον ὁ κατέχων ἡμῶν τὰς ἐπιθυμίας ἀπεριόριστος οὑτοσὶ πόλεμος, Trans. Russell: "but consider—perhaps it is not the peace of the world which is the ruin of great natures, but rather this unlimited warfare which lays hold on our desires and all the passions which garrison and utterly lay waste to our modern life."

archy on the art of the orator. A second argument is that warfare, conquest, empire result in the deterioration of the art. This is important in the debate about imperialism. The first argument reflects the continued frustration of some Romans with the monarchy, in itself the product of a venerable tradition: the monarchy and the lack of freedom are responsible for the deterioration of the art of the orator. The idea goes back to fifth-century Greek literature and its value judgments about the monarchies of the East. The second argument is less common in this form. It argues for a connection between warfare, conquest, and the concomitant reinforcement of greed and luxury which destroy us.[73] From greed, vanity, and luxury spring in turn cupidity, pride, and softness. This then should explain the deterioration of eloquence in Rome. Essentially, however, this is the usual fear that successful conquest and increased luxury will cause decline, further to be discussed below. In any event, it is either servitude or luxury and wealth which undermine the art of the orator in Rome.

Servitude is a central motive in Cicero's thinking about contemporary Greeks. The first of Cicero's letters to his brother, appointed proconsul of Africa for a third year, is a sort of tract containing advice. He warns him to be cautious in his dealings with the Greeks in his province: "And further among the Greeks themselves there are certain intimacies against which you must be strictly on your guard, except intimacy with the very few, if any, who are worthy of ancient Greece. In your province, however, there are a great many who are deceitful and unstable, and trained by a long course of servitude to show an excesss of sycophancy."[74] We recognize here the disdain of some Romans, Cicero among them, towards contemporary Greeks,[75] in combination with the certainty that a state of subjugation distorts and degenerates character. It applies to a collective the idea which we recognized in Plato's *Laws* at the individual level.

This effect of conquest is emphasized again in the speech which Josephus attributes to Agrippa II, when he attempts to dissuade the Jews from war in A.D. 66.[76] One of Agrippa's arguments is that an attempt to regain liberty could not succeed: "There was, to be sure, a time when you should have strained every nerve to keep out the Romans; that was when Pompey invaded this country [i.e. in 63 B.C.]. But our forefathers and their kings, though in wealth and in vigour of body and soul far your superiors, yet failed to withstand a small fraction of the Roman army; and will you to whom thraldom is hereditary, you who in resources fall so far short of those who first tendered their submission, will you, I say, defy the whole Roman empire?"[77] To Agrippa—or to Josephus and his

---

[73] The idea that luxury destroys empires is encountered already in Herodotus 9.122, see above, chapter 1, and below, chapter 4.

[74] Cicero, *ad Quintum fratrem* 1.1.16: nunc vero fallaces sunt per multi et leves et diuturna servitute ad nimiam adsentationem eruditi.

[75] See below, chapter 9.

[76] Josephus, *BJ* 2.16.4 (345)–2.16.4 (401).

[77] Josephus, *BJ* 2.16.4 (356–358, trans. Thackeray, Loeb): τότε τοιγαροῦν ἐχρῆν πάνθ᾽ ὑπὲρ τοῦ μὴ δέξασθαι Ῥωμαίους ποιεῖν, ὅτε ἐπέβαινεν τῆς χώρας Πομπήιος. ἀλλ᾽ οἱ μὲν ἡμέτεροι πρό-

intended readers—it is obvious here that wealth, mental and physical strength of the Jews in Judaea deteriorate after their incorporation in the empire.

This theme is very prominent in the work of Tacitus: "The Britons, however, exhibit more spirit, as being a people whom a long peace has not yet enervated. Indeed we have understood that even the Gauls were once renowned in war; but, after a while, sloth following on ease crept over them and they lost their courage along with their freedom. This too, has happened to the long-conquered tribes of Britain; the rest are still what the Gauls once were."[78] Thus it is assumed as a matter of course that the conquest of a people and their subjection to another inevitably set in motion a process whereby they increasingly lose their belligerency, their sense of freedom, and their virility, the longer they are subjects. Cicero, Josephus, and Tacitus agree that it is an irreversible process. Above we saw that the Elder Pliny also saw it as part of the task of an empire to soften the customs of the subject peoples. His aim, however, was to praise Italy, rather than express disdain for the provinces.

A related but not quite identical concept is found in Caesar's assertion that the Gauls who live nearer the Roman province are more decadent than those who live in contact with or among the Germans: "Upon the Gauls, however, the neighbourhood of our provinces and acquaintance with oversea commodities lavishes many articles of use or luxury; little by little they have grown accustomed to defeat, and after being conquered in many battles they do not even compare themselves in point of valour with the Germans."[79] The cause of the deterioration of some Gauls is here not only their servitude, but also the corrupting effect of Roman wealth.

These two notions are combined in the claim of *On the Sublime*: "It is the love of riches and of pleasure which enslaves us." Tacitus also combines the two ideas in the description of Agricola's policy of what we often call Romanization in Britain: "For, to accustom to rest and repose through the charms of luxury a population scattered and barbarous and therefore inclined to war, Agricola gave private encouragement and public aid to the building of temples, courts of justice and dwelling houses. . . . He provided a liberal education for the sons of the chiefs . . . Roman dress became fashionable. Step by step they were led to things which dispose to vice, the lounge, the bath, the elegant banquet. All this in their ignorance, they called civilization, when it was but a

---

γονοι καὶ οἱ βασιλεῖς αὐτῶν καὶ χρήμασιν καὶ σώμασιν καὶ ψυχαῖς ἄμεινον ὑμῶν πολλῷ διακείμενοι πρὸς μοῖραν ὀλίγην τῆς Ῥωμαίων δυνάμεως οὐκ ἀντέσχον· ὑμεῖς δὲ οἱ τὸ μὲν ὑπακούειν ἐκ διαδοχῆς παρειληφότες, τοῖς πράγμασιν δὲ τῶν πρώτων ὑπακουσάντων τοσοῦτον ἐλαττούμενοι, πρὸς ὅλην ἀνθίστασθε τὴν Ῥωμαίων ἡγεμονίαν;

[78] Tac., Agr. 11.5: plus tamen ferociae Britanni praeferunt, ut quos nondum longa pax emollierit. nam Gallos quoque in bellis floruisse accepimus; mox segnitia cum otio intravit, amissa virtute pariter ac libertate. quod Britannorum olim victis evenit: ceteri manent quales Galli fuerunt.

[79] Caesar, *BG* 6.24: Ac fuit antea tempus, cum Germanos Galli virtute superarent, ultro bella inferrent, . . . nunc quoniam in eadem inopia egestate patientiaque Germani permanent, eodem victu et cultu corporis utuntur, Gallis autem provinciarum propinquitas et transmarinarum rerum notitia multa ad copiam atque usum largitur, paulatim adsuefacti superari multisque victi proeliis ne se quidem ipsi cum illis virtute comparant.

part of their servitude."[80] Tacitus thus ascribes to Agricola—whom he had known intimately—a dual and combined policy of undermining possible British resistance to Roman rule: encouraging a soft, Roman lifestyle robbing them of their virility, and the longer it lasted, the less they would be capable of reverting to their previous qualities as a warrior people. Slavery is always believed to cause degeneration. The Britons were being undermined by a soft servitude.

These ideas are found again, explicit or a little less so in other passages. The revolt of Boudicca was initiated by "the Trinobantes and others who, not yet cowed by slavery, had agreed in secret conspiracy to reclaim their freedom."[81] The Romans supplied the Germans with alcoholic drinks: "In quenching their thirst they are not equally moderate. If you indulge their love of drinking by supplying them with as much as they desire, they will be overcome by their own vices as easily as by the arms of an enemy."[82] Here as elsewhere in Roman texts we encounter the conviction that their own, Roman, culture was basically corrupt, combined with the notion that Rome uses this corruption to corrupt its subjects and hence to ascertain its continued domination. Tacitus attributes a speech of the unoccupied Tencteri to the occupied Agrippinenses in 69: "Resume the manners and customs of your country, renouncing the pleasures, through which, rather than through their arms, the Romans secure their power against subject nations."[83] He could not be more explicit. Another speech, attributed to the Batavian leader Civilis is equally telling: "Let Syria and Asia serve, the East is used to kings, but in Gaul there are still many who were born before the imposition of tribute."[84] Tacitus attributes here to the Batavian leader Civilis Roman prejudices against the Orient, discussed extensively in this work.[85] In the present passage, that is combined with the idea that those who are born under Roman rule deteriorate and cannot resist, unlike those born in freedom.

---

[80] Tacitus, *Agricola* 21: namque ut homines dispersi ac rudes eoque in bella faciles quieti et otio per voluptates adsuescerent, hortari privatim, adiuvare publice, ut templa fora domos extruerent, . . . ; paulatimque discessum ad delenimenta vitiorum, porticus et balinea et conviviorum elegantiam. idque apud imperitos humanitas vocabatur, cum pars servitutis esset.

[81] Tacitus, *Ann.* 14.31: . . . Trinobantibus et qui alii nondum servitio fracti resumere libertatem occultis coniurationibus pepigerant, . . .

[82] *Germ.* 23: proximi ripae et vinum mercantur. . . . adversus sitim non eadem temperantia. si indulseris ebrietati suggerendo quantum concupiscunt, haud minus facile vitiis quam armis vincentur. Parallels for this attitude and practice can, I think, easily be found in European colonial history. For drinking habits of various peoples: Plato, *Legg.* 1.637d–e. Gauls and Germans are accused of excessive drinking in various sources; see below p. 415f.

[83] *Hist.* 4.64.3: instituta cultumque patrium resumite, abruptis voluptatibus, quibus Romani plus adversus subiectos quam armis valent. sincerus et integer et servitutis oblitus populus aut ex aequo agetis aut aliis imperitabitis. See also chapter 1.

[84] Tac. *Hist.* 4.17: servirent Syria Asiaque et suetus regibus Oriens: multos adhuc in Gallia vivere ante tributa genitos.

[85] Cf. R. H. Barrow, *Slavery in the Roman Empire* (New York and London 1928, repr. 1968), 215: ". . . and it is the verdict of all antiquity, written plainly on every page of Greek and Roman literature." It seems to be also the verdict of Barrow: "(Rome) was to fall a victim to the insidious poison of Oriental languor, which rouses itself only to domineer, of Oriental vanity, which swells the more as the object of its pride drops from its failing grasp."

In fact, only those who are born in freedom have a chance of regaining it after they have been subjected. It is a sentiment echoed by Cassius Dio in the pre-battle speech which he attributes to the rebel queen Boudicca: "—let us, I say, do our duty while we still remember what freedom is, that we may leave to our children not only its appellation but also its reality. For, if we utterly forget the happy state in which we were born and bred, what, pray, will they do, reared in bondage?"[86] Cassius Dio had read Tacitus, undoubtedly, and he remembered his Tacitus when writing Boudicca's speech. However, the appearance of this phrase also shows that, in the third century, when Dio wrote, such ideas were enough of a commonplace to be inserted in a long literary speech which does not contain a single original thought.

An interesting variant of these assumptions has been cited already in a different connection. The second-century Favorinus argues that the hereditary material of children is passed on to them through the seed of the father and the milk of whoever nurses them, their mother or another woman.[87] For this reason Favorinus strongly argues for the mother to nurse her own children. According to Favorinus, it is especially damaging if the wet nurse "is either a slave or of servile origin and, as usually happens, of a foreign and barbarious nation." Favorinus thus regards it as obvious that a slavish nature is hereditary. Even a free woman would pass on the slavish character that she inherited from her slave ancestor to any child that she nurses.

There clearly is a widespread view that slaves and subjugated peoples are dangerous when they have recently lost their freedom, but over time slavery causes deterioration and this is believed to be true for individuals and for entire peoples. It is therefore essential to make subject peoples adapt to imperial rule at an early stage, and one of the means to do so is to corrupt them into adopting a Roman (degenerate) lifestyle. When they have been subject for a generation or two, they can no longer successfully rebel. Perhaps this was often true, but it was in any case a stereotype and that may be one of the reasons why the Romans were invariably surprised when rebellion broke out in the provinces.

As we shall see below, in chapter 11, Tacitus's fear of the Germans lies in the fact that they have not yet been subjected. A belligerent people which has not been subjugated and lives not far from Italy is particularly threatening.

We started this chapter with Aristotle's theory of natural slavery. Even though the theory may be traced in Cicero's work and in those of later, mostly Christian authors, it did not as such become widely popular. It was impractical as an ideology for the Hellenistic monarchies with their non-Greek majorities, and the prevalent Roman ideas about imperial rule were quite different from Aristotle's theory. Unlike Aristotle and other Greeks, the Romans did not declare all foreigners inferior by nature. Although Romans had a fair share of

[86] Dio 62.4.3 (trans. E. Cary, Loeb): τὰ προσήκοντα πράξωμεν, ἕως ἔτι τῆς ἐλευθερίας μνημονεύομεν, ἵνα καὶ τὸ πρόσρημα καὶ τὸ ἔργον αὐτῆς τοῖς παισὶ καταλίπωμεν. ἂν γὰρ ἡμεῖς τῆς συντρόφου εὐδαιμονίας παντελῶς ἐκλαθώμεθα, τί ποτε ἐκεῖνοι ποιήσουσιν ἐν δουλείᾳ τραφέντες;
[87] Aulus Gellius, Noctes Atticae 12.1; cf. above, chapter 1, n. 103.

imperial arrogance, their ideas about foreigners were more differentiated and integration was too much a reality for Aristotle's bipolar view to become generally accepted.[88] Furthermore, most authors did not feel an urgent need to justify and rationalize slavery in the manner in which Aristotle attempted to do this.

Yet the theory was known among intellectuals and there were elements of it which became firmly entrenched in mainstream Roman thinking. These are, first, the unquestioned assumption that it is possible and reasonable to relate to entire peoples in the same manner as to individuals. Second, masters and slaves, rulers and subject peoples live in a symbiosis beneficial to both parties. Third, this relationship and these differences are essentially stable from one generation to the next. The fundamental difference is that most Roman authors did not hold that all foreigners were inferior by nature. The Romans may have regarded themselves as superior, but other peoples were seen as having different and distinct qualities. Some indeed were "born for slavery," but others were not. There was indeed a clearcut idea that long-term imperial rule reduces a people to a state almost identical to that of natural slavery, and this was very influential. Thus, paradoxically, what is seen in our days as a remarkable success of the Roman Empire, namely its integration of subject peoples, is represented by at least some of the important Roman authors as a process which reduces those peoples from fierce and free humans to degenerate slaves. Since the common assumption is that this is an irreversible process, we end up with the image of something rather akin to Aristotle's natural slaves.

Florentinus writes in book nine of his *Institutiones*: "Freedom is the natural status of someone who is free to do whatever is not forbidden by force or law. Slavery is a condition determined by the *ius gentium* whereby someone is subject to a foreign master against nature."[89] Here we see the Roman legal definition which in fact denies the existence of natural slavery. It regards slavery as based on law or convention rather than nature, and states that it rests on force.[90] Slaves by convention are war captives, held to be slaves by law, the very argument which Aristotle attempted to neutralize by his theory of natural slavery.

It is interesting to observe, although this falls outside the scope of this work and of my competence, that the theory of natural slavery was taken up and echoed by a few Muslim Aristotelians.[91] Some of these also combined it with elements of environmental determinism. Thus Avicenna (980–1037) asserts that "God, in his providential wisdom had placed, in regions of great heat or great

---

[88] See Part 2.

[89] *Dig.* 1.5.4: Florentinus libro nono institutionum. Libertas est naturalis facultas eius quod cuique facere libet, nisi si quid ui aut iure prohibetur. Seruitus est const<it>utio iuris gentium, qua quis dominio alieno contra naturam subicitur. Cf. *Inst.* 1.3.2: Servitus autem est constitutio iuris gentium, qua quis dominio alieno contra naturam subicitur; and see John Chrysostom, *Homilia 24 in ep. ad Ephesios* 22.2 (*PG* 62, pp.155–160). I owe these references to Dr. Youval Rotman.

[90] *Dig.* ibid.: serui ex eo appellati sunt, quod imperatores captiuos uendere ac per hoc seruare nec occidere solent.

[91] Bernard Lewis, *Race and Slavery in the Middle East: An Historical Enquiry* (New York and Oxford, 1990), 37f., 54f.

cold, peoples who were by their very nature slaves, and incapable of higher things—for there must be masters and slaves."[92] Over time a religious version of the theory became a commonplace in that it was claimed that slavery was a road to the blessings of Islam.[93]

As stated in the Introduction, one of the major aims of this work is to clarify part of the underlying assumptions and attitudes of ancient imperialism and of the integration or nonintegration of foreigners into Graeco-Roman society. It is assumed that an understanding of negative attitudes towards other peoples may be instructive in this respect. This should be true, first of all, for the stage where one nation or empire sets out to subjugate and annex or incorporate another people or nation. It is also interesting to take into account what was the image in ancient sources of peoples that were not subjugated. The present chapter represents an attempt to illuminate this subject by tracing ancient views of conquered peoples as slaves. This does not so much clarify any explicit and verbalized imperialist policy, strategy, or ideology; rather, it shows the attitudes towards others which are part and parcel of imperialism as a state of mind.

We have seen that inferior foreigners and slaves are to some extent approximated to animals. Aristotle regularly compares natural slaves with animals and concludes that in some aspects slaves are closer to animals than to their masters. It is therefore interesting that a number of Roman moralizing and philosophical texts tend to associate the experience of pleasure with the servile and the animal. To give way to the uncontrolled pursuit of pleasure is to enslave one's mind to one's body.[94] Comparisons of human beings with animals will therefore be a fitting subject for the next chapter.

BRUTES AND ANIMALS

Art thou a man? Thy form cries out thou art.
Thy tears are womanish, thy wild acts denote
The unreasonable fury of a beast.
Unseemly woman in a seeming man,
And ill-beseeming beast in seeming both!
—*Romeo and Juliet*, 3.3.108–112

"Whether during the construction of an anti-tank ditch ten thousand Russian women collapse from exhaustion or not, interests me only in so far as the ditch is finished for Germany. We shall never be hard and heartless when that is unnecessary. So much is clear. We Germans are the only people on earth that has a decent attitude towards the animal and we will also assume a decent

---

[92] Ibid., 55 and note 7 on p.123, where reference is made to E.I.J. Rosenthal, *Political Thought in Medieval Islam* (Cambridge, 1958), 154f.

[93] Lewis, *Race and Slavery*, 38.

[94] Catharine Edwards, *The Politics of Immorality in Ancient Rome* (Cambridge, 1993), 195–198.

attitude towards these human animals, but it is a crime against our own blood to worry about them."[95] The metaphorical reduction of foreigners and minorities to animals is frequent in the nineteenth century. Friedrich Engels, for instance, observes that the "lowest savages can revert to an animal-like condition."[96] Himmler, cited here, does not say that the Russian women should be exterminated because they were animals or even vermin, although that was a familiar line taken by Nazi propaganda.[97] The women were, for Himmler, slave labor working for Germany, and as such he calls them human animals and orders his men to treat them like work animals, no better and no worse.

It is, however, not necessary to descend to this level in considering such notions. Thomas Jefferson, in his discourse about the differences between whites and blacks, repeatedly describes the latter as being closer to animals.[98] He is assured of "the preference of the Oran-ootan for the black women over those of his own species," an idea which, as we saw above, also occurred to Voltaire. Blacks "have a disposition to sleep when abstracted from their diversions, and unemployed in labour. An animal whose body is at rest, and who does not reflect, must be disposed to sleep of course." This example from Jefferson is more instructive than that of Himmler, since Jefferson combined such an attitude with a genuine democratic outlook and a firm belief in the equality of men, which, after all, is generally considered to be the Greek heritage. It has already been seen that not only Jefferson, but many authors in the eighteenth and nineteenth centuries such as Buffon, Voltaire, Le Bon, and Rousseau, were preoccupied with, or rather, confused as regards the differences between various groups of humans and animals, especially blacks and apes.[99] In

[95] Himmler's speech on 4 October, 1943 in Posen for senior SS-cadre. My translation from the German as cited in L. de Jong, *Het Koninkrijk der Nederlanden in de Tweede Wereldoorlog* 8.1 (The Hague, 1978), 7.

[96] *Dialectics of Nature*, trans. from the German by Clemens Dutt (Moscow, 1964), 173, cited by Poliakov, *The Aryan Myth*, 244 and n.89.

[97] Already in the 1890s a small anti-semitic faction in the Reichstag called upon the German nation: "Rotten sie diese Raubtiere aus!" cited by R. Hilberg, *The Destruction of the European Jews* (New York, rev. ed., 1985), 18. Cholera germs are also referred to which clearly implies that it is best to exterminate them. Cf. the ramblings of H. S. Chamberlain, *The Foundations of the Nineteenth Century*, English trans., 2 vols. (London and New York, 1911), 1.495: "At any rate it is only shameful indolence of thought, or disgraceful historical falsehood, that can fail to see in the entrance of the Germanic tribes into the history of the world the rescuing of agonising humanity from the clutches of the everlastingly bestial." The "everlastingly bestial" here refers to "the Asiatic and African slave, . . . the Syrian mongrel, . . . the Jew, the Egyptian, . . . the savage bloodthirsty Mongolian, and the Bedouin with his mad delusions . . ." etc., who together were undermining the world of classical Rome and its Indo-European heritage. It should be observed that the attitude is still encountered today. In a Dutch paper, *NRC-Handelsblad*, of August 19, 2002, Joris Luyendijk contributes a supposedly amusing piece about driving habits in the Middle East: "Libanese drive like hyenas, Israelis like dogs and Egyptians like lemmings." The implication is that this is also typical of the collective character of these peoples.

[98] Thomas Jefferson, in the chapter on Laws in his *Notes on the State of Virginia* (1787, ed. 1955).

[99] Shulamit Volkov, "Exploring the Other: The Enlightenment's Search for the Boundaries of

this connection it is engaging to observe that Diderot wrote in 1772: "And it was at the time when the wild beast known as the Roman people was either devouring itself or busy devouring other nations that historians wrote and poets sang."[100] It is not my intention to engage in crude comparisons between modern racism and ancient literature. However, it is instructive to consider ancient ideas about the difference between animals and human beings and to trace expressions in ancient literature which show that then too some peoples were described in terms suggesting that they resembled animals or actually *were* animals.[101]

In this chapter we are concerned with ideas at two conceptual levels: the individual and the collective. We shall see that Greek and Latin literature compares human beings with animals either because of their qualities as individuals or because of essential shortcomings perceived in their social organization. As formulated by Dover: "The difference between humans and animals lay, in the Greek view, not only in the obvious superiority of human reasoning but in the extent to which man had used his powers or reasoning to ameliorate his own condition and ensure his survival by growing crops (Isocrates, *Pan.* 28) and by forming communities operating under laws for the restraint of aggression."[102] The latter is brought out specifically in a pronouncement by Demosthenes: "If laws were abolished and each individual were given power to do what he liked, not only does our communal organisation vanish but our very life would be in no way different from that of the animals."[103]

It will not be the concern of this chapter to trace the antecedents of ideas, popular in the sixteenth and seventeenth centuries, which held that some for-

---

Humanity," in R. S. Wistrich (ed.), *Demonizing the Other* (1999), 148–167, esp. 153f. Note also Le Bon, who states that "The primitive races are those in which no trace of culture is met with. They have remained in that state bordering on animality which was traversed by our ancestors of the age of stone instruments": Gustave Le Bon, *Lois psychologiques de l'évolution des peuples* (Paris, 1894), translated as *The Psychology of Peoples* (1924, repr. New York, 1974), 27; see also p.43, where Le Bon asserts that "the superior grades of a population [are] separated intellectually from the inferior grades by a distance as great as that which separates the white man from the negro, or even the negro from the monkey."

[100] Diderot, "Pensées détachées ou fragments politiques échappés au portefeuille d'un philosophe," *Œuvres complètes* 10 (Paris 1971), 81–83, here cited from P. Vidal-Naquet and Nicole Loraux, "The Formation of Bourgeois Athens," in Pierre Vidal-Naquet, *Politics Ancient and Modern* (Cambridge, 1995), 82–140.

[101] Léon Poliakov (ed.), *hommes et bêtes: entretiens sur le racisme, actes du colloque tenu du 12 au 15 mai 1973* (Paris and the Hague, 1975) includes contributions by J. Mélèze-Modrzejewski, P. Vidal-Naquet, and M. Benabou which deal with the period considered in the present study. However, the focus of these papers is quite different. In Greek literature comparison of people with animals seems to be less common. See, however, Aeschylus, *Supplices* 751; 758; 762; 887; 895 and cf. Hall, *Inventing the Barbarian* (1989), 126.

[102] K. J. Dover, *Greek Popular Morality in the Time of Plato and Aristotle* (Oxford, 1974), 74f.

[103] Demosthenes 25.20 (as translated by Dover, loc. cit.): . . . ἐπεὶ λυθέντων γε τούτων, καὶ ἑκάστῳ δοθείσης ἐξουσίας ὅ τι βούλεται ποιεῖν, οὐ μόνον ἡ πολιτεία οἴχεται, ἀλλ᾿ οὐδ᾿ ὁ βίος ἡμῶν τοῦ τῶν θηρίων οὐδὲν ἂν διενέγκαι. Dover refers also to Xenophon, *An.* 5.7.32, equating human lawlessness with the behaviour of beasts.

eigners, such as American Indians, were not descendants from Adam, but represented a species generated spontaneously from the earth.[104] Admittedly, such theories were ultimately inspired by Aristotle, who postulates that certain primitive animals spring from rotting earth. This subject, however, is not relevant for the present chapter, for Aristotle speaks of animals, not of men, and he nowhere claims that some human beings actually *were* animals. Other ideas, however, might have had some influence, namely the old and traditional belief that in an early stage human beings were "earthborn" (γηγενεῖς). This has been discussed in chapter 1, where it was seen to be mostly associated with the claim of some cities that their earliest inhabitants were literally autochthonous. That, however, was an indication of nobility, while the later ideas regarding foreign peoples supposedly generated from the earth were developed in order to deny them equal status as sons and daughters of Adam and Eve. The second idea that definitely was influential is Aristotle's assimilation of slaves to animals.

The first work to be mentioned in this connection is that of Semonides of Amorgos, a seventh-century poet (not to be confused with Simonides of Ceos, 556–468 B.C.).[105] It is an iambic poem which describes ten types of women, seven of those made out of animals: a sow, vixen, bitch, ass, ferret, mare, and a monkey. All of these are disagreeable types: "In the beginning, the god made the female mind separately. One he made from a long-bristled sow. In her house everything lies in disorder, smeared with mud, and rolls about the floor; and she herself unwashed, in clothes unlaundered, sits by the dungheap and grows fat. Another he made from a bitch, vicious, own daughter of her mother, who wants to hear everything and know everything," and so on.[106]

This text is, of course, important for the information it gives about the manner in which archaic Greek men viewed women,[107] but that is not the topic of the present study. It is relevant here for its description of human individual types in terms of animals. It has already been observed that these ideas often go together: man and animal, male and female, different types of peoples. As a literary exercise in stereotyping, the comparison with animals has been mentioned above because it is the first known example of a literary genre which was to become famous through Theophrastus's *Characters*. We have seen already that there are two methods whereby people are described as or compared with animals. First, there is the technique applied by Himmler, described above, whereby people are called animals in order to deny their humanity. Second,

---

[104] See chapter 1, above. For people "bred in the soil," in ancient and early modern literature, see also J. W. Johnson, *Journal of the History of Ideas* 21 (1960), 465–480.

[105] Martin West, *Iambi et elegi Graeci* (Oxford 1972), vol. 2, 97–109; 111–112; Hugh Lloyd-Jones, *Females of the Species: Semonides on Women* (London, 1975).

[106] (trans. Lloyd-Jones, p. 36): χωρὶς γυναικὸς θεὸς ἐποίησεν νόον / τὰ πρῶτα. τὴν μὲν ἐξ ὑὸς τανύτριχος, / τῆι πάντ' ἀν' οἶκον βορβόρωι πεφυρμένα / ἄκοσμα κεῖται καὶ κυλίνδεται χαμαί· / αὐτὴ δ' ἄλουτος ἀπλύτοις ἐν εἵμασιν / ἐν κοπρίηισιν ἡμένη πιαίνεται. / τὴν δ' ἐξ ἀλιτρῆς θεὸς ἔθηκ' ἀλώπεκος / γυναῖκα πάντων ἴδριν· οὐδέ μιν κακῶν / λέληθεν οὐδὲν οὐδὲ τῶν ἀμεινόνων·

[107] For the relationship of Semonides' poem to the views of women in the work of Hesiod, see Lloyd-Jones, pp. 18–21.

there is the manner in which fables look at people, describing animals as if they were humans, whereby those people in turn are given the presumed characteristics of the relevant animal: thus a tale about a fox actually describes a foxy type of person. As observed above, the comparison of specific human types with animals is a popular form of stereotyping, because all animals of a given sort are alike. The inference is then that something similar is the case with human beings.

Semonides' poem represents an intermediate variety. It claims that the specific type of woman is literally made out of an animal. The woman is then described as if she has the presumed characteristics of this animal, just as is being done in fables. However, in Semonides' poem the woman made from a sow *is* a sow, lives like one and has a sow's character. Another ancient text based on a related idea is an Aesopic fable, undated like all of them, which tells how Zeus ordered Prometheus to make men and animals. When Prometheus created too many animals he was forced to re-shape some animals into men, but as a result some men have a human shape, but a bestial soul.[108] The point of this is the same: some men, thought to have bestial characters, essentially *are* beasts. There is no immediate connection here with the physiognomic approach which assumes that people who somehow look like certain animals must have characters like those animals.[109]

As noted, one of the essential qualities of humanity lay, in the Greek view, in the formation of social communities operating under laws for the restraint of aggression. Political ideology could therefore play a role in comparisons of human beings with animals. Lysias asserts that the Athenians established a democracy, "because they considered it to be the business of animals to be subject to others by force."[110] As distinct from the sources cited so far, this concerns not man as an individual, but his organization at a social level. In the social sphere too Plato uses animal analogy to justify and explain eugenics in his *Republic*, an integral part of his proposed utopia. As seen above, he suggests applying to the breeding of the guardians, the highest class in his projected state, the

---

[108] *Corpus fabularum Aesopicarum*, ed. A. Hausrath, No. 228: ΠΡΟΜΗΘΕΥΣ ΚΑΙ ΑΝ-ΒΡΩΠΟΙ. Προμηθεὺς κατὰ πρόσταξιν Διὸς ἀνθρώπους ἔπλασε καὶ θηρία. ὁ δὲ Ζεὺς θεασάμενος πολλῷ πλείονα τὰ ἄλογα ζῷα ἐκέλευσεν αὐτὸν τῶν θηρίων τινὰ διαφθείραντα ἀνθρώπους μετατυπῶσαι. τοῦ δὲ τὸ προσταχθὲν ποιήσαντος συνέβη τοὺς ἐκ τούτων πλασθέντας τὴν μὲν μορφὴν ἀνθρώπων ἔχειν, τὰς δὲ ψυχὰς θηριώδεις. πρὸς ἄνδρα σκαιὸν καὶ θηριώδη ὁ λόγος εὔκαιρος.

[109] Lloyd-Jones, *Females of the Species*, 29–33 discusses "characters." "The whole point of Semonides' poem is that certain types of women do resemble certain animals" (p. 29). It is a work of art intended to give entertainment. The author "wished to entertain his audience by exploiting an observed resemblance between certain kinds of woman and certain kinds of animal, and by making use of this to argue the case in favour of the familiar thesis that the biggest plague to man is woman." All this may be true, but it remains a fact that the characterization of human beings as animals has emotional and intellectual consequences which need to be considered.

[110] Lysias, *Epitaphios* 19: ἡγησάμενοι θηρίων μὲν ἔργον εἶναι ὑπ' ἀλλήλων βίᾳ κρατεῖσθαι, F. J. Snell, *Lysias: Epitaphios* (Oxford, 1887), 16, refers to Plato, *Prot.* 321. Suzanne Saïd, "The Discourse of Identity in Greek Rhetoric from Isocrates to Aristides," in Malkin (ed.), *Ancient Perceptions of Greek Ethnicity* (2001), 275–299, esp. 279, observes that, in Greek rhetoric, barbarians in general are often compared or indirectly assimilated with animals.

methods which are applied naturally to hunting dogs, horses, and fighting birds in order to prevent deterioration of stock.[111]

However, the conceptual basis for the description of human beings as animals is analyzed by Aristotle, who asserts that "a bestial character is rare among human beings; it is found most frequently among barbarians, and some cases also occur (among Greeks) as a result of disease or arrested development. We sometimes also use 'bestial' as a term of opprobrium for a surpassing degree of human vice."[112] The reference to disease and arrested development and the remark about the special use of the term clearly is intended to explain the phenomenon when it occurs among Greeks. It also implies that, when applied to non-Greeks, the term is meant literally and not as a metaphor. Later in the same work Aristotle explains what he means by "bestial," arguing that there are two kinds of folly: "people irrational by nature and living solely by sensation, like certain remote tribes of barbarians, belong to the bestial class, others who lose their reason because of a disease or insanity, belong to the diseased."[113] Although Aristotle does not say so explicitly, it follows that he considers some foreign peoples collectively bestial. A little earlier Aristotle gives examples of what he means by unnatural pleasures or inclinations. He means a female (τὴν ἄνθρωπον) who is said to tear to pieces pregnant women and eats the offspring, or savages around the Black Sea, who are said to enjoy eating raw meat or human flesh[114] "and others among whom each in turn provides a child for the common banquet . . ."[115] These are instances of bestiality." The entire discussion is theoretical, but the examples are concrete, even though totally fictitious. Eating uncooked meat is one of the most obvious marks of lack of civilization in the opinion of the Greeks, as we see frequently in this study.[116] It is well known, however, that Aristotle was not the only Greek of his age preoccupied with notions of cannibalism.[117] More will be said about this below. In any event, it is clear that bestiality is a symptom or description of well-defined mental pathology in Greeks or a collective description of some particular inferior non-Greek peoples.

People were considered bestial if controlled by feelings and passions rather

[111] Cf. H. D. Rankin, *Plato and the Individual* (1964), 51–54 on the animal analogy in *Resp.* 459.

[112] Aristotle, *Eth. Nic.* 1145a, 29–33: οὕτω καὶ ὁ θηριώδης ἐν τοῖς ἀνθρώποις σπάνιος· μάλιστα δ' ἐν τοῖς βαρβάροις ἐστίν, γίνεται δ' ἔνια καὶ διὰ νόσους καὶ πηρώσεις· καὶ τοὺς διὰ κακίαν δὲ τῶν ἀνθρώπων ὑπερβάλλοντας οὕτως ἐπιδυσφημοῦμεν.

[113] Aristotle, *Eth.Nic.* 1149ag: καὶ τῶν ἀφρόνων οἱ μὲν ἐκ φύσεως ἀλόγιστοι καὶ μόνον τῇ αἰσθήσει ζῶντες θηριώδεις, ὥσπερ ἔνια γένη τῶν πόρρω βαρβάρων, οἱ δὲ διὰ νόσους, οἷον τὰς ἐπιληπτικάς, ἢ μανίας νοσηματώδεις. 1149a, 4–7: πᾶσα γὰρ ὑπερβάλλουσα καὶ ἀφροσύνη καὶ δειλία καὶ ἀκολασία καὶ χαλεπότης αἳ μὲν θηριώδεις αἳ δὲ νοσηματώδεις εἰσίν· On a closely related topic, see Keith Bradley, "Animalizing the Slave: the Truth of Fiction," *JRS* 90 (2000), 110–125.

[114] Cf. below the chapter on attitudes towards Egyptians with Juvenal's 15th satire on Egyptian cannibals eating their human flesh uncooked.

[115] The text here is problematic. I follow the Loeb translation.

[116] One of the early instances is Thucydides 3.94, who has heard this of some of the Aetolians, but will not vouch for the accuracy of the information.

[117] See, for instance, Isocrates, *Busiris* 5 (222).

than rational processes, and thus indulged in unnatural behavior. This is thought typical of distant foreigners and of pathological Greeks. The further implication of this is that the foreigners who do not control their powers of reasoning lack this capacity collectively, by nature and not through illness, and they are therefore incapable of forming orderly communities together. This is one of the reasons why foreigners are regarded as natural slaves. As already seen above, the "natural slaves" of Aristotle's *politics* are not quite identified with the brutish peoples of Aristotle's *Nicomachean Ethics*, although the natural slaves definitely are subhuman.[118] By contrast, the individual Greeks who are bestial are merely sick individuals who lack essential qualities. Their existence does not affect the whole of society.

It is worth considering also what Aristotle's observations tell us about contemporary ideas about animals. In his view excessive emotional patterns such as cowardice and ill-temper are either bestial or morbid.[119] We should note the automatic assumption here that animals normally yield to unnatural pleasures or inclinations, as if this were an obvious fact. This is especially remarkable since Aristotle and his followers made a point of observing nature as it is. They ought to have known or could have known that most animals do not practice the sort of acts they attribute to brutish people. Obviously, the Greeks, like other peoples, did not care whether what they said about animals was true or false.[120]

Aristotle himself does not try to give an explanation for the presumed bestialities of some foreign peoples which he describes. However, a Ps.Aristotelian text asks: "Why are those who live in conditions of excessive cold or heat beast-like both in habits and in appearance? Are both results due to the same cause?" The answer is in the affirmative. "For the best mixture benefits the mind but excesses disturb it, and just as they cause distortion to the body, so do they also affect the mental temperament."[121] This is yet another example of Aristotle's and his followers' firm belief in the environmental theory. It also shows a related conviction that this theory applies to both physical and mental characteristics in comparable fashion. Thus they reached the conclusion that people living in extreme climates are brutes in mind and body, and this conclusion is a generalization, for climate affects entire peoples, not individuals.

For the continued application of these theories it may be interesting here to note that they were considered relevant in justifying the enslavement of the American Indians. In 1512 Ferdinand II of Aragon summoned a *junta* to meet at Burgos and decide on the legitimacy of the conquest and the employment of native labor. Two of the opinions offered are extant. Both of these rested their arguments for the subjugation of the Indians on the claim that the Amerindian peoples were obviously barbarians and thus the natural slaves described by

---

[118] See Garnsey, *Ideas of Slavery*, 114, for a tentative explanation.

[119] *Eth. Nic.* 1149a 4–7. See above, n. 113.

[120] Cf. Dover, *Greek Popular Morality*, 75, n. 2.

[121] Ps. Aristotle, *Probl.* 909a: Διὰ τί θηριώδεις τὰ ἔθη καὶ τὰς ὄψεις οἱ ἐν ταῖς ὑπερβολαῖς ὄντες ἢ ψύχους ἢ καύματος; ἢ διὰ τὸ αὐτό; ἢ γὰρ ἀρίστη κρᾶσις καὶ τῇ διανοίᾳ συμφέρει, αἱ δὲ ὑπερβολαὶ ἐξιστᾶσι, καὶ ὥσπερ τὸ σῶμα διαστρέφουσιν, οὕτω καὶ τὴν τῆς διανοίας κρᾶσιν.

Aristotle in the *Politics,* "where it appears," said one of the two, called Gil Gregorio, "that through the barbarity and wicked disposition of the people of the Antilles they may, and should, be governed as slaves." Tyranny is the appropriate mode of government for the Indians because "slaves and barbarians . . . are those who are lacking in judgment and understanding as are these Indians who, it is said, are like talking animals."[122] Thus we see here that Aristotle's theories about natural slavery, barbarism, and brutishness were used as arguments to justify the Spanish treatment of the local population in the American colonies.

The point at issue in the passage of Aristotle's *Politics* 1253a, cited below, is that he quite explicitly classifies groups of people as bestial. Aristotle is not the first and certainly not the only one to do so, as is clear from the commonplace about non-Greek speech, regularly compared with animal noises.[123] The next question to consider then is what consequences this had for the way people considered bestial by Greeks or Romans were treated. The equation: they are animals and must therefore be destroyed, is never encountered in ancient sources. Although mass murder was not uncommon in antiquity, it is clear that there was no emotional need to portray the victims as animals in order to justify large-scale extermination. What concerns us here are not comparisons of individuals and their specific behavior,[124] but comparisons of groups and nations with animals, and whether there was a relation between viewing groups as animal-like and the way they were treated by the Greeks and, particularly, the Roman authorities. It should be noted that there are almost innocent forms of calling a human being an animal which we encounter regularly in daily life, when one person calls another "an ass," "a dog," or "a swine." Although such expressions are meant to be negative and crude, it is not really implied that the other has lost his humanity. The suggestion is that the named person has specific negative qualities which are, for some reason, almost always incorrectly associated with the named animal.

"In the beginning Africa was inhabited by the Gaetulians and Libyans, rude and uncivilized folk, who fed like beasts on the flesh of wild animals and the

---

[122] A. Pagden, *The Fall of Natural Man* (1982), 47–50; cf. 93, where he cites García de Loaysa's belief that they were "soulless parrots in human guise." See Lewis Hanke, *Aristotle and the American Indians: A Study in Race Prejudice in the Modern World* (Bloomington, IN, 1955), 15; see chapter 5 for the great debate in 1550–1551 at Valladolid between Las Casas and Sepúlveda about the application of Aristotle's theory of natural slavery to the American Indian and see especially pp. 55–61 for the interpretations of Aristotle's theory at the time.

[123] First attested in Aristophanes, Karl Deichgräber, *Parabasenverse aus Thesmophoriazusen II des Aristophanes bei Galen,* Sitzungsberichte der Deutschen Akademie der Wissenschaften zu Berlin, Klasse für Sprachen, Literatur und Kunst, Jahrg. 1956, Nr. 2

[124] Cf. Dominique Goguey, "Les Romains et les animaux: regard sur les grands fauves, liens affectifs entre l'homme et l'animal," in *Homme et animal dans l'antiquité romaine: actes du colloque de Nantes 1991* (Tours, 1995), 52–66, which is mostly concerned with relationships between men and animals as depicted in the literature of the Principate, but also pays some attention to comparisons of individual behavior with animals in ancient literature. See further the older study: A. Sauvage, *Étude de thèmes animaliers dans la poésie latine* (Brussels, 1975).

fruits of the earth. They were not governed either by institutions or law, nor were they subject to anyone's rule. A restless, roving people, they had their abodes wherever night compelled a halt."[125] Sallust informs his readers that he gives his account based on a translation from the Punic books said to have been written by king Hiempsal (sc. king of Numidia, father of Pompey's ally Juba), and in accordance with what the inhabitants of that land believe. This reminds us of the later scholarly treatise on Arabia, dedicated to Gaius Caesar by King Juba of Mauretania.[126] There were thus at least two geographical books written by learned North African client kings. The passage has also been mentioned above because of the interesting idea that there were original inhabitants mixed with newcomers resulting in the existing population. For the present discussion the comparison with beasts is noteworthy. What made those living in Africa in the beginning brutish or animal-like was their lifestyle of roving without institutions, law, or governments like the later Nomads, of whom the Romans also do not usually approve. Nomadic peoples are more often regarded as brutish or animal-like. Thus, Marius is said to have told his troops not to fear the shape or voices of the Cimbri and Teutones, which were absolutely strange and brutish.[127] This follows the Greek tradition, outlined above, which holds that one of the essential differences between humans and animals is their capacity for social organization. Tacitus tells of reports that the ultimate German tribes have the faces and visages of men and the bodies and limbs of wild beasts, but he does not vouch for the truth of this information (*Germania* 46.4).

Comparison of individuals with animals is a concomitant and closely related phenomenon. It is a favorite derogatory term in rhetoric. We find it occasionally in the speeches of Demosthenes.[128] Cicero uses it very frequently in his orations: the word *belua* occurs sixty-five times in his work, *bestia* as often, usually of course in connection with persons he fiercely attacked, such as Verres,[129] and Marcus Antonius: "You are not now dealing, Romans, with a man merely criminal and base, but with a monstrous and abominable beast."[130] These instances are interesting, for such people are of course not called animals because they suffered from a lack of literary culture or foreign lifestyle. Cicero wants to deny his targets, not culture, but any basic humanity by calling them "animals." This

---

[125] Sallust, *Iug.* 18.1: Africam initio habuere Gaetuli et Libyes, asperi incultique, quis cibus erat caro ferina atque humi pabulum uti pecoribus. ii neque moribus neque lege aut imperio quoiusquam regebantur: vagi palantes quas nox coegerat sedes habebant. See also above for discussion of other points of interest in the same passage. Diodorus describes some of the peoples who live in the remoter parts of Africa as "living like animals": 3.16.7, 3.31.4.

[126] Pliny, *NH* 6.31.141.

[127] Plutarch, *Marius* 16.2: τὴν μορφὴν . . . καὶ τὴν φωνὴν . . . ὅλως οὖσαν ἀλλόκοτον καὶ θηριώδη . . . also: 20.2.

[128] Demosthenes 24.143: τοῖς θηρίοις; 25.8; 58.49.8.

[129] Cicero, *in Verrem* 2.5.109: Cum homine [enim] crudeli nobis res est an cum fera atque immani belua?

[130] Cicero, *Philippic* 4.5.12: Non est vobis res, Quirites, cum scelerato homine ac nefario, sed cum immani taetraque belua quae, quoniam in foveam incidit, obruatur. *Passim* throughout the Philippics.

resembles modern custom more than the texts discussed so far, for the persons whose humanity is denied are not strange or frightening foreigners, but Romans belonging to the same social class.

A first- or second-century author, Cleomedes, attacks the vulgar language of Epicurus and mentions the Jews incidentally. In his criticism of Epicurus's language he mentions brothels, the Thesmophoria, and the synagogue. ". . . in part these (expressions) issue from the midst of the synagogue and the beggars in its courtyards. These are Jewish and debased and much lower than reptiles."[131] The description as lower than animals here refers to expressions, not to a people. Yet the implication is that such people spoke a language baser than reptiles. This belongs to the tradition which associates barbarian speech with animal noises.

Aristotle's observations and those of his predecessors and followers derive from tales about imagined peoples at the edge of the world or about an early form of human existence. The latter form is clearly echoed by Cicero, where he describes early human society as he believes it must have been. "Men wandered around in the open, like animals and lived on uncultivated food. Not reason but brute force determined action, there was no religion, no social obligations, no marriage or family-life, no law" etc.[132] It is a bleak view of early humanity, quite different from the idealizing tendency, which we found in Plato's description of humanity after the Great Flood or in the vision of the Golden Age.

Cicero influenced medieval authors such as Albertus Magnus, already mentioned several times, who cites Cicero and speaks of the "wild men leading the life of animals with the wild beasts . . ." and adds that "bestial men eat raw flesh and drink blood, and are delighted to drink and eat from human skulls."[133] Eating raw flesh is, as we have seen, an important theme in Greek and Roman culture. Drinking blood and eating from human skulls may be a later, Christian preoccupation. Following Albertus Magnus, Aquinas further developed the concept of the "Great Chain of Being,"[134] which represents a hierarchy of nature in

---

[131] Cleomedes, *De Motu Circulari* 2.1.91, Stern, No. 333, comments on 2.157f.: τὰ δὲ ἀπὸ μέσης τῆς προσευχῆς καὶ τῶν ἐπ' αὐλαῖς προσαιτούντων, Ἰουδαικά τινα καὶ παρακεχαραγμένα καὶ κατὰ πολὺ τῶν ἑρπετῶν ταπεινότερα. See also below, Part 2, chapter 13.

[132] Cicero, *De Inventione* 1.2: cum in agris homines passim bestiarum modo vagabantur et sibi victu fero vitam propagabant. nec ratione animi quicquam, sed pleraque viribus corporis administrabant, nondum divinae religionis, non humani officii ratio colebatur, nemo nuptias viderat legitimas . . .

[133] Albertus Magnus, *Ethicorum* 7.1.1 ed. Borgnet, vol. 7, p. 464, cited by Pagden, *The Fall of Natural Man*, 21.

[134] Thomas Aquinas, *Summa contra gentiles* 2.68. Cf. Arthur O. Lovejoy, *The Great Chain of Being: A Study of the History of an Idea* (Cambridge, MA, 1936). It was a key concept in the eighteenth century and, towards the end of this century, served as a tool to justify classifying blacks as less than human by Edward Long, *Candid Reflections upon the Judgement Lately Awarded by the Court of King's Bench in Westminster-Hall On What is Commonly Called the Negroe-cause / by a Planter* (London, 1772), which I have not seen; cf. Anthony J. Barker, *The African Link: British Attitudes to the Negro in the Era of the Atlantic Slave Trade, 1550–1807* (London, 1978), 41–58. Long's racist views were widely cited in the United States as a source for arguments in favor of slavery. In the nineteenth century, representatives of the "American School" of anthropology, J. C.

which the highest member of a species always approaches in form to the lowest of the next. This allowed the assumption that there is a low form of man who is so close to the border with the animal that he is not fully recognizable by other men as a fellow man.

As indicated in chapter 1, this idea influenced and was further developed by Paracelsus and others in the sixteenth and seventeenth centuries. The claim was that beings such as pygmies or the American Indians had no soul and descended from another, second Adam or generated spontaneously from the earth. They were *similitudines hominis* rather than real men. As already indicated above, there is an immediate link between such ideas and nineteenth-century racial determinism in the work of the French zoologist Georges Cuvier (1769–1832), mentioned repeatedly in these chapters. He assumed that there was a direct connection between the proportions and esthetic qualities—as he saw them—of the skull and the intellectual and moral qualities of human races. His aim was to establish a hierarchy, whereby "facial angle" was the instrument which indicated the relative proximity or remoteness of a human race to animals. Blacks and orang-utans were assumed to be particularly close.[135] The famous case study, used to prove this, was the "Hottentot Venus," a black woman from South Africa, displayed in a cage in London and Paris for some time, and examined by Cuvier before and after her death in 1814.[136]

The views held regarding mountain dwellers are discussed, below in chapter 10. For present purposes, however, we may cite Strabo (5.2.7 [224]) describing the mountaineers of Corsica. The author asserts "that those who occupy the mountains and live from brigandage are more savage than animals (ἀγρι- ωτέρους εἶναι θηρίων). At any rate, whenever the Roman generals have made a sally, and, falling suddenly upon the strongholds, have taken a large number of the people as slaves, you can at Rome see, and marvel at, the extent to which the nature of wild beasts, as also that of battening cattle (τὸ θηριῶδες καὶ τὸ βοσκηματῶδες ἐν αὐτοῖς), is manifested in them." His description of the mountaineers of Northern Iberia has already been cited. He goes on to tell how the Roman presence has changed their nature for the better. However, where this happens less, the people are more intractable and brutish (χαλεπώτεροί εἰσι καὶ θηριωδέστεροι) (3.3.8 [c. 156]). It is clear, however, that Strabo is referring here to a way of life and a culture which can be changed, not to a racial classification, with pretensions to describing these people in biological terms. The former means that they can improve, the latter that they are doomed by nature to an unchangeable inferior status. This follows, for instance, from his observation that the Celtiberians were the most fully adapted to a Roman way of life of all the Iberians, even though they were once considered the most

---

Nott and G. R. Gliddon, defended slavery on the argument that it was the most humane condition of life for an inferior race; cf. M. Harris, *The Rise of Anthropological Theory* (1968), 91. This of course is precisely an argument encountered already in the fourth century B.C.

[135] G. Jahoda, *Images of Savages* (1999), 76–79; Shulamit Volkov, "Exploring the Other," in Wistrich (ed.), *Demonizing the Other* (1999), 148–167, esp. 153f.

[136] Jahoda, *Images*, 79–81; C. Rawson, *God, Gulliver and Genocide* (2001), 113–130.

brutish of all (νομισθέντες ποτὲ θηριωδέστατοι).[137] These observations by Strabo are therefore not proto-racist, for they clearly posit the possibility of change. He describes social culture, not fixed nature.

Manilius, writing also in the reign of Tiberius, could not forgive the Germans for their successful revolt. Germany was therefore "fit only to breed wild beasts."[138] Josephus, in Agrippa II's catalogue of subjects of Rome, describes the Germans "as scorning death and having a temper fiercer than the wildest beasts."[139] Seneca returns to this theme, but more in the spirit of an intellectual. He says of the Germans and the Scythians that they are peoples, living wild and free "in the manner of lions and wolves who can neither serve nor command, for they do not have the power of a human intellect but a wild and unmanageable one. Indeed nobody can rule who cannot also be ruled. Generally empires have been among those peoples who live in a milder climate."[140]

This is part of the tradition encountered first in the work of Aristotle, cited above, who speaks in general terms of people "irrational by nature and living solely by sensation, like certain remote tribes of barbarians."[141] We have seen that Aristotle considers such barbarians, people irrational by nature, as belonging to the bestial class. This is true particularly of those living in conditions of excessive cold or heat and who are beastlike both in habits and in appearance. If they are not sociable, they are lower animals. All this is familiar as part of the environmental theory. Aristotle, like Seneca, already claimed that those fit to rule were living in the ideal mid-type climate. This well-known theme was taken over by Seneca, who applied it to the Germans. Seneca's tone is fairly detached. He compares the Germans with lions and wolves, being free and wild like them, but he can see some merit in these qualities. Unlike Tacitus, however, Seneca could comfort himself with the conclusion that the Germans were capable neither of ruling nor of being ruled.

An attitude more in line with that of Strabo is expressed by Eusebius in his *Life of Constantine.* (Constantine) "very soon subdued them all (sc. the Goths

---

[137] It may be proper to mention Ptolemy the Geographer, whose attitudes seem more Alexandrian than Roman and therefore had best be restricted to a footnote. In *Tetrabiblos* 2.3.15 he describes Britannia, Gaul, Germania, and Bastarnia as fiercer, more headstrong, and bestial (θηριώδεις). Note also 2.3.50: the people of Arabia, Azania and Middle Ethiopia are flesh-eaters, fish-eaters, and nomads, living a rough, bestial life (ἄγριον καὶ θηριώδη βίον ξῶντες).

[138] Manilius 4. 794: teque feris dignam tantum, Germania . . .

[139] Josephus, *BJ* 2.16.4 (377): καὶ τὴν μὲν ψυχὴν θανάτου καταφρονοῦσαν, τοὺς δὲ θυμοὺς τῶν ἀγριωτάτων θηρίων σφοδροτέρους . . .

[140] Seneca, *de ira* 2.15 *(dialogi* 4.15.4f.*)*: Deinde omnes istae feritate liberae gentes leonum luporumque ritu ut seruire non possunt, ita nec imperare; non enim humani uim ingenii, sed feri et intractabilis habent; nemo autem regere potest nisi qui et regi. Fere itaque imperia penes eos fuere populos qui mitiore caelo utuntur: in frigora septemtrionemque uergentibus "inmansueta ingenia" sunt, ut ait poeta, suoque simillima caelo. For another aspect to the same passage, below, chapter 12.

[141] These ideas were taken over, lock, stock, and barrel by some authors of the enlightenment. See, for instance, Jefferson's observations on blacks, as formulated in the chapter on Laws in the *Notes on the State of Virginia*, excerpts published in E. C. Eze, *Race and the Enlightenment* (1997), 95–103: "In general, their existence appears to participate more of sensation than reflection."

and Sarmatians), sometimes taming the refractory with the military arm, sometimes pacifying the rest by reasonable negotiations, converting them from a lawless animal existence to one of reason and law (ἐξ ἀνόμου καὶ θηριώδους βίου ἐπὶ τὸ λογικὸν καὶ νόμμον μεθαρμοσάμενος). In this way the Goths learnt at last to serve Rome."[142] Again, what was considered bestial were not their genes, but their way of life. This, however, was of essential importance in the view of those authors, for they had a clear sense of the comparative merits of peoples and those who were bestial stood lowest on the ladder. It was not a metaphor, but a term used for people who were essentially unsociable, which is how animals were conceived to be.

Later in the same century, Libanius divided humanity in two groups, Hellenes and barbarians. The latter, "in his pride, rages and raves like a wild beast; he slays his kinsman at his table and drinks a toast over his dead body."[143] He returns to this topic: "In this respect in particular I find the Greeks also to be superior to barbarians. These approximate to brutes in despising pity, while the Greeks are quick to pity and get over their wrath" (Or. 19.13)."[144] Libanius explicitly denies that the barbarians honored fundamental moral laws. A decent man does not kill relatives and guests, but barbarians murder relatives when they are guests and continue drinking. We may note here a topic to be discussed later, namely that Libanius was also a local patriot, as a citizen of Antioch in Syria. Ammianus regularly uses animal comparisons, both to disparage individuals and groups.[145]

Examples of the latter are his descriptions of attacking foreigners: Isaurians raiding the provinces,[146] Germans about to invade Gaul (16.5.17), both groups driven by hunger. The Saracens raiding are like rapacious kites.[147] After their victory at Adrianople the Goths attack the city "like wild beasts maddened all the more by the taste of blood."[148] However, such comparisons are not fully relevant for our discussion, since it is not these peoples in general, but only

[142] Eusebius, vita Constantini 4.5, trans. Averil Cameron and Stuart G. Hall, Eusebius. Life of Constantine (Oxford, 1999), 155, with comments on p. 311.

[143] Libanius, Or. 15.25; trans. A. F. Norman, Loeb: ὁ μὲν βάρβαρος μέγα λυττῶν καὶ ἀγριαίνων καὶ τὰ τῶν θηρίων μιμούμενος καὶ σφάττων ἐν δείπνῳ τὸν ὁμόφυλον καὶ πίνων ἐπὶ τοῦ νεκροῦ, κἂν ἱκετεύῃ τις, ὁ μὲν [τις] οὐδὲν ἤνυσεν, ὁ δὲ καὶ προσπαρώξυνεν.

[144] Or. 19.13: ᾧ μεγίστῳ καὶ τοὺς Ἕλληνας εὑρίσκω τῶν βαρβάρων διαφέροντας. οἱ μέν γε ἐγγύς εἰσι τῶν θηρίων ἀτιμάζοντες ἔλεον, οἱ δὲ ὀξεῖς τε ἐλεεῖν καὶ ὀργῆς περιόντες. See also ep. 1120: τὸ μὲν γὰρ καὶ τῶν βαρβάρων καὶ τῶν θηρίων, τὸ δὲ Ἑλληνικὸν καὶ Ἀθηναίων καὶ θεοῖς ἐοικότων; sp. 1430.

[145] T.E.J. Wiedemann, "Between Men and Beasts: Barbarians in Ammianus Marcellinus," in I. S. Moxon, J. D. Smart, and A. J. Woodman (eds.), Past Perspectives: Studies in Greek and Roman Historical Writing, 189–201; Timothy D. Barnes, Ammianus Marcellinus and the Representation of Historical Reality (Ithaca and London, 1998), 108–110.

[146] Ammianus 14.2.2 citing a comparison which appears in Cicero, Pro Cluentio 67: iam hoc non ignoratis iudices, ut etiam bestiae fame monitae plerumque ad eum locum ubi aliquando pastae sunt revertantur..

[147] 14.4.1: milvorum rapacium similes. For more examples along these lines, Barnes, p. 110. To the examples cited there, add 19.5.3, 19.6.4, 31.8.9.

[148] 31.15.2: ut bestiae sanguinis irritamento atrocius efferatae

specific actions of theirs which are described in animal terms. More relevant is his pronouncement that most of the Scythians know no agriculture, but wander over desert lands, which never knew the plough or seed, but are desolate and frosty. They feed in the foul manner of wild beasts—a reference, presumably, to the consumption of uncooked meat.[149] Here we encounter the familiar association of nomads, who are unsociable, with animals. This pronouncement is significant, because it is one of a number of comparisons Ammianus ascribes to others. Julian parades captive Persian soldiers before his troops and calls them "not men, but merely ugly she-goats disfigured with filth."[150] In this connection it is worth noting that the anti-Persian rhetoric was much fiercer in the later Roman Empire than it had ever been in the time of warfare between the two powers during the first two or three centuries of their confrontations.[151] Regarding the Christians, he is reported as claiming that no wild animals are so hostile to human beings as most Christians are to one another (22.5.4).

There is no need here to discuss the seventeen books of Aelian (A.D. 165/70–230/35) *On the Nature of Animals*. These contain curious stories about animals and their habits, intended to entertain rather than instruct. They are full of the paradoxical and miraculous and not relevant for the present topic, for animals may show traits marvelously recognized also in human beings, but the reverse is not true.

Cannibalism

One of the most obvious marks of brutish peoples is their habit of consuming human flesh. It is a central feature in Isocrates' *Busiris*, a speech about a fictitious Egyptian king, briefly discussed below and illustrated in figure 1.[152] Above it was noted that Aristotle was preoccupied with notions of cannibalism. Fantastic stories about cannibalism practiced by savage peoples or lunatics occur in serious texts, not only Aristotle's *Nicomachean Ethics,* but also in his *Politics.*[153] The reason Aristotle is mentioned here extensively is the fact that he rationalizes and generalizes. Yet, his views are in fact quite traditional. As already observed, when he asserts that those who live in conditions of excessive cold or heat are beastlike both in habits and in appearance, this is a well-known extension of the environmental theory. He says of the peoples of the Pontus area that they show "an inclination to murder and cannibalism" and speaks of their "bes-

[149] 22.8.42: quarum pars exigua frugibus alitur, residuae omnes palantes per solitudines uastas nec stiuam aliquando nec sementem expertas, sed squalentes et pruinosas ferarum taetro ritu uescuntur eis que caritates et habitacula uiles que supellectiles plaustris impositae sunt corticibus tectis | et, cum placuerit, sine obstaculo migrant eodem carpenta, quo libuerit, conuoluentes. See also Jerome, *Adversus Iovinianum* 2.7: nomades, et troglodytae, et scythae, et hunnorum noua feritas, semicrudis uescuntur carnibus.

[150] 24.8.1: deformes illuvie capellas et taetras

[151] See below, for a brief section on Romans and Persians.

[152] Chapter 7 on the Egyptians.

[153] See also Euripides, *Hec.* 1057f.; 1070–1072, discussed by Hall, *Inventing the Barbarian* (1989), 126.

tial dispositions" (θηριώδεις).[154] Herodotus already calls one tribe in this area the "Man-eaters" (Ἀνδροφάγοι). "Their customs are utterly bestial; they do not observe justice nor do they have any law. They are nomads . . . they alone of these peoples, eat human flesh" (4.106). This neatly sums up all the qualities assumed to distinguish man from beast, while ignoring the fact that most animals do not eat their own species. However, ancient attitudes to animals is a subject in its own right not to be discussed here. The mad Persian king Cambyses only gave up his Ethiopian campaign, says Herodotus, when the troops became so desperate from hunger that they began to eat every tenth man, selected by lot. Cambyses, who was afraid of nothing, "feared cannibalism."[155] The fourth-century historian Ephorus says of the Scythians that "some of them [as distinct from others] are so cruel that they even eat human flesh."[156] Horror stories were popular, such as that regarding Apollodorus, tyrant of Cassandreia in the early third century B.C., who slaughtered a boy as sacrificial victim and shared his flesh and blood, mixed with wine, with others.[157] In Rome rumors circulated about Catilina and his co-conspirators that they drank blood mixed with wine (Sallust, *Cat.* 22) or even slaughtered a man, or even a child, and ate his flesh (Plutarch, *Cic.* 10.4; Florus *ep.* 2.12.3; Dio 37.30).[158] We may safely attribute to these reports the level of credibility which medieval blood accusations against the Jews deserve. According to Diodorus, the Druids in Gaul sacrificed human beings in order to predict the future.[159] As usual, the farther north people lived, the wilder they were. Diodorus knows of the remotest of the northern peoples "who live beneath the Bears and on the borders of Scythia" that they ate human flesh and so do the Britons who live on Iris / Ireland (5.32.3f.).[160]

---

[154] Aristotle, *Politics* 1338b, 19–22: πολλὰ δ' ἐστὶ τῶν ἐθνῶν ἃ πρὸς τὸ κτείνειν καὶ πρὸς τὴν ἀνθρωποφαγίαν εὐχερῶς ἔχει; cf. comments by Kraut, p. 186f.; *Ethica Nicomachea* 1148b, 19–25.

[155] Herodotus 3.25: δείσας τὴν ἀλληλοφαγίην. The Taurians of the Crimea were reputed to have sacrificed foreigners to their local goddess, cf. Rives, *JRS* 85 (1995), 67f.

[156] Ephorus, in *FGrH* 70 F 42 = Strabo 7.3.9 (c.302). Jacoby, comm. ad loc., p. 51f., observes that this is a description of Scythia which is not based on Herodotus's sometimes idealizing views, but on Hecataeus and the Ionian ethnography. The inhabitants of the remote parts of the earth are often described as being particularly uncivilized and even bestial. Diodorus, 3.8.2, says of the Ethiopians: καὶ ταῖς μὲν ψυχαῖς παντελῶς ὑπάρχουσιν ἄγριοι καὶ τὸ θηριῶδες ἐμφαίνοντες, οὐχ οὕτω δὲ τοῖς θυμοῖς ὡς τοῖς ἐπιτηδεύμασιν. This may or may not be based on the observations of the Hellenistic author Agatharchides, as is often assumed.

[157] Diodorus, frg. of book 22. Cf. Rives, *JRS* 85 (1995), 72.

[158] Cf. Rives, *JRS* 85 (1995), 72.

[159] Diodorus 31.3. There is no indication that Posidonius is the source of this information. The story about human sacrifice by Jews, reported by Josephus, *contra Apionem* 2.92–96 and 121, need not be discussed here, for it is propaganda originating in Seleucid Hellenistic circles which falls outside the scope of this study. See E. Bickerman, "Ritualmord und Eselskult: Ein Beitrag zur Geschichte antiker Publizistik. I: Tempelopfer," reprinted in his *Studies in Jewish and Christian History* 2 (Leiden, 1980), 225–255, esp. 225–245.

[160] Similarly, Strabo reports that in his time the inhabitants of Ireland and some of the Scythians practised cannibalism (4.5.4 [c. 201]).

Livy attributes to a Roman commander, speaking after the battle of Cannae (216 B.C.), the accusations that Carthaginian soldiers used to feed upon human bodies (Livy 23.5.12). Pliny, describing the land east of the Caspian, writes: "This is the country of the man-eating Scythians who feed on human bodies; therefore the adjacent regions are waste deserts full of wild beasts menacing people equally savage as they are."[161] Pliny here reflects a long tradition. As observed above, Aristotle already describes those in the region of the Black Sea as savages who are said to enjoy eating raw meat or human flesh. The region where these horrors lived had shifted eastward in Pliny's time, from the Black Sea to the Caspian (but Jerome, cited above, again mentions the Scythians among those who eat their meat half-cooked). Clearly, the same associations return again and again: man must be sociable; unsociable beings cannot be human and are cannibals.

Occasionally, however, such accusations are directed towards regular, settled peoples in the provinces. Juvenal describes a conflict between two Egyptian comunities which resulted in cannibalism.[162]

Josephus, too, is full of gory details: the mother who ate her child during the siege of Jerusalem (BJ 6.3.3 [199]–3.5 [219]), "an act without precedent among Hellenes or barbarians, horrible to tell and unbelievable to hear." Yet Josephus rather enjoyed telling it. He relates both atrocities among the Jews themselves[163] and mass slaughter and cruelties by the Romans.[164] There is no need to reproduce the details here. Cannibalism, or the suggestion of it, is said to have been used as a means to terrorize the enemy. Josephus cites to this effect Nicolaos and Strabo on the invasion of Ptolemy Lathyrus in Judaea.[165] Ptolemy had villagers, women, and children killed, chopped to pieces, and cooked. He then instructed his soldiers to eat of them. "He gave this command so that the fugitives from the battle, coming home, would assume that the enemies were cannibals and so would be more terrified when seeing this." Frontinus, Strategemata 3.5 has a similar account on Clearchus from Sparta while fighting in Thrace in 402/1 B.C. These two accounts are not concerned with Romans, but with Greek and Seleucid armies, but they are related in texts of the Roman period. It is clear that these texts do not suggest that cannibalism was considered normal, but they do show that there were stories about invading armies prepared to go so far in their efforts to terrorize the defending troops.

---

[161] Pliny, NH 6.20.53: Anthropophagi Scythae insident humanis corporibus vesentes; ideo iuxta vastae solitudines ferarumque multitudo haut dissimilem hominum inmanitatem obsidens. Cf. 7.9–11. See also Josephus, Contra Apionem 2.8.37 (269), who says that the Scythians enjoy killing people and are little better than wild beasts (Σκύθαι δὲ φόνοις χαίροντες ἀνθρώπων καὶ βραχὺ τῶν θηρίων διαφέροντες).

[162] Juvenal, Satire 6.78–83; see below, chapter 7, p. 364, where it is observed that eating meat raw or uncooked was considered an essential difference between man and animal.

[163] BJ 5.10.3 (429–438); 6.1.1 (1–4).

[164] BJ 5.13.4 (548–552); 5.11.1 (449–451); 6.8.5 (404–407); 6.9.2 (414–419). Cf. Jonathan J. Price, Jerusalem under Siege: The Collapse of the Jewish State, 66–70 CE (Leiden, 1992), 172 and appendix 14.

[165] Josephus, Ant. 13.12.6 (345–7); cf. Stern, 1. nos. 89 and 101 with comments on 101.

Cannibalism seems to have been a favorite horror for Dio: he accuses Jews of cannibalism and excessive cruelty during the revolt in Cyrene, Egypt, and Cyprus under Trajan (Dio 68.32.1).[166] He is not, however, particularly anti-Jewish. The surviving description of the Bar-Kokhba revolt contains no gruesome details and his comments in 37.16f. are distant, but not hostile. However, Dio also reports Egyptian rebels in 171 as having practiced cannibalism, sacrificing and consuming a centurion (Dio 71.4.1). Dio does not tell whether the rebels cooked the meat. The second-century Christians were accused of incest. They organized common feasts which included the killing of babies. They supposedly dipped bread in their blood and drank it, which was followed by sexual orgies.[167] These slanders were started by Hellenized Jews, according to Origen and Justin. We have no non-Christian sources which prove that the Jews indeed were the origin of such accusations. It seems doubtful, for the same slanders were used by the Christians themselves against their own sectarians: Carpocratians,[168] Montanists, and against the Jews. Jerome accuses the Britons and Massagetae of cannibalism, claiming that the latter ate their dead relatives.[169] So far the discussion of cannibalism, a common theme and closely associated with that which associates foreigners with brutish and inhuman characters. Finally it is important here to mention that a very famous anthropological study doubts the very existence of cannibalism, except perhaps in circumstances of near-starvation.[170] This, it is said, goes too far, but it will still be salutary to remember that accusations of cannibalism more often than not have their roots in hostile imagination, like the blood libel, witchcraft, and sorcery.[171] In a sense, therefore,

---

[166] A note in ths Suda s.v. ἀτάσθαλα et παρείκοι reports that Trajan "was determined above all, if this were possible, to destroy the people altogether, but if not, then at least to crush it and to halt its excessive arrogant wickedness." This must refer either to the Parthians or, more likely, to the Jewish rebels in 117, see M. Stern, *GLAJJ*, No. 322a, with comments on pp.152–155.

[167] J.-P. Waltzing, "Le crime rituel reproché aux chrétiens du IIème siècle," *Bulletin de la Classe des Lettres de l'Académie Royale de Belgique* sér. 5, 11 (1925), 205–239; on alleged Dionysiac and Christian orgies: M. Gelzer, "Die Unterdrückung der Bacchanalien bei Livius" *Hermes* 71 (1936), 275–287, esp. 285f., who compares accusations of horrible deeds aimed at the *Bacchanalia* with similar ones targeted later at the Christians; one of the best known sources is Fronto, cited by Minucius Felix, *Octavius* 9.8; for allegations of cannibalism: F. J. Dölger, *Ant. u. Chr.* 4 (1934), 188–228. See further J. Rives, "Human Sacrifice among Pagans and Christians," *JRS* 85 (1995), 65–85, and more references and discussion below, chapter 12.

[168] Irenaeus, *adversus Haereses* 1.20.2; Clemens, *Stromata* 3.2.10.1.

[169] Jerome, *Adversus Iovinianum* 2.7; see also Isidore *Etymologiae* 9.2; 15.3; Tertullian, *Adversus Marcionem* 1.1.

[170] The seminal work was W. Arens, *The Man-Eating Myth: Anthropology and Anthropophagy* (Oxford, 1979); it has been criticized by I. M. Lewis, *Religion in Context* (Cambridge, 1986); see now: *The Anthropology of Cannibalism,* edited by Laurence R. Goldman (Westport, CT, 1999), with several essays which claim that Arens went too far in his scepticism; Jahoda, *Images of Savages* (London and New York, 1999), 104–127, provides numerous examples of clearly fraudulent or bogus reports on cannibalism.

[171] See Michael Pickering, "Consuming Doubts: What Some People Ate? Or What Some People Swallowed?" in Goldman (ed.), *The Anthropology of Cannibalism* (1999), 51–74. Pickering discusses the widely popular and uncritically accepted belief in the cannibalism of Australian aborigines. See p. 67: "There has been a tendency, usually not deliberate, among many researchers who

these phenomena are related to the central theme of the present work, which is the irrational in ideas about foreigners.

Cannibalism, like incestual relationships, has been deeply repugnant in the western literary tradition while, at the same time, stimulating a morbid interest.[172] It is a theme found frequently in later literary fiction.[173] As soon as Columbus set foot on the American continent in 1492, he began making enquiries about cannibalism and accusations of it became a permanent fixture in the arsenal of dehumanizing characterizations of the Amerindians.[174] In this case, too, this particular obsession was combined with other ideas so as to form a fixed pattern. Cannibalism was combined with human sacrifice: drunken feasts, sexual orgies including incest, ended in the frenzied consumption of the victim. In short, they broke elementary human laws and were therefore antisocial and thus virtually inhuman.[175] Here it is immediately obvious how little influence reality has on such perceptions. While it is true that human sacrifice was practiced in pre-Columbian America, the imaginary claims of cannibalism and other deviances were taken just as seriously.

Slaves and Animals

Related to the idea of cannibalism is the association of slaves with animals, which had an obvious appeal, for it is convenient to deny slaves their humanity. In the *Politics* Aristotle does not identify the natural slave with animals, but the natural slave is subhuman and in some respects approaches animals, notably in their practical functions: "The ox serves instead of a servant for the poor" (1252b, 12). "The use which is made of the slave diverges but little from the use made of tame animals; both he and they supply their owner with bodily help in meeting his daily requirements" (1254b, 25–29). "Tame animals have a better nature than wild, and it is better for all such animals that they should be ruled by man because they then get the benefit of preservation" (1254b, 11–14), a statement which is further clarified as follows: "We may thus conclude that all men who differ from others as much as the body differs from the soul, or an animal from a man (and this is the case with all whose function is bodily service)—all such are by nature slaves, and it is better for them, on the very same principle as in other cases just mentioned, to be ruled by a master. A man

---

rely heavily on historic texts for information about Aboriginal people to avoid the critical consideration of the original . . . contexts of their sources." (68): "In all societies where cannibalism is a belief, one aspect of the belief is to demarcate symbolic boundaries between the religious and the secular, between 'us' and 'them,' and between humans and nonhumans."

[172] Jahoda, *Images*, 109–112; Norman Cohn, *Europe's Inner Demons: An Enquiry Inspired by the Great Witch-Hunt* (London, 1975). For cannibalism in antiquity: M. Detienne, "Between Beasts and Gods," in R. L. Gordon (ed.), *Myth, Religion and Society: Structuralist Essays* (Cambridge, 1981), 215–228.

[173] Rawson, *God, Gulliver and Genocide*, 24–55: barbarism and cannibalism, 72–78: eating food fit for beasts, uncooked; 79–91: bestiality and cannibalism.

[174] Pagden, *The Fall of Natural Man*, 80–90.

[175] Pagden, 82.

is thus by nature a slave if he is capable of becoming (and this is the reason why he also actually becomes) the property of another, and if he participates in reason to the extent of apprehending it in another, though destitute of it himself. Herein he differs from animals, which do not apprehend reason, but simply obey their instincts."[176] Then Aristotle states that the use made of slaves and of animals is similar, being physical in both cases. Thus, the slave is as inferior to the master as the body to the soul or the lower animals to (all) men. The popularity of black slaves in fifth-century Athens may have something to do with their visible physical difference from the local population. This is an hypothesis, but it fits the desire expressed by Aristotle, to see in slaves an essentially different category of people (see figs. 5 and 6).

Aristotle asserts that nature makes nothing without aim or in vain and therefore has made all the animals for the sake of men (1256b, 21–23). This approach is reinforced by the sentence already cited. "From this it follows that even warfare is by nature a form of acquisition—for the art of hunting is part of it—which is applied against wild animals and against those men who are not prepared to be ruled even though they are born for subjection, in so far as this war is just by nature." In the *Metaphysics* he also assimilates slaves to animals, comparing their function in the household "where the free persons have the least liberty to act at random, and have all or most of their actions preordained for them, whereas the slaves and animals have little common responsibility and act for the most part at random."[177]

While Aristotle thus approximates slaves and animals, he does not assert that they *are* animals or that they are no better than animals.[178] The slave is a man, and a man differs from the animals in having *logos,* the faculty of articulate speech and that of forming concepts, while animals are guided only by perceptions.[179] The sole reservation is that Aristotle asserts that the slave "participates in *logos* (only) in so far that he understands it, but does not possess it."[180] The theory of natural slavery is discussed above. For the present it is significant to observe that Aristotle recognizes a a series of linear hierarchies: within man

---

[176] Aristotle, *Pol.* 1254b (trans. Ernest Barker): τὸν αὐτὸν δὲ τρόπον ἀναγκαῖον εἶναι καὶ ἐπὶ πάντων ἀνθρώπων. ὅσοι μὲν οὖν τοσοῦτον διεστᾶσιν ὅσον ψυχὴ σώματος καὶ ἄνθρωπος θηρίου (διάκεινται δὲ τοῦτον τὸν τρόπον ὅσων ἐστὶν ἔργον ἡ τοῦ σώματος χρῆσις, καὶ τοῦτ᾽ ἐστ᾽ ἀπ᾽ αὐτῶν βέλτιστον), οὗτοι μέν εἰσι φύσει δοῦλοι, . . . καὶ ἡ χρεία δὲ παραλλάττει μικρόν· ἡ γὰρ πρὸς τἀναγκαῖα τῷ σώματι βοήθεια γίνεται παρ᾽ ἀμφοῖν, παρά τε τῶν δούλων καὶ παρὰ τῶν ἡμέρων ζῴων. Cf. comments by Jean Aubonnet, *Aristote, Politique Livres I et II* (Paris, 1968), 116.

[177] Aristotle, *Metaph.* 1075a 22 (trans. H. Tredennick, Loeb): ἀλλ᾽ ὥσπερ ἐν οἰκίᾳ τοῖς ἐλευθέροις ἥκιστα ἔξεστιν ὅ τι ἔτυχε ποιεῖν, ἀλλὰ πάντα ἢ τὰ πλεῖστα τέτακται, τοῖς δὲ ἀνδραπόδοις καὶ τοῖς θηρίοις μικρὸν τὸ εἰς τὸ κοινόν, τὸ δὲ πολὺ ὅ τι ἔτυχεν·

[178] Garnsey, *Ideas of Slavery*, 110–114. Garnsey explores the boundary between slaves and animals. As he observes, the distinctions between human an animal, and slave and animal, do not coincide. It turns out that in the *Politics* the line between human and animal is usually firmly drawn, but that between slaves and animals is fuzzy.

[179] 1253a, 10f.; 1254b, 21ff. Cf. P. A. Brunt, "Aristotle and Slavery," in *Studies in Greek History and Thought* (1993), 343–388, esp. 360f.

[180] 1254b, 20–23: ἔστι γὰρ φύσει δοῦλος ὁ δυνάμενος ἄλλου εἶναι (διὸ καὶ ἄλλου ἐστίν), καὶ ὁ κοινωνῶν λόγου τοσοῦτον ὅσον αἰσθάνεσθαι ἀλλὰ μὴ ἔχειν.

there is soul and body, among human beings there are superior and inferior types—the women and children occupy a well-defined inferior place in the hierarchy—and below humanity are the animals. Aristotle assumes that nature has established this hierarchy for a purpose, whereby the lower elements have been created to serve and profit the higher ones. Somehow, this will profit both in different ways. Whatever the internal logic and moral justifications by modern standards, this is a rationalization of inequality which has been highly influential. Here it will suffice to note that the approximation between inferior man and animal has been instrumental in denying certain categories of people equal status as human beings. It is a concept that has been exploited eagerly during many centuries for the justification of the inequality of humanity.

Physiognomics

There is yet another fashion of comparing human beings with animals which, however, is irrelevant for the present chapter. It is found in the works of the physiognomists, discussed above. Here one finds elaborate analogies between characteristics attributed to animals and to human beings said to have both physical features and mental characteristics in common with those animals.[181] "The horse is a proud and dashing animal, courageous in battle, eager for victory, a hard worker. Men who correspond to this type of animal, have therefore straight and red hair, rather broad cheeks, a fairly long neck, rather open nostrils, a drooping lower lip, they are hot in love, boastful, very obstinate, less sensible."[182] While this is a way of stereotyping people and dividing them into types, the comparison with animals is not intended to deny the objects of comparison their quality as human beings. It is a psychologically complex process, but not of the kind discussed in this chapter.

Brutes and Animals—Conclusions

It may be concluded that comparisons and metaphors identifying people with animals are common in the ancient literature. It is, moreover, not certain that all such passages should be interpreted as comparisons or metaphors. Some of them seem to be intended quite literally. When that is the case we must conclude that this belongs to the arsenal of ideas familiar to us from modern racism, for in calling people animals we deny them humanity in every respect and place them in a category apart. The implication of such expressions in ancient literature is not that these people should be killed without further ado. That attitude would rest on the assumption that killing people is forbidden but killing animals is allowed or even desirable. As we saw in the first part of the present

---

[181] E.g., *De Physiognomonia* 118–132.

[182] *De Physiognomonia* 118: Equus animal erectum est atque exultans, in certando animosum, victoriae cupidum, non impatiens laboris. Homines ergo qui ad huius animalis speciem referuntur, capillo erunt tenso rubeo, genas habebunt maiores, collum longius, nares magis patulas, labium inferius demissum, erunt calidi in venerem, iactantes sui, contentiosi nimium, sapientem minus.

214   · C H A P T E R   2 ·

study, there was no need to justify the killing of large numbers of people in
antiquity by claiming they were animals. There appears to have been a genuine
feeling, however, that some people who were lacking in the basic elements of
civilization, as understood by the Greeks and Romans, were closer to animals
than to human beings. This was particularly the case when people were regarded as unsociable. Even if contact between peoples may be dangerous—the
topic of the previous section—it is still a necessary component of civilized
society. Nomads are the unsociable people par excellence, and it is such people
who are regarded as brutish. Cannibalism is a theme that also comes up fairly
frequently in this connection. It is questionable whether this attitude should
always be described as proto-racist, for the implication is, for a number of
authors at least, that they can be improved. In such cases we should regard the
phenomenon as an extreme case of ethnic prejudice. A well-governed empire,
says Strabo, could help transform such peoples into genuine human beings and
in this sense the approach served a practical purpose in the ideology of empire.[183]
However, the alternative was to destroy them as being harmful to the empire.

Graeco-Roman antiquity, c.q. Aristotle and the peripatetic treatise *Problemata*, also considered these questions at a more abstract level, in attempting
to formulate the relationship between humanity and animals. An integral part of
this problem is the status of slaves, whereby their approximation to—but not
identification with—animals served as model for many later thinkers—Buffon,
Voltaire, Le Bon, and Rousseau—but also Jefferson, who needed an intellectual
concept which reconciled a belief in equality with a firm conviction in the
existence of a hierarchy of humanity. Ancient thinking about slaves was to be a
useful tool for those who were in search of concepts rationalizing slavery and
racism. It is clear then that the animal comparison is a phenomenon common in
Greek and Roman thinking about presumed inferiors.

We may end this topic pointing out that it is not marginal for the issue of
imperialism. Aristotle regards some distant barbarians as belonging to the bestial class because they are "irrational by nature and living solely by sensation."
Some Greek authors reach the conclusion that people living in extreme climates
are brutes in mind and body. So far we see merely that some foreigners are
described as bestial. Strabo, however, asserts "that those who occupy the mountains and live from brigandage are more savage than animals." Here he is discussing peoples who inhabit Roman provinces. The connection with imperialist
thinking becomes clear when Strabo argues that Roman subjugation may turn
such people into proper human beings. Thus he informs his readers that the
Celtiberians were the most fully adapted to a Roman way of life of all the
Iberians, even though they were once considered the most brutish of all. Roman
authors, then, could use the accusation of bestiality of foreigners as an argu-

---

[183] For Strabo on the Roman Empire: Daniela Dueck, *Strabo of Amasia: A Greek Man of Letters
in Augustan Rome* (London, 2000), chapter 4.

ment in favor of subjugation and conquest because they would be improved into regular human beings.[184]

MASS MURDER, BLOODSHED, AND CLEMENCY

Mass death is frequent in our times.[185] The question to ask in the last part of this chapter is to what extent it was an instrument of ancient imperialism and, more relevant for the present study, to what extent such practices were justified by the claim of inferiority of the enemy. Furthermore, it is an essential part of every people's attitude towards foreigners whether it is regarded as permitted or useful to kill them in large numbers. In this respect the topic is relevant for this book.

An early and unambiguous expression that a people ought to be exterminated may be found in two parallel passages which describe the friends of Antiochus Sidetes as advising the king "to wipe out completely the Jewish people, since they alone of all nations avoided dealings with other people and looked upon all men as their enemies."[186] The first point to make is that the king did not follow the advice and the Jews were not exterminated; the second is that the information may not be reliable. The king's friends may not have given such advice. Even if they did not, the historical tradition regarded it as credible that they would have done so. This means that the idea as such was conceivable. This then is the first instance, known to me, of a clearly formulated plan of full-scale ethnic eradication for ideological reasons.[187]

As already observed, although mass murder was not uncommon in antiquity, it is not clear that there was an emotional need to portray the victims as animals. This is the case both for the period of the Roman republic and for the empire, as one would expect. True, Quinctus Flaminius claimed in 197 that the Romans never exterminated their enemies at once, the first time they fought them.[188] According to Vergil, Rome should remember to spare the vanquished, but also to subject the proud utterly (*Aen.* 6.853 *parcere subiectis et debellare*

---

[184] Dueck, op. cit., 115–19.

[185] Note Steven T. Katz, "Mass Death under Communist Rule and the Limits of 'Otherness'," in R. S. Wistrich, *Demonizing the Other: Antisemitism, Racism and Xenophobia* (Amsterdam, 1999), 267–293.

[186] Diodorus 34–35.1.1f.; Jos., *Ant.* 13.8.2 (245); cited in full below, chapter 13, notes 45 and 46.

[187] The Book of Esther is relevant in this connection, but this book is limited to Greek and Latin literature.

[188] Polybius 18.37: οὔτε γὰρ ʽρωμαίους οὐδενὶ τὸ πρῶτον πολεμήσαντας εὐθέως ἀναστάτους ποιεῖν τούτους· Livy 33.12.7 reports him as saying that it was an age-old Roman tradition to spare the vanquished. (vetustissimum morem victis parcendi). For Roman "clemency," see P. A. Brunt, "Laus Imperii," originally in P.D.A. Garnsey and C. R. Whittaker (eds.), *Imperialism in the Ancient World* (Cambridge, 1978), 159–91, reprinted as Chapter 14 in *Roman Imperial Themes* (Oxford 1990), 288–323; esp. 314–316; for Roman brutality: William V. Harris, *War and Imperialism in Republican Rome, 327–70 BC* (Oxford, 1979), 50–53; 263f.

superbos). This should not be interpreted to mean that the proud were to be spared once they were vanquished. "*Debellare*" clearly means that they would be vanquished and not spared, that is, exterminated. Augustus implies that he spared the vanquished when he writes in his *Res Gestae,* 3: "foreign peoples which could safely be pardoned, I preferred to preserve rather than exterminate."[189] This is another way of saying that Augustus naturally exterminated those he felt it was not safe to pardon. Polybius, describing the capture of Carthago Nova by Scipio Africanus in 209, says it was customary for the Roman troops to kill all inhabitants of a city they subdued. Pillaging started afterwards, after a signal had been given. He adds that he thinks the Romans did this to strike terror (καταπλήξεως χάριν, 10.15.5). As a result one often sees in towns taken by the Romans not only dead people, but "dogs cut in half, and the limbs cut off from other animals." If this observation by Polybius reflects actual Roman considerations, then such practices were in fact part of their method of warfare. These ideas and approaches are illustrated in figures 7–10. Indeed, it is quite conceivable that the Romans wanted to inspire terror. Whether they wanted to or not, they certainly did. Polybius says that the cause of the war with the Gauls in 231 B.C. was the conviction of the Gauls that the Romans "no longer made war on them for the sake of supremacy and sovereignty, but with a view to their total expulsion and extermination."[190] This is indeed what happened in the subsequent period.[191] A relatively minor skirmish between Macedonians and Romans in 200 B.C. resulted in forty fallen Macedonian cavalry. However, the extreme violence exerted by the Roman arms caused panic among the Macedonians, who were not used to it.[192] Livy clearly describes the scene with pride. Even so, it is still possible to say that this was the result of the Romans' fighting with more effective—hence bloodier—arms.[193] The Romans, however, are on record as resorting to mutilation of live victims,[194] while the details of animal slaughter which Polybius himself gives also suggest a form

[189] Externas gentes, quibus tuto ignosci potuit, conservare quam excidere malui.

[190] Polybius 2.21.9: νομίσαντες οὐχ ὑπὲρ ἡγεμονίας ἔτι καὶ δυναστείας ῾ρωμαίους τὸν πρὸς αὐτοὺς ποιήσασθαι πόλεμον, ἀλλ᾽ ὑπὲρ ὁλοσχεροῦς ἐξαναστάσεως καὶ καταφθορᾶς.

[191] Polybius 2.35.4: περὶ ὧν ἡμεῖς συνθεωρήσαντες μετ᾽ ὀλίγον χρόνον αὐτοὺς ἐκ τῶν περὶ τὸν Πάδον πεδίων ἐξωσθέντας, πλὴν ὀλίγων τόπων τῶν ὑπ᾽ αὐτὰς τὰς ἄλπεις κειμένων. F. W. Walbank, *A Historical Commentary on Polybius* 1 (Oxford, 1957), 211f. observes that Polybius, like Strabo, 5.1.6 (c.213); 10 (c.216), has exaggerated the extent to which the Gauls were physically expelled from Italy. Livy 36.39.3 reports more moderate measures, which in itself proves nothing, for Livy may be wrong. However, as Walbank mentions, with further references: "Hundreds of tombstones with Celtic names dating mainly from imperial times are only the most striking of the evidence proving that the Gauls were not expelled, but romanized." These matters might need reconsideration. Between the large-scale expulsions of around 200 B.C. and the burial of hundreds of people with Celtic names in imperial times, much may have happened.

[192] Livy 31.34: "[T]hey saw bodies decapitated by the Spanish sword, arms cut off with the shoulder, or heads detached from bodies, with all of the neck severed, entrails exposed and other horrible wounds."

[193] In the same chapter Livy describes Perseus's admiration when he first saw a Roman marching camp with its systematic layout.

[194] Florus 1.39.7: hands cut off.

of social pathology. Plutarch gives a graphic account of Sulla's plunder and slaughter in Athens, based on the stories of elderly Athenians who could still testify in his days (*Sulla* 14.3–7). In the Roman visual arts, mass executions were presented on monuments celebrating imperial victories, as seen in figure 9.

Large-scale expulsions were the norm, as implied, for instance, by Polybius's remark that the Romans hoped in 224 B.C. that they would be able entirely to expel the Celts from the plain of the Po (Polybius 2.31.8). At least there seems to be no inhibition in the sources when slaugher is described: Velleius succinctly reports that Marius killed more than a hundred and fifty thousand Teutons and that their people was exterminated.[195] Appian excels in his graphic description of the storming by Scipio of Byrsa in 146 B.C. (*Pun.* 128–130). Julius Caesar himself is quite open in his description of the slaughter of the Usipetes and Tencteri (*BG* 4.14f.): "the rest, a mass of children and women— for the Germans had left home and crossed the Rhine with all their people— began to flee in all directions. Caesar sent cavalry to pursue them." The whole crowd of Germans, children and women presumably included, were then pushed towards the junction of the Meuse and the Rhine where they were slain or perished in the river. Shortly afterwards the Nervii were almost entirely wiped out (*BG* 2.28). During the civil war he totally destroyed the Thessalian town of Gomphi (*BC* 3.80f.). In 25 B.C. Strabo records that the entire population of the Salassi, thirty-six thousand noncombatants and eight thousand fighting men, was sold as slaves; Dio adds that all men of military age were sold.[196] "Other small (Alpine) peoples, brigandish and impoverished, controlled Italy in former times; but now some of those have been totally wiped out, and others have been fully subdued" so that the passes through their territories are now safe.[197] Here then we have a passing mention of small anonymous tribes that have been totally wiped out. He "utterly destroyed (ἀνέστησεν ἄρδην) the Maltese and Corcyraeans, because they practised piracy, putting the young men to death and selling the others into slavery" (Appian, *Ill.* 47.7). Farther east, in Dalmatia, the Ardiaeoi (Vardaei) paid the price in an earlier stage. Appian says they attacked "Roman Illyria" in 135 B.C. and were punished by the consul Ser. Fulvius Flaccus (Appian, *Ill.* 10). Livy says Flaccus subdued them (*Per.* 56). Pliny records they were seriously reduced (*NH* 3.143). Strabo has more information (7.5.6 [c. 315]). He relates that the Romans "pushed them back into the interior and forced them to cultivate the soil. However, the land is rough, poor, and unsuitable for farmers, so that the people were destroyed and has almost

---

[195] Velleius 2.12.4: amplius centum quinquaginta milia hostium priore ac postero die ab eo trucidata gensque excisa Teutonum.

[196] Strabo 4.6.7 c.205; Dio 53.25; L.J.F. Keppie, *Colonisation and Veteran Settlement in Italy 47– 14 BC* (Rome, 1983), 206f. According to Strabo 4.6.6 (204) several other Alpine peoples were also wiped out entirely.

[197] Strabo 4.6.6 (c.204): καὶ ἄλλα πλείω μικρὰ ἔθνη κατέχοντα τὴν Ἰταλίαν ἐν τοῖς πρόσθεν χρόνοις λῃστρικὰ καὶ ἄπορα· νυνὶ δὲ τὰ μὲν ἐξέφθαρται τὰ δ' ἡμέρωται τελέως,

been wiped out."[198] Thus they suffered the treatment Marcus Aurelius later meted out to the Quadi (see below). The Pannonian revolt of A.D. 6–9 was initiated by Bato, leader of the Daesitiates in the region of Sarajevo in Central Bosnia (Dio 55.29.2–3). Velleius, who served himself in the region, says that this people and the Perustae "who were almost unconquerable because of the nature of the terrain and the mountains, their fierce temper, their remarkable fighting skills and, most of all, the narrow passes, were now, not only under the command, but by the hands and arms of Caesar [sc. Tiberius] himself, pacified, but only after they were almost entirely wiped out."[199]

An important question which can never be answered is how many minor and not so minor groups of peoples were "wiped out" without even such a summary record.[200] One further point to note here is that there are occasional passages which explain why a given people was *not* wholly exterminated. For instance, Plutarch, *Aemilius Paulus* 6.2, observes that the commander "allowed the subjugated Ligurians humane and accommodating terms. Indeed the Romans did not wish to wipe out the Ligurian people altogether, since it was situated, like a wall or bulwark against the movements of the Gauls, who were always threatening Italy."[201]

Tacitus's descriptions of Germanicus's campaigns in Germany in A.D. 14–16 are well known. In 14 he "ravaged a space of fifty miles with fire and sword. Neither sex nor old age inspired compassion. Both profane and sacred was utterly destroyed, including the best known sanctuary of these peoples, which they call Tamfana" (*Ann.* 1.51).[202] In A.D. 16 Germanicus obtained "a great victory and without bloodshed to us. From nine in the morning to the evening the enemy were slaughtered, and ten miles were covered with bodies and arms."[203] Germanicus set up a monument boasting that he had utterly subjected

---

[198] 7.5.6: ὥστ' ἐξέφθαρται τελέως [τὸ ἔθνος], μικροῦ δὲ καὶ ἐκλέλοιπε.

[199] Velleius 2.115.4: quippe Perustae et Desidiates Dematae, situ locorum ac montium, ingeniorum ferocia, mira etiam pugnandi scientia et praecipue angustiis saltuum paene inexpugnabiles, non iam ductu, sed manibus atque armis ipsius Caesaris tum demum pacati sunt, cum paene funditus eversi forent. For these peoples and events, see J. J. Wilkes, *Dalmatia* (London, 1969), 75f., 155–157, 274f.

[200] The terminology is there: *excidere, internecio, internicio, funditus evertere* and *debellare* in Latin, ἐκφθείρω, ἐκκόψαι, ἀφανίξω, ἀφανισμός, ἀνίστημι in Greek. A remarkable phrase is Domitian's Νασαμῶνας ἐκώλυσα εἶναι, reported by Dio, 67.4.6. When the Nasamones rebelled against extortion they were annihilated, combatants and noncombatants alike. A brief description of Lepidus massacring in Dalmatia in 15 B.C. leaves us wondering how many of the enemy survived: Velleius 2.115.2: . . . magna cum clade obsistentium excisis agris, exustis aedificiis, caesis viris . . .

[201] Plutarch, *Aemilius Paulus* 6.2: διέδωκε λόγον φιλάνθρωπον καὶ συμβατικόν· οὐ γὰρ ἦν βουλομένοις τοῖς Ρωμαίοις παντάπασιν ἐκκόψαι τὸ Λιγύων ἔθνος, ὥσπερ ἕρκος ἢ πρόβολον ἐμποδὼν κείμενον τοῖς Γαλατικοῖς κινήμασιν, ἐπαιωρουμένοις ἀεὶ περὶ τὴν Ἰταλίαν. Tiberius and Drusus partially depopulated Rhaetia in 15 B.C., leaving enough men to populate the land but not enough to start a rebellion (Dio 54.22.4–5).

[202] For similar complacent descriptions of massacres: 1.56.3, 2.25.4, 12.17. See also *Hist.* 1.63.

[203] Tac. *Ann.* 2.18: Magna ea victoria neque cruenta nobis fuit. quinta ab hora diei ad noctem caesi hostes decem milia passuum cadaveribus atque armis opplevere . . .

(*debellatis*, the verb used by Vergil, above) the Germans.[204] This followed a battle in which he asked his men "to engage in slaughter: they needed no prisoners and only the extermination of the people would mean the end of the war."[205] No less telling is Tacitus's own statement about another event: "More than sixty thousand (Germans) fell, not beneath the Roman arms and weapons, but, grander far, before our delighted eyes. May the tribes, I pray, ever retain if not love for us, at least hatred for each other; for while the destinies of empire bear hard upon us, fortune can give no greater boon than discord among our foes."[206] Tacitus records the extermination of the Germanic Bructeri by the Chamavi and Angrivarii and neighboring tribes. This is undoubtedly the classic statement expressing Roman delight in massive slaughter of the enemy—it is particularly festive if they do the work themselves, as illustrated vividly in figure 9. The style of the last sentence should be noted: it is in the form of a prayer. The phrase *urgentibus imperii fatis* seems ambiguous; however, it is hard to see it as anything but a negative phrase.[207] If so, it expresses fear for the fate of the empire and contains a prayer to fortune that she should assist survival by sowing discord among the Germans. This is one of many passages which make it impossible to claim that the Roman authors of the first and second centuries felt absolute certainty about the relationship of the empire with its neighbors, as asserted by Sherwin-White. Such fears can very well co-exist with strongly felt imperial ambitions, which is one of the themes of this book. Generally speaking, it is quite possible to be afraid of losing what one has, while still aiming to obtain much more. Finally, it is always possible that our sources exaggerate the number of victims and the blood actually shed. That does not alter the fact that the intended readers of the texts had no objections to reading that Roman armies had been carrying on in this manner.

It is relevant to note a further point, namely that there are definite elements of fear of at least some foreign peoples in our texts. We should see the copious descriptions of excessive cruelty and bloodshed on the part of the enemy in

[204] Tac. *Ann.* 2.22: Caesar congeriem armorum struxit, superbo cum titulo: debellatis inter Rhenum Albimque noationibus exercitum Tiberii Caesaris ea monimenta Marti et Iovi et Augusto sacravisse. Cf. E. A. Thompson, *The Early Germans* (Oxford, 1965), 91f. I am not sure why Thompson considers Tacitus "a comparatively humane Roman."

[205] 2.21: nil opus captivis, solam internicionem gentis finem bello fore.

[206] Tac. *Germ.* 33.2 super sexaginta milia non armis telisque Romanis, sed, quod magnificentius est, oblectationi oculisque ceciderunt. maneat, quaeso, duretque gentibus, si non amor nostri, at certe odium sui, quando urgentibus imperii fatis nihil iam praestare fortuna maius potest quam hostium discordiam.' For the phrase "urgentibus imperii fatis" cf. Livy 5.36.6 ibi iam urgentibus Romanam urbem fatis legati contra ius gentium arma capiunt; 22.43: <ex> maioris partis sententia ad nobilitandas clade Romana Cannas urgente fato profecti sunt. Cf. D. Timpe, *Romano-Germanica: Gesammelte Studien zur Germania des Tacitus* (Stuttgart and Leipzig, 1995), 203–228: "Die Germanen und die *fata imperii*," as observed by Timpe, p. 203: this sentence is the most discussed during the twentieth century of all of the *Germania* or perhaps even all of Tacitus.

[207] See references in R. Much, *Die Germania des Tacitus* (erste Auflage 1937; dritte Auflage, ed. by H. Jankuhn & W. Lange, Heidelberg, 1967), 399f.; Timpe, op. cit., cf. 204, n.6. The alternative is to understand it as "hurry on," "stimulate." Thus, for instance, A. A. Lund, *P. Cornelius Tacitus: Germania* (Heidelberg, 1988), 201f. See also below, chapter 12, p. 432.

various sources in this context. As Florus says: "It is a horrible thing to describe the savagery and cruelty of the Moesians and their barbarity exceeding that of all other barbarians" following which he supplies some details (2.26).[208] Since it is indeed a horrible thing to describe murder and torture in detail, I shall leave it to the reader to consult the original texts. These include the Arvernian Critognatus's speech as given by Caesar (cannibalism),[209] as well as Florus on Arminius's victims in A.D. 9 (2.30). In a speech composed by Livy for a Roman commander after Cannae, Hannibal's army is said to have been encouraged to eat human flesh (23.5.12), as cited above.

Cassius Dio delights in descriptions of excessive cruelty and perverse bloodthirstiness by rebellious natives, for instance, in his story about the rebellion of Boudicca (62.7). This does not occur in the parallel description in Tacitus's *Annals*, who only mentions 70,000 victims and "*caedes patibula ignes cruces*" (*Ann.* 14.33). However, Tacitus obviously enjoys the description of Romans slaughtering Britons: "Our soldiers spared not to slay even the women, while the very beasts of burden, transfixed by the missiles, swelled the piles of bodies." (Polybius, cited above, also mentions the animals as usual victims.) "Great glory, equal to that of our old victories, was won on that day. Some indeed say that there fell little less than eighty thousand of the Britons, with a loss to our soldiers of about four hundred, and only as many wounded."[210] It is noteworthy that Tacitus finds it unproblematic to tell of the slaughter of women and animals. It is usual for him, too, to consider a victory great as long as large numbers of enemy soldiers have been killed.[211] For Tacitus this is clearly part of the old-fashioned glory of which there was so much in earlier times and not enough in his own. These are rare instances in Tacitus *Annals* where he is positive without reserve, where his rhetoric contains no cynicism or sarcasm and acquires a religious overtone.

A remarkable historiographical phenomenon to be mentioned here is the foreign rebel's speech in historical accounts, and the most impressive example may well be the address which Tacitus composed for the British leader Calgacus. "(The Romans) robbers of the world, having by their universal plunder exhausted the land, they rifle the deep. If the enemy be rich, they are rapacious; if he be poor, they lust for dominion; neither the east nor the west has been able to satisfy them. Alone among men they covet with equal eagerness poverty and riches. To robbery, slaughter, plunder, they give the lying name of empire; they

---

[208] Also: 2.13; 22.

[209] Caesar, *BG* 7.77.

[210] *Ann.* 14.37 et miles ne mulierum quidem neci temperabat, confixaque telis etiam iumenta corporum cumulum auxerant. clara et antiquis victoriis par ea die laus parta: quippe sunt qui paulo minus quam octoginta milia Britannorum cecidisse tradant, militum quadringentis ferme interfectis nec multo amplius vulneratis.

[211] E.g., *Ann.* 2.18: "Magna ea Victoria neque cruenta nobis fuit." The slaughter lasted from morning until sunset. It was, in fact, one of Germanicus's bloody but undecisive engagements in Germany.

make a solitude and call it peace."[212] The speech is justly famous for its indictment of Roman imperialism from the perspective of its victims, but it has
weight beyond that. We cannot know what first-century Britons thought and
said about the Romans, and we can be certain that we have here the best possible speech which a brilliant Roman historian could compose. So much is obvious. There is, however, an additional element in Tacitus's account which
makes these points particularly significant: namely that they are nowhere contradicted or debated. The reader is being made aware that, in the eyes of rebellious provincials, Rome makes a solitude and calls it peace, but no effort is
made anywhere to counter these accusations. The Roman commander Agricola
delivers a parallel speech to his troops in the subsequent chapters. This is a
purely military speech. Nothing is said about the meaning or importance of
empire, nothing about the justice of the Roman cause. The enemy is there to be
beaten once and for all. The aim is to finish the campaign. "Crown your fifty
years' service with a glorious day; prove to your country that her armies could
never have been fairly charged with protracting a war or with causing a rebellion."[213] Thus, inevitably, the reader is left with the conviction that the accusations of the enemy commander are true, but, in Roman eyes irrelevant. This
may be further illustrated by the insouciance with which the Elder Pliny echoes
Calgacus's words: "Nevertheless it was not the arms of Rome that made (Ethiopia) a desert" (for this was the result of wars with Egypt).[214] One of the difficulties in understanding ancient imperialism is that it was not felt to require
explanations or justification.

Fourth-century panegyrics loved to describe massacres, and celebrated genocide, for instance Panegyric 12 of Constantine (A.D. 313): "With the whole bed
of the Rhine filled with ships you descended and devastated their lands and
mourning and sorrowful homes, and you inflicted destruction and desolation so
extensive on the perjured nation (sc. of the Franks) that in time to come it will
possess scarcely any name.[215] "What is lovelier than this triumphal celebration
in which he employs the slaughter of enemies for the pleasure of us all, and
enlarges the procession of the games out of the survivors of the massacre of the
barbarians?" (23.3). Earlier Constantine had acted agains the Bructeri. According to *Panegyric* 6, delivered in 310, "countless numbers were slaughtered,

[212] Tacitus, *Agricola* 30.4–6 (trans. Moses Hadas) : . . . et infestiores Romani, quorum superbiam
frustra per obsequium ac modestiam effugias. raptores orbis, postquam cuncta vastantibus defuere
terrae, mare scrutantur: si locuples hostis est, avari, si pauper, ambitiosi, quos non Oriens, non
Occidens satiaverit: soli omnium opes atque inopiam pari adfectu concupiscunt. auferre trucidare
ra- pere falsis nominibus imperium, atque ubi solitudinem faciunt, pacem appellant. Cf. the words
attributed to the Roman ally Boiocalus (*Ann.* 13.55.7): modo ne vastitatem et solitudinem mallent
quam amicos populos.
[213] *Agricola* 34.4: transigite cum expeditionibus, imponite quinquaginta annis magnum diem, ad-
probate rei publicae numquam exercitui imputari potuisse aut moras belli aut causas rebellandi.
[214] Pliny, *NH* 6.25.182: nec tamen arma Romana ibi solitudinem fecerunt
[215] *Pan. Lat.* 12 (9).22.6 (trans. Nixon and Rodgers). Toto Rheni alueo oppleto nauibus deuectus
terras eorum ac domos maestas lugentesque populatus es, tantamque cladem uastitatemque periurae
gentis intulisti ut post uix ullum nomen habitura sit.

and very many were captured. Whatever herds there were were seized or slaughtered; all the villages were put to the flame; the adults who were captured, whose untrustworthiness made them unfit for military service and whose ferocity for slavery, were given over to the amphitheatre for punishment; and their great numbers wore out the raging beasts."[216] Vegetius 3.10 praises the competence of Scipio Africanus in training his troops so that "he eventually captured the city of Numantia, and so cremated the inhabitants that none escaped."[217] Ammianus describes frequently without comment how the Romans, under Julian's command, indiscriminately killed men, women, and children: "they butchered everyone they found, men and women without distinction of age, like sheep."[218]

It should not surprise us that a society which developed the amphitheatre as a form of entertainment should also enjoy graphic descriptions of slaughter in war and, more important, have armies willing to engage in them. Polybius may, of course, be right in his belief that it had a function. This is made probable by the combination of uninhibited violence with discipline: first systematic slaughter without robbery, then, upon a signal, systematic pillage. It is also quite likely that causing terror was the intention and the actual result. Furthermore, to return to the previous topic, there was no emotional need for the Romans to declare their victims animals or inferior humans. None of our sources express a need to justify such acts, unlike the alleged behavior by rebels described above. Unlike genocide, cannibalism is not permitted whatever the circumstances.[219] It is therefore a common accusation directed at the enemy.

It is important to note that large-scale massacres were not really a moral issue. One commander was more interested in killing than another was, but it was quite possible for a commander to be a gentle philosopher and also to exterminate entire peoples, as we hear in the case of Marcus Aurelius. According to Cassius Dio, Marcus wanted to exterminate the Iazyges (ἐπίπαν ἐξελεῖν ἠθέλησεν) "because he knew this people to be untrustworthy" (71.13). In 16 Dio again notes that Marcus had wanted to exterminate them utterly (παντάπασιν ἐκκόψαι) but regretfully had to come to terms because of the attempt at usurpation by Avidius Cassius. In the case of the Quadi, Marcus ordered his troops to prevent the tribes from pursuing their normal economic life, and yet the Quadi were not allowed to emigrate. "In acting thus," says Dio "(the emperor) desired not to confiscate their lands, but to punish the people."[220] We already saw that this sort of treatment resulted in the virtual extinction of the

---

[216] *Pan. Lat.* 6 (7).12.3f. See also 8 (6).17.1 (A.D. 297) about soldiers of Constantius who reached London "and massacred indiscriminately all over the city whatever part of that multitude of barbarian hirelings had survived . . . Your men not only gave safety to your provincials by the slaughter of the enemy, but also the pleasure of the spectacle" (trans. Nixon and Rodgers).

[217] Cum ipsis denique Numantinos capta civitate sic concremavit, ut nullus evaderet.

[218] 16.11.9; also: 17.13.13, 24.2.3, 28.2.14, 30.5.14.

[219] For exceptional references in ancient sources: Widemann, "Barbarians in Ammianus Marcellinus," 189f.

[220] Dio 71.20. For the interpretation of this passage, see Isaac, *Limits of Empire*, 391 and n. 91.

Ardiaeoi (Vardaei) in Dalmatia. Yet, Marcus is on record as a man who was wont to treat even his greatest enemies humanely, or so Cassius Dio asserts (71.14). From the examples given it appears, however, that this refers to enemy rulers only. Those whom Marcus treated generously, according to Dio, were a satrap who had stirred up trouble in Armenia and Ariogaesus, king of the Iazyges, the very people Marcus had wanted to exterminate. This quality comes out again in 26, where Marcus, in a speech, allegedly says that he hopes the prize of the war will be for him to forgive Cassius, after gaining victory. The sequel is in the same vein. Marcus never abused Cassius and Cassius never uttered or wrote anything insulting to Marcus (27). After Cassius's death, Marcus refrains from punishing his supporters (28f.), clearly in contrast to other emperors. Marcus refused to see the severed head of Avidius Cassius (Dio 72.28.1), yet on the column celebrating his German wars he is depicted as receiving soldiers who bring him the heads of enemies killed (Marcus Column, scene 66).

These are interesting notions of chivalry. Perhaps there could be a special sort of interaction between enemies who know each other, or there may have been an enormous gap between impersonal warfare, between armies and peoples, and personalized conflict, between leaders. In any case, what we call genocide and the humane treatment of an enemy ruler are not mutually exclusive. Dio does not judge Marcus by his treatment of conquered peoples, but by that of conquered foreign rulers and Roman enemies. Even so, however, the evidence seems to contain paradoxes. According to Dio (71.29), Marcus was so averse to bloodshed that he did not accept gladiatorial games in earnest. Yet Dio fails to explain how this could be reconciled with Marcus's role as commander-in-chief of a fighting army who, like other Roman commanders, sometimes found it desirable to exterminate an enemy people. It is a paradox which becomes even more acute if one studies the gruesome images on Marcus's Column in Rome, two scenes of which are reproduced in this work (figs. 9 and 10).

Some victorious commanders preferred to seem to be gallant towards their vanquished enemies. If they fled and were executed, this was a cause for demonstrative indignation and declarations of regret. Thus Alexander treated the body of the murdered Darius with respect,[221] Aemilius Paulus spared Perseus (Plutarch, *Aemilius Paulus* 37), and Caesar shed tears over Pompey's seal-ring (Plutarch, *Caesar* 48). The life of Bato, instigator of the Pannonian revolt of AD 6–9, was spared while his people, the Daesidiates, were almost wiped out. He himself, however, was sent to Ravenna by Tiberius, after being presented with rich gifts (Suetonius, *Tiberius* 20). Zenobia of Palmyra enjoyed retirement in a villa in Tivoli after being exhibited in Aurelian's triumph over her.[222] This is not to suggest that such behavior was common or the norm, only that it oc-

---

[221] Arrian, *An.* 3.22.1; Quintus Curtius 5.13.25. Plutarch, *Alexander* 43. Cf. Arrian 6.29 for Alexander's care for the tomb of Cyrus.

[222] Richard Stoneman, *Palmyra and its Empire: Zenobia's Revolt against Rome* (Ann Arbor, MI, 1992), 187f.

curred and was considered praiseworthy when it did. Plutarch saw Titus Flaminius, Manius Acilius, and Aemilius Paulus as commanders "kingly in spirit" because they spared Greek sanctuaries and even made gifts. He contrasts these with later warlords, notably Sulla, who bought their soldiers to use them against their Roman competitors (*Sulla* 12). In later periods too, some warlords liked noble gestures—Napoleon, when he entered Vienna, is reported to have placed a guard of honor outside Haydn's house—and others did not.

Fears and Suppression

Vincendo Victi Sumus: The Problem of Immigrants and Minorities

"Captive Greece took her savage victor captive and brought the arts to rustic Latium."[1] This represents satire in the age of Augustus. As noted in the Introduction, we cannot use satire as considered reflection. The satire is a literary form, first developed in Rome, in which prevailing human vices, follies, abuses, or shortcomings are held up to censure by means of ridicule, irony, or related methods. It should not be treated as portraying daily life in an accurate manner. Yet it must be taken seriously as a form of commentary on the opinions of the speaker and, hence, of the current views of many of his readers. Quite clearly Horace really meant to say that Rome's Greek subjects had taught her the arts and in that sense were victors rather than captives.

"Through conquering we have been conquered" is the expression Pliny uses when he complains about Greek doctors.[2] It is a paraphrase of Horace's famous dictum, which shows that it made quite an impression on Roman readers. We also encounter a similar expression in Cicero's lament that unhappy revenue-farmers had been handed over "as slaves to Jews and Syrians, themselves peoples born to be slaves."[3] This is judicial rhetoric, clearly a sarcastic exaggeration, but the fact that Cicero expressed himself in this manner shows he expected it to be received as he intended. More important, Cicero's expression could not be understood if a popular version of Aristotle's doctrine of natural slavery had not been common ground for at least a large number of people in antiquity. Seneca, complaining about the Jews proselytizing, exclaims, equally sarcastic, that "the vanquished have given laws to their victors."[4] Seneca would not have expressed himself the way he did if he had not been certain his readers

---

[1] Horace, *Ep.* 2.1.156: Graecia capta ferum victorem cepit et artis intulit agresti Latio. For the phrase: Niall Rudd (ed.), *Horace, Epistles Book II and Epistle to the Pisones ('Ars Poetica')* (Cambridge, 1989), 101f.: "The phrase takes a very long view, telescoping events from the capture of Greek cities in Sicily during the first Punic war (264–241) to the sack of Corinth in 146."

[2] Pliny, *NH* 24.5.5: ita est profecto, magnitudine popul<us> R. perdidit ritus, vincendoque victi sumus. Cf. Florus, *epitoma* 1.47.7. For thoughts on Pliny's attitude toward the Greeks: Andrew Wallace-Hadrill, "Pliny the Elder and Man's Unnatural History," *Greece and Rome* 37 (1990), 80–96, at 92–96.

[3] Cicero, *de prov. cos.* 5.10: Iam vero publicanos miseros me etiam miserum illorum ita de me meritorum miseriis ac dolore! tradidit in servitutem Iudaeis et Syris, nationibus natis servituti. Discussed further below, in chapter 5.

[4] See also below pp. 322, 459 for this passage. Cf. in another context, Livy 21.1.3: Odiis etiam prope maioribus certarunt quam viribus, Romanis indignantibus quod victoribus victi ultro inferrent arma . . .

would have recognized the phrase as an allusion to Horace's dictum. Such statements are important, not because they reflect the reality of the time, but because they may show us something about tensions in Rome.

In this chapter we shall deal with such sentiments from the perspective of Roman authors who responded to the presence of large numbers of foreign immigrants from conquered lands who settled in Italy and the City of Rome. Another, related topic will be treated below, in chapter 5: the effects of the conquest of the East on Roman imperial attitudes. These resulted in various forms of fear, anxiety, and hostility that have to be considered separately.

To return to the elder Pliny's complaints about Greek doctors, the first of them came to Rome in 219 B.C., he tells us. He was at first very popular, but after some time lost his popularity (*NH* 29, 6.12–13). Pliny goes on to cite Cato Maior, *De Medicina* on this:

> I shall speak about those Greek fellows in their proper place, son Marcus, and point out the result of my enquiries at Athens, and convince you what benefit comes from dipping into their literature and making close study of it. They are a quite worthless people, and an intractable one, and you must consider my words prophetic. When that people gives us its literature it will corrupt all things and even all the more if it sends hither its physicians. They have conspired together to murder all foreigners with their physic, but this very thing they do for a fee, to gain credit and to destroy us easily. They are also always dubbing us barbarians, and to fling more filth on us than on others they give us the foul nickname of Opici.[5] I have forbidden you to have dealings with physicians.[6]

[5] For the term "Opici," e.g., Fronto's letter to Marcus Aurelius, 1.9.8, where Fronto asks Marcus to correct possible errors in a letter that he wrote to Marcus's mother in Greek: *Nolo enim me mater tua ut Opicum contemnat*; also: 2.8.2; 3.6.1. Cf. Alan E. Astin, Cato the Censor (Oxford, 1978), 173 and n.43. I am not aware of any passages in Greek literature where the term "Opici" is used in this manner (as distinct from its use for the Oscan people, which is neutral and regular, e.g., *Anthologia Graeca* 5.132.7; Schol. Plato, Rep. 353e).

[6] Pliny, *NH* 29.7.14: Dicam de istis Graecis suo loco, Marce fili, quid Athenis exquisitum habeam, et quod bonum sit illorum litteras inspicere, non perdiscere. uincam nequissimum et indocile esse genus illorum. et hoc puta uatem dixisse, quandoque ista gens suas litteras dabit, omnia conrumpet, tum etiam magis, si medicos suos huc mittet. iurarunt inter se barbaros necare omnis medicina, sed hoc ipsum mercede facient, ut fides iis sit et facile disperdant. nos quoque dictitant barbaros et spurcius nos quam alios Opicon appellatione foedant. interdixi tibi de medicis. Cf. Plutarch, *Cato Maior* 23.3: Rome would lose her empire when she had become infected with Greek letters. All Greek physicians had taken an oath never to treat barbarian enemies. See on these passages Astin, *Cato the Censor*, 170–173; Jean-Louis Ferrary, *Philhellénisme et impéialisme: Aspects idéologiques de la conquête romaine du monde hellénistique* (Rome, 1988), 537–539; Erich S. Gruen, Culture and National Identity in Republican Rome (Ithaca, NY, 1992 and London, 1993), ch. 2: "Cato and Hellenism," 52–83, esp. 54f., 75–80; Albert Henrichs, "Graecia Capta: *Roman Views of Greek Culture*," HSCP 97 (1995), 243–261, at 246–248. Henrichs disagrees with Astin and Gruen, who feel that Cato's words are not as fierce as they seem to be. Note also the earlier study by G. Walser, *Rom, das Reich und die fremden Völker in der Geschichtsschreibung der frühen Kaiserzeit: Studien zur Glaubwürdigkeit des Tacitus* (Baden-Baden, 1951), 67–72. Walser claims that the Romans did not by themselves develop any sense of superiority vis-à-vis other peoples.

Thus in Cato's view Greek literature is a corrupting influence, but Greek doctors are acutely dangerous. Pliny carries on about this, emphasizing how right Cato was. "For this reason even when Aesculapius was brought as a god to Rome, they are said to have built his temple outside the city, and on another occasion upon an island, and when, a long time too after Cato, they banished Greeks from Italy, to have specifically included physicians."[7] Both Cato and Pliny combine a strong sense that Rome was losing vigor and vitality through its luxuries and a fear of being undermined by foreign immigrants from among the subjugated peoples. Pliny's formulation is interesting: "We walk with the feet of others, we recognise our acquaintances with the eyes of others, rely on others' memory to make our salutations, and put into the hands of others our very lives; the precious things of nature, which support life, we have lost. We have nothing else of our own save our luxuries."[8] It expresses disapproval of a perceived total, physical dependency on slaves and frivolous lifestyle which result in a total loss of vitality. "They have ruined," says Pliny, "the morals of the Empire."[9] The Greeks, says Pliny, are the "parents of all vices" because they used olive oil at their gymnastics.[10] We see here, as elsewhere in this study, the extent to which many Romans feared that the empire which had been acquired served as a source of luxury and foreign influence that would corrupt and degenerate Roman society.

Elsewhere Pliny writes that traditional Roman medicine was cheap and effective,[11] but later quacks invented expensive imported medicines from Arabia,

---

Nationes exterae were politically dependent, but the Latin term had none of the pejorative meanings of Greek *barbaros*. The equation of *gens externa* with *barbari* penetrated in Rome exclusively under the influence of Greek literature. It is a peculiar view of the influence of literature to claim that people develop chauvinistic feelings only when they read foreign texts. For the image of doctors in Rome: Alice Gervais, "Que pensait-on des médecins dans l'ancienne Rome?" *Bulletin de l'Association Guillaume Budé* 4/2 (1964), 197–231.

[7] 29.8.15: ideo templum Aesculapii, etiam cum reciperetur is deus, extra urbem fecisse iterumque in insula traduntur et, cum Graecos Italia pellerent, diu etiam post Catonem, excepisse medicos.

[8] Pliny, *NH* 29.9.19 (trans. W.H.S. Jones, Loeb): alienis pedibus ambulamus, alienis oculis agnoscimus, aliena memoria salutamus, aliena et vivimus opera, perieruntque rerum naturae pretia et vitae argumenta. nihil aliud pro nostro habemus quam delicias. For Pliny's protests against luxury: M. Beagon, *Roman Nature: The Thought of Pliny the Elder* (Oxford, 1992), 190–194; Wallace-Hadrill, "Pliny the Elder," 85–92, concluding that it is rooted in unease about untraditional ways of marking social status, and so of defining the social hierarchy. An early attempt to evaluate the merits of Cato as distinct from those of Pliny may be found in T. Clifford Albutt, *Greek Medicine in Rome* (London, 1921), 62f., who thinks historians have done Cato some injustice. "In no small part we, as physicians, have derived our impressions of Cato from the babbling of Pliny, who had the vanity and garrulity of Boswell without his reverential sincerity." He goes on to compare Cato with Petrarch, "whose diatribes against physicians were no less unmeasured and indiscriminate."

[9] 29.8.26: 'illa perdidere imperii mores.' For the Roman preoccupation with (im)morality: Edwards, *The Politics of Immorality* (1993).

[10] Pliny, *NH* 15.19.1: usum eius ad luxuriam vertere Graeci, vitiorum omnium genitores, in gymnasiis publicando. See p. 395.

[11] For Cato and other Roman authors on traditional Roman medicine, see Gervais, "Que pensait-on des médecins," 202–204; for the early development of the profession in Rome: 204–206; for a

India, and the Red Sea, none of them better than the old Roman prescriptions. "It is perfectly true that owing to their greatness the Roman people have lost their usages, and through conquering we have been conquered. We are subjects of foreigners, and in one of the arts they have mastered even their masters."[12]

In understanding these texts we have to keep in mind that the work before us is a letter from the second century B.C. cited in a work of the second half of the first century A.D. It is an authentic letter which gives a conservative Roman's views on Greeks, doctors, and especially Greek doctors. Cato imagines that Rome is being corrupted by Greek culture, and threatened and fleeced by its doctors. Curiously, the Greeks are accused of being xenophobic. This is an old technique, resembling the anti-semitic claim that Jews hate gentiles, a claim made by Tacitus, among others. It is the reaction of people who detect their own faults and unacceptable intentions in others. This is significant for Cato's time, but it is no less important that the letter is quoted in full, with extensive comments, by Pliny the Elder. It is further interesting to note that Greeks, including expressly Greek doctors, were actually banished from Rome at some stage. This represents a third link in the evidence about hostility to these people and allows us to state that this sort of hostility occurred both in the second century B.C. and in the second half of the first century A.D. and afterwards, as will be seen below. It is perhaps relevant to note also that Tiberius banned druidism in Gaul, "both their soothsayers and their doctors."[13]

This is not to suggest that there was a continuous pattern of hatred among every Roman in all of this period. Suetonius reports that Julius Caesar granted citizenship to all those who practiced medicine at Rome and to all teachers of the liberal arts, so that they would be more eager to live in the city and in order to persuade others to attempt to acquire such knowledge.[14] Of course, an ambivalent attitude towards doctors is a phenomenon of all times.[15] Physical health is

---

survey: Elizabeth Rawson, *Intellectual Life in the Late Roman Republic* (London, 1985), chapter 12: "Medicine"; for a skeptical evaluation of Pliny's thoughts about medicine: V. Nutton, "The Perils of Patriotism: Pliny and Roman Medicine," in *Science in the early Roman Empire: Pliny the Elder, his sources and influence*, 30–58. The conclusion is that Pliny's own prescriptions were more likely to cause harm than the best contemporary medical care. See also V. Nutton, "Roman Medicine: Tradition, Confrontation, Assimilation," in *ANRW* 2.37.1, 393–444 on Greek influence on Roman medicine. Danielle Gourevitch, *Le trangle Hippocratique dans le monde gréco-romain: le malade, sa maladie et son médecin* (Rome, 1984), 347f. for Pliny's (and Cicero's) suspicions of doctors as poisoners. See also Beagon, *Roman Nature*, chapter 6: "*Ars Medicinae*: Man's Use of Nature in Medicine," pp. 202–240; for Pliny's attitude to Greek doctors: 203–208.

[12] Pliny, *NH* 24. 1.4–5 (trans. W.H.S. Jones, Loeb) ita est profecto, magnitudine popul<us> R. perdidit ritus, vincendoque victi sumus. paremus externis, et una artium imperatoribus quoque imperaverunt.

[13] Pliny, *NH* 30.13: namque Tiberii Caesaris principatus sustulit Druidas eorum et hoc genus vatum medicorumque.

[14] Suetonius, *Divus Iulius* 42.1. Note that Isocrates, *Busiris* 22 (225), claims that the Egyptians are the healthiest people of all because their priests are such excellent doctors.

[15] Petronius, *Satyricon* 42: "The doctors killed him off—or the truth is it was his bad luck, because a doctor does nothing but set your mind at rest" (trans. P. G. Walsh); Martialis 1.30: Chirurgus fuerat, nunc est vispillo Diaulus. Coepit quo poterat clinicus esse modo; also: 1.47; 6.53;

a vital need and doctors either can or cannot preserve and restore it; if they cannot, this causes resentment.[16] What is not universal, however, is widespread hostility to the profession, especially when practiced by foreigners. It has been argued that one should not take Cato's words entirely seriously.[17] However, Cato and Pliny's harangues raise curious associations with Stalin's "Doctors' Plot."[18] In 1953 nine doctors who had attended major Soviet leaders were arrested. They were charged with poisoning two of these leaders and with attempting to murder several marshals of the Soviet army. The doctors, at least six of whom were Jewish, were also accused of being in the employ of the U.S. and British intelligence services, as well as serving the interests of international Jewry. The Soviet press reported that all the doctors confessed their guilt. Here too we see doctors belonging to a resident minority being accused of conspiring to murder their upper-class patients. In the case of Stalin this was the culmination of a paranoid form of anti-semitism which only ended with his death. The trial and the rumored purge that was to follow did not occur because the death of Stalin intervened. Thereafter it was announced that a re-examination of the case showed the charges against the doctors to be false and their confessions to have been obtained by torture. In Rome, suspicions about Greek doctors were clearly a long-term phenomenon, which may tell us something about the attitudes of some Roman aristocrats towards doctors and towards Greeks. Greek superiority in this field and the dependence of the patients on the profession caused feelings of acute fear and hostility. The key sentence is Pliny's: "through conquering we have been conquered (vincendo victi sumus). We are the subjects of foreigners." As mentioned, this clearly is a paraphrase of Horace's famous dictum which demonstrates that it touched on an issue of central importance in Rome.

Jerome, *in Isaiam* 18 Praef. 1.63: alioquin ubi cibus, sequuntur et morbi; ubi morbi, adhibendus est et medicus; ubi medici, frequenter interitus; rursumque resurrectio, et noua ex integro conuersatio.

[16] Astin, *Cato*, 172, argues that Cato's rejection of Greek medicine is understandable as a rational conclusion: Greek doctors were unreliable and dangerous. He goes on to point out that the passage nevertheless does not present a rational assessment of that kind. Astin seems to overestimate the rationality of Cato's assessment, for the point is that Cato rejects *Greek* doctors, not their Roman colleagues. Quite possibly the latter were as unreliable and dangerous as the former or, perhaps, more so.

[17] Astin, *Cato*, 172: "Account must be taken of Cato's propensity for expressing himself in colourful hyperbole." Colorful hyperbole often is a quality displayed by genuine xenophobes and racists. See the comments in Elisabeth Rawson's review of Astin in *JRS* 70 (1980), 197–199. Gruen, "Cato and Hellenism," offers a subtle revision of Cato's attitudes. Indeed, there is no reason to doubt that he was a complex and intelligent figure, himself thoroughly familiar with classical and contemporary Greek culture. Gruen concludes: "Cato's mission was neither to resist Hellenism nor to liberate Rome from its influence but to highlight its features, both admirable and objectionable, in order to give clearer definition to the qualities and values that set Rome apart" (83). On p. 270 Gruen asserts: "The stereotypes would be taken seriously only by the literally minded." Ultimately our judgment depends on how we believe hostile language aimed at foreigners was understood by contemporary readers. I believe one should not underestimate the impact of forceful stereotypes or the strength of ambivalent emotions, even in subtle and intelligent characters.

[18] Cf. "Doctor's Plot," *Encyclopaedia Britannica* CD, version 1997.

A complementary perspective, no less relevant here, is offered in the writings of Galen (129–?199/216), notably his work *On Prognosis*:[19] Good, well-trained doctors who make good prognoses thereby stir up such envy against themselves that his incompetent colleagues conspire against him. He gives the example of Quintus, the best physician of his generation, who was expelled from Rome on a charge of murdering his patients (1.8f.). The best practicioners, therefore, either leave Rome, or they keep quiet, leaving it to scoundrels to gain a popular reputation (1.11f.). Competent Greek doctors in Rome are in danger of being poisoned by their Roman colleagues (4.16). At least, Galen mentions one such case. He tells at length of his confrontations with incompetent local doctors in Rome and their attacks on him (2-4.4). The philosopher Eudemus, his teacher and patient, contrasts the city of Rome with the small *poleis* of the Greek world, where there are no great gains to be had and everyone knows all about his neighbor's behavior (4.9). The wealthy of Rome honor the learned only to the extent that they can use them; unable to tolerate true experts or real philosophers, they are flattered by impostors who are enticed by the prospect of large profits.[20] In this connection it is only fair to observe that the Greek doctors also had a loyal clientele in Rome; the younger Pliny, for instance, had different views. He went to a good deal of trouble to get Roman citizenship for his medical therapist of Egyptian origin and to obtain the same favor for the relatives of his eastern doctor, Postumius Marinus.[21] That should not modify the impression derived from Cato's and Pliny's stated opinion, for Roman public opinion was not monolithic and there was no censorship which forced authors into uniform pronouncements.

To return to the elder Pliny for a related topic, we may briefly note his statements about trade with the east: "In no year does India absorb less than fifty million sesterces of our empire's wealth, sending back merchandise to be sold with us at a hundred times its prime cost" (NH 6.26.101). Elsewhere he gives another round sum: "And by the lowest reckoning India, China and that peninsula [Arabia] take from our empire a hundred million sesterces each year. That is the sum which our luxuries and our own women cost us. What fraction of these imports, I ask, gets to the gods or the lower world?" (*NH* 12.41.84)[22] These complaints of Pliny have been discussed by Sidebotham, who points out

[19] Galen, *de Praecognitione*, ed., trans., and comm. by Vivian Nutton, *Corpus Medicorum Graecorum* 5.8.1 (Berlin, 1979).

[20] Galen, *De Praecognitione* 1.13–15, 4.9, 4.14 (charlatans), 4.17 (Rome). Cf. Simon Swain, *Hellenism and Empire: Language, Classicism and Power in the Greek World, AD 50–250* (Oxford, 1996), 357–379, esp. 360–363.

[21] Pliny, *ep.* 10.5–7, 10, 11. Other supporters of medical science were Cicero, Varro, Lucretius, Caesar, Augustus, and Horace; cf. Gervais, *Bull. Ass. Budé* 4/2 (1964), 209–217. From Lucian, *Podagra* 265, it seems that many physicians were impoverished Syrians.

[22] Cf. S. E. Sidebotham, *Roman Economic Policy in the Erythra Thalassa, 30 BC–AD 217* (Leiden, 1986), 33–45. For Pliny's attitude towards luxury: Beagon, *Roman Nature*, 190–194. Beagon sees Pliny's attitude as determined by the extravagances of the reign of Nero.

that they are untrustworthy for two reasons.[23] First, the idea of a balance of trade did not exist in antiquity. Second, there are and were no statistics on volume of trade. Pliny cannot have known whether Rome imported more than it exported. Pliny's anger is almost certainly based on an undefined feeling that Rome should not be paying for imported luxury, just as Romans should not pay a lot of money for fancy eastern medicaments, but use traditional local prescriptions. The outburst also has a misogynous flavor. Luxuries and women are the favorite targets of conservatives of all ages. However, in its hostility towards eastern peoples it is again an example of the reaction of people who detect their own faults and unacceptable intentions in others, similar to people of doubtful honesty, who are quick to blame others for dishonest behavior.

In fact, these themes had in this period become so banal that Petronius inserted them in his satire of an epic poem, a "monstrous deluge of words" (*Satyricon* 124.3):

> I shrink from words evoking future ruin
> From tender boys adopting Persian ways,
> We stole their manhood the knife's cutting edge
> Exploited for men's lust. Without success
> Nature sought ways to encompass brief delay
> Of years fast fleeting: hence all sought their joy
> In harlots, in effeminates' mincing steps,
> In flowing hair, in novel garb oft changed,
> In all that captivates men's minds.[24]

The poem which appears in the *Satyricon* contains what Petronius clearly felt were hackneyed themes in epic poems of his time. The opening describes Rome's imperial ambition, driven by greed. Then follows the passage cited here, which expresses Roman fears of being morally corrupted by eastern subjects. The subjects are familiar: Persian wealth, homosexuality, and homosexual relations with castrated slaves, prostitution, and so on. The poem goes on to describe the decadent luxury of imperial Rome.

In the second century, Juvenal expresses a sentiment related to that of Horace in several of his satires, typically in anger, rather than in irony (after 118). *Sat.* 3. 60–72:

I cannot stand, Quirites, a Greek city of Rome; and yet what part of the dregs comes from Greece? The Syrian Orontes has long since flowed into the Tiber, bringing

---

[23] Sidebotham, op. cit., 38f.

[24] Petronius, *Satyricon* 119.19–27 (trans. P. G. Walsh): heu, pudet effari perituraque prodere fata: / Persarum ritu male pubescentibus annis / surripuere viros exsectaque viscera ferro / in venerem fregere, atque ut fuga nobilis aevi / circumscripta mora properantes differat annos . . . / quaerit se natura nec invenit. omnibus ergo /scorta placent fractique enervi corpore gressus / et laxi crines et tot nova nomina vestis, /quaeque virum quaerunt. Cf. Lucan, *BC* 10.133f. (describing a meal offered by Cleopatra to Caesar in Alexandria): Nec non infelix ferro mollita iuventus / Atque execta virum.

with it its language and its habits, its flutes and its loud harps; bringing too the tambourines, and the prostitutes who are ordered to do their job at the Circus. . . . One comes from lofty Sicyon, another from Amydon or Andros, others from Samos, Tralles or Alabanda; all are making for the Esquiline, or for the hill that takes its name from osier-beds; all are ready to worm their way into the houses of the great and become their masters.[25]

Whether or not this represents Juvenal's own angle of vision is not really important here. What is significant for us is that it represents the perspective of some Romans, presumably that of typically querulous citizens without wealth. The implications of this are clear. The image of one river flowing into another suggests that the two cultures have become inseparable. The imported culture is corrupt and despicable and the great houses have been taken over by foreign prostitutes, not merely Greek, but even worse: immigrants from Anatolia and Syria.

Juvenal elaborates on this elsewhere in the same poem: "They are experts in flattery, dishonest, lecherous and promiscuous. They take over the city with their money. Here in Rome the son of free-born parents has to give the wall to some rich man's slave" (3. 131).[26] Once again we find here the notion of the victor being subdued and at the same time corrupted by the corrupt subject. A variant is introduced in 2.163–170:

But what we now do in our victorious city, those whom we vanquished will not do. And yet they say that one Armenian, Zalaces, more effeminate than all our young men, has given himself to a passionate tribune. See what foreign contacts do! He came as a hostage, here they are turned into men. For if these boys stay longer in Rome, there will always be lovers. They will throw away their trousers, knives, bridles and whips. Thus they carry back to Artaxata the customs of the Romans.[27]

I have found no parallel for this way of thinking. The point of the passage is that Rome corrupts its effeminate eastern subjects even more than they were

[25] ". . . viscera magnarum domuum dominique futuri." See W. J. Watts, "Race Prejudice in the Satires of Juvenal," *Acta Classica* 19 (1976), 83–104; S. H. Braund, "Juvenal and the East: Satire as an Historical Source," in D. H. French and C. S. Lightfoot, *The Eastern Frontier of the Roman Empire*, 45–52; E. Courtney, *A Commentary on the Satires of Juvenal* (London, 1980).

[26] 3.131: divitis hic servo claudit latus ingenuorum filius. Courtney, p. 174: It is a sign of respect to walk on the left of another or on his outside. Sherwin-White, *Racial Prejudice*, 62–71, discusses Lucian. Not all of this is relevant for Sherwin-White's topic, but the comparison between Lucian and Juvenal is not uninteresting. The main theme, says Sherwin-White, is the jealousy felt by the native professional person for his too successful foreign rival. But he agrees that sometimes Juvenal expresses a dislike that is not motivated by fear or rivalry. He concludes: "So in Juvenal there is an active if minor strain of national and cultural prejudice at work." If this is a minor strain one wonders what a major strain would be like.

[27] sed quae nunc populi fiunt victoris in urbe, / non faciunt illi quos vicimus. et tamen unus / Armenius Zalaces cunctis narratur ephebis / mollior ardenti sese indulsisse tribuno./ aspice quid faciant commercia: uenerat obses, / hic fiunt homines. nam si mora longior urbem / †indulsit† pueris, non umquam derit amator. / mittentur bracae, cultelli, frena, flagellum:/ sic praetextatos referunt Artaxata mores. Cf. Courtney, comm. ad loc. and Braund, "Juvenal and the East," 50.

corrupted already. Zalaces is effeminate, as all Orientals are held to be by definition, but in Rome, he is turned into a homosexual by a Roman.[28] This then is
a paradox: the victor corrupts the subject, because he is now even more degenerate than his proverbially degenerate (eastern) subject. This is a step further
than the suggestion that Romanization turns the vanquished into slaves, as described by Tacitus in *Agricola*. Juvenal combines two approaches: Rome is
overwhelmed by its eastern inhabitants, becomes corrupt, and thus corrupts
others. Juvenal's satire, whether it expresses his own feelings or those of others,
is one of many Roman literary works that betray a sense of insecurity, which is
surprising for a representative of the ruling class of a major empire.[29] Even if
this is satirical exaggeration, it exaggerates feelings widely present; otherwise it
would not have been effective as satire.

This sentiment is depicted in Lucian's *Hirelings* from another perspective.[30]
The Syrian Greek satirist describes the reactions of local Romans in the city to
the presence of a Greek at dinner: "That was still left for us in addition to our
other afflictions, to play second fiddle to men who have just come into the
household, and it is only these Greeks who have the freedom of the city of
Rome. And yet, why is it that they are preferred to us? Is it not true that they
think they confer a tremendous benefit by turning phrases?"[31] This passage is
particulaly interesting because it shows the way in which Greeks in Rome experienced the confrontation with native Romans. Lucian does not give us the
point of view of the Greeks, but cites the local Romans as they express their
grudges. He does not render their complaints verbatim; he writes satire and
therefore exaggerates. The essence of his words, however, is earnest. It would
have been easy to show that the Greeks were indeed better educated and could
offer superior social skills, but he does not do so.

The idea that victorious Rome is conquered spiritually by its subjects occurs
as late as the fifth century, in an anti-Jewish tirade by Rutilius Namatianus:
"And would that Judaea had never been subdued by Pompey's wars and Titus'
military power! The infection of this plague, though excised, still creeps abroad
the more: and 'tis their own conquerors that a conquered race keeps down."[32]

The sense that Rome was undermined and corrupted by the enemy it had

---

[28] Cicero assumed homosexuality in Rome was of Greek origin, deriving from the gymnasium:
Cicero, *Tusculanae Disputationes* 4.70: mihi quidem haec in Graecorum gymnasiis nata consuetudo
videtur, in quibus isti liberi et concessi sunt amores; 5.58 (more Graeciae). Cf. *RE* 11.905f.

[29] For Juvenal's insecurity: N. Rudd, *Themes in Roman Satire* (1986), 191.

[30] Cf. Swain, *Hellenism and Empire*, 319–322.

[31] Lucian, *Merc. cond.* 17: Τοῦτο ἡμῖν πρὸς τοῖς ἄλλοις δεινοῖς ἐλείπετο, καὶ τῶν ἄρτι
εἰσεληλυθότων εἰς τὴν οἰκίαν δευτέρους εἶναι, καὶ μόνοις τοῖς Ἕλλησι τούτοις ἀνέῳκται ἡ
Ῥωμαίων πόλις· καίτοι τί ἐστιν ἐφ' ὅτῳ προτιμῶνται ἡμῶν; οὐ ῥημάτια δύστηνα λέγοντες οἴον-
ταί τι παμμέγεθες ὠφελεῖν; Cf. C. P. Jones, *Culture and Society in Lucian* (1998), 78–89.

[32] *De Reditu Suo* i, 381–398: Atque utinam numquam Iudaea subacta fuisset Pompei bellis imperioque Titi! Latius excisae pestis contagia serpunt victoresque suos natio victa premit (Stern,
Greek and Latin Authors, ii, No. 542, pp. 660–664). See on this now A. Cameron, "The last Pagans
of Rome," in *Transformation of* Urbs Roma *in Late Antiquity*, ed. W. V. Harris (Portsmouth, RI,
1999), 117f. More will be said about the Jews in chapter 13.

defeated will be discussed extensively below. That discussion, however, focuses on the ways Greeks and Romans saw other peoples collectively in their own lands. The prejudices and stereotypes expressed operated from a distance and the fear was that the Roman army there would degenerate and, upon its return, infect the Romans at home. This chapter attempts to show how Romans responded to the presence of substantial numbers of immigrants from foreign lands in Italy and Rome. The sources discussed do not relate to distant peoples, but to large numbers of minorities living among them in Italy and Rome, which is quite a different relationship, as everybody living in Europe and America in our times knows very well. This is not to suggest that Roman prejudices regarding, for instance, Syrians as people in their own land were radically different from those regarding the Syrian immigrants living in the city of Rome. For lucid analysis, however, it is necessary to be aware that there may be a difference. It is, in fact, likely that there is a difference, for the common response of people to their neighbors in town is different from their response to distant peoples.

As has been stressed above, it is characteristic of proto-racist and racist tensions that they combine, or alternate between, feelings of superiority and inferiority, attributing to the others both exaggerated powers or gifts and moral or mental shortcomings. These emotions tend to be particularly fierce where immigrants and minorities are concerned, even though they may occur with varying intensity towards other peoples, living elsewhere. The phrase "vincendo victi sumus" sums up this emotional paradox and it does so even if it is meant sarcastically. Such a mentality is self-contradictory, but characteristic of all forms of group-hatred.[33] It is typical, for instance, of nineteenth- and twentieth-century anti-semitism. The anti-semite sees himself both as victim and victor. The Jew is both superior and inferior. The non-Jew is both triumphant and in terrible danger from whatever the anti-semite believes the Jews to be doing in order to harm and undermine civilized society.[34] It is an attitude that satisfies both fantasies of superiority and fears of inferiority and will explain satisfactorily whatever happens in reality and can be used to justify many forms of discrimination or aggression. As will be seen below, in chapter 13, a similar pattern may be discerned in Roman attitudes to the Jews in Rome. As already noted, chapter 5 considers the related but separate topic of the effects of the Roman conquest of the East on Roman imperial sentiment.

It seems fair to conclude that the evidence of ambivalent feelings about foreigners, particularly subject foreigners in Rome and Italy, represent the sort of tension that is often engendered by the presence of substantial groups of immi-

---

[33] "As is so often the case in history, Nemesis ordained that the consequences of victory should be destructive to the victors, who were first engulfed and finally disappeared in the mass of the vanquished." Martin P. Nilsson, *Imperial Rome* (London, 1926; reprinted without change in New York, 1962), p. 363. It is interesting to see how Pliny's phobic exclamation is taken up by a scholar in the twentieth century as the climax and conclusion of a racist treatise. See also chapter 1, p. 110.

[34] Ritchie Robertson, *The 'Jewish Question' in German Literature 1749–1939: Emancipation and its Discontents* (Oxford, 1999), 185.

grants in an urban civilization. It is no coincidence that many of the disparaging comments derive from satire, for satire deals with the daily environment while history focuses on emperors, the court, armies, and foreign peoples. The historians undoubtedly are influenced by the presence of aliens in their own society and vicinity, but they do not necessarily write about it. The disparaging or hostile reactions to foreigners in satire are not to be played down because they occur in satire. They should be taken as reflecting real social stresses and tensions. These tensions frequently resulted in actual steps to remove the undesired aliens, as will be discussed in the next section.

EXPULSIONS

Ancient Greeks and Romans did not refrain from large-scale slaughter at times. The Roman army occasionally indulged in it, as seen in chapter 2. Inner-urban tensions could explode and result in massive slaughter, such as recorded by Josephus in Syrian cities in the period of the Jewish revolt and at other times in Eastern cities.[35] There was, however, never a doctrine resembling the Nazi "final solution." However fierce a group of foreigners are disliked, no ancient author argues that the other people should be exterminated in toto for ideological reasons. The Romans, however, regularly made attempts to get rid of foreigners from the city of Rome when they considered them undesirable. When Rome developed into the capital of an empire, many representatives of the subject peoples came to settle there, causing various forms of tension. From time to time, such tensions became threatening enough for the authorities to expel minorities from the city. It should be understood very clearly that these were measures which regarded Rome and Italy, not the empire as a whole.

According to Livy, those who introduced foreign cults were frequently expelled from the city. He attributes a statement to this effect to a consul who spoke in 186 B.C. when taking action against the Bacchanalia: "How often, in the times of our fathers and our grandfathers, has the task been assigned to the magistrates of forbidding the introduction of foreign cults, of excluding dabblers in sacrifices and fortune-tellers from the Forum, the Circus, and the City, of searching out and burning books of prophecies, and of annulling every system of sacrifice except that performed in the Roman way."[36] The first to suffer such treatments were the Latins and the Italian allies, between 187 and 172 B.C.[37] In 171 B.C., when war was declared on Macedonia, the envoys from the Macedonian king and all their compatriots resident in the city were given thirty days

---

[35] For riots in eastern cities, see Isaac, *Limits of Empire* (2d ed. 1992), 270–280.

[36] Livy 39.16.8 (trans. Evan T. Sage, Loeb): quotiens hoc patrum auorumque aetate magistratibus negotium est datum, uti sacra externa fieri uetarent, sacrificulos uates que foro circo urbe prohiberent, uaticinos libros conquirerent comburerentque, omnem disciplinam sacrificandi praeterquam more Romano abolerent? More on this affair below.

[37] See Balsdon, *Romans & Aliens*, 99f. See in general his chapter eight: "Expulsion from Rome, Italy or your Homeland."

to leave the city.[38] In 161 a *senatus consultum* authorized the praetor to remove Greek philosophers and rhetors from the city.[39] In either 173 or 154, another senatus consultum banished two Epicureans.

Gruen argues that these acts were either insignificant or unenforceable. Either way their effect was symbolic only. This may be true or not—the evidence is not very good—but one should not underestimate the importance of symbolic acts. At least they represent a strong feeling, widely present among those with political influence that those expelled should not be there. However, it is also possible that the measures were in fact intended to have long-term practical consequences, even though this did not actually happen. From other periods we know that communities may be involved in a constant struggle to prevent the arrival of foreigners perceived as unwelcome and remove those present. The expulsion of a number of them on one occasion removes neither the dynamics of migration nor the tension engendered among the host community. As with acts of war, one has to distinguish between the original intent or plan of a campaign and the final result. It is too often assumed that the result of a campaign was the one originally intended. That may be the case when an unexpected result leads to a wider campaign than planned, resulting in a major war, or when an unexpected failure leads to claims, after the event, that only modest results were intended. The same may be true with internal politics. An action, publicly announced, may have a temporary or limited effect only, but that need not imply it always was planned to be modest in scale. As John North concluded, "The really important conclusion is quite secure: 186 established both new religious possibilities and a new pattern of authoritarian response."[40]

In 156/5 Cato took steps to speed up the departure of an embassy from Greece which included the philosophers Carneades, Critolaos, and Diogenes, who had become too popular in Cato's eyes.[41] Pliny, after describing these events, adds that Cato "always on other occasions recommended the banishment of all Greeks from Italy."[42] In 139 B.C. the *praetor peregrinus* expelled all the astrologers from Rome and ordered them to leave Italy within ten days to prevent them from "offering for sale their foreign science."[43] At the same time he banished the Jews from Rome, "because they attempted to transmit their sacred rites to the Romans, and he cast down their private altars from public

---

[38] Polybius 27.6; Livy 42.48.3; Appian, *Mac.* 11.9 with details of the consternation and anxiety caused by the sudden decree.

[39] Gruen, *Studies in Greek Culture and Roman Policy* (Leiden, 1990), 171–178.

[40] J. A. North, "Religious Toleration in Republican Rome," *PCPS* 25 (1979), 85–103, esp. 98. See also Peter Garnsey, "Religious Toleration in Classical Antiquity," in: W. J. Sheils (ed.), *Persecution and Toleration* (Oxford, 1984), 1–27.

[41] Plutarch, *Cato Maior*, 22.5; Pliny, *NH* 7.112f.; cf. Cic., *de Oratore* 2.155–7 with comm. A. D. Leeman and H. Pinkster, M Tullius Cicero, De Oratore libri III (Heidelberg, 1985), 94f. The affair is also discussed in the chapter on Roman attitudes toward Greeks, below, p. 386.

[42] Pliny, *NH* 7.30.113: ille semper alioquin universos ex Italia pellendos censuit Graecos.

[43] ne peregrinam scientiam venditarent. Astin, *Cato the Censor*, 169, thinks Pliny exaggerates, but that seems unlikely. Cato is on record as having advocated drastic steps on other occasions.

places."[44] At an uncertain date, Greeks were expelled, including Greek doctors (Pliny, *NH* 29.8.15). The Jews were expelled again in A.D. 19, together with Isis-worshippers. 'Four thousand descendants of enfranchised slaves, tainted with that superstition and suitable in point of age, were to be shipped to Sardinia and there employed in suppressing brigandage: 'if they succumbed to the pestilential climate, it was a cheap loss (*vile damnum*)'."[45] We should note that, according to Tacitus, it was the emperor's view that this would be a cheap loss, although Tacitus presumably agreed. The rest had orders to leave Italy, unless they had renounced their impious ceremonial by a given date.[46] Between the middle of the first century B.C. and the reign of Tiberius, measures were regularly taken to suppress the Isis-cult.[47] There was another order by Claudius expelling the Jews in A.D. 41 or 49, "because they all the time made disturbances at the instigation of Chrestus."[48] Cassius Dio cites a harangue sup-

[44] Valerius Maximus 1.3.3 (Stern, no. 147a): Chaldaeos igitur Cornelius Hispalus urbe expulit et intra decem dies Italia abire iussit, ne peregrinam scientiam venditarent. Iudaeos quoque, qui Romanis tradere sacra sua conati erant, idem Hispalus urbe exterminavit arasque privatas e publicis locis abiecit. Stern, no. 147b: Idem Iudaeos, qui Sabazi Iovis cultu Romanos inficere mores conati erant, repetere domos suas coegit. Cf. comments in Stern, I, 358–360; Servius, *Commentarii in Vergilii Aeneida* 8.187 (Stern, No. 537a). Three subjects have been much discussed: (1) The meaning of the reference to Jupiter Sabazius. (2) The question whether there was a permanent Jewish presence in Rome by that time. (3) An hypothesis that there may have been a connection between this measure and the appearance in Rome, possibly at that time, of an embassy from Simon the Hasmonean. M. Goodman, Mission and Conversion: Proselytizing in the Religious History of the Roman Empire (Oxford, 1994), 68, 82f., argues that these passages are not reliable evidence of proselytism in the second century B.C. See E. Mary Smallwood, *The Jews under Roman Rule from Pompey to Diocletian: A Study in Political Relations* (Leiden, 1976), 128–130; H. Solin, 'Juden und Syrer im westlichen Teil der der römischen Welt," *ANRW* 2.29.2 (1983), 587–789, esp. 607f.; for references to earlier discussions: notes 25 and 26 and Schürer, vol. 3, p.74f. For these and related events, see now Gruen, *Diaspora* (2002), chapter 1.

[45] The normal situation in Sardinia, according to Cicero's rhetoric, *De Prov. Consularibus* 14: "a campaign in Sardinia against bandits in sheepskins, waged by a propraetor with one auxiliary cohort" (*res in Sardinia cum mastrucatis latrunculis a propraetore una cohorte auxiliaria gesta*).

[46] Tacitus, *Ann.* ii 85, 4 (Stern, no. 284); also: Suetonius, *Tiberius* 36 (Stern, no. 306); Dio 57.18.51 (Stern, no. 419); Jos. *Ant.* 18.3.5.(81ff.). Dio connects the expulsion with their attraction of proselytes, a factor not mentioned by Tacitus, but implied in Josephus. Solin, *ANRW* 29.2, 686–688, accepts that the measure was primarily a reaction to proselytism. M. H. Williams, "The Expulsion of the Jews from Rome in A.D. 19," *Latomus* 48 (1989), 765–784, has argued that proselytism was not a significant factor in this affair. She seeks a connection with problems in the corn supply and the poverty of many of the Jews in Rome at that time. Goodman, *Mission and Conversion* (1994), 68, agrees with Williams and disagrees with Stern and others on this source as evidence for large-scale proselytizing activities. The affair has now again been discussed by Gruen, Diaspora, 29–34. See also below, the discussion of attitudes towards the Jews, chapter 13.

[47] H. Sonnabend, *Fremdbild und Politik: Vorstellungen der Römer von Ägypten und dem Partherreich in der späten Republik und frühen Kaiserzeit* (Frankfurt, 1986), 136f. with references.

[48] Suetonius, *Claudius* 25.4 (Stern, no. 307): Iudaeos impulsore Chresto assidue tumultuantis Roma expulit; cf. Orosius, *Adversus Paganos* 7.6.15; Dio 60.6.6 (Stern, no. 422); Acts 18:2. See Stern's comments, ii, pp. 114–117. The scholia on Juvenal refer to this expulsion or to the one by Tiberius or to yet another one, unrecorded in other extant sources: *Scholia in Iuvenalem Vetustiora* (Wessner, p. 64; Stern, no. 538): *Dignus Aricinos qui mendicaret ad axes:* Qui ad portam Aricinam sive ad clivum mendicaret inter Iudaeos, qui ad Ariciam transierant ex urbe missi. See Stern's

posedly addressed to Vespasian by his minister Licinius Mucianus (Dio 66.13.1a). It contains a fierce attack on the Stoics. Consequently, Vespasian immediately banished all philosophers from Rome. The reasons for this hostility and the measures taken are less clear. Did it stem from enmity towards Greek intellectuals and philosophers, or was there a political motive? Dio lists arrogance and presumption, but does not give a rational motive for the expulsion. Perhaps none was needed. Below, more will be said about Jewish and Christian proselytism. Here it may be instructive also to observe how easily the sentiments analyzed in this chapter were adapted by the authors of racist works in the Nazi period, for instance von Eickstedt, who explains the ruinous effect on a higher civilization of biological contamination. "Rome was undermined by strangers and became the plaything of rulers of foreign races, while hardly a drop of the blood of the old Roman patriciate of indo-german extraction remained in the veins of its citizens. For whom had Rome conquered the world? Not for itself but for all those countless foreigners who, eager for success, flowed to the capital."[49] This parallel leads to a call for eugenics, the liquidation of criminal and pathological stock, necessary if Europe is to be saved.

To sum up: expulsions from the city of Rome occurred fairly regularly. When a reason is given, this is usually that the expelled represented practitioners of foreign cults, dabblers in sacrifices and fortune-tellers, or even simply philosophers. As argued in the first section of this chapter, hostile feelings about foreigners, particularly subject foreigners in Rome and Italy, are those that are often engendered by the presence of substantial groups of immigrants in an urban civilization. In this case these immigrants came from the provinces of the empire and they therefore represented peoples subjugated by the Romans. This would have labeled them as inferior in some sense at least. Clearly the presence of certain groups of such foreigners was occasionally deemed undesirable by some groups of senators, if these foreigners were believed to influence traditional religion, culture, and values. It is probably legitimate to see a connection between the feelings of hostility or even insecurity, discussed in the previous section of this chapter, and the period steps taken to expel aliens from the city of Rome and Italy. However, these were expulsions, not killings, and they had no long-term effect. Yet they are indicative of the tensions that existed in Rome from the time it ceased to be a mid-size city-state.

So far the response to groups of migrants in Rome and Italy. We should now consider a different theme in the complex of Greek and Roman attitudes towards foreign peoples. After considering the day-to-day response of urban Romans to the presence of immigrants in their midst, we now turn to ancient ideas about contact between peoples, seafaring, travel and the like. In other words,

---

comments (no. 2, p. 655); Schürer, 3.77f.; Solin, *ANRW* 2.29.2, 688–690; and, again, Gruen, *Diaspora*.

[49] Egon Freiherr von Eickstedt, *Rassenkunde und Rassengeschichte der Menschheit* (Stuttgart, 1934), 906, my translation of the German. Eickstedt's note 6 cites various scholarly works, some respectable, others not. For Eickstedt, see also above, Introduction, note 86.

we now move to Greek and Roman ideas about the effect of interaction with remote foreigners.

CONTACT BETWEEN PEOPLES: A BLESSING AND A CURSE

As observed above, the view that pure lineage is better than mixed ancestry occurs often in the ancient literature. In this connection it is frequently asserted in ancient Greek literature that contact with other peoples, seafaring, trade and commerce, lead to social evolution and consequent moral decline. Corruption and contamination are ever-present preoccupations. The idea is attested first in a fragment of Xenophanes (sixth century B.C.): [50] "And having learned unprofitable luxuries from the Lydians, as long as they were free of hateful tyranny, they used to go into the agora wearing robes all of purple, not less than a thousand in all, boastful, exulting in their gorgeous long-flowing hair, drenched in the scent of prepared unguents."[51] Xenophanes is referring to the Colophonians, who, being originally austere, became degenerated by their luxurious lifestyle, taken over from the Lydians. This passage is particularly interesting, because Xenophanes is speaking here of his hometown, which he felt was corrupted by the wealth of the Lydians. Not only is this a very early occurrence of the syndrome, it is applied to wealthy inhabitants of the East by an eastern Greek himself.

The concept may be found again in the fifth century, not surprisingly, in the Constitution of the Athenians which says, among its long list of complaints about contemporary Athens, that "by virtue of their naval power, the Athenians have mingled with various peoples and discovered types of luxury. Whatever the delicacy in Sicily, Italy, Cyprus, Egypt, Lydia, Pontus, the Peloponnese, or anywhere else,—all these have been brought together into one place by virtue of naval power."[52] The author means to say that the rabble profits from this affluence which, like so much else, is bad for the city as a whole, notably for the good people. A rather different argument is presented in characteristic fashion in Aristotle's Politics, where he observes that "It is a hotly debated question whether connexion with the sea is to the advantage, or the deteriment of a well-

---

[50] Xenophanes F3B (Diels Kranz) = F3 (West) = 3 (Lesher) = Athenaeus, *Deipnosophistae* 526a.

[51] Trans. J. H. Lesher, *Xenophanes of Colophon: Fragments, a Text and Translation with a Commentary* (Toronto, 1992), comments on pp. 61–65, 73–77. ἀβροσύνας δὲ μαθόντες ἀνωφελέας παρὰ Λυδῶν, / ὄφρα τυραννίης ἦσαν ἄνευ στυγερῆς, / ἤιεσαν εἰς ἀγορὴν παναλουργέα φάρε᾽ ἔχοντες, / οὐ μείους ὥσπερ χείλιοι ὡς ἐπίπαν, / αὐχαλέοι, χαίτησιν †ἀγαλλομεν εὐπρεπέεσσιν, / ἀσκητοῖς ὀδμὴν χρίμασι δευόμενοι. For lines 3–4 West refers to Cicero, *De Republica* 6.2 and for the entire fragment to Aristotle, *Politica* 1290b14.

[52] Ps.-Xenophon, *Constitution of the Athenians* (trans. G. W. Bowersock, Loeb) 2.7: τὴν ἀρχὴν τῆς θαλάττης πρῶτον μὲν τρόπους εὐωχιῶν ἐξηῦρον ἐπιμισγόμενοι ἄλλη ἄλλοις· ὥστε ὅ τι ἐν Σικελίᾳ ἡδὺ ἢ ἐν Ἰταλίᾳ ἢ ἐν Κύπρῳ ἢ ἐν Αἰγύπτῳ ἢ ἐν Λυδίᾳ ἢ ἐν τῷ Πόντῳ ἢ ἐν Πελοποννήσῳ ἢ ἄλλοθί που, ταῦτα πάντα εἰς ἓν ἤθροισται διὰ τὴν ἀρχὴν τῆς θαλάττης.

ordered state. There are some who maintain that the introduction of strangers, who have been born and bred under other laws, and the consequent increase of population, is prejudicial to good order. They argue that such an increase is inevitable when numbers of merchants use the sea for the export and import of commodities; and they regard it as inimical to good government" (trans. Ernest Barker).[53] If these results are avoided, however, Aristotle sees advantages in good communications with the sea. These lie in the military sphere, he says, and in facilitating commerce; "for the state ought to engage in commerce for its own interest, but not for the interest of the foreigner."

It is relevant here to consider ancient doubts about the desirability of intercourse with foreigners.[54] Fear of strangers and their ideas, corresponding fantasies about a golden past in which there was no need to travel elsewhere and no foreigners disturbed peace at home, are clearly present in Greek and Latin literature. Indeed, no concrete steps were ever taken by the Greeks or the Romans to limit contact with the outside world, such as the Japanese policy of national seclusion, which lasted from the seventeenth till the nineteenth century. Yet it is important for a study on Greek and Roman attitudes towards others to recognize that many authors considered intercourse with others harmful. It is interesting to observe that in modern times, too, there have existed and perhaps still exist ideas that true cultural self-definition is reinforced by isolation.[55]

Plato's Laws, book 3, contains a description of an imaginary state of affairs after the Flood. With no technology to speak of, there was little intercourse between men (678c), no civil strife (στάσις) or war, and men were kindly disposed and friendly towards one another, for there was food in abundance and men were genuinely good (678e–679c). Later in the work the question arises whether a city is better situated on the seashore or farther away from it. It is then argued it should not be too near the coast (*Leges* 704d: ATH): "For the sea is, in very truth, 'a right briny and bitter neighbour,'[56] although there is sweet-

[53] Aristotle, *Pol.* 1327a: Περὶ δὲ τῆς πρὸς τὴν θάλατταν κοινωνίας, πότερον ὠφέλιμος ταῖς εὐνομουμέναις πόλεσιν ἢ βλαβερά, πολλὰ τυγχάνουσιν ἀμφισβητοῦντες· τό τε γὰρ ἐπιξενοῦσθαί τινας ἐν ἄλλοις τεθραμμένους νόμοις ἀσύμφορον εἶναί φασι πρὸς τὴν εὐνομίαν, καὶ τὴν πολυανθρωπίαν· γίνεσθαι μὲν γὰρ ἐκ τοῦ χρῆσθαι τῇ θαλάττῃ διαπέμποντας καὶ δεχομένους ἐμπόρων πλῆθος, ὑπεναντίαν δ᾽ εἶναι πρὸς τὸ πολιτεύεσθαι καλῶς. Newman, comm. ad loc., 3.356–8, agrees with Aristotle's assessment and gives various references which reputedly show that many Greek cities suffered from overexposure to the influence of aliens: "many of the aliens who crowded to Greek seaports were Asiatics of a type the reverse of satisfactory." He also points out that "We know that the seaports of Dundee and Leith were the channels through which the Reformation found its way into Scotland" (with reference to Knox). It is not clear whether Newman cites this as a more recent example of bad influence of aliens.

[54] This is not a significant topic in the major work by Peregrine Horden and Nicholas Purcell, *The Corrupting Sea: A Study of Mediterranean History* (Oxford, 2000).

[55] See, for instance, Frederik Barth in F. Barth (ed.), *Ethnic Groups and Boundaries: The Social Organization of Culture Difference* (Bergen, 1969), 9: "Though the naïve assumption that each tribe and people has maintained its culture through a bellicose ignorance of its neighbours is no longer entertained, the simplistic view that geographical and social isolation have been the critical factors in sustaining cultural diversity persists."

[56] Cf. Alcman, fr.108, Page: ἁλμυρὸν τὸ γειτόνημα.

ness in its proximity for the uses of daily life; for by filling the markets of the city with foreign merchandise and retail trading, and breeding in men's souls knavish and tricky ways, it renders the city faithless and loveless, not to itself only, but to the rest of the world as well." Cities which lie near the sea tend to have all sorts of bad habits.[57] Plato considers traveling dangerous for impressionable young men. He would therefore forbid it to persons under forty and to anyone traveling in a private capacity, while allowing traveling only to people doing so in a public capacity and with special permission (*Leges* 950d).[58] The returning travelers would have to remain for some time subject to a supervisory body, in a sort of intellectual quarantine to prevent them from spreading dangerous ideas. If they returned corrupted and tried to influence others, they should die (*Leges* 950d; 952b–d).[59] Visiting strangers are kept under supervision to prevent them from unnecessary intercourse with the population and from introducing innovations, unless they are visitors on official journeys who are receive fitting honors and treatement (952e–953). Aristotle would not go as far as that, but as already noted, he too sees dangers as well as advantages for a city in accessibility from the sea (*Pol.* 1327a).

Among the Roman authors, Seneca has been cited, but there is a great deal more. For example, the poets assert that the Golden Age did not yet know the wicked art of seafaring (Lucretius, *DRN* 5. 1004–6; Ovid, *Met.* 1.94–6).[60] Cicero too, makes the younger Scipio praise the location of Rome at some distance from the sea, for cities on the coast are exposed to danger from attack by sea, and moreover, "maritime cities are prone to a certain moral degeneration, for they receive a mixture of strange languages and customs, and import foreign ways as well as foreign merchandise; so that none of their ancestral institutions could possibly remain unchanged . . . Many things, too, that cause ruin to states, as reinforcing the taste for luxury, are imported by sea."[61] The elements present in this condemnation of maritime cities are thus a combination of a general lack of safety with a tendency to moral decay which is the result of

---

[57] See *Leg.* 706 for the disastrous influence of proximity to the sea on the army: a force of infantry is good, large numbers of men serving in a navy leads to bad habits. Not Salamis saved Greece from Persia, but Marathon and Plataea (707 b–c).

[58] Military expeditions are not regarded as official visits abroad, it is suggested. Upon their return the travelers will teach the young that the political institutions of others are inferior to their own (951a).

[59] E. R. Dodds, *The Ancient Concept of Progress and other Essays on Greek Literature and Belief* (Oxford, 1973), 98, compares this with Nazi and Russian policy. Isocrates, *Busiris* 18 (225), claims that the Lacedaemonians have imitated the Egyptian customs in some aspects, notably a provision that no citizen fit for military service could leave the country without official authorization.

[60] Romm, *The Edges of the Earth*, 74f.

[61] Cicero, *Rep.* 2.6f. Est autem maritimis urbibus etiam quaedam corruptela ac demutatio morum; admiscentur enim novis sermonibus ac disciplinis et inportantur non merces solum adventiciae, sed etiam mores, ut nihil possit in patriis institutis manere integrum. Iam qui incolunt eas urbes, non haerent in suis sedibus, sed volucri semper spe et cogitatione rapiuntur a domo longius, atque etiam cum manent corpore, animo tamen exulant et vagantur. Nec vero ulla res magis labefactatam diu et Carthaginem et Corinthum pervertit aliquando quam hic error ac dissipatio civium, quod mercandi cupiditate et navigandi et agrorum et armorum cultum reliquerant. Cf. Cic. *de offic.* 1.150.

influence from foreign languages, customs, and trade. In fact, Cicero here follows Plato's arguments in the Laws, cited above. Cicero, however, takes this one step further when he attributes the origins of luxury in Greece to Phoenician traders,[62] thus explaining the political and social instability of Greek cities by their proximity to the sea.[63] By contrast, Romulus, in his wisdom, assured for Rome the advantages of a port city without the disadvantages of one (10). Cicero characteristically uses Plato's ideas about these matters to explain the failure of Greece and the success of Rome.[64] The idea recurs in *de lege agraria* 2.95, cited above. The Carthaginians are liars and frauds, not by origin, but because of the nature of their site with its port, merchants, and foreign languages, which leads to the desire to cheat. The idea that foreign languages should have a corrupting influence is particularly remarkable. It may well illuminate an aspect of the point which Momigliano makes throughout his *Alien Wisdom*, the fact that classical Greek culture (but not Hellenistic Greek culture) was monolingual. Maybe learning foreign languages was actually considered undesirable. Indeed, the moral tradition against navigation can be traced right back to the Greek literature of the fourth century.

In imperial Rome related ideas are found in Strabo: Scythians are more straightforward, frugal, and independent than we are.

> And yet our mode of life has spread its change for the worse to almost all peoples, introducing amongst them luxury and sensual pleasures and, to satisfy these vices, base artifices that lead to innumerable acts of greed. So then, much wickedness of this sort has fallen on the barbarian peoples also, on the Nomads as well as the rest; for as the result of taking up a seafaring life they not only have become morally worse, indulging in the practice of piracy and of slaying strangers, but also, because of their intercourse with many peoples, have partaken of the luxury and the peddling habits of these peoples. But though these things seem to conduce strongly to gentleness of manner, they corrupt morals and introduce cunning instead of the straightforwardness which I just now mentioned.[65]

This is interesting for several reasons, first because it is, in a sense, the reversal of the idea, common in Roman texts, that foreigners corrupted the Romans. Here we see, on the contrary, that Strabo sees his own culture as corrupting foreigners. Strabo here speaks of Greeks, but he emphatically describes them as the Greeks of his own age, when they had been living under Roman rule for more than a century and a half.[66] Second, it touches on Tacitus's

---

[62] Cicero, *De Re Publica* fr.3 ap. Nonius 431.11, p. 695, Lindsay: "Poeni primi mercaturis et mercibus suis avaritiam et magnificentiam et inexplebiles cupiditates omnium rerum importaverunt in Graeciam."

[63] 9: quae causa perspicua est malorum commutationumque Graeciae propter ea vitia maritimarum urbium, quae ante paulo perbreviter adtigi.

[64] There is no trace here of the usual view that Rome itself suffered moral decline through its contact with Greece and the East, an idea that does not fit the aims of Cicero in this particular work. Cf. Nicholas Petrochilos, *Roman Attitudes to the Greeks* (Athens, 1974), 89–92.

[65] Strabo 7.3.7 (c301f.); cf. Dueck, *Strabo of Anasia* (2000), 119f.

[66] There is no reason to believe Strabo copied such sentiments from Posidonius.

views of Romanization, with the difference that Tacitus links this process directly with the reduction to slavery under Roman rule and increased docility. For him it is an instrument of empire. For Strabo, on the other hand, the corruption seems to be merely a result of Romanization, not an instrument that helps in maintaining Roman superiority. Finally, the idea of a loss of masculinity resulting from this contact with luxury is not present in Strabo. The basic idea that wealth corrupts is there, however, as well as the idea that trade and communication are destructive processes. The reason for this moral condemnation of seafaring and communication is clear. There was a deeply ingrained sense that the moral quality of people of pure lineage was particularly high. The idea is attested first in the fragment of Xenophanes of the sixth century B.C., cited above.

Corruption and contamination are ever-present preoccupations. Thus it is clearly felt that communication across the sea is a cause of mutual deterioration, for it attacks the original purity and isolation of peoples. It is remarkable that the idea that communication could only be negative in its influence recurs so frequently. Ultimately it is closely connected with the questions regarding the idea of progress in antiquity. The very notion of a Golden Age excludes an idea of linear progress.[67] It is therefore no coincidence that Hesiod and later pessimistic authors, cited above, hold the Golden Age to be ignorant of navigation.[68] According to these views then, decline and dissolution are inevitable and communication between peoples reinforces these processes.[69]

However, the opposite idea, namely that people could be positively influenced through contact, also existed, although it was far less prominent than the belief that intercourse was harmful. Not surprisingly we find it in the optimistic Strabo, who expresses a positive approach clearly in a passage already cited because of its relevance for the environmental theory: "The Romans, too, took

---

[67] The Prometheus myth, as related by Hesiod, *Theogony*, 510–616; *Works and Days* 42–89, also precludes progress or at least implies that the gods do not wish men to possess arts and crafts. Aeschylus, *Prometheus Vinctus* has a different message, cf. Dodds, *The Ancient Concept of Progress*, 5–7, 31–43.

[68] The literature on progress in antiquity is extensive: Ludwig Edelstein, *The Idea of Progress in Classical Antiquity* (Baltimore, MD, 1967), argues that the idea of progress did exist throughout antiquity; Dodds, op. cit., chapter 1, 1–25, agrees with Edelstein that the idea was not wholly foreign to antiquity, but argues that only during a limited period in the fifth century was it widely accepted by the educated public at large. Thereafter all the major philosophical schools were more or less hostile to the idea. Where it was accepted, this is found in the works of scientists or works on science. A different view, briefly stated and not really argued, is represented by E. Gabba, "Literature," in M. Crawford (ed.), *Sources for Ancient History: Studies in the Uses of Historical Evidence* (Cambridge, 1983), 7. Gabba assumes that there was an assumption of linear progress in the past, leading up to the present, which forms the highest point in development. This is followed by decline and there is no prospect of a further growth in power or of a higher cultural level. It is hard to see what the basis is for the first of these assumptions other than, perhaps, the opening statements of Herodotus and Thucydides in their histories. See also the brief observations by Paul Veyne, "*Humanitas: les Romains et les autres*," in A. Giardina (ed.), *L'homme romain* (Paris, 1992), 421–459, esp. 423.

[69] For this idea, see also below, chapter 5.

over many nations inhabiting unfavourable regions, brought them in contact with each other and taught them how to live under forms of government." He then continues explaining that all of Europe is level and has a mild climate. Since nature is thus beneficial for its inhabitants, European countries tend to be peaceful. This, curiously, is the reverse of the assessment in *Airs*, 23, 3–4, cited above. In hard countries, continues Strabo, people are courageous and belligerent. "And so both kinds of country receive benefits from each other, for the latter helps with arms, the former with products of the soil, with arts and with character-building" (2.5.26 [c. 126]). It is interesting to see that, in Strabo, both ideas are present: the destructive effect of Rome on its subjects as well as the beneficial and stabilizing influence. He states the latter more strongly and more frequently than the former. There is also another approach to be found in the literature, the view that Rome profited through learning from others. Arrian considers this highly laudable. He writes (*Tactica* 33, trans. James G. DeVoto): "The Romans have many foreign (Iberian, Celtic) terms for formations, for they used Celtic cavalry. For, if on something else, also on this [matter], the Romans are worthy to be praised because they do not embrace [only] their own native things. Thus, having chosen noble things from everywhere, they made them their own. You would thus find that they take some armaments from others— and indeed they are called 'Roman,' because the Romans especially use them. [They take] soldierly exercises from others and the thrones of rulers and [their] purple-edged dress. Taking even gods from others, they worship them [as their own]." He mentions some foreign cults adopted by Rome. The laws of the Twelve Tables are taken from Athens, he tells us. This is not, of course, Romanization, but a related, opposite phenomenon, another aspect of integration of subjugated peoples. The second-century Greek senator Arrian was aware of this and could describe it; he clearly found it a significant pattern. Pliny the Elder combined a patriotic interest in the conquest of the seas with a personal interest in navigation, which is clear from his *Historia Naturalis*.[70] Undoubtedly, however, the authors who regard contact with foreigners as having deleterious effects are far more numerous and influential than those who emphasize its salutary aspects. The latter are a few Greek writing authors of the Roman period, the former range from the sixth century B.C. till late antiquity.

Conversely, there is a clear sense that unsociable people are not desirable. Thus the treatise Airs, Waters, Places already states that wildness, unsociability and bad temper occur in the European climate. The crucial importance of intercourse or sociability, among human beings is brought out repeatedly by Aristotle when he says: "a man who is incapable of entering into partnership (κοιν-ωνεῖν), or who is is so self-sufficing that he has no need to do so, is no part of a state, so that he must be either a lower animal or a god."[71] Of course, Aristotle

---

[70] Cf. Beagon, *Roman Nature*, "The Imperial Idealism of Pliny on Seafaring," pp. 183–190, comparing Pliny with Manilius and Seneca.

[71] Aristotle, *Pol.* 1253a: ὁ δὲ μὴ δυνάμενος κοινωνεῖν ἢ μηδὲν δεόμενος δι᾽ αὐτάρκειαν οὐθὲν μέρος πόλεως, ὥστε ἢ θηρίον ἢ θεός. This passage also contains the statement that man is a

here refers to man as part of a state and the isolation he means is a man who does not live in contact with his fellows. Aristotle emphasizes this when he says: "For man is not only a political (πολιτικὸν) but also a house-holding animal (οἰκονομικὸν ζῷον), and does not, like the other animals, couple occasionally and with any chance female or male, but man is in a special way not a solitary but a gregarious animal, associating with the persons with whom he has a natural kinship; accordingly there would be partnership, and justice of a sort, even if there were no state (πόλις)."[72] Thus the norms in this respect between individuals and groups are not essentially different and clearly there is a sense that peoples and states should not cut themselves off from other peoples and states. To do so is unnatural for any human being. There is a widespread assumption that the first criterion whereby human beings have to be judged is elementary sociability. It is humanity living in the remote parts of the world which is often thought to be unsociable, for instance the eastern Ethiopians: Diodorus, citing Agatharchides of Cnidus (c. 115 till after 145 B.C.) says of them they have no contact at all with other peoples; they are entirely emotionless in the face of horrors, they speak no language (Diodorus 3.18.5–6). Strabo says of Northern Iberia that it is extremely cold, but lies next to the ocean and thus has acquired its characteristic of inhospitability and aversion to intercourse with other countries (2.1.2 [c. 137]). He returns to this topic later (3.3.8 [c. 156]) "The quality of intractability and wildness in these people has not resulted solely from their engaging in warfare, but also from their remoteness; for the trip to their country, whether by sea or by land, is long, and since they are difficult to communicate with, they have lost the instinct of sociability (τὸ κοινωνικόν) and humanity (τὸ φιλάνθρωπον)."[73] Herodotus (2.35) already said about Egypt that the climate, rivers, and the manners and customs of the people are exactly the reverse of those in the rest of the world. It was one of the most serious reproaches against the Jews that they keep themselves apart from other people. Tacitus asserts that Moses himself introduced religious practices opposed to those of all other religions. They are extremely loyal towards each other, but they keep apart and, he continues, they feel only hate and enmity toward every other people (*Hist.* 5.4.1, Stern, no. 281). Interesting in this con-

---

political animal (ζῷον πολιτικόν) for which, see Wolfgang Kullmann, "Man as a Political Animal in Aristotle," in David Keyt and Fred D. Miller (eds.), *A Companion to Aristotle's* Politics (Oxford and Cambridge, MA, 1991), 94–117; Trevor J. Saunders, *Aristotle,* Politics. *Books I and II* (Oxford, 1995), 69. Note also the opening sentence of the *Politics* 1252a, 1, which states that every *polis* is a form of community and every community is formed towards some good. Cf. Cicero, *De Republica* 1.25.

[72] Aristotle, *Ethica Eudemia* 1242a: ὁ γὰρ ἄνθρωπος οὐ μόνον πολιτικὸν ἀλλὰ καὶ οἰκονομικὸν ζῷον, καὶ οὐχ ὥσπερ τἆλλά ποτε συνδυάζεται καὶ τῷ τυχόντι [καὶ] θήλει καὶ ἄρρενι ἀλλ' αἱ διὰ δύμον αὐλικόν, ἀλλὰ κοινωνικὸν ἄνθρωπος ζῷον πρὸς οὓς φύσει συγγένεια ἐστίν· καὶ κοινωνία τοίνυν καὶ δίκαιόν τι, καὶ εἰ μὴ πόλις εἴη·. I cite the Loeb translation by H. Rackham. In the present discussion it may be slightly confusing to translate ζῷον with the English "animal." "Being" might be more suitable.

[73] τὸ φιλάνθρωπον = Latin Humanitas on which see Veyne, "*Humanitas,*" 421–459; Greg Woolf, *Becoming Roman: the Origins of Provincial Civilization in Gaul* (Cambridge, 1998), 54–60.

nection is Plutarch's comment on the Teutones and Cimbri, in his life of Marius (*C. Marius* 11.3), where we read that their origin was unknown, because they had no intercourse with others and had traveled a long way. This, as already observed, is a novel variant: a people which was of pure lineage, but not autochthonous. Plutarch does not say these peoples were primitive nomads and he does not call them brutes, but this is clearly the category he was thinking of when he wrote as he did. As already noted, Strabo (7.2.3 [c. 294]) says they practice human sacrifice, which is another characteristic of primitives belonging to this category. The Elder Pliny sees little difference between sacrificing human beings and eating them.[74]

Admittedly, there is an obvious ambivalence regarding the desirability of communication between peoples. Trade and commerce are the vehicles for the corruption of much that is valuable, but peoples who are entirely cut off from the rest of the world have no merit either. They may even be brutes or almost animals, as emphasized by Aristotle. With this comparison we touch upon a sensitive and significant topic, for this has, through the ages, served as an excuse or justification to treat the objects of the comparison as less than human beings. These ideas, it may be noted, were taken over by Christian authors in the Middle Ages, such as Albertus Magnus (c. 1206–1280), who also accepted the theories of physiognomics from classical authors. The mediaeval authors, it may be noted, apply the term "barbarian" to non-Christians. It is characteristic of such barbarians that they do not observe the laws and participation in the community according to the principles of justice.[75]

Thus it is clear that there is a remarkable feeling among both Greeks and Romans that close communication with foreigners is a highly dubious process. The sense is that such intercourse corrupts and degrades the structure of society. This is, perhaps, less surprising for the Greeks than the Romans, for the Greeks before Alexander never extended an empire over non-Greeks. In their colonies contact with the local populations was ideologically, if less in practice, restricted. The Romans, however, continuously absorbed other peoples into their empire and yet there was an obvious ambivalence. There was a notion that strangers corrupted Rome, and the reverse is also found, but rarely: Roman rule degraded the vanquished. At the same time another, contradictory, idea was also important: isolated peoples who did not have contact with others were uncivilized. A lack of sociability is condemned. Those living in the Golden Age may have been pure in their isolation, but the nomads in the present were regarded as miserable because of their presumed unsociability.

The ideas traced here were influential in later periods. Above we saw that

---

[74] Pliny, *NH* 7.9 et nuperrime trans Alpis hominem immolari gentium earum more solitum, quod paulum a mandendo abest.

[75] Albertus Magnus, *Politicorum* 1.1.i–k, ed. A. Borgnet (Paris, 1890–1899), vol. 8, p. 10; *Ethicorum* 7.1.1 ed. Borgnet, vol. 7, p. 464, as cited by A. Pagden, *The Fall of Natural Man: The American Indian and the Origins of Comparative Ethnology* (Cambridge, 1982), 20f. Albertus Magnus refers to Cicero, *De Inventione* 1.2, discussing early humanity, when there was no law, order, and religion.

Machiavelli (1469–1527) attributes the integrity and piety of the Germans of his time partly to the fact that they had no contact with their corrupt neighbors. The ideas described were taken over in the sixteenth century by Jean Bodin: "As for the inhabitants upon the Sea coast, and of great townes of traffique, all writers have observed, That they are more subtill, politike, and cunning, than those that lie farre from the sea and traffique."[76]

[76] Jean Bodin, *The Six Bookes of a Commonweale*, ed. Kenneth Douglas McRae (Cambridge, MA, 1962), 564.

Conclusions to Part 1, Chapters 2 and 3

THESE TWO CHAPTERS aim to illuminate some aspects of Greek and Roman views of other peoples and how these affected their attitudes towards conquest, rule over others, and empire. They do not "explain" how ancient Empires worked, but they attempt to analyze aspects of relationships between peoples that should be part of any analysis of empire. The chapters relate extensively to the primary theme of this book: various forms of stereotyping and proto-racism are traced, some of which became influential in later periods, while others belong to the Graeco-Roman world only.

As is well known, the difference between the words "free" and "slave" originates in the private sphere and was applied by the Greeks to the national level after the Persian wars of the early fifth century. The idea that a subject people became subject to its victors in the same way as when a master bought a slave developed in this period. Chapter 2 starts with a discussion of Aristotle's theory of natural slavery, the only systematic discussion of the essence of slavery that has come down to us from antiquity. The subject is important for the present study for two reasons: first, there is the idea that part of humanity is born with the inherent qualities of slaves and thus should be enslaved; they are even better off as slaves. This division between natural slaves and natural free men in fact coincides with the division between Greeks and non-Greeks. As noted, this division must not be confused with the other contrast described by Aristotle: the distinction between Asiatics, Europeans, and those in the middle, the Greeks. Through the division of humanity into Greeks and non-Greeks, as seen by Aristotle, a slavish nature is acquired collectively and through heredity. Such a theory is a proto-racist justification of imperial expansion. It is therefore relevant for both major subjects of this study: the appearance of proto-racist ideas and ethnic stereotypes in Graeco-Roman antiquity as well as the role such ideas played in the shaping of a climate of imperial expansion.

Although Aristotle's theory may be traced in Roman literature, in Cicero's work, where it is applied to non-Romans as well, and in those of later, mostly Christian authors, it did not gain popularity as such later on. It was impractical as an ideology for the Hellenistic monarchies with their non-Greek majorities. The prevalent Roman practice of imperial rule was in fact quite different from Aristotle's theory. Unlike Aristotle and other Greeks, the Romans did not declare all foreigners inferior by nature. Although Romans had a fair share of imperial arrogance, their ideas about foreigners were more differentiated, and integration was such a practical reality that Aristotle's bipolar view could not be generally accepted.[1] As argued in chapter 1, the environmental theory was pop-

[1] See Part 2.

ular in Rome as well, and this was responsible for the assumption of "northern" and "southern" types, but that is a different topic. Most Greek and Roman authors did not feel an urgent need to justify and rationalize slavery in the manner in which Aristotle attempted to do this. Slavery was a fact of life and not a topic for active contemplation and discussion.

Yet the theory was known among intellectuals and there were elements of it which became entrenched in mainstream Roman thinking. These are, first, the unquestioned assumption that it is possible and reasonable to relate both to entire peoples and to individuals in the same manner, as either being naturally free or slavish. Second, masters and slaves, rulers and subject peoples live in a symbiosis beneficial to both parties. Third, this relationship and these differences are stable from one generation to the next. The fundamental difference is that most Roman authors did not hold to the same extent as the Greeks that all foreigners were inferior by nature. The Romans may have regarded themselves as superior, but other peoples were seen as having different and distinct qualities. Some indeed were "born for slavery," but others were not. As we shall see in Part 2, there was, in Roman eyes, a sliding scale from peoples who were regarded as being extremely slavish by nature (Syrians) to people who were naturally fierce fighters and protectors of their own independence (Germans).

The idea, however, that long-term imperial rule reduces peoples virtually to a condition of natural slavery was very influential. Thus, paradoxically, what is seen in our days as a remarkable success of the Roman Empire, namely its integration of subject peoples, is represented by at least some of the important Roman authors as a process which reduces those peoples from fierce and free humans to degenerate slaves. Since the common assumption is that this is an irreversible process, we end up with the image of something rather akin to Aristotle's natural slaves. A related topic considered instructive for present purposes is the image in ancient sources of peoples that were not subjugated. There naturally was a tendency for emperors and generals ambitious to make foreign conquests, to select a target that could be managed. Why initiate a war against a people thought to be virtually invincible?

The second part of chapter 2 goes on to discuss one specific way of looking at foreigners, namely comparisons of human beings with animals. This occurs in two different ways: first people are called animals in order to deny their humanity. This is particularly common in the case of far-away peoples. Second, there are fables, describing animals as if they were humans, whereby the presumed characteristics of the relevant animals are applied to people: thus a tale about a fox actually describes a foxy type of person. The comparison of specific human types with animals is a popular form of stereotyping. As animals of a given sort are very much alike, the inference is that something similar is the case with human beings. All of this was widespread in antiquity. An additional idea which is not now fashionable, but was important in medieval and later thinking, was the sense that slaves or foreigners are less than human and therefore to be categorized in between animals and full-fledged human beings. It should be noted, however, that in antiquity the idea usually is that people, when they are less than human, are "bestial," that they come close to being animals, but they are not regarded as animals proper. All in all, this way of looking at foreigners is a common ancient form of proto-racist thinking.

A specific topic which fascinated quite a number of authors are the eating habits of foreign peoples: the consumption of uncooked flesh is considered to be particularly bestial[2] and, even more so, cannibalism—in spite of the fact that the Greeks and Romans must have known that animals do not normally eat their own species. However, it has been observed more often that the Greeks and Romans often refer to animals and their behavior without actually looking at them.

The argument that some peoples are subhuman or bestial is never used to justify large-scale killings as has happened in recent history. It may be concluded, however, that the animal-comparison was important in ancient imperialist thinking, as one of the imageries determining ideas about foreigners.

The last section of chapter 3 discusses large-scale killings and genocide. Although these happened not infrequently, it is clear that there was no accompanying proto-racist justification. It appears the perpetrators of such deeds felt no need to justify their actions.

Chapter 3 discusses various phenomena indicating ambivalence of the Romans towards their own empire and subject peoples. The first topic of chapter 3 is the response of Roman authors to the presence of large numbers of foreign immigrants from conquered lands in Italy and in the city of Rome. Many of these came from the civilized countries east of Italy: Greece, Asia Minor, Syria, Judaea, and Egypt. The reactions to each of these peoples are discussed more specifically in Part 2. Here it is traced how the presence of subject foreigners in Italy and Rome resulted in the well-known tension that is often engendered by the settling of substantial numbers of immigrants in an urban evironment. One aspect is highlighted, namely the sense that these vanquished peoples somehow dominate the social and intellectual climate in Rome. This went hand in hand with a fear that Rome was undermined and corrupted by the enemy it had defeated. According to the usual scale of qualities, many of the immigrants came from peoples seen as decadent, soft, corrupt, and corrupting. These tensions frequently resulted in actual steps to remove the undesired aliens.

At another level, the third and last section of chapter 3 considers ancient doubts about the desirability of contact with foreigners. Fear of strangers and their ideas, corresponding fantasies about a golden past in which there was no need to travel elsewhere and no foreigners disturbed peace at home, are frequently encountered in Greek and Latin literature. There is a connection with the view, discussed in the first chapter, that pure lineage is better than mixed ancestry. So it is frequently asserted in ancient Greek literature that any contact with other peoples, seafaring, trade and commerce, not only endangers safety, but may also have social results: moral decline through the influence of foreign languages, customs, and trade is to be expected. This line of thought is present

---

[2] See above, p. 199.

in both Greek and Latin literature, even though clearly it did not prevent Greeks and Romans from traveling. Part of this complex of ideas is the feeling that wealth and luxury undermine strength and stability. We encountered this in chapter 1, as early as the fifth century B.C. and throughout Greek and Roman antiquity. It is one of the themes taken up again in early modern literature. Thus we find that the French philosopher Helvétius, one of the few who explicitly and at length rejects environmental determinism, sees a causal inverse connection between the vitality and courage of people and the level of their wealth.[3] The idea was taken up by numerous English authors, such as Temple, Clarendon, Milton, and Defoe.

The opposite idea, that people could be positively influenced through mutual contact, also existed, but it is far less prominent than the feeling that communication was harmful. On the other hand, there is a clear sense that unsociable people are undesirable. Thus it appears that both Greeks and Romans were ambivalent about communication with foreigners.

---

[3] Claude-Adrien Helvétius, *De l'esprit* (Paris 1758, repr. 1988), 392–394: "Le courage n'est, dans les Animaux, que l'effet de leurs besoins: ces besoins sont-ils satisfaits? Ils deviennent lâches: le Lion affamé attaque l'homme, le Lion rassasié le fuit." For this author, see above. He also agrees with ancient authors on another factor as being essential, namely the constitution. People will not be courageous living under a tyrant. Cf. J. W. Johnson, *The Formation of English Neo-Classical Thought* (1967), 48–50.

FIGURE 1. Caeretan black-figure hydria, Late Archaic Greek, c. 510 B.C. Vienna Kunsthistorisches Museum, ANSA IV 3576. Drawing: A. Furtwängler und K. Reichhold, *Griechische Vasenmalerei; Auswahl hervorragender Vasenbilder* (München, 1904), Pl. 51. Busiris was a legendary king in the Delta who, according to a Greek tradition, habitually slaughtered foreigners entering his country and sacrificed them to Zeus, until he vainly tried to do this to Heracles. The vase shows Heracles destroying Busiris and his priests. Various details refer to the customs and clothing of Egypt with remarkable precision. Heracles is raging near the altar, flinging two Egyptians around and trampling on two others. A group of black Nubians hastens to come to the aid of the king, shown on the back of the vase. They have the usual equipment of Egyptian guards. Busiris's henchmen are often depicted as black on such images. Some of the priests are black and Heracles himself is dark. Greek vases do not always make an effort to render skin color realistically, as may be seen also on figures 5 and 6. Busiris himself, identified by the *uraeus*, the royal symbol of Lower Egypt, has fallen in front of the altar. The hydria intentionally reminds of familiar Egyptian images of a huge pharaoh smiting his tiny foreign enemies. Thus it is a caricature of Egyptian formal art expressing the superiority of the ruler over foreigners, substituting instead the Greek hero who destroys the powerless Egyptians and ends their sacrilegious custom of sacrificing strangers.

Cf. Margaret C. Miller, "The Myth of Bousiris: Ethnicity and Art," in Beth Cohen (ed.), *Not the Classical Ideal: Athens and the Construction of the Other in Greek Art* (Brill, 2000), 414–442, fig. 16.1, p. 417f.

FIGURE 2a, 2b. Attic red-figure oinochoe, unattributed, Early Classical Greek, c. 465 B.C. Hamburg, Museum für Kunst und Gewerbe inv. no. 1981.173. Photos courtesy of the Museum. A Greek is preparing sexually to assault a terrified Persian, exotically dressed. This image parodies the familiar depictions of erotic pursuit. The Greek has an erection and runs towards the Persian, grasping his penis in his right hand like a weapon. The bearded foreigner presents his buttocks to the Greek. In an inscription which refers to the victory of the Athenian fleet at the Eurymedon river in 465 B.C., the Persian says: "I am Eurymedon; I stand bent over" (Εὐρυμέδων εἰμί κυβά[δε] ἕστηκα). For κυβά[δε] other readings are possible. K. Dover, *Greek Homosexuality* (1978), 105: "This expresses the exultation of the 'manly' Athenians at their victory over the 'womanish' Persians . . . ; it proclaims: 'We've really buggered the Persians.'" This victory is represented by "rape" of the defeated, thereby feminizing him. This form of sexually explicit representation becomes common, in a characteristically modified form, in Roman art. Like the images of the Egyptian Busiris, this representation shows the Persian foreigner as the helpless and impotent victim of Greek superiority.

Publication: K. Schauenburg 'ΕΥΡΥΜΕΔΩΝ ΕΙΜΙ' *AM* 90 (1975), 97–121. For the representation of victory as rape of a woman, see E. Hall, "Asia unmanned," in J. Rich and G. Shipley, *War and Society in the Greek World* (London, 1993), 108–133.

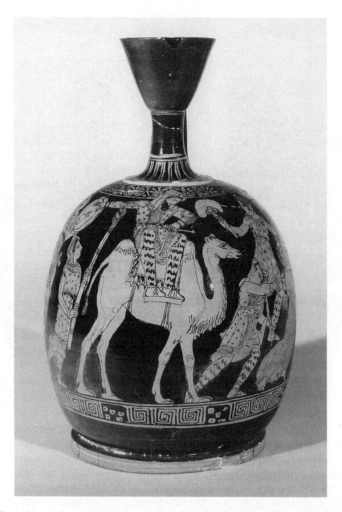

FIGURE 3. Attic red-figure lekythos, c. 400 B.C., Copyright The British Museum #695, photo courtesy of the Museum. The central figure is an oriental ruler, probably the King of Persia, riding a camel. Like the men around him he wears oriental dress: notably the jacket, trousers, chiton, shoes, and headdress. Around him are men and women, musicians, male and female dancers, and fan-bearers. The scene has sometimes been interpreted incorrectly as Dionysos (or the Phrygian god Sabazius) with an ecstatic band of followers. While there can be no doubt that an oriental court is depicted, the association with a group engaged in ritual license and revelry is no coincidence. Oriental courts were seen as a hotbed of orgiastic dissipation and that is the impression conveyed by this image. It reminds us of the accounts of Ktesias, in his *Persica* of the Persian court, as dominated by harem intrigues and punishment (*FGrH* 688 F 1–44). See the comments by Wulf Raeck, *Zum Barbarenbild in der Kunst Athens* (1981), 151f.

FIGURE 4a, 4b. Attic red-figure oinochoe, towards the end of the first half of the fifth century. British Museum, London #1912.7-9.1, photos courtesy of the Museum. The two images together represent Persian soldiers, one of whom rides side-saddle on a mule, while the other acts as drover. This is obviously a caricature. The mule stands still and the two soldiers are making attempts to move ahead. The rider makes a gesture with his left hand urging the other to do something about it, while the latter is lashing the animal with a whip, apparently without success. As on figure 2, the Persians are shown as being ineffectual or even ludicrous. This is a visual representation of the Greek attitude towards Persia after the Persian wars early in the fifth century, an attitude which gradually evolves from one of respect for a great power into a sense of disdain, as described in chapter 4.

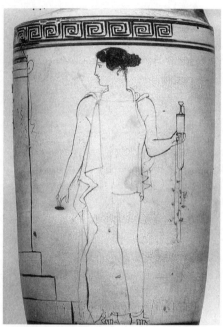

FIGURE 5a, 5b. Attic white-ground lekythos, Bosanquet painter, 450–440 B.C. Antiken-sammlung, Staatliche Museen zu Berlin–Preussischer Kulturbesitz-, v.i 3291. Photos courtesy of the Museum. A stately, well-clothed woman to the right of the tomb stands holding a lekythos in her left hand with her gaze directed toward a female figure left of the tomb who wears a burden on her head and an alabastron in her right hand. The latter undoubtedly represents a black slave. This is clear not only from the task she performs, but also from her short stature and simple garment. She may be identified not by the color of her skin (which is white), but by her physiognomy and hair. The noble appearance of the mistress is meant to contrast with the blunt features of the slave. It is to be noted that the latter is not characterized by skin color. In fifth-century Athens it was fashionable to keep black men and women as house slaves and as such they appear in Attic vase painting. Cf. F. M. Snowden, "Iconographical Evidence on the Black Popula-tions in Greco-Roman Antiquity," in J. Vercoutter, ed. *L' Image du Noir dans L'art occidental,* i; (Lausanne 1976), 133–245, at 164.

FIGURE 6. Attic red-figure belly amphora. Department of Classical and Near Eastern Antiquities, National Museum of Denmark, Copenhagen, Chr. VIII 320 Ptr., c. 470 B.C. Photo courtesy of the Museum. Nude black boy attending Athenian older man out of doors. The difference in stature is even more remarkable than in fig. 5. Again the boy is identified as black, not by the color of his skin, but by his physical features.

FIGURE 7. From a series of Roman imperial reliefs found in the Sebasteion at Aphrodisias by courtesy of the New York University Excavations at Aphrodisias. Photo: the New York Excavations. Cf. R.R.R. Smith, "The Imperial Reliefs from the Sebasteion at Aphrodisias," *JRS* 77 (1987), 88–138, at 115–120 with plates 14,16. The inscribed base identifies this as the Emperor Claudius and Britannia. Smith, p.116f.: "Claudius stands over the sprawling, defeated figure of Britannia. He pulls her head back by the hair for the death blow. . . . Britannia raises her right hand in vain defence or to appeal for clemency . . . With her left hand, she struggles to prevent her dress from falling off her shoulder. . . . The action of the panel as a whole is reminiscent of ideal Greek battle compositions, most obviously Amazonomachies, but without being closely based on any known group. . . . In art and imperial ideology at Rome, the emperor did not [usually] kill defeated provinces and peoples. He received their submission, extended clemency to them, or had them already incorporated in his train. Although we may know that Claudius will not actually kill Britannia, the received language and compositional logic of such groups certainly arouses that expectation." However we interpret and explain this, this is provincial art meant to evoke the Roman military power exercised by the Julio-Claudian dynasty in subjugating and controlling various foreign peoples. Even if the action is reminiscent of ideal Greek battle compositions, it shows an imagery never seen in Greek art and typically Roman: the confrontation of two peoples illustrated as two single individuals who represent their respective collectives. Also entirely Roman is the view of the Roman victor as man and the vanquished enemy as a woman.

FIGURES 8a–b, 8c–d. Judaea Capta: the imagery of military subjugation. Coins issued in the reign of Vespasian in A.D. 71 and later celebrate the suppression of the Jewish revolt (A.D. 66–70). (*a–b*) Israel Museum Inv. No. 140, silver denarius. Photos courtesy of the Museum. Obverse: Head of Vespasian with laurel crown; reverse: a veiled woman sits to the right of a palm tree with five branches and two bunches of dates. There are reasons to identify the woman, not as the land, or province of Judaea, but as the Jewish people. The palm tree, a vignette, is the equivalent of the inscription "Iudaea" on the next coin. She is seated on the ground, weeping. To the left of the palm tree stands a Roman military figure, facing right, his left foot on a helmet and holding a spear in his right hand, a short honorary sword (*parazonium*) in his left hand. This kind of imagery was invented by the Romans. They began to depict foreign peoples as single persons, thus stressing the collective stereotype rather than the individual. Enslaved peoples are typically, though not always, shown as women on the ground, dominated by the Roman soldier standing. The victorious emperor is identified by name on the obverse, the soldier (sometimes thought to be Titus) represents the conquering Roman army. (*c–d*) Israel Museum Inv. No. 139. Photos courtesy of the Museum. Silver denarius has a similar obverse. The reverse shows again a veiled, weeping woman, seated on the ground, leaning her head on her left hand, right hand on her knee. The inscription, like the palm tree on the other coin, identifies her as (the people of) Judaea. Behind her is a trophy, the weapons of the defeated enemy set up as a memorial of victory, here comprising a helmet and cuirass, one oblong and one round shield, two greaves and two shields on the ground. While the subject people is depicted twice in a similar manner, the military defeat is in this coin represented by the fact that the woman sits in front of captured arms. This emphasizes that she represents a people which was disarmed and made harmless.

The result of a military defeat by the Romans is helpless misery. Such is the straight-forward message of the coinage and victory monuments.

FIGURE 9a, 9b. Mass execution. The column of Marcus Aurelius was erected in Rome after A.D. 175 and before 193 to celebrate and depict in relief the emperor's successful wars against the Germans beyond the Danube. Its purpose was to convey an impression of unambiguous and virtually unopposed Roman superiority. This includes scenes depicting arbitrary slaughter and executions, the extermination of unarmed people, including women. The devastation of villages contributes to the impression of a war of extermination. A sense that the enemy was justly punished for his pride in resisting Rome is conveyed. Here shown is scene 61. Photo courtesy of Eugen Petersen, *Die Marcus-Säule auf Piazza Colonna in Rom*, eds. Eugen Petersen, Alfred von Domaszewski, and Guglielmo Calderini, Text (1 Band).–Tafeln (2 Port.), (Munich, 1896), Tafel 70. It represents the execution of German prisoners (*Quadi*). The place of the execution is

surrounded by guards on foot and on horseback. Two Germans, belonging to a tribe
which had remained loyal, brandish swords in order to behead two other Germans who
resisted Rome. Two more are already on the earth with their heads cut off, while four
others are waiting in line. Four Germans bind or hold the hands of those waiting on their
backs. A German, also armed with a sword, is in command of the execution. There are
several such scenes on the column and in one of them Marcus himself supervises (scene
20). This scene also shows how Rome used its subjects to fight and subdue others, often
belonging to the same culture. The monument conveyed to the citizens of Rome a sense
that Roman superiority was such that it used German troops to execute their vanquished
compatriots.

FIGURE 10. Marcus Aurelius and vanquished Germans, Inv. 809/S, Rome, Musei Capitolini, photo: Archivio Fotografico dei Musei Capitolini.

Three Aurelian panels on the stairs landing of the Museo del Palazzo dei Conservatori depict scenes of conquest and clemency, triumph and sacrifice. The present panel shows the emperor on horseback, dressed in a cuirass, his general's cloak (*paludamentum*) billowing out behind him. Beside him, also on horseback, his companion, senior commander and son-in-law Ti. Claudius Pompeianus. They are surrounded by a Roman officer and soldiers. One of the soldiers presents to the emperor two vanquished Germans who stretch out their arms as an act of formal submission and in a plea for mercy. The emperor extends his right arm towards them to indicate that he accepts their submission. The trees in the background and the military standards (*vexilla*) indicate that the scene takes place on the battlefield.

The composition is derived from the pictorial convention which shows an equestrian emperor trampling the enemy. Here, however, he is represented both as victor and dispensing clemency. The element of clemency is emphasized also by contemporary coinage, for in the reign of Marcus the legend CLEMENTIA AUG appears on a type which shows the cuirassed emperor extending clemency to a kneeling barbarian. The same theme is found on other works of sculpture: the famous equestrian statue of Marcus on the Campidoglio also represents him as trampling an enemy, while also dispensing clemency. This column of Marcus, scene 49, portrays Marcus standing while representatives from a vanquished people stretch out their arms covered with their cloaks as an act of submission, begging to be spared.

Unlike the images on coins, such as those on figure 8 and the reliefs from Aphrodisias, figure 7, reliefs such as these do not represent a form of symbolic or idealizing propaganda, but images meant to evoke the reality of a war, fought by the emperor in person with the Germans, such as the Romans would want it to be fought. Moreover, this image and the previous one are displayed on monuments which were meant to convey a positive message to the Roman public. They are vivid illustrations of what Virgil means when he encourages Rome "to spare the vanquished, but also to subject the proud utterly" (*Aen.* 6.853). The Germans are represented as either humiliated and submitting to Rome or being slaughtered, the emperor as a resolute and virtuous conqueror.

Cf. Inez Scott Ryberg, *Panel Reliefs of Marcus Aurelius* (New York, 1967), Plates ii and iii; pp. 9–15; Elizabeth Angelicoussis, "The Panel Reliefs of Marcus Aurelius," *MDAI Röm. Abt.* 91 (1984), 141–204, at 147f., Pl.63.2. Diana E. Kleiner, *Roman Sculpture* (New Haven, Conn. 1992), 292.

Greek and Roman Attitudes towards

Specific Groups: Greek and Roman

Imperialism

THE DISCUSSION so far has dealt with a number of general themes and questions regarding ancient prejudices, preconceptions, stereotypes, and collective judgments. It seemed proper to discuss first of all the emotional and intellectual processes which produced these views among Greeks and Romans. It also seemed relevant to consider similarities and differences between ancient ideas and comparable modern phenomena. It was concluded that it would be reasonable to speak of ancient proto-racism, as defined in the Introduction. There are patterns of thinking in antiquity that have features in common with modern forms of racial and group prejudices which justify applying the term "proto-racism." Two aspects come to mind: first, the clear sense that large groups of human beings show common characteristics determined by natural factors, such as climate and geography. Second, there is a strong belief held by many authors, both Greek and Roman, that mixed ancestry is undesirable. There was clearly a consensus that mixed marriages would result in offspring of lower quality. The ancient literature shows unequivocal trends of hostility towards specific foreign nations and towards immigrants from these nations.

The insistence in the first part of this work on the intellectual processes that are at work behind such views may have obscured to some extent the actual views which Greeks and Romans held of specific groups. It will therefore be useful to continue with a survey of various groups and the ideas presented about them in the ancient sources. This will elucidate the specific nature of the hostility or ambivalence towards the different groups and will also show the variations over time. The first chapters in this second part deal with Greek views of the Persians and other eastern peoples, and with Roman views of the East. In these two chapters particular emphasis will be placed on the connection between these views and the concepts of ancient imperialism. It will become clear that there was a a relationship between the nature of Greek views on Persia and the development of Greek military ambitions vis-à-vis Persia. As the Greeks became more aggressive and ambitious, they tended to disparage their eastern neighbor more and more. This is not to say that there was a direct causality, but at least a correspondence which is not coincidental. Roman views of the East derive from Greek ideas to a large extent, but the nature of Roman imperialism in the Late Republic and Early Empire is entirely different from Greek imperial designs. It will be argued that the nature of Roman imperialism will be better understood if Roman ideas regarding the subject peoples and enemies are carefully considered in this context. The Romans naturally regarded themselves as superior to any people they succeeded in defeating. Some of those, however, they regarded as essentially inferior. These views, it will be argued, also affected Roman ideas of the vulnerability of their own superiority and their faith in the stability of their empire, because of their belief that the inferiority of the others sapped Rome's native strength.

Following this, there is a discussion of the image of various specific peoples in the ancient literature: the Syrians, Phoenicians, and Carthaginians, which are often treated as one group in the sources. Next come the Egyptians, another specific eastern people whom the Greeks and Romans found it hard to cope with. References to Egypt in the ancient literature are very numerous and the present discussion will focus only on a few relevant aspects. Roman views of Parthia and Parthians are important for three reasons: first because the Romans were very much aware of the conflict between Greece and Persia in the fifth and fourth centuries, second because Parthia was the only rival empire which Rome had to face from the first century B.C. onward, and third because this was the only nation that was not represented in large numbers in the empire itself. There were few Parthians in any of the provinces of the Roman Empire, and the impressions of them in the literature are therefore distant and based to a large extent on hearsay. Thus it will be illuminating to compare views of the Parthians with those of peoples seen every day in Rome. In recent times we have seen how the growing intensity of contact with other peoples can be a factor which determines feelings of hostility and politics of discrimination.[1] A relatively brief section on Romans and Persians will focus on the enmity in the Early Empire which turned into fierce hostility in the Later Roman Empire. Special attention will then be paid to the Greeks in Roman eyes, a topic of crucial importance. Next we shall look at two western groups: the Gauls and the Germans.[2] Finally, a separate chapter will consider Roman hostility towards the Jews. In all these cases we shall see to what extent the patterns observed in the first part of this study are applicable to the current views of the peoples discussed.

---

[1] George L. Mosse, *Toward the Final Solution: A History of European Racism* (London, 1978), 12–14.

[2] There is no satisfactory name in English for the *Germani*. Germans raises associations with a later period, but still seems the best translation of Latin *Germani*.

Greeks and the East

The Fifth Century: The Attitudes of the Victors

Now that Hellas was to become a satrapy of the Persian
Empire, the issue was of the highest and ultimate
importance, it was the question whether the Greek people
would develop its strength in full freedom, or face a
gradual process of orientalisation under the pressure of the
oriental empire, coupled with spiritual slavery and the rule
of priests. This endows the struggle with Xerxes with a
singular significance in the history of the world, for Greek
culture, which after this siege developed in such a
marvellous manner and which has stimulated the entire
European civilization till our own days, could reach
this character of its own and this level only thanks to
this victory.[1]

The theme of Herodotus—the struggle of Greece with the
Orient—possessed for him (sc. Herodotus) a deeper meaning
than the political result of the Persian war. It was the contact
and collision of two different types of civilisation; of
peoples of two different characters and different political
institutions. In the last division of his work, where the final
struggle of Persia and Greece is narrated, this contest
between the slavery of the barbarian and the liberty of the
Greek, between Oriental autocracy and Hellenic
constitutionalism, is ever present and is forcibly brought out.
But the contrast of Hellenic with Oriental culture pervades
the whole work; it informs the unity of the external theme
with the deeper unity of an inner meaning. It is the keynote
of the History of Herodotus.[2]

---

[1] U. Wilcken, *Griechische Geschichte im Rahmen der Altertumsgeschichte* (München, 9th ed.
1962), 137, my translation.

[2] J. B. Bury, *Ancient Greek Historians* (Harvard lectures, s.i. 1909, new ed.: New York, 1958),
lecture ii.

(Herodotus) ". . . in depicting the heroic effort of the Greek complex to save itself—and thereby to save Europe, as yet unborn—for freedom, for science, for civilization."[3]

In 480–79 the Greeks saved themselves and the future of European civilization from Oriental conquest.[4]

The subject in Greek eyes was the most important event of their past, the vindication of the freedom of the city-state against oriental despotism.[5]

But they [sc. the Persian wars] also closed an old [epoch]. Greek culture had been created from the fruitful interchange between east and west; that debt was now forgotten. An iron curtain had descended: east against west, despotism against liberty.[6]

The battles of the wars against Persia were assimilated to the mythical archetypes of the Amazonomachy and Centauromachy, and began to appear alongside them in the self-confident art of fifth-century Athens as symbols of the victory of democracy, reason, and Greek culture over tyranny, irrationality, and barbarism.[7]

[3] R. W. Macan in *CAH* 5 (1927), 400; cf. 410: "the great deliverance, that concrete expression of the unity of Hellas, that proof, once for all, of the dynamic and ethical superiority of European culture." M. Pohlenz, *Herodot: Der erste Geschichtsschreiber des Abendlandes* (Leipzig, 1937), 203, quotes with approval from Hermann Stegemann's *Weltwende: der kampf um die zukunft und Deutschlands gestaltwandel* (Stuttgart 1934), a work "which aims at pointing out the road for the future of the West": . . . "Wir dürfen der kommenden Entscheidung nicht ins Auge sehen, ohne uns bewusst zu werden, dass diese Auseinandersetzung zwischen Asien und Europa die Jahrtausende füllt. . . . Es is nichts Kleines und bezeichnend für den griechischen Geist wie für Herodot, dass gleich in dem ersten abendländischen Geschichtswerk dieser Gegensatz erfasst ist, ja den Aufbau bestimmt." Stegemann, we may note, was a prolific author whose works include a title: *Das Trugbild von Versailles* (Stuttgart, 1926). Politically correct German classicists in the thirties had no difficulty in quietly dropping the celebration of freedom and democracy, guaranteed by Marathon and Salamis, while still enjoying the victory over an oriental empire.
[4] P. A. Brunt, "The Hellenic League against Persia" (1953), reprinted in *Studies in Greek History and Thought* (Oxford, 1993), 47–83, esp. 47.
[5] Oswyn Murray, *Early Greece* (London, 1980), 268.
[6] Op. cit. 279.
[7] Edith Hall, *Inventing the Barbarian: Greek Self-Definition through Tragedy* (Oxford, 1989), 102. Note also Chester G. Starr, *A History of the Ancient World* (New York, 1965), 294f.: "When . . . Herodotus . . . looked back on the stirring events of 480–79, he viewed the war between the Greeks and the Persians as one between freedom and tyranny. . . . That Greek civilization would have continued to progress under Persian rule seems more than doubtful." This is a textbook, but one written by a distinguished scholar in the field.

Such views go back further than the scholars of the past century, cited here. They are already present in the work of the eighteenth-century French philosopher and revolutionary Condorcet (1743–1794): "The battle of Salamis was one of those events, so rare in history, in which the struggle of a single day decides the destiny of the human race for centuries to come."[8] What Condorcet means is clear from another pronouncement: "It is to that same revolution that the human race owes its enlightenment and will owe its liberty. It has had a far greater influence upon the destiny of the present nations of Europe than events which are much closer to us, in which our own ancestors were actors and for which their country was the theatre: in a sense it constitutes the first page of our history."[9] It should be noted that not all authors of the time shared this view. Sismondi (1773–1842) writes: "In the Republics of Antiquity, there was no such thing as civil liberty: a citizen recognized himself to be a slave of the nation to which he belonged; he abandoned himself entirely to the decisions of the sovereign, never challenging the legislator's right to control all his actions and constrain his will in every respect; but, on the other hand, he was himself, in his turn, that sovereign and that legislator."[10] He was followed in this ambiguous approach by Benjamin Constant, but[11] it was the idealizing approach of Condorcet which most influenced thinking about Greek liberty during the centuries that followed.

According to these assessments, Herodotus and his contemporary fellow-Greeks all saw this war as more than merely one of the many conflicts between political enemies. It was not a fight for political independence, but one for the highest of values with consequences for our own times. Only by defeating Persia, it is felt, could Greece come into her own and thus make it possible for our own western civilization to develop. It is then taken for granted that the two sides in these wars represent opposite poles. While Greece equals Europe and the West (Wilcken, Murray, Brunt), liberty and constitutionalism (Condorcet, Burn, Murray), European civilization (Condorcet, Brunt), Persia stands for the slavery of the barbarian and Oriental autocracy (Bury). Alternative expressions

---

[8] Jean-Antoine-Nicolas de Condorcet, *Fragments de la quatrième époque*, part of the *Esquisse d'un tableau historique des progrès de l'esprit humain*, originally published in 1795; I have seen the edition published in Paris, 1904, 191. The work has been translated into English as *Sketch for a Historical Picture of the Progress of the Human Mind* (London, 1955). I cite this from P. Vidal-Naquet and Nicole Loraux, "The Formation of Bourgeois Athens" in Pierre Vidal-Naquet, *Politics Ancient and Modern* (Cambridge, 1995), 96, with references to the work of Condorcet and literature about this author on p. 95 f. and notes 71–83 on pp. 126f. Condorcet, it will be clear, was a firm believer in the superiority of European civilization, both a pioneer of the social sciences and a typical representative of the chauvinism of the Enlightenment.

[9] *Fragments*, 292, cited here from Vidal-Naquet, 96.

[10] J.-C.-L. Simonde Sismondi, *Histoire des républiques italiennes du Moyen-Âge* (Zürich, 1807), 4.369, here cited from P. Vidal-Naquet and Nicole Loraux, "The Formation of Bourgeois Athens," in Pierre Vidal-Naquet, *Politics Ancient and Modern* (Cambridge, 1995), 115.

[11] See Vidal-Naquet, "The Place of Greece in the Revolution," in *Politics Ancient and Modern*, 141–169, at 160.

are "oriental despotism" (Murray) and even the claim that "Aryan Persia was expelled to the Orient,"[12] a curious variation of the use of the term "Aryan," which in modern times has been employed for all sorts of ideas that need not concern us here.[13] The view that we, in our age, are what we are thanks to this victory is brought out explicitly by Condorcet and Wilcken, but they are by no means alone, and it is implied in the use of twentieth-century concepts by Murray.[14] Momigliano too, in a short essay, essentially agrees with these assessments.[15] There seems to be general agreement that the conceptual opposition of Greeks and others did not exist in the archaic period[16] and was engendered by the Persian wars.[17]

Thus it appears that many modern historians confidently associate Greek civilization with all or many of the most important values which contemporary

[12] E. Bayer, *Grundzüge der griechischen Geschichte* (Darmstadt, 1964), 60: "Die Scheidelinie zwischen Orient und Okzident war von den Griechen deutlich markiert, das arische Persien von ihnen in den Orient verwiesen."

[13] In Bayer's phrase "Aryan" seems to have an unusual, negative connotation, associated with the Orient rather than the West. For the development of the concept: Léon Poliakov, *Le mythe aryen: essay sur les sources du racisme et des nationalismes* (Paris 1971), trans.: *The Aryan Myth* (New York, 1996).

[14] It would be a futile exercise to list all the works on Herodotus which express such sentiments. The books cited here represent a sample. It will be obvious that I am referring to these authors solely to point out the similarity in their views on this particular matter. It should be noted that the views described here are still present in some of the latest works of reference, for instance: *The Cambridge Ancient History*, IV second edition (1988), 475 (O. Murray), and 515 (N. Hammond).

[15] A. Momigliano, "Persian Empire and Greek Freedom," in *The Idea of Freedom: Essays in Honour of Isaiah Berlin*, ed. A. Ryan (Oxford, 1979), 139–151, esp. 145f. See now Martin Ostwald, *Oligarchia: The Development of a Constitutional Form in Ancient Greece* (Stuttgart, 2000), 21. Ostwald, 19f., suggests that it may "be part of Herodotus' strategy to interpret the Persian Wars as a moral issue in which the ὕβρις of the Persian monarchy faced the more open society of the Greeks."

[16] Irad Malkin, *The Returns of Odysseus: Colonization and Ethnicity* (Berkeley, Los Angeles, London, 1998), 18; in general: I. Malkin (ed.), *Ancient Perceptions of Greek Identity* (Washington, DC, and Cambridge, MA, 2001).

[17] E. Hall, *Inventing the Barbarian*, esp. 56–100; S. Hornblower, *The Greek World 479–323 BC* (London, 2d ed. 1991), 11: "Persia gave the Greeks their identity, or the means for recognizing it." See also the similar arguments by Giovanni Pugliese Carratelli, "Le guerre mediche ed il sorgere della solidarietà ellenica," in *Atti del convegno sul tema: la Persia et il mondo greco-romano 1965*, Accademia Nazionale dei Lincei 363 (Rome, 1966), 147–156; Claude Mossé, 'Les rapports entre la Grèce et la Perse au IVème siècle avant Jesus-Christ," ib., 177–182, with a slight variation: "Il faut d'ailleurs souligner que cette supériorité du Grec sur le barbare était surtout éprouvée sur le plan *politique*. Ni la race, ni la culture n'intervenaient pour justifier ce mépris." See also Pericles Georges, *Barbarian Asia and the Greek Experience: From the Archaic Period to the Age of Xenophon* (Baltimore, 1994), chapter 6. An exception is Gerold Walser, *Hellas und Iran* (Darmstadt, 1984), who argues that the pejorative views of the barbarians are not found in the sources from the period of the Persian wars. Herodotus, he believes, is only partly influenced by the Athenian and chauvinistic views which developed in the mid-fifth century. According to Walser, Herodotus's own and original views were free from hostility toward foreigners. John Gould, *Herodotus* (New York, 1989), does not see Herodotus's views as determined by the polarity of East and West or Hellas and Persia, nor does he discuss the works of other modern authors who adhere to this characterization of Herodotus.

western culture cherishes for itself, while Persian civilization represents the opposite. They further assume that this was also Herodotus's view of the conflict in his time and—a third assumption—that Herodotus represents fifth-century common thinking in Greece on these matters. I would claim that these assumptions are not self-evident and should be reconsidered. This is highly relevant for the present study, besides being an important subject in its own right. It is relevant because ideas about the respective moral and social values of east and west played a considerable role in antiquity and hence influenced modern scholarship. It is therefore appropriate here to trace the origins of these ideas in Greek antiquity.

The first question to ask here, then, is whether the assessments of the Graeco-Persian wars in the fifth century, cited above, do indeed represent those current in contemporary Greece and especially in the work of Herodotus. Second, it is definitely worth considering whether Herodotus and his contemporaries really thought of the Persians in terms of spiritual slavery, the rule of priests, and oriental autocracy. More generally, did they view "east" and "west" or Europe and Asia as opposite poles? At another level we must see whether Herodotus and his contemporaries saw the issue of the war not just as determining the independence of the states on the Greek mainland, but also as defining their culture and spiritual values. This topic fits the general theme of this book for several reasons.

Did the Greeks who were attacked by the Persians in the early fifth century feel that their enemy was inferior, as assumed by some modern scholars? If so, was their sense of superiority cultural, political, or military? Did they feel that they were fighting, not so much for independence as for a better society than the Persians were expected to impose on them? Indeed, did they expect the Persians to do so? These are questions of immediate relevance to the general themes of this book, which traces such sentiments in antiquity.

Although it is obvious that Herodotus identified with Greece and saw Persia as the enemy, it is important to see how he describes Persia in moral and ideological terms. A dispassionate review is required all the more as so many modern interpreters are carried away by their own preconceptions.[18] Take for

---

[18] This is not to suggest that all commentators saw Herodotus and his writings in such terms. For recent works: Lateiner, cited below; Walser, cited above. On Iranians and Greeks before the Persian wars: A. Momigliano, *Alien Wisdom* (Cambridge, 1975), 123–129; for some thoughts on Herodotus in this connection: 129–132. Note David M. Lewis, *Sparta and Persia* (Leiden, 1977), 149: "Herodotus leaves us in no doubt that there are many admirable features about the Persians." H. Erbse, *Studien zum Verständnis Herodots* (Berlin, 1992) and G. Nagy, *Arethusa* 20 (1987), 175–184, both argue that Herodotus was far more influenced by epic poetry than by any contemporary views of other peoples and the imperialism of the age. David Konstan, "Persians, Greeks and Empire," *Arethusa* 20 (1987), 59–74. For a skeptical and critical view: Robin Osborne, *Greece in the Making, 1200–479 BC* (London and New York, 1996), 318–343. Above all, see now the different treatment by Rosalind Thomas, *Herodotus in Context: Ethnography, Science and the Art of Persuasion* (Cambridge, 2000), chapter 3, esp. 79–86, concluding that Herodotus sees the conventional geographical division into continents as meaningless, criticizing it in terms of *nomos*. See also the

example a comment on Herodotus 5.113, reporting the desertion of Salaminian charioteers to the Persians, during the battle near Salamis on Cyprus (497 B.C.). "Indeed it is tempting to see in the treacherous charioteers an oriental element in the population."[19] It should be needless to say, but there is in fact a need to show, that there is nothing in Herodotus to suggest this line of thought, nor is it obvious that he thought he was writing the history of the world.[20]

A start may be made with the famous opening passage of the entire work.[21] "This is the account of the investigation made by Herodotus of Halicarnassus written so that the past will not be forgotten and to prevent the great deeds of the Greeks and the barbarians from remaining without glory; and more particularly, [to show] why they fought each other."[22] The point to note here is that Herodotus states as a matter of course that the great deeds of both the Greeks and their enemies are to be recorded for posterity. This is not merely a recognition that there had been great deeds by the Persians, but also that it was one of the major aims of the work to record them no less than those of the Greeks.[23] Herodotus could have said, but did not say, what so many of his successors claimed, that the justification for writing his history was the unprecedented scale of the war. If he felt that the scale of the war, and what was at stake in terms of moral values, were the reasons for writing its history, he did not say so in this passage.

Obviously, Greeks are held to be more intelligent than barbarians, or at least,

---

conclusion on p. 99: "the idea that the continents as such, as part of their inherent character, are inevitably hostile to one another seems less well borne out by the *Histories* than one might have expected." See also the recent book by James Romm, *Herodotus* (New Haven, 1999), chapter 12, arguing that Herodotus does not have simplistic views; for Herodotus's description of the continents, see also Reinhold Bichler, *Herodots Welt: Der Aufbau der Historie amd Bild der fremden Länder und Völker, ihrer Zivilisation und ihrer Geschichte* (Berlin, 2000), 16–21.

[19] W. W. How and J. Wells, *A Commentary on Herodotus* (Oxford, 1912), vol. 2.62. The argument of the authors is that chariots were not common in Greek warfare after Homer. So, while these were Greek forces, they speculate that the "survival of the chariot in Cyprus may be due to oriental influence." In the next sentence this influence is then taken to be represented by an oriental element in the population.

[20] For an extreme statement along such lines: H. R. Immerwahr, *Form and Thought in Herodotus* (Cleveland, OH, 1966), 45, who claims: "The treatment of Eastern history and of the wars of Asia with Greece is thus developed intuitively (sc. by Herodotus) from a general conception of what the Greek struggle for freedom really meant for the history of the world."

[21] This is discussed in almost every study of Herodotus and forms the starting point for part of a recent book on Herodotus: J.A.S. Evans, *Herodotus: Explorer of the Past, Three Essays* (Princeton, 1991); cf. the remarks in Charles W. Fornara, *The Nature of Ancient History* (Berkeley and Los Angeles, 1983), 47; also: P. Nagy, *Arethusa* 20 (1987), 175–184. Further references: D. Asheri, *Erodoto Le storie. Libro I: La Lidia e la Persia* (Milano, 2d ed. 1989), 261f.

[22] Herodotus 1.1 Ἡροδότου Ἁλικαρνησσέος ἱστορίης ἀπόδεξις ἥδε, ὡς μήτε τὰ γενόμενα ἐξ ἀνθρώπων τῷ χρόνῳ ἐξίτηλα γένηται, μήτε ἔργα μεγάλα τε καὶ θωμαστά, τὰ μὲν Ἕλλησι, τὰ δὲ βαρβάροισι ἀποδεχθέντα, ἀκλέα γένηται, τά τε ἄλλα καὶ δι' ἣν αἰτίην ἐπολέμησαν ἀλλήλοισι.

[23] Thomas, *Herodotus in Context*, 101, notes that it is precisely the distinction between Greeks and barbarians with which Herodotus begins the *Histories,* and this is certainly true, but, after all, his subject was a war between Greeks and non-Greeks.

they have been so from very ancient times (1.60.3).[24] Herodotus assumes that other peoples see all peoples other than themselves as barbarians.[25] Greece, of course, has the best climate in the world, but Herodotus is prepared to believe that the "extreme regions of the earth" are equally lucky in their climate and natural resources. (3.106).[26] Herodotus does not express any anti-oriental sentiments.[27] In fact he nowhere goes as far as later Greek authors, discussed below, in polarizing Greeks versus others. He describes opportunism and treason on both sides. A number of examples should suffice.[28] Herodotus recognizes the Persians and some of their allies as great warriors: "In all Asia there was not at that time a braver or more warlike people (sc. than the Lydians)" (1.79, end). This description of the Lydians is particularly interesting, because they are described in pejorative terms in various sources.[29] To return to Herodotus's image

[24] Note the context of this passage: the Athenians let themselves be duped by a foolish trick of Pisistratus. This is remarkable, says Herodotus, for the Greeks have from the oldest times been more sagacious and free from simplicity than barbarians. And then he adds that the trick was not just played on Greeks, but on Athenians, who are always thought to surpass the Greeks in cleverness. One suspects that the reason for the phrasing of these lines is that Herodotus rather enjoys pointing out the foolishness of the Athenians, just as he does in 5.97.

[25] Herodotus 2.158: βαρβάρους δὲ πάντας οἱ Αἰγύπτιοι καλέουσι τοὺς μὴ σφίσι ὁμογλώσσους. It is interesting to note that the matter of language is here considered essential. This is also the case in 1 Cor. 14.11: ἐὰν οὖν μὴ εἰδῶ τὴν δύναμιν τῆς φωνῆς, ἔσομαι τῷ λαλοῦντι βάρβαρος καὶ ὁ λαλῶν ἐν ἐμοὶ βάρβαρος. Thomas, Herodotus in Context, 131, interprets the statement in comparison with the fragment of Antiphon, On Truth, 44, which also emphasizes the relativity of being a barbarian. See above, chapter 2, p. 173. Each people has its barbarians. E. Hall, Inventing the Barbarian, 178–180, describes the development of the use of the term. The OED² gives the following useful reference: 1549 Compl. Scot. xiii. 106 Euere nation reputis vthers nations to be barbariens, quhen there tua natours and complexions ar contrar til vtheris [i.e. each other]. In fact it is not the case that every nation has a term to indicate all the others collectively. The Greeks and Jews had one and so, apparently, did the Chinese, but it is not a universal feature. For the Chinese see references in Hall, op. cit., 60–62, for terms for "foreigner" in oriental languages: p. 4 nn. 4 and 5. See also below.

[26] James S. Romm, The Edges of the Earth in Ancient Thought: Geography, Exploration and Fiction (Princeton, 1992), 38–41; see also Klaus E. Müller, Geschichte der antiken Ethnographie und Ethnologischen Theoriebildung, 2 vols. (Wiesbaden, 1972); esp. vol. 1, 120–127.

[27] B. Laurot, "Idéaux grecs et barbarie chez Hérodote," Ktema 6 (1981), 39–48; G. Nenci (ed.), Hérodote et les peuples non grecs (Vandoeuvres–Genève, 1990), esp. P. Briant, "Hérodote et la société perse," pp. 69–113; Alan B. Lloyd, "Herodotus on Egyptians and Libyans," 215–244.

[28] See Donald Lateiner, The Historical Method of Herodotus (Toronto, 1989), 152f.

[29] How and Wells, A Commentary on Herodotus I, 95, comment: "H. adds this, because the Lydians of his own day were a proverb for effeminacy." In Appendix I, p. 372, these commentators explain that this was caused by a mixture of races. 'Such a process has happened repeatedly in India; such a process is conjectured to explain the disappearance from modern France of the race of tall, fair Gallic warriors, once so terrible to the Romans." For the Gauls in French historiography: Poliakov, The Aryan Myth, 21–35. For ancient views of Lydians: Antony Spawforth, "Shades of Greekness: A Lydian Case Study," in Malkin (ed.), Ancient Perceptions of Greek Ethnicity (2001), 375–400; for Lydians in Attic vase painting: Keith De Vries, "The Nearly Other: The Attic Vision of Phrygians and Lydians," in Beth Cohen (ed.), Not The Classical Ideal, 338–363, esp. 358–363. De Vries concludes that the the pejorative judgments held about the Lydians found expression in both literature and art. By contrast, the Phrygians are accused of cowardice in some literary passages, while this theme absent in vase painting; see pp. 342–357.

of the Persians: they honored those who showed themselves courageous in battle more highly than any people Herodotus knew (7.238) and Herodotus has no difficulty in describing them as fighting valiantly (8.86; 9.71). There is one passage in which the Persian troops are described in rhetorical and derogatory terms. It appears in the description of the battle of Thermopylae which the Persians won (7.210).[30]

Herodotus does not deny the relatively benevolent nature of the Persian empire. The Ionian cities are well treated by the Persians (6.42) and re-organized as democracies (6.43). The Persians are decent victors: "For the Persians are wont to honour those who show themselves valiant in fight more highly than any nation that I know" (7.238). Among the Persians nothing is more disgraceful than to lie, a statement which is particularly significant given the later habit of accusing one's enemies of being liars, discussed more extensively below.[31] Herodotus emphasizes the true magnanimity (μεγαλοφροσύνη) of Xerxes (7. 136).[32] "Among all this multitude of men there was not one who, for beauty and stature, deserved more than Xerxes himself to wield so vast a power" (7.187).[33] When angry, Herodotus tells us, Xerxes could behave excessively: when the bridges over the Hellespont were destroyed he gave orders that the Hellespont should receive three hundred lashes and that a pair of fetters should be cast into it. However, Herodotus considered it possible that the king afterwards repented of having scourged the Hellespont (7.54). It is easy to interpret this as the megalomaniac behavior of a tyrant, suffering from *hybris* or even madness, as did the Roman historians when Caligula behaved in a similar manner on the shores of the North Sea (Suetonius, *C. Caligula* 46). The question is whether this is how Herodotus meant it to be interpreted. Stories were obviously told depicting Xerxes as a caricature of a capricious despot, but Herodotus does not believe them (8.118f.). He describes a sumptuous meal prepared for Mardonios in Xerxes' luxurious tent after his defeat at Plataea, and cites the Spartan victor's caustic comments, but the point he makes is only that it is futile for rich nations to subjugate poor ones (9.81).[34]

Herodotus's rendering of the remarkable consultation between Xerxes and the exiled Spartan king Demaratus, as rendered by Herodotus, is particularly

[30] 7.210: At Thermopylae it became clear to the king that he had plenty of people, but few real men: Δῆλον δ' ἐποίευν παντί τεῳ καὶ οὐκ ἥκιστα αὐτῷ βασιλέϊ ὅτι πολλοὶ μὲν ἄνθρωποι εἶεν, ὀλίγοι δὲ ἄνδρες. After Thermopylae Xerxes mutilated Leonidas's body, but this was an individual act, contrary to Persian custom. See also 3.16 and 9.78 for similar observations.

[31] Herodotus 1.138: αἴσχιστον αὐτοῖσι τὸ ψεύδεσθαι νενόμισται. For accusations of other peoples as liars, see below, chapter 5.

[32] Similarly: 7.27–29, 146f., 181.

[33] Compare this with E. H. Blakeney's statement: "As a ruler he was arbitrary and unscrupulous; as a man, effeminate, extravagant, and cruel." *The History of Herodotus*, trans. George Rawlinson, ed. E. H. Blakeney (London, 1910), vol. 2, 214.

[34] This is a theme that recurs elsewhere: Croesus, 1.71; Persians, 9. 122. It was apparently a significant element in Herodotus's thinking. Thucydides 1.130—and not Herodotus—reports that the same Spartan commander later started wearing Persian dress, traveled through Thrace with a bodyguard of Persians and Egyptians, ate Persian meals, and was generally difficult to approach.

illuminating in this connection (7.101–5).[35] Xerxes asks how the Greeks will resist his attack. Demaratus, warning Xerxes that he is speaking the truth, responds that he is speaking only of the Spartans: "I praise all the Greeks who live in the Dorian lands, but I am going to speak now not about all, but only about the Lacedaemonians. First, they will never in any way accept your demands, which bring slavery to Greece, furthermore they will definitely join battle with you, even if all the other Greeks submit to you."[36] Xerxes' answer is relevant in one respect: he asserts the superiority of an army fighting under one commander: "How could a thousand men, or ten thousand, or even fifty thousand, being all of them equally free, and not commanded by one man,—how could they withstand such an army as mine?" Apart from the Persian numerical superiority, which is not in question, Xerxes continues: "If, indeed, they were commanded by one man like our army, they might out of fear fight better against their natural inclination and they might be forced by the lash to battle against an enemy superior in number. But left free, they definitely will not do anything like that."[37] First, it is essential to note that Demaratus praises only the Dorians and then speaks only of the Spartans. He considers it quite possible that all the other Greeks would submit. Herodotus knew, and so did his audience, that this did not happen, but Demaratus's argument reflects the perspec-

[35] The debate has been much discussed: David Lewis, *Sparta and Persia*, 148f.; A. Dihle, "Herodot und die Sophistik," *Philologus* 106 (1962) 207–220, analyzes Herodotus's use of sophistic technique in the dialogue; Martin Ostwald, "Freedom and the Greeks," in R.W. Davis (ed.), *The Origins of Modern Freedom in the West*, 35–63, esp. 46–48, discusses the meaning of "freedom" in the debate. He argues that Herodotus wants his readers to take the colloquy as contrasting Greek with Persian political values, whereby Persian ideas of "freedom," he suggests, do not go beyond absence of foreign domination, but the Greeks realize that even political freedom has parameters, but parameters set by a social norm rather than by an autocrat. However, Ostwald also observes that this account was written at least three or four decades after the end of the Persian Wars. See also Ostwald, "Shares and Rights: 'Citizenship' Greek Style and American Style," in J. Ober and C. Hedrick (ed.), *Demokratia* (Princeton, 1996), 49–61, esp. 54. Note further the two major studies by Kurt Raaflaub, "Zum Freiheitsbegriff der Griechen. Marterialien und Untersuchungen zur Bedeutungentwicklung von ἐλεύθερος / ἐλευθερία in der archaischen und klassischen Zeit," in E. C. Welskopf (ed.), *Untersuchungen ausgewählter altgriechischer sozialer Typenbegriffe und ihr Fortleben in Antike und Mittelalter* (Berlin, 1981), 180–405, esp. 225–228; *Die Entdeckung der Freiheit: Zur historischen Semantik und Gesellschaftsgeschichte eines politischen Grundbegriffes der Griechen* (Munich, 1985); D. Boedeker, "The Two Faces of Demaratus," *Arethusa* 20 (1987), 185–201; D. Lateiner, *The Historical Method of Herodotus* (Toronto, 1989), 160 and ch. 8; Thomas, *Herodotus in Context*, 109–111, an analysis in terms of *nomos* (Spartan *arete*) and *physis* (Greek poverty).

[36] 7.102: Αἰνέω μέν νυν πάντας τοὺς Ἕλληνας τοὺς περὶ ἐκείνους τοὺς Δωρικοὺς χώρους οἰκημένους, ἔρχομαι δὲ λέξων οὐ περὶ πάντων τούσδε τοὺς λόγους, ἀλλὰ περὶ Λακεδαιμονίων μούνων· πρῶτα μὲν ὅτι οὐκ ἔστι ὅκως κοτὲ σοὺς δέξονται λόγους δουλοσύνην φέροντας τῇ Ἑλλάδι, αὖτις δὲ ὡς ἀντιώσονταί τοι ἐς μάχην καὶ ἢν οἱ ἄλλοι Ἕλληνες πάντες τὰ σὰ φρονέωσι.

[37] 7.103; Κῶς ἂν δυναίατο χίλιοι ἢ καὶ μύριοι ἢ καὶ πεντακισμύριοι, ἐόντες γε ἐλεύθεροι πάντες ὁμοίως καὶ μὴ ὑπ' ἑνὸς ἀρχόμενοι, στρατῷ τοσῷδε ἀντιστῆναι; ... Ὑπὸ μὲν γὰρ ἑνὸς ἀρχόμενοι κατὰ τρόπον τὸν ἡμέτερον γενοίατ' ἂν δειμαίνοντες τοῦτον καὶ παρὰ τὴν ἑωυτῶν φύσιν ἀμείνονες, καὶ ἴοιεν ἀναγκαζόμενοι μάστιγι ἐς πλέονας ἐλάσσονες ἐόντες· ἀνειμένοι δὲ ἐς τὸ ἐλεύθερον οὐκ ἂν ποιοῖεν τούτων οὐδέτερα.

tive of the Spartans as Herodotus saw it: the Spartans alone were not going to submit and in chapter 104 he gives a specific reason for this. "The Spartans may be free, but not in every respect, for they always obey the law which is their lord whom they fear more than your subjects fear you. The law always commands the same thing: it forbids the Spartans to flee in battle, whatever the number of the enemy, but they maintain their battle order to conquer or die." Demaratus, like the authors of the epigrams for fallen Spartans, referred to below, thus considers the Spartans—unlike the other Greeks—superior because of their discipline, not because they are free. Xerxes, on the other hand, has no doubt that his army is better, because he believes that an army fighting under a single commander performs better through fear, unlike free men who are not forced into battle. It may be less important for the present discussion what the Persian king thought or is believed to have thought, but it is definitely of crucial importance why the non-Athenian allies considered it essential to resist Persia. Herodotus leaves no doubt that the most important of those allies, the Spartans, resisted the Persians because of their sense of honor and duty on the battlefield. We may add to this that Herodotus says explicitly that it was the privilege of the Spartan kings to declare war on whomever they thought fit (6.56).[38] Thus, the kings sent the Spartans to war and once on the battlefield, the Spartans would fight to victory or death. Clearly, Herodotus does not imply at all that the Spartans were fighting for freedom or democracy. They fought because it was their duty. Indeed, personal or collective motivation is regarded as irrelevant. In this connection, it is important to remember that, despite Herodotus's praise of Athens, it is Sparta which for him was Persia's principal antagonist.[39]

In a recent work Peter Hunt says that "Herodotus on a number of occasions emphasises that the Greeks were fighting against a Persian army consisting of slaves. This is a mistranslation of the word δοῦλος. When a Persian aristocrat is called the king's δοῦλος this does not mean that he is regarded in the same light as a domestic slave in an Athenian household. As observed by Gomme, when the Greeks called the barbarians δοῦλοι (not πολῖται), this meant 'servants' (of the one man, the king), rather than 'slaves,' which would be ἀνδράποδα but the ambiguity of the word δοῦλος was made much use of for political ends."[40] Indeed, Herodotus states that the Persian commanders were "servants, just like the rest of the troops" (7.96).[41] That makes sense in Persian society, but it would be wholly pointless to call a senior commander a slave, for, in Greek eyes, there is an essential contradiction between the presumed temperament of a slave and

[38] Lewis, Sparta and Persia, 43–49, for the position of the Spartan kings: "the kings were little more than hereditary generals" (48). This agrees with Aristotle, Politics 1285b–1286a, who asserts that Spartan kingship was really a military office. This may be accepted, but it was no mean role in Sparta, or in any other state, for that matter.

[39] Charles W. Fornara, Herodotus: An Interpretative Essay (Oxford, 1971), 50; Lewis, Sparta and Persia, 148.

[40] A. W. Gomme, A Historical Commentary on Thucydides: The Ten Years' War (Oxford, 1956), 3.646.

[41] Peter Hunt, Slaves, Warfare, and Ideology in the Greek Historians (Cambridge, 1989), 48f.

the necessary characteristics of a military commander. It should also be noted that Herodotus refers only to the ἐπιχώριοι ἡγεμόνες, that is, the native commanders of subject peoples,[42] although other passages may imply that all Persians are servants of the king, even including high nobles.[43] For instance in 7.19: Xerxes dreams and the Magi explain: "all mankind would become his servants" (δουλεύσειν τέ οἱ πάντας ἀνθρώπους). This is the terminology for conquest which is generally used in Greek sources: it has nothing to do with the Persians in particular. More important, it is clear that Herodotus himself never intended to convey the message that the Persian army functioned as an army of slaves.

Xerxes assumes, as a matter of course, that an army with one supreme commander, whom it fears, fights better than a Greek army—or at least this is Xerxes as represented in a speech by Herodotus.[44] Such an assumption, however, could be encountered anywhere. Xerxes was by no means the last military commander with such an opinion, nor did all commanders who held such views lose battles. In a famous passage, Herodotus observes that the Athenians fought no better than their neighbors when they were ruled by tyrants, but when they had freed themselves, they became by far the best. "This shows that, while suffering oppression they allowed themselves to be defeated since they toiled for a despot, but when they were freed, each of them did his best for himself."[45] This is an observation about a peculiarly Athenian situation: when ruled by a despot the Athenians were poor soldiers. It is echoed by Plato, who says the reverse about the Persians under Cyrus and afterwards, as shown below. Undoubtedly Herodotus means to say that tyranny is bad for morals, but the alternative is not democracy, but any form of constitutional rule in an independent *polis*.

Elsewhere, again, Herodotus himself observes (5.3): "The Thracians are the most powerful people in the world, except, of course, the Indians; and if they had one head, or were agreed among themselves, it is my belief that their match could not be found anywhere, and that they would very far surpass all other

---

[42] Herodotus explains that there was no need to mention them, for they were many and slaves like the remainder of the στρατευόμενοι. The real commanders were the Persian generals, who were at the head of the several nations which composed the army.

[43] 49, n. 19. 7.38: Xerxes, in anger, addresses a Lydian subject; 7.135: Two Spartans in argument with a Persian nobleman; 8.68: the Greek Artemisia makes derogatory remarks about peoples subject to the Persians; 8.116: The king of the Thracian Bisaltians and of Crestonia had refused to become the willing slave of Xerxes: ὃς οὔτε αὐτὸς ἔφη τῷ Ξέρξῃ ἑκὼν εἶναι δουλεύσειν. In 8.102 the Persian commander Mardonios is described as the king's servant, but this occurs for the sake of argument in another speech by Artemisia. The Loeb translation correctly renders this as "servant," which could be used for a free man.

[44] 7.103–4; cf. Tacitus, *Germania* 30, on the Chatti who were unusual among the Germans in that they had "more confidence in their military leaders than in the armed mass, a quality characteristic of Roman discipline."

[45] Herodotus 5.78: εἰ καὶ Ἀθηναῖοι τυραννευόμενοι μὲν οὐδαμῶν τῶν σφέας περιοικεόντων ἦσαν τὰ πολέμια ἀμείνονες, ἀπαλλαχθέντες δὲ τυράννων μακρῷ πρῶτοι ἐγένοντο. Δηλοῖ ὦν ταῦτα ὅτι κατεχόμενοι μὲν ἐθελοκάκεον ὡς δεσπότῃ ἐργαζόμενοι, ἐλευθερωθέντων δὲ αὐτὸς ἕκαστος ἑωυτῷ προεθυμέετο κατεργάζεσθαι.

nations."[46] Herodotus clearly would not subscribe to the view that an army with a single commander cannot be successful. Later Aristotle observes: "the quality of an army consists partly in the order and partly in the commander, but particularly in the latter, for it is he who determines the order and not the other way around."[47] In other words, even if Herodotus considers the Persian army an army of slaves, this does not mean they were poor fighters. As we know from other periods, slave armies can be remarkably effective. Just to mention one example: in the later Middle Ages the mamluks of Egypt defeated and expelled the Crusaders and halted the Mongol advance across the Middle East.[48]

This may be a suitable point for a brief mention of the Constitutional Debate, attributed by Herodotus to Persian noblemen, which is itself one of the most frequently debated sections in Herodotus's work.[49] The first point to make here is that Herodotus—rightly or not—considered it possible that such a debate could have taken place in Persia, and that a group of Persian noblemen were once in a position to decide on the proper form of government for their nation, with the result that they voted for a monarchy. The implication is that Herodotus did not believe that absolute monarchy was inevitable for the Persian nation. In other words, Persia was not ruled by monarchs because of the unalterably servile nature of its inhabitants—as claimed by later Greek authors— but through a conscious decision following rational debate. As pointed out by Ostwald, his main objection, which is brought forward repeatedly against monarchy (and democracy), is the degree to which these forms of government lead to ὕβρις (excess).[50] It is also fair to argue that Herodotus saw the failure of the Persian campaigns against Greece as being caused by the ὕβρις of two Persian kings, who thus suffered from a deficiency inherent in the monarchy.[51] However, at least one speaker in the debate saw democracy as suffering from the same weakness and it is dubious whether we can argue that Herodotus himself shared the view of one speaker rather than that of one of the others. The Constitutional Debate, therefore, cannot be used to argue that Herodotus saw the Persian wars as a conflict between East and West in which the former represents

[46] Θρηίκων δὲ ἔθνος μέγιστον ἐστι μετά γε Ἰνδοὺς πάντων ἀνθρώπων. εἰ δὲ ὑπ᾽ ἑνὸς ἄρχοιτο ἢ φρονέοι κατὰ τὠυτό, ἄμαχόν τ᾽ ἂν εἴη καὶ πολλῷ κράτιστον πάντων ἐθνέων κατὰ τὴν ἐμήν.

[47] Aristotle, Metaphysics 1075a: καὶ γὰρ ἐν τῇ τάξει τὸ εὖ καὶ ὁ στρατηγός, καὶ μᾶλλον οὗτος· οὐ γὰρ οὗτος διὰ τὴν τάξιν ἀλλ᾽ ἐκείνη διὰ τοῦτόν ἐστιν.

[48] Patricia Crone, Slaves on Horses: the Evolution of the Islamic Polity (Cambridge, 1980); Bernard Lewis, Race and Slavery in the Middle East: an Historical Enquiry (New York and Oxford, 1990), chapter 9: "Slaves in Arms."

[49] 3.80–3. See now Ostwald, Oligarchia, 17–20.

[50] Ostwald, Oligarchia, 19f. In 3.80 Otanes, arguing against monarchy, uses the term four times; in 81, Megabyzus, who is in favor of oligarchy, agrees with Otanes, but also applies it to democracy. See also Laurot, "Idéaux grecs," 46; Erbse, Studien zum Verständnis Herodots, 90f.; R. Bichler, Herodots Welt, 223–225.

[51] Cf. by contrast Aristotle, Pol. 1313b with its sweeping generalizations regarding the "devices of Persian and barbarian tyranny" (καὶ τἆλλα ὅσα τοιαῦτα Περσικὰ καὶ βάρβαρα τυραννικά ἐστιν (πάντα γὰρ ταὐτὸν δύναται)·) The "monarchy that aims at the common advantage, usually designated 'kingship'" (1279a: καλεῖν δ᾽ εἰώθαμεν τῶ μὲν μοναρχιῶν τὴν πρὸς τὸ κοινὸν ἀποβλέπουσαν συμφέρον βασιλείαν), apparently exists only among the Greeks, according to this view.

tyranny and the latter an open society. Herodotus says no more than that two specific Persian kings failed in their attempts to subjugate Greece because of a state of mind such as is often induced by the monarchy.

While there can be no doubt that Herodotus, like many of his contemporaries, saw the war between Greece and Persia as a struggle for freedom, there is never an indication in his work that he saw this as more than freedom for the Greek states from foreign domination.[52] It is worth noting also that classical Greek lacked a notion of "freedom of the individual" to do as he pleases, that is, to pursue his own life, liberty, and happiness. Even the most extreme expression of a personal liberty in this period by Xenophon is couched in terms of the collective δῆμος, of the people, not of the individual.[53] It is no different in the fourth century. Plato's *Menexenus* has a lot to say about ἐλευθερία / freedom (239–246: *passim*), but in all instances the meaning is clear: it means the collective freedom of Greek states from foreign domination by other states, be it Greeks subjugating other Greeks or barbarians ruling Greeks.[54]

This may seem a truism, but clearly there is a tendency in the commentaries and books cited above—and in numerous others not cited—to interpret Herodotus's position in terms of a struggle for the freedom of the individual in the broadest sense of the term, against a system which transformed human beings into collective subjects of the monarch. Neither in Herodotus's work nor in any other fifth-century sources is there any indication that they believed the war against Persia had been more than a war against a foreign invader. They may not have had a high opinion of one-man rule, but that was not the reason for their resistance to Persia. If Persia had been an aristocratic city-state, this would not have changed their attitudes.[55] The options were: subjugation by a foreign power—any foreigner—and hence slavery, or defeat of the foreigners and hence freedom. When the Athenians tell Spartan envoys why they would not support Persia, they give two reasons: the burning and destruction of Athenian temples by the Persians, and their own common brotherhood with the other

---

[52] See M. Ostwald, "Freedom and the Greeks," 44f.: "by far the greatest number of 'freedom' passages in Herodotus have a political thrust of which we do not hear before the Persian Wars. . . . a people is said to be 'free' when it is not ruled by—or has overthrown the rule of—a single potentate. . . . A second political use of 'freedom' in Herodotus describes the freedom of a state from domination by an alien power. . . . In most instances, however, it refers to the independence and freedom of particular tribes or cities, predominantly Greek, from Persian domination."

[53] Xenophon, *Hell.* 1.7.12: δεινὸν εἶναι εἰ μή τις ἐάσει δῆμον πράττειν ὃ ἂν βούληται. I owe this observation to Martin Ostwald.

[54] *Menex.* 239b οἰόμενοι δεῖν ὑπὲρ τῆς ἐλευθερίας καὶ Ἕλλησιν ὑπὲρ Ἑλλήνων μάχεσθαι καὶ βαρβάροις ὑπὲρ ἁπάντων τῶν Ἑλλήνων. The *Menexenus* is a difficult text to analyze for such purposes, but the use of the term ἐλευθερία seems clear; cf. S. Tsitsiridis, *Platons Menexenos* (Stuttart, 1998), 242.

[55] Freedom, not democracy, was the issue for the Greeks. Most of the states that took part in the struggle against Persia were not democracies, and for Athens itself becoming a democracy was a gradual process which was by no means complete at the time of the Persian wars, cf. M. Ostwald, "Popular Sovereignty and the Problem of Equality," *SCI* 19 (2000), 1–13. For a useful discussion of the sovereignty of the state: Mogens Herman Hansen, Polis *and City-State: An Ancient Concept and its Modern Equivalent* (Copenhagen, 1998), chapter 3: "The Concept of State," esp. 40–42.

Greeks (8.144). Thus the essence, according to Herodotus, was a combination of religious wrath[56] and loyalty towards the Greeks, but there he says nothing about freedom of the individual or hostility towards an eastern monarchy. Even if there had been claims that the Greek states were resisting Persia for the sake of a higher ideal of freedom, we should have every reason to doubt whether this was a genuine motive. After all, the immediate sequel to the Persian wars was a process whereby Athens started to restrict the freedom of its allies and continued to do so ever more. The Spartans, who fought the Persians alongside other Greek states, were themselves no model egalitarians, and after defeating the Athenians they themselves became an oppressive power.

Those Greeks who united for the war with Persia were fighting for freedom from being ruled by non-Greeks. These Greeks sent envoys to Gelon of Syracuse in an attempt to gain his support.[57] Gelon was a tyrant who had subjugated many Greek cities on Sicily, moved some part of their inhabitants to Syracuse, and sold others as slaves in the belief, says Herodotus, "that a people (*demos*) is a most unpleasant companion. Thus Gelon became a great tyrant."[58] The Greek envoys exhorted Gelon to support them because Persia intended to "subjugate all of Greece, and therefore we ask you to assist those who aim to liberate Greece and and join in liberating her."[59] It would be ludicrous to interpret this "freedom" as referring to anything like democracy or individual freedom. The Spartans who sent these envoys had no interest in individual liberty, and a struggle for democracy would have been the last argument to appeal to Gelon. Gelon answers that the Greeks of the mainland had failed to support him in his struggle with the barbarians, when he was fighting Carthage (7.158). However, he would be prepared to support the Greeks if they would make him commander-in-chief of the army. It is clear from this episode that the Greeks easily found a common language and mutual understanding when the issue was a war with non-Greeks, and this was also true for Greeks who had no sympathy at all for democracy.

In Athens itself, there were authors who disapproved of democracy for its excessive love of freedom, as they saw it. The earliest is the author often curiously called "The Old Oligarch," who wrote at an uncertain date in the fifth century, presumably in the forties and no later than 423.[60] The entire treatise is

[56] Cf. Diodorus 11.293f., who cites an oath sworn by all the Greeks before the battle of Plataea which included a promise not to rebuild any of the sanctuaries, but to leave them as a reminder to coming generations of the impiety of the barbarians. See below on other aspects of this passage in Herodotus's work. Cf. Walser, *Hellas und Iran*, chapter 9: "Die Perser und die griechischen Tempel," who points out that the destruction of Greek temples by Xerxes did not constitute a policy of religious suppression, but was part of a general pattern of behavior in ancient warfare.

[57] P.A. Brunt, "The Hellenic League against Persia," 47–83, esp. "The Hellenic League and Gelon," 75–80.

[58] Herodotus, 7.156: . . . νομίσας δῆμον εἶναι συνοίκημα ἀχαριτώτατον. τοιούτῳ μὲν τρόπῳ τύραννος ἐγεγόνεε μέγας ὁ Γέλων.

[59] 7.157: ἐν νόῳ δὲ ἔχων πᾶσαν τὴν Ἑλλάδα ὑπ' ἑωυτῷ ποιήσασθαι. Σὺ δὲ . . . βοήθεέ τε τοῖσι ἐλευθεροῦσι τὴν Ἑλλάδα καὶ συνελευθέρου.

[60] See G. W. Bowersock in the Loeb ed. *Pseudo-Xenophon: Constitution of the Athenians* in vol. 7 of Xenophon, 463–465, for discussion of the date, bibliography on pp. 470–473; also Jennifer T.

meant to show how the Athenian democracy is destructive of orderly government in favoring the rabble to the detriment of the upper class (χρηστοί). The word "freedom" (ἐλευθερία) is nowhere mentioned.

In the fourth century the famous enemies of democracy are Isocrates and Plato. Isocrates approved of the Athenian constitution as it used to be in the past, in his view:

> For those who directed the state in the time of Solon and Cleisthenes did not establish a polity which in name merely was hailed as the most impartial and the mildest of governments, while in practice showing itself the opposite to those who lived under it, nor one which trained the citizens in such fashion that they looked upon insolence as democracy, lawlessness as freedom, impudence of speech as equality, and licence to do what they pleased as happiness, but rather a polity which detested and punished such men and by so doing made all the citizens better and wiser.[61]

Thus Isocrates equates the democracy of his day with indiscipline, freedom with lawlesness, and political equality with the license to say anything you please. He is particularly concerned with the decline of morality, contrasting the upright religiosity, and the rejection of foreign cults in ancient times, with the loss of values in his own days (*Areopagiticus* 30, 37–50). The best governed people in the world are the Spartans because they are ruled most democratically.[62] However, the fiercest attack on the Athenian democracy is found in Plato's *Republic*: " 'And is not democracy's insatiable desire for what it defines as the good also what destroys it?' 'What do you say it defines as the good?' 'Freedom: Surely you would hear a democratic city say that this is the finest thing it has, so that as a result it is the only city worth living in for someone who is by nature free.' 'Yes, you often hear that.' 'Then, as I was about to say, does not the insatiable desire for freedom and the neglect of other things change this constitution and put it in need of a dictatorship?' "[63] In both attacks on contemporary democracy the idea of "freedom" is prominent. According to

---

Roberts, *Athens on Trial: The Antidemocratic Tradition in Western Thought* (Princeton, 1994), 52–54.

[61] Isocrates, *Areopagiticus* 7.20 (trans. George Norlin): Οἱ γὰρ κατ' ἐκεῖνον τὸν χρόνον τὴν πόλιν διοικοῦντες κατεστήσαντο πολιτείαν οὐκ ὀνόματι μὲν τῷ κοινοτάτῳ καὶ πραοτάτῳ προσαγορευομένην, ἐπὶ δὲ τῶν πράξεων οὐ τοιαύτην τοῖς ἐντυγχάνουσι φαινομένην, οὐδ' ἣ τοῦτον τὸν τρόπον ἐπαίδευε τοὺς πολίτας ὥσθ' ἡγεῖσθαι τὴν μὲν ἀκολασίαν δημοκρατίαν, τὴν δὲ παρανομίαν ἐλευθερίαν, τὴν δὲ παρρησίαν ἰσονομίαν, τὴν δ' ἐξουσίαν τοῦ ταῦτα ποιεῖν εὐδαιμονίαν, ἀλλὰ μισοῦσα καὶ κολάζουσα τοὺς τοιούτους βελτίους καὶ σωφρονεστέρους ἅπαντας τοὺς πολίτας ἐποίησεν. See also *Panathenaicus* 12.131; *Nicocles* 3.14. Cf. Roberts, *Athens on Trial*, 67–69.

[62] Isocrates, *Areopagiticus* 61: Οἶδα γὰρ τούς τε προγόνους τοὺς ἡμετέρους ἐν ταύτῃ τῇ καταστάσει πολὺ τῶν ἄλλων διενεγκόντας καὶ Λακεδαιμονίους διὰ τοῦτο κάλλιστα πολιτευομένους, ὅτι μάλιστα δημοκρατούμενοι τυγχάνουσιν.

[63] Plato, *Rep.* 557b; 562b–564a, esp. 562b–c (trans. G.M.A. Grube, revised by C.D.C. Reeve): ᾿Αρ' οὖν καὶ ὁ δημοκρατία ὁρίζεται ἀγαθόν, ἡ τούτου ἀπληστία καὶ ταύτην καταλύει; Λέγεις δ' αὐτὴν τί ὁρίζεσθαι; Τὴν ἐλευθερίαν, εἶπον. τοῦτο γάρ που ἐν δημοκρατουμένῃ 562.c πόλει ἀκούσαις ἂν ὡς ἔχει τε κάλλιστον καὶ διὰ ταῦτα ἐν μόνῃ ταύτῃ ἄξιον οἰκεῖν ὅστις φύσει ἐλεύθερος. Λέγεται γὰρ δή, ἔφη, καὶ πολὺ τοῦτο τὸ ῥῆμα. ᾿Αρ' οὖν, ἦν δ' ἐγώ, ὅπερ ἦα νυνδὴ ἐρῶν, ἡ τοῦ τοιούτου ἀπληστία καὶ ἡ τῶν ἄλλων ἀμέλεια καὶ ταύτην τὴν πολιτείαν μεθίστησίν τε καὶ παρασκευάζει τυραννίδος δεηθῆναι; Πῶς; ἔφη.

Isocrates, freedom degenerated into lawlessness; according to Plato it is the essence of democracy—a democracy, however, which prepares the way for dictatorship. In both cases liberty, which they describe as excessive in skeptical or even scornful terms, refers to the political status of the individual citizen. They do not discuss here the freedom from foreign rule which the Greeks maintained for themselves by defeating Persia. Of this they naturally approved. Isocrates was an enthusiastic enemy of Persia, and the fourth century is rich in texts celebrating freedom from foreign domination.[64] For Plato, in the *Laws,* Greece was saved by its victories over Persia. This represented a consensus.[65] However, the expressions used are "saving Greece" (τὴν Ἑλλάδα σῶσαι) and "the salvation of the Greeks" (τῆς σωτηρίας τοῖς Ἕλλησι). Greek liberty, personal or collective, is not mentioned.[66]

It will be relevant, en passant, to mention two of the other states that decided not to support the Greek resistance to Persia: Argos remained neutral because of her conflict with Sparta (Herodotus, 7.148–152). In fact the inhabitants declared themselves willing to participate if Sparta agreed to a thirty-year truce and if they were given joint command of the Greek army together with Sparta. When the latter was turned down in this form, they declared that they "could not suffer the insolence of the Lacedaemonians and rather than suffer that, they would be ruled by the barbarians."[67] This, then, is a case where a state remained neutral for clearly opportunistic reasons. To be ruled by barbarians was undesirable indeed, but there were worse things. The conflict with the Spartan neighbors was deemed more threatening to survival than a possible Persian conquest. The failure of Corcyra to participate in the Greek struggle is similarly instructive. The Corcyraeans promised to join the struggled to so, declaring: "the destruction of Greece they could not allow to happen, for if Greece fell, they themselves would be enslaved the next day" (7.168).[68] They then sent ships which kept their distance while the war continued, for purely opportunistic reasons, according to Herodotus, who describes this as a particularly crude form of hypocrisy, given the gap between rhetoric and actual behavior. Finally, the Cretans allowed themselves to be persuaded by the oracle at Delphi to keep their distance, the arguments being once again entirely opportunistic (7.169). If we see the reasons why several states decided not to support the Greeks, we

[64] As observed by Ostwald, "Freedom and the Greeks," 60. See note 97 for references in fourth-century orators to the Persian Wars of the fifth century; note 98 for references to conflict with other Greek states, and note 99 for passages where "freedom of the Greeks" or "of Greece" is invoked against Philip of Macedon; note 100 for Greek freedom as the rallying cry for Philip's campaign against Persia.

[65] Plato *Leges* 706b: A matter of disagreement in the dialogue between the Cretan and the Athenian is the relative importance of the sea battles and those on land. The Athenian is attacking everything to do with the fleet, naval power, and the men who served in the navy.

[66] See 562d, where democracy is represented as leading to excessive liberty: ἆρ᾽ οὐκ ἀνάγκη ἐν τοιαύτῃ πόλει ἐπὶ πᾶν τὸ τῆς ἐλευθερίας ἰέναι;

[67] Herodotus, 7.149: Οὕτω δή οἱ Ἀργεῖοί φασι οὐκ ἀνασχέσθαι τῶν Σπαρτιητέων τὴν πλεονεξίην, ἀλλ᾽ ἑλέσθαι μᾶλλον ὑπὸ τῶν βαρβάρων ἄρχεσθαι ἤ τι ὑπεῖξαι Λακεδαιμονίοισι·

[68] Herodotus, 7.168: φράζοντες ὡς οὔ σφι περιοπτέη ἐστὶ ἡ Ἑλλὰς ἀπολλυμένη· ἢν γὰρ σφαλῇ, σφεῖς γε οὐδὲν ἄλλο ἢ δουλεύσουσι τῇ πρώτῃ τῶν ἡμερέων·

may at least consider the possibility that many others, who did do so, were similarly driven by equally practical motives.

Herodotus never suggests that he considered the Athenian support for the Ionian revolt in 499 a moral obligation, in spite of the fact that it was the *casus belli* for the war between Athens and Persia. Herodotus goes to a great deal of trouble to portray the Ionian revolt as the exclusive result of intrigues by treacherous tyrants (5.28–35).[69] The expulsion of tyrants from various cities by Aristagoras of Miletus was, according to Herodotus, a purely opportunistic act in his view (5.37f.). Before turning to Athens, Aristagoras attempted to persuade Cleomenes of Sparta to lend him support with arguments based on the assumption of greed on Cleomenes' part (5.49) and while Cleomenes' refusal once again had nothing to do with principle (5.50). When the Athenians subsequently agreed to support them, that was again in response to fraudulent arguments—"it is easier to deceive a multitude than one man," says Herodotus (5.97).[70] Aristagoras, who is consistently described as the tyrant of Miletus, calls the Ionians "slaves instead of free men" only because they lived under Persian, that is, under foreign rule. In Herodotus's opinion, the twenty ships which Athens sent in support of the Ionians "were the beginning of disaster for Greeks and barbarians."[71]

So far the evidence from Herodotus. It will be clear that, in Herodotus's view, those who resisted Persia fought for their political independence. He does not suggest that this was a battle for any other spiritual value, for personal liberty or any of the other moral ideals which the modern scholarship claim he wishes to convey. Moreover, there is no support for the claim that Herodotus sees this as a war between West and East. He does not disparage Persia at all, but sees the Greek victory as one achieved in spite of the immense power of the enemy. It is interesting to note that Plutarch's essay against Herodotus contains an extensive attack on the author's sympathy for barbarians. He is a "barbarophile."[72] This, according to Plutarch, shows in his positive attitude towards the Egyptians: "He says there is a strong sense of religion and justice amongst all Egyptians."[73] As an example of his excessive appreciation of the Persians, Plutarch writes: "he says that the Persians learnt 'sexual intercourse with boys'

[69] See Walser, *Hellas und Iran*, 28 with references in note 67.

[70] For Aristagoras's mission as a case of "kinship diplomacy," see Christopher Jones, *Kinship Diplomacy in the Ancient World* (1999), 25f. Herodotus, 7.150, also says that there were reports claiming that Xerxes sent an embassy to Argos with arguments based on the kinship between Persia and Argos.

[71] 5.97.3: Αὗται δὲ αἱ νέες ἀρχὴ κακῶν ἐγένοντο Ἕλλησί τε καὶ βαρβάροισι. It is a peculiarity of many works on ancient history that the authors do not make it clear whether they are paraphrasing ancient sources or actually agree with them. For instance: Stewart Flory, *The Archaic Smile of Herodotus* (Detroit, 1987), 146: The Ionians "do not possess sufficient self-discipline to tolerate military training let alone endure the rigors of combat (6.12) and not even the threat of enslavement moves them." Is this Herodotus's opinion according to Flory or Flory himself?

[72] Plutarch, *The Malice of Herodotus (De Malignitate Herodoti)*, introduction, trans., and comm. by A. J. Bowen (Warminster, 1992), 12/857a–18/858e.

[73] Loc. cit.: καὶ πᾶσιν Αἰγυπτίοις ὁσιότητα πολλὴν καὶ δικαιοσύνην μαρτυρήσας,. Plutarch refers here to Herodotus 2.37.1 and 65.1. See Bowen's comments on all this.

from the Greeks."[74] Plutarch rejects this assertion by noting the Persians practiced castration "before they ever saw the Aegean." Whatever Plutarch might have meant when he used this argument,[75] these are the only issues related to realities of Herodotus's own time. The rest of Plutarch's quarrels with Herodotus are based on the interpretation and presentation of myths or distant history. Admittedly, this is only a minor part of Plutarch's criticism of the historian. The essence of his attack rests on Herodotus's presumed anti-Greek bias.

We must now consider the evidence from other fifth-century texts. One problematic document of this century which requires brief mention is the so-called Decree of Themistocles, found on a marble stele at Damala (ancient Troizen). Its lettering dates it to the end of the fourth century or the beginning of the third, but it purports to be a text of the decree ordering mobilization in 480 for the Athenian navy before the battles of Salamis and Artemisium in 480 B.C., as proposed by Themistocles.[76] Significant for our topic are lines 12–18: "all other Athenians and foreigners of military age shall embark on the two hundred ships prepared for this and fight the barbarian for their own freedom and that of the other Greeks with the Lacedaemonians, Corinthians, Aeginetans and and the others who are prepared to share the danger."[77] If these lines were indeed contained in the original decree, then this is additional evidence that the freedom of Athens and the other Greeks was the expressed war aim at the time of the wars itself. If this is the case, this could still be taken to mean freedom from being ruled by non-Greeks rather than individual freedom vis-à-vis the state.[78]

We are on firmer ground with Aeschylus's play *Persae*, produced in 472, which is the earliest extant literary work relating to the subject of the wars between Persia and Greece.[79] The first chorus describes the Persian host that has

---

[74] παισὶ μίσγεσθαι παρ' Ἑλλήνων μαθόντας; cf. Herodotus 1.135: καὶ δὴ καὶ ἀπ' Ἑλλήνων μαθόντες παισὶ μίσγονται. Herodotus mentions this as an example of his statement that the Persians easily adopt foreign customs, such as the Median dress and the Egyptian breastplate.

[75] Castration and homosexuality are also confused, or associated, in Juvenal, *Sat.* 2.111–6, discussed below.

[76] R. Meiggs and D. Lewis, *A Selection of Greek Historical Inscriptions to the End of the Fifth Century BC* (revised ed., Oxford, 1988), no. 23, with references to the extensive literature about this text and its degree of authenticity.

[77] τοὺς δὲ ἄλλους Ἀθη[ναίους ἅπαντας καὶ τοὺς ξέ]νους τοὺς ἡβῶντας εἰσβαίνειν ε[ἰς τὰς ἑτοιμασθ]ε[ί]σ[α]ς διακοσίας ναῦς καὶ ἀμύνεσ[θαι] τ[ὸμ βάρβαρον ὑπὲρ τῆ]ς ἐλευθερίας τῆς τε ἑαυτῶν [καὶ τῶν ἄλλων Ἑλλήνων] μετὰ Λακεδαιμονίων καὶ Κοριν[θίων καὶ Αἰγινητῶν] καὶ τῶν ἄλλων τῶμ βουλομένω[ν] κοινω[νήσειν τοῦ κινδύνο]υ· Precisely these lines have been accused of representing fourth-century rhetoric. However, Meiggs and Lewis refer for comparable formulation to Herodotus 5.64.2, 7.144.3, 178.2.

[78] Ostwald, "Freedom and the Greeks," 50, also points out that there is good evidence that cults of Zeus Eleutherios (guarantor of freedom) were established in several Greek states to celebrate the victory over the Persians.

[79] See, extensively, E. Hall, *Inventing the Barbarian*, chap. 2, with particular attention to the *Persae*, where the play is read along lines rather different from the views briefly indicated here. See, for instance, p. 67: "the cultural messages being disseminated: order over irrationality, democracy over tyranny, Hellas over barbarism." See also her edition of the play: E. Hall, *Aeschylus' Persae* (Warminster, 1996). For a different view: Walser, *Hellas und Iran*, 5: "Jeder unbefangene

departed for Greece. It contains an impressive description of the main components of the army. The commanders are "marshals of the Persians, kings themselves, yet vassals of the Great King, they press on, commanders of a vast host,
skilled to manage bow and steed, formidable of aspect and terrible in battle
through the valiant resolve of their souls" (23–28). The description continues in
this vein, emphasizing the wealth and power of the force. The adjective "rich in
gold" (πολύχρυσος) recurs four times. Some of the constituent peoples, such as
the Lydians, are also described as particularly wealthy[80] and their chariots are
terrible to see. The emphasis on the wealth of the Persians and Lydians here is
not, as in later texts, intended to convey a sense of weakness and softness—that
would make no sense on the part of a chorus consisting of Persian elders—but
it impresses on the audience the vast power of the army. Asia is mentioned
frequently—it is mighty, rich, and populous. The king himself, "the raging
leader of populous Asia drives his godlike flock against every land in two
movements: an equal of the gods, a hero of golden origin, he trusts in his
stalwart and stubborn commanders both on land and on the sea."[81]

The Persian army is terrifying: "No-one is so renowned for valour that they
can withstand such a huge flood of men, and ward them off with sturdy defences. A sea-wave is invincible. The Persians' army is irresistible and its people are brave of heart."[82] It is an army expert in the storming of cities. Their aim
is "to cast the yoke of slavery upon Hellas."[83] For the Greeks the issue is clear:
"On, you sons of Hellas! Free your native land, free your children, your wives,
the sanctuaries of your fathers' gods and the tombs of your ancestors. Now you
battle for all."[84]

Then there is Queen Atossa's remarkable dream, which I will not venture to

---

Leser des Aischylos wird zugeben, dass der Mitkämpfer von Marathon und Salamis seinen Gegnern
kein verächtliches Urteil zollt." Earlier J. Jüthner, *Hellenen und Barbaren* (Leipzig, 1923), 18f.
takes a position in the middle: the Persians, he says, are described with great sympathy and almost
like Greeks, yet the contrast between the slavishness of the Barbarian and Hellenic love of freedom
is already present. For another perspective: A. J. Podlecki, *The Political Background of Aeschylean
Tragedy* (Ann Arbor, 1966), 12f., who emphasizes the contemporary Athenian political situation.
The struggle between Cimon, son of Miltiades, the hero of Marathon and Themistocles, the architect of the victory at Salamis, explains the emphasis, in the *Persae* on Salamis, to the exclusion of
other victories in those wars. See also Georges, *Barbarian Asia and the Greek Experience*, chapter
4. Note also Marie Simon, "Die Anschauungen der Antike vom Morgenland," *Wissenschaftliche
Zeitschrift der Humboldt-Universität zu Berlin, gesellschaftliche-und sprachwissenschaftliche Reihe*
9 (1959/60), 139–143, which, however, is brief and imprecise.

[80] ἁβροδιαίτων δ' ἕπεται Λυδῶν ὄχλος, Xenophanes, in the sixth century, already describes the
Lydians as wealthy in comparable terms: F3B (Diels Kranz) = F3 (West) = 3 (Lesher):
ἁβροσύνας . . . παρὰ Λυδῶν.

[81] *Persae* 73–80 (trans. E. Hall, apart from 1.80): πολυάνδρου δ' Ἀσίας θούριος ἄρχων | ἐπὶ
πᾶσαν χθόνα ποιμανόριον θεῖον ἐλαύνει | διχόθεν, πεζονόμοις ἔκ τε θαλάσσας | ὀχυροῖσι
πεποιθὼς | στυφελοῖς ἐφέταις, χρυ | σογόνου γενεᾶς ἰσόθεος φώς.

[82] 87–92: δόκιμος δ' οὔτις ὑποστὰς | μεγάλῳ ῥεύματι φωτῶν | ὀχυροῖς ἕρκεσιν εἴργειν | ἄμ
αχον κῦμα θαλάσσας· | ἀπρόσοιστος γὰρ ὁ Περσᾶν | στρατὸς ἀλκίφρων τε λαός.

[83] 50: ζυγὸν ἀμφιβαλεῖν δούλιον Ἑλλάδι,

[84] 402–405: Ὦ παῖδες Ἑλλήνων, ἴτε, | ἐλευθεροῦτε πατρίδ', ἐλευθεροῦτε δὲ | παῖδας, γυν
αῖκας, θεῶν τε πατρῴων ἕδη, | θήκας τε προγόνων· νῦν ὑπὲρ πάντων ἀγών.

explain: "Two beautifully dressed women seemed to appear to me, one decked out in Persian robes, the other in Doric clothing. In stature they were conspicuously larger than people are today, and they were faultlessly lovely; they were sisters of the same kin. One of them lived in her fatherland, Greece, which she had obtained by lot, the other in the land of the barbarians."[85] The Greeks fought for the freedom of their fatherland, children, wives, native temples, and the graves of their fathers. That is to say: they were fighting foreigners to keep all that was theirs, they fought for liberty in the sense of "exemption or release from captivity, bondage, or slavery." There is nothing in Aeschylus comparable to the words which Euripides attributes to Helen (dated 412), exiled in Egypt: "A slave am I, the daughter of free parents, for among the barbarians all are slaves except one."[86] There is no evidence that their aim was individual liberty in the sense of "natural liberty," that is "the state in which every one is free to act as he thinks fit, subject only to the laws of nature."[87] Even in Aristotle's *Politics* the concept of liberty is complex.[88] It appears there first in contrast with slavery,[89] a contrast which applies both to individuals and to states. Individuals or states are free when they have no master.[90] This is a general view of liberty, unconnected with political liberty. The conceptual connection between political liberty and democracy is far more ambiguous. Aristotle claims that the democracies define liberty wrongly.[91] However, fourth-century disagreements about the merits of democracy should not concern us here, although it is worth noting that the equation of freedom with political liberty was considered problematic in the fourth century, and will therefore not have been evident to fifth-century authors writing about the Persian war.

There is no evidence that in fifth-century Greece Persia was seen as inferior: the Persians were indeed barbarians, but, as shown in the work of Hall, the meaning of the term "barbaros" itself changed, like the Latin term *superstitio*. In the early fifth century a *barbaros* was not inferior. There was thus a sense that this was a battle against a mighty foreigner whose aim was subjugation, but

---

[85] 181–7 (trans. E. Hall, 1.185 adapted): ἐδοξάτην μοι δύο γυναῖκ᾽ εὐείμονε, ἡ μὲν πέπλοισι Περσικοῖς ἠσκημένη, ἡ δ᾽ αὖτε Δωρικοῖσιν, εἰς ὄψιν μολεῖν, μεγέθει τε τῶν νῦν ἐκπρεπεστάτα πολύ, κάλλει τ᾽ ἀμώμω, καὶ κασιγνήτα γένους ταὐτοῦ· πάτραν δ᾽ ἔναιον ἡ μὲν Ἑλλάδα κλήρῳ λαχοῦσα γαῖαν, ἡ δὲ βάρβαρον. Cf. Hall, p.124, on the phenomenon of Greece and Persia as sisters.

[86] Euripides, *Helen* 275f.: δουλή καθέστηκ᾽ οὖσ᾽ ἐλευθέρων ἄπο· τὰ βαρβάρων γὰρ δοῦλα πάντα πλὴν ἑνός.

[87] Definitions 1a and 2b in *OED*². See above, p. for the question of personal and political freedom in this period.

[88] J. Barnes, "Aristotle and Political Liberty," in G. Patzig (ed.), *Aristoteles' "Politik,"* 249–263; R. Sorabji, "Comments on J. Barnes," ib., 264–276.

[89] Aristotle, *Pol.* 1253b4: οἰκία δὲ τέλειος ἐκ δούλων καὶ ἐλευθέρων. Cf. Newman, 2.131f. with relevant references.

[90] Barnes, op. cit., 253, referring to 1310b, 1327b, 1328a.

[91] 1310a, 28–36: αἴτιον δὲ τούτου ὅτι κακῶς ὁρίζονται τὸ ἐλεύθερον. Cf. Barnes, 253–6.

there is no differentiation between subjugation by westerners or northerners. The Orient is not mentioned[92] and in the *Prometheus* Asia is called "holy."[93]

The image of non-Greeks in Greek tragedy is the subject of Edith Hall's study,[94] which formulates rather different conclusions on some matters that are relevant here, notably in the statement cited at the beginning of this chapter.[95] In Hall's view, "The opposite of barbarian despotism is not a vague model of the generalized Greek city-state, but quite specifically democracy, and rhetoric in praise of democracy was an Athenian invention" (16). The present book is based on explicit statements in ancient prose, while Hall interprets Greek, or rather, Athenian tragedy which expresses views only via actors and chorus. These are undoubtedly an important source for the reconstruction of the contemporary social and religious ideas. Yet their interpretation necessarily results only in conclusions based on implicit judgments expressed on the stage. These are expressed by actors playing the roles of figures from Greek mythology. Since the material is so unequal, it will be best only to make a few general observations.

It seems possible that a review of the material discussed by Hall would show a marked development over time. In other words, it would be worth considering whether some of the views expressed by Hall are truer for Euripides' later work than for Aeschylus's earlier tragedies, for this is precisely the period which, in my view, saw a marked change in the opinions of Greeks about Persians.[96] Thus

---

[92] Needless to say, there is no lack of commentators who sought precisely this in the play and thus duly found it; for instance, W. Kranz, *Stasimon: Untersuchungen zu Form und Gehalt der griechischen Tragödie* (1933, repr. 1988), 77f.: "Allein es wäre Verkennung, ja Verfälschung, wenn man glauben wollte, dass diese verstehende Liebe zu fremdem Volkstum das Hochgefühl des Hellenen und Atheners Aischylos, des Kämpfers von Marathon, herabgemindert hätte. Grundgedanke seiner Seele ist und bleibt vielmehr, dass das Hellenische das Freie, zugleich aber auch das Zucht— und Massvolle, das Formende und Begrenzende ist, das Ausserhellenische dagegen das Sklavische, aber zugleich das Masslose, Formen Sprengende . . . die weiche, unterwürfige Art des persischen Volkes und Königs zerbricht an der Härte hellenischer Form und Kraft." Kranz reads into the play all the usual fourth-century stereotypes about Persians and phrases it in the terms of ideological German of the 1930s. He interprets the *Supplices* and *Septem* in comparable terms. Alles Weichliche, Schmeichelnde, Erniedrigende ist etwas Barbarisches (p.78). See the introduction to the edition of the *Persae* by E. Hall, with a view quite different from the one here proposed, and references to other modern authors.

[93] *Prometheus* 411f. ἁγνᾶς ’Ασίας ἕδος. If the play is not by Aeschylus, this still is an authentic line by someone else, whether it is Euphorion or not.

[94] E. Hall, *Inventing the Barbarian*.

[95] Hall, chapter 1, discusses the non-Greek world as seen in archaic literature before the Persian wars and concludes that in this period there is no marked polarization and contradiction between Greek and non-Greek found in the literature. C. Tuplin, "Greek Racism? Observations on Greek Ethnic Prejudice," 54–57, expresses reservations about this conclusion.

[96] The opposite view is advanced by Robert Schlaifer, "Greek Theories of Slavery from Homer to Aristotle," *HSCP* 47 (1936), 165–204, at 169. Schlaifer claims that Euripides "for dramatic reasons often lets his characters express the opposite view, [but] it is clear that his own sentiments are shown in the fragment Frg. 902 N²: τὸν ἐσθλὸν ἄνδρα, κἂν ἑκὰς ναίῃ χθονός, κἂν μήποτ’ ὄσσοις εἰσίδω, κρίνω φίλον. cf. 777 and 1047." I cannot see how we can be so certain that a fragment from a dramatic work, cited out of context, reflects the poet's own sentiments.

we find that the contrast between free Greeks and slavish barbarians occurs as a theme in one of Euripides' last plays, *Iphigeneia at Aulis* (Agamemnon): "no, it is Hellas, for whom I must sacrifice you whether I will or not; to this necessity I bow my head; for her freedom must be preserved, as far as any help of yours daughter, or mine can go; or they, who are the sons of Hellas, must be pillaged of their wives by barbarian robbery."[97] And later Iphigeneia herself: "And it is right, mother, that Hellenes should rule barbarians, but not barbarians Hellenes, those being slaves, while these are free."[98] In the first passage Menelaus suggests that the recapture of Helen is for the Greeks a matter of freedom or slavery for the Greeks. If the Greeks cannot go on their expedition, then the barbarians will make a habit of stealing Greek wives. Whatever the logic of the statement, it is clear that there is here an unbreakable link between freedom / slavery and Greeks / barbarians. In the second passage, the assumption is that Greeks are free, while barbarians are slaves and therefore it is taken for granted that the former should rule the latter. This is a combination of three ideas: the unquestioned assumption of the superiority of Greek over barbarian, the use of this idea for a doctrine of imperialism, which itself is linked with a doctrine of natural slavery.[99]

When Hall argues that Greek tragedy consistently and from the start draws a contrast between Greek democracy and barbarian despotism, it would follow that Athenian audiences were thus offered an Athenian projection, not Greek reality, which they accepted. Most Greek states were not democracies and did not want to be. The common ground between Greeks was that one should live in *poleis* with a proper constitution of its own, not that this should be a democracy in the Athenian sense.

Contemporary epigrams for the fallen express various sentiments: the Spartan dead at Thermopylae are praised for their courage, discipline, and obedience.[100] We are certainly not told that they fought for cultural freedom of the west. Athenian epigrams are slightly different in tone. They mention valor and glory rather than obedience. The fallen had kept all of Greece from seeing the day of slavery.[101] Panhellenic merit rather than discipline is the keynote. At Plataea

---

[97] Euripides, *Iphigeneia at Aulis* (trans. E. P. Coleridge), 1272–1275: ἐλευθέραν γὰρ δεῖ νιν ὅσον ἐν σοί, τέκνον, / κἀμοὶ γενέσθαι, μηδὲ βαρβάρων ὕπο / Ἕλληνας ὄντας λέκτρα συλᾶσθαι βίαι.

[98] Ibid., 1400–1401: βαρβάρων δ' Ἕλληνας ἄρχειν εἰκός, ἀλλ' οὐ βαρβάρους / μῆτερ, Ἑλλήνων· τὸ μὲν γὰρ δοῦλον, οἱ δ' ἐλεύθεροι. Cf. comments by Walter Stockert, *Euripides, Iphigenie in Aulis*. Band 2, *Detailkommentar* (Vienna 1992), 591, with references to Euripides, *Andromacha* 665f.: βάρβαροι δ' ὄντες γένος Ἕλλησιν ἄρξουσ'; frg. 719: Ἕλληνες ὄντες βαρβάροις δουλεύσομεν; *Helen* 276: τὰ βαρβάρων γὰρ δοῦλα πάντα πλὴν ἑνός.

[99] Hence Aristotle, *Politics* 1252b, where he expounds the doctrine of natural slavery, cites this line of Euripides, as noted above, chapter 2.

[100] Herodotus 7.228; D.L.Page, *Epigrammata Graeca* (Oxford, 1975), Fr. 6; cf. J. P. Barron, "The liberation of Greece," *CAH* iv, 2d ed. (1988), 592–622, esp. 619.

[101] ἡελλά[δα μ]ὲ πᾶσαν δούλιο[ν ἐμαρ ἰδεν]. R. Meiggs and D. Lewis, *A Selection of Greek Historical Inscriptions to the End of the Fifth Century BC* (revised ed., Oxford, 1988), no. 26; Frs. 8–9; *Anthologia Palatina* 7.251, 253 ap. P. Waltz, *Anthologie Grecque* I (Paris, 1960). Cf. Barron,

ceremonies commemorating the battle of 479 were instituted and maintained for centuries. The Spartan leader Pausanias offered to Zeus the Deliverer (Διὶ ἐλευθερίῳ) on the *agora* of Plataea.[102] A new altar was set up for this god.[103] Plutarch says these offerings were still made in his day by the Plataeans, whereby "the Hellenic council assembles in Plataea, and the Plataeans sacrifice to Zeus the Deliverer for victory."[104] The chief magistrate of the town pours a libation, saying: "I drink to the men who died for the freedom of the Greeks."[105] Similar, less famous cults were established after Persian Wars in other cities— in Athens, Himera, and Troezen.[106] Again, there is no difficulty in interpreting this as meaning freedom from foreign domination. In fact, the concept is first attested in poetry of the sixth century. In a fragment of a song attributed to Anacreon (born c. 570 B.C.), a certain Alcimon addresses the memory of Aristocleides, "who had lost his young life fighting to avert slavery from his country."[107]

Pindar, from pro-Persian Thebes, has complex feelings about the Greek victory over Persia. The first Pythian Ode, for Hieron of Aetna, winner of the chariot race in 470, mentions, in the fourth antistrophe and epode, the Battle of Himera (480) and that of Cyme (474). The implication of the passage is that Hieron's contributions to Greek freedom are as great as those of the mainland Greeks at their battles of Salamis and Plataea: "I pray thee, Cronos' son, let no Phoenician | or Tuscan war-cry stir from home, who saw | Their pride of ships wrecked before Cumae—| That ruin laid upon them by the leader | Of Syracusan warriors, who hurled | Their flower of youth from their swift ships of war | Down to the ocean wave, and saved Hellas | From grievous slavery etc."[108]

---

op. cit., 621f.; K.-W. Welwei, "Die 'Marathon'-Epigramme von der Athenischen Agora," in *Polis und Arché: Kleine Schriften zu Gesellschafts- und Herrschaftsstrukturen in der griechischen Welt*, Mischa Meier (ed.) (Stuttgart, 2000), 180–190. Cf. *IG* 7.53: Ἑλλάδι καὶ Μεγαρεῦσιν ἐλεύθερον ἆμαρ ἀέξειν | ἱέμενοι θανάτου μοῖταν ἐδεξάμεθα. See also Ostwald, "Freedom and the Greeks," 49.

[102] As claimed by the Plataeans in a speech they made in 429, attributed to them by Thucydides 2.71.2

[103] Plutarch, *Aristides* 20.4; *de Herodoti malignitate* 873b; Pausanias 9.2.5–7 and cf. *Anthologia Palatina* 6.50 for the verses said to have been inscribed on it.

[104] Plutarch, *Aristides* 19.7:

[105] Plutarch, *Aristides* 21; cf. Thuc. 3.58; Diodorus Siculus 11.29.1; cf. A. E. Raubitschek, "The Covenant of Plataea," *TAPA* 91 (1960), 178–183.

[106] Ostwald, "Freedom and the Greeks," 50 and note 48; K. Raaflaub, *Die Entdeckung der Freiheit* (Munich, 1985), 125–135. The cult at Troezen was in honor of Helios Eleutherios.

[107] ὤλεσας δ' ἥβην ἀμύνων πατρίδος δουλήιην. D. L. Page, *Poetae Melici Graeci* (Oxford, 1962), 419 (*Anth. Pal.* 13.4); M. L. West, *Iambi et elegi Graeci ante Alexandrum Cantati*, vol. 2 (Oxford, 1972), 32, iamb. 2; cf. Ostwald, "Freedom and the Greeks," 49: this is "the earliest surviving example of the idea that a country is "enslaved" when it is occupied by an alien power; it does not yet express the idea that a country not so occupied is 'free'."

[108] Pindar, *Pyth.* 1.71–5 (trans. G. S. Conway in G. S. Conway and Richard Stoneman, *The Odes and Selected Fragments* [London 1997]): λίσσομαι νεῦσον, Κρονίων, ἥμερον ὄφρα κατ' οἶκον ὁ Φοίνιξ ὁ Τυρσανῶν τ' ἀλαλατὸς ἔχῃ, ναυσίστονον ὕβριν ἰδὼν τὰν πρὸ Κύμας, οἷα Συρακοσίων ἀρχῷ δαμασθέντες πάθον, ὠκυπόρων ἀπὸ ναῶν ὅ σφιν ἐν πόντῳ βάλεθ' ἁλικίαν, Ἑλλάδ' ἐξέλκων βαρείας δουλίας. Hieron had "won . . . such honour as no man in all Hellas has reaped

Freedom, in this poem, refers to an absence of foreign rule and has nothing to do with democracy. Earlier, Pindar celebrates Hieron's foundation of the city of Aetna. This city replaced Catana and Naxos, which he depopulated not long after 480. To the new city he brought colonists from the Peloponnesos and from Syracuse and gave it "the laws of Hyllus," in other words, an aristocratic or oligarchic constitution. "Come then, | For Aetna's king | Let us unfold a song to charm his soul. | For him has Hieron founded his fair city | In freedom built of heaven's will, | Within the pattern of the laws of Hyllus;"[109] Obviously, freedom here does not represent democracy. The eighth Isthmian Ode was composed for Cleandrus of Aegina (478), who won victories at both the Isthmian and the Nemean Games. The Persian Wars are referred to as "great sorrow," because Thebes, where the Nemean Games took place, supported the Persian side, while Aegina was a fierce opponent of Persia: "I too, though heavy grief weighs on my heart, | Am bidden to invoke the glorious Muse. | From great sorrow released let us not languish | Bereft of victors' crowns, nor brood upon our woes."[110] Pindar alludes to the Theban disaster as the "stone of Tantalus" (10:Ταντάλου λίθον) and as "treacherous years, twisting life's track," but continues: "Yet even these things can be healed for mortals, so there be freedom; a man must keep good hope."[111] Freedom here is obviously freedom from Persian rule, but probably also freedom from suspicion and hostility among the Greeks themselves.[112]

Pindar's eighth Pythian Ode (446) opens with lines often discussed: "Peace, goddess of friendly intent, | Daughter of Justice, you who make cities great, | Holding the supreme keys of counsel and of wars—."[113] The reason for the opening invocation of Peace (ἡσυχία) is not quite certain, but usually assumed to be connected either with civil strife or with the presumed end of the

ever now" (47–49). L. R. Farnell, *Critical Commentary to the Works of Pindar* (London, 1931, repr. 1965), 114: "A passage of some historical value, but hardly in his best style."

[109] *Pyth.* 1.60–63 (trans. G. S. Conway): ἔπειτ' Αἴτνας Βασιλεῖ φίλιον ἐξεύρωμεν ὕμνον· τῷ πόλιν κείναν θεοδμάτῳ σὺν ἐλευθερίᾳ Ὑλλίδος στάθμας Ἱέρων ἐν νόμοις ἔκτισσε. Cf. Farnell, *Commentary*, 113: "The Lycurgean constitution, of which Hieron may have imposed the shadow upon his new city, might be euphemistically called ἐλευθερία, as the power of the king was constitutionally limited."

[110] *Isth.* 8.5–8: τῷ καὶ ἐγώ, καίπερ ἀχνύμενος θυμόν, αἰτέομαι χρυσέαν καλέσαι Μοῖσαν. ἐκ μεγάλων δὲ πενθέων λυθέντες μήτ' ἐν ὀρφανίᾳ πέσωμεν στεφάνων, μήτε κάδεα θεράπευε· Cf. Christopher Carey, *A Commentary of Five Odes of Pindar, Pythian 2, Pythian 9, Nemean 1, Nemean 7, Isthmian 8* (Salem, NH, 1981); for the historical background: 184f. Cf. J. H. Finley Jr., "Pindar and the Persian Invasion," *HSCPh* 63 (1958), 121–132.

[111] *Isth.* 8.14–17: δόλιος γὰρ αἰὼν ἐπ' ἀνδράσι κρέμαται, ἑλίσσων βίου πόρον· ἰατὰ δ' ἐστὶ βροτοῖς σύν γ' ἐλευθερίᾳ καὶ τά. χρὴ δ' ἀγαθὰν ἐλπίδ' ἀνδρὶ μέλειν.

[112] Cf. Finley, op. cit., p.128.

[113] *Pyth.*8.1: Φιλόφρον Ἡσυχία, Δίκας ὦ μεγιστόπολι θύγατερ, βουλᾶν τε καὶ πολέμων ἔχοισα κλαῖδας ὑπερτάτας. Cf. Farnell, *Commentary*, 192, observes that Pindar is the first to personify Ἡσυχία in Greek literature; I. L. Pfeijffer, *The Aeginetan Odes of Pindar: A Commentary on Nemean V, Nemean III & Pythian VIII* (Leiden, 1999); for the meaning of ἡσυχία, see pp. 426–429, 467; for the historical setting, 429–431. Pfeijffer places the poem against the background of the maritime rivalry between Athens and Aegina in those years and considers it likely that there was a threat of internal discord.

Persian Wars. The former, although not attested in other sources, is more likely, for ἡσυχία quiet, or peace, is the term Pindar used for absence of internal conflict, for instance in Frg. 109, addressed to the Thebans during the Persian War: "Let someone bring the community of the citizens into clear day by seeking out the bright light of noble-hearted Tranquillity, and take quarrelsome civil discord out of our hearts for it is a bringer of poverty and inimical to the rearing of children."[114] One of the Athenian victories over Persia is mentioned in one fragment: Frg. 76: O glorious Athens, | shining, violet-crowned, | celebrated in song, | bulwark of Hellas, | city of the gods . . . Frg. 77: when the sons of Athens | established the shining foundation of freedom.[115] "The shining foundation of freedom" in this fragment may again be assumed to be freedom from foreign rule without any connotation of personal or internal liberty.[116] Pindar, whose feelings must have been shared by those for whom he made his poetry, considered internal strife disastrous, and the Persian Wars were for him a source of grief because they engendered discord. Quite clearly they did not represent a struggle for the liberty of the individual, which did not interest him.

There can be no doubt when democratic ideology is first attested in Greek politics. This happened in connection with the Corcyraean affair in 427 B.C., as stated explicitly in highly critical terms by Thucydides: "The cause of all this was a desire for power fed by greed and ambition, and from that arose the passion among the contenders for victory. The leading men in the cities used respectable-seeming names on each side, claiming to value the political equality of democracy or the discipline of aristocracy, and while nominally cherishing public interests they in fact set them up as prizes."[117]

An intriguing impression emerges from a recent investigation of fifth-century

[114] Frg. 109: τὸ κοινόν τις ἀστῶν ἐν εὐδίᾳ τιθεὶς ἐρευνασάτω μεγαλάνορος Ἡσυχίας τὸ φαιδρὸν φάος, στάσιν ἀπὸ πραπίδος ἐπίκοτον ἀνελών, πενίας δότειραν, ἐχθρὰν κουροτρόφον. For ἡσυχία in this sense, cf. also Ol. 4.16.

[115] Dithyramb frgs. 76–7: ὦ ταὶ λιπαραὶ καὶ ἰοστέφανοι καὶ ἀοίδιμοι, Ἑλλάδος ἔρεισμα, κλειναὶ Ἀθᾶναι, δαιμόνιον πτολίεθρον. Dith.77 ὅθι παῖδες Ἀθαναίων ἐβάλοντο φαεννάν κρηπῖδ' ἐλευθερίας. The historical background may be the Athenian naval victory over the Persians at Artemisium, as indicated by Plutarch, who quotes frg. 77 (Them. 8.2.1; De glor. Athen. 350). It could also be later, after the Battle of Eion 475, for instance. Plutarch read frg. 77 as part of the same dithyramb as that to which frg. 76 belonged; cf. Farnell, Commentary, 418. Farnell also notes that the phrase κρηπῖδ' ἐλευθερίας implies the figure of a temple and a half-personification of ἐλευθερία.

[116] As observed by Ostwald, Oligarchia, 15f. regarding Pyth. 2.86–8, Pindar's rare mention of "tyrants" and "tyranny" suggests that these terms are taken as value-neutral. No opprobrium is attached to "tyranny," which refers unequivocally to one-man rule.

[117] Thucydides 3.82.8: οἱ γὰρ ἐν ταῖς πόλεσι προστάντες μετὰ ὀνόματος ἑκάτεροι εὐπρεποῦς, πλήθους τε ἰσονομίας πολιτικῆς καὶ ἀριστοκρατίας σώφρονος προτιμήσει, τὰ μὲν κοινὰ λόγῳ θεραπεύοντες ἆθλα ἐποιοῦντο. P. J. Rhodes (ed., trans., and comm.), Thucydides, History III (Warminster, 1994), trans. on p. 135, comm. ad loc., p. 238: "The contenders emphasized the aspect of their preferred constitution which was stressed by those who claimed that that was the best form of constitution, while what they actually wanted was a régime that would secure their own supremacy." Simon Hornblower, A Commentary on Thucydides vol. 1 (Oxford, 1991), 486, translates: "the one party professing to uphold equality before the law, the other the moderation of aristocratic government."

material culture: archaeology and iconography reveal a consistent pattern of Athenian receptivity to Achaemenid Persian culture.[118] "On analogy with the early modern European cultural phenomena of Chinoiserie and especially Türkerei, the response in classical Athens can be termed 'Perserie'."[119] The Perserie is then analyzed to evoke a diverse and complex response to Persian inspiration in various fields.

To sum up: attitudes towards Persia in the authors who wrote in the first half of the fifth century are oddly at variance with those ascribed to them as a matter of course by many scholars over the past century. Quite a few of the latter have a strong desire to read into those texts support for their own European sense of superiority, sometimes tainted with anti-eastern prejudices such as have been common ever since Europeans regularly traveled to the Ottoman Empire and described it as a backward and degenerate part of the world.[120] The former describe a war with a powerful enemy, led by strong monarchs, in which they were defending their political and economic independence. Those who claim that Herodotus wrote about a war between the moral values of the west against the tyranny of the east attribute to him a concept which was not his.[121] He certainly preferred to live in a *polis* with a proper constitution rather than a monarchy, let alone a tyranny. It is possible that he feared that the Greek way of life would be threatened if Persia conquered the mainland, although this clearly cannot as such be said of the Greek cities in Asia Minor which lived under Persian rule. However, he nowhere suggests that the allied Greeks (as distinct from the Athenians) were fighting Persia for the sake of democracy, let alone that Persia was resisted because it was an oriental power.

Herodotus and his contemporaries as well as later ancient authors divided the world into three parts: Europe, Asia, and Libya (2.16f.), not in two.[122] Thus, Herodotus and others found that there was much to celebrate in the Greek victory over the Persian invader, primarily the maintenance of independence for the Greek states. That Persia was a monarchy is recognized, but that was not the reason for resistance. Persia was a monarchy, but a very powerful one.

[118] Margaret C. Miller, *Athens and Persia: A Study in Cultural Receptivity* (Cambridge, 1997).
[119] Ibid., 1.
[120] To mention one of the most famous: C. F. Volney, *Voyage en Syrie et en Egypte pendant les années 1783, 1784, et 1785* (Paris, 1787). It should be added that Volney was no more impressed by contemporary Greece than he was by the Near East.
[121] Hartog, *Le miroir d'Hérodote* (1980), 213f., 329–345, suggests as an hypothesis that in Herodotus's work barbarians are invariably ruled either by monarchs or by despots except if they are nomads: "un pouvoir nomade est impensable." However, Hartog does not quite suggest that Herodotus sees the conflict between Persia and the Greeks in terms of a conflict between tyranny and individual freedom.
[122] As claimed, for instance, by H. Diller, 'Die Hellenen-Barbaren Antithese im Zeitalter der Perserkriege," in *Grecs et Barbares* Ent. Hardt 8, 39–68, at 58, where he argues that Herodotus is characterized by bipolarity: Asia (i.e., Persia) versus Europe (= Hellenes). This would be a peculiar view for a Hellene from Asia. The world was usually regarded as being divided into three parts or continents; see, e.g., Strabo 1.4.7 (c.65f.); Manilius 4.658–695; Pomponius Mela 1.9–24. Cf. R. Thomas, *Herodotus in Context*, 76–86.

There is no evidence in Greek sources of the first half of the fifth century for the view of many modern authors that Persia was seen as culturally or morally inferior, because it was a state ruled by a monarch. To put it differently: this book traces patterns of ethnic prejudice and proto-racism in Greco-Roman antiquity. In early fifth-century Greece there is no trace of this vis-à-vis Persia, in spite of the arguments by many contemporary scholars who ascribe such attitudes to the sources, mainly Herodotus. The focus on ethnic conflict, the entire complex of ideas about the cultural superiority of Greeks over Persians, or Europeans over Asiatics, is absent before the middle of the fifth century B.C. As seen in chapter 1, the concept of Europe versus Asia, hard as opposed to soft, poor to rich and all that implies is encountered first in the medical treatise *Airs, Waters, Places*, which is undated, but certainly later than Herodotus. We do not find it otherwise in the fifth century.

It is still possible to assert that the Greek victories over Persia were all that the modern authors, cited at the beginning of this chapter, claim them to have been: the salvation of Europe for freedom, civilization, and science; the victory of democracy, reason, and Greek culture over tyranny, irrationality, and barbarism, and so on. It must be admitted, however, that this is a modern assessment of the merits of the two powers and a modern assessment of the significance of the conflict. All the Greeks at the time claimed is that they were fighting against foreign rule.

This is not to assert that hostility towards the inhabitants of Asia is a recent phenomenon. It can be found in ancient literature, but in that of a later period, to which we now shall turn our attention.

THE FOURTH CENTURY: THE NEW SPIRIT

Authors writing after Herodotus are much fiercer about the opposition they see between Greeks and others. Gorgias is reported to have said that "Triumphs gained over barbarians demand victory hymns, those over Greeks dirges."[123] In his Olympic (408) he inserted the theme "barbarians," pleading against strife among the Greek cities and in favor of an attack on the land of the barbarians.[124] Lysias, too, is often described in the modern literature as favoring an attack on Persia. However, the surviving speeches only lament Greek discord and the resulting advantages to Persia. There is no suggestion that Lysias argued for a Persian expedition by Greek states.[125] In his funeral oration, composed sometime between 392 and 386, he recapitulates the wars fought by Athens and, in his references to the Persian Wars, it is striking how he tends to speak of "the barbarians from

[123] Diels-Kranz, Fr. 5b (Philostratus, *VS* 1.9.5): τὰ μὲν κατὰ τῶν βαρβάρων τρόπαια ὕμνους ἀπαιτεῖ τὰ δὲ κατὰ τῶν Ἑλλήνων θρήνους.
[124] Testimonia 1: στασιάζουσαν γὰρ τὴν Ἑλλάδα ὁρῶν ὁμονοίας ξύμβουλος αὐτοῖς ἐγένετο τρέπων ἐπὶ τοὺς βαρβάρους καὶ πείθων ἆθλα ποιεῖσθαι τῶν ὅπλων μὴ τὰς ἀλλήλων πόλεις, ἀλλὰ τὴν τῶν βαρβάρων χώραν.
[125] Lysias, *Olympic Oration* (Or. 33, 384 B.C.) and the *Epitaphios* (Or. 2) are the relevant texts.

Asia," of "the King of Asia" and of "Europe" rather than of "Persia" and of "Greece."¹²⁶ Thus we encounter here the concept first formulated in *Airs, Waters, Places*. Again and again Lysias proclaims that the Athenians have established freedom for Greece and, in most cases, he means freedom from foreign rule, but, as a secondary theme, he also introduces democracy in his praise of Athens.¹²⁷ The Athenians "compelled all to live as equals."¹²⁸

Later, Plato writes: " 'I say that the Greek people is its own and akin, but is strange and foreign to barbarians.' 'That is right.' 'Then when Greeks do battle with barbarians or barbarians with Greeks, we shall say that they are natural enemies and that such hostilities are to be called war. But when Greeks fight with Greeks, we shall say that they are natural friends and that in such circumstances Greece is sick and divided into factions and that such hostilities are to be called civil war (στάσις)' "¹²⁹ Plato wrote after the Peloponnesian war and was, therefore, more aware of the possible scale of fighting between the Greeks themselves. This is clear, too, from the *Menexenus*, where the sense is expressed that the Athenians felt that with Greeks they should wage war only until they gained a victory over them, . . . but that with barbarians they should war to the death, or until the destruction of the enemy in the full sense of the term (μέχρι διαφθορᾶς).¹³⁰

Herodotus and Plato may largely agree about the difference between internal

¹²⁶ Lysias, *Epitaphios* 21: ὁ τῆς Ἀσίας βασιλεύς . . . ἐλπίζων καὶ τὴν Εὐρώπην δουλώσεσθαι; 27: ὁ τῆς Ἀσίας βασιλεύς; 40, τῷ πλήθει τῷ τῆς Ἀσίας; 43, the Athenians "taught the barbarians from Asia that their courage was genuine and native born" (autochthonous, a significant concept, as seen above, in chapter 1): γνησίαν καὶ αὐτόχθονα τοῖς ἐκ τῆς Ἀσίας βαρβάροις τὴν αὑτῶν ἀρετὴν ἐπεδείξαντο; 47, they secured "a firm freedom for Europe": βέβαιον τὴν ἐλευθερίαν τῇ Εὐρώπῃ κατειργάσαντο. Cf. John Ziolkowski, "National and Other Contrasts in Athenian Funeral Orations," in H.A. Khan (ed.), *The Birth of the European Identity*, 1–35, with comments by J. Roy, ibid., 36–43. Ziolkowski, in his analysis of Athenian funeral orations, concludes that the funeral oration of Lysias is the first to bring out the polarity of Europe and Asia and the only one to emphasize this theme (p. 23). He observes: "One antithetical expression that does not appear (sc. in the funeral orations) is the convention, very common today, of speaking of East and West as representing two opposing worlds" (25). Roy, in his comments, p.38, notes that the reason for this is that the context of the *epitaphios* is military. "Barbarians are primarily the Persians, sometimes with their subjects, and they appear as military and political opponents." Little stress is therefore laid on their moral or cultural weakness.

¹²⁷ *Epitaphios* 18: πρῶτοι δὲ καὶ μόνοι ἐν ἐκείνῳ τῷ χρόνῳ ἐκβαλόντες τὰς παρὰ σφίσιν αὐτοῖς δυναστείας δημοκρατίαν κατεστήσαντο, ἡγούμενοι τὴν πάντων ἐλευθερίαν ὁμόνοιαν εἶναι μεγίστην,. Snell, *Lysias: Epitaphios* (1887), suggests that Plato, *Menex.* 238D may be a criticism on this. However, there is no need to assume that Plato, when he is critical of democracy, should be thinking of Lysias more than of any other adherent of the system.

¹²⁸ 56: ἀλλὰ τὸ ἴσον ἔχειν ἅπαντας ἀναγκάσαντες, see also 59–60; 61: ὑπὲρ τῆς δημοκρατίας στασιάσαντες.

¹²⁹ *Rep.* 470c–d: φημὶ γὰρ τὸ μὲν Ἑλληνικὸν γένος αὐτὸ αὑτῷ οἰκεῖον εἶναι καὶ συγγενές, τῷ δὲ βαρβαρικῷ ὀθνεῖόν τε καὶ ἀλλότριον. Καλῶς γε, ἔφη. Ἕλληνας μὲν ἄρα βαρβάροις καὶ βαρβάρους Ἕλλησι πολεμεῖν μαχομένους τε φήσομεν καὶ πολεμίους φύσει εἶναι, καὶ πόλεμον τὴν ἔχθραν ταύτην κλητέον· Ἕλληνας δὲ Ἕλλησιν, ὅταν τι τοιοῦτον δρῶσιν, φύσει μὲν φίλους εἶναι, νοσεῖν δ᾽ ἐν τῷ τοιούτῳ τὴν Ἑλλάδα καὶ στασιάζειν, καὶ στάσιν τὴν τοιαύτην ἔχθραν κλητέον. Cf. Plato, *Ep.* 8. 354A: φιλέλλην

¹³⁰ *Menex.* 242d: πρὸς μὲν τὸ ὁμόφυλον μέχρι νίκης δεῖν πολεμεῖν . . . πρὸς δὲ τοὺς βαρβάρους μέχρι διαφθορᾶς. Cf. for further parallels: V. Tsitsiridis, *Platons Menexenos* (1998), 308f.

and external conflict, but Herodotus nowhere goes so far as to say that war between Greeks and barbarians is necessary and natural.

Isocrates, *Panegyricus* (380 B.C.), writes:

It is impossible for people raised and governed as they are [sc. the Persians] to have any virtue, and, in combat, to put up a trophy over the enemies. How could there exist a competent commander or a courageous soldier with the habits of these people, of whom the majority is a crowd without discipline or experience of danger, which has lost its motivation for war and is better educated for slavery than our servants? Those who have the highest reputation among them have, without exception, never any care for the interest of other people or the state, but they spend all their time offending some and acting as slaves to others, in a manner whereby people are most corrupted. They indulge their bodies in the luxury of their riches. They have souls humiliated and terrified by the monarchy. They let themselves be inspected at the palace gates, prostrate themselves, practice every form of humility, fall on their knees for a mortal man whom they address as god, caring less for divinity than for men. (150–151)[131]

These are the words of an orator, addressing the Athenians in the early fourth century, a century after the Persians had failed in their attempt to conquer the Greek mainland and generations after the authors discussed above had celebrated their victory over an enemy considered formidable. In the meantime, Athens herself had failed in her attempt to acquire and maintain an empire. It is interesting to compare Isocrates' description of the Persian monarchy here with another address, written ten years later, for delivery by Nicocles, King of Cyprus. This contains a passage condemning oligarchies and democracies and praising the monarchy, because it is the only system which distributes privileges according to merit.[132]

To return to Isocrates' *Panegyricus,* in this text we find, for the first time in Greek rhetoric, although to some extent anticipated in *Airs, Waters, Places* and

---

[131] Isocrates, *Pan.* 150f.: Πῶς γὰρ ἐν τοῖς ἐκείνων ἐπιτηδεύμασιν ἐγγενέσθαι δύναιτ' ἂν ἢ στρατηγὸς δεινὸς ἢ στρατιώτης ἀγαθός, ὧν τὸ μὲν πλεῖστόν ἐστιν ὄχλος ἄτακτος καὶ κινδύνων ἄπειρος, πρὸς μὲν τὸν πόλεμον ἐκλελυμένος, πρὸς δὲ τὴν δουλείαν ἄμεινον τῶν παρ' ἡμῖν οἰκετῶν πεπαιδευμένος; 151 Οἱ δ' ἐν ταῖς μεγίσταις δόξαις ὄντες αὐτῶν ὁμαλῶς μὲν οὐδὲ κοινῶς οὐδὲ πολιτικῶς οὐδεπώποτ' ἐβίωσαν, ἅπαντα δὲ τὸν χρόνον διάγουσιν εἰς μὲν τοὺς ὑβρίζοντες, τοῖς δὲ δουλεύοντες, ὡς ἂν ἄνθρωποι μάλιστα τὰς φύσεις διαφθαρεῖεν, καὶ τὰ μὲν σώματα διὰ τοὺς πλούτους τρυφῶντες, τὰς δὲ ψυχὰς διὰ τὰς μοναρχίας ταπεινὰς καὶ περιδεεῖς ἔχοντες, ἐξεταζόμενοι πρὸς αὐτοῖς τοῖς βασιλείοις καὶ προκαλινδούμενοι καὶ πάντα τρόπον μικρὸν φρονεῖν μελετῶντες, θνητὸν μὲν ἄνδρα προσκυνοῦντες καὶ δαίμονα προσαγορεύοντες, τῶν δὲ θεῶν μᾶλλον ἢ τῶν ἀνθρώπων ὀλιγωροῦντες. For Isocrates' attitude toward Persia: E. Buchner, *Der Panegyrikos des Isokrates* Historia Einzelschriften 2 (Wiesbaden, 1958), where the present passage is not discussed in any detail (143f.); K. Bringmann, *Studien zu den politischen Ideen des Isokrates* (Göttingen, 1965), 17, 21f., 24; S. Perlman, "Panhellenism, the Polis and Imperialism," *Historia* 25 (1976), 1–30; Walser, *Hellas und Iran,* chapter 14; Stephen Usher, "Isocrates: Paideia, Kingship, and the Barbarians," in H. A. Khan (ed.), *The Birth of the European Identity* 131–145, at 141–145, comments by Paul Cartledge, pp. 146–153, at 149–151.

[132] Isocrates, 3, *Nicocles* 15: Αἱ δὲ μοναρχίαι πλεῖστον μὲν νέμουσι τῷ βελτίστῳ, δευτέρῳ δὲ τῷ μετ' ἐκεῖνον, τρίτῳ δὲ καὶ τετάρτῳ καὶ τοῖς ἄλλοις κατὰ τὸν αὐτὸν λόγον. Cf. Ostwald, *Oligarchia,* 28f.

in Attic vase painting (see figure 4 and, especially figure 2), an insistence on presumed oriental deficiencies such as a lack of discipline, softness, servility combined with arrogance, luxury, and corruption.[133] While the idea that Asiatics[134] were soft and not belligerent is also found in *Airs,* Isocrates is the earliest and most outspoken Athenian author to insist on this for political purposes. The second point to be noted here is the Greek insistence on the corrupting influence of wealth and luxury. As noted frequently in this book, the idea that luxury corrupts and even destroys empires was a commonplace in antiquity and hence fully accepted in some late periods such as that of the Enlightenment.[135] In chapter 2, we saw how common it is in Roman literature. In Greek literature it is the East, Asia Minor, and Persia which suffer from this weakness, not the Greeks themselves. Roman preoccupation is quite different: Roman moralists accuse Rome itself of being corrupted by Asiatic wealth and luxury.[136] According to Isocrates the Persians are also faithless to their friends, are swindlers,[137] and are impious towards the gods (*Pan.* 152). These deficiencies are found very often in later ancient sources hostile to peoples from the East.

While Aeschylus and Herodotus still found the Greek victory over Persia a marvel which required explanation, Isocrates wanted to instill in the public the idea that Persia was a power easy to defeat. A similar point is made briefly in the *Menexenus,* where it is stated: "And so the soldiers of Marathon and the sailors of Salamis became the schoolmasters of Hellas; the one teaching and habituating the Hellenes not to fear the barbarians at sea, and the others not to fear them by land."[138] The idea is present also in vase painting of around 400 B.C., as shown by figure 3. This idea is not found in Herodotus or Thucydides. It should be noted here that ideas about Phoenicians appear in earlier sources as well as later ones and these, being somewhat different, will be discussed below.

[133] Hall, *Inventing the Barbarian,* 128, sees references to barbarian luxury and softness also in fifth-century tragedy.

[134] As already noted, I use the term "Asiatics" as a problematic rendering of several Greek terms. Curiously, the anti-semitic scholar Ernst Renan argues that the Assyrian empire and civilization cannot have been the achievement of Semites, but must be attributed to the indo-european Persians, for only they and not the Chinese, Egyptians, or Semites have ever been capable of establishing a true empire, he believes: *Histoire générale et système comparé des langues Sémitiques* (1878), 67. His solution is a claim that the Assyrian upper class was Arian, as he calls it. For Renan's racist views: T. Todorov, *Nous et les autres: La Réflexion française sur la diversité humaine* (Paris, 1989), translated as *On Human Diversity: Nationalism, Racism, and Exoticism in French Thought* (Cambridge, MA, 1993), 107–113.

[135] Above, chapters 1–3, pp. 189f., 227, 241. For the influence of the ancient idea of the necessary decline of nations in later periods, Johnson, *The Formation of English Neo-Classical Thought* (1967), 49–68. At the background is the view of nations as living organisms.

[136] Prosperous living in Greece is now a subject in its own right: O. Murray, "Sympotic History," in idem (ed.), *Sympotica: A Symposium on the Sumposion* (Oxford, 1990), 3–13; Murray, "Histories of Pleasure," in Murray and M. Tecusan (eds.), *In Vino Veritas* (London, 1995), 3–16; J. Davidson, *Courtesans and Fishcakes: The Consuming Passions of Classical Athens* (London, 1997).

[137] Greed is also found as a characteristic of Phoenicians in Plato's *Republic,* as noted below.

[138] *Menex.* 241b: ὑπ᾽ ἀμφοτέρων δὴ συμβαίνει, τῶν τε Μαραθῶνι μαχεσαμένων καὶ τῶν ἐν Σαλαμῖνι ναυμαχησάντων, παιδευθῆναι τοὺς ἄλλους Ἕλληνας, ὑπὸ μὲν τῶν κατὰ γῆν, ὑπὸ δὲ τῶν κατὰ θάλατταν μαθόντας καὶ ἐθισθέντας μὴ φοβεῖσθαι τοὺς βαρβάρους.

There is no doubt in Isocrates' mind that a monarchy, such as that in Persia, makes it impossible for a nation to produce a good army, an assumption often echoed by modern scholars, although the opposite idea has also been defended with equal assurance.[139] Like the fifth-century authors, Isocrates recalls the destruction of the Athenian temples as a central event in the war (*Pan.* 156). Unlike them, however, he insists on the need to hate the Persians (*Pan.* 157ff.) "So naturally comes our hostility to them, that we most enjoy those of our stories which deal with the Trojan and Persian wars, for through them we learn of their disasters."[140] "Towards all other peoples with whom [the Greeks] waged war, they forget their past hostility when they stop fighting, but towards the Asiatics[141] they are not grateful even when they receive favours" (*Pan.* 157). He constantly repeats that the Greeks should unite to fight Persia (*Pan.* 106, 134, 160–166, 168, 181). Interestingly, the same text both calls for war and insists on the inferiority of the enemy and the need to punish him for past injuries.[142] Even in a text written as a "sportive essay" (παίγνιον) in c. 370 B.C., the *encomium of Helen,* Isocrates insists on seeing the conflict between the Greeks and Persia as a chronic one, which is really a struggle between Europe and Asia. Moreover, this chronic tension can result in one of two possibilities only: either the Greeks rule Asia or the reverse has to happen. Isocrates, in fact, reinterprets Herodotus in the sense that the Trojan War is represented as the first victory of Europe over Asia. Thanks to the Greek victory over Troy, the Greeks are not slaves of the barbarians.[143] Finally, it should be observed that Isocrates' hostility towards Persia, fierce as it is, cannot be called "proto-racist" by the definition given above. Although he consistently thinks in terms of an opposition Europe-Asia, his descriptions of the Persians all lie within the social and political spheres. The Persians are inferior because of the way they are ruled and because of their social relationships. The causes are not said to be hereditary or caused by physical traits.

---

[139] L. Poliakov, *Le mythe aryen* (1971), 45, cites J. Michelet, *Histoire de la France*, 2d ed. 1835, Introduction of 1831, about the Germans : "Le caractère de cette race, qui devait se mêler à tant d'autres, c'est la facile abnégation de soi. Le vassal se donne au seigneur, l'étudiant, l'artisan à leurs corporations. . . . Rien en d'étonnant si c'est en Allemagne que nous voyons, pour la première fois, l'homme se faire l'homme d'un autre, mettre ses mains dans les siennes et jurer de mourir pour lui. Ce dévouement sans intérêt, sans conditions . . . a pourtant fait la grandeur de la race germanique."

[140] Isocrates, *Pan.* 158: Οὕτω δὲ φύσει πολεμικῶς πρὸς αὐτοὺς ἔχομεν ὥστε καὶ τῶν μύθων ἥδιστα συνδιατρίβομεν τοῖς Τρωϊκοῖς καὶ Περσικοῖς. Hatred of foreigners in general and of Persians in particular as a virtue is brought out again in Plato, *Menexenus* 245d: ὅθεν καθαρὸν τὸ μῖσος ἐντέτηκε τῇ πόλει τῆς ἀλλοτρίας φύσεως which echoes Sophocles, *Electra* 1311: μῖσός τε γὰρ παλαιὸν ἐντέτηκε μοι. cf. Tsitsiridis, *Platons Menexenos* (1998), 361. See also the discussion of this text above, chapter 1.

[141] ἠπειρώταις = those dwelling on the continent. As mentioned before, I use the term "Asiatics" as a problematic rendering of several Greek terms.

[142] Cf. F. W. Walbank, "The Problem of Greek Nationality," in *Selected Papers* (1985), 1–19, esp. 2f.

[143] Isocrates, *Helen* 67f., discussed also above: δικαίως ἂν καὶ τοῦ μὴ δουλεύειν ἡμᾶς τοῖς βαρβάροις Ἑλένην αἰτίαν εἶναι νομίζοιμεν.

It is clear, then, that in Isocrates we find the bipolar world view, opposing Asia to Europe, with its contrast between a masculine and free Greece opposed to a weak and slavish Persia fully developed. The views which various modern authors attribute to Herodotus's history are in fact encountered only in Isocrates' political rhetoric and, to some extent, in earlier Attic vase painting. See figures 2, 3, and 4.

Isocrates (436–338) and Xenophon (428–354) were contemporaries, but their attitudes towards Persia were radically different. Isocrates was an ideologue, Xenophon was not. Indeed, he shows considerable respect for Persia, based on his personal experience of the country, and he expresses his admiration of Cyrus the Great: "he was so different from the other kings, both those who acquired their thrones from their fathers and those who gained them by their own efforts; the Scythian king, for instance, would never be able to expand his rule over any other people, although the Scythians are very great in number, for he would be pleased if only he could continue ruling his own people, so the Thracian king with the Thracians, the Illyrian with his Illyrians and all the other peoples, as I hear" (*Cyropaedia* 1.1.4). The younger Cyrus, like all subjects of the King, was a slave (*An.* 1.9.29, 2.5.38), but Xenophon makes it clear that this did not detract from his remarkable virtues. Following his account of the death of Cyrus the Younger in 401, Xenophon offers his readers very lengthy praise (*Anabasis* 1.9). He was "a man most kingly and of all the Persians after Cyrus the Great the most worthy man to rule, as all agree who seem to have known him well (1.9.1)." "In my judgment no man, either Greek or barbarian, was ever loved by a greater number of people" (1.9.28). Being king is difficult work, but, if done well, kingship is not an undesirable method of government in itself, as Xenophon tells us explicitly (e.g., *Cyropaedia* 1.1.3).

It is undoubtedly true that Xenophon's description of Mesopotamia and of the relative weakness of the Persian army may have contributed to the Greek perceptions of Persia as a force which could be defeated.[144] He observes that "while the King's rule was strong because of the extent of his territory and the number of its inhabitants, it was weak because of the length of the distances and the distribution of his forces" (1.5.9). There are indeed many scenes in the *Anabasis* which convey the message that the Greeks were better soldiers.[145] In

[144] Whether it was Xenophon's intention to convey this message to his Greek readers is another matter. For a survey and discussion of theories about Xenophon's aim in writing the *Anabasis*, see Steven W. Hirsch, *The Friendship of the Barbarian: Xenophon and the Persian Empire* (Hanover and London, 1985), 14–17. Hirsch himself traces the theme of trust and deceit in the *Anabasis* (18–38) and concludes that the work "is not about Persian deceit, but about deceit in human affairs. All parties to the events narrated by Xenophon—Greeks and Persians, friends as well as enemies—practice deceit, with dire consequences for the Greek army." For Xenophon's views on Persia: Walser, *Hellas und Iran*, chapter 13, "Das Persienbild Xenophons." John Dillery, *Xenophon and the History of His Times* (London and New York, 1995), does not contain extensive discussion of this aspect of Xenophon's works.

[145] Xenophon, *An.* 1.2.17f. describing the effect of the phalanx on the Persian troops; 1.8.18–20: the phalanx in action at Cunaxa and its effect on the enemy; 3.4.35: the Persians cannot fight during

his speech to his fellow officers he claims that the bodies and souls of the Greeks are superior to those of the enemy (3.1.23). However, the tone of all this is radically different from the rhetoric of Isocrates and others. Xenophon insists on the good discipline among Cyrus's aristocratic officers. In one of his speeches Xenophon encourages his men and tells them it is their duty to return to Greece and relate how rich a country Persia is. "They could bring here those who are now living in hardship at home and see them enjoying prosperity" (3.2.26). That, however, is one speech that meant to persuade the men to continue their journey home. Nowhere is there an explicit call in the *Anabasis* to start a war with Persia.

For such a call there is, indeed, a well-known precedent: In his account of the Ionian revolt Herodotus claims that Aristogoras of Miletus attempted to persuade Cleomenes of Sparta, and succeeded in persuading the Athenians, with such arguments. The Persians are worthless soldiers and easy to vanquish and the constituent parts of the Persian empire, described with the aid of a map, are extraordinarily wealthy and worth conquering (5.49; 97). Xenophon is nowhere so explicit as this. On the contrary, in the *Agesilaos* there is evidence of respect for the Persian cavalry and the forces led by Tissaphernes.[146] This is Xenophon's most panhellenic work and even so is quite different in spirit from Isocrates' speeches. To take one important point, while there is hostility towards Persia, there is no contempt to be found. Agesilaos, the hero of the work, was a "Greek-lover" (φιλέλλην) and a "Persian-hater" (μισοπέρσης) (7.4–7). The reason given for the latter are the attacks in the early fifth century, a theme which is found also in Isocrates and other authors and which would be taken up by Alexander again. Furthermore, he had objections against Persia's current politics. These reasons, however, do not resemble the fierce ideological hostility towards Persia of Isocrates' speeches.

I am aware of only one passage in Xenophon's *Anabasis* which might reflect traces of a common anti-oriental attitude. In 3.26–32 he describes at length a disagreement with an officer, Apollonides, thought to be a Boeotian, who, unlike, Xenophon, argued that they should try to come to an understanding with the King. In the end he is found out, because "he has both ears pierced like a Lydian," which proves him to be a traitor, according to his peers.[147]

---

the night. In 1.7.3 Cyrus tells his Greeks troops that they are better fighters I cannot agree with Dillery, *Xenophon,* 60f., that Xenophon "by putting [this panhellenic broadside] in the mouth of an 'easterner' . . . gives the point an authority that surpasses that spoken by a Greek." This interpretation rests on a misunderstanding of the function of rhetoric in history. Xenophon attributes to Cyrus a speech such as a good commander would be expected to deliver, namely one which extols the qualities of the soldiers whom he addresses. Even today commanders still give their units pep talks of this kind. I certainly cannot see in this passage "a call to panhellenic action" against Persia, as argued by Dillery. See also 1.10.10f. Walser, *Hellas und Iran,* 102f. points out that there are features in his description of Persia that are indubitably based on autopsy, which is important but not surprising, since Xenophon was there himself.

[146] *Agesilaos* 1.13; 1.23; cf. Hirsch, *The Friendship of the Barbarian,* chapter 3.

[147] Cf. Juvenal, *Sat.* 1.102–11: (trans. Braund) But a freedman is in front. "I was here first," he says. "Why should I be afraid or hesitate to hold my place, although I was born on the Euphrates—

Xenophon's *Cyropaedia* is largely an imaginary portrait of the ideal ruler, Cyrus the Great of Persia. Although it focuses on Cyrus, its setting is Persia, and a Persia that is sometimes said to resemble Sparta more than any other country.[148] This may be surprising, for Xenophon knew both Persia and Sparta. Whatever the aim of the work, it had great influence on Greek ideas about kingship. Xenophon may have been the first to ask himself how an empire functioned, as an admirer, not as one of Persia's Greek enemies. Even if the Persia of the *Cyropaedia* is in many respects a fiction, it is a sympathetic view of Persia as a successful empire. So far it must be concluded that the contemporaries Isocrates and Xenophon have remarkably different views toward Persia. Why this should be the case is a matter of speculation. There are obvious differences: Isocrates disliked the monarchy and Xenophon did not. Isocrates was an aggressive patriot and Xenophon was not. However, one major difference is clear: Xenophon traveled in Persia and he served with Persians in the army, under a commander whom he greatly admired. Whatever his experiences with various Persians after the death of Cyrus, he knew Persia from the inside. Isocrates hated it from afar.

The last chapter of the entire *Cyropaedia* (8.8), however, is fiercely hostile and critical. Its primary aim is to show that the Persians were no longer a reputable enemy. They had been great once, but only thanks to Cyrus. This chapter, 8.8, was written after 362/1.[149] As a result there has been an ongoing discussion about the authenticity of this chapter. Many earlier authors argued that Xenophon did not write it;[150] many, but by no means all recent scholars accept Xenophon's authorship.[151] This is not the place to summarize all the

a fact which the effeminate windows in my ears would prove although I personally deny it? The theme returns in the work of Petronius, *Satyricon* 102.14: "'Quidni?' inquit Giton 'etiam circumcide nos, ut Iudaei videamur, et pertunde aures, ut imitemur Arabes.'" and again in that of Tertullian, *De Pallio* 4.2: Feras, si in puero, matris sollicitudinem patiens; certe iam histriculus, certe iam uirum alicui clanculo functus adhuc sustinet stolam fundere, comam struere, cutem fingere, speculum consulere, collum demulcere, aurem quoque foratu effeminatus, quod illi apud sigeum strongyla seruat. For this passage of Petronius, see also below, chapter 6, note 81, chapter 13, note 158.

[148] Modern scholars often argue that Xenophon's Persia resembles Sparta more than it resembles Persia, but see Steven W. Hirsch, "1001 Iranian Nights: History and Fiction in Xenophon's Cyropaedia," *The Greek Historians: Literature and History, Papers presented to A. E. Raubitschek* (Saratoga, CA, 1985), 65–85; id., *The Friendship of the Barbarians*, chapter 4. See also Walser, *Hellas und Iran*, 112–114; Georges, *Barbarian Asia and the Greek Experience*, 228–241.

[149] Paragraph 4 refers to datable events, reported also by Diodorus 15.9.2.

[150] For references: Breitenbach, *RE* 9, col.1741. An early exception seems to be Gustave Eichler, *De Cyropaediae capite extremo* (Diss. Leipzig, non vidi).

[151] Genuine Xenophon: J. K. Anderson, *Xenophon* (London, 1974), 78n.1, see also 152, n.1; James Tatum, *Xenophon's Imperial Fiction* (Princeton, 1989), ch. 10, 215–239 ; Bodil Due, *The Cyropaedia: Xenophon's Aims and Methods* (Aarhus, 1989); Deborah L. Gera, *Xenophon's Cyropaedia: Style, Genre and Literary Technique* (Oxford, 1993), 299f.; C. Mueller-Goldingen, *Untersuchungen zu Xenophon's Kyropädie* (Stuttgart and Leipzig 1995), 262–271. Not Xenophon: Hirsch, *The Friendship of the Barbarians*; M. Bizos, editor of the Budé ed. *Cyropédie*, vol. 1 (Paris, 1971–1978), comm. ad loc., but E. Delebecque, the editor of vol. 2, believes it to be a later addition by Xenophon. Georges, *Barbarian Asia and the Greek Experience*, assumes as a matter of course

arguments in favor of or against Xenophon's authorship of this chapter. However, we may note that J. K. Anderson not only takes it for granted that the chapter was written by Xenophon, but also that the chapter is historically correct in describing Persia as degenerate: modern historians often seem ready to believe that any people who lost a war against an invading force must have been weak and degenerate. The hypothesis has also been proposed that Xenophon wrote this chapter as a call upon the Greeks to organize a Panhellenic campaign against Persia under Spartan leadership.[152] This does not affect the question of authorship; another author could equally well have made such a call. For our purposes it is not important who wrote the chapter, as long as it is agreed that it reflects the views of a Greek writing not long after 361. The chapter is important for its view of Persia. This may be summarized as follows.

The Role of the Monarch. The first point to emphasize here is the mighty role ascribed to the personality of the monarch in this chapter. "Cyrus' kingdom was the fairest and greatest in all of Asia" and, "in spite of its size, it was ruled only by the will of Cyrus (8.8.1). However, after his death his children immediately quarrelled, cities and peoples began to revolt and everything began to deteriorate."[153] Here, then, we have a Greek author who believes that one monarch can maintain and expand an ideal empire while his children could convert it into the opposite. Isocrates, on the other hand, firmly denies that those living under the Persian monarchy could ever have any merit.

Moral Degeneration. The Persians used to be trustworthy. They are so no longer. "Not a single man now trusts them, since their lack of piety is well known."[154] "Seeing this, all the inhabitants of Asia now have lost their piety and have become depraved."[155] "For like the masters, so are mostly the subjects. Thus they are now even more immoral than they used to be."

Financial Corruption. People who have done nothing wrong are arrested and forced to pay fines. As a result the well-to-do avoid relations with the authorities. Therefore they do not even dare to enlist in the royal army (8.8.6). The author adds that the country is therefore defenseless and any invader can march through the country at will.

---

that the chapter represents Xenophon's views of Persia when he wrote the text, see 213 and 231: Xenophon was "repelled by the degenerate spectacle of Cyrus II's rule." I have not seen Christopher Nadon, *Xenophon's Prince. Republic and Empire in the Cyropaedia* (Berkeley, 2001).

[152] Mueller-Goldingen, loc. cit. with reference to E. Schwartz, *Fünf Vorträge über den griechischen Roman* (Berlin, 2d ed. 1943), 69 (non vidi).

[153] 8.8.2: ἐπεὶ μέντοι Κῦρος ἐτελεύτησεν, εὐθὺς μὲν αὐτοῦ οἱ παῖδες ἐστασίαζον, εὐθὺς δὲ πόλεις καὶ ἔθνη ἀφίσταντο, πάντα δ' ἐπὶ τὸ χεῖρον ἐτρέποντο.

[154] 8.8.3: ὥσπερ οὐδὲ νῦν πιστεύει οὐδὲ εἷς ἔτι, ἐπεὶ ἔγνωσται ἡ ἀσέβεια αὐτῶν.

[155] 8.8.5 ταῦτ' οὖν ὁρῶντες οἱ ἐν τῇ Ἀσίᾳ πάντες ἐπὶ τὸ ἀσεβὲς καὶ τὸ ἄδικον τετραμμένοι εἰσίν·

Physical Deterioration. They do not care for their physical strength as they used to. "For example, it used to be their custom not to spit or blow their nose" (8.8.8). They eat and drink too much (9–10) and do not exercise (11–12). The boys are not properly educated and instructed (13–14).

Effeminacy (15–17). They are much more effeminate (θρυπτικώτεροι) now because they have adopted the softness of the Medes instead of the abstinence of the Persians. They live in comfort, eat rich food, and acquire dishonest wealth.[156] The opposition between Persians and Medes will be found again in Roman sources by the contrast between Parthians and Medes. The idea of a people being effeminate appears frequently in this work and is illustrated vividly by figure 2. It is therefore appropriate to recognize at the outset that this represents a specific set of values whereby men judge other men as weak or even impotent, calling them "effeminate." It is also interesting to note here that the effeminacy is the result of a way of life, not of an external factor. This also is an important theme which recurs above and below.

Deterioration of the Army (19–26). In the past the landed aristocracy would provide fine cavalry (19–22). Now they furnish useless servants who do not function in combat. Various types are listed, such as "cosmeticians who paint their eyes and cheeks for them and otherwise take care of their make-up." They do not fight in hand-to-hand engagements, nor does the infantry do this (23). Cyrus the Great made the charioteers an elite, but now they are untrained and useless (26). The Persians themselves know their troops are ineffectual and therefore they never go to war without the help of Greek mercenaries, either in internal conflicts or in wars with Greeks.

This description is rather different in tone and detail from Isocrates' harangue, cited above. The main difference is that Isocrates holds that "it is impossible for people raised and governed as they are to have any virtue, and, in combat, to put up a trophy over the enemies," while the author of the last chapter of the *Cyropaedia* is prepared to believe that the ideal monarch (Cyrus the Great) could rule over an ideal empire, but any lesser successor would immediately cause things to deteriorate to a situation comparable with that described by Isocrates. For the author of the last chapter of the *Cyropaedia*, Persia was a nation that had known excellence, but had now deteriorated. He gives no reason, apart from asserting that Cyrus's successors were bad kings. In contrast, the implication of Isocrates' description is that Persia could never have been a

---

[156] The idea that luxury breeds softness and destroys military quality did not die in antiquity. P. Gay, *The Cultivation of Hatred* (London, 1994), 121, writes about Theodore Roosevelt, who was a great partisan of manliness. He considered it an essential element of good character and feared that pampered modern living was damaging it fatally. "One of the prime dangers of civilisation," he told an audience at the University of Berlin in 1910, "has always been its tendency to cause the loss of virile fighting virtues, of the fighting edge. When men get too comfortable and lead too luxurious lives, there is always danger that the softness eats like an acid into their manliness of fibre."

serious power. In fact, the attitudes of the two authors toward the monarchy are almost the opposite: while Isocrates asserts that no monarchy could be successful, the author of the last chapter of the *Cyropaedia* holds that the perfect ruler can rule over a perfect nation, while the weak ruler will cause deterioration. This betrays a strong belief in the omnipotence of the ruler. Otherwise the two passages have various features in common. Both combine moral denunciation with criticism of other aspects. Both insist on the physical deterioration that has taken place, Persian riches leading to softness. The aim of both passages is to persuade the public that the Persian army is powerless.[157] In the case of Isocrates this is the prelude to a call to arms (*Pan.* 160–167). Xenophon, or the author who used his name, does not call for an attack on Persia, but the entire passage implies that such an attack would result in an easy success. The enemy is inferior, which implies that he could be attacked successfully. Finally, it is worth noting that, like Isocrates' observations, the disparagement of the Persians in this chapter is not proto-racist. Although the chapter is one long list of negative stereotypes, it does not claim that the Persians are weak by nature, through physical causes or inherited features. The causes are social and political and represent a form of degeneration, which is not racist. Racism assumes that racial qualities are fixed and stable.[158]

There are two more passages which may be profitably compared with the observations by Isocrates and (pseudo-?)Xenophon; the first of these appears in the third book of Plato's *Laws*, the second in Aristotle's *Politics*. *The Laws* was

---

[157] Note also Xenophon, *Hell.* 7.1.38: Ambassadors to Persia return to Greece. The ambassador from the Arcadian league reports "that the King had bakers, and cooks and wine-pourers, and doorkeepers in great numbers, but men who could fight with Greeks he had looked for carefully without being able to find any." The suggestion is, again, that wealth and the art of war are mutually contradictory.

[158] C. Bérard, "L'image de l'Autre et le héros étranger," *Sciences et Racisme* 67 (1985–1986), pp. 5–22, republished in English in Beth Cohen, ed., *Not The Classical Ideal: Athens and the Construction of the Other in Greek Art* (Leiden, 2000), argues that Athenian images of "orientals" (Persians and others) are essentially not racist. Athenian iconography, he argues, shows a form of "cultural, not a political racism—passive, rather than aggressive; while it may not be inoffensive, it is certainly not dangerous nor perverse." (409). This view has been criticized by Peter Stewart in his review of Cohen, *Bryn Mawr Classical Review* of January 2001, as unduly generous. For present purposes it is worth observing that "cultural racism" as opposed to "political racism" are confused concepts that had better be dropped. Cultural chauvinism can, but need not be, an aspect of racist attitudes, while racism can never be cultural only. Furthermore, the study of iconography may be illuminating in the discovery of specific forms of self-perception and the perception of others, but it should not be used to the exclusion of other evidence, which exists in abundance for fifth-century Athens, to give the Athenians marks for the quality of their racism. For a far more cautious interpretation of the representation of Persians in Attic art of the fifth century: Wulf Raeck, *Zum Barbarenbild in der Kunst Athens im 6. und 5. Jahrhundert v. Chr.* (Bonn, 1981), chapter 5, 221–231, at 225–228. He sketches a development whereby battles with Persians become immediately popular and are depicted in increasingly realistic fashion towards the middle of the fifth century, although there are also some caricatures of Persians in this period. In the second half of the century Raeck sees an increase of stereotypes in the depiction of Persians: elements of oriental luxury, standard ways of presenting eastern rulers. Barbarians in general are portrayed in increasingly uniform fashion with negative overtones, according to Raeck.

Plato's last work, composed during the decade before his death in 347 B.C. It cannot therefore have been written long after the last chapter of Xenophon's *Cyropaedia*. As described by the anonymous Athenian, the Persians maintained

> a judicious blend of liberty and subjection, and after gaining their own freedom they became the masters of a great number of other people. As rulers, they granted a degree of liberty to their subjects and put them on the same footing as themselves, with the result that soldiers felt more affection for their commanders and displayed greater zeal in the face of danger. The king felt no jealousy if any of his subjects was intelligent and had some advice to offer; on the contrary, he allowed free speech and valued those who could contribute to the formulation of policy; a sensible man could use his influence to help the common cause. Thanks to freedom, friendship, and the practice of pooling their ideas, during that period the Persians made progress all along the line.[159]

This passage is taken from a discussion about the principles of monarchy and democracy, where the point is argued that the two extremes, Persia and Athens, are bad, and a mixture is best. The latter is represented by Persia under Cyrus. Thus it rejects the frequent claim that the Persians are all slaves of a despotic king and all the accompanying notions of their resulting weaknesses. Deterioration followed under Cambyses, Cyrus's successor, restoration under Darius, followed by decline again under the next kings (694c–695). The reason adduced is the background of those kings. Cyrus and Darius were not kings' sons, but raised in simple circumstances and well disciplined. They themselves, however, allowed their sons to be educated "by women and eunuchs," over-pampered and in luxury. "Our verdict was that their corruption increased year by year; and the reason we assign for this is that they were too strict in depriving the people of liberty and too energetic in introducing authoritarian government, so that they destroyed all friendship and community of spirit in the state."[160] "When (the kings) come to need the common people to fight on their behalf, they discover the army has no loyalty, no eagerness to face danger and fight."[161] This, representing Plato's own times, comes closer to the familiar judgment, best illustrated by figure 3, but it is still free from the extreme anti-oriental stereotypes

[159] *Leg.* 694a–b (trans. Trevor J. Saunders): Πέρσαι γάρ, ὅτε μὲν τὸ μέτριον μᾶλλον δουλείας τε καὶ ἐλευθερίας ἦγον ἐπὶ Κύρου, πρῶτον μὲν ἐλεύθεροι ἐγένοντο, ἔπειτα δὲ ἄλλων πολλῶν δεσπόται. ἐλευθερίας γὰρ ἄρχοντες μεταδιδόντες ἀρχομένοις καὶ ἐπὶ τὸ ἴσον ἄγοντες, μᾶλλον φίλοι τε ἦσαν στρατιῶται στρατηγοῖς καὶ προθύμους αὑτοὺς ἐν τοῖς κινδύνοις παρείχοντο· καὶ εἴ τις αὖ φρόνιμος ἦν ἐν αὐτοῖς καὶ βουλεύειν δυνατός, οὐ φθονεροῦ τοῦ βασιλέως ὄντος, διδόντος δὲ παρρησίαν καὶ τιμῶντος τοὺς εἴς τι δυναμένους συμβουλεύειν, κοινὴν τὴν τοῦ φρονεῖν εἰς τὸ μέσον παρείχετο δύναμιν, καὶ πάντα δὴ τότε ἐπέδωκεν αὐτοῖς δι' ἐλευθερίαν τε καὶ φιλίαν καὶ νοῦ κοινωνίαν. Cf. Hirsch, 97–100.

[160] Plato, *Leg.* 697c–d (trans. Saunders): ἀνευρίσκομεν δὲ ἐπὶ ἔτι χείρους αὐτοὺς γεγονότας, τὴν δὲ αἰτίαν φαμέν, ὅτι τὸ ἐλεύθερον λίαν ἀφελόμενοι τοῦ δήμου, τὸ δεσποτικὸν δ' ἐπαγαγόντες μᾶλλον τοῦ προσήκοντος, τὸ φίλον ἀπώλεσαν καὶ τὸ κοινὸν ἐν τῇ πόλει. Excessive liberty as found in democratic Athens, finds Plato, has the same result (*Leg.* 699e).

[161] *Leg.* 697d–e: ὅταν τε εἰς χρείαν τοῦ μάχεσθαι περὶ ἑαυτῶν τοὺς δήμους ἀφικνῶνται, οὐδὲν κοινὸν ἐν αὐτοῖς αὖ μετὰ προθυμίας τοῦ ἐθέλειν κινδυνεύειν καὶ μάχεσθαι ἀνευρίσκουσιν.

encountered in other fourth-century texts. It may be observed that Plato's thoughts about the lack of motivation of soldiers living in a state of oppression echo those of Herodotus, when he describes the Athenian soldiers under Peisistratus and afterwards (5.78). Plato here talks about external and internal freedom. From his statement it is clear that he considers freedom from external rule good and to rule others is also good. Internal freedom is good only if enjoyed in moderation. The language is remarkable: what is required is the middle between slavery and freedom (τὸ μέτριον δουλείας τε καὶ ἐλευθερίας).

Although Plato discusses Persia in stereotypes, his views cannot be described as proto-racist, for he views the functioning of the monarchy as a determining factor. It describes a process of deterioration, which does not fit any racist complex of ideas, for those by definition posit stability and the impossibility of change. The only form of change regarded as possible is one for the worse, caused by racial mixture, but that is not Plato's point. Plato sees the proper functioning of a state as the result of its constitution and the relationship between rulers and the people. Climate, geography, and environment in general play no role here. There may be elements, however, of another common theme in Greek and, particularly, Roman thought, namely the idea of the inevitability of imperial decline as a result of the loss of toughness and drive.

Another underlying assumption here, as in the last chapter of the *Cyropaedia*, is that the monarchy is not necessarily a bad thing, but the person of the monarch determines all. Cyrus and Darius were ideal kings (the *Cyropaedia* does not mention Xerxes) but under their successors the state deteriorated. As distinct from Isocrates' views, it is not the Persian people as such or the monarchy which was responsible for this development, but the way the kings were raised, which happens to be the subject also of Xenophon's *Cyropaedia*. Elsewhere in the *Laws* Plato lists the Persians among the warlike peoples (πολεμικὰ γένη), the others being the Carthaginians, Celts, Iberians and Thracians (637d). Thus Xenophon and Plato share both a belief in the virtual omnipotence of the ruler and in the idea that the education of the monarch could determine the wellbeing of his nation. This emphasis on the centrality of the king means that there is no trace of proto-racism here, for the people are, as it were, a tool in the hands of the king and their fate is not determined by their own qualities.

Aristotle's *Politics*, Book 7, contains an important discussion of the ethics of war and imperialism of which only one element should be mentioned here.[162] As he says, "All the uncivilized peoples which are strong enough to conquer others pay the highest honours to military prowess; as witness the Scythians, the Persians, the Thracians, and the Celts."[163] So, both Plato and Aristotle regard the Persians as one of the most belligerent peoples they know.

---

[162] Aristotle, *Pol.* 1324b, writing at an uncertain date between the middle of the fourth century and his death in 322 B.C., lists exactly the same peoples as Plato as warlike. He first mentions the Scythians, Persians, Thracians, and Celts and then goes on to single out the Carthaginians as encouraging military valor and gives a description of a related practice among the Iberians.

[163] Trans. E. Barker. ἔτι δ᾿ ἐν τοῖς ἔθνεσι πᾶσι τοῖς δυναμένοις πλεονεκτεῖν ἡ τοιαύτη τετίμηται δύναμις, οἷον ἐν Σκύθαις καὶ Πέρσαις καὶ Θραξὶ καὶ Κελτοῖς.

Yet it is clear that the other attitude described, dismissing the Persians as a military power, coincides and is connected with the voices which supported a major Greek attack on Persia. It is far from certain that Plato and Xenophon themselves would have been in favor of such action. All the same, the view of Persia as immoral, degenerate, and weak was part of the complex of ideas which served to reinforce Greeks in their aggressive designs. The increasing influence of such ideas were the ideological basis for Alexander's march eastward. As observed in the Introduction, it is assumed here that an understanding of negative attitudes towards other peoples will clarify part of the underlying assumptions and mechanisms of ancient imperialism and of the integration or nonintegration of foreigners into Graeco-Roman society. This should be true, first of all, for the stage where one nation or empire sets out to subjugate and annex or incorporate—"enslave" is the simple ancient term—another people or nation. It can now be seen that the gradual transformation of the Greek perception of Persia was part of the mentality that led to Alexander's onslaught. Similar patterns will be discerned below in the attitudes of Romans towards foreigners.

I observed above that it is not profitable to discuss what the world would look like if Persia had won at Marathon and Salamis, or even how Greece would have developed under such circumstances. At this stage in the development of the argument it is only fair to say that Plato did in fact find it profitable.[164] In *Laws* 693a the following view is presented: "If it had not been for the joint determination of the Athenians and the Spartans to resist the slavery that threatened them, we should have by now virtually a complete mixture of the peoples—Greek with Greek, Greek with barbarian, and barbarian with Greek. We can see a parallel in the nations whom the Persians lord it over today: they have been split up and then horribly jumbled together again into the scattered communities in which they now live."[165]

This is instructive both for what it says and what it does not say. The disastrous result would have been a loss of identity for the individual Greek states and the end of separation between Greeks and non-Greeks. This implies a

---

[164] I should admit also that some modern scholars find it profitable, see: Robert Cowley (ed.), *What If? Military Historians Imagine What Might Have Been* (New York, 1999; paperback, London, 2001). Victor Davis Hansen discusses the consequences of a hypothetical Persian victory at Salamis. Quite sensibly he focuses not on the hypothetical Persian victory, but on the results, as he sees them, of the historical Greek victory. His views are a variant of the familiar: "Themistocles and his poor Athenians not only saved Greece and embryonic Western civilization from the Persians, but also redefined the West as something more egalitarian, restless—and volatile—that would evolve into a society that we more or less recognize today." Josiah Ober, in the next essay, regards Alexander's conquests as another essential ingredient for the development of world history as we know it.

[165] *Leg.* 692e–693a (trans. Saunders): ἀλλ᾽ εἰ μὴ τό τε Ἀθηναίων καὶ τὸ Λακεδαιμονίων κοινῇ διανόημα ἤμυνεν τὴν ἐπιοῦσαν δουλείαν, σχεδὸν ἂν ἤδη πάντ᾽ ἦν μεμειγμένα τὰ τῶν Ἑλλήνων γένη ἐν ἀλλήλοις, καὶ βάρβαρα ἐν Ἕλλησι καὶ Ἑλληνικὰ ἐν βαρβάροις, καθάπερ ὦν Πέρσαι τυραννοῦσι τὰ νῦν διαπεφορημένα καὶ συμπεφορημένα κακῶς ἐσπαρμένα κατοικεῖται.

strong belief in the importance of social and ethnic separation, an approach discussed extensively in Part 1 of this study. It is also an early example of the virtual consensus that existed in antiquity regarding mixed marriages, which were generally considered to result in the deterioration of the offspring, a view shared by many racists in other periods. However, there is no suggestion that the resulting loss of liberty at any level was a major consideration for the speaker, as is clear from Plato's assessment of Persia under Cyrus the Great in the same work cited above.

It can no longer be denied that there is a thorough shift in attitude from the late fifth century onwards. It is less easy to provide an explanation for it. The "imperialist ideology" is easy to discern even though it was not adopted by all Greek authors that we know. That was not to be expected, for Greek civilization was by no means a monolith. At an individual level it may not be too difficult to account for the sharp differences we encounter: Isocrates was an Athenian orator, who spoke for Athenian audiences and was involved in Athenian politics. He had no personal ties with Persia and, more important, he was a fiercely anti-monarchical orator, not a career officer. Xenophon, who represents a totally different attitude, had spent much time in Persia fighting along Persian troops. As opposed to Isocrates he could see the benefit of a monarchy and had his doubts about democracy. Whatever his loyalty as an Athenian, he fought for Sparta and lived as an exile. Both men may represent a broader public in Athens, but there can be no doubt that Isocrates, not Xenophon, was the man to influence Athenian politics. At a rather more conceptual level it should suffice to note that (a) attitudes in general became more and more confrontational; (b) increased self-confidence and a much enhanced sense of the opposition of Greeks and non-Greeks went hand in hand; (c) the result is, not surprisingly, imperialist ambition. Again, it has to be said that imperialism is as much an attitude of mind as a specific policy.

What all these sources have in common, however, as distinct from Herodotus and the other authors of the first half of the fifth century, is a marked disdain for Persia and the Persians. Whether it may be termed proto-racist, as in the treatise on *Airs*, or merely replete with ethnic prejudice, it is remarkable in its emphasis on the collective inferiority of Asia. Some, but not all, authors also display an ideology of fierce imperialist aggression. The overall impression, however, is unavoidable: increased self-confidence, expansionist drive, and various forms of proto-racism and ethnic prejudice formed the spiritual climate for Alexander's conquests in the East. Furthermore, it is clear that the tone of these passages formed the model for anti-eastern attitudes through the ages. The association of the East with despotism, effeminacy, moral degeneration, and lack of discipline is first encountered in the literature of the fourth century. The accusation that the East was marked by a paradoxical combination of softness and servility combined with arrogance, luxury, and corruption has had a long history which began in the fourth century. Even if this is not quite proto-racism in all authors of the fourth century, it was easy to reinterpret these phenomena along proto-racist lines. Yet another concept with a long history first appears in the work of

Isocrates, namely that of "total war." The conflict between the Greeks and Persia is more than simply a fight for hegemony; it is really a struggle between Europe and Asia. Moreover, this struggle can result in one of two possibilities only: either the Greeks rule Asia or the reverse has to happen. The concept was later formulated in theory by Clausewitz, in his analysis of "Absolute War and Real War,"[166] and elaborated by Ludendorff.[167]

ALEXANDER

Arrian writes that Alexander spoke as follows to his troops before the battle of Issus: "We Macedonians," he stated, "are to fight Medes and Persians, nations long steeped in luxury, while we have now long been inured to danger by the exertions of campaigning. Above all, it will be a fight of free men against slaves.[168] . . . As for our barbarian troops, Thracians, Paeonians, Illyrians, Agrianians, the most robust and warlike races of Europe, will be ranged against the most indolent and softest tribes of Asia"[169] (trans. Brunt, Loeb).

This is taken from one of those usual set pieces written by ancient historians for commanders who address their troops before a battle. It contains themes that are by now familiar: Persian luxury and softness. Weak slaves as opposed to sturdy, free men have been encountered before too, and so has the idea of a robust Europe against a soft Asia (in the treatise on *Airs* . . . and in Isocrates' work). However, this was to become far more prominent in Roman thinking. Since this is a speech composed by an author who lived in the second century A.D., more than four centuries after Alexander, we must consider the question whether this is Arrian's concept or Alexander himself. P. A. Brunt considers the speech not necessarily Arrian.[170] This is only one example of the difficulties facing the study of Alexander, for which we depend on sources of the Roman

---

[166] Carl von Clausewitz, *Vom Kriege* Book 8, chapter 2: "Absoluter und wirklicher Krieg"; see also the introductory note (Nachricht) written in 1827 and Michael Howard on "The Influence of Clausewitz" in the English translation, *On War*, ed. and trans. by Michael Howard and Peter Paret (reprint, New York, 1993), 29–49.

[167] Erich Ludendorff, *Der Totale Krieg* (Munich, 1935).

[168] Arrian, *An.* 2.7.4 Μακεδόνας τε γὰρ Πέρσαις καὶ Μήδοις, ἐκ πάνυ πολλοῦ τρυφῶσιν, αὐτοὺς ἐν τοῖς πόνοις τοῖς πολεμικοῖς πάλαι ἤδη μετὰ κινδύνων ἀσκουμένους, ἄλλως τε καὶ δούλοις ἀνθρώποις ἐλενθέρους, εἰς χεῖρας ἥξειν·

[169] Arrian, *An.* 2.7.5 βαρβάρων τε αὖ Θρᾷκας καὶ Παίονας καὶ Ἰλλυριοὺς καὶ Ἀγριᾶνας τοὺς εὐρωστοτάτους τε τῶν κατὰ τὴν Εὐρώπην καὶ μαχιμωτάτους πρὸς τὰ ἀπονώτατά τε καὶ μαλακώτατα τῆς Ἀσίας γένη ἀντιτάξεσθαι·

[170] Arrian, *History of Alexander and Indica*, Loeb edition, vol. I (Cambridge, MA, 1976), p. 147, n.4. cf. Vol. 2, Appendix xxvii: Arrian's speeches and letters. A. B. Bosworth, *A Historical Commentary on Arrian's History of Alexander*, I (Oxford, 1980), 204–206, notes that opinions vary about the authenticity of the speech and tends to accept it as authentic. Bosworth argues that the parts in *oratio obliqua*, that is, the paragraphs considered here, are derived from Arrian's main source, probably Ptolemy. On p. 206 Bosworth describes the contrast between European and Asiatic barbarians as solidly Aristotelian. It seems better to say that it could, but need not at all be, fourth century. It looks like Livy in Greek more than it looks like Isocrates.

period.[171] There is at least one passage in which Arrian explicitly disapproves of
the way Alexander "imitated Median and Persian opulence and inequality of
barbarian kings towards their subjects in daily life" (4.7.4). He disapproves—
and gives this as his personal opinion—of physical punishment as well as of
Alexander's adoption of Median dress and the Persian tiara.[172] The only text for
comparison is a different speech which Quintus Curtius gives.[173] Here we read
only that Alexander, "when he came to Greek troops, reminded them that it was
by these nations that war had been made upon their country." He refers to the
attack on Greece by Darius and Xerxes and the need to punish Persia for the
destruction of temples. "The obligations of human and divine law had been
violated."[174] The Illyrians and Thracians are mentioned only as "men used to
live by robbery." Thus there was need for revenge, but we find no trace of the
polarization between Europe and Asia as present in the speech given by Arrian.
It seems safe, therefore, to assume that Arrian inserted his own ideas about east
and west into a speech assigned to Alexander. It is remarkable—and to some
extent reinforces my point—that Alexander's words, as attributed to him by
Arrian, are echoed in the anonymous Panegyric of Constantine of A.D. 312.
"Alexander, again, accomplished his undertaking by the outcome of a single
battle against weak Medes, unwarlike Syrians, the Parthans' flighty arms and
Asians desirous of a change of servitude."[175] The rhetoric about eastern armies
did not change over the centuries, but there is no good evidence that Alexander
himself used this sort of language.

Indirect testimony of the Roman period to Alexander's ideology may be
found in Strabo's geography and Plutarch's *On the Fortune of Alexander*.
Strabo comments on the views of Eratosthenes (third century B.C.) and the
advisers of Alexander regarding the difference between Greeks and barbarians.
It is worth citing Strabo in full:

> Now, towards the end of his [sc. Eratosthenes'] treatise—after withholding praise
> from those who divide the whole multitude of mankind into two groups, namely

[171] Cf. P. Vidal-Naquet, "Flavius Arrien entre deux mondes," in *Arrien, Histoire d'Alexandre* (Paris 1984), 330–343 ("Alexandre le Romain").

[172] There is no need to doubt the historicity of this criticism. As noted above, the Spartan commander Pausanias behaved similarly and this was considered unacceptable as well (Thuc. 1.130). Quintus Curtius is more critical than Arrian of Alexander's adoption of Persian customs and dress: 6.2.1–4; 6.6.1–12 (quem arma Persarum non fregerant vitia vicerunt); also: 10.3.11–10.4.3. Note also the ferocious attack on Alexander by Lucan, BC 10.20–46 for which cf. M.P.O. Morford, *The Poet Lucan: Studies in Rhetorical Epic* (Oxford, 1967), chapter 2, "Lucan and Alexander the Great," who argues that this indirectly refers to Julius Caesar.

[173] 3.10.8, undated, first or second century. Brunt, op. cit., 157 n.2, says of this speech: "QC here interpolates a speech by Alexander, which seems to derive from a source common to Justin 11.9.3ff., not followed in Arrian 6.3.ff."

[174] foedera divini humanique iuris violata.

[175] *Pan. Lat.* 12 (9)5, trans. C.E.V. Nixon and Barbara Saylor Rodgers, *In Praise of Later Roman Emperors* (Berkeley, 1994), 303: Et ille quidem contra leues Medos et imbelles Syros et Parthorum arma uolatica et Asiaticos optantes mutare seruitium rem gessit proeliis unius euentu. I am not suggesting that the author had read Arrian (cf. Nixon and Rodgers, introduction, p. 289).

Greeks and Barbarians, and also from those who advised Alexander to treat the Greeks as friends but the Barbarians as enemies—Eratosthenes goes on to say that it would be better to make such divisions according to good qualities and bad qualities; for not only are many of the Greeks bad, but many of the Barbarians are refined—Indians and Arians, for example, and, further, Romans and Carthaginians, who carry on their governments so admirably. And this, he says, is the reason why Alexander, disregarding his advisers, welcomed as many as he could of the men of fair repute and did them favours—just as if those who have made such a division, placing some people in the category of censure, others in that of praise, did so for any other reason than that in some people there prevail the law-abiding and the political instinct, and the qualities associated with education and powers of speech, whereas in other people the opposite characteristics prevail! And so Alexander, not disregarding his advisers, but rather accepting their opinion, did what was consistent with, not contrary to, their advice; for he had regard to the real intent of those who gave him counsel.[176]

This is part of Strabo's lengthy criticism of Eratosthenes' work. In Strabo's passage therefore we have Strabo criticizing Eratosthenes' criticism of Alexander's advisers. It is clear from the text that Alexander ignored his advisers' recommendations to treat Greeks and non-Greeks as two groups, the former being his own people, the latter representing the enemy. Eratosthenes, so we understand from Strabo, argues against the division of mankind into Greeks and non-Greeks and prefers one which distinguishes between civilized peoples with good government and those who are uncivilized and poorly governed. Strabo claims that Eratosthenes misrepresents Alexander's advisers. Like Alexander, he says, they distinguish between good and bad peoples. However we interpret Strabo, he is clearly inconsistent in his attempt to reconcile the views of the two parties: Alexander / Eratosthenes and Alexander's advisers / Strabo himself.[177] Strabo adheres to the old division of Greeks and Barbarians and so did Alexander's advisers. Eratosthenes, following Alexander, as represented in this text, rejected this division.

Strabo has to be interpreted in conjunction with a passage in Plutarch,[178] who

---

[176] Strabo 1.4.9 (66–7) (trans. H. L. Jones, Loeb): Ἐπὶ τέλει δὲ τοῦ ὑπομνήματος οὐκ ἐπαινέσας τοὺς δίχα διαιροῦντας ἅπαν τὸ τῶν ἀνθρώπων πλῆθος εἴς τε Ἕλληνας καὶ βαρβάρους, καὶ τοὺς Ἀλεξάνδρῳ παραινοῦντας τοῖς μὲν Ἕλλησιν ὡς φίλοις χρῆσθαι τοῖς δὲ βαρβάροις ὡς πολεμίοις, βέλτιον εἶναί φησιν ἀρετῇ καὶ κακίᾳ διαιρεῖν ταῦτα. πολλοὺς γὰρ καὶ τῶν Ἑλλήνων εἶναι κακοὺς καὶ τῶν βαρβάρων ἀστείους, καθάπερ Ἰνδοὺς καὶ Ἀριανούς, ἔτι δὲ Ῥωμαίους καὶ Καρχηδονίους οὕτω θαυμαστῶς πολιτευομένους. διόπερ τὸν Ἀλέξανδρον ἀμελήσαντα τῶν παραινούντων, ὅσους οἷόν τ᾽ ἦν ἀποδέχεσθαι τῶν εὐδοκίμων ἀνδρῶν καὶ εὐεργετεῖν· ὥσπερ δι᾽ ἄλλο τι τῶν οὕτω διελόντων τοὺς μὲν ἐν ψόγῳ τοὺς δ᾽ ἐν ἐπαίνῳ τιθεμένων, ἢ διότι τοῖς μὲν ἐπικρατεῖ τὸ νόμιμον καὶ τὸ παιδείας καὶ λόγων οἰκεῖον, τοῖς δὲ τἀναντία. καὶ ὁ Ἀλέξανδρος οὖν οὐκ ἀμελήσας τῶν παραινούντων, ἀλλ᾽ ἀποδεξάμενος τὴν γνώμην τὰ ἀκόλουθα, οὐ τὰ ἐναντία ἐποίει, πρὸς τὴν διάνοιαν σκοπῶν τὴν τῶν ἐπεσταλκότων.

[177] For a somewhat different interpretation of Strabo in this passage: Daniela Dueck, *Strabo of Amaseia: A Greek Man of Letters in Augustan Rome* (London and New York, 2000), 76.

[178] Plutarch, *Mor.* 329 b–d (= *De Fort. Alex.* 6, trans. F. C. Babbitt, Loeb): οὐ γάρ, ὡς Ἀριστοτέλης (fr. 658) συνεβούλευεν αὐτῷ (τῷ Ἀλεξάνδρῳ), τοῖς μὲν Ἕλλησιν ἡγεμονικῶς τοῖς δὲ βαρ-

says that Alexander "did not follow Aristotle's advice to treat the Greeks as if he were their leader, and other peoples as if he were their master; to have regard for the Greeks as for friends and kindred, but to conduct himself toward other peoples as though they were plants or animals; for to do so would have been to cumber his leadership with numerous battles and banishments and festering seditions." Whatever Plutarch's source, this has usually been accepted as reflecting genuine advice from Aristotle, because it is similar in approach to Aristotle's views on natural slavery in his *Politics,* discussed in chapter 2.[179] Thus we have fairly good evidence that Aristotle advised Alexander to pursue a policy of sharp differentiation between Greeks and (eastern) enemies, who were to be ruled and treated "like plants and animals." It is clear also that Alexander rejected this advice. According to Plutarch, who may have drawn for this on Eratosthenes, Alexander distinguished Greeks from barbarians, not by dress or armament, but by the criterion of virtue and vice. There is no further solid information on Alexander's views of Greeks and barbarians, antedating the Roman period. Even if we accept that Plutarch is reliable here, it still remains the case that he is an author writing in the Roman period.

These are merely two examples of why it did not seem profitable to me to discuss Alexander's attitude toward Persians at length, as observed in the Introduction. There is a good deal that would be interesting if we could understand it, but the sources are almost all of the Roman period. The extant authors, as we know, did draw on historians who were contemporary, or near contemporary, with Alexander. However, in each instance it needs to be considered whether the texts we have represent fourth-century attitudes, or a mixture of Greek attitudes and Roman interpretation, as suggested for Arrian, above. Since this study aims at analyzing attitudes, based on contemporary text, it seemed best not to make the attempt.[180] It is quite clear, however, that the subjects discussed

---

βάροις δεσποτικῶς χρώμενος, καὶ τῶν μὲν ὡς φίλων καὶ οἰκείων ἐπι μελόμενος τοῖς δ' ὡς ζῴοις ἢ φυτοῖς προσφερόμενος, πολεμοποιῶν φυγῶν ἐνέπλησε καὶ στάσεων ὑπούλων τὴν ἡγεμονίαν, ἀλλὰ κοινός. This is V. Rose, *Aristotelis qui ferebrantur librorum fragmenta* (Stuttgart, 1886, repr. 1967), Fr. 658; W. D. Ross, *Aristotelis Fragmenta Seclecta* (Oxford, 1955), 63.

[179] I am not sure why E. Badian, "Alexander the Great and the Unity of Mankind," *Historia* 7 (1958), 425–44, esp. 443, considers the advisers' views cited by Strabo as differing widely from those cited by Plutarch. The former speaks of "friends" versus "the enemies," the latter of "friends and relatives" as opposed to "plants and animals." Since both texts represent paraphrases of whatever was said, there is no reason to deny that the anonymous advice, cited by Strabo, could also represent Aristotle's advice to Alexander, as handed down through various intermediaries: Strabo cites Eratosthenes who cites anonymous advisers, and there may have been another unknown intermediary. However, the aim of Badian's article is the fanciful interpretation by Tarn of these and other passages. Badian himself is prepared to agree that "there is a common train of thought in the two passages: we may say it is to the effect that Alexander, despite advice to the contrary, did not discriminate between Greeks and barbarians as such" (435). Badian, p.437, also agrees that Plutarch may have had Eratosthenes in mind in the passage here discussed.

[180] For the opposition between Greeks and barbarians in this connection: Andreotti, *Historia* 5 (1956), 257–263; Badian, *Historia* 7 (1958), 440–444. Cf. Susan I. Rotroff, "The Greeks and the Other in the Age of Alexander," in John E. Coleman and Clark A. Walz (eds.), *Greeks and Barbarians* (Bethesda, MD, 1997), 221–236.

in this study should be taken up for all of the Hellenistic period whether or not this would affect the conclusions drawn so far from Greece and Rome in earlier and later periods.

CONCLUSIONS

In spite of assertions to the contrary in the modern literature, the fifth-century authors who wrote about the wars with Persia did so in a spirit of respect for the Persians. They were proud of their victory over a major empire which had sought to subject the Greek mainland, but they did not attempt to belittle the enemy, nor is there any trace of thinking along lines of bipolarity: Europe versus Asia represented simple geographical concepts only.

In the later fifth century we first encounter the view that Asiatics are basically different from Europeans. The characteristics ascribed to Asiatics are softness, servility, and luxury. Political institutions are sometimes part of the equation: a monarchy necessarily reduces its subject to slaves in every respect. The Europeans are the opposite: strong, free, and independent. The Greeks combine the best of these worlds, for they have the courage and independence of Europeans, but are also skillful and intelligent, like the Asiatics, according to these later sources.

To sum up, outspoken and irrational anti-Oriental attitudes occur among Greek authors of the fourth century who had an imperialistic ideology, such as Isocrates. These attitudes are not yet found among the authors who described the wars with Persians or had fought or traveled themselves in the East, such as Herodotus, Aeschylus, and Xenophon. Forms of fierce hostility towards Persia are found first, not in the historical literature, but in rhetoric and philosophy. Gorgias, Lysias, Plato as well as Isocrates and, among the tragedians, Euripides, emphasize the opposition between Greece and the barbarians more than any previous literature. The concept of a natural enemy, who must be hated, first occurs in these authors and not, as claimed by many scholars, in Herodotus and his contemporaries. By the late fifth century Persia was not merely an enemy power—it was Asia, the opposite of Europe. No compromise was possible, desirable, or necessary, for the Asiatics were inferior and could be defeated. Thus we may discern here a direct correlation between imperialist conceptions and the way in which the enemy is perceived. The desire to defeat and conquer goes hand in hand with the perception of the enemy as weak, immoral, and contemptible.

The themes that come up are similar to those found in Roman literature from the late Republic onwards. These attitudes represent collective judgments and extreme stereotypes, as is clear from the way they are formulated. They are extreme in their imperialist hostility. However, the texts discussed so far cannot be said to contain features in common with modern racism. We have observed the application of generalizations (negative or positive) to minorities and foreigners and the role these play in the rhetoric of imperialism. Such collective judgments or stereotypes are sometimes but not always explained by the assumption that the characteristics described are the result of environmental influences exerted by climate and geography. The effect of heredity is not emphasized, although it is assumed that acquired characters may become hereditary, just as social factors (notably institutions) may have an impact. Generalizations are applied not only to the eastern neighbors of the Greeks, but also to other peoples, such as the Scythians in the north and the Egyptians in the south.

None of the texts discussed so far, however, can properly be said to show a proto-racist mentality, as defined above, for they do not describe foreigners as inferior through heredity or unalterable exterior influences. The presumed causes of qualitative differences are human actions or social relations within a person's own control. The constitution and form of government play a role and change is possible in principle, so that we should define these attitudes as displaying ethnic prejudice or preconceptions, rather than proto-racism. Above, in chapter 1, however, it has been seen that other writers in late fifth- and fourth-century Greece did, in fact, produce views which show essential characteristics of proto-racism. Significantly, in this period such views are found not in historical literature, but in medical and philosophical treatises. As will be seen below, historical writers adopted these ideas in a later stage. Moreover, the texts discussed here contain various themes which became part of the standard package of anti-eastern attitudes, and these were eventually incorporated by those with proto-racist views.

Roman Imperialism and the Conquest of the East

VERGIL'S ROMAN EMPIRE had no boundaries and was to be eternal.[1] This was written in the age of Augustus, with its state-sponsored belief in progress—a belief rare for any period of Graeco-Roman antiquity.[2] Not everyone was so sanguine. Even while the empire was expanding, some Romans were worried about the peoples they incorporated—or failed to subjugate. In their old prayer the Censors asked for the aggrandizement of Rome, but Scipio Africanus changed it: it was large enough and he prayed that it would be preserved forever (Valerius Maximus 4.1.10). The old and superior cultures of the East, the Greek world, and Asia were often felt to be daunting. Oracles foretold that power would return to the East.[3] In Caesar's time there were rumors among the population of Rome that Julius Caesar "planned to move to Alexandria or Ilium, take the wealth of the empire with him, exhaust Italy by levies and leave the care of the city to his friends."[4] Thus, before Antony established himself in Alexandria with Cleopatra, Alexandria could be the subject of such rumors, while the presumed choice of Ilium shows that, long before the transformation of Byzantium into Constantinople, this was seen as an area from where the empire could conceivably be ruled.[5] As we have already seen, at times there was a preoccupation in Rome with the idea of the cultural and intellectual superiority of some of the subject peoples. Below we shall see further testimony regarding fear of a possible decline and demise of the Roman Empire, a preoccupation that in fact coincided with the period of most aggressive expansion. Even then the end of the Empire was thinkable and there existed ideas that the center of power would move back to the East. Egypt was formally incorporated only in the reign of Augustus, but Greeks and Romans had by that time had centuries of ambivalent interaction.

This chapter will attempt to trace some of the aspects of Roman imperialism and its attitude to the eastern neighbors and subject peoples. It will be seen how

---

[1] Vergil, *Aen.* 1.278: ego nec metas rerum nec tempora pono: imperium sine fine dedi.

[2] For the absence of a belief in progress in antiquity, see Dodds, cited in chapter 3, n. 59.

[3] Lactantius, *Div. Inst.* 7.15.11: "Cujus vastitatis et confusionis haec erit causa, quod Romanum nomen, quo nunc regitur orbis (horret animus dicere: sed dicam, quia futurum est) tolletur de terra, et imperium in Asiam revertetur, ac rursus Oriens dominabitur, atque Occidens serviet."

[4] Suetonius, *Divus Iulius* 79, 3: Quin etiam varia fama percrebruit migraturum Alexandream vel Ilium, translatis simul opibus imperii exhaustaque Italia dilectibus et procuratione urbis amicis permissa . . .

[5] As Erich Gruen suggests, the rumor about a transfer to Ilium may allude also to Troy as mother-city of Rome, but that does not, I think, discount Suetonius's interpretation. Suetonius clearly suggests that this was connected with a putative takeover of the empire by the eastern part of it, for he mentions both Ilium and Alexandria as possible imperial capitals.

Romans considered themselves superior in various ways and entitled to rule eastern peoples regarded as militarily inferior. Roman views of these peoples, however, could also stimulate ideas of the vulnerability of their own leadership and their faith in the stability of empire because of their belief that the weakness of the other sapped Rome's native military and political strength. The essence of Roman identity and the source of its greatest strength was felt to be the moral distinction of the Romans in comparison with other peoples.[6] If this particular superiority was diminished by foreign influence, the very existence of the empire was in danger.

In Rome such misgivings regarding contacts with foreigners were particularly keen when the army was involved. The Elder Cato, as quaestor, attacked his commander Scipio in 204 B.C. for corrupting his soldiers with excessive pay and pleasures.[7] More relevant for the present discussion is the following pronouncement by Sallust: "Besides all this, Lucius Sulla, in order to secure the loyalty of the army which he led into Asia, had allowed it a luxury and license contrary to the warlike spirit of his soldiers. There it was that the army of the Roman people first learned to indulge in women and drink; to admire statues, painting, and chased vases, to steal them from private houses and public places, to pillage shrines, and to desecrate everything, both sacred and profane" (trans. J. C. Rolfe, Loeb).[8] Sallust, writing in the mid-first-century B.C., raises very serious accusations against three targets: the Dictator Sulla, who allowed it to happen; the army, which had become a source of corruption and contamination; and, of course, the inhabitants of Asia Minor, who inspired all this evil.[9] Asia is a land of luxury, softness, and lack of morals, as first claimed by Isocrates in the early fourth century B.C. This fits Sallust's general view that imperial conquest put an end to an age when men were still free from greed. Sallust believes

---

[6] Hor. *Carm.* 1.1; Livy 1 *pr.* 11; Pliny, *NH* 7.130; cf. Nathan S. Rosenstein, *Imperatores Victi: Military Defeat and Aristocratic Competition in the Middle and Late Republic* (Berkeley, 1990), for the Roman belief in a connection between divine favor and military success; Catharine Edwards, *The Politics of Immorality in Ancient Rome* (Cambridge, 1993), 20–22 for the insistence of the Romans on their virtue.

[7] Plutarch, *Marcus Cato* 3.5–7. Cf. Livy 29.19 for similar attacks on Scipio in Rome, cited below in the discussion of Roman attitudes towards Greeks.

[8] Sallustius, *Cat.* 11.5: huc adcedebat, quod L. Sulla exercitum, quem in Asia ductaverat, quo sibi fidum faceret, contra morem maiorum luxuriose nimisque liberaliter habuerat. loca amoena, voluptaria facile in otio ferocis militum animos molliverant: ibi primum insuevit exercitus populi Romani amare potare, signa tabulas pictas vasa caelata mirari, ea privatim et publice rapere, delubra spoliare, sacra profanaque omnia polluere. Elsewhere Sallust is concerned with the moral decline of Rome for internal reasons: Sallustius, *Catilina.* 37.7; *Jug.* 41.7–8; Florus 1.47. See A.W. Lintott, "Imperial Expansion and Moral Decline in the Roman Republic," *Historia* 21 (1972), 626–638 and further sources asserting the internal causes of decline cited in n.10 on p. 627. Note also the earlier article F. Hampl, 'Römische Politik in republikanischer Zeit und das Problem des "Sittenverfalls",' *HZ* 188 (1959), 497–525. See now Edwards, *The Politics of Immorality* (1993) for the political use made in Rome of the presumed moral characteristics of current politicians and leaders.

[9] Echoed by some modern scholars, e.g., R. H. Barrow, *Slavery in the Roman Empire* (New York and London, 1928; repr. 1968), "Heredity, climate, institutions have always proved fatal to the Western race rash enough to ally itself too closely with the East."

the first imperialists in history to have been Cyrus in Asia and the Athenians and Lacedaemonians in Greece (*Cat.* 2.1–2).

Here it should be noted, as will be clear also from chapter 9 on Roman attitudes towards the Greeks, that there was a shift over time. The Romans first felt that their conquest of the wealthy regions of Southern Italy exposed them to corrupting luxury, next these feelings were transferred to Greece proper, and then, when Asia Minor and the Near East were gradually taken over, these became the regions most explicitly felt to be a source of corruption.

It is interesting to observe that, a century after Sallust wrote these lines, the Elder Pliny still accepted such ideas and he was convinced that the beginning of this process of degeneration of the Romans themselves was the first entry of Roman troops in Asia Minor in 189 B.C.: "It was the conquest of Asia that first introduced luxury into Italy."[10] The next stage was the incorporation of Pergamum through the bequest of Attalus III (133 B.C.): 'But receiving Asia also as a gift dealt a much more serious blow to our morals . . . and the bequest of it that came to us on the death of King Attalus was more disadvantageous than the victory of Scipio. For on that occasion all scruples entirely disappeared in regard to buying these articles."[11] Other disasters were the conquest of Achaea with the sack of Corinth in 146 B.C., and that of Carthage in the same year. All this is part of a much longer section lamenting the degrading effects of increased wealth in Rome, caused by successes in warfare. Cicero is another respectable Roman who disapproved—or assumed that his target audience disapproved—of Asiatic morals. Men with an Asiatic background are *saltatores*, dancers.[12] In this respect, as in others we have already seen, the Elder Pliny's opinions were typically those of the very conservative Roman upper class. Essential features in this highly charged complex of emotions are fears about the contamination of Roman moral integrity through pollution with morally corrupt subject peoples; the debilitating effect of increased wealth resulting from the subjugation of wealthy foreigners; and, ultimately, the destruction of the Roman Empire by its very success.[13]

Such ideas are also found in the work of Florus: "It was the conquest of Syria which first corrupted us, followed by the Asiatic inheritance bequeathed

[10] Pliny, *NH* 33.53.148: Asia primum devicta luxuriam misit in Italiam. In an interesting variant on this theme Cicero claims that the Phoenicians first introduced greed, luxury, and the uninhibited desire for everything into Greece. *de re publica* 3. fr.3: 3: Poeni primi mercaturis et mercibus suis avaritiam et magnificentiam et inexplebiles cupiditates omnium rerum inportaverunt in Graeciam.

[11] loc. cit.: at eadem Asia donata multo etiam gravius adflixit mores . . . tum enim haec emendi Romae in auctionibus regiis verecundia exempta est urbis . . .

[12] *Pro Murena* 13: Saltatorem appellat L. Murenam Cato; *Piso* 20–22; 89 (Aulus Gabinius); *Deiotarus* 28; also *De Domo sua* 60; *Phil.* 5.15: atque ego de notis iudicibus dixi; quos minus nostis nolui nominare: saltatores, citharistas, totum denique comissationis Antonianae chorum in tertiam decuriam iudicum scitote esse coniectum.

[13] Clearly there is more to be said about Roman luxury than the qualms and criticism expressed by moralists, but that is not the subject of this study. See, for instance, Andrew Dalby, *Empire of Pleasures: Luxury and Indulgence in the Roman World* (London and New York, 2000), a work which follows the interest expressed in such studies by Oswyn Murray.

by the king of Pergamon. The resources and wealth thus acquired spoiled the morals of the age and ruined the State, which was engulfed in its own vices as in a common sewer."[14] For Juvenal the Syrian immigrants in Rome had turned the Tiber into the Orontes. Florus goes a step further and descends to the level of a sewer. Another frequent image is that of corruption, moral and material. Juvenal combines these commonplaces in one of his fierce diatribes: in the past women were modest and chaste. "We are now suffering the calamities of long peace. Luxury, more deadly than any foe, has laid her hand upon us, and avenges a conquered world."[15] Here Juvenal combines the idea, frequently encountered in this work, of the corrupting effects of luxury and wealth and the demoralizing impact of peace. He then introduces a third common variety of social frustration—xenophobia: "Filthy lucre first brought in amongst us foreign ways."[16]

Florus, we may add, does not write satire or judicial rhetoric. He is bitter, but literally means what he says. The common conviction is that Roman morals have been fatally undermined, but from the outside, not from within. One might legitimately ask what was the innate quality of morals if they were so easily destroyed by outsiders, for the essence of morals, after all, is that they can withstand a strong challenge, but that line of thinking did not appeal to the authors we are considering here.

The Macedonians who rule Alexandria in Egypt, who rule Seleucia and Babylon and other colonies spread all over the world, have degenerated into Syrians, Parthians and Egyptians; Massilia, situated among the Gauls, has taken over some of the characteristics of its neighbours; what have the Tarentines preserved of that hard and terrible Spartan discipline? Whatever grows in its own soil, prospers better; transplanted to alien soil, it changes and it degenerates to conform to the soil which feeds it. . . .[17] You, by Hercules, being men of Mars, must take care and escape as quickly as possible from the amenities of Asia: such power have these foreign pleasures to smother vigour of character; so powerful is the impact of contact with the way of life and customs of the natives.[18]

[14] Florus, *epitoma* i 47, 7: Syria prima nos victa corrupit, mox Asiatica Pergameni regis hereditas. Illae opes atque divitiae adflixere saeculi mores, mersamque vitiis suis quasi sentina rem publicam pessum dedere.

[15] Juvenal 6.292–3: nunc patimur longae pacis mala, saeuior armis I luxuria incubuit uictumque ulciscitur orbem.

[16] Juvenal, *Satire* 6.294–300: nullum crimen abest facinusque libidinis ex quo I paupertas Romana perit. hinc fluxit ad istos I et Sybaris colles, hinc et Rhodos et Miletos I atque coronatum et petulans madidumque Tarentum. I prima peregrinos obscena pecunia mores I intulit, et turpi fregerunt saecula luxu I diuitiae molles.

[17] 38.17.12: Macedones, qui Alexandream in Aegypto, qui Seleuciam ac Babyloniam, quique alias sparsas per orbem terrarum colonias habent, in Syros Parthos Aegyptios degenerarunt; Massilia, inter Gallos sita, traxit aliquantum ab accolis animorum; Tarentinis quid ex spartana dura illa et horrida disciplina mansit? generosius in sua quidquid sede gignitur; insitum alienae terrae in id quo alitur, natura uertente se, degenerat. . . . For Massilia different statements are cited below, p. 311.

[18] 38.17.16: eosdemne hos creditis esse, qui patres eorum auique fuerunt? . . . 17: uberrimo agro,

This is a passage from a speech attributed by Livy to the commander Cn. Manlius, addressing his troops in 189 B.C. before the victory which, as we just saw, Sallust and the Elder Pliny considered so harmful to Roman morals. It combines several relevant elements at different levels, not all of them familiar. Livy was writing in the reign of Augustus. We need not assume that the republican commander said anything like what Livy reports. It is safe, however, to regard the text as one which Livy felt should represent the words spoken by a Roman commander about to go to battle against eastern troops. It contains several ideas important for the present study. The idea that some people are effeminate, feeble, and soft, while others are masculine, strong, and virtuous, has been encountered frequently, both in Greek and Roman texts, even though the modern literature seems to associate it more with Romans than with Greeks. Softness, *mollitia*, was part of a complex of invariably undesirable qualities.[19] It was associated with homosexuality, passivity, indolence, but also with a lack of self-control or indulgence. In chapter 6, we shall see how entire peoples are seen in terms of these weaknesses, or their opposites: masculinity, activity, aggression, and self-control. Aristotle unambiguously introduces the contrasting pairs of association: man, light, good as opposed to woman, darkness, left, evil (*Metaphysics* 1.986a 22). Ultimately femininity became the characteristic of any people vanquished by a masculine victor, as shown in figures 7 and 8.

Another of the ideas present in the passage cited here has been discussed at length above, in chapter 1: the view that the physical and mental characteristics of groups of human beings are determined by the environment, by climate, and geography more than by heredity or social culture.[20] However, there are other significant features: the expansion of an empire contains in itself the seeds of the dissolution of that empire: contamination with the inferior values and qualities of the subject population will inevitably lead to decay.[21] Related to this is the conviction that emigration leads to deterioration and this deterioration is a one-way process. Those moving from a sturdy environment to a weak one degenerate, but the reverse is not true. On the contrary: those corrupted will, upon their return home, corrupt others. Thus no Roman source ever claims that the Roman troops in Britain or Germany gained in strength, while we read again and again that those in Syria deteriorated. In fact, the implication of the

---

mitissimo caelo, clementibus accolarum ingeniis omnis illa, cum qua uenerant, mansuefacta est feritas. uobis mehercule, Martiis uiris, cauenda ac fugienda quam primum amoenitas est Asiae: tantum hae peregrinae uoluptates ad extinguendum uigorem animorum possunt; tantum contagio disciplinae morisque accolarum ualet. Josephus, *BJ* 2.16.4 (362), attributes to Agrippa II, in his address to the Jews in Jerusalem before they start their revolt in A.D. 66, the question: "Do you really suppose that you are going to war with Egyptians or Arabs?"

[19] Edwards, *The Politics of Immorality*, chapter 2: "*Mollitia:* reading the body," 63–97 and chapter 5 on "pleasure," which here includes prosperity.

[20] E. Norden, *Die germanische Urgeschichte in Tacitus Germania* (Stuttgart, 4th ed. 1959), 156–160, in his enthusiastic discussion of this passage in Livy, has no doubt that Livy follows Posidonius in his observations.

[21] See chapter 1, for decline as a result of migration; chapter 2, as a result of contact between peoples.

words Livy attributes to the Roman commander is that migration can never be healthy: "Whatever grows in its own soil, prospers better."

At another level there are various important features of Roman imperialism involved: (1) Because wealth corrupts and natural advantages, such as a favorable climate and abundant resources, rob men of fighting qualities, Rome's strength was undermined by its conquered possessions in the East. Of course, Rome was not the only expanding empire that found it difficult to cope with its own material wealth, but it definitely regarded this as an extremely important issue and it emphasized, more than other periods, the immediate connection between luxury and degeneration. (2) The army was the vehicle of this corruption. The former is a theme that recurs frequently in authors of this period. The idea of the empire being corrupted by wealthy Asiatics is clearly related to the older notion that prosperity (*eudaimonia*) corrupts. It is also encountered in Polybius (c. 200–c. 118 B.C.).[22] Polybius, who follows standard notions of decline from Greek political theory, has no doubt that a successful empire will eventually decline because of its very success and prosperity. For Polybius, however, this is not merely theory, it is theory applied to the Roman Empire. Wealth will lead to ambition and strife, conflict between the leaders and the population, mob-rule. Polybius sees the beginning of individual corruption in Rome as coinciding with the first campaigns overseas (18.35), although he also believes that their *mores* were as such unimpaired at the time of the battle of Cannae, in the Second Punic war (6.56.1). The idea that all empires must come to an end is given expressive form in Scipio Aemilianus's tearful comments while seeing Carthage being destroyed.[23] It is worth observing that all this anguish antedates by some three centuries the reign of Marcus Aurelius and this is where Gibbon began his work. It is a theme that continues to fascinate in our times.

There are, apparently, two processes at work, at least in the conceptual world we are considering here: there is the influence of the environment, producing sturdy and stupid people, or intelligent and soft ones. Second, there is the matter of contamination guaranteeing deterioration whenever there is migration and

---

[22] E.g., 6.57.5–8, cf. C.W. Fornara, *The Nature of Ancient History in Ancient Greece and Rome* (Berkeley and Los Angeles, 1983), 85–87. See Lintott, "Imperial Expansion," 638: in his view the tradition which ascribed the political failure of the Republic to moral corruption derived from wealth and foreign conquest, developed from the propaganda of the Gracchan period.

[23] Polybius's description, 38.21 and 22 and Scipio's quotation of *Iliad* 6.448f. have been preserved by Appian, *Pun.* 132 and have led to divergent interpretations in recent scholarship; cf. A. E. Astin, *Scipio Aemilianus* (Oxford, 1967), 251f., 282–287, at 285f., questioning the intensity of the emotional experience; A. Momigliano, *Alien Wisdom*, 22f., regards Astin's assessment as troubled by public school prejudices. Eduard Fraenkel, who did not suffer from such prejudices, was untroubled by the tears and more romantically inclined. He regarded Scipio's attitude as "a Greek outlook on life and a Greek conception of history, the theory of the necessary vicissitudes of human fate and of the cycle in the life of nations, which that great man has made so much his own that it overshadows all else in that hour of his greatest success": "Rome and Greek Culture" (his Oxford oration), reprinted in *Kleine Beiträge zur klassischen Philologie* (Rome, 1964), vol. 2, 583–598, at 597; see more recently, Albert Henrichs, *HSCP* 97 (1995), 250–254.

contact. We may note that this concept exists in Greek literature, as seen above, in chapter 1, but it played no significant role in Greek colonization for the Greeks did not fear that their *apoikiai* would fail to maintain the values of the mother-city. The reason for this distinction is clear. The Greek *apoikiai* were Greek *poleis* which did not intend to incorporate large numbers of foreigners. Where there was no integration there was no fear of contamination.

Thus there is the basic assumption that any change resulting from contact with others must be a change for the worse and cannot be an improvement. This is part of the ancient tendency to regard all forms of change as bad by definition—*res novae*, "new things," revolution, can only lead to deterioration. Because change must always be deterioration, there exists no passage which says that Asiatics transplanted to a northern climate become tough or that when they come into contact with Germans they are influenced by the latter and become tough warriors. The most significant feature of this whole complex is the idea of contamination or pollution, also present in the passage from Sallust discussed above. This idea was adhered to very consistently. The army of the Cimbri failed to capture Rome because they let themselves go soft in Venetia, according to several sources, Venetia, "the region in which the Italian climate is almost at its softest."[24] But it was not only the sky and the soil which sapped their vigor; they learned to eat bread and cooked meat and drink wine. In other words, both the idea of the climate and the acquisition of a more developed lifestyle by contact with others were responsible for their deterioration. This is regarded as true for all armies, not just that of the Romans. It is interesting to see that there was no conceptual difficulty in believing that the Cimbri lost their vigor in circumstances which did not prevent the Romans from acquiring an empire.

In later periods the idea of degeneration is one of the basic characteristics of racist attitudes, although these show many variants.[25] Decline and degeneration was a significant theme for many intellectuals in the nineteenth and early twentieth centuries. The best known expression of the idea is found, of course, in the works of de Gobineau, Oswald Spengler, and Arnold Toynbee.[26] Whether the Roman sources here discussed contain elements of what we call racism is a delicate question, central to the subject of this book. There is the certainty of Roman superiority being undermined by contact with inferior foreigners, which we find also in modern racist attitudes. Furthermore, the conviction that the

[24] Florus 1.28.13: quo fere tractu Italia mollissima est, ipsa soli caelique clementia robur elanguit. Orosius 5.16.14; Cassius Dio 27 fr. 94.2 lists the same causes as Florus and adds warm baths. These are mentioned also by the *Historia Augusta* in its complaints about the Roman troops in Syria: SHA *Avidius Cassius* 5.11.

[25] For instance, Buffon's *Natural History* with its theory of degeneracy (G-L. Leclerc, Comte de Buffon, *Histoire Naturelle* "de la dégénération des animaux"), originally published in 1766, cited above, in the Introduction.

[26] It is also relevant to mention in this connection the theory of degeneration among biologists, cf. P. J. Bowler, "Holding your head up high: degeneration and orthogenesis in theories of human evolution," in James R. Moore (ed.), *History, Humanity and Evolution* (Cambridge, 1989), 329–353.

foreigners are incapable of improvement fits the definition, proposed in the Introduction. There it was posited that the essence of racism is that it regards individuals as superior or inferior because they are believed to share imagined physical, mental, and moral attributes with the group to which they are deemed to belong, and it is assumed that they cannot change these traits individually. The Roman sources cited so far certainly establish a hierarchy of groups of human beings, and these are certainly based on a belief that they share common characteristics that cannot be changed individually. These characteristics are not necessarily inherited. They are caused by the environment, that is climate and soil, as expressed emphatically by Livy: "Whatever grows in its own soil, prospers better; transplanted to alien soil, it changes and it degenerates to conform to the soil which feeds it." This indubitably may be called a proto-racist complex of ideas, whereby there is a remarkable insistence on the idea that each people prospers best in its own environment and changes for the worse when transplanted. Change, in fact, is always for the worse. This, of course, is not a modern attitude. Modern racism is deeply concerned with progress, yet it is an anxious and troubled mind-set and so is its ancient predecessor.

This is essential: as observed also in chapter 3, the idea of progress was not common in Greek and Roman culture and the view that there is a constant decline so common that it hardly needs explanation. To give a random example: the elder Pliny says that it is "almost a matter of observation that with the entire human race, the stature on the whole is becoming smaller daily, and that few men are taller than their fathers, as the conflagration that is the crisis towards which the age is now verging is exhausting the fertility of the semen."[27] He says that Homer already said so and gives examples of bodies of ancient men which were discovered and proved to be extraordinarily tall.

Obviously, we have to take into account the fact that the passage under discussion is taken from a speech and has to be interpreted as such. Livy himself adopts a rather different line in another speech of the same year, where the Rhodians address the senate. There the Rhodians assert that Greek colonies remain Greek in spite of being surrounded by barbarians. "Moving to another land does not change one's origin or customs."[28] Massilia is given as an example of a colony that had remained Greek under such circumstances.[29] Thus it was possible to build a case proving the opposite if that was expedient.

It will therefore be both illuminating and engaging to look forward briefly to

---

[27] Pliny, *NH* 7.73.1: in plenum autem cuncto mortalium generi minorem in dies fieri propemodum observatur rarosque patribus proceriores, consumente ubertatem seminum exustione, in cuius vices nunc vergat aevum.

[28] Livy 37.54.18: nec terra mutata mutavit genus aut mores.

[29] See for Massilia and the Celts A. Momigliano, *Alien Wisdom*, 50–57. On p. 56 he concludes: "The general impression of Massalia in ancient sources is of a city which had decided to remain unchanged in its archaic Hellenic shape." Note Florus's comments on Massiliote resistance to Caesar: 2.24: Graecula civitas non pro mollitia nominis et vallum rumpere et incendere machinas ausa, etiam congredi navibus. Cicero, *Pro Flacco,* 63, claims in judicial rhetoric that Massilia in civilization and solidity is the superior not only of Greece, but apparently of the entire world. Yet the contrary has also been asserted: Livy 38.17.12, cited above, n. 17.

312 • CHAPTER 5 •

the fate awaiting Cn. Manlius upon his triumphant return to Rome as reported, once again, by Livy. In spite of the warnings which Livy attributes to him in his speech, the troops were, according to Livy, indeed influenced by their contact with the delights of the cities of Asia, the abundance of its wealth, and the feebleness of its inhabitants which "made armies richer rather than stronger" (39.1.3).[30] Discipline was slack when the army was in Asia. When it returned to Rome, it brought with it all sorts of undesirable luxuries. Expensive banquets became fashionable. "At that time the cook, for the ancients the cheapest of slaves, began to be appreciated and exploited and to be valuable and what had been a service became an art" (39.6.7–9).[31]

At this stage we may sum up the argument as follows: the sources cited here consider religious, moral, political, and social values and may be regarded as representing Roman ethnic prejudice and proto-racism. These are embedded in their own views of the acquisition of empire and its effect on the imperial power. It will be useful to consider these further, in particular the notion that conquest inevitably results in the corruption of the victor, through contamination with the weakness of the vanquished.

In 211 B.C., M. Marcellus plundered Syracuse and transported its works of art to Rome, an act which was for Polybius a subject of serious doubt, as he explains. When leading simple lives the Romans had constantly been victorious over peoples who possessed numerous works of art. "To abandon the habits of the victors and to imitate those of the conquered, not only appropriating the objects, but at the same time attracting that envy which is inseparable from their possession, which is the one thing most to be dreaded by superiors in power, is surely an incontestable error."[32] According to Livy, Cato described the works of art from Syracuse in an untranslatable pun as "hostile standards."[33] Polybius regards the victory over Perseus (167 B.C.) as a particularly corrupting event. At that time Roman youth was infected with Greek homosexuality, pros-

[30] ditiores quam fortiores exercitus faciebat. The idea that Asia was rich was common in Livy's times as it was before, see, e.g., Manilius 4.671: inde Asiae populi divesque per omnia tellus.

[31] Pliny, NH 9.67, for a similar complaint. A different view is expressed by Aristotle, Politics 1255B: "and indeed there might be more advanced scientific study of such matters, for instance a science of cookery and the other such kinds of domestic service (τῶν τοιούτων μάθησις, οἷον ὀψοποιικὴ καὶ τἆλλα τὰ τοιαῦτα γένη τῆς διακονίας)—for different servants have different functions" (trans. H. Rackham, Loeb).

[32] Polybius 9.10.5–11: τὸ γὰρ ἀπολιπόντας τὰ τῶν νικώντων ἔθη τὸν τῶν ἡττωμένων ζῆλον ἀναλαμβάνειν, προσεπιδραττομένους ἅμα καὶ τὸν ἐξακολουθοῦντα τοῖς τοιούτοις φθόνον, ὃ πάντων ἐστὶ φοβερώτατον ταῖς ὑπεροχαῖς, ὁμολογούμενον ἄν εἴποι τις εἶναι τῶν πραττόντων παράπτωμα. Cf. F. W. Walbank, A Historical Commentary on Polybius, vol.1 (Oxford, 1957), 134f. Polybius's criticism had already been voiced by Cato. fr. 224 Malc.: Miror audere atque religionem non tenere, statuas deorum, exempla earum facierum, signa domi pro supellectile statuere. See also Jean-Louis Ferrary, Philhellénisme et impérialisme: Aspects idéologiques de la conquête romaine du monde hellénistique (Rome, 1988), 572–578.

[33] Livy 34.4.4: "Infesta, mihi credite, signa ab Syracusis illata sunt huic urbi."

titution, excessive dining, and general extravagance.[34] It is clear that the connection between moral corruption caused by their victories over the Greeks precedes similar ideas regarding the conquest of Asia, even though the latter gained in strength afterwards.[35]

Polybius's strictures may represent the earliest occurrence in ancient literature of the idea that not just Rome's masculinity and strength but also its morals were affected by the acquisition of the wealth and luxury of the vanquished. This was later echoed by Livy, who adds that the license "to despoil all kinds of buildings, sacred and profane, finally turned against the Roman gods."[36] Elsewhere Polybius cites Romans critical of the destruction of Carthage and the dissolution of the kingdom of Macedonia. These were betrayals of the traditional moral principles guiding Rome in war. They predicted Roman supremacy would end the way Athenian and Spartan domination had been destroyed (36.9.5–10).

Such worries are found also in Cicero's *De Re Publica,* as voiced by Laelius. Violating the treaty rights of allies and Latins, as Ti. Gracchus did, would cause hatred, and an empire cannot survive if it is based on force and fear alone.[37] Generally speaking this sort of decline is a Roman obsession, not a Greek one for which there may be a logical explanation: the Romans, in building their empire, had themselves destroyed other empires. They were also aware of the destruction of the Achaemenid Empire by Alexander and the brevity of Alexander's own empire. However, there may also be a deeper difference in mentality. As expressed by Lucan (A.D. 39–65): "But among the people there were hidden causes of war—the causes which have ever brought down ruin upon imperial peoples. For when Rome had conquered the world and Fortune showered excess of wealth upon her, virtue was dethroned by prosperity, and the spoil taken from the enemy lured men to extravagance" etc.[38]

The opposite idea, that of an eternal empire or an eternal Rome exists in Roman, literature, but it is in fact not a very significant theme.[39] "Eternity,"

[34] Polybius 31.25.3–5; Diodorus 31.26.7 . After his victory Aemilius Paulus celebrated a magnificent festival to show that "the man who knew how to be victorious in war could also organize a festive meal and games" (Livy 45.32.11).

[35] As observed by Petrochilos, *Roman Attitudes* (1974), 73.

[36] Livy 25.40.2: "hostium quidem illa spolia et parta belli iure; ceterum inde primum initium mirandi Graecarum artium opera licentiaeque huius sacra profanaque omnia vulgo spoliandi factum est, quae postremo in Romanos deos . . . vertit." See also Plutarch, *Marcellus* 21.

[37] Polybius himself also is of the opinion that moral standards of warfare and tactics declined in Greece while in Rome some ancient principles survived (13.3). Cicero, *De Re Publica* 3.41.1 (LAEL.) * Asia Ti. Gracchus, perseveravit in civibus, sociorum nominisque Latini iura neclexit ac foedera. quae si consuetudo ac licentia manare coeperit latius, imperiumque nostrum ad vim a iure traduxerit, ut qui adhuc voluntate nobis oboediunt, terrore teneantur, etsi nobis qui id aetatis sumus evigilatum fere est, tamen de posteris nostris et de illa immortalitate rei publicae sollicitor, quae poterat esse perpetua, si patriis viveretur institutis et moribus.

[38] Lucan *BC* 1.158–162: namque, ut opes nimias mundo fortuna subacto / intulit et rebus mores cessere secundis / praedaque et hostiles luxum suasere rapinae, /.

[39] B. Isaac, "Roma Aeterna," *Historia* 2 (1998), 19–31 (in Hebrew).

applied to the empire, to the state and its glory and renown, is a recurrent theme in Cicero's work. The only period in Roman history which saw a carefully orchestrated departure from the always present gloom and pessimism about the future was the age of Augustus, with its proclamation of a new Golden Age.[40] The best-known celebration of the boundlessness of Rome's empire is found in Vergil's *Aeneis:*[41] "For these I set neither bounds nor periods of empire; dominion without end have I bestowed."[42] Thereafter the idea occurs, but is not a significant one in the literature.[43] Even authors in the reign of Augustus were steeped in fear of possible harmful effects caused by contacts with Greece and the East. Propertius is quite specific: "Happy and in peace lived the youth of the country in those far off days, whose riches consisted of the harvest and the tree . . . Gold has banished faith, for gold judgements can be bought, gold is courted by the law, and soon the conscience that requires no law goes the same way . . . I shall speak out, and may my country accept me as a true seer! Proud Rome is being destroyed by its own prosperity."[44] Livy himself, ruminating on a hypothetical war between Alexander and Rome, concludes that Alexander would have come with an army demoralized and corrupted by its presence in Persia.[45] It is the Roman historian Livy who says so, not a Greek author.

Several Latin authors, and a Greek one writing for Romans, tell us that Hannibal's troops in winter-quarters in Campania became so effeminate because of the pleasures afforded them, that Hannibal said they were not his men, but women.[46] A similar story has been cited above of the Cimbri losing their

---

[40] P. Zanker, *The Power of Images in the Age of Augustus* (Ann Arbor, 1988), chapter 5.

[41] Vergil, *Aen.* 1.278 (trans. Fairclough, Loeb): his ego (sc. Iuppiter) nec metas rerum nec tempora pono: imperium sine fine dedi; cf. R. G. Austin, *P. Vergili Maronis Aeneidos Liber Primus* (Oxford, 1971), comm ad loc. on p.106.

[42] Sometimes the phrase is misunderstood and "sine fine" interpreted in a spatial sense. That is clearly an error, as will be obvious, if not from the text itself, then from the comments in Servius, *in Vergilii Aeneidos Libros* (Servii Grammatici Qui Feruntur in Vergilii Carmina Commentarii. Vols. 1–2, ed. G. Thilo, 1878–1884). 1.278 nec metas rervm nec tempora pono 'metas' ad terras rettulit, 'tempora' ad annos; Lavinio enim et Albae finem statuit, Romanis tribuit aeternitatem, {quia subiunxit 'imperium sine fine dedi'.}. Clearly, *metas rerum* refers to the physical aspect, *tempora* and *sine fine* to the temporal element.

[43] For instance: Pliny, *NH* 2.18.2; Pliny, *Pan.* 67.3; Suetonius, *Nero* 11.2; Tacitus, *Hist.* 1. 84; *Ann.* 3.6. I am referring here to passages which describe the Empire, rather than the city, as eternal.

[44] Propertius 3.13.25f.: felix agrestum quondam pacata iuuentus, / diuitiae quorum messis et arbor erant! / . . . 48f.: aurum omnes uicta iam pietate colunt. / auro pulsa fides, auro uenalia iura, / aurum lex sequitur, mox sine lege pudor. / . . . 59f. proloquar (atque utinam patriae sim uerus haruspex!): / frangitur ipsa suis Roma superba bonis./

[45] Livy 9.17.16: Non cum Dareo rem esse dixisset, quem mulierum ac spadonum agmen trahentiem, inter purpuram atque aurum oneratum fortunae apparatibus suae, praedam verius quam hostem . . . 18.3: Dareo magis similis quam Alexandro in Italiam venisset et exercitum Macedoniae oblitum degenerantemque iam in Persarum mores adduxisset. It has been suggested that Vergil was inspired by these lines: Vergil, *Aen.* 9.602: non hic Atridae nec fandi fictor Ulixes. Cf. N. Horsfall, "Numanus Remulus: Ethnography and Propaganda in *Aen.* ix, 598f.," *Latomus* 30 (1971), 1108–1116, esp. 1108. Horsfall observes that Vergil's debt is tempting but cannot be proved.

[46] Strabo 5.4.13 (c. 250–251) and Cicero, *de lege agraria* 2.95, cited below; Livy 23.18.10–16;

strength in Venetia. It is interesting also to see Cassius Dio's description of how the army was corrupted in 187 by the effects of Asiatic luxury (τῆς τρυφῆς τῆς Ἀσιανῆς γευσάμενοι). "Having spent some time among the possessions of the vanquished amid the abundance of spoils and the licence granted by success in arms, they rapidly came to emulate the prodigality of these peoples and ere long to trample underfoot their own ancestral traditions. Thus this terrible influence, starting in that quarter, invaded the city as well" (Dio 19.64). "These peoples" were Dio's own ancestors.

It is worth noting that such ideas represent a view of society which ascribes a major cause of change or negative influence to lifestyle rather than climate. The opinions cited here resemble the last chapter of the *Cyropaedia* rather than the treatise on *Airs*. People become effeminate, greedy, and immoral through contact with other effeminate and wealthy people, not through the influence of climate or geography. These other peoples, however, are assumed to be effeminate, soft, and luxurious through the effect of climate and geography. We may thus recognize a complex pattern of xenophobia: the subject peoples themselves are viewed as they are in terms of the environment, climate, often in combination with their form of government. The stereotypes are thus a form of proto-racism. When the Roman troops are believed to be affected by these weaknesses, this is no longer a simple form of proto-racism, but an—equally irrational—fear of contamination by the subject peoples. This is an essential feature of modern racism which has found its most pathological expression in the Nürnberger laws and apartheid. In any case, these notions occur so often in the ancient literature that it is impossible to discard them as a rhetorical fancy.[47]

Apparently there was a strong sense among the Romans that their very successes carried the seed of decline. The hostility and contempt they felt towards some of their subjects were often coupled with fear of becoming like them. Clearly the conquering armies are seen as having been polluted by their victims and then passing on the pollution to the citizens at home, as Lucius Verus's troops in Babylonia are reputed to have done in a physical sense when they brought the plague back with them.[48] Another explanation of this phenomenon may be to suggest that there was a discrepancy in Rome between a traditional moral demand for sobriety, temperance, and modest lifestyle and

---

Valerius Maximus 9.1.1. Cf. E. L. Wheeler, "The Laxity of the Syrian Legions," in D. L. Kennedy (ed.), *The Roman Army in the East* (Ann Arbor, MI, 1996), 229–276, esp. 238f.

[47] It is interesting to note, as P. Gay observes in *The Cultivation of Hatred* (London, 1994), 96, that William James dramatized the waning energies of the middle classes by pitting them against classical antiquity: The Greeks' "spirit was still too essentially masculine for pessimism to be elaborated or lengthily dwelt on." Modern races were "more complex, and (so to speak) more feminine than the Hellenes" of the classical age [note: William James, *The Varieties of Religious Experience: A Study in Human Nature* (1902), 142n.]. Thus the same people may be called essentially masculine by a modern author and essentially effeminate by an ancient Roman writer.

[48] J. F. Gilliam, "The Plague under Marcus Aurelius," *AJP* 82 (1961), 225–251.

the reality of life in a wealthy imperial society. The tensions engendered by this discrepancy were best resolved by blaming the victims of imperial expansion for the results.

So far we have dealt with texts which describe Roman troops affected by contact with Asiatics as the agents of dissolution of the empire. The passages cited here are undeniably expressions of xenophobia. The expansion of the empire into Asia brought individuals from the new provinces to Rome. It cannot be overemphasized that these attitudes were widespread. It may be useful to conclude this chapter by citing a number of variants or derivatives of this mode of thinking.

> Then, too, there are those unhappy revenue-farmers—and what misery to me were the miseries and troubles of those to whom I owed so much!—he [sc. Gabinius, the governor of Syria] handed them [sc. the revenue farmers] over as slaves to Jews and Syrians, themselves peoples born to be slaves.[49]

Like other pronouncements in rhetoric aimed at the law courts, this has to be interpreted cautiously. The phrases are all meant to contribute to the larger aim of winning the cause. Still, it is legitimate to assume that Cicero expected his audience and readers to agree with the feelings expressed about Jews and Syrians. Writing in 1974, Momigliano observed: "Books, and there are so many of them, on Cicero's political thought might at least note the desperate vagueness of his ideas on the provincials, which in the case of the Gauls amounted to contempt" (*Alien Wisdom*, 71). If there is any group of provincials Cicero admires, I am not aware of it.[50] Moreover, if Cicero operated at this level, the least we may suspect is that many Roman aristocrats shared his ignorance and hostile attitude. As regards the present pronouncement, first we must note that here again the idea is conveyed that "the victor is subjugated by the conquered." It clearly anticipates Horace's famous "Captive Greece took her savage victor captive and brought the arts to rustic Latium," discussed in chapter 3. There are important differences, however, for Horace wrote satirically about the influence of Greek culture on Rome and Italy. Cicero, on the other hand, is speaking in a judicial context of the position of Roman tax collectors in a province. Still, this pronouncement may be cited as one of many in which the spectre is raised of Roman imperial weakness vis-à-vis its subject peoples.

[49] Cicero, *de prov. cos.* 5.10: Iam vero publicanos miseros me etiam miserum illorum ita de me meritorum miseriis ac dolore! tradidit in servitutem Iudaeis et Syris, nationibus natis servituti. Cited by Stern, *Greek and Latin Authors on Jews and Judaism*, I, no. 70, p. 202. I cannot agree with Stern's comments: "This emphasis on the Jews' being born to slavery may have suggested itself to Cicero due to the large number of Jewish slaves who were brought to Rome after the capture of Jerusalem by Pompey." Even if large numbers of Jewish (and Syrian?) slaves were brought to Rome at the time—although we do not know that this was the case—the language of the expression does not reflect rational observation, but irrational antagonism. Note the recent article J.-E. Bernard, "Philosophie politique et antijudaïsme chez Cicéron," *SCI* 19 (2000), 113–131. See further the discussion of anti-Jewish attitudes, below, chapter 13.

[50] R. Syme, *The Provincial at Rome* (Exeter, 1999), 39–41, cites examples to show that Cicero speaks of aristocrats from Gaul however it suits his purpose.

Second, we should ask what exactly Cicero means by *servituti nati,* a people 'born for slavery.'[51] As observed above, in chapter 2, Aristotle already holds that the essence of slavery is not merely a social condition, but also an inborn characteristic. This, surely, is the background of the idea. Some people are born slaves. As already discussed, the Romans extended this concept by assuming that slavery in the long term has a corrupting, enfeebling, and emasculating effect which is irreparable and irreversible.

Thus the expression *servituti nati* suggests that these characteristics were seen as being transmitted to the next generation. This would have been no problem in Cicero's mind, for he, like other Greeks and Romans, believed in the transmission of acquired characters, discussed in chapter 1. The relationship between imperialism and views on slavery is dealt with in chapter 2. For the present, it is important to note that in Cicero's attack on Syrians and Jews we again encounter the claim that the vanquished have reversed their proper role. It is a theme we encounter again and again. While it is possible to claim that each instance must be understood in context, it cannot be denied that the frequency with which it occurs in a string of authors of different generations indicates that it was alive as a topic. The underlying uncertainty which such pronouncements betray is occasionally expressed in so many words by Roman authors.

It is relevant to note that Cicero is not the only one to describe eastern peoples as "born for slavery." Livy does so too in a speech to his troops which he attributes to the consul Manius Acilius (191 B.C.): "There, as you know, there were Macedonians and Thracians and Illyrians, all most warlike nations, here Syrians and Asiatic Greeks, the most worthless peoples among mankind and born for slavery."[52] Seneca sees no difference between the peoples of Asia Minor and the Parthians in this respect. The wise man will not mind if the "King of the Medes" (the Parthians) or "King Attalus of Asia" is arrogant. "You, O king, have under you Parthians and Medes and Bactrians, but you hold them in check by fear; they never allow you to relax your bow; they are your bitterest enemies, open to bribes, and eager for a new master."[53] This, of course, is the traditional attitude towards easterners, current since the late fifth century B.C. It is, however, more remarkable to see it expressed by Nero's chief advisor than by Isocrates.

The term *"Asiatici Graeci"* used by Livy is noteworthy. The distinction be-

[51] Bernard, "Philosophie politique," 123, discusses this pronouncement by Cicero, but not the phrase *servituti nati.* Note a curious variation on this theme in Tac. *Agr.* 31.2 (Calgacus's speech): nata servituti mancipia semel veneunt, atque ultro a dominis aluntur: Britannia servitutem suam cotidie emit, cotidie pascit.

[52] Livy 36.17.4–5: quippe illic Macedones Thracesque et Illyrii erant, ferocissimae omnes gentes, hic Syri et Asiatici Graeci sunt, uilissima genera hominum et seruituti nata. Cf. Livy 35.49.8: (speech by Roman consul Quinctius in 192 B.C.).

[53] Seneca, *de Constantia* 13.4: Habes sub te Parthos et Medos et Bactrianos, sed quos metu contines, sed propter quos remittere arcum tibi non contigit, sed hostes teterrimos, sed venales, sed novum aucupantes dominum. See also Lucan 7.442f.: *Felices Arabes Medique Eoaque tellus, Quam sub perpetuis tenuerunt fata tyrannis.* The Arabs, Medes, and Eastern peoples are fortunate because fate *always* kept them under tyrants, while the Romans had known freedom.

tween contemporary—as distinct from ancient—Greeks from the mainland and the Greek-speaking inhabitants of Asia Minor sometimes seems to lose its importance to Roman authors.[54] It is clearly present, to some extent, in Juvenal's famous lines: "I cannot stand, Quirites, a Greek city of Rome. Yet how small a part of the dregs is from Greece proper? The Syrian Orontes has long been discharging into the Tiber."[55] Greeks are undesirable, but most of the Greeks in Rome are from Syria. The implication is that Juvenal regards them all as Greeks, but there are Greeks from Greece proper and from elsewhere. The latter are Greeks of even lower quality. In the remainder of the satire all Greeks are treated alike.[56]

The distinction between several kinds of Greeks is not always made, however. This may be illustrated by Tacitus's comments on the garrison at Trapezus (Pontus on the Black Sea) in 69. This was a cohort, "once a part of the royal contingent. They had afterwards received the privileges of citizenship, and while they carried their arms and banners in Roman fashion, they still retained the indolence and licence of the Greek."[57] Tacitus apparently finds indolence and license[58] typical of the Greeks wherever they lived. And, unlike some of the other foreigners he does not like, these particular foreigners were not at all respectable. A remarkable pronouncement to this effect occurs in a speech which Tacitus attributes to the Batavian leader Civilis: "Let Syria, Asia and the Orient, used to kings as it is, be slaves. In Gaul still live many of those born before the (imposition of) tribute."[59] In other words, Tacitus attributes the usual Roman upper-class ideas about the Orient to the Batavian leaders. These are a combination of the fourth-century Greek views of Asia which we have already encountered together with the Roman ideas about imperialism and slavery discussed in the first chapter.

There may be another such case in the work of Tacitus, where he describes the Parthian rebellion against their king Vonones, a hostage in Rome, whom Augustus had given as king to the Parthians at their request. "Soon they felt shame at Parthians having become degenerate, at their having sought a king from another world, one too infected with the training of the enemy, at the

[54] For a different view: A. Spawforth, "Shades of Greekness," in Malkin (ed.), *Ancient Perceptions of Greek Ethnicity* (2001), 375–400, esp. 376–379. My impression is that the Romans distinguished first and foremost between the ancient, fifth-, and fourth-century Greeks and their descendants whom they had defeated.

[55] Juvenal, *Satire* 3.60–65: non possum ferre, Quirites, Graecam urbem. quamuis quota portio faecis Achaei? iam pridem Syrus in Tiberim defluxit Orontes et linguam et mores et cum tibicine chordas obliquas nec non gentilia tympana secum uexit et ad circum iussas prostare puellas. The distinction is implied also by the younger Pliny, *Ep.* 8.24.2: Cogita te missum in provinciam Achaiam, illam veram et meram Graeciam etc.

[56] N. Rudd, *Themes in Roman Satire* (1986), 184.

[57] Tac., *Hist.* 3.47: mox donati civitate Romana signa armaque in nostrum modum, desidiam licentiamque Graecorum retinebant.

[58] Possibly "indiscipline and idleness" is a better translation of *desidia* and *licentia*.

[59] Tacitus, *Hist.* 4.17: servirent Syria Asiaque et suetus regibus Oriens: multos adhuc in Gallia vivere ante tributa genitos.

throne of the Arsacids now being possessed and given away among the provinces of Rome."[60] Vonones is said to have been despised also because of his untraditional attitudes. He was not interested in hunting and horses, he let himself be carried in a litter, and scorned the traditional feasts. He had Greek companions (a quality which the Romans did not always like in their own rulers) and was accessible. "And because his customs were alien from theirs, they hated both his good and his bad qualities."[61] It is impossible to say how much Tacitus really knew about Parthian opinions regarding this king, but it is quite interesting to see that he describes Parthian feelings in the standard terms. Vonones, through his prolonged stay in Rome, had become tainted by strange customs. He was as unacceptable to the Parthians as a Roman emperor with Parthian habits and customs would have been. The qualities which Tacitus describes as being usual in Parthia are not those he usually attributes to Greeks and orientals: they are those of a nomad king. The subjects of the nomad king regarded Rome in the same light in which Romans regarded Syrians.

It is quite possible that there was a development after the integration of the eastern provinces whereby the distinction between "Asiatic" and other Greeks was sometimes seen as less significant. The section on separate groups of peoples below offers some support for this assumption. Finally, however, it is worth observing again that Roman rhetoric did not change over time in its attitude towards eastern peoples. This is clear, for instance, from the Panegyric of Constantine Augustus from 312, describing the eastern armies Alexander the Great had faced (12.5). It does so in precisely the same terms that we find in Arrian's second-century account: weak Medes, unwarlike Syrians, the Parthians' flighty arms, and Asians desirous of a change of servitude. The same text (12.6.1) despises the Greek citizens of Gomphi in Thessaly as *Graeculi*.

One author may be mentioned here, even though he is neither Greek nor Roman, but a Hellenistic Egyptian scholar writing in the mid-second century A.D. Ptolemy the Geographer, astrologer and mathematician, reversed the commonplace about east and west. In his handbook of astrology, *apotelesmatica* or *Tetrabiblos,* he gives a brief survey of the different characters of peoples, from north to south and east to west.[62] Like other authors he divides the world into three parts. Those in the south are burnt by the sun and therefore mostly savage (ἐπὶ πᾶν ἄγριοι) and the same goes for the animals in the region. Those living in the north also are savage in their habits, because it is too cold. Again, the same is said of the fauna and flora. Those in the middle, according to Ptolemy, are civilized and sociable. Of these the southern group are the elite, being more intelligent and inventive and better in investigating things divine.[63] They are

---

[60] Tacitus, *Ann.* 2.2.3: mox subiit pudor: degeneravisse Parthos; petitum alio ex orbe regem, hostium artibus infectum; iam inter provincias Romanas solium Arsacidarum haberi darique.

[61] ib.2.2.6: et quia ipsorum moribus aliena, perinde odium pravis et honestis.

[62] Ptolemy, *Tetrabiblos* 2.2.8; for this passage, cf. K. E. Müller, *Geschichte der antiken Ethnographie* 2 (1980), 172f.

[63] 2.2.8: τούτων δὲ οἱ πρὸς νότον ὡς ἐπίπαν ἀγχινούστεροι καὶ εὐμήχανοι μᾶλλον καὶ περὶ τὴν τῶν θείων ἱστορίαν ἱκανώτεροι.

investigative and good at mathematics. The author leaves it to the reader to work out that he means here his native Egypt and thus himself. So far this is not surprising. We encounter a division between north, south, and the middle and this, being the region in which the author finds himself, is the best of all. This idea, the division between north, middle, and south, and similar ideas are attested from the fifth century B.C. in texts discussed above, in chapter 1. Ptolemy then goes on to describe the difference between east and west and it is here that he is entirely unconventional: his astrological approach leads him to declare that "the eastern group are more masculine, vigorous of soul, and frank in all things . . . This region therefore is diurnal, masculine, and right-handed. . . . Those to the west are more feminine, softer of soul, and secretive."[64]

Ptolemy, being an Egyptian, simply has reversed the age-old stereotypes about East and West to his own satisfaction, for he considers Egypt as part of the East. It is only fair to point out, however, that Ptolemy's approval of the eastern group does not extend far beyond the border of his native land. Below, we shall see what he thinks of Syrians, Arabs, Jews, and others: they are despicable cowards, treacherous, servile, and in general fickle.[65]

A last note on Ptolemy: his views that the peoples, animals, and even flora of specific regions resemble one another because they originate in the same environment, or rather, under the same stars, is interesting. Above, we have seen that comparisons of human beings with animals is an important feature in physiognomics. Here, however, these parallels are extended to the environmental theory and that is remarkable. We find the same notion again in the eighteenth-century author Blumenbach.[66] As seen in chapter 1, Blumenbach follows many of the elements of the classical environmental theory, applying them to his theories about the differences between peoples. He claims that the northern Lapps resemble bears and the blacks, monkeys.[67]

---

[64] 2.2.9 (trans. F. E. Robbins, Loeb): καθόλου δὲ πάλιν οἱ μὲν πρὸς ἕω μᾶλλόν εἰσιν ἠρρενωμέ-νοι καὶ εὔτονοι τὰς ψυχὰς καὶ πάντα ἐκφαίνοντες, . . . καὶ τὸ μέρος ἐκεῖνο ἡμερινόν τε καὶ ἀρρενικὸν καὶ δεξιόν, καθ᾽ ὃ καὶ ἐν τοῖς ζῴοις ὁρῶμεν τὰ δεξιὰ μέρη μᾶλλον ἐπιτηδειότητα ἔχοντα πρὸς ἰσχὺν καὶ εὐτονίαν. οἱ δὲ πρὸς ἑσπέραν τεθηλυσμένοι μᾶλλόν εἰσι καὶ τὰς ψυχὰς ἁπαλώτεροι, καὶ τὰ πολλὰ κρύπτοντες,

[65] Much of Ptolemy's second book consists of a collection of stereotypes about various peoples in astrological terms. There is very little consistency here. The familiar pattern of the soft East versus the hard West is also encountered elsewhere in this confused work; see 2.3.13 ff. Similarly, Appian, another Alexandrian author who wrote in the second century, describes in the Preface to his *Roman History,* 9, the Roman subjugation of Asia as easy, "because of the weakness and cowardice of its peoples" (δι᾽ ἀσθένειαν καὶ ἀτολμίαν τῶν ἐθνῶν), while the conquest of Africa and of Europe was in many instances very hard.

[66] Johann Friedrich Blumenbach, *Über die natürlichen Verschiedenheiten im Menschengeschlecht* (Leipzig, 1798, first published in 1776), 139f.

[67] The Laplanders are often mentioned in seventeenth-century literature as the northern opposite of the southern blacks. This reminds us somewhat of the old, Greek habit of contrasting peoples living in the northern and southern extreme regions, such as the Scyths and Ethiopians. See, for instance, the references by Buffon, cited in chapter 1.

In the late Roman period the antiquarian Vegetius conveyed his views on the differences between the Romans and their subjects: 1.1:

> The Romans conquered all peoples solely because of their military training. How else could small Roman forces have availed against hordes of Gauls? How could small stature have ventured to confront Germanic tallness? That the Spaniards surpassed our men not only in numbers but also in physical strength is obvious. To Africans' treachery and riches we have always been unequal. No one has doubted that we are defeated by the arts and intelligence of the Greeks. But what succeeded against all of them was careful selection of recruits, instruction in the rules, so to speak of war, toughening in daily exercises.[68]

We have here a clear and explicit statement—not meant as satire or sarcastically—of the (late) Roman view of the reason for the success of Roman imperialism, coupled with a series of traditional stereotypes about aliens, among them some positive ones. The Spaniards are strong, the Africans treacherous and rich, the Greeks intelligent and great artists, but the Romans were militarily superior and that determined the outcome.

This passage may remind us of a statement by Cicero: "We cannot pretend to ourselves, however much we would like to, that we are superior to the Hispani in number, to the Gauls in strength, to the Phoenicians in cleverness, to the Greeks in the arts . . . ; it is by our piety and religion, yes, by this unique wisdom of ours, which has made us understand that all is ruled and guided by the power of the gods, that we have triumphed over all peoples and nations."[69] Cicero, as suitable in a speech about religious matters, ascribes their excellent religiosity as the true source of Roman superiority. Other Roman authors are

---

[68] Vegetius, *ep.*1.1 (trans. N. P. Milner): Nulla enim alia re uidemus populum Romanum orbem subegisse terrarum nisi armorum exercitio, disciplina castrorum usu que militiae. Quid enim aduersus Gallorum multitudinem paucitas Romana ualuisset? Quid aduersus Germanorum proceritatem breuitas potuisset audere? Hispanos quidem non tantum numero sed et uiribus corporum nostris praestitisse manifestum est; Afrorum dolis atque diuitiis semper impares fuimus; Graecorum artibus prudentia que nos uinci nemo dubitauit. Sed aduersus omnia profuit tironem sollerter eligere, ius, ut ita dixerim, armorum docere, cotidiano exercitio roborare, quaecumque euenire in acie atque proeliis possunt, omnia in campestri meditatione praenoscere, seuere in desides uindicare.

[69] Cicero, *De haruspicum responsis* 19: Quam volumus licet, patres conscripti, ipsi nos amemus, tamen nec numero Hispanos nec robore Gallos nec callidate Poenos nec artibus Graecos . . . sed pietate ac religione atque hac una sapientia, quod deorum numine omnia regi gubernarique perspeximus, omnis gentis nationesque superavimus. Cicero to some extent echoes Polybius, 6.56.6 (trans. W. R. Paton, Loeb): "But the quality in which the Roman commonwealth is most distinctly superior is, in my opinion, the nature of their religious convictions. I believe that it is the very thing which among other peoples is an object of reproach, I mean superstition (δεισιδαιμονία), which maintains the cohesion of the Roman state." Cf. F. Walbank, *Commentary on Polybius* 1 (Oxford, 1957), 741f., who points out that Polybius's interpretation of Roman religion is that of a Greek rationalist, not of a native Roman. Cf. before Cicero: Sallust, *Jugurtha* 14.19; and later: Horace, *Odes* 3.6.5; Vergil, *Aen.* 6.791. For Cicero's thoughts on religion: Mary Beard, "Cicero and Divination: the Formation of a Latin Discourse," *JRS* 76 (1986), 33–46.

convinced that the essence of Roman superiority in comparison with other peoples was to be found in their morals.[70] Vegetius, however, who writes about the Roman army, concludes that only in the art of war was Rome stronger than its subject peoples and only thanks to this quality was it victorious.

If so much was at stake, and Rome, victorious only thanks to one specific quality, was faced with such formidable enemies, it was easy to imagine that all could be lost. In this chapter we have seen that ancient authors suffered occasionally from anxiety regarding the stability and safety of the empire. With regard to the Jews, Seneca the Philosopher expresses this too in vehement form: "Meanwhile the customs of this accursed people (the Jews) have gained such influence that they are now received throughout all the world. The vanquished have given laws to their victors."[71] It will be clear that Seneca here means the religious observances of the Jews, for that was what made them remarkable in Roman eyes. This, too, confirms the importance of the link between religion and empire. Cicero claims that the empire owed its existence to piety and religion. Seneca says that the influence of Jewish customs undermines it.

CONCLUSIONS

This chapter discusses the impact of stereotypical thinking on Roman imperial policy with particular reference to the East, the East being a shifting concept through the centuries: first it was Greece, then Asia Minor, then what is now called "the Near East," particularly Syria. As we saw in chapter 3, in the second century B.C. we encounter hostility towards Greek literature, influential as it was, and Greek medicine, both described as threatening in various ways. Greek literature corrupted morals, Greek doctors fleeced and killed their patients. It must be admitted that the sources for all this are limited. It is an hypothesis of the present work that they are an indication of the mood among the Roman establishment. Better attested is the fear of the Roman army conquering and occupying Asia as a corruptible and corrupting agent. Having been exposed to vast luxury, lack of morals, and sexual excess, it would spread these vices in Rome and Italy. The presumed causes of these defects in Asia itself have been discussed above and will be discussed again below, in chapters 6 and 9. We are faced with the usual environmental theory. Asia Minor and Syria had natural advantages, such as a favorable climate and abundant resources, which were thought to have enfeebled the population. These defects, however, were also seen as infectious. The victorious army was affected and infected and would undermine Roman strength in turn.

There are several further important concepts at the root of these fears. First, there is the idea, familiar throughout antiquity, that traveling and contact with

---

[70] See above, nn. 6, 8.

[71] Seneca, *de Superstitione* ap. Augustinus, *de Civitate Dei* 6.11: "Cum interim usque eo sceleratissimae gentis consuetudo convaluit, ut per omnes iam terras recepta sit; victi victoribus leges dederunt" (Stern, *Greek and Latin Authors*, I, no.186, p. 431f.).

foreigners are hazardous because doing so may impair the traditional integrity of a people. Second, there is the idea that a change of environment can only lead to deterioration and never to improvement. As seen above: Gauls who move to Asia Minor deteriorate and lose their old qualities as warriors, but we never hear of effeminate men who migrate to a harsh climate and become true fighters. Third, there is the elementary absence of any idea of progress. Change can only be for the worse. Fourth, and connected with the third concept, we have seen that, ever since the second century B.C., at least some Romans were preoccupied with the decline and fall of their empire, a process they thought inevitable. The main cause was thought to be a loss of masculinity, integrity, and patriotism, caused by the combination of factors just listed. Thus the expansion and growth of empire carried with it its destruction. Finally there is to be mentioned the common attitude to slavery: slavery as a natural condition of some peoples has been discussed above. Influential in Rome was a related idea that the state of slavery or collective subjection after conquest resulted in an irreversible decline of masculinity and fighting spirit. Once a people is subject to another, it will inevitably lose its capacity for independence. If, at the same time, such a people has an attractive culture, its feebleness will corrupt the victor and thus destroy the empire.

Thus we see that there is a direct and immediate connection between Roman stereotypes of others and the self-perception of Romans as conquerors and masters.

Phoenicians, Carthaginians, Syrians

Go seek alliance with the heathen Saracen,
To share his filthy rites, and try to snatch
Forgetfulness in his libidinous courts,
Oblivion in the fountain by the date-tree

—T. S. Eliot, *Murder in the Cathedral,* 600

PHOENICIANS AND CARTHAGINIANS[1]

The Phoenicians, as distinct from the Syrians, are familiar from the Iliad and even more from the Odyssey. "At once the son of Peleus set out prizes for the foot-race: / a mixing-bowl of silver, a work of art, which held only / six measures, but for its liveliness it surpassed all others / on earth by far, since skilled Sidonian craftsmen had wrought it / well, and Phoenicians carried it over the misty face of the water."[2] In the Odyssey the Phoenicians appear on one occasion as honest sailors who do what they can to keep their side of a bargain (*Od.* 13.271–286), but they are also depicted as deceitful, greedy merchants: "Then there came a man of Phoenicia, well versed in guile, / a greedy knave, who had already wrought much evil among men. / He prevailed upon me by his cunning, and took me with him until / we reached Phoenicia, where lay his house and his possessions . . . He set me on a seafaring ship bound for Libya / having given lying counsel to the end that I should convey a cargo with him / but in truth that, when there, he might sell me, and and get a vast price."[3]

---

[1] For ancient attitudes towards Phoenicians and Carthaginians: F. Mazza, "The Phoenicians as seen by the Ancient World," in S. Moscati (ed.), *The Phoenicians* (New York, 1988), 548–567; F. Mazza et al. (eds.), *Fonti classiche per la civiltà fenicia e punica* (Rome, 1988).

[2] *Il.* 23.740–744 (trans. R. Lattimore): Πηλεΐδης δ' αἶψ' ἄλλα τίθει ταχυτῆτος ἄεθλα / ἀργύρεον κρητῆρα τετυγμένον· ἓξ δ' ἄρα μέτρα / χάνδανεν, αὐτὰρ κάλλει ἐνίκα πᾶσαν ἐπ' αἶαν / πολλόν, ἐπεὶ Σιδόνες πολυδαίδαλοι εὖ ἤσκησαν, / Φοίνικες δ' ἄγον ἄνδρες ἐπ' ἠεροειδέα πόντον, W. Leaf, in his commentary, notes that the distinction between the Sidonians as craftsmen and the Phoenicians as traders is always observed in Homer. The Phoenicians are not mentioned elsewhere in the Iliad; for the Sidonians, see also 6.289–291. See also George F. Bass, "Beneath the Wine Dark Sea: Nautical Archaeology and the Phoenicians of the *Odyssey*," in John E. Coleman and Clark A. Walz (eds.), *Greeks and Barbarians: Essays on Interactions between Greeks and Non-Greeks in Antiquity and the Consequences for Eurocentrism* (Bethesda, MD, 1997), 71–101.

[3] *Od.* 14.287–297 (trans. A. T. Murray, Loeb): δὴ τότε Φοῖνιξ ἦλθεν ἀνὴρ ἀπατήλια εἰδώς, / τρώκτης, ὃς δὴ πολλὰ κάκ' ἀνθρώπους ἐεόργει· / ὅς μ' ἄγε παρπεπιθὼν ᾗσι φρεσίν, ὄφρ' / ἱκόμεσθα / Φοινίκην, ὅθι τοῦ γε δόμοι καὶ κτήματ' ἔκειτο./ . . . /ἐς Λιβύην μ' ἐπὶ νηὸς ἐφέσσατο ποντοπόροιο, / ψεύδεα βουλεύσας, ἵνα οἱ σὺν φόρτον ἄγοιμι, / κεῖθι δέ μ' ὣς περάσειε καὶ ἄσπετον ὦνον ἕλοιτο. /

This is Odysseus speaking; in the next book Eumaeus has a similar story: "One day thither came Phoenicians, men famed for their ships, / greedy knaves in their black ships./ Now there was in my father's house a Phoenician woman, / comely and tall, and skilled in glorious handiwork."[4] In the Homeric epic, then, the Phoenicians are skilful craftsmen and sailors[5] but they are also treacherous merchants. Polybius writes in similar terms of the sea power of the Carthaginians and of their navigating skills (1.20.12, 6.52.1). Diodorus, writing in the first century B.C., describes the Phoenicians as pioneer sailors and traders (5.20) while Pliny claims they invented trade.[6] Cicero asserts that the Etruscans and the Phoenicians (*Poeni*: Phoenicians or Carthaginians?) were the only barbarians with a naval tradition, the former as merchants, the latter as pirates.[7] It is slightly unusual to find them described as pirates for, as we will see below, the Phoenicians are more often described as thieving merchants. Cicero, here as elsewhere, uses conventional prejudices in an original manner. He attributes the origins of luxury and greed in Greece to the influence of Phoenician traders.[8] Here he is adopting ideas expressed by Plato about contacts between peoples (discussed in chapter 3), and using them to explain the failure of Greece and the success of Rome.

However, there are exceptions. The geographer Pomponius Mela, writing in the mid-first century, is generally less judgmental and more appreciative of foreign peoples than most ancient authors. However, even by his own standards his praise for the Phoenicians is lavish: they are "an intelligent people, successful in war and peace: outstanding in literature and also in other arts, they devised navigating the seas, fight sea battles, rule peoples."[9] In contrast, as we

---

[4] *Od.* 15.415–8: ἔνθα δὲ Φοίνικες ναυσικλυτοὶ ἤλυθον ἄνδρες, / τρῶκται, μυρί᾽ ἄγοντες ἀθύρματα νηΐ μελαίνῃ. / ἔσκε δὲ πατρὸς ἐμοῖο γυνὴ Φοίνισσ᾽ ἐνὶ οἴκῳ, / καλή τε μεγάλη τε καὶ ἀγλαὰ ἔργα ἰδυῖα·

[5] Mazza, op. cit., 553f. refers to parallels in the Old Testament.

[6] Pliny, *NH* 7.57.199. See also Diodorus 5.35.4f.; 5.38.3: "For the Phoenicians, it appears, were from ancient times clever men in making discoveries to their gain, and the Italians are equally clever in leaving no gain to anyone else." Pliny's claim that the Phoenicians were the first traders does not agree with Herodotus, who credits the Lydians with the initiative of using coin and trading (1.94): Πρῶτοι δὲ ἀνθρώπων τῶν ἡμεῖς ἴδμεν νόμισμα χρυσοῦ καὶ ἀργύρου κοψάμενοι ἐχρήσαντο, πρῶτοι δὲ καὶ κάπηλοι ἐγένοντο.

[7] Cicero, *de re publica* 2.9.8: ita barbarorum agris quasi adtexta | quaedam videtur ora esse Graeciae; nam e barbaris quidem ipsis nulli erant antea maritumi praeter Etruscos et Poenos, alteri mercandi causa, latrocinandi alteri.

[8] Cicero, *de re publica* fr.3 ap. Nonius 431.11, p.695 Lindsay: Poeni primi mercaturis et mercibus suis avaritiam et magnificentiam et inexplebiles cupiditates omnium rerum inportaverunt in Graeciam.

[9] Pomponius Mela 1.65: Phoenicen inlustravere Phoenices, sollers hominum genus et ad belli pacisque munia eximium: litteras et litterarum operas aliasque etiam artes, maria navibus adire, classe confligere, inperitare gentibus, regnum proeliumque conmenti. See now Roger Batty, "Mela's Phoenician Geography," *JRS* 90 (2000), 70–94. In another period Diderot, *Encyclopédie* IV, *Oeuvres complètes* 8 (Paris, 1976), 108, writes: "Voici un peuple intéressé, turbulent, inquiet, qui ose le premier s'exposer sur des planches fragiles, traverser les mers, visiter les nations, leur porter ses connaissances & ses productions, prendre les leurs, & faire de sa contrée le centre de l'univers habité. Mais ces entreprises hardies ne se forment point sans l'invention des sciences & des

saw in chapter 1, Ptolemy, the second-century geographer and astronomer, is particularly hostile towards all the peoples living east of Egypt. He can be assumed to represent an Alexandrian perspective, even though he claims scientific objectivity in assigning the stars as the reason why they are good at trade but unscrupulous, treacherous, despicable cowards, and more. While the Phoenicians, even in Roman times, were still famous for various positive qualities and for their purple and glass, the positive stereotypes mostly faded away over time,[10] while the negative ones, later transferred to "Lebanese" or "Levantine merchants," were never to disappear.

Negative views of Phoenicians recur in the fourth century B.C. in the work of Plato. In his *Laws* 747c–e we find Egyptians, Phoenicians, "and many other peoples" being accused of "having an approach to wealth and life in general which shows a narrowminded outlook."[11] He then considers that there may be two reasons for this which need not concern us here. In the *Republic* 435c–436a he again mentions the greed (τὸ φιλοχρήματον) of the Egyptians and Phoenicians. He also uses the term "Phoenician story" as proverbial for a persuasive lie.[12] While fifth-century sources knew of some eastern peoples as fabulously rich, this is possibly the first source since Homer which associates peoples from the East with unfair and greedy trading. Interestingly, as we shall see below, wealth and greed were not considered characteristics of the Jews in antiquity. This was a stereotype which was attached to various eastern peoples in antiquity, but not to the Jews.

Phoenician cities and their foundations all over the Mediterranean are usually considered as having the same characteristics as those attributed specifically to the Phoenicians. This is true for the city of Carthage, which is naturally more important as a major enemy in Roman sources than any city of Phoenicia proper or any of its other colonies. Carthage is usually regarded as Phoenician and therefore distinct from the neighboring peoples of North Africa.[13] A remarkable early reference to Carthage specifically, as distinct from Phoenicia,

---

arts. L'astronomie, la géométrie, la mécanique, la politique sont donc fort anciennes chez les Phéniciens."

[10] Tyrian purple is still praised by Strabo 16.2.23 (c. 757); Pliny, *NH* 9.60.127. Strabo, loc. cit., states that the Sidonians are skilled in many arts (citing *Il.* 23.743), each of them concerning the merchant and the shipowner. Glass: Strabo 16.2.25 (c. 758); Pliny, *NH* 36.65.190–91; 66.193.

[11] *Leg.* 747c (trans. Saunders): καθάπερ Αἰγυπτίους καὶ Φοίνικας καὶ πολλὰ ἔτερα ἀπειργασμένα γένη νῦν ἔστιν ἰδεῖν ὑπὸ τῆς τῶν ἄλλων ἐπιτηδευμάτων καὶ κτημάτων ἀνεγευθερίας, The idea that Orientals are swindlers is also represented in Isocrates' *Panegyricus* 150f. (380 B.C.), cited above. A direct reference to Plato, with explanation in terms of the usual environmental theory, may be found in Ps. Dionysius Hal., *Ars Rhetorica* 11.5.23: some peoples are keen on learning: the Greeks; some keen on earning money: the Phoenicians and Egyptians; some have fierce tempers: those barbarians who are dedicated to warfare.

[12] Plato, *Resp.* 414c: Μηδὲν καινόν, ἦν δ' ἐγώ, ἀλλὰ Φοινικικόν τι, πρότερον μὲν ἤδη πολλαχοῦ γεγονός, ὥς φασιν οἱ ποιηταὶ καὶ πεπείκασιν, ἐφ' ἡμῶν δὲ οὐ γεγονὸς οὐδ' οἶδα εἰ γενόμενον ἄν, πεῖσαι δὲ συχνῆς πειθοῦς. The phrase could mean that the story truly originates among Phoenicians, but this is not very likely.

[13] Vergil, *Aen.* 1.338: sed fines Lybici, genus intractabile bello; 4.40: hinc Gaetulae urbes, genus insuperabile bello, et Numidae infreni cingunt . . . lateque furentes Barcaei.

may be found in Greek literature, in the work of Aristotle, who praises the
Carthaginian constitution at length and says that it is comparable to those of
Crete and of Sparta.[14] Such praise of Carthage is rare in the work of any ancient
author. Both Plato and Aristotle mention the Carthaginians among the warlike
peoples.[15] Plautus's *Poenulus* contains some passages which show that the negative stereotypes of Phoenicians were applied without change to the Carthaginians. "Besides, this fellow knows every language, but cunningly pretends not
to: he is a true Carthaginian (*Poenus*), and what more needs one say?"[16]

Lucilius refers to a Syrophoenician as a usurer.[17] This is significant, for the
attitudes of Lucilius (active in the final third of the second century, died 102/1)
reflect those of a landed family of senatorial status and corresponding morality.
He is likely to have visited Greece, but did not serve in Asia Minor.[18] This
means that he was probably echoing the common views of Roman aristocrats
on Phoenicians resident in republican Rome at a period long before the incorporation of the region into the empire. This need not surprise us, since some of
these views go back to Homer, as we have seen. There must have been a good
deal of hostile rhetoric against Carthage, especially at the time when the two
powers, Rome and Carthage, fought one another. An example from the remaining fragments of Cato Maior: "Who are the ones that frequently broke treaties?
The Carthaginians. Who are the ones that waged war most cruelly? The Carthaginians. Who are the ones that ravaged Italy? The Carthaginians. Who are
the ones that demand to be forgiven? The Carthaginians. You see therefore how
fitting it is to conquer them."[19] Here then we have the standard themes of
treacherousness and cruelty. However, this was not the only approach in republican times.

It is useful to look at the way the Carthaginian leader Hannibal is described
by various historians. Polybius (c. 200–after 118 B.C.) lists both good and bad
qualities, describing him as an enemy of Rome, without adding anti-Punic gen-

[14] *Pol.* 1272b–1273b; Strabo 1.4.9 (c.66), cites Eratosthenes (third century B.C.) as mentioning the
Romans and Carthaginians in a similar sense; cf. Polybius 6.43.1; 51.1–5. Polybius praises the
Carthaginian consitution, but says it had degenerated by the time of the Hannibalic war. Rome was
in its prime at that time and therefore won the war. See Newman, 2.401–8, Appendix B, "On the
Carthaginian Constitution."

[15] Plato, *Leg.* 637d–e; Aristotle, *Pol.* 1324b.

[16] Plautus, *Poen.* 112f.: et is omnis linguas scit, sed dissimulat sciens se scire: Poenus plane est.
quid verbis opust?

[17] Lucilius, *Sat.* 15.497f.: ac de ist<o> sacer ill<e> toco<glyph>os ac S<y>ro<pho>enix
quid facere est solitus? When the term "Syrophoenician" is used there is, of course, no ambiguity as
to the origin of the person: he is not a Carthaginian, but a Phoenician from the original homeland.

[18] E. Gruen, *Culture and National Identity in Republican Rome* (1992/93), ch. 7.

[19] *Rhet. Her.* 4.20 *Oratorum Romanorum Fragmenta* ed. E. Malcovati (Turin, 4th ed. 1976),
195b: Qui sunt, qui foedera saepe ruperunt? Carthaginienses. qui sunt, qui crudelissime bellum
gesserunt? Carthaginienses. qui sunt, qui Italiam deformaverunt? Carthaginienses. qui sunt, qui sibi
postulent ignosci? Carthaginienses. videte ergo quam conveniat eos impetrare. As an example of
their extraordinary cruelty Cato, elsewhere cited by Aulus Gellius, *Noctes Atticae* 3.14.19, relates
that they "buried the men halfway down into the earth and lighted a fire around them and so they
killed them." See also 9.14.10.

eralizations or stereotypes (9.22.7; 24–6). The same is true for Cornelius Nepos (c. 99–24 B.C.): "If it be true, as no one doubts, that the Roman people have surpassed all other nations in valour, it must be admitted that Hannibal excelled all other commanders in skill as much as the Roman people are superior to all nations in bravery. For as often as he engaged with that people in Italy, he invariably came off victor; and if his strength had not been impaired by the jealousy of his fellow-citizens at home, he would have been able, to all appearances, to conquer the Romans."[20] However, a drastic change in the depiction of Hannibal and the Carthaginians occurs in the work of Livy (59 B.C.–A.D. 17 or 64 B.C.–A.D. 12). In Livy's writings Hannibal is demonized and so are his compatriots: 'These admirable qualities of the man were equalled by his monstrous vices: his cruelty was inhuman, his perfidy worse than Punic; he had no regard for truth, and none for sanctity, no fear of the gods, no reverence for an oath, no religious scruple.' All these negative qualities are attributed to the Carthaginians in general in Latin sources.[21] This then reflects the tone of the Augustan age. The old negative stereotypes regarding the Phoenicians were now combined with a particularly hostile tendency to characterize the Carthaginians as especially treacherous enemies. As observed elsewhere in this study, there were similar changes in style and ideology on other topics and towards other peoples.

The most persistent stereotypes attached to Phoenicians in general and Carthaginians in particular are their guile, unreliability, and treacherousness. Reporting on a disagreement between Greeks and Phoenicians about Tyrian activity in the region of the Strait of Gibraltar, Strabo cites Posidonius, who also "believes this to be the most plausible account of the matter, but that the oracle and the many expeditions from Tyre are a Phoenician lie,"[22] a phrase also used by Plato.[23] Livy has a report of a dispute in the Senate in 172, apparently based on Polybius, in which older and more traditional senators spoke of Punic crafti-

---

[20] Nepos, *Hannibal* 1.1: Si verum est, quod nemo dubitat, ut populus Romanus omnes gentes virtute superarit, non est infitiandum Hannibalem tanto praestitisse ceteros imperatores prudentia quanto populus Romanus antecedat fortitudine cunctas nationes. Nam quotienscumque cum eo congressus est in Italia, semper discessit superior. Quod nisi domi civium suorum invidia debilitatus esset, Romanos videtur superare potuisse. Also: 5.4r. Nepos similarly praises Hamilcar in his *Life* of him. 13: Sic vir fortissimus, multis variisque perfunctus laboribus, anno adquievit septuagesimo.

[21] 21.4.9: has tantas uiri uirtutes ingentia uitia aequabant, inhumana crudelitas, perfidia plus quam Punica, nihil ueri, nihil sancti, nullus deum metus, nullum ius iurandum, nulla religio. Hannibal's cruelty is represented as proverbial by Valerius Maximus, also 9.2.1; 9.2.2E (Valerius Maximus wrote in the reign of Tiberius, but the dates of his sources are unknown). Carthaginian cruelty towards Regulus: id. 9.2.1E; and see also: 1.1.14; 7.6.2; 9.i.1. For Hannibal's treachery: Valerius Maximus 3.8.1; 9.6.2E. Punic treachery: 7.4.2E: "fontem perfidiae." For Fabius's *pietas* and Hannibal's *vafri mores*: 7.3.8.

[22] Strabo 3.5.5 (170): ψεῦσμα Φοινικικόν. Cf. p. 125.

[23] J. Romm, *The Edges of the Earth* (1992), 18, seems to take this at face value: "Furthermore, there is speculation that the Phoenicians deliberately exaggerated reports of dire perils beyond the Straits in order to scare away competitors (the legend behind the proverbial expression 'Phoenician lie')."

ness and Greek artfulness.[24] It is extremely common for people to consider another people liars, be it their enemies, or merely rivals or neighbors. As noted above, Herodotus is unusual in his observation that the Persians regard it as disgraceful to lie. It is therefore interesting to trace in brief the history of such accusations in antiquity. We have already seen that they appear in Homer and in the works of Roman republican authors.[25] The proverbial idea of *Punica fides*, Punic faith, as implying lying is common, although we find the actual expression less than one might expect, given the familiarity of the phrase. Here, in this quotation by Strabo from Posidonius, we should interpret it as representing the Roman attitude, rather than that of the Greeks, for Posidonius, the friend and protégé of Pompey, was writing for Rome.[26]

The accusation of Asiatic faithlessness, however, was as such not a Roman but a Greek invention. Homer's description of Phoenicians has already been quoted. Isocrates, as cited above, says the Persians are swindlers and faithless to their friends. In Latin literature, Sallust mentions *Punica fides* once, using the term in a clearly proverbial sense.[27] Cicero, not surprisingly, asserts that the *Puni* are the most treacherous of all peoples.[28] He says so on several occasions, once explaining that they are liars, "not by origin, but because of the nature of their site, with its port, which brought them in contact with merchants and strangers speaking foreign languages" (*de lege agraria* 2.95). This particular argument has already been discussed, as is proper, in the chapter on the Roman tradition of environmental determinism. We find the term *Punica fides* three times in Livy, twice employed in a rhetorical manner.[29] An interesting variation is offered by Lucan, who represents the Numidians of the time of the civil war as the heirs of Carthage in their unreliability: "Next I fear the two-faced cunning of the fickle Moor; for that impious son of Carthage, mindful of his pedigree, threatens Italy."[30] Valerius Maximus, writing in the reign of Tiberius, may usually be counted upon to echo existing and older prejudices and he duly

[24] Livy 42.47.7: *versutiae Punicae* and *calliditas Graeca*; cf. fr. Diodorus 30.7.1: ἔλεγον μὴ πρέπειν Ῥωμαίοις μιμεῖσθαι Φοίνικας ὥστε δι᾽ ἀπάτης ἀλλ᾽ οὐ δι᾽ ἀρετῆς τῶν πολεμίων περιγίνεσθαι.

[25] Horace calls the Parthians deceitful; see below, chapter 8, n. 33.

[26] A. Momigliano, *Alien Wisdom* (Cambridge, 1975), 72.

[27] sed ego conperior Bocchum magis Punica fide quam ob ea, quae praedicabat, simul Romanos et Numidam spe pacis adtinuisse (*Jugurtha* 108.3).

[28] Cicero, *Pro Scauro* 19.42: Fallacissimum genus esse Phoenicum omnia monumenta vetustatis atque omnes historiae nobis prodiderunt. Also *de officiis* 1.38.

[29] Livy 22.6.12: "quae Punica religione servata fides ab Hannibale est." *Punica religio* here replaces *Punica fides* in the same rhetorical sense. 21.4.9, cited below. 30.30.27: . . . suspectam esse vobis Punicam fidem . . . This is from a speech attributed to Hannibal. It will be noted that in Livy the phrase always occurs in connection with Hannibal. Note also: *versutiae Punicae* (42.47.7); Horace, *carm.* 4.4.49: *perfidus Hannibal*; Vergilius, *Aen.* 661: *Tyriosque bilingues*. T. E. Page, comm. ad loc., notes that the word *bilinguis* refers primarily to the forked tongue of the serpent.

[30] Lucan, *BC* 8.283 (trans. J.D. Duff, Loeb): hinc anceps dubii terret sollertia Mauri; namque memor generis Carthaginis inpia proles inminet Hesperiae, multusque in pectore uano est Hannibal, obliquo maculat qui sanguine regnum et Numidas contingit auos.

mentions "that Punic craftiness, notorious throughout the world."[31] The Carthaginians were also remarkably wealthy, as emphasized in several passages by the same author.[32] Similarly, somewhat later in the first century, Silius Italicus, in his *Punica* describes the young men of Carthage and Tyre as "skilled in deceiving and ever ready to prepare stratagems in the dark."[33] The claim that Hannibal was a particularly treacherous enemy occurs as self-evident in poetry of the Flavian era. Statius, in his poem to celebrate the paving of the *via Domitiana* in Italy (A.D. 95), expresses his joy that "no Libyan hordes" would use it and that "no foreign commander" was "scouring the fields of Campania in treacherous warfare."[34] Appian's *Punic Wars*, written in the second half of the second century A.D., contains a pair of speeches, held after the battle of Zama (202 B.C.). The Carthaginian ambassador is apologetic. Scipio Africanus in his reply is said to have asserted that the Carthaginians do not deserve any pardon, "you, who have so often violated your treaties with us."[35] Afterwards in the senate such assertions are repeated: "What treaty, what oath, have they not trampled under foot? . . . As long as we treat with them they will violate the treaties as they have heretofore, always making some excuse that they were overreached, for doubtful points always provide plausible grounds for dispute."[36] It is for us, of course, impossible to decide whether Phoenicians and Carthaginians were less honest than Greeks or Romans or more so, but it is easy to understand that the Carthaginians would be described in such terms, for the Phoenicians were depicted as dishonest merchants ever since Homer, and the Carthaginians were, in addition, a major enemy of Rome. The stereotype did not disappear altogether in antiquity: a fourth-century source still calls the Africans "somewhat deceitful."[37] A recent parallel is "perfidious Albion," which renders the French original *la perfide Albion*.[38]

Momigliano has written that:

---

[31] Valerius Maximus 7.4.4: ita illa toto terrarum orbe infamis Punica calliditas Romana elusa prudentia Hannibalem Neroni, Hasdrubalem Salinatori decipiendum tradidit. Cf. 7.4.2: haec fuit Punica fortitudo, dolis et insidiis et fallacia instructa.

[32] Valerius Maximus 4.4.6.

[33] Silius Italicus *Punica* 3.231–4: princeps signa tulit Tyria Carthagine pubes, / membra levis celsi que decus fraudata superbum / corporis, at docilis fallendi et nectere tectos / numquam tarda dolos.

[34] Statius, *Silvae* 4.3.4–6: certe non Libycae sonant catervae, / nec dux advena peierante bello / Campanos quatit inquietus agros, / Cf. 4.6.77f: semper atrox dextra periuroque ense superbus.

[35] Appian, *Libyca* 8.53.229 (trans. H. White, Loeb): ἐστὲ μὲν οὐδεμᾶς συγγνώμης ἄξιοι, πολλάκις ἐς σπονδὰς ἡμῶν ὑβρίσαντες. Similarly: 9.58.253; 9.59.258f.

[36] *Lib.* 9.64.284f.: τίς σπονδή, τίς ὅρκος, ὃν οὐκ ἐπάτησαν; τίς δὲ συνθήκη καὶ χάρις, ἐς 285 ἦν οὐχ ὕβρισαν; . . . 287: μέχρι μὲν συντίθενται, παραβήσονται, καθάπερ καὶ πάλαι, πρόφασιν αἰεί τινα τῶν συνθηκῶν φέροντες ὡς ἐν αὐταῖς ἠλαττωμένοι· τὰ δ᾿ ἀμφίλογα εὐπροφάσιστα·

[37] Firmicus Maternus, *Mathesis* 1.2.3: *Afri subdoli*, but note the reservations made in 1.10.12: *Afrorum . . . subdolas mentes honestae fidei ornamenta condecorant.*

[38] *OED*² s.v. Albion': the phrase "la perfide Albion" is said to have been first used by the Marquis de Ximenès (1726–1817) (*N & Q.* (1932) CXLII. 107/2).

Vilification of the character of the Carthaginians was to be found in the Sicilian-born historian Timaeus even before some Roman orators and writers made *"Punica fides"* into a catchword. But it is doubtful whether many Greeks were taken in by such propaganda. Polybius refused to believe it . . . Notwithstanding Cato and Cicero, and perhaps Ennius, there were even Latin writers who refused to join in the chorus: there is nothing very wrong in the *Poenulus* of Plautus; Cornelius Nepos wrote a most sympathetic sketch of Hannibal;[39] Vergil came near to transferring *"Punica fides"* to Aeneas. Only Greek imperial writers such as Plutarch and Appian accepted what had become the conventional literary description of the Carthaginians without reflecting that *Punica fides* had its counterpart in *"Graeca fides."* (*Alien Wisdom*, 4)[40]

I would not accept this judgment without modification. Momigliano's sources, in my opinion, show what he does not recognize himself, namely that this was not really a difference between Greek and Roman. This is all the more obvious if we add Posidonius and his "Phoenician lie."[41] Moreover, Polybius did not really refuse to believe it, for if he did, he would not say of Hannibal that he "adopted a typically Punic artifice."[42] I should add that the Greeks are indeed occasionally accused of being untrustworthy, but I know of only one occurrence of the expression *Graeca fides*, in Plautus, of whose *Poenulus* Momigliano approves.[43] Similarly, there is no evidence of the use of *Germanica fides*, yet Strabo, Velleius, and Manilius, all of them authors writing not long after Varus's disastrous defeat in A.D. 9, describe the Germans as utterly untrustworthy.[44] The use of a term like *"Punica fides"* or *"Graeca fides"* is certainly significant, but it is of some interest to check how often it is used. More importantly, its absence in the work of any given author does not mean this author is free of

[39] But, we may add, Nepos was a model of "xenophilia." He defended the Greeks in a passage cited below, chapter 9, n. 124.

[40] Cf. J. H. Thiel in Erich S. Gruen (ed.), *Imperialism in the Roman Republic* (New York, 1970), 23: "For the Romans were great masters both of patriotism and hypocrisy and the *fides Romana* was not better than the *fides Punica*, perhaps even worse: the Romans used to *speak* far too much of *fides*, which is a very bad sign."

[41] The two authors who clearly avoid crude stereotypes and attempt to be even-handed in general are Polybius and Nepos. Hostile epithets and descriptions of Phoenicians and Carthaginians are found in Homer, Plato, Strabo (citing Posidonius), Sallust, Cicero. They become the norm and increase in number and strength in the works of Livy, Lucan, Valerius Maximus, and Silius Italicus.

[42] Polybius 3.87.1: Ἐχρήσατο δέ τινι καὶ Φοινικικῷ στρατηγήματι τοιούτῳ κατὰ τὴν παραχειμασίαν. F. W. Walbank, *A Historical Commentary on Polybius,* vol.1 (Oxford, 1957), 412, sees this in connection with the proverbial *Punica fides*. Polybius relates that Hannibal, fearing that his Gallic allies would make an attempt on his life, disguised himself with wigs and various costumes.

[43] Plautus, *Asinaria* 198: Diem aquam solem lunam noctem, haec argento non emo: / Cetera quae uolumus uti Graeca mercamur fide. Cicero, *Pro Flacco* 12.13 is not a suitable passage for consideration here, because it was Cicero's aim to discredit Greek testimony in court.

[44] Strabo 7.1.4 (c.291); Velleius 2.118: natumque mendacio genus; Manilius 1.896–903, speaking of "clandestinis surgentia fraudibus arma . . . foedere rupto." The Frisians are said to have claimed that "nobody excelled the Germans in arms or in loyalty," nullos mortalium armis aut fide ante Germanos esse (Tac., *Ann.* 13.54.5).

332 · *CHAPTER 6* ·

stereotypes or xenophobia. It probably is true to say that enemies in general, more often than not, genuinely believe the other side to be treacherous. This is illustrated very nicely by Plutarch's account of the final moments of Crassus in Parthia, in 53 B.C. When he was leading him into a trap, the Surenas told Crassus that he wanted to have the agreement between the two of them in writing; "'for you Romans at least,' said he, 'are not very mindful of agreements'."[45]

This is the place to cite an important text that is sometimes mis-interpreted. Statius, writing in the reign of Domitian, dedicated an ode in Horatian style to his friend Septimius Severus. This was not the future ruler of that name, but probably his grandfather and, like the Emperor, he came from Leptis in Africa. Although written in Statius's usual flattering style, the references to Severus's African background are slightly condescending.

> Did Leptis that loses itself in the distant Syrtes beget you? . . . Who would not think that my sweet Septimius had crawled an infant on all the hills of Rome? Who would not say that he had drunk, his weaning done, of Juturna's fountain? Nor is your prowess to be wondered at: straightaway, still ignorant of Africa and its shallows, you entered the havens of Ausonia, and sailed, an adopted child, on Tuscan waters. . . . Neither your speech nor your dress is Punic, yours is no stranger's mind: Italian are you, Italian! Yet in our city and among the knights of Rome Libya has sons who would adorn her.[46]

Here, as in various texts dealing with the inhabitants of overseas provinces, no obvious and sharp difference is made between the fully Romanized and aristocratic provincials and those, mostly belonging to the lower classes, who adhered to the local culture. Hence the poet rather overemphasizes how un-African or Punic Severus is. Was he really born in Leptis? One would have thought he had been a baby in Rome. This is only natural for he had hardly lived in Africa and therefore he does not speak or dress like a Phoenician. His mind is not foreign: he is Italian! (twice repeated). The implication is that it was normal

---

[45] Plutarch, *Crassus* 31.3: Οὐ γὰρ ὑμεῖς γε, ἔφη, πάνυ μνήμονες ὁμολογιῶν οἱ Ῥωμαῖοι. See also below, Justinus 41.3.5 calls the Parthians treacherous.

[46] Statius, *Silvae* 4.5.29–48 (trans. J. H. Mozley, Loeb): tene in remotis Syrtibus avia / Leptis creavit? . . . / quis non in omni vertice Romuli / reptasse dulcem Septimium putet? / quis fonte Iuturnae relictis / uberibus neget esse pastum? / nec mira virtus: protinus Ausonum portus vadosae nescius Africae intras adoptatusque Tuscis gurgitibus puer innatasti./ . . . / non sermo Poenus, non habitus tibi, externa non mens: Italus, Italus. / sunt Vrbe Romanisque turmis / qui Libyam deceant alumni. The *sermo Poenus* may refer to dialect or accent or both, but F. Vollmer, *P. Papinii Statii: Silvarum Libri herausgegeben und erklärt* (Leipzig, 1898, repr. Hildesheim, 1971), 471, takes this as meaning: "you are not a Punic liar," *sermo Poenus* being the equivalent of *punica fides*. This does not seem to be a satisfactory interpretation. The present line describes external appearance and emphasizes that Severus was not recognizably foreign in Rome. It is hardly a compliment to state that, unlike his compatriots, someone is *not* a liar. Vollmer claims the phrase raises associations with Hannibal. The latter, however, is described in the same poem in quite different terms, cited above. For the interpretation here accepted, see, e.g., A. R. Birley, *The African Emperor: Septimius Severus* (London, 2d ed. 1988), 18–20.

for equestrians from a place like Lepcis with the status of a *municipium* to be regarded as foreign in appearance, speech, and spirit.[47]

It may be a joke when the *Historia Augusta* claims that the Emperor Septimius Severus was ashamed of his sister from Leptis because she could scarcely speak.[48] This is all the more probable if we compare this assertion with a phrase from a letter by Fronto, written in Greek to the mother of the Emperor in 143: "I am a Libyan of the Libyan nomads."[49] Fronto was born in Cirta in Numidia, a Roman colony from the time of Julius Caesar,[50] and his *nomen gentis* Cornelius indicates a grant of citizenship to ancestors in the republican period. Thus his remark that he was a nomad is an affectation. He was no more a nomad than the Emperor himself was, as everybody around him and he himself knew very well, for he was one of the most respected senators of his generation.[51] It shows, however, that even the most distinguished Romans felt ambivalent, and presumably were made to feel so, if they originated in provinces of relatively lower status.

It is therefore undoubtedly true that native Roman aristocrats tended to blur the distinction between a provincial Roman aristocrat and a native Phoenician, Syrian, or other provincial, even if we do not believe that Septimius Severus had a sister who spoke no Latin. Statius's condescension towards the inhabitants of North Africa is evident again when he says that in Rome there are persons and equestrians, who are a credit to Libya, their homeland.[52]

To return to the views of Phoenicians and Carthaginians in Rome, it is relevant here to note that the diminutive *Poenulus*, unlike its equivalent *Graeculus*, is not very common. Apart from Plautus only Cicero uses it once (*de finibus*

[47] For Lepcis Magna as the home-city of Septimius Severus: Birley, 1–22. For full bibliography on the city, R.J.A. Talbert (ed.), *Barrington Atlas of the Greek and Roman World* (Princeton, 2000), Gazetteer, Map 35.

[48] SHA, *Severus* 15.7. According to the same source, 1.4, the Emperor himself was drilled in the Latin and Greek literatures as a child.

[49] Fronto, *Epist. Graecae* 1.10 Naber 239–42 (trans. C. R. Haines, Loeb): εἴ τι τῶν ὀνομάτων ἐν ταῖς ἐπιστολαῖς ταύταις εἴη ἄκυρον ἢ βάρβαρον ἢ ἄλλως ἀδόκιμον ἢ μὴ πάνυ Ἀττικόν, ἀλλὰ . . . τοῦ ὀνόματος σ' ἀξιῶ τήν γε διάνοιαν σκοπεῖν αὐτὴν καθ' αὑτήν· οἶσθα γὰρ ὅτι ἐν αὐτοῖς ὀνόμασιν καὶ αὐτῇ διαλέκτῳ διατρίβω. καὶ γὰρ τὸν Σκύθην ἐκεῖνον τὸν Ἀνάχαρσιν οὐ πάνυ τι ἀττικίσαι φασίν, ἐπαινεθῆναι δ' ἐκ τῆς διανοίας καὶ τῶν ἐνθυμημάτων. παραβαλῶ δὴ ἐμαυτὸν Ἀναχάρσιδι οὐ μὰ Δία κατὰ τὴν σοφίαν ἀλλὰ κατὰ τὸ βάρβαρος ὁμοίως εἶναι. ἦν γὰρ ὁ μὲν Σκύθης τῶν νομάδων Σκυθῶν, ἐγὼ δὲ Λίβυς τῶν Λιβύων τῶν νομάδων.

[50] Full bibliography: *Barrington Atlas* Gazetteer, Map 31.

[51] Fronto returns to this theme several times, again with reference to his Greek: he is "a breathing barbarian." *ad M. Caes.* 2.8.2: Igitur paene me Opicum animantem ad Graecam scripturam perpulerunt "homines". . . Cf. 1.6.1; 3.9.8. The term "*Opicus*," "Oscan," however, does not refer to a provincial in Rome, but is said to have been used by Greeks in a negative sense for Romans in general.

[52] Mozley, in the Loeb edition, prefers to translate the last line cited: "Yet in our city and among the knights of Rome are men who might well be foster-sons of Libya." Vollmer: "es giebt leider Römer, die wegen ihrer Treulosigkeit verdienten nicht als Römer, sondern als Libyer geboren zu sein." Again, Statius may be patronizing towards Severus and full of the superiority of Italian birth, but the poem is meant to flatter him, not to emphasize that he comes from a land inhabited by liars and crooks.

4.56)—for a true Phoenician, not a Carthaginian. Like the famous *Brittunculi*
from the Vindolanda tablets, these expressions are clearly derogatory.[53] They do
not refer to the physical size of people, for most Britons were taller than most
Romans, but to their status as subject people. The diminutive raises associations
with slavery. In the visual arts slaves are of course often depicted as smaller
than their masters.

Besides being untrustworthy liars, the Phoenicians and Carthaginians are also
accused of being extraordinarily cruel. Livy attributes this speech to a Roman
commander, speaking after the battle of Cannae (216 B.C.): "Cruel and ferocious
by nature and custom, these soldiers have been rendered more cruel still by the
commander himself, in making bridges and dykes with human bodies piled up,
and—horrible to relate—by habituating them to feed upon human bodies."[54]
Cannibalism is one of the favorite accusations aimed at enemies who are both
hated and feared. The least that can be said, as observed above, is that it is far
more often reported than reliably attested in reality.[55] In yet another literary
speech, composed by Appian, we read: "They cast our men, whom they had
taken prisoners, into ditches and rivers, making bridges of their bodies to pass
over. They had them trodden under foot by elephants etc."[56] The accusation of
cannibalism is emotionally connected with another taboo custom, practiced regularly in fact by the Phoenicians and Carthaginians, namely, human sacrifice.
Human sacrifice, or accusations of such a practice, are mentioned frequently in
this study. Greeks and Romans regarded the custom with particular disapproval,
although they practiced it themselves at some stage. It has been argued recently
that there is very little solid evidence for actual human sacrifice practiced by
Greeks in historical times.[57] For Rome there are clear indications that it at least
existed till late Republican times. Greek and Latin authors attribute the custom
to, among others, Britons, Gauls, Jews, and Christians. The earliest reference in
classical literature to such practices among the Phoenicians and particularly the
Carthaginians is by Cleitarchus (late fourth century B.C.).[58] Diodorus describes

[53] A. K. Bowman and J. David Thomas, *The Vindolanda Writing Tablets (Tabulae Vindolandenses
II)* (London, 1994), 106–108, no. 164; Alan K. Bowman, *Life and Letters on the Roman Frontier:
Vindolanda and its People* (London, 1994), 29, 106. The context is military: nec residunt Brittun-
culi ut iaculos mittant: "nor do the *Brittunculi* mount in order to throw javelins."

[54] Livy 23.5.12: Hunc natura et moribus inmitem ferumque insuper dux ipse efferavit pontibus ac
molibus ex humanorum corporum strue faciendis et, quod proloqui etiam piget, vesci corporibus
humanis docendo. For accusations of cannibalism, see above, chapter 1.

[55] See above, chapter 2, and below, chapters 11, 12, and 13.

[56] Appian, *Lib.* 9.63.281: τοὺς δ' αἰχμαλώτους ἡμῶν τοὺς μὲν ἐς τάφρους καὶ ποταμοὺς
ἐμβαλόντες ὡς γεφύραις ἐπέβαινον, τοὺς δὲ τοῖς ἐλέφασιν ὑπέβαλλον,

[57] Dennis D. Hughes, *Human Sacrifice in Ancient Greece* (London and New York, 1991) has
collected the evidence and argues that there is very little evidence of actual human sacrifice among
Greeks. The references in Greek texts regard it as an unholy and unlawful practice associated with
contemporary non-Greeks and Greeks of a remote past.

[58] Schol. Plato, *Rep.* 337a. (*FGH* 137 F9): a graphic description of children burned alive as
offering to the bronze statue of Kronos (Molokh); cf. Quintus Curtius 4.3.23 for which see Jacoby's
commentary, p. 489, on Cleitarchus, *FGrH* loc. cit. For the accusations of Christian infanticide in
the second century: J.-P. Waltzing, "Le crime rituel reproché aux chrétiens du 2ᵉ siècle," in *Aca-*

large-scale child sacrifice at Carthage in an emergency in 310 B.C. (20.4) and Plutarch adds that on such occasions mothers watched without weeping or lamenting (*de superstitione* 13.171c–d).[59] The Phoenicians and Carthaginians seem to have been unique in their practice of sacrificing their own children.[60]

On another subject, Plutarch devotes a full page to the incomprehensible parsimony of Perseus of Macedonia. "And he acted thus although he was no Lydian or Phoenician, but one who claimed that he shared in the virtue of Alexander and Philip because he was a descendent of them" (Plutarch, *Aemilius Paulus* 12.5). The remark about Lydians or Phoenicians is entirely Plutarch's addition and shows that those peoples were, in his eyes, not merely rich, but also miserly. Rich people of all ages are often described as either extravagant or miserly or combining those faults, being extravagant for themselves and miserly towards others.

I would conclude that there is a good deal of rhetoric and hostility to Phoenicians and Carthaginians in both Greek and Latin authors, early and late. The tone and style of both changed in the reign of Augustus, with Livy giving the first example of the new style. Vergil may be more nuanced and, a little later, Mela may be an exception, but generally the tone is negative. It is essential to note here that the Phoenicians, as described so far, are both gifted and immoral. They are wealthy and cruel, but, unlike Syrians or inhabitants of Asia Minor, they are not weak or effeminate.

SYRIANS

It is not always clear what is meant when we read about Syrians in ancient literature, for it could refer to various things: origin, language, culture, or even the inhabitants of the province of Syria whatever their origin. This is best illustrated by the Greek autobiographical poem of Meleager of Gadara: "Tyre of the godlike boys and Gadara's holy earth made me a man; lovely Kos of the Meropes took care of me in my old age. So if you are a Syrian, Salaam! If you are a Phoenician, Naidios! If you are Greek, Chaire! And do you say the same

---

démie Royale de Belgique, Bull. de la Classe des Lettres, ser. 5, vol.11 (1925), 205–239; Franz Joseph Dölger, "Sacramentum infanticidii*,*" *Antike und Christentum* 4 (1934), 188–228, with extensive discussion of the sources, notably Tertullian, *Ad nationes* 1.7.23, 31, 33; *Apologeticum* 8.7 and others, cited on p.197. See most recently: J. Rives, "Human Sacrifice among Pagans and Christians," *JRS* 85 (1995), 65–85, with further literature cited on p. 66, n. 6. Waltzing points out that the early Christian authors claim the slanderous accusations are initiated by Jews. Dölger argues that the accusation of the Christians had its origins in similar accusations of Jewish human sacrifice. As is well known, Christians regularly accused Jews of the ritual slaughter of infants, the first instance being *Matthew* 2:16 on the Slaughter of the Innocents. See also below, chapter 13.

[59] Cf. Shelby Brown, *Late Carthaginian Child Sacrifice and Sacrificial Monuments in their Mediterranean Context* (Sheffield, 1991), collecting the literary and archaeological evidence attesting regular practice of child sacrifice.

[60] Brown, conclusion in chapter 7.

[to me]."[61] So here we have a Greek poem that plays with the multicultural background of the poet and his multilingual environment in Syria in the second–first centuries B.C.[62] In another poem there is a suggestion of an apologetic or defensive attitude towards his background: he describes his place of origin as "An Attic fatherland in Assyria (sc. Syria) . . . Gadara" and exclaims: "What wonder if I am a Syrian? We all inhabit one fatherland, one world."[63] The sentiment reminds us of Democritus who, in the fifth century B.C., claimed: "To the wise man every land is to be travelled; for the whole world is the native land of the good soul."[64] However, Meleager's own background, unlike that of Democritus, is ambiguous. He may be an accomplished Greek poet from an "Attic" city, which was also the birthplace of Menippus and Philodemus, but he remains a Syrian and feels a need to emphasize that this does not diminish his worth.

An obscure text has been analyzed recently by Fergus Millar.[65] This is a marginal note inserted in a manuscript of Photius's *Bibliotheca,* which contains the summary of a novel *Babyloniaca* by Iamblichus (2d century A.D.):[66] "This Iamblichus was a Syrian by origin on both his father's and his mother's side, a Syrian not in the sense of the Greeks who have settled in Syria, but of the native ones (*autochthones*), familiar with the Syrian language and living by their customs." For present purposes it is important to see that Syrians could be one of two kinds: those of native origin who spoke Syriac and lived according

---

[61] *The Greek Anthology: Hellenistic Epigrams,* edited by A.S.F. Gow and D. L. Page (Cambridge, 1965), vol. 1, p. 217, no. 4 (*Anthologia Palatina* 7.419): ὃν θεόπαις ἤνδρωσε Τύρος Γαδάρων θ᾽ ἱερὰ χθών, / Κῶς δ᾽ ἐρατὴ Μερόπων πρέσβυν ἐγηροτρόφει. / ἀλλ᾽ εἰ μὲν Σύρος ἐσσί, σαλάμ· εἰ δ᾽ οὖν σύ γε Φοῖνιξ, / ναίδιος· εἰ δ᾽ Ἕλλην, χαῖρε· τὸ δ᾽ αὐτὸ φράσον. See also p. 216, nos. 2 (*AP* 7.417) and 3 (*AP* 7.418) and cf. the comments, vol. 2, pp. 606–609. For Tyre see also C 12.59: Ἀβρούς, ναὶ τὸν Ἔρωτα, τρέφει Τύρος· ἀλλὰ Μυΐσκος ἔσβεσεν ἐκλάμψας ἀστέρας ἠέλιος; Gow and Page, vol. 1, pp. 237f. no.78 (12.256): ὀλβίστη νήσων ἱερὰ Τύρος, ἣ τὸ μυρόπνουν ἄλσος ἔχει παίδων Κύπριδος ἀνθοφόρον. Cf. Joseph Geiger, "Language, Culture and Identity in Ancient Palestine," in Erik Nis Ostenfeld (ed.), *Greek Romans and Roman Greeks: Studies in Cultural Interaction* (Aarhus, 2002), 233–246, at 233f.

[62] D. L. Page in Emile Rostain (ed.), *Miscellanea di studi alessandrini in memoria di Augusto Rostagni* (Torino, 1963), 544–547; T.B.L. Webster, *Hellenistic Poetry and Art* (London, 1964), 208–215.

[63] *The Greek Anthology,* ed. Gow and Page (1965), 1, p. 216, no. 2 (*Anthologia Palatina* 7.417): Νᾶσος ἐμὰ θρέπτειρα Τύρος· πάτρα δέ με τεκνοῖ Ἀτθὶς ἐν Ἀσσυρίοις ναιομένα Γαδάρα· Εὐφράτεω δ᾽ ἔβλαστον ὁ σὺν Μούσαις Μελέαγρος πρῶτα Μενιππείοις συντροχάσας Χάρισιν. εἰ δὲ Σύρος, τί τὸ θαῦμα; μίαν, ξένε, πατρίδα κόσμον ναίομεν, ἐν θνατοὺς πάντας ἔτικτε Χάος. For the reading Γαδάρα see Gow and Page, 2.607.

[64] Democritus, fr. 247 (Diels); C.C.W. Taylor, *The Atomists Leucippus and Democritus* (Toronto, 1999), p. 37, D111: ἀνδρὶ σοφῶι πᾶσα γῆ βατή· ψυχῆς γὰρ ἀγαθῆς πατρὶς ὁ κόσμος. Cf. above, chapter 2, n. 32.

[65] Fergus Millar, *The Roman Near East: 31 BC–AD 337* (Cambridge, MA, 1993), 491.

[66] R. Henry (ed. and trans.), *Photius, Bibliothèque* II (Paris 1960), p. 40, n.1 for the Greek text of the note: Οὗτος ὁ Ἰάμβλιχος Σύρος ἦν γένος πατρόθεν καὶ μητρόθεν, Σύρος δὲ οὐχὶ τῶν ἐπῳκότων τὴν Συρίαν Ἑλλήνων, ἀλλὰ τῶν αὐτοχθόνων, γλῶσσαν δὲ σύραν εἰδώς. I cite part of Millar's translation of the note, with minor variations. See also: S. Swain, *Hellenism and Empire* (1996), 303f.

to local customs, and the descendants of Greek settlers who spoke Greek and lived like Greeks. Besides origin, the factors determining social identity were thus language and culture or way of life. The emphasis on origin on both the father's and the mother's side suggests that mixed marriages were very common, which shows that, as so often, matters of origin cannot have been clearcut, centuries after the Seleucids founded their cities there. Of Iamblichus we are told that he also learned Babylonian and Greek, the latter well enough to become a skilled orator. When Jerome, writing at the end of the fourth century, says of Malchus that he was *Syrus natione et lingua*[67] he probably means that he belonged to the same categories as Iamblichus: he was a Syrian of local origin and spoke Syrian. In this connection it is confusing that a *natio,* or Greek ἔθνος can also indicate a Roman province.[68] Important though they are, such problems concerning social identity are not the concern of the present study, which asks how people were seen by Greeks and Romans, not how they saw or described themselves. Since there is such ambiguity, however, about what it means to be Syrian, this means that there may be ambiguity in the texts considered here and this is relevant for present purposes. In each of the texts concerned we must carefully consider what precisely is meant when Syrians are mentioned. The case of Iamblichus is especially relevant, for it shows that, in terms of social identity, a man could belong to the native, or rather, non-Greek sector of the population of Syria and continue to be regarded as such, even if he had learned Greek well enough to become a skilled Greek orator, which clearly was the ultimate test.

The passages cited above and those analyzed below show how complex and confusing the linguistic and cultural backgrounds of the Hellenized Syrians were, and it is clear that this must have been confusing to the Greeks and Romans who had little sympathy for Syrians. It is also important to see how ambivalent the Hellenized Syrians themselves were about their origin, an ambivalence that will have been reinforced by the attitudes of Greeks and Romans and, at the same time, must have reinforced the negative stereotypes current in the Greek and Roman world.

Posidonius (c. 135–c. 51 B.C.) describes the wealth of Syria in the later Seleucid period.[69] Since the quotations have been transmitted by Athenaeus, the information deals with sumptuous banquets. It is clear, however, that Posidonius, himself a Syrian Greek from Apamea, and a contemporary of Meleager of Gadara, considered this luxury degenerate (ἐτρύφων = to live luxuriously, with a suggestion of effeminacy and license). The Syrians, he writes, were forever meeting for a life of continual feasting. The *gymnasia* were turned from centers for exercise into baths. They spent the greater part of the day overeating (γαστριζόμενοι) at their clubs. It must be remembered that Posidonius

[67] Hieronymus, *vita Malchi* 41–2 (*PL* 23.54); P. Edgardo M. Morales, *Edición crítica de 'de Monacho captivo' (vita Malchi) de San Jerónimo* (Roma, 1991), 90.
[68] Isaac, *The Near East under Roman Rule* (1998), 264f.
[69] Posidonius F61a, b Kidd (Athenaeus, *Deipnosophistae* 12.540B–C; 5.210C–D); F62a,b (Athenaeus, *Deipnosophistae* 12.527E–F; 5.210E–F).

was indeed a Syrian Greek by origin, but he was educated in Athens and settled in Rhodes, where his School became the leading center of Stoicism. His judgment of Syria under the Seleucids can therefore hardly be regarded as a view from within, unless perhaps it represents a case of ethnic self-hatred. However that may be, we may assume that his expressed opinion was influential.

When we now turn to the Greeks and Romans giving their views of Syrians, we see that they were not only deemed faithless. They were "born for slavery," an expression discussed above, in chapter 2. Livy uses this idea twice in speeches which he attributes to republican commanders. In a speech by the Roman consul Quinctius in 192 B.C., the latter is reported as saying: "the forces of King Antiochus, about which there had been so much bragging a little while ago; the different kinds of weapons, the many names of unheard-of peoples, Dahae and Medes and Cadusians and Elymaeans—these were all Syrians, far better fitted to be slaves, on account of their servile dispositions, than to be a race of warriors" (Livy 35.49.8).[70] We have here a juxtaposition of oriental and servile, and an opposition between Orientals and warriors. This text makes it clear quite emphatically that there is no distinction between various kinds of Syrians. All subjects of the Seleucid king are the same. The second passage is a speech to his troops by the consul Manlius Acilius in 191 B.C.: "that hostile army was both larger in number and composed of a somewhat better grade of soldiers; there, as you know, there were Macedonians and Thracians and Illyrians, all most warlike nations, here Syrians and Asiatic Greeks, the most worthless peoples among mankind and born for slavery."[71] Here too it is probably pointless to ask what kind of Syrians are meant. All Syrians are inferior, whether they speak Greek or a Semitic language.

There were, however, even more disturbing feelings about Orientals. Their men were not really men, a quality brought out by Vergil, who describes Paris "with his half-male (eunuch) train, supporting his chin and reeking lovelocks with a Maeonian bonnet."[72] Paris was the accepted type of a warrior whose conquests are only over women. The reference to his "eunuch train" raises associations with the popular view of oriental courts at the time and with the eunuch priests of the Phrygian Cybele, for which see below. The Maeonian (i.e., Lydian or Phrygian) mitra was a headgear fastened with strings under the chin. "Phrygian" is here as often elsewhere used contemptuously.[73] Note the

---

[70] uaria enim genera armorum et multa nomina gentium inauditarum, Dahas <et Medos> et Cadusios et Elymaeos, Syros omnes esse, haud paulo mancipiorum melius propter seruilia ingenia quam militum genus.

[71] Livy 36.17.4–5.

[72] *Aen.* 4.215–7: "et nunc ille Paris [sc. Aeneas], cum semiviro comitatu, / Maeonia mentum mitra crinemque madentem / subnixus, rapto, potitur;

[73] See the comments by T. E. Page, *The Aeneid of Virgil* (London, 1964, 1st ed. 1894/1900), ii, 287: "the Phrygians . . . for whose stupidity, effeminacy, and orgiastic worship they [sc. the Romans] had a national contempt." Cf. 12.99: "semiviri Phrygis." Page writes: "The term 'Phrygian' is often used by Vergil contemptuously with a suggestion of Oriental cowardice and effeminacy." For comments at another level: N. Horsfall, "Numanus Remulus: Ethnography and Propaganda in *Aen.* ix 598f.," *Latomus* 30 (1971), 1108–1116, at 1109. Note that the cowardice of the Phrygians

pertinent remarks by N. Horsefall: "the *duritia* of the Italians is a dominating theme; they are a *durum genus* from birth and they are hardened in icy rivers. The repetition is prominent and deliberate. *Duritia* is peculiarly Roman—the product of hard toil in farm or army (references to many passages). The Trojans are marked by luxurious degeneracy. 'O vere Phrygiae neque enim Phryges'. The men are not even men." It is remarkable, however, that these men who are not men are, in fact, Trojans, future founders of Rome, being taunted in this manner first by a king in North Africa, later by a native Italian.[74]

Vergil's telling of the story of Dido and Aeneas is the classic rendition of the first Roman encounter with Carthage and the Punic world.[75] Yet, while Aeneas was the ancestor of the Romans, he himself was a Trojan from Asia Minor and Dido was a Phoenician who founded a city in Africa. The story explains the future enduring hostility between Rome and Carthage,[76] but it does not do so in terms of a struggle between East and West. In the tragedy of Dido and Aeneas the former was a victim, the latter fraudulent, and neither behaved in accordance with the stereotypes discussed in the present chapter. The ethnic and proto-racist stereotypes found in the work are incidental rather than an integral part of the story.[77] Moreover, where they occur in their most explicit form, Vergil attributes them not to the narrator, but to men speaking in anger. The message conveyed, therefore, is that there were people who would speak about easterners in this manner, but this does not necessarily represent Vergil's own views of them, nor does it suggest that these were the prevailing views of his time.

Above we saw that Juvenal is particularly rich in hostile jokes regarding foreigners in Rome. Several of those regarding the east are worth mentioning here. Juvenal 7.13–15: "How much better that [i.e. to sell your possessions] than to say before a judge 'I saw' what you did not see! Leave that to the Knights of Asia, [of Bithynia and Cappadocia too] and the gentry that were imported bare-footed from the other Gaul."[78] The equites Asiani are the nou-

---

was a stereotype already in fifth-century Greece: Euripides, *Orestes* 1351f. and in comedy, for which see T. Long, *Barbarians in Greek Comedy* (Carbondale, 1986), 141; Keith De Vries, "The Nearly Other: The Attic Vision of Phrygians and Lydians," in B. Cohen (ed.), *Not the Classical Ideal* (2000), 338–363, at 342–357. As shown in this paper, the theme of Phrygian cowardice is absent from Attic vase painting.

[74] Vergil, *Aen.* 4.215–7, already cited, for the words of Iarbas, King of Numidia; 9.598–620: a typical Roman commander's speech in verse before a battle with Easterners, of the sort encountered frequently in this study. Besides the decadent Phrygians the Greeks also are dealt with in one line (602): "non hic Atridae, nec fandi fictor Ulixes."

[75] N. M. Horsfall, "Dido in the Light of History," in Harrison (ed.), *Oxford Readings in Vergil's* Aeneid (1990), 127–144.

[76] Vergil, *Aen.* 4.622–9: Dido's curse and prayer for eternal hostility between the two peoples.

[77] Iuno says to Venus (103f.): "liceat Phrygio servire marito / dotalisque tuae Tyrios permittere dextrae." Thus Phoenician Dido will be the slave of a Phrygian and her Tyrians the dowry. This again occurs in a speech, but even so those who are despised in it are not the Phoenicians, but the Trojans, contemptuously called Phrygians.

[78] hoc satius quam si dicas sub iudice 'uidi' quod non uidisti; faciant equites Asiani, [quamquam et Cappadoces faciant equitesque Bithyni] altera quos nudo traducit gallica talo. Note that it is the

veaux riches who will lie before a judge. This is interesting, for we have seen that the stereotype of being habitual liars was attributed to the Phoenicians, while Herodotus still claims that, among Persians, lying was considered the ultimate disgrace (Herodotus 1.138). The others who are now wealthy upstarts come from "the other Gaul," that is Galatia in Asia Minor. 8.159–61: Nero's legate Lateranus frequents a bar run by a Syrophoenician: "The Syrophoenician runs out to meet him, continually drenched in perfume, an inhabitant of the Idumaean gate, the Syrophoenician (Syrophoenix) greets him with host's gestures as lord and master" (trans. S. Braund).[79] The expression "Syrophoenician" occurs also in Mark 7,26, where it is used for a woman from the district of Tyre and Sidon who is described as "Greek and of Syrophoenician origin."[80] The Syrophoenician appears here more as the standard stereotype of a man from the East than as the typical Phoenician of earlier sources, where he would have been a clever and deceitful trader. It is possible that the distinction between the stereotypical Phoenicians and Syrians had become blurred by this time. It is also possible that stereotypes attributed to immigrants in the city of Rome were somewhat different from the traditional ethnic stereotypes towards foreigners living in their homeland.

In another context Braund has pointed out that Lateranus is going to the bar when he is of the proper age to serve in the army along the Rhine and the Danube and the rivers of Armenia and Syria. Lateranus ought to be in the East as a commander, but instead he is in Rome as a degenerate. This is considered to be the ultimate form of dissolution, comparable to the image, cited above, where an effete Asiatic is turned into a homosexual by a Roman. Easterners are both insolent pushers and effeminate: "But a freedman is in front. 'I was here first,' he says. 'Why should I be afraid or hesitate to hold my place, although I was born on the Euphrates—a fact which the effeminate windows in my ears would prove although I personally deny it?'"[81] If there is anything worse, it is described in the second satire, where effeteness and perversion are combined with superstition. In 2.111-6: self-castration *Phrygio more* is advocated to the

---

other Gaul, Galatia, which Juvenal finds objectionable, not the western Gauls. *Equites Asiani* is a sneering joke for *equites* could only be *Romani.*

[79] S. H. Braund, "Juvenal and the East," 49. For this passage, see also below, chapter 13, n. 109.

[80] ἡ δὲ γυνὴ ἦν Ἑλληνίς Συροφοινίκισσα τῷ γένει. In Matthew 15,21 she is described as a Canaanite woman (Χαναναία). Cf. Isaac, *The Near East under Roman Rule*, 261. An early reference is Lucilius, *Sat.* 15.496. See also above, chapter 1, p. 145 on Lucian, *Deor. Conc.* 4, where Kadmos, the grandfather of Dionysus, is said to be a Syrophoenician trader. For the term "Syrophoenician" see Joseph Geiger, "Graecolatini" in L. Sawicki and D. Shalev, *Donum grammaticum: Studies in Latin and Celtic Linguistics in Honour of Hannah Rosén* (Leuven, 2002), 153: "it means rather a Syrian (in the wider connotation of the term) from the particular part of Syria called Phoenicia."

[81] S. H. Braund, "Juvenal and the East," 49. Juvenal, *Sat.* 1.102–11 (trans. S. Braund): Sed libertinus prior est. "prior" inquit "ego adsum. cur timeam dubitemve locum defendere? quamvis natus ad Euphraten, molles quod in aure fenestrae arguerint licet ipse negem? Cf. Xenophon's account of Apollonides, the traitor who was found out, because "he has both ears pierced like a Lydian," above, chapter 4, n. 147 and below, chapter 13, n. 158. Cf. Tertullian, *De Pallio* 4.2; for the expression *molles*, cf. Manilius 754: "et millis Arabas, silvarum ditia regna."

homosexuals of Rome as if it were the logical conclusion to their effeminate conduct.[82] This allusion to Vergil, cited above, is a reference to the cult of Cybele and her priests, the Galli, who castrate themselves.[83] The association of Near Eastern rites and sexual perversion appears again in 6.511-6 about the eunuch priest of Bellona and the mater deum: "And now, behold! In comes the chorus of the frantic Bellona and the mother of the Gods, attended by a giant eunuch to whom his obscene inferiors must do reverence, who has cut off his effeminate genitals with a shard. Before him the howling herd with the timbrels give way; his plebeian cheeks are covered with a Phrygian tiara."[84] To do reverence to a eunuch is the ultimate disgrace and once more this is closely associated with the East, for that is where most eunuch-slaves were imported from and that is where some of them had cultic functions.[85] Other targets in this satire are fortune-tellers and astrologers—often of eastern origin and old targets of dislike for conservative Romans. These hostile feelings were reinforced by the circumstance that these eastern cults were not only present in Rome, but also had an obvious appeal for Romans. Efforts to ban foreign cults are reported frequently, and anger at seeing people adhering to foreign cults or converting to Judaism are topics to which we shall return.

A Greek-writing author who must be considered here with care is Lucian, who came from Samosata in Commagene (born c. A.D. 120).[86] His satires, writ-

---

[82] The confusion of homosexuality with castration is found also in Plutarch, *De malignitate Herodoti* 13/ cited above. It is, perhaps, comparable with the association of castration with circumcision, in a pun by Cicero, *Vita Ciceronis* 7.6; Stern, 1.no.263. Roman legislation equated circumcision of non-Jews with castration, cf. E. M. Smallwood, "The Legislation of Hadrian and Antoninus Pius against Circumcision," *Latomus* 18 (1959), 334–347; and "The Legislation of Hadrian and Antoninus Pius against Circumcision: Addendum," *Latomus* 20 (1961), 93–96; A. Linder, *The Jews in Roman Imperial Legislation* (Detroit and Jerusalem, 1987), p. 101, n.108.

[83] Courtney, *A Commentary*, p.142. For Cybele and her cult the first extensive reference in Latin literature is Lucretius 2.610–660. This description lacks the hostility found in the satirical works of other poets. A scornful description of the cults in Rome of Cybele and of Isis can be found also in Seneca, *De Vita Beata* 2.26.8.

[84] Trans. G. G. Ramsay, except for line 3, for which, cf. Courtney, p.142. ecce furentis | Bellonae matrisque deum chorus intrat et ingens | semivir, obsceno facies reverenda minori, | mollia qui rapta secuit genitalia testa | iam pridem, cui rauca cohors, cui tympana cedunt | plebeia et Phrygia vestitur bucca tiara. |

[85] M. K. Hopkins, "Eunuchs in Politics in the Later Roman Empire," *PCPS* (1963), 62–80; Hopkins, "The Political Power of Eunuchs," *Conquerors and Slaves* (1978), 172–196; *RE* Supp. 3. cols. 449f. (A. Hug); Balsdon, *Romans and Aliens*, 227–230. For self-castration and religious eunuchs: L. H. Gray, "Eunuch," *Encyclopaedia of Religion and Ethics*, ed. J. Hastings (New York, 1951), 5.579–84; A. D. Nock, "Eunuchs in Ancient Religion," *Essays on Religion in the Ancient World* 1 (Oxford, 1972), 7–15; G. M. Sanders, *Rivista di Archeologia Christiana* 8 (1972) 984–1034; P. Bilde, "Atargatis/Dea Syria: Hellenization of Her Cult?" in P. Bilde et al., (eds.) *Religion and Religious Practice in the Seleucid Kingdom* (Aarhus, 1990), 151–187.

[86] Jonas Palm, *Rom, Römertum und Imperium in der griechischen Literatur der Kaiserzeit* (Lund, 1959), 45–51, contains comments on Lucian, notably on *Nigrinus*. Here, as elsewhere in the book, the sole purpose is to show that Lucian is not "anti-Roman." Here, as elsewhere, he fails to see the difference in the literature between the Roman Empire and Rome, the city. The book contains full references to earlier literature. For Lucian: Jennifer Hall, *Lucian's Satire* (New York, 1981); C. P.

ten for a Greek-reading public, are concerned with society in contemporary Rome and the provinces. The importance of satire for the present study has been emphasized in the Introduction and there is no need to repeat the arguments here. When Lucian calls himself a Syrian, there are various emotional filters to understand: he was a satirist, a provincial from the far East of the Empire, and an author writing satire. This was a genre developed in Rome but Lucian wrote in the second, not the first language of the empire. Clearly, in terms of the description cited at the beginning of the section, Lucian was "a Syrian in the sense of the Greeks who have settled in Syria, not one of the native ones (*autochthones*), a speaker and writer of Greek." Was he familiar with the Syrian language? What role did Aramaic play in his life? He does not tell.[87] He presumably did not live by Syrian customs, but by those of the Hellenistic cities. His subject was life in Greece and in the capital, and his own position there. We do not even know whether he would call himself a "Syrian" if he was not writing satire. He was a Greek by choice. His works are relevant for us insofar as they depict the position of a Greek-speaking Syrian in contemporary Greek and Roman society and in particular the attitudes of that society towards someone like Lucian, as he himself experienced them.

Matters of social identity are not the subject of this study, although they are indirectly relevant. Modern scholarship sometimes assumes that there was an easy distinction between a "Semitic" and a "Greek" population as if the two were obviously separate, be it by origin, religion, or culture or a combination of these.[88]

In the case of Lucian, the first point to note are the frequent apologetic allusions to his origin which, as suggested for Meleager and Posidonius, may suggest if not a degree of ethnic self-hatred, then at least a measure of ambivalence at his ethnic identity.[89] A good example is a passage in *The Ignorant Book-Collector*: Lucian asks why this unlettered rich man collects books. Perhaps it is to display his wealth. "Come now, as far as I know—and I too am a Syrian—if you had not smuggled yourself into that old man's will with all speed, you would be starving to death by now, and would be putting up your books at auction!"[90] The implication seems to be that Lucian understands the

Jones, *Culture and Society in Lucian* (Cambridge, MA, 1986); Christopher Robinson, *Lucian and his Influence in Europe* (London, 1979); R. Bracht Branham, *Unruly Eloquence: Lucian and the Comedy of Traditions* (Cambridge, MA, 1989); Graham Anderson, *The Second Sophistic: A Cultural Phenomenon in the Roman Empire* (London, 1993); Simon Swain, *Hellenism and Empire: Language, Classicism, and Power in the Greek World, AD 50–250* (Oxford, 1996), 298–329 and esp. 298–308 about Lucian and his Syrian background. Sherwin-White, *Racial Prejudice*, 62–71, also discusses Lucian.

[87] Jones, *Culture and Society in Lucian*, 6–8; Fergus Millar, *The Roman Near East*, 454–456.

[88] On these matters, Fergus Millar, *The Roman Near East*, Part II and the polemic work by Warwick Ball, *Rome in the East: The Transformation of an Empire* (London and New York, 2000).

[89] Swain, *Hellenism and Empire*, 307, on Lucian's somewhat bitter references to his origin.

[90] *adversus Indoctum* 19.20 to 20.1: καὶ μὴν ὅσα γε κἀμὲ Σύρον ὄντα εἰδέναι, εἰ μὴ σαυτὸν φέρων ταῖς τοῦ γέροντος ἐκείνου διαθήκαις παρενέγραψας, ἀπωλώλεις ἂν ὑπὸ λιμοῦ ἤδη καὶ ἀλοράν προυτίθεις τῶν βιβλίων. In *de Syria dea* 1.12 Lucian calls himself "Assyrian." γράφω δὲ

matter, because the other too is a (Greek speaking) Syrian.[91] Thus Lucian has known him a long time and is informed of his situation, but it is clearly also implied that the man got his riches in a typically Syrian manner, not by honest toil, but by legal though dishonest behavior through an inheritance from someone who was not a relative. It is the sort of remark that a person might make who identifies with the prejudices of the establishment towards the minority of which he is part. We must keep in mind, however, that this is satire and not necessarily Lucian speaking in earnest. Alternatively, Lucian's comments may be taken as a parody of normal attitudes, both those of the establishment and those of Hellenized Syrians in Greek-speaking cities. However we wish to read Lucian, the negative stereotypes are undeniable. Lucian may also have meant to convey that this was how his readers envisaged fellow Syrians speaking to each other. The least that can be said is that Lucian, himself a Syrian, associates being Syrian in this passage with a lack of morals and rectitude. If none of this would appeal to a contemporary public, the entire passage would be pointless.

Another ambivalent passage may be found in "The Scythian," where Lucian compares his situation with that of the Scythian Anacharsis: "—and please do not resent my likening myself to a man of regal stature, for he too was a barbarian, and no one could say that we Syrians are inferior to Scythians. It is not on grounds of royalty that I compare my situation with his, but rather because we are both barbarians. For when I first came to live in your city, I was utterly terrified as soon as I saw its size, its beauty, its high population, its power and general splendour."[92] Despite the emphatic apology, the comparison with Anacharsis—who is also the subject of another work by Lucian—is meant seriously. It is hardly possible to argue that Lucian in comparing himself with Anacharsis offers a parody of widespread attitudes. Anacharsis was the traditional example of a wise barbarian, although he was later seen as more of a critic of the Greeks than in the early treatment by Herodotus.[93] Both Lucian, then, and Anacharsis were wise but both were barbarians. This is interesting in the case of Lucian. A citizen of the empire who functioned at the highest intellectual level in Greek could apparently be called a barbarian if he came from a Greek city in a remote province. Another intellectual who compares himself with Anacharsis is Fronto, in the letter already cited, written in Greek in 143 to

---

Ἀσσύριος ἐών, For this work and its authorship: Jones, *Culture and Society,* 109f.; Jaś Elsner, "Describing Self in the language of Other: Pseudo (?) Lucian at the temple of Hierapolis," in S. Goldhill (ed.), *Being Greek under Rome* (2001), 123–153.

[91] The Loeb edition, vol. 1, by A. A. Harmon, 1953, adds by way of clarification: "he may or may not have been of Semitic stock."

[92] *Scyth* 9.6ff. φημὶ δὴ ὅμοιόν τι καὶ αὐτὸς παθεῖν τῷ Ἀναχάρσιδι-καὶ πρὸς Χαρίτων μὴ νεμεσήσητέ μοι τῆς εἰκόνος, εἰ βασιλικῷ ἀνδρὶ ἐμαυτὸν εἴκασα· βάρβαρος μὲν γὰρ κἀκεῖνος καὶ οὐδέν τι φαίης ἂν τοὺς Σύρους ἡμᾶς φαυλοτέρους εἶναι τῶν Σκυθῶν. ἀτὰρ οὐδὲ κατὰ τὸ βασιλικὸν εἰσποιῶ τἀμὰ ἐς τὴν ὁμοιότητα, κατ' ἐκεῖνα δέ. ὅτε γὰρ πρῶτον ἐπεδήμησα ὑμῶν τῇ πόλει, ἐξεπλάγην μὲν εὐθὺς ἰδὼν τὸ μέγεθος κἀὶ τὸ κάλλος καὶ τῶν ἐμπολιτευομένων τὸ πλῆθος καὶ τὴν ἄλλην δύναμιν καὶ λαμπρότητα πᾶσαν."

[93] For Herodotus on Anacharsis: François Hartog, *Le miroir d'Hérodote: Essai sur la représentation de l'autre* (Paris, 1980), 82–102.

Domitia Lucilla, the Emperor Antoninus's mother. Fronto apologizes for any possible infelicities in his Attic and adds that Anacharsis is also said to have been imperfect in Greek, "but he was praised for his meaning and his thoughts. I will compare myself, then, with Anacharsis, not, by heaven, in wisdom, but as being like him a barbarian. For he was a Scythian of the nomad Scythians" and then follows the phrase discussed above: "I am a Libyan of the Libyan nomads."[94] Both Fronto and, a little later, Lucian, were apparently ambivalent about their provincial background and they overcompensated a little by comparing themselves with the classic case of the wise barbarian. The essence of this passage is that once again Lucian associates being a Greek-speaking Syrian with being considered a barbarian in Greek cities. Even if this appears in a satire, it would be effective as satire only if his readers recognized some form of reality in it.

Lucian's description of the city does not suggest cultural or linguistic superiority, but the feelings of a villager when first confronted with a metropolis. Whatever the case, it is clear that here too Lucian mentions his Syrian identity as an inferior status. Syrians may not be inferior to Scythians, but the passage implies that they clearly feel inferior to Athenians.

Lucian returns to this topic in *Fisherman*: "I am a Syrian, Philosophy, from the banks of the Euphrates. But what of that? I know that some of my opponents here are just as barbarian as I: but in their manners and culture they are not like men of Soli or Cyprus or Babylon or Stagira.[95] Yet as far as you are concerned it would make no difference even if a man's speech were foreign, if only his way of thinking were manifestly right and just."[96] Parresiades, who is addressing Philosophy here, calls himself a Syrian. Since he mentions the banks of the Euphrates, this means the region of Lucian's own fatherland, Commagene. Once again he calls people of this sort barbarians, in spite of their high level of culture. Perhaps Lucian would have called anyone who did not come from a major city a barbarian. In any event, the meaning of being barbarian is that one does not belong to the real community of Athenians, Romans, etc.

---

[94] Fronto, *Epist. Graecae* 1.10 Naber 239–42 (trans. C. R. Haines, Loeb): εἴ τι τῶν ὀνομάτων ἐν ταῖς ἐπιστολαῖς ταύταις εἴη ἄκυρον ἢ βάρβαρον ἢ ἄλλως ἀδόκιμον ἢ μὴ πάνυ Ἀττικόν, ἀλλὰ . . . τοῦ ὀνόματος σ' ἀξιῶ τήν γε διάνοιαν σκοπεῖν αὐτὴν καθ' αὑτήν· οἶσθα γὰρ ὅτι ἐν αὐτοῖς ὀνόμασιν καὶ αὐτῇ διαλέκτῳ διατρίβω. καὶ γὰρ τὸν Σκύθην ἐκεῖνον τὸν Ἀνάχαρσιν οὐ πάνυ τι ἀττικίσαι φασίν, ἐπαινεθῆναι δ' ἐκ τῆς διανοίας καὶ τῶν ἐνθυμημάτων. παραβαλῶ δὴ ἐμαυτὸν Ἀναχάρσιδι οὐ μὰ Δία κατὰ τὴν σοφίαν ἀλλὰ κατὰ τὸ βάρβαρος ὁμοίως εἶναι. ἦν γὰρ ὁ μὲν Σκύθης τῶν νομάδων Σκυθῶν. See above, p. 145.

[95] The meaning behind these specific place-names is not entirely clear to me. Soli and Stagira are impeccably Greek cities, the latter even being the birthplace of Aristotle. Why these are coupled with Cyprus and Babylon and what the four geographical names have in common, I cannot understand. One would expect four names of obviously Greek cities or obviously barbarian regions.

[96] *Revivescentes sive piscator* 19.6: Σύρος, ὦ Φιλοσοφία, τῶν Ἐπευφρατιδίων. ἀλλὰ τί τοῦτο; καὶ γὰρ τούτων τινὰς οἶδα τῶν ἀντιδίκων μου οὐχ ἧττον ἐμοῦ βαρβάρους τὸ γένος· ὁ τρόπος δὲ καὶ ἡ παιδεία οὐ κατὰ Σολέας ἢ Κυπρίους ἢ Βαβυλωνίους ἢ Σταγειρίτας. καί τοι πρός γε σὲ οὐδὲν ἂν ἔλαττον γένοιτο οὐδ' εἰ τὴν φωνὴν βάρβαρος εἴη τις, εἴπερ ἡ γνώμη ὀρθὴ καὶ δικαία φαίνοιτο οὖσα.

Then follows a claim which would never find universal approval in Greece, namely that one could be a philosopher in a barbarian tongue. However, here, clearly, barbarian is being used in its original sense of non-Greek. In the *Double Indictment,* Lucian himself appears as a nameless "Syrian" whom "Rhetoric" claims to have found as a young man, barbaric in speech and dress and then to have civilized.[97] The Syrian himself acknowledges being a barbarian, but claims to have dressed his dialogue in Hellenic clothing: "As far as the rest of it goes, he cannot complain, I am sure, that I have stripped him of that Greek mantle and shifted him into a foreign one (βαρβαρικόν τι), even though I myself am considered foreign (βάρβαρος)."[98]

Whenever Lucian brings Syrians into his works, there is always a note of apology or criticism, which must either represent his own views, or refer satirically to what many others think of Syrians. Lucian's Syrians are impoverished wandering doctors,[99] or serve as doormen in great houses in Rome, with the suggestion that there, with their "vile Syrian accent,"[100] they abuse their position towards less exalted visitors (*On Hirelings* 10.13). They exorcise spirits for a large fee,[101] and it is clearly suggested that they are greedy quacks. A Syrian slave named Syros takes part in a temple robbery in Egypt (*Toxaris* 28). The overwhelming impression from Lucian's work is that he describes Graeco-Syrians as the sort of men who were ambivalent about their origins, and both suffered from and identified with the prejudices they encountered in Greece and Rome. One might possibly claim that the satirical genre leads Lucian to exaggerate. Even if he exaggerates, the essence is still there.

A remarkable example of this sort of attitude may be found also in Dio Chrysostom's thirty-third oration in which he addresses the Tarsians, criticizing their appearance, manners, and accent: "And would anyone call you colonists from Argos, as you claim to be, or more likely colonists of those abominable

---

[97] *Bis Acc* 27: Ἐγὼ γάρ, ὦ ἄνδρες δικασταί, τουτονὶ κομιδῇ μειράκιον ὄντα, βάρβαρον ἔτι τὴν φωνὴν καὶ μονονουχὶ κάνδυν ἐνδεδυκότα εἰς τὸν Ἀσσύριον τρόπον . . . Cf. R. B. Branham, *Unruly Eloquence*, 34–37.

[98] *Bis Acc.* 34 (trans. A. M. Harmon, Loeb): ἐπεὶ τῶν γε ἄλλων ἕνεκα οὐκ ἂν οἶμαι μέμψαιτό μοι, ὡς θοἰμάτιον τοῦτο τὸ Ἑλληνικὸν περισπάσας αὐτοῦ βαρβαρικόν τι μετενέδυσα, καὶ ταῦτα βάρβαρος αὐτὸς εἶναι δοκῶν·

[99] *Podagra* 265: Σύροι μέν ἐσμεν, ἐκ Δαμασκοῦ τῷ γένει, λιμῷ δὲ πολλῷ καὶ πενίᾳ κρατούμενοι γῆν καὶ θάλασσαν ἐφέπομεν πλανώμενοι· ἔχομεν δὲ χρῖσμα πατροδώρητον τόδε, ἐν ᾧ παρηγοροῦμεν ἀλγούντων πόνους.

[100] It is tempting to think in this connection of the objections many assimilated Jewish Germans used to raise against fellow-Jewish Germans who spoke a German that had a distinct accent and character of its own.

[101] *Philopseudes* 16. Stern, *Greek and Latin Authors, No.* 372, p. 221, believes that the "the Syrian from Palestine" (τὸν Σύρον τὸν ἐκ τῆς Παλαιστίνης) here should be a Jew. His reason is that Ovid, *Ars Amatoria* 1.416: *Palaestino . . . Syro* definitely refers to a Jew. However, Stern, Vol. 1, p. 349, himself observes that the man in Tibullus 1.7.18 *Palaestino . . . Syro* obviously is not a Jew. It could be relevant also that Lucian wrote when the formal name of the province of Judaea had been changed to Syria-Palaestina (the *Philopseudes* was composed between A.D. 166 and 170), which was not the case in Ovid's time. How would one call a non-Jewish inhabitant of the province of Syria-Palaestina? For other aspects of this passage: Jones, *Culture and Society in Lucian*, 48.

Aradians? Would he call you Greeks, or the most licentious of Phoenicians?"[102] Tarsus, capital of Cilicia in Western Asia Minor, had been hellenized at least since the second century B.C. Like other hellenized cities it duly rediscovered pure hellenic origins for itself. Aradus was an important island-city off the Phoenician coast, also hellenized.[103] Apparently, the worst that a man from Prusa in Bythinia could say to a city in Cilicia is that they were "Phoenician colonists." The adjective "licentious" is not among those usually applied to Phoenicians, but comes from the anti-Syrian and anti-Asiatic sphere. If this means anything, it may be another earlier instance of the blurring of the distinction between Phoenicians and their vicinity over time which we noted above. Below we shall again encounter Dio's contempt for the Phoenicians, when he expresses his fury at the Athenians for having crowned a man from Phoenicia as Olympian poet.

It is curious to see how some slurs disappear for centuries, to reappear again in unexpected places. Philostratus attributes to Apollonius the following remark: "Apollonius answered thus: 'We must make allowance for the very timid remarks which Damis has made about the situation; for he is a Syrian and lives on the border of Media, where tyrants are worshipped and where no one entertains a lofty ideal of freedom.'"[104] This sounds more like the fourth century B.C. than the second century A.D. It could have been said by Isocrates. The criticism here is not aimed against language or the general level of culture, but against the slavish nature attributed to the Syrians.

A third-century Greek from Asia Minor who clearly despised Syrians (as well as Gauls, Egyptians, and Africans) was Cassius Dio, as we saw in his description of the Emperor Caracalla already cited.[105] "From his Syrian mother he had acquired his wickedness." The pejorative applied here to the Syrians, τὸ πανοῦργον, "cunning," "craftiness," has a history which goes back to the fifth century B.C., when the author of *Airs, Waters, Places* first describes the Asiatics as clever. Unreliable cleverness is the one feature which Syrians and Phoenicians are thought to have in common, although they are otherwise rather differently portrayed in the sources.

Prejudices and slurs against peoples in the East in the fourth century A.D. were the subject of a paper I published some years ago.[106] The Jews are dis-

---

[102] Dio Chrysostom, *Or.* 33.41 (trans. J. W. Cohoon and H. Lamar Crosby, Loeb): καὶ πότερον ὑμᾶς Ἀργείων ἀποίκους, ὡς λέγετε, φήσει τις ἢ μᾶλλον ἐκείνων Ἀραδίων; καὶ πότερον Ἕλληνας ἢ Φοινίκων τοὺς ἀσελγεστάτους; cf. C. P. Jones, *The Roman World of Dio Chrysostom* (Cambridge, MA, 1978), 71–82.

[103] For Aradus: H. Seyrig, "Arados et Baetocaece," *Syria* 28 (1951), 191–220; J.-P. Rey-Coquais, *Arados et sa Pérée aux époques grecque, romaine et Byzantine* (Paris, 1974), for its legends regarding its origins: 250f.

[104] Philostratus, *vita Apol.* 7.14: Ἀσσύριος γὰρ ὢν καὶ Μήδοις προσοικήσας, οὗ τὰς τυραννίδας προσκυνοῦσιν, οὐδὲν ὑπὲρ ἐλευθερίας ἐνθυμεῖται μέγα,

[105] Dio 78 (77) 6.1a. It recurs in 10.2: πρὸς δὲ τούτοις εἶχε καὶ τό πανοῦργον τῆς μητρὸς καὶ τῶν Σύρων, ὅθεν ἐκείνη ἦν.

[106] "Orientals and Jews in the Historia Augusta: Fourth-Century Prejudice and Stereotypes," in I. M. Gafni, A. Oppenheimer, *The Jews in the Hellenistic-Roman World: Studies in Memory of Men-*

cussed in the present work in chapter 13 below. The speech by Livy writing in the reign of Augustus attributed to the commander Cn. Manlius addressing his troops in 189 B.C., has been discussed at length above. The point allegedly made by the commander is that eastern armies cannot fight, while western troops, transplanted to the east, will quickly degenerate. This immediately reminds us of another literary speech, the one attributed by Cassius Dio to Marcus Aurelius encouraging his western troops when they were about to fight the eastern army of Avidius Cassius: "You at least, fellow soldiers, ought to be of good cheer. For Cilicians, Syrians, Jews and Egyptians have certainly never proved superior to you and never will, even if they should muster as many tens of thousands more than you as they now muster fewer" (Dio 71.25.1). This is essentially the same point Dio, a Greek senator from Asia Minor, wrote more than two centuries after Livy.[107] This shows the strength of this stereotype, which we first encountered in the fourth century B.C. We also find it in another third-century Greek author, Herodian, in his report of the events of A.D. 193.[108] This is remarkable, for the author came from the Greek part of the empire and yet, like Lucian, has a low opinion of Syrians.[109] Apparently these two authors viewed the non-Greek inhabitants of Asia Minor, the Near East, and Egypt in the third century with the same reservations and prejudices as a historian writing in Rome in the reign of Augustus.

It is quite possible that respectable Greek-speaking citizens from the eastern provinces distanced themselves from other easterners, in order to identify more completely with western members of the establishment in the hope of gaining their approval. It is even questionable whether Herodian meant it as an unambiguous compliment when he called Easterners "fairly sharp-witted," for the idea that Asiatics or Southerners are intelligent but spineless is a familiar commonplace, found in Aristotle, Cicero, Vitruvius, and Vegetius.[110] We still en-

---

ahem Stern, eds. I. M. Gafni, A. Oppenheimer, D. R. Schwarz (Jerusalem, 1996), 101–118, reprinted with postscript in *The Near East under Roman Rule*, 268–282.

[107] Josephus, *BJ* 2.16.4 (362), interestingly makes essentially the same point when he attributes to Agrippa II, addressing the Jews in Jerusalem in AD 66, the question: "Do you really suppose that you are going to war with Egyptians or Arabs?"

[108] 2.10.6–7: The troops in Syria live in luxury. "It is elegant, witty remarks that the Syrians are good at, particularly the people of Antioch"; cf. 3.1.3; 3.4.1 on the presumed poor quality of Niger's supporters; Syrians are by nature erratic (2.7.9).

[109] C. R. Whittaker, *Herodian* (Cambridge, MA, 1969), I, xxiv–xxviii, at xxvii: "By an unsatisfactory process of elimination either Greece or Asia Minor present themselves for consideration." Note that H. Sidebottom, "The Date of the Composition of Herodian's History," *L'antiquité classique* 66 (1997), 271–276, argues for a later date than is usually assumed (the 60s of the third century).

[110] As translated by Whittaker. In this passage a tribune is described as "not without sense—he was a Syrian, and Easterners are fairly sharp-witted." 3.11.8 ἀλλ' ἄτε ἀνὴρ οὐκ ἔξω φρενῶν καθεστώς (καὶ γὰρ ἦν τῷ γένει Σύρος, δριμύτεροι δ' ὡς πρὸς τὰς ἐννοίας οἱ ὑπὸ τὴν ἀνατολὴν ἄνθρωποι). The views of Aristotle, Vegetius, and Vitruvius on these matters have been discussed extensively in chapter 1, above. For Cicero on the Phoenicians, *de finibus* 4.56: Postea tuus ille Poenulus—scis enim Citieos, clientes tuos, e Phoenica profectos—, homo igitur acutus.

counter the same attitude towards eastern troops in Crusader sources.[111] The idea that eastern peoples are not courageous survived into recent times.[112]

The *Historia Augusta* contains several passages with emphatic anti-Syrian slurs. The Syrians are degenerate, frivolous, and poor soldiers. There are several themes which recur in this source: the soldiers in Syria "live like Greeks." It is interesting to see that the hostility towards Syria is here amalgamated with the older enmity towards Greeks.[113] The soldiers have sex, drink, bathe, and live in luxury. The last element goes back to the fourth century B.C., to be taken over by the Romans when they conquered the East. It is the old fear that Roman troops on campaign in the East are contaminated by Asiatic luxury, which included bathing. By the time the *Historia Augusta* echoed these sentiments, they had been around for some eight centuries, the Roman Empire was about to split in two parts, the eastern part surviving the western for many centuries.

The luxury of bathing appears as a theme already in Posidonius, cited above, where he says that in Syria *gymnasia* turned into baths. It is a curious preoccupation of well-to-do Romans; witness the nostalgic verbosity in Seneca's description of Scipio Africanus's squalid, dark little bath-house (*Ep.* 86.4ff.). In fact, every Roman military base in northwestern Europe had a bath-house as a matter of course, so it should not have surprised or worried Romans if the troops in Syria had their baths.[114] The *Historia Augusta* also mentions Syrian Antioch as the location of Lucius Verus's dissipations when others were fighting his Parthian war for him, stating explicitly that low forms of entertainment are characteristic of this city, of Syria in general, and of Alexandria in Egypt (SHA *Verus* 8.11; *Marcus Antoninus* 8.12). This echoes earlier accusations of similar behavior by Pescennius Niger (Herodian, cited above).

The *Historia Augusta,* in one of its least reliable lives, goes to much trouble to depict Severus Alexander as one of the finest emperors of the entire series. The *Life* emphasizes this emperor's Syrian background: "He [Alexander] preferred it to be thought that he derived his descent from the Roman people, for he was ashamed at being called a Syrian, particularly because on the occasion of a certain festival, the people of Antioch, the Egyptians, and the people of Alexandria had irritated him with taunts, as they are wont to do, calling him a

---

[111] William of Tyre, *Historia in partibus transmarinis gestarum* xxii 15, in *Recueil des Historiens des Croisades, Historiens Occidentales* 1 (1844), p. 1091: "Syri, qui apud nos effeminate et molles habentur"; Jacques de Vitry, *Historia orientalis seu hierosolymitana*, in *Gesta dei per Francos*, i, ed. J. Bongars (1611), 1089: "Prorsus imbelles et praeliis velut mulieres nutiles." This is taken at face value by R. C. Smail, *Crusading Warfare 1097–1193* (Cambridge, 1956), 53.

[112] An exception, as in so much else, may be found in the work of Claude-Adrien Helvétius, *De l'esprit* (Paris 1758, repr. 1988), 401–404 who argues strongly against the stereotype.

[113] SHA *Avidius Cassius* 5.11: Graecanicis militibus; *Severus Alexander* 53.7: milites Romani, vestri socii, mei contubernales et commilitones amant, potant, la<v>ant Graecorum more[m] et <ad luxuriam> quidem se instituunt.

[114] For the legionary baths: H. von Petrikovits, *Die Innenbauten römischer Legionslager während der Prinzipatszeit* (Opladen 1975), 102–4; the auxiliary forts along the Antonine wall had bath-houses in Scotland: Anne S. Robertson, revised and ed. by L. Keppie, *The Antonine Wall* (Glasgow, 1990), *passim;* G. Webster, *The Roman Imperial Army* (London, 3rd ed. 1985), 227f., 259.

Syrian *archisynagogus* and a high priest (using the Greek *archiereus*, not the Latin *Pontifex Maximus* which was part of the imperial titulature).[115] Whether Severus Alexander was ever taunted in this manner, and whether he really was ashamed of being Syrian, is impossible to verify. If he was ashamed he was neither the first nor the last to suffer such feelings about his background. More specifically, we have seen that for Lucian of Samosata his Syrian origin was quite an important and ambiguous topic. It is also very interesting to see that Syrians here are linked not only with Greeks, but also with Jews, for there can be no doubt that *archisynagogus* raises associations with a Jewish function. It is furthermore remarkable that by the late fourth century it is evident that there is a contradiction between being Syrian and being Roman. Severus Alexander is represented as being ashamed of his origins. The author expresses the implications of being Syrian in one of his spurious exchanges with the emperor Constantine. There the latter is supposed to have asked what could have made a man who was a Syrian and a foreigner into such a good emperor, unlike so many others who were of Roman origin.[116] Again, the implication is that Syrians are not Romans but foreigners, and that they are supposed to be an inferior people. It should be emphasized that expressions of such sentiments are neither incidental nor confined to this particular *Life*. Elsewhere, Claudius Pompeianus, Marcus's son-in-law and an Antiochene, is described as a foreigner (*peregrinus*).[117] Syrians are not only degenerate, they lack the basic qualities that characterize Romans: *fides*[118] and *gravitas*.[119] This is also applied to Africans whose *Punica fides* is brought against them.[120]

The *Historia Augusta* is a remarkable text with more jokes, word-play, and slurs than most, but it is certainly not the only text of the second half of the fourth century to express derogatory feelings about Syria. Eunapius, for instance, still considers the Syrians obsequious.[121] Julian accused the citizens of

[115] SHA *Severus Alexander* 28.7: volebat videri originem de Romanorum gente trahere, qu<ia> eum pudebat Syrum dici, maxime quod quodam tempore frust<r>a, ut solent Ant[h]ioc<h>enses, Aegyptii, Alexandrini, lacessi[t]v[s]era<n>t convi[n]ciolis, et Syrum archisynagogum eum vocantes <et> archiereum. Cf. Stern, ii, 630 ; Isaac, *The Near East under Roman Rule*, 274, n. 24.

[116] 65.1: Soles quaerere, Constantine maxime, quid sit quod hominem Syrum et alienigenam talem principem fecerit, cum tot Romani generis, tot aliarum provinciarum reperiantur improbi, impuri, crudeles, abiecti, iniusti, libidinosi.

[117] SHA, *Avidius Cassius* 10.4: (epistula Faustinae ad Marcum): . . . Pompeianus gener et senior est et peregrinus. Marcus Antoninus 20,6: filiam suam . . . grandaevo equitis Romani filio Claudio Pompeiano dedit [sc. Marcus] genere Antiochensi . . .

[118] SHA, *Aurelian* 31: Rarum est ut Syri fidem servent, immo difficile. This, obviously, is related to the old tradition accusing Phoenicians/Carthaginians of *perfidia*.

[119] SHA, *Tacitus* 3.5: iam si nihil de Persicis motibus nuntiatur, cogitate tam leves esse mentes Syrorum ut regnare vel feminas cupiant potius quam nostram perpeti sanctimoniam.

[120] See above, p. 329.

[121] Eunapius *Vit. Soph.* 16.2.2: καὶ ὃ πάντες οἱ Συροφοίνικες ἔχουσιν κατὰ τὴν κοινὴν ἔντευξιν ἡδύ καὶ κεχαρισμένον, . . . Cf. the conclusions along similar lines by Nicole Belayche, "L'Oronte et le Tibre: l'«Orient» des cultes «orientaux» de l'Empire romain," in Mohammad Ali Amir-Moezzi et John Scheid, *L'Orient dans l'histoire religieuse de l'Europe: l'invention des origines* (Turnhout, 2000), 1–36, at 34f.

Antioch, asserting: "What constitutes for you the true beauty of mind, that is a voluptuous life."[122] Two sources in the fourth century surprisingly call the Syrians greedy, a feature usually attributed to the Phoenicians.[123] We may conclude this section with a warning that all this obviously does not mean that all Syrians themselves agreed with such assessments. Unlike Lucian of Samosata, Libanius of Antioch was proud of his origins. "Syria," he says, "is a factory of the Muses: for a long time now it has fashioned orators . . . and there is a mass of students from many quarters that sharpens a teacher and itself gets what it has come for" (*Ep* 441.5. cf. Or. 11.181ff.).

CONCLUSIONS

To conclude this chapter it will be instructive to see how Greek and Roman views of Phoenicians and Syrians fit into the general theme of this book. It will be immediately clear that these eastern peoples were the target of particularly fierce forms of dislike and disapproval. Their merits and gifts are regarded as morally dubious, their faults are the opposite of the merits decent people ought to display. The Phoenicians are deceitful merchants already in the work of Homer. They were also skillful craftsmen and sailors, but these qualities are not generally recognized, for they are by themselves dubious, particularly the sailing, as we saw in chapter 3. They are greedy sharpers in the eyes of both Greeks and Romans. They practice cannibalism and human sacrifice. Rome was more in conflict with them than the Greeks, through their wars with Carthage. Thus we find the Phoenicians and Carthaginians described as treacherous and cruel in the works of Cicero and Livy. Here it is noteworthy that Cicero does not regard these faults as theirs by nature, but as the result of Carthage being a port city. That still means it is an environmental factor and thus inevitable, which makes it a proto-racist argument according to the definition accepted in this study. Sometimes the Phoenicians are assimilated to the Syrians in the texts, but usually they are not. The factor that determines much of the Roman attitude is the old enmity between Rome and Carthage and their important role in the sea-trade. Otherwise they are less of a presence in the city or Rome than the Syrians.

The Syrians are good at feasting, they tend to go to the baths rather than exercise, and they overeat. They are servile, effeminate, and perverted. They may be clever, a dubious quality, but like the Phoenicians, they are unreliable. Above all, they are born for slavery, which is the classic example of a proto-racist claim. Of course, not all of the negative views cited are proto-racist; most of them reflect simple ethnic prejudice. All this appears in Greek and Latin

[122] Julian, *Misopogon* 20: Ἔστι μὲν γάρ, ὡς ὑμεῖς κρίνετε, ψυχῆς ἀληθινὸν κάλλος ὑγρότης βίου·

[123] *De Physiognomonia* 14; Firmicus Maternus, *Mathesis* 1.1; 1.4. Note, however, 1.10.12, where, for the sake of argument it is claimed that "Syrian cupidity has been transformed into a sudden generosity."

sources alike and, among the Greeks, it is found already in Posidonius and still present in Ptolemy and Herodian. Those Syrians who themselves are intellectual Greeks, like Lucian, are defensive and ambivalent. Even if we prefer to read Lucian as writing in a spirit of satirical exaggeration, then we still must accept that he offers a perspective of serious negative stereotypes attached to Hellenized immigrants from Syria in Greece and Rome. The Syrians and other easterners from the same general region are present in some considerable number in Rome, and Roman attitudes are clearly influenced by the immediate contact with them. Much of the hostility is marked by a fear of contamination with the presumed Syrian effeminacy, perversion, superstition, and servility.

Egyptians

REFERENCES TO EGYPT AND THE EGYPTIANS are very numerous in ancient sources,[1] and this chapter will therefore focus only on a few aspects which are especially relevant to the present discussion, looking at hostility and stereotypes as well the theme of the Egyptians in their natural environment.[2] This study, given its subject matter in general, will focus on the Egyptians proper, the "native Egyptians" as they are called in many contemporary works, rather than the city of Alexandria or the Ptolemaic rulers and Hellenized Egyptians.[3] Here, as elsewhere in this study, we are concerned with current attitudes towards contemporary Egyptians. Literary discussions of historical or legendary Egyp-

[1] Consequently, or correspondingly, the bibliography on ancient attitudes towards Egypt is quite substantial: G. Nenci (ed.), *Hérodote et les peuples non grecs* (Vandoeuvres–Genève, 1990), esp. Alan B. Lloyd, "Herodotus on Egyptians and Libyans," 215–244; id. *Herodotus Book II* 3 vols. (Leiden, 1975); Claire Préaux, "La singularité de l'Égypte dans le monde gréco-romain," *Chronique d'Égypte* 49 (1950), 110–123; "Les raisons de l'originalité de l'Égypte," *Museum Helveticum* 10 (1953), 203–221; P. Lambrechts, "Augustus en de Egyptische Godsdienst," *Mededelingen van de Koninklijke Vlaamse Academie voor Wetenschappen . . . van België*, Klasse der Letteren 18.2 (1956), 3–32; Meyer Reinhold, "Roman Attitudes Toward Egyptians," *Ancient World* 3 (1980), 97–103; K.A.D. Smelik and E. A. Hemelrijk, "Opinions on Egyptian Animal Worship in Antiquity," *ANRW* 2.17.4 (1984), 1852–2000; H. Sonnabend, *Fremdenbild und Politik: Vorstellungen der Römer von Ägypten und dem Partherreich in der späten Republik und frühen Kaiserzeit* (Frankfurt, 1986); forthcoming: Gideon Bohak, "The Ibis and the Jewish Question: Ancient 'Anti-semitism' in Historical Perspective," in M. Mor and A. Oppenheimer (eds.), *Jewish-Gentile Relations in the Second Temple, Mishnaic and Talmudic Periods* (Jerusalem). Note also: I. Shatzman, "The Egyptian Question in Roman Politics (59–54 B.C.)," *Latomus* 30 (1971), 363–369. I have not yet seen Erik Hornung, *Das esoterische Aegypten* (Munich, 1999) or its translation into English: *The Secret Lore of Egypt. Its Impact on the West*, Ithaca and London, 2001. This work clearly covers other aspects of the impact of Egypt on the West and it does so for a much longer period than is treated in the present book. See now: Phiroze Vasunia, *The Gift of the Nile: Hellenizing Egypt from Aeschylus to Alexander* (Berkeley, 2001). It is important to note that there is, in this section, nothing like an attempt to cover the subject fully or list all the relevant sources. That would be unnecessary, given the accessibility of the information in the literature cited. My only aim here is to give an honest impression of the ambivalence found in Greek and Latin sources regarding Egypt and the Egyptians.

[2] Egypt is also admired in Greek and Latin sources, but this is not a topic for discussion in the present work; cf. C. Froidefrond, *Le mirage égyptien dans la littérature grecque d'Homère à Aristote* (Gap, 1971); Sonnabend, *Fremdenbild und Politik*, chapter 4; Phiroze, op. cit.

[3] For Alexandria the major study by P. Fraser, *Ptolemaic Alexandria* (Oxford, 1972), does not discuss the Roman period; indirectly relevant are O. W. Rheinmuth, *The Prefect of Egypt from Augustus to Diocletian* (1935); D. Delia, *Alexandrian Citizenship during the Roman Principate* (Atlanta, GA, 1991). For some specific aspects, Isaac, *Limits of Empire*, 277–279. There is an abundance of hostile pronouncements regarding Alexandria in sources of the Roman period, but these had better be studied in the context of a general work about this city after the Hellenistic period.

tians, such as Isocrates, *Busiris*, are relevant only insofar as they might tell us something about ideas about contemporary Egyptians. In other words, if we assume that Isocrates, in his remarks about the legendary king Busiris, expresses ideas about Egypt in the fourth century B.C., then this work becomes relevant for this study. It will be seen that there are numerous and varied negative stereotypes, but also a number of constantly recurring themes. There were early contacts between Greeks and Egyptians attested in the literature and through inscriptions from Egypt.[4] An early contact at a higher level was Solon's visit to Pharaoh Amasis, probably between 570 and 560.[5]

The first reference, possibly coined by Hecataeus for the Egyptians, has been discussed above.[6] It describes the Egyptians as resembling only themselves and no other people. The claim is repeated for the Egyptians in combination with the Scythians in *Airs, Waters, Places* 19: "As regards the seasons and their physical shape, the Scythian people is very different from other men and, like the Egyptian people, it resembles only itself."[7] The Scythians and Egyptians, regarded as the extreme peoples of the North and the South, are separate and different from all other peoples. Herodotus (2.35) wrote that the climate and rivers of Egypt, as well as the manners and customs of its people, are exactly the reverse of those in the rest of the world. For Herodotus this was a cause of wonder and special interest; there is no hostility anywhere in his extensive report on the country. "The Egyptians follow their ancestral customs and adopt no foreign ones."[8] Herodotus also reports that the Egyptians believed themselves to be the most ancient of mankind, but this belief had been shaken by an experiment which need not be discussed here.[9] So far this has no obviously negative connotations. In a study such as this, concerned with racist concepts, it is important to note also that the Egyptian physical characteristics as such do not interest Herodotus.[10] He provides this long treatment of Egypt "because it has so many wonders and works that are too impressive to describe." Moreover, in Herodotus and in *Airs* these descriptions are not accompanied by slurs, pejorative adjectives, or collective condemnation, such as are already to be found in some other fifth-century authors.

A fragment from Aeschylus states that "The Egyptians are excellent in devis-

[4] Greek mercenaries in Egyptian service (591 B.C.): R. Meiggs and D. Lewis, *A Selection of Greek Historical Inscriptions to the End of the Fifth Century* B.C. (Oxford, 2d ed. 1989), no. 7.

[5] Herodotus 1.30; Plutarch, *Solon* 26.

[6] Parmenides, fr. 8.57: ἑωυτῶι πάντοσε τωὐτόν, τῶι δ' ἑτέρωι μὴ τωὐτόν. See above, chapter 1, pp. 58, 110.

[7] *Airs* 19: Περὶ δὲ τῶν ὡρέων καὶ τῆς μορφῆς, ὅτι πολὺ ἀπήλλακται τῶν λοιπῶν ἀνθρώπων τὸ Σκυθικὸν γένος, καὶ ἔοικεν αὐτὸ ἑωυτέῳ, ὥσπερ τὸ Αἰγύπτιον . . .

[8] 2.79; 91. Cf. Pomponius Mela 1.57: cultores regionum multo aliter a ceteris agunt. For symmetry and inversion in Herodotus' description of Egypt: Vazunia, *The Gift of the Nile*, 92–100.

[9] Herodotus 2.2. Cf. Plato, *Timaeus* 22b, where an Egyptian priest is cited as calling the Greeks a young people. For the experiment described by Herodotus, see the Introduction, n. 15.

[10] As observed by Alan B. Lloyd, "Herodotus on Egyptians and Libyans," in *Herodote et les peuples non grecs* (Geneva, 1990), 215–244, at 221.

ing tricks."[11] In the *Supplices* Egyptian men are characterized by the choir as "a people abominably lustful and insatiate of battle,"[12] and again as 'intolerable in their wantonness."[13] Their bread and beer are inferior and less conducive to manliness than the Greek diet.[14] Sophocles makes Oedipus describe his sons as living like Egyptians because they stay at home, while his daughter bears her father's burdens: "O true image of the ways of Egypt that they show their spirit and their life! For there the men sit weaving in the house, but the wives go forth to win the daily bread!"[15] While this literally echoes Herodotus,[16] it is worth observing that the idea of the reversal of male and female roles occurs also in the Hippocratic treatise *Airs*, but there it is described as a characteristic of the Scyths, the extreme northern people, corresponding to the Egyptians who live farthest to the south.[17] The idea that generally everything in Egypt is different or even perverse is presumably responsible for the examples of eccentric behavior cited by Sophocles and other authors. The expression αἰγυπτιάζειν is used in the sense of "to act deceitfully" in Old Comedy.[18]

The fourth century as represented by Plato has been discussed above in the section on Syrians and Phoenicians, where the Egyptians and others are characterized as greedy sharpers. Elsewhere Plato describes Egyptian priests as addressing Solon in an arrogant manner.[19] Yet there was respect for them and their ancient society and culture. Plato attributes to Socrates remarks about the ancient wisdom of the Egyptians. The God Theuth (Thoth) was the one "who first

[11] Aeschylus, fr. 373 Radt: δεινοὶ πλέκειν τοι μηχανὰς Αἰγύπτιοι. The line is cited by the Scholiast to Aristophanes, *Nubes* 1130: ἐλέγετο γὰρ ληιστεύεσθαι ἡ Αἴγυπτος. Αἰσχύλος· δεινοὶ πλέκειν τοι μηχανὰς Αἰγύπτιοι. καὶ Θεόκριτος ἐν Ἀδωνιαζούσαις οὐδεὶς κακοεργὸς δαλεῖται τὸν ἰόντα παρέρπων Αἰγυπτιστί. καὶ αἰγυπτιάζειν τὸ ὕπουλα πράττειν. "Egypt is said to be infested with robbers" Aeschylus [. . .]. And Theocritus (15.48): "We do not get scoundrels creeping up on passers-by to rob them in Egyptian fashion." And αἰγυπτιάζειν means: to act deceitfully (Cratinus, fr.378). See references in S. Radt, *Tragicorum Graecorum Fragmenta* (Göttingen 1971–), 3, comm. ad loc. and A.S.F. Gow, *Theocritus* (Cambridge, 1965), 2, p. 280.

[12] Aeschylus, *Supp.* 742: ἐξῶλές ἐστι μάργον Αἰγύπτου γένος μάχης τ' ἄπληστον καὶ λέγω πρὸς εἰδότα. For Aeschylus's *Supplices* and Egypt, see now Vazunia, *The Gift of the Nile* (2001), 68–74, 143–146; see 33–40, 58–64 for his discussion of Euripides' *Helen* and Egypt.

[13] Aeschylus, *Supp.* 817f.: γένος γὰρ Αἰγύπτιον ὕβριν δύσφορον ἀρσενογενὲς.

[14] 761; 953; cf. Hall, *Inventing the Barbarian* (1989), 133.

[15] Sophocles, *OC* 337–341: Ὦ πάντ' ἐκείνω τοῖς ἐν Αἰγύπτῳ νόμοις φύσιν κατεικασθέντε καὶ βίου τροφάς· ἐκεῖ γὰρ οἱ μὲν ἄρσενες κατὰ στέγας θακοῦσιν ἱστουργοῦντες, αἱ δὲ σύννομοι τἄξω βίου τροφεῖα πορσύνουσ' ἀεί. Cf. the observations of Vasunia, *The Gift of the Nile*, 98.

[16] Herodotus 2.35: τὰ πολλὰ πάντα ἔμπαλιν τοῖσι ἄλλοισι ἀνθρώποισι ἐστήσαντο ἤθεά τε καὶ νόμους. Ἐν τοῖσι αἱ μὲν γυναῖκες ἀγοράζουσι καὶ καπηλεύουσι, οἱ δὲ ἄνδρες κατ' οἴκους ἐόντες ὑφαίνουσι.

[17] See above, chapter 1, p. 66.

[18] Eustathius, *Od.* 1.149.14 citing Cratinus as using αἰγυπτιάσαι καὶ αἰγυπτιάζειν in the sense of τὸ πανουργεῖν καὶ κακοτροπεύεσθαι. See also Aristophanes, *Thesm.* 922.

[19] *Timaeus* 22a–b: ὦ Σόλων, Σόλων, Ἕλληνες ἀεὶ παῖδές ἐστε, γέρων δὲ Ἕλλην οὐκ ἔστιν. Cf. Ps. Dionysius Hal., *Ars Rhetorica* 11.4.6. As noted above, Solon's visit to Egypt is reported also by Herodotus, 1.30. This is not the proper venue to discuss the image of an old and mostly fictional Egypt which appears in Plato's *Timaeus* and *Critias*, for we are concerned with Greek views of contemporary Egyptians. For recent discussion: Vasunia, *The Gift of the Nile*, chapter 6.

discovered number and calculation, geometry and astronomy, as well as the games of checkers and dice, and, above all else, writing."[20] That, however, was ancient history. In contrast, the fourth-century Athenian orator Hyperides describes a certain contemporary Anthogenes as a "speechwriter, a man of affairs and, most significant of all, an Egyptian."[21] The implication is that Hyperides could assume that his audience accepted the commonplace that Egyptians were dishonest merchants. There are a few exceptions in this list of consistently hostile commonplaces. Isocrates, *Busiris* (390–385 B.C.) is an exercise in rhetoric in defense of the legendary first king of Egypt which has to be read with special caution, for the author himself admits (*Busiris* 9) that his topic is not a serious one.[22] The central element in the works is the sacrifice of foreigners, practiced regularly by the fictitious King Busiris. It is indeed worth mentioning that the text contains positive elements in its description of Egypt and its inhabitants. Egypt has the best climate in the world (12), a good constitution, poorly imitated by the Lacedaemonians (15–17), and the Egytians are very pious (24–29). Yet, the bottom line is that the Egyptian king is depicted in the most extreme xenophobic terms, as one who constantly practices human sacrifice, his victims are foreigners, and he is ultimately subdued by Heracles (see fig. 1).[23]

Then there is Aristotle, who disparages Persia but is less critical of Egypt. In his *Politics* he observes: "The history of Egypt attests the antiquity of all political institutions. The Egyptians are generally accounted the oldest people on earth; and they have always had a body of law and a system of politics."[24] Again, there is no doubt regarding the antiquity of their culture and that is important in itself. Contemporary Egyptians, however, have to be judged by their own merits. When referring to Egypt, he is sometimes neutral and sometimes negative, but occasionally even respectful.[25] He does not belong in the category of those who totally disparaged the Egyptians.

[20] Plato, *Phaedrus* 274c–d (trans. A. Nehamas and P. Woodruff): τοῦτον δὴ πρῶτον ἀριθμόν τε καὶ λογισμὸν εὑρεῖν καὶ γεωμετρίαν καὶ ἀστρονομίαν, ἔτι δὲ πεττείας τε καὶ κυβείας, καὶ δὴ καὶ γράμματα. The point of Socrates' story is that the invention of letters was a mixed blessing, as argued by the Egyptian King Thamos.

[21] Hyperides, *Against Athenogenes* 2.1, cited by Smelik and Hemelrijk, *ANRW* 2.17.4 (1984), 1877 and n.164.

[22] Cf. Margaret C. Miller, "The Myth of Bousiris: Ethnicity and Art," in Beth Cohen (ed.), *Not the Classical Ideal,* 413–442, which traces the transformation of the Busiris myth in vase-painting after the Persian wars, showing how the story shifts from an Egyptian to a Persian setting. See now Vasunia, *The Gift of the Nile* chapter 5.

[23] Vasunia, p. 215.

[24] Aristotle, *Pol.* 1329b (trans. Ernest Barker): ὅτι δὲ πάντα ἀρχαῖα, σημεῖον τὰ περὶ Αἴγυπτόν ἐστιν· οὗτοι γὰρ ἀρχαιότατοι μὲν δοκοῦσιν εἶναι, νόμων δὲ τετυχήκασιν ἀεὶ καὶ τάξεως πολιτικῆς. See comments by Newman, 3.388f.: "In the reference to the Egyptians it is evidently assumed with much *naïveté* that as a race is when it first comes into being, so it will remain." As seen in the introduction, the assumption that people are unchangeable and unchanged is one of the essential characteristics of racism.

[25] *Pol.* 1286a; 1329b; *Probl.* 909a asserts that the Ethiopians and Egyptians are bandy-legged because of the heat, like planks which warp when drying; *EE* 1215b on the Apis; 1235b on mummification. See, however, *Pol.* 1313b, where the pyramids are listed among various examples of the devices of tyrants to keep people poor and busy, so they have no leisure to plot against the ruler.

Other negative generalizations about Egypt are found in the works of various authors, but apart from their being negative there does not seem to be much continuity. Some themes recur through the ages, for instance greed and dishonesty, wantonness, presumption, and rebelliousness. It is interesting to note that the combined accusation of cunning and rebelliousness was still aimed at the Armenians by German racists who supported the Turkish policy against the Armenian minority.[26] There is, however, a great variety of negative characterizations of Egyptians. Thus Polybius says, in a specific context, that "the cruelty of the Egyptians is terrible when they are in anger."[27] Elsewhere he speaks of "Egyptian extravagance and carelessness" (ἀσωτία καὶ ῥᾳθυμία Αἰγυπτιακή 39.7.7). These are negative qualities that do not recur in other authors. Quintus Curtius calls them an idle people, "more inclined to revolt than to achieve something," which again is rather familiar.[28] Seneca describes Egypt as a province, "talkative and good in insulting its governors."[29] Elsewhere he instructs Lucilius that pleasures are "like the robbers whom the Egyptians call 'lovers,' who embrace us in order to strangle us."[30] This shows that there was an idea that Egyptian robbers are more pernicious than those in other countries. Clearly, this is a ragbag of stereotypes with few common features.

The Egyptians, however, were best known in antiquity for their unusual religion: the cult of animals and the practice of mummification made a strong impression on the Greeks and Romans, particularly on the latter.[31] The animal

---

Physiogn. 812a: "Those who are too swarthy are cowardly; this applies to Egyptians and Ethiopians." 812b: "Those whose eyes are excessively black are cowardly." And: "Those with very woolly hair are cowardly; this appplies to the Ethiopians." The idea that dark people are cowards and light people courageous fighters is found already in *Airs, Waters, Places* discussed above. This is an exception to Frank M. Snowden, *Before Color Prejudice* (1983), who concludes that generally there were no such prejudices in antiquity. Note, however, the different views of Lloyd A. Thompson, *Romans and Blacks* (1989). The least that can be said is that ancient views of the Ethiopians were not uniform. Herodotus certainly gives a different perspective, cf. Reinhold Bichler, *Herodots Welt: Der Aufbau der Historie am Bild der fremden Länder und Völker, ihrer Zivilisation und ihrer Geschichte* (Berlin, 2000), 31–35.

[26] See Hilmar Kaiser, *Imperialism, Racism and Development Theories: The Construction of a Dominant Paradigm on Ottoman Armenians* (Ann Arbor, MI, 1997), 10, citing a German foreign ministry document.

[27] 15.33.10; cf. F. W. Walbank, "Egypt in Polybius," in John Ruffle et al. (eds.), *Glimpses of Ancient Egypt: Studies in Honour of H.W. Fairman* (Warminster, 1979), 180–189.

[28] 4.1.30: vana gens et novandis quam gerendis aptior rebus.

[29] Seneca, *Consolatio ad Helviam Matrem, Dial.* 12 [11].19.6: Itaque loquax et in contumelias praefectorum ingeniosa prouincia. O. Seeck, *Geschichte des Untergangs der antiken Welt* 4, 2d ed. (Stuttgart, 1922), 331, accepts without question all the ancient stereotypes: "Der Ägypter verstand es meisterlich, sich zu ducken und Mächtigen zu schmeicheln. Aber weil er sie ängstlich und tückisch belauerte, hatte er auch ein scharfes Auge für ihre Schwächen und rächte sich gern für seine Unterdrückung durch giftigen Spott."

[30] Seneca, *Ep.* 51.13: Voluptates praecipue exturba et invisissimas habe; latronum more, quos φιλητάς Aegyptii vocant, in hoc nos amplectuntur, ut strangulent.

[31] M. Malaise, *Les conditions de pénétration et de diffusion des cultes égyptiens en Italie* (Leiden, 1972) ; see the detailed treatment by Smelik and Hemelrijk; Sonnabend, *Fremdenbild und Politik,* 118–142. The Egyptians are described as very pious by Isocrates, *Busiris* 24–29.

cult attracted a good deal of attention, mostly negative. We may start with Cicero: "Who does not know of the custom of the Egyptians? Their minds are infected with degraded superstitions and they would sooner submit to any torment than injure an ibis or asp or cat or dog or crocodile, and even if they have unwittingly done anything of the kind there is no penalty from which they would recoil."[32] The language here is rather extreme: Egyptian ideas represent not merely erroneous ideas, but *pravitas,* depravity, a term which Cicero uses frequently when he calls something not just mistaken, but utterly wrong. "With the errors of the poets may be classed the monstrous doctrines of the magi and the insane mythology of Egypt, and also their popular beliefs."[33] That is to say: Egyptian religion is a form of *dementia,* insanity. "[S]ome bull is regarded as a god, which the Egyptians call Apis, and many monsters and beasts of every sort are held by them sacred to the gods."[34] These pronouncements by Cicero have the advantage of not appearing in speeches. It is therefore likely that they represent Cicero's true opinion, rather than his special pleading for the law courts. The vehemence of the language employed is remarkable. The disapproval rests on two points: first, the very notion that gods should bear the shape of animals or partly animals, and second, the fact that live animals are deemed holy. Both are complete reversals of traditional Greek and Roman values, which hold that gods are superior to men and men superior to animals. It is the reverse of the natural hierarchy, in both senses of the word natural. In fact, in the western tradition animal worship was long regarded one of the more serious transgressions against elementary morality and, in Christianity, it became a feature of devil worship.

If the Egyptian religion had merely been a remote aberration it might have been regarded as mildly amusing or somewhat ridiculous and would not have stimulated such a particularly hostile response. There can be no doubt that this reaction was caused by the fact that Egyptian cults exerted some influence in Rome and attracted followers, possibly many of them, for Cicero did not really care what happened in far-away countries, but he was sensitive to the mood in Rome. Confirmation of this is found in the record of a series of measures taken in these years. In fifty-eight altars for Serapis, Isis, Arpocrates, and Anubis were destroyed by order of the Senate and erected again through the influence of the *populares.*[35] Lambrechts argues, not without plausibility, that there was

---

[32] Cic., *Tusc.* 5.78 Aegyptiorum morem quis ignorat? quorum inbutae mentes pravitatis erroribus quamvis carnificinam prius subierint quam ibim aut aspidem aut faelem aut canem aut crocodillum violent, quorum etiamsi inprudentes quippiam fecerint, poenam nullam recusent. Negative comments about Alexandria in *Pro Rabirio* 12.35 are less relevant here.

[33] *de natura deorum* 1.16.43: Cum poetarum autem errore coniungere licet portenta magorum Aegyptiorumque in eodem genere dementiam, tum etiam vulgi opiniones . . . See also 1.29.81, 1.36.101, 3.19.47, all of them negative pronouncements on the Egyptian animal cult, cf. comments by Smelik and Hemelrijk, 1956f.

[34] Cicero, *De Republica* 3.9.14: bovem quendam putari deum, quem Apim Aegyptii nominant, multaque alia portenta apud eosdem et cuiusque generis beluas numero consecratas deorum;

[35] Tertullian, *Ad Nat.* 1.10; *Apol.* 6; Arnobius, *Adv. Nat.* 2.73; cf. Lambrechts, *Mededelingen* . . . *Vlaamse Academie voor Wetenschappen* 18 (1956),10f.

support for the Egyptian cults among the *populares* because of their widespread
popularity among the city population, while the *optimates* considered them a
focus of dangerous political activity.[36] In 53 B.C. there followed a decree to tear
down the temples of Serapis and Isis, which private individuals had built in
Rome, although outside the pomerium (Dio 40.47.3).[37] According to Dio 47.16,
however, the *triumviri* ordered a temple for Serapis and Isis to be built towards
the end of 43 B.C. Afterwards Augustus had his doubts on this matter. Among
measures taken in 28 B.C. for the benefit or pleasure of the urban population,
Dio relates that Augustus 'did not allow the Egyptian rites to be celebrated
inside the pomerium—which would have implied the adoption of the Egyptian
gods amongst the official Roman divinities. However, he made provision for the
temples; those which had been built by private individuals he ordered their sons
and descendants, if any survived, to repair, and the rest he restored himself'
(Dio 53.2.4). Although Dio does not say so, this clearly means that Augustus
definitely rescinded the decree issued twenty-five years earlier.[38] Octavian's own
attitude towards Egyptian cults was, apparently, relatively tolerant. When in
Egypt, he claimed to have a high regard for the god Serapis although he refused
to worship Apis and the remains of the Ptolemies.[39] In the city of Rome the
result of his policy was apparently a rapid flourishing of Egyptian cults, for in
21 B.C. Agrippa took measures restricting their performance in the city.[40]

While Egyptian religion is noted frequently by hostile Roman commentators,
this is by no means the only criticism made of this people in Roman authors.
Their presumed lack of credibility, first found in Aeschylus, is repeated by the
anonymous author, perhaps Hirtius, of Caesar's Alexandrian war: "Yet, as far as
I am concerned, had I now the task of defending the Alexandrians and proving
them to be neither untrustworthy nor hot-headed, it would be a waste of many
words: indeed when one gets to know both the people and its nature there can
be no doubt whatever that their kind is extremely prone to treachery."[41]

---

[36] Lambrechts, 10–12.

[37] Measures taken in 50 B.C.: Valerius Maximus 1.3–4; in 48 B.C.: Dio 42.26. See also Dio
40.47.2–4.

[38] It is thus an error to list this as an instance of Octavian's aversion to Egyptian gods and rites, as
stated by M. Reinhold, *Ancient World* 3 (1980), 98. For the Isis temple 'antiquo quae proxima surgit
ovili: Juvenal 6.529.

[39] 51.16.3. Cf. Julian, *Ep.* 111: ἄνδρες, εἶπεν, Ἀλεξανδρεῖς, ἀφίημι τὴν πόλιν αἰτίας πάσης
αἰδοῖ τοῦ μεγάλου θεοῦ Σαράπιδος . . . Sarapis is not mentioned in the parallel passage from
Plutarch, *Antonius* 80.3. Reinhold, loc. cit., and others cited ibid. note 20, believe that Augustus's
expression of veneration for Serapis was only a political expedient of the moment, for in fact, they
say, Augustus harbored a deep antipathy toward Egyptian cults. Whether true or not, it does not
matter. What matters is not what Augustus thought but what he said. Lambrechts, *Mededelingen
. . . Vlaamse Academie voor Wetenschappen* 18 (1956), has argued that Octavian / Augustus's
policy as regards the Egyptian cult changed considerably over time, between 43 and 10 B.C. It
evolved and became increasingly hostile, even though it was always determined by a policy of
caution, moderation, and opportunism. I am not sure that the sources really show an increased
hostility over the years.

[40] Dio 54.6.6.

[41] Bellum Alexandrinum 7.2 At mihi si defendendi essent Alexandrini neque fallaces esse neque

Possibly the idea that Egypt was treacherous was widespread and encouraged at the time of the conflict between Antony and Octavian. We also find it in Propertius in a vituperation of Cleopatra: "Guilty Alexandria, land ever ready for treason."[42] Not all authors of the republican period are equally hostile. Diodorus describes the Egyptian animal cults in some detail and relates that he himself saw a Roman who had killed a cat being lynched around 59 B.C. (1.83). He says the animal cult appears to be extraordinary, but worthy of investigation.[43] Diodorus's first book is entirely devoted to Egypt and no deeply felt hostility is noticeable anywhere. He even praises their morals occasionally (1.93.4).

So far the sources on Egypt from the Greek and republican periods. For the imperial period Livy's speech attributed to Manlius in 189 B.C. has been cited several times and discussed at length. It is worth returning to it once more: "The Macedonians who rule Alexandria in Egypt, who rule Seleucia and Babylon and other colonies spread all over the world, have degenerated into Syrians, Parthians and Egyptians." The point to note here is the general and overall disparagement of the three major eastern peoples: Syrians, Parthians, and Egyptians, without distinction. Another literary speech may be cited here, attributed by Cassius Dio to Octavian and supposedly made to the troops at Actium: "Alexandrians and Egyptians (what worse or what truer name could one apply to them?), who worship reptiles and beasts as gods, who embalm their own bodies to give them the semblance of immortality, who are most reckless in effrontery but most feeble in courage and who, worst of all, are slaves to a woman and not to a man."[44] The Egyptians are here, as in other sources, depicted as soft, cowardly, yet arrogant, the sort of opposed negative qualities, so often attributed to minorities and foreigners.[45] The familiar accusation of their being slaves is here amplified by the claim that they are slaves to a woman. Egyptian religion and, in particular, the custom of mummification are singled out here as particularly objectionable. Seneca also had a thorough dislike of the cults of Cybele and Isis in Rome, or at least of those who practiced these cults.[46] As with Judaism and the cults from Asia Minor, the reason for the anger which these religions aroused among conservative Romans is the obvious appeal they

---

temerarii, multa oratio frustra absumeretur; dum vero uno tempore et natio eorum et natura cognoscatur, aptissimum esse hoc genus ad proditionem dubitare nemo potest. Cf. Florus 2.13.60 in his account of Caesar in Alexandria: *de inbelli ac perfida gente.*

[42] Propertius 3.11.33: noxia Alexandria, dolis aptissima tellus

[43] Diodorus 1.83.1: εἰκότως φαίνεται πολλοῖς παράδοξον τὸ γιγνόμενον καὶ ζητήσεως ἄξιον.

[44] Dio 50.24.6: Ἀλεξανδρεῖς τε καὶ Αἰγύπτιοι ὄντες (τί γὰρ ἂν ἄλλο τις αὐτοὺς χεῖρον ἢ ἀληθέστερον εἰπεῖν ἔχοι;) καὶ τὰ μὲν ἑρπετὰ καὶ τἆλλα θηρία ὥσπερ τινὰς θεοὺς θεραπεύοντες, τὰ δὲ σώματα τὰ σφέτερα ἐς δόξαν ἀθανασίας ταριχεύοντες, καὶ θρασύνασθαι μὲν προπετέστατοι ἀνδρίσασθαι δὲ ἀσθενέστατοι ὄντες, καὶ τὸ μέγιστον γυναικὶ ἀντ' ἀνδρὸς δουλεύοντες, Cf. Smelik and Hemelrijk, op. cit., 1928f., where it is observed that many of the hostile stereotypes regarding Egypt were coined by the poets in the reign of Augustus.

[45] For the Egyptians as a soft people, see Lucan 8.543: Et Pelusiaci tam mollis turba Canopi; 10.54: Rex puer inbellis populi sedaverat iras; Florus 2.13.60: . . . de inbelli ac perfida gente . . .

[46] Seneca, *De Vita Beata* 26.8.

had for many citizens in Rome and Italy. This is a topic that will be discussed again in the chapter on attitudes towards Jews.

Statius, consoling Melior upon the death of his foster son, says: "No outlandish revolving stage turned thee about, no slave-boy wert thou amid Egyptian wares, to utter studied jests and well-conned speeches, and by impudent tricks to seek and slowly win a master."[47] It is interesting to observe that there were norms of approved behavior even for slaves offered for sale. The Egyptians and—one may assume—Syrians and other slaves of eastern origin had the name of being dishonest and using trickery and artifice to attract the attention of a possible buyer. Although it is not spelled out in this passage, the idea that these people were born for slavery was undoubtedly at the back of the poet's mind, for he seems to imply that a German on the slave market would preserve his dignity. A contemporary of Statius, Martial is revealing in his praise of the new Flavian palace on the Palatine in Rome. "Laugh, Caesar, at the royal wonders of the pyramids! Barbarian Memphis is now silent about eastern work. How small a part of the Parrhasian palace is equalled by Mareotic labour! The day sees nothing more famous in the entire world!"[48] The pyramids were traditionally counted among the Seven Wonders of the World.[49] When Martial invites Caesar to laugh at the pyramids and the city of Memphis, now that he himself has a sumptious palace in Rome, we discern something of the old jealousy and inferiority the new rulers apparently felt towards the old cultures they had conquered. The palace in Rome now dwarfed the traditional Wonders in Egypt, so that Rome has replaced Egypt as the foremost producer of astonishing feats of engineering.

An even more acute expression of imperial discomfort is found in Pliny's *Panegyricus,* delivered to Trajan in A.D. 100. It contains an instructive passage which lashes out against Egypt. Four chapters of Pliny's speech are devoted to the corn supply. The immediate occasion was a year of drought in Egypt, when the Nile failed to rise as usual. Crops failed, and Trajan sent supplies to help Egypt in her emergency. "This conceited and impudent nation used to brag that they still had to feed their conquerors, that their river and their ships determined our plenty or our famine."[50] Pliny goes on to claim that Egypt and Rome were now even. The lesson to be learned by Egypt is that 'she does not provide us with food, but pays tribute. Let her know that she is not indispensable to the

---

[47] Statius, *Silvae* 2.1.74 (reign of Domitian, late first century A.D.; trans. J. H. Mozley): Non te barbaricae versabat turbo catastae, nec mixtus Phariis venalis mercibus infans compositosque sales meditataque verba locutus quaesisti lascivus erum tardeque parasti. See also 5.5.67.

[48] Martial, *Ep.* 8.36.2: Regia pyramidum, Caesar, miracula ride;| Iam tacet Eoum barbara Memphis opus: | Pars quota Parrhasiae labor est Mareoticus aulae? Clarius in toto nil videt orbe dies. Memphis was earlier described as barbarian by Martial's friend Lucan 8.542: 'O superi, Nilusne et barbara Memphis . . .'

[49] Diodorus 1.63.2–64; Ammianus 22.15.28, where reference is made to Herodotus's description (2.124–7).

[50] Pliny, *Pan.* 31.2: Superbiebat ventosa et insolens natio, quod victorem quidem populum pasceret, tamen quodque in suo flumine in suis navibus vel abundantia nostra vel fames esset.

Roman people and yet is Rome's slave."[51] "We do not need Egypt, but Egypt cannot do without us. She is finished, this country which could have been most fertile had she been free." This is a good example of the fear of dependence on the subject nations. The reality is well known: Rome could not function without imported grain. This was a constant reason for worry, ever since the annexation of Egypt as a province.[52] The sense of dependency must have been reinforced after Vespasian cut off the supply from Alexandria in 69. Pliny therefore builds an elaborate and comforting construction suggesting that the reverse was now true, merely because Egypt had a single bad harvest and had to be supported by Rome. This is a striking exhibition of anger towards a subject nation that has been supplying much-needed produce to its conqueror and is considered to be presumptuous about it. This presumption probably existed only in Roman minds, for senators did not visit Egypt. However, in Pliny's eyes a principle was at stake: a slave-nation cannot claim to supply a necessity; it only pays what it owes. Pliny sees Egypt here from the perspective of a Roman senator and administrator. His objections do not resemble those that we have encountered in the writings of private Greek and Roman authors. As with them, however, the bottom line is dislike and disapproval.

A different line of thought is expressed by Tacitus, who relates that "in the past Italy used to dispatch supplies for the legions in far-away provinces, and even now it is not unproductive. But we prefer to exploit Africa and Egypt, and the life of the Roman people is entrusted to ships and all their risks" (*Ann.* 12.43.4). Tacitus thus suggests that Rome depended on imported grain because of the irresponsibility of Roman government. Yet Pliny and Tacitus have an important feeling in common: their dislike of distant parts of the empire and their fear of dependency on them. Tacitus, moreover, joins many others cited above in his dislike of shipping.[53] On Egypt Tacitus is entirely characteristic: "Ever since the reign of the Divine Augustus, knights instead of kings have governed Egypt and the troops by which it has to be kept in subjection. It has been thought best thus to keep under the Emperor's control a province so difficult of access, so productive of corn, ever in conflict and fickle through its superstition and licentiousness, ignorant of the laws and unmindful of its magistrates."[54] Here we find the majority of the standard slurs against Egypt as en-

---

[51] Non alimenta se nobis sed tributa praestare; sciat se non esse populo Romano necessariam, et tamen serviat.

[52] G. Rickman, *The Corn Supply of Ancient Rome* (Oxford, 1980); P. Garnsey, *Famine and Food Supply in the Graeco-Roman World: Responses to Risk and Crisis* (Cambridge, 1988); id., *Food and Society in Classical Antiquity* (Cambridge, 1999).

[53] Cf. *Ann.* 3.54.6: (Tiberius speaking) "at hercule nemo refert, quod Italia externae opis indiget, quod vita populi Romani per incerta maris et tempestatum cotidie volvitur."

[54] Tacitus, *Hist.* 1.11: Aegyptum copiasque, quibus coerceretur, iam inde a divo Augusto equites Romani obtinent loco regum: ita visum expedire, provinciam aditu difficilem, annonae fecundam, superstitione ac lascivia discordem et mobilem, insciam legum, ignaram magistratuum, domi retinere. Interestingly, another second-century author Apuleius, *Florida* 6, describes the Egyptians as erudite, the Nabataeans as merchants, but the Jews as superstitious: ". . . super Aegyptios eruditos et Iudaeos superstitiosos et Nabathaeos mercatores."

countered in the sources, expressed with typical Tacitean brevity. As already noted, the Egyptian religion was particularly despised, and this continued to be so after the annexation of the country as a province. The Egyptians prayed to "monstrous gods of every sort and to barking Anubis."[55] According to Tacitus they were a "people devoted to superstitions."[56]

This may also be a suitable occasion to refer once again to Tacitus's comments on the four thousand descendants of enfranchised slaves of Jewish origin, together with Isis worshippers. These were to be shipped to Sardinia and employed there in suppressing brigandage: "if they succumbed to the pestilential climate, it was a cheap loss (*vile damnum*)," according to Tacitus (*Ann.* 2.85).[57] Other sources report repression of the cult of Isis at this time. A temple was destroyed again, having been destroyed earlier in 53 B.C. and subsequently restored by order of Octavian, and the cult-statue was thrown in the Tiber.[58] The Egyptian cults in the city of Rome, then, were a subject of ever recurring tension between those who fiercely disapproved of them and their adherents among the city populace.

It is important to realize that the dislike of Egypt and the Egyptians was not confined to those Roman aristocrats who had never been to Egypt but disliked the presence of Egyptians and their cults in the city of Rome. Plutarch, born in Greek Chaeronea in the mid-first century, had visited Egypt himself, although he does not seem to know much about it. Yet he attacks Herodotus as a "barbarophile"[59] because of his positive attitude towards Egyptians: Herodotus "says there is a strong sense of religion and justice amongst all Egyptians."[60] Like other authors before and after him, it was precisely Egyptian religion which Plutarch found repugnant. In his essay about Isis and Osiris he discusses the animal cult at great length. He finds it ridiculous and dangerous, for it makes the naïve superstitious and the cynical atheist and brutish.[61] He writes that the Egyptians had wily and artful kings. One of those observed that Egyptians were by nature frivolous and inclined to change and novelty, but because of their number their strength was invincible. He therefore established among them an everlasting superstition, a ground for continuous quarrelling.[62] This story com-

---

[55] Vergil, *Aen.* 8.698: omnigenumque deum monstra et latrator Anubis.

[56] Tacitus, *Hist.* 4.81: dedita superstitionibus gens; cf. 1.11: , superstitione ac lascivia discordem et mobilem.

[57] Cf. R. Syme, *Tacitus* (Oxford, 1958), 1.468. Cited above, chapter 3, p. 237.

[58] Suetonius, *Tiberius* 36.1; Josephus, *Ant.* 18.3.4.(79); not mentioned by Tacitus. As observed by Syme, loc.cit., this is a paradoxical omission.

[59] Plutarch, *The Malice of Herodotus (De Malignitate Herodoti)*, introduction, trans. and comm. by A. J. Bowen (Warminster, 1992), 12/857a–18/858e; 12/857a. Οὕτω δὲ φιλοβάρβαρός ἐστιν. . .

[60] 857a καὶ πᾶσιν Αἰγυπτίοις ὁσιότητα [or: θειότητα] πολλὴν καὶ δικαιοσύνην μαρτυρήσας,. Plutarch refers here to Herodotus 2.37.1 and 65.1. See Bowen's comments on all this.

[61] *De Iside et Osiride* 371.

[62] 380a: ἄλλοι δὲ [τῶνδε] τῶν δεινῶν τινα καὶ πανούργων βασιλέων ἱστοροῦσι τοὺς Αἰγυπτίους καταμαθόντα τῇ μὲν φύσει κούφους καὶ πρὸς μεταβολὴν καὶ νεωτερισμὸν ὀξυρρόπους ὄντας, ἄμαχον δὲ καὶ δυσκάθεκτον ὑπὸ πλήθους δύναμιν ἐν τῷ συμφρονεῖν καὶ κοινοπ-

bines many of the slurs and criticisms that we encountered above. Syrians are also accused of being frivolous (in the *Historia Augusta*). The evils of a monarchy are an old Greek notion, allowing Plutarch to assume that the entire range of Egyptian beliefs and associated customs had been imposed on the nation by one monarch. The Jews, too, are accused of extreme superstition, and several authors ascribe their particular variety to a single individual, the person of Moses who, according to Tacitus, also had his political agenda when he introduced his laws.[63]

While it is true that there are only so many different ways of disliking and disparaging others, the choice of negatives still says something about the emotional character of the hatred. Other Greek authors of the Roman period echo Plutarch's dislike. Dio Chrysostom, like Plato, reports a conversation in which a remarkably arrogant Egyptian priest disparages the Greeks, claiming that the Greeks are "ignorant in most things" and saying "that they are pretentious, considering themselves highly learned, while in fact they are totally ignorant."[64] Lucian, in his *Assembly of the Gods*, 10 and elsewhere, makes fun of the Egyptian gods. In his *Philopseudes* he gives an extensive caricature of an Egyptian priest. He considers the Egyptians "the most superstitious of all people."[65] In the same century Philostratus attacks the Egyptians along similar lines (*vita Apollonii* 3.32).

To return to an author from the city of Rome, Juvenal (c. A.D. 110–130), as usual, gives expression to the most fearful hatred of foreigners who have reached a position in Roman society which should have been reserved for the locals. An Egyptian wearing a Tyrian cloak as well as an equestrian gold ring is appalling. "When a guttersnipe of the Nile like Crispinus—a slave-born denizen of Canopus—hitches a Tyrian cloak on to his shoulder, whilst on his sweating finger he airs a summer ring of gold, unable to endure the weight of a heavier gem—it is hard *not* to write satire."[66] The physical repugnance of the *eques* of Egyptian origin is noteworthy: unlike his Italian fellow equestrians, he has a sweating finger. The physical expression of this hatred of the Egyptians

---

ραγεῖν ἔχοντας, ἀίδιον αὐτοῖς ἐγκατασπεῖραι δείξαντα δεισιδαιμονίαν διαφορᾶς ἀπαύστου πρόφασιν.

[63] A rare positive assessment of Moses occurs in the anonymous *De Sublimitate* 9.9 (Stern, No. 148), first century A.D.. Other pagan writers who approve of Moses are Hecataeus, ap. Diodorus 40.3 (Stern , No. 11) and Strabo 16.2.35f (Stern, No. 115).

[64] Dio Chrysostom, *Or.* 11.37 ἐγὼ οὖν ὡς ἐπυθόμην παρὰ τῶν ἐν Αἰγύπτῳ ἱερέων ἑνὸς εὖ μάλα γέροντος ἐν τῇ Ὀνούφι, ἄλλα τε πολλὰ τῶν Ἑλλήνων κατα γελῶντος ὡς οὐθὲν εἰδότων ἀληθὲς περὶ τῶν πλείστων, . . . (39) λέγων ὅτι ἀλαζόνες εἰσὶν οἱ Ἕλληνες καὶ ἀμαθέστατοι ὄντες πολυμαθεστάτους ἑαυτοὺς νομίζουσι·

[65] Lucian, *Pro Imaginibus* 27: τοὺς Αἰγυπτίους, οἵπερ καὶ δεισιδαιμονέστατοί εἰσιν πάντων,

[66] Juvenal, *Sat.* 1.26–29 (trans. G. G. Ramsay) cum pars Niliacae plebis, cum uerna Canopi Crispinus Tyrias umero reuocante lacernas uentilet aestiuum digitis sudantibus aurum nec sufferre queat maioris pondera gemmae, difficile est saturam non scribere. In 4.1–33 he rants against the same Crispinus for buying a very expensive fish. Compare Juvenal's anger at the *equites Asiani* (7.13–16).

who were adopted into the Roman governing class is also embodied in his advice not only to urinate on the statues of Tiberius Julius Alexander.[67]

Besides worrying about the penetration of the governing class by Egyptians, Juvenal, like many other Roman authors, is angered by the influence of Egyptian cults in Rome. His sixth satire has already been cited for its hostility towards Asiatic cults and Judaism in Rome. Egyptian cults fare no better in this satire (6.522–41). The Isis and Osiris cults and that of Anubis in Rome are said to attract hysterical women; their priests secretly mock their followers; they take bribes and encourage immoral behavior. Juvenal, who dislikes any and all foreigners, is particularly inventive in his fifteenth satire on the conflict between two neighboring towns in Egypt in A.D. 127.[68] "Who knows not, O Bithynian Volusius, what monsters demented Egypt worships?"[69] Egyptian banquets are excessive: "Egypt, doubtless, is a rude country; but in indulgence, so far as I myself have noted, its barbarous rabble yields not to the ill-famed Canopus."[70] The climax here is the description of cannibalism in lines 78–83, with the poignant detail that the body was eaten uncooked.[71] As has been shown, eating meat cooked is often considered the essential difference between man and animal.[72] "Man is not an animal that eats raw flesh."[73] Eating human flesh uncooked is thus the ultimate in brutish barbarism. It is remarkable too, but not difficult to understand, that an Alexandrian-born author, Achilles Tatius, also expresses himself in the most hostile terms about the Egyptian. He is "subject to the most slavish cowardice when he is afraid and the most foolhardy rashness when he is encouraged by his position."[74]

---

[67] *Sat.* 1.129–131. . . . atque triumphales inter quas ausus habere nescio quis titulos Aegyptius atque Arabarches, cuius ad effigiem non tantum meiere fas est. Cf. Courtney, p.110f. From the text we must understand that for Juvenal Tiberius Alexander was an Egyptian. His Jewish origin is not referred to here. Sherwin-White, *Racial Prejudice*, 74–76 concludes from texts like these: "So in Juvenal there is an active if minor strain of national and cultural prejudice at work." I cannot understand why he calls it minor.

[68] Juvenal, *Satire* 15. Courtney's commentary has remarks about this (pp.590f.).

[69] *Sat.*15.1–2: Quis nescit, Volusi Bithynice, qualia demens Aegyptos portenta colat?

[70] *Sat.* 15.44–6: horrida sane / Aegyptos, sed luxuria, quantum ipse notavi, / barbara famoso non cedit turba Canopo.

[71] Courtney has some good comments on this (pp. 590f.); cf. J. Moreau, "Une scène d'anthropophagie en Égypte en l'an 127 de notre ère (Juvenal satire XV)," *CE* 15 (1940), 279–285; G. Highet, "A Fight in the Desert: Juvenal XV and a Modern Parallel," *ClJ* 45 (1949/50), 94–96; B. B. Powell, "What Juvenal saw: Egyptian Religion and Anthropophagy in Satire 15," *RhM* 122 (1979), 185–189. Egyptian rebels in 171 also are reported to have practiced cannibalism, sacrificing and consuming a centurion (Dio 71.4.1). Dio does not tell whether the rebels cooked the meat. As observed above, cannibalism is more often a fantasy than a fact attested in real life. For accusations of human sacrifice, see also the observations on bestiality as expounded by Aristotle, *Eth. Nic.* 1149a, and the chapter on hostility towards the Jews, below. See also Isocrates, *Busiris* 5 (222).

[72] M. Detienne, "Between Beasts and Gods," in R. L. Gordon (ed.), *Myth, Religion and Society* (Cambridge, 1982), 215–228, at 218f.

[73] Porphyrius, *de abstinentia* 1.13: οὐ γὰρ ἦν ὠμοφάγον ζῷον ὁ ἄνθρωπος·

[74] *Leucippe and Clitophon* (trans. S. Gaselee) 4.14.9: ἀνὴρ γὰρ Αἰγύπτιος καὶ τὸ δειλόν, ὅπου φοβεῖται, δεδούλωται, καὶ τὸ μάχιμον, ἐν οἷς θαρρεῖ, παρώξυνται· ἀμφότερα δὲ οὐ κατὰ μέτρον, ἀλλὰ τὸ μὲν ἀσθενέστερον δυστυχεῖ, τὸ δὲ προπετέστερον κρατεῖ.

It is even more interesting to see that the historian Cassius Dio had his doubts about the handling of Egyptian cults in Rome. When he discusses various portents which frightened the Romans in the year 52 B.C., he adds his own opinion: "But it seems to me that that decree passed the previous year, near its close, with regard to Serapis and Isis, was a portent equal to any; for the senate had decided to tear down their temples, which some individuals had built on their own account. Indeed, for a long time they did not believe in these gods, and even when the rendering of public worship to them gained the day, they settled them outside the pomerium." Dio, then, considered it a dangerous act of sacrilege to tear down temples in Rome to Egyptian gods, an indication that he himself, a Greek senator from Asia Minor, had no doubts as to the power of these gods. Indeed, in general Dio seems to have been free from hostile feelings towards Egyptian cults, and ambivalent about the people.[75] In one passage he describes them as "the most religious people on earth in many respects" which surely is not meant as criticism, even if he does go on to explain that they fight each other on religious matters (42.34.1–2). He expresses himself in strong language about the Alexandrians (Dio 39.58) and elsewhere calls Egypt heavily populated, easy, and fickle.[76]

Following this author there is quite a gap in the Greek and Latin sources. From the second half of the fourth century, however, there are several authors with relevant pronouncements on Egypt: the anonymous treatise on *Physiognomonia,* Ammianus, and the Historia Augusta. The treatise claims that people with curly hair resemble the Egyptians and are therefore very deceitful, greedy, fearful, and grasping.[77] Deceitfulness and greed are familiar and timidity is also attested in earlier periods (e.g., Dio 50.24.6). As argued in chapter 1, this sort of argument in physiognomics must be considered a form of proto-racism because it sees a direct connection between collective physical and mental characteristics.

Ammianus describes the Egyptians, at the time of a visit by Julian

---

[75] M. Reinhold, *Ancient World* 3 (1980), 97f., asserts that "next to Juvenal no other Greek or Roman author was as obsessed with prejudice against and contempt for the Egyptians as Cassius Dio," but this rests partly on misinterpretations. Dio 39.58 is fiercely disparaging of the Alexandrians, but not to the same degree of the Egyptians in general. In 42.3.4 Dio says that those who treacherously murdered Pompey "brought a curse upon themselves and all Egypt." The Egyptians "were first delivered to be slaves of Cleopatra, which they particularly disliked, and later were enrolled among the subjects of Rome." Dio does not assert that the Egyptians collectively were guilty of this act, but that they paid for it. In fact, he observes that the Egyptians regarded Pompey with very kindly feelings (42.4.4). 50.24.6, cited above, is a literary pre-battle speech composed by Dio for Octavian. This certainly contains negative stereotypes commonly believed in the age of Augustus and, presumably, of Dio, but it does not necessarily reflect Dio's own attitudes. Dio records the marriage of Cleopatra with her brother, but expresses no opinion on it and explains that it was only a formal marriage, imposed by Caesar (42.35.4).

[76] Dio 51.17.1: πρὸς τὸ πολύανδρον καὶ τῶν πόλεων καὶ τῆς χώρας, καὶ πρὸς τὸ ῥᾴδιον τό τε κοῦφον τῶν τρόπων αὐτῶν. Cf. Tacitus, *Hist.* 1.11, cited above (*mobilis*); Dio 78 (77) 6.1a uses the term κοῦφον also for Gaul.

[77] *De Physiognomonia* 14: nimium subdolum, avarum, timidum, lucri cupidum . . .

as a quarrelsome sort of men, always most happily engaged in intricate litigation and most eager in demanding excessive restitution for any payment they have made to a collector of debts either in order to be relieved of the debt or at least to obtain postponement of payment. Or they threaten wealthy men with prosecution for extortion which they anxiously prefer to avoid. All these, crowding together and chattering like jackdaws interrupted the Emperor himself and the praetorian prefects, demanding sums they declared to have paid, justly or not, seventy years before to various people.[78]

Ammianus then tells with approval how Julian stopped all these procedures and "put an end to this obstinate attempt at blackmail."[79] The Egyptians were told to report to the emperor at Chalcedon, where he was going himself, while at the same time the emperor issued orders not to transport any Egyptian from Chalcedon to Constantinople. Since the Egyptians were stuck in Chalcedon, they returned home. This description clearly contains elements of satire. It may not be going too far to compare it with descriptions of European colonial officials among the natives. At any rate, the comparison of the Egyptians with chattering birds, the suggestion that they go to so much trouble in order to avoid paying just debts, the phrase regarding payments made seventy years earlier, and the manner in which Julian made fools of the obstreperous Egyptians—these are all matters of style and detail which convey a good deal of contempt.[80]

Two literary passages come to mind, the one because of a certain resemblance, the other for its contrast: the first is Ammianus's description of Marcus's visit to Palestine on his way to Egypt, which immediately precedes the present passage. Ammianus describes Marcus as "being often annoyed by the malodorous and unmanageable Jews."[81] The second is Strabo's description of Petra, as related to him by Athenodorus (xvi 4,21 [779]): at Petra there were

---

[78] Ammianus 22.6.1–2: Per hoc idem tempus rumoribus exciti uariis Aegyptii uenere complures, genus hominum controuersum et assuetudine perplexius litigandi semper laetissimum maximeque auidum multiplicatum reposcere, si compulsori quidquam dederit, ut leuari debito possit, uel certe commodius per dilationem inferre, quae flagitantur, aut criminis uitandi formidine diuites pecuniarum repetundarum interrogare. hi omnes denseti in unum principem ipsum et praefectos praetorio gracularum more strepentes interpellabant incondite modo non ante septuagensimum annum extorquentes, quae dedisse se iure uel secus plurimis affirmabant. Cf. J.den Boeft et al., *Philological and Historical Commentary on Ammianus Marcellinus XXII* (Groningen, 1995), 63–67.

[79] evanuit pertinax calumniandi propositum

[80] Note the phrase *genus hominum controuersum et assuetudine perplexius litigandi semper laetissimum.* den Boeft et al. observe that this "fulsome characterization testifies to Ammianus' wish to make perfectly clear what kind of people Julian had to deal with: not bona fide litigants, but inveterate abusers of justice."

[81] Ammianus, 22.5: "Ille enim cum Palaestinam transiret, Aegyptum petens, Iudaeorum fetentium et tumultuantium saepe taedio percitus." Cf. the comments and references by Stern, *Greek and Latin Authors on Jews and Judaism* 2 (1980), 606f. The context is Ammianus's description of Julian's dissatisfaction with the squabbles of the Christians. Ammianus then explained that Julian misquoted Marcus.

many Romans and other foreigners, and those were often engaged in lawsuits, both between themselves and with the locals, but none of the natives prosecuted one another in any way, for they kept peace with one another.

Ammianus's Antiochene contemporary Libanius has a similar description of an Egyptian: "Yet of all the people who resented being compelled to pay, everyone would have been glad to get his money back home, especially an Egyptian, for we see them nothing loth to refer to any payments of money they have made and, in fact, only too prone to reclaim payments not made at all."[82]

Ammianus's description of Egypt as given in this passage may contain obvious traditional stereotypes, but it is almost certainly his own work: at any rate, it cannot be attributed to an earlier source. The same cannot be said with any certainty of his longer description of Egypt in 22.15–16.[83] This contains one paragraph characterizing the Egyptians that is worth citing here:

> The Egyptians are most of them rather swarthy and dark and somewhat gloomy (or: gloomier than *magi*). They are lean and dryish, easily excitable in their gestures, quarrelsome, and most persistent, importunate creditors. Among them a man blushes if he cannot show several weals on his body incurred while refusing to pay tribute. And nobody has yet been found capable of devising a torture which succeeds in eliciting from a hardened bandit of that region his own name against his will.[84]

It is immediately clear that this is not the usual stock of slurs against Egyptians. The common accusation of fraudulence may be found in Ammianus's other passage, but is not present in the second. Other features such as wantonness, arrogance, cowardice, and especially superstition, are missing. What we do find here are the traditional accusations of greed and stubborn resistance to the authorities. The idea that the Egyptians are quarrelsome is found in at least one other place in the work of Plutarch and it recurs in Ammianus's other description. Unlike his predecessors, Ammianus does not disparage the Egyptian religion: the reason for this silence may be due to the fourth-century cir-

[82] Libanius, *Or.* 14.56 (trans. A. F. Norman): καίτοι τίς οὐκ ἂν τῶν ἡνίκα ἠναγκάζοντο δοῦναι λελυπημένων ἡδέως ἂν πάλιν ἤνεγκε τὸ χρυσίον οἴκαδε, καὶ ταῦτα Αἰγύπτιος; οὓς οὐκ ὀκνοῦντας ὁρῶμεν ὧν ἔδοσαν μνησθῆναι, ἀλλὰ μάλ' εὐχερῶς εἰσπράττοντας ἃ μὴ δέδοται.

[83] Ammianus, 22.15.1, says he described Egypt at length in the (now lost) parts of his history, dealing with Hadrian and Severus. Here, he says, he told mostly what he had seen himself (*visa pleraque narrantes*). John Matthews, *The Roman Empire of Ammianus* (London and Baltimore, 1989), 14, 27f., 111, 462, assumes Ammianus's description in book 22 reflects his own experience of the country. Note also Ammianus's critical attitude towards the Arabs, a people with which he undoubtedly was familiar. See the discussion by Irfan Shahîd, *Byzantium and the Arabs in the Fourth Century* (Washington, 1984), 239–250.

[84] Ammianus 22.16.23: Homines autem Aegyptii plerique suffusculi sunt et atrati magisque maestiores, gracilenti et aridi, ad singulos motus excandescentes, controuersi et reposcones acerrimi. erubescit apud eos, si qui non infitiando tributa plurimas in corpore uibices ostendat. et nulla tormentorum uis inueniri adhuc potuit, quae obdurato illius tractus latroni inuito elicere potuit, ut nomen proprium dicat. Cf. den Boeft et al., *Commentary*, 310f.

cumstances.[85] Thus while Ammianus does repeat some of the standard commonplaces on Egyptians, others are missing and the impression is that these two short passages are not borrowed from other authors.

Still in the later fourth century, the *Historia Augusta,* as we saw above, has quite a lot to say against the Syrians. However, the longest and most hostile tirade against a people of the East may be found in the *Quadrigae Tyrannorum,* in a spurious letter about the Egyptians attributed to Hadrian, preceded by lavish disparagement: "Among them, indeed, are Christians and Samaritans and those who are always dissatisfied with the present although they enjoy excessive liberty."[86] The letter continues in a similar vein:

> Those who worship Serapis there, are [in fact] Christians, and those who call themselves bishops of Christ are [in fact] devotees of Serapis. There is no Jewish *archisynagogus,* no Samaritan, no Christian presbyter, who is not an astrologer, a soothsayer, or a master of wrestlers. When the Patriarch himself visits Egypt, he is forced by some to worship Serapis, by others to worship Christ. They are a most seditious sort of people, most deceptive, most injurious; their city is wealthy, rich, and [their land] fertile and no one is idle. . . . Their only god is money, and this the Christians, the Jews, and all people adore.[87]

There are several points of interest in this text. The author disapproves of eastern religions among which he still includes Christianity. He insists on the confusion which he claims was characteristic of these people. This reminds us of the alleged taunts of the people of Antioch against the Egyptians and the people of Alexandria, who are supposed to have called Severus Alexander a Syrian *archisynagogus* and a high priest. The view that eastern peoples are seditious and frivolous was also encountered above among the sources regarding the Syrians.[88] Astrologers and soothsayers were already considered undesirable elements in republican Rome. Thus, while the identification of Orientals with astrologers and the like goes back to the republican period, the notion that easterners and Jews, in particular, are avaricious and grasping occurs in ancient

---

[85] Julian himself was greatly influenced by Neoplatonic circles where Egypt was considered a land of ancient wisdom; see Smelik and Hemelrijk, 1953; Matthews, *Roman Empire,* chapter 7.

[86] SHA, *Quadrigae Tyrannorum* 7,4–5: Sunt enim Aegyptii, ut satis nostri, <in>venti ventosi, furibundi, iactantes, iniuriosi atque adeo vani, liberi, novarum rerum usque ad cantilenas publicas cupientes, versificatores, epigrammatarii, mathematici, haruspices, medici. Nam <in> eis C<h>ristiani, Samaritae et quibus praesentia semper tempora cum enormi libertate displiceant. Another tirade against Egyptians: *Tyr. Trig.* 22, 1–3.

[87] SHA, *Quadrigae Tyrannorum* 8, 2 ff.: Illic qui Serapem colunt, C<h>ristiani sunt et devoti sunt Serapi, qui se C<h>risti episcopos dicunt. Nemo illic archisynagogus Iudaeorum, nemo Samarites, nemo C<h>ristianorum presbyter non mathematicus, non haruspex, non aliptes. Ipse ille patrarcha cum Aegyptum venerit, ab aliis Serapidem adorare, ab aliis cogitur Christum. Genus hominum. seditiosissimum, vanissimum, iniuriosissimum, civitas opulenta, dives fecunda, in qua nemo vivat otiosus. . . . Unus illis deus nummus est. Hunc Christiani, hunc Iudaei, hunc omnes venerantur et gentes . . . Cf. the comments in Stern, *Greek and Latin Authors,* ii, 638–641 and R. Syme, *Ammianus and the Historia Augusta* (Oxford, 1968), 61. For the accusation of greed, see above.

[88] Herodian ii 7,8–9; SHA, *Tacitus* 3,5.

texts from the time of Plato at least and has lasted till the present day, although, as noted below, the Jews are not regularly accused of being greedy in ancient sources.

CONCLUSIONS

To conclude this chapter: the negative stereotypes found about Egypt throughout antiquity are remarkably varied. We find hostile stereotypes already in several Greek authors of the fifth century B.C.. Herodotus, however, is not negative and some later sources, particularly Diodorus Siculus, show respect. The question then is whether this should count for more than the briefer and more isolated negative references that appear in so many other sources. It seems fair to suggest that the two authors who were on balance favorably impressed with the Egyptians are also the two who were most interested in their civilization and history. As such they always were a minority, for we have no information that there are many more such accounts that are lost. All the others who did not take the trouble to write extensively about the Egyptians, but who expressed themselves in critical and stereotypical terms, are almost certainly far more representative of the common attitudes of their times that Herodotus and Diodorus were. Yet we must keep in mind that these two authors went to a good deal of trouble to give a balanced account of the country and they probably convinced at least part of their readers.

Over the centuries one particular feature seems to have been dominant in the Greek and Roman view of the Egyptians, when they considered their religion and cults, namely the element of fraudulence. This goes back at least to Aeschylus and the Old Comedy. Other features are promiscuity, greed, arrogance, fickleness, cowardice, stubborn resistance to the authorities, and superstition. The most notable and controversial aspect of Egyptian culture for both Greeks and Romans was their religion with its animal cult. It constantly attracted followers in Rome, which aroused resistance, and countermeasures were taken from time to time. The essence of the alleged shortcomings of the Egyptians, like those of the Syrians, may be summed up as being a lack of *fides* and of *gravitas*. These were the values which the Romans always ascribed to themselves, irrespective of their actual behavior. They also judged all other peoples by the presumed absence or presence of these characteristics, for these were the qualities whose absence saved their self-esteem when they were faced with culturally superior subjects. Like other foreign peoples, the Egyptians were viewed by Romans in their own Roman terms. As such they were regarded as lacking the most important positive qualities.

Other forms of ambivalence are expressed, for instance, when Martial claims that the new Flavian palace in Rome allowed the Emperor to laugh at the pyramids of Egypt. Similarly, in another sphere, there is the younger Pliny's happiness when Egypt, one year, has a poor harvest: this teaches them that Rome does not really need all their grain. Generally, however, the peoples of the East represented to the Romans the opposite of the essential features they imagined themselves to have—or to have had in the good old days. Yet there are obvious differences between the image of the Egyptians and that of other eastern peoples, the latter being generally wicked and decadent, the former wicked and odd. At the opposite end of the scale of values there are the Gauls and Germans who had their weaknesses, but they were not perfidious, frivolous, or effeminate according to our texts (although, as observed above, several authors writing not long after A.D. 9 found the Germans treacherous). Some of the stereotypes encountered among Greeks and Romans reflect not only ethnic prejudice, but also proto-racism, for instance when it is asserted that their bread and beer are less conducive to manliness than the food of the Greeks, furthermore there is the regular insistence on their servile nature or on the opposite quality also frequently attributed: their obstreperousness. Their negative character features are connected with physical characteristics according to the fourth-century treatise on physiognomics, which is per definition a form of proto-racism. Many of the peoples of the East could conveniently be despised for lacking the qualities which the Romans thought they should have themselves. However, it can perhaps be said that there was no other people which so irritated many Greeks and Romans as Egyptians.

This might have been the natural place in this work to discuss hostility towards the Jews who were, after all, of eastern origin like the Syrians and Egyptians. There are, however, a number of recent important books which deal with this complex subject. The aspect this work can offer which these other works have not attempted is to consider this hostility in the context of the antagonism towards other foreign peoples and minorities and to see how it fits in the theoretical framework set forth in the Introduction. It will therefore be best to consider some other peoples first: Persians, Greeks, Gauls, Germans, and some remoter peoples, all as seen by Roman authors. A separate chapter on the Jews will follow at the end of this part of the work.

Parthia/Persia

THE ATTITUDE OF THE GREEKS towards the Persians has been considered extensively above. The fact that it played a major role in Greek history may be one reason why the theme of Persia is echoed in Roman literature as well. There are several other reasons why Parthia should have been prominent among foreign peoples discussed by Roman authors.[1] Parthia, as the only major empire facing Rome, was important enough to guarantee it a special place in the Roman perception of foreigners. On the other hand, Parthia and the Parthians do not seem to be mentioned as frequently as one might expect. Of course, the historians pay attention to the many wars between Rome and Parthia and, no less significantly, we know that works have been lost, especially Arrian's seventeen-book *Parthica* with its detailed narrative of Trajan's campaigns. Had they been preserved we might have had different impressions.[2] However this may be, the Parthians seem remote, as they were indeed geographically. There were no great numbers of Parthians in Rome, to impress their foreign appearance and manners on the inhabitants in their daily life. Thus there was no day-to-day friction and no cause for jealousy, fear, or incomprehension. The Parthian as an enemy was more abstract than real in the perception of Romans living in Italy.[3] Parthia was indeed "another world" in the words of Manilius.[4] "It is a vast land surrounded by vast coasts. Over the ages the Parthians vanquished the Bactrians and Ethiopians,[5] Babylon and Susa and Nineveh, and places whose names could scarcely be conveyed because of countless forms of language [i.e. because the names are so outlandish]."[6]

Romans never gave up the idea that Parthia ought to be incorporated into the

---

[1] Cf. Holger Sonnabend, *Fremdenbild und Politik: Vorstellungen der Römer von Aegypten und dem Parterreich in der späten Republik und frühen Kaiserzeit* (Frankfurt/Main, 1986). Note also the interesting paper, dealing with an aspect not discussed in the present book: R. F. Schneider, "Die Faszination des Feindes: Bilder der Parther und des Orients in Rom," Wiesehöfer (ed.), *Das Partherreich und seine Zeugnisse* (1998), 95–146.

[2] For Parthian history: N. C. Debevoise, *The Political History of Parthia* (Chicago, 1938); K. Schippmann, *Grundzüge der parthischen Geschichte* (Darmstadt, 1980); M.A.R. Colledge, *The Parthian Period* (1986); Ehsan Yarshater (ed.), *The Cambridge History of Iran* 3.1–2 (1983).

[3] For the relationship between Rome and Persia/ Parthia: Isaac, *Limits of Empire*, chapter 1. See now Engelbert Winter and Beate Dignas, *Rom und das Perserreich: Zwei Weltmächte zwischen Konfrontation und Koexistenz* (Berlin, 2001).

[4] Manilius 4.674–5: Parthique vel orbis alter; cf. Tacitus, *Annales* 2.2: petitum alio ex orbe regem..

[5] These are Ethiopians in Asia, mentioned also in *Od.* 1.23 and Herodotus 3.94.1; 7.70.

[6] Manilius 4.802–5 (trans. G. P. Goold): magna iacet tellus magnis circumdata ripis Parthis et <a> Parthis domitae per saecula gentes, Bactraque <et> Aethiopes, Babylon et Susa Ninosque, nominaque innumeris vix complectenda figuris.

empire and there were times, perhaps, when they thought this would be easy, first when Crassus undertook his Parthian campaign and was trounced thoroughly: Crassus's soldiers "had been fully persuaded that the Parthians were not different at all from the Armenians or even the Cappadocians, whom Lucullus had robbed and plundered till he was weary of it."[7] The same appears to have been the attitude when Julius Caesar,[8] and later Augustus, made preparations for an eastern campaign: "War is divine Caesar planning against rich India, and to cleave with his navy the waters of the pearl-bearing ocean. Great is the reward, O citizenry of Rome: the most distant of lands is preparing triumphs for you; Tigris and Euphrates will flow under your dominion; late though it be, it shall pass as a province beneath the rule of Italy, and Parthian trophies will grow accustomed to Latin Jupiter."[9] In the reign of Augustus, war with Parthia appeared an imminent reality, as may be illustrated by various passages in the work of Propertius[10] and Horace.[11] The Parthians are usually called "Medes" and they are typically referred to as cavalry and bowmen,[12] known for their tactic of shooting while withdrawing.[13] Sometimes the tone is one of triumphalism, as in some of Horace's odes: "Come, crush one hundred cups for life /Preserved, Maecenas; keep till day / The candles lit; let noise and strife / Be far away. / Lay down that load of state-concern; /The Dacian hosts are all o'erthrown; / The Mede, that sought our overturn, / Now seeks his own; / A servant now, our ancient foe, / The Spaniard, wears at last our chain; / The Scythian half unbends his bow / And quits the plain."[14] In 28 B.C. Horace is

---

[7] Plutarch, *Crassus* 18: πεπεισμένοι γὰρ οὐδὲν ᾿Αρμενίων διαφέρειν Πάρθους οὐδὲ Καππαδοκῶν, οὓς ἄγων καὶ φέρων Λεύκολλος ἀπεῖπε, . . .

[8] Nicolaos (Jacoby, FGH 90F 130.95); Plutarch, *Caesar* 58.3.

[9] Propertius 3.4 (trans. C. P. Goold, Loeb): Arma deus Caesar dites meditatur ad Indos, / et freta gemmiferi findere classe maris. / magna, uiri, merces! parat ultima terra triumphos; / Tigris et Euphrates sub tua iura fluent; / sera, sed Ausoniis ueniet prouincia uirgis; / assuescent Latio Partha tropaea Ioui. /. See also 4.6.83f.

[10] Propertius often links Parthian warfare with love affairs in Rome. 2.13.1–2: Non tot Achaemeniis armantur Susa sagittis,/ spicula quot nostro pectore fixit Amor (whereby, as usual, no difference is made between Parthians, Persians, or Achaemenids); 2.14.21–3: winning a girl is a greater victory than defeating the Parthians; 3.12: Propertius berates Postumus for abandoning the faithful Galla on an eastern campaign. See also: 2.10.13–18.

[11] Horace, *Carm.* 1.2.51f. (Winter 28 B.C.) calls for revenge on the Parthians, described, as usual, in Horace's work as "Medes": neu sinas Medos equitare inultos / te duce Caesar. For the date see the commentary by Adolf Kiessling and Richard Heinze, *Q. Horatius Flaccus: Die Oden und Epoden* (Dublin and Zürich, 1966), 10f.; 1.12.53–56 (25 B.C., according to Kiessling and Heinze, p. 59). Horace is confident of victory, first over the Parthians, then over the peoples of the Far East: "ille seu Parthos Latio imminentis / egerit iusto domitos triumpho / sive subiectos Orientis orae / Seras et Indos."

[12] E.g. Ovid, *Fasti* 5.590f.: quid rapidi profuit usus equi? Parthe, . . .

[13] Horace, *carm.* 1.19.9–12; 2.13.17; Plutarch, *Crassus* 24.

[14] Horace, *carm.* 3.8.16–24: mitte civilis super urbe curas: / occidit Daci Cotisonis agmen, / Medus infestus sibi luctuosis / dissidet armis, / servit Hispanae vetus hostis orae / Cantaber sera domitus catena, / iam Scythae laxo meditantur arcu / cedere campis. For the date: Kiessling and Heinze, 298. The translation is by John Conington, *Horace. The Odes and Carmen Saeculare of Horace* (London, 1882).

satisfied because there is internal strife among the Parthians.[15] The return of the legionary eagles in 20 B.C. is cheered as a major victory.[16] In 15 B.C. all the existing enemies of Rome have been defeated by Augustus: By grace of Caesar's high command. / Thee Spanish tribes, unused to yield, / Mede, Indian, Scyth that knows no home, / Acknowledge, sword at once and shield / Italy and queenly Rome."[17]

However, the Parthians were not usually seen in the same light as the inhabitants of Asia Minor or Syria. There was a clear sense that they were of nomadic origin and it was commonly believed that they were related to the Scythians. According to Strabo, some said that Arsaces, the first Parthian king, "derives his origin from the Scythians, whereas others say that he was a Bactrian" (11.9.3 [c. 515]).[18] According to the epitome of Pompeius Trogus, the Parthians were originally "exiles from Scythia."[19] He describes Arsaces, the founder of the Parthian dynasty, as "a man of obscure origins but proven courage. He had made a living by robbery and banditry."[20]

Unlike the Augustan poets cited above, Roman prose authors in the reigns of Augustus and Tiberius such as Strabo frequently acknowledge that the Parthian empire rivals their own: ". . . and at the present time they rule over so much land and so many tribes that in the size of their empire they have become, in a way, rivals of the Romans. The cause of this is their mode of life, and also their

---

[15] See also: Horace, *carm.* 1.26.5; 2.16.6–8.

[16] Horace, *carm.* 4.5.25–8 (c.14 B.C., Kiessling and Heinze, p. 414): quis Parthum paveat, quis gelidum Scythen, / quis Germania quos horrida parturt / fetus, incolumi Caesare? quis ferae / bellum curet Hiberiae? These Parthians, Scythians, Germans and Spanish are Rome's most dangerous enemies. For this passage, see Kiessling and Heinze, p. 417f. Horace, *carm.* 4.15.6 (13 B.C.): "et signa nostro restituit Iovi / derepta Parthorum superbis / postibus." Ovid, *Fasti* 5.580–91.

[17] Horace, *carm.* 4.14.41–4: "te Cantaber non ante domabilis / Medusque et Indus, te profugus Scythes / miratur, o tutela praesens / Italiae dominaeque Romae," etc.

[18] Cf. Jan Willem Drijvers, "Strabo on Parthia and the Parhians," in Josef Wiesehöfer (ed.), *Das Partherreich und seine Zeugnisse: Beiträge des internationalen Colloquiums, Eutin (27.–30. Juni 1996)* (Stuttgart, 1998), 286–293.

[19] Justinus, ep. Pompeius Trogus 41.1: Parthi, penes quos velut divisione orbis cum Romanis facta nunc Orientis imperium est, Scytharum exules fuere. 2 Hoc etiam ipsorum vocabulo manifestatur, nam Scythico sermone exules "parthi" dicuntur; also: 2.1.3; 2.3.6; cited by Isidore, *Etymologiae* 9.2. See also Strabo, 11.9.3 (c. 515): τῆς Μαιώτιδος Σκυθῶν· ἀπὸ τούτων δ' οὖν ἕλκειν φασὶ τὸ γένος τὸν Ἀρσάκην, οἱ δὲ Βακτριανὸν λέγουσιν αὐτόν. For more sources asserting the Scythian origin of the Parthians: Sonnabend, *Fremdenbild und Politik*, 276–279. As observed by Sonnabend, 277f., 280, Scythia and Parthia are sometimes used as synonyms and the Parthians and Scythians are frequently mentioned in the same passages. See also Ettore Paratore, "La Persia nella letteratura latina," in *Atti del convegno sul tema: la Persia et il mondo greco-romano 1965*, Accademia Nazionale dei Lincei 363 (Rome, 1966), 505–558. A major disadvantage of this paper is that it does not distinguish between passages referring to ancient Persia and those related to contemporary Parthia / Persia. While it is clear that the Latin literature sometimes associated contemporary Parthia with fifth-century, Achaemenid Persia, this is no reason for us to blur the distinction. Moreover, the numerous references to the fifth century are not presented in relation to the Greek literary tradition from which they derive.

[20] Justinus 41.4.6: Erat eo tempore Arsaces, vir sicut incertae originis, ita virtutis expertae. Hic solitus latrociniis et rapto vivere accepta opinione.

customs, which contain much that is barbarian and Scythian in character, though more that is conducive to hegemony and success in war."[21] Indeed this fits the spirit of the reign of Tiberius better than most of that of Augustus.[22] Pompeius Trogus, writing in roughly the same period, observes rather more reluctantly: "Today the Parthians rule the East, the world being partitioned, as it were, between them and the Romans; but originally they were exiles from Scythia." They were obscure and "one may well feel surprise that they should, through their valour, have achieved such success as to rule the nations in whose empires they had been like a herd of slaves."[23] The same work notes that "the Parthians were attacked by Rome in three wars in which they faced Rome's greatest commanders, while she (Rome) was at the height of her power and of all peoples in the world the Parthians alone emerged not merely as equals but as victors" (41.1.7).

In the reign of Augustus, only Livy seems to have resisted the conclusion that the Parthians ought to be recognized as a match for the Romans. For Livy it is "the most worthless of the Greeks who favour the glory of even the Parthians over that of the Roman people."[24] Who were those absolutely worthless Greeks? One of them, and perhaps the most significant, must have been Strabo.[25]

A little later in the first century A.D. Lucan complains: "Shame is it that the peoples of the East shrank more from contact with the phalanx than they shrink now from contact with the legion. Though Roman rule extends to the North and the home of the West wind, though we oppress the lands that lie behind the burning South wind, yet in the East we shall yield precedence to the lord of the Parthians. Parthia, that brought doom on the Crassi, was a mere peaceful prov-

---

[21] 11.9.1 (c. 514)ff. (= Posidonius, F233 Kidd): description of Parthia. Strabo 11.9.2 (c. 515): καὶ νῦν ἐπάρχουσι τοσαύτης γῆς καὶ τοσούτων ἐθνῶν ὥστε ἀντίπαλοι τοῖς Ῥωμαίοις τρόπον τινὰ γεγόνασι κατὰ μέγεθος τῆς ἀρχῆς. αἴτιος δ' ὁ βίος αὐτῶν καὶ τὰ ἔθη τὰ ἔχοντα πολὺ μὲν τὸ βάρβαρον καὶ τὸ Σκυθικόν, πλέον μέντοι τὸ χρήσιμον πρὸς ἡγεμονίαν καὶ τὴν ἐν τοῖς πολέμοις κατόρθωσιν. At the end of this chapter Strabo refers to works of his own, now lost, for Parthian customs. Cf. Lucan, *BC* 8.300–2: Nec pila timentur / Nostra nimis Parthis, audentque in bella venire / Experti Scythicas Crasso pereunte pharetras.

[22] For Strabo as a Tiberian author: Sarah Pothecary, "Strabo, the Tiberian Author: Past, Present and Silence in Strabo's *Geography*," *Mnemosyne* 55 (2002), 387–438.

[23] Justinus (trans. J. C. Yardley) 41.1.1: Parthi, penes quos velut divisione orbis cum Romanis facta nunc Orientis imperium est, Scytharum exules fuere. 2 Hoc etiam ipsorum vocabulo manifestatur, nam Scythico sermone exules 'parthi' dicuntur. . . . 5 Postremum Macedonibus triumphato Oriente 6 servierunt, ut cuivis mirum videatur ad tantam eos felicitatem per virtutem provectos, ut imperent gentibus, sub quarum imperio veluti servile vulgus fuere. Similarly, writing in the first century, Curtius Rufus 6.2.12: Tunc ignobilis gens, nunc caput omnium qui post Euphraten et Tigrem amnes siti Rubro mari terminantur.

[24] Livy 9.18.6: . . . quod levissimi ex Graecis, qui Parthorum quoque contra nomen Romanum gloriae favent . . .

[25] It is one of the paradoxes of classical philology that the tremendous geographical work of Strabo is among the few ancient works in this field that have been preserved even though it had so little impact on later Latin authors. Apparently Strabo's contemporary Livy regarded him as one of the "levissimi ex Graecis." Livy either ignores or was unacquainted with Pompeius Trogus's assessment already cited.

ince of little Pella."²⁶ The rhetorical force of these lines lies in the play on North, East, South, and West, for as shown frequently in this study, the inhabitants of the North were considered good fighters, while Easterners were thought to be soft and natural slaves. In the third century, after numerous wars, Cassius Dio still arrives at essentially the same assessment: ". . . finally they advanced to so great glory and power as to wage war even against the Romans at that time, and ever afterward down to the present day to be considered a match for them. They are really formidable in warfare, but nevertheless they have a reputation greater than their achievements . . ." for they have not gained anything and given up some parts of their empire. Yet "they have not yet been enslaved, but even to this day hold their own in the wars they wage against us, whenever they become involved in them." (40.14–15).

Thus the Parthians seem to have been considered the descendants of lowly but combative nomads, not quite respectable themselves. They should have been part of the Roman Empire, but their military and political strength and the extent of their own empire were highly regarded. Many sources describe Parthian tactics and most authors are considerably impressed:²⁷ "Their one passion is for war" and "Would that my belief in the power of the cruel sons of Arsaces were not so strong!"²⁸ They were also clearly perceived as the successors of the Achaemenid empire—in spite of the intervening rule of Alexander and the Seleucids. Strabo observes that the Persians were the only foreign power based in Asia ("barbarians") which had ruled Greeks for any length of time (15.3.23 [c.735f.]). The Parthians are sometimes called Medes, more often in poetry than in prose,²⁹ which shows to what extent they were associated with the Achaeme-

---

²⁶ Lucan, *BC* 10.47–52 (trans. J. D. Duff, Loeb): pro pudor, Eoi propius timuere sarisas / quam nunc pila timent populi. / licet usque sub Arcton / regnemus Zephyri que domos terras que premamus / flagrantis post terga Noti, cedemus in ortus / Arsacidum domino. / non felix Parthia Crassis / exiguae secura fuit provincia Pellae. /

²⁷ The famous line: "Murus erit quodcumque potest obstare sagittae" (Lucan, *BC* 8.379), is just one of the various rhetorical descriptions of Parthian fighting in this work: Pompey's speech is full of opportunistic admiration, 294–308; Lentulus's response emphasizes weaknesses: 371–388. Dio 40.15 also depicts Parthian tactics. The most vivid description is Plutarch's account of Crassus's defeat near Carrhae: *Crassus* 24–28. Pliny, *NH* 16.159–62, discusses a reed from which arrows are made. All of the East "lives subject to the sway of the reed." He mentions the Ethiopians, Egyptians, Arabs, Indians, Scythians, and Bactrians, and the numerous peoples of the Sarmatians and all the realms of the Parthians, almost one-half of mankind in the whole world. However, when all is said and done, the best reed grows in Italy, in the river at Bologna, the Reno. E. Gabba, "Sulle influenze reciproche degli ordinamenti militari dei Parti e dei Romani," in *Atti del convegno sul tema: la Persia et il mondo greco-romano 1965,* Accademia Nazionale dei Lincei 363 (Rome, 1966), 51–73, argues that the Roman imperial army was reorganized over time after the impact of the battle of Carrhae. Units of cavalry and archers in the *auxilia* were built up during the first three centuries A.D., above all by the need to cope with the Parthian / Sassanian army, in Gabba's opinion.

²⁸ Lucan, *BC* 8.294: "Pugnandi sola voluptas." 306f.: "O utinam non tanta mihi fiducia saevis / Esset in Arsacidis!" Note that *pugnandi* is a generally accepted correction for *Regnandi MSS*.

²⁹ Horace, *Odes* 1.27.5; 2.2.17–21; 3.8.19f; 4.14.41–2; *carmen saeculare* 53; Lucan, *BC* 8.216; 354; also: 8.226: *arva Cyri*; Pliny, *NH* 6.40: "Persarum regna, quae nunc Parthorum intellegimus." Plutarch, *Crassus* 24, brings out the difference between the commander, Surena, whose valor contrasted oddly with his "effeminate beauty," his Median dress, and painted face, while the other

nids. As a result, Romans transferred to the Parthians some of the old stereo-types, encountered from the fourth century B.C., regarding the Persians.[30] Thus the old Greek opposition between Persians and Medes is echoed in Roman sources by a literary contrast between Parthians and Medes.

The stereotypes focus particularly on the place of the monarch in society.[31] Cicero was told that the "barbarian kings of the Persians and Syrians have several wives and give them entire cities as dowry."[32] The Parthians are deceit-ful,[33] but that is an accusation aimed at most enemies.[34] More interesting is a speech attributed by Tacitus to Claudius advising the Parthian prince Meher-dates who was going to be king in 49. The Roman monarch "told him not to conceive himself as a despot with his slaves, but rather as a governor among freemen, and to practise clemency and justice which barbarians would like the more for being unused to them."[35] To the members of the Parthian embassy he added wise words: "they must bear with the whims of kings, and frequent changes were bad."[36] Assuming that Claudius really spoke along these lines, we have here an emperor teaching civic wisdom to the Parthians, as if he were a

---

Parthians looked like Scythians, to make themselves more impressive. Surena is described as treacherous (31) and decadent with his wagon-loads of concubines (21; 32), but Plutarch has to admit that he was an extraordinary commander (21) and, in the end, highly successful.

[30] I cannot agree with Sonnabend, *Fremdenbild und Politik*, 280–288, that the view of the Par-thians as representative of the Orient was the dominant one.

[31] Horace, *carm.* 2.2.17–21: Phraates has been restored to the throne of Cyrus, is an absolute monarch, but only virtue, not power and riches, gives happiness.

[32] Cicero, *in Verrem* 3.76: solere aiunt reges barbaros Persarum ac Syrorum plures uxores habere, his autem uxoribus civitates attribuere hoc modo: haec civitas mulieri in redimiculum praebeat, haec in collum, haec in crinis. For an extraordinarily long account of the polygamy of Parthian kings: Metellus in Lucan, 8.396–411 (myriad wives, including sisters and mothers). Lucan, 8.406f.: "Parthorum dominus quotiens sic sanguine mixto / nascitur Arsacides!" is misunderstood by Para-tore, "La Persia nella letteratura latina," p. 526, as referring to the presumed mixed origin of the Parthians from Scythians.

[33] Horace, *Ep.* 2.1.112: invenior Parthis mendacior.

[34] As observed above, Phoenicians, Egyptians, Germans, and women are similarly accused.

[35] Tacitus, *Ann.* 12.11.2: addidit praecepta (etenim aderat Meherdates), ut non dominationem et servos, sed rectorem et civis cogitaret, clementiamque ac iustitiam, quanto ignota barbaris, tanto laetiora capesseret. Norbert Ehrhardt, "Parther und parthische Geschichte," in Wiesehöfer (ed.), *Das Partherreich und seine Zeugnisse* (1998), 295–307, at 302, views Claudius's speech as if it simply reflects Tacitus's own views and does not reflect anything Claudius could have said or might have said. However, if Tacitus elsewhere based himself on a real Claudian address in Lyons, he could have done the same in the present case. Erhardt furthermore cites, e.g., *Ann.* 6.31; 12.44–51 and 13.38 as evidence that Tacitus considers the Parthians typically cruel, arrogant, and treacherous. Tacitus may have regarded them so, but the present passages seem too specific to warrant such generalizations. At most they concern the actions and hence the character of individual rulers and aristocrats. While Tacitus may indeed describe those as typically barbarian (13.38.3: "barbarae astutiae"), he nowhere suggests that their actions and character are typically Parthian, a necessary precondition if we are to speak of ethnic prejudice. The same may be said of Erhardt's analysis of other passages (ibid., 304). I do not agree therefore with his statement: "Die Kapitel über Parther und römisch-parthische Beziehungen sind massiv mit Beurteilungen und Wertungen seitens des Tacitus angereichert" (302). We must be wary of overinterpretation.

[36] *Ann.* 12.11.3: ac tamen ferenda regum ingenia neque usui crebras mutationes.

Solon visiting Croesus. It is quite clear that the absence of a sense of justice "among the barbarians" was a matter of course to Claudius.

Martial can always be relied upon to support the chauvinist view: "Flatteries, you come to me in vain, you poor creatures with your shameless lips. I am not about to speak of 'Lord and God.' There is no place for you any more in this city. Go far away to turbaned Parthians and kiss the soles of gaudy monarchs— base, abject suppliants. There is no lord here, but a commander-in-chief and the most just of all senators, through whom rustic, dry-haired Truth has been brought back from the house of Styx."[37] Seneca addresses the Parthian king: ". . . but you hold them [sc. your subjects] in check by fear; they never allow you to relax your bow; they are your bitterest enemies, open to bribes, and eager for a new master."[38] Like Claudius, Seneca, advisor and mentor to the Emperor Nero, regards Parthia with the superiority of a modern veteran parliamentarian facing the members of a military junta ruling a distant country. Yet these stereotypes are rather distant. They lack the feeling of immediacy conveyed by the expressions of hatred towards those peoples of the East whose presence was felt daily in Rome. Catullus mocks what he knows by hearsay of the "impious religion of the Persians."[39] On the whole, as already noted, the Parthians are not a very obvious presence in the literature, except in the texts specifically dealing with eastern wars.[40] Justinus's epitome of Pompeius Trogus has one chapter full of stereotypes and this may be worth citing here:

The Parthians are all very devout with regard to religion and the worship of the gods. Their national character is impetuous, truculent, devious and insolent; they consider violence appropriate for males, and passivity for females. They are always restless and ready to create trouble, either at home or abroad; and they are naturally taciturn, more given to action than words, keeping a veil of silence over success as well as failure. They obey their leaders from fear rather than respect. They are unrestrained in their sexual pleasures, but sparing with food; and no reliance can be placed on their word or their promises, except when keeping them is in their own interest.[41]

[37] 10.72.5–7 (trans. Shackleton Bailey, Loeb): Frustra, Blanditiae, venitis ad me / attritis miserabiles labellis: / dicturus dominum deum que non sum. / iam non est locus hac in urbe vobis; / ad Parthos procul ite pilleatos / et turpes humiles que supplices que / pictorum sola basiate regum. / non est hic dominus sed imperator, / sed iustissimus omnium senator, / per quem de Stygia domo reducta est / siccis rustica Veritas capillis. /

[38] Seneca, de Constantia 13.4: Habes sub te Parthos et Medos et Bactrianos, sed quos metu contines, sed propter quos remittere arcum tibi non contigit, sed hostes teterrimos, sed venales, sed novum aucupantes dominum. See also Posidonius F57 Kidd (= Athenaeus, Deipnosophistae 4.152F–153B), describing the special position of the king at Parthian banquets, separate from the others and higher. See above, p. 317.

[39] Catullus 90.4: si vera est Persarum impia religio.

[40] Drijvers, in Wiesehöfer (ed.), Das Partherreich und seine Zeugnisse, 290–292, observes that the work of Strabo even conveys a sense of ignorance on Parthia and the Parthians.

[41] Justinus (trans. J. C. Yardley), 41.3.6–9: In superstitionibus atque cura deorum praecipua omnibus veneratio est. Ingenia genti tumida, seditiosa, fraudulenta, procacia; quippe violentiam viris, mansuetudinem mulieribus adsignant. Semper aut in externos aut in domesticos motus inquieti,

It is impossible to say whether this long string of stereotypes reflects general trends or just Pompeius Trogus's own vague ideas about the Parthians. However, it is clear from the epitome that he wrote extensively about them and it is therefore not impossible that this text gives us more than a random collection of negative characteristics. On the assumption that this is the case, it is worth comparing these adjectives with the Roman judgments of other peoples, traced above and below.[42] *Tumidus,* that is: impetuous, restless, violent, is a quality often ascribed to Gauls, although this particular adjective does not seem to be attested elsewhere. *Seditiosa,* truculent, quarrelsome, is often used of the Egyptians. *Fraudulentus,* devious, deceitful, fraudulent—like "cruel" and "arrogant"—is too commonly used to describe foreigners, both enemies and subjects, for it to be significant in any way. However, it is worth remembering that no people has so consistently been accused of lying as the Phoenicians, discussed above. It is definitely more often said of eastern peoples than of others that they are unreliable and with regard to the Persians, for instance, we find the same assertion in Ammianus.[43] *Procax,* insolent, impudent, audacious is a description familiar from the younger Pliny, who accuses the Egyptians of being a *ventosa et insolens natio,* which is conceptually similar. The violence ascribed to them is also typical of the Germans, according to Tacitus, and *inquieti,* restless, is used to describe the Gauls, according to the *Historia Augusta.* It is also a quality sometimes ascribed to nomads. Taciturn is used less often for foreigners, but its opposite, loquacity, is considered typical of Greeks and Egyptians. The Parthian attitude of fear towards their rulers is a characteristic often recorded of eastern peoples. "Unrestrained in their sexual pleasures" is similar to Tacitus's report of the Jews, at least among themselves. Tacitus says the opposite of the Germans, and further reports that the Germans and the Gauls are enthusiastic eaters, unlike the Parthians. If there is a pattern in all this, it is that the Parthians are *not* typically eastern, except in their attitudes towards their kings. They do share some presumed unpleasant characteristics with the Egyptians, but in other respects they resemble the Gauls and Germans, notably in their belligerence. None of this fits the usual pattern offered by adherents of the environmental theory. The reason for this, presumably, is the persistent ability by the Parthian Empire to remain independent of Roman power. This made it impossible to describe them as effeminate, fickle, weak, and subject to debilitating practices.

It is significant that the literature of the Byzantine period reflects attitudes of

---

natura taciti, ad faciendum quam ad dicendum promptiores; proinde secunda adversaque silentio tegunt. Principibus metu, non pudore parent. In libidinem proiecti, in cibum parci. Fides dicti promissique nulla, nisi quatenus expedit. For this source on Parthia: Bernard van Wickevoort Crommelin, "Die Parther und die parthische Geschichte bei Pompeius Trogus-Iustin," in Wiesehöfer (ed.), *Das Partherreich und seine Zeugnisse* (1998), 259–277. As pointed out on p. 272f., nothing is known about the sources for this work. There is therefore no point in speculating whether the present statement is due to Pompeius Trogus or his source. Inevitably it used to be claimed that Pompeius Trogus heavily relied on Timagenes of Alexandria or Posidonius. Cf. Claude Nicolet, *Space, Geography and Politics in the Early Roman Empire* (Ann Arbor, MI, 1991), 33 and note 25.

[42] Full references are found in the relevant chapters and not repeated here.

[43] Ammianus calls Persia a *fallacissima gens* (21.13.4).

far greater hostility towards Persia than was apparent in earlier centuries.[44] Let me give a few examples. Agathias is remarkable for his extreme anti-Persian rhetoric,[45] but he is not the only one: Procopius also shows violent hostility to Khusro.[46] The Persians were considered perverted, as is clear from various accusations of incest.[47] They did not bury their dead properly, and they exposed the sick.[48] They were incapable of understanding or producing genuine philosophy.[49]

An interesting case is the recurring accusations of savage and barbaric punishment inflicted by Persian kings, particularly on their own generals. We read this about Khusro and his generals Nakhoragan[50] and Shahin. Of the latter we read that he was flayed and his skin made into a bag—"a painful and violent death," as Nicephoros helpfully explains.[51] Elsewhere, however, we learn that Shahin in fact remained in service another ten years.[52] Agathias further claims that Shapur was the first to inflict this form of punishment on the captive Roman Emperor Valerian, which was "confirmed by the testimony of several historians." In fact, none of the earlier extant historians mentions this at all.[53] Zosimus mentions only Valerian's capture.[54] The *Epitome de Caesaribus* (late fourth–early fifth century) and Orosius (early fifth century) say Valerian grew old in shameful captivity: the Parthian king used him as footstool.[55] Two Christian authors have Valerian flayed *after* his death.[56] A gruesome end for Valerian would have appealed to Christian authors because Valerian had been an active persecutor of the Christians. Thus, when Agathias claims that Valerian was flayed alive, this must be seen as a bogus horror story, designed to portray the Persian king as particularly cruel and barbaric. This is not to deny that generals may have been treated shabbily by their monarchs: that happened in the Roman Empire as well.[57]

---

[44] These observations have been published before. See *The Near East under Roman Rule* (1998), 439–441. For the fourth century there is now Alain Chauvot, *Opinions romaines face aux barbares au ive siècle ap. J.-C.* (Paris, 1998), which, however, does not say much about Persia; see 32–34; 45, 109f.

[45] *Hist.* 2.22.

[46] *BP* 2.9.8–9; cf. the comments by Averil Cameron, *Agathias* (Oxford, 1970), 44; 116.

[47] Agathias 2.24, 1; 31, 6–9; comments: Cameron, *Agathias*, 92.

[48] Cf. Averil Cameron, "Agathias on the Sassanians," *Dumbarton Oaks Papers* 23–24 (1969–1970), 67–183, at 78—80 with comments on 90f.

[49] Agathias, 28–30. King Khusro was interested, but a naïve barbarian all the same; Cf. Cameron, op. cit., 114f.

[50] Agathias, 4.23, 2.

[51] Nicephoros, *Breviarium*, 7 (Cyril Mango, *The Patriarch Nicephorus: Short History*, ed., comm. and trans. [Washington, DC, 1990], with comments at p. 177).

[52] Theophanes, *Chron.*, 315 de Boor 315.

[53] *RE* xiii s.v. Licinius (Valerianus), cols. 492 for full references.

[54] Zosimus 1.36.2.

[55] *Epitome de Caesaribus* 32. 6; Orosius, *Adversus Paganos* 7.22.4.

[56] Lactantius, *De mortibus persecutorum* 5.3–6 (late third–early fourth century); Petrus Patricius (A.D. 500–565), 13 (*FHG* iv 188).

[57] In Byzantium: Justinian's treatment of Belisarius and that of Narses by Justin II. In Persia Hormizd's humiliation of his general Bahrām caused a civil war (Theophylact 3.8.1–3).

To sum up: the Parthians appear in the sources as redoubtable but distant enemies. We encounter stereotypes and disapproval, but these are different from the ones attached to other eastern peoples. Sometimes the stereotypes usually associated with Asiatics and Syrians are transferred to the Parthians, but this is not very common. There is therefore no obvious pattern of ethnic prejudice, let alone proto-racism. The difference from Greek attitudes towards Persians, at least from the late fifth century B.C. onwards, could not be greater, but that is not surprising. For the Greeks, Persia was the neighboring empire which dominated a number of their cities and was a constant presence in their political life till Macedonia destroyed Achaemenid Persia as an empire. The Greeks developed the first manifestations of clear-cut proto-racism and a rich store of ethnic prejudices in their confrontation with this people which dominated much of their political life. This was far less true of Rome, which adopted many of the attitudes and anti-Persian prejudices developed by the Greeks, but attributed them to other eastern peoples, closer to the Mediterranean, which played a larger role in their existence. The Romans in Rome did not feel Persian religion or culture exerted any direct influence on them. No less important, Rome never succeeded in incorporating the rival empire. These combined factors determined their own attitude.

Roman Views of Greeks

THE RELATIONSHIP BETWEEN GREECE AND ROME and their mutually ambivalent attitudes have attracted great attention in the scholarly literature.[1] Greece occupied a unique position among all the peoples which were integrated into the Roman Empire over time. Their influence on Roman culture and religion was greater than that of any other people and was felt to be so by the Romans themselves. This has led to familiar manifestations of philhellenic attitudes of a number of emperors: Nero,[2] Hadrian,[3] and Marcus Aurelius, who wrote his meditations in Greek. That will not be our topic. Anticipating the conclusions of this chapter, I would argue that the resistance to Nero's and—to some extent—Hadrian's philhellenism was not so much directed against their admiration for classical Greek culture, but against their identification with contempo-

---

[1] The manner in which Rome absorbed or responded to Greek culture and religion is the subject of a large number of important publications: Eduard Fraenkel, "Rome and Greek Culture" (his Oxford oration), reprinted in *Kleine Beiträge zur klassischen Philologie* (Rome, 1964), vol. 2, 583–598; G. W. Bowersock, *Augustus and the Greek World* (Oxford, 1965); Nicholas Petrochilos, *Roman Attitudes to the Greeks* (Athens, 1974); J.P.V.D. Balsdon, *Romans & Aliens* (1979), 30–54, bibliography on 265f; P. A. Brunt, "Laus Imperii," in *Roman Imperial Themes* (Oxford, 1990), 316f.; J. Palm, *Rom, Römertum und Imperium in der griechischen Literatur der Kaiserzeit* (Lund, 1959); Sherwin-White, *Racial Prejudice* (1967), chap. 3; Y.-A. Dauge, *Le Barbare* (1981), 546–554, "Barbarie du monde grec" concludes, remarkably, that for the Romans "the Greek world was quite often a significant part of the barbarian universe." M. Beard and M. Crawford, *Rome in the Late Republic* (Ithaca, 1985); on the Hellenization of Roman education and literature: Elizabeth Rawson, *Intellectual Life in the Late Roman Republic* (Baltimore, MD, 1985); Andrew Wallace-Hadrill, "Greek Knowledge, Roman Power: Review article of Elizabeth Rawson," op. cit., *CPh* 83 (1988), 224–233. For the influence of Greek architecture: Pierre Gros, "Les premières générations d'architectes hellénistiques à Rome," in *Mélanges Huergon* (Rome, 1976), 387–410. See also Wallace-Hadrill, "Roman Arches and Greek Honours: the Language of Power at Rome," *PCPS* 36 (1990), 143–181: arguing that the manner in which Roman aristocrats were honored in the Late Republic represents a form of Hellenization; Erich S. Gruen, *Culture and National Identity in Republican Rome* (1992/93), chap. 6, 223–271: "The Appeal of Hellas"; John Scheid, "*Graeco Ritu*: A Typically Roman Way of Honoring the Gods," *HSCP* 97 (1995), 15–31. For Greeks, Greek culture, and Greek attitudes towards Rome in the late republic and early empire: C. P. Jones, *Plutarch and Rome* (Oxford, 1971); id., *Culture and Society in Lucian* (Cambridge, MA, 1986); Greg Woolf, "Becoming Roman, Staying Greek," *PCPS* 40 (1994), 116–143; Simon Swain, *Hellenism and Empire* (1996). See in general: Momigliano, *Alien Wisdom* (1975).

[2] Miriam T. Griffin, *Nero: the End of a Dynasty* (London, 1984), 208–213, and, for the background in Nero's family: 213–215. Those who read Hebrew will not deny themselves the pleasure of reading Zvi Yavetz, *Claudius and Nero: From Systematisation to Dilettantism* (Tel Aviv, 1999), esp. 111–117.

[3] Anthony R. Birley, *Hadrian: the Restless Emperor* (London and New York, 1997), 175–188.

rary Greeks. First-century Romans did not accept an emperor with a beard.[4] The present chapter then is concerned with common Roman views of Greeks and not opinions of Greeks about Rome, except that it will be useful occasionally to see what Greeks thought of Roman attitudes towards themselves.[5] More specifically, the aim here is to trace Roman views of the contemporary Greeks as a subject people, rather than the culture of classical Greece, its religion, mythology, literature, philosophy, rhetoric, and arts. As we shall see, the Romans themselves made a clear distinction between classical Greece and its heritage and their subjects, the contemporary Greeks.

Indeed, it is quite clear that the Romans of the late republic and early empire were very much aware of the influence Greece had exerted on Rome also in the past. One may cite the tale of Roman delegates going to Greece to inspect the laws of Solon as a model for the Twelve Tables (Dionysius, *Ant.* 10.51.5; 52.4; 54.3), or Fabius Pictor's trip to the Delphic Oracle when Rome needed guidance in the Hanibalic war (Livy 22.57.5). Such stories are definitely part of the status of historical Greece and its influence upon republican Rome in the first century. This status is also one of the reasons why inconsistent, seemingly contradictory, views could be held by Roman writers in the same period—or even by the same person (Cicero, for instance). The contribution and influence of historical Greece could not be denied, but would not prevent many Romans from disliking and disparaging contemporary Greeks. The topic is complex. See, for instance, Syme's brief comments on the age of Augustus: "Here as elsewhere the Principate of Caesar Augustus is double-faced. It stands as the firm champion of Italy against the East, yet it is a monarchy in the East. Nor can Rome even pretend to be hostile to everything that is Greek. In arts and letters the age is all for classical Hellas against contemporary Hellenism. In fact Caesar Augustus disdains old Hellas, now weak and impoverished, and extends his favour to the chief men among the Greeks in Asia."[6] For present purposes therefore we need to focus on contemporary Greeks in the eyes of Romans. This is not a study of history and memory in Rome, but of Roman views of other peoples in their own times.

Even this is a large topic, for the sources are relatively rich—although uneven for the various periods under review. Also, modern authors have written much on the subject while their attitudes are inevitably colored by current social patterns and ideology. This is amply illustrated by the literature of the past

---

[4] Cf. Seneca, *Ep.* 5.2, expressing disapproval of conspicuous attire which includes an unkempt beard (*neglegentiorem barbam*); see also 48.7. When Julian was emperor in the fourth century his beard was again an issue, see his satire μισοπώγων. The fourth-century emperors were again clean-shaven.

[5] For the attitudes of the Greeks themselves under Roman rule, see Suzanne Saïd, "The Discourse of Identity in Greek Rhetoric from Isocrates to Aristides," in Malkin (ed.), *Ancient Perceptions of Greek Ethnicity* (2001), 275–299.

[6] Syme, *Tacitus* (1958), 507, adding: "The one exception is noteworthy, Eurycles the dynast of Sparta." See also 512: "Honour rendered to the classics, however, might absolve a man from recognizing anything that had subsequently been done by Greeks in the kingdoms founded by the successors of Alexander."

forty years cited in note 1 and even better by comparing those studies with, for instance, the essay by W. Kroll, writing in 1924: "As the Romans gained deeper insight in the internal situation in Hellas, both the people and their leaders necessarily were seen to be correspondingly more despicable."[7] Furthermore, given the framework of the present study, the emphasis will necessarily be on the negative or ambivalent aspects of the relationship and the treatment will therefore inevitably be incomplete.

As already observed, a further complicating factor in discussing the period after the first century B.C. is that the texts sometimes make no real difference between Greeks from the mainland and those from the eastern provinces.[8] It usually matters even less whether they were descendants of Greek and Macedonian settlers or descendants of the Hellenized inhabitants of the Seleucid and Ptolemaic Kingdoms. This may or may not reflect their own views of themselves. Lucian does not call himself a Hellene but a Syrian. However, the ethnicity of the population in the eastern provinces is not our topic.[9] For us the question is how the Romans in Rome and elsewhere saw Greeks. When they make no difference between a Greek from Chaeronea and one from Samosata, this means that we must consider both as Greeks for our present purposes. Tacitus's comments on the garrison at Trapezus (Pontus on the Black Sea) in 69 ignore the difference.[10] When they do make such a difference, then we have to follow them. If Livy makes a commander refer to "Asiatic Greeks," then these are obviously considered a special brand of Greeks. Juvenal, as observed above, finds there are too many Greeks in Rome, but he finds the Greeks from outside Greece proper especially undesirable.[11]

One of the earliest Hellenophiles in Rome was Claudius Marcellus, an outstanding commander of the third century. As Plutarch remarks, he loved Greek learning, but because of his activities as a military man he had little time to devote to it (*Marcellus* 1.2). The most tangible result of this affection, therefore, was the removal to Rome of numerous works of art from Syracuse, which he sacked in 212.[12] Polybius and, following him, Livy considered this case of large-scale art theft the beginning of a habit which would ultimately backfire, as indicated above. There were others of that generation and the next with sympathy for the Greek language, for Fabius Pictor wrote his history of Rome in that

---

[7] W. Kroll, "Römer und Griechen," in *Studien zum Verständnis der römischen Literatur* (1924, repr. Darmstadt, 1964), 1–23, at 1. Kroll observes also: "Die Erfahrungen, die man bei den politischen Berührungen mit der hellenischen Welt seit dem Beginn des 2. Jhdts. machte, konnten nicht anders als zu einer Verachtung dieser im Erfolg ebenso aufgeblasenen wie im Misserfolg würdelosen Gernegrosse führen."

[8] Above, chapter 5, pp. 317–318 and nn. 54–58.

[9] Fergus Millar, *The Roman Near East: 31 BC–AD 337* (Cambridge, MA, 1993), Part II; *Identities in the Eastern Mediterranean in Antiquity, Mediterranean Archaeology* 11 (1998).

[10] Tac., *Hist.* 3.47.

[11] Pliny, *Ep.* 8.24.2, also implies that there is a difference between Greeks from Greece proper and those from the East who originate in perviously non-Greek regions. See above, chapter 5.

[12] For extensive discussion: Gruen, *Culture and National Identity in Republican Rome* 94–103, 241f.; see also Swain, *Hellenism and Empire,* 141f. for Plutarch on Marcellus.

language.[13] Among many aristocrats, however, contemporary Greeks were despised. When M'. Acilius Glabrio rebuked an Aetolian embassy in 191 for being preposterous, he said they were "acting like Greeks."[14] Livy reports a dispute in the Senate in 172, apparently based on genuine contemporary sources, in which older and traditional senators rebuke Roman envoys to Macedon for trickery. Their terms for this sort of behavior were "Punic craftiness and Greek artfulness."[15]

The earliest body of fully preserved texts in Latin, Plautus's comedies, shows how the Greeks were seen at another level of society. In Plautus's Latin *pergraecari* and *congraecari* are common terms for "to revel" and "debauchery."[16] Roman comedy also first introduces into Roman literature the figure of the parasite, a theme taken over from Greek comedy and the subject of much discussion. This is to some extent really relevant here, for the parasite as depicted in literature might be but was not always Greek, and Greek stereotypes were often but not necessarily attributed to him.[17] As already seen above, in chapter 1, the idea that Rome was being corrupted by the wealth and decadence of Greece preceded views, more commonly attested afterwards, that such corruption was the result of the conquest of Asia. In this connection a few words may be said about the action against the Bacchanalia in 186 B.C., related at length by Livy and the subject of a decree of the senate, the substance of which is transmitted in an inscription.[18] Livy attributes the introduction of what he considers a

---

[13] R. Mellor, *The Roman Historians* (London, 1999), 16f.; Gruen, op. cit., 230f. Roman receptivity to Hellenism predated Fabius Pictor; for the evidence: Gruen, 227–230. For Roman comparisons of the Greek and Latin languages and their respective merits: Petrochilos, *Roman Attitudes* (1974), 23–33.

[14] Polybius 20.10.6f.: ἔτι γὰρ ὑμεῖς ἑλληνοκοπεῖτε; cf. Livy 36.28.4f.

[15] Livy 42.47.7: *versutiae Punicae* and *calliditas Graeca*; cf. fr. Diodorus 30.7.1. Cf. Petrochilos, *Roman Attitudes* (1974), 43.

[16] Cf. Fronto, Frg. 12.1: nostrarum variarum fortunarum subsidium. parentum tuorum. Et pergraecari potius amoenis locis quam coerceri carcere viderentur. See Petrochilos, 74f.; Gruen, op. cit., 262, for Plautus on Greeks. Gruen argues that Plautus is not endorsing anti-Greek stereotypes, but lampooning them. Petrochilos believes that Plautus usually, but not always, intends to depict Greek society and sometimes selects or slants his material to give a reflection of attitudes and feelings at Rome. It appears more significant that the stereotypes existed, than to establish whether Plautus himself believed them. The same principle of interpretation applies here as in the case of satire, cf. the Introduction. See also Petrochilos, 45, 69–88 on luxury and moral decline. Petrochilos, however, does little to distinguish, even where this would be possible, between Roman attitudes towards Asiatics, Asiatic Greeks, and other Greeks.

[17] Cf. Cynthia Damon, "Greek Parasites and Roman Patronage," *HSCP* 97 (1995), 181–195. Note the examples from Juvenal. In *Satire* 1 he describes typical Roman *clientes* as parasites. In *Satire* 3 they are Greeks competing in this capacity with local Romans who are jealous of their successes, a subject found afterwards in the work of Lucian, as will be seen below.

[18] Livy 39.8–18; *CIL* 1.196; *ILS* 18; A. Degrassi (ed.), *Inscriptiones Latinae Liberal Re: Publicae* 2 vols. (Florence, 1963), 511. For critical discussion: M. Gelzer, "Die Unterdrückung der Bacchanalien bei Livius," *Hermes* 71 (1936), 275–287, at 285f., who compares accusations of horrible deeds aimed at the *Bacchanalia* with similar ones targeted later at the Christians; Gelzer argues for an early and later phase in the sources, whereby the later one is responsible for the reports of horrors; J. A. North, "Religious Toleration in Republican Rome," *PCPS* 25 (1979), 85–103; Jean-

degenerate and dangerous cult to a Greek, and yet he explicitly dissociates Greece from any guilt, direct or indirect. The man who introduced the practice was an anonymous Greek, "without any of those arts which this people, the most learned of all, has brought to us in great numbers for the care of mind and body."[19] The manner in which it is said to have spread is interesting: the Greek was "a hierophant of nocturnal rites" which "in the beginning he divulged only to a few" (39.8.5). Thereafter it began to spread widely through Italy "like a contagious disease" (39.9.1). The fears of secrecy and of contamination by foreign evils are familiar by now. Indeed, as described by Livy, the cult contained many of the elements often attributed to foreigners by Romans: there was secret debauchery, fraud, crime, forced initiation, and conspiracy, and the initiated formed a huge number, "almost another people within the Roman people" (39.13.14). In this case, however, the source of evil was not sought among foreigners. Although it is quite clear that Livy's account of the affair is highly distorted,[20] it is, for present purposes, interesting to see how he distorts it.

Another bizarre affair, to some extent comparable, took place in 181 B.C., when ancient books, some of which contained Pythagorean writings, were reputedly discovered in a chest belonging to King Numa Pompilius.[21] The books were read by Q. Petilius, urban praetor, who considered them dangerous and persuaded the Senate they should be burned because they undermined traditional religion.[22] However we interpret this, it certainly represents an assertion of Roman traditional values against Hellenistic ideas and beliefs.

The first major author in any consideration of this subject must be the Elder Cato. His remarkable harangue about Greek doctors has been cited and discussed extensively above.[23] His hatred of foreign doctors was matched by his hostility towards philosophers (*Cato Maior*, 22f.) and Greek culture in general (*Cato Maior* 23).[24] Cato thought the Greek people *nequissimum et indocile,*

Marie Pailler, *Bacchanalia: La répression de 186 av. J.-C. à Rome et en Italie: vestiges, images, tradition* (Rome 1988); E. S. Gruen, *Studies in Greek Culture and Roman Policy* (Leiden, 1990), 34–78.

[19] Livy 39.8.3: Graecus ignobilis in Etruriam primum uenit nulla cum arte earum quas multas ad animorum corporumque cultum nobis eruditissima omnium gens inuexit, sacrificulus et uates . . . See also Cicero, *De Legibus* 2.36f.: omnia nocturna.

[20] Gruen, op. cit., 72, argues that Rome had little reason to fear the cult as a threat to religion, society, or public order. Bacchic sectarians supplied convenient victims for purposes that had little to do with the sect itself, he says.

[21] Livy 40.29.2–14; Pliny, *NH* 13.84–8; Valerius Maximus 1.1.12; Plutarch, *Numa* 22.2–5; Augustine, *CD* 7.34.

[22] See the discussion by Pailler, *Bacchanalia* (1988), Part 4, chap. 12; and Gruen, *Studies in Greek Culture and Roman Policy*, 163–170; references to modern literature on p. 164, n.28.

[23] Chapter 3, p. 226f.

[24] Momigliano, *Alien Wisdom*, 99, says that Cato made jokes in Rome against the Greeks. That may be too mild a description of what Cato did. Plutarch, *Cato Maior* 23, uses the verb προπηλακίζω, which Liddle and Scott translate as "treat with contumely," i.e., with scornful or contemptuous insolence. R. Syme, *Tacitus* (1958), 2.511: "the hostility of Cato to all things Greek has been uncritically exaggerated." Syme refers to D. Kienast, *Cato der Zensor: Seine Persönlichkeit und seine Zeit* (1954), 101–116, at 115f. Kienast, however, does not claim that Cato's hostility has

"utterly vile and unruly."[25] "When that people gives us its literature it will corrupt all things," writes Cato to his son. The idea of corruption and deterioration has been encountered frequently in our consideration of xenophobic attitudes. Notable is Plutarch's story about the famous embassy to Rome in 156/5, which included the philosophers Carneades, Critolaos, and Diogenes. Cato took steps to complete the senatorial debate as quickly as possible so that the philosophers would go home. He felt that they were becoming too popular.[26] As formulated by Plutarch, he had two fears: he thought young men would come to prefer a reputation based on talking rather than on achievements in war, and he wanted education to be geared towards law and the magistracies rather than philosophy.[27] The philosophers were not in fact expelled, as has sometimes been claimed, but Pliny, after describing these events, adds that Cato "always on other occasions recommended the banishment of all Greeks from Italy."[28] However, attitudes could change fairly quickly, even within one family. "What a change of morals!" writes Pliny, "Cato's grandson brought home one philosopher from his military tribunate and another from his mission to Cyprus." The next item to be mentioned here is Plutarch's description of Cato's visit to Athens, when he dealt with the Athenians through an interpreter, although he

---

been exaggerated, he agrees with Cato: "Wie Cato als Politiker und Feldherr einen scharfen Blick für das Wesentliche bewiesen hatte, so erkannte er auch in der geistigen Auseinandersetzung mit dem Griechentum rasch die Grösse und die Gefahr der griechischen Kultur. Cato war viel zu selbstbewusst und geistig beweglich, um sich der hellenistischen Kultur rückhaltlos hinzugeben." In a similar spirit he argues (104f.) that Cato's attack on Greek doctors was justified, because Pliny agrees with him. Kienast, with Syme's approval, claims that Cato's xenophobia was justified.

[25] Astin, *Cato the Censor* (1978), 172f., comments: "The latter term surely refers to the constant restlessness and political instability of Greece, the former very probably to the endemic corruption and venality which Polybius himself attests." This is yet another example of the common tendency to explain irrational hostility and prejudice in terms of real and actual defects and faults on the part of the group that is hated. In assessing Cato's attitude it is immaterial that he, like Cicero, may have thought of the contemporary Greeks in those terms, while respecting the ancient Greeks. It is poor reasoning to claim that ethnic hatred of an existing group is cancelled or offset by admiration for their dead ancestors. For more examples, see the chapter on the Jews.

[26] Plutarch, *Cato Maior*, 22.5; cf. Cic., *de Oratore* 2.155–7 with comm. A. D. Leeman and H. Pinkster, 3 (Heidelberg, 1985), 94f. See discussion by Astin, *Cato the Censor*, 174–177. Like Kienast, Astin finds Cato's hostility understandable. J.-L. Ferrary, *Philhellénisme et impérialisme* (1988), 351–363, at 357f. Gruen, *Studies in Greek Culture and Roman Policy*, 174–177, argues that the affair has been misinterpreted. Far from showing anti-Greek action, it proves the popularity of Greek philosophers in Rome, who successfully completed their mission. See also above, in the section on expulsions.

[27] Plutarch concludes: "This he did not do, as some think, because of personal hostility to Carneades but because he was hostile to philosophy and in rivalry spoke abusively of all Greek culture and training" (πᾶσαν Ἑλληνικὴν μοῦσαν καὶ παιδείαν ὑπὸ φιλοτιμίας προπηλακίζων). Astin, *Cato*, 176, believes this is a generalization of Plutarch and not to be accepted as such. He argues that it would be a mistake to attach great weight to or to interpret too literally the reference to laws and magistrates. It is also possible to argue that it would be a mistake to understimate the impact of hostile rhetoric. If Plutarch interpreted Cato the way he did, based on more texts of Cato than we have, why would Cato's contemporaries have interpreted him along the lines proposed by Astin?

[28] Pliny, *NH* 7.30.113: ille semper alioquin universos ex Italia pellendos censuit Graecos.

was perfectly capable of speaking to them directly (*Cato Maior*, 4f.).[29] Cato concluded from his own brevity and from the verbosity of the translation that the words of the Greeks were born on their lips, but those of the Romans in their hearts. Cato also criticized Romans who wrote Greek, declaring that Rome would lose her empire when she had become infected with Greek letters (23.3). In a sense, all this seems curiously modern and similar to the attitudes of conservatives and nationalists over the past century or two. More to the point: this is the defensive attitude of someone who feels threatened by a foreign culture. The fear comes out particularly well in the assumption of a doctor's plot to murder Romans (for gain) and in the claim that Greek intellectual influence could destroy the Roman Empire.[30] It bears emphasizing again, however, that even anti-Hellene Romans probably resisted the influence of their own, contemporary Greeks without rejecting the values and achievements of classical Greek literature and culture.

As is well known, there were others with a good deal of sympathy for the Greeks and they came under attack by Cato and like-minded aristocrats. The charismatic Scipio Africanus was attacked by Cato, then his quaestor in Spain (204 B.C.), for extravagant living, for pampering his troops and giving too much time to the *palaestra* and the theater.[31] In Rome too, Scipio was censured for wearing Greek dress, visiting the gymnasium, reading books in Greek, attending the *palaestra*, etc.[32] This suggests that material indulgence and various aspects of a Greek lifestyle were seen to be incompatible with true Roman values by some aristocrats.

Another Roman aristocrat taken to task by both the Elder Cato and Polybius for his philhellenism was Aulus Postumius: talkative, loquacious, and vainglorious, he even attempted to produce a poem and a work of history in Greek. The Greek Polybius himself, interestingly, notes "that he had adopted the worst qualities of the Greeks, for he sought pleasure and avoided labour."[33] Such anti-

[29] For Cato's visit to Greece, cf. Astin, *Cato*, 55–59 and for his refusal to speak Greek, 160; Gruen, 64f., 68f., 81.

[30] Livy attributes to Cato a speech on the status of women which suggests similar sentiments in this domain. It shows an acute fear of female dominance (34.2–4): nunc domi victa libertas nostra impotentia muliebri hic quoque in foro obteritur et calcatur, et quia singulas non continuimus universas horremus. However, this is Livy rendering what he thought his readers expected Cato to have said.

[31] Plutarch, *Cato Maior* 3.5. Cf. Astin, *Cato*, 13–15; Catharine Edwards, *The Politics of Immorality in Ancient Rome* (Cambridge, 1993), chap. 3.

[32] Livy 29.19.12: cum pallio crepidisque inambulare in gymnasio; libellis eum palaestraeque operam dare. See also 38.51.1. Cf. Balsdon, *Romans and Aliens*, 34f.; Gruen, *Culture and Identity in Republican Rome*, 242f. asserts that these reproaches were not directed "at the Hellenism as such but at the unseemliness of a Roman commander and Representative of the *res publica* behaving in an undignified and inappropriate fashion." That is possible, but it still remains the case that Roman aristocrats felt it unseemly for a commander regularly to read Greek books.

[33] Polybius, 39.1: ἐξηλώκει τὰ χείριστα τῶν Ἑλληνικῶν καὶ γὰρ φιλήδονος ἦν καὶ φυγόπονος. Cf. Walbank, *Historical Commentary* vol. 3 (1979), 726f., who notes that "such an apology from someone writing in Greek was perhaps little more than a commonplace; . . . It was Cato's comment that drew popular ridicule on Postumius."

Hellenic attitudes were not, it seems, determined by political groupings or social background. Polybius's own ambivalence is also expressed in his comments on the untrustworthiness of the Greeks as compared with the Romans.
The latter are unequalled in their religiosity which, in his view, truly preserves
the state. Unlike Roman magistrates, who are honest, he says, Greek civic officers can never be trusted with any money.[34] In 154, construction of the first
stone theater was halted following a speech by the former consul, P. Scipio
Nasica, who considered theater harmful to Roman morals. "It was absolutely
unacceptable for Romans to accustom themselves to Hellenic pleasures."[35] Another aristocrat, T. Albucius, a senator in the second half of the second century
B.C., who was also deemed too enthusiastic in his love of Greek, was mocked
by Lucilius and criticized by Cicero.[36]

As noted above, the Elder Cato refused to speak Greek in Athens. Marius
was as suspicious of the penetration of Greek culture in Rome as was the Elder
Cato,[37] but unlike Cato he is said to have refused even to study Greek literature
properly and he never used the language for any serious purpose, because he
considered it ridiculous to study a literature taught by teachers who were enslaved to others.[38] In this respect Marius merely followed the customs of the
magistrates in early times, who would never give their legal *responsa* in Greek
and obliged Greeks to speak Latin or employ interpreters.[39]

Of course we must distinguish between a desire to maintain proper style and
linguistic chauvinism. The Emperor Tiberius spoke fluent Greek without
qualms, but would not tolerate the use of Greek words in official documents in

[34] Polybius 6.56.6–15, discussed above, chapter 5, n. 69. There the focus was on what it says
about Roman religiosity. This is to a certain extent echoed by Cicero, *De haruspicum responsis* 19.
It must be observed here that Polybius, a Greek in Rome, idealizes Roman integrity and generalizes
about Greek dishonesty. W. Kroll, *Studien zum Verständniss der römischen Literatur* (1924, repr.
Damstadt, 1964), 1, n.2, takes these statements of Polybius at face value.

[35] Appian, *BC* 1.4.28: οὐ χρήσμον ὅλως Ἑλληνικαῖς ἡδυπαθείαις Ῥωμαίους ἐθίζεσθαι.

[36] Lucilius 88–94 (Marx), cited by Cicero, *De Finibus* 1.9; Cicero, *Brut.* 131.3: "virtually a
Greek" *(doctus etiam Graecis T. Albucius vel potius paene Graecus).*

[37] For Cato, v.supra.

[38] Plutarch, *Marius* 2.2; Sallust, *Iug.* 85.32; also: 63.3; 85.12–13; Cicero, *Pro Arch.* 19; Val. Max.
2.2.3. Cf. T. F. Carney, *A Biography of C. Marius* (Chicago, 2d ed. 1970), 9–14; Gruen, op. cit.,
268f., for the argument that Marius was not so much ignorant of Hellenic culture and language as
intent on reaffirming Roman mastery and superiority. As in the case of Cato, it could be argued that
the public message, claiming Roman superiority, is no less important than the fact that the man may
have had no personal dislike of the Greeks. "The stereotypes would be taken seriously only by the
literal-minded," writes Gruen, p. 270. Perhaps there were not a few of those? In a similar vein,
Gruen, 259f., argues that the expulsion of Greek intellectuals had only symbolic significance. Even
if this is true, it remains a fact that the Senate found it worthwhile to engage in frequent symbolic
acts of this sort.

[39] Valerius Maximus 2.2.2: Magistratus uero prisci quantopere suam populique Romani maie-
statem retinentes se gesserint hinc cognosci potest, quod inter cetera obtinendae grauitatis indicia
illud quoque magna cum perseuerantia custodiebant, ne Graecis umquam nisi latine responsa
darent. quin etiam ipsos linguae uolubilitate, qua plurimum ualent, excussa per interpretem loqui
cogebant non in urbe tantum nostra, sed etiam in Graecia et Asia, quo scilicet Latinae uocis honos
per omnes gentes uenerabilior diffunderetur.

Latin.[40] Thus, it is possible to argue, as does Erich Gruen, that the focus of these criticisms was the behavior and attitudes of Romans rather than the Greeks and their culture. Cato and Marius, in this view, aimed to maintain a public image reinforcing Roman superiority in moral and other senses, even though they were willing in practice to borrow positive elements from Greek intellectuality and civilization. In spite of much hostility among some of the aristocrats, as is well known, educated Romans absorbed the Greek language, literature, and culture very thoroughly.[41] However, even those who did so were often hostile at the same time. Gruen has pointed out that the anti-Greek stereotypes encountered in the literature of the Republic insist on Roman superiority and are all aimed at supposed personal characteristics of contemporary Greeks—not at Roman taste and interest in Hellenic culture.[42]

It is possible also that there was a change in the course of the first century B.C. The literature seems to indicate a more straightforward form of hostility towards Greeks in that period and, especially, during the reign of Augustus.[43] However, it is also possible that this impression is due to the availability of more relevant texts. In the last years of the republic, Cicero was highly ambivalent about contemporary Greeks.[44] Cicero defended Octavian against Antony's jibes regarding his ancestors. His mother came from Aricia, a city 25 kilometers southeast of Rome. "You might think he [sc. Antony] was speaking of a woman from Tralles or Ephesus! See how we who come from the *municipia* are all looked down upon, that is, obviously, all of us, for how few of us do not come from the *municipia*?"[45] It is clear what he thinks, and how he knows his audience would think, about a man whose mother came from Tralles or Ephesus. Like several others he clearly distinguished between the old Greece, which was admirable, and contemporary Greeks,[46] both in his correspondence and in rhetoric.[47] Indeed, the sort of inquiry which takes a minute at most, thanks to modern

[40] Suetonius, *Tiberius* 71. Tiberius on a certain occasion would not allow a soldier to give testimony in Greek. This makes good sense, for it was practical for a unified and integrated empire to maintain Latin as the sole language used in the army. Similar care for the avoidance of Greek expressions in Latin is expressed by Cicero, *Tusc.* 1.15; *Academica* 1.24f.; Horace, *Sat.* 1.20.27–30.

[41] Balsdon, *Romans and Aliens*, 43–51; Gruen, *Culture and Identity in Republican Rome*, passim, esp. chap. 6.

[42] Ibid., 264.

[43] Gruen, loc. cit., asserts that attitudes at the turn of the first century B.C. show continuity and consistency.

[44] Harold Guite, "Cicero's Attitude to the Greeks," *Greece & Rome* 9 (1962), 142–159; I have not seen J. P. Mahaffy, *The Silver Age of the Greek World* (Chicago, 1906), chap. 7: "The Hellenism of Cicero and his Friends."

[45] Cicero, *Philippicae* 3.15: "Aricina mater." Trallianam aut Ephesiam putes dicere. Videte quam despiciamur omnes qui sumus e municipiis id est, omnes plane: quotus enim quisque nostrum non est?

[46] Cicero, *ad Quintum fratrem* 1.1.28: non enim me hoc iam dicere pudebit, praesertim in ea vita atque iis rebus gestis in quibus non potest residere inertiae aut levitatis ulla suspicio, nos ea quae consecuti simus iis studiis et artibus esse adeptos quae sint nobis Graeciae monumentis disciplinisque tradita. For a similar sentiment: Pliny, *ep.* 8.24, discussed below, p. 398.

[47] *Pro Flacco* 62f. with a remarkable praise of historic Athens, Sparta, various other regions, and

technology, shows that Cicero is the first author frequently to use the condescending term "*Graeculus*"—it became very popular immediately afterwards, although its use is not evenly distributed.[48] Curiously, Cicero himself is reported as having been written off as a "Greek" and "scholar" in his early years in Rome, because he was cautious in suing for office. He was called thus because those were the names "which the low and ignorant classes at Rome were wont to give so readily," according to Plutarch.[49] If correct, this might indicate that Cicero later distinguished himself by using to good effect in court the sort of popular prejudices and social hostilities which other upper-class Romans preferred to leave unsaid, or reserved for informal contact, because they were regarded as belonging to the sphere of lowly and ignorant people. In other words, there is reason to suspect that Cicero, having experienced its sting personally, introduced the language of popular prejudice into the law courts.

Cicero himself, as said already, was ambivalent. In an early letter to Atticus he said of himself and his brother that he was a *Philhellene*.[50] He bought Greek art for his home.[51] Rome owed her culture to the classical Greeks, as he often admits: "I shall not be ashamed to say that I am indebted for whatever I have accomplished to the pursuits and accomplishments transmitted to us in the writings and teachings of Greece. Wherefore, beyond the common honesty which we owe to everybody, more than that, it seems to me that we owe a special debt to this people, namely, among those men whose precepts have instructed us, willingly to exhibit the lessons we have learnt from them."[52] However, at pres-

---

even Massilia. Athenian prestige "is so great that even the present shattered and ruined name of Greece is sustained by the glory of this city": auctoritate autem tanta est ut iam fractum prope ac debilitatum Graeciae nomen huius urbis laude nitatur. As observed by Syme, *Tacitus* (1958), 2.512: "Honour rendered to the classics . . . might absolve a man from recognizing anything that had subsequently been done by Greeks in the kingdoms founded by the successors of Alexander."

[48] It is found once in Varro, fr. 243 ap. H. Funaioli, *Grammaticae Romanae Fragmenta* (Stuttgart, 1969), 269, in a purely grammatical discussion. It occurs sixteen times in Cicero's work, more than in that of any other author, but this may not be decisive, since there is so much of it. It appears four times in Petronius: 38.3, 46.5, 88.10, and 76.10 (*Graeculius*), which is significant because he satirizes daily conversation. The fifth-century author Macrobius still uses it frequently: *Saturnalia* 2.4.31; 7.9.26. Cf. M. Dubuisson, "*Graecus, Graeculus, Graecari*: L'emploi péjoratif du nom des Grecs en Latin," in Ἑλληνισμός: Quelques jalons pour une historie de l'identité grecque, ed. S. Said (Leiden, 1991), 316–335, at 322–329. Dubuisson argues that its meaning is usually not pejorative, a conclusion that might have to be reconsidered. See also Petrochilos, *Roman Attitudes*, 48–54.

[49] Plutarch, *Cicero* 5.2.1: καὶ τόν γε πρῶτον ἐν Ῥώμῃ χρόνον εὐλαβῶς διῆγε καὶ ταῖς ἀρχαῖς ὀκνηρῶς προσῄει καὶ παρημελεῖτο, ταῦτα δὴ τὰ Ῥωμαίων τοῖς βαναυσοτάτοις πρόχειρα καὶ συνήθη ῥήματα Γραικὸς καὶ σχολαστικὸς ἀκούων. See below for Cassius Dio's explanation of the term Γραικός.

[50] *ad Atticum* 1.15.2: Nunc, quoniam et laudis avidissimi semper fuimus et praeter ceteros φιλέλληνες et sumus et habemur . . . See Guite, *Greece & Rome* 9 (1962), 143f. for thoughts about what Cicero may have meant.

[51] Cicero, *ad Atticum* 1.8.

[52] Cicero, *pro Flacc.* 62; *ad Quintum fratrem* 1.1.27ff.; *de rep.* 2.34; *Tusc. disp.* 1.1–7. Cf. Brunt, "Laus Imperii," 316f. Roman respect for the old Greece: Balsdon, *Romans and Aliens*, 38–40.

ent the Greeks were for the most part morally inferior and degenerate, he says.[53] Peoples like the Mysians and Phrygians he considered much inferior even to the Greeks of the mainland. He warned his brother Quintus against close contact with Greeks when he was governor of Asia "except with the very few, if any, who are worthy of the ancient Greeks. Those in your province indeed are treacherous, very many of them, and worthless, and trained by a long servitude to show excessive flattery."[54] A contemporary Greek intellectual who was an associate of Piso may be criticized, says Cicero, in his attack on Piso, but he was a decent man and he should therefore be dealt with gently, "not as an infamous reprobate, not as presumptious, but as a *Graeculus*, a flatterer, a poet."[55]

In Cicero's work we also encounter, for the first time, an explicit suggestion that the Greeks in Rome are both hostile and unduly influential, a classic example of a xenophobic attitude: "They are presumptious in this city, which they hate, among those they hate seeing, and in a state which they failed to destroy, not for want of desire, but of strength."[56] This is the sort of complaint we encounter frequently when it comes to substantial minorities in Rome. Cicero expresses himself in similar terms about the Jews, and in the literature of the imperial period such animosities towards Asiatics, Syrians, and Jews were particularly strong. Whether Cicero himself believed what he said in court we cannot know and do not need to know, for it is significant for us only that he had reason to assume that his audience would be persuaded by such insinuation.

Cicero's speeches, where these accusations are repeated very often, cannot, of course, be taken as straightforward expressions of his own views. They were a combination of rhetoric and special pleading. However, this cannot be said of his treatises. These have a much better claim of representing Cicero's genuine views, for they are not meant to impress a large audience. They are intended to persuade the single reader and, occasionally, to portray as faithfully as possible a conversation between distinguished men. For the latter we might start with *de oratore*, which contains a fair number of pronouncements that may be considered representative of Roman upper-class ideas about the Greeks in the last years of the republic. First, Greeks are described as *inepti*, a term which, ac-

---

[53] *pro Flacco* 9, 16, 57, 61; *ad Quintum fratrem* 1.2.4; *pro Sest.* 141; *pro Lig.* 11.

[54] *ad Qf* 1.1.16: Atque etiam e Graecis ipsis diligenter cavendae sunt quaedam familiaritates praeter hominum perpaucorum si qui sunt vetere Graecia digni; nunc vero fallaces sunt permulti et leves et diuturna servitute ad nimiam adsentationem eruditi. Cf. D. R. Shackleton Bailey, *Cicero: Epistulae ad Quintum Fratrem et M. Brutum* (Cambridge, 1980), 151. Shackleton Bailey cites, without comment, Tyrrell and Purser: "the whole sentence would serve as a good description of the natives of India under British rule." See also *ad QF* 1.1.19. For the Greeks as *leves*, see also Firmicus Maternus, *Mathesis* 1.2.4; 1.10.12, where it is asserted against the stereotype that *Graecorum levitas frequenter modestae gravitatis pondus accepit.*

[55] Cicero, *in Pisonem* 70: in quo reprehendat eum licet, si qui volet, modo leviter, non ut impurum, non ut improbum, non ut audacem, sed ut Graeculum, ut adsentatorem, ut poëtam.

[56] *Pro Flacco* 61: In hac igitur urbe se iactant quam oderunt, apud eos quos inviti vident, in ea re publica ad quam opprimendam non animus eis, sed vires defuerunt . . .

cording to Wilkins, "is untranslatable: 'impertinent' often comes nearest to it: 'wanting in tact' is sometimes more exact."[57] Cicero writes:

> The Greek nation, with all its learning, abounds in this fault, and so, as the Greeks do not perceive the significance of this plague, they have not even bestowed a name upon the fault in question, for, search where you may, you will not find out how the Greeks designate the "tactless" man. But, of all the countless forms assumed by want of tact, I rather think that the grossest is the Greeks' habit, in any place and any company they like, of plunging into the most subtle dialectic concerning subjects that present extreme difficulty, or at any rate do not call for discussion.[58]

It is an interesting form of collective disapproval to say that a nation suffers from a fault for which they have no term. It is the sort of disapproval that Romans could express because they knew Greek well. It is also remarkable that it should be considered a serious defect of all Greeks that they are willing to discuss any topic anywhere. It is precisely the quality of Greek intellectuality that preoccupies the discussants in *de oratore*: "In fact controversy about a word has long tormented those Greeklings, fonder as they are of argument than of truth."[59] "How now?" exclaimed Crassus, "Do you think I am some idle talkative Greekling, who is also perhaps full of learning and erudition, that you propound me a petty question on which to talk as I will?"[60] "And upon my word, he was right, for what better example of prating insolence could there be than for a Greek, who had never seen a foeman or a camp, or even had the slightest connection with any public employment, to lecture on military matters to Hannibal, who all those years had been disputing empire with the Roman people, the conquerors of the world?"[61] The tone is sometimes different, depending on the speaker: ". . . and perceiving that the Greeks, men not only

---

[57] Cicero, *de oratore libri III*, ed. A.S. Wilkins (Oxford, 1892); 1. Band, Buch I, A. D. Leeman and H. Pinkster (Heidelberg, 1981); 2. Band: Buch I; Buch II (1985). Leeman, ad 1.102.2: Der locus classicus für die hier zum Ausdrück gebrachte Auffassung über die Griechen ist 2.17–18, cited by Augustine, *de civ. dei* 9.5; *contra Cresc.* 1.12.15. Cf. Petrochilos, *Roman Attitudes*, 35f.

[58] 2.18 Trans. E. W. Sutton and H. Rackham. Hoc vitio cumulata est eruditissima illa Graecorum natio; itaque quod vim huius mali Graeci non vident, ne nomen quidem ei vitio imposuerunt; ut enim quaeras omnia, quo modo Graeci ineptum appellent, non reperies. Omnium autem ineptiarum, quae sunt innumerabiles, haud sciam an nulla sit maior quam, ut illi solent, quocumque in loco, quoscumque inter homines visum est, de rebus aut difficillimis aut non necessariis argutissime disputare. For comments, see Leeman and Pinkster, vol. 2, p. 211f.

[59] 1.47f.: Verbi enim controversia iam diu torquet Graeculos homines contentionis cupidiores quam veritatis.

[60] 1.102: "Quid? mihi vos nunc" inquit Crassus "tamquam alicui Graeculo otioso et loquaci et fortasse docto atque erudito quaestiunculam, de qua meo arbitratu loquar, ponitis?" Comm. Leeman, ad loc.

[61] 2.76 quid enim aut adrogantius aut loquacius fieri potuit quam Hannibali, qui tot annis de imperio cum populo Romano omnium gentium victore certasset, Graecum hominem, qui numquam hostem, numquam castra vidisset, numquam denique minimam partem ullius publici muneris attigisset, praecepta de re militari dare? See also 1.105; 2.19.

abounding in genius and learning, but also amply endowed with leisure and the love of study."[62]

There is another failing which Cicero was the first to blame the Greeks for, namely their *levitas,* that is, their inconstancy or even worthlessness.[63] It is a term which Cicero often uses quite generally, but the Greeks are singled out— and not only in his forensic speeches[64]—for having this quality, the opposite of *gravitas,* which was a typically Roman merit.[65] The Romans generally regarded themselves as morally superior in comparison with other peoples,[66] but this was particularly true in the case of Romans and Greeks. Like some other authors, Cicero makes no real distinction between Greeks from the mainland and Asiatics.[67] Although it is often claimed that *levitas* was a proverbial quality of the Greeks in Roman eyes,[68] it is not usually encountered among later authors. It appears to have impressed itself as proverbial on modern readers mainly through Cicero's repeated use. As will be seen below, the Gauls were also accused of being *leves.* A related reproach: all Greeks tend to be irresponsible.[69] On balance, then, it seems that the Greeks were regarded with some respect for their intellectual curiosity and learning, but their faults were more serious: they were called excessively talkative, dishonest, intellectually presumptuous and uninhibited and, at least according to Cicero, inconstant.

Hostility is also extended to Romans who are too close to Greek culture, for instance in a quotation from Cicero's grandfather: "The old M. Cicero, father of that excellent man, our friend, said that our generation is like Syrian slaves: the better they know Greek, the worse is their character" (2.265).[70] This is a pro-

---

[62] 1.22: et quod Graecos homines non solum ingenio et doctrina, sed etiam otio studioque abundantis . . . And cf. 2.36f., with Antonius attacking Greek influence and Catulus defending it.

[63] Aulus Gellius, *NA* 6.11.1–4 observes that *levitas* in his time generally is used to indicate *inconstantia* and *mutabilitas,* but was, in Cicero's time and in his work, used for *viles* or people considered *nullo honore dignos.* For Greek *levitas* see Petrochilos, *Roman Attitudes,* 40–42.

[64] *Brutus* 96: hoc in oratore Latino primum mihi videtur et levitas apparuisse illa Graecorum et verborum comprensio et iam artifex, ut ita dicam, stilus; *De Finibus* 2.80: Sit ista in Graecorum levitate perversitas, qui maledictis insectantur eos a quibus de veritate dissentiunt.

[65] *Pro Sestio* 75.141: . . . quod si aput Atheniensis, homines Graecos, longe a nostrorum hominum gravitate diiunctos . . . See further, *Pro Flacco* 57: levitas propria Graecorum; also 24; 36; 61; 71: Graecorum luxuria et levitate; 37; 66 (Asiatic *levitas*); fr.2 (Hieron. ad Gal. 1,3 et epist. 10,3): ingenita levitas et erudita vanitas; *Pro Ligario* 11; Livy 9.18.6: levissimi ex Graecis (cited above); Lucan, *BC* 3.302: non Graia levitate.

[66] Edwards, *The Politics of Immorality,* 20–22.

[67] Cic. *Pro Flacco* 37: levitatem totius Asiae; see also 60f. for Cicero on Greeks from Asia Minor.

[68] E.g. V. Hunnink, *M.Annaeus Lucanus, Bellum Civile Book III: A Commentary* (Amsterdam, 1992), 145.

[69] *ad familiares* 16.4.2: Lyso enim noster, vereor, ne neglegentior sit; primum, quia omnes Graeci . . .

[70] nostros homines similis esse Syrorum venalium: ut quisque optime Graece sciret, ita esse nequissimum; cf. Leeman, Pinkster, and Rabbie, *De Oratore Libri III: Kommentar* 3 (Heidelberg, 1989), 294, with references to Turnebus (1594, 2d ed.) and to *Fam* 7.24.2: Sardos venales, alium alio nequiorum.

nouncement for which I have seen no parallel: the claim that Syrian slaves are worse, the better their Greek is. It suggests that Syrian slaves, in themselves despicable, are even more so if they are Hellenized. Even so Romans, Cicero included, used Greek words and phrases in their spoken and written language all the time.[71] Cicero is ambivalent about the language itself, occasionally insisting on the superiority of Latin over Greek,[72] an attitude which may reflect concern for the status of Latin in Rome rather than a genuine belief that Latin was a better instrument of philosophical thought.[73] Thus his attitude may represent a desire to defend the use of Latin and not simplistic jingoism. Greeks, however, were seen as inferior when it came to the highest values in society, and Cicero definitely fears that Romans who were overinvolved in their culture would be affected by their lack of values.

In spite of all this condescension, Horace, as mentioned above, expresses the essence of the Roman dilemma: "Captive Greece took her savage victor captive and brought the arts to rustic Latium."[74] This is the clearest expression anywhere of Roman ambivalence with regard to a subject people with a superior cultural tradition, for no Roman could have read with equanimity that a subject nation took Rome captive. There was a complement to this complex relationship: as we see frequently in these pages, the Greeks under Roman rule tend to identify with their rulers' negative judgments of themselves. Polybius wrote an attack of two pages, already cited, on Aulus Postumius, the philhelene "who had acquired the worst of Greek characteristics." Strabo calls the Greeks "the most talkative of all men."[75] In the first century Dio Chrysostom had complex feelings about this subject. "The Athenians," he said, "have now proclaimed someone an 'Olympian' poet, while he was no Athenian by birth, but Phoenician, and one, at that, who did not come from Tyre or Sidon, but from some village or from the countryside, and it is someone who has his arms depilated and wears a corset."[76] Here we see a descending scale of status as seen by a first-century orator with nostalgic feelings about classical Athens, who himself came from Prusa in Asia Minor: (1) Athenian, (2) not Athenian by birth, but Greek, (3) Phoenician from an old and respectable city, (4) Phoenician from the countryside. This is the ultimate in disgrace. However, we are informed that the Olympian was also effeminate in oriental fashion, a traditional stereotype, although the physical details mentioned would not occur in Greek texts of the

[71] Balsdon, *Romans and Aliens*, 48.

[72] E.g., Cicero, *de Finibus* 1.10; 3.5; *Tusc.* 3.10. Cf. Petrochilos, *Roman Attitudes*, 27–31.

[73] As argued by Petrochilos, 28f., on the basis of *de Finibus* 1.4; 1.8; *Brut.* 247; *De Officiis* 1.1; *N.D.* 1.7–8.

[74] Horace, *Ep.* 2.1.156: Graecia capta ferum victorem cepit et artis intulit agresti Latio.

[75] 3.4.19 (c.166): τῶν Ἑλλήνων, οἳ λαλίστατοι πάντων γεγόνασι

[76] Dio Chrysostom *Or.* 31.116: ἤδη τοίνυν ἤκουσά τι καὶ τοιοῦτόν τινος ἀποσχεδιάζοντος, ὅτι καὶ παρ' ἑτέροις ἰδεῖν ἔστι τοῦτο γιγνόμενον· πάλιν δὲ ἑτέρου, ὡς καὶ παρ' Ἀθηναίοις πολλὰ πράττεται νῦν, οἷς οὐκ ἀπεικότως ἄν τις ἐπιπλήξειεν, οὐ περὶ τὰ ἄλλα μόνον, ἀλλὰ καὶ περὶ τὰς τιμάς· οἵ γε τὸν δεῖνα μὲν Ὀλύμπιον κεκλήκασιν οὐδὲ φύσει πολίτην ἑαυτῶν, Φοίνικα δὲ ἄνθρωπον οὐκ ἀπὸ Τύρου καὶ Σιδῶνος, ἀλλ' ἀπὸ κώμης τινὸς ἢ τῆς ἠπείρου, καὶ ταῦτα πιττούμενον τοὺς βραχίονας καὶ περιδήματα φοροῦντα·

fourth century B.C. Greek decline is an important theme in Dio's work and
the example is meant to show how low Athens had sunk. "Greek failings"
(Ἑλληνικὰ ἁμαρτήματα), he says, is a term the Romans use when they talk of
the Greek love of honorary titles for their cities (38.38). His stance regarding
the Phoenician would be indistinguishable from many Roman pronouncements
if it had been written in Latin. This attitude recurs in another oration, where he
tells the Tarsians their manners are such that one would think them colonists
from Arados (in Phoenicia).[77] His words about Athens are more ambiguous.

Hostile Roman feelings toward the Greeks did not decrease during the principate.[78] In this period, Seneca expresses a combination of insecurity and dislike
in the following statement: "Whatever Roman eloquence has that it can set
against and display before arrogant Greece flourished about the time of Cicero."[79]
A single but perhaps significant view of poetry in these terms is expressed by
Martial.[80] The Elder Pliny cherished a firm antipathy for all Greeks, as has
already been seen in his pronouncements about Greek doctors. They are the
source of all vice because they use olive oil in the gymnasium.[81] They are an
excessively self-congratulatory people,[82] admire all their own achievements,[83]
and spread extraordinary falsehoods (*mendacia*),[84] another keyword being *vanitas*.[85] Other authors agreed with this assessment.[86] It is remarkable to see how
the Roman assessment of the Greeks here echoes pronouncements once made
by Greeks about Persians, whom Isocrates had called faithless and swindlers.

   As one might expect, Juvenal, writing satire, descends to a much murkier
level. When he writes in his third satire: "I cannot stand, Quirites, a Greek city
of Rome,"[87] he immediately continues to make it clear that his enmity in this

---

[77] Dio Chrysostom, *Or.* 33.41, discussed above, p. 345f.

[78] For Greek culture and identity in the Roman Empire: Simon Goldhill (ed.), *Being Greek under Rome* (2001).

[79] Seneca, *controv.* 1 praef. 6: quidquid Romana facundia habet quod insolenti Graeciae aut op-
ponat aut praeferat circa Ciceronem effloruit. One of the possible reasons Seneca gives for the
decline is luxury. The idea that luxury causes deterioration is seen again and again and is closely
connected with the manner in which Romans see their Empire. For the "*arrogantia*" of the Greeks:
Petrochilos, *Roman Attitudes*, 39.

[80] Martial 2.86.3–5: nusquam Graecula quod recantat echo | nec dictat mihi luculentus Attis |
mollem debilitate galliambon . . . Here we find poetry discredited in terms like "Greekling" and
effeminate.

[81] Pliny, *NH* 15.19: vitiorum omnium genitores; cf. Silius, *Punica* 14.136–8: "pigro luctandi
studio certamen in umbra / molle pati docta et gaudens splendescere olivo / stat, mediocre decus
vincentum, ignava iuventus. /

[82] Pliny, *NH* 3.42: genus in gloriam suam effusissimum.

[83] 4.4: omnia sua mirantibus. Cf. Tac., *Ann.* 2.88.3, cited below.

[84] 5.4: portentosa Graeciae mendacia; 2.248; 28.112 mendaciis Graecae vanitatis; 37.41.

[85] 37.31 Occasio est vanitatis Graecorum detegendae; also 36.79.

[86] Tacitus, *Hist.* 2.4. Valerius Maximus 4.7.4: illa gentis ad fingendum paratae monstro similia
mendacia.

[87] Juvenal, *Satire* 3.60–5: non possum ferre, Quirites, Graecam urbem. quamuis quota portio
faecis Achaei? iam pridem Syrus in Tiberim defluxit Orontes et linguam et mores et cum tibicine

case really concerns residents in Rome who come from the eastern provinces. He does not differentiate between Greeks from the mainland and Greeks from the eastern provinces. Both kinds are undesirable. Later he mentions Greeks from various places, some of them classical Greeks, others in Asia Minor: they have a quick intelligence, are incredibly impertinent, and more talkative than Isaeus.[88] Juvenal's third *satire* also introduces the topic of parasites and represents the Greek immigrants as taking over from the native Romans by their superior social versatility and causing resentment thereby. They do not just penetrate Roman society, they also corrupt it, particularly Roman women, which is one of the topics of the sixth satire. "What can be more offensive than this, that no woman believes in her own beauty unless she has converted herself from a Tuscan into a Greekling (*Graecula*), or from a maid of Sulmo into a true maid of Athens? They talk nothing but Greek, though it is a greater shame for our people to be ignorant of Latin; . . . their very loves are carried on in Greek fashion,"[89] and this is true for young and old alike. Juvenal's complaints focus on language and erotic encounters. Niall Rudd has observed quite rightly that the resentment which Juvenal so pungently conveys must come, to some extent at least, from feelings of insecurity. As always, it needs to be remembered that the lines quoted here are but a few in a poem of more than six hundred, all savaging the morals and habits of contemporary women.

Juvenal's reproaches resemble those made by Cicero more than a century before, cited above. "To be a language teacher, rhetorician, mathematician, painter, wrestler, soothsayer, rope-dancer, doctor, and magician: everything our hungry *Graeculus* knows. Tell him to go to heaven and he will."[90] In the eighth satire, Juvenal shows again that he does not like Greeks. Explaining to a weak young nobleman that the Romans have not left much to steal in the provinces, he continues: "You despise perchance, and deservedly, the unwarlike Rhodian and the scented Corinthian: what harm will their resined youths do you, or the smooth legs of the entire breed? But keep clear of rugged Spain, avoid the land of the Gaul and the Dalmatian shore."[91] In other words, Greeks from Rhodes

---

chordas obliquas nec non gentilia tympana secum uexit et ad circum iussas prostare puellas. Cf. N. Rudd, *Themes in Roman Satire* (1986), chapter 5: "Greek and the Greeks."

[88] Ibid. 69–74: hic alta Sicyone, ast hic Amydone relicta, hic Andro, ille Samo, hic Trallibus aut Alabandis, Esquilias dictumque petunt a uimine collem, uiscera magnarum domuum dominique futuri. ingenium uelox, audacia perdita, sermo promptus et Isaeo torrentior.

[89] Juvenal, *Satire* 6.185–191 (trans. G. G. Ramsay, Loeb): nam quid rancidius quam quod se non putat ulla | formosam nisi quae de Tusca Graecula facta est, | de Sulmonensi mera Cecropis? omnia Graece: | [cum sit turpe magis nostris nescire Latine.] hoc sermone pauent, hoc iram, gaudia, curas, | hoc cuncta effundunt animi secreta. quid ultra? | concumbunt Graece. Sulmo was the birthplace of the poet Ovid.

[90] *Satire* 3. 76–8: grammaticus, rhetor, geometres, pictor, aliptes, | augur, schoenobates, medicus, magus, omnia nouit | Graeculus esuriens: in caelum iusseris ibit.

[91] *Satire* 8.116: forsitan inbellis Rhodios unctamque Corinthon despicias merito: quid resinata iuuentus cruraque totius facient tibi leuia gentis? horrida uitanda est Hispania, Gallicus axis Illyricumque latus; The presence or absence of hair on legs is noted more often: Juvenal 2.11ff.; 9.12ff; Martial 10.65.6.

and Corinth are effeminate and soft.[92] They are despicable, unlike the inhabitants of Spain, Gaul, and Dalmatia. It is, again, engaging to see that the Greeks
are now described in the very terms which they themselves invented for their
eastern neighbors, as has been seen above, in the discussion of *Airs*, and Aristotle. It is worth observing that these particular faults are not stressed in the
work of Cicero who was, perhaps, less preoccupied with masculinity and martial achievement.

Furthermore, Juvenal says nothing against the Africans (ibid., 117–120).
Elsewhere he refers to Gaul and Africa as boasting fine schools of rhetoric
(7.147–9). Juvenal compares the Greeks as one group with the inhabitants of
Spain, Gaul, Dalmatia, and he is less critical of Africa as well. Tacitus also
found the Greeks in Rome inadequate. In the *Dialogus* he offers a discussion
about the reasons for the decline of rhetoric. Messala gives one view: Education
is at fault. In the past mothers reared their children with devotion and strict
discipline. "But in our day we entrust the infant to a little Greek servant-girl
(*Graecula ancilla*) who is attended by one or two, commonly the worst of all
the slaves, creatures utterly unfit for any important work."[93] Curiously, this is a
traditional idea derived from Greek literature. Plato asserts that the sons of the
Persian kings Cyrus and Darius were not fit to be kings because they allowed
their sons to be educated "by women and eunuchs," overpampered and in luxury (*Leges* 695a). Tacitus also despises the Greek historians of his days: Arminius is unknown to them "who admire only their own achievements."[94]

A remarkable piece of rhetoric is the speech which Tacitus attributes to Cn
Piso, visiting Athens in A.D. 18. It is, of course, impossible to say whether Piso
said anything like this, or whether Tacitus merely thought he might have spoken
like that, which in itself would not diminish its significance. Piso was aggra-
vated at Germanicus's courtesy towards Athens—"not the people of Athens,
who indeed had been exterminated by repeated disasters, but a miserable medley of tribes."[95] Here then an absolute distinction is made between historical
Athens and the contemporary people of Athens which was but a medley, an
"impure mixture" as the dictionary of Lewis and Short translates *conluvies*.
Another point of interest in this passage: there is no doubt regarding the immediate association of this description for any Roman well read in Greek literature, and for Piso's Athenian audience. The old Athenians were *autochthones*,
of pure lineage, but the city population in the first century was a mixture, a

[92] Roman ideas about a Greek lack of manliness: Petrochilos, *Roman Attitudes*, 46.

[93] Tac. *Dialogus* 29.1: At nunc natus infans delegatur Graeculae alicui ancillae, cui adiungitur
unus aut alter ex omnibus servis, plerumque vilissimus nec cuiquam serio ministerio accom-
modatus. Cf. Balsdon, *Romans and Aliens,* 36. See especially Syme, *Tacitus*, 2.505–519: "Tacitus
and the Greeks." See also below, chapter 12, n. 37.

[94] Tacitus, *Ann.* 2.88.3: Graecorum annalibus ignotus, qui sua tantum mirantur. Cf. Syme, *Tacitus*,
2.513, n.5.

[95] Tacitus, *Ann.* 2.55: At Cn.Piso . . . civitatem Atheniensium turbido incessu exterritam oratione
saeva increpat, oblique Germanicum perstringens, quod contra decus Romani nominis non Athenienses tot cladibus extinctos, sed conluviem illam nationum comitate nimia coluisset . . .

rabble of good-for-nothings. This shows both how the old idea of Athenian autochthony was alive and accepted in the Roman period and to what extent the proto-racist thrust of the concept was taken for granted, half a millennium after it began to circulate.[96]

It is interesting to see one reference to the Greeks in Trajan's correspondence with Pliny, where the subject is construction work in Nicaea. Trajan writes that "those *Graeculi* all are fond of the gymnasia. That is perhaps why they have undertaken their project with too much ambition."[97] This is far milder in tone than the criticism of Scipio already cited, but still the object is the same, so this represents three full centuries of Roman objections to the gymnasium. Again, it should be noted that for Trajan and Pliny the citizens of Nicaea are *Graeculi.* The fact that it is a city beyond the region of classical Hellas is irrelevant. The younger Pliny took his cue from the attitude of the Emperor. In his *Panegyricus* to Trajan he indulges in one of the familiar complaints about deterioration: "But now that the handling of arms has been transformed into a spectacle instead of a personal skill, and has become entertainment instead of work, when exercises are not longer directed by a veteran crowned with the mural or civic crown, but by a little Greek trainer."[98] The point is obvious: Greeks play and Romans fight. When Romans deteriorate, they allow themselves to be trained by Greeklings instead of victorious veterans, but Trajan himself was a Roman of the old type. It is not farfetched to assume that Pliny writes this because that was how Trajan wanted to be praised. Yet the Younger Pliny himself displays an attitude, quite different from that of the Elder Pliny and which might best be characterized as a combination of admiration for ancient Greece and patronizing or condescending benevolence for the contemporary Greeks.

This, at least, is apparent from a lengthy letter of advice written to a certain Maximus who was going to Achaea as *corrector,* that is, as a special official responsible for the cities of free status in the province (8.24): "Keep in mind that you have been sent to the province of Achaea, to that true and genuine Greece, where first *humanitas* and literature as well as agriculture are believed to have originated; that you have been sent to organize the constitution of free cities . . . Respect the founding gods and their names, respect their ancient glory and their very antiquity, qualities which are in a man venerable, in cities revered. . . . To take away the remaining shadow and what is left of the name of their freedom is hard, cruel and barbarous."[99] This culminates in a compari-

---

[96] For Athenian autochthony, see chapter 1.

[97] Pliny, *ep.* 10.40.2 Gymnasiis indulgent Graeculi; ideo forsitan Nicaeenses maiore animo constructionem eius adgressi sunt.

[98] Pliny, *Pan.* 13.5: Postquam uero studium armorum a manibus ad oculos, ad uoluptatem a labore translatum est, postquam exercitationibus nostris non ueteranorum aliquis cui decus muralis aut ciuica, sed Graeculus magister adsistit . . .

[99] Pliny, *ep.* 8.24: Cogita te missum in prouinciam Achaiam, illam ueram et meram Graeciam, in qua primum humanitas litterae, etiam fruges inuentae esse creduntur; missum ad ordinandum statum liberarum ciuitatum . . . Reuerere conditores deos et nomina deorum, reuerere gloriam ueterem et hanc ipsam senectutem, quae in homine uenerabilis, in urbibus sacra. . . . quibus reli-

son: "You see that doctors treat free clients more gently and with greater compassion than slaves, even though there is no difference between the illness of a slave and that of a free man."[100] The implications of this comparison are remarkable: the Greeks are not, like Syrians and other easterners, regarded as "natural slaves." They are free and have the nature of free men, but even so they are compared with patients suffering from an illness while the imperial rulers act as doctor.[101] That is to say, they deserve the respect due to their status, but they are certainly not fully functional as a people.

It is interesting to note that the term "Greekling" recurs once again in imperial correspondence. Fronto writes to Marcus Aurelius as Caesar about a possible lawsuit against Herodes Atticus, where he would call him "a Greekling and uneducated, yet that will not mean blood being shed."[102] This, however, did not preclude good relations between the two afterwards. Greeks, presumably, had learned to live with these forms of hostility on the part of the Romans, who clearly felt there was nothing much wrong with such behavior.

Above I explained briefly why I felt this section on Greeks should include some inhabitants of the eastern provinces. Whatever they called themselves, and many indeed did call themselves "Greeks," they were often—but not always—considered Greeks by Latin-speaking Romans. It is therefore appropriate to include the Greek author Lucian among the Greeks, even though he originated from Samosata, capital of Commagene. The question how Lucian saw himself has been raised by Palm. When Lucian speaks of Marcus's war with the Marcomanni and Quadi, the Roman troops are referred to as "ours" (*Alex* 48.19). Palm considers this highly significant.[103] I am not certain that this

---

quam umbram et residuum libertatis nomen eripere durum ferum barbarum est. Cf. Cicero, *ad Q.Fr.* 1.1, cited above, chapter 2, n. 74. F. Zucker, "Plinius epist. VIII 24—ein Denkmal antiker Humanität," *Philologus* 84 (1928), 209–232, at 221–223, points to the parallel, also referring to *pro Flacco* 61f. As Zucker observes, Pliny speaks as a member of the philhellenic circle of Sosius Senecio and Minicius Fundanus. It is interesting to see how Zucker without any reservations approves of Cicero's and Pliny's attitude toward their contemporary Greeks: "Sehr stark tritt bei Cicero die Zwiespältigkeit zutage, in die viele dem Griechentum der Vergangenheit sich verpflichtet fühlende Römer durch die moralische Minderwertigkeit der zeitgenössischen Griechen versetzt wurden" (230). A. N. Sherwin-White, *The Letters of Pliny: A Historical and Social Commentary* (Oxford 1966), 477–479 and cf. interesting observations by G. Woolf, *PCPS* 40 (1994), 116–143, at 119–121 (misquoting Vergil).

[100] Vides a medicis, quamquam in adversa valetudine nihil servi ac liberi differant, mollius tamen liberos clementiusque tractari.

[101] A long comparison of lawgivers with doctors already occurs in Plato's *Laws*. He makes a distinction between a slave doctor and a free doctor. The former usually treats slaves and imposes a standard treatment which he learned from his master without checking, thinking, or consultation. In contrast, the free doctor, who usually treats free men, first tries to understand the nature of the patient's illness, discusses it with the patient and with his friends, and only then prescribes whatever is needed. (*Leges* 4.720a–e; 9.857c–e). The emphases and points of comparison are obviously not the same in Plato and Pliny. The former discusses lawgiving, the latter an imperial relationship. Both, however, are considering the necessary differences in attitude toward free men and slaves.

[102] Fronto, *ad M. Caes.* 3.3.3, p. 38 (van den Hout); p. 41 (Naber): sicubi graeculum et indoctum dixero, non erit internecivum.

[103] J. Palm, *Rom, Römertum*, 54. See also *Hist. conscr.* 29, 5: "nobody would dare attack us—we

is the case. Apart from the genre, which makes it difficult to determine whether the author is speaking in earnest, the present passage rules out anything else. When the emperor is fighting Marcomanni and Quadi, with whom would one expect the Graeco-Syrian Lucian to identify?

Lucian's work is highly instructive on contemporary attitudes if context and background are taken into account. He has already been cited when satirizing common hostile attitudes to people with a mixed background (*Deor. Conc.* 7). There the mixture in question concerned only mainland Greek and eastern elements: Lucian was reacting to attitudes in Greece or among Greeks in Greece, not to attitudes in Rome or Italy. This is interesting in itself, for we have seen that at least some upper class Romans considered the distinction between Greeks from Greece and Hellenized inhabitants of the eastern provinces unimportant. Elsewhere, however, Lucian satirizes the reactions of local Romans to the presence of a Greek at dinner (*Hirelings* 17, cited above): the Romans feel that the Greeks, who are clever talkers, undermine their social position, a theme also present in Juvenal's *Satire* 3. This sort of hostility affords us a good impression of social tension. Later in the same work a man has been fired from his post in the house: "Your accuser is trustworthy even when he says nothing, while you are a Greek, and relaxed in manner and prone to all sorts of wrongdoing. That is how they think we [i.e. Greeks] all are, of course" (40).[104] This is an indication of an automatic presumption that every Greek is less reliable than any local person.

Palm, in his search for Greeks who consider themselves Romans, has also attempted to draw conclusions from a number of passages in the medical treatises of Galen from Pergamum (A.D. 129–c. 199). First, he emphasizes that this work presents the opposition: barbarians versus us, the Greeks.[105] I cannot agree with Palm that this is remarkable. By the time Galen wrote, the Greeks had been calling themselves "Hellenes" and everybody else "barbarians" for more than six centuries. Palm notes that Galen also speaks of "our emperor Severus."[106] What else would Severus be called? Palm concludes: "Thus Galen creates the impression of a man who wants to emphasise his Hellenic origin, and, at the same time, his close relationship with the emperor. He is directly subject to the

---

have beaten everybody already." See, however, Bowersock, *JRS* 58 (1968), 262; Jones, *Lucian*, 89.

[104] *Merc. Cond.* 40: ὁ μὲν γὰρ κατήγορος καὶ σιωπῶν ἀξιόπιστος, σὺ δὲ Ἕλλην καὶ ῥάδιος τὸν τρόπον καὶ πρὸς πᾶσαν ἀδικίαν εὔκολος. τοιούτους γὰρ ἅπαντας ἡμᾶς εἶναι οἴονται, καὶ μάλα εἰκότως· δοκῶ γάρ μοι καὶ τῆς τοιαύτης δόξης αὐτῶν, ἣν ἔχουσι περὶ ἡμῶν, κατανενοηκέναι τὴν αἰτίαν.

[105] *De sanitate tuenda* 6.51; cited by Palm, p. 75 as I 10.17.

[106] *De antidotis* 4.65.9: τοῦ νῦν ὄντος ἡμῶν αὐτὸ κράτορος Σεβήρου; *De anatomicis administrationibus* 2.215: ἄρχειν ἡγημένου τοῦ καὶ νῦν ἡμῖν ἄρχοντος Ἀντωνίνου, Palm observes that this is the first use of the expression "our emperor" in Greek, apart from Dionysius Periegetes, who wrote a century earlier in Greek (Müller, *Geogr. Gr. Min.* II; V. 355), but this is "a demütige Verbeugung des Verfassers"; cf. the Scholia, ibid. II 444: Ῥώμην τιμήεσσαν, ἐμῶν μέγαν οἶκον ἀνάκτων, μητέρα πασάων πολίων. Admittedly, this is humble, but why is it therefore insignificant that Dionysius Peregetes calls Rome "the large house of my rulers" and meaningful when Galen speaks of "our present ruler"?

emperor and the Roman people do not exist as intermediary authority."[107] This does not follow. "Our emperor" is neither more nor less of a fixed formula than "the Roman Empire," which Palm says has no significance.[108] Also, Galen more often than not refers to emperors without adding "ours."[109] This is not to deny that he sees the emperor as his legitimate ruler, but it must be recognized that the essence of monarchy is that there is no people as *Zwischeninstanz* between ruler and subject.[110] Plutarch was born before A.D. 50 and died after 120, which is before Galen was born. He never calls the Romans "barbarians," although he had a marked dislike of all strangers, but he employs the term "barbarian" without distinction for non-Greeks and for the enemies of Rome.[111] In his historical observations and approach he fully identifies with Rome, even if he would not call himself "a Roman." I cannot therefore agree with Palm in his attempt to show that the early second century saw a significant change in the self-perception of the Greeks as subjects of the Roman emperor.

Cassius Dio, himself a Roman from the Greek East says, as a matter of course, that the Romans call a Hellene Γραικός, "*Graecus*" (or, perhaps, rather *Graeculus*) "and they use this term in disapproval against them for their lowly origin."[112] Apparently, the image of the Greeks in Rome did not necessarily undergo a metamorphosis.

Latin rhetoric, at any rate, does not show any change. The Panegyricus of Constantine Augustus of A.D. 312 reminds the emperor that "C. Caesar destroyed Gomphi, a city in Thessaly, in one day because it refused obedience. But he attacked Greeklings, you subalpine men."[113] While the orator reminds his audience of events in the time of Julius Caesar, he clearly considers the difference between Greeks and Italians as relevant for Constantine as he thought it had been in the first century B.C.

The Roman Emperor Julian, although of Thracian origin, was a proud Greek. He addresses the people of Antioch as follows: "nay, since I thought that you

[107] "er steht unmittelbar unter dem Kaiser; das römische Volk existiert nicht als Zwischeninstanz."

[108] *De rebus boni malique suci* 6.749: πολλὰ τῶν Ῥωμαίοις ὑπακουόντων ἐθνῶν, *De antidotis* 14.77: ἄπασαν τὴν ὑπὸ Ῥωμαίοις γῆν. I would say that these are not "feststehende Formeln," but phrases that translate "*Imperium Romanum*," which was very much a relevant entity for everybody concerned, at the time.

[109] E.g., *de antidotis* 2.14.24; 64; *de praenotione ad Posthumum* 14.650. Should we assume these texts were written in a Hellenic chauvinist mood?

[110] This point is made by Z. Yavetz, *Plebs and Princeps* (Oxford, 1969).

[111] Plutarch frequently calls non-Greeks barbarians. For the enemies of Rome as barbarians, see *Camillus* 18.4; 6 (Gauls); *Marcellus* 4.3; 8.1 (Insubres); *Lucullus* 29.2: Greeks rise against barbarians (= Armenians) in support of Romans; also: 32.1; *Sertorius* 3.2 (Cimbri and Teutones); 6.3 (Alpine population); 6.5 (Iberians); *Pompey* 35; 51.2 (Gauls); *Caes.* 16.3 (Britons) 19.2 (Germans). Cf. Jones, *Plutarch*, 124.

[112] Cassius Dio 11.161 (Zonaras 8.13): Γραικὸν . . . οὕτω γὰρ καλοῦσι τοὺς Ἕλληνας, καὶ εἰς ὄνειδος δυσγενείας τῷ προσρήματι κατ᾽ αὐτῶν χρῶνται. Note, above, Plutarch's explanation of Cicero's nickname Γραικός.

[113] *Pan. Lat.* 12.6 (trans. Nixon and Rodgers): Gomphos, urbem Thessaliae, quoniam abnueret obsequium, C. Caesar uno die sustulit. Sed ille Graeculos homines adortus est, tu Subalpinos. (cf. *Caes. BC* 3.80).

were sons of Greeks, and I myself, though my family is Thracian, am a Greek in my habits, I supposed that we should regard one another with the greatest possible affection." (*Misopogon* 40). Here then we have a Roman emperor who claims to be Greek, even though he admits his Thracian origin. He is Greek by culture. He also accepts Syrian Antioch as a Greek city and assumes that the common bond of Greek language and culture is itself a sufficient reason for affection between this city and an emperor. Julian, however, had peculiar ideas about Greek identity. In his fourth oration ("To Helios the King," 153a ff.), he states that Greek colonies had made it easier for the world to be governed by the Romans. "For the Romans themselves not only belong to the Greek people,[114] but also the sacred ordinances and the pious belief in the gods which they have established and maintain are, from beginning to end, Greek. . . . For which reason I myself recognise that our city is Greek, both in descent and as to its constitution."[115] Julian, a Roman Emperor, seeks a common identity for all that is Greek and Roman. The Greek colonies paved the way for the integration of the Roman Empire; Roman law and religion are essentially Greek in his eyes. It is difficult to believe that many fourth-century Romans would have agreed with him, but Julian was emperor. Libanius, Julan's teacher, at any rate, does not go so far, but agrees that Julian was a Greek and ruled over Greeks,[116] although he realizes that some people, "the descendants of Aeneas," may not approve of such sentiments (*Or.* 15.25).

It is most interesting to see that these sentiments were not shared by Julian's western troops in Gaul (A.D. 358). When there was a food shortage they attacked him, "calling him an Asiatic, a *Graeculus*, a fraud and a nitwit with a show of wisdom."[117] Here then we have a Roman emperor who himself sought to be both Roman and Greek, who argued that the Roman Empire *was* Greek and yet he was called a *Graeculus* by his soldiers, more than four centuries after we first find it in the writings of Cicero and more than two centuries after Hadrian was called by this name.[118] Yet Julian had a perfect command of Latin as well as of Greek.[119] It is an important question whether these tensions had increased in the fourth century, or had remained the same but appear more widespread because we have more texts for this period. In any case, Julian considered himself a proud Hellene, but it is obvious that soldiers in the west cherished all the old prejudices against Greeks from the Asiatic provinces, even if they served as supreme commander. Even in the fourth century, almost five

[114] Julian, *Or.* 4.153a: τὰ πλεῖστα τῆς οἰκουμένης, παρεσκεύασε δὲ ῥᾷον ὑπακοῦσαι Ῥωμαίοις ἔχουσι καὶ αὐτοῖς οὐ γένος μόνον Ἑλληνικόν, . . .

[115] ἀνθ' ὧν οἶμαι καὶ αὐτὸς ἔγνω τὴν πόλιν Ἑλληνίδα γένος τε καὶ πολιτείαν.

[116] πρῶτον μὲν Ἕλλην τις εἶ καὶ κρατεῖς Ἑλλήνων.

[117] Ammianus 17.9.3: extrema minitans Iulianum compellationibus incessebat et probris, | Asianum appellans, Graeculum et fallacem et specie sapientiae stolidum.

[118] *Epitome de Caesaribus* 14: Hadrianus a plerisque Graeculus appellatus est.

[119] Libanius, *Or.* 12. 92, who admits that he could not judge Julian's Latin, but he relied on "the Karchedonian." On Julian's Latin, see also Ammianus 16.5.7. Libanius used a translator when he had to write a letter in Latin (*ep.* 434 to Themistius).

centuries after much of Asia Minor was incorporated in the empire, "Asiatic" could still be used as a term of abuse without it being necessary to add a qualifying adjective, Greeks remained Greeklings, considered pretentious frauds. The fifth-century author Macrobius still uses the term *Graeculus*[120] and he still uses the same commonplaces: "Can even the notorious glibness of you Greeks find an excuse for this reckless contradiction?"[121]

A passage from Procopius shows that this was even the case in the sixth century, more than seven centuries after Scipio was attacked for his philhellene behavior. Procopius is explaining how poorly Justinian treated the soldiers, who were at the mercy of the *logothetes*. "Furthermore, they kept grinding down the soldiers with many other forms of penalties, as though to requite them thus for the dangers incurred in the wars, charging some with being 'Greeks,' as though it were wholly impossible for any man from Greece to be a decent man" (trans. H. B. Dewing, Loeb).[122] The difference here is that Procopius does not appear to accept this attitude towards Greeks.

We shall end this section with two observations: first, there were some defenders of the Greeks in Rome. Cornelius Nepos, the earliest extant biographer in Latin (c. 110–124), did his best to create understanding for the Greeks among the Romans.[123] He was clearly a model of tolerance: we have already noted that he described Hannibal and Hamilcar in positive terms. The preface to his *de excellentibus ducibus exterarum gentium*, dedicated to Atticus, speaks in favor of tolerance towards Greeks. "Critics will for the most part be men unfamiliar with Greek letters, who will think no conduct proper which does not conform to their own habits. If these men can be made to understand that not all peoples look upon the same acts as honourable or base, but that they judge them all in the light of the usage of their forefathers, they will not be surprised that I, in giving an account of the merits of Greeks, have borne in mind the usage of that nation."[124] He then gives examples: Cimon had his sister for a wife; in Crete it is considered praiseworthy for young men to have many love affairs; it is an honor to be proclaimed victor at Olympia and to appear on the stage. "On the other hand, many actions are seemly according to our code

---

[120] *Saturnalia* 2.4.31; 7.9.26.

[121] 7.9.9 potest ne excusare huius contrarietatis ausum vel vestri oris nota volubilitas?' Cf: *Saturnalia* 1 praef. 14: nam sum, inquit, homo Romanus, natus in Latio, et eloquium Graecum a nobis alienissimum est.

[122] Procopius, *Anecdota* 24.7: Ἔτι μέντοι καὶ ἄλλαις ζημιῶν ἰδέαις πολλαῖς τοὺς στρατιώτας ἀπέκναιον, ὥσπερ ἀμειβόμενοι τῶν ἐν τοῖς πολέμοις κινδύνων, ἐπικαλοῦντες τοῖς μὲν ὡς Γραικοὶ εἶεν, ὥσπερ οὐκ ἐξὸν τῶν ἀπὸ τῆς Ἑλλάδος τὸ παράπαν τινὶ γενναίῳ γενέσθαι, . . .

[123] J. Geiger, *Cornelius Nepos and Ancient Political Biography* (Wiesbaden, 1985); F. Millar, "Cornelius Nepos 'Atticus' and the Roman Revolution," *Greece & Rome* 35 (1988), 40–55; A. C. Dionisotti, "Nepos and the Generals," *JRS* 78 (1988), 35–49. Nepos wrote for a Roman public who did not read much Greek and wanted basic instruction.

[124] Nepos, *Liber de Excellentibus Ducibus Exterarum Gentium, Prologus*, 1.2–4: sed ii erunt fere, qui expertes litterarum Graecarum nihil rectum, nisi quod ipsorum moribus conueniat, putabunt. hi si didicerint non eadem omnibus esse honesta atque turpia, sed omnia maiorum institutis iudicari, non admirabuntur nos in Graiorum uirtutibus exponendis mores eorum secutos.

which the Greeks look upon as shameful." Romans take their wives to dinner-parties, unthinkable in Greece; Greek women stay in the 'women's apartment' [*gynaeconitis*]. Here we have a rare case of a Roman author who speaks out in favor of tolerance and understanding, and his examples focus on the relationship between men and women.

The second observation concerns the self-perception or ethnicity of the inhabitants of the eastern provinces, which is not the subject of this book, but should at least be mentioned. Many cities and groups living in the Roman East were proud to call themselves Hellenes. The citizens of Hadrian's Antinoopolis were *Neoi Hellenes*.[125] In the New Testament the term "Hellenes" or "Hellenists" (Ἑλληνισταί) can mean various things. In Judaea it usually refers to Greek-speaking Jews, as a term denoting language, not ethnic origin. Outside Judaea it usually refers to Greek-speaking non-Jews.[126] Here, as in Herodotus, use of the term is based on language. Cities in Syria called themselves Hellenic, as appears from a remarkable inscription found in Scythopolis.[127] An inscription from Trachonitis in Southern Syria is dedicated by "The Hellenes in Danaba."[128] Thus it would appear that many inhabitants of the Greek-speaking East claim to be Greeks or Hellenes, just like those in Greece and elsewhere, even though others may not have recognized them as such. In the eastern provinces there were Hellenes and non-Hellenes and this difference was important to them. While some Romans, including two emperors, were Hellenophiles, many more continued to feel highly uncomfortable or worse with Greeks through the centuries, wherever they came from.

Conclusions

This is not an easy chapter to sum up, for Roman attitudes towards the Greeks were complex and ambivalent through the centuries. The Greeks, with their language and culture, made more of an impact on Rome than any other people, and the Romans knew them better than they knew any other people. Often the Romans distinguish between the Greeks of the classical period and their con-

[125] H. I. Bell, "Antinoopolis: A Hadrianic Foundation," *JRS* 30(1940), 133–147; P. V. Pistorius, *Indices Antinoopolitani* (Leiden, 1939).

[126] B. Isaac, "Ethnic Groups in Judaea under Roman Rule," reprinted in *The Near East under Roman Rule* (1998), 257–267, at 261–263.

[127] The city of Nysa-Scythopolis is referred to as "one of the Hellenic cities in Coele-Syria" on an inscription published by G. Foerster and Y. Tsafrir, "Nysa-Scythopolis. A New Inscription and the Titles of the City on its Coins," *Israel Numismatic Journal* 9 (1986–1987), 53–58: τῶν κατὰ Κοίλην Συρίαν Ἑλληνίδων. See the comments by P.-L. Gatier, "Décapole et Coelé-Syrie: deux inscriptions nouvelles," *Syria* 67 (1990), 204–206, at 205f.; Alla Stein, in her unpublished Ph.D. thesis (Tel Aviv, 1991).

[128] M. Sartre, in *L'epigrafia del villaggio*. Actes du VIIe colloque international Borghesi à l'occasion du cinquantenaire d' *Epigraphica* (Forli, 27–30 septembre 1990), A. Calbi et al. (ed.) (Faenza, 1993), 133–135; *AE* 1993.1636 from Dhunaybeh (Danaba): Οἱ ἐν Δαναβοις Ἕλληνες Μηνοφίλῳ εὐνοίας ἕνεκεν. This phrase, it has been proposed, might suggest a connection with the Herodian settlers in Trachonitis.

temporary Greeks who were a subject people. Thus, classical Greek objects of art were admired and therefore stolen when the Romans conquered Greek cities. This is the reason why inconsistent, seemingly contradictory, views could be held by Roman writers of the same period—or even by the same person. Attitudes were highly ambivalent towards their own contemporary Greeks. The Greek language was learned, used, and admired by many, but also greatly resisted by others, some of them highly influential. Ethnic stereotypes abound from the second century B.C. at least: the Greeks are artful; they indulge in revelry and debauchery. Greek cults and philosophy attracted followers and were banned. The Elder Cato first asserted that Greece corrupted Rome: he singled out Greek literature and language (and doctors). Rome would lose her empire when she had become infected with Greek letters. Here we see that more than ambivalence is at work: Greek influence was sometimes even thought to affect the stability of Roman society. These feelings were never to disappear and expressed themselves in a multitude of negative qualifications: the Greeks are degenerate and morally inferior; they are both hostile and influential; they are intellectually arrogant and inconstant (*leves*). The Romans aimed some of the old Greek anti-Persian stereotypes against the Greeks themselves: Greeks are faithless, swindlers, effeminate, and soft. There was not just one attitude towards the Greeks, there were many of them, just as there were several kinds of Greeks: those from Athens, those from other mainland cities, Greeks from Asia Minor, from Syria, and from Alexandria in Egypt. What they have in common is that almost nobody in Rome describes any of the Greeks as fully functional in Roman terms and they are never described in the way Romans describe some northern or wilder peoples: they are not virile, courageous, or fierce. They do not have the simple, masculine values or Roman *gravitas*. Otherwise, attitudes vary from hostility (Cato, Cicero in much of his work, the Elder Pliny) to patronizing (the Younger Pliny). The classic statement is that of Horace. Rome may have subdued Greece, but Greek culture conquered Rome.

Such attitudes have been discussed in chapter 3, where it has been stressed that they are characteristic of proto-racist and racist tensions, in the sense that they combine or alternate between feelings of superiority and inferiority, attributing to the others both exaggerated powers or gifts and moral or mental shortcomings. It must be admitted, however, that the stereotypes about Greeks as such are not usually expressed in proto-racist terms. They represent value judgments about the Greeks, but do not usually emphasize that the Greeks are the way they are because they are born like that, or because the environment has made them so. It is probably safe to conclude that Roman attitudes towards the Greeks represent a complex relationship. It is marked by admiration and high regard, combined with a pattern of prejudices and xenophobic responses that often approaches proto-racism, but has far less of this than, for example, attitudes towards Syrians or Egyptians.

Mountaineers and Plainsmen

HERODOTUS 9.122 explains that the Persians followed Cyrus's advice "and chose rather to live in a rough land and be rulers, than to cultivate plains and be the slaves of others." This is the first instance of the common ancient notion of the opposition between rugged mountain and fertile plain. The inhabitants of the former tend to rule and the latter to cultivate and serve. It is found with more details in *Airs, Waters, Places*, 24.2–3 and it recurs in the work of the sixteenth-century author Jean Bodin.[1] We are concerned here with the division between two of the four significant social groups recognized in antiquity: Urban peoples and nomads, mountaineers and plainsmen.

The account of the history of mankind after the great flood, found in the third book of Plato's *Laws*, has been cited above. It further considers the characteristics of life in the mountains as opposed to that on the coast and in cities, but along different lines.[2] Because the flood had destroyed all life at lesser heights, only simple herdsmen survived on the mountaintops. They were unskilled in the arts, had no cities, no technology. Since they had almost nothing, there was hardly any social intercourse, no commerce. Although society was primitive, life was also blessed, for there was no warfare and civil strife. People were well supplied with food, clothing, and other necessities. Since they were neither poor nor rich, they were kind to one another, honest and good. As there were no cities and no warfare and society was simple, there was no need of constitutions and legislation. Plato cites Homer on the Cyclopes: "Neither assemblies nor council have they, nor appointed laws, but they dwell on the peaks of lofty mountains in hollow caves, and each one is lawgiver to his children and his wives, and they reck nothing one of another."[3]

These mythical mountaineers are a brand different from those mentioned by Herodotus and the author of *Airs,* who are hard and savage warriors. Plato's mountaineers fit the idea of the noble savage better than that of the poor but savage mountaineers who live in conflict with the wealthier cultivators of the plain. In fact, Plato's mountain-dwellers do not live in conflict with the plainsmen, because the latter were assumed not to exist anymore after the Great Flood. However this may be, they were mythical people. They have some features in common with humanity in Hesiod's Golden Age and some with the idealized inhabitants of the far North and South, Scythians and Ethiopians,

---

[1] Jean Bodin (1530–1596), *The Six Bookes of a Commonweale* (Cambridge, MA, 1962), p. 564.
[2] Plato, *Leges* 677a–682.
[3] Homer, *Od.* 9.112–115 (Trans. A. T. Murray): τοῖσιν δ᾽ οὔτ᾽ ἀγοραὶ βουληφόροι οὔτε θέμιστες, ἀλλ᾽ οἵ γ᾽ ὑψηλῶν ὀρέων ναίουσι κάρηνα ἐν σπέεσι γλαφυροῖσι, θεμιστεύει δὲ ἕκαστος παίδων ἠδ᾽ ἀλόχων, οὐδ᾽ ἀλλήλων ἀλέγουσι.

mentioned frequently above. Plato's prehistory of the human civilization was adopted without much change by Cicero, Lactantius, Augustine, and other Christian authors.[4] These are views of people living in isolation in a distant past or an unknown far-away region. Such ideas do not belong to the subject matter of the present work, which attempts to understand Graeco-Roman responses to actual rather than imagined peoples.

The alternative tradition regarding mountaineers who are known and who interact with the cultivators of the plain is also significant in later authors, as one would expect, since here we are dealing with actual peoples, sometimes real enemies of the Greeks and Romans. We find this theme in the work of Cicero, where he refers to the Ligurians as "mountaineers, hard and boorish because of the nature of their land." These are compared with the Campanians, who have "the best land imaginable, fertile with an abundance of crops, a healthy and beautiful town."[5] The Campanians lived in such an ideal environment that even Hannibal's army became soft when it spent the winter there. These are the usual *topoi* of the time.

In the work of Strabo the opposition between mountain and plain is a significant theme, and he deserves special attention here. Strabo, 2.5.26 (c.126) has been cited twice, once for his special adaptation of the environmental theory to Europe and once for the effect of contact between peoples, which it considers. Strabo's own contribution to the environmental theory—or the one we know through him—consists of two elements: (1) the insistence on the opposition between mountain and plain, already present in *Airs, Waters, Places*,[6] which he expands and elaborates; and 2) the idea that a benevolent and strong empire can help restore and maintain the correct balance between the two. Strabo says of Europe that it is particularly suitable for the development of excellence in men and governments. Of the inhabitable part of Europe, the cold mountainous regions furnish by nature only a wretched existence to their inhabitants, yet even the regions of poverty and piracy become civilized as soon as they get good administrators. The Greeks are his example. Another natural advantage of Europe is the fact that "it is diversified with plains and mountains, so that throughout its entire extent the agricultural and civilised elements dwell side by side with the warlike element; but . . . the peace-loving element is more numerous and therefore keeps control over the whole body. . . . and the leading nations, too—formerly the Greeks and later the Macedonians and the Romans—have taken hold and helped."

His views on the social tension between mountains and plains recur in several passages. As will be seen, they often come up in combination with praise for Roman conquest and policing and thus become part of Strabo's theory of imperialism. A start may be made with his description of the Lebanon and

---

[4] Cicero, *de Officiis* 1.11–14; 2.11–15; Lactantius, *Divinae institutiones* 6.10; Isidore, *Etymologiae* 14.2.4–6; Augustine, *de civitate Dei* 14ff. passim. For the later adaptations: A. Pagden, *The Fall of Natural Man* (1982), 19.

[5] Cicero, *De lege agraria* 2.95.

[6] V. supra, chapter 1, pp. 86, n. 114, and 89, n. 122.

Southern Syria, 16.2.18 (755): "Now all the mountainous parts are held by Ituraeans and Arabians, all of whom are robbers, but the people in the plains are farmers; and when the latter are harassed by the robbers at different times they require different kinds of help." He then explains that Pompey destroyed the strongholds of the mountaineers, which they used as bases of operation.[7]

Another troublesome area in those parts is the lava-plateau of Trachonitis, from which region raids were held against the inhabitants of Damascus and the merchants from South Arabia. "But this is less the case now that the gang of bandits has been broken up through the good government established by the Romans and the security guaranteed by the soldiers that are in garrison in Syria" (16.2.20 [c. 756]).

The second region which Strabo places in this category includes the islands Corsica and Sardinia (5.2.7 [c. 224]). Corsica has already been mentioned. It was poor and rough and we saw above that according to Strabo those who occupied the mountains and lived from brigandage were more savage than animals. The Roman army made occasional attacks upon their strongholds and then took large numbers of people as slaves. In Rome, people would marvel at their bestiality. Sardinia was also partly rugged and dangerous, but other parts were very fertile and cultivated, especially with grain. These fertile districts were continuously raided by mountaineers who lived in caves (like the inhabitants of Trachonitis) and refrained from cultivation even where they could do so profitably. They also sailed against the people on the opposite coast, the Pisatae in particular. "Now the military governors who are sent to the island resist the mountaineers part of the time, but sometimes they grow weary of it—when it is not profitable continuously to maintain a camp in unhealthful places, and then the only thing left for them is to employ stratagems (i.e. attack them when they are celebrating)." An episode, more extensively discussed below for other reasons, tells of four thousand adherents of foreign cults, Jews and worshippers of Isis, who were drafted into the army and sent to combat bandits in Sardinia in A.D. 19, that is, not long after Strabo wrote. "If they succumbed to the pestilential climate, it was a cheap loss (*vile damnum*)," according to Tacitus (*Ann.* 2.85). "Usually," explains Strabo, (4.6.4 [203]), "a praefect of equestrian rank is sent to the mountaineers—as is done in the case of other peoples who are absolute barbarians."[8]

Northern Spain has already been mentioned as a region with difficult mountaineers, kept under control by Rome, but there we do not find the contrast between mountains and plain expressed. We do find it, however, in the account of several Alpine peoples: the Ligures who barred the passes to southern France and made raids by sea and land,[9] smaller peoples who were partly wiped out, partly subjugated,[10] and the Salassi, already mentioned, who were in fact subju-

---

[7] Cf. Isaac, *Limits of Empire*, 60–65.

[8] Strabo 4.6.4 (c.203) ἐπὶ δὲ τοὺς ὀρεινοὺς πέμπεταί τις ὕπαρχος τῶν ἱππικῶν ἀνδρῶν, καθάπερ καὶ ἐπ᾽ ἄλλους τῶν τελέως βαρβάρων.

[9] Strabo 4.6.3 (c. 203); Dio 54.24.3.

[10] Strabo 4.6.6 (c. 204): smaller peoples.

gated in two stages, according to Strabo.[11] At first, they were established closer
to the plain, where they exploited gold mines and were in conflict with those
who cultivated the plain. The Romans twice attempted to push them back, but
left them in partial control of the rivers and full control of the passes. After
years of conflict this led to the drastic steps taken in 25 B.C. All mountain
peoples east of the Salassi used to overrun the neighboring plains in all directions, it is reported, murdering all male villagers, including boys, and women
known by divination to be pregnant with male offspring (Strabo 4.6.8f., [c.
206]; Dio 54.22.2). However, Tiberius and Drusus put a stop to this and made
them pay tribute (in their Alpine campaign 15 B.C.).[12] All the same, Strabo adds
some information about the trade which had been carried on between the poor
mountaineers and the plainsmen before the Roman campaign, the only point
where Strabo, perhaps, takes a little distance from the Augustan propaganda
which emphasizes the definite need for the campaign.[13] On the *Tropaeum Alpium* at La Turbie, Augustus claimed to have made war on none of the peoples
without just cause or provocation (Pliny, *NH* 3.136–8; *CIL* 5.7817), "a protesta-
tion," says Syme, "which might perhaps have been spared."

It would be easy to go on listing similar cases, but no point would be served
for the present discussion. There were also several such regions to be added to
the empire after Strabo's time, such as Thrace, with its Mt. Haemus, home of
the Bessoi, "who are called bandits by the bandits themselves."[14] It will be clear
by now that we have in Strabo an interesting combination of his own application of the environmental theory and the achievements of Augustan imperialism
as he presented them throughout his work. However, he was a fine scholar and
we may assume that there was also a good deal of reality in his information.[15]

We do not have to believe in the Hippocratic idea of environment to accept
that mountaineers are poorer than farmers working fertile lowlands. Banditry
and social unrest quite likely existed in many areas where the two lived in close
proximity. Whether these conflicts were always as fierce as the Roman propa-
gandists claim, we cannot know, nor is it obvious that Roman successes in
combating banditry were always as impressive as Strabo reports for his own

[11] Syme, *CAH* 10 (1934), 348: "Terentius Varro applied the ruthless measures that were here and
elsewhere necessary and all but blotted out the very name of the Salassi." Gruen, cited in the next
note, gives various reasons for the campaign. He does not suggest it was necessary to blot out the
very names of any peoples.

[12] Dio 54.22.3–4; Velleius 2.95.1–2; Strabo 4.6.9 (c. 206); Suetonius, *Aug*.21; *Tib.* 9; cf. E. S.
Gruen, *CAH²* 10 (1996), 169–171.

[13] The salutary effect of Augustus's expansion of the empire is one of the constant themes in
Strabo's work.

[14] Strabo 7.5.12: καὶ ὑπὸ τῶν λῃστῶν λῃσταὶ προσαγορεύονται, Tacitus, *Ann.* 4.46 . . .
Thraecum gentibus, qui montium editis sine cultu atque eo ferocius agitabant. The text is somewhat
problematic: incultu MSS. Another emendation: incultius. Furneaux ad loc.: " 'Cultus' is used of
luxuries and refinements of life in 3.30.4."

[15] Susan E. Alcock, *Graecia Capta: The Landscapes of Roman Greece* (Cambridge, 1993), offers
a synthesis, based on interpretations of both the texts and archaeological material. This shows what
can be done if such information is available in sufficient quantities.

time.[16] It is clear, however, that there was a firm conviction that those dwelling in the mountains were a separate and special kind of people. This tradition goes back to the fifth century B.C. and is continued by authors of the Roman period. Such peoples are found all over the empire and all they allegedly have in common is based on the fact that they live in mountainous territory. It is part and parcel of the environmental theory, but represents a remarkable variation of it, since it is applied, not to people living in different parts of the world, but to peoples living in close proximity: mountaineers and plainsmen. Since people living in one and the same part of the world are thus placed firmly in distinct social spheres, due to factors beyond their control, it is proper to describe this approach as proto-racist. As is often the case, Strabo has his own views. He follows the tradition, but argues that the mountaineers are people who require various forms of treatment on the part of the Roman Empire. If they are treated properly, they can be transformed into useful subjects of the empire.

Like so many of the stereotypical forms of thought discussed in this study, this particular determinism was taken over in early modern times. Jean Bodin (1529/30–1596), cited extensively above, discusses the character of mountaineers as opposed to plainsmen at length.[17]

---

[16] Cf. Isaac, *Limits of Empire*, chap. 2; B. D. Shaw, "Banditry in the Roman Empire," *Past and Present* 105 (1984), 3–52; id. "Bandit highlands and lowland peace: the mountains of Isauria-Cilicia," *JESHO* 33 (1990), 199–233; also ib. 237–270; id. "The Bandit," in A. Giardina (ed.), *The Romans* (Chicago and London, 1993), 300–341.

[17] Bodin, *The Six Bookes of a Commonweale*, 563f. with references to antiquity. For Bodin, see above, chapter 1.

Gauls

WE CANNOT KNOW from contemporary sources how the Romans saw the Gauls in the centuries of the greatest Celtic strength. Plato mentions the Celts among the warlike peoples of his time—the others being the Persians, Carthaginians, Iberians, and Thracians (637d). Aristotle lists the same people, while omitting the Iberians (*Pol.* 1324b).[1] Plato and Aristotle, like other contemporaries, knew of the military successes of the Celts in many parts of the Mediterranean world, although they did not know too much about them as a people,[2] while they were hardly or not at all aware of the existence of the Germans.[3] Clearly, Romans must have viewed the Gauls who sacked Rome in 390 B.C. in a different light from those who were provincials after Caesar's conquest.[4] The fear they could inspire in the early encounters is evident from the accounts of some of the later authors who describe these events. Plutarch says that the Romans feared the Gauls more than they feared any other people.[5] The Celtic invasion of Italy in 231 was "the most serious that had ever occurred; all the Italians and especially the Romans had been exposed to great and terrible peril."[6] The subsequent war was "second to no war in history."[7]

The first ancient author to deal with the Celts extensively is Polybius, referring mostly to the conflict between Rome and the Gauls in Northern Italy in the later third century, before and during the Second Punic War.[8] Of Gallia Cis-

---

[1] Newman, 3.326: Aristotle has before him Hdt. 2.167, ὀρέων καὶ Θρήικας καὶ Σκύθας καὶ Πέρσας καὶ Λυδούς (he substitutes the Celts for the Lydians) . . . He probably also has before him Plato, *Laws* 637d . . . and perhaps Xen. *Mem.* 2.1.10. See also *Pol.* 1269b26.

[2] A. Momigliano, *Alien Wisdom* (Cambridge, 1975), 59f.

[3] The first author to use the name *Germani* is Caesar, see below, chapter 12, p. 427.

[4] For discussion of the invasion: T. J. Cornell, *The Beginnings of Rome* (London, 1995), 313–316.

[5] *Marcellus* 3.2: . . . τῶν Γαλατῶν· οὓς μάλιστα Ῥωμαῖοι δεῖσαι δοκοῦσιν, ἅτε δὴ καὶ τὴν πόλιν ὑπ᾿ αὐτῶν ἀποβαλόντες. Plutarch adds that their fear, at the time of the war in Cisalpine Gaul, following the First Punic War, was also clear from the preparations for the war. "Never before or afterwards, it is said, were so many men in arms." See also Polybius 2.20.8; 2.23.7.

[6] Polybius 2.31.7.

[7] 2.35.2: Ὁ μὲν οὖν πρὸς τοὺς Κελτοὺς πόλεμος τοιοῦτον ἔσχε τὸ τέλος, κατὰ μὲν τὴν ἀπόνοιαν καὶ τόλμαν τῶν ἀγωνιζομένων ἀνδρῶν, ἔτι δὲ κατὰ τὰς μάχας καὶ τὸ πλῆθος τῶν ἐν αὐταῖς ἀπολλυμένων καὶ παραταττομένων οὐδενὸς καταδεέστερος τῶν ἱστορημένων, F. W. Walbank, *A Historical Commentary on Polybius*, vol.1 (1957), 211, comments that this is a common τόπος of ancient historians, referring to Thucydides 1.1.2; 21.2, as the first instance. For Thucydides it was of course no τόπος. Walbank notes that Polybius uses it repeatedly.

[8] P. Berger, "Le portrait des Celtes dans les *Histoires* de Polybe," *Ancient Society* 23 (1992), 105–126; É. Foulon, "Polybe et les Celtes (I)," *Les Études Classiques* 68 (2000), 319–354; for the characterization of Celts in Polybius: 341–354, which does not distinguish between Galatians of

alpina he says the population is populous, tall, beautiful, and courageous in war.[9] Although courageous, however, they are led more by passion then calculation (2.35.2f.). They had a habit of excessive drinking, were fond of booty (2.19.4; 3.78.5) and, according to Polybius, had the reputation that they would betray for gain (2.7.5f.). They were unruly (3.49.2) and notoriously fickle, as Polybius says repeatedly.[10] In battle and in raiding they were particularly efficient at the first onslaught (2.33.1–3), but they are said to have had no staying power (2.35.6), an observation which is not confirmed by all of Polybius's own descriptions of battles (e.g., 2.30). These characteristics developed over time into stereotypes, as will be seen.

The first extant Latin author to mention the Celts is Cato the Censor. "Most of Gaul is very actively engaged in two things: the art of war and witty speaking."[11] Although this is not much to go on, it is rather a mild statement when compared with Cato's ranting against the Greeks. Presumably, he felt that Roman society was less threatened by humorous fighters than by the superior culture of the Greeks. At any rate, this is only one passage and there is not much else to cite during the subsequent century. The point regarding their wit is quite unusual. The next author to be mentioned is Posidonius (c. 135–c. 51 B.C.), who wrote a lost Celtic ethnography which is cited by the authors Athenaeus and Strabo. He was almost certainly read by Diodorus, probably also by Caesar, and possibly by Ammianus, who once claims to be using Timagenes.[12]

The next authors whose pronouncements on Gauls are preserved are Cicero and Caesar. Cicero speaks with contempt of all provincials including the Gauls, both in his speeches and in his correspondence.[13] Thus "the most eminent of Gauls are not to be compared with the meanest of Romans; they were an arro-

---

Asia Minor and Celts of western Europe, surely a serious error. In this chapter, we are concerned with the western Celts (Gauls). Foulon makes no clear distinction either between general characterization and between descriptions of isolated incidents in Polybius's account.

[9] Polybius 2. 15.7: τό γε μὴν πλῆθος τῶν ἀνδρῶν, καὶ τὸ μέγεθος καὶ κάλλος τῶν σωμάτων, ἔτι δὲ τὴν ἐν τοῖς πολέμοις τόλμαν, ἐξ αὐτῶν τῶν πράξεων σαφῶς ἔσται καταμαθεῖν. See also: 3.34.2f.

[10] Polybius, 2.32.8: τὴν Γαλατικὴν ἀθεσίαν; 3.70.4: τὴν τῶν Κελτῶν ἀθεσίαν. 3.78.2: Hannibal, himself while using a "Punic artifice" feared τὴν ἀθεσίαν τῶν Κελτῶν.

[11] Cato, Origines fr. 34 (Peter), fr. 2 (Iordan): Pleraque Gallia duas res industriosissime persequitur, rem militarem et argute loqui. Cf. Momigliano, Alien Wisdom, 65. I am not sure why Momigliano says that the Celts loomed large in Cato's Origines. They loomed larger in Polybius's Histories.

[12] There has been a tendency in the modern scholarship to attribute without due caution many passages in these authors to Posidonius, even when there is no explicit evidence; see the discussion by I. G. Kidd, Posidonius II, The Commentary (1988), 308–310. The relevant fragments in Kidd's compilation are 67 (Athenaeus 4.151E–152F), on gladiatorial contests during dinner; 68 (Athenaeus 4.154A–C), and 69 (Athenaeus 6.246C–D), on companions, joining Celts in war, whom they call parasites; 274 (Strabo 4.4.5 [c. 198]); 276 (Strabo 4.4.6 [c. 198]). Ammianus 15.9 claims to be using Timagenes' History (FGrH 88.F2). For discussion, see J. J. Tierney, "The Celtic Ethnography of Posidonius," Proceedings of the Royal Irish Academy no. 60 (1960), 189–275, ascribing far too much to Posidonius; Daphne Nash, "Reconstructing Posidonius' Celtic Ethnography: some Considerations," Britannia 7 (1976), 111–126, offering a critical and realistic re-assessment.

[13] P. A. Brunt, "Laus Imperii," in Roman Imperial Themes (Oxford, 1990), 316f.

gant and faithless people, bound by no religious scruples, the true descendants of those who had burned down the Capitol" (*pro Font.* 27–36). In a letter to his brother he writes: "If fate places you in command of Africans, Spaniards or Gauls, savage and barbarian nations, then your civilisation (*humanitas*) will yet oblige you to take care of their interests, advantage and preservation."[14] Cicero's attitude towards such peoples was distant, as might be expected from a man whose perspective was formed in the capital, the senate, and the law courts. However, he does not apply to them his favorite epithet *levitas*, frivolity, which he uses so often when disparaging Greeks, even though Polybius and later authors, such as Cicero's contemporary Caesar, often call the Gauls fickle.

Caesar's views of the Gauls developed during years of direct military experience in Gaul. He wrote an ethnographic excursus on the Gauls after spending eight years there, when he visited all parts of it. It has already been noted that Caesar could be unconventional in his observations, for instance in his description of the Suebi.[15] He attributes their characteristics, as he sees them, to lifestyle and diet, rather than to external factors such as climate and geography. It is therefore not clear, as has been argued, that he wrote under the influence of the traditional view of the inhabitants of northwestern Europe, notably that represented in Posidonius and Varro.[16] If he follows any ancient authority, Polybius might be the better choice if literary influence has to be posited, which is uncertain. However, it is important to note that he does not write in the spirit of disdain that marks his contemporary Cicero's approach. There are not many passages where Caesar speaks with contempt of the Gauls. "The Gallic mentality was ready and eager to rush into wars, but very bad at enduring defeats" (3.19.6). This clearly corresponds with Polybius's description. Caesar talks of impulsiveness and inconstancy (*levitas*) of the Gauls,[17] their sudden and impetuous plans,[18] and, again, their fickleness.[19] All this is uninformative and amounts to the same thing: the Gauls were impulsive, but it echoes Polybius' qualifica-

---

[14] Cic., *ad Quintum fratrem* 1.1.27: quod si te sors Afris aut Hispanis aut Gallis praefecisset, immanibus ac barbaris nationibus, tamen esset humanitatis tuae consulere eorum commodis et utilitati salutique servire; for this passage see Greg Woolf, "Becoming Roman, Staying Greek," *PCPS* 40 (1994), 116–143, at 119; for *humanitas* see id., *Becoming Roman: The Origins of Provincial Civilization in Gaul* (Cambridge, 1998), 54–60. The idea of *humanitas* was taken up by the authors of the Enlightenment, notably Voltaire, from Cicero: Peter Gay, *The Enlightenment: An Interpretation* (New York, 1966), 107–109.

[15] chapter 1, p. 97.

[16] J. J. Tierney, *Proc. Roy. Irish Acad.* 60 (1960), 189–275; Momigliano, *Alien Wisdom*, 71. Momigliano could not have seen the salutary re-assessment by Daphne Nash, *Britannia* 7 (1976), 111–126, at 126: "It is time that Caesar was recognized as a primary authority on the Celts, and not regarded as a plagiarist of Poseidonios." Kidd, *The Commentary* (1988), 309: "To suggest that Caesar in vi.11–28, simply rehashed material observed by Posidonius perhaps fifty years earlier (even if supplemented later) is improbable."

[17] *BG* 2.1.3: mobilitate et levitate animi. Cf. Livy 22.1.3. Tacitus applied the term to the Arabs (*Tac. Ann.* 12.14). Paradoxically, Cicero, who is so persistent in calling the Greeks *leves*, does not describe the Gauls in such terms.

[18] 3.8.3: Gallorum subita et repentina consilia.

[19] 4.13.3: Gallorum infirmitas.

tions.[20] Yet, if there was one aspect of Gallic culture which Caesar knew from personal experience, it was their behavior in battle. It is not credible that he would have copied Polybius's assessment of them as fighters if he had not agreed with it. Whether he also wants to emphasize their cruelty is not so clear.[21] This may be the appropriate point to note that the range of negative qualities applicable to foreigners is necessarily limited, for they depend on the positive characteristics which people attribute to themselves. Just as the Gauls were inconstant, so were the Greeks. Inconstancy, *levitas*, is important, for, as noted above, it is the opposite of one of the best Roman qualities, *gravitas*. When considering the Gauls, Caesar speaks with admiration of Vercingetorix (e.g., 7.89.1–2). However, admiration for an enemy leader is common, as we have seen repeatedly, and does not necessarily include respect for the people as a whole. Yet such respect is not altogether absent. Caesar emphasizes that the Gauls were fighting for their freedom, and that subjection to Rome meant *servitus* (3.8.4). This is a mark of respect, the opposite of the description "born for slavery" which some authors apply to eastern peoples.

Even so, Caesar emphasizes the contrast between the warlike *Germani* and the deteriorating Gauls. This is best seen in his remarks about the Volcae Tectosages, a Gallic people who had established themselves in the heart of the southern Germanic area.[22] The Volcae, he says, live in the same economic conditions as the Germanic tribes, so that their pattern of life and personal phy-

---

[20] Momigliano, *Alien Wisdom*, 72, refers to Michel Rambaud, *La déformation historique dans les Commentaires de César* (Paris, 1953), 326, who, interestingly, calls these utterances typical examples of "déformation historique." "If it was a deformation," writes Momigliano, "it was anticipated by Posidonius. Caesar found in him not only valuable factual information about places and institutions, but an encouraging analysis of the weakness of Celtic society." I think Momigliano goes too far if he considers such phrases "an analysis of society." Furthermore, I am not certain why Momigliano is so certain that these judgments derive directly and only from Posidonius. They are not found in any of the indubitably Posidonian passages which have been preserved. Diodorus 5 is, according to Momigliano, p. 67, also based partly on Posidonius, a peculiar idea, for it contains a quite different view of the Gauls. In any event, the essence of these judgments is that they are commonplaces, whether taken from Posidonius or not. Another observation that I find hard to understand is Momigliano's statement: "It is certainly a paradox that Posidonius, the friend and *protégé* of Pompey should help Caesar through his historical work to conquer Gaul and therefore to destroy his rival." If Caesar took all the commonplaces about Gauls in his work from Posidonius— which is far from clear to me—then it is preposterous to say that this helped him in conquering Gaul. Wars are not won on a diet of prejudices. The most one can say is that the commonplaces he may have found in Posidonius did not affect Caesar's judgment when it counted. Also, any attempt to understand Caesar's account of the Gauls in perspective should be taken seriously and Rambaud, pp. 325–327, seems to make sense.

[21] Zeitler in H. Jankuhn and D. Timpe, *Beiträge zum Verständnis der Germania des Tacitus*, Teil I: *Bericht über die Kolloquien der Kommission für die Altertumskunde Nord- und Mitteleuropas im Jahr 1986* (Göttingen, 1989), 49f., notes that Caesar in his excursus on the Gauls emphasizes their cruelty It is true that he describes their human sacrifices with disapproval (6.16) and their manner of treating widows if there are doubts about the manner of death of the husband (6.19). Otherwise, however, and throughout the work he does not say much about their cruelty. Exceptions are 7.38 and 7.77, not an impressive harvest for eight books of accounts of a war with the Gauls.

[22] See also chapter 1, p. 96f.

sique and condition are the same as those of the Germans (6.24.2–5). These Gauls maintain their sober lifestyle and military prowess and he contrasts them with the Celts of Gaul, who had developed their economic life through the propinquity of the Roman province and its supplies of consumer goods, and thus gradually lost their supremacy in the skills of war (24.5–6). The processes described here are familiar. The Gauls lose their manhood through the contaminating influence of Roman prosperity, but a single group, which remained free from this effect, did not change. Here, then, we recognize the familiar pattern: soft societies undermine strong groups through association.

Caesar could be independent in his observations, but some passages also make it clear that Caesar was influenced by traditional ideas. For example, the Belgae were better fighters than other peoples in Gaul. Caesar gives different reasons for this in two separate passages. In the first he says it was because most of them were of German origin.[23] However, they had moved across the Rhine long ago and were closely connected by proximity and intermarriage with the Remi. So here the move to Gaul, a better land, and the tendency to mixed marriages did not affect their military capacities, as should have happened according to the common belief that migration to a rich environment leads to deterioration.[24] Perhaps Caesar was less impressed with the notion of pure lineage and the corrupting effect of wealth than some other Roman authors, which would again be a sign of independent thinking on his part. However, in the second passage Caesar says that the Belgae were the most valorous, "because they are the most distant from the culture and civilisation of the (Roman) province, and because the merchants visit them least, who import the wares that induce effeminacy, while they are closest to the Germans who live across the Rhine, with whom they continuously fight."[25] Among the Belgae, he says, "the Nervii were particularly fierce and courageous; they did not allow any wine or other luxuries to be imported and hence traders had no access to them."[26] These two passages represent various entirely traditional ideas: the

---

[23] 2.4: plerosque Belgas esse ortos ab Germanis Rhenumque antiquitus traductos propter loci fertilitatem ibi consedisse.

[24] Sherwin-White, *Racial Prejudice,* 20 concludes about Caesar and the Gauls: "Because of this [Roman] sense of superiority the question of racial feeling inspired by fear simply did not arise." As I mentioned earlier, I do not agree that racial feeling occurs only when inspired by fear. More important: when it is inspired by fear this may be irrational fear. However, Caesar and the Gauls are a special case. He had subjected them successfully, so he really may not have been afraid of them. Furthermore, his *Gallic War* contains a political message and the message certainly is not that the Romans should fear their newly conquered subjects. Even so, Caesar's work contains many of the traditional commonplaces about northern foreigners.

[25] *BG* 1.1 quod a cultu atque humanitate provinciae longissime absunt, minimeque ad eos mercatores saepe commeant atque ea quae ad effeminandos animos pertinent important, proximique sunt Germanis, qui trans Rhenum incolunt, quibuscum continenter bellum gerunt. Cf. Strabo 4.4.3f. (c. 196), who says that all the Gallic people are fighters by nature, but those who live more to the north and along the ocean are more bellicose. Thus the *Belgae* are the bravest and among them the *Bellovaci* and *Suessiones* the most outstanding.

[26] 2.15.4: nullum aditum esse ad eos mercatoribus; nihil pati vini reliquarumque rerum inferri, quod eis rebus relanguescere animos eorum et remitti virtutem existimarent. For the evidence of

corrupting influence of trade as opposed to the salutary effect of isolation (cf. Tacitus on the Germans) and the softening effects of good living and wine.

Caesar reports that the Suebi also did not import wine because it makes men soft and effeminate.[27] Whatever the truth of these claims or, rather, wherever Caesar found this information, there is no confirmation of it anywhere.[28] Posidonius confirms that some Germans at least "drink milk and their wine unmixed."[29] Tacitus says that "the Germans produce liquor out of barley or wheat, which was fermented into something like wine. Those living on the bank of the Rhine also buy wine."[30] They are also known to have been avid consumers of a sort of mead made from honey.[31] Of course, Germans who lived farther to the north would have found it more difficult to acquire wine. The one point that we should not doubt, clearly, is Caesar's assessment of the military capabilities of the various Gallic peoples. This represents personal experience as commander in the field. It is probably also true, as he says, that the Belgae and Helvetii[32] were fighting continuously with the Germans and it is reasonable that this would have contributed to their military prowess. His other explanations are a different matter and should be considered critically.

The first author to write extensively about the Gauls after Caesar is Diodorus.[33] He relates at length how addicted the Gauls are to wine (5.26.2–3). They are extremely greedy,[34] an accusation repeated later by Plutarch (see below) and

---

bronze, glass, and silver cups (i.e., luxury goods) found beyond the Roman frontier: C. R. Whittaker, *Frontiers of the Roman Empire* (Baltimore and London, 1994), 122–125; L. Hedeager, "A quantitative Analysis of Roman imports in Europe north of the limes," in K. Kristiansen and D. Paludan-Müller (eds.), *New Directions in Archaeology* (Copenhagen, 1977), 191–216.

[27] 4.2.6: Vinum ad se omnino importari non sinunt, quod ea re ad laborem ferendum remollescere homines atque effeminari arbitrantur. Caesar's excursus about the Suebi: Trzaska-Richter, *Furor Teutonicus* (1991), 82–87.

[28] Ancient literature contains peculiar ideas about the effect of wine. Plutarch, *Camillus* 15, informs us that when the Gauls invaded Italy in the early fourth century they tasted wine for the first time. They were so obsessed with the taste of it that they decided to move to the land that produced it.

[29] Jacoby, *FGH* 87 F22; Theiler 188; Edelstein and Kidd, 73: Γερμανοὶ δέ, ὡς ἱστορεῖ Ποσειδώνιος ἐν τῇ τριακοστῇ, ἄριστον προσφέρονται κρέα μεληδὸν ὠπτῇ μένα καὶ ἐπιπίνουσι γάλα καὶ τὸν οἶνον ἄκρατον. The identity of these Germans has been much discussed, but cannot concern us here. Cf. W. Theiler, *Poseidonios: die Fragmente* II *Erläuterungen* (Berlin, 1982), 111; I. G. Kidd, *Posidonius* II. *The Commentary* I (Cambridge, 1988), 323–326. As already mentioned, abstention from wine, or drinking wine, mixed or unmixed, drinking blood, and drinking milk, were all considered significant customs for foreigners as early as Herodotus in his description of the customs of the Scythians; cf. F. Hartog, *Le miroir d'Hérodote* (1980), 179–184.

[30] Tac., *Germ.* 23: Potui umor ex hordeo aut frumento, in quandam similitudinem vini corruptus; proximi ripae et vinum mercantur. Cf. comments ad loc. A. A. Lund, *P. Cornelius Tacitus. Germania* (1988), 174f.

[31] "A drink known to all Aryan-speaking peoples," says Anderson, *Cornelii Taciti, De Origine et Situ Germanorum* (Oxford, 1938), 124. This leaves us with the question whether speakers of Turkish or Semitic languages failed to discover it, or had no taste for it.

[32] *BG* 1.1: Qua de causa Helvetii quoque reliquos Gallos virtute praecedunt.

[33] For Diodorus's presumed use of Posidonius, see above, n. 20.

[34] 5.27.4: καίπερ ὄντων τῶν Κελτῶν φιλαργύρων καθ' ὑπερβολήν.

which is slightly unusual to be aimed at western peoples. Like others, he is impressed with their external appearance: tall, blond, strong (5.28.1; 32.2). They are courageous, aggressive warriors who invade other peoples' lands (5.32.4–5).

Strabo has much to say about the Gauls, far more than can be treated seriously here, but a few themes should be discussed. "The barbarians beyond the Massiliotes became more and more subdued over time on account of the military superiority of the Romans and instead of carrying on war have already turned to civic life and farming."[35] This is one of many passages in Strabo where he depicts the military superiority of Rome as the root of stability and prosperity. It is also a positive version of two traditional concepts: the opposition between warrior peoples and farming peoples and the common idea, discussed in chapter 2, that Romanization is a form of adaptation to being slaves. However, Strabo does not use these terms here.

"The whole people is war-mad and both high-spirited and quick for battle, although otherwise simple and not ill mannered,"[36] they are naïve and easy to defeat with stratagems. "As for their might, it arises partly from their large physique and from their numbers." Because they are so naïve and impulsive they always support neighbors whom they feel have been maltreated. The statement about Gallic belligerence and impulsiveness much resembles Caesar's repeated pronouncements; their belligerence is also mentioned by Cato. However, in Caesar's work there is no suggestion that there is any direct connection between the belligerence of a people, their physical size, and the numbers of their population. The large number of Gauls is brought out earlier, by Polybius. While it is an obvious fact that the Gauls and Germans were taller on average than the inhabitants of Italy, it is also quite clear that Strabo is here presenting a traditional motive. *Airs, Waters, Places* (24) already says that Europeans are wild, courageous, and belligerent, especially those in the mountains, who also happen to be light of skin and tall. Those living on poor land in particular are "hard in physique and steady, blonde rather than dark, stubborn and independent in character and in temper" (24).[37] In late antiquity Vitruvius (6.1.4), possibly, but not certainly citing Posidonius, applies this to all of those living in the North: they are better fighters but slow-witted.

These parallels show how even a fine scholar like Strabo could mix facts with traditional commonplaces that had circulated for centuries. Next follow

---

[35] Strabo 4.1.5 (c. 180): ἐξημερουμένων δ᾽ ἀεὶ τῶν ὑπερκειμένων βαρβάρων καὶ ἀντὶ τοῦ πολεμεῖν τετραμμένων ἤδη πρὸς πολιτείας καὶ γεωργίας διὰ τὴν τῶν Ῥωμαίων ἐπικράτειαν.

[36] Strabo 4.4.2 (c. 195): τὸ σύμπαν φῦλον . . . ἀρειμάνιον ἐστι καὶ θυμικόν τε καὶ ταχὺ πρὸς μάχην, ἄλλως δὲ ἁπλοῦν καὶ οὐ κακόηθες; this passage is considered by Theiler to derive from Posidonius and therefore included among his fragments as No. 33. There is no real evidence in support of this attribution. The only part of Strabo's Celtic ethnography expressly referring to Posidonius is the passage on head trophies collected by Gauls: F274.5–7, Edelstein and Kidd (Strabo 4.4.5 [c. 197f.]); Diodorus 5.29.4–5; see Kidd, *Posidonius: the Commentary* I (ii) 936–938.

[37] Note also Herodotus 4.108, part of his description of Scythia: Βουδῖνοι δὲ, ἔθνος ἐὸν μέγα καὶ πολλόν, γλαυκόν τε πᾶν ἰσχυρῶς ἐστι καὶ πυρρόν. And, of course, Tacitus, *Germania* 4.

418 · *CHAPTER 11* ·

various other generalizations which echo Caesar's repeated descriptions: Strabo notes the simplicity and straightforwardness of the Gauls.[38] He then repeats that at present "they are all at peace, since they have been enslaved and are living according to the commands of the Romans who subdued them."[39] This is one of the numerous passages in which Strabo attempts to contribute to Augustan and Tiberian propaganda—whether he ever was thanked for it, like some Latin poets and prose writers we do not know. Strabo continues, saying that he derives his account of the Gauls from the way they used to live in earlier times as well as from customs that still exist among the Germans. "For these peoples are by nature and in their institutions similar and related to each other; they also live in a country with a common boundary, as it is divided by the river Rhine, and most parts are similar, although Germania is further to the North . . . And therefore it is easy for them to migrate."[40] This passage is significant in what it says about Strabo's view of river boundaries as barriers, but that is not a topic to be discussed here. Strabo finds that the Gauls and Germans "are related" and he states unequivocally that there was easy movement by both peoples. This in fact denies Tacitus's later view that the Germans were autochthonous.

The next text to be considered here is Tacitus's report on the arguments for and against admission of Gauls from Gallia Comata into the Senate (*Ann.* 11.23–25). A fragment of Claudius's original speech on this subject has been found in Lyons (*ILS* 212).[41] The arguments against the inclusion of Gauls in the Senate as seen in these two sources are of interest. To begin with, there was resistance to the inclusion of any provincials in the Senate, which, it was argued, ought to remain a body of Roman citizens from Italy. "Is it not enough that Veneti and Insubres have already burst into the Senate-house, without having a mob of foreigners inflicted on us as if we were a captured city?"[42] The Veneti and Insubres were Gauls from Gallia Transpadana who had received Roman citizenship in 49 B.C. That measure had clearly been unpopular with some influential people in Rome. Now Gauls from across the Alps were regarded as worse. "The Roman Senate will be swamped with foreigners and Rome will be, as it were, a captive city." This language belongs to the category of expressions analyzed in some detail above (*vincendo victi sumus,* the victors

[38] τὸ ἁπλοῦν καὶ αὐθέκαστον.
[39] 4.4.2 (c. 195): νυνὶ μὲν οὖν ἐν εἰρήνῃ πάντες εἰσὶ δεδουλωμένοι καὶ ζῶντες κατὰ τὰ προστάγματα τῶν ἑλόντων αὐτοὺς Ρωμαίων,
[40] 4.4.2 (c. 196): καὶ γὰρ τῇ φύσει καὶ τοῖς πολιτεύμασιν ἐμφερεῖς εἰσι καὶ συγγενεῖς ἀλλήλοις οὗτοι, ὅμορόν τε οἰκοῦσι χώραν διοριζομένην τῷ Ρήνῳ ποταμῷ καὶ παραπλήσια ἔχουσαν τὰ πλεῖστα. ἀρκτικωτέρα δ᾽ ἐστὶν ἡ Γερμανία, κρινομένων τῶν τε νοτίων μερῶν πρὸς τὰ νότια καὶ τῶν ἀρκτικῶν πρὸς τὰ ἀρκτικά. διὰ τοῦτο δὲ καὶ τὰς μεταναστάσεις αὐτῶν ῥαδίως ὑπάρχειν συμβαίνει,
[41] M. T. Griffin, "The Lyons Tablet and Tacitean Hindsight," *CQ* 32 (1982), 404–418, and see now Ronald Syme, *The Provincial at Rome* and *Rome and the Balkans 80 BC–AD 14*, Anthony Birley, ed. (Exeter, 1999), containing a monograph, written by Syme in 1934. Analysis of the speech in Tacitus: chapter 11; analysis of the text from Lyons: chapter 12.
[42] an parum quod Veneti et Insubres curiam inruperint, nisi coetus alienigenarum velut captivitas inferatur? Cf. Syme's comments, p. 91.

are vanquished by the conquered). This was the usual response to the influence of immigrants amidst Roman aristocratic society. There will be no honor left for the remaining aristocrats or any poor senator from Latium. "Everything will be full of those rich Gauls."[43] Other texts also describe Gaul as particularly wealthy. In the present context the emphasis placed on it makes the argument sound familiarly xenophobic. In our own times it is one of the standard arguments against immigration that foreigners appropriate positions which should go to local people who deserve them better. The last point made is that the ancestors of these Gauls fought Caesar and, in the remote past, besieged the Capitol—an argument used already by Cicero in *Pro Fonteio*, cited above. To hold the deeds of their forefathers against a people is another form of discrimination with reference to group characteristics. At the same time, it is worth noting what is *not* said. The Gauls are not described as inferior or unworthy per se. Thus, the thrust of the argument is that the Roman aristocrats are afraid of competition and of losing their dominance in the Senate to provincials. There is no hostility toward the Gauls as persons or denigration of them as barbarians, but there is jealousy of their riches. There is no fear that the lineage of Roman aristocrats or Romans in general would be compromised by foreign intrusions.[44]

Claudius, in his speech, observes that immigrants joined the aristocracy in Rome from the beginning and that Rome never excluded foreigners. "What was the ruin of Sparta and Athens, but this, that mighty as they were in war, they spurned as aliens those whom they had conquered?"[45] Various peoples have been at war with Rome and were then integrated into the empire. The Gauls were subjected in a relatively short war. "Thereafter was a continuous and firm peace. Now they are linked to us through customs, education and marriage; let them therefore bring us their gold and their riches, rather than keep them separate."[46]

This clear expression of the principle of the integration of subject peoples is made explicit here in an important imperial address. We know that it happened in practice, and it is therefore valuable to see that there was a conscious idea of doing so. Claudius also formulates what is needed: a long-term habit of peaceful behavior, the adoption of a Roman way of life, education as well as social integration. Claudius ignores, as a matter of convenience, the revolt of A.D. 21,

---

[43] oppleturos omnia divites illos. An unusual accusation appears in Plutarch, *Pyrrhus* 26.6, where the author tells of Pyrrhus's Gallic troops who plundered royal graves, "the Gauls being a people inordinately greedy." Diodorus 5.27.4 says the same (see above). See also Manilius, *Astronomica* 4.793: quot fert Gallia dives. Manilius wrote in the reigns of Augustus and Tiberius. Josephus, *BJ* 2.16.4 (372) emphasizes the great wealth and productivity of the Gauls.

[44] Syme, *The Provincial at Rome* (1999), 41f.: "The literary sources for the history of the early Principate will be scrutinized in vain for evidence of the contention that senators from Spain and Narbonensis represented a scandalous innovation."

[45] *Ann.* 11.24: quid aliud exitio Lacedaemoniis et Atheniensibus fuit, quamquam armis pollerent, nisi quod victos pro alienigenis arcebant?

[46] *Ann.* 11.24.10: continua inde ac fida pax. Iam moribus artibus adfinitatibus nostris mixti aurum et opes suas inferant potius quam separati habeant.

led by Julius Florus and Julius Sacrovir.[47] Furthermore, Claudius's measures did not prevent the revolt of Vindex[48] and the large-scale support in Gaul for the Batavian Revolt in 69.[49] Finally, it has been pointed out that Claudius's decision had little effect, for the record shows hardly any senators from Gallia Comata,[50] an indication, perhaps, that Claudius's liberal views were not shared by his successors. Whatever the results, it is interesting that in this debate nothing worse was said of the Gauls than that they were foreigners and had been recent enemies.

No less remarkable in this respect is Juvenal, whom we have noted as one of the fiercest enemies of Greeks, Egyptians, Jews, and Syrians in Rome. One of his attacks on these peoples occurs in the beginning of his seventh satire (7.13, discussed above). The same satire contains one of the few references in his work to Gauls, in a section on the poor state of rhetoric in Rome. "Better go to Gaul or to Africa, that nursing mother of lawyers, if you would make a living by your tongue!"[51] The reason is that Rome is too expensive. Thus all Juvenal has to say here about Gaul is that, like Africa, it has good schools of rhetoric. This may remind us to some extent of Cato, who found the Gauls witty speakers. Strabo also observed that the Gauls, if coaxed, would be practical and engage in study and languages.[52] Other occasions for Juvenal to mention Gallia again refer to the study of rhetoric there.[53] East and West are placed in marked contrast in a passage already cited: "You despise perchance, and deservedly, the unwarlike Rhodian and the scented Corinthian: what harm will their resined youths do you, or the smooth legs of the entire breed? But keep clear of rugged

---

[47] *Ann.* 3.40–7; R. Syme, *Tacitus* (Oxford, 1958), 458–463; A. J. Christopherson, "The provincial assembly of the Three Gauls in the Julio-Claudian period," *Historia* 17 (1968), 351–366; E. M. Wightman, *Roman Trier and the Treveri* (London, 1970); Woolf, *Becoming Roman*, 21f.; 31f.

[48] P. A. Brunt, "The revolt of Vindex and the Fall of Nero," reprinted with revisions in *Roman Imperial Themes*, 9–32, 481–487; J. B. Hainsworth, "Verginius and Vindex," *Historia* 11 (1962), 86–96; S. L. Dyson, "Native revolts in the Roman empire," *Historia* 20 (1971), 239–274; id., "Native revolt patterns in the Roman Empire," *ANRW* 2.3, 138–175; E. M. Wightman, "Il y avait en Gaule deux sortes de Gaulois," in D. M. Pippidi (ed.), *Assimilation et résistance à la culture gréco-romaine dans le monde ancien* (Paris, 1976), 407–419.

[49] Tacitus, *Hist.* 4.12–37; 54–79; 5.14–26; Brunt, "Tacitus on the Batavian Revolt," *Latomus* 19 (1960), 494–517, reprinted with revisions in *Roman Imperial Themes*, 33–52; 481–487. See also the earlier discussion by Walser, *Rom, das Reich und die fremden Völker* (1951), 86–128. Walser argues that Tacitus misrepresents this revolt and other provincial revolts by re-interpreting them in Roman terms. These revolts are no response to maladministration, but resistance against taxation, according to Walser.

[50] Syme, *Tacitus*, 461–462; Sherwin-White, *Racial Prejudice*, 52–61; W. Eck, "Die Struktur der Städte in den nordwestlichen Provinzen und ihr Beitrag zur Administration des Reiches," in W. Eck and H. Galsterer (eds.), *Die Stadt in Oberitalien und in den nordwestlichen Provinzen des römischen Reiches* (Mainz, 1991), 73–84; J. F. Matthews, *Western Aristocracies and Imperial Court: AD 364–425* (Oxford, 1975), 349f.; K. Hopkins, *Death and Renewal* (Cambridge, 1982), 184–193.

[51] 7.147: accipiat te Gallia vel potius nutricula causidicorum Africa, si placuit mercedem ponere linguae.

[52] Strabo 4.4.2 (c. 195); Courtney, p. 368, also refers to 4.1.5 (c. 181), but that is not so relevant, for it mentions Gauls studying Greek in Massilia.

[53] 7.214; 15.111f.

Spain, avoid the land of the Gaul and the Dalmatian shore" (8.116). This is the old contrast between an effeminate East and manly West which we first encountered in the Hippocratic treatise. Over the centuries it was sometimes transformed in more of a north–south opposition, but in Juvenal's eyes the east–west contrast was far more significant. It is clear, at any rate, that Juvenal's xenophobia focused on the immigrants from the eastern part of the empire, wherever they came from, while Gallia, Hispania, and Africa could evoke some admiration.[54]

It is likely too that the Gauls formed less of a conspicuous presence in the city of Rome than the immigrants from the East and therefore annoyed Juvenal and people like him not as much. Cassius Dio should be mentioned again here, with his comments about the triple origins of Caracalla and his corresponding faults.[55] Possibly one should not read too much into this statement and not take it too literally. However, Caracalla was an important figure in Dio's life and he felt strongly about him. The comments on him seem spontaneous and serious. Born in Lyons, Caracalla had the inconstancy, cowardice, and impulsiveness of Gaul.[56] Inconstancy and impulsiveness are familiar terms since Polybius, but Dio's accusation of "cowardice" is unexpected, for three earlier authors, Polybius, Caesar, Diodorus, and later Strabo and Ammianus, variously describe them as enthusiastic fighters. It may be a random accusation, or a commonplace of Dio's time. The latter is not so likely, for Dio describes the Emperor Claudius as a coward without attributing this to the fact that he too had been born in Lyons. Furthermore, it has already been observed, but may be worth repeating, that Dio applies these age-old stereotypes to a man who had been born in Lyons, but did not grow up in Gaul, and that Lyons was the prosperous capital of a major Roman province. The implication is that, somehow, the location of one's birth gave one the presumed characteristics of the local inhabitants, which was a basic assumption of Ptolemy the Geographer.[57] It also shows that, centuries after Claudius wanted to enroll them in the Roman senate, a serious, aristocratic historian still applied the old stereotypes associated with Gauls.

Well-known, but not so commonly mentioned in the ancient literature as one might have expected, is the influence in Gaul of the Druids.[58] Gallic religion

[54] Cf. Syme, *The Provincial at Rome*, 43f. explains Juvenal's lack of hostility towards senators from the western provinces: "all the great names in Roman letters from Tiberius to Hadrian, with the solitary exception of Juvenal [but see the editor's note 30], and many of the lesser, are contributed by the provinces and by a quasi-provincial region of Italy, the Transpadana." Syme returns to this in *Tacitus* (1958), 609f.: "Juvenal could have turned the edge of his satire against the successful upstarts from the western provinces. . . . Juvenal refrains, seeking easier topics, and more congenial—decayed noblemen or indigent Greek adventurers."

[55] See above, chapter 1, p. 146 n. 359.

[56] Dio 78 (77) 6.1a: τῆς μὲν Γαλατίας τὸ κοῦφον καὶ τὸ δειλὸν καὶ τὸ θρασύ. τὸ κοῦφον clearly translates *levitas* and τὸ θρασύ presumably renders *mobilitas animi*.

[57] See chapter 1.

[58] It is not clear when the Druids became known to Greek and Latin authors. Diogenes Laertius 1.6 refers to them as ancient philosophers among the barbarians, paired with the Gymnosophists. This may go back to a relatively early source.

was regarded as full of superstition, condoning the ultimate barbarism, human sacrifice. Diodorus writes that the Gauls practiced human sacrifice and it may be relevant to consider his formulation: in a well-known passage he explains that the Gauls had bards and "a sort of philosophers and experts in religion, highly honoured among them whom they call Druids. The Gauls also use seers whom they regard as respectable and these men predict the future."[59] This raises the question whether the Druids or another class of dignitaries were responsible for the human sacrifices. Caesar, however, does not know of separate classes of bards and seers and attributes to the Druids responsibility for worship, sacrifice, and full authority in religious and judicial matters.[60] Strabo lists three classes held in special honor: Bards, Vates, and Druids. Of these the Vates deal with religion and are natural philosophers, while the Druids study not only natural but also moral philosophy. They are regarded as the most just of men and therefore are entrusted with private and public arbitration.[61] In any case, the Romans looked askance at Druidism and they banned it in the reigns of Tiberius[62] and perhaps again in that of Claudius.[63]

[59] Diodorus 5.31.2: φιλόσοφοί τέ τινές εἰσι καὶ θεολόγοι περιττῶς τιμώμενοι, οὓς δρουίδας ὀνομάζουσι. χρῶνται δὲ καὶ μάντεσιν, ἀποδοχῆς μεγάλης ἀξιοῦντες αὐτούς· οὗτοι δὲ διά τε τῆς οἰωνοσκοπίας καὶ διὰ τῆς τῶν ἱερείων θυσίας τὰ μέλλοντα προλέγουσι, καὶ πᾶν τὸ πλῆθος ἔχουσιν ὑπήκοον. There is no indication anywhere in the text that this information derives from Posidonius. The bards are mentioned also by Athenaeus, who cites Posidonius, but that is no basis for the attribution of Diodorus's information about the Druids to Posidonius; cf. Athenaeus 6.246c–d = Posidonius F69 Kidd, commentary: Edelstein and Kidd, *Posidonius* II: *The Commentary:* (i) *Testimonia and Fragments 1–149* (Cambridge, 1988), 316–318. Nash, *Britannia* 7 (1976), 123–126, convincingly argues (against Tierney) that the information of Caesar about Druids did not derive from Posidonius in particular and should be taken seriously. Note also Cicero, *pro Fonteio* 31.

[60] Caesar, *BG* 6.13.4: illi rebus divinis intersunt, sacrificia publica ac privata procurant, religiones interpretantur. . . . 5: nam fere de omnibus contro versiis publicis privatisque constituunt

[61] Strabo 4.4.4 (c. 197): Παρὰ πᾶσι δ᾽ ὡς ἐπίπαν τρία φῦλα τῶν τιμωμένων διαφερόντως ἐστί, βάρδοι τε καὶ ὀυάτεις καὶ δρυΐδαι· βάρδοι μὲν ὑμνηταὶ καὶ ποιηταί, ὀυάτεις δὲ ἱεροποιοὶ καὶ φυσιολόγοι, δρυΐδαι δὲ πρὸς τῇ φυσιολογίᾳ καὶ τὴν ἠθικὴν φιλοσοφίαν ἀσκοῦσι· δικαιότατοι δὲ νομίζονται καὶ διὰ τοῦτο πιστεύονται τάς τε ἰδιωτικὰς κρίσεις καὶ τὰς κοινάς

[62] See below, reference to Pliny.

[63] Suetonius, *Claudius* 25.5, where it is noted that under Augustus this religion had been prohibited to Roman citizens. Cf. Caesar, *BG* 6.13f.; 16; 18; Pomponius Mela 3.2.19; Aurelius Victor, *liber de Caesaribus* 4.2. Cf. H. Last, "Rome and the Druids: a Note," *JRS* 39 (1949), 1–5, argues that the Roman explanation has to be accepted. The Druids were truly savage and disgusting. A. Momigliano, *Claudius, the Emperor and his Achievement* (Cambridge, 1961), 92f., n.18 with references to older literature. Momigliano perhaps tends to systematize the Roman measures too much. On the Druids in general: S. Piggott, *The Druids* (London, 1968); Anne Ross, "Ritual and the Druids," in Miranda J. Green (ed.), *The Celtic World* (London and New York, 1995), 423–444 and, in general, Barry Cunliffe, *The Ancient Celts* (Oxford, 1997); Ramsay McMullen, *Romanization in the Time of Augustus* (New Haven, 2000), chapter 4, at 88f. On religion in Roman Gaul: G. Woolf, *Becoming Roman*, chapter 8 and the works by P. M. Duval, *Les dieux de la Gaule* (Paris, 2d ed. 1976); J.-J. Hatt, *Mythes et dieux de la Gaule* (Paris, 1989). As for Rome and human sacrifice: it was a source of embarrassment that Rome itself followed instructions by the Sibylline books and buried alive two Greeks and two Gauls, not only at the time of the war with the Insubres after the First Punic War (Plutarch, *Marcellus* 3.7.1), but still in the late second century (*Quaestiones Ro-*

The prohibition was in any event not fully effective, for Druids were involved in the revolt of Boudicca (Tac., *Ann.* 14.30.3) and in that of A.D. 69.[64] It is not clear, therefore, how active the Romans were in suppressing Druidism, or even why they thought it desirable to do so.[65] It may not be very wrong to accept the Elder Pliny's explicit statements about the reason for their persecution. In chapters discussing *magicae vanitates* and *ars portentosa*, which he dislikes, he includes human sacrifice as a particularly abominable rite, even in Rome not abolished until 97 B.C., "so that down to that date it is manifest that such abominable rites were practised."[66] It should be remembered that these rites were not necessarily seen as merely inhuman, they may well have been regarded as positively dangerous. Among the many peoples who indulged in them even in living memory are the two Gallic provinces. "Hence Tiberius Caesar as emperor suppressed their Druids and that sort of seers and medicine men."[67] Pliny then continues saying that the practice still exists in Britain in a very active way.[68] He wrote this certainly after Claudius's reputed measures

---

manae 83/283f). Plutarch is puzzled: "It definitely seems illogical that they themselves do this and yet reproach barbarians that they practice sacrilege." It is perhaps not so illogical if the Romans truly believed in the efficacy of such rites. The Elder Pliny notes that not until 97 B.C. a senatus consultum was passed banning human sacrifice (*NH* 30.2.12); yet in his time too foreigners were buried under the supervision of the *XVviri sacris faciundis* (*NH* 28.12); cf. A. Fraschetti, "Le sepolture rituali de Foro Boario," in *Le délit religieux dans la cité antique* (Table ronde, Rome 1978) (Rome, 1981), 51–115, at 83; North, *PCPS* 205 (1979), 99, n.5. Rumors were spread also that Catilina and his co-conspirators drank blood mixed with wine (Sallust, *Cat.* 22) or even slaughtered a man and ate his flesh (Plutarch, *Cic.* 10.4; Florus ep. 2.12.3); cf. for a similar report, related to an earlier period: Plutarch, *Publicola* 4.1. Human sacrifice is associated with barbarian communities in Greek tragedy, although in Greek myth human victims are regularly sacrificed by Greeks: Hall, *Inventing the Barbarian* (1989), 146–148. The Cimbri are typically the sort of people associated with human sacrifice: Strabo 7.2.3 (c. 294).

[64] Tac., *Hist.* 4.54. Note also, a little earlier, the prophet who gathered eight thousand fanatical followers among the Aedui (*Hist.* 2.61) and, in roughly the same period: the priestess Veleda, venerated among the Germans: Tacitus, *Hist.* 4.65; 5.24.5; *Germania* 8.3.2; Statius, *Silvae* 1.4.90.

[65] Momigliano, *The Emperor Claudius*, 28, sees in the Druids an anti-Roman element. Syme, *Tacitus*, 457f., asks whether ritual murder among the Gauls was the true reason or only the inevitable pretext for the banning of Druidism. He criticizes H. Last, *JRS* 39 (1949), 1ff. for according undue importance to Roman humanitarian ideals and suggests the Druids may have been seen as a subversive force. Similarly, Martin Goodman has suggested that it was not Druidic practices but the Druids' authority with the Celtic population that shocked Romans: *The Ruling Class of Judaea: The Origins of the Jewish Revolt against Rome AD 66–70* (Cambridge, 1987), 240–247. For a different emphasis: Woolf, *Becoming Roman*, 220–222.

[66] Pliny, *NH* 30.12 (trans. W.H.S. Jones, Loeb): palamque in tempus illut sacra prodigiosa celebrata. See below, p. 467.

[67] Pliny, *NH* 30.13: namque Tiberii Caesaris principatus sustulit Druidas eorum et hoc genus vatum medicorumque. Syme, *Tacitus* (1958), 457, n.6, asserts: "Pliny was close to the event, and he knew Gaul. Suetonius, who assigns to Claudius the abolition of Druidism (*Divus Claudius* 25.5), cannot compete. It is therefore unsound to admit his testimony to equal rank with that of Pliny" (as does Momigliano). Suetonius's evidence, however, should not be discarded altogether.

[68] Pliny, *NH* 30.13: Britannia hodieque eam adtonita celebrat tantis caerimoniis, ut dedisse Persis videri possit. adeo ista toto mundo consensere, quamquam discordi et sibi ignoto.

against the Druids[69] and probably after the extermination of many of them on the island of Mona (Anglesey) in A.D. 60 as well, where the Roman army also "destroyed their groves, devoted to savage superstitions, for they regarded it as a religious obligation to honour the altars with the blood of captives and to consult the gods with the aid of human intestines."[70] The Druids reappear in Gaul in A.D. 70, when they predict a universal empire for the rebellious Transalpine nations, as recorded by Tacitus (*Hist.* 4.54). Pliny, however, is not preoccupied so much with the Druids as with the practice of magic[71] and, especially, of human sacrifice, which he regards as part of magic. In this connection, he concludes that it is impossible to estimate how great a debt is owed to the Romans who have abolished the monstrous rites in which it was the ultimate religious act to kill a man while it was even considered most healthful to eat him.[72]

Druids recur in a digression on Gaul by Ammianus (15.9–12). This contains three sections on the Gauls. The first, on the origin of the Gauls, cites Timagenes of Alexandria (first century B.C.) as an authority.[73] It is a sympathetic description without slurs: "In these regions men gradually grew educated and the study of the liberal arts prospered, stimulated by the Bards, the Euhages and the Druids."[74] The second, brief, section (15.11), embedded in a geographical description, contains qualifications which derive mostly from Caesar.[75] The third (15.12.1–4) has some of the age-old stereotypes: Gauls are tall, have loud voices, and are fierce fighters and good soldiers. Like Cicero, Livy, Diodorus, and Athenaeus, Ammianus claims they drink to excess.[76] They frequently have opulent dinner parties (16.8.8).[77] Ammianus, however, does not repeat some other commonplaces: he does not call the Gauls impulsive and fickle or greedy. He is one of the few authors to insist on their cleanliness and neat appearance,[78] which may therefore represent his personal impression. Finally, he inserts a

[69] Pliny's *Naturalis Historia* was dedicated to Titus *sexies consul* (1 praef. 3), i.e., in 77. Book 30 cannot have been written many years before.

[70] Tacitus, *Ann.* 14.30: excisique luci saevis superstitionibus sacri: nam cruore captivo adolere aras et hominum fibris consulere deos fas habebant.

[71] According to Pliny, *NH* 29.54, Claudius put to death a Roman knight from the Vocontii who kept a serpent's egg with him during a lawsuit, a practice known as a form of Druidic magic.

[72] Pliny, *NH* 30.13: nec satis aestimari potest, quantum Romanis debeatur, qui sustulere monstra, in quibus hominem occidere religiosissimum erat, mandi vero etiam saluberrimum.

[73] Timagenes' *History of the Gauls*; *FGrH* 88, F2.

[74] Ammianus 15.9.8: Per haec loca hominibus paulatim excultis, viguere studia laudabilium doctrinarum, inchoata per bardos et euhagis et drysidas.

[75] 15.11.4: Horum omnium apud veteres Belgae dicebantur esse fortissimi, ea propter quod ab humaniore cultu longe discreti nec adventiciis effeminati deliciis, diu cum transrhenanis certavere Germanis etc.

[76] Ammianus cites Cicero, *pro Fonteio* fr.9: Gallos post haec dilutius esse poturos, quod illi venenum esse arbitrabuntur. Drinking Gauls also: Livy 5.33.2–3; Diodorus 5.26.3 both cited above; Athenaeus 4.34.

[77] Athenaeus, loc. cit.; Diodorus 5.28.4. Cf. Woolf, *Becoming Roman*, 174–205.

[78] Ptolemy, *Tetrabiblos* 2.3.16 comments on the cleanliness (φιλοκάθαρον) of Tyrrhenia, Celtica, and Spain.

remarkable description of a Gallic wife, supporting her man and stronger than he, fierce and unbeatable in a fight, "levelling blows like a catapult." This reads like a caricature, almost as if taken from the adventures of *Astérix le Gaulois* rather than from real life, and raises a further question as to the nature of this and at least one other geographic digression. When Ammianus describes *Galli*, this suggests that he is talking about the ethnic Gauls of the first century and much of the material, as has been shown here, derives from sources which were more than four centuries old by the time he wrote. When other fourth-century sources mention contemporary Gauls, they mean the inhabitants of the Romanized Gallic provinces, not the historic tribes.[79] Much of the digression has an anachronistic flavor and, remarkably, the same is true for that on the Near Eastern provinces. Here, for instance, the description of Arabia would almost seem to have been written two and a half centuries before Ammianus, shortly after the annexation of the province of Arabia by Trajan (14.8.13).[80] An early fourth-century source, Firmicus Maternus, is unusual in calling the Gauls stupid.[81]

CONCLUSIONS

To conclude this chapter: in considering the Gauls we see that the Roman attitudes towards them are entirely different from those towards any people discussed so far. While allowing for variations and exceptions, we encounter a number of stereotypes that remained rather constant from the second century B.C. onward. The Gauls were tall, blonde, strong, and courageous in war, but they were also heavy drinkers, fickle and unruly. In war they were efficient at the first onslaught, but had no staying power. Whatever the truth—and Caesar clearly wrote as an expert about the Gauls as fighters—this combination of features fits the environmental theory precisely, as formulated already in *Airs, Waters, Places* 24. Many Gauls may have been taller and blonder than many Romans and they may have been fine warriors, but the essence for this study is that they were assumed to be so collectively and under the determining influence of the environment.

There is, however, at least in Caesar's writings, another factor at work: their proximity to the Roman Empire and the influence of trade in luxury goods had a corrupting effect. Hence they were far less redoubtable than the Germans.

---

[79] *Pan.Lat.* 2 (12) 23: *triumphis tuis Galli . . . irascimur.* The *Panegyrici Latini* hardly ever use the term *Galli.* Cf. 5 (8) 3–5: Aedui.

[80] Cf. Matthews, *The Roman Empire of Ammianus*, 343f., 463f., who says the the anomaly is best explained by the supposition that Ammianus was compiling his digression from earlier sources.

[81] Firmicus Maternus, *Mathesis* 1.2.3: Galli stolidi. For the sake of his argument Firmicus Maternus declares in 1.10.12 that in Gaul people gain strength through their prudent sagacity, but that still means that their stupidity was a commonplace to begin with at the time. The only comparable qualification I am aware of is Strabo 4.4.2 (c. 195), who calls the Gallic people ἁπλοῦν.

This line of thinking also goes back to the fifth century, as has been seen in chapter 1.

Yet it is quite clear as well that, generally speaking, the Gauls aroused far less hostility than the Greeks and the various peoples of the Near East, whether Hellenized or not. Most of the commonplaces found through the ages appear first in the work of Polybius, who relates the wars between Celts and Romans in the fourth and third centuries. The Gauls were, or had been once, fierce and virile fighters, among the most redoubtable enemies of Rome, but thanks to various weaknesses, they could be reduced to a state of safe subjection. It is clear that the stereotypes determined by the environmental theory: East versus West and North versus South, played a significant role in Roman attitudes towards the Gauls. The Gauls were fine fighters, but not too good. Even if they were still capable of military resistance (in A.D. 21 and 69), they did not offer an existential threat to the empire. They could be dangerous, but they were not feared like the Germans, for, since the second century B.C., Rome had always been militarily superior. We cannot avoid the conclusion, however, that the "eastern" or "southern" stereotypes aroused more emotional hostility than the "western" or "northern" forms, while the latter are sometimes described with disdain. The Gauls, it should be noted, are the first people discussed in this part of the study who belonged to the northwestern area of the empire.

One might speculate that the cultural or social competition either in Rome or in the provinces also was important. Romans did not have to feel that the Gauls were their masters in a cultural sense, while Greeks and some eastern peoples clearly were superior in some essential aspects. Thus we saw that Gauls annoyed Juvenal far less than Greeks, Syrians, Egyptians, and the inhabitants of Africa. Indeed, their religion was regarded as barbaric and steps were taken to suppress the Druids, perhaps not altogether successfully, but there is no indication that the Druids and Gallic religion were regarded as an irritant in Rome itself. Indeed, no decisive answer can be given to the question why Rome wished to wipe out Druidism. The motive may have been political, religious, or moral, or a combination. It would have been interesting if we knew, because we might then be able to conclude whether the reason belongs to the sphere of what we would call *realpolitik* or more to that of religious prejudice or even ideology. Finally, when Claudius wanted to accept Gauls into the Senate there was resistance, and the arguments cited are typically xenophobic but not particularly anti-Gallic. The same arguments could have been used against many other foreigners. Generally speaking, Gauls are often described in terms of stereotypes and commonplaces and these are a mixture of the familiar themes of the environmental theory and ethnic prejudice. This brings us to the Germans, who were not hated and were even respected to some extent, but they were dangerous and feared.

Germans

THE GERMANS HAVE already been mentioned frequently, since it is impossible to discuss attitudes towards Gauls without referring to Germans, especially since the two are rather similar in some descriptions.[1] The name as such is used first by Caesar.[2] According to Caesar one distinction that stands out is that the Germans had no Druids.[3] Tacitus's ideas about the pure lineage of the Germans required discussion under that heading and will not be repeated. It is not my subject to discuss the Germans as such, their internal, social, and economic history, or the specifics of trade or Romanization. What we do need to understand, as far as possible, are the Roman views of the Germans vis-à-vis the empire.[4]

Consider all the tribes whom Roman peace does not reach—I mean the Germans and all the nomad tribes that assail us along the Danube. They are oppressed by eternal winter and a gloomy sky, the barren soil grudges them support, they keep off the rain with thatch or leaves, they range over ice-bound marshes, and hunt wild beasts for food. Are they unhappy, do you think? There is no unhappiness for those

[1] For a sensible analysis of what the ancient sources mean when they speak of Germani: D. Timpe, "Ethnologische Begriffsbildung in der Antike," in Heinrich Beck, Germanenprobleme in heutiger Sicht (Berlin, 1986), 22–40, at 37–40.

[2] Caesar, BG 1.1.3f; 1.2.3 etc. Diodorus 5.32 calls the Gauls in Gallia Κελτοί and the peoples farther away whom we know as Germani Γαλάται, adding that the Romans call all of them Γαλάται.

[3] Caesar, BG 6.21: nam neque druides habent, qui rebus divinis praesint, neque sacrificiis student.

[4] See R. Chevallier, Rome et la Germanie au 1er siècle de notre ère (Brussels, 1961), especially chap. 1: "La Germanie dans la littérature et l'opinion publique romaines au 1er siècle de notre ère", 2: "L'opinion romaine et la Germanie à Rome," and see especially pp. 10–15 on the depiction of Germans on Roman victory monuments, showing respect; K. von See, Barbar, Germane, Arier: die Suche nach der Identität der Deutschen (Heidelberg, 1994), 31–60: "Der Germane als Barbar," an attempt to analyze the Germania in terms of cultural theories, which are, however, too schematic and therefore rather confused; A. A. Lund, Germania: Interpretiert, herausgegeben, übertragen, kommentiert. (Heidelberg, 1988); H. Jankuhn and D. Timpe, Beiträge zum Verständnis der Germania des Tacitus, Teil I: Bericht über die Kolloquien der Kommission für die Altertumskunde Nord- und Mitteleuropas im Jahr 1986 (Göttingen, 1989); G. Neumann and H. Seemann (eds.), Beiträge . . . Teil II . . . Kolloquien . . . im Jahre 1986 und 1987 (Göttingen, 1992); C. Trzaska-Richter, Furor Teutonicus: Das römische Germanenbild in Politik und Propaganda von den Anfängen bis zum 2. Jahrhunderts n. Chr. Bochumer Altertumswissenschaftliches Colloquium 8 (Trier, 1991); D. Timpe, Romano-Germanica: Gesammelte Studien zur Germania des Tacitus (Stuttgart and Leipzig, 1995). See also the older discussion by Walser, Rom, das Reich und die fremden Völker (1951), 77–82. Here Walser again claims that Tacitus sees the Germani in Roman terms. A. A. Lund, Zum Germanenbild der Römer. Eine Einführung in die antike Ethnographie (Heidelberg, 1990). See also above, chapter 1, n. 327.

whom habit has brought back to nature. . . . good men are shaken in order that they may grow strong. (trans. J. W. Basore)[5]

Seneca never faced Germans or their Roman patrons at court, except the Emperor's German bodyguards, and it may not have made much difference to the Romans at court whether those guards were Scyths, Germans, or Celts.[6] Although they were present in the city and elsewhere, he did not meet any clever Germans at banquets either in the city or in Italy outside Rome.[7] They were a distant people about whom he knew little or nothing and he did not see their martial qualities as threatening the empire, as Tacitus certainly did. This explains the surprisingly moderate tone of Seneca's words. In his work there is no echo of the pride of triumphs over the Germans or anger at the losses inflicted by them.[8] An interesting theme raised here is the happiness of living close to nature as propounded by an urban dignitary. Strabo, who wrote as a geographer after Caesar's campaigns in Gaul and during and after Augustus's wars across the Rhine, had more to say about them. He observes that all of them live in dire poverty and tend to live like nomads, even if they are not quite nomads. "In imitation of the Nomads, they load their household belongings on their wagons and with their beasts turn whithersoever they think best" (7.1.3 [c. 291]). The farther north they live, the poorer they are, it seems. Whatever the truth of the statement, it is obviously a traditional stereotype.[9]

In this brief survey of Roman views on the Germans, it seems best to start with the period when Romans and German peoples were in regular contact. Although there is a good deal to say about the traumatic impact of the war between Rome and the invading Cimbri and Teutones, essentially this was an isolated major clash which did not result in permanent and continuous contact between the various parties in the conflict.[10] The same may be said about Caesar's contact with the Germans—he was the first to use this name to indicate the peoples living east of the Gauls.[11] Writing during the reigns of Augustus and

[5] *de providentia* 4.14: Omnes considera gentes in quibus Romana pax desinit, Germanos dico et quidquid circa Histrum uagarum gentium occursat: perpetua illos hiemps, triste caelum premit, maligne solum sterile sustentat; imbrem culmo aut fronde defendunt, super durata glacie stagna persultant, 1.4.15 in alimentum feras captant. Miseri tibi uidentur? nihil miserum est quod in naturam consuetudo perduxit; . . . Quid miraris bonos uiros, ut confirmentur, concuti?

[6] Dio, 78.5.5–6, calls Caracalla's barbarian guards Scythians and Celts while Herodian, 4.7.3; 13.6 calls them Germans, which shows that some confusion regarding the ethnic identity of such guards could occur.

[7] According to Josephus (as attributed to Agrippa II, *BJ* 2.16.4 [376f.]), there were German captives everywhere in the empire.

[8] For victories, triumphs, and trophies: Chevallier, *Rome et la Germanie*, 10f.

[9] Strabo had no better understanding of the essence of nomadism than other Greek and Roman authors. Nomads were believed to wander around at random.

[10] For Roman views of the Cimbri and Teutones: C. Trzaska-Richter, *Furor Teutonicus*, 48–79. Views of the Germans in Caesar's work: 80–128.

[11] Cf. Trzaska-Richter, *Furor Teutonicus,* "Das Germanenbild bei Caesar," 80–128. For the name: *BG* 1.1.3: (Belgae) . . . proximique sunt Germanis, qui trans Rhenum incolunt, quibus cum conti-

Tiberius, Strabo is aware that most of the things said about the Cimbri are incorrect or highly improbable.[12] A good start for the present observations may be the work of Strabo himself, who wrote after the incorporation of Gaul had made the Germans permanent neighbors of the empire. In his view of their position towards the empire, Strabo invariably maintains his sunny views of the state of affairs in his days, even after the disaster of Varus. The Cherusci and their allies "all paid the penalty, and afforded the younger Germanicus a most brilliant triumph" (7.1.4 [c. 291]). True, Arminius was still keeping up the war, but most German leaders either were captured or had deserted Arminius.[13] Even the notorious Cimbri sent to Augustus a kettle most sacred to them with a plea for his friendship and amnesty for their past misdeeds. This petition was granted" (7.2.1 [c. 293]). Strabo does not say what he thinks of having the Rhine as a border. However, for a man who was cautious in matters of foreign conquest he seems to have had unusual ideas about the northeastern frontier Since Strabo wrote when the area between the Rhine and the Elbe had already been lost, some of his comments about the area even farther east of the Elbe are remarkable.

These tribes have become known through their wars with the Romans, in which they would either yield and then later revolt again, or else quit their settlements; and they would have been been better known if Augustus had allowed his generals to cross the Elbe in pursuit of those who emigrated thither. But as a matter of fact he supposed that he could conduct the war in hand more successfully if he should hold off from those outside the Elbe who were living in peace, and should not incite them to make common cause with the others in their enmity against him. (7.1.4 [c. 291])

Is it going too far to suggest that the geographer regrets the imperial decision not to campaign east of the Elbe for the loss of geographical information this entailed? However, all was not lost: "the lands beyond the Elbe are wholly unknown for none of the earlier travellers have gone there and the Romans

---

nenter bellum gerunt. The first attestation of the name occurs in two fragments of Posidonius: Kidd F73 (Athenaeus, *Deipn.* 4.153e): Γερμανοὶ δέ, ὡς ἱστορεῖ Ποσειδώνιος ἐν τῇ τριακοστῇ . . . ; commentary by Edelstein and Kidd, vol. II (i), 322–326; Kidd F277b (Eustathius, *Comm. ad Homeri Iliadem* 13.6). This has engendered much discussion of more than antiquarian interest. The question is whether Germani and Celts were regarded as ethnically distinct as early as the middle of the second century B.C., for there is no other author before Julius Caesar to distinguish Germani from Galli geographically, collectively, and ethnically (*BG* 1.1). Cf. D. Timpe, "Ethnologische Begriffsbildung," in *Germanenprobleme in heutiger Sicht* ed. H. Beck (Berlin/New York, 1986), 22–40.

[12] Strabo 7.2.1–2 (c. 292–3). Strabo rejects the theory that their way of life was caused by the inundation of their peninsula by a great floodtide and prefers Posidonius's hypothesis that the piratical and nomadic character of the Cimbri drove them as far as the Cimmerian Bosporus which, says Posidonius, owes its name to them (Edelstein and Kidd, fr. 272); Kidd, *Commentary* 2 (2), 922–932; cf. Plutarch, *Marius* 11.3; Pliny, *NH* 2.167; Tacitus, *Germania* 37.

[13] Cf.: Sarah Pothecary, "Strabo, the Tiberian Author: Past, Present and Silence in Strabo's *Geography*," *Mnemosyne* 55 (2002), 387–438.

have not yet [*sic*] advanced into the area beyond the Elbe."[14] Strabo clearly implies that he would have thought it a good idea if Rome had crossed the Elbe and that he expected this to happen eventually.

In matters of character, Strabo has little sympathy for the Germans. They tended to revolt and betray. In dealing with these peoples, distrust had been a great advantage, "whereas those who have been trusted have done the greatest harm, as, for instance, the Cherusci."[15] Strabo, Velleius, and Manilius all describe the Germans as utterly untrustworthy, "a nation born to lie."[16] This, however, seems not to have been a matter of consensus. It was more of a reaction to the Roman defeat in A.D. 9. The Romans, when defeated, often consider themselves the victims of treachery, but when victorious they see themselves as an example of courage. Tacitus does not hesitate to call the Germans "a people without either natural or acquired cunning, they disclose their hidden thoughts in the freedom of the festivity."[17] Strabo's views of the Germans do not appear to be influenced by any feeling that they formed one of the greatest challenges the Roman empire would be facing. Velleius and Tacitus saw them in a different light. Velleius uses *feritas Germana* as a proverbial term[18] and ridicules Varus for imagining that such men could be governed by the usages of law. "When placed in charge of the army in Germany, he entertained the notion that the Germans were a people who were men only in limbs and voice, and that they, who could not be subdued by the sword, could be soothed by the law."[19] Manilius, again, reflecting the mood after the successful revolt of the Germans, says that Germany is "fit only to breed wild beasts."[20]

This theme recurs in the works of various authors.[21] Josephus, in Agrippa II's catalogue of subjects of Rome, describes the Germans "as scorning death and having a temper fiercer than the wildest beasts."[22] Seneca, varying this somewhat, says of the Germans and the Scythians that they are peoples, living wild and free "in the manner of lions and wolves who can neither serve nor command, for they do not have the power of a human intellect but a wild and

---

[14] 7.2.4 (c. 294): οὔθ' οἱ Ῥωμαῖοί πω προῆλθον εἰς τὰ περαιτέρω τοῦ Ἄλβιος·

[15] 7.1.4 (c. 291): πρὸς οὓς ἡ μὲν ἀπιστία μέγα ὄφελος, οἱ δὲ πιστευθέντες τὰ μέγιστα κατέβλαψαν.

[16] Strabo 7.1.4 (c. 291); Velleius 2.118: At illi . . . in summa feritate versutissimi natumque mendacio genus . . . ; Manilius 1.896–903, cited above, chapter 6, p. 331 n. 44, for the enemy accused of lying. Trzaska-Richter, *Furor Teutonicus*, 118–122, argues that Caesar, for political reasons, already describes the Usipetes and Tencteri as treacherous.

[17] *Germania* 22: gens non astuta nec callida aperit adhuc secreta pectoris licentia loci.

[18] 2.106: Fracti Langobardi, gens etiam Germana feritate ferocior; for the Langobardi: cf. Strabo 7.1.3 (c. 291). See also Velleius 2, 119.5.

[19] Velleius 2.117.3: Is, cum exercitui qui erat in Germania praeesset, concepit esse homines, qui nihil praeter uocem membraque haberent hominum, quique gladiis domari non poterant, posse iure mulceri. Velleius gives a distorted description of Varus, see Isaac, *Limits of Empire*, 56f.

[20] Manilius 4. 794: teque feris dignam tantum, Germania . . . See also chapter 2, n. 138.

[21] See the discussion of "Brutes and Animals" in Part 1.

[22] Josephus, *BJ* 2.16.4 (377): καὶ τὴν μὲν ψυχὴν θανάτου καταφρονοῦσαν, τοὺς δὲ θυμοὺς τῶν ἀγριωτάτων θηρίων σφοδροτέρους . . . Above, p. 205.

unmanagable one."[23] Apparently, Seneca, could live with the thought that the Germans would remain unconquered.

Maroboduus and the Marcomanni are clearly described by Velleius as a threat to Italy and the Roman Empire.[24] After Varus's disaster, this author saw the Germans as an enemy posing a threat to Italy no less dangerous than the war with the Cimbri and Teutones in the late second century B.C.[25] The panic passed, but after Strabo no other author seems to have felt as much at ease about the Germans as he did. Seneca writes that the Germans were the most courageous of men, fiercest when attacking.[26] The Germans (and Scythians) were seen as the most irascible peoples, but that quality was immediately connected with their freedom. Seneca writes: " 'That you may be convinced,' says our opponent, 'that anger does have in it something noble, you will see that such nations as are free—for example, the Germans and Scythians—are most prone to anger'."[27] Seneca then continues to develop this theme in terms of the traditional stereotypes of the environmental theory, combined with the familiar views of the effect of subjugation. Those living in the north have wild tempers; they are brave and firm, prone to anger—the subject of Seneca's work—and they are therefore unconquerable, but because they have no staying power, they are not the type to subjugate others. "Even as they cannot submit to servitude, neither can they exercise dominion."[28] Elsewhere he observes how remarkable the Germans were because they were truly eager for war.[29] Unlike other authors, Seneca seems not to have regarded the Roman failure to subdue the Germans as a cause for serious concern. A variant of this attitude recurs, perhaps, much later, in Vegetius, who did not belittle Roman failures in subduing the Germans, but positively denied them: only Roman military skills and discipline were capable of defeating German tallness.[30] Plutarch wistfully reminds his readers that the civil wars were a waste, for the Romans could have fought the Parthians and the Germans.[31] A great task remained in the subjugation of Scythia and India. In this the Romans would not have failed, suggests Plutarch.[32] The implication seems to be that the Roman Empire in the age of Julius Caesar could have subdued the Parthians and the Germans, but not the Romans of the second

[23] Seneca, *de ira* 2.15 (*dialogi* 4.15.4f.): Deinde omnes istae feritate liberae gentes leonum luporumque ritu ut seruire non possunt, ita nec imperare; non enim humani uim ingenii, sed feri et intractabilis habent . . . For the same passage in another connection, see above, chapter 2, n. 140.

[24] Velleius 2.109: et nostro quoque imperio timendum. . . . Nec securam incrementi sui patiebatur esse Italiam . . .

[25] Velleius 2.120: . . . hostis . . . qui Cimbricam Teutonicamque militiam Italiae minabatur . . .

[26] Seneca, *De Ira* 1.11: Germanis quid est animosius? quid ad incursum acrius?

[27] *De Ira* 2.15: "Vt scias" inquit "iram habere in se generosi aliquid, liberas videbis gentes, quae iracundissimae sunt, ut Germanos et Scythas."

[28] ut servire non possunt, ita nec imperare.

[29] Seneca, *QN* 6.7: Germanos, auidam belli gentem.

[30] Vegetius 1.1.4 Quid aduersus Germanorum proceritatem breuitas potuisset audere? Cf. Columella, *De Re Rustica* 1; Plutarch and Tacitus have been cited above on this subject.

[31] For a different outlook: Horace 1.2.21–4; 49–52.

[32] Plutarch, *Pompey* 70.3.–5

century A.D. who, in Plutarch's view, apparently were less valiant and capable than their ancestors in the first century B.C. This is yet another example of the usual assumption in Greece and Rome of unavoidable general decline.

No Roman author has given more thought in his writings to the Germans than Tacitus. His delight when he could report on massive slaughter of Germans has been cited above.[33] His attitude is not easy to sum up, but obviously there is a good deal of both admiration and apprehension in his work. There is nothing petty about the Germans, they have enormous failings and great merit. This is not to deny that he also saw them in terms of traditional stereotypes. Because of their pure lineage they all look alike (*Germania* 4). This echoes the assertion in the fifth century B.C. that the Scythians are all alike.[34] Furthermore they all have blue eyes, red hair, and huge frames; they cannot stand hard work nor can they stand heat or thirst, but they are inured to cold and hunger. This is mostly the familiar Roman development of the old environmental theory, as seen most fully in Vitruvius. The observation that they are incapable of sustained labor does not occur in Vitruvius, but Strabo developed a rather similar thought. Tacitus repeats this in various forms. They love fighting, sleeping, and feasting; they hate peace and serious work.[35] Therefore they live in poverty. They have no cities and their villages are primitive and badly organized (16). To Tutor, leader of the Treveri, Tacitus attributes the statement that the Germans "do not follow orders, and cannot be governed, but always act according to their own whim."[36]

Tacitus, however, leaves no doubt as regards their remarkable virtues, the sum of which is that they may be poor, but as a result they are free from the corruption which undermined Rome, as Tacitus saw it. They maintain a strict marriage code. "Almost alone among barbarians they are content with one wife, except a very few among them" (*Germania* 18). "Thus, with their virtue protected, the women live uncorrupted by the allurements of public shows or the stimulant of feastings." Adultery is very rare and heavily punished by the husband. Tacitus does not say, but implies that all this is the opposite of what was found in contemporary Rome. They practice no birth control, and do not dispose of unwanted babies—an observation Tacitus also makes regarding the Jews (19). Every mother feeds her own offspring and never entrusts it to servants and nurses (20). As Tacitus says elsewhere of his own period, it was a sign of degeneration that mothers no longer took care of their own children in Rome.[37] As already observed, Tacitus describes them as "a people without ei-

---

[33] Above, chapter 2, p. 219, on the extermination of the Bructeri.

[34] *Airs, Waters, Places* 19; see above, chapter 1, n. 45.

[35] 14; 15.1: . . . cum idem homines sic ament inertiam et oderint quietem.

[36] Tacitus, *Hist.* 4.76.9: nam Germanos . . . non iuberi, non regi, sed cuncta ex libidine agere.

[37] *Dialogus* 28.4–29.1, cited also above, chapter 9, n. 93, where it is observed that the idea is encountered already in earlier literature. A. A. Lund, comm. ad loc., p.167, observes that the starting point of this discussion was that Romans believed children to be corrupted by the milk of wet-nurses, for which, see Aulus Gellius, *Noctes Atticae* 12.1.17 and discussion above, chapter 1, p. 81 and notes 103, 104; chapter 2, p. 192 and n. 87.

ther natural or acquired cunning: they disclose their hidden thoughts in the freedom of the festivity" (22), a generalization which contradicts both Strabo and Velleius, who describe the Germans as utterly untrustworthy, "a nation born to lie." They satisfy their hunger without elaborate preparation and without delicacies. Admittedly, they drink a lot (23). This statement gains significance if we remember Livy's complaint that degeneration started in Rome in the early second century with the rise in status of the cook. "At that time the cook, for the ancients once the cheapest of slaves, began to be appreciated and exploited and to be valuable, and what had been a service became an art."[38] The comparison with Rome is implicit throughout: the Germans are virtuous and the Romans decadent. "Freedmen are never of any weight in the state except in tribes ruled by kings. There indeed they rise above the freeborn and the noble. Among the others the unequal status of the freedman is a proof of freedom" (25).[39] They do not exploit capital to increase it with interest (26). This would remind Tacitus's readers and us, for instance, of the financial crisis in Rome, described in *Annales* 6.16f. The Germans, as seen by Tacitus, may be summed up by four character traits: *simplicitas, ira/iracundia, inertia,* and *libertas.*[40] The first and fourth qualities are held up as a mirror to the Romans.

In the second part of the *Germania,* Tacitus describes individual peoples or tribes. I cannot give a running commentary on that work, so I shall simply indicate a few statements relevant to the present discussion. The Chatti "are for a Germanic people much given to orderly judgement and sagacity. They have more confidence in their military leaders than in the armed mass, a quality characteristic of Roman discipline."[41] Tacitus describes how they do not indulge in mere raids, but go out on an orderly campaign. The traditional assumption is that northerners are courageous but dim, southerners clever but soft and cowardly. The Chatti have some of the positive characteristics of southerners while still being northern in their virtue. Tacitus does not say so, but the implication is that they were extremely dangerous neighbors to the Roman Empire. That this was in fact the case is obvious from their participation in the rebellion of Civilis and from Domitian's very partial success against them in his Germanic campaign.[42]

The Chauci, farthest to the North, are the best and prefer to maintain their

---

[38] Livy 39.6.7–9; cf. above chapter 2, n. 31.

[39] *Germ.* 25: liberti non multum supra servos sunt, raro aliquod momentum in domo, numquam in civitate exceptis dumtaxat iis gentibus quae regnantur. ibi enim et super ingenuos et super nobiles ascendunt: apud ceteros impares libertini libertatis argumentum sunt.

[40] Lund in Beck (ed.), *Germanenprobleme in heutiger Sicht* (1986), 62.

[41] *Germ.* 30.3: Multum ut inter Germanos rationis ac sollertiae . . . quodque rarissimum nec nisi Romanae disciplinae concessum plus reponere in duce quam in exercitu. See also *Ann.* 12.27f., describing a dangerous raid carried out by the Chatti.

[42] For the Chatti in 69: Tacitus, *Hist.* 4.37; for references in ancient sources: R. Much, *Die Germania des Tacitus* (Heidelberg, 3rd ed. 1967), 378–384; for Domitian's campaign against the Chatti, Schönberger, "The Roman Frontier in Germany: An Archaeological Survey," *JRS* 59 (1969), 144–197, at 158. It is interesting to consider that the Batavi themselves were said to be an offshoot of the Chatti.

greatness through justice.[43] They do not attack, expand, or harm others. This clearly is a schematic portrait of those living in the far North. They are idealized peoples living close to the edge of the world. In fact, correct information, contradicting this schematic portrait, would have been easily available to Tacitus.[44] The Elder Pliny describes the Chauci as people whose life in liberty is more miserable than that of slaves (*NH* 16.2). Tacitus describes another exemplary case in his next chapter (36), the Cherusci, good pacifists who lost out because they could not maintain their position against lawless and powerful neighbors.[45] Both Tacitus's report on the Chauci and that on the Cherusci are unhistorical and determined by didactic stereotypes.[46] Tacitus had no impartial interest in the Germans.[47] He wanted them to be conquered (*tam diu Germania vincitur*),[48] not only because Rome's martial honor required it, but because he considered the Germans more dangerous than any other people. "Not the Samnites, not the Carthaginians, not Spain, Gaul, or even the Parthians have given us warning more often: indeed the liberty of the Germans is more ferocious than the monarchy of Arsaces. With what else, indeed, can the East mock us with but with the death of Crassus, when it has itself lost Pacorus, and been crushed under Ventidius?"[49] Then follows a list of defeats, humiliations, or hard-won victories over the Germans. "Recently we have celebrated triumphs rather than victories over them."[50] If Tacitus wanted to impress on his readers the need for a full conquest of Germany beyond the Rhine, then he also made it clear that subjecting the Chatti would be one of the greatest challenges.

"To the Langobardi, however, their small numbers are a distinction. Although they are surrounded by numerous and most valorous peoples, they are safe, not by obedience, but by risking battles" (*Germania* 40). This contradicts both Tacitus's own remarks on their neighbors the peace-loving Chauci and the Cherusci whose prosperity and power had declined, as well as the remarks by Strabo and

---

[43] *Germ.* 35: populus inter Germanos nobilissimus quique magnitudinem suam malit iustitia tueri. Cf. Pliny 16.2.

[44] Cf. J.G.C. Anderson, *Cornelli Taciti, de origine et situ Germanorum* (Oxford, 1938), p. 167f.; Much, *Die Germania des Tacitus*, 406–411.

[45] Here again, Tacitus is far off the mark. For the reality: Anderson, p.171.

[46] Romm, *The Edges of the Earth in Ancient Thought*, 140–149, discusses Tacitus's information on these remote parts, but does not consider ethnic information.

[47] This does not mean that I would describe the *Germania* as a political pamphlet, arguing explicitly for military or other action. Tacitus describes the state of affairs as he sees it, resulting from the failure to incorporate the German peoples.

[48] Some German commentators find Tacitus too flippant. Much, *Die Germania des Tacitus*, 420, belabors the obvious: "Darin liegt gewiss ein Spott. So lange zu siegen ist unmöglich." The editors of the third edition, however, have a different sense of irony: "Der zu Rede stehende Satz darf nicht nur als ironisch gemeint aufgefasst worden."

[49] *Germ.*37.3: non Samnis, non Poeni, non Hispaniae Galliaeve, ne Parthi quidem saepius admonuere: quippe regno Arsacis acrior est Germanorum libertas. quid enim aliud nobis quam caedem Crassi, amisso et ipse Pacoro, infra Ventidium deiectus Oriens obecerit?

[50] *Germ.* 37.6 nam proximis temporibus triumphati magis quam victi sunt.

Velleius.[51] We may therefore deduce once again that it is the lesson, as much as the facts, which is important to Tacitus.

The Hermunduri are most loyal to Rome (41). In their territory originates the Elbe, "a river once famous and well known, now one only hears of it."[52] This is Tacitus's third bitter remark about Rome's failure to subjugate all of the Germans. "The fame and strength of the Marcomanni is foremost and they have acquired their very territory by valour, having expelled the Boii in the past. Nor are the Naristi and Quadi inferior to them."[53] "This is, as it were, the front of Germany where it is encircled by the Danube. They have their own kings, whose strength and power depend on Roman authority, rarely by arms, more often by money."[54] In the reign of Augustus, Maroboduus founded the most powerful empire ever created by any of the Germans. While Tacitus recognizes that they were a good ally, every well-informed Roman of his days might have felt apprehension at this powerful presence in Bohemia, and there was no need to spell this out, although the expression "this is as it were the front of Germany" is almost explicit in emphasizing the military danger. It evokes the idea of a battlefield with three especially powerful peoples facing Rome.[55] Behind them there are various peoples, including the most terrifying of all the Germans, the Harii, powerful fighters and masters at psychological warfare: "Their shields are black, their bodies are painted black; they pick dark nights for battles and cause terror by the very fearful shadow of a ghostly army. No enemy can bear this novel and infernal sight: for in all battles the eyes are first defeated."[56]

[51] Cf. *Cornelli Taciti*, Anderson 184f. For the Langobardi: Strabo 7.1.3 (c. 291); Velleius 2.106.

[52] *Germania* 41: flumen inclutum et notum olim; nunc tantum auditur. Anderson's puzzling comment (p.193): "The name of the Elbe evokes a sigh over the failure of a great scheme, but Tacitus would not have favoured a forward policy in Germany." If Tacitus's own writings, notably the *Germania*, are anything to go by, Tacitus wanted nothing better than a policy of active expansion in Germany.

[53] 42: praecipua Marcomanorum gloria viresque atque ipsa etiam sedes pulsis olim Boiis virtute parta. nec Naristi Quadive degenerant.

[54] Ibid.: eaque Germaniae velut frons est, quatenus Danuvio praecingitur.

[55] *Frons* is almost always used in a military context in the work of Tacitus, e.g., *Hist.* 2.25; *Ann.* 1.50; 51; 2.16. As a geographical expression it occurs in *Hist.* 4.12. H. W. Benario (ed., trans., and comm.), *Tacitus Germany / Germania* (Warminster, 1999), 107, misses the point in translating: "the frontier of Germany." Anderson, comm. on p. 195, rightly notes: "*Frons* in contrast to *terga claudunt*" (c. 43.1). This is battlefield imagery.

[56] *Germ.* 43.4: ceterum Harii super vires, quibus enumeratos paulo ante populos antecedunt, truces insitae feritati arte ac tempore lenocinantur: nigra scuta, tincta corpora; atras ad proelia noctes legunt ipsa que formidine atque umbra feralis exercitus terrorem inferunt, nullo hostium sustinente novum ac velut infernum aspectum; nam primi in omnibus proeliis oculi vincuntur. See Benario, op. cit., 109, for the evocative images in Tacitus's description. The geographical spread of all these peoples is explained extensively in the various commentaries. The specialism of the Harii as nightfighters reminds us of Xenophon's Thynoi, a Thracian people "who were said to be the best nightfighters of all": ἦσαν δ᾽ οὗτοι Θυνοί, πάντων λεγόμενοι εἶναι μάλιστα νυκτὸς πολεμικώτατοι (*An.* 7.2.22.; cf. 7.4.14). For the Thynoi: *RE* 6a, cols. 734ff. (Lenk); Christo Danov, *Altthrakien* (Berlin, 1976), index.

The status quo lasted till the reign of Marcus Aurelius with its great Marcomannic war. In the last chapter Tacitus discusses the Peucini (also named Bastarni), Veneti, and Fenni, wondering whether they should be assigned to the Germans or the Sarmatians, for their language is related to that of the Germans and they live like them in permanent settlements. They are all squalid and their leaders are indolent, which would make them typically German. However, by intermarriage they are said to be degenerating into a people resembling the Sarmatae.[57] Here, then, we have once again the undoubted assumption of the superiority of pure lineage: intermarriage between Germans and others would affect the quality of the offspring and turn them into lesser people than their German forefathers.

The essence of Tacitus's view of the Germans is that they were pure and unaffected by the corruption characteristic of Asiatics, Greeks, and the Romans themselves. They may have been lazy, poor, boorish, and violent, but they were not degenerate or feminine. They were powerful warriors, most of them disorganized and without staying power, but some, notably the Chatti, combined Germanic qualities with Roman organization. A Chattian Maroboduus, who would unite the Chatti and other peoples of the region, could spell disaster for the empire.[58] The Germans were both the ultimate northwesterners of the environmental theory and a model held up for the Romans who should recognize where they themselves were weakening. The message of Tacitus's *Germania,* therefore, is that the Germans are too dangerous for Rome to leave unconquered.[59] At the same time Tacitus is fully aware that this dangerous enemy has still not been vanquished after more than two centuries of occasional warfare. This is not an Isocrates explaining to his audience that the enemy is a pushover, soft, incapable of sustained resistance, but a cynic and a pessimist, who wants to impress upon his readers that there exists a major threat and disgrace. Prolonged conflict has still left the most dangerous enemy of Rome intact, a few hundred miles from Northern Italy.[60]

As argued in chapter 2, there clearly exists a conviction that long-term slaves or second-generation slaves are no longer dangerous. The idea is that slavery causes deterioration and this is true for entire peoples as well. It is therefore useful to make subject peoples adapt to imperial rule for a while. If they have been subject for a generation or two, they can no longer successfully rebel. This comes out also in the speech which Josephus attributes to Agrippa II, when he

---

[57] *Germ.* 46: Perucinorum Venethorumque et Fennorum nationes Germanis an Sarmatis adscribam dubito. quamquam Peucini . . . sermone cultu sede ac domiciliis ut Germani agunt. sordes omnium ac torpor procerum: conubiis mixtis nonnihil in Sarmatarum habitum foedantur. Cf. Strabo 7.3.17 (c. 306), who says they border on the *Germani* and are themselves of German descent.

[58] In the *Germania* Tacitus ignores Domitian's campaign against the Chatti and the defection of the Marcomanni and Quadi in 89, cf. Syme, *Tacitus,* 127f.

[59] Cf. Syme, *Tacitus,* 46–48.

[60] In the *Historiae* and *Annals* the Germans are described with more criticism; cf. Syme, *Tacitus,* 174.

attempts to dissuade the Jews from war in A.D. 66.[61] Tacitus's fear of the Germans lies in the fact that they have not yet been subjected. They have remained pure and uncontaminated, thus retaining their virility. The state of an enslaved people is a vicious circle: the longer people are dependent, the less they are capable of regaining and maintaining independence. The Roman Empire had failed in transforming the Germans into a subject people and Tacitus warns his readers that it might be a costly failure.

There were, of course, German peoples who did form part of the empire, so there were slaves of German origin in Rome. However, they are far less a subject of comments by Roman authors than various other peoples discussed in this work: Syrians, Greeks, Phoenicians, Jews and others. A well-attested German presence in Rome were the Emperor's *Germani custodes*.[62] These were dismissed in 69.[63] In 41 they reacted violently to the murder of Caligula and killed several of the conspirators, as described by Josephus. "It is an ancestral trait of them to act emotionally in a manner rarely if at all encountered among other barbarians, because they consider their actions less in advance. They are physically forceful and very successful in their first clash with any enemy."[64] Belligerence and impulsiveness are more often mentioned as characteristics of Gauls by Caesar and Strabo: conceivably it is relevant here that Josephus says the German bodyguards made up the "Celtic cohort." However, both the anger and the lack of staying power, which Josephus says are typically German, also fit their description by Seneca, cited at the start of this chapter. Unrelated to any ethnic or national stereotype and typical of the position of such guards is Josephus's insistence on their greed.

Another mention of a German in Rome occurs in a brief epigram by Martial: "Marcia leaps here, German, not the Rhine. Why do you stand in the way and keep the boy from the rain of the generous pool? Barbarian, it is not fitting that victorious water should relieve captive thirst and a citizen servant be elbowed aside."[65] This is an episode where two servants want to drink from a fountain

---

[61] Cited above, chapter 2, n. 77.

[62] References in F. Millar, *The Emperor in the Roman World* (London, 1977), 62 and n.24.

[63] Dismissed by Galba: Suetonius, *Galba* 12.2, but Dio 65.17.2 still mentions Germani as guards to Vitellius. Many of these guards were Batavians, according to the inscriptions (e.g., *ILS* 1725; 1727; 1729; 1730). If they were dismissed by Galba and sent home at that time, it is conceivable that this contributed to the dissatisfaction causing the Batavian revolt in 69, one of the numerous feasible hypotheses in ancient history which it is impossible to verify.

[64] Jos., *Ant.* 19.1.15 (120): θυμῷ δὲ χρῆσθαι πάτριόν ἐστιν αὐτοῖς, ὥσπερ σπάνιον εἴ τισιν ἑτέροις βαρβάρων διὰ τὸ ἡσσόνως λογισμὸν ἐπιδέχεσθαι τῶν ποιουμένων, ῥωμαλέοι τε τοῖς σώμασι καὶ τῇ πρώτῃ ὁρμῇ συνιόντες τοῖς πολεμίοις οὓς ἂν νομίσωσι, μεγάλα κατορθοῦντες. Cf. 19.1.18 (149); Suetonius, *Caligula* 58.3.

[65] Martialis, *ep.* 11.96: (trans. Shackleton Bailey, Loeb) Marcia, non Rhenus, salit hic, Germane: quid obstas / et puerum prohibes divitis imbre lacus? / barbare, non debet, summoto cive ministro, / captivam victrix unda levare sitim. / See the comments by N. M. Kay, *Martial Book XI: A Commentary* (London, 1985), ad loc.

fed by the *aqua Marcia* and a young, local ("citizen") slave is elbowed aside by
a German slave. The terminology evokes association with major conflict: "Rhenus," "Germane," "barbare," "cive." This is clearly meant to be humorous, but
at the same time shows how much the issue of the Germans was alive for
Romans in this period. At first this raises association with the familiar theme of
the vanquished conquering the victor. However, it is probably more significant
here that the hostility towards a German slave is described in terms of foreign
rather than local conflict. The Germans were a threat at an imperial level. As a
presence in the city of Rome they may have generated less antagonism than
representatives of other, major cultures and religions.

CONCLUSIONS

The Germans occupied a special place among Rome's foreigners. We should
summarize here in what sense that affects the questions asked in this study. The
Germans were not an obvious presence in the city of Rome and not felt to be
so. Unlike the Parthians, however, they were not distant either. The Hermunduri
and Marcomanni were closer to Italy than most Roman provinces. This both-
ered some Romans more than others. Seneca was not troubled, but Tacitus was
very much so.

   The Germans constitute more of an object of stereotypical thinking than almost any other people. They tend to be described as larger than life: after their
rebellion in A.D. 9 they are not merely liars, they are a "nation born to lie."
Germany was a land "fit only to breed wild beasts" according to Manilius. The
claim that they were of pure lineage has been discussed extensively in chapter
1. They may or may not have thought so themselves, but Tacitus was certain
they were. We know that this kind of theory implies proto-racist thinking. As
observed by Timpe, environmental theory also was highly serviceable for the
Romans in their views of the Gauls and the Germans. The Gauls had many of
the usual characteristics of northern peoples, living in a cold climate. The Germans even lived farther northwards, so they had the same qualities but to a
greater degree.[66] Indeed, the environmental theory is applied constantly in the
case of the Germans. Seneca observes that those living in the north have wild
tempers; they are brave and firm, prone to anger, and therefore unconquerable.
According to Tacitus, all Germans look alike because of their pure lineage.
They cannot stand hard work nor can they stand heat or thirst, but they are
inured to cold and hunger and so on. So, in the case of the Germans two forms
of stereotypical thinking were at work. We see that the theory of pure lineage
and environmental theory in combination resulted in a fully stereotypical view
of the Germans, which has therefore all the characteristics of a proto-racist
approach.

   [66] Chevallier, *Rome et la Germanie*, 27: "A vrai dire, pour les Romains, les charactéristiques des
Germains sont celles des Gaulois simplement poussées à l'extrême." D. Timpe in *Germanenprobleme in heutiger Sicht* (1986), 38f.

This is not to suggest that all German peoples are described in identical terms. Obvious distinctions were made between them, but these were in part determined by the classical mechanisms of ancient ethnography. Those living close to the empire or marrying non-Germanic peoples became softer and deteriorated (the Peucini, Veneti, and Fenni), while those living farther away became the topics of didactic stereotypes (the Chauci and Cherusci in Tacitus's description).

According to the environmental theory the Germans were therefore considered the opposite of most eastern peoples: they were *not* corrupt, decadent, or perverse. They were not clever, cunning or good traders, but they were sexually virtuous and raised their children properly. They lived simple lives, squalid perhaps, but squalor does not detract from virtue. Their leaders were indolent but that did not diminish their qualities as fighters, for they were proverbially fierce. Especially as described by Tacitus, they had preserved all the good qualities of the legendary early Romans. Their redeeming feature, as an enemy, was poor organization, but the Chatti combined an almost Roman organizational skill with northern virtue. In the eyes of Tacitus and other Romans, the failure to subdue all of the Germans was the single worst failure of the empire. It was a matter of safety as well as honor. The logic of ancient imperialism describes here a vicious circle: subject people eventually lose their independence of mind and become natural, born subjects; conversely those who are *not* subjected remain dangerous. Combine this with the essential pessimism and belief in inevitable decline of the ancient world, and the German presence is indeed a serious threat.

As observed above, the Gauls aroused far less emotional hostility than the Greeks and the various peoples of the Near East, whether Hellenized or not. The Gauls were, or had been once, fierce and virile fighters, but they had been reduced to a state of safe subjection. Although they could be dangerous they did not offer an existential threat to the Empire. In the case of the Gauls the stereotypes were determined by the environmental theory: East versus West and North versus South, played a significant role in Roman attitudes. This is true to a still larger extent of the Germans who did constitute an existential threat. The Germans were and remained fierce and virile fighters and they had not been conquered. They were not the object of the fierce emotional hostility which the peoples of the East aroused, but rather of some disdain for their lack of culture, discipline, and organization. In terms of Roman value judgments they are regarded as the opposite of Asiatics and Syrians. However, as an object of protoracist thinking and ethnic prejudice they are their equals.

Jews

Also in this period we encounter the characteristic hostility
of the Westerner to this so thoroughly Oriental race and its
strange opinions and customs.[1]

MOMMSEN OFTEN COMBINES many of the themes which were to determine and focus later views on the subject. He has no doubt that Roman enmity was essentially the same as the nineteenth-century phenomenon. It is a form of hatred to be understood in the broader context of the opposition between West and East. The more specific root of the enmity is found in the opinions and customs of the Jews. All of these assertions have been debated since, separately and in combination, in an ever increasing number of publications.

Hostility towards the Jews in antiquity is a more emotionally loaded subject than other comparable topics. A modern inquiry into these matters is therefore more likely to suffer from distortion, or from a distorted response, because of the emotional involvement of the author and his or her readers. Obviously, citizens of modern nation-states, such as the French, Germans, and British, studied the Roman Empire from their own perspective in the early modern period and presumably they still do, even if they no longer identify with the old Gauls, Germans, and Britons as they used to.[2] Consequently, ideas about Gauls, ancient Germans, and Britons affect the French, modern Germans, and British respectively in special ways. The study of the position of the Jews in ancient empires is even more complex. Those who study ancient Judaism tend to do so from their own perspective on Judaism and its recent history, as they themselves are the first to recognize.[3] However, even while recognizing this, they

An earlier version of this chapter was published as an article in Hebrew in *Zion* 66 (2001), 41–72.

[1] Mommsen, *Römische Geschichte* 3.549: Auch zu jener Zeit . . . begegnen wir der eigentümlichen Antipathie der Okzidentalen gegen diese so gründlich orientalische Rasse und ihre fremdartigen Meinungen und Sitten.

[2] Cf. Léon Poliakov, *The Aryan Myth* (1971), chap. 1: "early myths of origin," for the manner in which various European nations reconstructed their history over time.

[3] The two recent monographs are: Peter Schäfer, *Judeophobia: Attitudes toward the Jews in the Ancient World* (Cambridge, MA, 1997); Zvi Yavetz, *Judenfeindschaft in der Antike* (Munich, 1997), the former a work by a German, writing in English, the latter by an Israeli, writing in German. Among the many important earlier studies should be mentioned *honoris causa*: Léon Poliakov, *Histoire de l'Antisémitisme* vol. 1 *Du Christ aux Juifs de Cour* (Paris 1955), 21–29, which, however, has little to say about antiquity. Directly relevant are two further monographs: J. N. Sevenster,

still tend to feel that somehow judgment should be passed and blame appor-
tioned to a degree otherwise not quite common in academic publications. Unlike the other peoples who were part of the Roman Empire, the Jews still exist
as a people and as a minority in many countries. Their history in the later
Hellenistic and Roman empires is closely connected with the earliest history of
Christianity. Christian activity is responsible for the preservation of a good deal
of ancient source-material on Jews that is not available for other ethnic groups
in antiquity. In particular, the works of Josephus were transmitted by Christian
copyists.[4] The present work should do for the Jews what it attempts to do for
other groups, that is, to trace views of the Jews in Greece and Rome, particularly ambivalent or hostile feelings. The aim should be to determine to what
extent those feelings must be described as proto-racist or as expressions of
ethnic—or other—prejudice. This is a complex matter because it is almost
impossible to consider ancient attitudes without being aware of the manifestations of later anti-semitism. One cannot but compare and this will in fact prove
illuminating. One must, however, beware of false comparisons.

Greece is not relevant to us here, for, "as far as we know, the Greeks lived
happily in their classical age without recognizing the existence of the Jews."[5]
The origins of non-Jewish opinions about Jews in Rome are closely related to
the position and history of the Jews in the Seleucid and Ptolemaic kingdoms,

The Roots of Pagan Anti-Semitism in the Ancient World (Leiden, 1975); John G. Gager, *The Origins of Anti-Semitism: Attitudes toward Judaism in Pagan and Christian Antiquity* (New York and Oxford, 1983); Wolf Liebeschuetz, "The Influence of Judaism among non-Jews in the Imperial Pe-
riod," *JJS* 52 (2001), 235–252. Y.-A. Dauge, *Le Barbare* (1981), contains no systematic discussion
of Roman attitudes towards the Jews. There are frequent references in which the author expresses
his view—as distinct from, or in agreement with the sources—that the Jews were proud, unstable,
violent, fanatic, and so on. All this raised fear and hostility, according to Dauge (e.g., p.136f.; a
summary appears on p. 476); also: V. Nikiprowetzky (ed.), *de l'antijudaisme antique à l'antisémitisme contemporain* (Lille, 1979): Carlos Levy, "L'antijudaisme paien: essay de synthèse," 51–
86; J. Mélèze-Modrzejewski, "Sur l'antisemitisme païen," 411–439 in Maurice Olender (ed.), *Pour
Léon Poliakov, le racisme: mythes et sciences* (Paris, 1981); David Berger (ed.), *History and Hate:
The Dimensions of Anti-Semitism* (Philadelphia and New York, 1986): Louis H. Feldman, "Anti-
Semitism in the Ancient World," 15–42; see note 3 on p. 37f. for numerous references to modern
studies of the subject; Shaye J. D. Cohen, "Anti-Semitism in Antiquity: The Problem of Definition,"
43–47; Nicholas de Lange, "The Origins of Anti-Semitism: Ancient Evidence and Modern Interpretations," in Sander L. Gilman and Steven T. Katz, *Anti-Semitism in Times of Crisis* (New York,
1991), 21–37; Daniel R. Schwartz, 'Antisemitism and Other –ism's in the Greco-Roman World," in
Robert S. Wistrich, *Demonizing the Other: Antisemitism, Racism and Xenophobia* (Amsterdam,
1999), 73–78; see also Bruno Rochette, "Juifs et Romains, Y a-t-il un antijudaïsme romain?" *Revue
des Études juives* 160 (2001), 1–31. Arnaldo Momigliano, "Le judaïsme comme «religion-paria»
chez Max Weber," ibid., 201–208, is most interesting, but it is not concerned with antiquity. Other
works will be cited in the notes below. This book went to press before I could consult Ernst
Baltrusch, *Die Juden und das Römische Reich. Geschichte einer konfliktreichen Beziehung*
(Darmstadt, 2002) and René S. Bloch, *Antike Vorstellungen vom Judentum. Der Judenexkurs des
Tacitus im Rahmen der griechisch-römischen Ethnographie* (Historia Einzelschriften, 2002).

[4] See the observations by Gideon Bohak, "The Ibis and the Jewish Question: Ancient 'Anti-
semitism' in Historical Perspective," in M. Mor and A. Oppenheimer (eds.), *Jewish-Gentile Relations in the Second Temple, Mishnaic and Talmudic Periods* (Jerusalem, forthcoming).

[5] A. Momigliano, *Alien Wisdom*, chap. 4 and p. 78.

but this is a large topic which falls outside the scope of this book.[6] Nor is this the place to review the position of the Jews in Egypt and in Judaea. The latter, in particular, occupied an exceptional position and the conflict there undoubtedly had various distinctive causes and dynamics. This chapter will therefore attempt to describe Roman views of Jews using the perspective of the Roman views of other aliens and subject peoples we have described above, while keeping in mind that these are often derived from the opinions and attitudes of the Hellenistic world. That may seem obvious. Less obvious, or at least, less observed in practice is the essential difference between Roman comments on Jews in Rome and on those in Judaea or in general.[7] While it is quite possible to cherish hatred of far-away peoples, it is clearly the case that social friction caused by day-to-day contact is a different phenomenon from more abstract forms of hostility. The importance of this distinction is noted frequently in this study and it is particularly important to insist on it in connection with the Jews. Many texts deal with the Jews in Judaea, but their presence in other parts of the empire and in the capital also left its mark on their image in later Greek and Latin literature.

In considering enmity towards the Jews, all recent studies acknowledge that there is a problem of terminology: "anti-semitism" is a modern term with clearly racist connotations. Like so many racist concepts, it is confused and confusing. Those who take the book of *Genesis* seriously may believe all Semites are descendants of Sem. However, according to current usage "Semitic" indicates a language group.[8] Yet anti-semitism usually entails hostility only towards Jews. Anti-semites are not necessarily hostile to speakers of Arabic, while to hate Arabs but not Jews would not normally be called anti-semitism. Furthermore, it does not matter to anti-semites whether the Jews they dislike speak Hebrew or another language.[9] Those who called themselves anti-semites in the nineteenth

[6] See the works of Schäfer and Yavetz, already cited, and Momigliano, op. cit., chap. 5; A. Giovannini, "Les origines de l'antijudaïsme dans le monde grec," *Cahiers du Centre G. Glotz* 6 (1995), 41–60.

[7] Gager, *The Origins of Anti-Semitism*, insists on this point.

[8] See on this: Tzvetan Todorov, *On Human Diversity: Nationalism, Racism and Exoticism in French Thought* (Cambridge, MA, 1993), pp. 140–146, "Linguistic Races" dealing in particular with Ernest Renan. Renan regarded the Semites and Aryans as "linguistic races." Whatever this means, Todorov, 145, points out that Ernest Renan and Le Bon "simply transpose onto culture the prejudices that are commonly attached to race." Renan, *Histoire générale et système comparé des langues Sémitiques* (Paris 1878), 587, predicts that "The great Indo-European race is obviously destined to incorporate all the others."

[9] Some scholars attempt to give common characteristics of all the Semitic peoples: Renan, *Histoire générale*, 9–16; E. Meyer, *Geschichte des Altertums* 1.2, §330 ff., esp. §352: "Allgemeiner Charakter der Semiten"; see also the first edition of the *Cambridge Ancient History* 1, chapter 5, pp.181–237: the Semites. The term "anti-Semitism' was coined in 1879 by the German agitator Wilhelm Marr to designate the anti-Jewish campaigns under way in central Europe at that time. He began the publication of his *Antisemitische Hefte* in the following year. For Marr, cf. Moshe Zimmermann, *Wilhelm Marr, "the Patriarch of Anti-Semitism"* (Jerusalem, 1982). In English the term has been current since 1881 according to the *OED*. Cf. Yavetz, *Judenfeindschaft*, 49–51 for various definitions. Lucid observations by Bolkestein, cited in the next note, p.153f.

and early twentieth centuries usually had not met Arabs, or if they had, may not have disliked them, but they hated their own Jewish compatriots. For the sake of convenience, they imagined that these belonged to a different race, although the term was supposed to apply to language-use rather than origin. Anti-semitism is therefore a term which denotes hostility to an imaginary race.[10] The *OED* defines it as: "Theory, action, or practice directed against the Jews. Hence *anti-Semite*, one who is hostile or opposed to the Jews."

It has often been observed that fear is an inseparable part of modern anti-semitism.[11] Hence "Judeophobia," the term used by Zvi Yavetz as well as in Peter Schäfer's book on the subject. It is an evocative term, coined by the Russian doctor, Leon Pinsker, in his pamphlet *Auto-Emancipation*. The disadvantage of the term is that it only relates to one part of a complex of feelings and attitudes: it emphasizes the element of fear and ignores that of hostility and does not adequately describe the delusional nature of anti-semitism, whether or not this did exist in antiquity.[12] The term "xenophobia" has the same disadvan-

---

[10] H. Bolkestein, "Antisemitisme in de Oudheid," *Socialistische Gids* 21 (1936), 152–166 and A. G. Roos, "Joden en Jodenvervolging in het Oude Egypte," *De Gids* 110 (1947), 1–25 both argue that ancient hatred of the Jews was not racism, because there was no concept of "race" in antiquity and therefore no racism. They also argue that it was not economic in nature, but caused by religious and social tensions. Bolkestein argues that these were reinforced by Jewish religious arrogance. According to Roos an important cause of ancient hatred of the Jews was fear of proselytism. W. den Boer, in his review of Sherwin-White, *Classical Journal* 65 (1969), 184, criticizes Sherwin-White for overlooking these papers "presumably because they are written in Dutch." This is not quite fair. Even those who read Dutch without effort do not usually consult *De Socialistische Gids* and *De Gids* for publications on antiquity. The idea that ancient anti-semitism was a form of racism is already rejected by Johannes Leipoldt in his brief monograph: *Antisemitismus in der alten Welt* (Leipzig, 1933), 17–20. L. Poliakov, "L'antisémitisme est-il un racisme?," in M. Wieviorka (ed.), *Racisme et modernité* (Paris, 1993), 82–84, argues again that ancient antisemitism, which he calls by that name, was not racism because the latter did not exist in antiquity. He ignores not only Bolkestein and Roos but also den Boer, even though the latter wrote in English.

[11] Jean-Paul Sartre, *Réflections sur la question juive* (Paris, 1954), 62: (l'antisémite) "C'est un homme qui a peur. Non des Juifs, certes : de lui-même, de sa conscience, de sa liberté, de ses instincts, de ses responsabilités, de la solitude, du changement, de la société et du monde ; de tout sauf des Juifs." Similarly, Albert Memmi in his *Le racisme. Description, définition, traitement* (Paris, 1982), which I had to consult in the German translation: *Rassismus* (Frankfurt/Main, 1987), 100: "The racist is a person who is afraid; he is afraid because he is the aggressor and he is aggressor because he is afraid."

[12] Margaret H. Williams, in her review of Yavetz and Schäfer, in *JRS* 89 (1999), 213, doubts whether the term "Judeophobia," "with its clear implication of irrationality, is entirely appropriate." She considers that there is much evidence in ancient sources for gentile dislike of Jews in the Graeco-Roman world. She then states that this dislike does not appear to have been particularly phobic. "Irrational fear of Jews is surely the product of a much later age." The implication of this pronouncement would seem to be that gentile dislike of Jews in this period was rational. Schäfer, Yavetz, and Williams seem to agree with Sherwin-White that racial or group hatred has to be characterized by fear if it is to be recognized as such. Schäfer and Yavetz, however, would not agree with Sherwin-White that the cause of ancient hatred of the Jews lay in the attitudes and behavior of the Jews themselves. This view has been around in various forms for many years. See, e.g., Th. Mommsen, *Römische Geschichte* 5.519: "Der Judenhass und die Judenhetzen sind so alt wie die Diaspora selbst; diese privilegierten und autonomen orientalischen Gemeinden innerhalb

tage. There "misoxenia" might have been preferable to indicate hatred of foreigners. "Judenfeindschaft," which Zvi Yavetz uses in the title of his monograph, is a convenient German compound for which there is no English equivalent.[13] "Anti-judaism" raises associations with early Christian hostility, which will not be discussed here.[14]

Two definitions of anti-semitism offered in a recent work may also be considered in this connection:[15]

> 1. hostility towards Jews as a group which results from no legitimate cause or greatly exceeds any reasonable, ethical response to genuine provocation.
> 2. a pejorative perception of Jewish physical or moral traits which is either utterly groundless or a result of irrational generalization and exaggeration.

In the author's comments on these definitions I miss a firm rejection of them on the ground that any hostility towards a larger group of people or collective is a major error in judgment, whether there has been genuine provocation or not. In fact the author takes for granted that a large dose of collective intolerance has to be accepted as the norm in a healthy society. These definitions allow for an extremely broad range of group hostility as long as it is claimed that there has been a certain degree of provocation. To mention just one possibility: does it make sense at all to allow for the existence of "a pejorative perception of Jewish physical traits which is *not* groundless," as would follow from the first definition? Would this sort of statement be considered acceptable if applied to various other minorities in the United States? The essence of ethnic prejudice and racist hatred lies in the unjustifiably collective nature of the concept, not in the actual behavior or appearance of the target of the prejudices or hatred. Racism is a state of mind and any definition that places the onus of collective hostility on the target is a form of justification of such attitudes. Berger asks (p. 4): "At what point does a generalization become irrational?" The answer is

---

der hellenischen mussten sie so notwendig entwickeln wie der Sumpf die böse Luft." Leipoldt, *Antisemitismus in der alten Welt*, 20: "die religiöse Besonderheit des Juden erregte unangenehmes Aufsehen, und zwar um so mehr, als der Jude auf diese Besonderheiten stolz war." See also pp. 23 and 31: "Es fehlte dem Judentume an innerer Verbundenheit mit seinem Wirtsvolke." A recent example of the suggestion that, essentially, the Jews themselves are to be held responsible for anti-semitism can be found in C. Habicht, "Hellenismus und Judentum in der Zeit des Judas Makkabäus," in *Jahrbuch der Heidelberger Akademie der Wissenschaften für das Jahr 1974* (Heidelberg, 1974), 97–110, at 109. See also the introduction to part 2 of this book.

[13] Zvi Yavetz published an article in English, preceding his monograph entitled: "Judeophobia in Classical Antiquity. A Different Approach," *JJS* 44 (1993), 1–22. Schäfer, 6f. For psychiatric considerations of anti-semitism: Erik H. Erikson, *Childhood and Society* (New York, 1950), 332f., comparing Hitler's anti-Semitism with Syphilophobia; Rudolph M. Loewenstein, *Christians and Jews: a Psychoanalytic Study* (New York, 1963 [first published in 1951]).

[14] For Christian anti-semitism: Jules Isaac, *Jésus et Israël* (1948); English: *Jesus and Israel* (New York, 1971); M. Simon, *Verus Israel: A Study of the Relations between Christians and Jews in the Roman Empire (135–425)* (originally published in French in 1964, English translation, Oxford, 1986); R. Ruether, *Faith and Fratricide: the Theological Roots of Anti-Semitism* (New York, 1974).

[15] David Berger, "Anti-Semitism: An Overview," in Berger (ed.), *History and Hate: The Dimensions of Anti-Semitism* (Philadelphia and New York, 1986), 3–14, at 3.

simple: conceptually, generalizations are irrational by definition. Indeed Berger observes, regarding these definitions, that they "can place an atypical and sometimes unwelcome burden on historians, who must consequently make ethical judgments a central part of historical analysis."

There are two points to raise in response to this statement. First, if these definitions place such a burden on historians, that proves them to be faulty definitions, inviting a confused mixture of preaching and analysis. Second, it is quite clear that many historians do not find it an unwelcome burden at all to make ethical judgments. Studies in ancient history are replete with them as shown, for instance, in Sherwin-White's evaluation of ancient attitudes towards the Jews: "Here one notes the characteristic phenomenon of the subject of race prejudice showing an insufficient awareness of the traits that cause him to be disliked."[16] It appears that Sherwin-White in this case would define and interpret race prejudice as "justified collective dislike." He has no doubt that the Jews themselves were the cause of anti-semitism in antiquity. He writes further: "It would seem that Jewish communities outside Judaea were trying to have it both ways: to live as self-contained Judaic colonies, and at the same time to secure the private advantage of local citizenship, while refusing to share in the burdens and duties of local government. . . . It was not surprising if animosity intensified in such circumstances" (94). This represents a common line of thought, encountered in the writings of Jews and non-Jews in the nineteenth and twentieth centuries. To non-Jewish anti-semites it has the advantage of making Jews responsible for anti-semitism; to Jews it gives the advantage of a notion that they themselves could and should solve the problem of anti-semitism.[17] It may even be found in modified form in the writings of authors who emphatically reject racist discrimination of Jews. Theodor Mommsen concludes his famous essay against anti-semitism in Germany with a call for the Jews to give up their separateness and join the Christian German nation.[18] They had to give up their Jewishness, just like he, Mommsen, had given up his identity as a native from Holstein who became a citizen of the newly founded German state. This is an approach which denies any ethnic or religious minority the right to

---

[16] Sherwin-White, p. 87 n. 2: on Jos, *c. Ap.* 2.11 and *BJ* 2.17.3 (411–416). See also: "the separatism of the Jewish community within the very cities where they tried to infiltrate into the local franchise. Prejudice arising from this separatism continued to ferment between Greeks and Jews" (95). Note the terminology: "trying to infiltrate" rather than "settle" or "migrate."

[17] B. Rubin, *Assimilation and its Discontents* (New York, 1995), 55f.; Ritchie Robertson, *The "Jewish Question" in German Literature 1749–1939: Emancipation and its Discontents* (Oxford, 1999), chapter 4. The idea has been discarded succinctly in one sentence by Jean-Paul Sartre, *Réflections sur la question juive*, 18: "C'est donc l'idée qu'on se fait du Juif qui semble déterminer l'histoire, non la donnée historique qui fait naître l'idée."

[18] Theodor Mommsen, *Auch ein Wort über unser Judenthum* (Berlin, 1880), 15f.: "Ausserhalb dieser Schranken zu bleiben ist möglich, aber schwer und gefahrenvoll . . . es ist ihre Pflicht, so weit sie es können ohne gegen ihr Gewissen zu handeln, auch ihrerseits die Sonderart nach bestem Vermögen von sich zu thun und alle Schranken zwischen sich und den übrigen deutschen Mitbürgern mit entschlossener Hand niederzuwerfen."

exist. It takes an absolute form of social intolerance for granted as the natural state of affairs. The justification of intolerance towards minorities makes sense only if it is taken for granted that those minorities ought not to exist. Such attitudes were more common in previous generations than they are in our times, when the idea of multiculturalism has gained respectability if not universal acceptance.

To conclude this discussion, I would say there is nothing very wrong with the definition of anti-semitism found in the *OED,* cited above.[19] It is, however, possible to go at least one step further. Anti-semitism is defined properly only if it is recognized as a form of racism or collective prejudice. These terms have been defined in the Introduction to the entire work. We can speak of racist anti-semitism if it attributes to the Jews collective traits, physical, mental, and moral, which are unalterable by human will, because they are caused by hereditary factors or external influences, such as climate and geography. Anti-semitism is not racist, but a form of ethnic or religious prejudice if it does not deny in principle the possibility of change or variation at an individual or even collective level. The presumed group characteristics are not then held to be stable, unalterable, or imposed from the outside through physical factors: biology, climate, or geography.[20]

It may be useful to illustrate this with an example from recent history. In the nineteenth century it was possible for Jews in Germany and Austria to occupy certain high positions only if they were baptized. One of the better known cases is that of Gustav Mahler, who could become director of the Vienna Opera only after formal conversion. Such baptized Jews of course could remain the targets of anti-semitism, but formally they were counted as Germans and Austrians of good standing. According to the criteria here proposed this is ethnic and religious discrimination, not racism. Personal choice could determine one's identity.[21] By contrast, the Nürnberger race laws regarded baptized Jews or their baptized children still as Jews, which removes any scope for personal choice or variation. This makes them racist by definition, as they were intended to be. We shall have to see which form—if any—is applicable to the ancient forms of hostility towards the Jews.

I have arranged the subject matter here by topic, rather than in chronological order or by author, for in this manner we should get an impression of ideas current over the centuries. Obviously, no arrangement can be entirely satisfactory, since so many themes are interconnected or appear linked in the same

---

[19] The *Britannica* has "hostility toward or discrimination against Jews as a religious or racial group." This is not at all satisfactory for it leaves one wondering what is meant by "the Jews as a racial group." It is typical and worrying that a recent edition of a major work of reference still uses such terminology, for in using it, it accepts the conceptual premises of the racists. See also the discussion in Sevenster's introduction: *The Roots of Pagan anti-semitism,* 1–5.

[20] Cf. George M. Fredrickson, *Racism: a Short History* (2002), 7: "racism is not operative if members of stigmatized groups can voluntarily change their identities and advance to positions of prominence and prestige within the dominant group."

[21] Accordingly, Mommsen's demand of the Jews to give up their group identity and religion and join the Christian German nation, cited here, is ethnic and religious intolerance cautiously phrased. It should not be called racism.

texts, necessitating repeated cross-references. However, all the sources, except Josephus's *Jewish War* and *Antiquities* are easily accessible in Stern's three volumes on *Greek and Roman Authors on Jews and Judaism.*[22] Concepts and stereotypes about Jews are best grouped as follows: (1) The social sphere, a topic which will include some observation about converts to Judaism and sympathizers. (2) Religion. These two headings themselves will again be subdivided by topic.

First, however, it will be useful to go over the evidence for the formal status of the Jews in Rome and the provinces in the early empire.[23] Julius Caesar and Augustus in particular took various measures to confirm the formal recognition of the Jews in the Roman Empire. A considerable number of official documents have been preserved by Josephus.[24] Tessa Rajak has shown that these are not based on a charter protecting the legal status of the Jews throughout the empire. This form of legislation was not required in the existing circumstances.[25] Rajak argues that the documents cited by Josephus constitute a series of ad hoc measures taken to protect the Jews confirming the rights of Jewish communities in various locations and usually enacted in response to attacks on Jewish practices in the provinces.

Some of these documents represent *senatus consulta,* some exemptions by Julius Caesar and Augustus themselves, and some are similar documents from Roman magistrates or governors of the late republic or early empire. All of them are intended to ensure the Jews the right to practice their own religion and to retain their privileges. Caesar's policy was generally repressive of associations in Rome, since at that time they served various political ends, and for this reason "Caesar banned all *collegia* other than those existing from earlier times."[26] This was common practice in antiquity in monarchical states. Aristotle already explains this in detail as one of the means whereby tyrannies are preserved, namely the prohibition "of common meals, clubs, education, and anything of a

<hr>

[22] Stern's collection also includes many non nonfavourable or admiring comments about Jews by Greeks and Romans.

[23] E. Schürer, *The History of the Jewish People in the Age of Jesus Christ (175 BC–AD 135),* revised ed. by G. Vermes, F. Millar, M. Goodman (Edinburgh 1973–), vol. 1, p. 275; 3, chap. II2, pp. 107–125; W. Horbury, W. D. Davies, and J. Sturdy (eds.), *The Cambridge History of Judaism* vol. 3: *The Early Roman Period* (Cambridge 1999), chap. 6 (by E. Mary Smallwood), esp. 172–177.

[24] Josephus, *Ant.* 14.10 (185–267) and 16.6 (160–179); Suetonius, *Augustus,* 93. Cf. J. Juster, *Les Juifs dans l'empire romain* 1 (1914), 213–242; 391–408; 2. 1–27; Rabello: *ANRW* 2.13 (1980), 662–762; T. Rajak, "Was there a Roman Charter for the Jews?" *JRS* 74 (1984), 107–123 = *The Jewish Dialogue with Greece and Rome* (2001), 301–333; J.-E. Bernard, "Transferts historiographiques: Josèphe, César et les privilèges juifs," *Bull. du Centre de la Recherche français de Jérusalem,* CNRS Editions, 2, 1998, 13–24; see now M. Pucci Ben-Zeev, *Jewish Rights in the Roman World* (Tübingen, 1998).

[25] Rajak, op. cit., Rajak, p. 112, asks whether any of this material had, in the Roman perception, a general application or any validity as precedent, beyond the specific context. In spite of Josephus's suggestion to this effect, the conclusion is that this was not the case.

[26] Suet. *Div. Iul.* 42.3: cuncta collegia praeter antiquitus constituta distraxit; *Div Aug.* 32. For associations, permitted, and political clubs, forbidden from the time of Caesar and Augustus: Schürer, 1. p.112, n.23.

like character—or, in other words, a defensive attitude against everything likely to produce the two qualities of mutual confidence and a high spirit. A second measure is to prohibit societies for cultural purposes, and any gathering of a similar character: in a word, the adoption of every means for making every subject as much of a stranger as is possible to every other. (Mutual acquaintance always tends to create mutual confidence.)"[27]

While *collegia* had organized freely under the republic, this came to an end under Caesar, possibly as a result of the political role they had played in the years of unrest.[28] This then became a basic principle of Roman rule under the principate, both in Rome and the provinces. One document cited by Josephus seems to indicate that these measures did not apply to the Jews. They are said to have been excepted from this ban on *collegia* because of the antiquity of their institutions and previous precedent.[29] Caesar stipulates that the Jews are an *ethnos* ruled in Judaea by a recognized ethnarch/high priest, with the status of friend and ally.[30] These rulers are allowed to decide on all questions concerning the Jews' way of life.[31] Through Caesar's favor, Jews living outside Palestine may also have been granted important privileges.

Recently it has been argued that the document cited by Josephus is not reliable evidence of an exemption for the Jews.[32] Philo testifies to the toleration of the Jews in Rome in the reign of Augustus:[33]

[27] Aristotle, *Pol.* 1313a–b (trans. Ernest Barker): καὶ μήτε συσσίτια ἐᾶν μήτε ἑταιρίαν μήτε παιδείαν μήτε ἄλλο μηθὲν τοιοῦτον, ἀλλὰ πάντα φυλάττειν ὅθεν εἴωθε γίγνεσθαι δύο, φρόνημά τε καὶ πίστις, καὶ μήτε σχολὰς μήτε ἄλλους συλλόγους ἐπιτρέπειν γίγνεσθαι σχολαστικούς, καὶ πάντα ποιεῖν ἐξ ὧν ὅτι μάλιστα ἀγνῶτες ἀλλήλοις ἔσονται πάντες (ἡ γὰρ γνῶσις πίστιν ποιεῖ μᾶλλον πρὸς ἀλλήλους)·.

[28] Wendy Cotter, "The Collegia and Roman Law: State Restrictions on Voluntary Associations 64 BCE-200 CE," in J. S. Kloppenborg and S. G. Wilson, *Voluntary Associations in the Graeco-Roman World* (London, 1996), 74–89, at 74–76. As noted on p. 76, the first prohibition occurred in 64 B.C., when the senate dissolved all suspect collegia, but synagogues were exempt. Possible reasons for this exemption are discussed on p. 77.

[29] See *Ant.* 14.10.8 (213–216): The Jews alone were permitted to assemble, "or to collect contributions of money or to hold common meals. Similarly do I forbid other religious societies but permit these people alone to assemble and feast in accordance with their native customs and ordinances."

[30] *Ant.* 14.10.2 (194f.): Ὑρκανὸν Ἀλεξάνδρου καὶ τὰ τέκνα αὐτοῦ ἐθνάρχας Ἰουδαίων εἶναι ἀρχιερωσύνην τε Ἰουδαίων διὰ παντὸς ἔχειν κατὰ τὰ πάτρια ἔθη, εἶναί τε αὐτὸν καὶ τοὺς παῖδας αὐτοῦ συμμάχους ἡμῖν ἔτι τε καὶ ἐν τοῖς κατ' ἄνδρα φίλοις ἀριθμεῖσθαι, ὅσα τε κατὰ τοὺς ἰδίους αὐτῶν νόμους ἐστὶν ἀρχιερατικὰ φιλάνθρωπα, ταῦτα κελεύω κατέχειν αὐτὸν καὶ τὰ τέκνα αὐτοῦ· Also: 14.10.4 (199).

[31] ἄν τε μεταξὺ γένηταί τις ζήτησις περὶ τῆς Ἰουδαίων ἀγωγῆς, ἀρέσκει μοι κρίσιν γίνεσθαι [παρ' αὐτοῖς].

[32] Margaret Williams, "The Jewish Community in Rome," in Martin Goodman (ed.), *Jews in a Graeco-Roman World* (Oxford, 1998), 215–228, at 217–221, where the reliability of Josephus's document is questioned. Williams goes on to argue that the Romans did not formally classify the synagogues of the city of Rome as *collegia*. There was, she suggests, some form of supra-synagogal structure, a common council. The problem is discussed also by E. Gruen, *Diaspora: Jews amidst the Greeks and Romans* (Cambridge, MA, 2002), 24–26.

[33] Philo, *Leg.* 23 (155–7); cf. Cotter, "Collegia," 78f.

Augustus knew that the great region of Rome across the Tiber is occupied and inhabited by Jews, most of whom were emancipated Roman citizens. After having been brought as captives to Italy, they were liberated by their owners and they were not forced to violate any of their ancestral customs. He knew, therefore, that they have houses of prayer where they meet together, especially on the sacred sabbaths . . . He knew also that they collect money for sacred purposes from their firstfruits and send them to Jerusalem . . . Yet he neither banished them from Rome nor deprived them of their Roman citizenship.

After Caesar's death, his decisions regarding the Jews in the provinces were confirmed.[34] This included the right to send money to the Temple in Jerusalem which, as will be seen below, Cicero and Tacitus found objectionable.[35] The usual expression is that the Jews are permitted to follow "the laws of their fathers." The emphasis here always is on the *ethnarch* and the *ethnos,* and on children and their fathers. The Jews have these privileges because they were an *ethnos*, a people. At this point it is relevant to note that the Jewish religion is often described as a *religio licita* in the modern literature, an expression cited out of context from Tertullian's *Apologeticum,* which is not a legal or formal text but a Christian source and one in which Judaism is referred to with irony and even sarcasm.[36] The term *religio licita* is not attested anywhere else in ancient sources. Judaism is more often described as *superstitio* than as *religio,* and national cults were normally permitted, unless there were specific reasons to ban them. In a non-Christian Roman text, the expression *religio licita* would be irrelevant, for subject peoples normally had a right to practice their ancestral religion. A much discussed episode in the reign of Claudius may have led to temporary restrictions of the freedom of assembly for Jews, if we follow Cassius Dio.[37]

By the second century, legislation ruled that Jews were only permitted to circumcise their own sons, as stipulated in a rescript from Antoninus Pius, which adds that circumcision of non-Jews is punishable.[38] The rescript thus determines that Jewish identity is exclusively a matter of origin and it effectively makes full conversion a criminal act. This is further made explicit in

[34] *Ant.*14.10.10 (219–222); 14.10.11–12 (223); 14.10.20 (241).

[35] 16.6.1 (163).

[36] Tertullian, *Apologeticum* 21: . . . quasi sub umbraculo insignissimae religionis, certe licitae. . . . By contrast it is said about Christianity, *Apol.* 4.4: Iam primum cum dure definitis dicendo: Non licet esse vos! Cf. T. D. Barnes, *Tertullian: A Historical and Literary Study* (Oxford, 1971), 90f. See H. Castritius in *Judentum und Antisemitismus von der Antike bis zur Gegenwart,* Thomas Klein et al. (eds.) (Düsseldorf, 1984), 22.

[37] Dio 60.6.6, for which see below p. 458, note 82. Suetonius, *Claudius* 25.4, states that the Jews were in fact expelled, "because they all the time made disturbances at the instigation of Chrestus." See also *Acts* 18:2; Orosius 7.6.16 and references to modern literature, below, in the chapter on Christianity. For extensive discussion of the statement by Dio, with full references to secondary literature, H. Botermann, *Das Judenedikt des Kaisers Claudius: Römischer Staat und Christiani im 1. Jahrhundert* (Stuttgart, 1996), 103–140; H. Dixon Slingerland, *Claudian Policymaking and the Early Imperial Repression of Judaism at Rome* (Atlanta, GA, 1997).

[38] *Dig.* 48.8.11 (Modestinus), discussed also below.

another legal text: Roman citizens who allow themselves or their slaves to be circumcised in accordance with the Jewish custom, are to be exiled.³⁹ It has been argued that conversion was subject to criminal sanction as being in violation of the prohibition of atheism.⁴⁰ The proselyte was not punishable for worshiping the Jewish god, but because he failed to worship the proper gods, which was a criminal omission. Whether these laws actually prevented conversion as they were intended to is another matter, to be discussed below. What is clear, however, is that the Jews, as a recognized people—but only they themselves and their descendants—were allowed to practice their religion without hindrance, both in Judaea and elsewhere, and even in Rome. This did not change when Judaea was incorporated as a province, nor was the essence of this status affected by the Jewish revolts against Rome.⁴¹

THE SOCIAL SPHERE

Turning now to concepts and stereotypes about Jews, it is clear that they are accused of being antisocial, cutting themselves off from the rest of humanity.⁴² This idea is expressed by Diodorus, citing Hecataeus of Abdera,⁴³ and in two parallel passages in Diodorus and Josephus, which may or may not be based on Posidonius.⁴⁴ These describe the friends of Antiochus Sidetes as advising him

---

³⁹ Paulus, *Sententiae*, 5.22.3–4 ap. Linder, *The Jews in Roman Imperial Legislation* (1987), no.6, pp. 117–120.

⁴⁰ Juster, *Les Juifs dans l'Empire romain: leur condition juridique, économique et sociale,* vol. 1, 256, against Mommsen, *Gesammelte Schriften* 3.389ff. Cf. A. M. Rabello, "The Attitude of Rome Towards Conversions to Judaism" reprinted in *The Jews in the Roman Empire* (2000), xiv.47; "A Tribute to Jean Juster," ibid. xv.222f.

⁴¹ After the destruction of the Temple the money sent by Jews to Jerusalem was converted into the *fiscus Judaicus* and there is considerable uncertainty about Hadrian's possible prohibition of circumcision. At the most, it was a temporary measure. Simon, *Verus Israel,* 41, states that Roman attitudes towards the Jews were more positive after A.D. 70. "Among the sentiments the pagans express it is even possible to detect a new and more positive note. Little by little the old anti-Semitic spirit gives way, especially among the educated classes, to a distinct sympathy, nourished by a common hostility to the common enemy [sc. Christianity]." In support of this peculiar pronouncement he cites Porphyry and Iamblichus.

⁴² Sevenster, *The Roots of Pagan Anti-Semitism,* discusses under the heading "Strangeness" in chapter 3, both different behavior in the social sphere and unusual religious customs. He regards this as the "fundamental reason for pagan anti-Semitism" (chap. 3, pp. 89–144).

⁴³ Diodorus 40.3.4 (Stern, No. 11): ἀπάνθρωπόν τινα καὶ μισόξενον βίον εἰσηγήσατο. Cf. Jos., *contra Apionem* 2.258 (Stern, No. 258), which, however, represents the Alexandrian tradition not discussed here in detail; see below. Stern, 2, 39 also refers to the formulation of Paul in 1 Thess. 2.14f.: Ἰουδαίων . . . πᾶσιν ἀνθρώποις ἐναντίων.

⁴⁴ Diodorus, *Bibliotheca Historica* 34–35.1.1f. (Stern, No. 63, with comments on pp.183f.): μόνους γὰρ ἁπάντων ἐθνῶν ἀκοινωνήτους εἶναι τῆς πρὸς ἄλλο ἔθνος ἐπιμιξίας καὶ πολεμίους ὑπολαμβάνειν πάντας. μόνους γὰρ ἁπάντων ἐθνῶν ἀκοινωνήτους εἶναι τῆς πρὸς ἄλλο ἔθνος ἐπιμιξίας καὶ πολεμίους ὑπολαμβάνειν πάντας . . . συστησαμένους δὲ τὸ τῶν Ἰουδαίων ἔθνος παραδόσιμον ποιῆσαι τὸ μῖσος τὸ πρὸς τοὺς ἀνθρώπους· διὰ τοῦτο δὲ καὶ νόμιμα παντελῶς

"to wipe out completely the Jewish people, since they alone of all nations avoided dealings with any other people and looked upon all men as their enemies." Their ancestors having been expelled from Egypt because they were impious and detested by the gods, the Jews "made hatred of mankind into a tradition, and on this account had introduced utterly outlandish laws: not to break bread with any other race, nor to show them any good will at all." Josephus says the advisors urged the king "to extirpate this nation because of the separateness of their way of life."[45]

It is not easy to say whether these passages should be regarded as Hellenistic rather than Roman in spirit because the origin of the ideas is obscure. In any event, it is clear that the passage cited is the first occurrence of concepts which later became prominent among a number of Roman authors who wrote about the Jews. The essential phrase here appears to be that the Jews are unsociable (μόνους γὰρ ἁπάντων ἐθνῶν ἀκοινωνήτους). A variant appears in Philo's work, who defends the Jews against claims that their laws command misanthropic and unsociable practices.[46] This was repeated in rather similar terms by Celsus (second century A.D.), as cited by Origen: "they are proud and refuse the society of others."[47] It has been seen above that Greek authors from the treatise on *Airs* onward considered sociability an indispensable feature of a civilized people. In a passage already cited, Aristotle states: "The man who is isolated—who is unable to share (κοινωνεῖν) in the benefits of political association, or has no need to share because he is already self-sufficient—is no part of the polis, and must therefore be either a beast or a god."[48] Strabo and Diodorus, cited above, consider it a characteristic of remote barbaric people that they are cut off from other peoples. These, however, are wild and distant people, which the Jews are not.

According to Diodorus, the Jews are regarded as unique because they cut themselves off from other peoples by their own choice. In the text transmitted by Diodorus, the instruments by which the Jews keep themselves apart are bizarre customs: not sharing meals and hating all other peoples.[49] The idea is expressed in particularly fierce form by Philostratus in the third century in a speech which he attributes to the Stoic Euphrates:

> For the Jews have long been in revolt not only against the Romans but against humanity; and a people that has made its own a life apart and irreconcilable, that

---

ἐξηλλαγμένα καταδεῖξαι, τὸ μηδενὶ ἄλλῳ ἔθνει τραπέζης κοινωνεῖν μηδ᾽ εὐνοεῖν τὸ παράπαν.

[45] Jos., *Ant.* 13. 8.2 (245): ὁ δὲ ἀπωσάμενος τὴν ἐπι βουλὴν τῶν μὲν παραινούντων ἐξελεῖν τὸ ἔθνος διὰ τὴν πρὸς ἄλλους αὐτῶν τῆς διαίτης ἀμιξίαν οὐκ ἐφρόντιζεν. See above, chapter 2, n. 186, for another aspect regarding this tradition.

[46] Philo, *De Virtutibus* 141: τοὺς δὲ νόμους ὡς ἄμικτα καὶ ἀκοινώνητα παραγγέλλοντας . . .

[47] Celsus ap. Origenes, *Contra Celsum* 5.2.41 (Stern, No. 375, p. 256): εἰ δ᾽ ὥς τι σοφώτερον εἰδότες σεμνύνονταί τε καὶ τὴν ἄλλων κοινωνίαν. . . .

[48] Aristotle, *Pol.* 1253a (trans. Ernest Barker): ὁ δὲ μὴ δυνάμενος κοινωνεῖν ἢ μηδὲν δεόμενος δι᾽ αὐτάρκειαν οὐθὲν μέρος πόλεως, ὥστε ἢ θηρίον ἢ θεός.

[49] The themes of misanthropy and xenophobia are analyzed by Schäfer, *Judeophobia*, 170–177.

cannot share with the rest of mankind in the pleasures of the table nor join in their libations or prayers or sacrifices, are separated from ourselves by a greater gulf than divides us from Susa or Bactra or the more distant Indies. What sense then or reason was there in chastising them for revolting from us, whom we had better have never annexed?[50]

The assertion that it would have been better not to annex the Jews is new and relatively rare. We shall encounter it below in a statement by Rutilius Namatianus. The claim that they are unsociable is familiar, but it is interesting to see the specific reasons: the refusal to eat and worship together. Noteworthy is furthermore the assertion that the Jews are more remote than the farthest peoples of the world.

The pagan rejection of the Jews because of the customs that separate them from all other peoples may originate in Hellenistic Egypt, as has been argued forcefully by several scholars.[51] If so, this is remarkable, for the Egyptians themselves were regarded in this light by the Greeks and Romans. The Egyptian people "resembles only itself," says the treatise on *Airs, Waters, Places*, 19. Herodotus (2.35) writes about Egypt that the climate and rivers, as well as the manners and customs of the people, are the reverse of those in the rest of the world. As for the Jews, even if the idea of their separateness did originate in Egypt, it subsequently became firmly entrenched in Roman literature. Tacitus returns to these themes. He is one of the two Roman authors to repeat the Egyptian-Hellenistic tradition which claimed that the Jews were expelled from Egypt because they suffered from a plague.[52] This is a remarkable reversion of the exodus story, but as such not prominent in the Latin literature[53]—nor important as an anti-semitic theme in later periods. It is also, clearly, connected with a desire to explain the separateness of the Jews as caused by their original impurity rather than their social code.[54]

Tacitus, however, also gives another explanation for the Jewish social themes: "To establish his influence over this people for all time, Moses introduced new religious practices, quite opposed to those of all other religions. The Jews regard as profane all that we hold sacred; on the other hand, they permit

[50] Philostratus, *Vita Apollonii* 5.33 (trans. F. C. Conybeare, Loeb): ἐκεῖνοι μὲν γὰρ πάλαι ἀφεστᾶσιν οὐ μόνον Ῥωμαίων, ἀλλὰ καὶ πάντων ἀνθρώπων· οἱ γὰρ βίον ἄμικτον εὑρόντες καὶ οἷς μήτε κοινὴ πρὸς ἀνθρώπους τράπεζα μήτε σπονδαὶ μήτε εὐχαὶ μήτε θυσίαι, πλέον ἀφεστᾶσιν ἡμῶν ἢ Σοῦσα καὶ Βάκτρα καὶ οἱ ὑπὲρ ταῦτα Ἰνδοί· οὐκοῦν οὐδ' εἰκὸς ἦν τιμωρεῖσθαι τούτους ἀφισταμένους, οὓς βέλτιον ἦν μηδὲ κτᾶσθαι.

[51] Schäfer, 163–170, with discussion of previous literature.

[52] Tacitus, *Hist.* 5.3.1 (Stern, No. 281, comments, vol. 2.35); Pompeius Trogus, apud: Iustinus 36.2.12 (Stern, No. 137). Cf. Erich S. Gruen, *Heritage and Hellenism: The Reinvention of Jewish Tradition* (Berkeley, 1998), chap. 2: "The Use and Abuse of the Exodus," where it is argued that some of the classical texts dealing with the Exodus story have been interpreted in a simplistic manner under the influence of Josephus.

[53] Robertson, *The "Jewish Question" in German Literature*, 23f. notes that the tradition was taken over by authors of the Enlightenment, notably Giordano Bruno and Friedrich Schiller.

[54] Pompeius Trogus, op. cit., 36.1.15, says so explicitly.

all that we abhor.["55] The Jews are thought to have cut themselves off from the remainder of humanity by adopting religious customs and morals distinct from or even opposed to those of all other peoples. Tacitus essentially follows the same line as the source of Josephus and Diodorus, but re-interprets the origin of their customs in characteristic fashion. The historian of the Principate sees Moses as a sort of Lycurgus, or rather an Augustus who fashioned the constitution so as to leave his mark forever on the state he created. It was also ancient tradition among the Romans to claim that those whose religion they did not respect had morals that were not worthy of respect either. For example, Livy attributes to a witness against the Bacchanalia in 186 B.C. the claim that "To consider nothing wrong was the highest form of religious devotion among them [sc. the participants in the rites]."[56] Thus similarly, in the next chapter of his *Histories*, Tacitus repeats that the Jews, while maintaining strict loyalty towards one another, "feel hostility and hatred towards all others. . . . They instituted circumcision to distinguish themselves thereby from other peoples. Those who are converted to their way of life accept the same practice, and the earliest habit they adopt is to despise the gods, to renounce their country, and to regard their parents, children, and brothers as of little consequence."[57]

There are several themes here, but the essence of the passage is, again, that it is the Jews who erect a barrier between themselves and others. Tacitus refers to dietary laws[58] and circumcision, but also introduces sexual customs. Concerning the latter he combines the ideas of unsociability and moral corruption: they keep themselves apart, even in their sexuality, but have no morals among themselves, this in contrast with the incorrupt Germans who maintain the sanctity of marriage and of the relationship between husband and wife.[59] Tacitus twice says that proselytes to Judaism are the worst (*pessimus quisque*), for they are traitors to their religion, country, and family. In accepting the foreign cult they abandon their own and, with it, all the social obligations that every decent man respects.

In roughly the same period Juvenal also attacks proselytes along similar lines: "Having been wont to deride Roman laws, they learn and follow and revere Jewish law, and all that Moses passed on in his secret volume, prohibiting to point the way to anyone not following the same rites, and leading none but the circumcised to the desired fountain."[60] This part of his satire is aimed

---

[55] Tacitus, *Hist.* 5.4.1: Moyses quo sibi in posterum gentem firmaret, novos ritus contrariosque ceteris mortalibus indidit. Profana illic omnia quae apud nos sacra, rursum concessa apud illos quae nobis incesta.

[56] Livy, 39.13.11: nihil nefas ducere, hanc summam inter eos religionem esse.

[57] *Hist.* 5.5.1: et quia apud ipsos fides obstinata misericordia in promptu, sed adversus omnes alios hostile odium. (2) Separati epulis, discreti cubilibus, proiectissima ad libidinem gens, alienarum concubitu abstinent; inter se nihil inlicitum. Circumcidere genitalia instituerunt, ut diversitate noscantur. Transgressi in morem eorum idem usurpant, nec quidquam prius imbuuntur quam contemnere deos, exuere patriam, parentes liberos fratres vilia habere.

[58] Herodotus already uses diet as a criterium of ethnicity: 3.23.1; 9.82.

[59] Tacitus, *Germania* 17, 18, discussed also above, in the chapter on Germans.

[60] Juvenal, 14.100-104 (Stern, No. 301, comments on vol. 2, pp. 107): Romanas autem soliti contemnere leges | Iudaicum ediscunt et servant ac metuunt ius, | tradidit arcano quodcumque

against Jewish proselytes, but there are several characteristics Juvenal sees
these proselytes as sharing with born Jews, the most important of which is that
they deride Roman law while honoring Jewish law. The two sets of laws are
thus considered mutually exclusive. In becoming Jewish, Juvenal is saying,
Romans cut themselves off from civilized Roman society. This is further illustrated by the claims that proselytes refuse to point the way to gentiles and that
Moses had produced a secret book.[61] The fear of foreign secret cults was already prevalent in republican Rome.[62] The idea that Jews are exclusively loyal
towards each other occurs first in Cicero's work.

> There follows the odium that is attached to Jewish gold. This is no doubt the reason
> why this case is being tried not far from the Aurelian Steps. You procured this place
> and that crowd, Laelius, for this trial. You know what a big crowd it is, how they
> stick together, how influential they are in informal assemblies. So I will speak in a
> low voice so that only the jurors may hear; for those are not wanting who would
> incite them against me and against every respectable man. I shall not help them to
> do this more easily.[63]

This is, of course, judicial rhetoric: it was Cicero's brief to discredit the testimony of Jews against Flaccus, *improbatio testium,* according to the usual practice in Roman lawcourts.[64] But the orator had to strike a chord amongst his
audience.[65] When Cicero explicitly asserts that there were large numbers of
Jews in Rome who were hostile to the *optimates* and could influence public
meetings, this must have been at least credible to those present. What Cicero
himself really thought about Jews is indeed interesting, but not important for an

---

volumine Moyses: | non monstrare vias eadem nisi sacra colenti, | quaesitum ad fontem solos
deducere verpos. This is a passage from a satire whose main theme is the bad influence that the
vices of parents have on their children; cf. Courtney's comments ad loc., p. 571f.; J. P. Stein, *CP* 65
(1970), 34ff.; Edouard Will and Claude Orrieux, *«Prosélytisme Juif»? Histoire d'une erreur* (Paris,
1992), 111f. Possibly in response to accusations like these, Josephus, *Contra Apionem* 2.211, asserts that Jews must, among other services rendered to foreigners, point out the road. Cf. *Ant.* 4.8.31
(276).

[61] The meaning of *quaesitum ad fontem solos deducere verpos* is not quite certain, see Stern,
comm. ad loc.

[62] Livy describes the Bacchanalia, against which action was taken in 186 B.C., as *occulta et
nocturna sacra* (39.8.4).

[63] Cicero, *Pro Flacco* 66f.: Sequitur auri illa invidia Iudaici. Hoc nimirum est illud quod non
longe a gradibus Aureliis haec causa dicitur. Ob hoc crimen hic locus abs te, Laeli, atque illa turba
quaesita est; scis quanta sit manus, quanta concordia, quantum valeat in contionibus. Sic submissa
voce agam tantum ut iudices audiant; neque enim desunt qui istos in me atque in optimum quemque
incitent; quos ego, quo id facilius faciant, non adiuvabo.

[64] Yavetz, *Judenfeindschaft in der Antike*, 33–35; Schäfer, 180f.

[65] Anthony J. Marshall, "Flaccus and the Jews of Asia" (Cicero *Pro Flacco* 28.67–69), *Phoenix*
29 (1975), 139–154, at 142: "the most one can safely conclude is that Cicero counted on arousing
anti-Jewish prejudice in the juror's minds to colour their consideration of the charges against
Flaccus." It is not clear to me why this is "the most" one can safely conclude. This is what one can
and should conclude and it is enough.

understanding of this part of the *Pro Flacco*.[66] Jewish *concordia* was obviously a commonplace, as was the impression that there were many Jews in Rome, believed to number enough to form pressure groups. The former is not in doubt. Not long afterwards, after the assassination of Caesar in 44 B.C., large numbers of foreign residents in Rome, particularly Jews, showed up to express their grief.[67]

Some time later Horace wrote his much-discussed lines: "This is one of those lesser frailties I spoke of, and if you should make no allowance for it, then would a big band of poets come to my aid—for we are the big majority—and we, like Jews, will compel you to become one of our throng."[68] It has often been claimed that this refers to Jewish proselytizing practices.[69] Other scholars argue that it portrays Jews as prone to use pressure to achieve their political ends and that it implies nothing about gentiles being compelled to become Jewish.[70] Since the subjects of these lines are poets, and Jews are merely an object for comparison, it is hardly likely that Horace is speaking of forced conversion. It is, however, very probable that, like Cicero, he is referring here to the political pressure which Jews could exert thanks to their mutual loyalty. Tacitus asserts that the Jews take care to increase their number and therefore are not allowed to expose any of their children.[71] Here Tacitus turns into an object of criticism what we in our times would consider humane practice. However, Aristotle had already proposed that a law should be enacted demanding the

---

[66] Yavetz, 33f., argues against some earlier scholars, cited by Stern, 1, p. 199, that there is no evidence of any fierce anti-semitism in Cicero. He had no great sympathy and was mostly indifferent. Solin, *ANRW* 2.29.2 (1983), 608f. expresses a similar view. Cf. Marshall, *Phoenix* 29 (1975), 139–154, a paper which is mostly concerned with the background and intentions of Flaccus himself. See also the discussion above and the recent article by J.-E. Bernard, "Philosophie politique et antijudaïsme chez Cicéron," *SCI* 19 (2000), 113–131.

[67] Suetonius, *Iulius* 84: In summo publico luctu exterarum gentium multitudo circulatim suo quaeque more lamentata est praecipueque Iudaei, qui etiam noctibus continuis bustum frequentarunt. Again, in the reign of Augustus large numbers of Jews living in Rome assembled to welcome the man who impersonated Alexander, the son of Herod (Josephus, *BJ* 2.7.1 [101–110]; *Ant.* 17.12.1 [324–338]).

[68] *Sermones* 1.4.139–3 (Stern, No. 127): . . . Hoc est mediocribus illis | ex vitiis unum; cui si concedere nolis, | multa poetarum veniat manus, auxilio quae | sit mihi: nam multo plures sumus, ac veluti te | Iudaei cogemus in hanc concedere turbam. Cf. the translation of N. Rudd, *Satires of Horace and Persius* (Penguin, 1973): ". . . and, like the Jews, we make you fall in with our happy band."

[69] Stern, 1. 321; 323 with references to earlier literature.

[70] J. Nolland, "Proselytism or Politics in Horace, *Satires* I.4.138–143?" *Vigiliae Christianae* 33 (1979), 347–355, emphasizing the parallel with Cicero, *Pro Flacco* 6.6; Will and Orrieux, *Prosélytisme Juif?*, 103–105; M. Goodman, *Mission and Conversion: Proselytizing in the Religious History of the Roman Empire* (Oxford, 1994), 74; Schäfer, 107f.

[71] Tacitus, *Hist.* 5.5.3: Augendae tamen multitudini consulitur; nam et necare quemquam ex agnatis nefas . . . Cf. Stern's comments, vol. 2, p. 41 and Hecataeus, ap. Diodorus 40.3.8 (Stern, no. 11). Strabo 17.2.5 (c. 824) claims that the Egyptians rear every child that is born "and circumcise the males, and excise the females, as is also customary among the Jews." For Hecataeus's assessment of Moses, see above, 2, chapter 7, n. 63.

456   · CHAPTER 13 ·

exposure of deformed children.[72] Thus, from Cicero to Tacitus we notice a
strand of thinking which holds that the Jews are loyal to one another, form an
effective pressure group, and are hostile to all non-Jews. The same would hold
true for converts, who thereby become traitors to their country and family.

It is important to keep in mind that all these texts reflect reactions to the
presence of Jews in the city of Rome. They are not vague feelings about a
distant people or a minority in various provinces, but direct responses to a
significant element in the city population. The presence of Jews living according to their own customs in Rome on the other side of the Tiber was tolerated
by Augustus and Tiberius, according to Philo, *Leg.* 23 (156f.). From time to
time efforts were made to halt the spread of Judaism among Romans in Rome,
as mentioned above,[73] possibly in 139 B.C. and, better attested, in A.D. 19, when
four thousand descendants of enfranchised slaves "infected by this religion"
were expelled together with Isis worshippers.[74] This was decided upon in a
senatus consultum, according to Tacitus. Four thousand people were mobilized
and shipped to Sardinia for the suppression of brigandage, the others had to
leave Italy or "renounce the impious rites." As formulated by Tacitus, this concerns proselytes, for they were "infected" with foreign cults and required to
renounce them. Suetonius suggests that both proselytes and born Jews were
concerned.[75] He adds that "those who were caught by this superstition were

---

[72] Aristotle, *Pol.* 1335b. It is worth noting that this is part of a program of state-imposed eugenics
which Aristotle devises, as observed above, in chapter 1. Aristotle is against the exposure of children for the sake of population control. He prefers abortion for this purpose.

[73] See above, chapter 3, p. 236f.

[74] Tacitus, *Ann.* 2.85 (Stern, No. 284 with comments on pp. 69–73); Suetonius, *Tiberius* 36;
Josephus, *Ant.* 18.3.5. (81ff.); Dio 57.18.5a. Cf. E. M. Smallwood, "Some Notes on the Jews under
Tiberius," *Latomus* 15 (1956), 314–329, where it is argued that the affair was caused by Roman
anger about proselytism. E. Abel, "Were the Jews banished from Rome in AD 19?" *REJ* 127
(1968), 383–386, argues that the four thousand expelled were not born Jews but proselytes. A
different view: M. H. Williams, "The Expulsion of the Jews from Rome in AD 19," *Latomus* 48
(1989), 765–784, with further references to earlier literature on p. 765, n. 2; Williams suggests that
the Jews were expelled in an attempt to suppress unrest caused by problems with the corn supply;
L.V. Rutgers, "Roman Policy towards the Jews: Expulsions from the City of Rome during the First
Century C.E.," *Classical Antiquity* 13 (1994), 56–74, reprinted in *The Hidden Heritage of Diaspora
Judaism* (Leuven, 1998) and in K. P. Donfried and P. Richardson (eds.), *Judaism and Christianity in
First-Century Rome* (Grand Rapids, MI, 1998), finds Williams' suggestion attractive, but insists that
important questions remain unanswered. Slingerland, *Claudian Policymaking*, 53–62, strongly disagrees with Smallwood and Williams. Slingerland, p. 61f., concludes that "the fundamental cause of
Tiberius' 19 CE actions against Roman Jews was the fact that they were practicing the rites associated with the Jewish religion, and it is equally clear that the intention of these actions was the
eradication of these practices from the city." B. Rochette, "Tibère, les cultes étrangers et les astrologues (Suétone, *Vie de Tibère*, 36)," *Les Études Classiques* 69 (2001), 189–194, briefly discusses
Suetonius's language and concludes that the entire episode was undoubtedly part of a continuous
series of measures taken to maintain public order. There is no room for any suggestion, he says, that
this is evidence of any hostility towards the Jews in Rome on the part of Tiberius. The whole
question of the expulsions of the Jews from Rome is discussed extensively by Gruen, *Diaspora*,
15–41.

[75] This follows from the phrases "qui superstitione ea tenebantur" and "reliquos gentis eiusdem
vel similia sectantes."

compelled to burn their religious vestments and all equipment," a phrase which clearly refers to proselytes rather than born Jews. The fragment which derives from Dio states explicitly that Jews were actively engaged in converting non-Jews. Josephus also tells a story about Jews who defrauded an aristocratic lady proselyte. According to this source, Tiberius ordered as a result the entire Jewish community in Rome to leave the city. It is likely that at least Tacitus and Suetonius preserve some form of the *senatus consultum*. However that may be, in spite of the variations, there is a consensus in the sources that the cause of friction was the practice of Judaism and Egyptian cults in the city of Rome, even if we accept the argument that the former was not the result of proselytizing activities initiated and pursued by Jews.[76] Even if we accept the argument of Williams that not proselytism, but social and economic unrest was the reason for the expulsion, it is still the case that foreign cults and proselytism are portrayed by several authors as a significant factor in the affair. There may not in fact have been very many proselytes in Rome in this period,[77] but for our attempt to trace the Roman views of Judaism, it is no less significant when ancient sources say there were a large number. It is the popular perspective of reality which counts, not actual reality. Similarly, in modern wealthy countries, what determines policies towards foreign workers is not the question whether they really affect the employment of citizens of those countries, but whether this is thought to be the case. In such cases politicians respond to popular pressure more than to economic reality.[78]

There are probably few issues in the history of the Jews in Rome so extensively discussed as the treatment of the Jews by the Emperor Claudius. According to Suetonius there was an order by Claudius, expelling the Jews, "because they all the time made disturbances at the instigation of Chrestus."[79] The ap-

---

[76] As argued by Goodman, *Mission and Conversion,* 68, against Stern and others. Cf. Will and Orrieux, *Prosélytisme juif?* 105–109; Schäfer, *Judeophobia,* 109–111. The issue of Jewish proselytism is a hotly debated one. For major statements of the opposing views: L. Feldman, *Jew and Gentile in the Ancient World: Attitudes and Interactions from Alexander to Justinian,* (Princeton, 1993) advocates vigorous and successful Jewish proselytism; Scot McKnight, *A Light among the Gentiles: Jewish Missionary Activity in the Second Temple Period* (Minneapolis, 1991) challenges this view, arguing that "Judaism never developed a clear mission to the Gentiles that had as its goal the conversion of the world." It was not truly a "missionary religion," although there is evidence of conversion to Judaism through a variety of means. For criticism of Feldman, see also: L. V. Rutgers, "Attitudes to Judaism in the Greco-Roman Period," reprinted in *The Hidden Heritage of Diaspora Judaism* (Leuven, 1998), 199–234.

[77] Williams, *Latomus* 48 (1989), 769–172.

[78] Erich Gruen, *Diaspora,* 29–36, suggests a connection with the tensions engendered by the death of Germanicus in 19. He also points out that, three years earlier, astrologers and magicians were expelled from Italy, following the accusation of Libo Drusus of treasonable ambitions in which practitioners of obscure arts were involved (Tac. *Ann.* 2.27–32; Suetonius, *Tiberius* 36; Dio 57.15.8). All this may reflect a climate of increased suspicion of foreign cults and foreigners in general in those years.

[79] Suetonius, *Claudius* 25.4 (Stern, No. 307): Iudaeos impulsore Chresto assidue tumultuantis Roma expulit; Dio 60.6.6; Philo, *Legatio* 155–8; Orosius 7.6.15. See Stern's comments, 2.114–7; for references to earlier discussions: Schürer, *History* 3.1. p. 77f.; recent discussion: Will and Orrieux, *Prosélytisme juif?,* 109; L. V. Rutgers, *Classical Antiquity* 13 (1994), 65f.; two full-length

pearance of the name "Chrestus" has understandably been interpreted by many as referring to Jesus; however, this appears to be an untenable assumption.[80] In any case, the passage states explicitly that Claudius expelled the Jews from Rome. A brief statement in *Acts* also says Claudius expelled the Jews from the city.[81] Dio says a little more: "As for the Jews, who had again increased so greatly that by reason of their multitude it would have been hard without raising a tumult to bar them from the city, he did not drive them out, but ordered them, while continuing their traditional mode of life, not to hold meetings."[82] There are other sources too which provide information about Claudius's policy towards the Jews. According to Tacitus, Claudius considered foreign superstitions a danger because they threatened the old Italian religious institutions which were important in times of crisis for the State.[83] A famous papyrus, P. Lond. 1912 (*CPI* 153), contains a letter dated in 41 B.C. from Claudius to the city of Alexandria which deals also with the status of the Jews there and opposes any attempt to improve their status in the city. It is likely that the various sources refer to events in Rome in two different years, probably 41 and 49, the latter representing Suetonius's statement about an expulsion of the Jews from the city.

We hear an echo of first-century upper-class attitudes in the work of Seneca (the Philosopher, end of the first century B.C. to A.D. 65) who relates that he was under Pythagorean influence and hence a vegetarian for some time in his youth during the reign of Tiberius. Since this could be construed as interest in foreign rites which involved abstinence from certain animals, Seneca's father asked him to refrain from this practice, "not out of fear of prosecution, but because he hated philosophy."[84] May it be assumed that there was a fashion at the time of following the Jewish dietary laws, as an expression of interest in Judaism? Solid citizens like Seneca's father would strongly disapprove of such a fashion—although, confusingly, the explanation that the father "hated philosophy" would fit a dislike of a Pythagorean lifestyle more than a dislike of Judaism. Seneca himself engaged in philosophy and he hated Jews, a "*sceleratissima*

---

monographs deal with the problem: Helga Botermann, *Das Judenedikt des Kaisers Claudius* (1996), with extensive bibliography in the introduction, 23f.; Slingerland, *Claudian Policymaking*; Gruen, *Diaspora*, 36–41.

[80] If we assume that Jesus Christ is meant, this presupposes that Suetonius thought "Chrestus" was alive and in the city of Rome in the reign of Claudius and inciting the Jews, which is an unlikely set of assumptions. Tacitus knew that Jesus had been executed in the reign of Tiberius, cf. Stern, 2.116f. and the literature in the previous note. Suetonius would therefore have been aware of these facts as well.

[81] *Acts* 18:2: Καὶ εὑρών τινα Ἰουδαῖον ὀνόματι Ἀκύλαν, Ποντικὸν τῷ γένει προσφάτως ἐληλυθότα ἀπὸ τῆς Ἰταλίας καὶ Πρίσκιλλαν γυναῖκα αὐτοῦ, διὰ τὸ διατεταχέναι Κλαύδιον χωρίζεσθαι πάντας τοὺς Ἰουδαίους ἀπὸ τῆς Ῥώμης.

[82] Dio 60.6 (Stern, vol. 2, No. 422): τούς τε Ἰουδαίους πλεονάσαντας αὖθις, ὥστε χαλεπῶς ἂν ἄνευ ταραχῆς ὑπὸ τοῦ ὄχλου σφῶν τῆς πόλεως εἰρχθῆναι, οὐκ ἐξήλασε μέν, τῷ δὲ δὴ πατρίῳ βίῳ χρωμένους ἐκέλευσε μὴ συναθροίζεσθαι.

[83] Claudius on the College of Haruspices, Tac. *Ann.* 11.15.1. See also Orosius 7.6.15 (in the ninth year of Claudius, A.D. 49): Anno eiusdem nono expulsos per Claudium urbe Iudaeos Iosephus refert. Sed me magis Suetonius movet, qui ait hoc modo . . .'

[84] Seneca, *Ep.* 108.22 (Stern, No. 189).

gens." He considered their influence pernicious, as expressed in a statement transmitted by Augustine.[85] In this text Augustine says Seneca expressed criticism of Jewish customs, especially the sabbath, and he adds a direct quotation from Seneca: "Meanwhile the customs of this accursed race have gained such influence that they are now received throughout all the world. The vanquished have given laws to their victors."[86] The formulation of this phrase leaves no doubt as to the author's emotions on the subject. It is not of direct importance here to determine whether he refers to sympathizers or full converts or what we can learn from this passage about the spread of conversion to Judaism at the time.[87] Rather, the importance of it lies in the clear sense conveyed that the vanquished are conquering the victors. This is a concept which we have already encountered frequently with regard to other peoples: Gauls, Greeks, Syrians, and Easterners in general (chapter 3). Thus we have here yet another passage which shows how threatening Romans found some of their subjects as soon as they sensed some influence from them in the religious, social, or cultural sphere.

Juvenal's attack on proselytes, cited above,[88] in combination with the well-known claim that the Syrian Orontes is now flowing into the Tiber, shows that he harboured similar sentiments. Tacitus despised proselytes: "the worst elements (among other peoples) disregarded their ancestral religions and used to send tribute and contributed it to Jerusalem, thus increasing Jewish wealth."[89] Foreign cults penetrated the households of Roman magistrates, says Cassius Longinus in A.D. 61, in a speech attributed to him by Tacitus.[90] This referred to slaves, but senatorial families themselves were also affected. Under Nero a Roman matron, Pomponia Graecina, was accused of foreign superstition.[91] Her husband, A. Plautius, was ordered to investigate the matter (and found her innocent). Domitian, in a famous description by Suetonius, is reported to have

[85] Cf. Schäfer, pp. 111–113.

[86] Augustinus, *De Civitate Dei*, 6.11 (Stern, No. 186): Cum interim usque eo sceleratissimae gentis consuetudo convaluit, ut per omnes iam terras recepta sit; victi victoribus leges dederunt. See also above, chapter 3, for the earlier models for this pronouncement.

[87] Stern, 1.429–432, assumes this statement, derived from a work composed in the sixties of the first century, reflects Seneca's feelings "at the height of the Jewish proselytizing movement and the diffusion of Jewish customs throughout the Mediterranean world." Schäfer, 111–113, does not accept this and maintains that we cannot learn from this or other passages that there was proselytizing activity. Goodman does not discuss the present passage.

[88] P. 453 and above, chapter 3, p. 231f.

[89] Tacitus, *Hist.* 5.5.1: Nam pessimus quisque spretis religionibus patriis tributa et stipes illuc <con>gerebant, unde auctae Iudaeorum res.

[90] Tacitus, *Ann.* 14.44.3: postquam vero nationes in familiis habemus quibus diversi ritus, externa sacra aut nulla sunt . . . This is the speech in which Cassius Longinus argues for the execution of four hundred slaves because one of them had murdered their owner, the city-prefect. As observed by Syme, *Tacitus* (1958), 533, Tacitus furnishes through the oration of Cassius Longinus the arguments for severity, but none for mercy.

[91] Tacitus, *Ann.* 13.32.2: et Pomponia Graecina insignis femina, A. Plautio, quem ovasse de Britannis rettuli, nupta ac superstitionis externae rea, mariti iudicio permissa. She could have been accused of being involved in an Egyptian cult, in Judaism or Christianity.

gone to great lengths to identify Jews for the sake of the special tax on them.[92] This was the sort of judicial activism which gave Domitian his bad name, in contrast to Trajan, who ruled with regard to the Christians that they were not to be hunted out (*conquirendi non sunt*), emphasizing also that anonymous accusations were to be ignored (Pliny, *ep.* 97). Trajan here was responding to Pliny's account, from which it appeared that he had, in fact, put Christians on trial in response to an anonymous accusation.[93] Domitian, in his campaign, sought two categories in particular: non-Jews who lived as Jews without publicly acknowledging this, and born Jews who concealed their origin. The former are relevant here. Domitian is also on record as having put to death his relative Flavius Clemens and his wife Flavia Domitilla on the charge of atheism (ἔγκλημα ἀθεότητος). This, according to Cassius Dio, was a charge on which many who inclined to Jewish customs were condemned.[94] Elsewhere Cassius Dio, who is also unusual in his fairly tolerant description of the Jewish God, refers to both Jews by birth and proselytes as *Ioudaioi*: "I do not know how they obtained this appellation, but it applies also to other people, even if they are of alien descent, who adopt their customs. This group also exists among the Romans, and although it has been repressed often, it has increased very much and has succeeded in obtaining the right of freedom in its way of life."[95] The passage is important because it states explicitly that there was an increase in the number of proselytes by the early third century, which Dio mentions without disapproval in spite of the fact that "they are different from other people in virtually their entire way of life."[96] Dio has this idea of separateness in common with earlier,

[92] Suetonius, *Domitianus* 12.2 (Stern, No. 320). Dio, 68.1.2, notes that, after Nerva succeeded Domitian, he would not permit anyone to accuse anybody of *maiestas* or of adopting the Jewish mode of life. See E. M. Smallwood, "Domitian's Attitude towards the Jews and Judaism," *CP* 51 (1956), 1–13; M. Goodman, "Nerva, the *fiscus Judaicus* and Jewish Identity," *JRS* 79 (1989), 40–44. Goodman argues that after A.D. 96 the Roman definition of a Jew depended on his or her public declaration of Judaism only. Thus Jews were defined as such by their proclaimed religion alone rather than their birth. See also M. H. Williams, "Domitian, the Jews and the 'Judaizers'—A Simple Matter of Cupiditas and Maiestas?" *Historia* 39 (1990), 196–211.

[93] Pliny, *ep.* 96: Propositus est libellus sine auctore multorum nomina continens. Pliny, *ep.* 97: Sine auctore vero propositi libelli nullo crimine locum habere debent. This is followed by a reprimand: Nam et pessimi exempli nec nostri saeculi est.

[94] Dio 67.14.1–3, for which see Stern 435, with comments, pp. 380–384, on the question whether the two inclined to Judaism, as Dio himself asserts, or to Christianity. Cf. Smallwood, *CP* 51 (1956), 3f.; adherents of Judaism and atheism: 6f. As observed by Smallwood, p. 9, there is no evidence that born Jews were attacked in the reign of Domitian. See also T. Rajak, *JRS* 69 (1979), 192; Williams, op. cit., 206f. Williams, 208f., does not accept that proselytism in itself cannot have been a decisive factor in the action taken against Flavius Clemens, his wife Flavia Domitilla, and M'. Acilius Glabrio. She argues that political motives and Domitian's dislike of the Jews were the reasons.

[95] Dio 37.17.1: ἡ δὲ ἐπίκλησις αὕτη ἐκείνοις μὲν οὐκ οἶδ' ὅθεν ἤρξατο γενέσθαι, φέρει δὲ καὶ ἐπὶ τοὺς ἄλλους ἀνθρώπους ὅσοι τὰ νόμιμα αὐτῶν, καίπερ ἀλλοεθνεῖς ὄντες, ζηλοῦσι. καὶ ἔστι καὶ παρὰ τοῖς Ῥωμαίοις τὸ γένος τοῦτο, κολουσθὲν μὲν πολλάκις, αὐξηθὲν δὲ ἐπὶ πλεῖστον, ὥστε καὶ ἐς παρρησίαν τῆς νομίσεως ἐκνικῆσαι (Stern, No. 406).

[96] κεχωρίδαται δὲ ἀπὸ τῶν λοιπῶν ἀνθρώπων ἔς τε τἆλλα τὰ περὶ τὴν δίαιταν πάνθ' ὡς εἰπεῖν.

hostile authors, but he is unusual in that he considers Jewish proselytes to be just like Jews by birth. However, a different view of this aspect is expressed in the address which Dio assigns to Maccenas. The latter advises Augustus "to hate and punish those who are involved in foreign cults, not only for the sake of the gods—for if they do not respect them they will not honour any other being—but also because such people preferring new gods persuade many to adopt strange cults and this leads to conspiracies, factions, and political societies which do not profit the monarchy in the least."[97] Dio is explicit in his rejection of foreign cults: not only are they a threat to religion and religious values, but they are also a focus of political danger. We shall see below that this is precisely the argument Trajan uses for his prohibition of Christianity. The Jews were exceptional in being allowed to assemble for religious services while other foreign religions were forbidden to do so in Rome during the reigns of Caesar and Augustus.

Turning now to the legal sources themselves for the actual Roman legislation regarding the Jews, we see once more that the subject of conversion occupied the authorities both before and after the empire became Christian. First there is the rescript of Antoninus Pius which only permits Jews to circumcise their own sons, and states that circumcision of non-Jews is punishable.[98] The rescript determines in fact that Jewish identity is exclusively a matter of birth, as Jews are only permitted to circumcise their own sons. It should be noted, however, that it deals only with circumcision and not with other forms of Jewish tradition. Towards the end of the third century, the jurist Paul states that only Jews by origin are allowed to practice circumcision. Gentiles who allow themselves or their slaves to be circumcised voluntarily are to be exiled and their property confiscated, while the doctors involved in such acts are liable to capital punishment as well. Jews who circumcise non-Jewish slaves are liable to deportation or capital punishment.[99] According to the *Historia Augusta,* in a passage that may possibly be trusted, Septimius Severus again forbade conversion to Judaism and Christianity[100]—to little purpose, if we may believe Dio. Both the contents and the style of legislation regarding the Jews changed immediately in the reign of Constantine. A law of 329 prohibited proselytism and it imposed the death penalty on Jews persecuting Jewish converts to Christianity, indicating that

---

[97] Dio 52.36.2: τοὺς δὲ δὴ ξενίζοντάς τι περὶ αὐτὸ καὶ μίσει καὶ κόλαζε, μὴ μόνον τῶν θεῶν ἕνεκα, ὧν ὁ καταφρονήσας οὐδ᾽ ἄλλου ἄν τινος προτιμήσειεν, ἀλλ᾽ ὅτι καὶ καινά τινα δαιμόνια οἱ τοιοῦτοι ἀντεσφέροντες πολλοὺς ἀναπείθουσιν ἀλλοτριονομεῖν, κἀκ τούτου καὶ συνωμοσίαι καὶ συστάσεις ἑταιρεῖαί τε γίγνονται, ἅπερ ἥκιστα μοναρχίᾳ συμφέρει.

[98] *Dig.* 48.8.11 (Modestinus) Circumcidere Iudaeis filios suos tantum rescripto divi Pii permittitur: in non eiusdem religionis qui hoc fecerit, castrantis poena irrogatur. Cf. Amnon Linder, *The Jews in Roman Imperial Legislation* (Detroit, MI and Jerusalem, 1987), 99–102.

[99] Paulus, *Sententiae* 5.22.3f.: Cives Romani, qui se Iudaico ritu vel servos suos circumcidi patiuntur, bonis ademptis in insulam perpetuo relegantur: medici capite puniuntur. Iudaei si alienae nationis comparatos servos circumciderint, aut deportantur aut capite puniuntur. Cf. Linder, pp. 117–120.

[100] SHA *Severus* 17.1: Iudaeos fieri sub gravi poena vetuit. Idem etiam de Ch<h>ristianis sanxit. Cf. Stern, 2, p. 625 for comments.

such persecutions did indeed take place.[101] Legislation during the following centuries clearly shows that the matter of conversion to and from Judaism remained a subject which preoccupied the authorities.

Finally, the condemnation of Jewish proselytism recurs in particularly hostile form in the work of the fifth-century author Rutilius Namatianus: "And would that Judaea had never been subdued by Pompey's wars and Titus' military power! The infection of this plague, though excised, still creeps abroad the more": and "it is their own conquerors that a conquered race keeps down."[102] The claim that the Jews were an unfortunate acquisition is also expressed in the speech of Philostratus, cited above. The implication of such feelings is clear: a truly successful empire is superior in every respect, not just through arms and politics, and it should not be influenced at all by its subjects in religious and cultural matters. Undoubtedly, the way we read these texts is a subjective matter, but when seen in combination, it is hard not to be persuaded that the Roman establishment was very sensitive to cultural and religious influence exercised by its subjects. It is also hard not to conclude that this sensitivity was to some extent irrational.[103] If the Roman Empire was successful because it absorbed many different conquered nations, it must also be concluded that it did so in spite of strong xenophobic tendencies among the establishment in Rome. These people truly thought that the presence of provincials in the capital should be limited to the supply of willing slaves. As noted in chapter 3, such an ambivalent attitude is characteristic of the Roman attitude towards various subject peoples. It has been stressed there that it is illustrative of proto-racist and racist tensions, which combine, or alternate between, feelings of superiority and inferiority, attributing to the others both exaggerated powers and shortcomings. In any case, there are enough texts to conclude that there was a marked sensitivity to a perceived presence of Jewish proselytes in Rome which expressed itself in

[101] *CTh.* 16.8.1; *CJ* 1.9.3, cf. Linder, 125–132.

[102] Rutilius Namatianus, *De Reditu Suo* 1.395–8 (Stern, no. 542): Atque utinam numquam Iudaea subacta fuisset I Pompeii bellis imperiisque Titi! I Latius excisae pestis contagia serpunt I victoresque suos natio victa premit. Cf. Stern 2. p. 664; Schäfer, 87–89.

[103] From these conclusions it follows that I disagree with scholars who tend to interpret Roman attitudes toward the Jews and the policies that followed from these attitudes as generally rational and justified by reality: see, for instance, H. Solin, "Juden und Syrer im westlichen Teil der römischen Welt: Eine ethnisch-demographische Studie" *ANRW* 2.29.2, 607ff, esp. 686: the Jews in Rome were "ein ständiges Ferment der Unruhe," criticized by L.V. Rutgers, *Classical Antiquity,* 13 (1994), 56–74, at p. 63f. Rutgers himself, however, reaches general conclusions not so far removed from these views, see p. 68f: "Rome was of course capable of treating the Jews harshly, but usually it had good reasons when it did so." What does Rutgers mean when he writes: "At best, a dislike for Judaism served to justify on a subconscious level decisions that had essentially been reached on the basis of administrative and legal considerations"? It is anybody's privilege to speculate about the workings of the unconscious of Roman officials, but why would their unconscious have needed a dislike to justify decisions reached on the basis of administrative considerations? In our culture it normally is the conscious which rationalizes thoughts and acts determined by irrational impulses of the unconscious. As already observed, such arguments, justifying intolerance towards minorities, are reasonable only if it is taken for granted that the established majority has no reason to tolerate minorities with different beliefs and customs. It is a circular argument.

hostile reactions. It is quite clear that this happened in response to the novel forms of religious and social choice exhibited by some Roman citizens. They abandoned the traditional religion and the community of loyal citizens, committing themselves to a different conception of religion and a separate community. The paradoxical phrase "vincendo victi sumus" sums up this emotional dilemma and it does so even if it is meant sarcastically.

This brings us to yet another familiar topic in the social sphere, which is related to and yet the converse of the idea that the conquerors are being conquered, namely the claim that members of a subject people are born slaves. This is said frequently of precisely the same people who also are described as subjects conquering their conquerors: Greeks, Syrians, and assorted eastern peoples, and I have discussed it extensively in chapter 2. It represents a familiar pattern of polarity in discriminatory attitudes towards minorities. Cicero also describes the Jews once in such terms: "Then, too, there are those unhappy revenue-farmers—and what misery to me were the miseries of those to whom I owed so much!—he handed them over as slaves to Jews and Syrians, themselves peoples born to be slaves."[104] Momigliano asserts that when Cicero speaks of the Jews as a "natio nata servituti," he is actually repeating a judgment of Apollonius Molon (Jos. *c. Apionem* 2.148). This, he says, had been shown a false claim by the Jewish defense of their Temple against Pompey. "But the success of the cultural policy of Rome lent plausibility to Cicero's lie."[105] There is no need to assume Cicero needed Apollonius Molon for the production of such a phrase. Moreover, the latter, as represented by Josephus, does not describe the Jews as "born slaves," but accuses them of cowardice (δειλίαν ἡμῖν ὀνειδίζει). A born slave is not quite the same as a coward. As shown in chapter 2, it had been a significant concept for centuries when Cicero used the expression. Moreover, according to Cicero it is Syrians *and* Jews who are born slaves. More important still, it is only in this one speech by Cicero that the Jews are described in such terms. It is therefore doubtful whether Momigliano is right in his assertion that Cicero's lie was considered plausible. In spite of Cicero's influence, this particular theme does not appear again in any description of the Jews. Elsewhere Cicero comments on the Jews after Pompey's eastern campaign: "But now it is even more so, when that nation by its armed resistance has shown what it thinks of our rule; how dear it was to the immortal gods is shown by the fact that it has been conquered, let out for taxes, made a slave."[106] This does not imply that the Jews were born for slavery because they were cowards. What happens is that Cicero triumphantly declares

---

[104] Cicero, *De Provinciis Consularibus* 5, 10: Iam vero publicanos miseros—me etiam miserum illorum ita de me meritorum miseriis ac dolore! tradidit in servitutem Iudaeis et Syris, nationibus natis servituti (Stern, no. 70, with comments on 203f., discussed above).

[105] Momigliano, *Alien Wisdom,* 122.

[106] Cicero, *Pro Flacco* 28.69 (Stern, No. 68): nunc vero hoc magis quod illa gens quid de nostro imperio sentiret ostendit armis; quam cara dis immortalibus esset docuit quod est victa, quod elocata, quod serva.

that the gods wanted them to be slaves when they turned to armed resistance against Rome.

Moreover, it cannot be repeated too often—and has indeed been repeated almost too often—that we should be very cautious in using Cicero's judicial rhetoric as expressions of an opinion firmly held. Elsewhere Cicero refers to the contrast between "a campaign waged in Sardinia against bandits in sheepskins by a propraetor with one auxiliary cohort, and a war with the most powerful peoples and rulers in Syria carried out by a consular army."[107] From the context it is clear that Cicero is referring to the Jews here, although he does not mention them. Even Tacitus, with all his animosity, fails to take up the theme of "born slavery" in the case of the Jews. In fact, he implies the opposite, namely that the Jews scorn death, because they believe that the souls of those who are killed in battle, or through capital punishment, are immortal (*Hist.* 5.5.3). It would have made no sense to accuse the Jews of being cowards, for by Tacitus's time too many contemporaries were aware of their rebelliousness.[108] This follows, for instance, from Tacitus's words of explanation regarding the difficulty of the siege of Jerusalem. It was "hard because of the nature of the mountain-citadel and stubborn superstition and it was this, rather than sufficient forces, which enabled the besieged to suffer the hardships (of the siege)."[109] Whatever else the Jews were accused of, neither the Hellenistic nor the Roman authors who dislike them assert their nature is slavish. Similarly, although they originated in the East, they are not usually accused of softness or effeminacy, unlike many other peoples from Asia Minor and Syria. If the Jews were regarded as "born for slavery" at all they were so in the sense that all non-Roman peoples were destined to be subdued by Rome.

One further theme in the social sphere which recurs fairly often is that of the beggars found near the synagogues. This, however, is typically a phenomenon of the city of Rome in the late first and second centuries A.D. There were apparently many poor Jews in the city in this period. Martial describes various nuisances in the city of Rome. The noise is insufferable, one of the causes being "the Jew taught by his mother to beg."[110] Juvenal complains that the "holy fount and grove and shrine" near the Porta Capena have been taken over by

---

[107] Cicero, *De Prov. Consularibus* 7.15: . . . res in Sardinia cum mastrucatis latrunculis a propraetore una cohorte auxiliaria gesta et bellum cum maximis Syriae gentibus et tyrannis consulari exercitu imperioque confectum.

[108] Juvenal, *Sat.* 8.158–162, describes a *Syrophoenix* who lived near the "Idumaean gate" as servile in his behavior. Although there were Jews living in the quarter, his description as a Syrophoenician shows that he was not a Jew, but a Lebanese Syrian. See also above, chapter 3, n. 79, for this passage.

[109] Tacitus, *Hist.* 2.4.3: Profligaverat bellum Iudaicum Vespasianus, obpugnatione Hierosolymorum reliqua, duro magis et arduo opere ob ingenium montis et pervicaciam superstitionis quam quo satis virium obsessis ad tolerandas necessitates superesset.

[110] Martial, ep. 12.57.13 (Stern, No. 246): a matre doctus nec rogare Iudaeus. On Jewish beggars in Rome: H. J. Lewy, *Studies in Jewish Hellenism* (Jerusalem, 1960, 197ff., in Hebrew); L.V. Rutgers, *The Jews in Late Ancient Rome: Evidence of Cultural Interaction in the Roman Diaspora* (Leiden, 1995).

Jewish paupers.[111] Elsewhere he describes a particularly aggressive Jewish beggar near a synagogue (3.290–6 [Stern 297]). The sixth satire deals with Roman
women and is 661 lines long, so we should not overestimate the importance of
Jewish women in Rome if six lines deal with one of them, even though it is
probably presented as a typical case: "No sooner has that fellow departed than a
palsied Jewess, leaving her basket and her truss of hay, comes begging to her
secret ear; she is an interpreter of the laws of Jerusalem, a high priestess of the
tree, a trusty go-between of highest heaven. She, too, fills her palm, but more
sparingly, for a Jew will tell you dreams of any kind you please for the minutest
of coins."[112] In this case the beggar is a fraudulent soothsayer. The first- or
second-century author, Cleomedes, has already been mentioned because of his
reference to the beggars in its courtyards of the synagogues. "These are Jewish
and debased and much lower than reptiles." He attacks the vulgar language of
Epicurus and mentions the Jews only incidentally.[113] The description "lower
than animals" here refers to expressions, to the manner of speaking of these
people, not to people as such. Such a description belongs to the tradition which
associates barbarian speech with animal noises.

The synagogue is once again mentioned in connection with paupers in a
source from the second half of the second century.[114] To associate synagogues
with beggars is clearly an aspect of urban life in Rome. It is possible that there
were more beggars around synagogues than elsewhere because Jews were wont
to hand out charity to them there. However it may be, although interesting, this
does not tell us much about ancient views of Jews in general. It is certainly
significant that the Jews in the Roman Empire are not, like Jews in later periods, described as rich, greedy, and successful in business.[115] The Temple in
Jerusalem amassed wealth and this annoyed some Romans, but Jews are not
represented as typical traders. Above we saw that it is the Phoenicians who are
described in such terms in antiquity. Jews as usurers are a stereotype introduced
in the twelfth century only.

---

[111] Juvenal, *Sat.* 3.10–18 (Stern, No. 296 with comments; Courtney, p. 158).

[112] Juvenal, *Sat.* 6.542–7 (Stern, No. 299 with comments on 2. p.101): Cum dedit ille locum,
cophino fenoque relicto I arcanam Iudaea tremens mendicat in aurem, I interpres legum Solymarum
et magna sacerdos arboris ac summi fida internuntia caeli. I Implet et illa manum, sed parcius; aere
minuto I qualiacumque voles Iudaei somnia vendunt. Cf. Livy 39.8.4: sacrificulus et vates . . .
occultorum et nocturnorum antistes sacrorum.

[113] Cleomedes, *De Motu Circulari* 2.1.91, Stern, No. 333, comments on 2.157f. See also above,
chapter 2, n. 131, for this passage.

[114] Artemidorus (2d half of the 2d century .A.D.), *Oneirocritica* 3.53 (Stern 395, comments on p.
329f.).

[115] Mommsen, *Römische Geschichte,* 3.549, fails to recognize this: "Auch zu jener Zeit war das
vorwiegende Geschäft der Juden der Handel: mit dem erobernden römischen Kaufmann zog damals
der jüdische Händler ebenso überall hin wie später mit dem genuesischen und venezianischen, und
neben der römischen strömte das Kapital allerorts bei der jüdischen Kaufmannschaft zusammen."
For lucid observations: Juster, *Les Juifs dans l'Empire romain,* 2.291–313; I. Heinemann, *RE* Supp.
5, s.v. Antisemitismus (1931), col.39f.

The Jewish Religion

The importance of religion in Roman evaluations of other peoples and their influence on Roman religion and society should not be underestimated. It is clearly expressed, for instance, in the speech which Livy attributes to the consul who took action against the Bacchanalia in 186 B.C. Even if it does not reflect the actual words of the consul at the time, at least it shows what Livy felt he might have said. "Nothing is more deceptive in appearance than a false religion."[116] "For men wisest in all divine and human law used to judge that nothing was so potent in destroying religion as the replacement of native sacrifices by foreign ritual."[117] Foreign cults were definitely regarded as a potential threat to the stability of the state. The citizens were warned that it would be *superstitio* to fear action taken against the Bacchanalia.[118] For Romans to indulge in foreign superstition was punished as a criminal act in principle, even if foreign cults were not always prosecuted in practice.[119] As has often been observed, for the Romans the opposition *religio* and *superstitio* is a classical dichotomy.[120] The term *superstitio* has been discussed very often. It will suffice therefore to note here that Roman religion (or, in the Later Roman Empire, Christianity) is always called *religio* and never *superstitio*, while other religions are sometimes called *religio* and sometimes *superstitio*. The latter term was originally almost devoid of negative judgment—like the Greek *barbaros*—but became over time increasingly hostile. In the Later Roman Empire, only the Christian religion was a *religio* and all other religions were called *superstitio*. The term *Superstitio* often (but not always) suggests that a religion thus entitled is deemed to engage in immoral or excessive cult-practices; it contains an element of irra-

---

[116] Livy, 39.16.6: Nihil enim in speciem fallacius est quam praua religio.

[117] 39.16.9: iudicabant enim prudentissimi uiri omnis diuini humani que iuris nihil aeque dissoluendae religionis esse quam ubi non patrio sed externo ritu sacrificaretur.

[118] 39.16.10: haec uobis praedicenda ratus sum, ne qua superstitio agitaret animos uestros, cum demolientes nos Bacchanalia discutientes que nefarios coetus cerneretis.

[119] Tac., *Ann.* 13.32.2.

[120] Stern, No. 68, vol. 1. comm. 199; J.-E. Bernard, "Philosophie politique et antijudaïsme chez Cicéron," *SCI* 19 (2000), 113–131, at 124. On *superstitio*, see *RE* 28.1 s.v. superstitio, cols. 937–9 (Pfaff); R. C. Ross, "Superstitio," *CJ* 44 (1968–1969), 354–358; R. Freudenberger, *Das Verhalten der römischen Behörden gegen die Christen im 2. Jahrhundert dargestellt am Brief des Plinius und Trajan und den Reskripten Trajans und Hadrians* (Munich, 1967, repr.1969), 189–199; S. Calderone, "Superstitio," *ANRW* 1.2 (1972), 377–396; D. Grodzynski, "Superstitio," *REA* 76 (1974), 36–60, a lucid, chronological survey of the sense of the term in classical Latin literature and in Christian authors from Tertullian to the fourth century; W. Belardi, *Superstitio* (Rome, 1976); J. Scheid, "Religion et superstition à l'époque de Tacite: quelques réflexions," in *Religion, supersticion y magia en el mundo romano* (Cadiz, 1985), 19–34; A. Linder, *The Jews in Roman Imperial Legislation* (1987), 55–58; 105, n. 10; M. Beard, J. North, and S. Price, *Religions of Rome* (Cambridge, 1998), 214–227. As traced by Grodzynski, over the centuries "superstitio" had the following meanings: in the third century B.C. it was used for "fortune-telling," from the first century B.C. till the beginning of the second century A.D. it represented a deviation from the Roman religion, and from the second till the fifth century it indicated other peoples' inferior religions. For the etymology, see Belardi.

tional fear. For the Jewish religion Cicero uses both terms and he is the first to call it a *barbara superstitio*.[121] He makes it clear that the practice of Jewish religion (*istorum religio sacrorum*) is incompatible with Roman institutions,[122] for the organization of rites "is not only of concern to religion, but also to the well-being of the state."[123] The penetration of foreign superstition was a source of frequent worry. Naturally the Jews were not the only people whose religion was disapproved of, as already indicated.[124] Some of the religions which the Romans despised were influential in Rome. They were found threatening because of their appeal to Romans, such as some Egyptian and Asiatic cults, Judaism, and Christianity. Others were considered immoral, excessive, or primitive but not influential in Rome, such as the Gallic, British, or Germanic cults. A distinction should be made between attitudes towards religions and cults represented in Rome and Italy, and those that were actively practiced only in the provinces. Foreign cults such as those from Egypt and Judaism, which attracted attention in Roman society because they were a presence clearly felt in Rome, were regarded in a different light from those that were known only through indirect sources as a provincial phenomenon.

As an example of the latter category, Tacitus writes that the Britons practiced human sacrifice and were hence given to inhuman superstitions.[125] Gallic superstition under the spiritual guidance of the Druids has been much discussed, as observed above,[126] and so was that of many Germans.[127] As long as no human sacrifices were practiced or anti-Roman rebellion instigated, foreign cults were left alone in the provinces, especially if they could claim to be ancient. The antiquity of cult practices made them respectable. This is the reason Josephus devotes a considerable part of his work against Apion to the citation of records

---

[121] Cicero, *Pro Flacco* 67: Huic autem barbarae superstitioni resistere severitatis, multitudinem Iudaeorum flagrantem non numquam in contionibus pro re publica contemnere gravitatis summae fuit. The *barbara superstitio* could refer either to the Jewish religion in general or specifically to the custom of sending gold to the temple in Jerusalem.

[122] as stated explicitly in *Pro Flacco*, 29.69: "the practice of their sacred rites was at variance with the glory of our empire, the dignity of our name, the customs of our ancestors."

[123] Cic. *de legibus* 2.12.30: Quod sequitur uero, non solum ad religionem pertinet sed etiam ad ciuitatis statum ut sine iis qui sacris publice praesint, religioni priuatae satis facere non possint. Cf. *De Divinatione* 2.149 quam ob rem, ut religio propaganda etiam est, quae est iuncta cum cognitione naturae, sic superstitionis stirpes omnes eiiciendae. Seneca *De Clementia* 2.5: Ergo quemadmodum religio deos colit, superstitio violat . . . Tac., *Ann.* 11.15.1: According to Claudius the study of the ceremonies of the "haruspices" was less zealously practiced "quod nunc segnius fieri publica circa bonas artes socordia, et quia externae superstitiones valescant." For this passage, see also above, p. 458.

[124] Tac., *Hist.* 1.11.1 . . . provinciam aditu difficilem, annonae fecundam, superstitione ac lascivia discordem et mobilem, insciam legum, ignaram magistratuum . . . . also: *Hist.* 4.81. See above for additional relevant sources.

[125] Tac., *Ann.* 14.30.3 praesidium posthac impositum victis excisi que luci saevis superstitionibus sacri: nam cruore captivo adolere aras et hominum fibris consulere deos fas habebant. Also: *Agricola* 11.3; cf. Syme, *Tacitus* 1.457f. See above, p. 423.

[126] Above, chapter 11.

[127] Tac., *Germ.* 39.2; also Hist. 4.61.

468   · C H A P T E R   1 3 ·

demonstrating the antiquity of Judaism (*c. Apionem* 13.69–23.218). Conversely, it was the novelty of Christianity that made it despicable in Roman eyes. However, whatever their antiquity, all foreign cults that attracted followers in Rome were resisted, as noted above. Hatred of the Jewish people and hatred of their religion are sometimes combined and sometimes clearly distinct, but it is not always possible to distinguish between the two. Quintilian (second half of the first century A.D.) appears to combine the two in his statement that "founders of cities are hated for bringing together a people which is pernicious for others, such as the founder [sc. Moses] of the Jewish superstition."[128] It is also possible to argue that Quintilian considers the Jews pernicious because of the religion they practice and spread (whether actively or not).

Many Roman authors had a low opinion of the Jews and their religion. Their criticism extended to particulars of the Jewish religion, as far as they knew it, and to characteristics that were attributed to the Jews. There is no need here to discuss in detail how Roman authors viewed Jewish religion, since that has been done in modern works that are easily accessible.[129] It will suffice to review briefly various important subjects. The common denominator of all the practices that attracted the attention of non-Jewish authors is their otherness. It may be said at the outset that the Egyptian cults were regarded as strangely different as well, for reasons that were discussed in chapter 7. These are distinct from the objections against the Jewish religion. The first topic is the exclusive monotheism of the Jews with the concomitant absence of a cult-statue in the Temple in Jerusalem before its destruction.[130] Varro (116–127 B.C.) approved of this,[131] and it is the one feature of Judaism which gained a measure of respect from Tacitus (*Hist.* 5.5.4). He compares it favorably with the Egyptians and their numerous animals and "commingled images." Plutarch writes generally in a positive and respectful tone about it[132] and Cassius Dio also writes with understanding (37.17.2). These authors express respect for Jewish monotheism, but many others disapprove: they regard the Jewish concept of one God as an aberration.[133]

---

[128] Quintilian, *Institutio Oratoria* 3.7. 21 (Stern, No. 230). Et parentes malorum odimus: et est conditoribus urbium infame contraxisse aliquam perniciosam ceteris gentem, qualis est primus Iudaicae superstitionis auctor . . . As observed by Williams, *Historia* 39 (1990), 206, this appears in a passage from the chapter "De Laude et Vituperatione," which probably was written after the execution of Flavius Clemens for his Jewish tendencies. He was Quintilian's patron and Quintilian may have wanted to demonstrate that he did not want to be identified with his patron's Jewish sympathies. This may be true, but it is an hypothesis which cannot be proved or disproved.

[129] All the sources are available in Stern's major work. Gager, *The Origins of Anti-Semitism*, 55–66, contains a succinct discussion. Peter Schäfer, *Judeophobia* (1997), Part I, contains separate chapters on each and every topic which features prominently in the Hellenistic and Roman literature: the Jewish God, Abstinence from Pork, Sabbath, and Circumcision.

[130] Schäfer, 34–65.

[131] Stern, No. 72, vol. 1, pp. 207–212.

[132] Plutarch, *Quaestiones Convivales* 4.6 "Who the god of the Jews is" (Stern, No. 258).

[133] Julian, *ep.* 20.454a *Ad Theodorum* No. 89a (Stern, No. 483), respects the Jewish God for the qualities ascribed to him, but rejects the idea that he should be the only god. Among modern anti-

It was even suggested that monotheism fitted their antisocial attitudes, described above: their God refuses to associate with other gods, as asserted by Numenius of Apamea (second half of the second century A.D.), who says that the Jewish God is ἀκοινώνητος, "not sociable, exclusive."[134] This is precisely the expression used by Diodorus and others to describe the Jews themselves, as cited above. In peoples this was a quality which Greeks and Romans rejected, and the same was true for their divinity.

A particularly hostile tradition claims that the Jews really worshipped an ass, whose statue stood in the Temple.[135] In the second century this accusation was leveled at the Christians too, according to Christian sources.[136] As observed in the chapter on Egypt, animal worship has for long been a particularly sensitive topic in the western tradition. It is often associated with human sacrifice, cannibalism, and collective sexual aberration. The Christians consistently accused witches, doctrinal deviants, foreigners such as American Indians and the Jews of acts of cannibalism, animal worship, and sexual deviance.[137] These are

---

semites Jewish monotheism is not usually a subject of reproach. This would be awkward, since most of them are Christians. An exception is Ernst Renan, who associated monotheism with simple-mindedness and an absolute monarchy: *Histoire générale et système comparé des langues Sémitiques* (Paris, 1878), 5: "Cette race n'a jamais conçu gouvernement de l'univers que comme une monarchie absolue; sa théodicée n'a pas fait un pas depuis le livre de Job," p. 9: "L'absence de culture philosophique et scientifique chez les Sémites tient, ce me semble, au manque d'étendue, de variété et, par conséquent, d'esprit analytique, qui les distingue. Les facultés qui engendrent la mythologie sont les mêmes que celles qui engendrent la philosophie." As an expert in semitic languages and like other racists, he is selective in his generalities and fails to note that the classic monarchy for Greek historians would be Persia, yet Persian religion was not monotheistic and the Persians spoke no Semitic language. For Renan on Jews and Greeks in the history of Christianity, see Tessa Rajak, "Jews and Greeks: The Invention and Exploitation of Polarities in the Nineteenth Century," reprinted in *The Jewish Dialogue with Greece and Rome* (2001), 545–58.

[134] Numenius of Apamea, ap. Lydus, *De Mensibus* 4.53, pp.109f. (Stern, No. 367): ὁ δὲ Νουμήνιος ἀκοινώνητον αὐτὸν καὶ πατέρα πάντων τῶν θεῶν εἶναι λέγει, ἀπαξιοῦντα κοινωνεῖν αὐτῷ τῆς τιμῆς τινα.

[135] See in particular E. J. Bickerman, "Ritualmord und Eselskult: Ein Beitrag zur Geschichte antiker Publizistik," in *Studies in Jewish and Christian History* 2 (1980), 225–255, at 245–255; Stern, vol. 1. pp. 97f.; bibliography on p. 98; 184; 530; 563; vol. 2. p. 18; 36; Schäfer, 55–62. It appears that this tradition originated either in Egypt or as Seleucid anti-Jewish propaganda. It is found in Roman sources in derivative form, but does not play a significant role in Roman ideas about Jewish religion.

[136] The principal sources: Minucius Felix, *Octavius* 9f.; Tertullian *ad Nationes* 1.14; cf. *id. Apologeticum.* 16.12; Eusebius, *HE* 5.1.14 and below. Cf. J-.P. Waltzing, "Le crime rituel reproché aux chrétiens du 2ᵉ siècle," in *Académie Royale de Belgique*, Bull. de la Classe des Lettres, ser. 5, vol. 11 (1925), 205–239; Franz Joseph Dölger, "Sacramentum infanticidii," *Antike und Christentum* 4 (1934), 188–228; T. F. Mathews, *The Clash of Gods: A Reinterpretation of Early Christian Art* (Princeton, 2d ed. 1999) 27f.; 45f; *RAC s.v.* Esel: Christlich (I. Opelt); *DACL s.v.* Âne: Calumnie de l'onolatrie (H. Leclerq). The celebrants of the Eucharist were said to venerate the head of a donkey, slaughter, and eat a child and then to engage in a sexual orgy.

[137] Norman Cohn, *Europe's Inner Demons: An Enquiry Inspired by the Great Witch-Hunt* (London, 1975).

among the features of traditional, delusional anti-semitism which never quite faded away.

Dietary Restrictions

The second subject that appears frequently in the sources are the dietary restrictions, notably the abstinence from pork.[138] It was not in itself remarkable for peoples to have their own specific diet. As already mentioned, Herodotus uses diet as a criterion of ethnicity (3.23.1; 9.82) and Caesar pays attention to dietary habits of the peoples he describes (*BG* 4.1.8–9). In the case of the Jews, their special diet is not in itself a subject of fierce criticism. What was criticized is the idea that the Jews would not share meals with non-Jews, but that has already been discussed under the heading of "sociability." One feature which, then as now, attracted attention is the abstinence from pork. A few satirists refer to this as a ridiculous custom. Petronius gives an unusual satirizing slant by the suggestion that the Jews worship pigs as a god. A related approach in a different style may be found in Plutarch, who asks in earnest whether the Jews abstain from pork because of reverence or aversion.[139] A similar perspective is found in numerous anti-semitic caricatures from the thirteenth through the nineteenth centuries.[140] In Germany, churches and public buildings very often depicted "die Judensau," and Jews in various intimate poses with a pig.[141] I would add a passage from the *Historia Augusta* (*HA*) which is not usually included as referring to this subject. When the *HA* describes Elagabalus's religious mania it says: "And sometimes at his banquets he served ostriches, saying that the Jews had been commanded to eat them."[142] This may be one of the many instances of deliberate obfuscation on the part of the author, for Jews are, in fact, forbidden to eat ostriches,[143] but he may not have known this. The point of the joke may have been merely that Jews are described as having been commanded to eat something exotic, while in fact they were known as people who abstained from

[138] Schäfer, 66–81.

[139] Petronius, *Frg.* 37 (Stern, No. 195); Plutarch, *Quaest. Conv.* 4.5.1 (Stern, No. 258); Juvenal, 14.96–106 (Stern, No. 301, comments on 2, pp.103–107).

[140] Eduard Fuchs, *Die Juden in der Karikatur: Ein Beitrag zur Kulturgeschichte* (Munich, 1921; repr. 1985), p. 8: "das grosse Judenschwein," here and on many other of these caricatures a pig is depicted as suckling Jews; nos. 15 and 16 ("die Judensau") on p. 9; no. 20 on p.13: a Jew riding a pig, found more often on these pages; no. 40 on p. 19; no. 42; no. 49; no. 50; no. 58 on p. 38; no. 67 on p. 47: an English caricature showing Jews eating a piglet for breakfast; no.7 1 on p. 51: kissing a piglet; no. 128 on p. 121. Cf. Joshua Trachtenberg, *The Devil and the Jews: The Medieval Conception of the Jew and Its Relation to Modern Anti-Semitism* (New Haven, CT. 1943; repr. Philadephia, 1983), 26.

[141] See previous note and op. cit., pp. 114; 118. Stefan Rohrbacher and Michael Schmidt, *Judenbilder: Kulturgeschichte antijudischer Mythen und antisemitischer Vorurteile* (Reinbeck bei Hamburg, 1991), 161–163; cf *DACL loc cit* above on Christians and the ass.

[142] SHA, *Heliogabalus* 28,4: "Struthocamelos exhibuit in cenis aliquotiens, dicens praeceptum Iudaeis ut ederent."

[143] R. Syme, *Ammianus and the Historia Augusta* (Oxford, 1968), 113, points out that the SHA "shows an abnormal interest in ostriches." They are mentioned eight times.

perfectly normal fare like pork. Their dietary laws, like their monotheism, were emphatically regarded as an aspect of the unsociability of the Jews.

The Jewish Sabbath

The third topic familiar from the sources is the Sabbath.[144] It is mentioned as a well-known institution without negative emphasis by several poets in the reign of Augustus,[145] another indication that there were enough Jews in the city of Rome in this period for their customs to be familiar in broad circles. A number of later authors consider the Sabbath wasteful and a proof of the idleness of the Jews.[146] Several others want to demonstrate the absurdity of the Sabbath by claiming that Jerusalem was conquered because the Jews would not defend themselves on that day.[147] Plutarch lists keeping of the Sabbath as one of the bad barbarian customs which are taken up by Romans, yet another critical remark about foreign customs penetrating contemporary society.[148] Several authors in the reign of Augustus and afterwards refer to the Sabbath erroneously and sometimes ironically as a fast day.[149] A curious late attack may be found in a letter from Synesius (c. 365–413/414) to his brother, where he describes how a Jewish skipper and his Jewish sailors stopped functioning at sunset on Sabbath eve and almost let the vessel go down.[150] It cannot be said that such mockery of Sabbath practices amounts to hostility. It is one of the numerous customs and habits which were seen to single out the Jews and raised little sympathy, if not criticism.

An unusual accusation found in the work of the fifth-century author Rutilius Namatianus is that the Jewish God is soft or effeminate, because he rested on

[144] Schäfer, 82–92.

[145] Tibullus, 1.3.15–18 (Stern, No. 126); Horace, *Serm.* 1.9.67–72 (Stern, No. 129); Ovid, *Ars Amatoria* 1.413–416 (Stern, No. 142).

[146] Seneca, *De Superstitione* ap. Augustinus, *De Civitate Dei* 6.11 (Stern, No. 186); Tacitus, *Hist.* 5.4.3 (Stern, No. 281, comments in Vol. 2, pp. 37f.). Tacitus adds that the appeal of idleness on the Sabbath made them introduce a seventh year of idleness as well. Juvenal 14.96f. (Stern, No. 301) mentions the day as one also revered by proselytes who have not fully converted; cf. Stern, comments in vol. 2, p. 103f. In the fifth century Rutilius Namatianus, *De Reditu Suo* 1.398–92 (Stern, No. 542), is one of the authors who describe the Sabbath as cold: see Stern's comments, 2. p. 663f. The Sabbath is described as cold because it is forbidden to light fire, see already Meleager from Gadara in the second-first century B.C.: Stern, vol. 1, No. 43, p. 140.

[147] Dio 37.16.2 (Stern, No. 406) on Pompey's capture of the city; Frontinus, *Stratagemata* 2.1.17 (Stern, No. 229 with comments on Vol. 1. pp. 510f.) on Titus's capture of Jerusalem (the passage is erroneous in several respects); Plutarch, *De Superstitione* 8 (Stern, No. 256); it is not quite certain what siege Plutarch has in mind, cf. Stern, comments on p. 549.

[148] Plutarch, *De Superstitione* 3 (Stern, No. 255), see also the previous note. Note also Seneca's hostile remark: *Ep. Mor.* 95.47 (Stern, No. 188): Accendere aliquem lucernas sabbatis prohibeamus, quoniam nec lumine dii egent et ne homines quidem delectantur fuligine. This may be yet another implied comment on the popularity of Jewish customs in Rome of his day.

[149] Pompeius Trogus, ap. Iustinus, *Ep.* 36.2.14 (Stern, No. 137) and other authors, cited by Stern in the commentary, vol. 1, pp. 341 and 277; Petronius, *Carmen* 50, *Frg.* 37 (Stern, No. 195); Martial, *Ep.* 4.4 (Stern, No. 239).

[150] Synesius, *Ep.* 5 (Stern, No. 569).

the seventh day.[151] Here criticism of the Jewish nation and their Sabbath is extended or transferred to their God, but, as argued above, the Jews, together with the Parthians, were the two eastern nations that were not normally regarded as soft or effeminate by Greek and Roman authors.

Circumcision

Finally, there is the particularly sensitive topic of circumcision.[152] This was the symbol of the Jewish male and the final step taken by a convert.[153] It is usually mentioned with great disapproval. Strabo mentions it as one of the bad customs of the Jews which were typical of their decline and adopted when, after Moses and his first successors, "superstitious men were appointed to the priesthood and then tyrannical people."[154] Tacitus, as already mentioned, says that the Jews "adopted circumcision to distinguish themselves from other peoples by this difference." The idea of the social separateness of the Jews has been described above. Circumcision was the one physical feature emphasizing this separateness. In spite of the circumstance that there were other peoples who also had this custom, it became the obvious distinguishing mark of a Jewish male, for the other peoples were not present in such numbers in Italy.[155] Jews could be referred to as simply "the circumcised."[156] Petronius lists it among other remarkable or even ludicrous physical characteristics of foreign peoples.[157] Petronius presents being circumcised as one of two shortcomings of an otherwise perfect slave, in the eyes of his master.[158] Martial repeatedly mentions circumcised

---

[151] Rutilius Namatianus, *De Reditu Suo* 1.391f. (Stern, No. 542): Septima quaeque dies turpi damnata veterno, tamquam lassati mollis imago dei. Cf. Celsus ap. Origenes, *contra Celsum* 6.61 (Stern, No. 375).

[152] Schäfer, 93–105; cf. Pierre Cordier, "Les Romains et la circoncision," *Revue des Études Juives* 160 (2001), 337–355, which offers a semantic analysis of the relevant terminology with conclusions rather different from those that follow here.

[153] Goodman, *Mission and Conversion* (1994), 67, 77, 81f.; Schäfer, 96f. See, for instance, Petronius, loc. cit., cited already in connection with the Sabbath; Juvenal, 14.99 (Stern, No. 301).

[154] Strabo 16.2.37 (c. 761) (Stern, No. 115), adding excision of the females, cf. Stern, comments on p. 306.

[155] As appears from the well-known story told by Suetonius, *Domitianus* 12.2 (Stern, No. 320).

[156] Horace, *Serm.* 1.9.70 (Stern, No. 129): "curti Iudaei"; Persius, *Sat.* 5.184 (Stern, No. 190): recutita sabbata. Cf. Will and Orrieux, *Prosélytisme Juif?*, 105.

[157] Petronius, *Satyricon* 102.14 (Stern, No. 194), a passage already cited, above, chapter 4, as it is one of several references in ancient literature to eastern men with pierced ears, describes people who are proposing nonsensical plans to deceive the enemies they want to escape. "Ita tamquam servi Aethiopes et praesto tibi erimus sine tormentorum iniuria hilares et permutato colore imponemus inimicis. 'Quidni?' inquit Giton 'etiam circumcide nos, ut Iudaei videamur, et pertunde aures, ut imitemur Arabes, et increta facies, ut suos Gallia cives putet: tamquam his solus color figuram possit pervertere.'" Thus they are going to paint themselves black to look like Ethiopian slaves, be circumcised to make them look like Jews, have pierced ears to masquerade as Arabs and chalk their faces white to be taken for Gauls. The text then continues to describe other physical features of Africans.

[158] Petronius, *Satyricon* 68.6–8 (Stern, No. 193). His other shortcoming is that he snores, while it does not matter that he did not go to school and is cross-eyed.

Jews, each time from the perspective of his persistent preoccupation with their sexuality.[159] He singles out the "circumcised Jews" among nine nations as being "lecherous," although all find favor with Caelia. She turns down only Romans. This is a sexual variant of the ever-returning sense that the victors are defeated by the vanquished.[160] Particularly angry is *ep.* 11.94 which accuses a circumcised poet, Anchialus, born in Jerusalem, of plagiarizing Martial's poems, even while criticizing them and having intercourse with Martial's boy.[161] Tacitus has quite a different impression of the behavior of Jewish men: "although as a people, they are extremely given to lust, they refrain from intercourse with foreign women; among themselves, however, nothing is forbidden."[162] Tacitus here displays a duality in his views which is familiar also from modern hostility towards minorities: they are accused of extremes which often are mutually exclusive. In any case, both Martial and Tacitus have ideas of strongly developed libidinous urges among the Jews, but disagree about the forms these take. Such accusations remind us of later forms of anti-semitism, but it is impossible to say how widespread they were in antiquity, since they are found only in these two authors.

A later, satirical reference to circumcision appears in the *Historia Augusta*: "At this time the Jews started a war because they were forbidden to mutilate their genitals."[163] This statement is famous because it is the only source which appears to state explicitly that the cause of the Bar Kokhba war in the reign of Hadrian was a prohibition of circumcision.[164] Whatever the merit of this theory,

---

[159] Martial, *Ep.* 7.30.5; 7.35 (with the elegant translation into Italian by Ker, LCL; Stern, No. 241, where the Italian translation is printed); 7.82.6 (Stern, No. 243); 11.94 (Stern No. 245), all extensively analyzed by Schäfer, 99–102. Williams, *Historia* 39 (1990), 205, observes that book 7 was specifically dedicated to Domitian and suggests that the hostility towards the Jews in the poems of this book was therefore aimed at delighting the emperor. She observes that Martial's Book 7 is notable for the greatest concentration of anti-Jewish poems anywhere in his work. See also Shaye J. D. Cohen, "Was Martial's Slave Jewish?" in *The Beginnings of Jewishness: Boundaries, Varieties, Uncertainties* (Berkeley, 1999), 351–357; and for 7.82: "Was Menophilus Jewish?" ibid., 358f.

[160] Martial 7.30: Das Parthis, das Germanis, das, Caelia, Dacis etc. . . . Qua ratione facis, cum sis Romana puella, quod Romana tibi mentula nulla placet?

[161] For 11.94, N. M. Kay, *Martial Book XI* (London, 1985), 267–261. See especially his comments on the repeated expression *verpe poeta:* "The jibe of 'verpe' is aimed both at the poet being a Jew and at his being a lustful *pedicator.* . . . the words *verpus* and *verpa,* alluding to erection of the penis, are elsewhere found in contexts suggesting aggressive homosexual acts . . . and excessive lustfulness."

[162] Tacitus, *Hist.* 5.5.2: proiectissima ad libidinem gens, alienarum concubitu abstinent; inter se nihil inlicitum. Cf. comments by Stern, 2. p. 40. See on these matters: Aline Rousselle, *La contamination spirituelle: science, droit et religion dans l'Antiquité* (Paris, 1998), chap. 7: "Vivre sous deux droits," 170–195.

[163] SHA, *Hadrian* 14.2: "moverunt ea tempestate et Iudaei bellum, quod vetabantur mutilare genitalia." See on this passage: B. Isaac, *The Near East under Roman Rule* (1998), 277f.

[164] The subject has been much debated. Cf. Schürer, i, 536–540; Smallwood, *The Jews under Roman Rule,* 429–531; Stern, ii, comments on pp. 619–621, all with extensive bibliography. Note also J. Geiger, "The Ban on Circumcision and the Bar-Kokhba Revolt," *Zion* 41 (1976), 139ff. (Heb.); Schäfer, *Der Bar Kokhba-Aufstand* (Tübingen, 1981); B. Isaac and A. Oppenheimer, "The

it is worth noting that the SHA does not use the word circumcision, but mutilation. The implication is that this was a ludicrous rebellion, for who in his right senses would go to war because he was forbidden to mutilate himself? The statement about the origins of the Bar Kokhba war puts the war as a whole in a ridiculous light and it is therefore worth considering whether this does not call into question the trustworthiness of this statement in a source which is anyway of dubious reliability. The equation of circumcision with mutilation, on the other hand, is found also in the work of a contemporary Christian author, John Chrysostom: "Watch out for the dogs, watch out for the evil-workers, watch out for those who mutilate the flesh. For we are the true circumcision, who worship God in spirit."[165]

Other Accusations

So far we have been faced with ancient views of actual characteristics of the Jews, even if they are sometimes distorted or maliciously reinterpreted. The Jews did indeed abstain from pork, rest on the Sabbath, and so on. We must now consider to what extent total fabrications or other forms of hostile representation occur in the sources. The subject that requires attention in this connection is the accusation of human sacrifice.[166] As has been remarked several times above, the practice of human sacrifice was considered the ultimate barbarism by Greeks and Romans, even though there are embarrassing reports about such practices in Rome.[167] Pliny observes that "not until the 657th year of the City (i.e. 97 B.C.) did the senate ban human sacrifice; so that clearly till that

---

Revolt of Bar Kokhba: Ideology and Modern Scholarship," = B. Isaac, *The Near East Under Roman Rule* (1998), 220–252, at 233f.; additional bibliography on pp. 254–256; Schäfer, *Judeophobia*, 103–105.

[165] John Chrysostom, *Homilia adversus Judaeos*, PG 48. col. 845. Chrysostom is here quoting Paul: *Philippians* 3, 2: βλέπετε τοὺς κύνας, βλέπετε τοὺς κακοὺς ἐργάτας, βλέπετε τὴν κατατομήν. ἡμεῖς γὰρ ἐσμεν ἡ περιτομή, οἱ πνεύματι θεοῦ λατρεύοντες. On Chrysostom and the Jews: Robert L. Wilken, *John Chrysostom and the Jews: rhetoric and reality in the late 4th century* (Berkeley, 1983).

[166] J. Rives, "Human Sacrifice among Pagans and Christians," *JRS* 85 (1995), 65–85.

[167] For accusations of human sacrifice, see also the observations on bestiality as expounded by Aristotle, *Eth.Nic.* 1149a, discussed above. The evidence for human sacrifice in Greece has been discussed once more by Dennis D. Hughes, *Human Sacrifice in Ancient Greece* (London and New York, 1991), who concludes that there is very little sound evidence for historical Greece (v. supra, chapters 2 and 6). Human sacrifice is associated with barbarian communities in Greek tragedy, even though in Greek myth human victims are regularly sacrificed by Greeks: E. Hall, *Inventing the Barbarian*, 146–148. Theophrastus regarded human sacrifice not as a primitive custom, but as a form of corruption, which he traced back to the discovery of fire: *de pietate,* cited by Porphyry, *de abstinentia,* 2.5ff. See Plutarch, *Marcellus* 3.3f., for human sacrifices of pairs of Greeks and Celts, buried alive, on the Forum Boarium after the First Punic War, clearly considered embarrassing an embarrassing episode, and *Quaestiones Romanae* 83/283F, discussed above, chapter 11, n. 63. See also Minucius Felix, *Octavius* 30: Romani Graecum et Graecam, Gallum et Gallam, sacrificii viventes obruere. Minucius Felix also mentions other peoples who practiced human sacrifice.

time such unnatural rituals were practised."[168] Human sacrifice is associated with the Druids in Britannia and Gaul.[169] The Thracians are thought to have practiced it.[170] The Carthaginians were notorious for it and so were the Scythians.[171] The first such accusation aimed at the Jews is reported by Josephus.[172] The Jews are again accused of the practice by Damocritus, who wrote a work *On Jews* (in Greek):[173] "he states that they used to worship an asinine golden head and that every seventh year they caught a foreigner and sacrificed him. They used to kill him by carding his flesh into small pieces." There are no other instances. Thus, although the accusation is found a few times, it cannot be said to have been a common belief and, while originating in Hellenistic culture, it was not taken over by the Romans. Still, the fact that such reports existed may not be ignored, like the accusations of a related horror: cannibalism.[174] It is at least worth noting that there is a precedent in antiquity for the blood libel which became so common in later periods.[175] The blood libel as such was apparently first aimed at Christians and only later by Christians at the Jews. While the accusations of human sacrifice attested in Josephus and the fragment of Damocritus refer to an adult, the later blood libel always concerns ritual infanticide.[176] It is perhaps significant that the accusation of human sacrifice was aimed at the Jews by Hellenistic authors, but not in Roman literature. The reality of human sacrifice—unlike that of cannibalism—is not in doubt, but as we know perfectly well, the reports that Jews practiced it in the Hellenistic period are based on hostile phantasy. It is fair to conclude that antagonism

---

[168] Pliny, *NH* 30.12: DCLVII demum anno urbis Cn. Cornelio Lentulo P. Licinio Crasso cos. senatusconsultum factum est, ne homo immolaretur, palamque fit, in tempus il<l>ut sacra prodigiosa celebrata.

[169] See above and Strabo 4.4.6 (c. 198).

[170] Jerome, ep. 60.4, *ad Heliodorum:* The savage Bessians and their host of skin-clad peoples, who used to offer human sacrifice to the dead, have now dissolved their rough discord into the sweet music of the Cross, and the whole world with one voice cries out, "Christ."

[171] Plutarch, *de Superstitione* 13.

[172] Josephus, *contra Apionem* 2.89 (Stern, No. 171). Cf. Bickerman, "Ritualmord und Eselskult," in *Studies in Jewish and Christian History* 2 (Leiden, 1980), 225–255, at 245–255 and discussion by Rives, *JRS* 85 (1995), 70–72.

[173] Damocritus (I AD?) Suda, s.v. (Stern, No. 247), comments on p. 531.

[174] Cassius Dio: accusations of Jewish cannibalism and excessive cruelty during the revolt in Cyrene, Egypt, and Cyprus under Trajan (Dio 68.32.1). W.H.C. Frend, *Martyrdom and Persecution in the Early Church* (Oxford, 1965), 223, is prepared to believe that these reports are "not perhaps entirely myth." Accusations of cannibalism are discussed above, chapter 2.

[175] For the accusations of ritual murder in the Middle Ages and afterwards: R. Po-chia Hsia, *The Myth of Ritual Murder: Jews and Magic in Reformation Germany* (New Haven and London, 1988), for references to older literature on the blood libel: p. 2, note 3; Rohrbacher and Schmidt, *Judenbilder* (1991), 274–291. See also the older work: Trachtenberg, *The Devil and the Jews*, Part 2.9: "Ritual Murder," 10: "The Blood Accusation"; R. Po-chia Hsia, *Trent 1475: Stories of a Ritual Murder Trial* (New Haven, 1992).

[176] Waltzing, *Académie Royale de Belgique, Bull.* Lettres, ser. 5, vol. 11 (1925), 205–239, F. J. Dölger, *Antike und Christentum* 4 (1934), 188–228.

towards the Jews in the Hellenistic literature is marked by a far greater measure of irrationality and imagination than Roman hostility towards them.

Negative Stereotypes

Finally, there are several negative stereotypes related to the Jewish religion, which was considered absurd by many non-Jews. Therefore, the Jews themselves could be regarded as being credulous. This is best known through Horace's "Apella the Jew may believe it, not I."[177] From here it is only one step to making the Jews themselves frauds and impostors, an accusation frequently aimed also at Greeks, at other eastern peoples, and at Egyptians. Thus we find a "Syrian from Palestine" as fraudulent exorcist in Lucian, *Philopseudes* 16 (perhaps no Jew). And elsewhere: "Some purge themselves with sacred medicine; Others are mocked by chants impostors sell, and other fools fall for the spells of Jews."[178] Juvenal has similar objections, as already mentioned.[179] Also mentioned above is the case which Josephus reports as well of Jews who defrauded an aristocratic lady convert. So there was definitely a popular image of fraudulent Jews. This does not exclude the possibility that such Jews indeed existed, but we have no way to determine what are hostile stereotypes and what reflects reality.[180] Perhaps there was a related idea that the Jewish religion was secret. At least, we find allusions to this notion in Juvenal's assertion already cited: "all that Moses handed down in his secret tome, forbidding to point out the way to any not worshipping the same rites."[181] Accusations of fraudulence and secrecy represent an old tradition: they are found already in Livy's report of the scandal concerning the Bacchanalia, three centuries before Juvenal criticized the alleged secrecy of the Jews. Secrecy was regarded as making a foreign cult particularly dangerous because it raised associations with political conspiracy. It may not have been a frequent charge against Jews, but the fact that it occurs at all has some significance.

Another hostile claim that appears in the writings of several authors is worth noting: [Apollonius Molon] "adds that we are the most witless of all barbarians, and are consequently the only people who have contributed no useful invention to civilization."[182] It is repeated by Apion who, again according to Josephus, claims that the Jews "have not produced any remarkable men, for instance inventors in the arts and crafts or men remarkable for their wisdom."[183] It occurs

---

[177] Horace, *Sermones* 1.5.100: credat Iudaeus Apella, non ego (Stern, 128, comments: 1.p. 324).

[178] Lucian, *Podagra* 171–173 (Stern, No. 374); see also *Alexander Pseudopropheta* 13 (Stern, No. 373), where the false prophet utters meaningless words "like Hebrew or Phoenician."

[179] See above, p. 465.

[180] M. Simon, *Verus Israel*, 341f., goes remarkably far in accepting these attacks: "[Judaism] exercised a more murky influence on the masses by its reputed ability to ward off the Powers. This aspect of Jewish influence, which was older than Christianity, continued to make itself felt even within the Christian ranks." See p. 504, n.120 with, altogether, two references.

[181] Above, p. 454.

[182] Josephus, *Contra Apionem* 2.148 (Stern, No. 49).

[183] *Contra Apionem* 2.135 (Stern, No. 175).

also in a quotation from Celsus[184] and, with a different emphasis, in the writings of the Emperor Julian,[185] who says that the Hebrews did not originate any science or any philosophical study, nor did they have a single commander like Alexander or Caesar. Anyone inferior to those two great men deserves more admiration than all the commanders of the Jews put together. It should be noted that this particular idea is not found in the central works of Roman literature. It originated in Alexandrian circles and recurs in a second-century Middle-Platonic philosopher and in the writings of a fourth-century emperor with a mostly Greek education. Given that it occurs four times over a lengthy period it is worth mentioning, since the accusation that the Jews do not contribute to civilization is familiar from recent anti-semitism.[186] Although not found very frequently in antiquity, the idea was there.

Did the Romans Advocate Genocide?

We have already seen that the Romans did not in principle reject the idea of genocide and in fact practiced it when this seemed useful. Do we encounter in Roman literature any idea that Jews should be exterminated as a people? At the beginning of this chapter we saw the advisors of the Seleucid King Antiochus proposing "to wipe out completely the Jewish people, since they alone of all nations avoided dealings with any other people and looked upon all men as their enemies." Philo of Alexandria claims that Seianus "wished to destroy" the Jewish people. It is not clear whether we should take this literally or merely as an indication of a hostile policy, but the least this says is that the idea, or the fear of the idea, existed.[187] One source reports that Titus, in 70, decided to destroy the Temple in Jerusalem "in order that the religion of the Jews and the Christians should be more completely exterminated. For those religions, though opposed to one another, derive from the same founders; the Christians stemmed from the Jews and the extirpation of the root would easily cause the offspring to perish."[188] This text is independent of Josephus's account of Titus's campaign. It is based on another source, usually assumed to be Tacitus. The report that the destruction of the Temple was the result of a deliberate Roman decision is quite convincing. It is also possible that it was hoped this would mean the end of the Jewish religion. No pagan religion could exist without sanctuaries where their cult was practiced and it cannot have been expected that Judaism would suc-

---

[184] Celsus, ap. Origenes, *Contra Celsum* 1.16; 4.31 (Stern, No. 375).

[185] Julian, *Contra Galilaeos* 176; 178; 218B–C (Stern, No. 481a).

[186] Ritchie Robertson, *The "Jewish Question" in German Literature* (1999), 192–195, traces the conception of Jews as devoid of creativity. It is applied to all of the Semites by E. Renan, *Histoire generale* (1878), 9–16, at 16: "Ainsi la race sémitique se reconna?t presque uniquement à des charactères négatifs: elle n'a ni mythologie, ni épopée, ni science, ni philosophie, ni fiction, ni arts plastiques, ni vie civile; en tout, absence de complexité, de nuances, sentiment exclusif de l'unité."

[187] Cf. E. Mary Smallwood, "Some Notes on the Jews under Tiberius," *Latomus* 15 (1956), 314–329; *The Jews under Roman Rule* (Leiden, 1976), 165–167; 201f. Smallwood has shown that this was not the affair of A.D. 19, but a later episode, towards the end of Seianus's career, c. A.D. 30.

[188] Sulpicius Severus, *Chronica* 2.30.4 (Stern, No. 282). See Stern's comments, 2.65–7.

ceed in maintaining itself without its central sanctuary. Sulpicius Severus thus attributes to the Romans the desire to wipe out the Jewish and Christian religions. This is, of course, not the same as planning to destroy a people in a physical sense. In his *Parthica* Arrian says that "Trajan was determined above all, if it were possible, to destroy the nation utterly, but if not, at least to crush it and to stop its presumptuous wickedness."[189] Taken together, these sources, particularly those regarding Titus and Trajan, make clear that some commanders and rulers wanted to be rid of the Jews. However, on the whole, there is little evidence for intentions of whole-scale genocide.

THE JEWS — DISCUSSION AND CONCLUSIONS

This chapter aims at describing the most significant characteristics of Roman feelings about the Jews, but it does not attempt to trace the full development of ideas about the Jews over time in Alexandria, Palestine, and Rome. Roman feelings about Jews are often hostile, as is clear from the language used: *sceleratissima gens* (Seneca), *taeterrima gens* (Tacitus), *perniciosa gens* (Quintilian), "much lower than reptiles" (Cleomedes), "a graceless people" (γένος ἔκσπονδον) (Synesius).[190] The works of Juvenal and Martial speak for themselves. Most of these belong to the mainstream of Latin literature and are representative of a broad section of Roman upper-class opinion. It is essential to note that these attitudes reflect responses to the presence of Jews inside the city of Rome. When the empire became Christian, an even stronger hostility towards Jews became the norm. Constantine refers to the Jews as "bloodstained men (who) are, as one might expect, mentally blind" and "a detestable mob," a "deadly" or a "nefarious sect."[191]

The hostility towards Jews focuses on a number of topics, partly in the social sphere, partly religious, or a combination of these two. The main objection is

---

[189] Arrian, *Parthica* ap. Suda, s.v. ἀτάσθαλα et παρείκοι (Stern, No. 332a): Ὁ δὲ Τραϊανὸς ἔγνω μάλιστα μέν, εἰ παρείκοι, ἐξελεῖν τὸ ἔθνος εἰ δὲ μή, ἀλλὰ συντρίψας γε παῦσαι τῆς ἄγαν ἀτασθαλίας. It has been argued, entirely convincingly, that the people Trajan desired to destroy could not have been the Parthians, but must have been the Jewish people, who rebelled ferociously during Trajan's Parthian war. Cf. Stern's comments on 2.152–5. Eusebius, *HE* 4.2.5: Trajan instructed Lusius Quietus to remove the Jews from the province of Mesopotamia; cf. Jerome, *Chronica* (Helm), p.196 and other sources, cited by Stern, p.152. These may support the fragment of Arrian.

[190] Synesius, *ep.* 5 (Stern, No. 569). The full description is: "a graceless people and fully convinced of the piety of sending to Hades as many Greeks as possible."

[191] Constantine's letter about the date of Easter, Eusebius, *Life of Constantine* (trans. Averil Cameron and Stuart G. Hall, Oxford 1999): 3.18.2. οἳ τὰς ἑαυτῶν χεῖρας ἀθεμίτῳ πλημμελήματι χράναντες εἰκότως τὰς ψυχὰς οἱ μιαροὶ τυφλώττουσιν. . . . 3.18.3: τοῦ ἐχθίστου τῶν Ἰουδαίων ὄχλου. Cf. *CTh* 16.8.1; *CJ* 1.9.3: feralem sectam; nefariam sectam. See the comments by G. Stemberger, *Juden und Christen im Heiligen Land: Palästina unter Konstantin und Theodosius* (Munich, 1987), 45f. It is for our purposes irrelevant whether Constantine himself formulated this or an advisor. We are interested, not in what Constantine thought, but what he stood for, and we know that such language was not used in official documents of previous emperors.

that the Jews are an antisocial people who purposely cut themselves off from the rest of the world. This is considered the ultimate in barbarism, unforgiveable in the case of the Jews, because they are not a remote mountain people or nomads, but live among civilized peoples. It is true that there are Roman authors who flirt, in a very abstract way, with the idea that the world would have been better if people were to live in isolation, as seen in chapter 7, but this line of thought was never pursued in any consistent manner. It is claimed that the Jews live apart, are loyal to each other, and hate all others. Connected with these objections is the idea that Jewish morals and their way of life are the reverse of those of normal people. These ideas originated in some form in the East, notably in Alexandria, but developed in Rome through the influence of contact with Jews living in Italy and in the capital. The Romans adopted some, but by no means all, of the traditional anti-Jewish ideas, put their own slant on them, and developed more.

A particularly aggravating factor was the obvious popularity of Judaism in some Roman circles. Recently it has been argued that Jews in the first century favored an apologetic mission to win gentile sympathizers, but were not interested in winning new Jews. It is quite possible that the actual number of such people was not large, but even so, the sympathizers were also viewed as a dangerous phenomenon, while full conversion was regarded with hostility by various Roman authors. Proselytes were considered traitors, because in converting to Judaism—if that is what they did—they not only accepted a religion regarded with aversion and customs considered ridiculous or worse, but they actually abandoned their ancestral religion, customs, and laws. In this sense, conversion to Judaism was seen as a change, not merely of cult practice, but of ethnic identity and all that this entailed in the sphere of loyalties and obligations. Not only were the Jews, in Roman eyes, a separate and exclusive community in Rome as well as elsewhere, they are sometimes even seen as forming a pressure group, loyal to each other and hostile to others—a suggestion that is present in the literature from Cicero on. The combination of the real or presumed attraction of proselytes and the sense that the Jews formed a pressure group resulted in the familiar anxiety that the victors were subdued by the vanquished, discussed under a separate heading above, where it is applied to Greeks, Asiatics, Syrians, Gauls, and others. The language used in various texts is familiar again from the attacks on Greek culture and Asiatic customs, for instance: we encounter expressions like "infection" and "contamination," which suggest the transmission of disease or pollution. Through conversion both the numbers and the wealth of the Jews were believed to increase. Whether this was true or not, such statements are found in the literature from the late republic till the third century and they definitely reflect various degrees of discomfort or worse. A different phenomenon which belongs to life in urban Rome is the presence of numbers of impoverished Jews who, apparently, were found in the vicinity of synagogues.[192] There are accusations that some of these people acted

[192] For the Jews in the city of Rome: Schürer, *History* 3.1, 73–81; David Noy, *Jewish Inscriptions*

as fraudulent soothsayers and exorcists. It is important to note that, unlike most other peoples from the same general area, the Jews are not commonly seen as effeminate or born slaves.

In the religious sphere there are related animosities. Some authors speak of secrecy, which raises associations with the mystery cults forbidden in Rome. Monotheism itself was rejected by some of the writers. In spite of a small number of thinkers who had some respect for the consistency and logic of the concept, the Jewish God was viewed, like the Jewish people, as being exclusive. This in itself made the religion incompatible with Roman religion. The dietary laws meant that Jews did not share meals with others, which was part of their image as unsociable. The Sabbath was regarded with little sympathy. Circumcision emphasized and marked the otherness of Jewish men and meant a decisive step for converts to take; it was abhorred. We also encounter notions concerning uninhibited lust or sexually extravagant behavior among the Jews.

The evaluation of these matters will always depend on the attitude of the evaluator. Those who cherish their antipathies towards other nations, groups, or minorities always claim that their dislike is based on objective realities. There are similar patterns in the analysis of antiquity. Those who dislike Jews in the present will conclude that there were objective reasons for the Greeks and Romans to dislike them.[193] One difficulty in understanding the relationships in antiquity properly is that we have no numerical information. There is no way of knowing how many Jews there were in the various provinces and in Rome, and how many proselytes. However this may be, it is clear that people of every period are guided more by emotions than by numbers and facts when thinking about social groups, and it should not be difficult to accept that most of the ancient authors discussed in this chapter were not guided by rational considerations in their judgments and fears.

Yet, in spite of all this hostility, Judaism was permitted in Judaea, in Rome, and in the provinces. It was permitted although the religion as such was regarded by many with highly negative feelings, because the Jews had the status of a recognized people and a people had a right to its religion, whatever it was.

---

of Western Europe. 2. The City of Rome (Cambridge, 1995); M. Williams, "The Structure of the Jewish Community in Rome," in M. Goodman (ed.), Jews in a Graeco-Roman World (Oxford 1998), 215–228.

[193] Ruth Benedict wrote her monograph Race and Racism (London, 1942) with the clear intention of clarifying the concept of race and attacking racism in a time which saw extravagant abuse of the concept. She strongly insists that racism is a creation of our own time. However, on p. 103, she states: "The Hebrew law and the prophets also contributed to the foundations of Jesus's teaching. The ancient Mosaic law lays down gracious rules: . . . After the Assyrian (sic) captivity, however, an opposition party arose which advocated separatism. . . . Fanatical racism therefore occurred in Israel long before the days of modern racism, but no trace of it is to be found in the words of Christ. His teachings of a great community of peoples without regard to race agreed with the older Hebraic law, and were given a solid basis, also, by the achievements of the Roman Empire." It is curious that we should find such a traditional form of Christian anti-semitism and bigotry in an American anthropologist and thinker, writing in 1939 and publishing in 1942 precisely to combat racism.

481

It did not have a right to accept foreigners into its midst and when this happened, as was seen to happen among the Jews, countermeasures were taken
from time to time. Thus, religion was made an inseparable part of ethnic identity, and in this way the Romans seriously restricted freedom of religion. Children had the right and duty to practice the religion of their parents, but nobody
had an automatic right to practice the religion of another people. That was
considered a politically significant act. In the case of Roman citizens it was also
regarded as a breach of the required loyalty, for religion was an inseparable part
of the state.

Under the empire, the imperial cult became part of this complex. Rome accepted that the Jews had a peculiar fanaticism which made it impossible to
demand of them what was demanded of everybody else, but they were suffered
as an exception. On the part of the Romans, this was a realistic policy, rather
than an expression of tolerance, for they were aware that Jews would rather let
themselves be killed than revere a mortal ruler as if he were a god. For the
same reason Jews were exempted from army service and other duties which
impinged on their customs. The Romans succeeded in building an empire because they were realists and they did not usually attempt to enforce the unenforceable. The result of Caligula's demand to have his statue placed in the Temple in Jerusalem provides a notorious example of what could happen if Roman
leaders lost their sense of realism. In other cases of friction and the sanctions
which resulted, the evidence may not be enough to determine cause and effect.[194]

Above, it was emphasized that the Jews are not described as soft or effeminate in Roman sources, unlike other peoples from the same area. Cicero is the
only one who ever calls them "born slaves." Apparently this was not a theme
that caught the imagination either. The stereotypes of Jews did not correspond
with those applied to most eastern peoples and Jews were not classified with the
weak and spineless peoples.

Conclusions

So, where do we agree with the views of Mommsen, cited in the beginning of
this chapter? Roman enmity, says Mommsen, was essentially the same as the
nineteenth-century phenomenon. It is a form of racial hatred and the broader
context is one of West against East. The more specific root of the enmity is to
be found in the opinions and customs of the Jews. Only the last part seems
convincing, in view of the discussion above. Roman hostility towards the Jews
did not resemble later anti-semitism, nor was it similar to Roman hatred of the
East. It was not racist in character, but did indeed focus on some elements of

---

[194] The various instances of expulsion from Rome in the first century, for instance, have been
much debated and no consensus has been reached. Rutgers, *Classical Antiquity* 13 (1994), 68:
"Rome was of course capable of treating the Jews harshly, but usually it had good reasons when it
did so." This sounds more like the conclusion of an official enquiry, appointed to whitewash a
scandal, than as a scholarly evaluation of brief and one-sided reports.

482 · CHAPTER 13 ·

the Jewish religion and customs. The subject of proselytism is not prominent in Mommsen's brief statements on the Jews.

Finally, we ought to assess these attitudes in the light of the views of other peoples discussed in this part of the book. In Greek and Roman eyes, eastern peoples tend to be seen as clever and cunning, degenerate and effeminate, born slaves—qualities which are often attributed to two major factors: the environment and monarchy. Various other negative factors are often added, such as wealth, which undermines collective strength. All this is not true of notions about the Jews. While they are described as frivolous, lying, treacherous, libidinous, and generally morally depraved, they are not usually regarded as a typical eastern people and no reason for their negative qualities is given in terms of environment or constitution. Their worst social characteristic is their separateness and this, insofar as any explanation is given, fits their most remarkable feature, their religion. Some authors have an historical explanation for this, notably Tacitus, who considers Moses the man responsible for some of their institutions, and asserts that he imposed on the Jews religious practices opposed to those of all other religions in order to establish his influence over this people for all time.

Still, it must be emphasized that those forms of hostile prejudice or stereotypes which might be described as proto-racist do not apply to the Jews. The negative characteristics described in the sources are not seen as unalterable, in the sense that they result from climate or are inherited. The latter would not have been unthinkable, for the separateness of the Jews and the fact that, according to Tacitus, they abstain from intercourse with foreign women, might have resulted in a view of the Jews as being of pure lineage. Such a description is never found in the literature, for being of pure lineage is considered a positive thing in antiquity—which is why the Jews of Babylonia made this claim for themselves. It would have been possible for ancient authors to claim that the bad qualities of the Jews were the result of inherited factors, but in fact such a claim is never made. In this connection it is noteworthy that Jews are never described as animals or brutes in Greek and Roman literature, while this is one of the most convenient forms of dehumanizing others.[195] Thus, while there is a good deal of hostility towards the Jews, this represents ethnic hatred and cannot be described as ancient racism or proto-racism.

It is especially remarkable that the Jews do not appear as merchants, rich, greedy, and grasping, unlike the Phoenicians in antiquity and unlike the Jews in post-medieval periods.[196] In this connection it may be interesting to mention

[195] To the best of my knowledge the first authors who compare Jews with animals are S. Bernard of Clairveaux (1090–1153), and Petrus Venerabilis of Cluny (1122–56): Bernard de Clairveaux, Migne, *PL* 183. col. 1068; Petrus Venerabilis, Migne, *PL* 189. col. 602.

[196] As noted by Jules Isaac, *Genèse de l'antisémitisme: essai historique* (Paris, 1956), 122. Approval of this conclusion of his does not mean I agree with the further assessment of ancient antisemitism proposed by this author. J. Leipoldt, *Antisemitimus in der alten Welt* (1933), 34–37, recognizes that the Jews in antiquity were not a people of traders, let alone *the* trading people, but he then argues at length that there were numerous Jewish traders who were partly responsible for

Immanuel Kant, who believed the Jews in ancient Palestine to have been an entire nation of fraudulent merchants whose Diaspora was a great benefit for them because it enabled them to grow into the richest people of the world.[197] He not only believed that all Jews in his time were wealthy merchants, he also was certain they always must have been merchants, even in Biblical times. This was not the Roman view. If the Jews in Rome were regarded by Roman aristocrats as unduly influential, this was not because of their presumed financial power, but because of the influence of their religion and social habits.

It can, however, be said that some of the elements of later anti-semitism are clearly present in ancient Rome, while others are not. Some of the later anti-semitic prejudices are encountered, not in connection with Jews in particular, but rather with other eastern peoples. It is essential to keep in mind that most of the texts referred to reflect attitudes of Romans to Jews inside the city of Rome. It is probably fair to say that Tacitus's dislike of the Jews represented feelings of a man for a people whom he frequently encountered. Far less is known about

---

the bad reputation of the Jewish people. Sevenster, *The Roots of Pagan Anti-Semitism*, chap. 2, also argues that the economic status of the Jews, or their presumed economic status, was not the root for ancient anti-Semitism. This, he believes, is related to the lack of racial discrimination in antiquity (for which, see his chap. 1). He accepts the familiar claim that there existed no racism in antiquity. He is vague about the meaning of 'race': ". . . attention must be paid to the distinction . . . between the concept 'race' formed on the grounds of a biological theory and the term 'race' used to designate a totality of national and social characteristics. The first connotation of the concept 'race', goes no further back than the last century and was certainly not known in the ancient world" (p. 42). What is "a totality of national and social characteristics" doing in an academic work? This distinction he has adopted from M. Radin, *The Jews among the Greeks and Romans* (1915), chap. 3. Radin's definition of pre-nineteenth century race is "a sum of national and social traits which it might be difficult to acquire in one generation, but which could readily be gained in two" (p. 48). For Radin, then, a race is formed in a couple of decennia and racism is in fact the equivalent of ethnic prejudice and xenophobia. Radin's definitions of race and racism have been taken over word for word (without acknowledgment) by Simon Davis, *Race-Relations in Ancient Egypt: Greek, Egyptian, Hebrew, Roman* (New York, 1952), xi–xiii.

[197] I. Kant, *Schriften zur Anthropologie Geschichtsphilosophie Politik und Pädagogik* (repr. Darmstadt, 1970), chapter: Anthropologie in pragmatischer Hinsicht, Vom Erkenntnisvermögen, p. 517f. note: "Die unter uns lebenden Palästinenser sind durch ihren Wuchergeist seit ihrem Exil, auch was die grösste Menge betrifft, in den nicht unbegründeten Ruf des Betruges gekommen. Es scheint nun zwar befremdlich, sich eine Nation von Betrügern zu denken; aber eben so befremdlich ist es doch auch, eine Nation von lauter Kaufleuten zu denken, deren bei weitem grösster Teil, durch einen alten, von dem Staat, darin sie leben, anerkannten Aberglauben verbunden, keine bürgerliche Ehre sucht, sondern dieser ihren Verlust durch die Vorteile der Überlistung des Volks, unter dem sie Schutz finden, und selbst ihrer untereinander ersetzen wollen. Nun kann dieses bei einer ganzen Nation von lauter Kaufleuten, als nicht-produzierenden Gliedern der Gesellschaft (z.B. der Juden in Polen), auch nicht anders sein." He continues to give a possible explanation: ". . . vom Ursprunge dieser sonderbaren Verfassung (nämlich eines Volks von lauter Kaufleuten)." Following the destruction of Jerusalem these merchants spread all over the world. In fact their diaspora must be seen not as a curse, but as a blessing for this people "zumal der Reichtum derselben, als Individuen geschätzt, wahrscheinlich den eines jeden anderen Volks von gleicher Personenzahl jetz übersteigt." For the association of Jews with finance by anti-semites: Rohrbacher and Schmidt, *Judenbilder*, 41–136; Robertson, *The "Jewish Question" in German Literature*, 120f. Kant places early Judaism outside the moral scale, calling it a mere political religion, cf. Yirmiahu Yovel, *Kant and the Philosophy of History* (Princeton, 1980).

relationships in other parts of the empire. It is clear that widespread hostility did not normally affect the formal status of the Jews in the empire, although there was an obvious hostile response to any real or assumed increase in the number of proselytes. Christians, however, were in a different position and it will be instructive briefly to consider their status.

Jews and Christians

The available sources do not make it easy to say anything about Roman views on the Christians in the early empire, for in the Latin literature of the period explicit references to Christians, as opposed to those to Jews, are very few in number. Thus, while we know that it was forbidden to be a Christian, there is no explanation of why this was so. It could be argued that this question is not relevant for the present study. There are two reasons, however, why it must be dealt with. First, any explicit prohibition "to be" or "to belong to" a specific group of people is interesting in a discussion of how the Greeks and Romans related to others. Second, in view of the observations on the position of the Jews above, it is important to see how that of the Christians differed. It has been seen that the Jews were allowed to practice their religion because it was the religion of their ancestors and Jewish identity was inherited, not acquired, since conversion was prohibited. By contrast, Christianity was never an inherited, and always an acquired religion. The Christians were not a people, even if there existed a tendency, among some of their authors, to describe themselves as a people. Thus, while the Christians were, at best, "a kind of men" (*genus hominum*), the Jews were always called "a people" (*gens*), even by those who disliked them. The status of the Jews and of the Christians in the empire is thus immediately connected with problems of ethnicity and of group status.

The secondary literature is extensive.[198] As already observed, any new religion or cult like Christianity would have been considered inferior to any old and established religion like Judaism. The Roman sources themselves must be the starting point of this specific discussion of attitudes towards Christians and I shall therefore refrain from discussing the events in Judaea during Jesus's lifetime and the process that ended with his execution.[199] The earliest testimony is

---

[198] A lucid treatment: G.E.M. de Ste. Croix, "Why were the Early Christians Persecuted?" *Past and Present* 26 (1963), 6–38; also: A. N. Sherwin-White, *Past and Present* 27 (1964), 23–27; de Ste. Croix's rejoinder, 28–33; W.H.C. Frend, *Martyrdom and Persecution in the Early Church: A Study of Conflict from the Maccabees to Donatus* (Oxford, 1965), chapters 4, 6, 7, 8; R. Freudenberger, *Das Verhalten der römischen Behörden gegen die Christen im 2. Jahrhundert dargestellt am Brief des Plinius und Trajan und den Reskripten Trajans und Hadrians* (Munich, 1967, repr. 1969). This is essentially an extensive commentary on the two letters in Pliny; for "die drei Rechtsfragen," see 73–76; T. D. Barnes, "Legislation against the Christians," *JRS* 58 (1968), 32–50. See also the older G. La Piana, "Foreign Groups in Rome During the First Centuries of the Empire," *HTR* 20 (1927), 183–403.

[199] The sources for these events are all found in the New Testament, apart from the highly problematic passages in Josephus, *Antiquities* 18.3.3 (63–4); 20.9.1 (200), cf. Schürer, *History* 1, 430–441. There are no proper Latin sources, apart from the few lines in Tacitus, cited below.

often considered to appear in Suetonius: there was an order by Claudius, expelling the Jews in A.D. 41 or 49, 'because they all the time made disturbances at the instigation of Chrestus.'[200] However, it seems that this must be rejected as evidence of measures against Christians. The earliest indubitable information on persecution of the Christians in Rome depicts how Nero made them responsible for the great fire of Rome. Tacitus relates:

> Consequently, to get rid of the report, Nero fastened the guilt and inflicted the most exquisite tortures on a class hated for their abominations, called Christians by the populace. Christus, from whom the name had its origin, suffered the extreme penalty during the reign of Tiberius, at the hands of one of our procurators, Pontius Pilatus, and a most harmful superstition, thus checked for the moment, again broke out not only in Judaea, the first source of the evil, but even in Rome, where all things hideous and shameful from every part of the world find a centre and become popular.[201] Accordingly, an arrest was first made of all who pleaded guilty; then, upon their information, an immense multitude was convicted, not so much of the crime of firing the city, as of hatred against mankind.[202]

Suetonius refers briefly to the same events: "Punishment was inflicted on the Christians, a class of men given to a new and mischievous superstition."[203] Neither Tacitus nor Suetonius believe or want to suggest that the Christians really bore any guilt for the fire. They explain that the Christians merely seemed to be a useful target because they were hated by the urban population. Tacitus says that this hatred was caused by their abominations, *per flagitia*. This term usually refers to extreme acts like infanticide, cannibalism, and incest.[204] The term *exitiabilis superstitio* is similarly strong. Tacitus also accuses the Christians of "hatred of mankind," *odio humani generis*. Elsewhere he charges the Jews with a similar "hatred of mankind."[205] Suetonius merely mentions Christianity as a "new and harmful superstition." Tacitus and Suetonius both consider the religion of the Christians harmful, shameful, and hideous. This gives an impression of the unpopularity of the early Christians in Rome as well as their quite substantial presence in the city. Since both authors leave no doubt

---

[200] Suetonius, *Claudius* 25.4.

[201] Tacitus detested the populace of Rome: Syme, *Tacitus* (1958), 2.531f.

[202] Tacitus, *Ann.* 15.44: ergo abolendo rumori Nero subdidit reos et quaesitissimis poenis adfecit quos per flagitia invisos vulgus Christianos appellabat. auctor nominis eius Christus Tiberio imperitante per procuratorem Pontium Pilatum supplicio adfectus erat; repressaque in praesens exitiabilis superstitio rursum erumpebat, non modo per Iudaeam, originem eius mali, sed per urbem etiam quo cuncta undique atrocia aut pudenda confluunt celebranturque. igitur primum correpti qui fatebantur, deinde indicio eorum multitudo ingens haud proinde in crimine incendii quam odio humani generis convicti sunt. In 66/7 the Jews of Antioch were falsely accused of responsibility for a fire: Jos. *BJ* 7.2.3 (41–53). For Tacitus's comments on the Christians, see also Freudenberger, *Das Verhalten der römischen Behörden*, 180–189; Botermann, *Das Judenedikt des Kaisers Claudius* (1996), 177–182; Botermann argues that at the time the Christians still were considered a Jewish sect, while the name of "Christians" was first used in the Flavian period.

[203] Suetonius, *Nero* 16.2: afflicti suppliciis Christiani, genus hominum superstitionis nouae ac maleficae.

[204] Freudenberger, *Das Verhalten der römischen Behörden*, 78.

[205] Tacitus, *Hist.* 5.5.2: adversus omnis alios hostile odium.

that Nero punished the Christians as scapegoats, these events do not show the standing of Christianity when the judicial system functioned in terms of its own genuine legal code.[206]

For this we may turn to Pliny the Younger's famous exchange of letters with Trajan, written when he was the emperor's governor of Bithynia-Pontus in Asia Minor, c. 110.[207] Consulting Trajan about the Christians in his province, Pliny writes: "The question is whether a pardon ought to be granted to anyone retracting his beliefs, or, if he once professed Christianity, he shall gain nothing by renouncing it; and whether it is the mere name of Christian which is punishable, even if innocent of crime, or rather the crimes associated with the name."[208] Pliny asks the Emperor various questions: (1) Is it possible to repent, retract and be pardoned? (2) Is being a Christian criminal in itself, or only when carrying out misdeeds (*flagitia*, the term also used by Tacitus) in association with this group of people? (3) Is he, Pliny, correct in not searching actively for Christians, but only investigating people who are accused of being Christian? Trajan answers that this is correct, but rebukes Pliny for investigating suspects who were the target of an anonymous accusation. If the people accused insisted that they were Christian, they were executed. If they were Roman citizens, Pliny sent them to Rome. When they denied they were, or ever had been Christians, they had to prove this by repeating after the governor "a formula of invocation to the gods and making offerings of wine and incense to an imperial statue brought there for this purpose and furthermore by reviling the name of Christ."[209] Some of them confessed that they had been Christians in the past, and these had to go through the same procedure: doing reverence to the imperial statue and the images of the gods and so on. If they recanted, they were pardoned, like the Jews and practitioners of the Isis-cult expelled from Rome in A.D. 19. Only if they kept insisting that they were Christians, having been asked three times, were they executed.[210] It is thus clear that the crime was inherent in

[206] Cf. Barnes, *JRS* 58 (1968), 34.

[207] Pliny, *ep.* 10.96 and Trajan's reply. Cf. A. N. Sherwin-White, *The Letters of Pliny: A Historical and Social Commentary* (Oxford, 1966; reissued 1985), 691–710; Appendix 5, 772–787, which is essentially a reprint of his article "The Early Persecutions and Roman Law Again," *JTS* NS 3 (1952), 199ff.; Barnes, op. cit., 36f.

[208] Pliny, *ep.* 10.96.2 (trans. Radice, Loeb): detur paenitentiae uenia, an ei, qui omnino Christianus fuit, desisse non prosit; nomen ipsum, si flagitiis careat, an flagitia cohaerentia nomini puniantur.

[209] Pliny, *ep.* 10.96.5f. Qui negabant esse se Christianos aut fuisse, cum praeeunte me deos adpellarent et imagini tuae, quam propter hoc iusseram cum simulacris numinum adferri, ture ac uino supplicarent, praeterea male dicerent Christo, quorum nihil cogi posse dicuntur qui sunt re uera Christiani, dimittendos putaui. The demand that those who were suspected of Christianity should bring offerings to pagan gods was also made *ceteris paribus* of the Jews in Antioch in 66/7 (Jos. *BJ* 7.2.3 (41–53), at (50f.); cf. Freudenberger, 141–154.

[210] Pliny adds that their *pertinacia* and *obstinatio* ought to be punished. Some authors have argued that the essence of their crime was thus stubbornness and obstinacy: see most recently A. N. Sherwin-White, *Past and Present* 27 (1964), 23–27; refuted by de Ste. Croix, *Past and Present* 26 (1963), 18f.; 27 (1964), 28–33; similarly, at length: Freudenberger, 99–110. Christian obstinacy is criticized also by Marcus Aurelius 11.3; cf. comments by A.S.L. Farquharson, *The Meditations of the Emperor Marcus Aurelius* (Oxford, 1951), 2. 859f.

being a Christian, not in any specific act associated with this status. Such a crime could be pardoned by giving clear proof of a change of heart.[211]

Pliny understood from those who had been Christians in the past that "they had met regularly before dawn on a fixed day to chant verses in honour of Christ as if to a god and to bind themselves by oath to abstain from theft, robbery and adultery and various other immoral acts. After this ceremony it had been their custom to disperse and reassemble later to take food of an ordinary, harmless kind but they had in fact given up this practice since my edict, issued on your instructions, which banned all political societies."[212] After torturing two slave-women who were still practicing Christians, he writes, "I found nothing but a perverse and extravagant cult."[213] There are many of them. "It is not only the towns, but villages and rural districts too which are infected through contact with this wretched cult" (*superstitionis istius contagio pervagata est*). This is the usual language of infection and illness. Pliny thinks the situation can be corrected, for people have begun to frequent the temples which had been almost entirely abandoned for a long time. In his reply (10.97), Trajan refuses to respond to Pliny's thoughts on the subject, but he confirms that being a Christian is itself a crime: if they are accused and found guilty they are to be executed.[214] There is implied criticism in Trajan's reply, for he firmly rejects any action based on anonymous accusations, such as Pliny had in fact taken.

From Pliny it may be understood that Christianity had become a cult specifically prohibited when Trajan banned all political societies (*hetaeria*).[215] This is made clear in the emperor's letter to Pliny 10.34 in which he prohibits the formation of a *collegium fabrorum* (firemen) at Nicomedia. The reason is, Trajan writes to Pliny, "that *factiones* like these [sc. like the college of firemen] have been responsible for the political disturbances in your province, particularly in its towns. If people assemble for a common purpose, whatever name we give them, and for whatever reason, they soon turn into a political society" (*hetaeriae eaeque brevi fient*). We have already seen above that such bans were common policy in antiquity, as analyzed in some detail by Aristotle. Caesar also prohibited political associations. Whether he made an exception for the

[211] de Ste. Croix, *Past and Present* 26 (1963), 19; Barnes, *JRS* 58 (1968), 37.

[212] 10.96.7: edictum meum, quo secundum mandata tua hetaerias esse uetueram

[213] 10.96.8: Nihil aliud inueni quam superstitionem prauam et immodicam.

[214] 10.97: si deferantur et arguantur, puniendi sunt. Barnes, p. 48, observes: "whereas all other criminals, once convicted, were punished for what they had done in the past, the Christian was punished for what he was in the present, and up to the last moment could gain pardon by apostasy." This is perhaps unnecessarily paradoxical. As Trajan states unequivocally: those who repent are pardoned (*veniam ex paenitentia impetret*). Their status is therefore no different from that of other pardoned criminals. It was a policy designed to prevent Christianity from spreading.

[215] There seems to be no reason to deny—as some scholars do—that it was precisely this measure which determined that Christianity would be illegal, for Pliny says explicitly that it had been the reason for some Christians to give up participating in meetings of the Church. Neither Pliny nor Trajan mention any other law or stipulation prohibiting such meetings. Pliny himself explains to Trajan that the activities carried out at Christian meetings were perfectly harmless, but they were not allowed all the same. As noted by Cotter, "The Collegia," 83f., with reference to *P.Oxy* 1029, evidence from Egypt confirms Trajan's close scrutiny of guilds.

Jews, because they were a recognized and friendly *ethnos*, is now disputed. In any case, this does not mean that the Jewish religion was regarded with approval by Romans. On the contrary, it is quite obvious that it was considered objectionable by many of them. This, however, was not the point. Judaism, hated by many Romans, was yet permitted because it was the religion of a people with a recognized status, while Christianity was not—hence Christian services were forbidden under the edict which banned all political associations.[216] Pliny explains at length that the actual ritual practice of the Christians was harmless. His statement that they took "food of an ordinary, harmless kind" suggests that he had heard rumors or accusations of ritual murder and cannibalism,[217] but had concluded that these were baseless. Even so, however, he describes Christianity as a perverse and extravagant cult which spreads like a contagious disease. It is undoubtedly this aspect, the rapid spread of support, which prompted the authorities to take measures against the Christians through officials like Pliny. At the end of his letter Pliny makes it clear that his policy against the Christians was designed to halt the spread of Christianity and reinforce the involvement of the population in the traditional cults which had apparently been in a state of crisis. Hence the aim was to return Christians to the traditional Roman religion, rather than to punish those who had been or still were adherents of Christianity.[218]

Christianity was not merely illegal, it was expansionist. Judaism was permitted, but it was not allowed to attract proselytes, although this happened anyway, perhaps in spite of Jewish reluctance—as argued now by some scholars. Christianity was forbidden, but it actively sought to spread the good news.

---

[216] Gibbon, *The Decline and Fall*: "The Jews were a people which followed, the Christians a sect which deserted, the religion of their fathers." Cf. Barnes, *Tertullian* (1971), 90; A. Momigliano, "The Social Structure of the Ancient City: Religious Dissent and Heresy," in S. C. Humphreys, *Anthropology and the Greeks* (London, 1978). In a variation on Gibbon's pronouncement, Voltaire notes: "The Jews did not want the statue of Jupiter in Jerusalem; the Christians did not want it in the Capitol" ("tolérance," *Dictionnaire philosophique*, ed. R. Naves (Paris, 1967), 401.

[217] Waltzing, *Académie . . . de Belgique, Bull.* 5/11 (1925), 210f.; Rives, *JRS* 85 (1995), 65–85. See above, nn. 174 and 175, for such accusations. The accusations are found primarily in indirect form, in the reactions to them in early Christian authors such as Justin and Origen. These also claim that the origin of the libel must be sought among the Jews. Justinus, *Dialogus cum Tryphone* 17.1.12: καταλέγοντας τε ταῦτα ἅπερ καθ' ἡμῶν οἱ ἀγνοοῦντες ἡμᾶς πάντες λέγουσιν·; also: 10.1; more specifically: Origenes, *Contra Celsum* 6.27: Καὶ δοκεῖ μοι παραπλήσιον Ἰουδαίοις πεποιηκέναι, τοῖς κατὰ τὴν ἀρχὴν τῆς τοῦ χριστιανισμοῦ διδασκαλίας κατασκεδάσασι δυσφημίαν τοῦ λόγου, ὡς ἄρα καταθύσαντες παιδίον μετα λαμβάνουσιν αὐτοῦ τῶν σαρκῶν, καὶ πάλιν ὅτι οἱ ἀπὸ τοῦ λόγου τὰ τοῦ σκότου πράττειν βουλόμενοι σβεννύουσι μὲν τὸ φῶς, ἕκαστος δὲ τῇ παρατυχούσῃ μίγνυται· For further sources of this period: Waltzing, 216–36. The earlier sources mention cannibalism. Eusebius, *HE* 5.1.1–4 records the earliest accusations, made in 177, of the sacrifice and ritual consumption of infants, mentioned in the later sources, notably Minucius Felix, *Octavius* 9, 30f.; Tertullian, *Apolog.* 7.1; *Ad nationes* 1.7.

[218] There is no need here to discuss the problematic rescript of Hadrian to Minucius Fundanus, cited by Eusebius, *HE* 4.8.6–4.9; Justin, *1Apol.* 68; H. Nesselhauf, "Hadrians Reskript an Minicius Fundanus," *Hermes* 104 (1976), 348–361, does not consider it authentic. Other scholars do: T. D. Barnes, *JRS* 58 (1968), 37, with references in note 59; see Frend, *Martyrdom and Persecution in the Early Church* (1965), 223–225, for further references in n. 111 on p. 233.

It is often asserted that Christianity was prohibited because of the attitude of the Christians: their exclusivity and their intolerance of any religion other than their own.[219] It is clear that this indeed presents the Christian attitude, for the New Testament leaves no doubt that it rejects all forms of paganism: "Except a man be born again, he cannot see the kingdom of God."[220] It must be admitted that, as regards the Roman response, this must remain a hypothesis, for the sources are all Christian. There are no Roman authors who confirm that this is the reason why Christianity was prohibited. Pliny, the main source, says Christian cult-practices are harmless, but that their cult is perverse and extravagant. The information we have from the Roman side is Pliny's assertion that Christian worship in the reign of Trajan had been made illegal when the emperor enforced a ban on the formation of all associations, while the Jews had been exempted from earlier measures in this sphere. Otherwise it is not immediately obvious whether the Romans who disliked Judaism found Christianity even more objectionable, or whether those who condemned Christianity had a better opinion of Judaism.

A good example from the second century is Lucian's *Peregrinus,* which contains a satirical description of an impostor who, for a while, passes for a leader among the Christians.[221] The description of this man, while he masquerades as a Christian, clearly contains Jewish elements: "It was then that he learned the wondrous lore of the Christians, by associating with their priests and scribes in Palestine. And—how else could it be?—in a trice he made them all look like children; for he was prophet, cult-leader, head of the synagogue, and everything, all by himself."[222] Clearly, it makes no difference to Lucian whether he is speaking of synagogues or churches. Both religions are equally ludicrous. Lucian's confusion of Christian and Jewish elements reminds us of another, later, satirizing passage, in the *Historia Augusta,* where it says that Severus Alexander was ashamed at being called a Syrian, particularly because on the occasion of a certain festival, the people of Antioch, the Egyptians, and the people of Alexandria had irritated him with taunts, as they are wont to do, calling him a Syrian *archisynagogus* and a high priest.[223] Lucian's Christians are as credulous as Horace's Apella the Jew, for they are easily taken in by Peregrinus. Thus, the claim that Christianity was prohibited because its attitude towards the Roman religion was more extreme than that of Judaism has to remain a speculation. There is no confirmation of this in any Roman source. The only point regarding foreign cults that we find recurrently is a consistent policy of trying

---

[219] de Ste. Croix, *Past and Present* 26 (1963), 25f.; Goodman, *Mission and Conversion,* 96f.

[220] John 3:3: ἀμὴν ἀμὴν λέγω σοι, ἐὰν μή τις γεννηθῇ ἄνωθεν, οὐ δύναται ἰδεῖν τὴν βασιλείαν τοῦ θεοῦ.; also: 5:21; Paul: 1 Cor. 10: 14; cf. 1 Cor. 5:10; 6:9–11; 1 Thess. 1:9; Rom 1: 18–25.

[221] For this work: Jones, *Culture and Society* (1986), chap. 11; for Lucian on the Christians: 121.

[222] Lucian, *The Passing of Peregrinus,* 11 (trans. A. M. Harmon, Loeb): ὅτεπερ καὶ τὴν θαυμαστὴν σοφίαν τῶν Χριστιανῶν ἐξέμαθεν, περὶ τὴν Παλαιστίνην τοῖς ἱερεῦσιν καὶ γραμματεῦσιν αὐτῶν ξυγγενόμενος. καὶ τί γάρ; ἐν βραχεῖ παῖδας αὐτοὺς ἀπέφηνε, προφήτης καὶ θιασάρχης καὶ ξυναγωγεὺς καὶ πάντα μόνος αὐτὸς ὤν,

[223] SHA *Severus Alexander* 28.7, cited above.

to prevent them from spreading among all classes of the Roman population. They were believed to weaken the loyalty of the aristocracy and incite the lower classes. They had no right to exist and were regarded as politically dangerous.

It is curious that the reason for the ban on Christianity should be a matter of dispute among scholars, since the Roman attitude towards religion ever since the republican period is well known. John North has put it in simple terms: "You might, of course choose to make your vow to one deity rather than another, but you could not make an act of commitment to a new cult, which would cut you off from the old ones; there are no alternative religious systems available."²²⁴ Or as formulated by J. Scheid: "Public religion may be defined as a social religion and a religion of cultic acts. Social religion is practised by a person as member of a community and not as a subjective individual, as a person."²²⁵ Or, Cicero expresses it even more succinctly: "Each people has its own religion and we have ours."²²⁶ The Jews were allowed to practice their religion, but they were forbidden to accept converts; the Christians were forbidden to do either. As argued by Scot McKnight and Martin Goodman, it is possible that the Jews were not very active in attracting proselytes, but there is no doubt that the early church held that all people must convert.²²⁷ It may not have made a difference—or it may have exacerbated hostility—that the Christians from Paul onwards claimed they were a community in their own right. He mentions the Jews and the Hellenists and then there is the Church.²²⁸ Eusebius even calls the Church a "people" (ἔθνος).²²⁹ Ultimately, of course, their lack of

²²⁴ J.A. North, *PCPS* 205 (1979), 85–103, at 85; "The Development of Religious Pluralism," in J. Lieu, J. North, and T. Rajak, *The Jews among Pagans and Christians* (London and New York, 1992), 177–180; Mary Beard and Michael Crawford, *Rome in the Late Republic* (Ithaca, NY, 1985), 30f.; 38f.; M. Beard, "Cicero and Divination: The Formation of a Latin Discourse," *JRS* 76 (1986), 33–46, at 34.

²²⁵ John Scheid, in: *Religion, supersticion y magia en el mundo romano* (Cadiz, 1985), 19; François Jacques and J. Scheid, *Rome et l'integration de l'Empire Romain* vol. 1 (Paris, 2d ed. 1992), 111–128 at 112: "Les religions du monde romain étaient communautaires, et les aspects sociaux jouaient toujours un role central dans l'expression religieuse. Un Romain pratiquait avant tout parce qu'il adhérait à la religion publique, tout comme il devenait membre de la communauté religieuse domestique par la naissance ou l'adoption;"

²²⁶ Cicero, *Pro Flacco* 69.4: Sua cuique civitati religio . . . est, nostra nobis.

²²⁷ For Jewish missionary activities: McKnight, *A Light among the Gentiles*; Goodman, *Mission and Conversion,* 91–108; Goodman, 106–108, argues that proselytizing by Christians may have been less predominant in the second half of the second century.

²²⁸ 1 Cor. 10:32: ἀπρόσκοποι καὶ Ἰουδαίοις γίνεσθε καὶ Ἕλλησιν καὶ τῇ ἐκκλησίᾳ τοῦ θεοῦ. In the late second century the Christians are said to have been called a *tertium genus* as distinct from the pagans and Jews: Tertullian, *Ad nationes* 1.8: Verum recogitate, ne quos tertium genus dicitis, principem locum obtineant, siquidem non ulla gens non Christiana; itaque quaecumque gens prima, nihilominus Christiana. Ridicula dementia, novissimos dicitis et tertios nominatis. Sed de superstitione tertium genus deputamur, non de ratione, ut sint Romani, Judaei, dehinc Christiani. 1.19: Habetis et vos tertium genus, etsi non de tertio ritu, attamen de tertio sexu.

²²⁹ Eus.*HE* 1.4.2: a new nation (νέον ἔθνος); which extended to wherever the sun shines. 10.4.19: τίς ἔθνος τὸ μηδὲ ἀκουσθὲν ἐξ αἰῶνος οὐκ ἐν γωνίᾳ ποι γῆς λεληθός, ἀλλὰ καθ' ὅλης τῆς ὑφ' ἥλιον ἱδρύσατο; for this concept: Dionysius of Halicarnassus, 1.3.3: "she [sc. Rome] is the first and

any ethnic association assured the Christians their success in the empire. Christianity and empire found each other in the belief in universal conversion and the ideology of universal rule, in monotheism and monarchy, an idea nowhere better expressed than by Origen (c. 185–c. 254): "'Go therefore and make disciples of all nations.' It is clear that Jesus is born in the reign of Augustus who had, so to speak, united into one kingdom most of the peoples of the earth. The existence of many kingdoms would have been an obstacle to the spread of Jesus' teaching all over the world."[230] However, that is another subject. For present purposes it is essential that the difference between legitimacy and prohibition of a religion was determined by birth and descent.

Religion, like citizenship, was inherited, not acquired—apart from the Roman citizenship and state-cult. This is significant if we want to understand Roman views of others and themselves. This is the reason why a brief discussion of Christianity is relevant in the present work which deals with proto-racism and ethnic prejudice. Roman views of other peoples practicing their ancestral religion, such as the Jews, varied from admiration to highly critical and could contain elements of prejudice or proto-racism. There was, however, no doubt as regards their legitimacy, while Christianity was definitely regarded as an illegitimate religion without proper historical roots.

---

only power ever to have made the risings and settings of the sun the boundaries of her power." Cf. Goodman, *Mission and Conversion*, 100f. An imperial edict, cited by Eus.*HE* 9.9a.1–6 refers in three ways to the Christians: τῷ ἔθνει τῶν Χριστιανῶν.; τῇ αὐτῇ δεισιδαιμονίᾳ; τῆς θρησκείας τοῦ θείου αὐτῶν. See Tessa Rajak, "Jews and Christians as Groups in a Pagan World," reprinted in *The Jewish Dialogue with Greece and Rome* (2001), 355–372. Cf. Guy G. Stroumsa, "Philosophy of the Barbarians: On Early Christian Ethnological Representations." in H. Cancik, H. Lichtenberger, and P. Schäfer (eds.), *Geschichte—Tradition-Reflexion: Festschrift für Martin Hengel zum 70. Geburtstag*, Band 2 (Tübingen, 1996), 339–368, at 340–32.

[230] Origen, *Contra Celsum* 2.30: "Πορευθέντες μαθητεύσατε πάντα τὰ ἔθνη." (Matt. 28.19) Καὶ σαφές γε ὅτι κατὰ τὴν Αὐγούστου βασιλείαν ὁ Ἰησοῦς γεγέννηται, τοῦ, ἵν' οὕτως ὀνομάσω, ὁμαλίσαντος διὰ μιᾶς βασιλείας τοὺς πολλοὺς τῶν ἐπὶ γῆς. Ἦν δ' ἂν ἐμπόδιον τοῦ νεμηθῆναι τὴν Ἰησοῦ διδασκαλίαν εἰς πᾶσαν τὴν οἰκουμένην τὸ πολλὰς εἶναι βασιλείας . . .

Conclusions to Part 2

IT WAS THE AIM of Part 1 to trace general concepts and approaches towards others in Greece and Rome in a roughly systematic manner. Part 2 represents an attempt to show how these ideas are applied to specific peoples. The selection contains peoples from various parts of the ancient world, all of them of importance to the Greeks and Romans for different reasons. The aim is not to trace interaction, but patterns of hostility, xenophobia, and early racism. Here, as elsewhere, I repeat that this is necessarily a very particular viewpoint that is nonetheless legitimate, because it exerted much influence on social relations at the time and determined future concepts throughout the post-classical periods. Before summing up what can be said about the specific peoples, it will be useful to review a few general patterns observed.

The views we now may consider as widely held by Greeks and Romans developed later than is often assumed. Herodotus, his predecessors, insofar as we know them, and contemporaries did not think in the usual stereotypical pairs of West–East, Asia–Europe, Greeks–barbarians, individual freedom–tyranny. Herodotus certainly saw the wars of the early fifth century between Greece and Persia as a struggle for freedom, but that was freedom in the sense of political independence, freedom from foreign rule, not the freedom of the individual, let alone democracy. Herodotus does not describe these wars as a battle for Greek values and culture. He does not disparage Persia nor deny its military power, and there is no indication that Greeks of this period would have disagreed with him.

The views ascribed so often to Herodotus are encountered in later authors, notably the Greek orators of the late fifth and the fourth centuries. The question of the development of the idea of δαιμόνιον, "individual freedom" is a complex one. It certainly does not antedate Socrates' and did not become a meaningful subject in Greek and Roman thought at all. An argument can be made that it only becomes significant in modern times, in the Romantic period (eighteenth–nineteenth centuries).[1] Late-fifth and early-fourth century authors speak of "barbarians from Asia," of "the King of Asia," and of "Europe" rather than of "Persia" and of "Greece." Conflict between Greece and Persia is regarded as self-evident and natural in this period. Persia represents the absolute monarchy, which Isocrates despises, claiming that it excludes the development of military virtue and power. In this period the image of eastern degeneration, financial corruption and luxury, physical deterioration, arrogance combined with servility and effeminacy is first found in the literature. Yet, these hostile and derogatory

---

[1] I am grateful to Martin Ostwald for clarification.

characteristics are seen as resulting from social and constitutional factors, not from environmental or external causes. The collective inferiority of Asia is a constant theme, but the views are not yet proto-racist in the proper sense of the term as defined in the Introduction. These attitudes are, however, clearly combined with the development of designs of war and conquest. At this stage they could be defined as "social and cultural imperialism." In a later stage they were combined with proto-racist ideas and as such we find them in the Roman attitudes towards eastern peoples.

Peculiarly Roman, however, is the ambivalence of such feelings. Unlike the Greeks of the fifth and fourth centuries, the Romans of the second century B.C. could not imagine that they enjoyed cultural, intellectual, and artistic superiority as a matter of course. They might claim that they represented moral, military, and social values of a higher sort, but that was not fully satisfactory. Several times we encounter the claim that the victors and the vanquished have reversed their proper roles. The conquests of Greece and Asia were seen as a source of moral and material corruption through the contact of the military with the subject peoples. Contamination was feared by the debilitating effect of increased wealth, resulting from the subjugation of wealthy and delicate foreigners.

Attitudes to various peoples of the empire are fairly consistent in this respect. There is the honest smell of manure opposite the femininity and degeneracy of perfume. Muscle is more respectable than brain although it is best to have both, combined with moral integrity and a sound respect for the gods. A minimum of culture is required and a minimum of social intercourse, a lack of the latter being typical of nomads and mountaineers. It has been seen in these chapters that the Greeks thought in terms of an opposition west/Europe/Greece versus east/Asia/Persia, while the opposition north (Scythia)—south (Egypt and Ethiopia) plays a secondary role. Rome, being itself farther west, translated this mostly in an opposition between north and east, while finding itself ideally in the middle. Ideas about what was east correspondingly vary. To the Greeks, Persia is a typically eastern power with all that that entails. To the Romans, the Greeks themselves show some of the dubious characteristics of the East, while the peoples east of Greece were later absorbed into the assemblage of eastern stereotypes.

The Phoenicians are encountered as clever traders and cheats already in the Homeric epic. These stereotypes remain with them throughout antiquity, and Carthaginians were seen as having the same characteristics. When they became Rome's enemies, this view was reinforced. It is quite usual for political and military enemies to regard one another as faithless. Thus the Carthaginians, in the Roman perspective, are bereft of *fides*. They are also particularly cruel—the practice of human sacrifice and related accusations of cannibalism are singled out. These characteristics represent moral and social stereotypes, not proto-racism. The Phoenicians and Carthaginians, it could be said, were bad by choice, not by nature. An interesting, secondary point is that city-Romans and Italians tended to blur the difference—which surely was important in those provinces themselves—between a provincial Roman aristocrat and a native

Phoenician, Syrian, or other provincials. Families may have held Roman citizenship for generations and lived perfectly assimilatory urban mediterranean lives; they still were Phoenicians, Syrians, Gauls, or other forms of half-strangers.

Like the Phoenicians, the Syrians are faithless. Unlike the Phoenicians, however, the Syrians were *born* for slavery according to the Aristotelian formula. The presumed qualities of the Syrians and other Asiatic peoples which earn them the description of having been born for slavery are servility, effeminacy, perversity. Homosexuality, self-castration, perverted cults are all associated with this presumed lack of masculinity. They were no fighters, it was thought. Connected with this is the accusation of luxurious living. The Syrians are good at feasting, they tend to go to the baths rather than exercise, and they overeat. Like the Phoenicians they may be competent at what they do, but they lack masculinity. This means that they represent the opposite of what Romans think real men ought to be. Yet, the Syrians were obviously subjects of the Roman Empire in precisely the same manner in which the Gauls and Hispani were, but no ancient author calls the latter *born* for slavery. These were regarded as good fighters, conquered in war. That, of course, was as much a stereotype as the ideas about Syrians, but a positive one. As emphasized in the Introduction, stereotypes can be positive just as they can be negative.

Roman ideas about Syrians constitute a complex of stereotypes with proto-racist characteristics. Their presumed qualities were also regarded as infectious. When effeminate Syrians and Romans are brought together, the Romans become soft and the Syrians remain as they are. The reverse would never apply: Syrians do not become sturdy fighters under the influence of Roman conquerors.

Other sentiments are also encountered, harder to define, expressed, for instance in the work of Lucian, himself of Syrian origin. They seem to indicate that there were various ethnic stereotypes associated with Syrians. A curious example which occurs in the work of Posidonius, himself born in Syria, is the claim that Syrians turned gymnasia into baths—an example of soft living. Such attitudes made it difficult for the most civilized Syrians to free themselves from the taint that they were barbarians. Syrians who themselves are intellectual Greeks, like Lucian and, perhaps, Posidonius and others are defensive and ambivalent about their identity. Over time the distinction between Phoenicians and Syrians became blurred. Furthermore, it is worth observing that the Roman attitudes towards Phoenicians and Syrians from the first century B.C. onward are a response partly to their presence in Rome and Italy and partly to the presence of Roman citizens and troops in Syria. The former leads to more direct forms of hostility, the latter to more general forms of stereotypes.

The Egyptians loomed large in both Greek and Roman literature. The antiquity of their civilization and state was well known and evoked mixed feelings. Herodotus, of course, wrote extensively about them, basing his observations on his visit to their country, and was not negative. There are later authors who also show respect, but hostile stereotypes are encountered already in the early fifth century and never disappear throughout the period under discussion. These stereotypes are quite varied, but the features that strike almost every author who mentions the Egyptians are their religion and cult practices. The latter were often considered insane and depraved. Only brutish people could regard some animals as holy and worship gods with the shape of animals, a custom that was all the more disturbing since some of the Egyptian gods attracted followers in Rome.

Negative stereotypes are Egyptian promiscuity, greed, arrogance, fickleness, cowardice, and constant resistance to the legitimate authorities. Yet the Egyptians differed from the Asiatics in the eyes of most Greeks and Romans from the sixth century B.C. onward. They were not considered decadent or effeminate, but they represented the opposite of Roman values in another respect: like the Syrians they lacked *fides* and *gravitas.* This was for the Romans the ultimate yardstick for the judgment of every foreign people and no people could match the Romans in this respect. However, some peoples lacked these essential qualities more than others. Egyptians were considered wicked, weird, and frivolous. Like the Phoenicians, they were regarded as having a bad character as it were by choice. The Greek and Roman stereotypes concerning Egyptians do not seem to fit the definition of proto-racism to the same degree as those associated with Syrians and peoples of Asia Minor, who were regarded born slaves. There is some proto-racism occasionally, for example in the frequent descriptions of the Egyptians as servile, especially when the fourth-century A.D. treatise on physiognomics connects this with their physical characteristics. However, most of the ancient stereotypes concerning the Egyptians seem to consist of social, religious, and behavioral generalizations that we would not classify as racist in character. They obviously had an ancient and impressive culture with its pyramids and other marvels of which some Romans were rather envious. A specially sensitive factor was the Roman dependence on Egyptian corn. The Egyptians, therefore, were not inferior by birth, but disturbing in their oddity in Roman eyes. They were the target of stereotypes that clearly belong to the category of social, cultural, and religious generalizations that were not proto-racist, but vehement all the same. The tone usually is one of dislike rather than contempt.

The Parthians appear in Roman literature as a people quite different from the Persians whom we meet in Greek literature. To Rome they were a redoubtable but distant enemy. We encounter stereotypes and disapproval, but these are different from the ones attached to other eastern peoples. The Parthians were regarded as a serious enemy, representing a genuine warrior nation, but having the usual barbarian attributes of nomadic peoples. Sometimes the stereotypes usually associated with Asiatics and Syrians are transferred to the Parthians, but this is not very common. There is therefore no obvious pattern of ethnic prejudice, let alone proto-racism. The difference with Greek attitudes towards Persians, at least from the late fifth century B.C. onward, could not be greater, but that is not surprising: for the Greeks Persia was the neighboring empire which ruled part of their cities and influenced many more. Persia was a constant presence in the political life of the Asiatic and mainland Greeks till Alexander. The Greeks, as we saw above, developed the first manifestations of proto-racism and numerous strong ethnic prejudices in their confrontation with this people which dominated the region till they themselves expanded eastward. For Rome, Persia did not become a factor of great interest until the first century B.C. Indeed, Rome took over many of the attitudes and anti-Persian prejudices developed by the Greeks, but it applied those stereotypes to other eastern peoples, closer to the Mediterranean, which played a larger role in their existence in an earlier phase, that is, the second and first centuries B.C. The Romans in Rome did not feel Persian religion or culture exerted any direct influence, and that was what determined their own attitude. For Rome, Parthia represented the only rival empire in existence from the first century B.C. onward, but it was remote. Consequently, Parthians do not normally appear in Roman literature as a typically Oriental people. They are depicted more often as a nomadic people related to the Scythians and as formidable bowmen and cavalry. This is easily understood, for, unlike other eastern peoples, the Parthians never were decisively beaten, let alone subjugated by the Romans. They were ruled by absolute monarchs, a rather important theme in the literature. There is no clear or obvious pattern in the stereotypes applied to them in the literature or if there is, it is that the Parthians are not typically eastern, except in their attitudes towards their kings. They do share some presumed unpleasant characteristics with the Egyptians, but in other respects they resemble the Gauls and Germans, notably in their belligerence. None of this fits the usual pattern offered by adherents of the environmental theory.

No culture had a deeper and longer lasting influence on Rome than that of classical Greece, and the Romans knew the Greeks, their language, and culture better than they knew any other foreign people. Many Romans distinguished between contemporary Greece and classical Greece which defeated the Persian attacks and produced the culture with which they closely associated. In this study care was taken to distinguish between Roman responses to the classical Greece of the past and the contemporary Greeks who became subjects of the Roman Empire. In the republican period, Greece played to some extent the role that Asia took over afterward. The objections were mainly directed towards matters of lifestyle, character, and culture regarded as incompatible with true Roman values. According to Cato the Censor, the Greeks were for the most part morally inferior and degenerate. For him such contempt was combined with a genuine fear of contamination. Rome would lose her empire if it became infected by Greek letters. These suspicions were not limited to literary matters. They were a response to the physical presence of Greeks in Rome and Italy and to their influence there. Much of Greek culture was dangerous: cults, language, philosophy, and medicine. It is particularly interesting to see that the Greeks are now described in the very terms which they themselves invented for their own eastern neighbors in the fifth and fourth centuries B.C. Later, upon further Roman expansion to the East, the peoples of Asia in the view of many Romans replaced the Greeks as the major corrupting influence. The conquered Greek cities were also a welcome source of objects of classical art, which was acquired without being paid for.

This pattern of attraction and resistance did not change or perhaps even sharpened in the first century B.C., as is apparent from the works of Cicero, who recognized Roman indebtedness to classical Greece but frequently criticizes the Greeks of his own times: they were arrogant and lacked *gravitas*. Cicero is the first author, but not the last, frequently to use the diminutive *Graeculus* (Greekling).

What Cato feared, Horace saw as an accomplished fact, except that he knew the Empire was not lost, nor was Latin literature: "Captive Greece took her savage victor captive and brought the arts to rustic Latium." Not everybody is so equanimous. When Juvenal speaks of "a Greek city of Rome," he clearly implies that Rome is no longer genuinely Roman. However, he speaks not of the ancient Greek (or Asiatic) culture, but of the impact on the city of the presence of foreigners living there in his own time. It is the contemporary Greeks who stir mostly negative feelings, not the culture of their ancestors. The list of negative qualifications is impressive: the Greeks are faithless, swindlers, soft, degenerate, and morally inferior; they are both hostile and influential; they are intellectually arrogant and inconstant (*leves*). The Greeks revel and engage in debauchery. They are like patients suffering from an illness, while the imperial rulers act as doctors. The Greeks are treacherous and trained by a long servitude to show excessive flattery. They are also described as dishonest, argumentative, and presumptious in Rome, a city which they would have wanted to destroy if only they could.

Yet, the Greeks are never, like Syrians and other easterners, regarded as "natural slaves." They are free and have the nature of free men, although they are sometimes called effeminate. What all these qualifications have in common is that almost none of them describes any of the Greeks as fully functional in Roman terms. Also they are never described in the way Romans describe some northern or wilder peoples: they are not virile, courageous, or fierce. They do not have simple, masculine values. That makes the obvious influence they had on Roman culture and society all the more doubtful, given the ancient hypersensitivity to influence.

The sum of these attitudes shows some elements characteristic of proto-racist and racist tensions, in the sense that they combine, or alternate between, feelings of superiority and inferiority, attributing to the others both exaggerated powers and infectious shortcomings which are part of their inherited nature. It is also clear, however, that other stereotypes about Greeks rather belong to the social and cultural sphere in which most ethnic prejudice is usually expressed.

It seems fair to conclude that Roman attitudes towards the Greeks represent an ambivalent relationship, marked by admiration and high regard, combined with a pattern of prejudices and xenophobic responses. These often approach proto-racism, but have far less of this than, for example, attitudes towards Syrians and Asiatics. According to some, the Greeks deserve some regard and compassion for what they once were, but no longer are.

Between the chapters on eastern and western peoples, a brief discussion is inserted of a special topic: the opposition between mountaineers and plainsmen, a significant division in the views of ancient authors. The contrast between the hard, tough, and undisciplined mountaineers and the diligent, wealthy, and obedient plainsmen represents a literary tradition that goes back to the fifth century B.C. and is present also in authors of the Roman period. Such peoples are found all over the empire and what they allegedly have in common is based on the fact that they live in mountainous territory or in plains. It is part and parcel of the environmental theory, but represents a remarkable variation of it, since it is applied, not to peoples living in different parts of the world, but to peoples living in close proximity: mountaineers and plainsmen. A specifically Roman imperial variant may be found in the work of Strabo. He repeatedly emphasizes the idea that a benevolent and strong empire can help restore and maintain the correct balance between these two types of subjects. Both can be useful to the ruling empire as long as they are handled properly. Thus an environmental *topos* or commonplace becomes part of the imperial ideology. Since people living in one and the same part of the world are thus placed firmly in distinct social spheres, due to factors beyond their control, it is proper to describe this approach as proto-racist.

The opposite of Asiatics and Egyptians are the Gauls and Germans. Unlike the Greeks, Syrians, and Egyptians, the Gauls are not a significant factor in the society and culture of the city of Rome, in spite of Claudius's decision to make them eligible for Senate membership. They do not form a competitive socio-economic factor in the city. Although they had once threatened the very existence of the city, they were by the second century B.C. no longer seen as a serious danger. They did not provoke feelings of great animosity, except, perhaps, the Druids and their custom of human sacrifice. For the present study it is important to note that the environmental theory contributes heavily to the Roman appreciation of Gallic culture. This is combined with repeated insistence on the occurance of degeneracy through contamination. The Gauls were neighbors of Rome and therefore they were exposed to the pernicious influence of Roman wealth and luxuries, the more so the closer their location. This particularly affected their supremacy in the skills of war. In other words, those living in the region corresponding to modern Belgium were less affected than those in the South. Yet, on balance, the Gauls are respected in most sources as belligerent, although impulsive. There are also various reports which make it quite clear that they were not regarded as primitive barbarians. Cato knows the Gauls for their wit and Juvenal is aware of Gaul's good schools of rhetoric. Other texts mention that the Gauls were good lawyers. In any case, the Gauls were not regarded with hostility. They had their faults, but they were not thought to be decadent or effeminate.

The Germans, ever since Varus's defeat, were a constant reminder of failure, and many authors regarded them as a major threat. Roman authors saw them as the ultimate northern people. Accordingly, a full assortment of environmental stereotypes was applied to them. They had many of the presumed characteristics which the Romans thought they recognized in the Gauls, but they had these characteristics in larger measure in every respect. Tacitus attributes this to their pure lineage, a significant idea, even if we ignore its influence in later history. Since Tacitus says they were not of mixed descent, they had preserved all their presumed characteristics free from contamination. They may have been "fit only to breed wild beasts" and hence ungovernable, but that was a proto-racist source of consolation only to some of the ancient authors. They were of pure blood because they lived far to the north and apart from others and therefore were not corrupted into civilized degeneracy of any kind, except those living closest to other peoples. However, those who remained true Germans answered to all the appropriate stereotypes. The Roman imperial view of itself and others saw here an unavoidable logic: subject people eventually lose their independence of mind. Conversely the Germans, if they are *not* subjected, remain dangerous. Combine this with the essential pessimism and belief in inevitable decline of the ancient world, and the German presence is indeed a serious long-term threat. They were tall, brave, and firm, prone to anger. They cannot stand hard work nor can they stand heat or thirst, but they are inured to cold and hunger. They love fighting, sleeping, and feasting; they hate peace and serious work and so forth. With all their weaknesses, however, the Germans represented the ultimate form of virility. Many of their virtues were the opposite of Roman decadence, especially in Tacitus's *Germania*. Being uncorrupted and powerful, they were the the most dangerous people that had not been conquered.

For this work it is important to note that, in the case of the Germans we encounter a strong combination of forms of proto-racism: environmental stereotypes are reinforced by the belief in pure lineage and sociocultural integrity. These notions in turn played a significant role in the ideas about the relationship between the empire and the Germanic peoples. Thus Roman views—and especially those of Tacitus—on the Germans are probably the best example to be found anywhere in ancient literature of a full integration of proto-racist stereotypes and imperialist ideology. To conquer and rule them was not only the ultimate test of a warrior-empire, it was also a necessity for its long-term survival. It so happens that these ideas were absorbed by a nation particularly susceptible to them in the early modern and modern periods.

The conclusions reached in considering attitudes towards the Jews are unexpected for those thinking in terms of later anti-semitism. Although Judaism and the Jews were strongly disliked by many authors, the forms this hostility took in Rome are *sui generis*. The Jews are described as frivolous, lying, treacherous, libidinous, and in general morally depraved, but the Romans did *not* regard the Jews as a typically eastern people, like the Phoenicians or the Syrians. They did not have the image of being clever, greedy, and unreliable traders and they are not usually viewed as soft, effeminate, or decadent, nor are they seen as particularly servile (Cicero only once calls them "born for servitude"). They are described as an antisocial people, a reproach otherwise ascribed to far-away and primitive nomads and mountaineers. The unappealing features of their social behavior and religion, however, are regarded as a matter of deliberate choice on their part. They are not the result of environmental or geographical influences. We find no claim anywhere that the Jews are born with these characteristics. This means that, in the terms of the definition adopted in the Introduction, Roman anti-Jewish feelings were a form of ethnic hostility only. Ancient hatred of the Jews cannot be described in terms of racism or proto-racism. In other words, Roman hostility towards this people is conceptually different from its later successors. It is also different from Hellenistic hatred, which was more irrational in disposition. Yet there also is a difference with hostile attitudes towards other peoples in antiquity.

This conclusion is reinforced by the attitudes towards converts. While the social attitudes and many features of the religion of the Jews are disliked, there is no doubt as to their legitimacy, for their religion is an ancestral tradition. Converts, however, betray their own heritage. In the Roman world, religion and ethnic loyalties were inseparable. Thus converts to Judaism are seen as people who deliberately abandon their ancestral loyalties and exchange them for the antisocial company and exclusive religion of the Jews.

End Conclusions

Ethnic Prejudice, Proto-Racism, and Imperialism in Antiquity

THE FIRST CHAPTER OF Part 1 attempted to describe and analyze the conceptual framework of Graeco-Roman attitudes towards other peoples, tracing patterns of proto-racism or pronounced forms of ethnic stereotypes, as defined in the Introduction. It will suffice here to note once again that the dominant approach, accepted in some form by almost all the available sources from the second half of the fifth century B.C. on,[1] is the environmental theory: an environmental determinism which made it possible for Greek and Roman texts to describe foreign peoples in terms of fixed physical and mental traits, determined by climate and geography. From the beginning this concept was connected with a bipolar world-view. It posits an essential contrast between a sturdy but mentally inadequate Europe and a soft Asia, the latter enjoying a good climate, with a healthy and wealthy population, suffering, however, from deficient masculinity and an insufficient sense of individual and collective independence. Aristotle developed the theory further, adding two elements which made it a useful conceptual tool for imperialists. He held that the Greeks occupied the ideal environment between Europe and Asia and were therefore supremely capable of ruling others. Aristotle's second addition is the claim that the inhabitants of Asia were servile by nature, or natural slaves, and therefore suited to be subjects of the Greeks. Roman authors took over these ideas, duly substituting themselves as the ideal rulers.

These concepts were combined with an almost generally accepted belief in the heredity of characteristics acquired by human beings during their lives. Assuming the environment to determine human character and quality, combined with a belief in the heredity of acquired characters, leads to an outlook almost as deterministic as modern racist theory. When applied to human groups, these two complementary ideas attribute to them characteristics which, in due course of time, become uniform and constant. Similarly, they are a powerful tool justifying imperial rule: those who have been conquered must, because of their defeat, be inferior by nature to their conquerors and then, once they have become subjects and slaves, they rapidly acquire and transmit to their descendants the qualities of being born slaves as formulated by Aristotle.

An important element for many Greek authors is the form of government. Here opinions vary, but for some authors monarchic rule by definition excludes

---

[1] As argued at length, it is not represented in the work of Herodotus who saw connections between climate, environment, and the character of peoples, but nowhere saw these as part of a theory or set of conditions determining collective character.

the presence of any merit in peoples so ruled. For other authors the quality of government is but one of the factors which determine overall merit.

A variant and particularly inflexible form of environmental determinism is astrology which, for instance in the work of Ptolemy of Alexandria, assumes that the character of entire peoples is decisively determined by their geographical location. Another conceptual device in the arrangement of a hierarchy of peoples is the belief in autochthony and pure lineage. Since this attaches particular value to pure blood, it should be defined as proto-racist. It implies the ultimate dream of perfection for those who feel that there is merit in marrying within one's group and that those marrying outside will produce offspring of lesser quality. This concept reflects a belief that the essence of a person is almost exclusively determined by his ancestry and far less or not at all by his own deeds and choices in life. It furthermore reinforces the gap in status between locals and foreigners.

In the fifth and fourth centuries B.C. the element of descent becomes increasingly important for the Athenians, who consider themselves as being of pure lineage and occupants of the same land from the beginning of time. It is clear that the Athenians were particularly fond of their presumed autochthony. This is meaningful for the present study. Athenian literature has had more influence through the ages than all of the rest of Greek literature together. Autochthony, being an Athenian idea and represented in many Athenian texts, is likely to have influenced a broad public of readers, wherever Greek literature was read. Modified forms of the Athenian idea of autochthony are indeed encountered in later periods and other cultures. The idea of pure versus mixed lineage proves to be one of essential importance to many peoples of all periods. Indeed, the idea that there is a permanent connection between race and soil is a concept revived with vigor in the nineteenth and twentieth centuries.

A theme immediately related to the belief in lineage and connection with the land, which occurs in authors of the fourth century, is that of eugenics. This was advocated by both Plato and Aristotle as a means of preventing a feared deterioration of citizens, especially of the best elements. In Plato it was presented as a system to be kept secret, whereby the upper class of "the Guardians" would maintain their racial superiority. Eugenics gained great influence as a racist concept in the later nineteenth and the twentieth centuries and those who spread the idea obviously were familiar with Plato's work. The concept never was as central to the thinking of any ancient author as it has been in racist theory in modern times. In both ancient and recent thinking, however, it should be noted, the idea of preventing degeneration was probably more important than the hope of improving race. The concept of eugenics, like racism, always was an aspect of—and a response to—the fear of decline and degeneration in society. The Romans did not claim pure lineage, let alone autochthony, for themselves, yet regarded the descent of other peoples as important. They shared with many others the assumption that mixed descent is a form of corruption and results in human beings of inferior quality.

While eugenics was never as popular in antiquity as it was in the nineteenth and twentieth centuries, physiognomics by contrast was highly popular both in antiquity and in more recent history. It seeks to detect through their external features the characters and destiny of individuals. The chapter on this subject illustrates the manner in which these concepts are used to rate the mental, physical, and moral levels, not only of individuals, but also of whole peoples. The approach is essentially an application of three widely accepted theories, combined here: first it is assumed that the environment has a direct, continuous impact on collective physical features, as extensively discussed above. Second, there is the assumption of a direct and stable connection between external, physical features and mental and moral qualities. Third, it is assumed that this connection between external factors and mental characteristics is stronger than individual variations. The result is a system of classifying people according to ethnic stereotypes, both physical and mental. One tool is comparisons with animals. This denial of individuality and variation, both between individuals and generations, is characteristic of racist thinking. In antiquity as in modern racist theory, these assumptions are not based on empirical observation or objective reasoning. They are based on belief or, rather, conviction. The system became particularly popular in the second century A.D. and was immensely influential in later periods.

Chapter 2 deals with the above topics in their connection with ancient imperialism. Three subjects are discussed: slaves and subject peoples, comparisons of human beings with animals, and mass death or genocide as practiced by states in antiquity. Greek and Roman conceptions of individual slavery were closely connected with attitudes towards conquered peoples as a whole: most slaves, not born as such, had lost their freedom through capture in war. Their status was in many respects seen as similar to that of entire peoples who had lost a war. Aristotle's *Politics* propounds the view that masters and slaves were essentially different and naturally fit for their respective functions in life. Masters and slaves are claimed to live in a symbiosis which is beneficial to both. The theory is particularly important for the present study because, in fact, the characteristics of natural slaves are applied to foreigners only, never to Greeks. Specific non-Greek peoples are described as collectively having qualities which designate them as the proper material for slaves of the Greeks. The arguments applied by Aristotle to individual slaves and masters are thus easily transmitted to entire groups and peoples. Both mind and body are claimed to suit the function in life of masters and slaves: According to Aristotle, "it is nature's intention also to erect a physical difference between the body of the freeman and that of the slave, giving the latter strength for the menial duties of life, but making the former upright in carriage and (though useless for physical labour) useful for the various purposes of civic life." Since masters and slaves are said to be born with these characteristics, this theory is proto-racist according to the definition adopted in the Introduction.

The usual method of acquiring slaves is war. War is described as a form of acquisition, just like hunting, and the object is the procurement of slaves from among those peoples who are already slaves by nature. Provided certain norms are respected, war is therefore a legitimate process aimed at reducing inferior foreigners to the state of slavery for which nature has designed them anyway. Thus this proto-racist ideology serves to justify wars of conquest. This does not mean it causes such wars, but it helps in justifying them. It is also noteworthy that slaves are thought to be closer in nature to animals than the masters. Aristotle's theory of natural slavery influenced later writers: they accept the natural inferiority of some peoples as a given fact and posit that this justifies their subjugation and enslavement.

A related idea about slavery and empire is encountered first in the work of Plato and thereafter in the writings of various Roman historians. It is the idea that a person, once he is enslaved, loses his strength, his will to fight for freedom, and becomes totally servile. In other words: it is an irreversible process. Although it is not the same as the theory of natural slavery, it claims that a person or a people, after a generation or two of slavery or subjugation, acquires a slavish personality unfit for a life in freedom. This claim is regularly applied to peoples living under Roman rule. There is a widespread conviction that recent slaves are still dangerous, but over time slavery causes deterioration, and this is thought to be true for entire peoples as well. It is therefore important to make subject peoples adapt to imperial rule for two or three generations. Thereafter they can no longer rebel successfully. As seen in chapter 11, Tacitus's fear of the Germans lies in the fact that they have not yet been subjected. Their freedom and independence means that they are not exposed to the corrupting influence of serfdom and Roman luxury. To sum up: the theory of natural slavery and related attitudes towards the vanquished are all geared to justify empire both from a moral and a functional perspective. This is not to say that such ideas were instrumental in promoting imperialism, but it is clear that they served to remove moral qualms or even prevent such qualms from becoming a significant factor in the public attitudes of many Greeks and Romans.

Then follows another subject, the response frequently encountered of peoples to foreign peoples or minorities, namely comparisons of human beings with animals. Comparisons and metaphors identifying people with animals are common in the ancient literature. There is a rich and varied literary tradition that uses animals as a literary device. However, not all literary passages that represent people as animals should be interpreted as comparisons or metaphors. Some of them seem to be intended quite literally. Thus Aristotle says that those who yield to unnatural inclinations are not natural, but bestial or diseased. He applies this also to entire peoples. Like the theory of natural slavery and related attitudes towards foreigners, the animal comparison was part of an attitude of mind, a way of thinking about oneself as distinct from a foreigner, which formed the framework in which imperialism could flourish unfettered by moral inhibitions or restraints.

In modern cultures this denial of the humanity of others can serve as an excuse to treat them in a brutish manner or even to exterminate them. This, however, is not a pattern encountered in the ancient world, when people presumably felt less of a need to justify large-scale slaughter in moral terms.

Chapter 3 focuses on a number of specific topics, seen to be relevant to the heart of the present discussion, namely ancient ways of looking at immigrant foreigners and members of minorities within society at large. While chapter 1 primarily considers attitudes in Greek and Roman literature towards other peoples living at a distance, in their own lands, chapter 3 attempts to clarify another important topic, namely the attitudes of Romans towards foreigners who settled in Italy and in the city of Rome. The subjects include fear of being influenced by, or even dominated by the vanquished, a particularly sensitive topic for Romans because of the tremendous influence exerted by Greek culture. The texts available suggest apprehension that the Romans would lose their ancestral physical and moral strength and be affected by Greek luxury and license. Their forceful masculinity would be affected by soft Mediterranean culture. The fear of being conquered by the vanquished is a self-contradictory mentality on the part of an imperial power, but it has the characteristics of many forms of group hatred. It is an attitude that satisfies both fantasies of superiority and fears of inferiority; it will explain equally well whatever happens in reality, and it can be used to justify aggression. It is well represented in Roman sources but also characteristic of modern racism with its constant fear of being contaminated by other inferior races. It suits the general Roman preoccupation with the decline of empire and civilization and, at the same time, makes outsiders responsible for this disastrous development. In tracing these tensions I do not want to imply that there is an easy connection between their presence and specific policies on the part of the Roman Empire. It is my aim to show that the attitudes of the Romans towards their empire and its inhabitants, as attested in the available literature, were complex and often contradictory.

This is not to say, of course, that such ambivalent or hostile feelings about foreigners occur only in imperial societies. As we know from contemporary Europe, societies without the least imperial ambition can still suffer from a good deal of xenophobia, particularly when they include substantial numbers of immigrants or minorities. Xenophobia and ethnic hatred can exist in any complex society, but imperial states by their very nature are confronted continuously with a variety of peoples which form part of the empire, and settle in urban centers. Thus two essentially different forms of ethnic stereotypes and proto-racism can be discerned: the first is aimed at foreign peoples, seen from a distance; the second at minority groups within their own society. The former is seen to be more aggressive in nature when it is combined with imperial or expansionist ambitions. The latter may, but does not have to, occur in imperial societies that see an influx of immigrants from the conquered nations.

In the next section of chapter 3, periodically returning efforts to ban the foreign presence from the city of Rome and Italy are considered. Expulsions from Rome were the result of social stresses or even collective hatred, but they were expulsions, not killings, and they had no long-term effect, as is easily understood, for even modern prosperous states with their bureaucracy and technology are unsuccessful in their attempts to keep out immigrants. The periodic Roman decisions to expel foreigners, it has been argued in this work, are indicative of the tensions that existed in Rome from the time it ceased to be a mid-size city-state. The fact that such expulsions took place at all means that we must take seriously the various sources which express hostility towards immigrant people. It is also clear, however, that Roman attitudes, like those of other peoples in comparable circumstances, were not consistent over time. Thus periods of hostility and expulsions were followed by periods of tolerance and inaction.

A related topic is the ambivalent attitude in both Greek and Roman sources regarding the effects, beneficial or harmful, of contact between peoples. I am not aware of any obvious parallel for this tendency in western cultures in recent centuries, unless we want to compare it with the fluctuations between isolationism and international engagement encountered in modern nations. Ancient literature, however, expresses an obvious ambivalence regarding the desirability of communication between peoples. Trade and commerce are seen as the vehicles for the corruption of much that is valuable or even essential. Like mixed marriages, they harm integrity and soberness. Yet peoples who are entirely cut off from the rest of the world have no merit either. It was only in a distant past, in the Golden Age, that people could live happily without traveling and trading. These feelings of reluctance in seeking contact with other nations did not, however, have much practical effect. Both Greeks and Romans did not allow such feelings to restrain their foreign ambitions.

At this point it bears repeating that the entire complex of ideas and attitudes here described derives from the extant Greek and Roman texts. As is well known, these do not represent a random selection, but have come to us through a process of transmission in antiquity and afterward, which itself was guided by fashions and trends in education, science, and the tastes of book collectors. It is therefore impossible to deny that there may have been other views on the subjects here discussed which are no longer accessible to the modern reader because they appeared in texts that have disappeared. This theory cannot be proved or disproved, but we may at least claim that the development, traced on the basis of the available literature, is fairly consistent. Furthermore, it is impossible to deny that even a full collection of ancient texts—had it been accessible—would still represent the views of those segments of society which produced and published literature. To mention just two examples: we have many texts that disapprove of eastern cults in Rome and hardly any that support them. It would be an interesting question how Roman supporters of the Isis cult would have judged Egyptians as a people. Second, there are quite a few passages that express disapproval of converts to Judaism, but we have no pronouncements by the converts themselves. The present study therefore analyzes the opinions we encounter in the sources, while allowing for the possibility that there may have been other views. We are concerned with long-term developments, and these appear to be quite consistent in the available material.

Part 2 considers various specific peoples as characterized in Greek and Roman literature, both those in their midst and distant peoples. This allows us to gain a more coherent impression of reactions to specific peoples, while keeping in mind the conclusions gained in the first part of this study.

Chapter 4 considers the attitudes of Greek authors towards the Persians and other inhabitants of Asia after the Greek victory over the Persians early in the fifth century B.C. Most important to consider here is Herodotus, but others are also relevant and discussed. In spite of assertions to the opposite in the modern literature, the fifth-century authors who wrote about the wars with Persia did so in a spirit of respect for the Persians and their military might. The Greeks were proud of their victory over a major power which had sought to subject the Greek mainland, but they did not attempt to belittle the enemy, nor is there any trace of thinking along lines of bipolarity: Europe versus Asia represented simple geographical concepts only. Herodotus and others do not view the war with the Persians as a conflict between continents, between political cultures or in any other obviously ideological perspective. They see it as a battle for independence, for freedom from foreign rule, but not as a struggle for the freedom of the individual, as so often claimed in the modern literature. The Persians are not belittled, nor are they described in derogatory stereotypical terms, and there is certainly no trace of proto-racism in the sources of this period.

Outspoken and irrational anti-Oriental attitudes occur among Greek authors of the fourth century who had an imperialistic ideology, such as Isocrates. These attitudes are not yet found among the authors who described the wars with Persians or had fought or traveled themselves in the East, such as Herodotus, Aeschylus, and Xenophon. Expressions of fierce hostility towards Persia are found first, not in the historical literature, but in rhetoric and philosophy. Gorgias, Lysias, Plato as well as Isocrates and, among the tragedians, Euripides, emphasize the essential opposition between Greece and the barbarians more than any previous literature. The concept of a natural enemy, who must be hated, first occurs in these authors and not, as claimed by many scholars, in Herodotus and his contemporaries. By the late fifth century Persia was not merely an enemy power—it was Asia, the opposite of Europe. No compromise was possible, desirable, or necessary, for the Asiatics were inferior and could be defeated. Thus we may discern here a direct correlation between imperialist conceptions and the way in which the enemy is perceived. The desire to defeat and conquer goes hand in hand with the perception of the enemy as weak, immoral, and contemptible.

Chapter 5 discusses the impact of stereotypical attitudes on Roman imperial thinking with particular reference to the East. The East was anything east of Italy and shifted eastward as the empire expanded: at first it was Greece, then, after the full incorporation of Greece as a province it shifted to Asia Minor—which had been East in Greek eyes. Only afterward the East in Roman eyes came to include what is "the Near East" in modern times. Wherever it was, it represented a source of conflicting emotions. The Romans, being conquerors, naturally considered themselves superior and entitled to rule eastern peoples regarded as militarily inferior. Yet, paradoxically, Roman views of these peoples could evoke a vision of their own vulnerability and threaten faith in the stability of empire because there was a strong belief that the inferiority of the other sapped Rome's moral fiber and native strength. Thus imperial expansion was believed to carry with it the seeds of disintegration.

The first clear expression of this ambivalence has been described in chapter 3, which traced the attitudes of Romans towards large numbers of foreigners from various parts of the empire who settled in Italy and in the city of Rome. We encountered hostility towards Greek literature, influential as it was, and towards Greek medicine, both described as threatening in various ways. A related phenomenon is the fear that the Roman army was corruptible and, conquering Asia, could become a corrupting agent. Exposed, as it was believed to be, to vast luxury, lack of morals, and sexual excess, it would spread these vices in Rome and Italy.

At the root of these fears was, first, the idea, familiar throughout antiquity, that traveling and contact with foreigners are bad because they impair the traditional integrity of a people. Second, it was thought that a change of environment can only lead to deterioration and never to improvement. Third, there is the elementary absence of a belief in progress. Change can only be for the worse. Fourth, and connected with the third concept, we have seen that, ever since the second century B.C., Rome was preoccupied with the decline of her Empire, a process considered inevitable by many Romans. Loss of masculinity, integrity, and patriotism, factors just listed, was frequently thought to be the main cause. Thus the expansion of empire carries with it the cause of its destruction. An interesting connection between Roman stereotypes of other peoples and the self-perception of the Romans as conquerors can be discerned.

These attitudes often go far in their imperialist hostility. There are elements for which there is no parallel in modern or early modern thinking, such as the almost total absence of any belief in long-term progress. Furthermore, the deep-seated mistrust of communication and contact between peoples is not common in modern western culture, nor do we encounter in the history of European colonialism anything like the Roman fear of corruption of the colonial armies by natives. In modern times, disapproval of individuals "who went native" was censure of an individual form of presumed degeneration, which could be avoided and was not regarded as a serious large-scale threat. On the whole the European colonial powers were confident of the superiority of their own Christian faith and they felt comfortable ruling masses of Moslem, Hindu, or Buddhist subjects without Old Cato's fear that these religions, or the native cultures in their colonies, would prove stronger than their own cultures. Such fears have increased in recent times. As I write these lines, parties in western Europe are in the ascendance which warn of the dangers supposedly posed to western cultural, moral, and social identity, by immigrants who do not identify with and accept the existing values.

A pattern of proto-racism in Greek and Roman views of subject peoples can be observed. We have seen the application of generalizations (negative or positive) to minorities and foreigners and the role these play in the rhetoric of imperialism. Stereotypes are rationalized by the assumption that the characteristics described are the result of environmental influences. It is also assumed that acquired characters may become hereditary, just as social factors (notably forms of government) may have an impact. The idea of collective, natural slavery served as a popular element in an ideology which justified conquest and subjugation of foreign peoples. It was in fact a circular argument: once a people was vanquished, this showed that they were inferior and, being inferior, they were fit only to be subject to the imperial power. Particularly in Rome this was reinforced by the belief that conquest and subjection by another power will rob a people over time of the qualities needed for independence. The constitution and form of government play a role, and change is in principle possible.

It might have been interesting to trace such ideas through the age of Alexander and his successors, but this is not really profitable for present purposes. The important sources on this subject all belong to the Roman period and may therefore represent Roman views rather than those of the fourth century B.C. Another topic of great interest is the way in which the Greeks (Demosthenes) saw Philip of Macedon and the Macedonians as non-Greeks. However, this again involves the very question of who and what was Greek, which this book does not address. The Hellenistic period has been omitted. Admittedly, this leaves out of account a whole range of attitudes and outlooks that might be different in approach from those encountered in the present study, but such a study would not clarify classical Greek and Roman attitudes.

Chapters 6 to 13 offer a survey of ancient views of specific, selected groups of foreigners. The aim here is, as it were, to reverse our point of view. The first part of the study attempted to analyze the ways in which Greeks and Romans saw foreigners and to describe the conceptual mechanisms at play. It was my aim to do so in a systematic way, adducing examples from the texts as appropriate. However, such a treatment, based as it is on thematic analysis, tends to obscure the distinct character of the attitudes towards specific peoples in various parts of the ancient world. Consequently, no coherent image of any one people as seen through Greek and Roman sources, in a given period, emerged there. The last part of this study therefore attempts to elucidate the specific attitudes and opinions regarding various peoples in the light of the concepts traced in the first. Moreover, it then emerges how various generalizations and preconceptions appear continuously through the ages, from the fifth century B.C. till the later Roman empire.

The results of these investigations have been summarized at the end of Part 2 and there is no need to recapitulate them here. It will be instructive, however, to integrate these results with the general conclusions reached in Part 1. In other words, we ought to see how the various conceptual mechanisms traced in Part 1 have been encountered in attitudes towards individual peoples studied in Part 2.

It may be asked whether there is any point or justification in attempting to classify stereotypes and generalizations. After all, we do not know to what extent some of those generalizations may actually have been based on facts, which is one of the difficulties of the present subject. There is, for instance, no reason to doubt that the average Gaul was taller than the average Syrian in the first century A.D., just as there is no reason to deny that most Nigerians have a darker skin than most Danes today. We can go a step further and agree that the ancient Phoenicians were more active in the Mediterranean trade than the ancient Gauls. Thus it is quite clear that it is possible to list various generalizations, ancient and modern, that are actually true. It is precisely an essential characteristic of stereotypes and generalizations that some of them are indubitably true, while more of them have very little basis in reality or no basis at all. It is the aim of the present study, not to determine what various peoples really were like, but how they are seen in Greek and Roman literature and how the stereotypes and generalizations we encounter are related and develop. Whether or not we accept as fact that eastern troops fought less well than western armies, the point is that this claim carries a value judgment: not whether they reflect reality is meaningful, but the implied value judgment inherent in generalizations.

We have seen that it is always important to consider the origin of generalizations: are we faced with members of a coherent society and their views of other, possibly distant peoples, or are we dealing with a multicultural urban society, where groups of immigrants mix with longer established strata of society? The obvious example is the difference between the fourth-century B.C. Greeks and their views of Persia and Asia Minor and the first-century A.D. Romans who were living in a city with numerous immigrants from Anatolia and Syria. The attitudes of the first group usually are part of an imperialist ideology. Views held about subject peoples or candidates of subjugation are largely characteristic of the mentality of an imperial power. The second group of attitudes are formed by social friction within a given society.

We have seen in Part 2 that in antiquity a good deal of proto-racism was found, as distinct from ethnic, cultural, and religious stereotypes. The two phenomena—proto-racism and stereotypical thinking—are usually combined, but the mix varies in the attitudes towards different peoples. Patterns of opposites can be distinguished. Throughout antiquity we see that the opposition between masculine and effeminate plays a dominant role. These opposite qualities both have strings of associated characteristics. Those who are typically masculine are courageous warriors but not particularly industrious or intelligent. Those who are effeminate tend also to be servile, poor fighters, but they may be diligent and clever. These characteristics are usually assumed to have been imposed by nature, in other words, they definitely belong to the proto-racist set of images.

A second pair of common contrasts betrays mostly sympathy or dislike: peoples are dishonest, cruel, rebellious, and fickle, or they are honest, independently minded, and constant. Although these are all issues of character, they are not qualities imposed by nature; they depend on human will, can be changed, and must therefore be considered as stereotypes. It is important to observe that the second group of opposites need not be milder or kinder than the first. Some proto-racist ideas are not quite so fierce, while some ethnic stereotypes betray

violent hatred. It is a phenomenon of recent history that racism should be associated with bloodshed, while ethnic stereotyping is seen as a more harmless
form of discrimination. We have now entered an age when racism is no longer
regarded as respectable by consensus, while it has become more accepted to
express prejudices in cultural terms.[2]

This study emphasizes the immediate connection that is frequently encountered between prejudice, proto-racist attitudes, and imperial ideology. The interrelationship between these phenomena has not been treated in any separate
chapter and it will be useful therefore to summarize once again the conclusions
formulated throughout this work.

1. Chronologically the first ethnocentric justification of imperialist expansion
is encountered in Greek literature, in the late fifth and early fourth centuries
when it is argued that Asiatics are feeble because they are ruled by monarchs,
while the Europeans are good fighters because of their institutions, for they are
not ruled by kings. This idea was further developed by Aristotle: In his view
the Greeks combine European spirit and freedom with Asiatic intelligence and
competence. They are therefore capable of ruling all mankind—an early-text, if
not the first one to suggest that Greeks could achieve universal rule.

2a. and 2b. The environmental theory and the belief in the heredity of acquired characters are concepts broadly accepted in Greece and Rome. First
formulated some time in the fifth century, they hold that collective characteristics of groups of people are permanently determined by climate and geography.
The implication is that the essential features of body and mind come from the
outside and do not occur through genetic evolution or conscious choice. Individuality and individual change are thereby ignored. When applied to human
groups, these ideas lead to a belief that their characteristics are uniform and
constant, once acquired. These presumed characteristics are then subject to
value judgments, in which the others are usually rejected as being inferior to
the observer, or, in rare instances, approved of as being untainted and superior.
It is furthermore true, as a general rule, that such descriptions are not based on

---

[2] See, for instance, Ehud Barak in an interview with Benny Morris in the *New York Review of Books* of June 13, 2002: "They [sc. the Palestinians] are products of a culture in which to tell a lie . . . creates no dissonance. They don't suffer from the problem of telling lies that exists in Judeo-Christian culture. Truth is seen as an irrelevant category. There is only that which serves your purpose and that which doesn't. They see themselves as emissaries of a national movement for whom everything is permissible. There is no such thing as 'the truth.' Speaking of Arab society, Barak recalls: 'The deputy director of the US Federal Bureau of Investigation once told me that there are societies in which lie detector tests don't work, societies in which lies do not create cognitive dissonance [on which the tests are based].'" We have seen in this study that there is a well-established tradition going back to antiquity of accusing other peoples, notably enemies, of being consistent liars: the Phoenicians, Carthaginians, the Romans, Cretans, all southern peoples, but also the German tribes, and Jews. In another period we hear of "Perfidous Albion." Such accusations are often mutual. Thus the representative of the League of Arab States refers to the "Israeli liar machine" in the General Assembly of the UN (August 16, 1982) and Ariel Sharon is "the biggest liar ever witnessed," according to the representative of Syria in the UNHCR debate on April 2, 2002.

direct observation. As a result, when another people is regarded as inferior, it is easy to argue that they have no claim to independence and should be conquered.

3. Aristotle developed the environmental theory further, adding two elements which made it an essential tool for imperialists. He claims that Greece occupies the very best environment between Europe and Asia and therefore produces people ideally capable of ruling others.

4. Aristotle's second addition is the claim that the inhabitants of Asia were servile by nature, or natural slaves, and therefore suited to be subjects of the Greeks. These ideas became popular and are found in the works of many Roman authors, who duly substitute themselves as the ideal rulers. The theory of natural slavery is expounded by Aristotle in his *Politics*. It became an essential concept in ancient imperialist thinking, as it can easily be applied to entire peoples.

5. Other relevant concepts are autochthony and pure lineage. The Athenians, in their period of imperial expansion, developed an emotional attachment to these interrelated ideas. Rome made no claim of being autochthonous or of pure blood, but applied those ideas to other peoples. Also important is the opposite attitude towards the idea of mixed blood. There is a firm conviction, encountered in numerous texts, that mixing leads to degeneration. The idea is not so much that purity of lineage will lead to improvement; the reverse is true: any form of mixture will result in something worse. This, as has been shown, is connected with the absence of a belief in progress in antiquity. As has been emphasised frequently in this book, all these concepts, by themselves and in combination, did not initiate and promote imperialism, but they definitely were essential in justifying it and as such their importance should not be underestimated. Successful imperialism requires a certain moral and social climate.

6. The last significant concept to be mentioned here in connection with imperialist ideas, closely related with the fifth point, is that of decline and degeneration through displacement and contamination. Just as there are believed to be environments which are good or even ideal for the creation of an imperial power, so there are those that are unfavorable. So much was clear already. A related idea, that also is part of the complex of environmental theory, is that of decline as a result of migration. A concomitant idea is deterioration through contamination. Both Strabo and Tacitus hold that what we call "Romanization" is essentially a process of corruption: "And yet our [Roman] mode of life has spread its change for the worse to almost all peoples, introducing amongst them luxury and sensual pleasures and, to satisfy these vices, base artifices that lead to innumerable acts of greed." Important in this connection was the idea that Roman troops stationed amongst effeminate and soft peoples will themselves become soft and transmit their softness to their fellow citizens upon their return home. Roman troops stationed near Germans will not themselves become stronger: their own inherent decadence will corrupt their neighbors. Clearly the an-

cient ideas about decline and degeneration did not give cause for conquest and subjugation. Indeed, they might rather have put brakes on imperial ambition, but this does not appear to have happened. Even so, such feelings show the complexity of Greek and Roman imperialism.

The Roman views—and especially those of Tacitus—on the Germans are probably the best example to be found anywhere in ancient literature of a full integration of proto-racist stereotypes and imperialist ideology. To conquer and rule them was not only the ultimate test of a warrior-empire, it was also a necessity for its long-term survival. As long as the Germans would remain independent and maintain their pure lineage—as emphasized by Tacitus—they would preserve their strength. Their subjugation and Romanization would corrupt them and remove the threat they represented. Romanization represented a successful process of ethnic decomposition and imperial integration, necessary for the establishment and maintenance of full control. Where this failed, the empire was under threat. There is a continuous preoccupation with the decline of Empire in antiquity. When Gibbon chose the title of his great work, this entirely reflected ancient views of history.

If the German fighting power was seen as such a threat, why did the Romans never seriously endeavour to conquer the Germans after the early first century A.D.? The reasons are not hard to find. Whatever the impact of ideas such as Tacitus tried to convey, the German public image in Rome did not make them an attractive target for imperial campaigns. They *were* fierce fighters and moreover inhabited a poor land. A brief raid in Mesopotamia promised more gain than years of fighting in Germany ever could. I would propose the hypothesis that Roman deliberations on such matters were guided as much by the common image of—and stereotypes associated with—the foreigners who were candidates for subjugation as by factual knowledge and accurate information.

I hope this study has succeeded in showing that proto-racism was a significant phenomenon in antiquity. The distinction between a proto-racist attitude and other forms of prejudice is intellectually far more important to us than it was to Greeks and Romans. Other prejudices have therefore been given their due, but particular attention has been paid to proto-racism for two reasons. First, the relevance of the concept had to be proven. There would be no disagreement as to the existence of ethnic prejudice or xenophobia in antiquity, even though there may be marked differences in the evaluation of these phenomena. However, the existence of proto-racism is not obvious. Second, proto-racism and racism in all its manifestations are conceptually and by definition the most extreme forms of prejudice. Ethnic, cultural, and similar prejudices may be quite vehement, but they do not deny in principle the possibility of change at an individual or collective level. Proto-racist or racist prejudice, however, regards the presumed group characteristics as unalterable. It therefore excludes individual variation or collective improvement. Moreover, it is based on an imaginary categorization: races do not exist in fact. Paradoxically, therefore, race tends to mean whatever the racist wants it to mean and this can focus on physical, moral, intellectual, and religious categories, in other words: it encompasses everything. Thus, as the most extreme form of stereotypical thinking, it has led also to the most extreme forms of hostile and violent discrimination. Consequently, while ethnic prejudice by its very nature represents irrational thinking, racism goes much further in its rigid denial of reality. If we speak in terms of mental health—which is not my field—then obviously racism is a more severe pathology than ethnic prejudice. While these developments reached their pinnacle in the nineteenth and twentieth centuries and not during Greek and Roman antiquity, it is the claim of this study that the ideas ultimately go back to these early periods.

This study therefore is an attempt to give the Greeks and Romans their due: if they have given us, through their literature, many of the ideas of freedom, democracy, philosophy, novel artistic concepts and so much else that we regard as essential in our culture, it should be recognized that the same literature also transmitted some of the elementary concepts of discrimination and inequality that are still with us. It is possible also that in considering these phenomena in their early shape, we may gain a better understanding of their contemporary forms.

SELECTED BIBLIOGRAPHY

BOOKS AND MONOGRAPHS

Adorno, F. et al. (eds.), *Corpus dei papiri filosofici greci e latini* I (Florence, 1989).

Adrados, Francisco Rodriguez, *History of the Graeco-Latin fable* 2 vols. (Leiden, 1999–2000).

Alcock, Susan E., *Graecia Capta: The Landscapes of Roman Greece* (Cambridge, 1993).

Allbutt, T. Clifford, *Greek Medicine in Rome* (London, 1921).

Amir-Moezzi, Mohammad Ali, and Scheid, John, *L'Orient dans l'histoire religieuse de l'Europe: l'invention des origines* (Turnhout, 2000).

Anderson, Benedict, *Imagined Communities: Reflections on the Origin and Spread of Nationalism* (London and New York, 1983).

Anderson, Graham, *The Second Sophistic: A Cultural Phenomenon in the Roman Empire* (London, 1993).

Anderson, J.G.C., *Cornelii Taciti, de origine et situ Germanorum* (Oxford, 1938).

Anderson, William S., *Essays on Roman Satire* (Princeton, 1982).

André, J. (ed., trans., and comm.), *Traité de physiognomonie par un anonyme latin* (Paris, 1981).

Arens, W., *The Man-Eating Myth: Anthropology and Anthropophagy* (Oxford, 1979).

Asheri, D., *Erodoto Le storie. Libro I: La Lidia e la Persia* (Milano, 2d ed. 1989).

Astin, Alan E., *Scipio Aemilianus* (Oxford, 1967).

———, *Cato the Censor* (Oxford, 1978).

Atti del convegno sul tema: la Persia et il mondo greco-romano 1965, Accademia Nazionale dei Lincei 363 (Rome, 1966).

Audin, A., *Lyons, miroir de Rome dans les Gaules* (Paris, 1965).

Babbitt, S. E., and Campbell, S., *Racism and Philosophy* (Ithaca and London, 1999).

Ball, Warwick, *Rome in the East: The Transformation of an Empire* (London and New York, 2000).

Balsdon, J.P.V.D., *The Emperor Gaius (Caligula)* (Oxford, 1934, repr. 1964).

———, *Romans & Aliens* (London, 1979).

Baltrusch, Ernst, *Die Juden und das Römische Reich. Geschichte einer konfliktreichen Beziehung* (Darmstadt, 2002).

Banton, M., *Race Relations* (London, 1967).

———, *The Idea of Race* (London, 1977).

———, *Racial Theories* (Cambridge, 1987).

Barigazzi, A. (ed.), *Favorino di Arelate, Opere: introduzione, testo critico e commento* (Florence, 1966).

Barker, Anthony J., *The African Link: British Attitudes to the Negro in the Era of the Atlantic Slave Trade, 1550–1807* (London, 1978).

Barnes, Jonathan, *The Presocratic Philosophers* (London, 1982).

Barnes, Timothy D., *Tertullian: A Historical and Literary Study* (Oxford, 1971).

———, *Ammianus Marcellinus and the Representation of Historical Reality* (Ithaca and London, 1998).

Barras, Vincent et al., *Galien: L'âme et ses passions* (Paris, 1995).

Barth, F. (ed.), *Ethnic Groups and Boundaries: The Social Organization of Cultural Difference* (Bergen, Oslo, London, 1969).

Barton, Tamsyn S., *Power and Knowledge: Astrology, Physiognomics, and Medicine under the Roman Empire* (Ann Arbor, MI, 1994).

Barzun, Jacques, *Race: A Study in Superstition* (first published in 1937; rev. ed.: New York, 1965).

Beagon, M., *Roman Nature: The Thought of Pliny the Elder* (Oxford, 1992).

Beard, M., and Crawford, M., *Rome in the Late Republic* (Ithaca, 1985).

Beard, M., North. J., and Price, S., *Religions of Rome* (Cambridge, 1998).

Beck, H. (ed.), *Germanenprobleme in heutiger Sicht* (Berlin, 1986).

Belardi, Walter, *Superstitio* (Rome, 1976).

Benario, Herbert W., *Tacitus Germany / Germania* (Warminster, 1999).

Benedict, R., *Race and Racism* (London, 1942).

Berger, David (ed.), *History and Hate: The Dimensions of Anti-Semitism* (Philadelphia and New York, 1986).

Bernasconi, Robert, and Lott, Tommy L., *The Idea of Race* (Indianapolis, IN, 2000).

Bichler, Reinhold, *Herodots Welt: Der Aufbau der Historie am Bild der fremden Länder und Völker, ihrer Zivilisation und ihrer Geschichte* (Berlin, 2000).

Bickerman, E. J., *Religion and Politics in the Hellenistic and Roman World* (Como, 1985).

Bilde, P. et al. (eds.), *Ethnicity in Hellenistic Egypt* (Aarhus, 1992).

Biraschi, Anna Maria, and Salmeri, Giovanni (eds.), *Strabone e l'Asia Minore* (Napoli and Perugia, 2000).

Birley, Anthony R., *The African Emperor: Septimius Severus* (London, 2d ed. 1988).

———, *Hadrian: the Restless Emperor* (London and New York, 1997).

Blumenbach, Johann Friedrich, *Über die natürlichen Verschiedenheiten im Menschengeschlecht* (Leipzig, 1798, first published in 1776).

Boas, Franz, *The Mind of Primitive Man* (New York, 1911).

———, *Kultur und Rasse* (Leipzig, 1914).

Bodin, Jean, *The Six Bookes of a Commonweale*, ed. Kenneth Douglas McRae (Cambridge, MA, 1962).

Boedeker, D., and Raaflaub, K. A., *Democracy, Empire, and the Arts in Fifth-Century Athens* (Cambridge, MA, 1998).

Bon, Gustave Le -, *Lois psychologiques de l'évolution des peuples* (Paris, 1894).

———, *The Psychology of Peoples* (English translation of the above, 1924; repr. New York, 1974).

Borchardt, F. L., *German Antiquity in Renaissance Myth* (Baltimore, 1971).

Bosworth, A. B., *A Historical Commentary on Arrian's History of Alexander*, I (Oxford, 1980).

Botermann, H., *Das Judenedikt des Kaisers Claudius: Römischer Staat und Christiani im 1. Jahrhundert* (Stuttgart, 1996).

Bowersock, G. W., *Roman Arabia* (Cambridge, MA, 1983).

Bowman, A. K., and Thomas, J. David, *The Vindolanda Writing Tablets (Tabulae Vindolandenses* II) (London, 1994).

Bowman, Alan K., *Life and Letters on the Roman Frontier: Vindolanda and its People* (London, 1994).

Branham, R. Bracht, *Unruly Eloquence: Lucian and the Comedy of Traditions* (Cambridge, MA, 1989).

Braund, D., *Georgia in Antiquity* (Oxford, 1994).

Bremmer, J. (ed.), *Interpretations of Greek Mythology* (London, 1987).

Bringmann, K., *Studien zu den politischen Ideen des Isokrates* (Göttingen, 1965).

Brown, Shelby, *Late Carthaginian Child Sacrifice and Sacrificial Monuments in their Mediterranean Context* (Sheffield, 1991).

Brunt, P. A., *Roman Imperial Themes* (Oxford, 1990).

———, *Studies in Greek History and Thought* (Oxford, 1993).

Buchner, E., *Der Panegyrikos des Isokrates* Historia Einzelschriften 2 (Wiesbaden, 1958).

Buffon, Georges-Louis Leclerc de -, *Histoire naturelle générale et particulière avec la Description du Cabinet du Roy*, vol. 4 (1766).

———, English translation of the above (London, 1817).

Bulmer, Martin, and Solomos, John (eds.), *Racism* (Oxford, 1999).

Cameron, Averil, *Agathias* (Oxford, 1970).

Cameron, Averil, and Hall, Stuart G., *Eusebius, Life of Constantine* (translated with introduction and commentary, Oxford, 1999).

Cancik, H., Lichtenberger, H., and Schäfer, P. (eds.), *Geschichte—Tradition-Reflexion: Festschrift für Martin Hengel zum 70. Geburtstag*, Band 2 (Tübingen, 1996).

Carey, Christopher, *A Commentary of Five Odes of Pindar, Pythian 2, Pythian 9, Nemean 1, Nemean 7, Isthmian 8* (Salem, NH, 1981).

Cartledge, P., Garnsey, P., and Gruen, E., *Hellenistic Constructs: Essays in Culture, History and Historiography* (Berkeley, 1997).

Cavalli-Sforza, L. L., Menozzi, Paolo, and Piazza, Alberto, *The History and Geography of Human Genes* (Princeton, 1994).

Chauvot, Alain, *Opinions romaines face aux barbares au ive siècle ap. J.-C.* (Paris, 1998).

Chevallier, R., *Rome et la Germanie au 1er siècle de notre ère* (Brussels, 1961).

Childs, Donald J., *Modernism and Eugenics: Woolf, Eliot, Yeats, and the Culture of Degeneration* (Cambridge, 2001).

Cohen, Beth (ed.), *Not the Classical Ideal: Athens and the Construction of the Other in Greek Art* (Leiden, 2000) .

Cohen, Edward E., *The Athenian Nation* (Princeton, 2000).

Cohn, Norman, *Europe's Inner Demons: An Enquiry Inspired by the Great Witch-Hunt* (London, 1975).

Coleman, John E., and Walz, Clark A., *Greeks and Barbarians: Essays on the Interactions between Greeks and Non-Greeks in Antiquity and the Consequences for Eurocentrism* (Bethesda, MD, 1997).

Colledge, Malcolm A. R., *The Parthian Period* (Leiden, 1986).

Conington, John, *Horace. The Odes and Carmen Saeculare of Horace* (London, 1882).

Cornell, T. J., *The Beginnings of Rome: Italy and Rome from the Bronze Age to the Punic Wars* (London, 1995).

Coudenhove-Kalergi, Count Heinrich, *Anti-semitism throughout the Ages* (London, 1935, originally published in German: *Das Wesen des Antisemitismus* (Vienna, 1901).

Courtney, E., *A Commentary on the Satires of Juvenal* (London, 1980).

Crawford, M. (ed.), *Sources for Ancient History: Studies in the Uses of Historical Evidence* (Cambridge, 1983).

Cunliffe, Barry, *The Ancient Celts* (Oxford, 1997).

Darwin, Charles, *The Variations of Plants and Animals Under Domestication*, 2 vols. (London, 1868).

———, *The Descent of Man, Selection in Relation to Sex* (London, 1877), reprinted as volume 21 of *The Works of Charles Darwin* ed. by Paul H. Barrett and R. B. Freeman (London, 1989).

Dauge, Yves Albert, *Le Barbare: Recherches sur la conception romaine de la barbarie et de la civilisation* (Brussels, 1981).

Davis, Simon, *Race-Relations in Ancient Egypt: Greek, Egyptian, Hebrew, Roman* (New York, 1952).

Debevoise, N. C., *The Political History of Parthia* (Chicago, 1938).

Detienne, M., *Dionysos mis à mort* (Paris, 1977).

————, *Dionysus Slain* (translation of the above, Baltimore, 1979).

D'Holbach, Paul-Henri Thiry, *La politique naturelle ou discours sur les vrais principes du gouvernement* (London, 1770, repr. Hildesheim-New York, 1971).

————, *Le Systeme social: Principes naturels de la morale et de la politique, avec un examen de l'influence du gouvernement sur les moeurs* (Paris, 1773).

Diderot, Denis, *Supplément au voyage de Bougainville* (written 1772, published 1796) ed. Gilbert Chinard (Oxford and London, 1935).

————, *Œuvres complètes* (Paris 1875, repr. 1966).

————, *Encyclopédie 3, Oeuvres complètes 7* (Paris, 1976).

Dijk, Gert-Jan van, *AINOI, LOGOI, MYTHOI. Fables in Archaic, Classical, and Hellenistic Greek Literature, with a Study of the Theory and Terminology of the Genre* (Leiden, 1997).

Dobesch, G., *Das europäische "Barbaricum" und die Zone der Mediterrankultur: Ihre historische Wechselwirkung und das Geschichtsbild des Poseidonios* (Vienna, 1995).

Dodds, E. R., *Plato, Gorgias: A Revised Text with Introduction and Commentary* (Oxford, 1959).

————, *The Ancient Concept of Progress and other Essays on Greek Literature and Belief* (Oxford, 1973).

Dorati, M., *Le storie di Erodoto: etnografia e racconto* (Pisa and Rome, 2000).

Dover, K. J., *Greek Popular Morality in the Time of Plato and Aristotle* (Oxford, 1974).

————, *Greek Homosexuality* (Oxford, 1978).

Due, Bodil, *The Cyropaedia: Xenophon's Aims and Methods* (Aarhus, 1989).

Dueck, Daniela, *Strabo of Amasia: A Greek Man of Letters in Augustan Rome* (London, 2000).

Duval, P. M., *Les dieux de la Gaule* (Paris, 2d ed. 1976).

Edelstein, Ludwig, *The Idea of Progress in Classical Antiquity* (Baltimore, MD, 1967).

Edelstein, Ludwig, and Kidd, I. G., *Posidonius* 3 vols. in 4 (Cambridge, 1972–1999), vols. 2–3 ed. by Kidd.

Edwards, Catharine, *The Politics of Immorality in Ancient Rome* (Cambridge, 1993).

Engels, Johannes, *Augusteische Oikumenegeographie und Universalhistorie im Werk Strabons von Amaseia* (Geographica Historica 12; Stuttgart, 1999).

Erbse, H., *Studien zum Verständnis Herodots* (Berlin, 1992).

Evans, Elisabeth C., *Physiognomics in the Ancient World* (Philadelphia, 1969).

Evans, J.A.S., *Herodotus: Explorer of the Past, Three Essays* (Princeton, 1991).

Eze, E. C., *Race and the Enlightenment* (Oxford, 1997).

Farnell, L. R., *Critical Commentary to the Works of Pindar* (London, 1931, repr. 1965).

Farquharson, A.S.L., *The Meditations of the Emperor Marcus Aurelius* (Oxford, 1951).

Feldman, L., *Jew and Gentile in the Ancient World: Attitudes and Interactions from Alexander to Justinian* (Princeton, 1993).

Ferrary, Jean-Louis, *Philhellénisme et impérialisme: Aspects idéologiques de la conquête romaine du monde hellénistique* (Rome, 1988).

Finley, M. I., *Slavery in Classical Antiquity* (Cambridge, 2d ed. 1968).

Flory, S., *The Archaic Smile of Herodotus* (Detroit, 1987).

Foerster, R., *Scriptores physiognomonici graeci et latini*, 2 vols. (Leipzig, 1893).

Fornara, Charles W., *The Nature of Ancient History in Ancient Greece and Rome* (Berkeley and Los Angeles, 1983).

Fournol, Etienne-Maurice, *Bodin, prédécesseur de Montesquieu: étude sur quelques théories politiques de la «république» et de «l'esprit des lois»* (Paris, 1896, repr. Genève, 1970).

Franck, Sebastian, *Germaniae Chronicon* or *Teütscher Nation, aller Teütscher Völcker, Herkommen, Namen, Händel, Thaten* etc. (Frankfurt am Main, 1539).

Fredrickson, George M., *Racism: a Short History* (Princeton, 2002).

French, Roger, and Greenaway, Frank (eds.), *Science in the Early Roman Empire: Pliny the Elder, His Sources and Influence* (London, 1986).

Freudenberger, R., *Das Verhalten der römischen Behörden gegen die Christen im 2. Jahrhundert dargestellt am Brief des Plinius and Trajan und den Reskripten Trajans und Hadrians* (Munich, 1967, repr.1969).

Froidefrond, C., *Le mirage égyptien dans la littérature grecque d'Homère à Aristote* (Gap, 1971).

Fuchs, Eduard, *Die Juden in der Karikatur: Ein Beitrag zur Kulturgeschichte* (Munich, 1921; repr. 1985).

Furtwängler, A., and Reichhold, K., *Griechische Vasenmalerei; Auswahl hervorragender Vasenbilder* (München, 1904).

Gafni, I. M., Oppenheimer, A., and Schwartz, D. R. (eds.), *The Jews in the Hellenistic-Roman World: Studies in Memory of Menahem Stern* (Jerusalem, 1996).

Gager, John G., *The Origins of Anti-Semitism: Attitudes toward Judaism in Pagan and Christian Antiquity* (New York and Oxford, 1983).

Garnsey, P.D.A., and Whittaker, C. R. (eds.), *Imperialism in the Ancient World* (Cambridge, 1978).

Garnsey, Peter, *Famine and Food Supply in the Graeco-Roman World: Responses to Risk and Crisis* (Cambridge, 1988).

———, *Ideas of Slavery from Aristotle to Augustine* (Cambridge, 1996).

———, *Food and Society in Classical Antiquity* (Cambridge, 1999).

Geiger, Joseph, *Cornelius Nepos and Ancient Political Biography* (Wiesbaden, 1985).

Gellner, E., *Nations and Nationalism* (Ithaca, NY, 1983).

Georges, Pericles, *Barbarian Asia and the Greek Experience: From the Archaic Period to the Age of Xenophon* (Baltimore, 1994).

Giardina, A. (ed.), *L'homme romain* (Paris, 1992).

Gilman, Sander L., and Katz, Steven T., *Anti-Semitism in Times of Crisis* (New York, 1991).

Glazer N., and Moynihan, D. P., *Ethnicity: Theory and Experience* (Cambridge, MA, 1975).

Gleason, Maud W., *Making Men: Sophists and Self-Presentation in Ancient Rome* (Princeton, 1995).

Glick, Thomas F. (ed.), *The Comparative Reception of Darwinism* (Austin, TX, 1972).

Goldhill, Simon (ed.), *Being Greek under Rome: Cultural Identity, the Second Sophistic and the Development of Empire* (Cambridge, 2001).

Goldman, Laurence R. (ed.), *The Anthropology of Cannibalism* (Westport, CT, 1999).

Gomme, A. W., *Essays in Greek History and Literature* (Oxford, 1937).

———, *A Historical Commentary on Thucydides*, 5 vols., vol. 5 by Gomme, A. Andrewes, and K.J. Dover (Oxford, 1956–1981).

Goodman, M., *The Ruling Class of Judaea: The Origins of the Jewish Revolt against Rome AD 66–70* (Cambridge, 1987).

————, *Mission and Conversion: Proselytizing in the Religious History of the Roman Empire* (Oxford 1994)..

———— (ed.), *Jews in a Graeco-Roman World* (Oxford, 1998).

Gould, John, *Herodotus* (New York, 1989).

Gourevitch, Danielle, *Le triangle Hippocratique dans le monde gréco-romain: la malade, sa maladie et son médecin* (Rome, 1984).

Graves, Joseph L., *The Emperor's New Clothes: Biological Theories of Race at the Millennium* (New Brunswick, NJ, 2001).

Green, Miranda J. (ed.), *The Celtic World* (London and New York, 1995).

Griffin, Miriam T., *Nero: the End of a Dynasty* (London, 1984).

Griffith, M., and Mastronarde, D. J. (eds.), *Cabinet of the Muses: Essays on Classics and Comparative Literature in Honor of Thomas G. Rosenmeyer* (Atlanta, GA, 1990).

Gruen, Erich S., *Studies in Greek Culture and Roman Policy* (Leiden, 1990).

————, *Culture and National Identity in Republican Rome* (Ithaca, NY, 1992; London, 1993).

————, *Heritage and Hellenism: The Reinvention of Jewish Tradition* (Berkeley, 1998).

————, *Diaspora: Jews amidst Greeks and Romans* (Cambridge, MA, 2002).

Guillaumin, Colette, *L'idéologie raciste: genèse et language actuel* (Paris and The Hague, 1972).

Guthrie, W.K.C., *A History of Greek Philosophy* 3 (Cambridge, 1962).

Hall, Edith, *Inventing the Barbarian: Greek Self-Definition through Tragedy* (Oxford, 1989).

Hall, Jennifer, *Lucian's Satire* (New York, 1981).

Hall, Jonathan M., *Ethnic Identity in Greek Antiquity* (Cambridge, 1997).

————, *Hellenicity: between ethnicity and culture* (Chicago 2002) (I have not seen this work).

Halperin, D. M., Winkler, J. J., and Zeitlin, F. I. (eds.), *Before Sexuality: The Construction of Erotic Experience in the Ancient Greek World* (Princeton, 1989).

Hansen, Mogens Herman, *Polis and City-State: An Ancient Concept and its Modern Equivalent* (Copenhagen, 1998).

Harris, William V., *War and Imperialism in Republican Rome, 327–70 BC* (Oxford, 1979).

Harrison, S. J. (ed.), *Oxford Readings in Vergil's* Aeneid (Oxford, 1990).

Hartog, François, *Le miroir d'Hérodote: Essai sur la représentation de l'autre* (Paris, 1980).

Hatt, J.-J., *Mythes et dieux de la Gaule* (Paris, 1989).

Heinimann, M., *Nomos und Physis: Herkunft und Bedeutung einer Antithese im griechischen Denken des 5. Jahrhunderts.* Schweizerische Beiträge zur Altertumswissenschaft 1 (Basel, 1945, repr. Darmstadt, 1978).

Helvétius, Claude-Adrien, *De l'esprit* (Paris, 1758, repr. 1988).

Henderson, John, *Writing down Rome: Satire, Comedy, and other Offences in Latin Poetry* (Oxford, 1999).

Hignett, C., *A History of the Athenian Constitution to the End of the Fifth Century B.C.* (Oxford, 1952 with subsequent reprints).

Hilberg, R., *The Destruction of the European Jews* (New York, rev. ed., 1985).

Hirsch, Steven W., *The Friendship of the Barbarians: Xenophon and the Persian Empire* (Hanover, 1985).

Hobsbawm, E. J., *Nations and Nationalism since 1780* (Cambridge, 1990).

Hobsbawm, E. J., and Ranger, T., *The Invention of Tradition* (Cambridge, 1983).

Hopkins, Keith, *Conquerors and Slaves* (Cambridge, 1978).

―――, *Death and Renewal* (Cambridge, 1982).

Horbury, W., Davies, W. D., and Sturdy, J. (eds.), *The Cambridge History of Judaism,* vol. 3: *The Early Roman Period* (Cambridge, 1999).

Horden, Peregrine, and Purcell, Nicholas, *The Corrupting Sea: A Study of Mediterranean History* (Oxford, 2000).

Hornblower, Simon, *A Commentary on Thucydides* vol. 1 (Oxford, 1991).

―――, *The Greek World 479–323 BC* (London, 2d ed., 1991).

How, W. W., and Wells, J., *A Commentary on Herodotus,* 2 vols. (Oxford, 1912).

Hsia, R. Po-Chia, *The Myth of Ritual Murder: Jews and Magic in Reformation Germany* (New Haven and London, 1988).

―――, *Trent 1475: Stories of a Ritual Murder Trial* (New Haven and London, 1992).

Hughes, Dennis D., *Human Sacrifice in Ancient Greece* (London and New York, 1991).

Hunnink, V., *M.Annaeus Lucanus, Bellum Civile Book III: A Commentary* (Amsterdam, 1992).

Hunt, Peter, *Slaves, Warfare, and Ideology in the Greek Historians* (Cambridge, 1998).

Isaac, Benjamin, *The Limits of Empire: the Roman Army in the East* (Oxford, 2d ed. 1992).

―――, *The Near East under Roman Rule: Selected Papers* (Leiden, 1998).

Isaac, Benjamin, and Oppenheimer, A., "The Revolt of Bar Kokhba: Ideology and Modern Scholarship," reprinted with additions in Isaac, *The Near East Under Roman Rule* (1998), 220–252.

Isaac, Jules, *Jésus et Israël* (1948); English: *Jesus and Israel* (New York, 1971).

―――, *Genèse de l'antisémitisme: essai historique* (Paris 1956).

Jahoda, Gustav, *Images of Savages: Ancient Roots of Modern Prejudice in Western Culture* (London and New York, 1999).

Jankuhn, H., and Timpe, D., *Beiträge zum Verständnis der Germania des Tacitus,* Teil I: *Bericht über die Kolloquien der Kommission für die Altertumskunde Nord- und Mitteleuropas im Jahr 1986* (Göttingen, 1989).

Jefferson, Thomas, *Notes on the State of Virginia* (1787) ed. W. Peden (Chapel Hill, 1955).

Johnson, James William, *The Formation of English Neo-Classical Thought* (Princeton, 1967).

Jones, Christopher P., *Plutarch and Rome* (Oxford, 1971).

―――, *The Roman World of Dio Chrysostom* (Cambridge, MA, 1978).

―――, *Culture and Society in Lucian* (Cambridge, MA, 1986).

―――, *Kinship Diplomacy in the Ancient World* (Cambridge, MA, 1999).

Jones, Siân, *The Archaeology of Ethnicity: Constructing Identities in the Past and Present* (London and New York, 1997).

Jones, W.H.S., *Philosophy and Medicine in Ancient Greece, Bull. Hist. of Medicine* Supp. 8 (1946).

Jouanna, J., *Hippocrate, Airs, eaux, lieux* (Paris, 1996).

Juster, J., *Les Juifs dans l'Empire romain: leur condition juridique, économique et sociale* 1 (Paris, 1914).

Jüthner, Julius, *Hellenen und Barbaren: Aus der Geschichte des Nationalbewusstseins* (Leipzig, 1923).

Kaiser, Hilmar, *Imperialism, Racism and Development Theories: The Construction of a Dominant Paradigm on Ottoman Armenians* (Ann Arbor, MI, 1997).

Kay, N. M., *Martial Book XI* (London, 1985).

Kames, Lord (Henry Homes), *Sketches of the History of Man* (Edinburgh, 2d ed. 1778; Dublin, 3rd ed. 1779, repr. of the second ed., London, 1993).

Kant, Immanuel, *Gesammelte Schriften* (Berlin, 1900–1966).

———, *Beobachtungen über das Gefühl des Schönen und Erhabenen* (Königsberg, 1764).

———, *Observations on the Feeling of the Beautiful and Sublime* (1764), English translation of the above by J. T. Goldthwait (Berkeley, CA, 1960).

———, *Schriften zur Anthropologie Geschichtsphilophie Politik und Pädagogik* (repr. Darmstadt, 1970).

Kennedy, D. L. (ed.), *The Roman Army in the East*. Journal of Roman Archaeology Suppl. 18 (Ann Arbor, MI, 1996).

Keppie, L.J.F., *Colonisation and Veteran Settlement in Italy 47–14 BC* (Rome, 1983).

Keyt, David, and Miller, Fred D. (eds.), *A Companion to Aristotle's Politics* (Oxford, 1991).

Khan, H. A. (ed.), *The Birth of the European Identity; The Europe-Asia Contrast in Greek Thought 490–322 B.C.* (Nottingham, 1994).

Kienast, Dietmar, *Cato der Zensor: Seine Persönlichkeit und seine Zeit* (Heidelberg, 1951; repr.).

Klein, Thomas et al. (eds.), *Judentum und Antisemitismus von der Antike bis zur Gegenwart* (Düsseldorf, 1984).

Kleiner, Diana E., *Roman Scultpure* (New Haven, CT, 1992).

Kloppenborg, J. S., and Wilson, S. G., *Voluntary Associations in the Graeco-Roman World* (London, 1996).

Kyrkos, Basileios A., *Antiphon-Kritias-Anonymus Iamblichi: Studienausgabe Ausgewählter Texte* (Ioannina, 1988).

Lang, Berel (ed.), *Race and Racism in Theory and Practice* (Oxford and Lanham, MD, 1999).

Leeman, A. D., and Pinkster, H., *M. Tullius Cicero, De Oratore libri III* (Heidelberg, 1981–).

Leipoldt, Johannes, *Antisemitismus in der alten Welt* (Leipzig, 1933).

Lévi-Strauss, Claude, *Race et Histoire* (Paris, 1952).

Lewis, Bernard, *The Jews of Islam* (Princeton, 1984).

———, *Race and Slavery in the Middle East: An Historical Enquiry* (New York and Oxford, 1990).

Lewis, David, *Sparta and Persia* (Leiden, 1977).

Lewis, I. M., *Religion in Context* (Cambridge, 1986).

Lewy, H. J., *Studies in Jewish Hellenism* (Jerusalem, 1960, in Hebrew).

Lieu, J., North, J., and Rajak, T., *The Jews among Pagans and Christians* (London and New York, 1992).

Lloyd, Alan B., *Herodotus Book II*. 3 vols. (Leiden, 1975).

Lloyd, G.E.R., *Magic, Reason and Experience* (Cambridge, 1976).

———, *Science, Folklore and Ideology: Studies in the Life Sciences in Ancient Greece* (Cambridge, 1983).

Lloyd-Jones, Hugh, *Females of the Species: Semonides on Women* (London, 1975).

Long, T., *Barbarians in Greek Comedy* (Carbondale, 1986).

Loraux, Nicole, *The Invention of Athens* (London, 1986).

———, *The Children of Athena: Athenian Ideas about Citizenship and the Division between the Sexes* (Princeton, 1993).

Lord, Carnes, *Education and Culture in the Political Thought of Aristotle* (Ithaca and London, 1982).

Luce, T. J., and Woodman, A. J., *Tacitus and the Tacitean Tradition* (Princeton, 1993).

Lund, Allan A., *Germania: Interpretiert, herausgegeben, übertragen, kommentiert* (Heidelberg, 1988).

———, *Zum Germanenbild der Römer. Eine Einführung in die antike Ethnographie* (Heidelberg, 1990).

———, *Gemanenideologie im Nazionalsozialismus: Zur Rezeption der 'Germania' des Tacitus im "Dritten Reich"* (Heidelberg, 1995).

Malkin, I., *The Returns of Odysseus: Colonization and Ethnicity* (Berkeley, 1998).

———, (ed.), *Ancient Perceptions of Greek Ethnicity* (Washington, DC and Cambridge, MA, 2001).

Mason, P., *Race Relations* (London, 1970).

Mathews, T. F., *The Clash of Gods: A reinterpretation of Early Christian Art* (Princeton, 2d ed. 1999).

Matthews, John F., *Western Aristocracies and Imperial Court: AD 364–425* (Oxford, 1975).

———, *The Roman Empire of Ammianus* (London and Baltimore, 1989).

Mazza, F. et al. (eds.), *Fonti classiche per la civiltà fenicia e punica* (Rome, 1988).

McKnight, Scot, *A Light among the Gentiles: Jewish Missionary Activity in the Second Temple Period* (Minneapolis, 1991).

Mellor, Ronald (ed.), *Tacitus: The Classical Heritage* (New York, 1995).

———, *The Roman Historians* (London, 1999).

Memmi, Albert, *Le racisme. Description, définition, traitement* (Paris, 1982).

———, *Rassismus* (German trans. of the above, Frankfurt/Main, 1987).

Miles, Robert, *White Man's Country: Racism in British Politics* (London, 1984).

Millar, F., *A Study of Cassius Dio* (Oxford, 1964).

———, *The Roman Near East: 31 BC–AD 337* (Cambridge, MA, 1993).

Molyneaux, Brian Leigh, *The Cultural Life of Images: Visual Representation in Archaeology* (London, 1997).

Momigliano, Arnaldo, *Claudius, the Emperor and his Achievement,* trans. W. D. Hogarth (Oxford, 1934), repr. with a new bibliography (1942–1959) (Cambridge, 1961).

———, *Alien Wisdom: the Limits of Hellenization* (Cambridge, 1975).

Mommsen, Theodor, *Auch ein Wort über unser Judenthum* (Berlin, 1880).

Montagu, Ashley, *Statement on Race* (New York, 1951).

———, *The Idea of Race* (Lincoln, NE, 1965).

———, *Man's Most Dangerous Myth: The Fallacy of Race* (New York and Oxford, 1974).

Montanari, Enrico, *Il mito dell'autoctonia: linee di una dinamica mitico-politica ateniense* (Rome, 2d ed. 1981).

Morales, P. Edgardo M., *Edición crítica de 'de Monacho captivo' (vita Malchi) de San Jerónimo* (Roma, 1991).

Morford, M.P.O., *The Poet Lucan: Studies in Rhetorical Epic* (Oxford, 1967).

Moscati, S. (ed.), *The Phoenicians* (New York, 1988).

Mosse, George L., *The Crisis of the German Ideology* (New York, 1964).

———, *Toward the Final Solution: A History of European Racism* (London, 1978).

Much, R., *Die Germania des Tacitus* (erste Auflage, 1937; dritte Auflage, ed. by H. Jankuhn and W. Lange, Heidelberg, 1967).

Müller, Klaus E., *Geschichte der antiken Ethnographie und Ethnologischen Theoriebildung*, 2 vols. (Wiesbaden, 1972).

Nenci, G. (ed.), *Hérodote et les peuples non grecs* (Vandoeuvres–Genève, 1990).

Newman, W. L., *The Politics of Aristotle*, 4 vols. (Oxford, 1887–1902).

Nicolet, Claude, *Space, Geography and Politics in the Early Roman Empire* (Ann Arbor, 1991).

Nikiprowetzky, V. (ed.), *de l'antijudaisme antique à l'antisémitisme contemporain* (Lille, 1979).

Norden, E., *Die germanische Urgeschichte in Tacitus' Germania* (Stuttgart, 5th ed. 1998).

Nutton, Vivian, *Corpus Medicorum Graecorum* 8.1 (Berlin, 1979).

Ogden, Daniel, *Greek Bastardy in the Classical and Hellenistic Periods* (Oxford, 1996).

Olender, Maurice (ed.), *Pour Léon Poliakov, le racisme: mythes et sciences* (Paris, 1981).

Oppenheimer, Aharon, *Babylonia Judaica in the Talmudic Period* (Wiesbaden, 1983).

Ostenfeld, Erik Nils (ed.), *Greek Romans and Roman Greeks: Studies in Cultural Interaction* (Aarhus, 2002).

Ostwald, Martin, *From Popular Sovereignty to the Sovereignty of Law: Law, Society, and Politics in Fifth-Century Athens* (Berkeley and Los Angeles, 1986).

———, *Oligarchia: The Development of a Constitutional Form in Ancient Greece* (Stuttgart, 2000).

Paassen, C. van, *The Classical Tradition of Geography* (Groningen, 1957).

Pagden, Anthony, *The Fall of Natural Man: The American Indian and the Origins of Comparative Ethnology* (Cambridge, 1982).

Page, D. L., *Poetae Melici Graeci* (Oxford, 1962).

———, *Epigrammata Graeca* (Oxford, 1975).

Pailler, Jean-Marie, *Bacchanalia: La répression de 186 av. J.-C. à Rome et en Italie: vestiges, images, tradition* (Rome, 1988).

Palm, Jonas, *Rom, Römertum und Imperium in der griechischen Literatur der Kaiserzeit* (Lund, 1959).

Patterson, C., *Pericles' Citizenship Law of 451–50 B.C.* (New York, 1981).

Patzig, Günther, *Aristoteles' "Politik", Akten des XI. Symposium Aristotelicum, 1987* (Göttingen, 1990).

Percival, Melissa, *The Appearance of Character: Physiognomy and Facial Expression in Eighteenth-Century France* (Leeds, 1999).

Petersen, Eugen, Domaszewski, Alfred von, and Calderini, Guglielmo (eds.), *Die Marcus-Säule auf Piazza Colonna in Rom* Text (1 Band).–Tafeln (2 Port.) (Munich, 1896).

Petrochilos, Nicholas, *Roman Attitudes to the Greeks* (Athens, 1974).

Piggott, S., *The Druids* (London, 1968).

Pippidi, D. M. (ed.), *Assimilation et résistance à la culture gréco-romaine dans le monde ancien* (Paris, 1976).

Podlecki, A. J., *The Political Background of Aeschylean Tragedy* (Ann Arbor, 1966).

Pohlenz, M., *Herodot: Der erste Geschichtsschreiber des Abendlandes* (Leipzig, 1937).

———, *Hippokrates und die Begründung der wissenschaftlichen Medizin* (Berlin, 1938).

Poliakov, Léon, *Le mythe aryen: essay sur les sources du racisme et des nationalismes* (Paris, 1971).

———, *The Aryan Myth* (translation of the above, New York, 1996).

——— (ed.), *hommes et bêtes: entretiens sur le racisme, actes du colloque tenu du 12 au 15 mai 1973* (Paris and the Hague, 1975).

———, *Le Racisme* (Paris, 1976).

————, *Histoire de l'Antisémitisme* (Paris, 1955); *The History of Antisemitism,* 4 vols. (London, 1974–1986).

————, *Ni Juif ni Grec: Entretiens sur le racisme* (Paris, The Hague, New York, 1978).

Popper, Karl R., *The Open Society and Its Enemies,* I, *The Spell of Plato* (Princeton, rev. ed., 1966).

Price, J., *Thucydides and Internal War: Stasis as a Model for the Peloponnesian War* (Cambridge, 2001).

Pucci Ben-Zeev, M., *Jewish Rights in the Roman World* (Tübingen, 1998).

Raeck, W., *Zum Barbarenbild in der Kunst Athens im 6. und 5. Jahrhundert v. Chr.* (Bonn, 1981).

Rajak, Tessa, *The Jewish Dialogue with Greece and Rome: Studies in Cultural and Social Interaction* (Leiden, 2001).

Rankin, Herbert D., *Plato and the Individual* (London, 1964).

Rawson, Claude, *God, Gulliver and Genocide: Barbarism and the European Imagination 1492–1945* (Oxford, 2001).

Rawson, Elizabeth, *The Spartan Tradition in European Thought* (Oxford, 1969).

————, *Intellectual Life in the Late Roman Republic* (London, 1985).

Rhodes, P. J. (ed., trans. and comm.), *Thucydides, History III* (Warminster, 1994).

Rickman, G., *The Corn Supply of Ancient Rome* (Oxford, 1980).

Ridé, Jacques, *L'image du Germain dans la pensée et la litterature allemandes de la redécouverte de Tacite à la fin du xvième siècle.* 3 vols., 1274 pp. (Lille and Paris 1977).

Rives, J. B., *Tacitus: Germania* (Oxford, 1999).

Roberts, Jennifer T., *Athens on Trial: The Antidemocratic Tradition in Western Thought* (Princeton, 1994).

Robertson, Ritchie, *The 'Jewish Question' in German Literature 1749–1939: Emancipation and its Discontents* (Oxford, 1999).

Robin, Christopher, *Lucian and his Influence in Europe* (London, 1980).

Rohrbacher, Stefan, and Schmidt, Michael, *Judenbilder: Kulturgeschichte antijudischer Mythen und antisemitischer Vorurteile* (Reinbeck bei Hamburg, 1991).

Romilly, J. de, *Thucydides and Athenian Imperialism* (Oxford, 1963).

Romm, James S., *The Edges of the Earth in Ancient Thought: Geography, Exploration and Fiction* (Princeton, 1992).

————, *Herodotus* (New Haven, 1999).

Rosenstein, Nathan S., *'Imperatores Victi: Military Defeat and Aristocratic Competition in the Middle and Late Republic* (Berkeley, 1990).

Rubin, B., *Assimilation and its Discontents* (New York, 1995).

Rudd, Niall, *Themes in Roman Satire* (London, 1986).

———— (ed.), *Horace, Epistles Book II and Epistle to the Pisones ("Ars Poetica")* (Cambridge, 1989).

Ruether, R., *Faith and Fratricide: the Theological Roots of Anti-Semitism* (New York, 1974).

Ruffle, John et al. (eds.), *Glimpses of Ancient Egypt: Studies in Honour of H.W. Fairman* (Warminster, 1979).

Rutgers, L.V., *The Jews in Late Ancient Rome: Evidence of Cultural Interaction in the Roman Diaspora* (Leiden, 1995).

————, *The Hidden Heritage of Diaspora Judaism* (Leuven, 1998).

Saïd, S. (ed.) ʿΕλληνισμός: *Quelques jalons pour une historie de l'identité grecque* (Leiden, 1991).

Sartre, Jean-Paul, *Réflections sur la question juive* (Paris, 1954).

Schäfer, Peter, *Judeophobia: Attitudes toward the Jews in the Ancient World* (Cambridge, MA, 1997).

Schellhase, Kenneth C., *Tacitus in Renaissance Political Thought* (Chicago, 1976).

Schippmann, Klaus, *Grundzüge der parthischen Geschichte* (Darmstadt, 1980).

Schürer, E., *The History of the Jewish People in the Age of Jesus Christ (175 BC–AD 135)*, rev. ed. by G. Vermes, F. Millar, M. Goodman (Edinburgh, 1973–1987).

Schwartz Cowan, Ruth, *Sir Francis Galton and the Study of Heredity in the Nineteenth Century* (New York and London, 1985).

See, K. von *Barbar, Germane, Arier: die Suche nach der Identität der Deutschen* (Heidelberg, 1994).

Selden, Steven, *Inheriting Shame: The Story of Eugenics and Racism in America* (New York, 1999).

Sevenster, J. N., *The Roots of Pagan Anti-Semitism in the Ancient World* (Leiden, 1975).

Shackleton Bailey, D. R., *Cicero: Epistulae ad Quintum Fratrem et M. Brutum* (Cambridge, 1980).

Shahîd, Irfan, *Byzantium and the Arabs in the Fourth Century* (Washington, 1984).

Sherwin-White, A. N., *The Letters of Pliny: A Historical and Social Commentary* (Oxford, 1966).

⸻, *Racial Prejudice in Imperial Rome* (Cambridge, 1967).

Sidebotham, S. E., *Roman Economic Policy in the Erythra Thalassa, 30 BC–AD 217* (Leiden, 1986).

Simon, M., *Verus Israel: A Study of the Relations between Christians and Jews in the Roman Empire (135–425)* (originally published in French in 1964, English trans.: Oxford, 1986).

Slingerland, H. Dixon, *Claudian Policymaking and the Early Imperial Repression of Judaism at Rome* (Atlanta, GA, 1997).

Smallwood, E. Mary, *The Jews under Roman Rule from Pompey to Diocletian: A Study in Political Relations* (Leiden, 1976).

Smeed, J. W., *The Theophrastan Character: The History of a Literary Genre* (Oxford, 1985).

Snell, F. J., *Lysias: Epitaphios* (Oxford, 1887).

Snowden, Frank M., *Before Color Prejudice: The Ancient View of the Blacks* (Cambridge, MA, 1983).

Sonnabend, H., *Fremdenbild und Politik: Vorstellungen der Römer von Ägypten und dem Partherreich in der späten Republik und frühen Kaiserzeit* (Frankfurt, 1986).

Sprague, R. K. (ed.), *The Older Sophists: a complete translation by several hands of the fragments in Die Fragmente der Vorsokratiker, edited by Diels-Kranz . . . with a new edition of Antiphon and Euthydemus.* (Columbia, SC, 1972).

Steinschneider, M., *Die arabischen Übersetzungen aus dem Griechischen* (Leipzig, 1897).

Stemberger, G., *Juden und Christen im Heiligen Land: Palästina unter Konstantin und Theodosius* (Munich, 1987).

Stern, Menahem, *Greek and Latin Authors on Jews and Judaism*, 3 vols. (Jerusalem, 1974–1984).

Stockert, Walter, *Euripides, Iphigenie in Aulis.* Band 2, *Detailkommentar* (Vienna, 1992).

Stocking, George W. (ed.), *The Shaping of American Anthropology, 1883–1911: A Franz Boas Reader* (Chicago, 1974).

Stoneman, Richard, *Palmyra and its Empire: Zenobia's Revolt against Rome* (Ann Arbor, 1992).

Swain, Simon, *Hellenism and Empire: Language, Classicism and Power in the Greek World, AD 50–250* (Oxford, 1996).

Syme, Ronald, *Tacitus* (Oxford, 1958).

———, *Ammianus and the Historia Augusta* (Oxford, 1968).

———, *The Provincial at Rome* and *Rome and the Balkans 80 BC–AD 14*, ed. by Anthony Birley (Exeter, 1999).

Tatum, James, *Xenophon's Imperial Fiction* (Princeton, 1989).

The Greek Historians: Literature and History, Papers presented to A. E. Raubitschek (Saratoga, CA, 1985).

Thomas, Rosalind, *Herodotus in Context: Ethnography, Science and the Art of Persuasion* (Cambridge, 2000).

Thompson, E. A., *The Early Germans* (Oxford, 1965).

Thompson, Lloyd A., *Romans and Blacks* (London and Oklahoma, 1989).

Timpe, D., *Romano-Germanica: Gesammelte Studien zur Germania des Tacitus* (Stuttgart and Leipzig, 1995).

Todorov, Tzvetan, *Nous et les autres: La Réflexion française sur la diversité humaine* (Paris, 1989).

———, *On Human Diversity: Nationalism, Racism, and Exoticism in French Thought* (English translation of the above, Cambridge, MA, 1993).

Trachtenberg, Joshua, *The Devil and the Jews: The Medieval Conception of the Jew and Its Relation to Modern Anti-Semitism* (New Haven, CT. 1943; repr. Philadephia, 1983).

Trzaska-Richter, C., *Furor Teutonicus: Das römische Germanenbild in Politik und Propaganda von den Anfängen bis zum 2. Jahrhunderts n. Chr.* Bochumer Altertumswissenschaftliches Colloquium 8 (Trier, 1991).

Trüdinger, Karl, *Studien zur Geschichte der griechisch-römischen Ethnographie* (Basel, 1918).

Vasunia, Phiroze, *The Gift of the Nile: Hellenizing Egypt from Aeschylus to Alexander* (Berkeley, 2001).

Vernant, Jean-Pierre, and Vidal-Naquet, Pierre, *Travail and Esclavage en Grèce ancienne* (Bruxelles 1985, 2d ed. 1988).

Vidal-Naquet, Pierre, *Politics Ancient and Modern* (Cambridge, 1995).

Vlastos, Gregory, *Platonic Studies* (Princeton, 2d ed. 1981).

Walser, G., *Rom, das Reich und die fremden Völker in der Geschichtsschreibung der frühen Kaiserzeit: Studien zur Glaubwürdigkeit des Tacitus* (Baden-Baden, 1951).

———, *Hellas und Iran: Studien zu den Griechischen-Persischen Beziehungen vor Alexander* (Darmstadt, 1984).

Wasserstein (ed.), A., *Galen's Commentary on the Hippocratic Treatise: Airs, Waters, Places in the Hebrew Translation of Solomon Ha-Me'ati;* edited with introd., English translation and notes (Jerusalem, 1982).

Weiss, Sheila Faith, *Race Hygiene and National Efficiency: The Eugenics of Wilhelm Schallmayer* (Berkeley, 1987).

Whitehead, David, *The Ideology of the Athenian Metic* (Cambridge, 1977).

Whitmarsh, Tim, *Greek Literature and the Roman Empire: The Politics of Imitation* (Oxford, 2001).

Wiesehöfer, Josef (ed.), *Das Partherreich und seine Zeugnisse: Beiträge des internationalen Colloquiums, Eutin (27.–30. Juni 1996)* (Stuttgart, 1998).

Wilken, Robert L., *John Chrysostom and the Jews: Rhetoric and Reality in the Late 4th Century* (Berkeley, 1983).

Will, Edouard, and Orrieux, Claude, *«Prosélytisme Juif»? Histoire d'une erreur* (Paris, 1992).

Winter, Engelbert, and Dignas, Beate, *Rom und das Perserreich: Zwei Weltmächte zwischen Konfrontation und Koexistenz* (Berlin, 2001).

Wistrich, Robert S. (ed.), *Demonizing the Other: Antisemitism, Racism and Xenophobia* (Amsterdam, 1999).

Woolf, Greg, *Becoming Roman: the Origins of Provincial Civilization in Gaul* (Cambridge, 1998).

Wuilleumier, P., *Lyons, métropole des Gaules* (Paris, 1953).

Yavetz, Zvi, *Plebs and Princeps* (Oxford, 1969).

———, *Slaves and Slavery in Ancient Rome* (New Brunswick, NJ, 1988).

———, *Judenfeindschaft in der Antike* (Munich, 1997).

———, *Claudius and Nero: From Systematisation to Dilettantism* (Tel Aviv, 1999 in Hebrew).

Zanker, P., *The Power of Images in the Age of Augustus* (Ann Arbor, 1988).

Zeitlin, F. I., *Playing the Other: Gender and Society in Classical Greek Literature* (Chicago and London, 1996).

Zimmermann, Moshe, *Wilhelm Mar: the Patriarch of Anti-Semitism* (New York, 1986).

ARTICLES

Abel, E., "Were the Jews banished from Rome in AD 19?" *REJ* 127 (1968), 383–386.

Amishai-Maisels, Z., "The Demonization of the 'Other' in the Visual Arts," in Wistrich (ed.), *Demonizing the Other: Antisemitism, Racism and Xenophobia* (1999), 44–72.

Angelicoussis, Elizabeth, "The Panel Reliefs of Marcus Aurelius," *MDAI Röm. Abt.* 91 (1984), 141–204.

Backhaus, W., "Der Hellenen-Barbaren-Gegensatz und die Hippokratische Schrift" ΠΕΡΙ ΑΕΡΩΝ ΥΔΑΤΩΝ ΤΟΠΩΝ,' *Historia* 25 (1976), 170–185.

Badian, E., "Alexander the Great and the Unity of Mankind," *Historia* 7 (1958), 425–444.

Barnes, Jonathan, "Aristotle and Political Liberty," in Patzig (ed.), *Aristoteles' "Politik"* (Göttingen, 1990), 249–263.

Barnes, T. D., "Legislation against the Christians," *JRS* 58 (1968), 32–50.

Beard, Mary, "Cicero and Diviniation: the Formation of a Latin Discourse," *JRS* 76 (1986), 33–46.

Belayche, Nicole, "L'Oronte et le Tibre: l'«Orient» des cultes «orientaux» de l'Empire romain," in Amir-Moezzi and Scheid, *L'Orient dans l'histoire religieuse de l'Europe* (2000), 1–36.

Bennett, H., "The Exposure of Infants in Ancient Rome," 18 (1923), 341–351.

Bérard, C., "L'image de l'Autre et le héros étranger," *Sciences et Racisme* 67 (1985–1986), pp. 5–22, republished in English in Cohen (ed.), *Not The Classical Ideal* (2000).

Berger, David, "Anti-Semitism: An Overview," in Berger (ed.), *History and Hate* (1986), 3–14.

Bernard, J.-E., "Transferts historiographiques: Josèphe, César et les privilèges juifs," *Bull. du Centre de la Recherche français de Jérusalem*, CNRS Editions, 2, 1998, 13–24.

Bernard, J.-E., "Philosophie politique et antijudaïsme chez Cicéron," *SCI* 19 (2000), 113–131.

Bickerman, E. J., "Ritualmord und Eselskult: Ein Beitrag zur Geschichte antiker Publizistik," *Studies in Jewish and Christian History* 2 (1980), 225–255.

——, "Origines Gentium," *CPh* 47 (1952), 65–81 = *Religion and Politics in the Hellenistic and Roman World* (1985), 399–417.

Bilde, P., "Atargatis/Dea Syria: Hellenization of Her Cult?" in Bilde et al. (eds.), *Religion and Religious Practice in the Seleucid Kingdom* (1990), 151–187.

Blackburn, Daniel G., "Why Race Is not a Biological Concept," in Berel Lang (ed.), *Race and Racism in Theory and Practice* (Lanham, MD and Oxford, 2000).

Bohak, Gideon, "The Ibis and the Jewish Question: Ancient 'Anti-Semitism' in Historical Perspective," in Mor and Oppenheimer (eds.), *Jewish-Gentile Relations in the Second Temple, Mishnaic and Talmudic Periods* (forthcoming).

Bolkestein, H., "Antisemitisme in de Oudheid," *Socialistische Gids* 21 (1936), 152–166.

Bradley, Keith, "Animalizing the Slave: the Truth of Fiction," *JRS* 90 (2000), 110–125.

Braund, D., "Greeks, Scythians and *Hippake*, or 'Reading Mare's-Cheese'," in Tsetskhladze (ed.), *Ancient Greeks West and East* (1999), 521–530.

Braund, S. H., "Juvenal and the East: Satire as an Historical Source," in: French and Lightfoot, *The Eastern Frontier of the Roman Empire: Proceedings held at Ankara in September 1988* (Oxford, BAR Series, 1989), 45–52.

Briant, P., "Hérodote et la société perse," in Nenci (ed.), *Hérodote et les peuples non grecs* (1990), 69–113.

Bringmann, K., "Topoi in der taciteischen Germania," in Jankuhn and Timpe, *Beiträge zum Vertändnis der Germania* I (1989), 59–78.

Brunt, P. A., "Laus Imperii," originally in Garnsey and Whittaker (eds.), *Imperialism in the Ancient World* (1978), 159–191, reprinted as chapter 14 in *Roman Imperial Themes* (1990), 288–323.

——, "The revolt of Vindex and the Fall of Nero," (1959), reprinted with revisions in *Roman Imperial Themes*, (1993), 9–32, 481–487.

——, "Tacitus on the Batavian Revolt," *Latomus* 19 (1960), 494–517, reprinted with revisions in *Roman Imperial Themes*, 33–52; 481–487.

——, "The Hellenic League against Persia" (1953), reprinted in *Studies in Greek History and Thought* (1993), 47–83.

——, "Introduction to Thucydides," in *Studies in Greek History and Thought* (1993), 137–180; Postscript. 'Thucydides' Funeral Speech," 159–180.

——, "Aristotle and Slavery," in *Studies in Greek History and Thought* (1993), 343–388.

Caizzi, F. Decleva, "Il nuovo papiro di Antifonte," *Studi di Filosofia preplatonica* (Naples, 1984), 191–208.

Calderone, S., "Superstitio," *ANRW* 1.2 (1972), 377–396.

Cambiano, Giuseppe, "Aristotle and the Anonymous Opponents of Slavery," in Finley (ed.), *Classical Slavery* (London, 1987), 22–41.

Cameron, A., "The Exposure of Children and Greek Ethics," *CR* 46 (1932), 105–114.

Carratelli, Giovanni Pugliese, "Le guerre mediche ed il sorgere della solidarietà ellenica," in *la Persia et il mondo greco-romano* (1966), 147–156.

Christ, Karl, "Römer und Barbaren in der hohen Kaiserzeit," *Saeculum* 10 (1959), 273–288.

Cohen, Shaye J. D., "Anti-Semitism in Antiquity: The Problem of Definition," in Berger (ed.), *History and Hate* (1986), 43–47.

——, "Was Martial's Slave Jewish?" in *The Beginnings of Jewishness: Boundaries, Varieties, Uncertainties* (Berkeley, 1999), 351–357.

532   · *S E L E C T E D   B I B L I O G R A P H Y* ·

————, "Was Menophilus Jewish?," in *The Beginnings of Jewishness*, 358f.

Coleman, J. E., "Ancient Greek Ethnocentrism," in Coleman and Walz (eds.), *Greeks and Barbarians* (1997), 175–220.

Cordier, Pierre, "Les Romains et la circoncision," *Revue des Études juives* 160 (2001), 337–355.

Cotter, Wendy, "The Collegia and Roman Law: State Restrictions on Voluntary Associations 64 BCE–200 CE," in Kloppenborg and Wilson, *Voluntary Associations* (1996), 74–89.

Couissin, J., "Suétone physiognomoniste dans les Vies des XII Césars," *Rev. Ét. Lat.* 31 (1953), 234–256.

Damon, Cynthia, "Greek Parasites and Roman Patronage," *HSCP* 97 (1995), 181–195.

Davies, J. K., "Athenian Citizenship: The Descent Group and the Alternatives," *CJ* 73 (1977–1978), 105–121.

Dihle, A., "Herodot und die Sophistik," *Philologus* 106 (1962) 207–220.

Diller, H., "Die Hellenen-Barbaren Antithese im Zeitalter der Perserkriege," in *Grecs et Barbares* Ent. Hardt 8 (Geneva, 1962), 39–68.

Dölger, Franz Joseph, "Sacramentum infanticidii," *Antike und Christentum* 4 (1934), 188–228.

Donfried, K. P., and Richardson , P. (eds.), *Judaism and Christianity in First-Century Rome* (Grand Rapids, MI, 1998).

Dubuisson, M., "*Graecus, Graeculus, Graecari*: L'emploi péjoratif du nom des Grecs en Latin," in S. Saïd (ed.), *Ἑλληνισμός: Quelques jalons pour une historie de l'identité grecque* (1991) , 316–335.

Ehrhardt, Norbert, "Parther und parthische Geschichte," in Wiesehöfer (ed.), *Das Partherreich und seine Zeugnisse* (1998), 295–307.

Eijk, Ph.J. van der, "'Airs, Waters, Places' and 'On the Sacred Disease': Two Different Religiosities," *Hermes* 119 (1991), 168–176.

Elsner, Jaś, "Describing Self in the Language of Other: Pseudo (?) Lucian at the temple of Hierapolis," in S. Goldhill (ed.), *Being Greek under Rome* (2001), 123–153.

Evans, Elisabeth C., "Roman Descriptions of Personal Appearance in History and Biography," *HSCP* 46 (1935), 43–84.

————, "The Study of Physiognomy in the Second Century AD," *TAPA* 72 (1941), 96–108.

————, "Galen, the Physician as Physiognomist," *TAPA* 76 (1945), 287–298.

————, "Physiognomics in the Roman Empire," 45 (1950), 277–282.

Faris, J., "Is Plato's a Caste State Based on Racial Differences?" *CQ* 44 (1950), 38–43.

Feldman, Louis H., "Anti-Semitism in the Ancient World," in Berger (ed.), *History and Hate* (1986), 15–42.

Finley J. H., Jr., "Pindar and the Persian Invasion," *HSCPh* 63 (1958), 121–132.

Foulon, É., "Polybe et les Celtes (I)," *Les Études Classiques* 68 (2000), 319–354.

Fraenkel, Eduard, "Rome and Greek Culture," Oxford oration reprinted in *Kleine Beiträge zur klassischen Philologie* (Rome, 1964) vol. 2, 583–598.

Freeman, Derek, "The Evolutionary Theories of Charles Darwin and Herbert Spencer," *Current Anthropology* 15 (1974), 211–237.

Gabba, E., "Sulle influenze reciproche degli ordinamenti militari dei Parti e dei Romani," in *Atti del convegno sul tema: la Persia et il mondo greco-romano 1965,* Accademia Nazionale dei Lincei 363 (Rome 1966), 51–73.

Garnsey, Peter, "Religious Toleration in Classical Antiquity," in W. J. Sheils (ed.), *Persecution and Toleration* (Oxford, 1984), 1–27.

Garnsey, P., "The Middle Stoics and Slavery," in Cartledge, Garnsey, and Gruen, *Hellenistic Constructs* (1997), 159–174.

Geiger, Joseph, "The Ban on Circumcision and the Bar-Kokhba Revolt," *Zion* 41 (1976), 139ff. (in Hebrew).

——, "Language, Culture and Identity in Ancient Palestine," in Ostenfeld (ed.), *Greek Romans and Roman Greeks* (2002), 233–246.

——, "Graecolatini," in L. Sawicki and D. Shalev, *Donum grammaticum: Studies in Latin and Celtic Linguistics in Honour of Hannah Rosén* (Leuven, 2002), 153.

Gelzer, M., "Die Unterdrückung der Bacchanalien bei Livius," *Hermes* 71 (1936), 275–287.

Gervais, Alice, "Que pensait-on des médecins dans l'ancienne Rome?" *Bulletin de l'Association Guillaume Budé* 4/2 (1964), 197–231.

Giovannini, A., "Les origines de l'antijudaïsme dans le monde grec," *Cahiers du Centre G. Glotz* 6 (1995), 41–60.

Gleason, M., "The Semiotics of Gender: Physiognomy and Self-Fashioning in the Second Century C.E.," in Halperin, Winkler, and Zeitlin (eds.), *Before Sexuality* (1989), 389–416.

Gigon, Olof, "Die Sklaverei bei Aristoteles," in *La «Politique» d'Aristote* Entretiens sur l'antiquité classique 11 (Geneva 1965), 247–276.

Goguey, D., "Les Romains et les animaux: regard sur les grands fauves, liens affectifs entre l'homme et l'animal," in: *Homme et animal dans l'antiquité Romaine: actes du colloque de Nantes 1991* (Centre de recherches A. Piganiol, Tours, 1995), 51–66.

Gomme, A.W., "The Law of Citizenship at Athens," in *Essays in Greek History and Literature* (Oxford, 1937), 67–88.

Goodman, Martin, "Nerva, the *fiscus Judaicus* and Jewish Identity," *JRS* 79 (1989), 40–44.

Greene, John L., "Darwin as a Social Evolutionist," *Journal of the History of Biology* 10 (1997), 1–27.

Grensemann, H., "Das 24. Kapitel von De aeribus, aquis, locis," *Hermes* 107 (1979), 423–441.

Griffin, M. T., "The Lyons Tablet and Tacitean Hindsight," *CQ* 32 (1982), 404–418.

Grodzynski, D., "Superstitio," *REA* 76 (1974), 36–60.

Gros, Pierre, "Les premières générations d'architectes hellénistiques à Rome," in *Mélanges Heurgon* (Rome, 1976), 387–410.

Guillaumin, Colette, "The Changing Face of 'Race'," in Bulmer and Solomos, *Racism* (1999), 355–362, reprinted from Guillaumin, *Racism, Sexism, Power and Ideology* (London, 1995).

Guite, Harold, "Cicero's Attitude to the Greeks," *Greece and Rome* 9 (1962), 142–159.

Hainsworth, J. B., "Verginius and Vindex," *Historia* 11 (1962), 86–96.

Hampl, F., "Römische Politik in republikanischer Zeit und das Problem des 'Sittenverfalls'," *HZ* 188 (1959), 497–525.

Henrichs, Albert, "Graecia Capta: *Roman Views of Greek Culture*," *HSCP* 97 (1995), 243–261.

Highet, G., "A Fight in the Desert: Iuvenal XV and a Modern Parallel," *CJ* 45 (1949/50), 94–96.

Hirsch, Steven W., "1001 Iranian Nights: History and Fiction in Xenophon's Cyropaedia," *The Greek Historians . . . Papers presented to A. E. Raubitschek* (1985), 65–68.

Hook, La Rue van -, "The Exposure of Infants at Athens," *TAPA* 51 (1920), 134–145.

Hopkins, M. K., "Eunuchs in Politics in the Later Roman Empire," *Proc. Cambridge Phil. Soc.* (1963), 62–80.

———, "The Political Power of Eunuchs," *Conquerors and Slaves* (1978), 172–196.

Horsfall, N., "Numanus Remulus: Ethnography and Propaganda in *Aen.* ix, 598f.," *Latomus* 30 (1971), 1108–1116.

———, "Dido in the Light of History," in S. J. Harrison (ed.), *Oxford Readings in Vergil's* Aeneid (Oxford, 1990), 127–144.

Isaac, Benjamin, "Orientals and Jews in the Historia Augusta: Fourth-Century Prejudice and Stereotypes," in Gafni, Oppenheimer, and Schwartz (eds.), *Studies in Memory of Menahem Stern* (1996), 101–118, reprinted with postscript in Isaac, *The Near East under Roman Rule*, 268–282.

———, "Ethnic Groups in Judaea under Roman Rule," reprinted in *The Near East under Roman Rule* (1998), 257–267.

Jacoby, F., "Zu Hippokrates" ΠΕΡΙ ΑΕΡΩΝ ΥΔΑΤΩΝ ΤΟΠΩΝ, *Hermes* 46 (1911), 518–567.

Jones, C. P., "ἔθνος and γένος in Herodotus," *CQ* 46 (1996), 315–320.

Kant, Immanuel, *Von den verschiedenen Rassen der Menschen* (1775), in *Kants Gesammelte Schriften,* Band 2, *Vorkritische Schriften* (Berlin, 1912), 429–443.

———, *Beobachtungen über das Gefühl des Schönen und Erhabenen*, ch. 4: "Von den Nationalcharakteren" (1764) in *Sämtliche Werken* 2.

Kelley, D., "*Tacitus Noster*: The *Germania* in the Renaissance and Reformation," in Luce and Woodman, *Tacitus and the Tacitean Tradition* (1993), 152–167.

Konstan, David, "Persians, Greeks and Empire," *Arethusa* 20 (1987), 59–74.

———, "To Hellēnikon ethnos," in Malkin (ed.), *Ancient Perceptions of Greek Ethnicity* (2001), 29–50.

Kroll, W., "Römer und Griechen," in *Studien zum Verständnis der römischen Literatur* (1924, repr. Darmstadt, 1964), 1–23.

Kullmann, Wolfgang, "Man as a Political Animal in Aristotle," in Keyt and Miller (eds.), *A Companion to Aristotle's* Politics (1991), 94–117.

Lambrechts, P., "Augustus en de Egyptische Godsdienst," *Mededelingen van de Koninklijke Vlaamse Academie voor Wetenschappen . . . van België,* Klasse der Letteren 18.2 (1956), 3–32.

Lange, Nicholas de, "The Origins of Anti-Semitism: Ancient Evidence and Modern Interpretations," in Gilman and Katz, *Anti-Semitism in Times of Crisis* (1991), 21–37.

Last, H., "Rome and the Druids: a Note," *JRS* 39 (1949), 1–5.

Lateiner, Donald, "The Empirical Element in the Methods of Early Greek Medical Writers and Herodotus: A Shared Epistemological Response," *Antichthon* 20 (1986) 1–20.

Laurot, B., "Idéaux grecs et barbarie chez Hérodote," *Ktema* 6 (1981), 39–48.

Levy, Carlos, "L'antijudaisme paien: essay de synthèse," in Nikiprowetzky (ed.), *de l'antijudaisme antique à l'antisémitisme contemporain* (1979) 51–86.

Liebeschuetz, Wolf, "The Influence of Judaism among non-Jews in the Imperial Period," *JJS* 52 (2001), 235–52.

Lintott, A.W., "Imperial Expansion and Moral Decline in the Roman Republic," *Historia* 21 (1972), 626–638.

Lloyd, Alan B. "Herodotus on Egyptians and Libyans," in Nenci (ed.), *Hérodote et les peuples non grecs* (1990), 215–244.

López Férez, J. A., "Los escritos Hipocráticos y el Nacimiento de la identidad Europea," in Khan (ed.), *The Birth of the European Identity* (1994), 90–123.

Lund, A. A., "Zum Germanenbegriff bei Tacitus," in Beck (ed.), *Germanenprobleme in heutiger Sicht* (1986), 53–87.

Marshall, Anthony J., "Flaccus and the Jews of Asia (Cicero *Pro Flacco* 28.67–69)," *Phoenix* 29 (1975), 139–154.

Mazza, F., "The Phoenicians as seen by the Ancient World," in Moscati (ed.), *The Phoenicians* (1988), 548–567.

McInerney, Jeremy, "Ethnos and Ethnicity in Early Greece," in Malkin (ed.), *Ancient Perceptions of Greek Ethnicity* (2001), 51–73.

Memmi, Albert, "Essai de définition du racisme," *La Nef* 19–20 (1964), 41–47.

Miles, Robert, "Theories of Racism," in Bulmer and Solomos, *Racism* (1999), 348f., reprinted from Miles, *Racism* (London, 1989).

Millar, Fergus, "Cornelius Nepos 'Atticus' and the Roman Revolution," *Greece and Rome* 35 (1988), 40–55.

———, "Ethnic Identity in the Roman Near East, AD 325–450," *Identities in the Eastern Mediterranean in Antiquity, Mediterranean Archaeology* 11 (1998), 159–176.

Miller, Margaret C., "The Myth of Bousiris: Ethnicity and Art," in Cohen (ed.), *Not the Classical Ideal* (2000), 413–442.

Momigliano, A., "Some Observations on Causes of War in Ancient Historiography," *Proceedings of the Second International Congress of Classical Studies*, I (Copenhagen, 1958), 199.

———, "The Social Structure of the Ancient City: Religious Dissent and Heresy," in S. C. Humphreys, *Anthropology and the Greeks* (London, 1978), 190f.

———, "Persian Empire and Greek Freedom," in *The Idea of Freedom*, ed. A. Ryan (1979), 139–151.

Moreau, J., "Une scène d'anthropophagie en Égypte en l'an 127 de notre ère (Juvenal satire XV)," *CE* 15 (1940), 279–285.

Morgan, Catherine, "Ethne, Ethnicity, and Early Greek States, ca. 1200–480 BC: An Archaeological Perspective," in Malkin (ed.), *Ancient Perceptions* (2001), 75–112.

Mossé, Claude, "Les rapports entre la Grèce et la Perse au IVème siècle avant Jesus-Christ," *la Persia et il mondo greco-romano* (1966), 177–182.

Nash, Daphne, "Reconstructing Posidonios' Celtic Ethnography: Some Considerations," *Britannia* 7 (1976), 111–126.

Nock, A. D., "Eunuchs in Ancient Religion," in *Essays on Religion in the Ancient World* (ed. Zeph Stewart) 1 (Oxford, 1972), 7–15.

Nolland, J., "Proselytism or Politics in Horace, *Satires* I,4,138–143?," *Vigiliae Christianae* 33 (1979), 347–355.

North, J. A. "Religious Toleration in Republican Rome," *PCPS* 25 (1979), 85–103.

———, "The Development of Religious Pluralism," in Lieu, North, and Rajak, *The Jews among Pagans and Christians* (1992), 177–180.

Nutton, V., "The Perils of Patriotism: Pliny and Roman Medicine," in French and Greenaway (eds.), *Science in the Early Roman Empire* (London, 1986), 30–58.

———, "Roman Medicine: Tradition, Confrontation, Assimilation," in *ANRW* 2.37.1, 393–444.

Ostwald, M., "*Nomos* and *Phusis* in Antiphon's περὶ ἀληθείας," in Griffith and Mastronarde (eds.), *Cabinet of the Muses* (1990), 293–306.

———, "Freedom and the Greeks," in R.W. Davis (ed.), *The Origins of Modern Freedom in the West* (Stanford, CA, 1995), 35–63.

———, "Shares and Rights: 'Citizenship' Greek Style and American Style," in J. Ober and C. Hedrick (ed.), *Demokratia* (Princeton, 1996), 49–61.

————, "Popular Sovereignty and the Problem of Equality," *SCI* 19 (2000), 1–13.

Øystergård, Uffe, "What Is National and Ethnic Identity?" in Bilde et al., *Ethnicity in Hellenistic Egypt* (Aarhus, 1992), 16–38.

Paratore, Ettore, "La Persia nella letteratura latina," in *Atti del convegno sul tema: la Persia et il mondo greco-romano 1965,* Accademia Nazionale dei Lincei 363 (Rome, 1966), 505–558.

Parker, Robert, "Myths of Early Athens," in Bremmer (ed.), *Interpretations of Greek Mythology* (1987), 187–214.

Perlman, S., "Panhellenism, the Polis and Imperialism," *Historia* 25 (1976), 1–30.

Piana, G. La "Foreign Groups in Rome During the First Centuries of the Empire," *HTR* 20 (1927), 183–403.

Pickering, Michael, "Consuming Doubts: What Some People Ate? Or What Some People Swallowed?" in Goldman (ed.), *The Anthropology of Cannibalism* (1999), 51–74.

Pirson, Felix, "Style and Message on the Column of Marcus Aurelius," *PBSR* 64 (1996), 139–179.

Poliakov, L., "L'antisémitisme est-il un racisme?" in Wieviorka, M. (ed.), *Racisme et modernité* (Paris, 1993), 82–84.

Pothecary, Sarah, "Strabo, the Tiberian Author: Past, Present and Silence in Strabo's *Geography*," *Mnemosyne* 55 (2002), 387–438.

Powell, B. B., "What Juvenal saw: Egyptian Religion and Anthropophagy in Satire 15," *RhM* 122 (1979), 185–189.

Préaux, Claire, "La singularité de l'Égypte dans le monde gréco-romain," *Chronique d'Égypte* 49 (1950), 110–123.

————, "Les raisons de l'originalité de l'Égypte," *Museum Helveticum* 10 (1953), 203–221.

Rabello, A. M., "The Attitude of Rome Towards Conversions to Judaism," reprinted in *The Jews in the Roman Empire* (2000), xiv.

————, "A Tribute to Jean Juster," reprinted in *The Jews in the Roman Empire* (2000), xv.

Radin, Max, "The Exposure of Infants in Roman Law and Practice," *CJ* 20 (1925), 337–342.

Rajak, T., "Was there a Roman Charter for the Jews?" *JRS* 74 (1984), 107–123 = *The Jewish Dialogue with Greece and Rome* (2001), 301–333.

————, "Jews and Greeks: The Invention and Exploitation of Polarities in the Nineteenth Century," reprinted in *The Jewish Dialogue with Greece and Rome* (2001), 545–548.

Raubitschek, A. E., "The Covenant of Plataea," *TAPA* 91 (1960), 178–183.

Rebenich, Stefan, "Der Fall Helmut Berve," *Chiron* 31 (2000), 457–496.

Reinhold, Meyer, "Roman Attitudes Toward Egyptians," *Ancient World* 3 (1980), 97–103.

Rives, J., "Human Sacrifice among Pagans and Christians," *JRS* 85 (1995), 65–85.

Rochette, Bruno, "Juifs et Romains, Y a-t-il un antijudaïsme romain?" *Revue des Études Juives* 160 (2001), 1–31.

————, "Tibère, les cultes étrangers et les astrologues (Suétone, *Vie de Tibère*, 36)," *Les Études Classiques* 69 (2001), 189–194.

Roos, A. G., "Joden en Jodenvervolging in het Oude Egypte," *De Gids* 110 (1947), 1–25.

Rosivach, V. J., "Autochthony and the Athenians," *CQ* 37 (1987), 294–306.

————, "Enslaving *Barbaroi* and the Athenian Ideology of Slavery," *Historia* 48 (1999), 129–157.

Ross, Anne, "Ritual and the Druids," in Green (ed.), *The Celtic World* (1995), 423–444.

Ross, R. C., "Superstitio," *CJ* 44 (1968–1969), 354–358.

Rotroff, Susan I., "The Greeks and the Other in the Age of Alexander," in Coleman and Walz (eds.), *Greeks and Barbarians* (1997), 221–236.

Rutgers, L.V., "Roman Policy towards the Jews: Expulsions from the City of Rome during the First Century C.E.," *Classical Antiquity* 13 (1994), 56–74.

———, "Attitudes to Judaism in the Greco-Roman Period," reprinted in *The Hidden Heritage of Diaspora Judaism* (Leuven,1998), 199–234.

Saddington, D. B., "Roman Attitudes to the External Gentes of the North," *Acta Classica* 4 (1961), 90–102.

———, "Race Relations in the Roman Empire," *ANRW* 2.3 (1975), 112–137.

Saïd, Suzanne, "The Discourse of Identity in Greek Rhetoric from Isocrates to Aristides," in Malkin (ed.), *Ancient Perceptions of Greek Ethnicity* (2001), 275–299.

Shapiro, H. Alan, "Autochthony and the Visual Arts in Fifth-Century Athens," in Boedeker and Raaflaub, *Democracy, Empire and the Arts* (1998), 127–151.

Salmon, P., "Racisme ou refus de la différence dans le monde gréco-romain," *DHA* 10 (1984), 75–98.

Schauenburg, K., "ΕΥΡΥΜΕΔΩΝ ΕΙΜΙ," *Athenische Mitteilungen* 90 (1975), 97–121.

Scheid, John, "Religion et superstition à l'époque de Tacite: quelques réflexions," in *Religion, supersticion y magia en el mundo romano* (Cadiz, 1985), 19–34.

———, "*Graeco Ritu:* A Typically Roman Way of Honoring the Gods," *HSCP* 97 (1995), 15–31.

Schlaifer, Robert, "Greek Theories of Slavery from Homer to Aristotle," *HSCP* 47 (1936), 165–204, repr. in Finley, *Slavery in Classical Antiquity* (1968), 93–132.

Schneider, Rolf Michael, "Die Faszination des Feindes: Bilder der Parther und des Orients in Rom," in Wiesehöfer (ed.), *Das Partherreich und seine Zeugnisse* (1998), 95–146.

Schofield, M., "Ideology and Philosophy in Aristotle's Theory of Slavery," in Patzig, *Aristoteles' "Politik"* (1990), 1–27.

Schul, Yaacov, and Zukier, Henri, "Why do Stereotypes Stick?" in Wistrich, *Demonizing the Other* (1999), 31–33.

Schwartz, Daniel R., "Antisemitism and Other –ism's in the Greco-Roman World," in Wistrich, *Demonizing the Other* (1999), 73–78.

Shatzman, I., "The Egyptian Question in Roman Politics (59–54 BC)," *Latomus* 30 (1971), 363–369.

Sherwin-White, A. N., "The Early Persecutions and Roman Law Again," *JTS* NS 3 (1952), 199ff.

Sidebottom, H., "The Date of the Composition of Herodian's History," *L'antiquité classique* 66 (1997), 271–276.

Simon, Marie, "Die Anschauungen der Antike vom Morgenland," *Wissenschaftliche Zeitschrift der Humboldt-Universität zu Berlin, gesellschaftliche-und sprachwissenschaftliche Reihe* 9 (1959/60), 139–143.

Smallwood, E. M., "Some Notes on the Jews under Tiberius," *Latomus* 15 (1956), 314–29.

———, "Domitian's Attitude towards the Jews and Judaism," *CP* 51 (1956), 1–13.

———, "The Legislation of Hadrian and Antoninus Pius against Circumcision," *Latomus* 18 (1959), 334–347.

———, "The Legislation of Hadrian and Antoninus Pius against Circumcision: Addendum," *Latomus* 20 (1961), 93–96.

Smelik, K.A.D., and Hemelrijk, E. A., "Opinions on Egyptian Animal Worship in Antiquity," *ANRW* 2.17.4 (1984), 1852–2000.

Smith, Nicholas D., "Aristotle's Theory of Natural Slavery," repr. in David Keyt and Fred D. Miller (eds.), *A Companion to Aristotle's Politics* (Oxford, 1991), 142–155.

Smith, R.R.R. "The Imperial Reliefs from the Sebasteion at Aphrodisias," *JRS* 77 (1987), 88–138.

Snowden, F. M. "Iconographical Evidence on the Black Populations in Greco-Roman Antiquity," in J. Vercoutter et al. (eds), *L'Image du Noir dans L'art occidental*, i: (Lausanne, 1976).

Snowden, Frank M., "Greeks and Ethiopians," in Coleman and Walz (eds.), *Greeks and Barbarians* (1997), 103–126.

Solin, H., "Juden und Syrer im westlichen Teil der der römischen Welt: Eine ethnisch-demographische Studie," *ANRW* 2.29.2 (1983), 587–789.

Sparkes, B., "Some Greek Images of Others," in Molyneaux, *The Cultural Life of Images: Visual Representation in Archaeology* (1997), 130–158.

Spawforth, Antony, "Shades of Greekness: A Lydian Case Study," in Malkin (ed.), *Ancient Perceptions of Greek Ethnicity* (2001), 375–400.

Ste. Croix, G.E.M. de, "Why were the Early Christians Persecuted?" *Past and Present* 26 (1963), 6–38; response: A. N. Sherwin-White, *Past and Present* 27 (1964), 23–27; de Ste. Croix's rejoinder, 28–33.

Stroumsa, Guy G., "Philosophy of the Barbarians: On Early Christian Ethnological Representations," in H. Cancik, H. Lichtenberger, and P. Schäfer (eds.), *Geschichte–Tradition-Reflexion: Festschrift für Martin Hengel zum 70. Geburtstag*, Band 2 (Tübingen, 1996), 339–368.

Swain, Simon, "Favorinus and Hadrian," *ZPE* 79 (1989), 150–158.

Thomas, Rosalind, "Ethnicity, Genealogy, and Hellenism in Herodotus," in Malkin (ed.), *Ancient Perceptions of Greek Ethnicity* (2001), 213–233.

Timpe, D., "Ethnologische Begriffsbildung," in H. Beck (ed.), *Germanenprobleme in heutiger Sicht* (Berlin/New York 1986), 22–40.

Triebel-Schubert, Charlotte, "Anthropologie und Norm: der Skythenabschnitt in der hippokratischen Schrift "Über die Umwelt,'" *Medizin Historisches Journal* 25 (1990), 90–103.

Tuplin, Christopher, "Greek Racism? Observations on the Character and Limits of Greek Ethnic Prejudice," in Tsetskhladze (ed.), *Ancient Greeks West and East* (Leiden, 1999), 47–75.

Usher, Stephen, "Isocrates: Paideia, Kingship, and the Barbarians," in Khan (ed.), *The Birth of the European Identity* (1994).

Veyne, Paul, "*Humanitas:* Les romains et les autres," in Giardina (ed.), *L'homme romain* (1992), 421–459.

Vidal-Naquet, P., "Flavius Arrien entre deux mondes," in *Arrien, Histoire d'Alexandre* (Paris 1984), 330–343.

——— , "The Place of Greece in the Revolution," in *Politics . . .* (1995), 141–169.

Vidal-Naquet, P., and Loraux, N., "The Formation of Bourgeois Athens," in Vidal-Naquet, *Politics Ancient and Modern* (1995), 82–140.

Vlastos, Gregory, "Slavery in Plato's Thought," in *Platonic Studies* (2d ed. 1981), 147–163; reprinted also in Finley (ed.), *Slavery in Classical Antiquity* (1968), 133–149.

——— , "Does Slavery Exist in Plato's Republic?" in: *Platonic Studies* (1981), 291–295.

Volkov, Shulamit, "Exploring the Other: The Enlightenment's Search for the Boundaries of Humanity," in Wistrich (ed.), *Demonizing the Other* (1999), 148–167.

Vries, Keith De, "The Nearly Other: The Attic Vision of Phrygians and Lydians," in Cohen (ed.), *Not The Classical Ideal* (2000), 338–363.

Walbank, F. W., "Egypt in Polybius," in Ruffle et al. (eds.), *Glimpses of Ancient Egypt* (1979), 180–189.

———, "The Problem of Greek Nationality," in *Selected Papers: Studies in Greek and Roman History and Historiography* (Cambridge, 1985), 1–19.

———, "Nationality as a Factor in Roman History," in *Selected Papers* (1985), 57–76.

Wallace-Hadrill, Andrew, "Greek Knowledge, Roman Power," *CPh* 83 (1988), 224–233.

———, "Pliny the Elder and Man's Unnatural History," *Greece and Rome* 37 (1990), 80–96.

———, "Roman Arches and Greek Honours: the Language of Power at Rome," *PCPS* 36 (1990), 143–181.

Waltzing, J.-P., "Le crime rituel reproché aux chrétiens du 2ᵉ siècle," in *Académie Royale de Belgique*, Bull. de la Classe des Lettres, ser. 5, vol.11 (1925), 205–239.

Watts, W. J., "Race Prejudice in the Satires of Juvenal," *Acta Classica* 19 (1976), 83–104.

West, Stephanie, "Herodotus in the North? Reflections on a Colossal Cauldron," *SCI* 19 (2000), 15–34.

Wheeler, E. L., "The Laxity of the Syrian Legions," in Kennedy (ed.), *The Roman Army in the East* (Ann Arbor, 1996), 229–276.

Wickevoort Crommelin, Bernard van, "Die Parther und die parthische Geschichte bei Pompeius Trogus-Iustin," in Wiesehöfer (ed.), *Das Partherreich und seine Zeugnisse* (1998), 259–277.

Wiedemann, T.E.J., "Between Men and Beasts: Barbarians in Ammianus Marcellinus," in: Moxon, Smart, and Woodman (eds.), *Past Perspectives* (Cambridge, 1986), 189–201.

Wightman, E. M., "Il y avait en Gaule deux sortes de Gaulois," in D. M. Pippidi (ed.), *Assimilation et résistance à la culture gréco-romaine dans le monde ancien* (Paris, 1976), 407–419.

Williams, Margaret H., "The Expulsion of the Jews from Rome in AD 19," *Latomus* 48 (1989), 765–784.

———, "Domitian, the Jews and the 'Judaizers'—A Simple Matter of Cupiditas and Maiestas?" *Historia* 39 (1990), 196–211.

———, "The Structure of the Jewish Community in Rome," in Goodman (ed.), *Jews in a Graeco-Roman World* (1998), 215–228.

Woolf, Greg, "Becoming Roman, Staying Greek," *PCPS* 40 (1994), 116–143.

Yavetz, Z., "Judeophobia in Classical Antiquity. A Different Approach," *JJS* 44 (1993), 1–22.

Ziolkowski, John, "National and Other Contrasts in Athenian Funeral Orations," in Khan (ed.), *The Birth of the European Identity* (1994), 1–35.

Zirkle, Conway, "The Early History of the Idea of the Inheritance of Acquired Characteristics and of Pangenesis," *Trans. Am. Phil. Soc.*, ns 35 (1946), 91–151.

Zucker, F., "Plinius epist. VIII 24—ein Denkmal antiker Humanität," *Philologus* 84 (1928), 209–232.

in Lyons, 418–420; on Egypt, 361; on environmental determinism, 95f.; Gauls, 190; on German family life, 432; his descriptions of large-scale killings, 220; his views on the Germans, 142–144, 432–436; on the import of grain, 361; on the Parthians as nomads, 319; on the pure lineage of the Germans, 137–142; regards Britons as superior to Gauls, 190; regards Germans as superior to Gauls, 141f.; regards Germans as superior to Sarmatae, 142. *See also* Jews

Taine, Hypolyte, 133

Tarsians, criticized by Dio Chrysostom, 345

Tencteri, 140f.

Tertullian, on environmental determinism, 78, 97f. *See also* germs

Teutones and Cimbri, compared with animals, 202; deteriorated in Venetia, 310, 313f.; of pure lineage but not autochthonous, 139; unsociable, 245f. *See also* wine

theatre, Roman criticism of, 388. *See also* Cimbri

Thebes, foundation myth of, 131. *See also* Pindar

Theophrastus, 162f., 197

Thrace, 409

Thracians, as fierce warriors, 99, 267, 295, 317; offered human sacrifice, 475. *See also* Herodotus; Plato; Xenophon

Tiberius, 223, 409

Timagenes of Alexandria, 136 n.320

Tom and Jerry, 152

total war, 297f.

Toynbee, A., 310

Trachonitis, 408

trade, eastern regarded as harmful, 136, 241; regarded as either harmful or advantageous, 240. *See also* contact, between peoples; Pliny (the Elder); wealth

Trajan, about a gymnasium for Nicaea, 398; on the treatment of Christians, 486–488

Tralles, 389

Trapezus, 318, 383

Trinobantes, 191

Tropaeum Alpium (La Turbie), 409

Twelve Tables, 382

uncooked meat, consumption of, 199, 310, 364

UNESCO, statement on race, 32

universal rule, and Greeks, 72; and Rome, 85; said to be a law of nature, 182, 184f.

Vegetius, 87, 222; on Roman military superiority, 321

Velleius Paterculus, on Germans, 430f.

Veneti, 418, 436, 439

Vercingetorix, 414

Vergil, on Africans, 148; on Phrygians, 338f.; the story of Dido and Aeneas by, 339

Verus, L., 348

Vespasian, bans philosophers from Rome, 237f.

Vitruvius, on environmental determinism, 83–85; on Italy and universal rule, 85

Volcae Tectosages, 96f.

Voltaire, 11

Vonones, King of Parthia, 318f.

warfare, as a means of acquiring slaves, 178f.; morally justified, 181f.; and the constitution, 264–268

warm baths, 310 n.24

wealth, as cause of collective deterioration, 91, 97, 188–192, 227, 241, 285f., 298f., 306f., 315, 414f. *See also* Arrian; Cassius Dio; Cato; Cicero; *Cyropaedia*, last chapter; Flavius Josephus; Gauls; Isocrates; Julius Caesar; Pliny (the Elder); Strabo; Tacitus; Xenophon

wind, 136

wine, reputed effects, 79 n.145, 81, 310, 415f. *See also* alcohol

Winny the Pooh, 152

witches, 34

women, Greek, 177f.; barbarian and slaves, 177f.

world, the edge of, 203, 263; divided into three parts, 282

xenophobia, in Athens, 119–121, 225–247; definition of, 38f., 443f.; in Rome, 225–247, 418f., 459f. *See also* Petronius

Xenophon, attitude towards Persia of, 288–293; on Cyrus the Great, 288, 290; on Cyrus the Younger, 288; last chapter of *Cyropaedia* of, 290–293; on monarchy, 288; on the location of Athens, 73; political message of his *anabasis*, 288f.; on the Scythians and Thracians, 288. See also *Cyropaedia*, last chapter

Xerxes, 264f.

Zenobia, 223